PARADISE OF PAPER ART

DESIGNERBOOKS

In the past few decades there have been several predictions and proclamations of a paperless world. This seems like a logical concept as computers and other devices become the primary methods to distribute and acquire information. But it hasn't happened. So why not? More commercial, office and desktop printing is done today than ever before and at the same time we spend more time in front of a screen than we ever have in the past. We can work without paper. Artists and designers can create until completion on a computer and in most cases this is how things are done in commercial design. In the past, pieces would have to be printed, cut, aligned, taped and photographed by hand. Being a designer was a physical job that satisfied both the intellectual and the physical demands of our brains and our bodies. This is no longer necessary. A designer can do a days work without getting up from a chair, without turning away from a screen, without ever holding a piece of paper in their hands.

It is this lack of necessity, the lack of paper, of a physical product, that provides an urge to return to the tactile and makes the idea of working with paper so intriguing and so new in today's design. It is a reaction against the flat screen. Paper is a flat surface to be printed or written on but in an environment where most of our information and ideas are created and consumed in a intangible digital world the materiality of a thin sheet of paper becomes pronounced and significant. Paper can become the bridge between the flat and the voluminous, between 2 dimensional and 3 dimensional, between a surface and an object. It is an object that can be held in our hands, folded and cut, shaped and sewn, pushed and manipulated to take on a wide range of properties and new meanings. Artists are turning to paper as well, working beyond the role of paper as a drawing surface and into the realm of its materiality. Paper can become sculpture. It can become architecture. It can become fashion, It can be light. It can imitate a variety of materials and replicate objects and scenes in our environment. Paper is normally thought of as waste and bad for the environment but the irony is that paper offers a more environmentally friendly way to construct new sculptures and scenes in lieu of more rigid or permanent materials in our throw away culture. Why use wood or plastic or fabric for a display, an installation or a dress that will be discarded in a few days, or even in a few decades? The fragility of paper suggests that it is a fleeting material yet it will last for thousands of years under the right conditions.

We don't need paper the way we used to. It is now unemployed and looking for work. In its job search, it has redefined itself in endless new ways and is now busier than ever. It is now free to be in the studio and explore the infinite options of its properties and the meanings hidden within its own material. The "paperless world", the digital age, has pushed it into new realms and territories it may not have gone otherwise.

The works in this book are not so much "works on paper" as they are "works of paper". Some of the work is based in craft, some is based in concept, some grow upon traditions that are centuries old and some are innovative, new ways to see the material. The material crosses and combines worlds of art, design, fashion, and architecture from the commercial to the conceptual. We use paper every day but we didn't really know what it was really capable of until now.

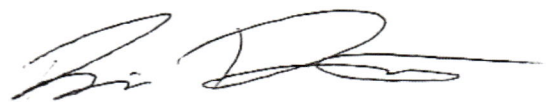

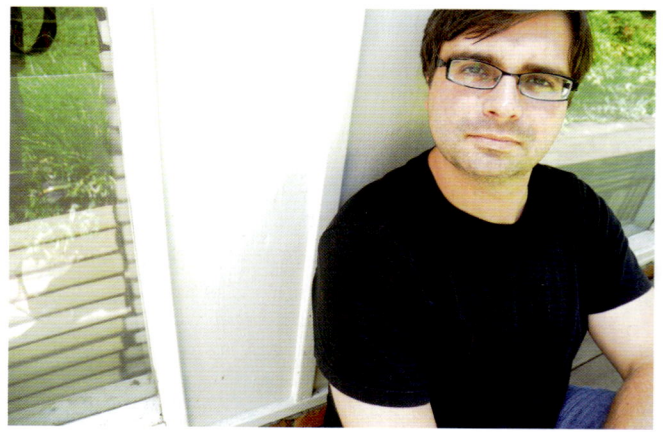

Photographer: Susan Rosmarin

Brian Dettmer

Paper, historically considered as a means with which to record our words, music, drawings and ideas, is currently regarded in the art world for its materiality.

Evolving concurrently with the invention and utilization of computers, the variety of applications of paper by artists and designers is expansive and diverse. Of course, a sheet of paper can be used to simply record information, but within the context of art and design, it is increasingly being used to create three-dimensional forms and worlds.

Paper works can simultaneously appear hyper-realistic, animated and whimsical, while others feel fantastical, grounded and sedentary. All this is accomplished by using a thin fragile sheet of material that is utilitarian in function and readily accessible in our culture that anyone can easily tear, burn and throw it away. This commonality illustrates the paradox of paper as an artistic medium.

Paper can simultaneously be a mundane and magical material for artists and designers. Although its surfaces and textures primary function began as a place to record words, notes, and illustrations, paper now holds limitless possibilities for the artists represented in this book. Constantly pushing the boundaries of what the material can do, they create worlds that invoke a new frontier in art making. What stands out for the viewer is how the processes of formation can be ethereal and magical transformations.

As an artist, I first approached paper as a material that could conduct and capture light. The photographic print began as a light-capturing piece of paper that produced a pictorial image of a moment in time. My work endeavors to channel light through paper to produce a sculptural moment in time. I use paper to create sculptures that hint at both mass and ephemerality, but are really textural paper illusions.

This book reduces paper to its primary form and function: recorded information to communicate to its reader. The true meaning of the book, its form, its function, is to share with you all the possibilities this material can produce within the unique vision of talented artists and designers.

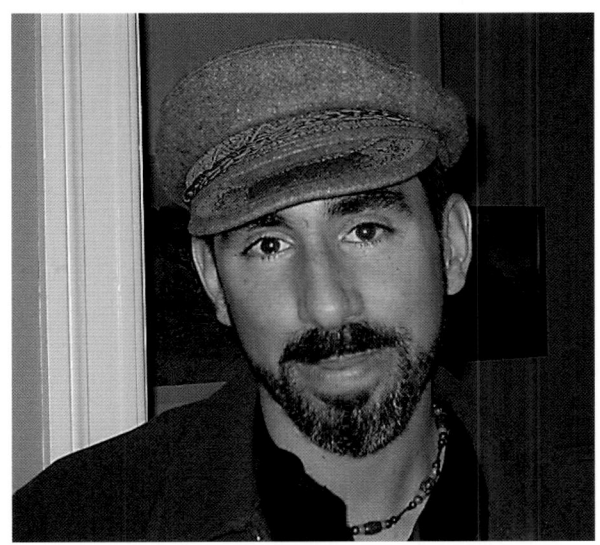

Christophe Piallat

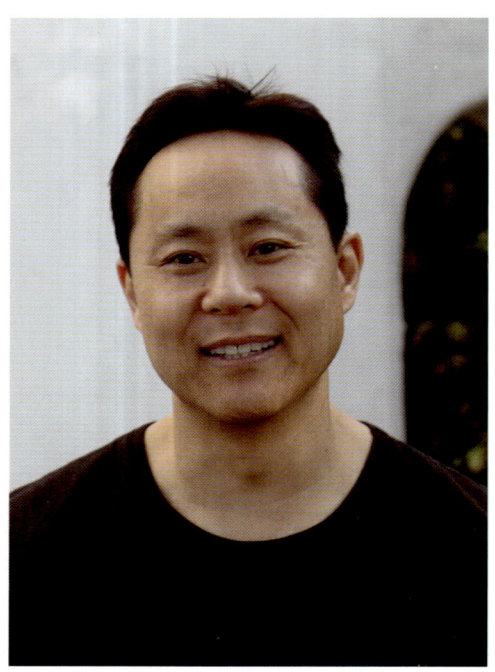

Jeff Nishinaka

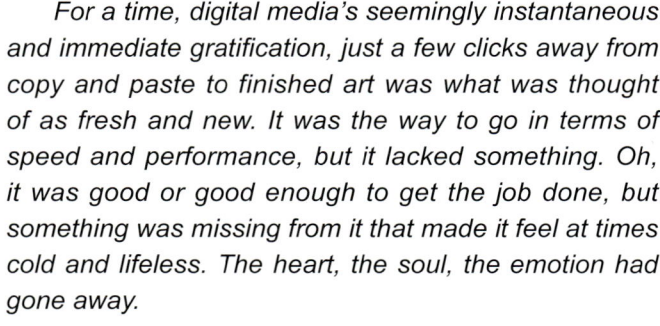

For a time, digital media's seemingly instantaneous and immediate gratification, just a few clicks away from copy and paste to finished art was what was thought of as fresh and new. It was the way to go in terms of speed and performance, but it lacked something. Oh, it was good or good enough to get the job done, but something was missing from it that made it feel at times cold and lifeless. The heart, the soul, the emotion had gone away.

Then there was a newfound appreciation for things that involved the long process of laborious hands-on manipulation. From humble beginnings to a celebration of masterful maneuvering, the endless possibilities that paper presented was like the rediscovery of a long lost treasure that was somehow misplaced and forgotten.

One can feel that paper has a life and energy of its own that can be redirected into something that is tangible and real, that has texture and depth, a heart and soul. Unlike something that is created with the click of a mouse or the swipe of a stylus on a tablet, paper needs to be touched, cut, folded, cast in molds, ripped and layered, crumpled and glued a thousand times and more. Only then can the life and energy of the artist be transferred to paper as well.

Paper can be used to "create an image that the public will remember and associate with a company or product." That is partly from a quote my friend Doyald Young wrote in his book describing the object of a design. Paper used as the medium to express a design is something that takes it beyond the cold calculated concept to sell something and gives to it warmth and humanity. In a world that wants to go "paperless" for the sake of the environment, it seems that the only way to save the environment is when humanity is put back into paper and the things we trust and love.

So this book is a celebration of rediscovering that what was thought of as old becomes new once again. That what we do with our hands "the good old fashioned way" is appreciated and even yearned for. And that art even if only for art's sake does matter.

CONTENTS

PART 1. PAPER + ART .... 20-203 pages

PART 2. PAPER + DESIGN .... 206-511 pages

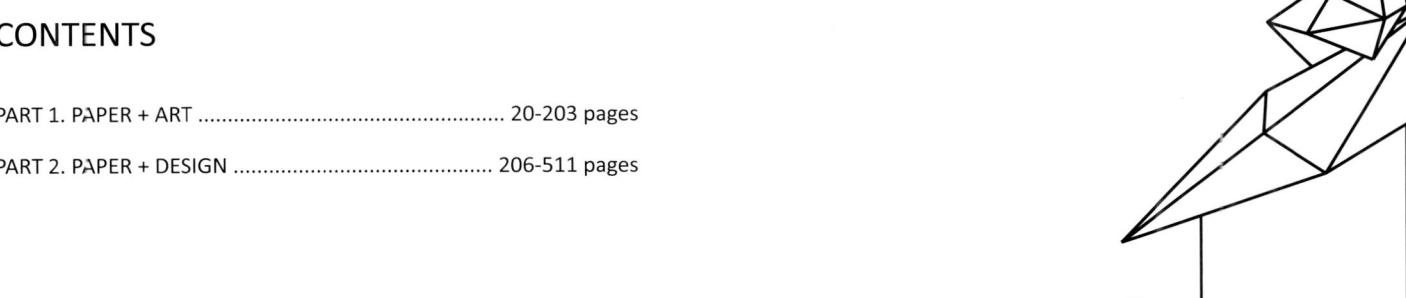

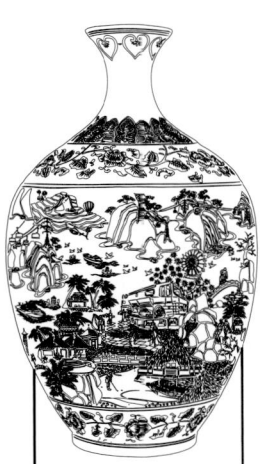

Bovey Lee

www.boveylee.com

Hong Kong–born, American artist Bovey Lee is internationally acclaimed for her cut paper. Her education includes University of California, Berkeley (MFA/painting); Pratt Institute, New York (MFA/digital arts); and the Chinese University of Hong Kong (EA/fine arts). Recent exhibitions include Nevada Museum of Art, USA; IFC Shanghai, China (presented by Hugo Boss); Fujikawa Kirie Art Museum, Japan; Museum Rijswijk, The Netherlands; and Museum Bellerive, Switzerland. Collections include the Ashmolean Museum of Art and Archaeology, Oxford University, UK; Hong Kong Museum of Art; The Chinese University of Hong Kong; Progressive Corporate Art Collection, USA; and Fidelity Investments, Hong Kong and USA.

20-27

Brian Dettmer

www.briandettmer.com

Dettmer is originally from Chicago. He currently resides in Atlanta, GA.
Dettmer has had solo shows in New York, Chicago, San Francisco, Atlanta and Barcelona. His work has been exhibited throughout North America and Europe at galleries and museums including the Museum of Art and Design (NY), MOCA (GA), the International Museum of Surgical Science (IL), and the Museum Rijswijk (Netherlands). Dettmer's bibliography includes The New York Times, ArtNews, The Guardian, Telegraph, Chicago Tribune, Modern Painters, Wired, The Village Voice and NPR.

28-39

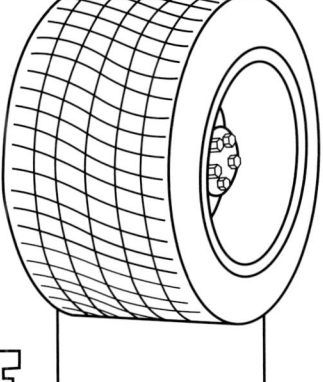

Chris Gilmour

www.chrisgilmour.com

Chris has chosen a simple but meaningful material for his work: in first place because corrugated cardboard is usually employed to pack and ship the artist's work, rather than physically representing the oeuvre itself (the container, in this case, becomes the content). Even more interesting is the gap between the cheap, discarded material and the height of the final output. It's an elegant operation that goes beyond the usual theme of recycling, and underlines the role of the modern artist as a new 'artisan virtuoso', at ease with the industrial material as much as the icons of an industrial culture. The end result is a "fragile perfection", a sober reflection on our own world, where the value of beauty is too often misunderstood with its price.
Text by Monica Turlot, senior writer, artist and critic at Brandpowder.

40-49

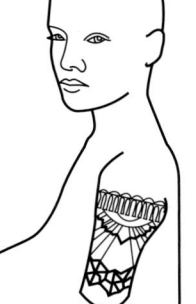

Christine Kim

www.christinekim.ca

Inspired by boundaries, I often use Victorian fences to illustrate the tension created at these borders. At once, sturdy and restrictive, the fence also stands as a decorative ornament to mark the line between private and public spaces. It is a stern warning and an intricate embellishment. The illustrations accumulate layers of fences, figures, and screens -- all cut and perforated with patterns to allow them to cast shadows and create distances, making new relationships from this displacement.

50-55

Christophe Piallat

www.christophepiallat.com

Christophe Piallat began his artistic career in the early 1990's as a travel and documentary photographer. From that time on the photographic medium has been the language he has used to understand a host of other disciplines. Light is the key instrument in his production and results in work that blends the realms of painting, drawing, photography and sculpture. His paper and light installations have been exhibited internationally, including the 2010 Holland Paper Biennale and most recently in 2012 with the 1st International Biennale of Santorini.

56-67

Clemens Behr

www.clemensbehr.com

Born 20.10.1985 in Koblenz, Germany.
Studied Graphic Design at the University of Applied Sciences Dortmund, Germany.
2008/09 Universitat de Barcelona, Facultat de Belles Artes, Spain.
Currently studying fine arts at UdK Berlin.
When he was around 18, he was really interested in futurism and dada art. Especially in showing a moving image through a single painting or drawing, like he saw in Marcel Duchamp's " Nude Descending A Staircase Nr.2". At this time he developed the more abstract part of his work.
This abstract compositions have been 2 dimensional for a couple of years, but then grew into the 3rd dimension slowly. His first real work with cardboard was made at an expo in Essen/Germany in 2006. He originally planed to build cardboard-frames for his illustrations, but quickly those frames started to grow and he discovered, that it could be much more fun to use different materials to create his shapes, instead of just painting on the wall. From that day on he started to work constantly with cardboard, tape and trash bags when creating sculptures.
He would say, in further installations and exhibitions the style developed itself through the technic and its process. He was just learning by doing, how to process shapes more quickly and how to get the most out of the chosen materials and tools. In terms of the installation, the image you get, should seem like a Transformer-Origami-like distortion of the space itself. This kind of image is surely leading the establishment of his style and work.

68-75

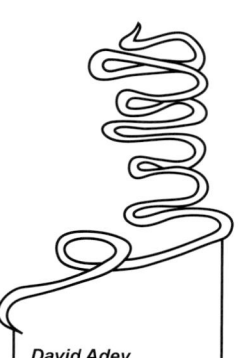

David Adey

www.davidadey.com

David Adey's work traverses between the perverse and the spiritual as it brings to the fore issues of religion, sexuality and desire, collecting and consuming of pop-culture and its obsession with celebrity. Adey invites the viewer to examine Western culture's fetishization of the flesh via the media's seemingly endless preoccupation with the "beautiful" bodies of female and male stars and starlets. There is an omnipresent touch of the macabre—a maniacal precision of the serial killer about his work—that makes it all the more prophetic. Adey's photo-sculptural strategies leave the viewer to ponder who and what will end up defining contemporary culture, historically, and to provoke questions into the very subject and essence of worship today.

Art critic and blogger Kevin Freitas has made this incisive examination of David Adey's work: "Using ordinary "craft punches", Adey pilfers today's fashion magazines and dissects hundreds of flesh tone shapes from the celebrities and models displayed within their glossy pages, and then resurrects the victims in works that are simply astounding in their complexity of design and simplicity of idea and construction. Each punched shape is pinned (crucified) like an entomological collection to a Styrofoam background and turned into some of the most sensual and sublime collages ever produced. Adey's transformations show that it is not any more bizarre to take a digital image of a "live" model, reproduce it and present it as an actual living breathing being—as truth—then it is to reverse that process, as he does, by bringing an idea or "impression" back into the realm of an object or fact. His work is the ultimate visual game of seduction and sensation, visually reproducing the pleasures of the surface time and time again."

76-85

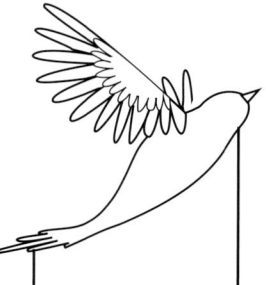

Diana Beltran Herrera

www.ppiinnee.com

Diana Beltran Herrera is a Colombian designer and artist. She uses the paper as a main technique of her work where spring her paper bird sculptures. This serie of works comes out on her experience with nature and the discovering process she has had in relation with the world in its real form.

Through the work Diana analyzes the movement in the relation between object-space. The birds provide her with quantity of information manifested in their activities and dynamism. This new space is externalized by the point of view of the artist on some major events of the birds and their environment, in which behaviors are represented, forms, qualities and intentions all related with movement.

The interest of the artist is to take the rol of the investigation and generate a document reinterpreting the traditional way to record a story in the paper: using items that are broken into pieces as if each were a word, which then come together and unite, representing a moment of time that consists in a visual poetry through a natural language .Is the visual record of an event, a text without words that turn into a material testimony to all information collected and supported in the paper.

Diana thinks that the paper as a temporal medium allows her to interpretation elements that has a life and she waits for the moment that the material generate its own transformations with the years coming.

86-89

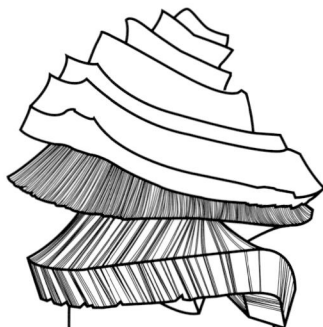

Doug Beube

www.dougbeube.com

Doug Beube is a mixed-media artist working in bookwork, collage, sculpture and photography. Since 1993, he has been curator of a private collection, The Allan Chasanoff Bookwork Collection: The Book Under Pressure, in New York City. Doug teaches classes at Parsons The New School in artists' books, collage, mixed-media, and photography and workshops at Penland, Haystack and The Center for Book Arts. He regularly lectures on his work throughout the US, Canada and Europe. Prior to receiving an MFA in Photography from the Visual Studies Workshop in Rochester, NY, graduating in 1983, he was darkroom assistant to Minor White in Arlington, MA. He exhibits extensively both nationally and internationally and his bookwork and photographs are in numerous private and public collections. In the fall of 2011 a monograph entitled, Doug Beube: Breaking the Codex: Bookwork, Collage and Mixed Media, was published. David Revere McFadden, chief curator of the Museum of Art and Design in New York City wrote the introduction. The in depth overview of Doug's artwork, with essay contributions from several well known writers, critics and curators, discuss his art made over the past thirty years.

90-95

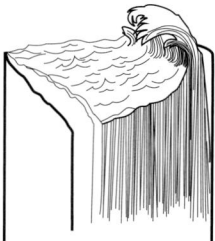

Guy Laramée

www.guylaramee.com

In the course of his 30 years of practice, inter-disciplinary artist Guy Laramée has created in such varied and numerous disciplines as theater writing and directing, contemporary music composition, musical instrument design and building, singing, video, scenography, sculpture, installation, painting, and literature. He has received more than 30 arts grants and was awarded the Canada Council's Joseph S. Stauffer award for musical composition. His work has been presented in United States, Belgium, France, Germany, Switzerland, Japan, and Latin America.

From 1984 to 1988 he composed music for contemporary dance. After 1988 he composed and designed sound scenography for theater. His research in non-tempered tunings and multiple layer polyrhythms led him to found TUYO in 1987, an ensemble performing microtonal and gestural music on invented instruments. He directed this ensemble until 1991.

Parallel to his artistic practice, he has pursued investigation in the field of anthropology. His fieldwork includes ethno-musicography of the Fetish ritual in Togo (1986), oracular imagination among healers in the Peruvian Amazon (1993-95), and concepts of creativity and imagination among contemporary artists (M.A. thesis, 2002). Ethnographic imagination is an important characteristic in his artistic work.

Although his work has been presented in museums and galleries, its appearance in the context of gallery exhibition is relatively new (2004). Nevertheless, at the end of 2011 his work will have been included in 15 solo and more than 20 collective shows. Half of these have been in international exhibits.

96-105

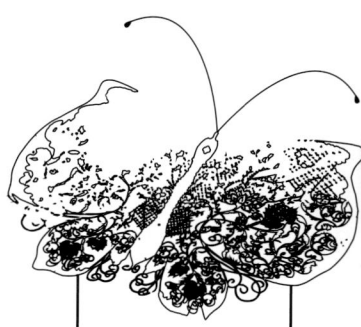

Hina Aoyama

www.hinaaoyama.com

Born 1970 in Yokohama, Japan

Started super fine Lacy-paper-cuttings since 2000. Currently lives and works in Ferney Voltaire, France.

106-109

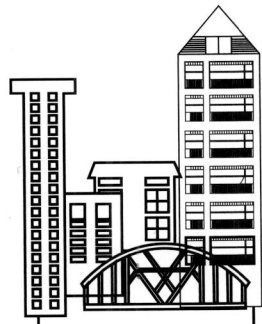

Laura Cooperman

www.lauracooperman.com

Due to people's increased mobility, the idea of home is no longer fixed in place, but rather constructed from collected memory, history and myth. Through the use of intricate layered paper cut outs and architectural installations, Cooperman's work addresses the fluid space where historical, geographical, and personal borders fluctuate, challenging one's sense of place, origin, and home. Traditional textile designs, architectural elements, wild vegetation and commercial products from different cultures find themselves pieced together in a new environment with new meaning and purpose attached.

110-115

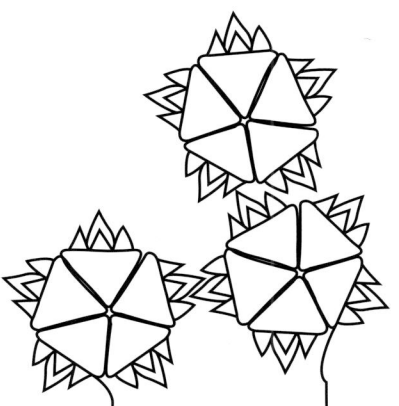

Lee Huey Ming

www.mingsrealm.com

Ming is a paper artist and graphic designer based in Auckland, New Zealand. She has a Master of Art and Design at Auckland University of Technology. Her works have been exhibited in various galleries in Auckland. Ming loves spending her time observing the intricacies of nature. Her love for tactility, curiosity to explore and to observe handmade craftsmanship and actual, physically built objects is expressed in her intricate paper cuttings and paper sculptures. Her works investigates the structure of nature whom she claims to be inspired by Ernst Haeckel.

116-119

Linus Hui

www.flickr.com/photos/linusishere/

Linus has determined to make people feel good (or bad) through his industrious attempts to photograph himself with props and paper cut-outs artworks, with or without quirky expressions.

Starting his humble photographic career with 2 series of Flickr's "365" daily photo projects, Linus has honed his talent expanded dramatically, while expanding his wardrobe of costumes and paper cut-outs.

120-123

Lisa Nilsson

www.lisanilssonart.com

Lisa Nilsson grew up in Avon Massachusetts. She is a graduate of the Rhode Island School of Design where she studied illustration, and also of the McCann Technical School's medical assisting program where her life-long interest in anatomy and cool-looking medical things grew a bit better informed. She lives in North Adams, Massachusetts.

124-129

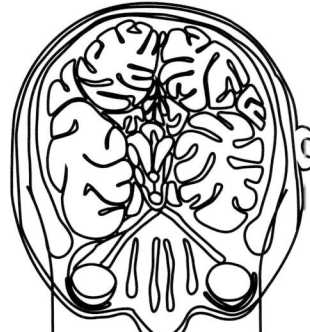

Lucas simões

www.lucassimoes.com.br

I'm an independent artist based in São Paulo, with a background in architecture, urbanism and design. My experience as an architect redefined my perceptions of art and opened new paths of discovery. This outlook has influenced my drawing process and his constructive approach to his work with images and sculpture.

I source many different materials which I then deconstructs into new forms. In my work materiality of the supporting medium is important. The process of making the support a part of the work is achieved through the experiences it is subjected to, such as burning, cutting, distorting or diluting, which, at its most extreme, can destroy the subject.

130-135

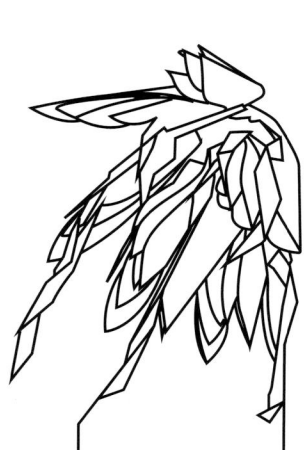

**Martin Böttger
Tsaworks**

www.tsaworks.com

The main focus of my work is on visual arts, in particular 3D animations, generative as well as interactive animations, club visuals, video installations, audio-visual performances, sculptures and installations. My number-one tool is the computer, which I use to create 3D animations and sculptural concepts. In addition, I use diferent kinds of materials to implement ideas. My works cover topics like time, space, deformation, deconstruction, rearrangement, layering, distortion, tensions, relations, harmony, mass- and swarm structuring/clustering. On these thematic contents, I work on three levels: firstly, video/animation work; secondly, installation/ sculptural work and lastly, the work with sound structures/audio-visual performance. In the last few years, I have been concentrating on merging the fields of animation and sculpture, thus taking animations to the real world and cutting their digital roots. This also required a new approach: the idea that stable objects are really moving when taking into account the two components time and position. To visualize this idea is my objective. Other projects deal with the combination of sound structures to form an installation, with different types of sounds and their harmonic and dis-harmonic elements playing together and becoming some sort of three-dimensional object.

136-143

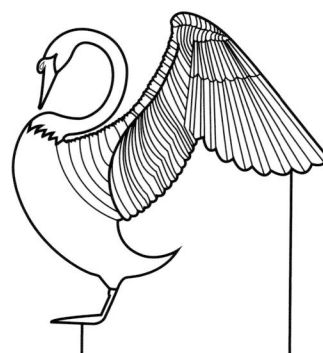

Michael Lomax

www.mjlomax.co.uk

UK based Michael Lomax is a paper cutting artist creating highly detailed works largely based around fairy tales and folklore.

144-149

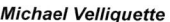

Michael Velliquette

www.velliquette.com

MICHAEL VELLIQUETTE (b. 1971 USA) is a mixed media artist known for his work with paper. He is represented by DCKT Contemporary (New York), David Shelton Gallery (San Antonio), and Blythe Projects (Los Angeles). His museum exhibitions include Slash: Paper Under the Knife at the Museum of Art and Design New York, Art on Paper at the Weatherspoon Art Museum, and Psychedelic at the San Antonio Museum of Art. His work is in the collections of The Progressive Corporation, The John Michael Kohler Art Center, and the San Antonio Museum of Art. He lives in Madison, Wisconsin USA.

150-159

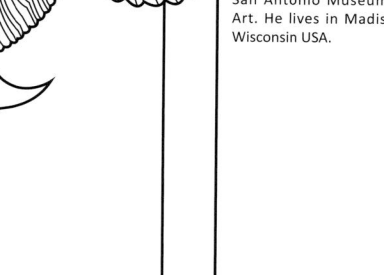

Nathalie Boutté

www.nathalieboutte.com

Nathalie Boutté was born in 1967, she lives and works in Montreuil, near Paris, France.

For over 20 years she has worked at the various stages of production in traditional paper-based publishing and in doing so acquired an in-depth knowledge of paper-based production work. Nathalie has been a freelance graphic and web designer since 2007 but she has always remained in manual contact with paper. It is paper that has been the basis of her works since she started creating in 2009.

Nathalie is neither a photographer nor a sculptor nor a painter, her collages are all of these things. Her creations are derived from her knowledge of paper and volumes. She cuts long narrow strips of paper that she patiently assembles, one by one thus creating a feather effect which constantly evolves. She uses colour and greys as well as tracing paper and sometimes she mixes Indian ink or gold sheets with the paper to create an even more varied effect.

Nathalie is self-taught, she has no specialist degree or training, what she knows she has taught herself through passion. She is not opposed to formal training, but she believes that the key to knowledge has always resided in the practical side of experimenting with materials. Her creations are always a beginning of something new, her technique is forever being enriched and improved. There is no certainty with her, no one truth, but there is always another experience, another achievement.

160-163

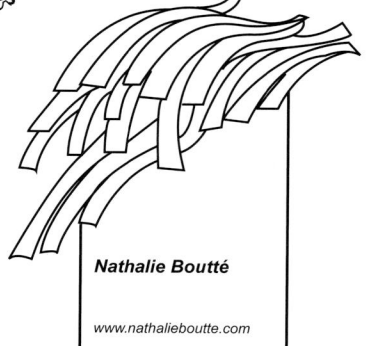

Peter Gentenaar

www.gentenaar-torley.nl

Paper has a memory according to Peter Gentenaar. A sheet of paper keeps and always returns to the form it first was made and dried in. The fact that most paper is made flat doesn't mean that paper, which has dried up in a 3-dimensional shape, will not be strong in that shape. The memory of paper goes back to its former plant life. It is this knowledge about paper, which Gentenaar uses in his sculptures.

164-171

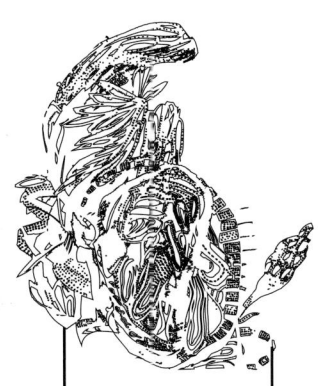

Simone Lourenço

www.simonelourenco.com

Simone Lourenco was born in 1974 in Rio de Janeiro, Brazil. She begun making art as a printmaker, specializing in monotypes and has since transitioned to making three-dimensional works and drawings. Simone works primarily with paper and creates multi-layered, labor intensive pieces with attention to detail. Her favorite subject is nature and its patterns, and how it often mirrors human life.

Her work has been widely exhibited in solo and group shows nationally and internationally. Exhibits include the Vincent Price Museum, CA; The Wignall Museum of Contemporary Art, CA; Scope New York; Pelham Art Center, NY; and the Prague Fringe Festival, Czech Republic. She was also a recipient of the Wall Street Gallery award from the Arts Connecticut 52nd Juried show, curated by Joaquim Pissarro. Simone lives and works in New York, New York.

172-175

Tahiti Pehrson

www.tahitipehrson.com

Tahiti Pehrson is a self taught artist working in hand-cut paper for over a decade. Living in Northern California with deep roots in the Bay Area. Pehrson continues to create prolific and ambitious bodies of work.

176-179

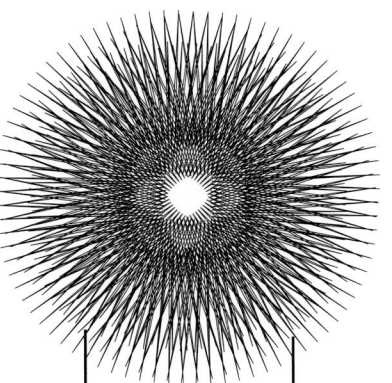

Valérie Buess

www.valeriebuess.com

Valérie Buess was born in Switzerland and is now based in Germany.

Experimenting with all kind of paper for over 20 years. Participating in many international juried exhibition all over the world.

180-193

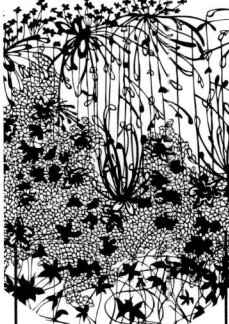

Vanessa Alarie

www.behance.net/ vanessaalarie

Vanessa Alarie was born in Sherbrooke (Quebec, Canada). She completed a Bachelor in arts at the University of Quebec in Outaouais, a Master in museum studies at the Montreal University and she begins a PhD in 2012. Greatly inspired by the nature surrounding her, Vanessa cuts her paper combining brittleness, gentleness and meditation.

194-203

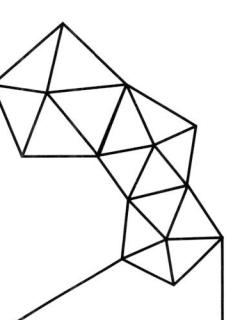

Amila Hrustic

www.amila.ba

Amila Hrustic (1987) Sarajevo, Bosnia and Herzegovina. Works mainly as graphic and product designer, but is also very active as a VJ. Her work appears regulary in different magazines, books and exhibitions around the globe. As a VJ, she explores and promotes aesthetic of analogue and digital artefacts and glitches. Amila is also contributing and wiritng for nonprofit SUB magazine which is focused on underground and sub culture and art.

206-207

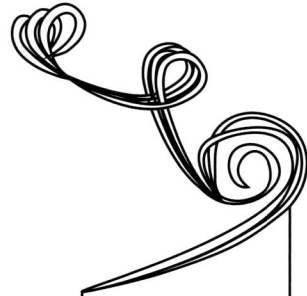

Amy Flurry and Nikki Nye

www.paper-cut-project.com

Paper-Cut-Project is a design collaboration by Amy Flurry and Nikki Nye that realizes a shared love of fashion and the fantasy in storytelling using expressive paper cutouts. The Atlanta-based duo make exquisite shapes in paper as an antidote to the ubiquity of mass-production in fashion, signaling an allegiance to hands-on design at the intersection of art and fashion.

The first installation in 2010 was a collection of wigs for Jeffrey New York and their three-dimensional sculptures have since been commissioned by Hermes, Christies, Cartier, Kate Spade, The Bay and featured in international publications including Italian Vogue.

208-215

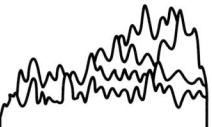

Andrew Bradford

www.be.net/W-I-P

I am a designer from the North East of England. My passions reside in the bosom of design and within that sphere my interests are broad and I enjoy all sides of the creative spectrum from character design to typography, Web Design to illustration, print to interactive and everything in-between.

216-217

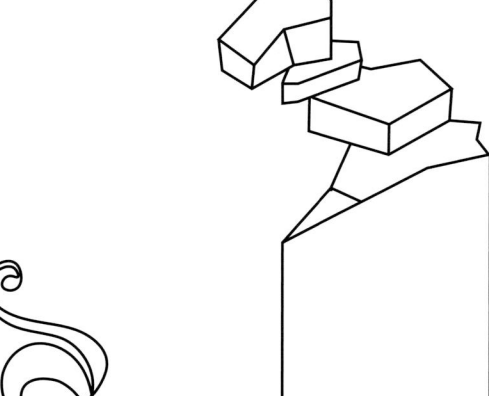

Andy Singleton

www.andysingleton.co.uk

Andy Singleton is a paper artist and illustrator based in Wakefield, England. He Studied Animation with illustration at Manchester Metropolitan University, graduating in 2006. His work is an exploration of the natural and manmade world through intricate paper cuttings, paper sculpture and hand drawn illustrations. Andy believes a hands on, pragmatic approach to producing work is the best way to fully realise the potential of new ideas. The crafting of an object to a high standard is an essenstial part of singletons practice. Andy currently works on commercial and personal projects from his studio in Wakefield, England.

218-229

Anna Härlin

www.annahaerlin.de

Anna Härlin is a Berlin based multidisciplinary freelance designer. Her work includes projects for miscellaneous public and private clients on a variety of national and international projects including conception, art direction, typography, design, illustration and interactive design. Clients are CUT magazine, Etsy, Fuenfwerken Design AG, Nordsonne Identity GmbH, MetaDesign, etc.

230-233

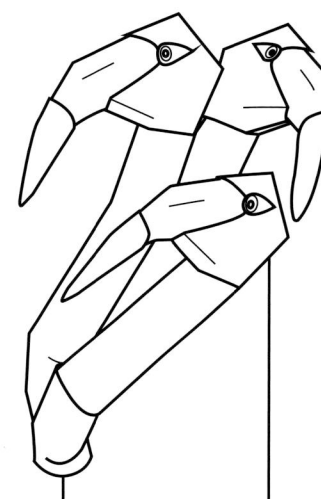

Benja Harney

www.paperform.com.au

I'm a self-taught Paper Engineer living and working in Sydney, Australia. Paper is my passion…I love the contradictions: strong/delicate_complex/simple.

Through my business, Paperform, I have been dedicated to engineering high-end pop-up books and crisp paper constructions professionally for 6 years now spanning a variety of applications: fine art, advertising, magazine illustration, fashion and packaging. Paper is such a humble medium to work with. It inspires and challenges me every time I sit down at my cutting mat. I strive for creativity and perfection in every project I undertake. I hope you enjoy my work.

234-247

Brian Li Sui Fong

www.studiotoki.ca

Kyosuke Nishida, Brian Li Sui Fong and Dominic Liu are designers based in Montréal and Toronto. They have worked together on several installation-based as well as commercial work and continue to collaborate, having graduated from the same university in Montréal Canada.

248-249

Chan Hwee Chong

www.behance.net/ Hweechong

Chan Hwee Chong is a Singaporean artist who loves experimenting with different fields of art and design to create street installations, typography, art direction and graphic design. His works have been recognised in many international award shows, exhibitions and publications. He currently works as an advertising creative director in China's cultural capital, Beijing.

250-253

Christian Tagliavini

www.christiantagliavini.com

Swiss-Italian, born in 1971, educated in Italy and Switzerland, where he lives and works as photographer. This provides him the perfect frame and background to invent, create and totally produce images that blend fine arts and craftsmanship. No, not simply images, as Christian Tagliavini loves designing stories with open endings (requiring observer's complicity) on unexplored themes or unusual concepts, featuring uncommon people with their lives and their thoughts made visible. This rich and exciting collision of circumstances results in photos as a final product.

254-257

CoupleOf

coupleof@coupleof.co.il
CoupleOf | Facebook

CoupleOf shoe brand was established in 2000 by designer couple; Shelly & Elon Satat-Kombor. The brand name originated from the many aspects of the designers collaboration; life and work as a couple, the intrinsic aspect of shoes, which come in pairs, and an interpretation of the term "one-off" as an expression of singularity and uniqueness.

CoupleOf shoes consist of a studio and 3 stores in Israel and are sold worldwide; at the well known 'Anthropologie' stores in the US and UK, as well as in boutiques in Europe. Recently the Brand received the Annual Design Award by the Ministry of Culture, Israel.

258-261

Davy & Kristin McGuire

www.davyandkristinmcguire.com

Davy & Kristin are an award winning director/designer duo whose projects range from music videos, commercials, animation films and installations to live theatre shows, dance performances, video projections and everything in between. They created The Icebook and directed, designed and performed a critically acclaimed stage adaptation of Howl's Moving Castle at the Southwark Playhouse in London. Their clients' list includes Cirque du Soleil, Microsoft Advertising, Canal+, NHK, Royal Shakespeare Company, The Guillemots, Partizan and others.

262-269

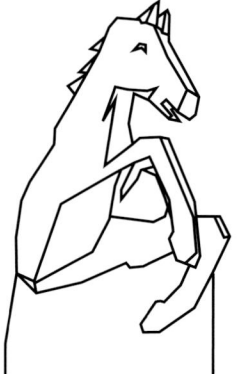
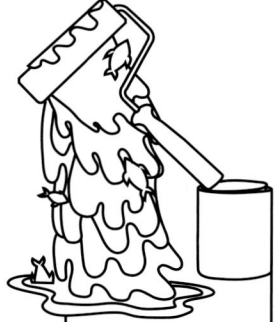
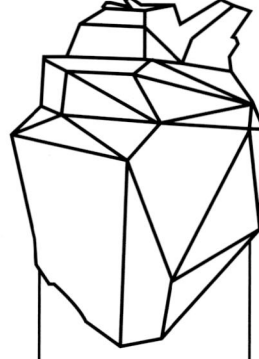
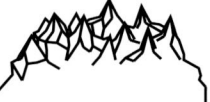

Eiko Ojala

www.ploom.tv

Eiko Ojala is freelance illustrator living in Estonia. He's illustrations are minimal colorful in paper-cut style. He likes how lights and shodows put motion into his illustrations and make it more living.

270-275

Fideli Sundqvist

www.fidelisundqvist.com

Fideli Sundqvist was born in the end of November 1987 in Uppsala, Sweden. She has been living in Stockholm since six years ago. In the spring of 2011 she took her degree from Konstfack, the University College of Arts, Crafts and Design, the education Graphic Design and Illustration. Since fall 2011, she is represented by Agent Molly & Co. Fideli Sundqvist is a papercut artist, illustrator and designer. Most of all she works with paper, including both two-dimensional and three-dimensional objects. She creates anything, from build abstracts, geometric shapes to constructed worlds and imaginary visions of reality. Fideli thinks that there is nothing as fun as working with her hands and cut the paper and figure out and tell stories and convey moods into paper or depict real things. There are endless of possibilities.

276-287

Foamagency

www.foamagency.com

FOAM is a branded content agency. We conceptualise and produce brilliant, talked–about content. We work in the medium that's best for the idea. We're experts in digital, film, print and events.

FOAM started within a global entertainment company. We're the perfect choice to develop that innovative music strategy you've been looking for – and we can partner you with some of the worlds leading recording artists. We've built a reputation as award winning innovators in creative content. We've created hugely successful and highly targeted earned media content for our clients.

All our work is based on detailed audience insight and our own creative methodology that's given us and our clients a fantastic success rate.

288-289

Happycentro

www.happycentro.it

The studio began in 1998 in Verona, the romantic city of Romeo and Juliet. In recent years we have worked with both large and small clients, for local agencies and major international companies. Our approach to design is always the same: designing a logo, an advertising page, a wall or directing a commercial offers the same opportunity to deal with a problem.

With time we have become quite good at solving problems. Mixing complexity, order and fatigue is our formula for beauty. Always, in addition to the commissioned work, we spend plenty of energy in research and testing. Visual art, typography, graphic design, illustration, animation, film direction and music. We like contamination between creative disciplines and diversity in general. We don't like to do the same thing twice and prefer to go beyond what we are already able to do. It is tiring but satisfied.

290-297

Hattie Newman

www.hattienewman.co.uk

Originally from beautiful West Devon countryside, Hattie studied Illustration at UWE, Bristol in the UK. After graduating with a first class degree, she now lives and works in London as an Image Maker and Set Designer. Combining her two and three dimensional imaginations, she loves making work inspired by all things charming and strange and has a particular passion for paper! She's worked on a breadth of projects including installations, animations, children's books and advertising campaigns. Clients include Sony, Honda, P&G, The Guardian, Macmillan Publishers, Cadbury and The Times.

298-299

Jeff Nishinaka

www.jeffnishinaka.com

Los Angeles native Jeff Nishinaka is the world's premier paper sculptor with a prolific career that spans 30 years. Nishinaka attended UCLA and graduated from the prestigious Art Center College of Design, where he first experimented with paper art and sculpture. Nishinaka's commercial portfolio includes Bloomingdale's, Galeries Lafayette, Sprint, The Peninsula Hotel, Visa, Penn State University, Paramount Pictures and Coca Cola, among others. Actor Jackie Chan, who is a close friend of the artist, owns the largest collection of Nishinaka's work. Nishinaka began working in paper quite by accident. "I have always wanted to be a painter, but while studying illustration at Art Center, I was given assignments in both a graphic design and fashion drawing class at the same time to experiment in different mediums, one of them being paper. That was my 'Ah-ha!' moment. I quickly developed a feel for working with paper. From then on, I began experimenting with different papers, finding ways to shape, bend, and round edges on it. I wanted to manipulate paper in the least invasive way, to keep the integrity and feel of it. Paper to me is a living, breathing thing that has a life of it's own. I just try to redirect that energy into something that feels animated and alive.

300-315

Julene Harrison

www.madebyjulene.com

Originally a textile designer Julene was made redundant in late 2008 and this changed the path of her creative career. She began making paper cuts as one-off gifts for friends, and realised they were hugely popular. Julene started getting commissions for her designs in May 2009. Since then she has set up a website and blog (madebyjulene.com) to deal with demand, and has created hand-made paper cuts and laser cuts for people all over the world.

The work is primarily text based but portraits and illustrations of all kinds are undertaken, for commercial customers as well as private. She has created paper-cut illustrations for brands such as O2, The Telegraph, Net-A-Porter, Virgin, The Wall St Journal and Nivea.

316-321

Julien Vallée

www.jvallee.com

Julien Vallée is a Montreal based director and designer. Since 2006, Vallée has been working in a broad range of fields including motion design, art direction and installation, creating a body of work mostly revolving around playfulness and experimentation. Along the way, he has been directing handcrafted stop-motion openings for the The New York Times, flying objects for Google, pink explosions for MTV-Hits, cell phone deconstructions for Nokia and celebrating the EURO 2012 for Coca Cola.

322-335

Kyle Bean

www.kylebean.co.uk

Kyle Bean is an Artist and Designer from Brighton specialising in hand made models, sets and tactile illustrations. Since graduating from a degree in Illustration from the University of Brighton in 2009 he has worked for a diverse range of clients on various projects. Kyle has created window displays for luxury brands such as Liberty, Selfridges and Hermes and editorial commissions for publications such as Wallpaper*, Financial Times, VMAN and Wired. Alongside his commercial work, Kyle has produced some personal projects that have gained him international recognition. These projects include 'Mobile Evolution' - a Russian doll style model depicting the miniaturisation of mobile technology, and 'What Came First?' - a sculpture of a chicken made from egg shells. Kyle has exhibited his work in London, at the International Design Biennial in France and most recently became a Young Gun winner at the Art Directors Club in New York.

336-347

LAVA

www.l-a-v-a.net

LAVA was founded by Chris Bosse, Tobias Wallisser and Alexander Rieck.
Chris Bosse is the director of LAVA Asia Pacific, based in Sydney, Australia. Chris is Adjunct Professor and Innovation fellow at the University of Technology, Sydney and lectures worldwide. For a number of years Chris was Associate Architect at PTW Architects in Sydney, completing many projects in China, Vietnam, the Middle-East and Japan. Chris's work on the Watercube swimming center in Beijing received the prestigious Atmosphere Award at the 9th Annual Venice Biennale and Chris was recently recognized as an emerging architect on the world stage by the RIBA London.
Tobias Wallisser and Alexander Rieck are the directors of LAVA Europe and are based in Stuttgart, Germany.
Tobias is Professor of Innovative Construction and Spatial concepts at the State Academy of Fine Arts Stuttgart. For 10 years Tobias was Associate Architect at UN Studio in Amsterdam, completing a series of high profile projects and master plans including the World Trade Center project in New York and the Arnhem Interchange. Tobias was instrumental in the emergence of the recent Stuttgart Mercedes-benz Museum which has attracted worldwide attention for its innovative spatial concept.
Alexander works as a senior researcher at the renowned Fraunhofer Institute in Stuttgart. He studied architecture in Stuttgart and Phoenix and worked for a number of high-profile architects in Germany before joining the field of research. He started his research career in the Virtual Reality environment. Alexander has led many of the Office 21 research projects that produced ground-breaking work in the field of future office organization. He is a renowned expert on innovations in the fields of office, hotel, living and future construction, and an author of many publications about working environments and building processes of the future.

348-355

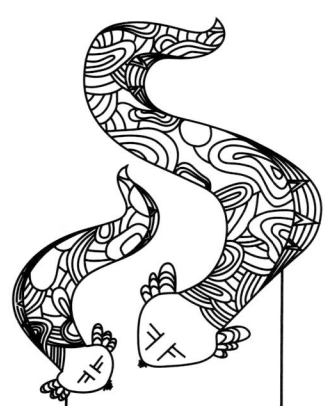

Lavanya Naidoo

www.behance.net/lavanya

Lavanya Naidoo is a 24 year old Visual Communicator based in Cape Town, South Africa. She works in the advertising industry as a below-the-line-designer and experiments with various media on personal projects.

356-357

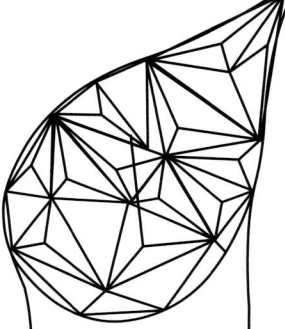

Lim Siang Ching

www.pattern-matters.com

Siang Ching is a Singapore based Graphic Designer/Illustrator. She graduated from Nanyang Academy of Fine Arts with a Diploma in Visual Communication, and a First Class Honors Bachelors in Design Communication from LASALLE College of the Arts. She is the founder of Pattern Matters who finds joy in patterns and everything handmade.

358-363

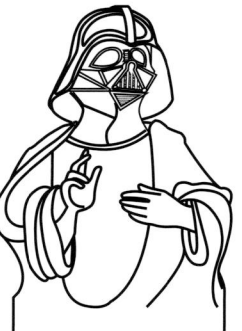

Lobulo Design

www.lobulodesign.com

I realised what I wanted to be when I grew up, while shopping with my mother at the supermarket. I would always make her pick the cereals for the picture on the cover, rather than for what was actually inside. Naturally, I ended up studying graphic design and marketing, learning that there's much more to a computer than just playing pacman.

A variety of unique, creative collaborations, as well as more than 8 years experience of working for various graphic design and marketing studios in Barcelona, have meant that I have filled the streets, and a few hard disks, with my designs, illustrations, editorial projects and concepts. Small or large, formal or informal, but always expressing emotions. Always sending out a message.

364-371

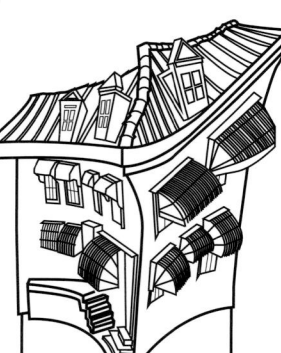

Mandy Smith

www.mandysmithwork.com

Recreating varied elements and worlds through challenging the inherent simplicity of paper, sculptural artist Mandy Smith combines intricate design with a unique craftsmanship.

Taking inspiration from both the fantastical and the every day, she creates magical sculptures for animation, fashion and theater that stir emotions and bring people into a world outside of their own.

372-385

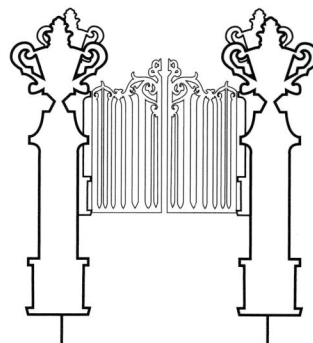

Mathilde Nivet

www.mathildenivet.com

I'm a 29 years old paper designer. During my studies of textile design 8 years ago, I started to work around the theme of mail, letters, which quickly lead me to manipulate paper by using amount of envelopes. I kept on experimenting around during until the end of my studies in 2007. When I started my own business, It became my special touch and expertness.

Working with paper allow me to reach very various sectors and to use different skills. Thus, I do art work, illustrations, scenography, set design, packaging and design products. I use cutting, folding, popup, computing and drawing. I share my time between my computer and mu cutting table. I'll say that my style is feminine, urban, decorative and obsessional.

Neat and precise, fleeting and fragile, ordinary, omnipresent, proximate and efficient. Create set design, offering small universes full of details where the spectator can virtually install himself, have a walk, invent an imaginary life in this world. I like also to realise item with several interpretation levels, whose occur a careful watching to exhaust all the details.

386-399

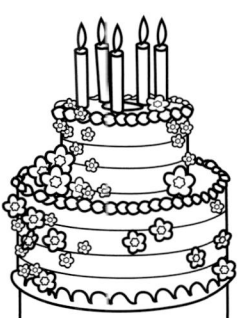

Matthew Sporzynski

www.mcardboard.tumblr.com

Born in Ann Arbor, Michigan in 1967. Attended Parsons School of Design, NYC. Founded Couturier de Cardboard Inc. in 1999. Work has appeared in Town & Country, Vogue, Harper's Bazaar, GQ, and Real Simple. Corporate clients have included The Estée Lauder Companies, Tiffany & Co. The Museum of Modern Art, Christian Dior, Target, Macy's, and Polo Ralph Lauren.

I am a designer and illustrator with a specialization in paper and cardboard. I think of myself as more a craftsman than an artist – I usually work to order and I have been very lucky in the projects my clients have asked me to undertake.
I have always been "crafty". I studied design and began my career before computers were common in the business. I was fortunate to get on-the-job training in Adobe Illustrator as well as to meet great contacts in printing, die-cutting, photography and publishing. I'm creative but pretty literal-minded – better at measuring than drawing.

I support myself doing paper-related projects. Sometimes I get nice messages from people saying they like my work – people I haven't even met.

400-411

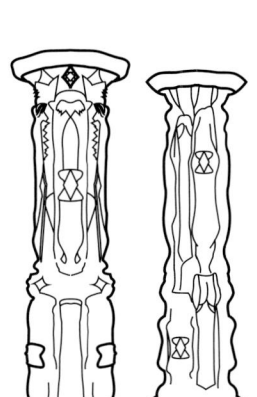

Michael Hansmeyer

www.michael-hansmeyer.com

Michael Hansmeyer is an architect and programmer who explores the use of algorithms and computation to generate architectural form. He is currently based in the CAAD group at ETH's architecture department in Zurich. He holds an MBA degree from Insead Fontainebleau as well as a Master of Architecture degree from Columbia University. He previously worked with McKinsey & Company, J.P. Morgan, and at Herzog & de Meuron architects.

412-417

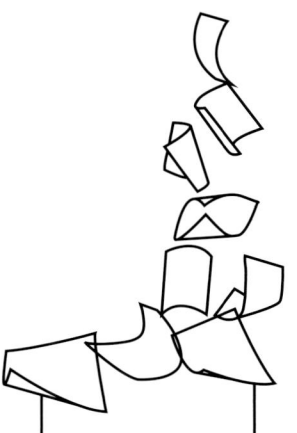

Paul Cocksedge Studio

www.paulcocksedgestudio.com

London based PAUL COCKSEDGE STUDIO is the internationally acclaimed design practice of partners Paul Cocksedge and Joana Pinho. Notable for inhouse design of concepts, installations, public interventions and exclusive interior objects, the Studio explores the limits of technology in order to create unique design experiences. With an interdisciplinary approach and an acute sense of quality, Paul Cocksedge Studio reinvents contemporary design as an event.

The Studio accepts commissions and occasional consultancy work for a wide range of companies and sectors, with a diverse catalogue of high-profile clients encompassing luxury fashion labels, exclusive interiors manufacturers and major cultural institutions. Paul Cocksedge Studio is dedicated to building a sophisticated portfolio of unique pieces and projects of international repute.

418-421

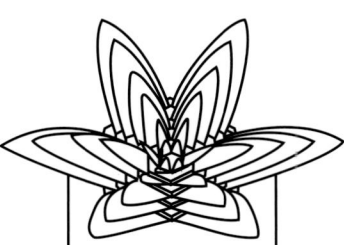

Peter Dahmen

www.peterdahmen.de

The graphic designer Peter Dahmen is specialized in the construction of pop up sculptures. He creates prototypes for serial production as well as unique single pieces. He lives as a self-employed designer in Dortmund/Germany.

422-425

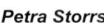

Petra Storrs

www.petrastorrs.com

We work with a wide and international client base to make new and interesting designs and concepts for costumes, props and sets for photo, film and stage. Our designs are often labours of love, from the initial drawing and ideas to the final building and creation.
Our Projects span: Creative/Art direction, Costume & Styling, Set Design, Music Videos/Films, Still life/Editorial.

"Petra Storrs is a surrealistic multi-disciplinary, London-based artist whose acclaimed art direction explores elaborate set, fashion and costume design with a penchant for an otherworldly, wonderland aesthetic through photography. Her work for the likes of Lady Gaga, Paloma Faith and Dazed & Confused magazine evokes the essence of craft with an escapist romanticism. Storrs was recently commissioned to create an augmented reality animation "SkyRise" for the Becks Green Box projects, fusing cheer-leading, architecture and synchronised swimming into a smart phone viewable art exhibition, along with the V&A Museum, and has just been recognised by the Independent Newspaper as one of 15 artists that will define the future of British art."

426-429

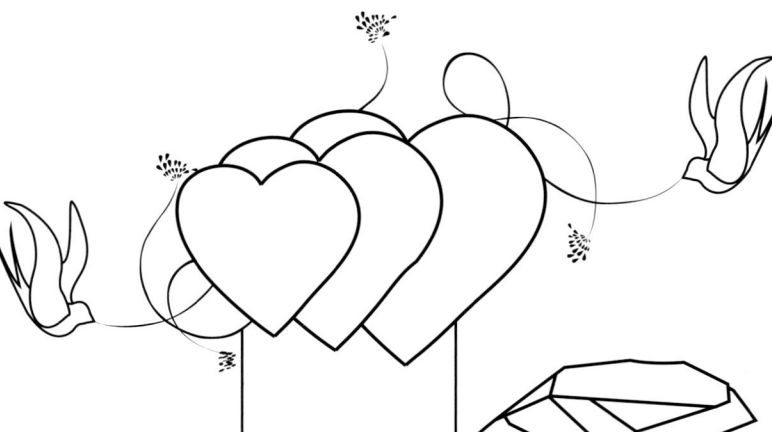
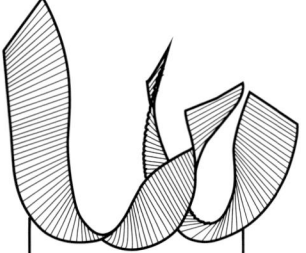
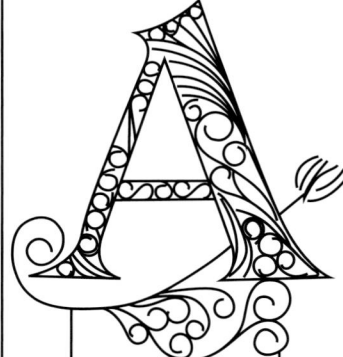
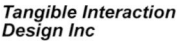
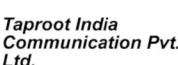

Richard Sweeney

www.richardsweeney.co.uk

Richard Sweeney was born in Huddersfield, England in 1984. He discovered a natural talent for sculpture at Batley School of Art and Design in 2002, which led him to the study of Three Dimensional Design at the Manchester Metropolitan University, where he concentrated on the hands-on manipulation of paper to create design models, which ultimately developed into sculptural pieces in their own right.

Richard's practice combines the disciplines of design, photography, craft and sculpture, resulting in a varied output of work including graphic design and public sculpture commissions. Combining hand-craft with computer aided design and CNC manufacturing techniques, Richard seeks to maintain an experimental, hand-on approach, utilising the unique properties of often mundane materials to discover unique sculptural forms. He has lectured at the University of Applied Arts, Vienna as part of the Sliver architecture lecture series 2009 and is a regular guest lecturer at the graphic design department at Sheffield Hallum University.
Richard is represented by Victor Felix Gallery, London.

430-435

Sabeena Karnik

www.be.net/sabeenu

The typography Designer is Sabeena Karnik. She resides in Mumbai, India and is a calligrapher and illustrator. She has specialized in paper typography.

Each letter was designed with inspiration from the jewellery, hence there was a small element of the jewel in each alphabet.

436-441

Shotopop

www.Shotopop.com

SHOTOPOP is a devout team of visual zealots who pride ourselves on conjuring the new, the unimagined and the fantastical. In our offices, furiously snipping silver scissors give birth to a thousand paper feathers, crazy caffeine dreams turn into flashing pixel rainbows and the most ambitious flights of fancy, become our proudest moments.

We've got micro brewery beer in the fridge, Cannes Lions in the window, Broadway market down the road and our very own surprise blend of coffee every day. So feel free to contact us with any kind of project or pop round for a chat. We'll even let you stroke our skull-in-a-jar.

442-449

Tangible Interaction Design Inc

www.tangibleinteraction.com

Tangible Interaction creates full-on sensory experiences people can interact with in the everyday physical world. Using leading-edge digital technologies, Tangible transforms ordinary spaces like sidewalks, retail spaces and concert venues into inspiring interactive environments people walk through, explore with their hands, or simply stand back and watch in amazement.

Founded by Alex Beim, Tangible takes design beyond the confines of print and digital, creating real world experiences people can interact with directly. Exploration, play, and entertainment are the focus of Tangible's projects, which are developed by a team of experts who unite graphic and structural design, programming, electronics engineering, music, lighting, architecture and production.

450-453

Taproot India Communication Pvt. Ltd.

www.taprootindia.co.in

Taproot India Communications Pvt. Ltd. established by Agnello Dias and Santosh Padhi, only recently opened its doors in 2009. In 2010, Taproot was ranked amongst the World's Top 20 Independent Agencies by Cannes Lions International Festival of Creativity, was the Best Performing Indian Agency at the Clio Awards and also led the race at Spikes Asia by bagging 7 metals. In 2011, Taproot entered into the rosters of multinationals such as PepsiCo giving them the most talked about campaigns of 2011 – 'Change the Game,' which went on to win the Grand Effie award. In 2012, Taproot bagged the title of the 2nd highest awarded agency at the Abby's. Needless to say, Taproot India has an unparalleled reputation for cutting-edge creative capability.

454-455

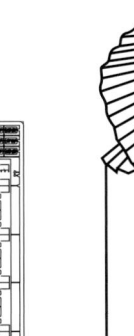

TERADA MOKEI

http://www.terada.mokei.jp/en/

TERADA MOKEI was established with a view to exploring the potential for modeling, which is created by scaling things down and giving them detail, through models. This reflects our belief that when real items are replaced with models, the latter have an essence of reality, stuffed with dreams, and the potential to become more vibrant -- better word in my opinion than their originals. We also consider it important to enjoy the process of assembling models.

TERADA MOKEI also hopes to convey the fun of assembling models and imagining the same.

456-469

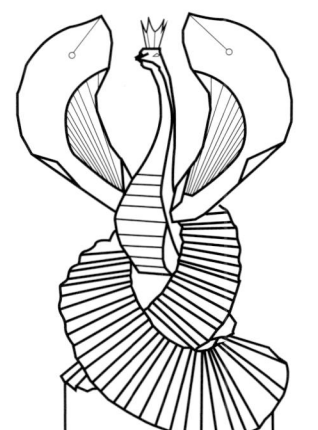

The Makerie Studio

www.themakeriestudio.com

The Makerie Studio are Julie Wilkinson and Joyanne Horscroft, award-winning paper sculpture designers, based in London and Milan. The pair collaborate to produce art pieces for advertising, display and editorial with designs inspired by nature and all things lost.

470-485

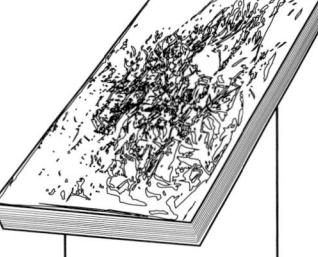

Tímea Andorka

www.andorkatimea.com

I'm a freelance graphic designer since 2009 from Budapest, Hungary. My work finds connections to the world of ideas and creativity – I am designing books, exhibition identities, theatre posters. I am experienced as identity designer and publication designer.

Somehow I prefer hand made objects than products made purely by computer; I am particularly enthusiastic over the possibilities of paper. Nevertheless, I am open for every kind of challenge.

486-491

United Fakes

www.unitedfakes.com

United Fakes is a multidisciplinary team who takes craftsmanship into a media industry level. We are a team of seven people plus two cats. Our names are Albert, Ana, Dario, Omaira, Oriol, Pano and Sergi, the two cats are called Xino and Sophie. We all belong to different working backgrounds ranging from graphics to product design and from photography to web design. In our work, we like to deliver a message that is rich in content and full of detail and we also like to switch roles in every project.

Although we've been working with computers all our lives and as much as we use them daily, we still love to get our hands dirty. United Fakes is fine bunch of people telling stories!

492-493

Zim&Zou

www.zimandzou.fr

Lucie Thomas teamed up with Thibault Zimmermann to form Zim&Zou, a french studio based in Nancy that explores different fields including paper sculpture, installation, graphic design, illustration. Both aged 25, they studied graphic design during 3 years in an artschool. Rather than composing images on a computer, they prefer creating real objects with paper and taking photos out of them. A number of intricate illustrations actually come from the three-dimensional installations made by Zim&Zou. Their choice of paper is due to the versatility and good quality of the material, especially when it is sculpted and photographed. Zim&Zou's strength is to be a complementary and polyvalent duo.

494-511

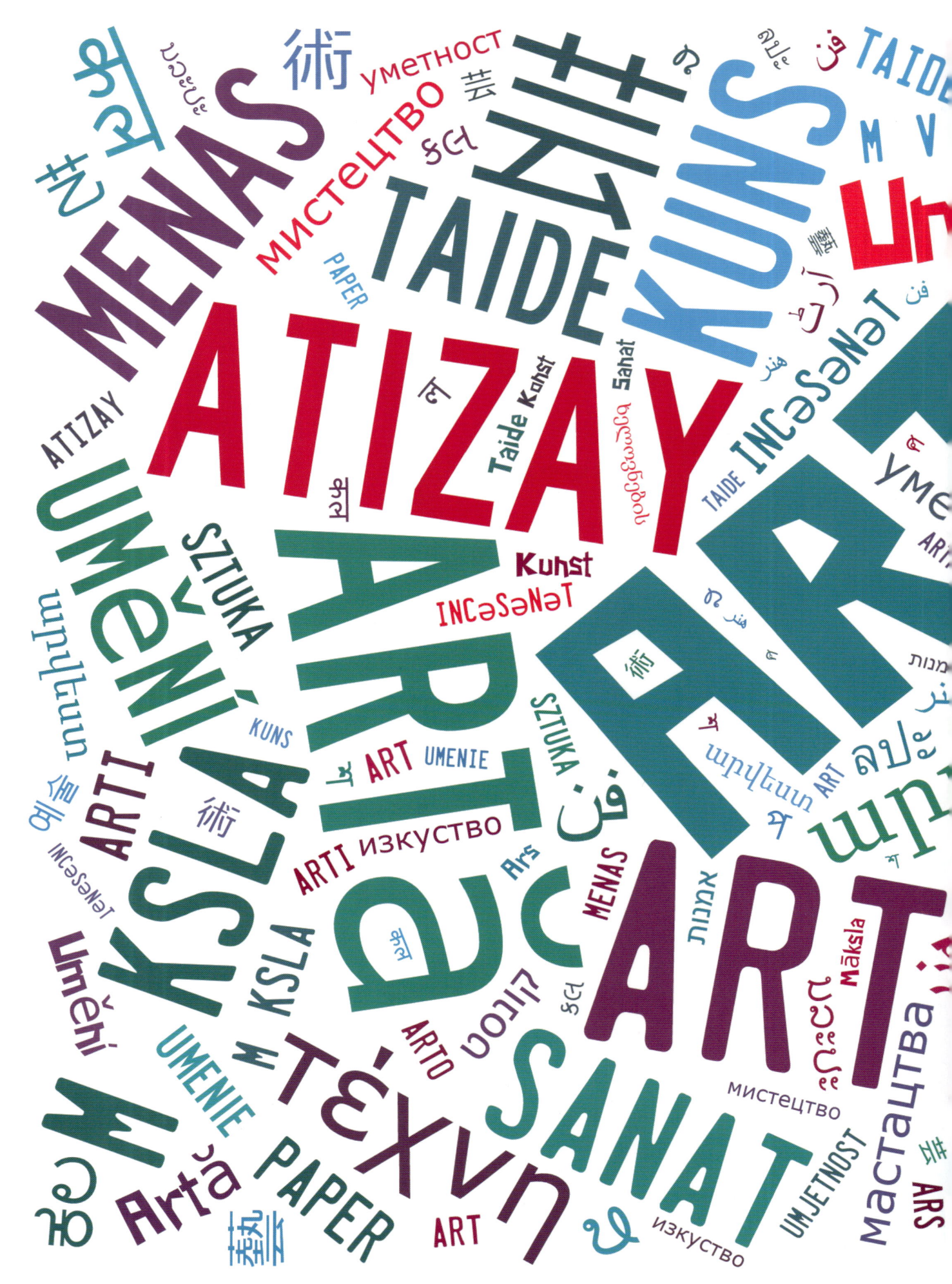

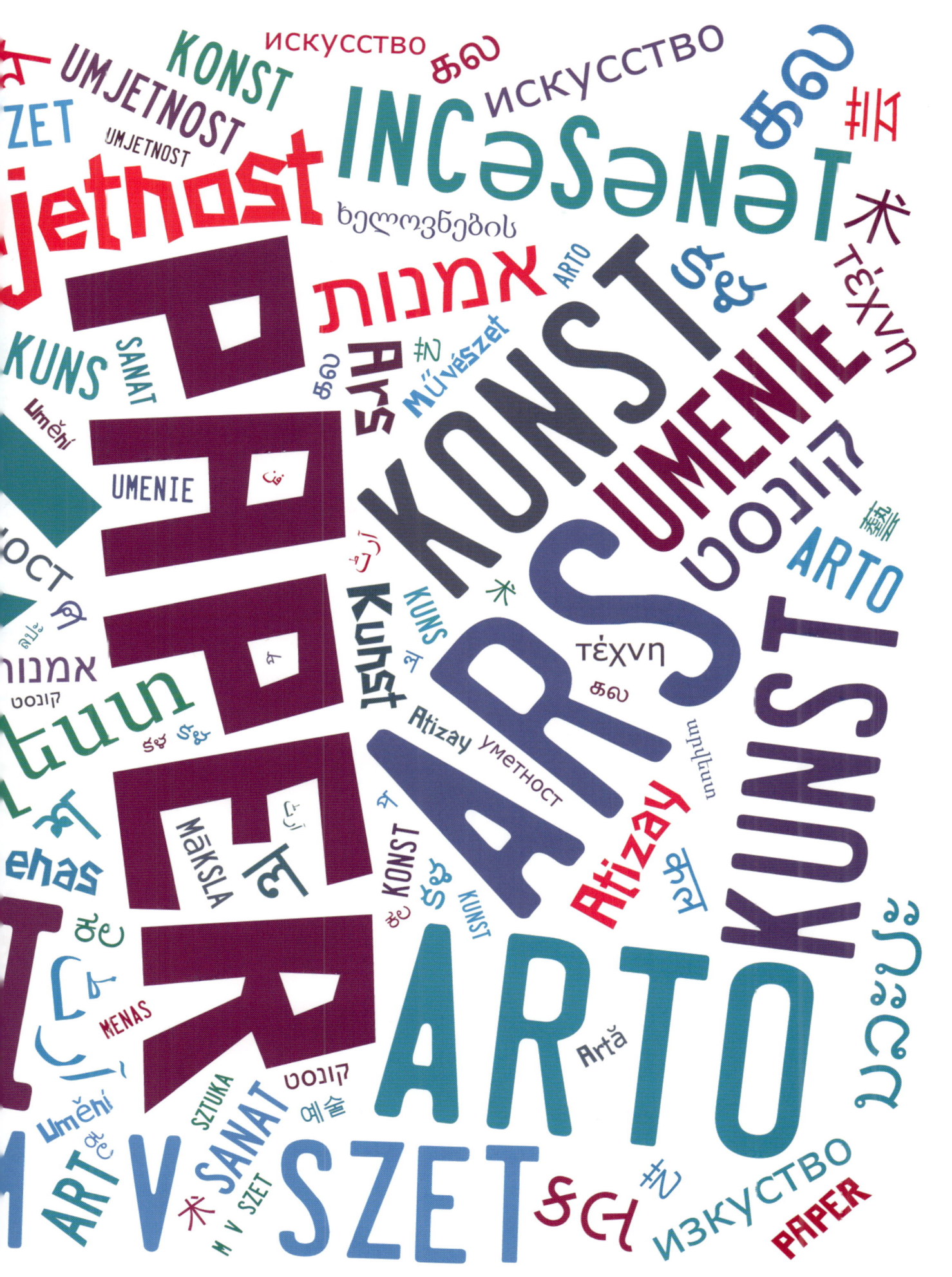

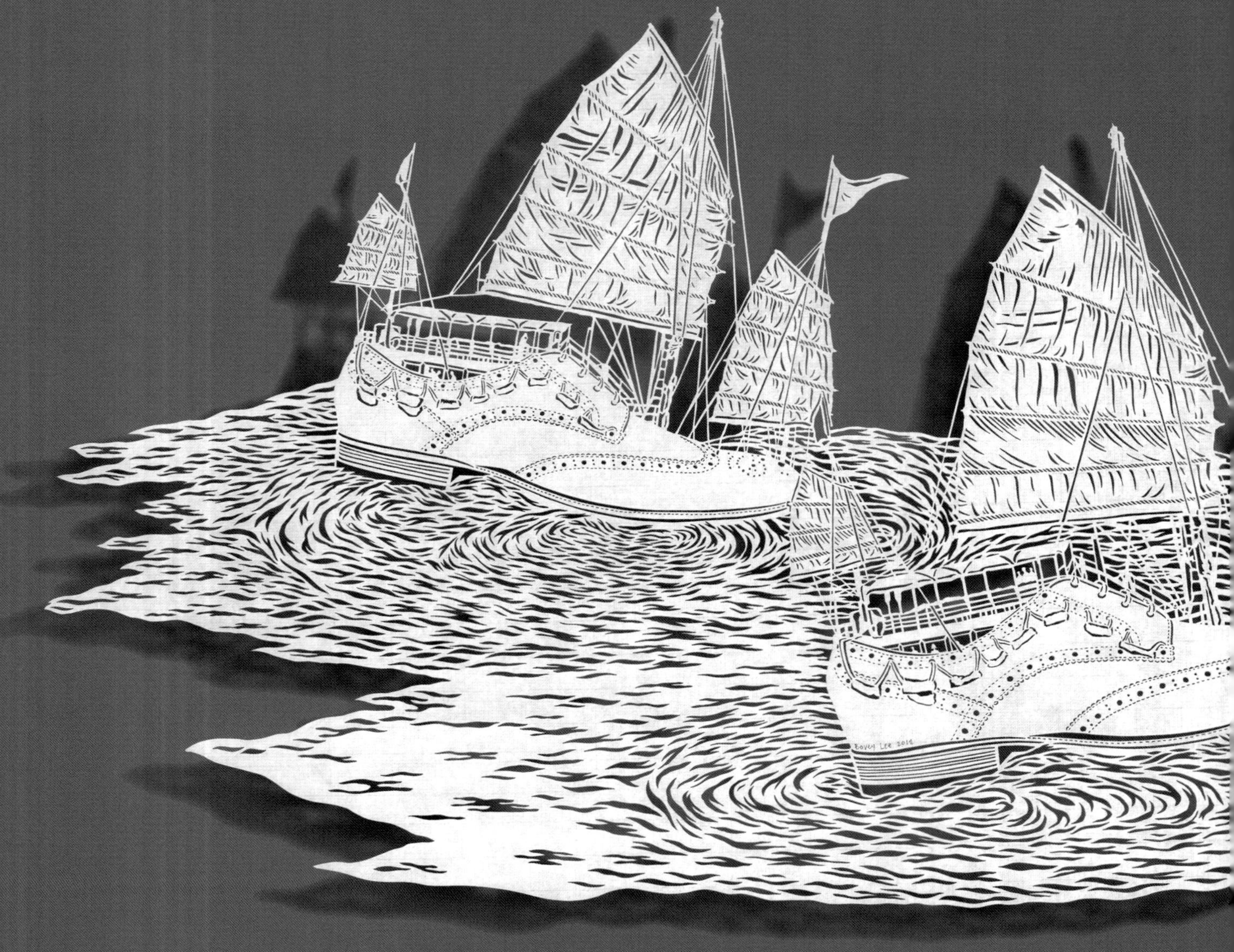

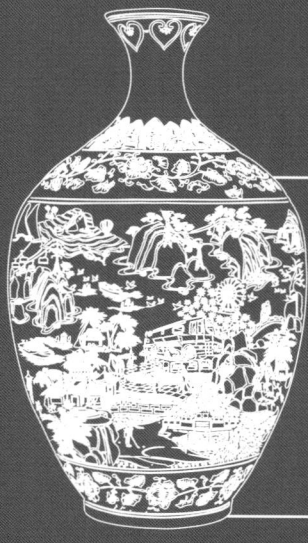

1. Wingtip Voyage
2. In the Same Boat
3. Dragging Cows Up a Tree
4. Pushing Mountains
5. Baking McMansion
6. Vase I
7. Vase II
8. Briefcase Vacation – Spring
9. Briefcase Vacation – Summer
10. Briefcase Vacation – Fall
11. Briefcase Vacation – Winter

—Bovey Lee

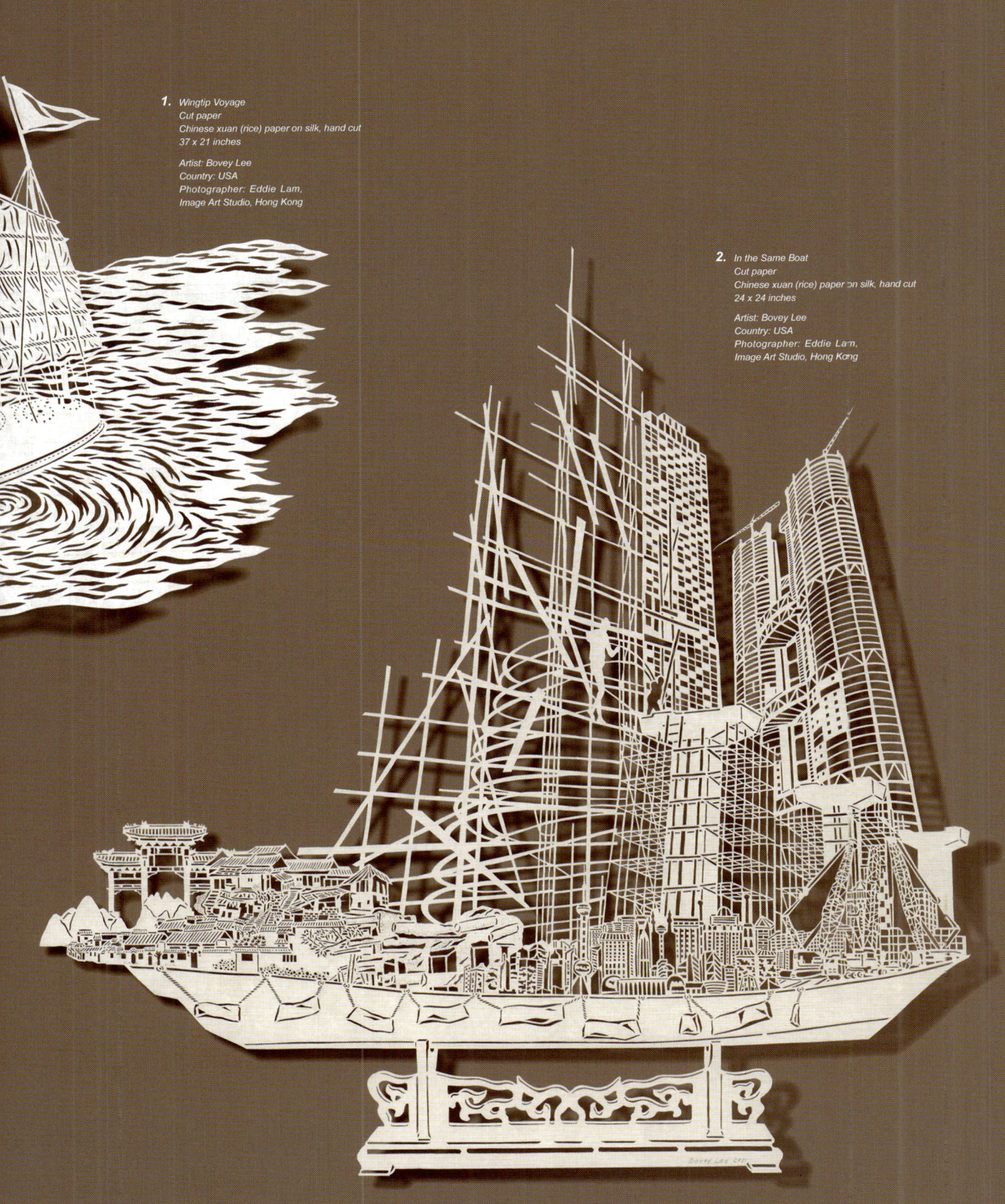

1. Wingtip Voyage
   Cut paper
   Chinese xuan (rice) paper on silk, hand cut
   37 x 21 inches

   Artist: Bovey Lee
   Country: USA
   Photographer: Eddie Lam,
   Image Art Studio, Hong Kong

2. In the Same Boat
   Cut paper
   Chinese xuan (rice) paper on silk, hand cut
   24 x 24 inches

   Artist: Bovey Lee
   Country: USA
   Photographer: Eddie Lam,
   Image Art Studio, Hong Kong

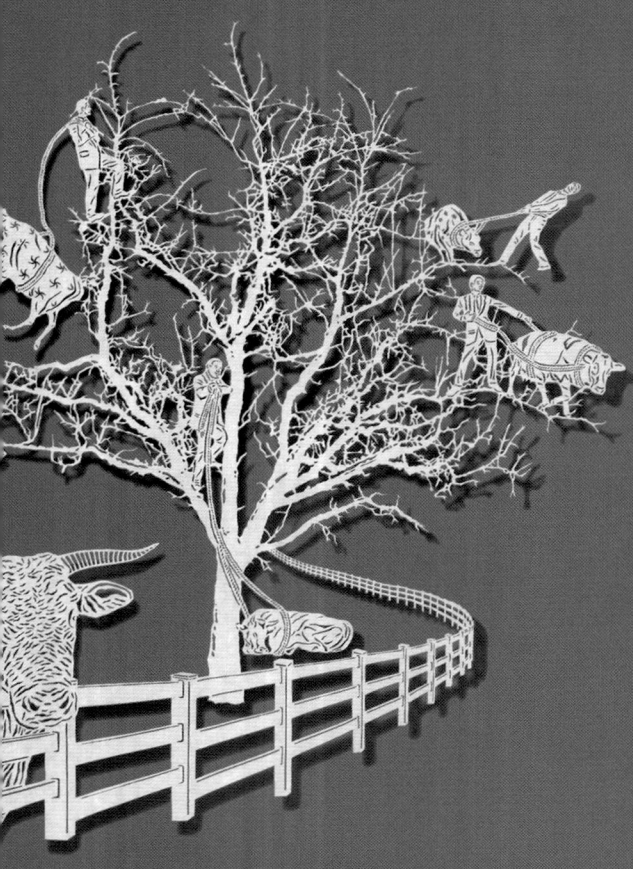

4. Pushing Mountains
Cut paper
Chinese xuan (rice) paper on silk, hand cut
12 x 27 inches

Artist: Bovey Lee
Country: USA
Photographer: Eddie Lam,
Image Art Studio, Hong Kong

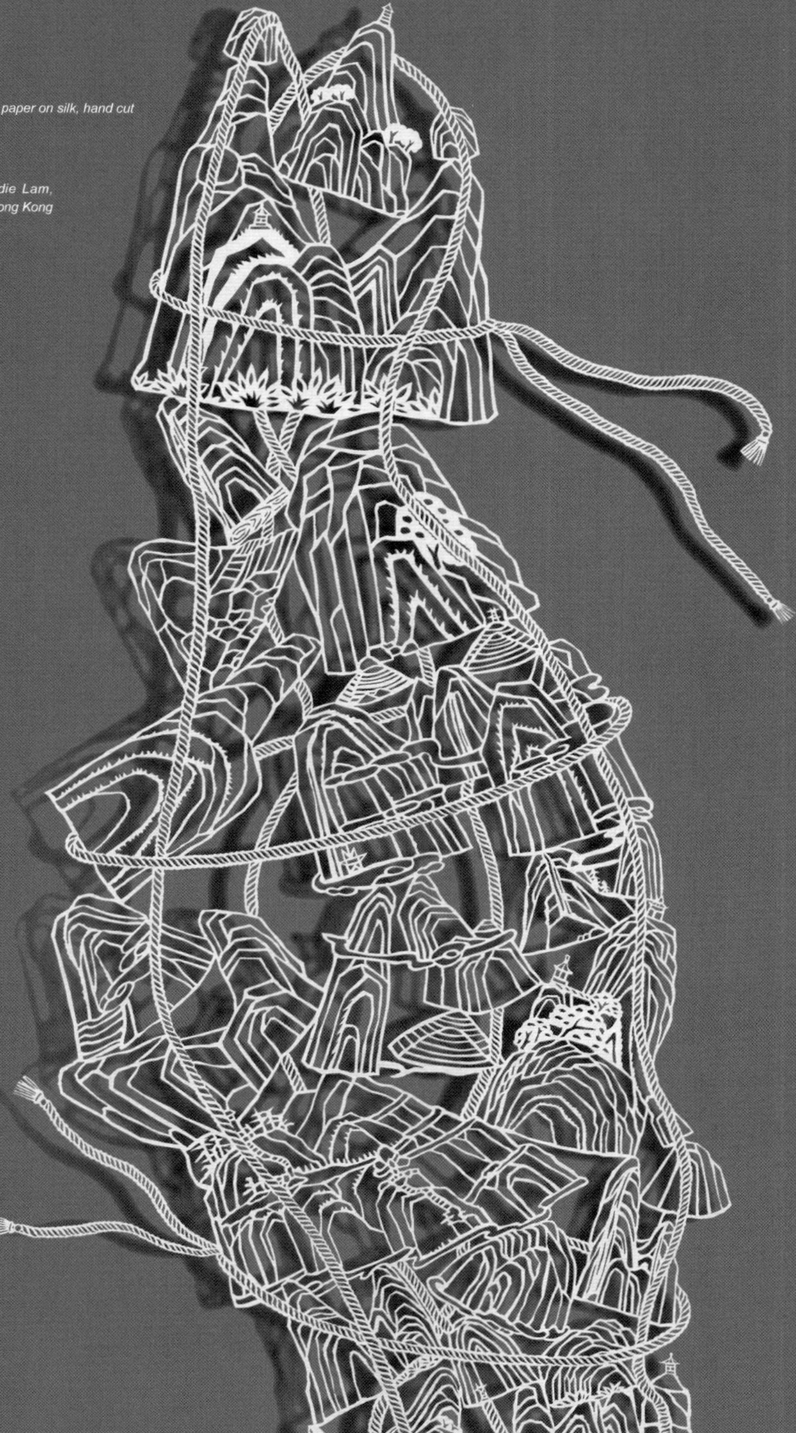

3. Dragging Cows Up a Tree
Cut paper
Chinese xuan (rice) paper on silk, hand cut
16.25 x 21.5 inches

Artist: Bovey Lee
Country: USA
Photographer: Eddie Lam,
Image Art Studio, Hong Kong

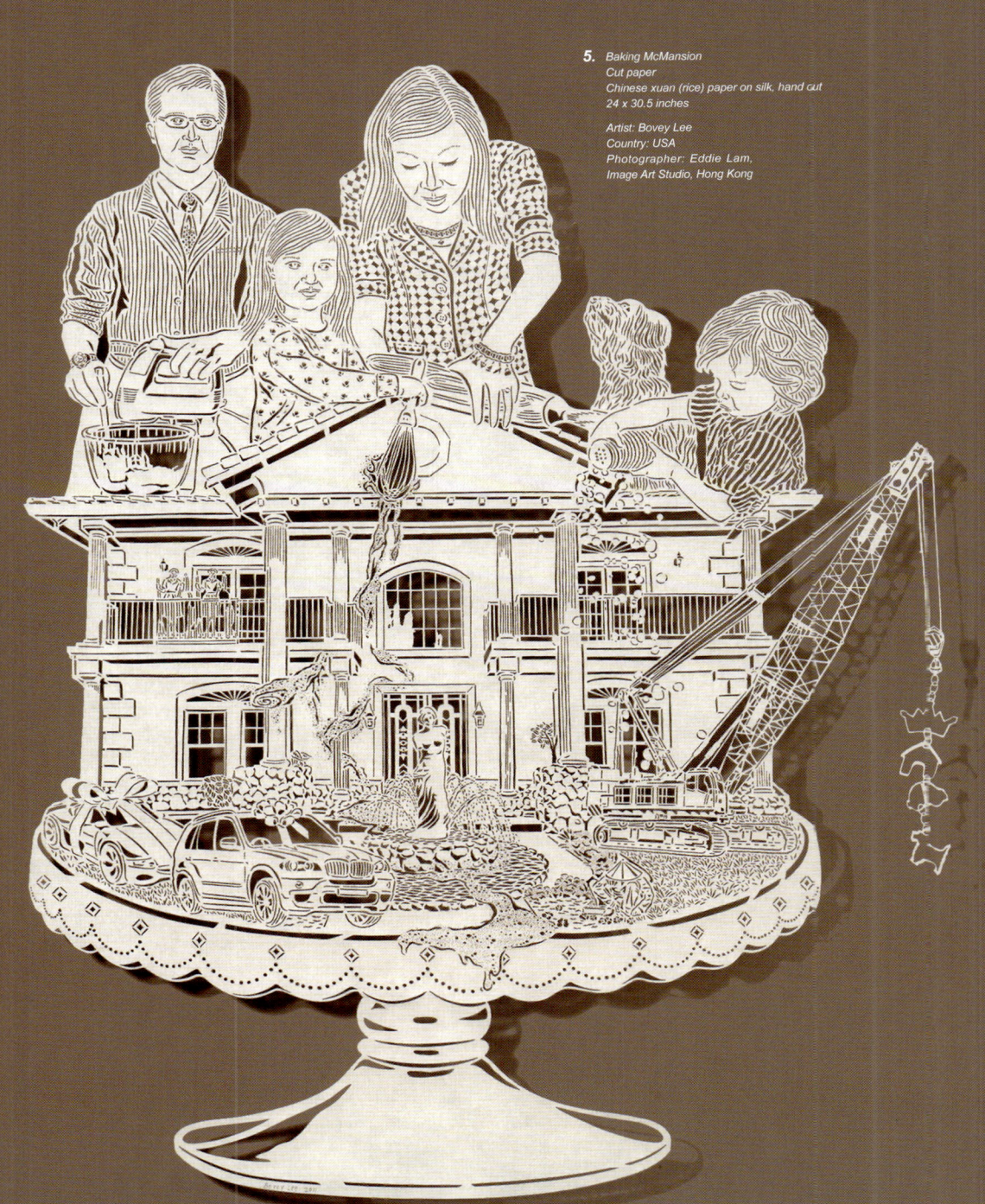

5. Baking McMansion
Cut paper
Chinese xuan (rice) paper on silk, hand cut
24 x 30.5 inches

Artist: Bovey Lee
Country: USA
Photographer: Eddie Lam,
Image Art Studio, Hong Kong

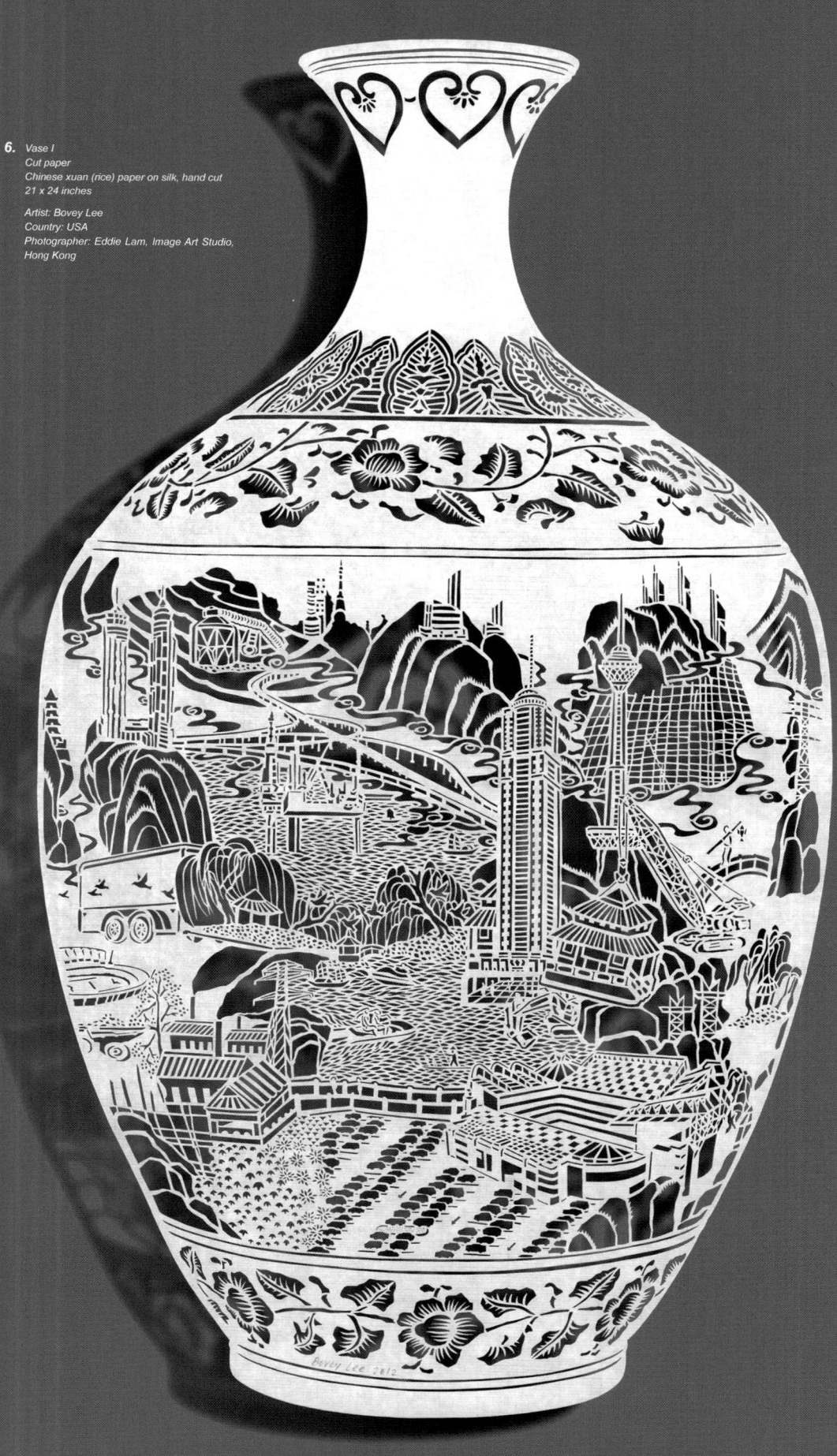

6. Vase I
Cut paper
Chinese xuan (rice) paper on silk, hand cut
21 x 24 inches

Artist: Bovey Lee
Country: USA
Photographer: Eddie Lam, Image Art Studio, Hong Kong

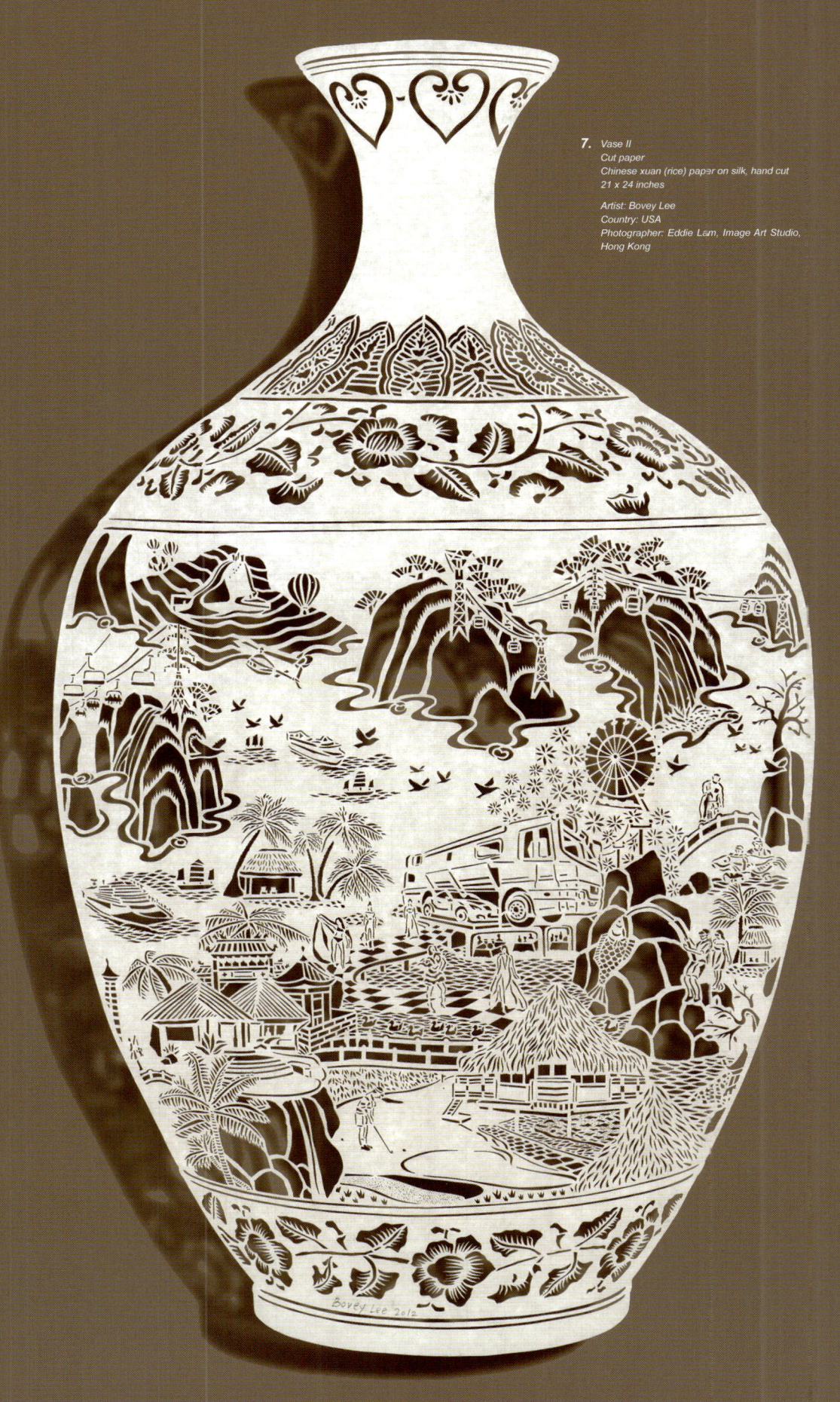

7. Vase II
Cut paper
Chinese xuan (rice) paper on silk, hand cut
21 x 24 inches

Artist: Bovey Lee
Country: USA
Photographer: Eddie Lam, Image Art Studio, Hong Kong

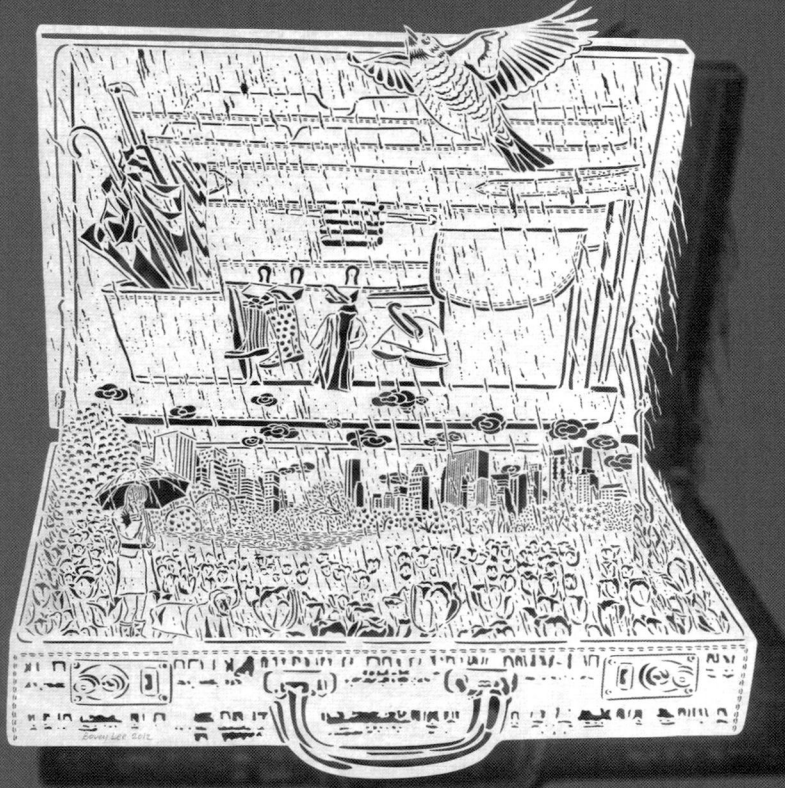

8. *Briefcase Vacation – Spring*
Cut paper
Chinese xuan (rice) paper on silk, hand cut
21.5x21.5 inches

Artist: Bovey Lee
Country: USA
Photographer: Eddie Lam, Image Art Studio, Hong Kong

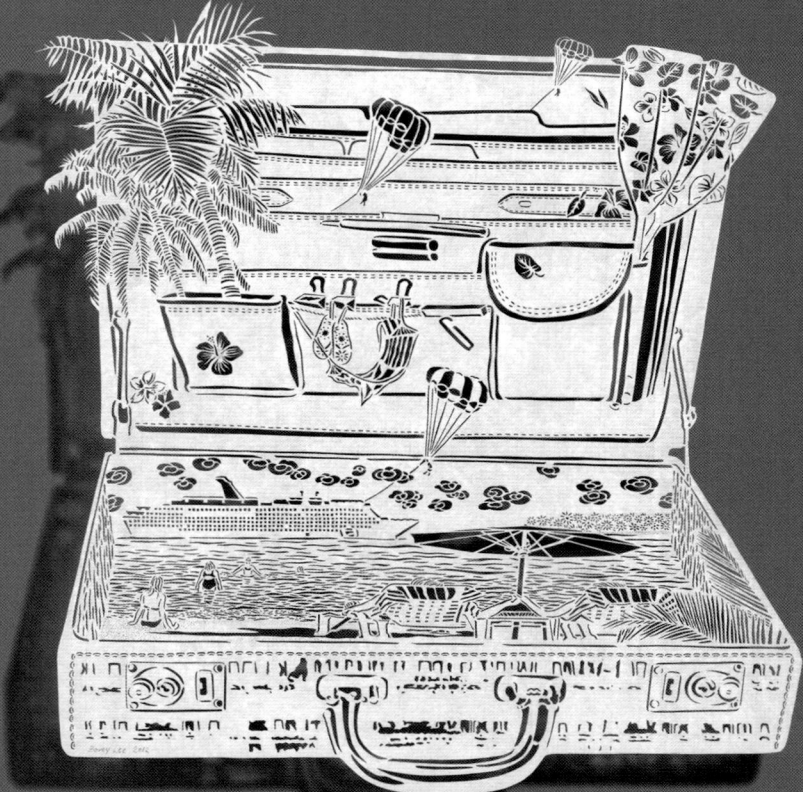

9. *Briefcase Vacation – Summer*
Cut paper
Chinese xuan (rice) paper on silk, hand cut
21.5x21.5 inches

Artist: Bovey Lee
Country: USA
Photographer: Eddie Lam, Image Art Studio, Hong Kong

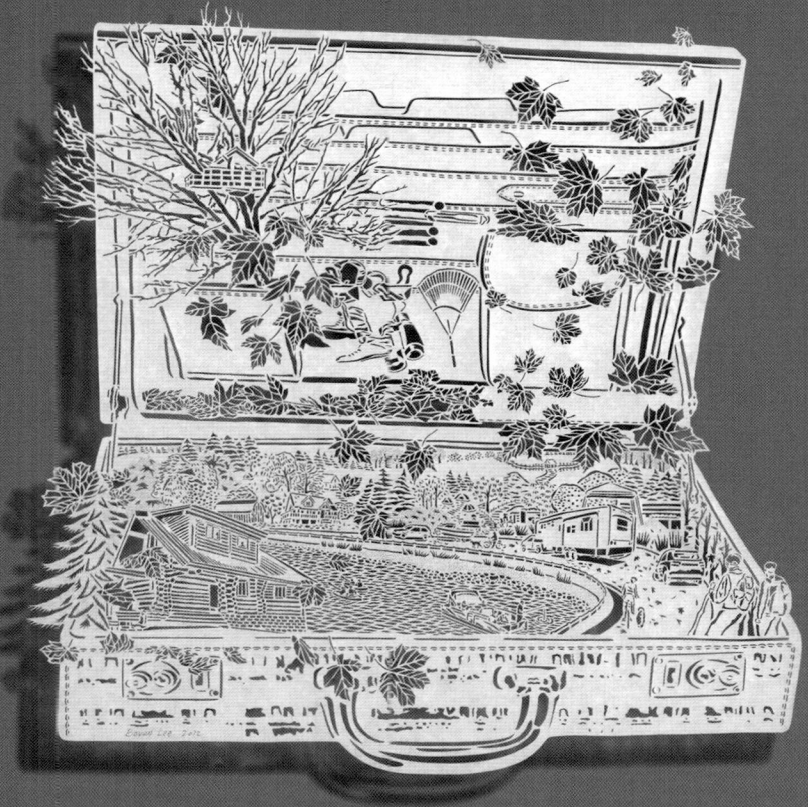

10. Briefcase Vacation – Fall
Cut paper
Chinese xuan (rice) paper or silk, hand cut
21.5x21.5 inches

Artist: Bovey Lee
Country: USA
Photographer: Eddie Lam, Image Art Studio, Hong Kong

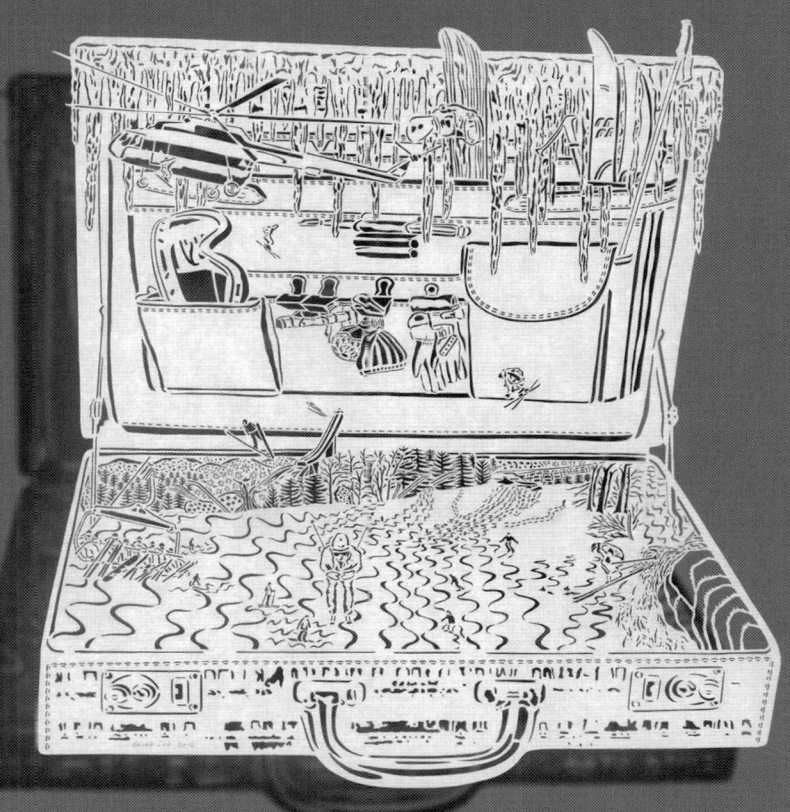

11. Briefcase Vacation – Winter
Cut paper
Chinese xuan (rice) paper on silk, hand cut
21.5x21.5 inches

Artist: Bovey Lee
Country: USA
Photographer: Eddie Lam, Image Art Studio, Hong Kong

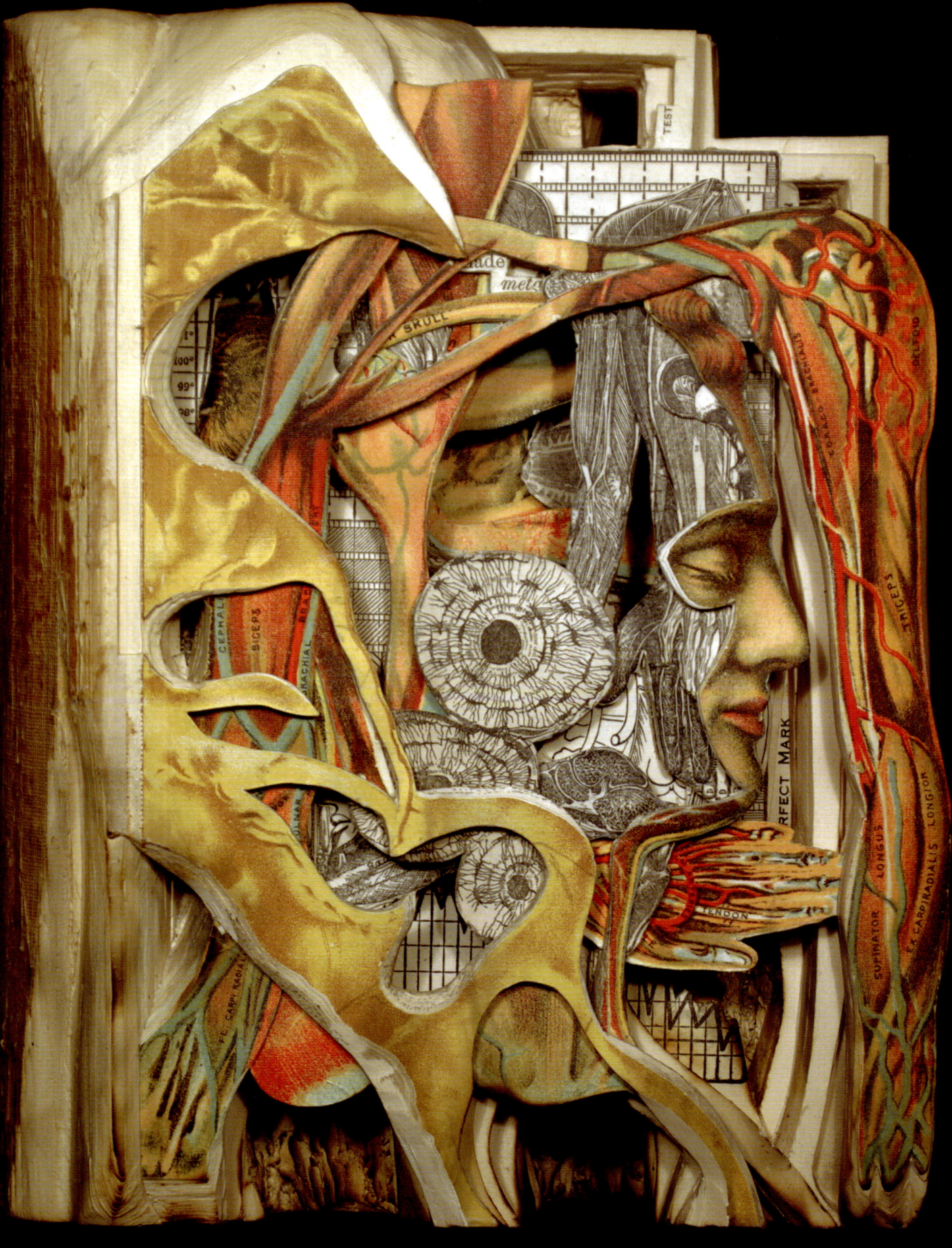

1. **Absolute Authority**
   Hardcover book, acrylic medium, 9-3/4" x 7-3/4" x 4" - Image Courtesy of the Artist and Wexler Gallery
   Artist: Brian Dettmer   Country: USA   Photographer: Brian Dettmer

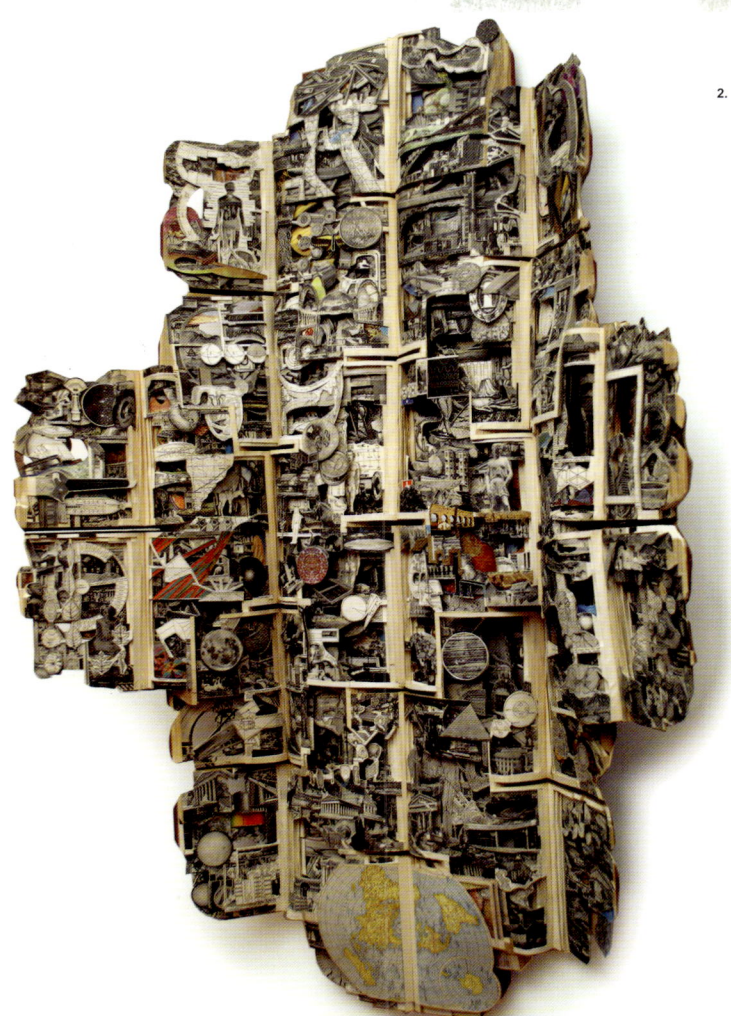

2. American Peoples

Hardcover books, acrylic medium, 61" x 39" x 14" (154 x 100 x 34 cm)
- Image Courtesy of the Artist and Toomey Tourell Fine Art

Artist: Brian Dettmer
Country: USA
Photographer: Brian Dettmer

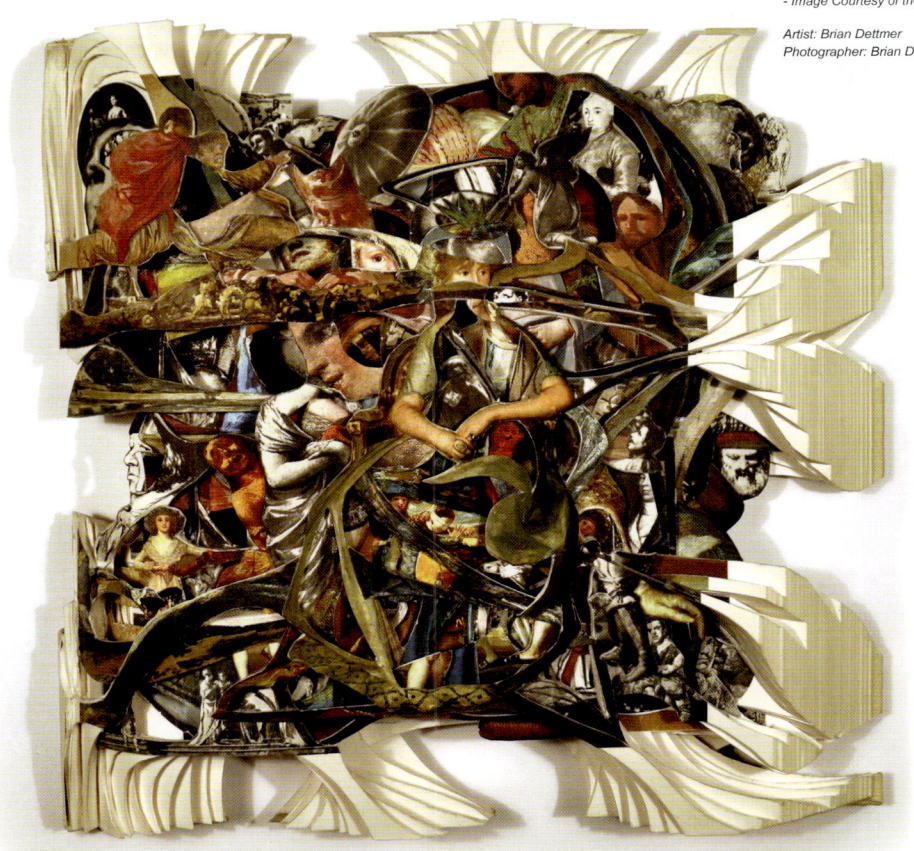

3. Goya

Altered Book, 13-1/8" x 13" x 2-3/8"
- Image Courtesy of the Artist and MiTO Gallery

Artist: Brian Dettmer   Country: USA
Photographer: Brian Dettmer

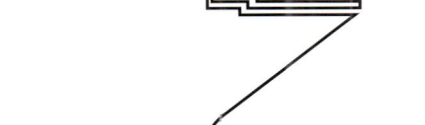

1. Absolute Authority
2. American Peoples
3. Goya
4. I Could Tell You
5. The March of Democracy
6. R.O.T.C Manual
7. Civilisation Part 1
8. Civilisation Part 3
9. Compiled Upon a New Plan
10. Complete Guide
11. Encyclopedias of World Travel
12. The Encyclopedia of Architecture
13. The Volume Library
14. We Kill One (detail)
15. Prose and Poetry of the World
16. Macmillan (detail)
17. Smith's Scientific Series
18. Totem
19. Tower of Babble

---Brian Dettmer

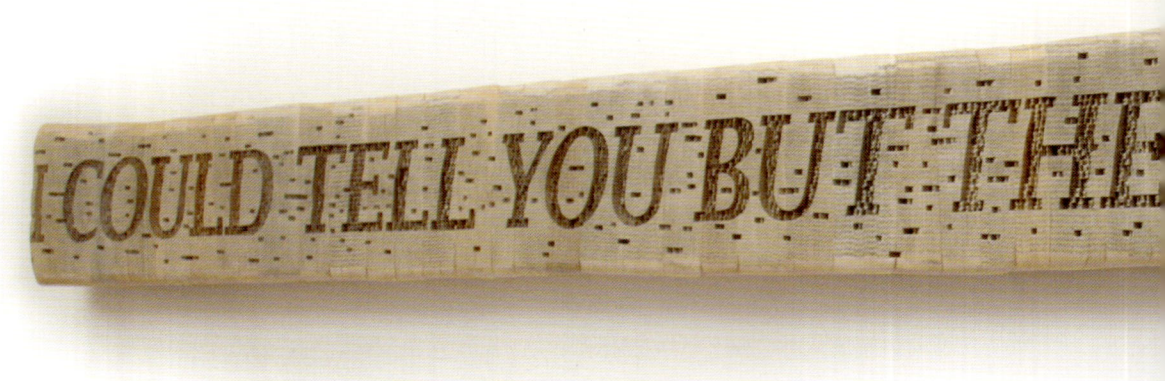

4. **I Could Tell You**
   Paperback books, a
   Artist: Brian Dettmer.
   Photographer: Briar

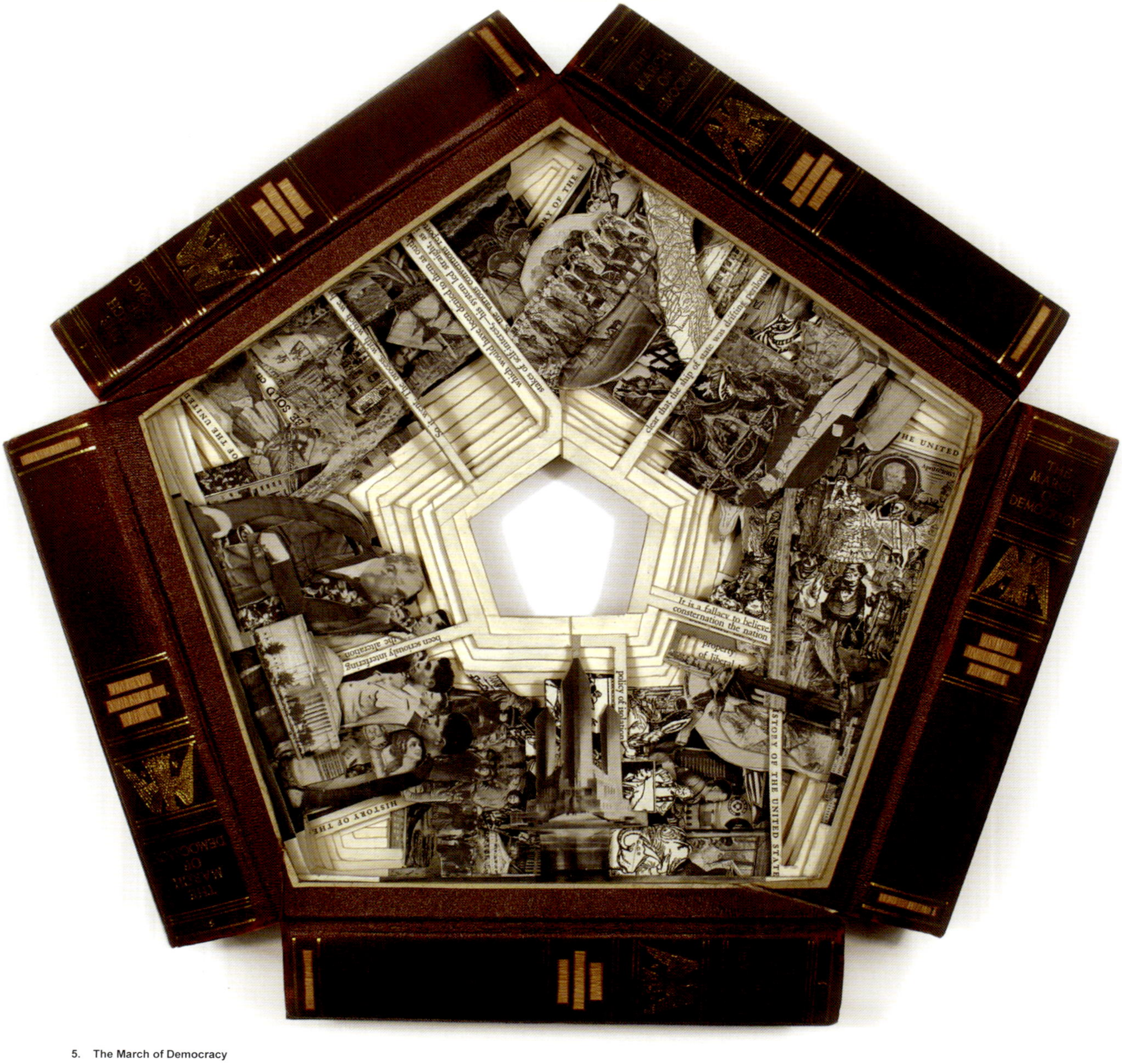

5. **The March of Democracy**
   Altered books, 18 1/2" x 19 1/2" x 4" - image Courtesy of the Artist and Saltworks
   Artist: Brian Dettmer   Country: USA
   Photographer: Brian Dettmer

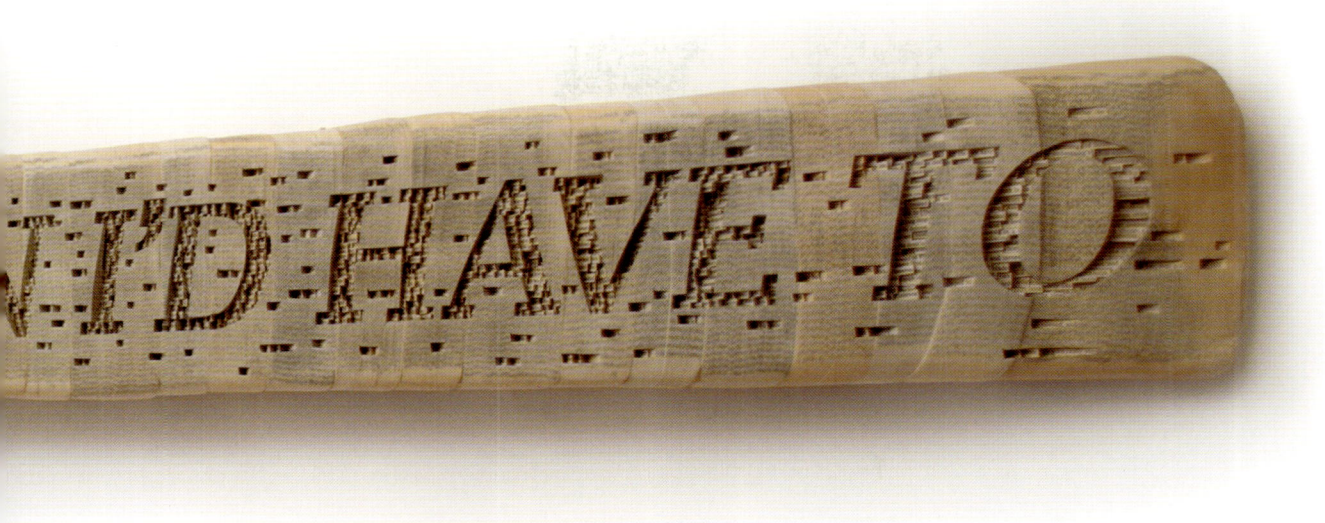

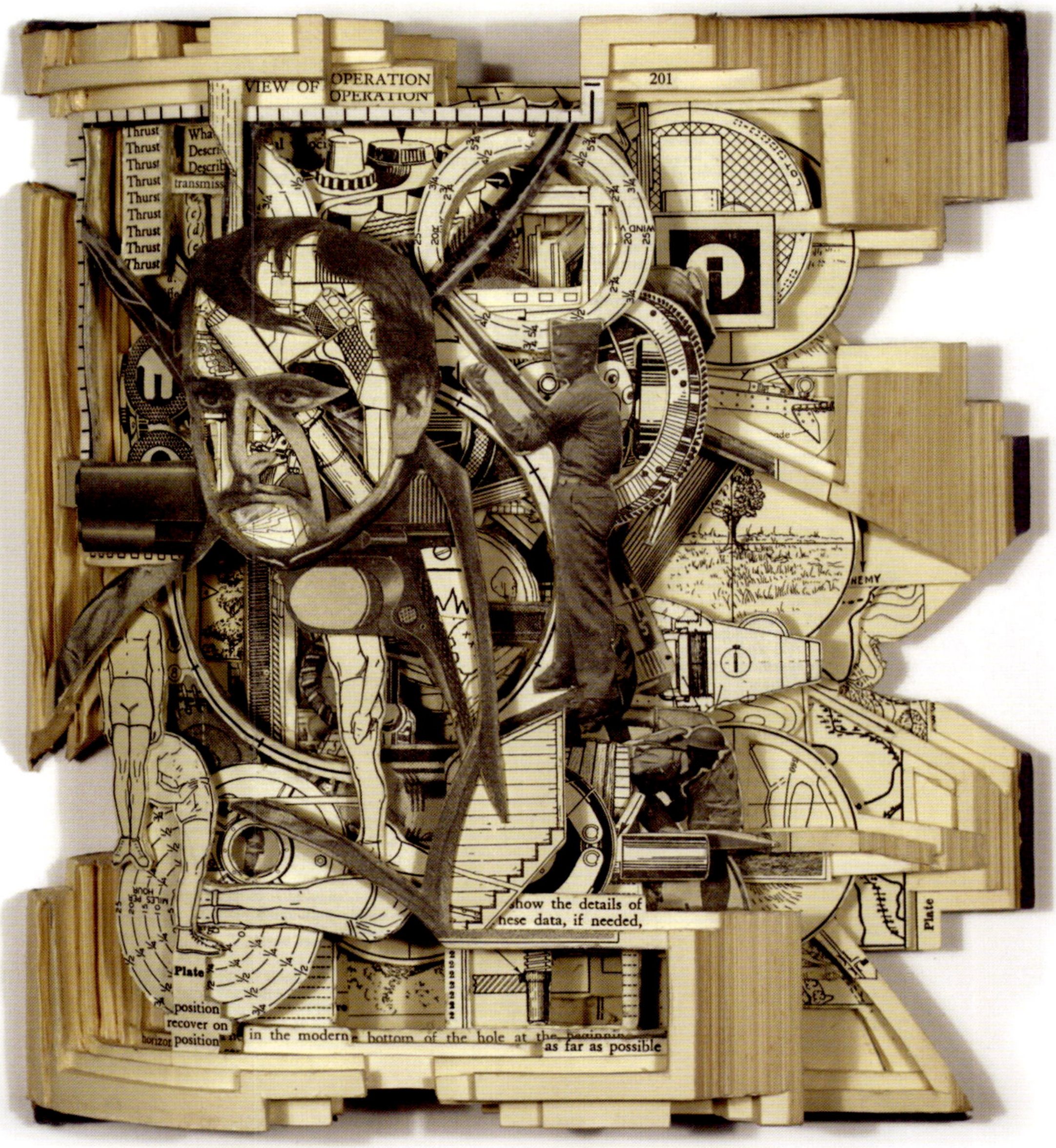

6. **R.O.T.C Manual**
 Altered Book, 9-5/8" x 8-1/2" x 2" - Image Courtesy of the Artist and Saltworks
 Artist: Brian Dettmer   Country: USA
 Photographer: Brian Dettmer

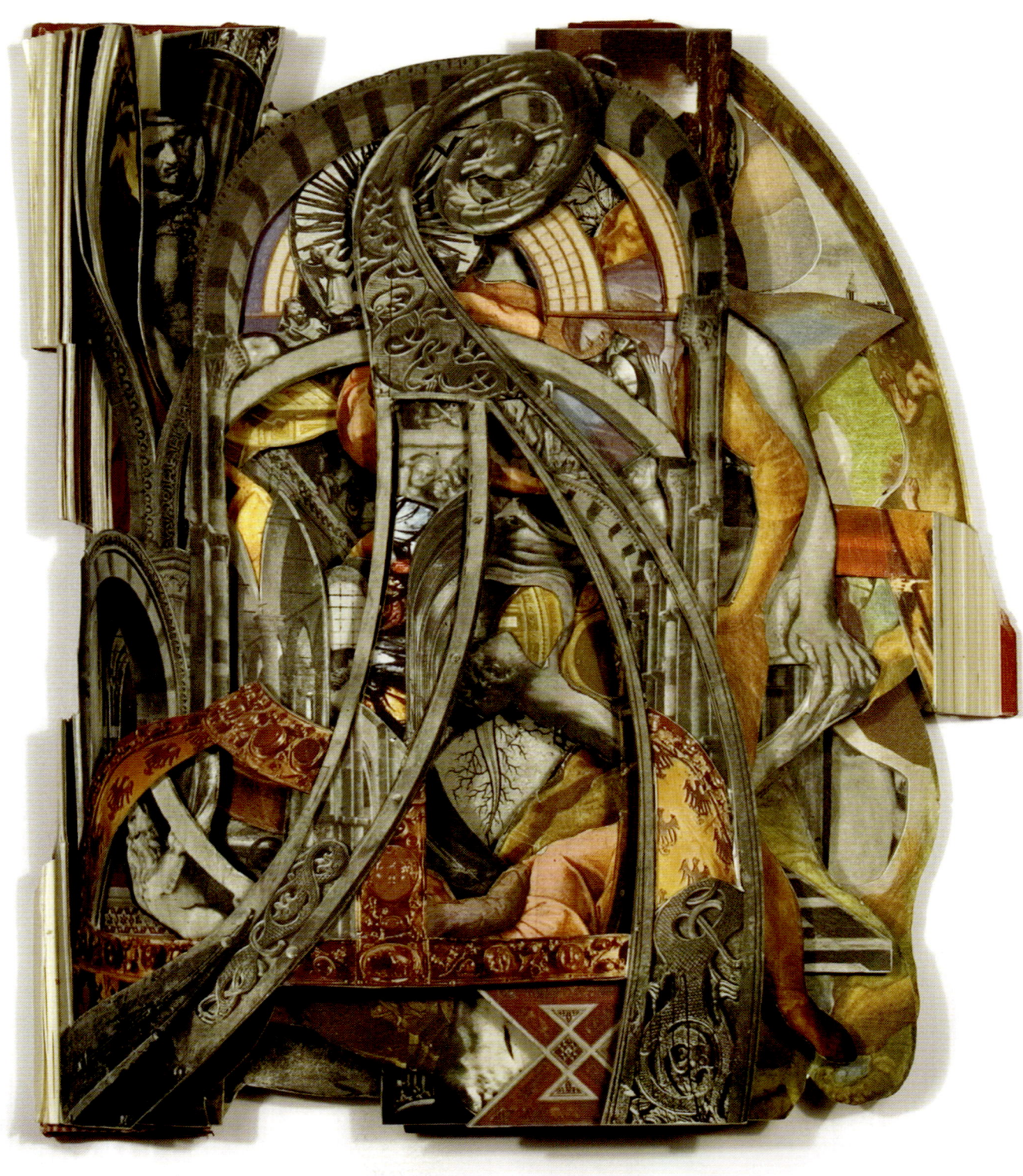

7. **Civilisation Part 1**

Altered Book, 10" x 8-1/2" x 1-5/8" - Image Courtesy of the Artist and Saltworks

Artist: Brian Dettmer
Country: USA
Photographer: Brian Dettmer

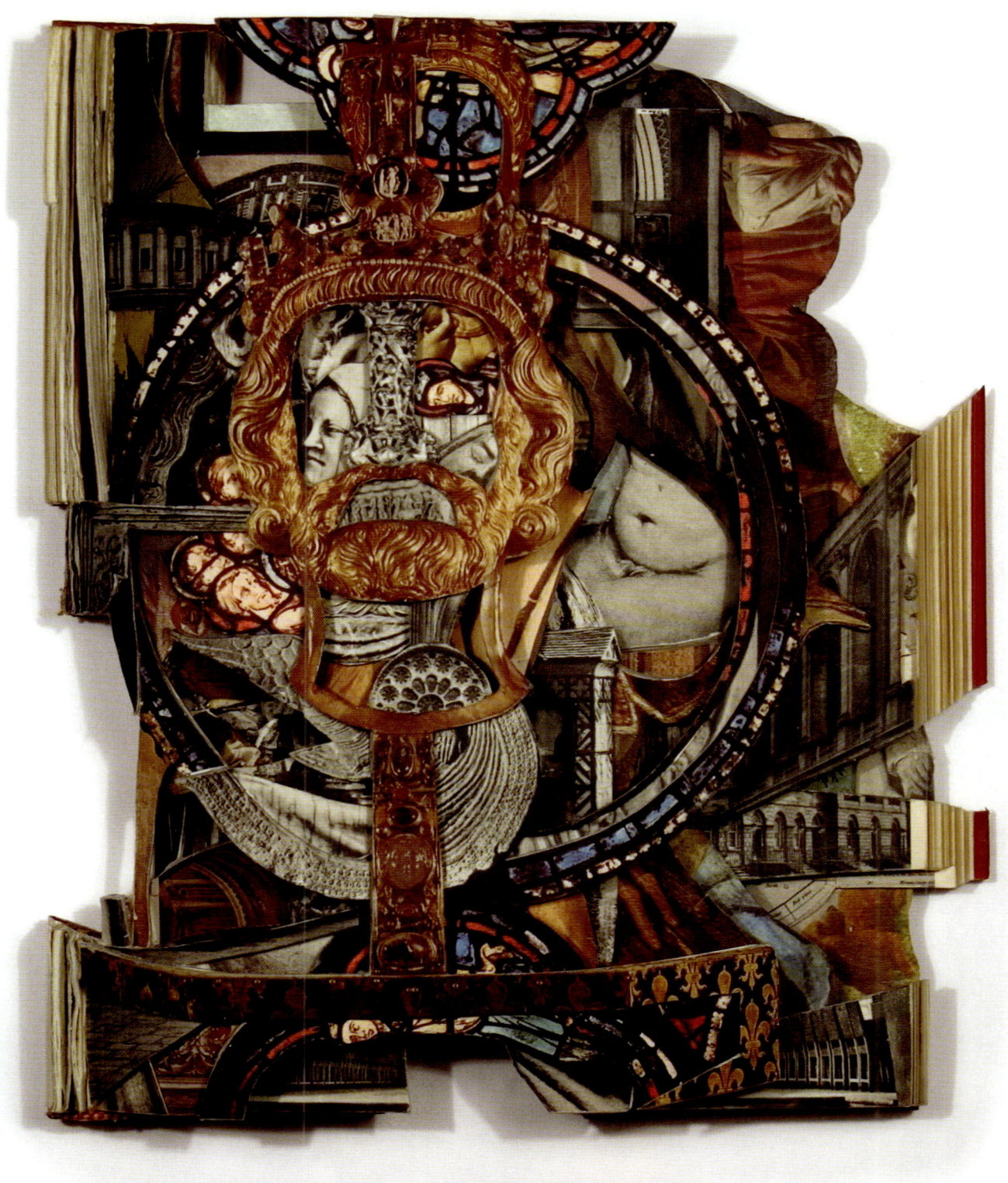

8. **Civilisation Part 3**

   Altered Book, 10" x 8-1/2" x 1-5/8" - Image Courtesy of the Artist and Saltworks

   Artist: Brian Dettmer
   Country: USA
   Photographer: Brian Dettmer

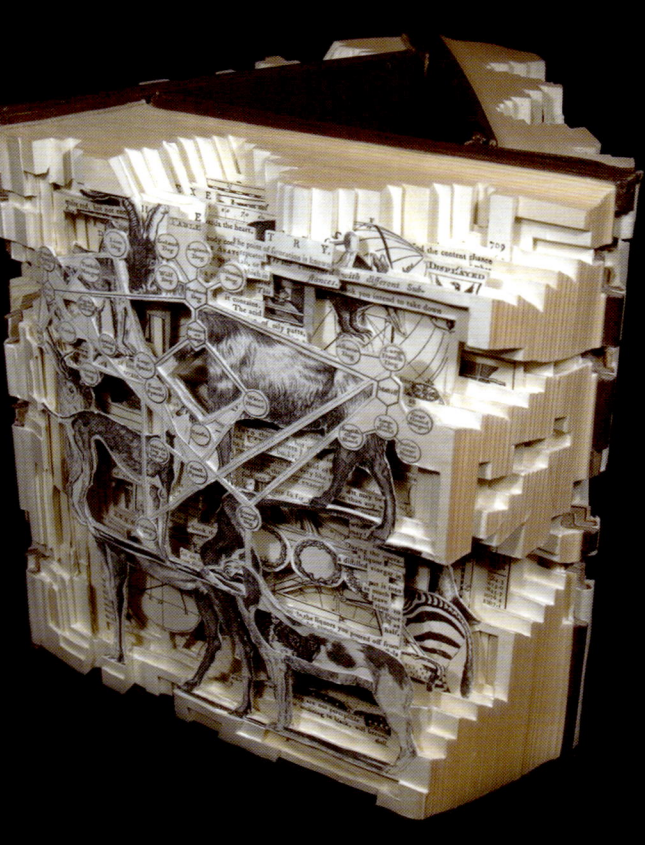

9. Compiled Upon a New Plan

Altered Books, 10-1/2" x 10" x 10-3/4" - Image Courtesy of the Artist and Packer Schopf
Artist: Brian Dettmer   Country: USA   Photographer: Brian Dettmer

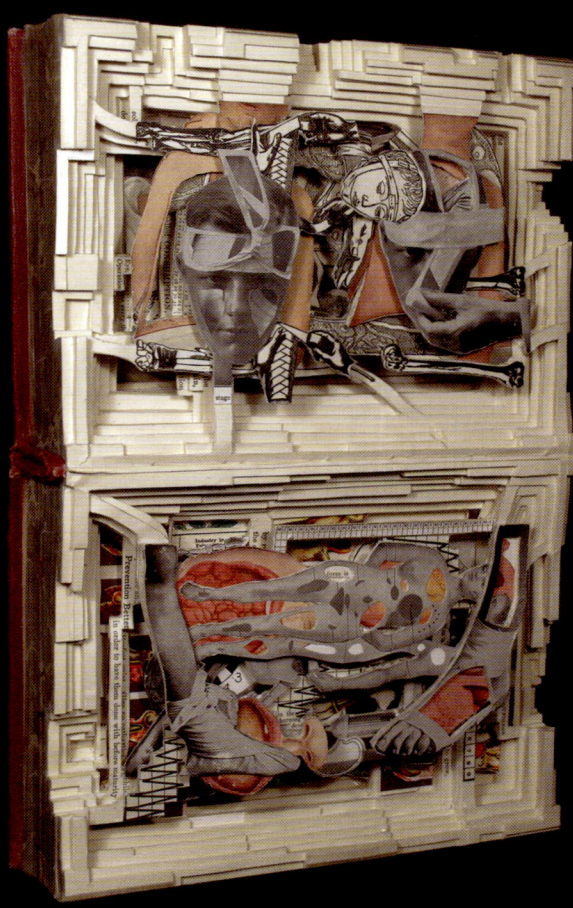

10. Complete Guide

Hardcover book, acrylic medium, 15" x 10-1/8" x 2-1/4" - Image Courtesy of the Artist and P
Artist: Brian Dettmer   Country: USA   Photographer: Brian Dettmer

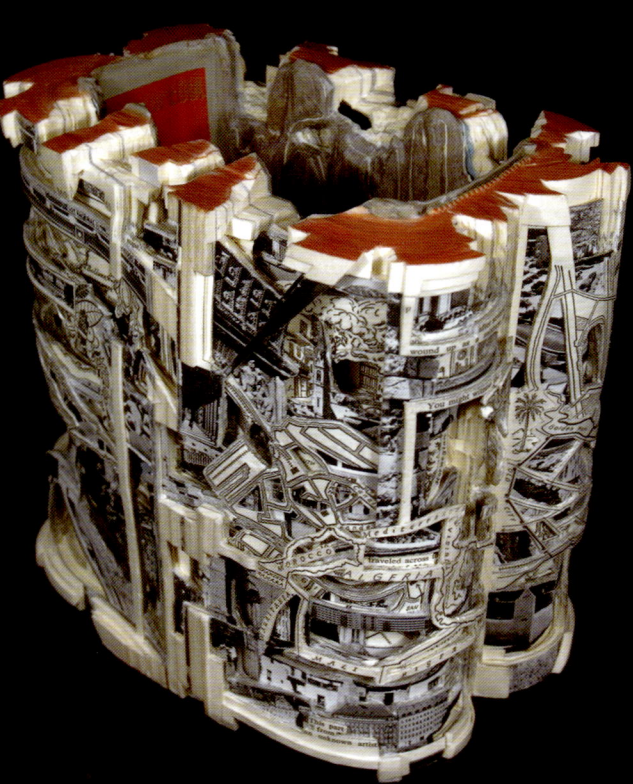

11. Encyclopedias of World Travel

Altered Book, 8 1/2" x 7 3/4" x 1 1/2" - Image Courtesy of the Artist and Saltworks
Artist: Brian Dettmer   Country: USA   Photographer: Brian Dettmer

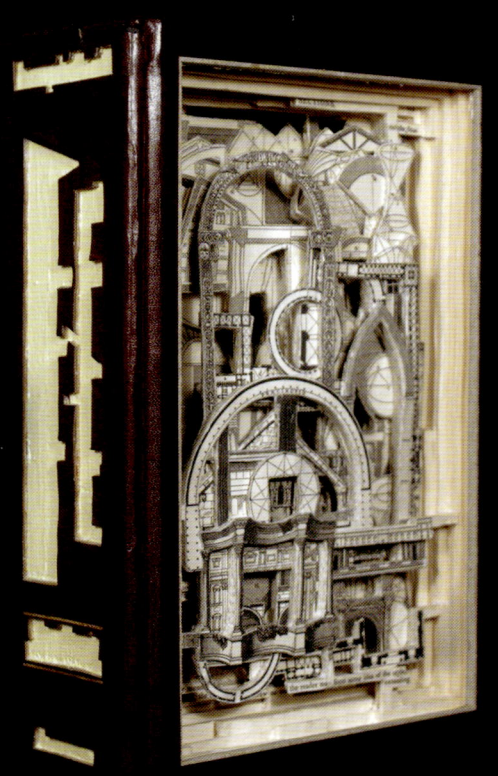

12. The Encyclopedia of Architecture

Altered Book, 9-3/8" x 6-1/8" x 2-7/8" - Image Courtesy of the Artist and Kinz + Tillou Fine Art
Artist: Brian Dettmer   Country: USA   Photographer: Brian Dettmer

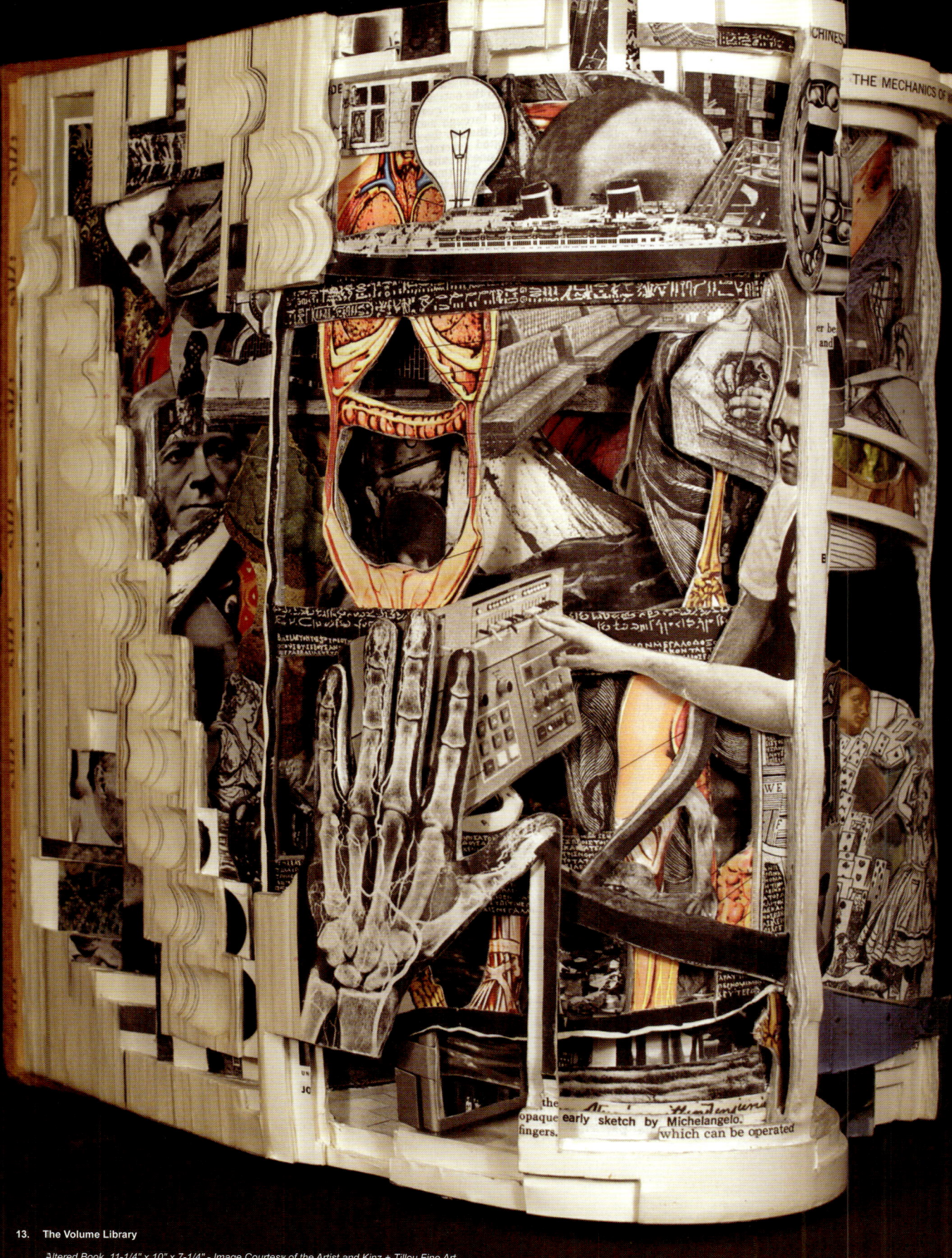

13. The Volume Library
Altered Book, 11-1/4" x 10" x 7-1/4" - Image Courtesy of the Artist and Kinz + Tillou Fine Art
Artist: Brian Dettmer   Country: USA   Photographer: Brian Dettmer

14. We Kill One (detail)
Hardcover book, acrylic medium, 9-1/4" x 6-1/4" x 1-1/4" - Image Courtesy of the Artist   Artist: Brian Dettmer   Country: USA   Photographer: Brian Dettmer

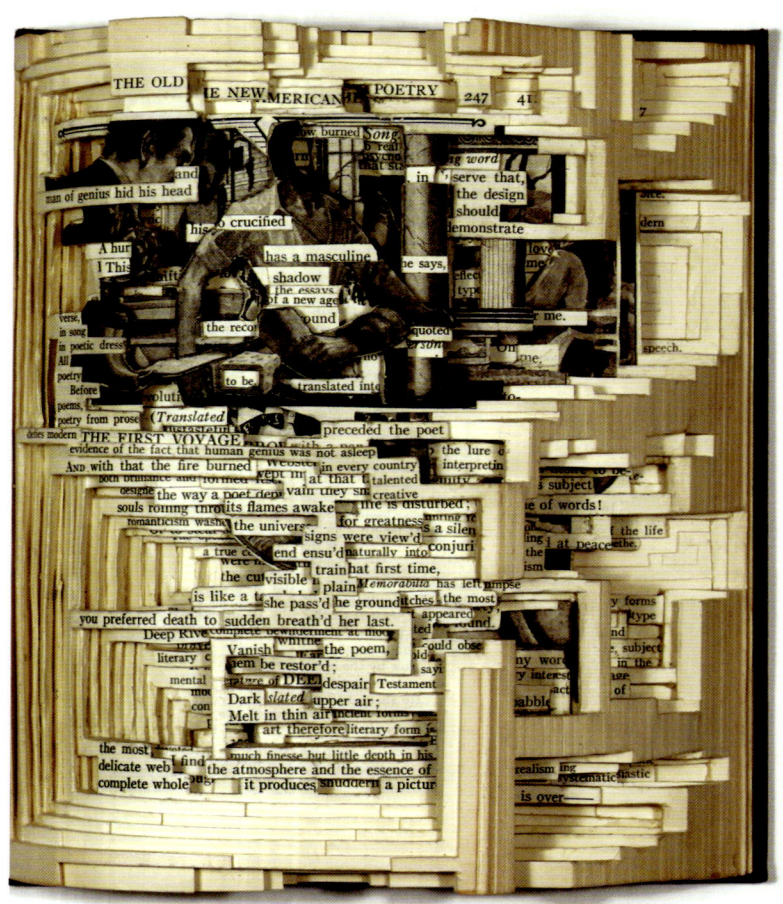

15. Prose and Poetry of the World
Hardcover book, acrylic medium, 8-1/2" x 7-1/2" x 2" - Image Courtesy of the Artist and Packer Schopf
Artist: Brian Dettmer   Country: USA   Photographer: Brian Dettmer

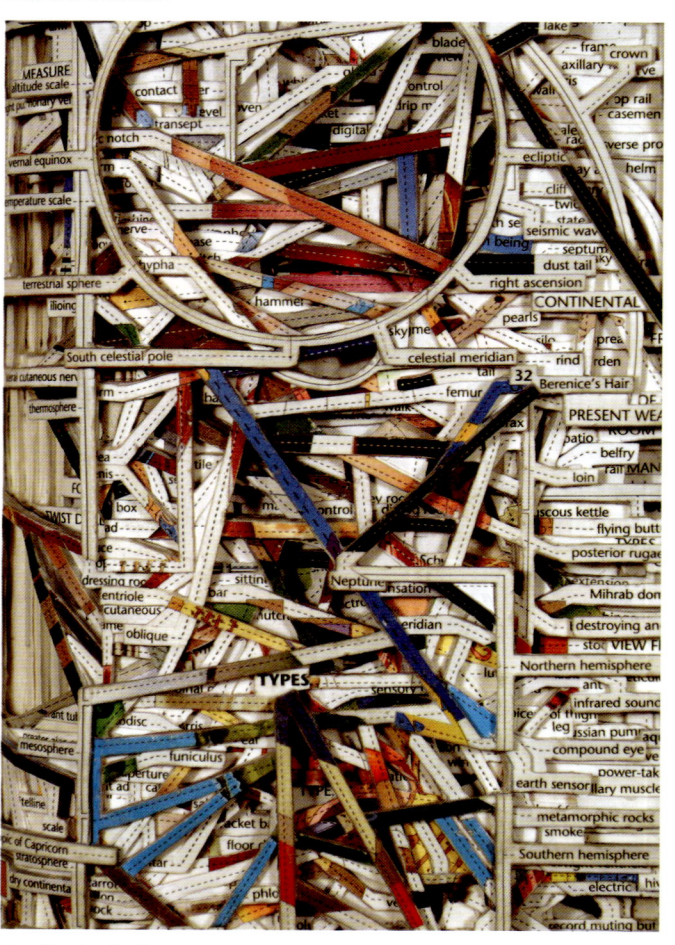

16. Macmillan (detail)
Hardcover book, acrylic medium, 11-1/8" x 9-1/2" x 2-1/8" - Image Courtesy of the Artist and Toomey Tourell Fine Art
Artist: Brian Dettmer   Country: USA   Photographer: Brian Dettmer

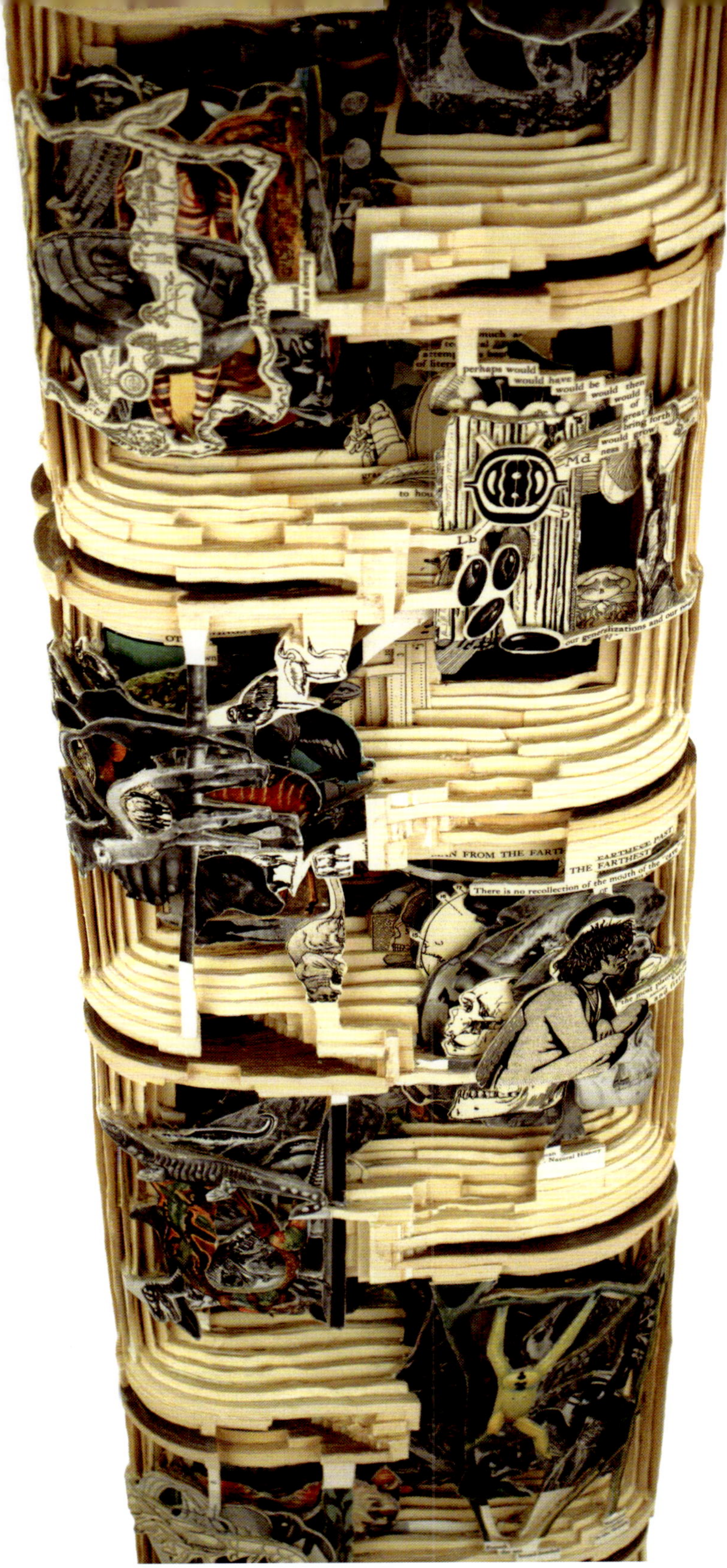

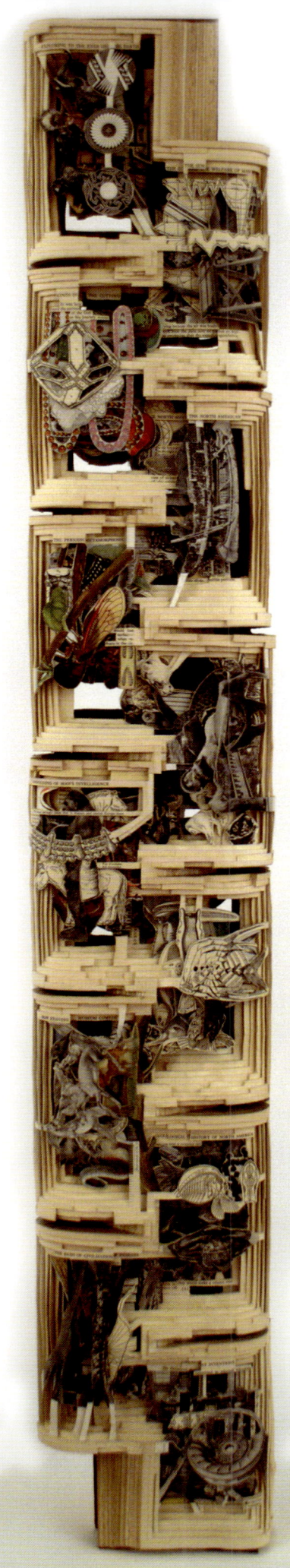

17. **Smith's Scientific Series**

Hardcover books with pedestal, 28" x 10-1/2" x 10-1/2" - Image Courtesy of the Artist and Kinz + Tillou Fine Art

Artist: Brian Dettmer
Country: USA
Photographer: Brian Dettmer

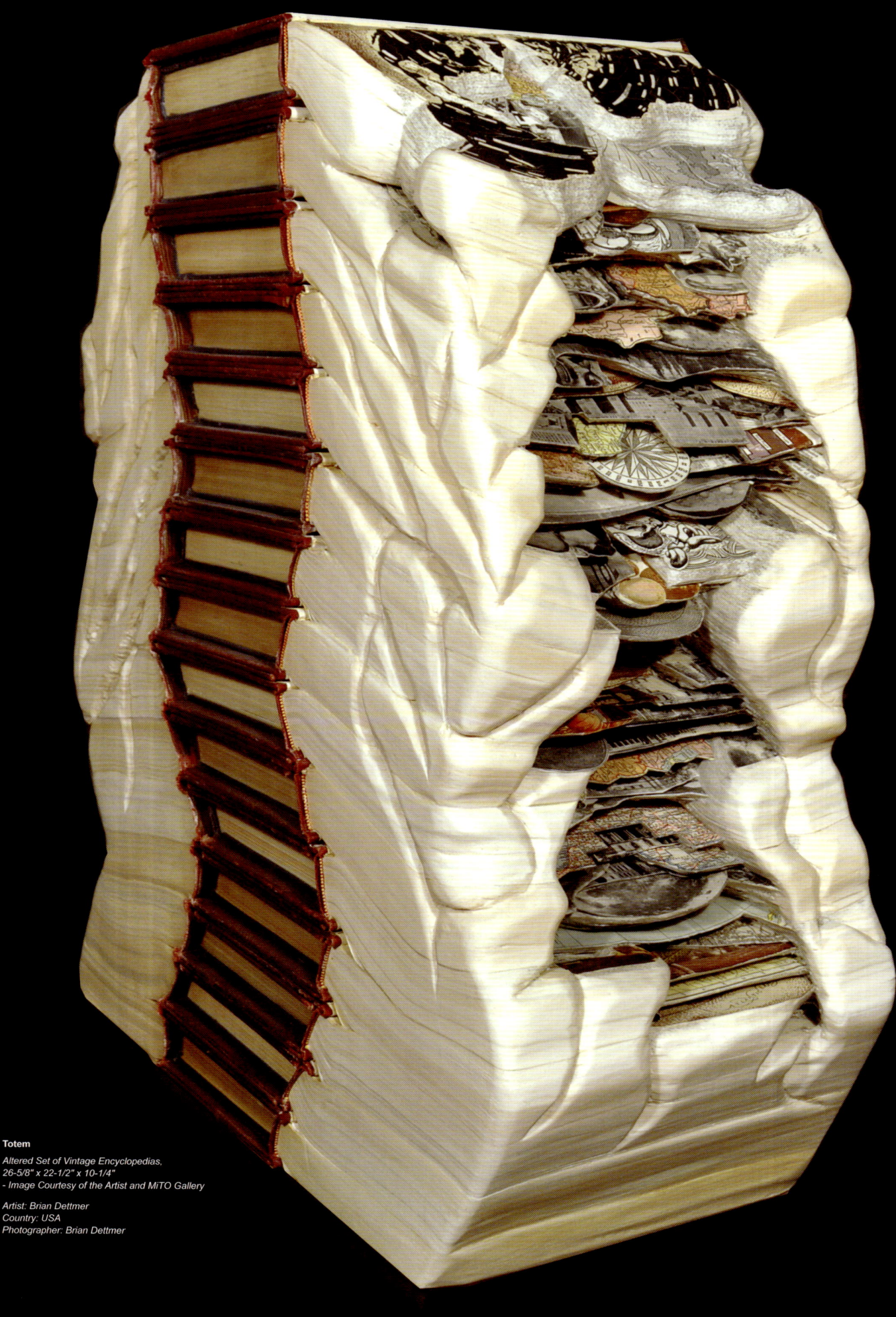

18. Totem
Altered Set of Vintage Encyclopedias,
26-5/8" x 22-1/2" x 10-1/4"
- Image Courtesy of the Artist and MiTO Gallery

Artist: Brian Dettmer
Country: USA
Photographer: Brian Dettmer

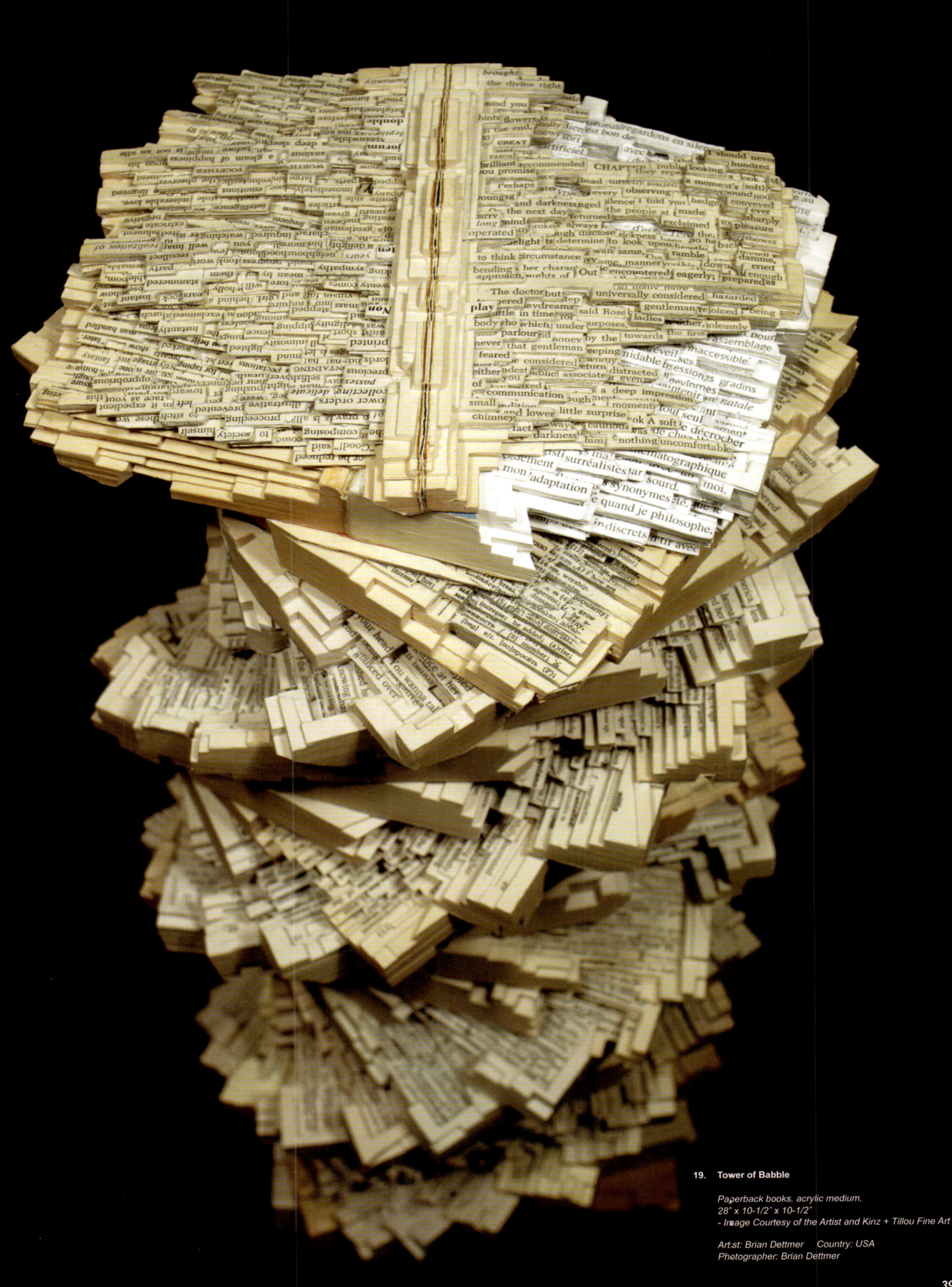

19. **Tower of Babble**

Paperback books, acrylic medium,
28" x 10-1/2" x 10-1/2"
- Image Courtesy of the Artist and Kinz + Tillou Fine Art

Artist: Brian Dettmer   Country: USA
Photographer: Brian Dettmer

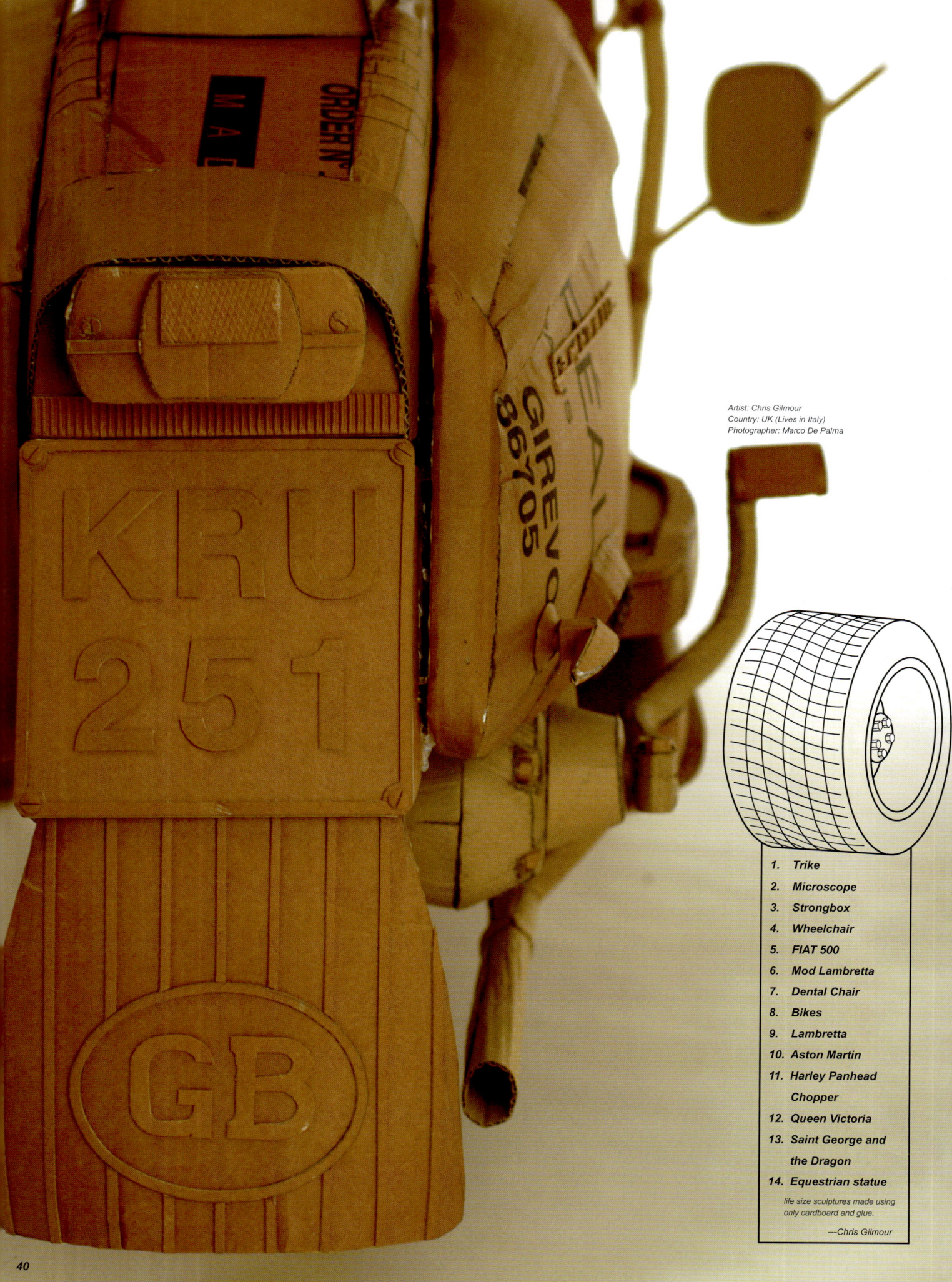

Artist: Chris Gilmour
Country: UK (Lives in Italy)
Photographer: Marco De Palma

1. Trike
2. Microscope
3. Strongbox
4. Wheelchair
5. FIAT 500
6. Mod Lambretta
7. Dental Chair
8. Bikes
9. Lambretta
10. Aston Martin
11. Harley Panhead Chopper
12. Queen Victoria
13. Saint George and the Dragon
14. Equestrian statue

life size sculptures made using only cardboard and glue.

—Chris Gilmour

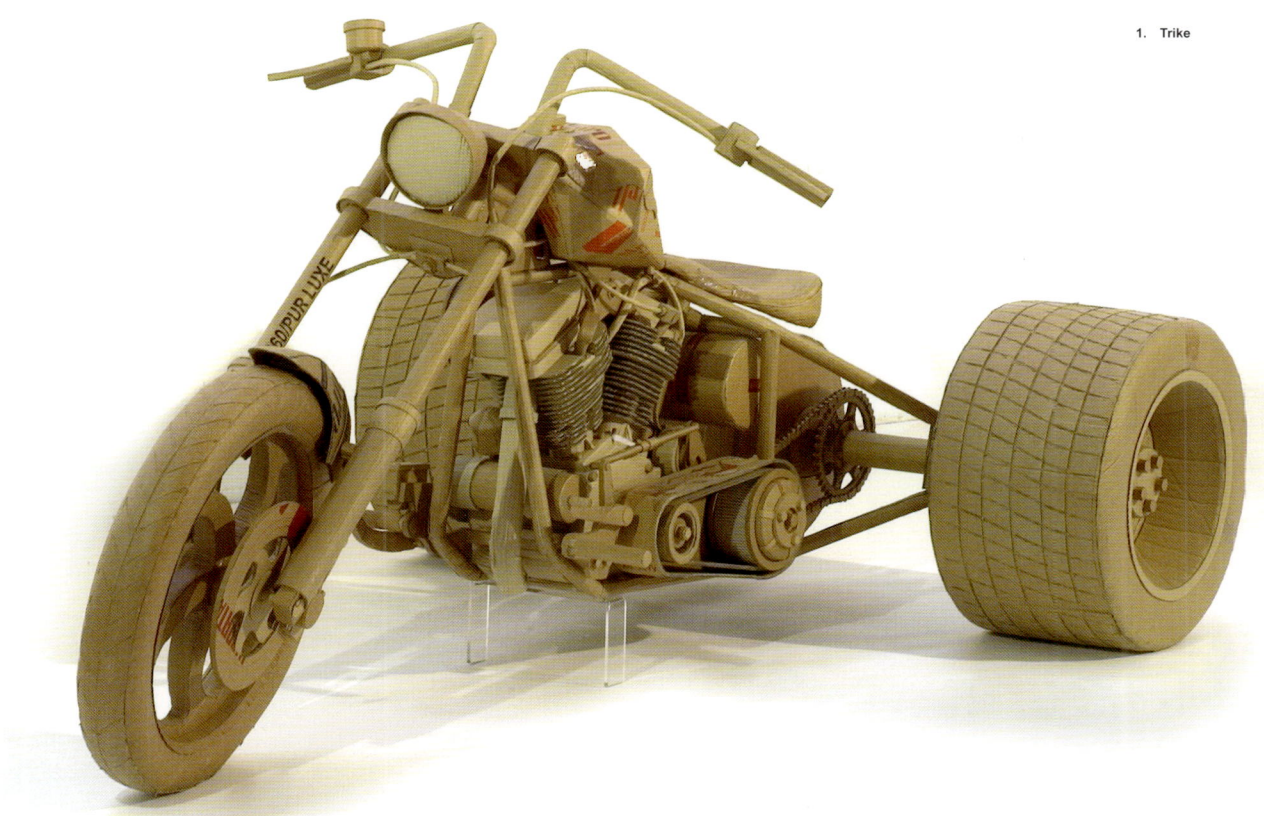

1. Trike

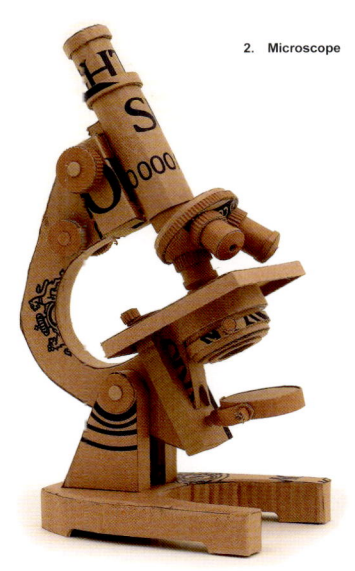

2. Microscope

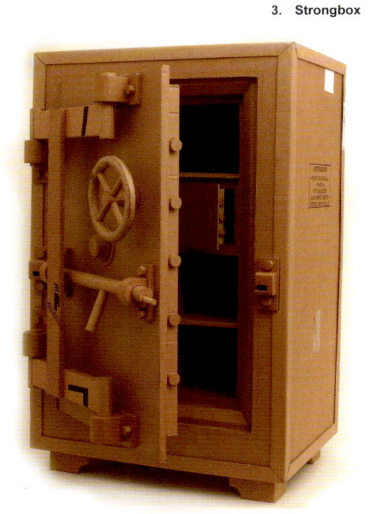

3. Strongbox

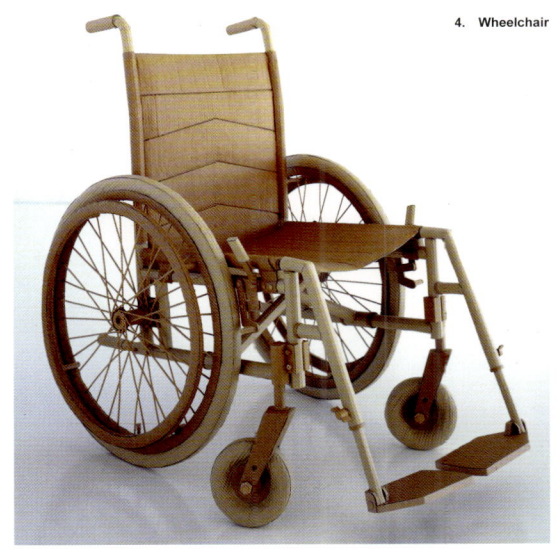

4. Wheelchair

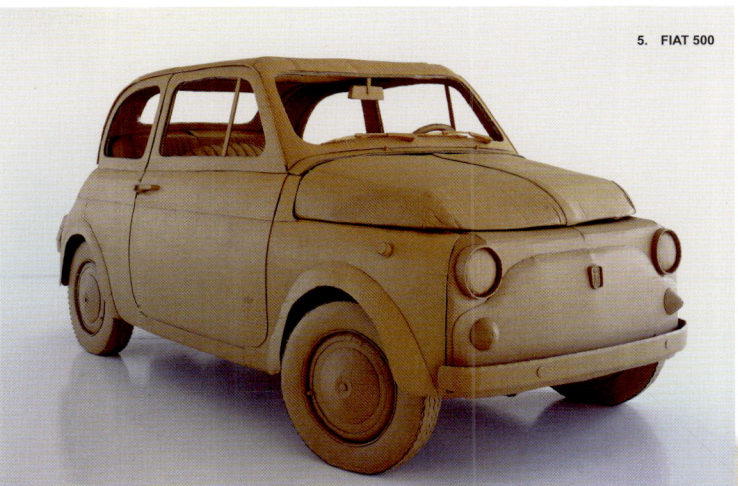

5. FIAT 500

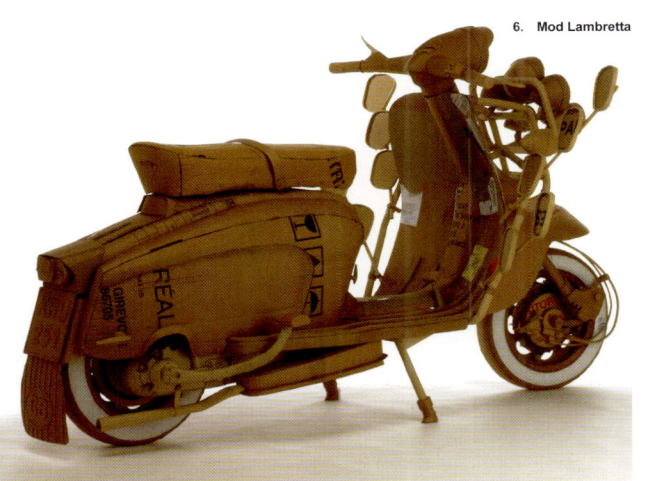

6. Mod Lambretta

7. Dental Chair

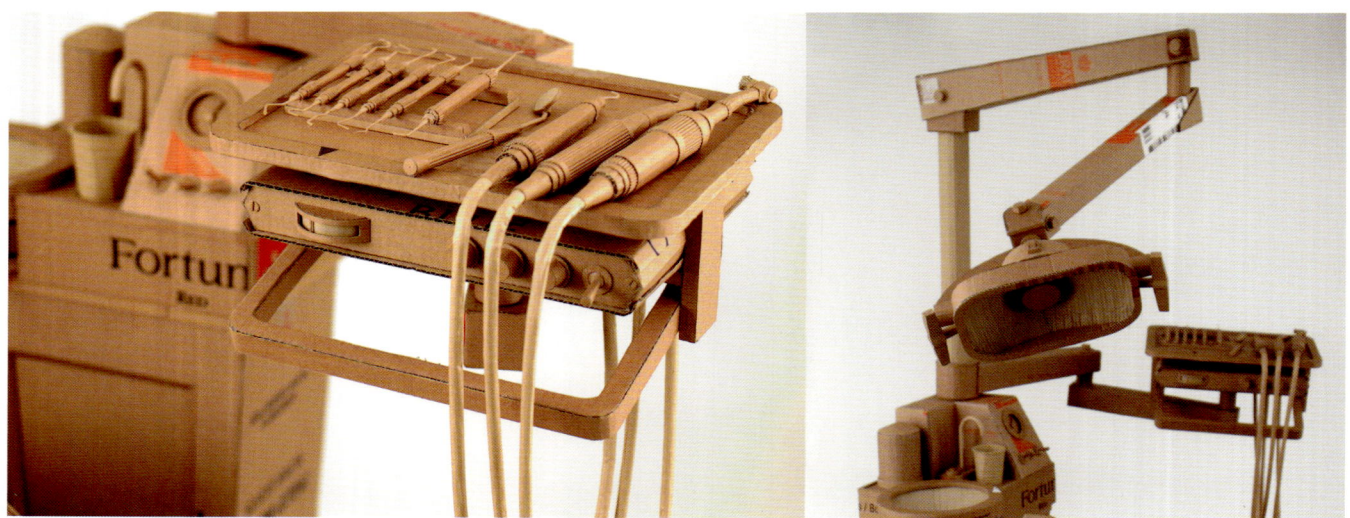

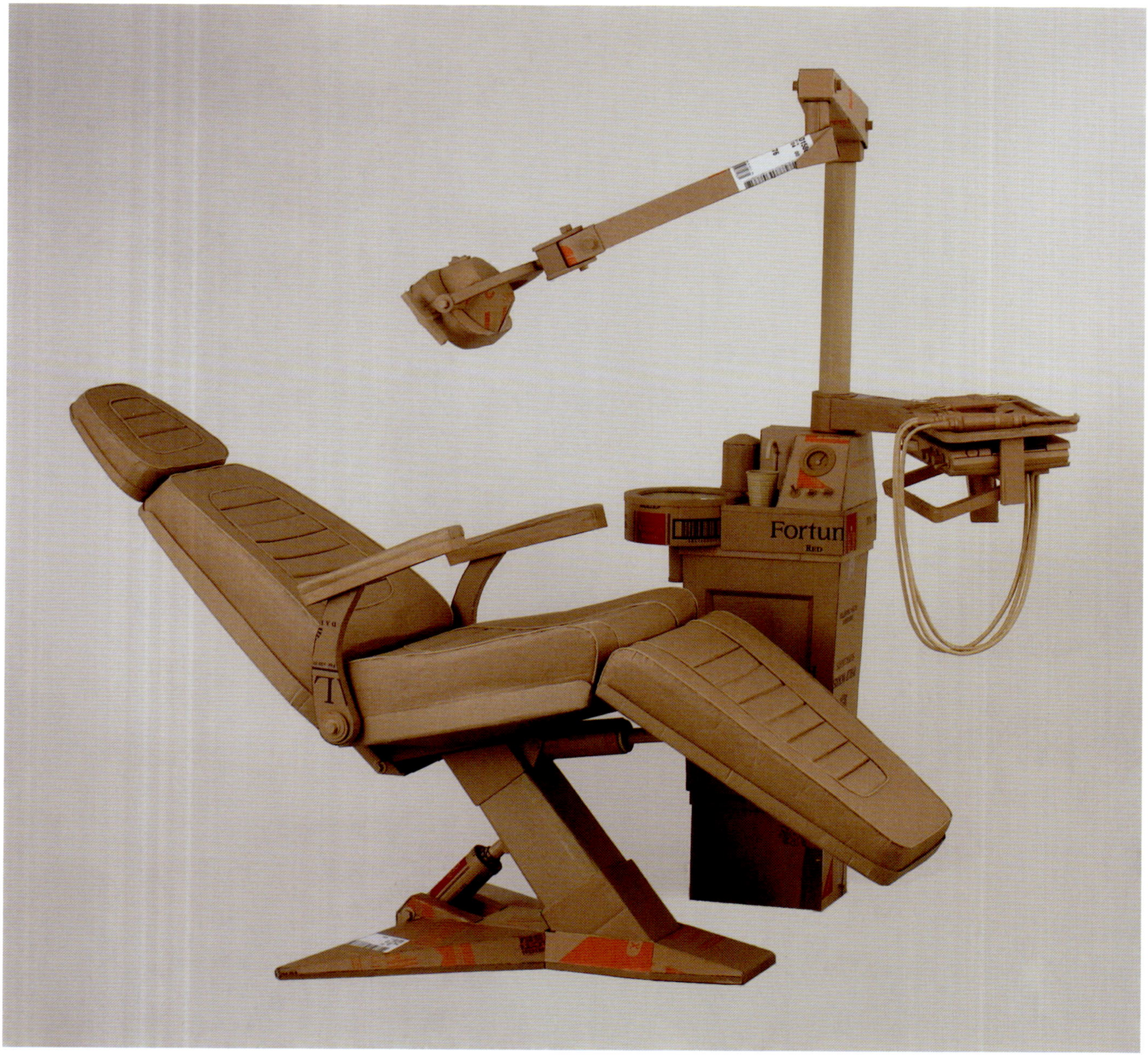

Artist: Chris Gilmour
Country: UK (Lives in Italy)
Photographer: Marco De Palma

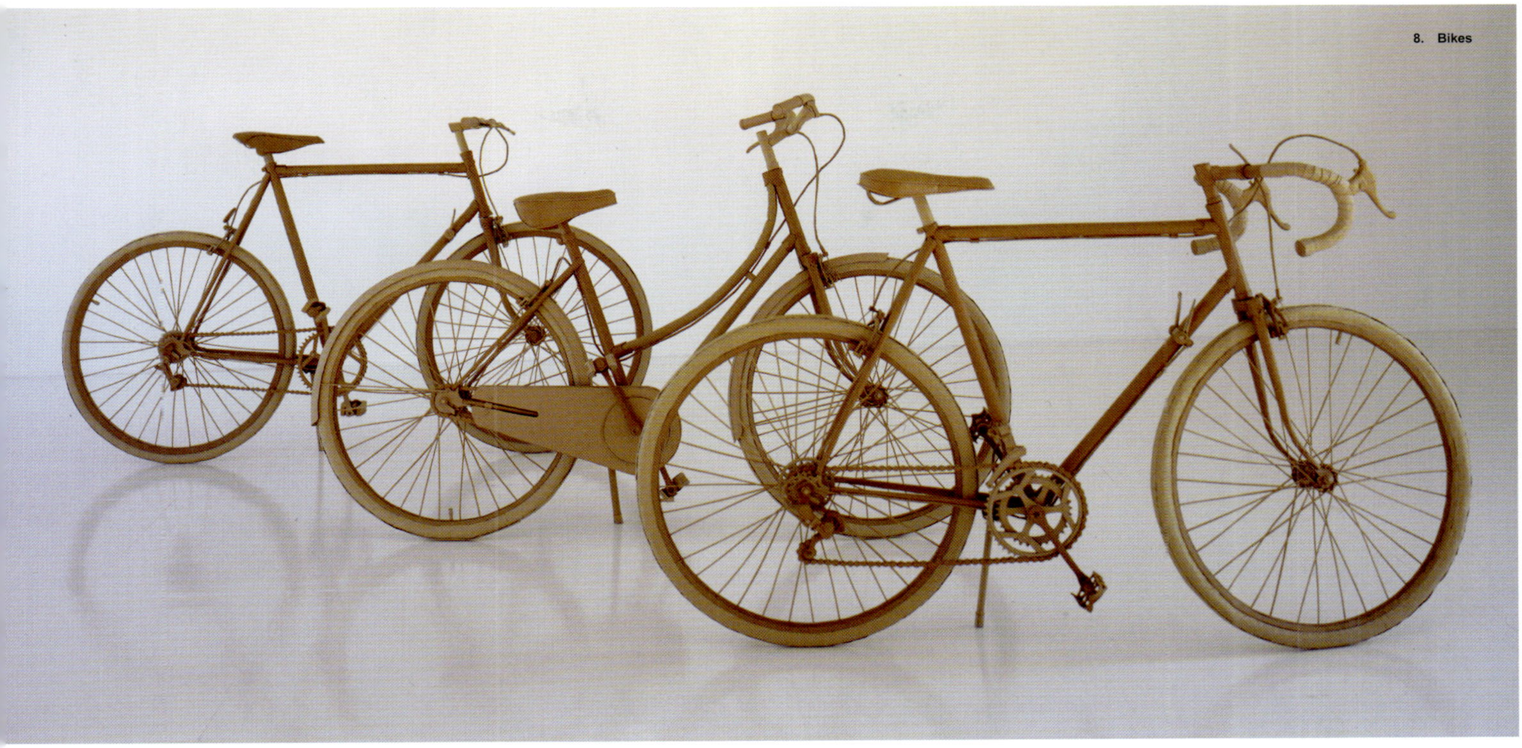

8. Bikes

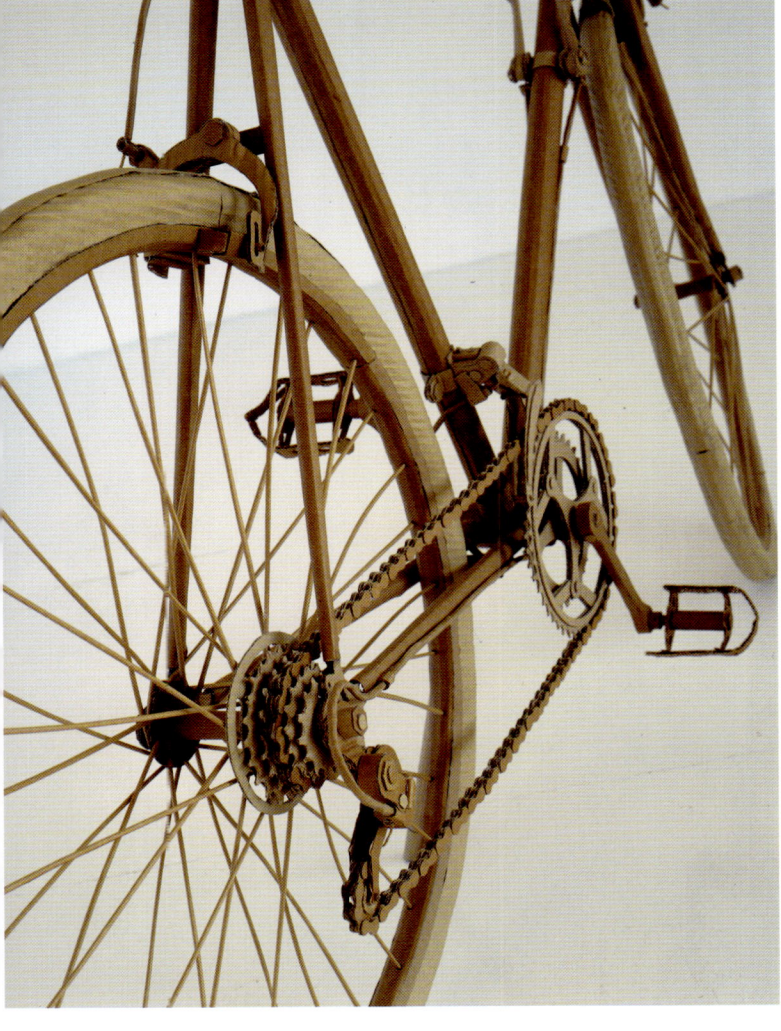
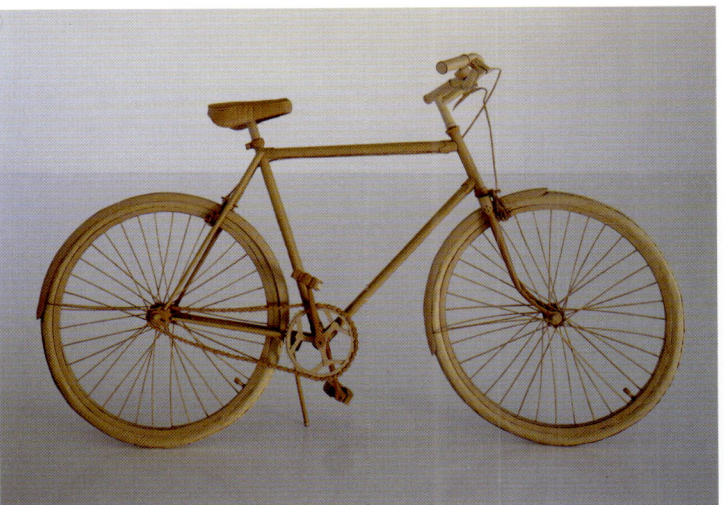
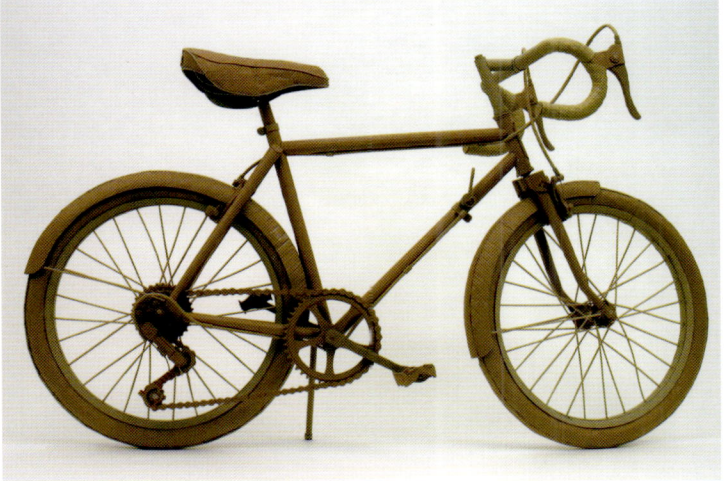

9. Lambretta

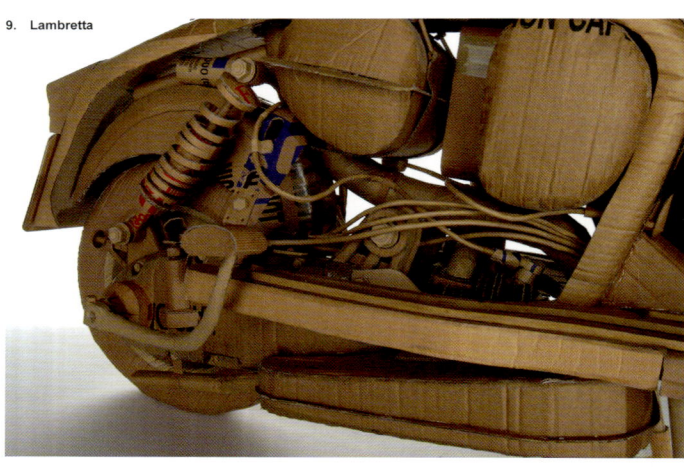
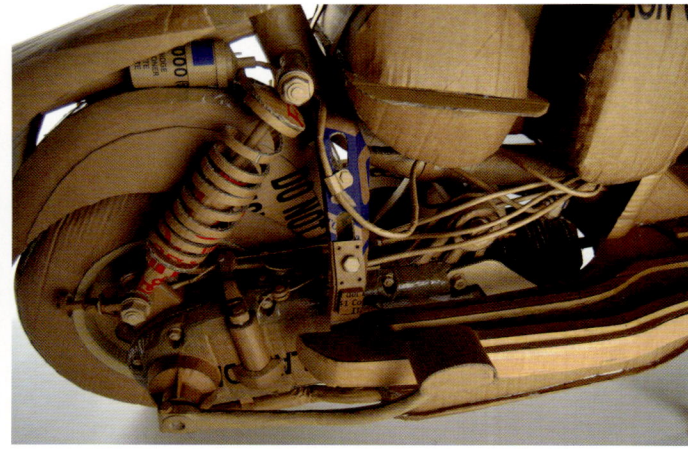
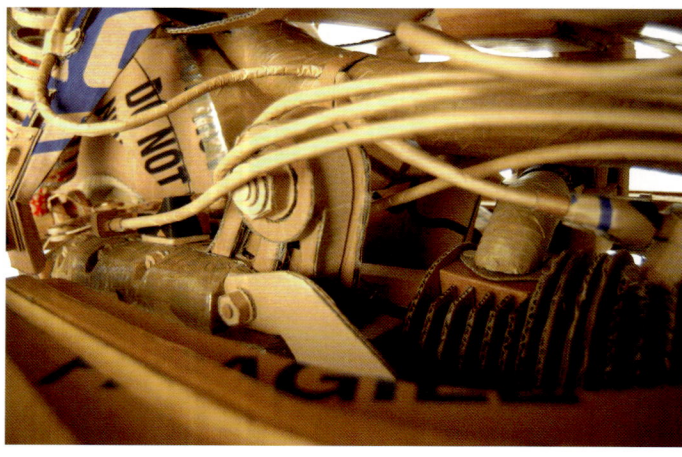
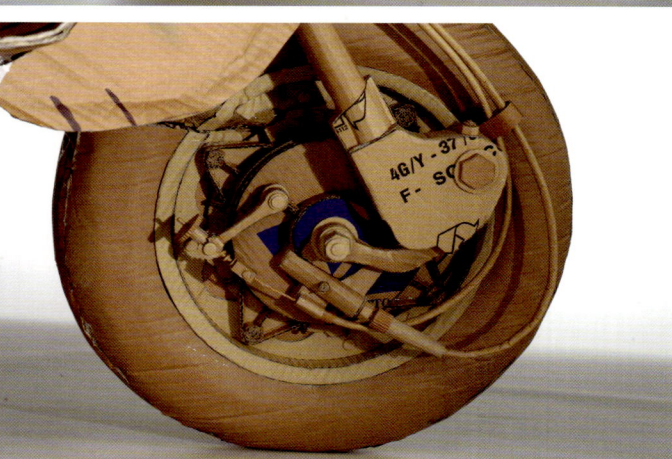

Artist: Chris Gilmour
Country: UK (Lives in Italy)
Photographer: Marco De Palma

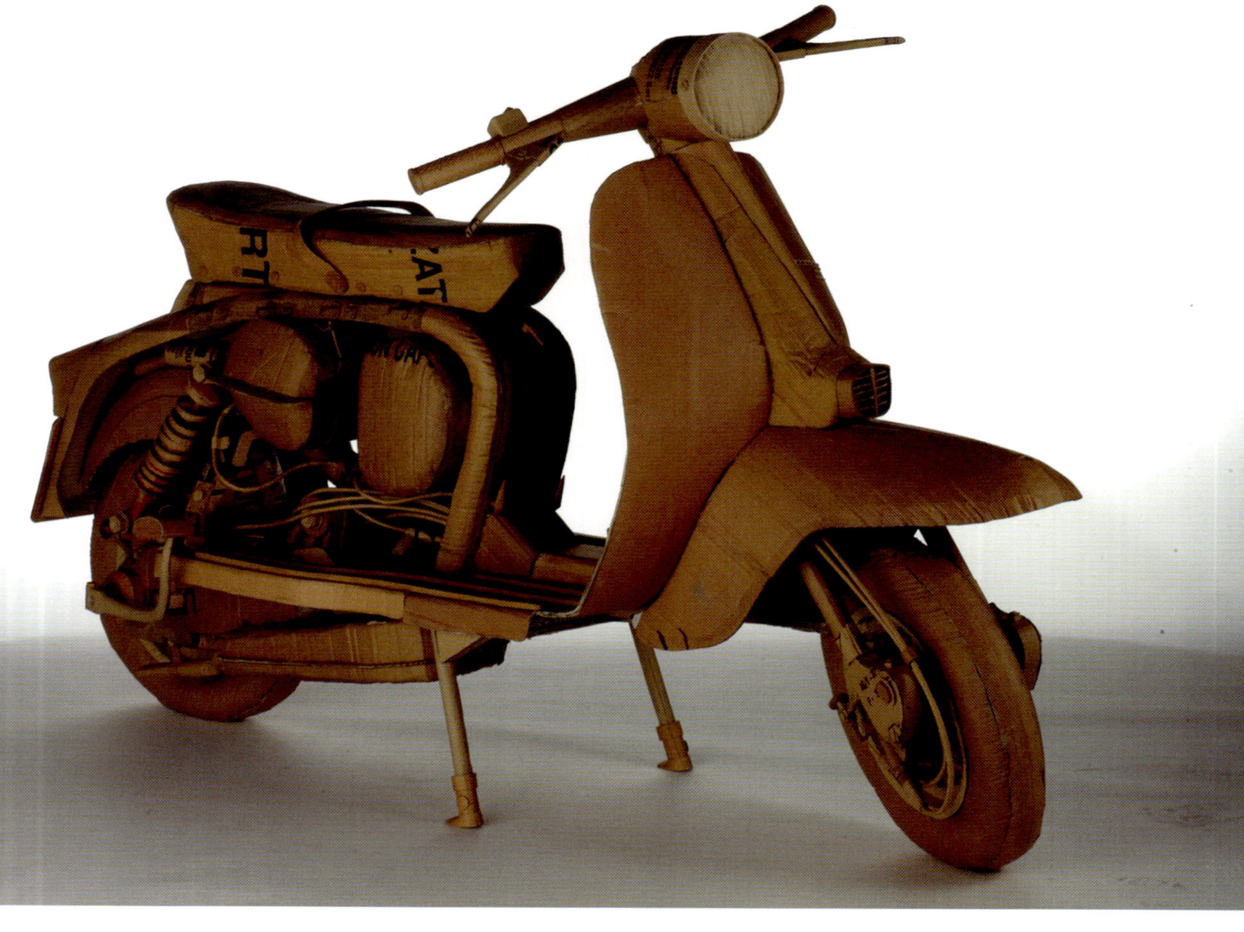

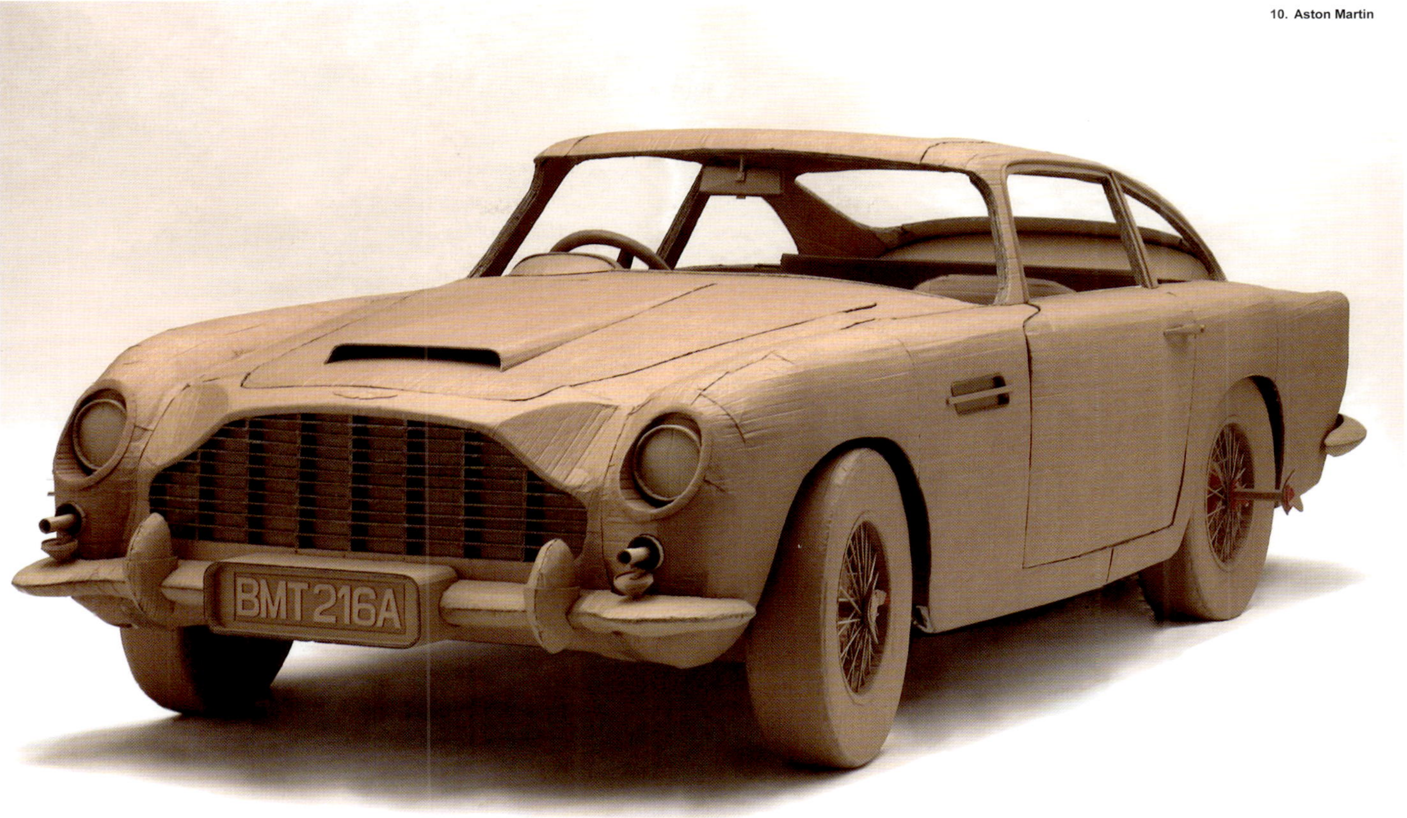

10. Aston Martin

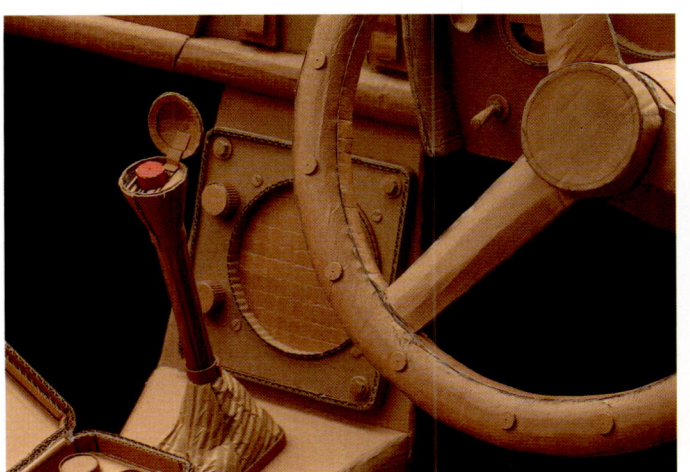
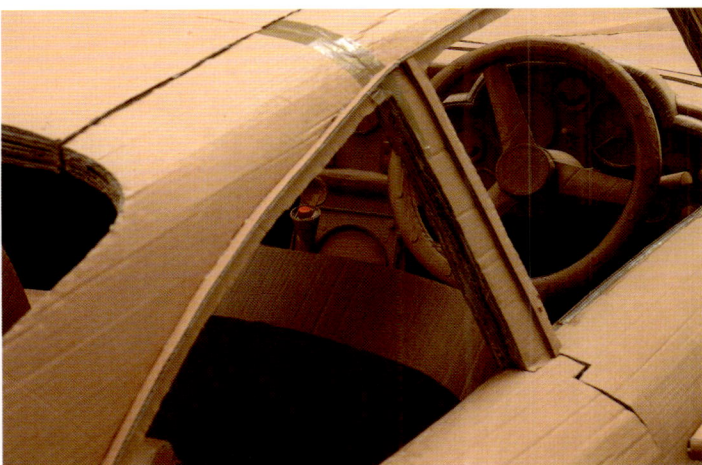
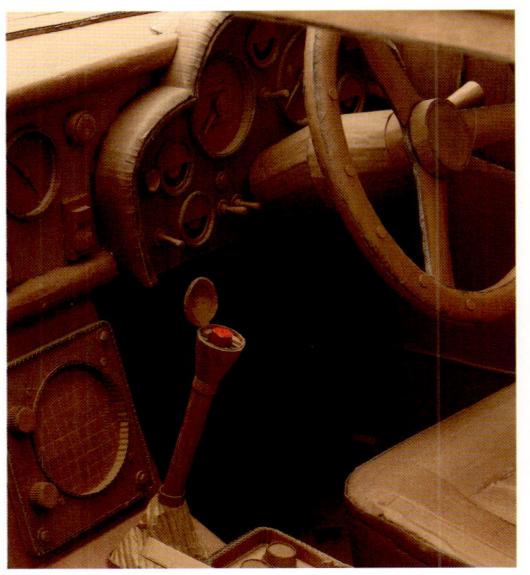
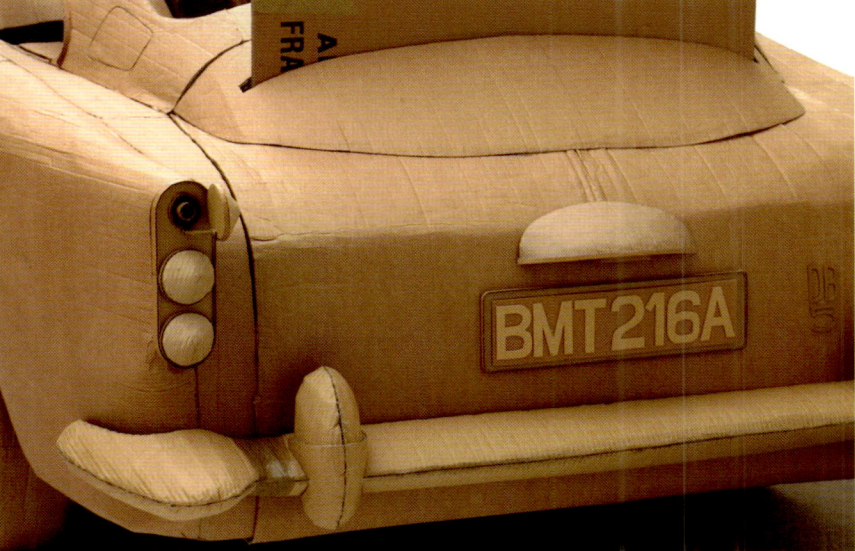

11. Harley Panhead Chopper

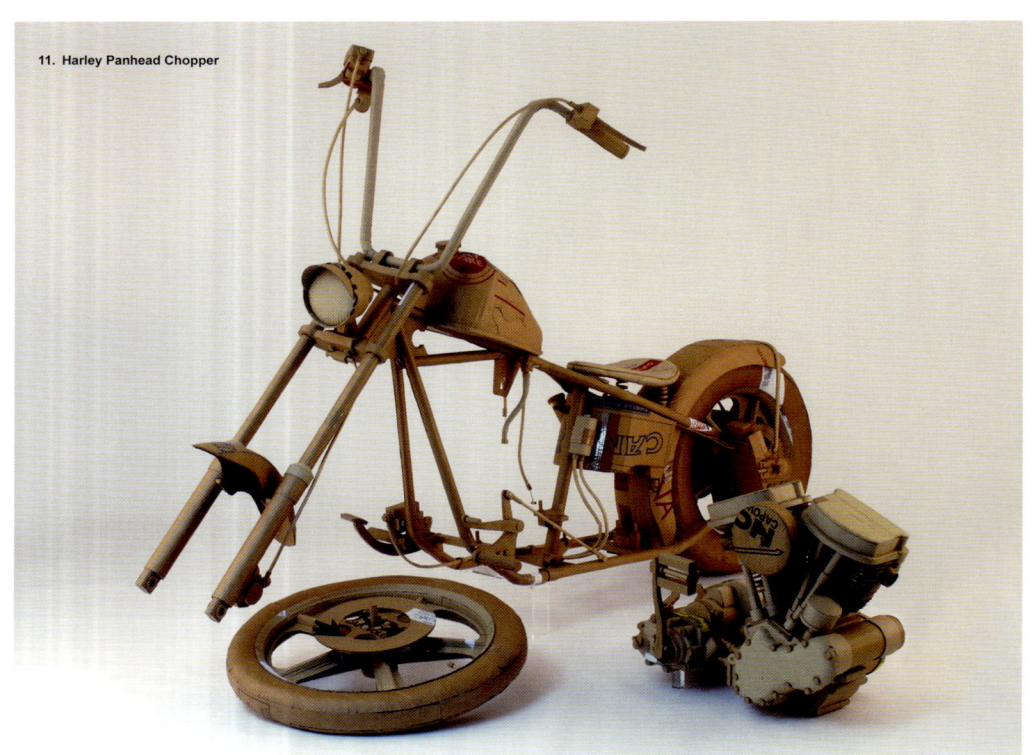
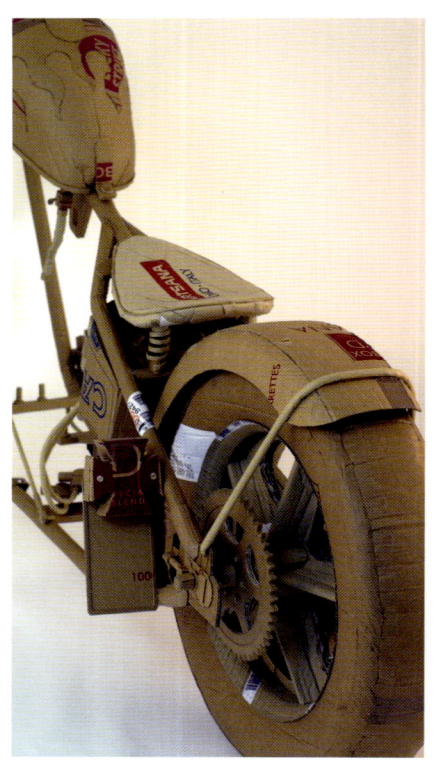
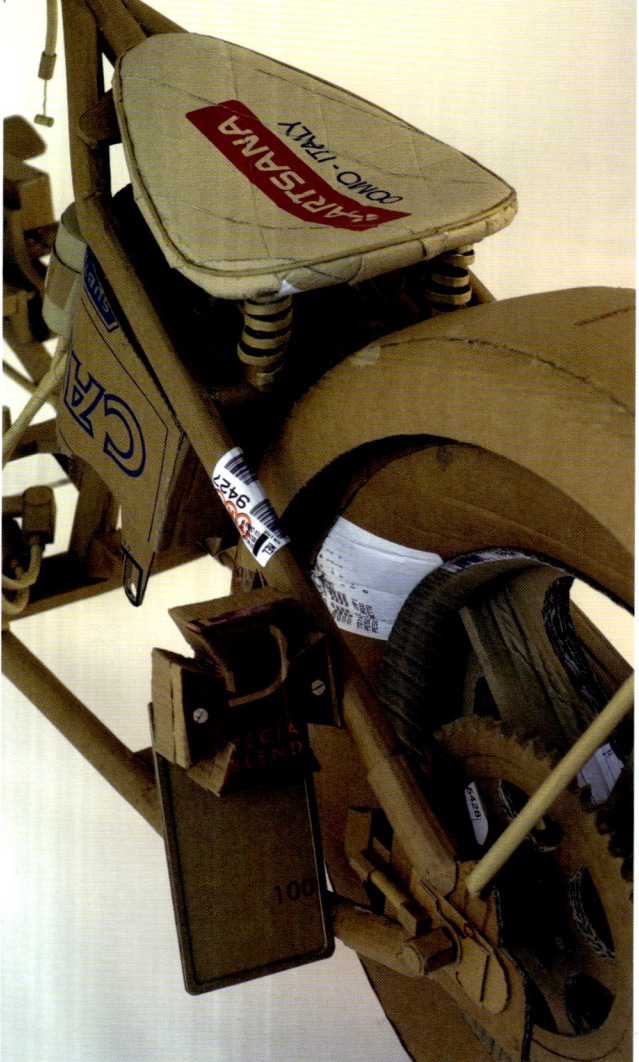
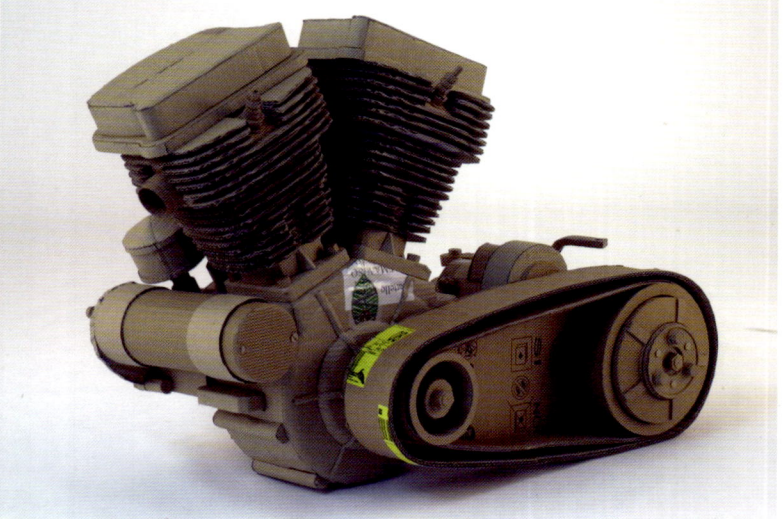
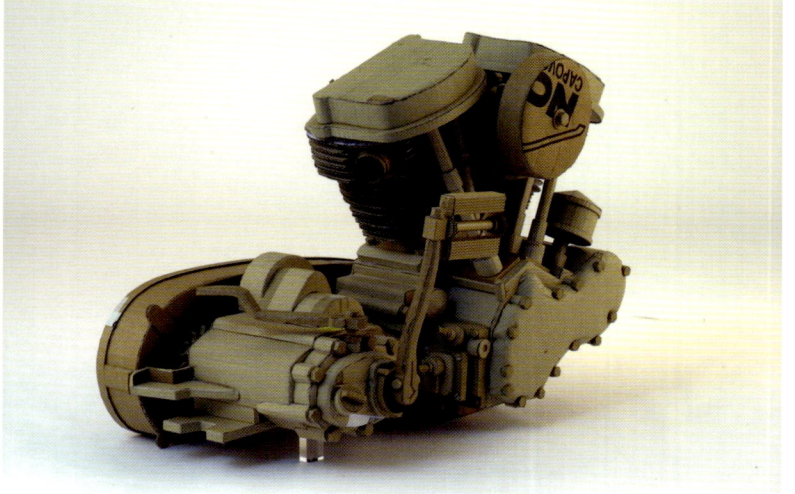

12. Queen Victoria

Artist: Chris Gilmour
Country: UK (Lives in Italy)
Photographer: Marco De Palma

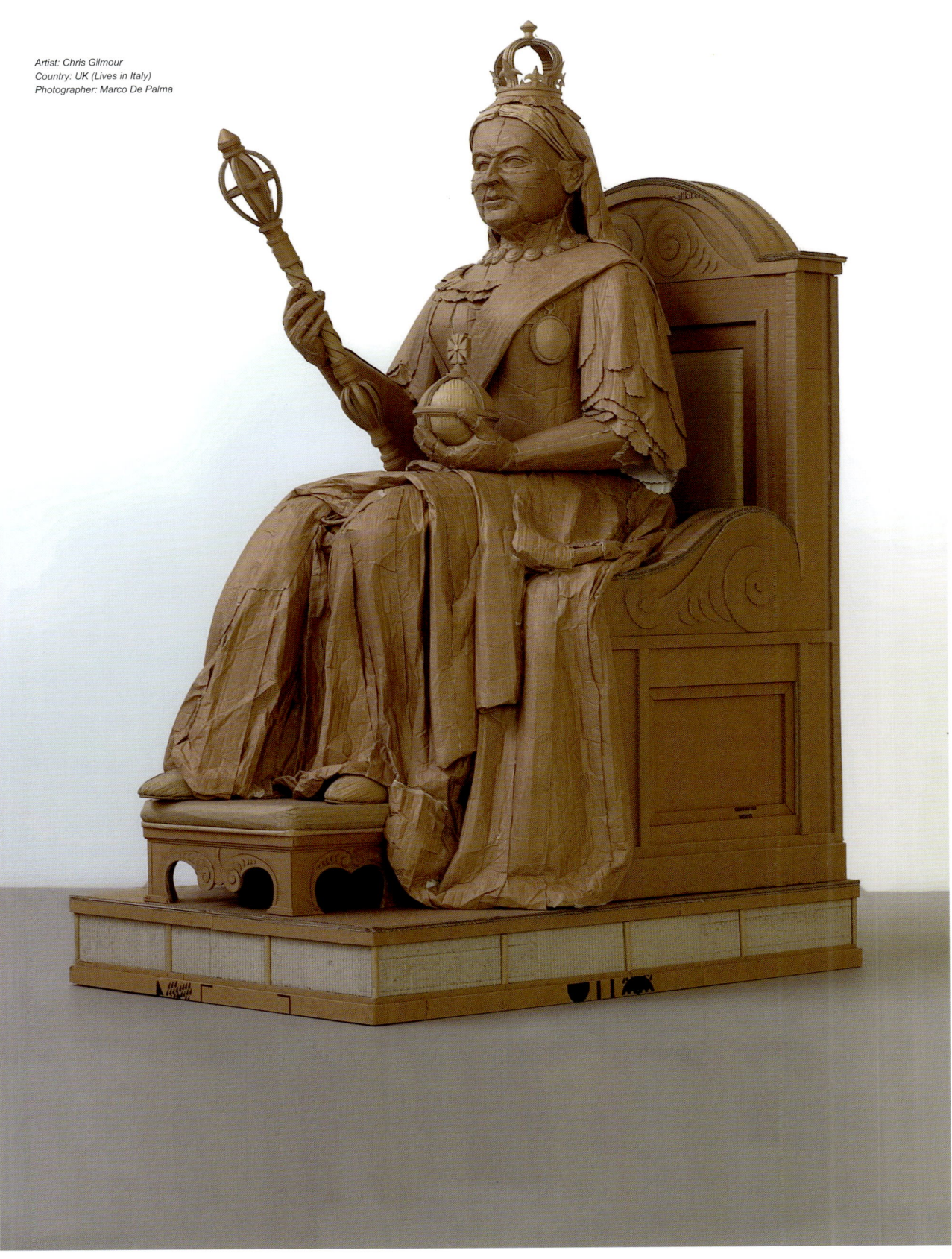

13. Saint George and the Dragon

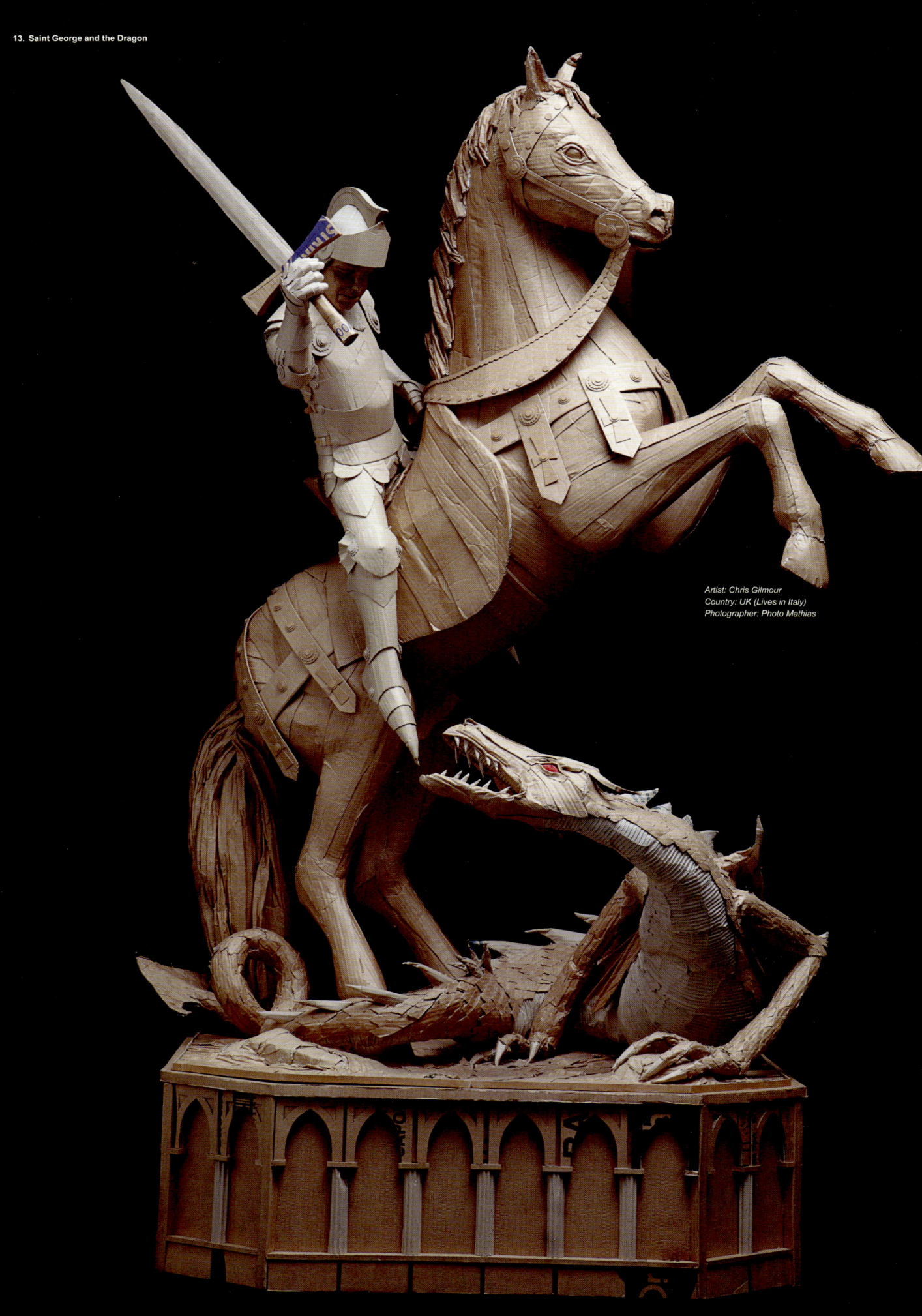

Artist: Chris Gilmour
Country: UK (Lives in Italy)
Photographer: Photo Mathias

14. Equestrian statue

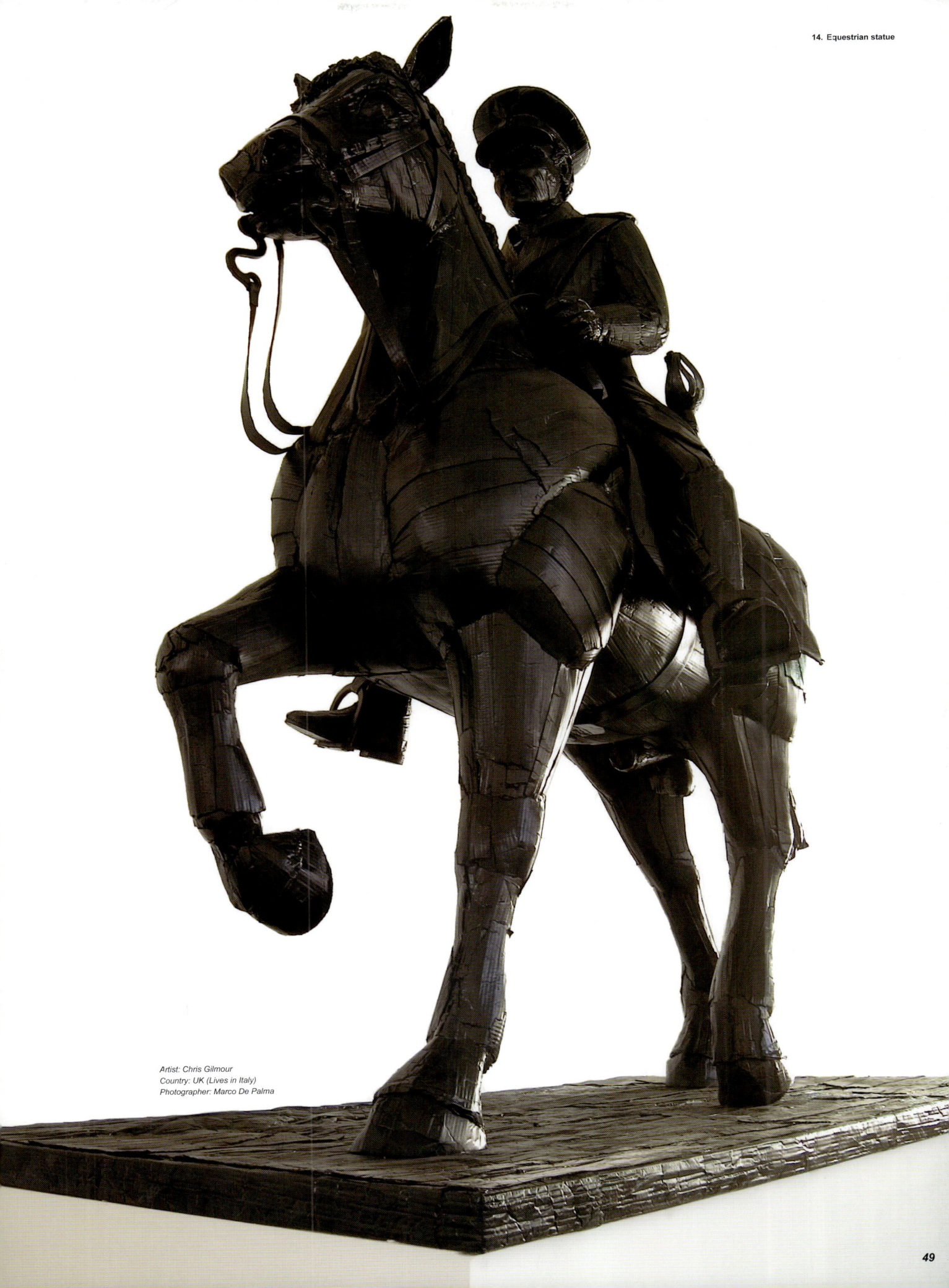

Artist: Chris Gilmour
Country: UK (Lives in Italy)
Photographer: Marco De Palma

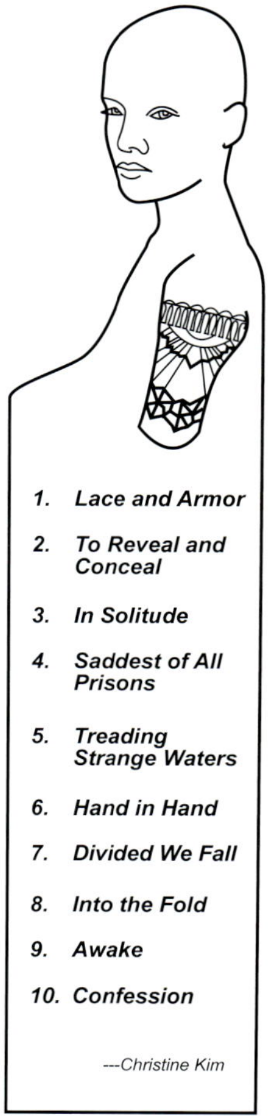

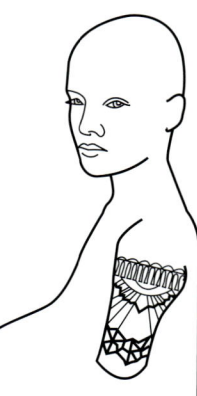

1. Lace and Armor
2. To Reveal and Conceal
3. In Solitude
4. Saddest of All Prisons
5. Treading Strange Waters
6. Hand in Hand
7. Divided We Fall
8. Into the Fold
9. Awake
10. Confession

---Christine Kim

1. **Lace and Armor**

A fence keeps out the unwanted. It protects, but also imprisons. Cut out of paper, the fence and screen become barriers; however, these ones are delicate, fragile, and paper-thin.

Artist: Christine Kim
Country: Canada
Photographer: Christine Kim

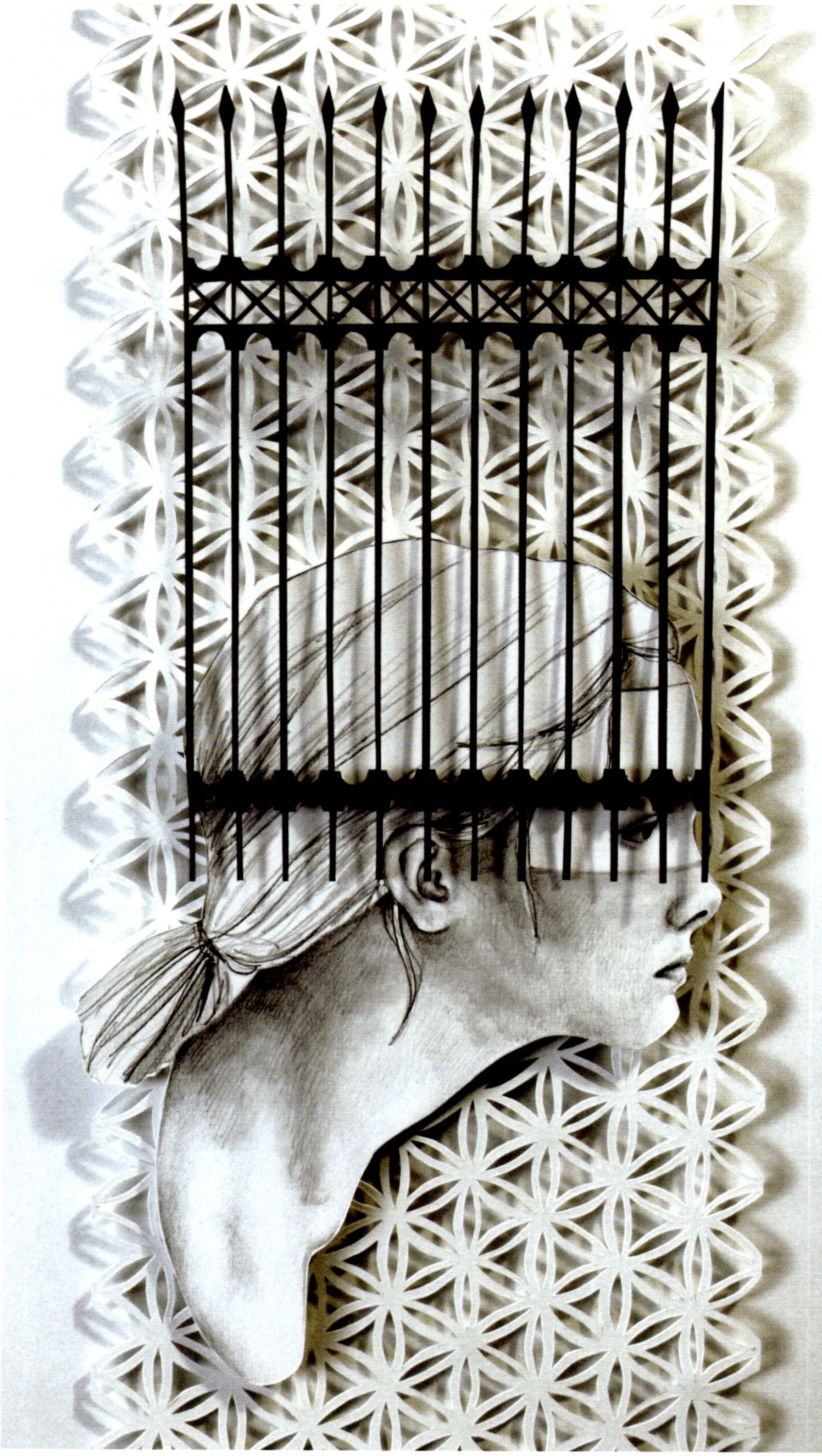

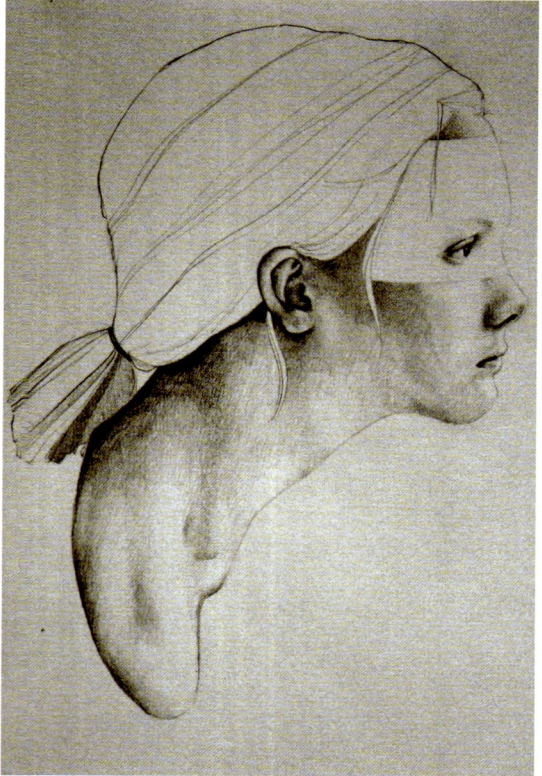

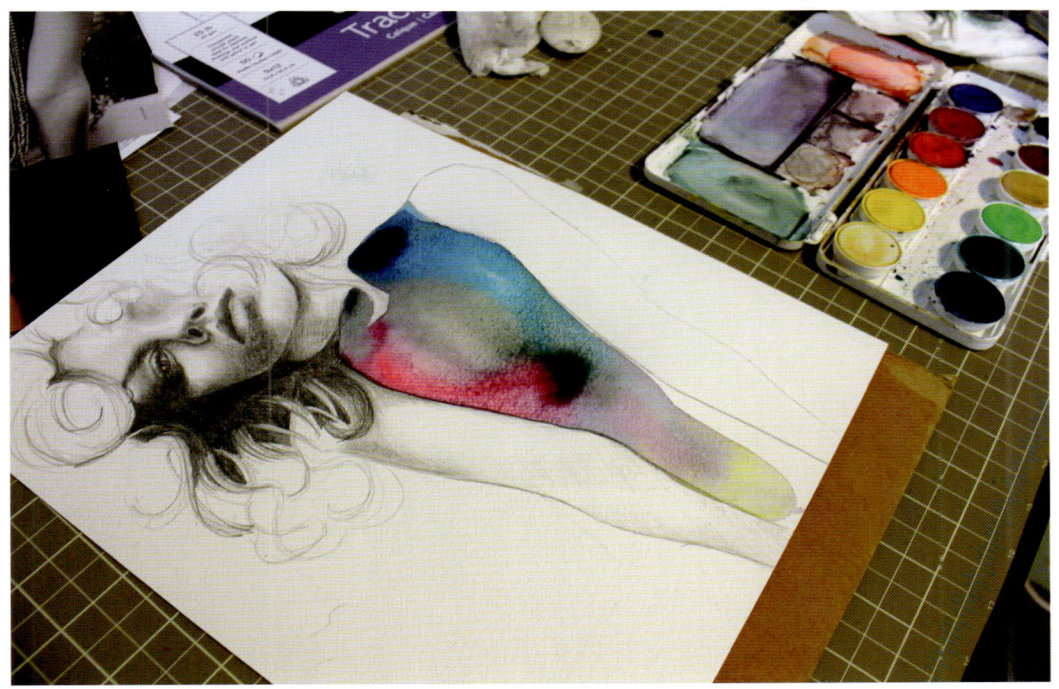

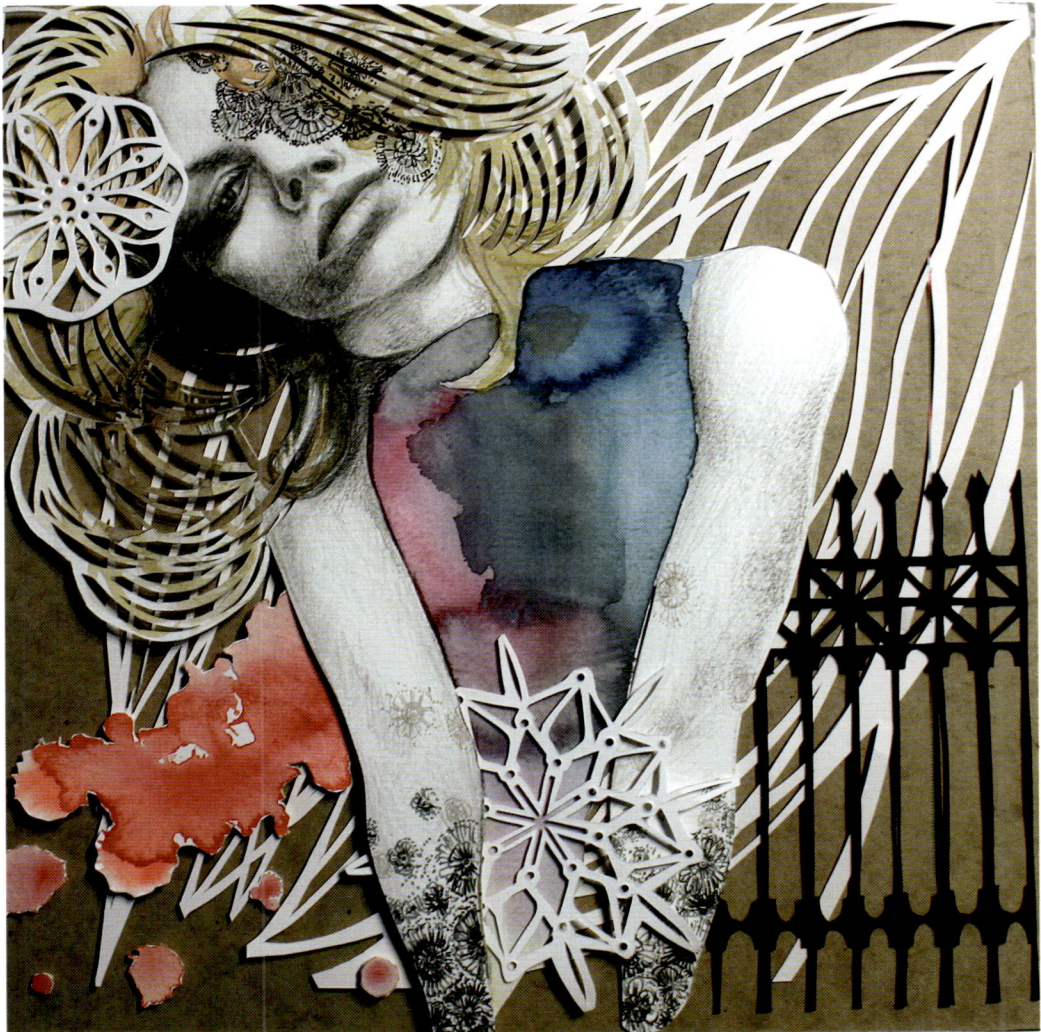

2. To Reveal and Conceal

Lace is also a fence. Both reveal and conceal through heavy ornamentation. Here, black lace is drawn on her face and arms as if they were tattooed. I'm interested in black lace because of its reference to funerals – a black lace mantilla worn against death, and for death. I am currently working on a new body of work focusing solely on lace veils.

Artist: Christine Kim
Country: Canada
Photographer: Christine Kim

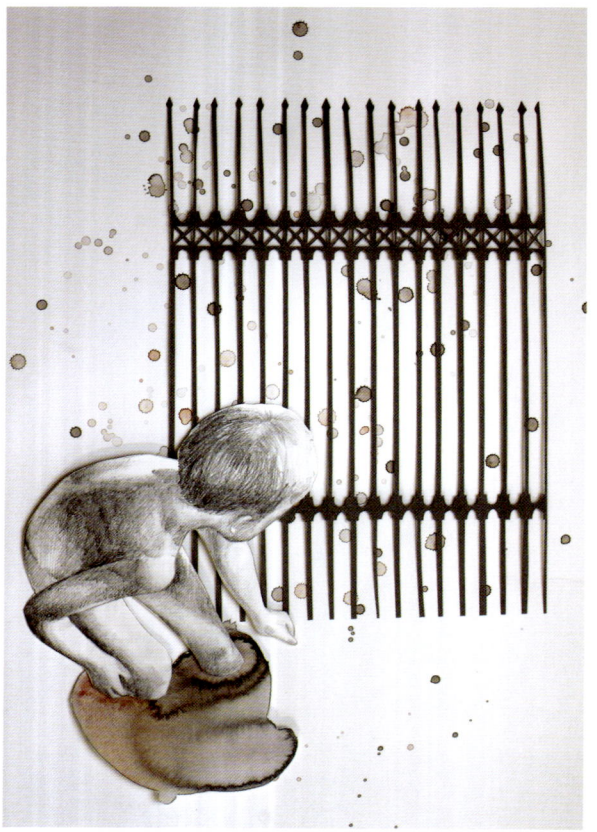

3. In Solitude

I wanted to play with the distance of the figure to the fence. The boy is wading in murky waters and bends down, peering more closely at this barrier. I wanted a fence to tower over him and create tension between the vulnerability of his youth and an unmoving barrier.

Artist: Christine Kim
Country: Canada
Photographer: Christine Kim

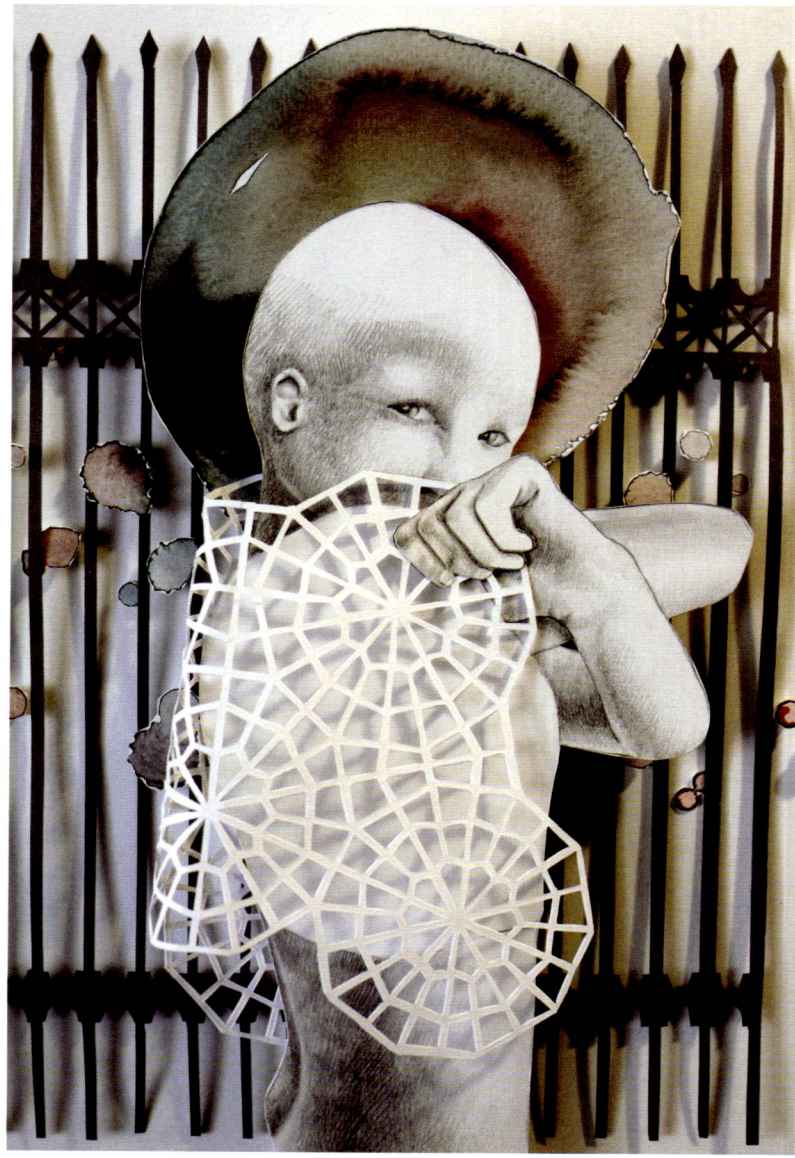

4. Saddest of All Prisons

I wanted to fold this paper screen and wrap it around the figure as if it were clothing; however, this is not soft and malleable. Instead, it is rigid and self-imposed.

Artist: Christine Kim
Country: Canada
Photographer: Christine Kim

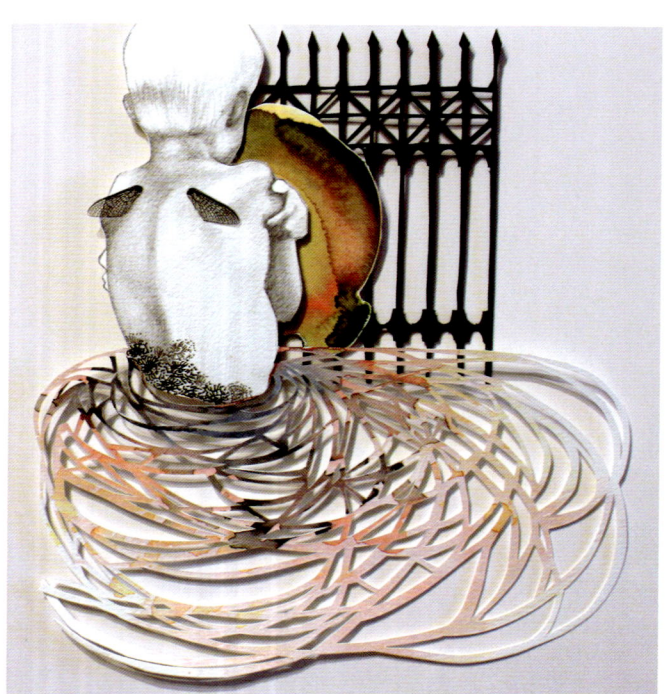

5. Treading Strange Waters

I drew this boy wading in water as a lithograph years ago. The image stayed with me because it reminded me of seeing the vast ocean in awe and in fear. The boy, however, sees a fence that protects, but also restrains.

Artist: Christine Kim
Country: Canada
Photographer: Christine Kim

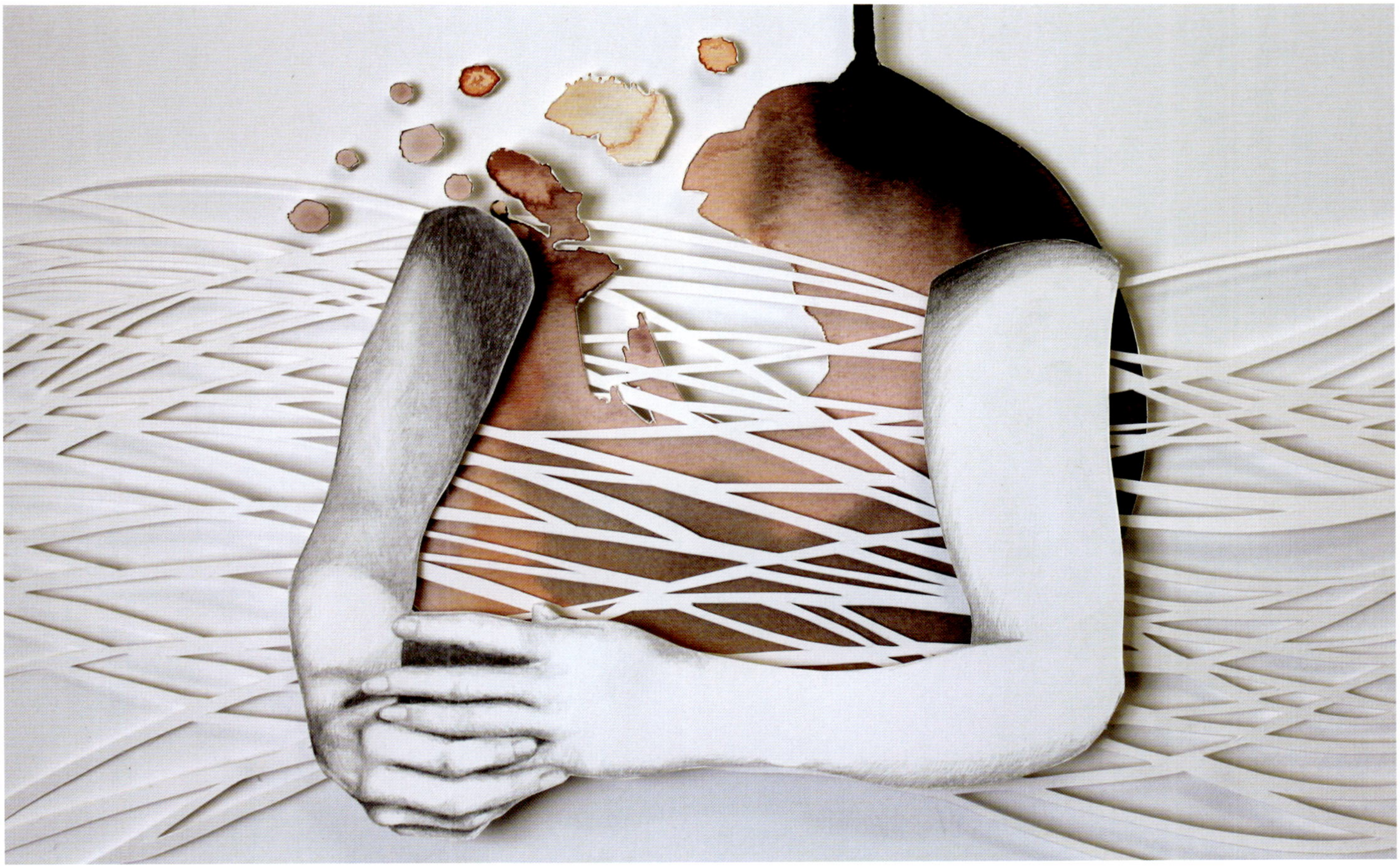

6. **Hand in Hand**
I wanted to isolate arms and hands to reveal an emotion. The hands here are nervous or uneasy. In the background, I wanted to play with stillness and movement in the looseness of gestural color and the precision of cut lines.

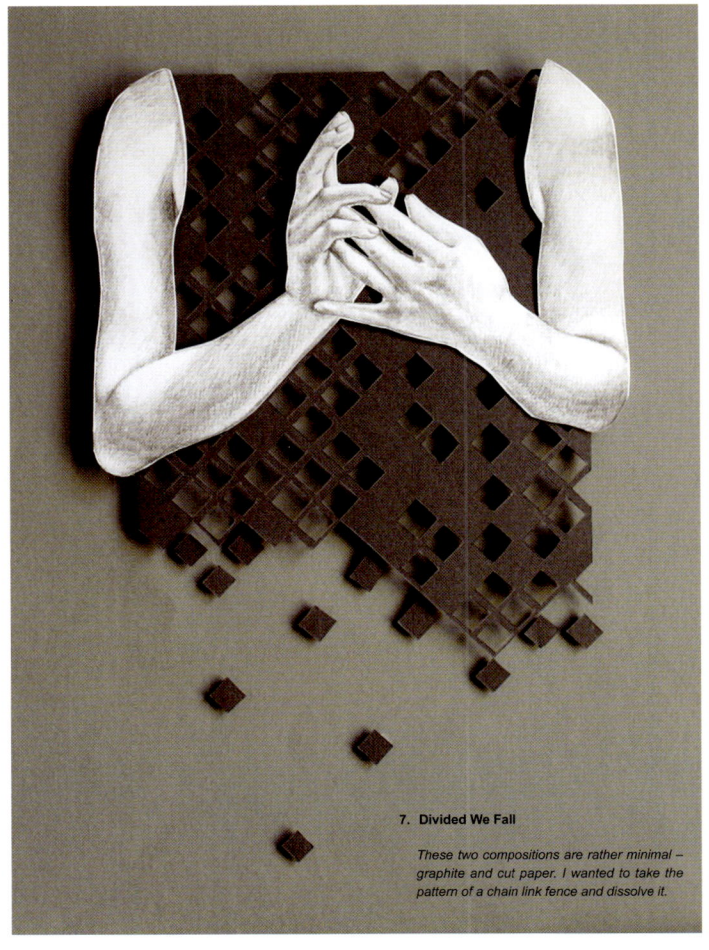

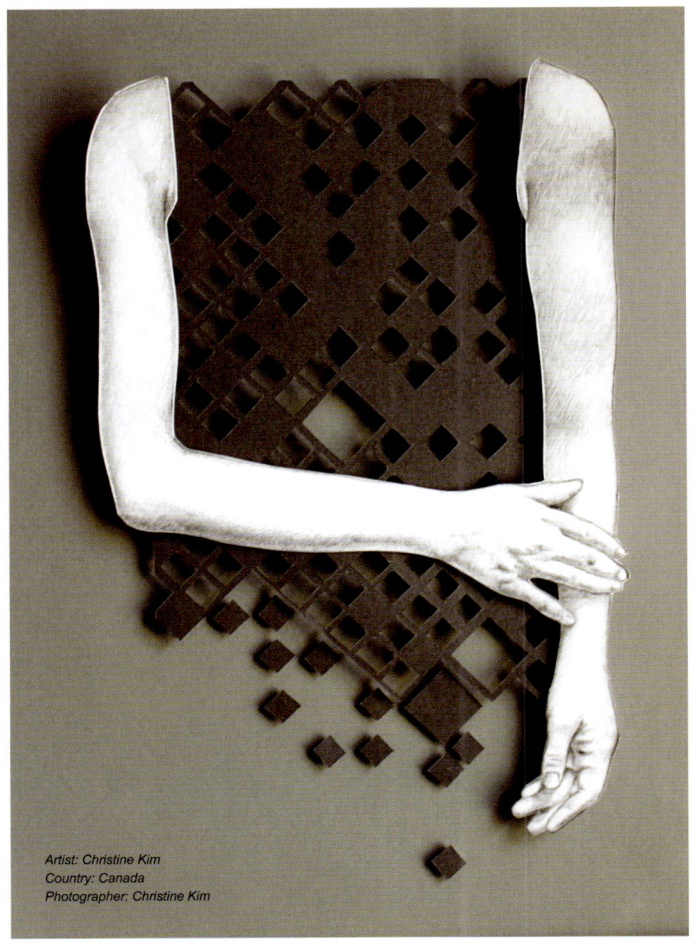

7. **Divided We Fall**
These two compositions are rather minimal – graphite and cut paper. I wanted to take the pattern of a chain link fence and dissolve it.

Artist: Christine Kim
Country: Canada
Photographer: Christine Kim

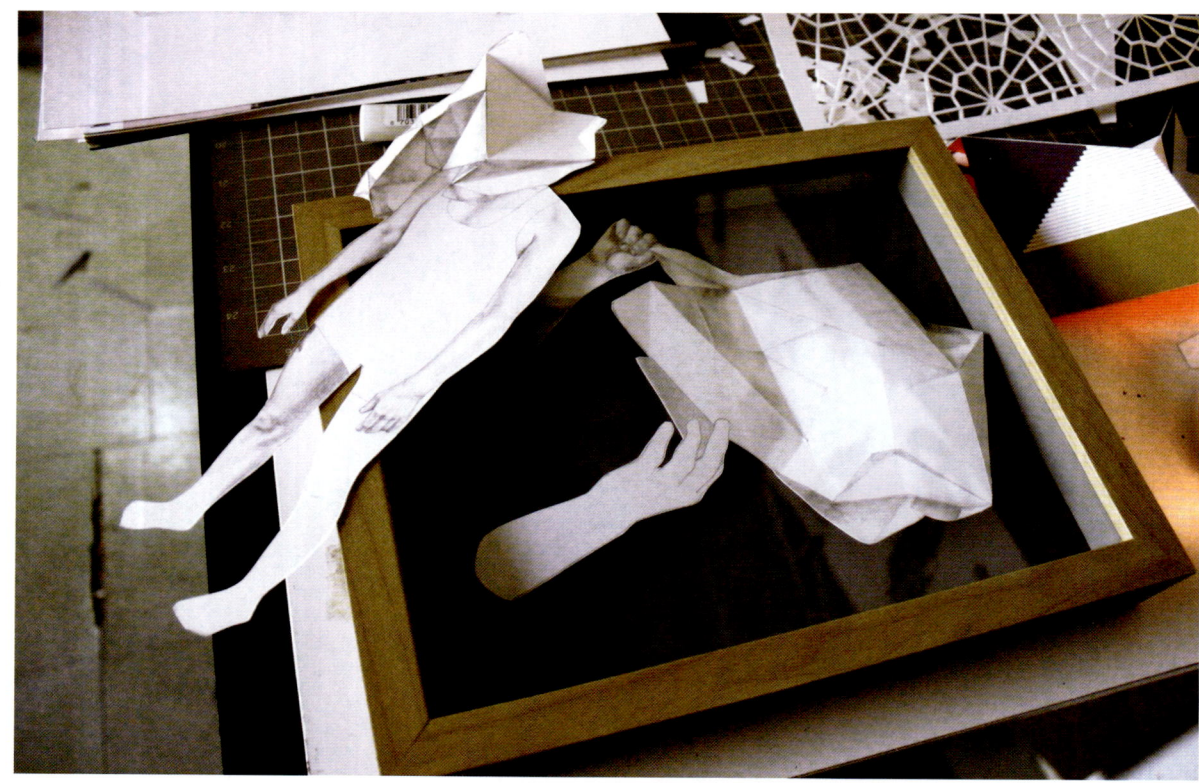

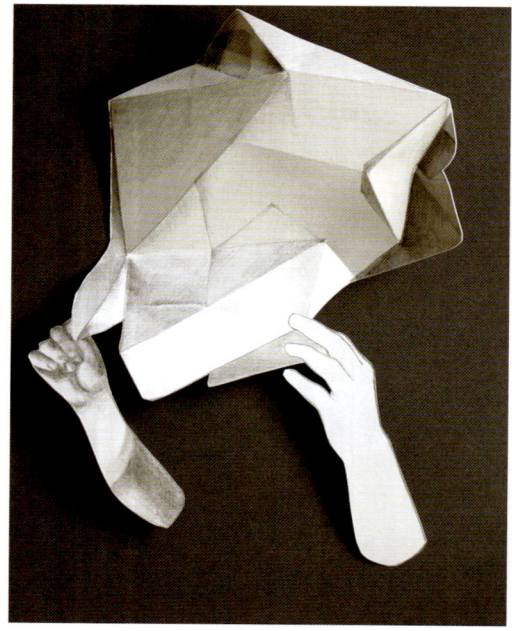

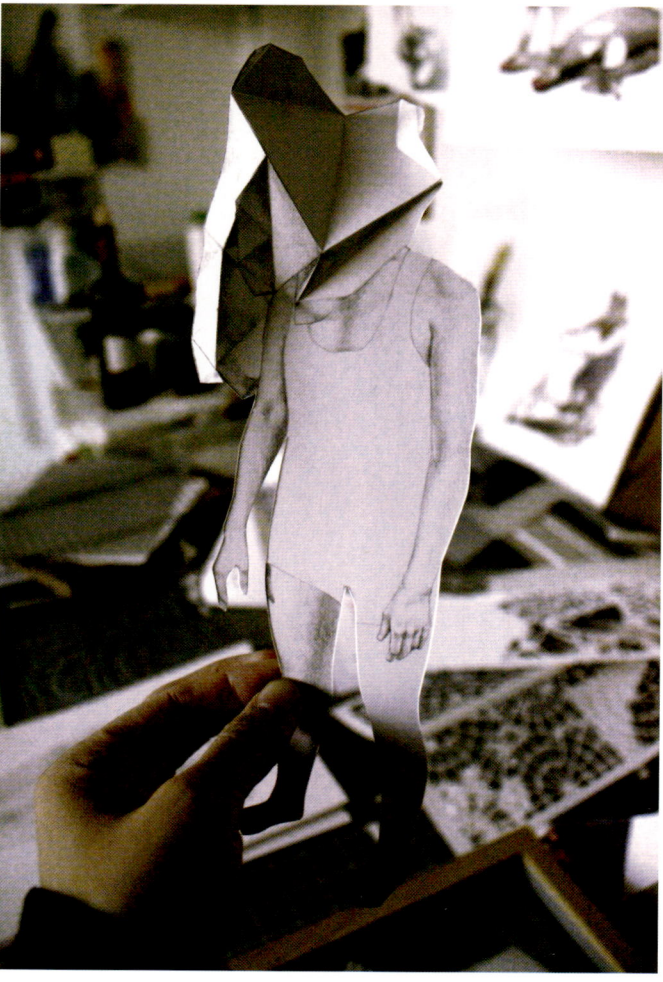

8. Into the Fold

This piece is based on a series of photographs of me wearing folded paper. I drew myself and folded the drawing afterwards to play with the geometric and organic, the light and shadow.

Artist: Christine Kim
Country: Canada
Photographer: Christine Kim

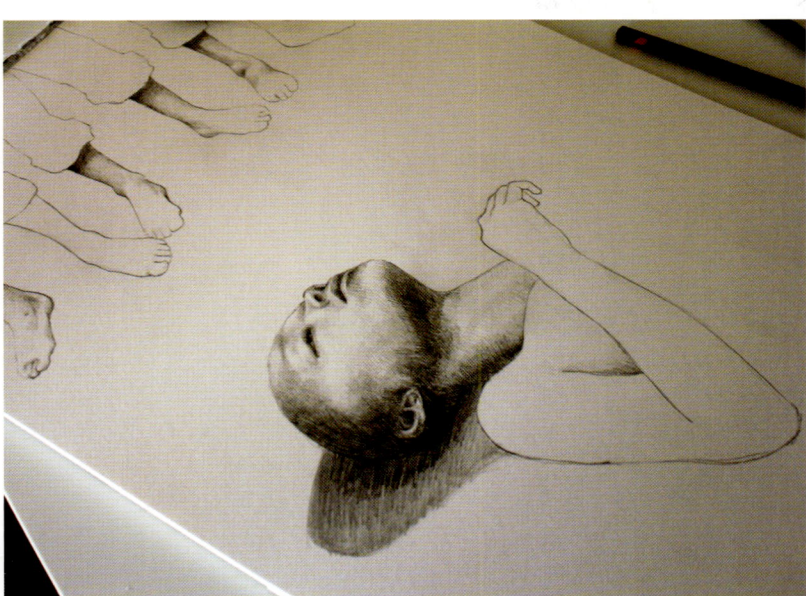

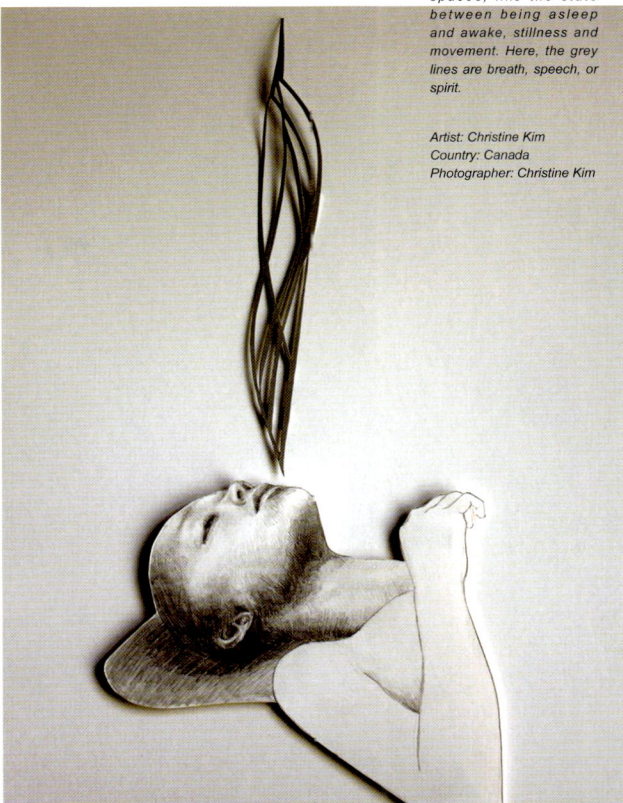

9. Awake

I am interested in interstitial spaces, like the state between being asleep and awake, stillness and movement. Here, the grey lines are breath, speech, or spirit.

Artist: Christine Kim
Country: Canada
Photographer: Christine Kim

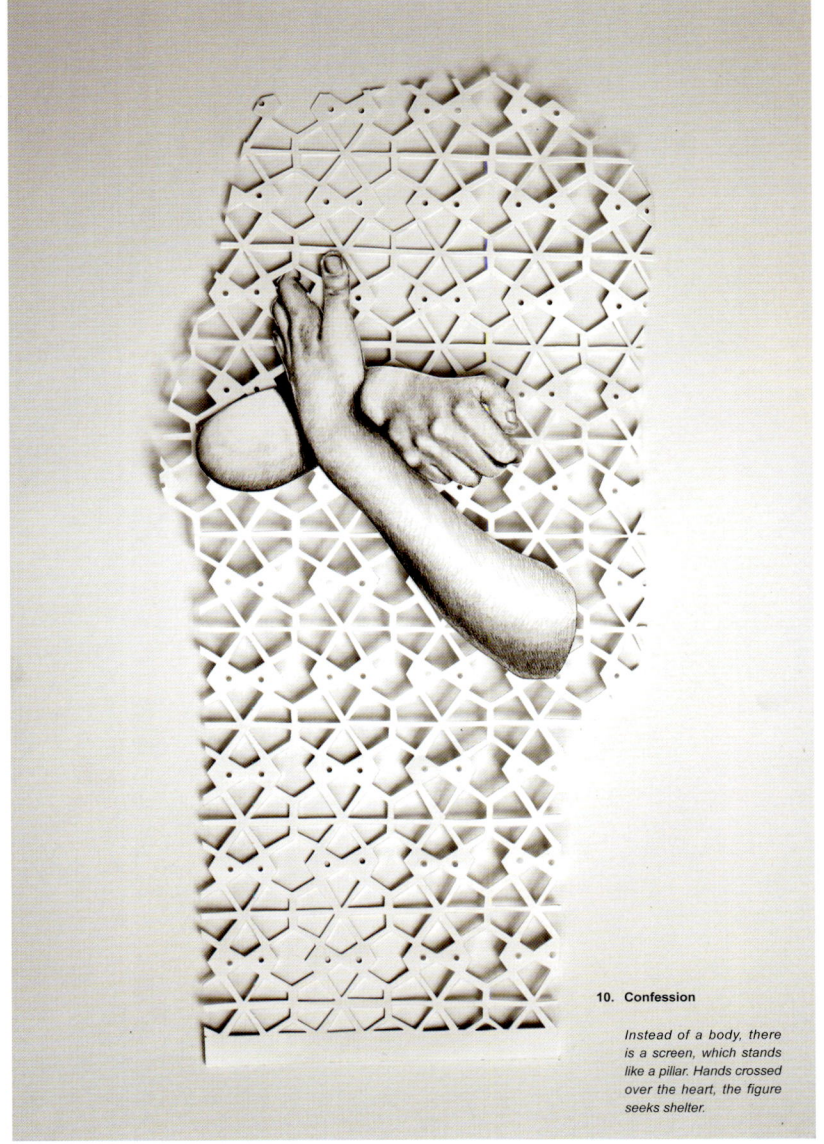

10. Confession

Instead of a body, there is a screen, which stands like a pillar. Hands crossed over the heart, the figure seeks shelter.

Artist: Christine Kim
Country: Canada
Photographer: Christine Kim

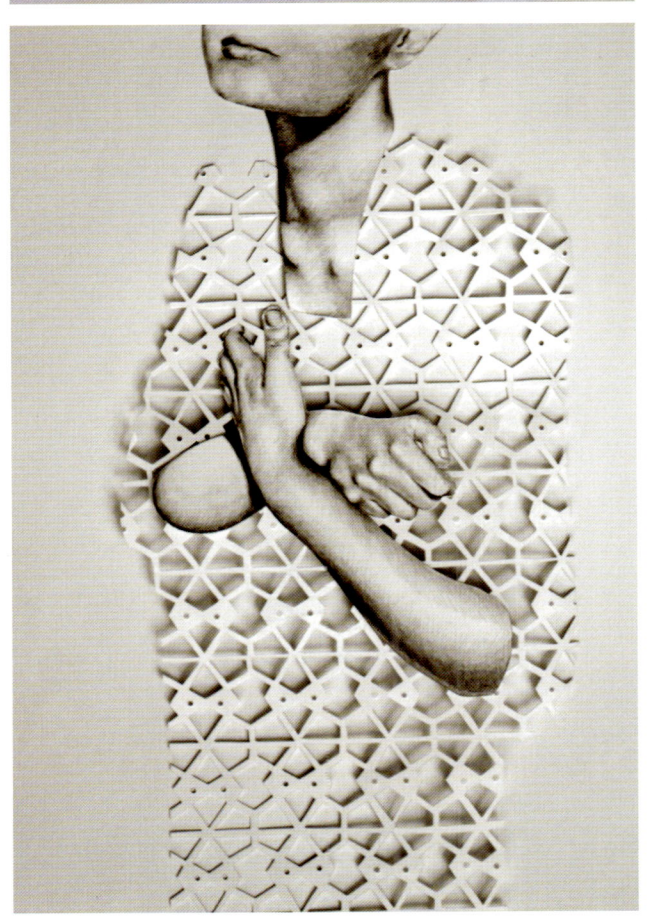

1. Epiliminion

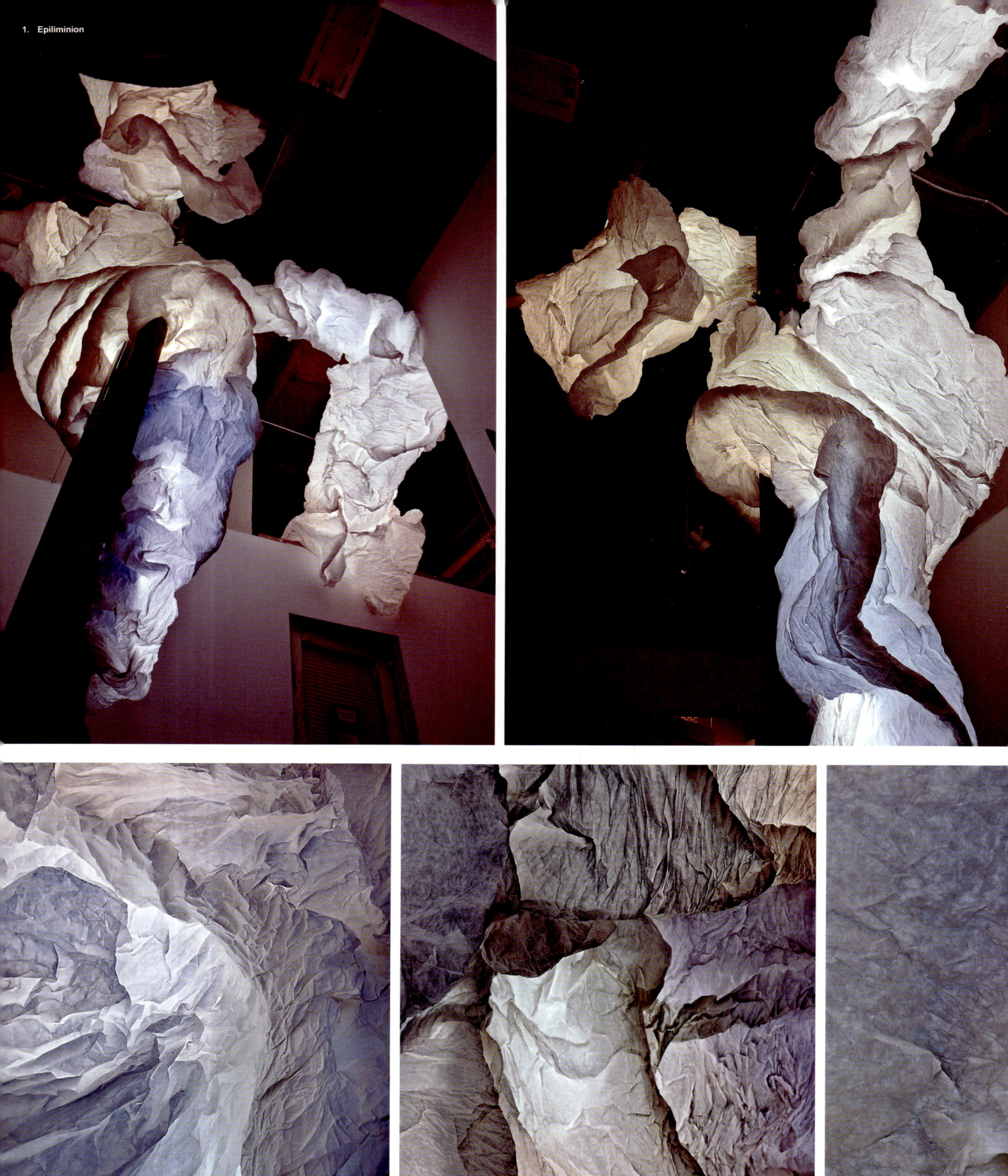

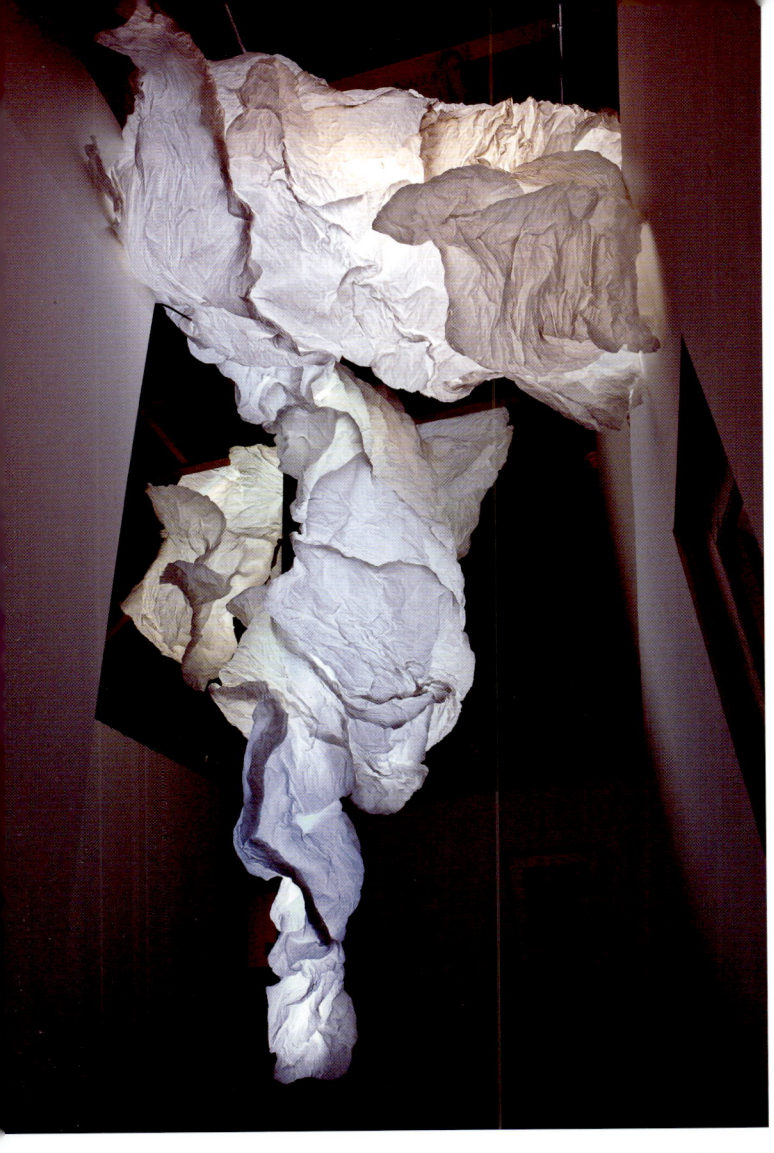
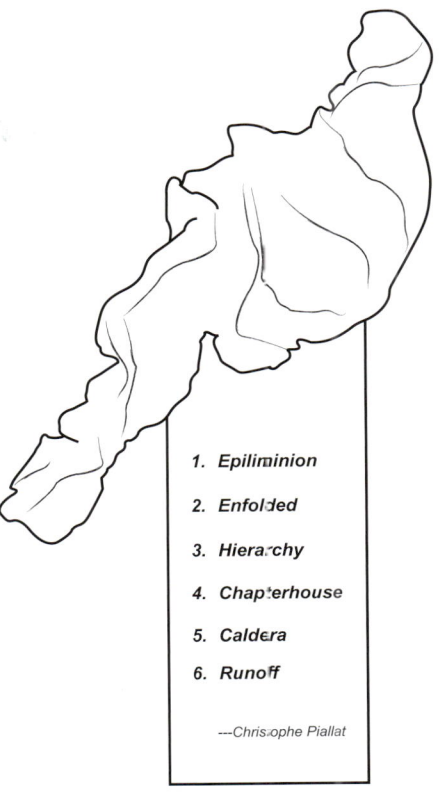

1. *Epiliminion*
2. *Enfolded*
3. *Hierarchy*
4. *Chapterhouse*
5. *Caldera*
6. *Runoff*

---Christophe Piallat

Artist: Christophe Piallat
Country: USA
Photographer: Christophe Piallat

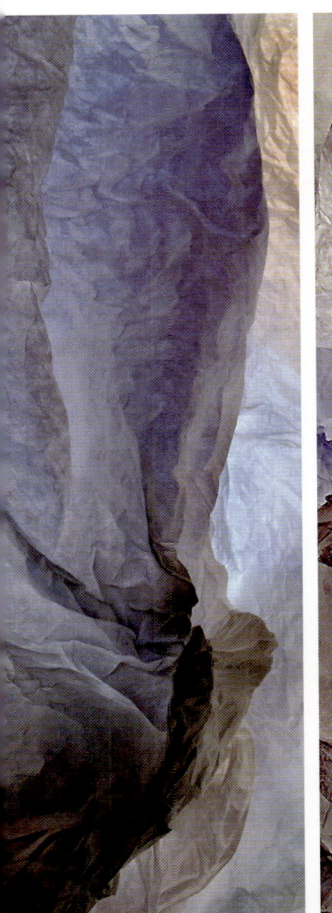
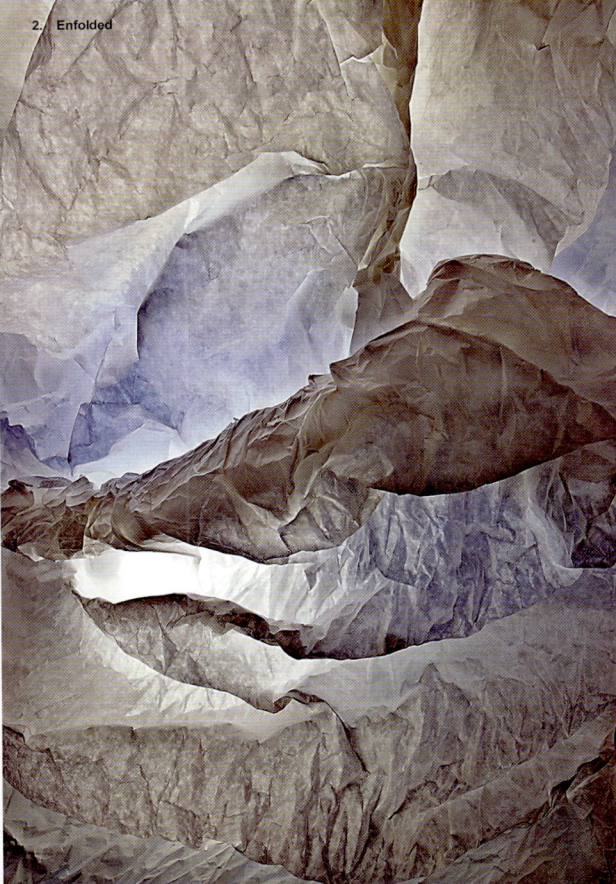

2. Enfolded

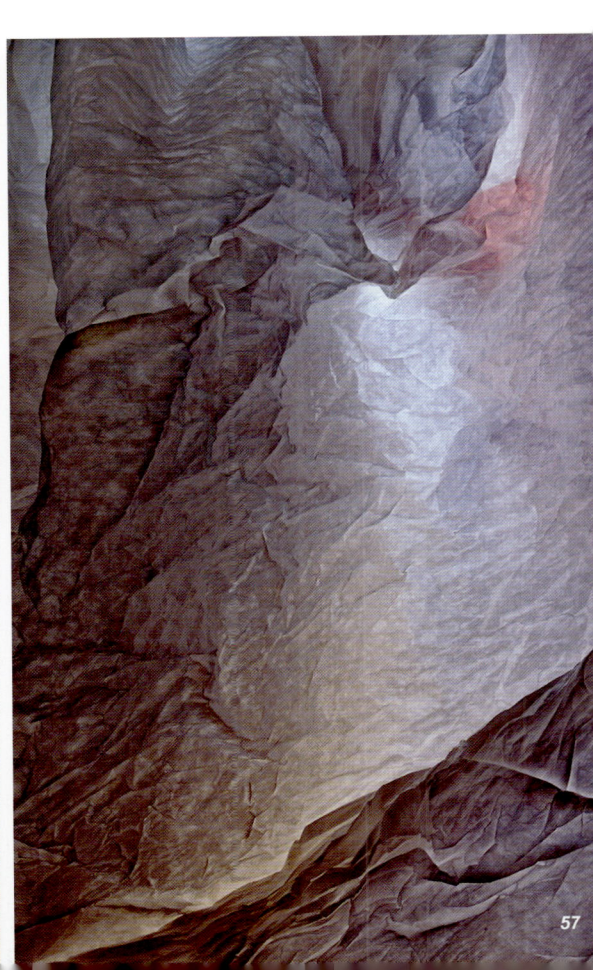

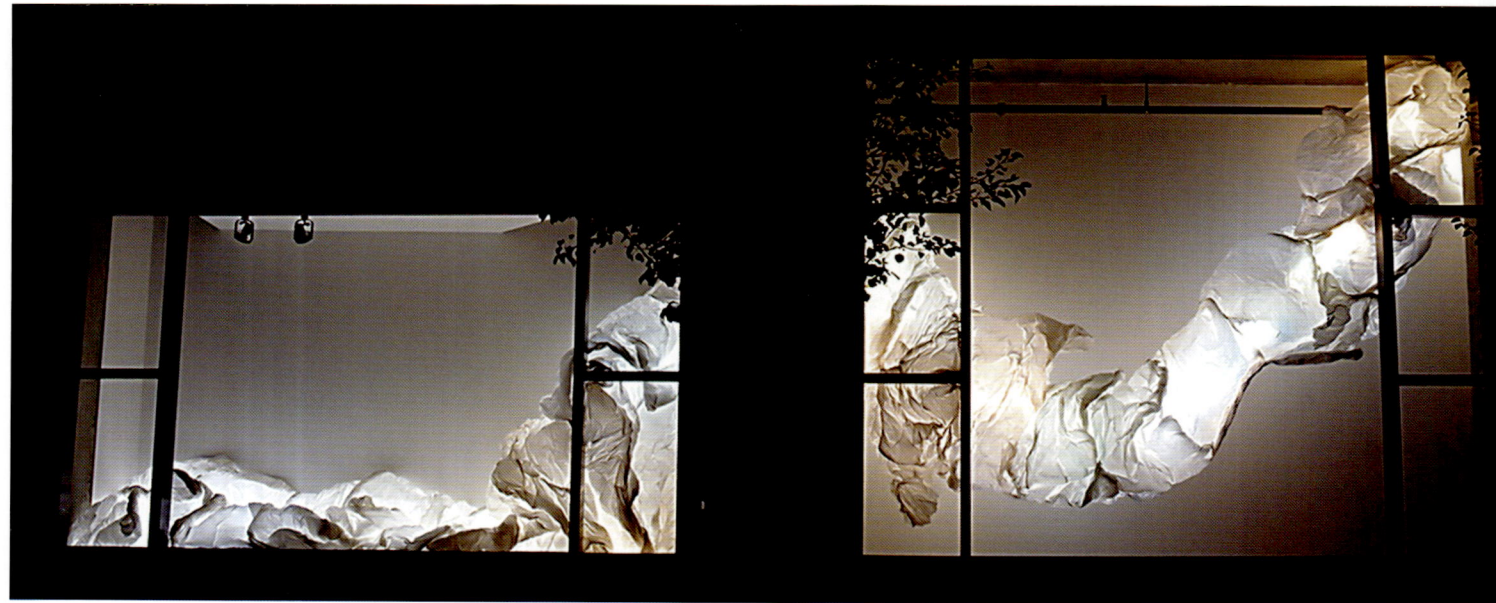

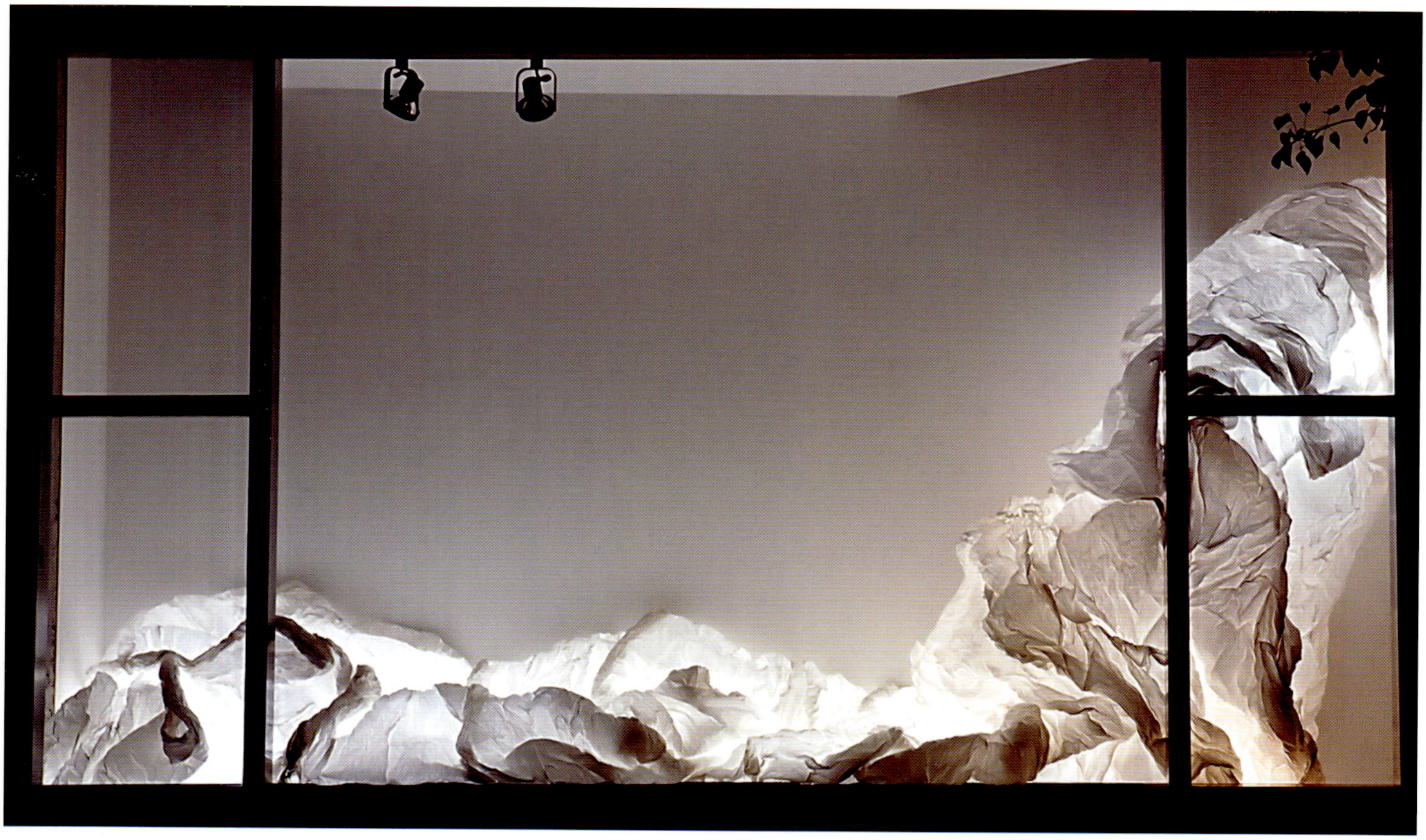

2. Enfolded

For the last five years my practice has focused on the amalgamation of three dimensional installation and photography. Light is the integral component at the heart of these media and represents the true foundation of my work. Similar to the photographic process, my installations seek to capture light, transform paper, and present a sculptural, as opposed to a pictorial, moment in time. Materials include: recycled, hand-crushed, butcher paper, wood, natural and artificial light sources.

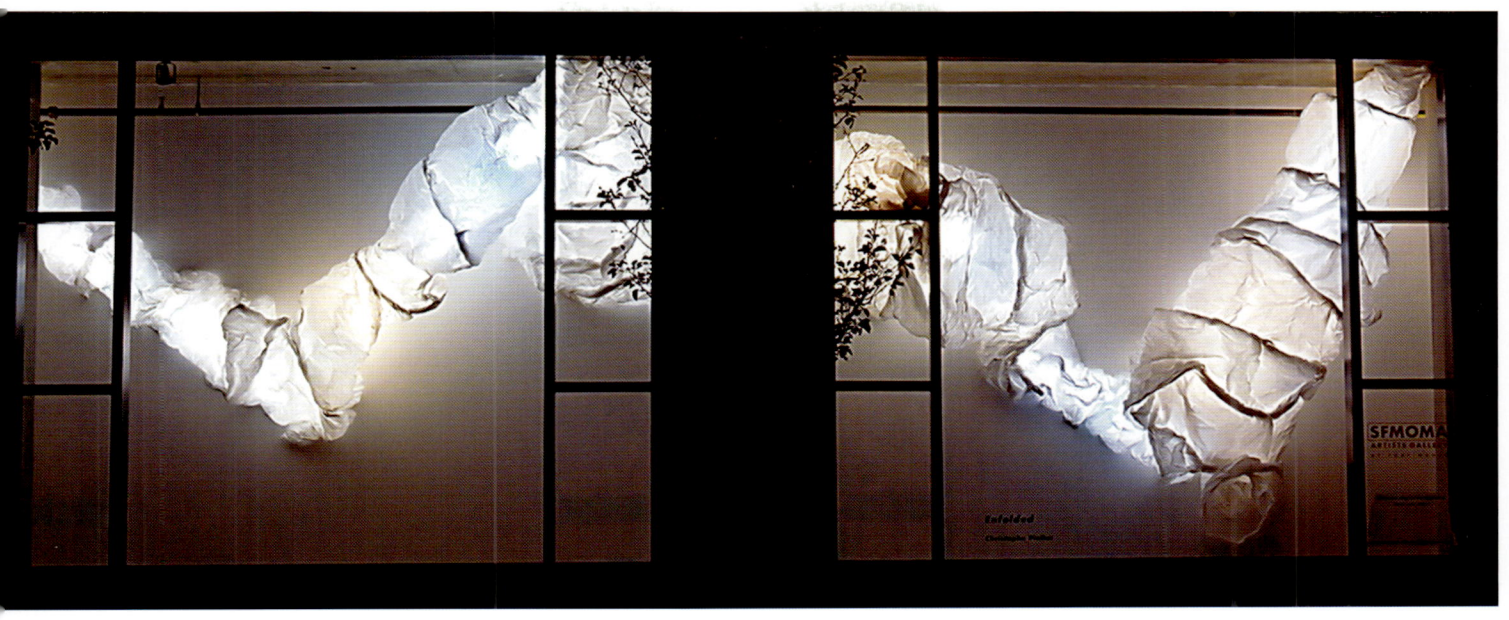

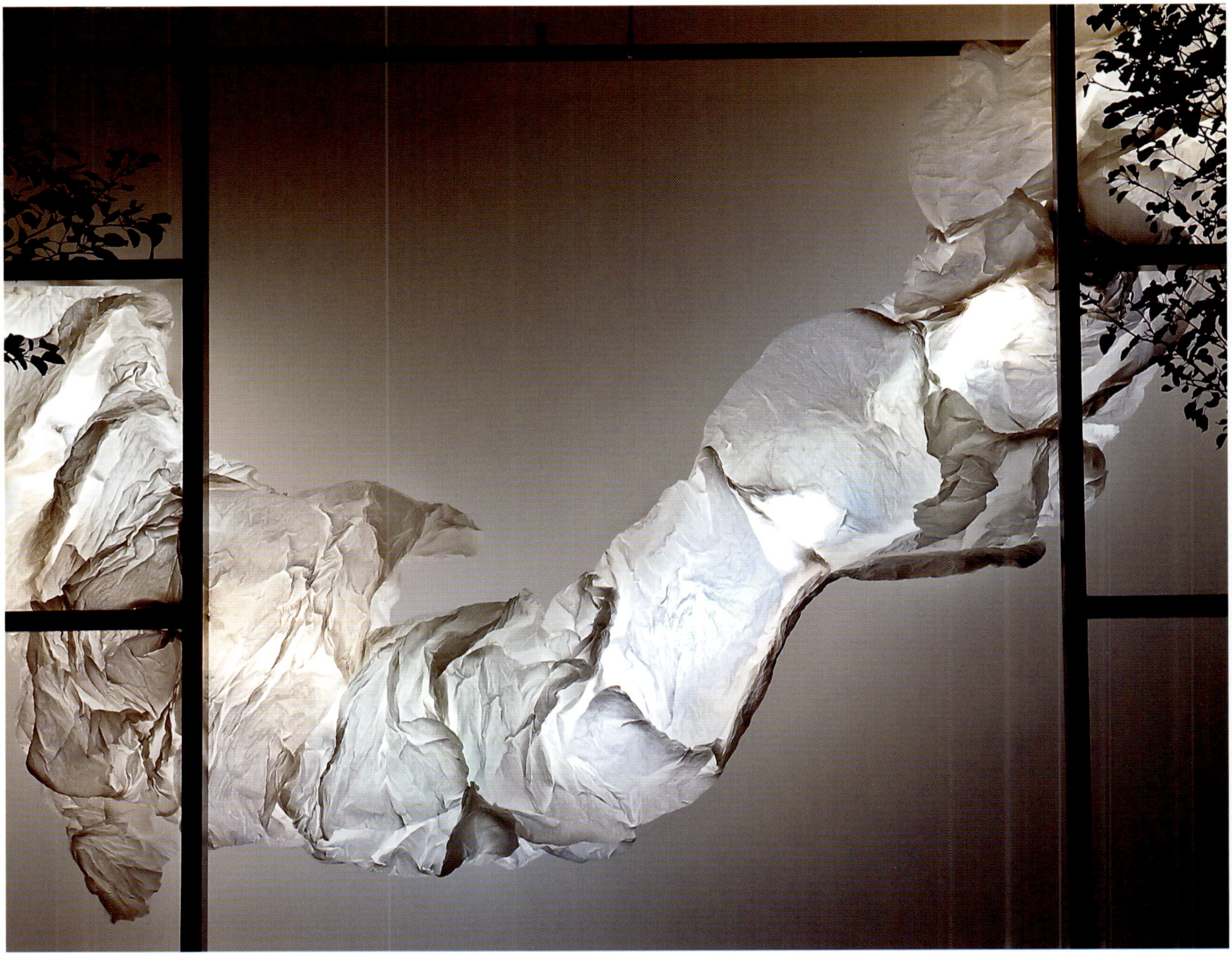

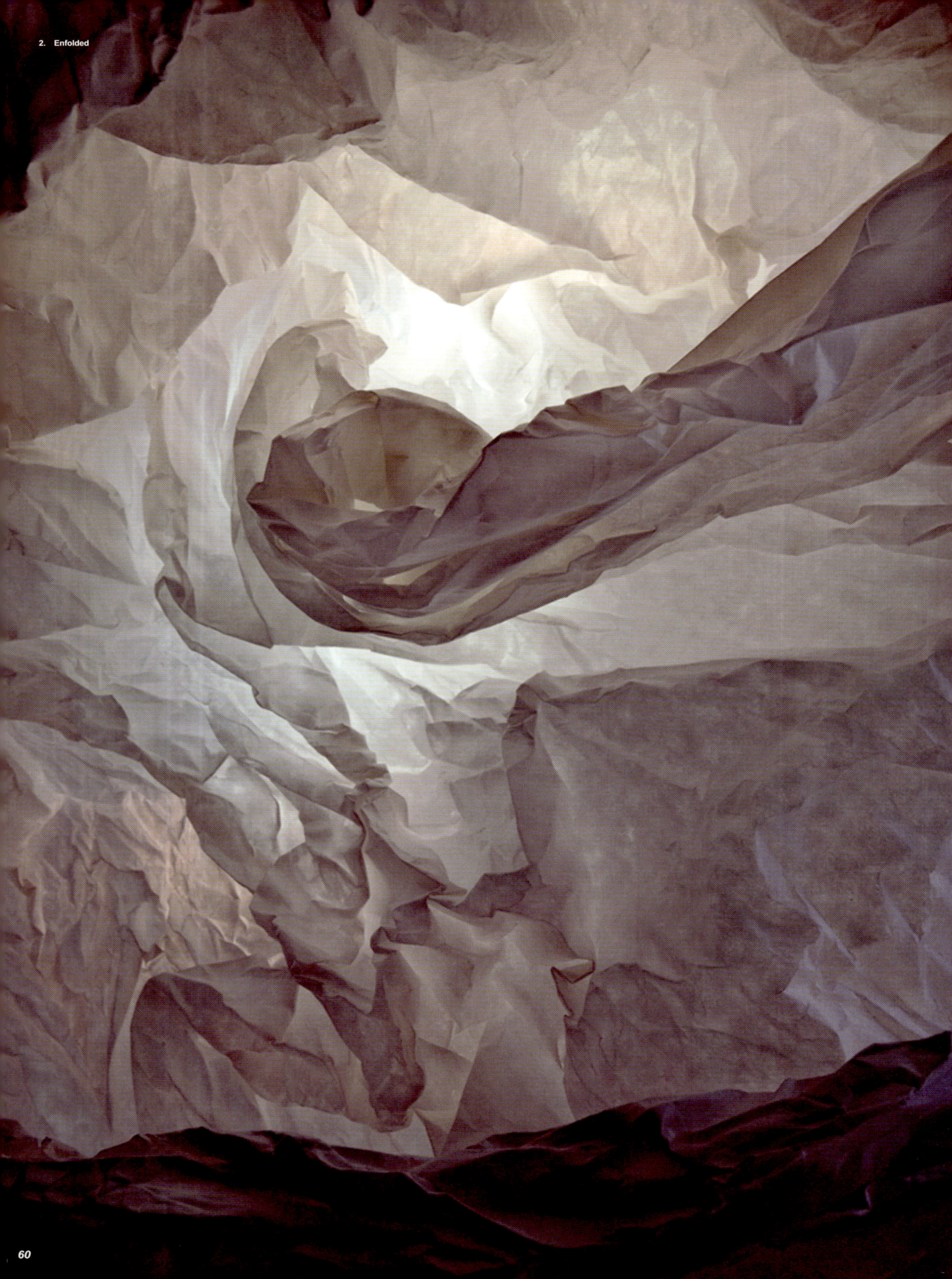

3. Hierarchy

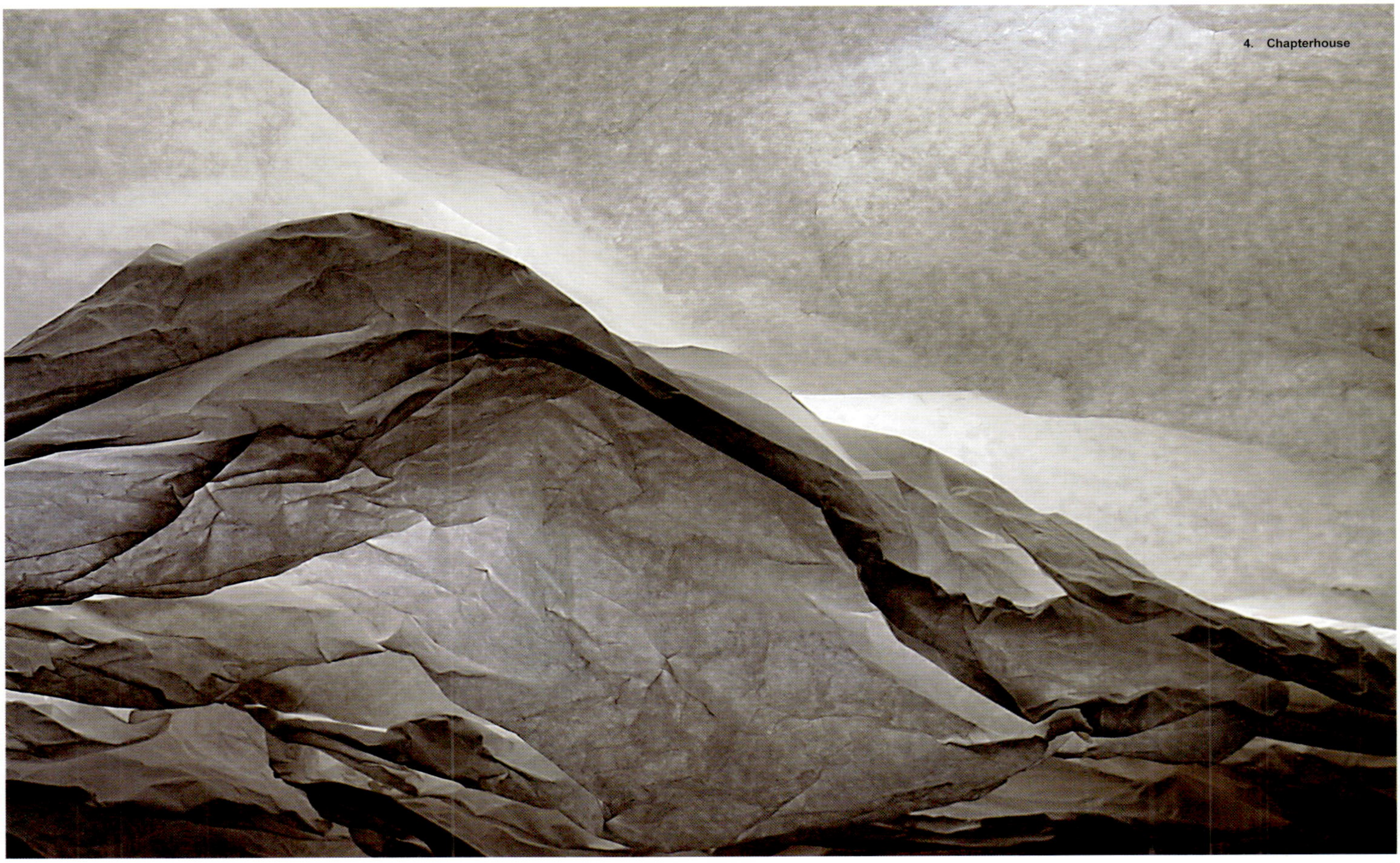

4. Chapterhouse

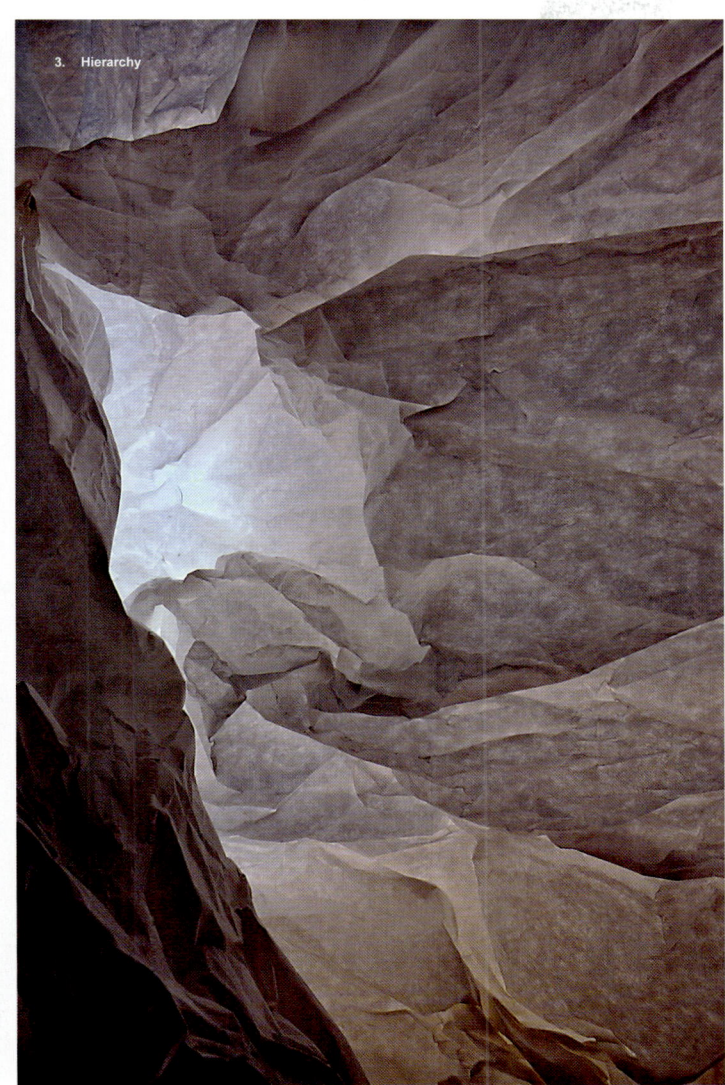
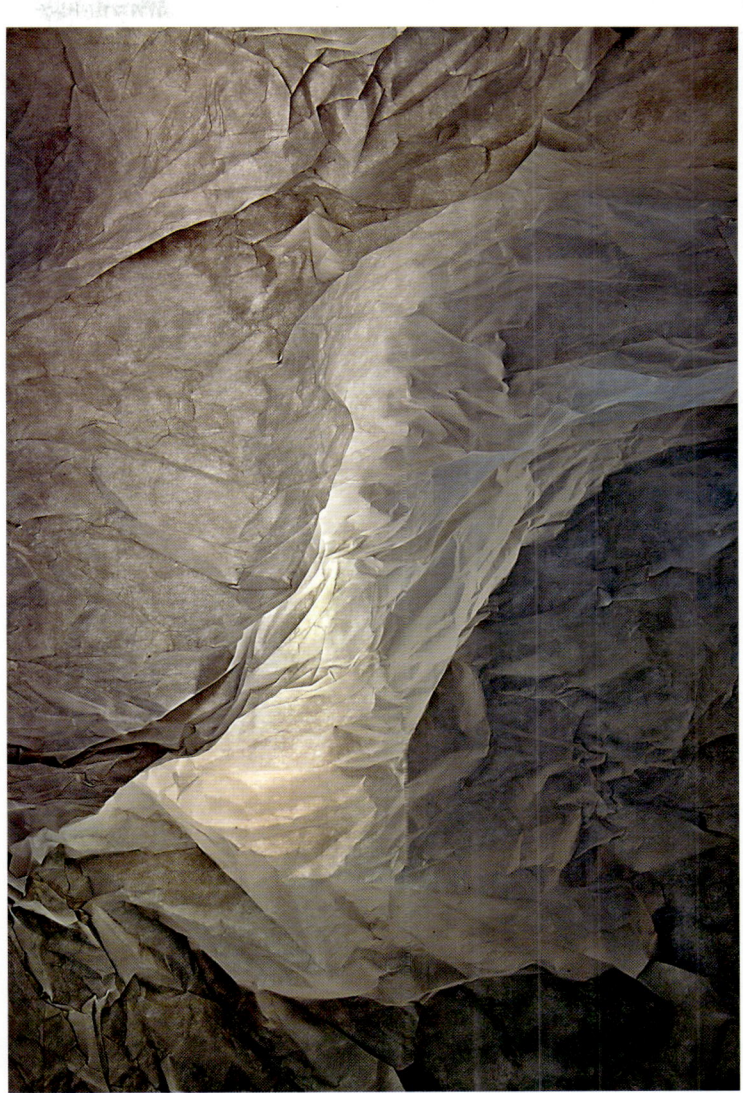

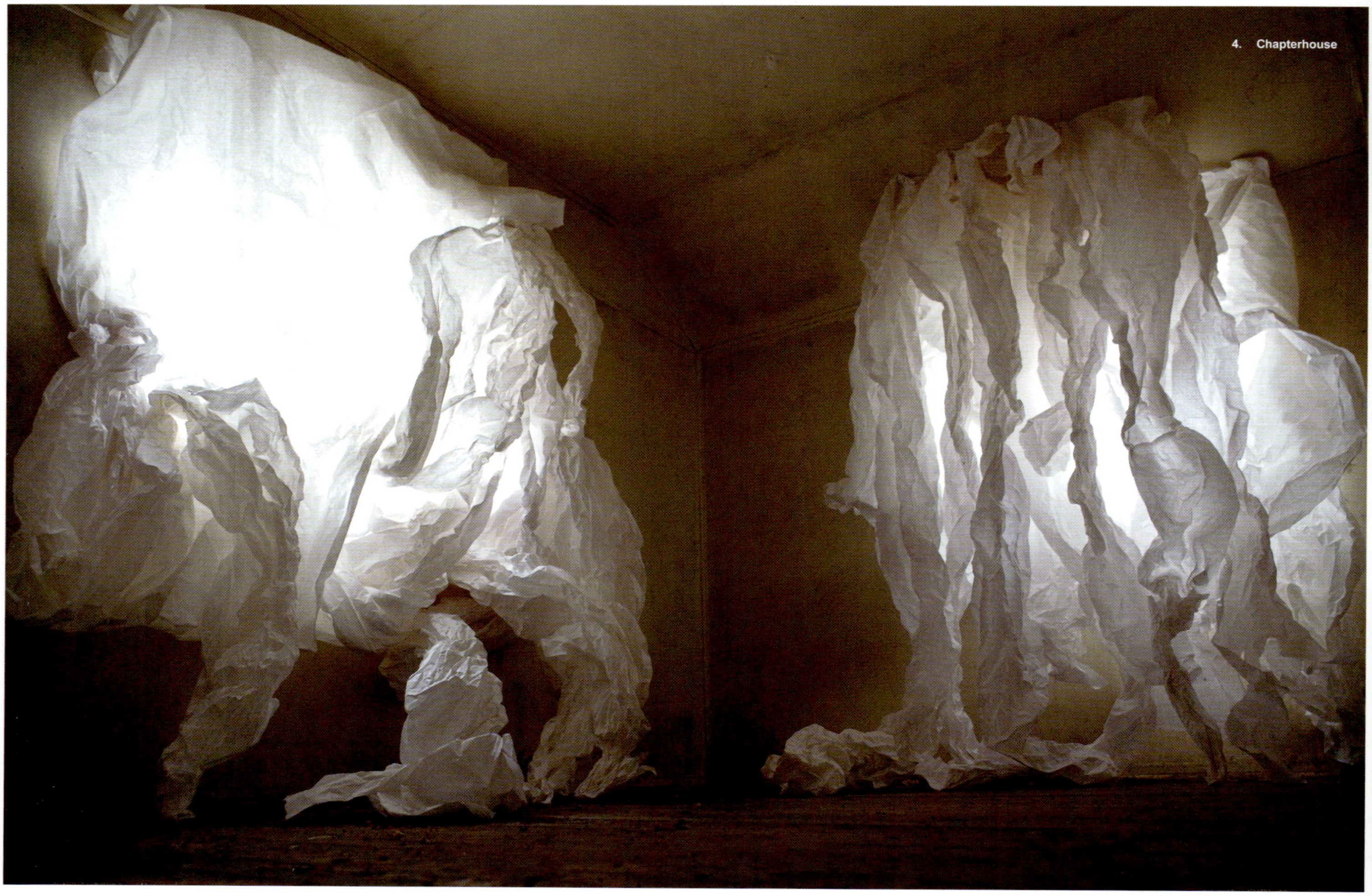

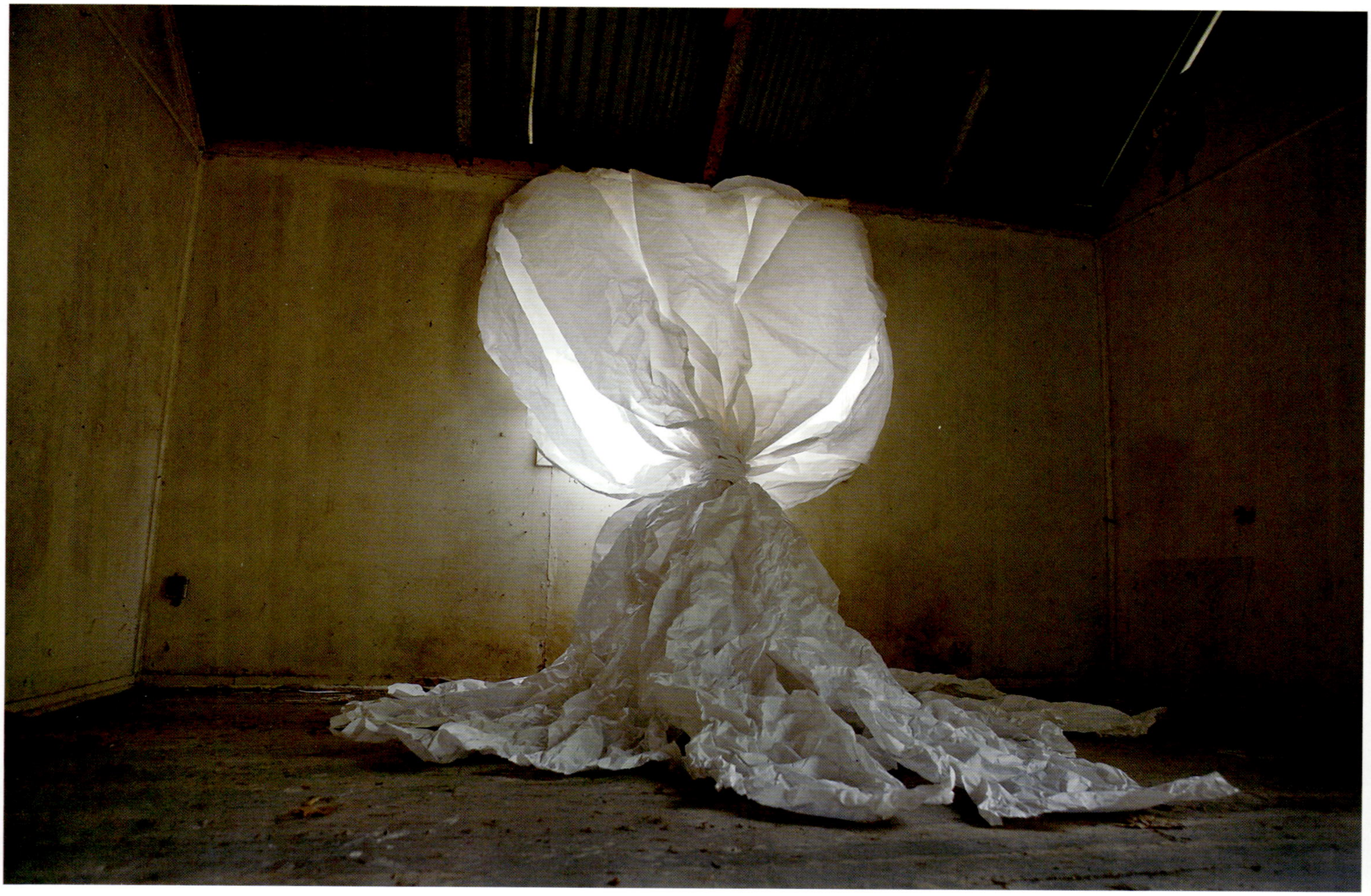

4. Chapterhouse

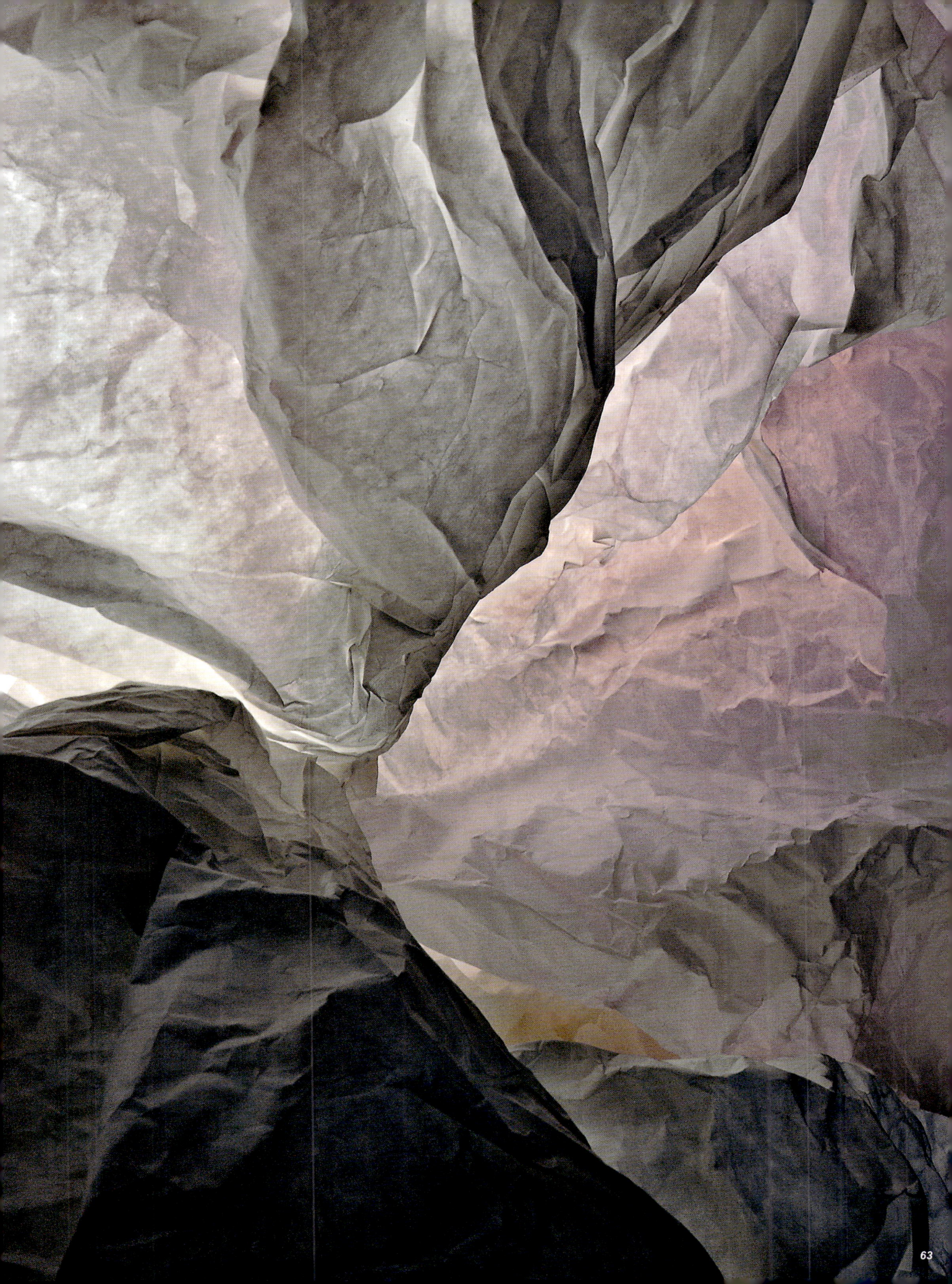

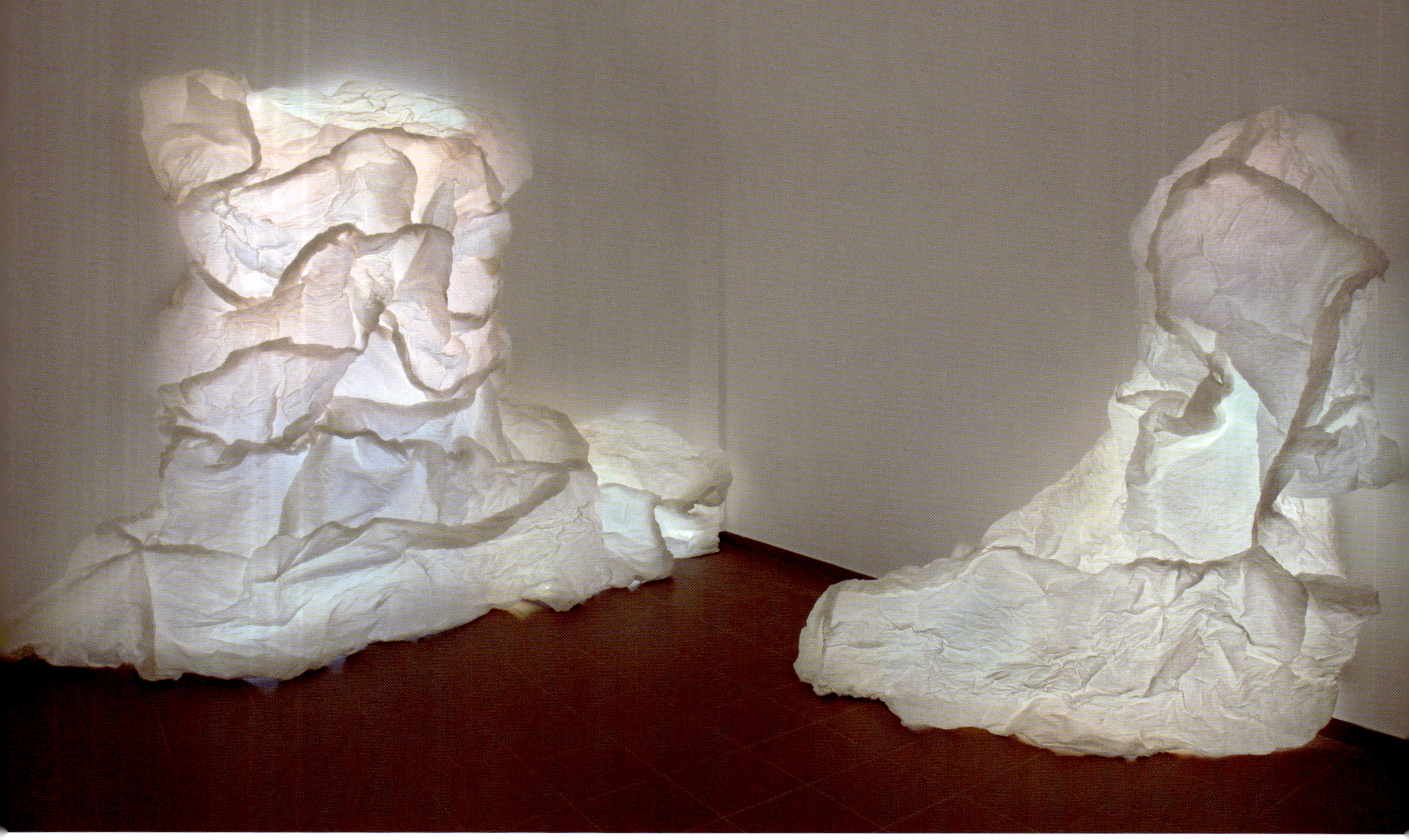

5. Caldera

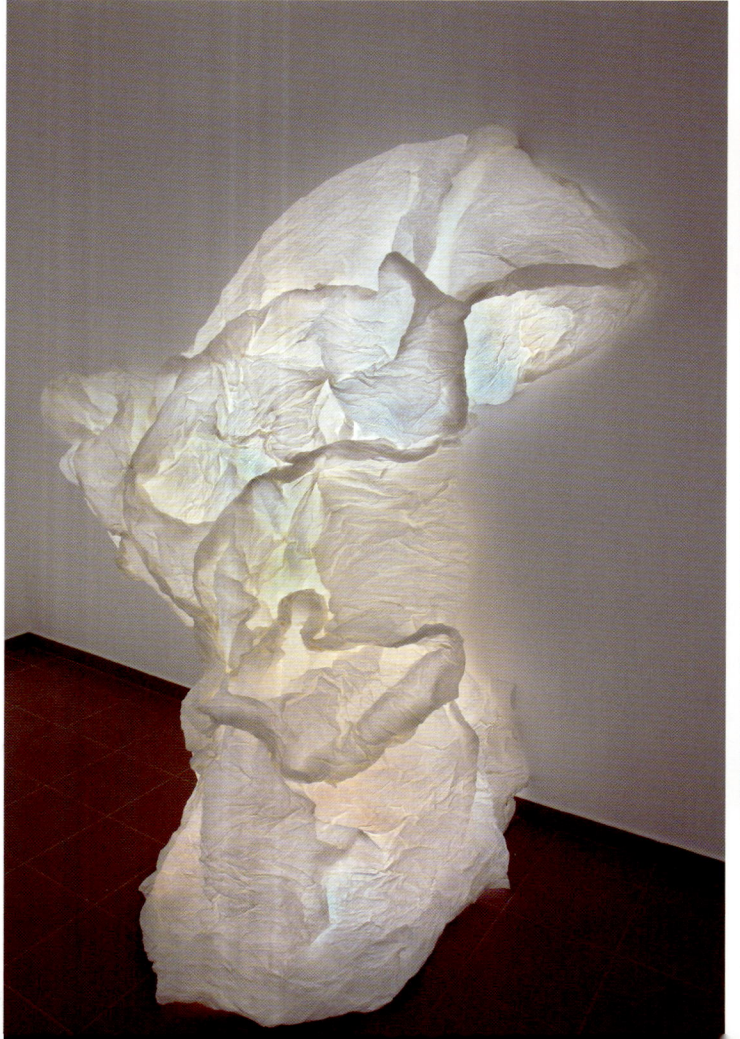
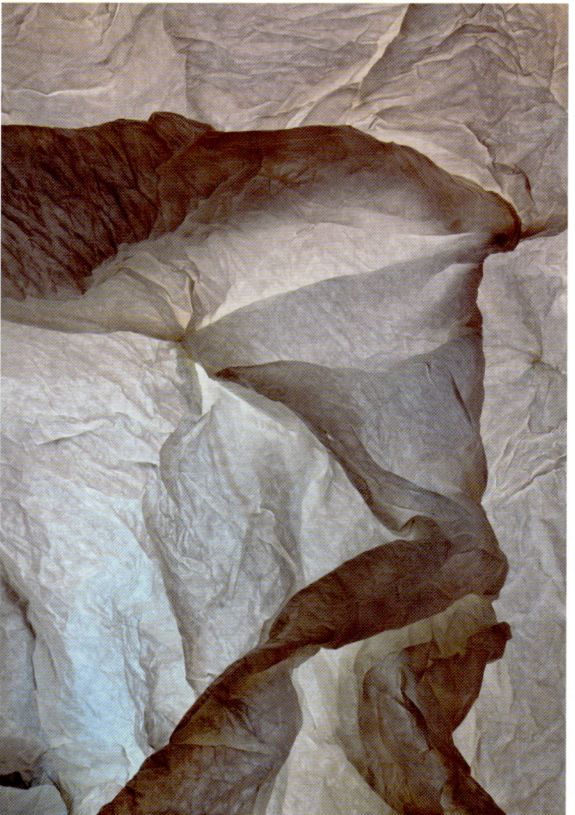
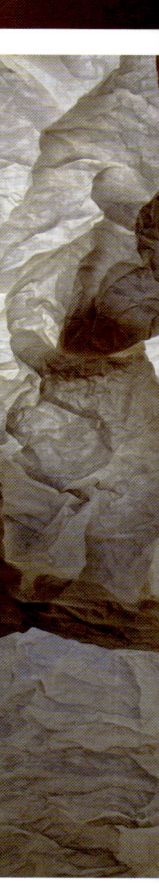

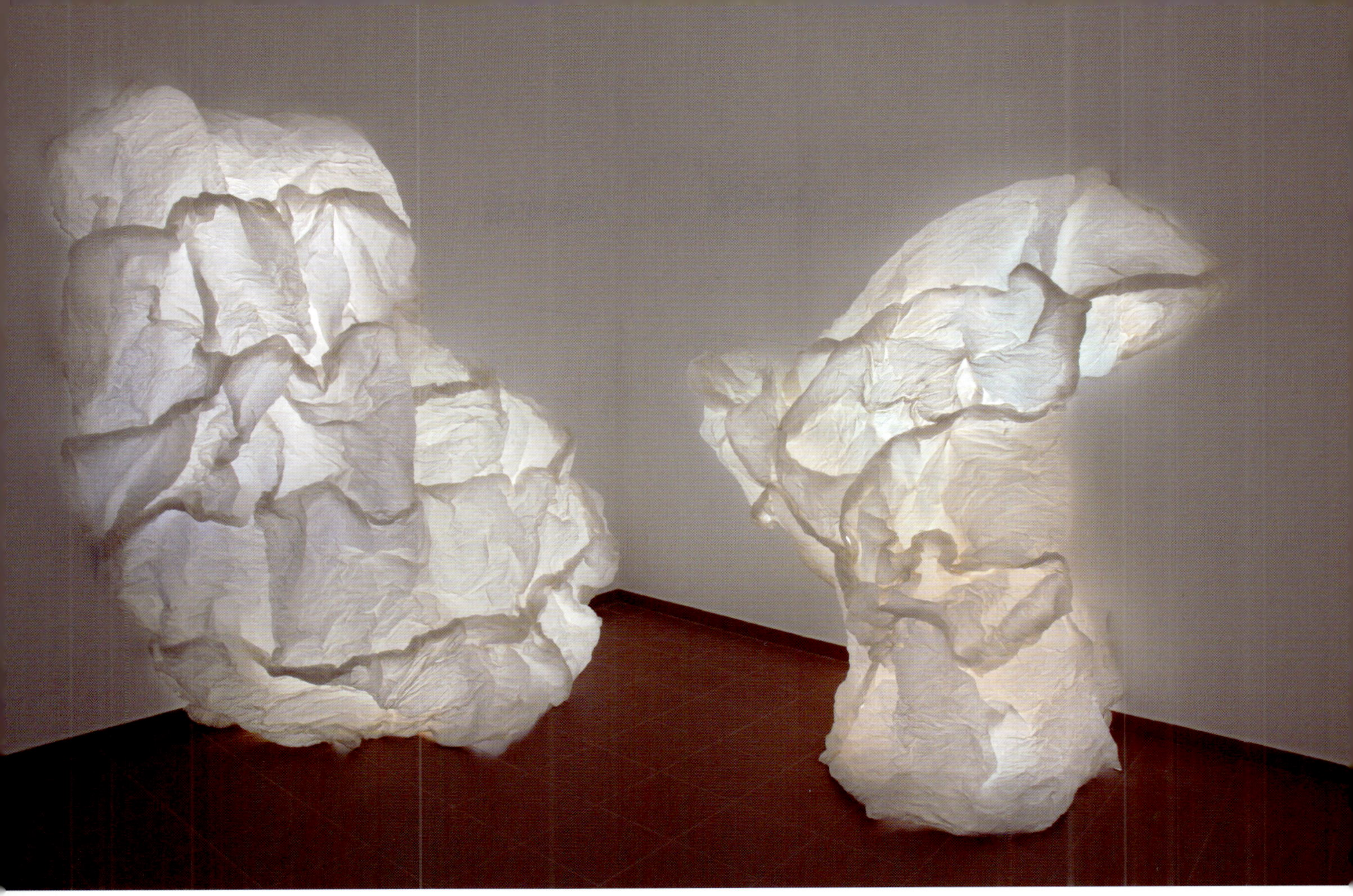

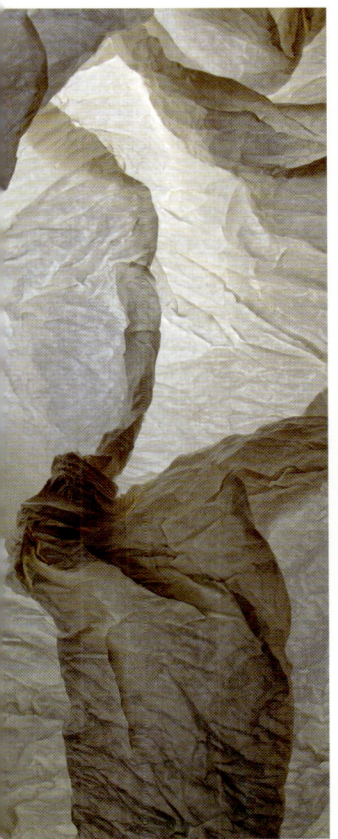
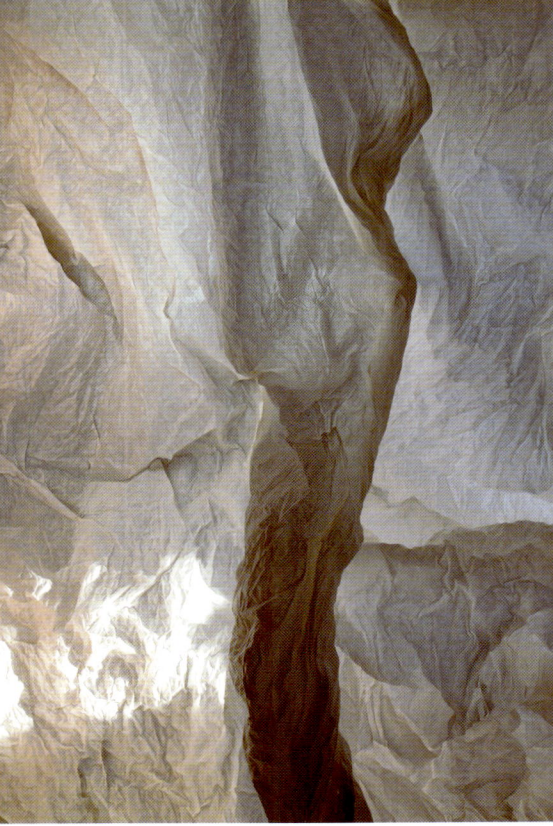
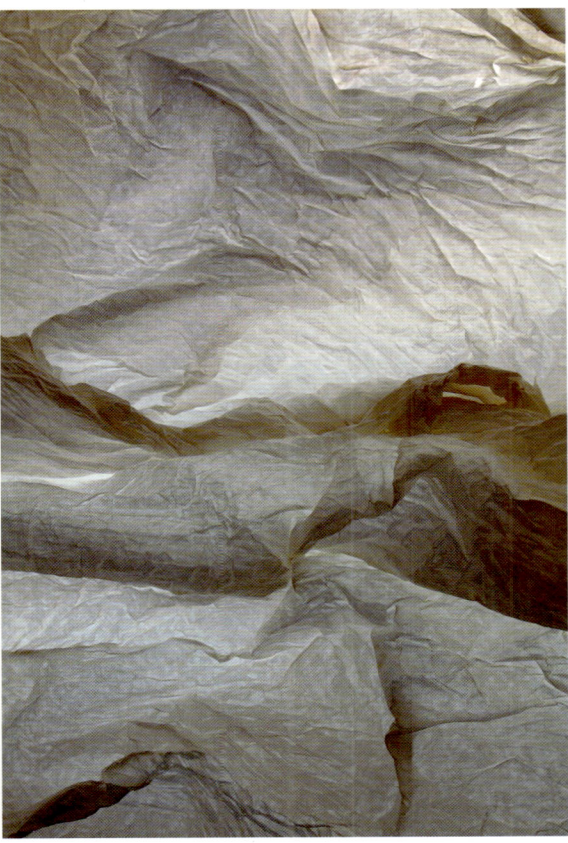

Once installed, photographic documentation records the details of these installations. The camera transforms small details (sometimes 15cm x 20cm total) into vast textural landscapes. These separate works are presented as translucent Giclee prints. Installations have been exhibited at the San Francisco Museum of Modern Art, the 2010 Holland Paper Biennial in The Netherlands, and most recently at the 1st International Biennale of Santorini Greece.

6. **Runoff**
   Hollande Paper Biennial

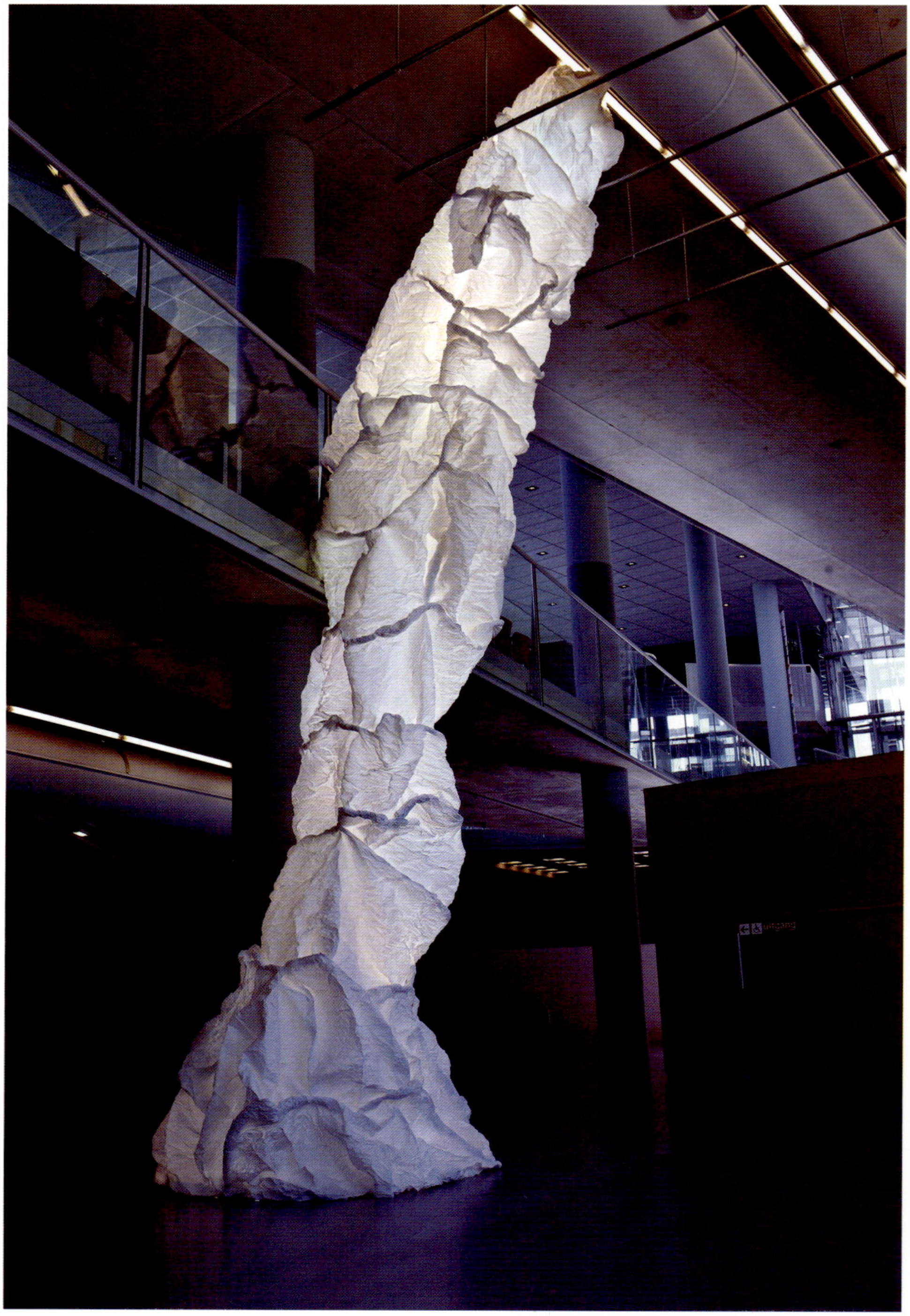

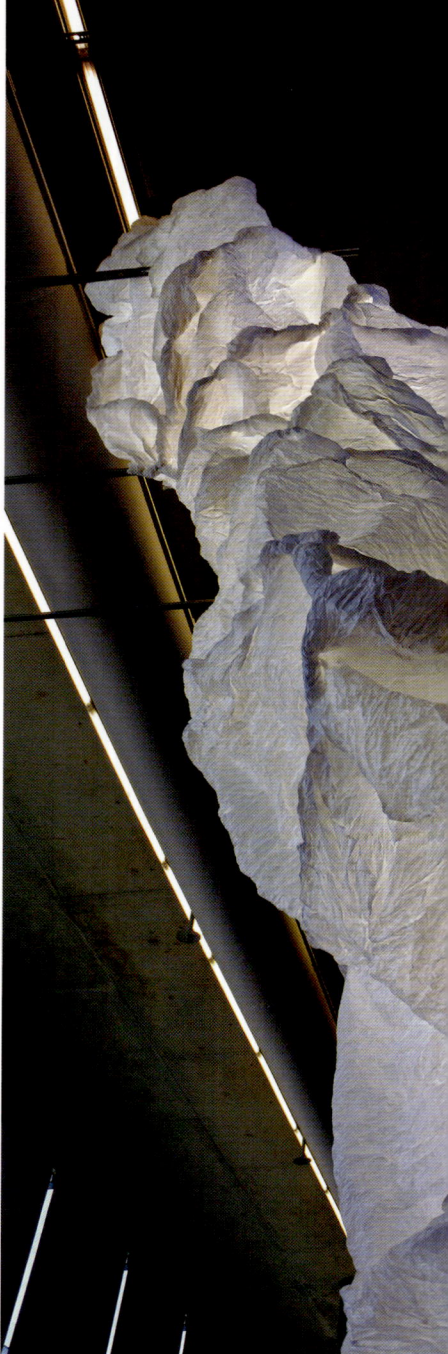

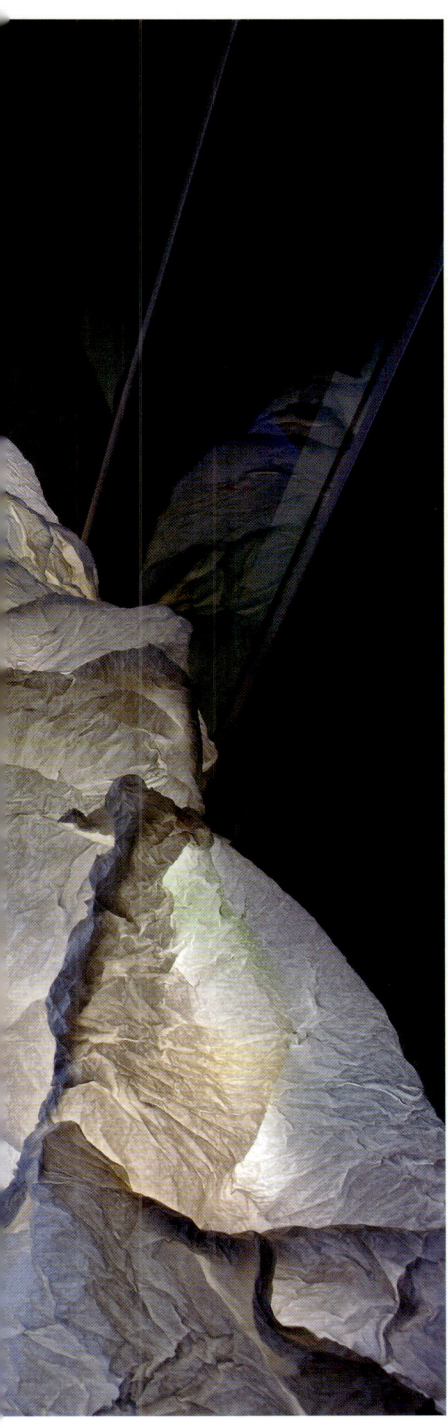

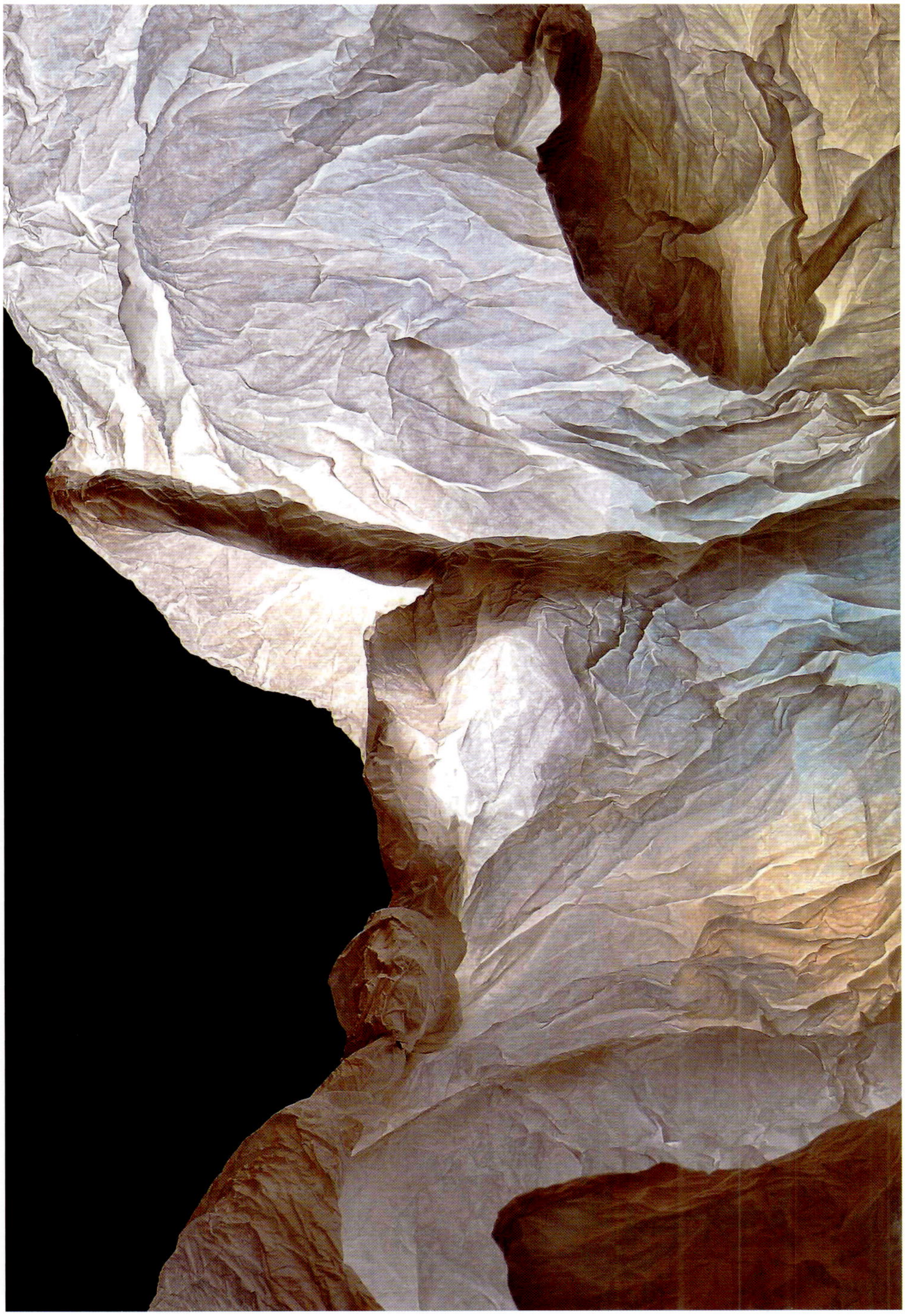

Artist: Christophe Piallat
Country: USA
Photographer: Christophe Piallat

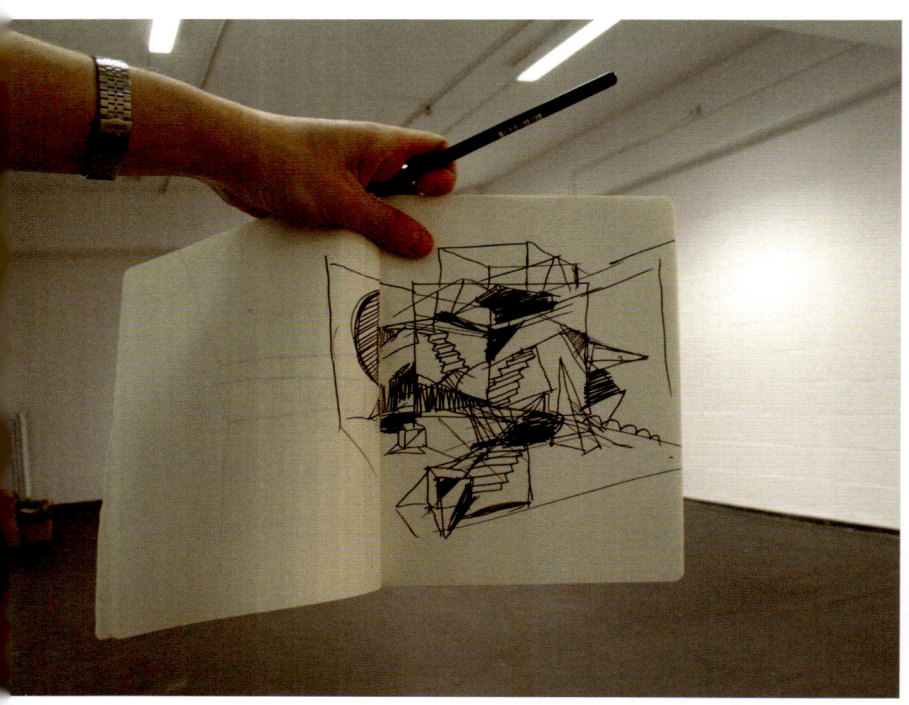
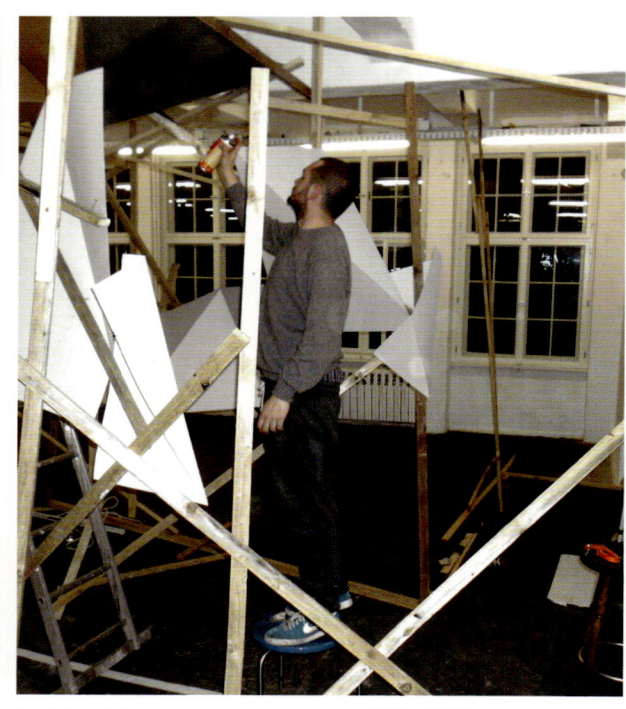
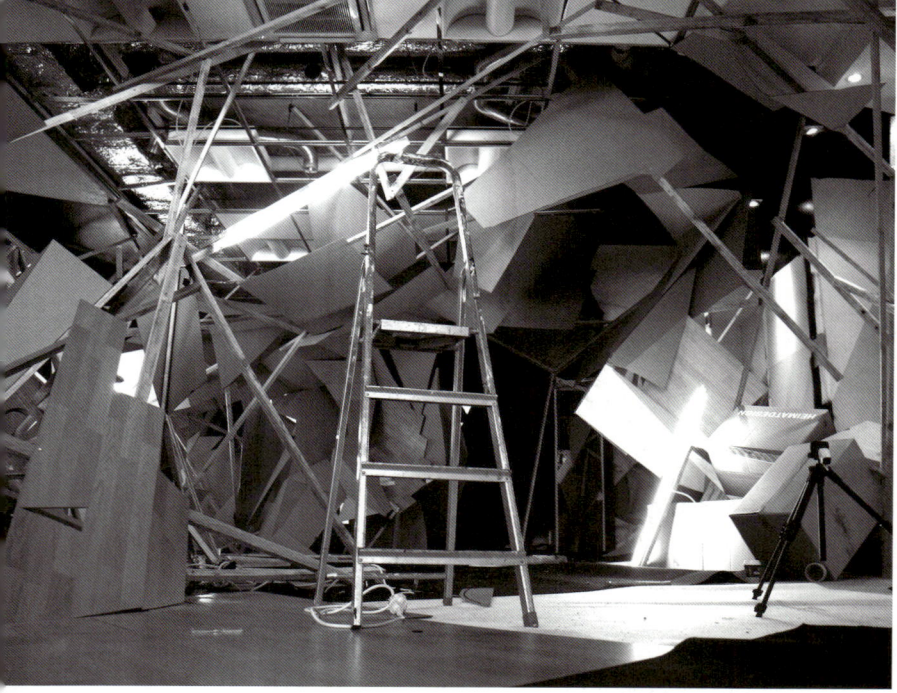
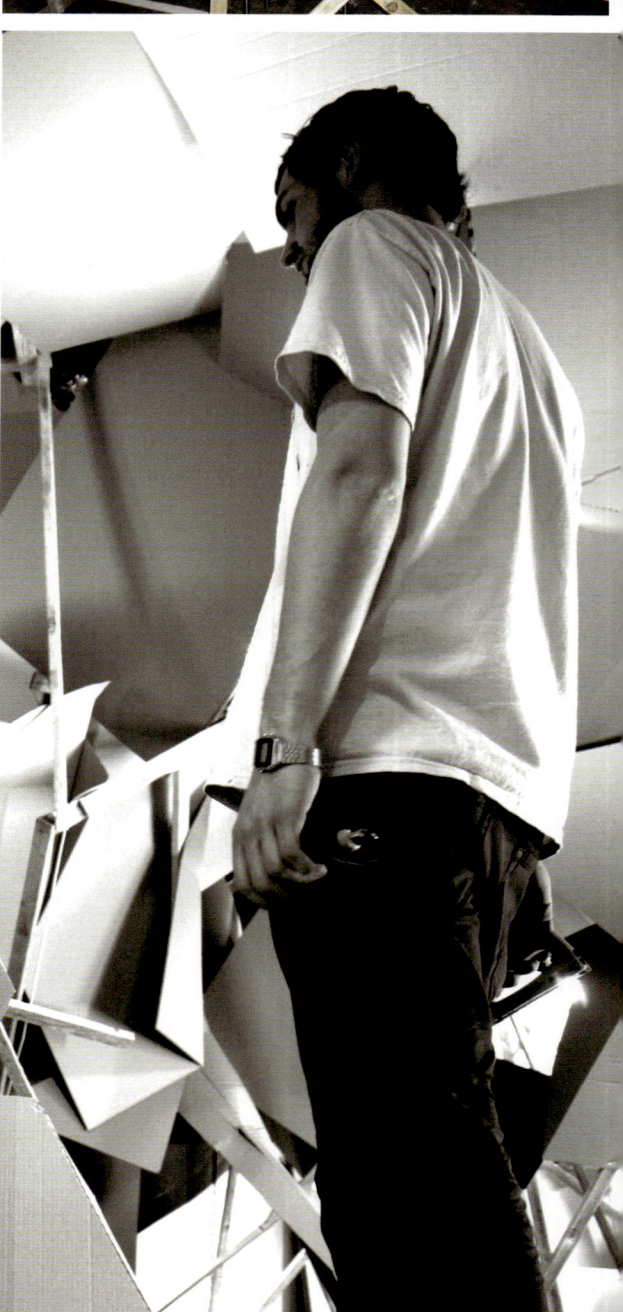
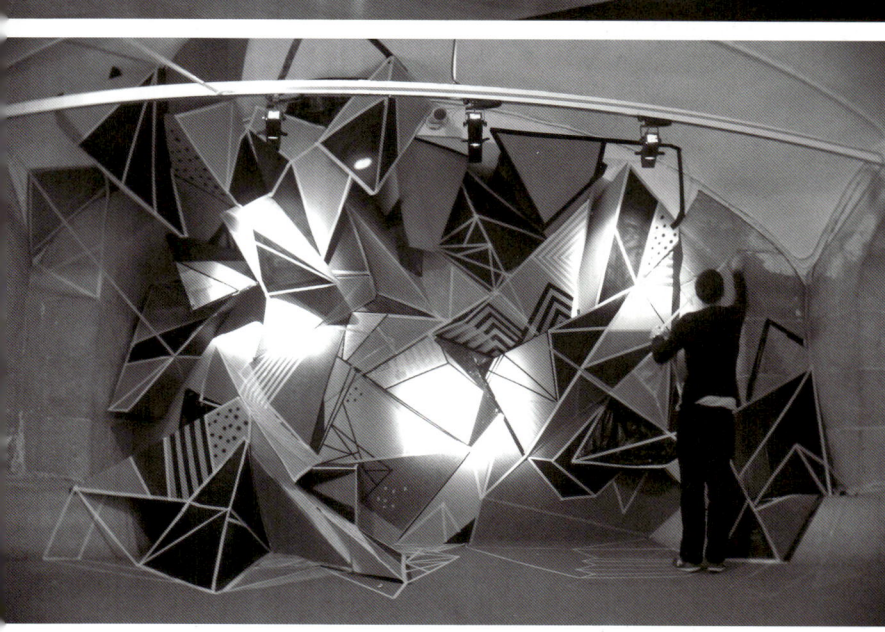

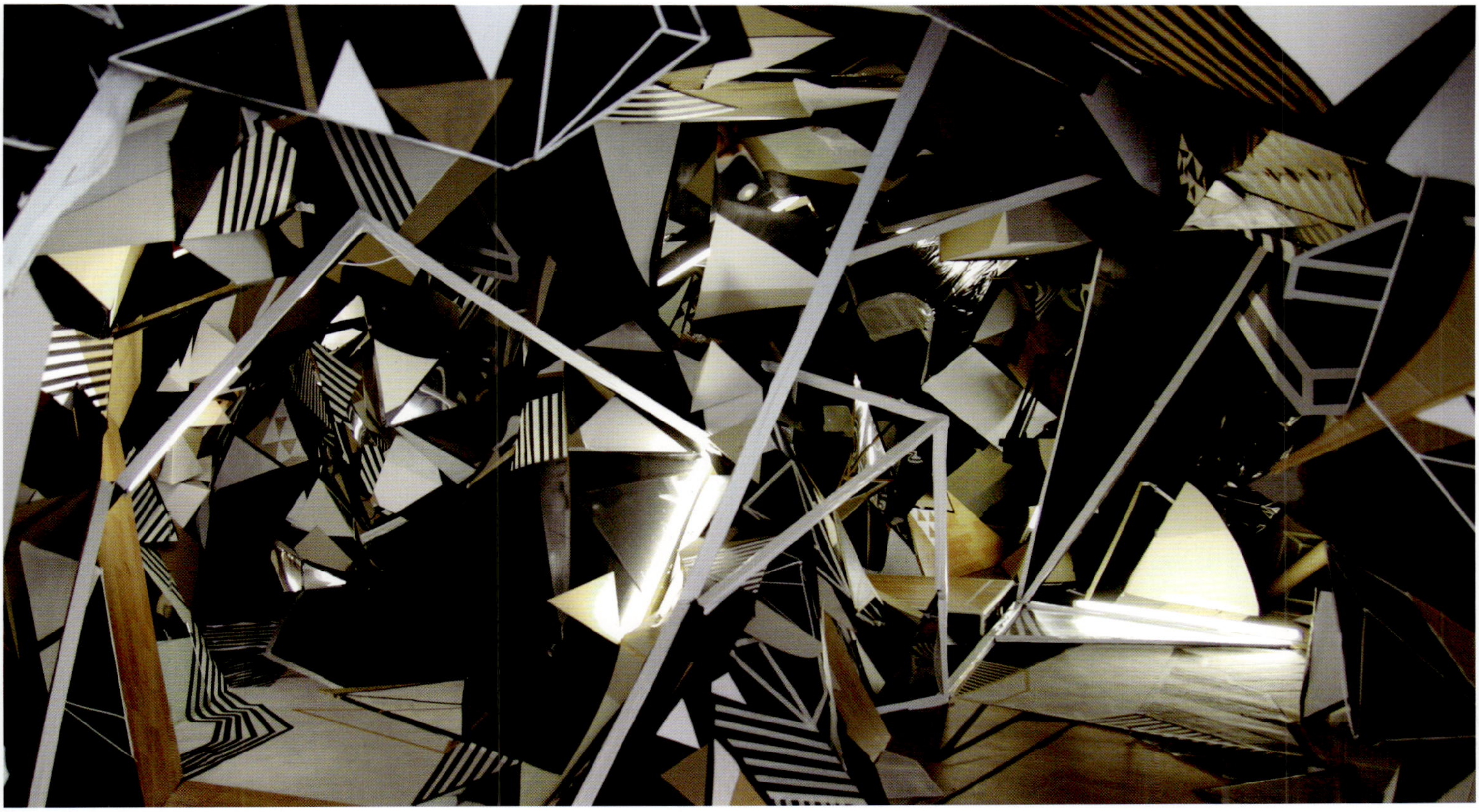

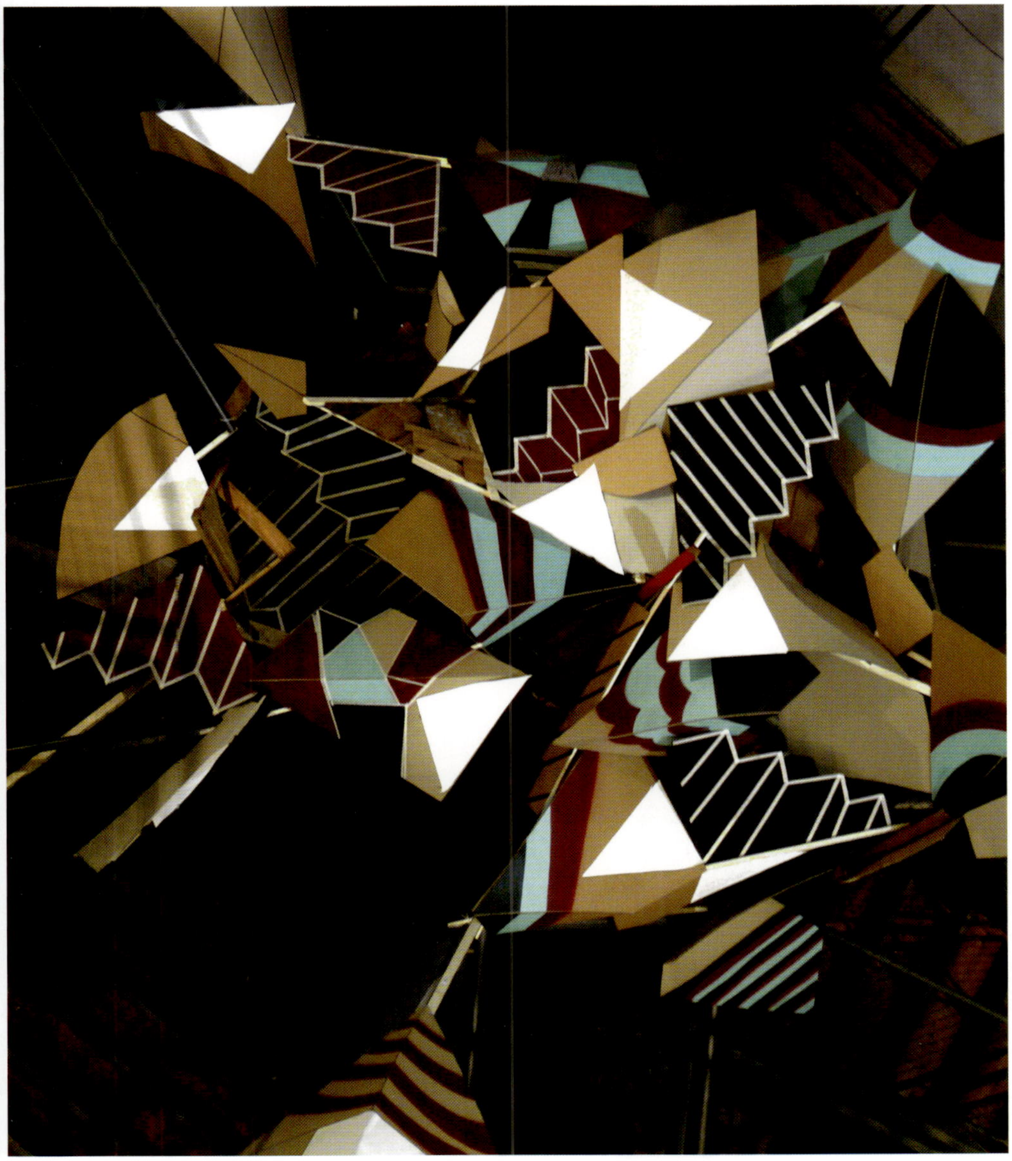

1. **Avalanche**

   Installation on 2 Floors built up over 7 weeks as. The avalanche had different states and shapes.
   One room with mirrors and another with sound-reactive projections..
   The used materials are cardboard, wood, tape, mirrors, paint, carpet and wallpapers.

   Artist: Clemens Behr
   Country: Germany

2. **Step 09**

   Installation at the Step 09 Art Fair in Milano.
   Leonardo da Vinci Museum of Science and Technology

   Artist: Clemens Behr
   Country: Germany

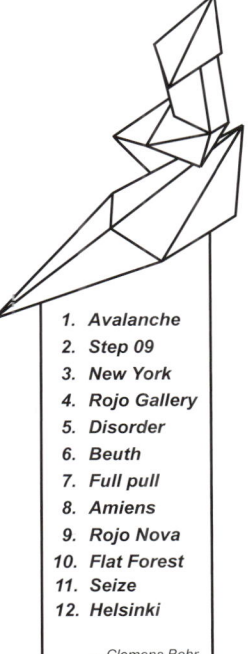

1. Avalanche
2. Step 09
3. New York
4. Rojo Gallery
5. Disorder
6. Beuth
7. Full pull
8. Amiens
9. Rojo Nova
10. Flat Forest
11. Seize
12. Helsinki

---Clemens Behr

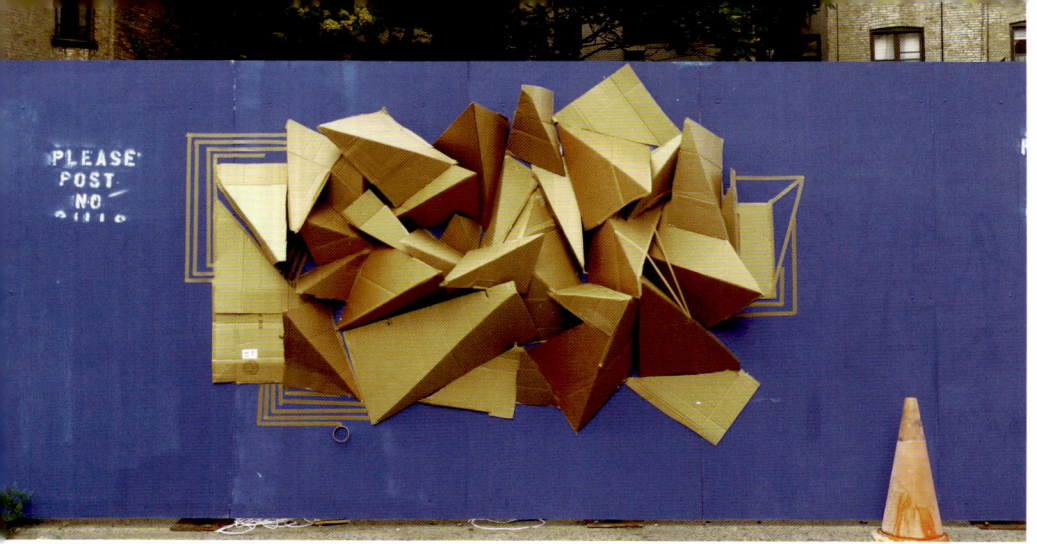

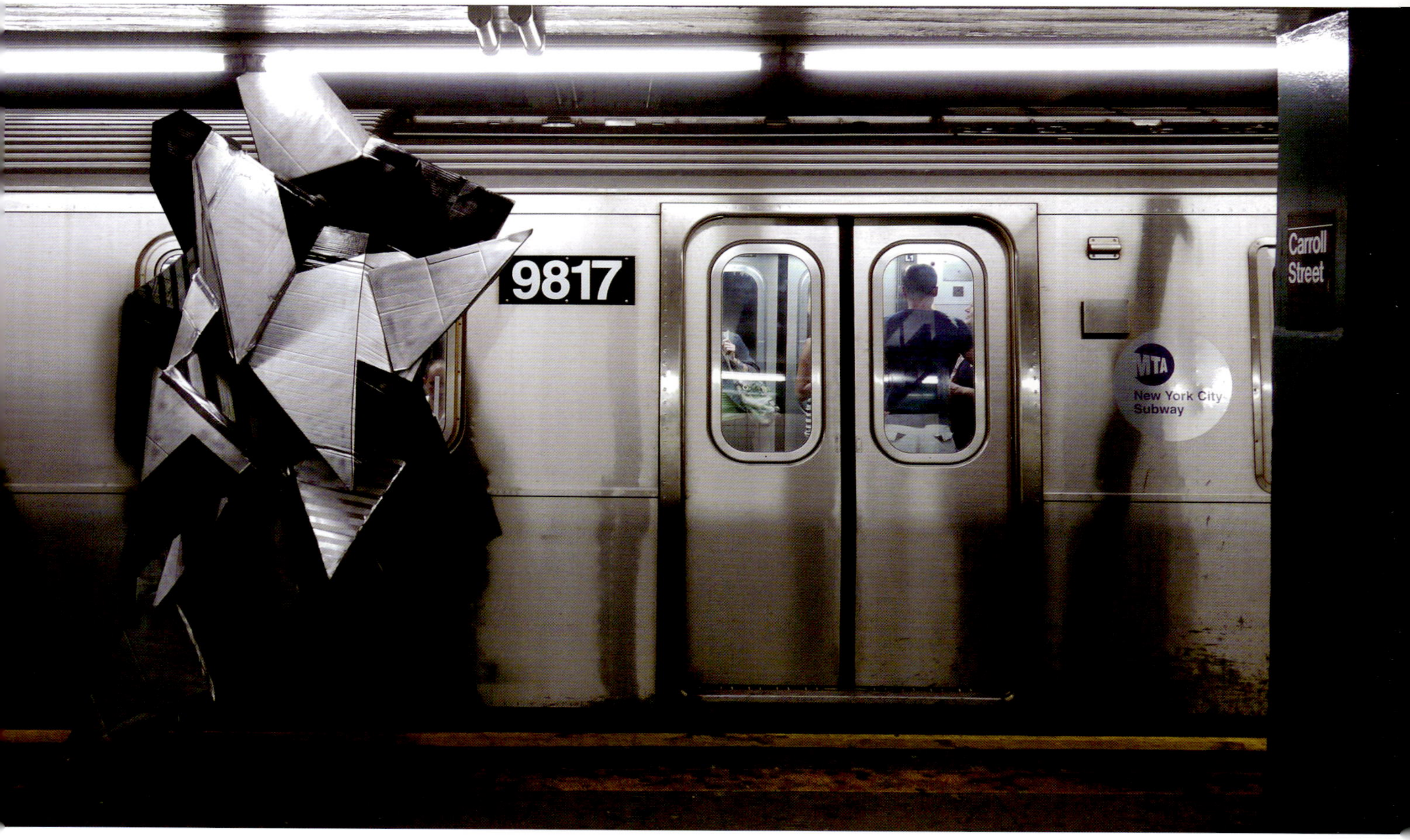

3. **New York**

Several uncommissioned public installations in East Village, China Town, Soho and Brooklyn. Materials: Cardboard, Wood, Tape and Paint.

Artist: Clemens Behr
Country: Germany

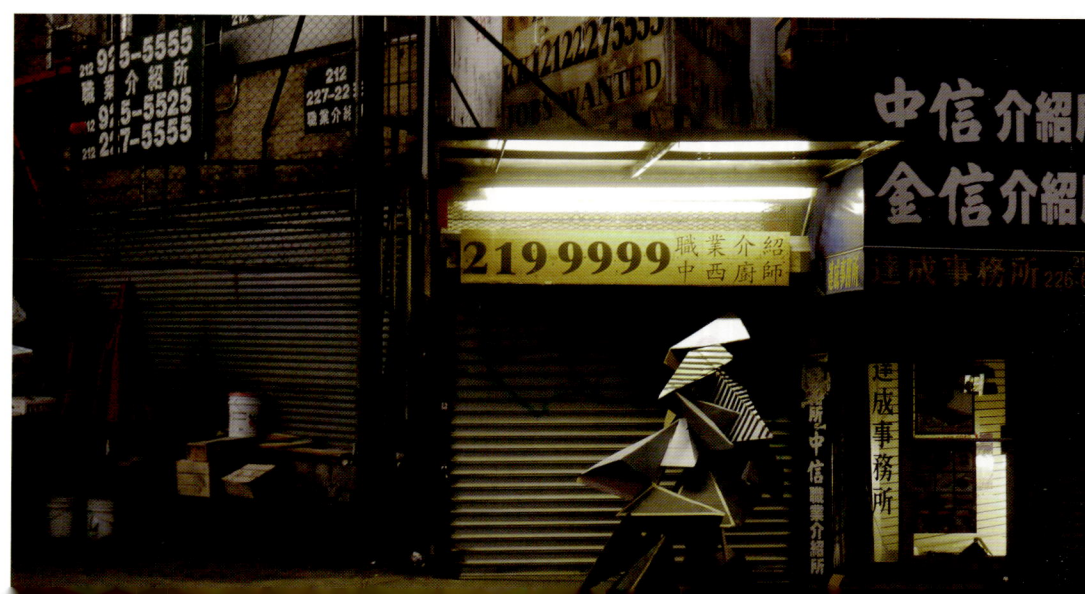

4. Rojo Gallery

Solo exhibition at rojo artspace in Barcelona.
Materials: Cardbaord Tape and Paint.

Artist: Clemens Behr
Country: Germany

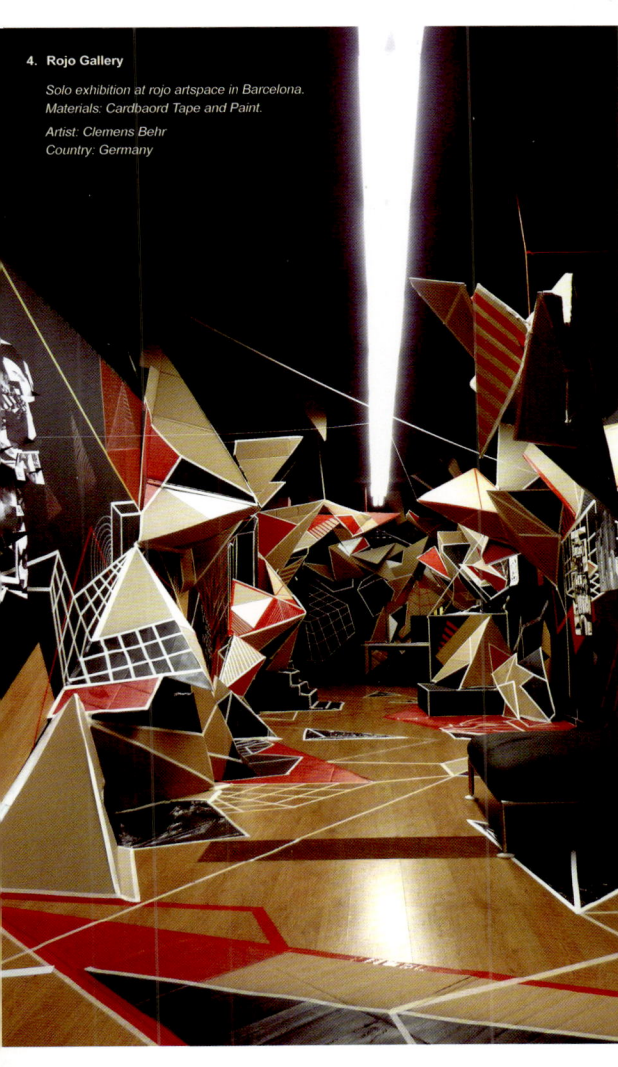
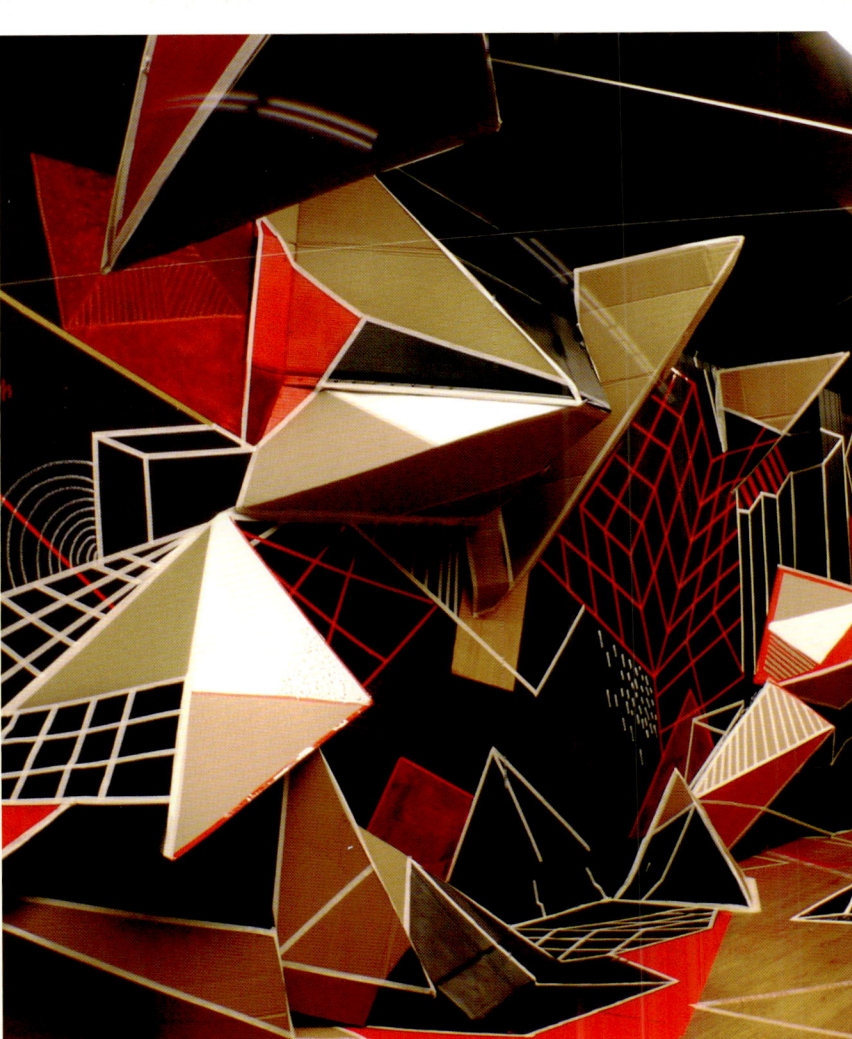

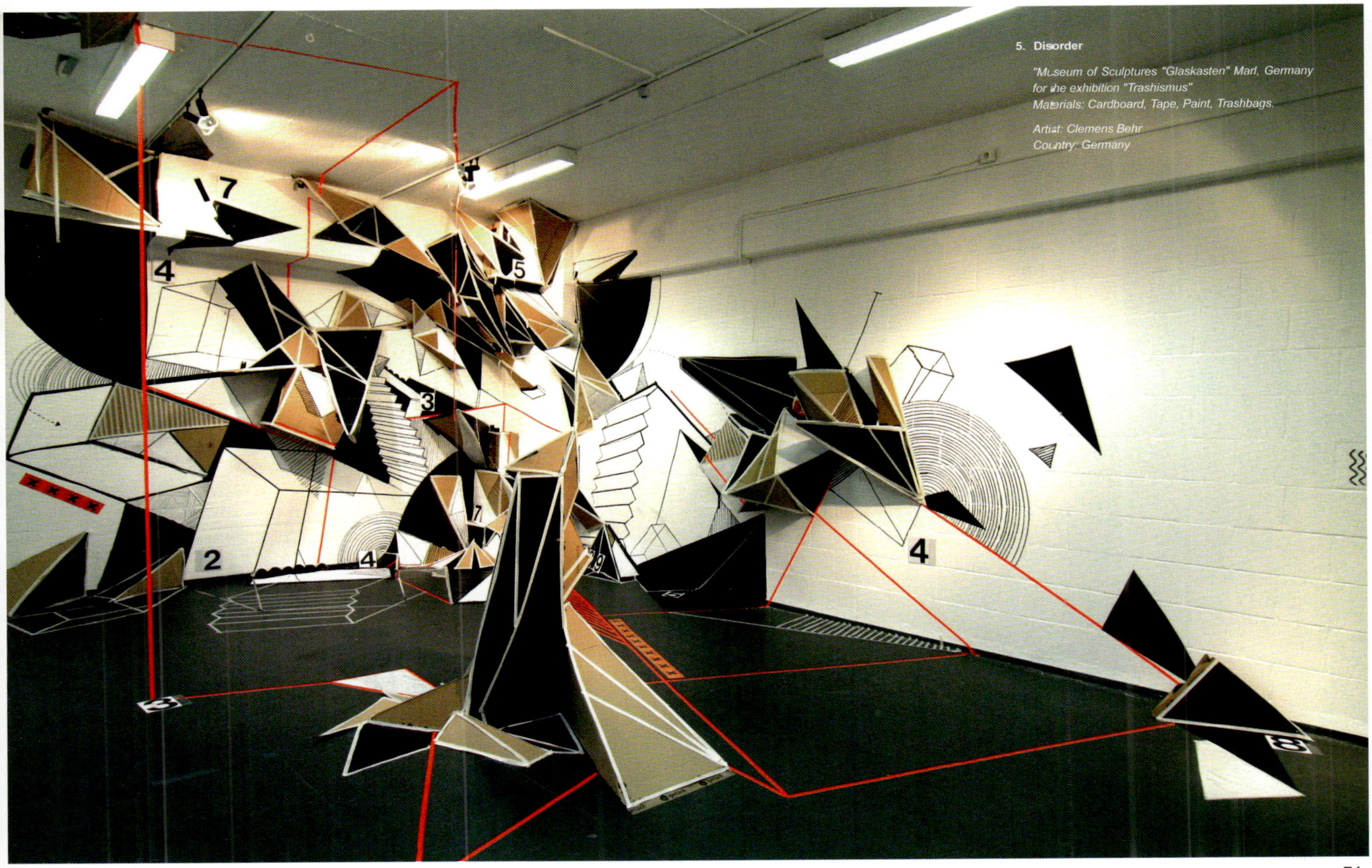

5. Disorder

"Museum of Sculptures "Glaskasten" Marl, Germany for the exhibition "Trashismus"
Materials: Cardboard, Tape, Paint, Trashbags.

Artist: Clemens Behr
Country: Germany

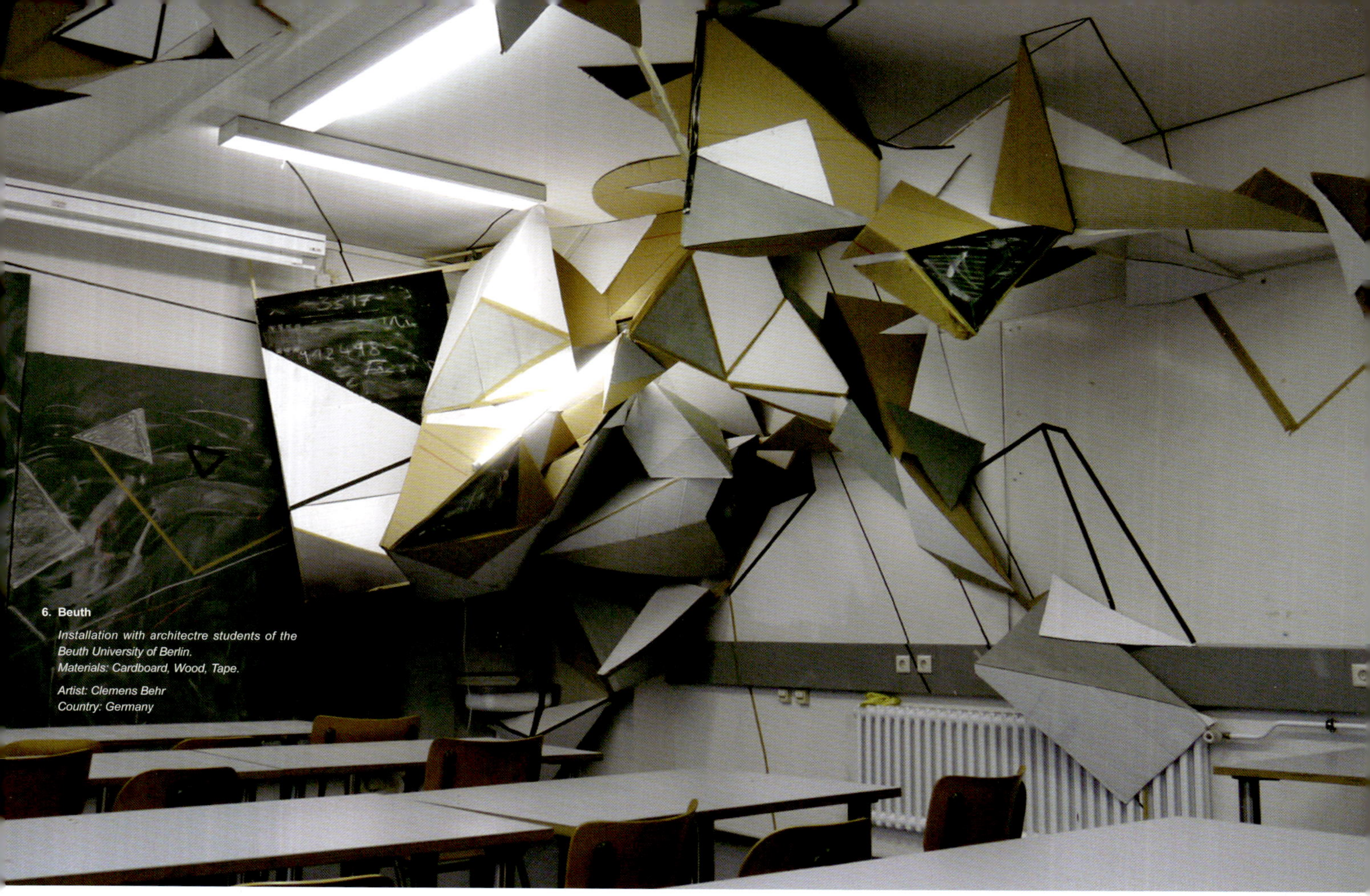

6. Beuth

*Installation with architectre students of the Beuth University of Berlin.
Materials: Cardboard, Wood, Tape.*

Artist: Clemens Behr
Country: Germany

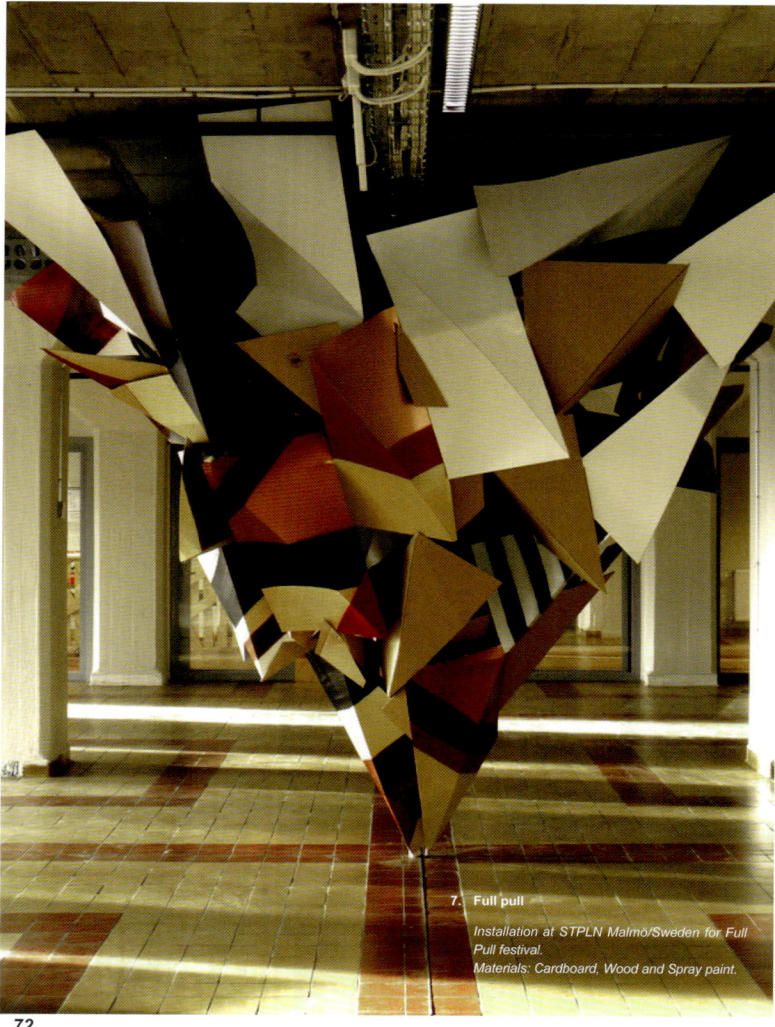

7. Full pull

*Installation at STPLN Malmö/Sweden for Full Pull festival.
Materials: Cardboard, Wood and Spray paint.*

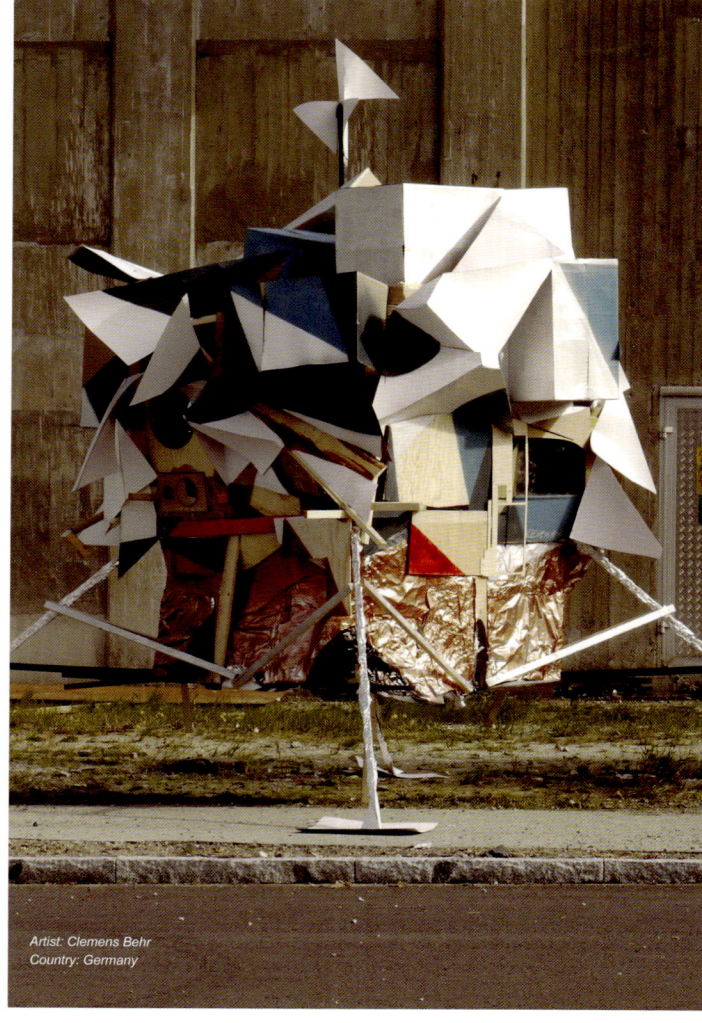

Artist: Clemens Behr
Country: Germany

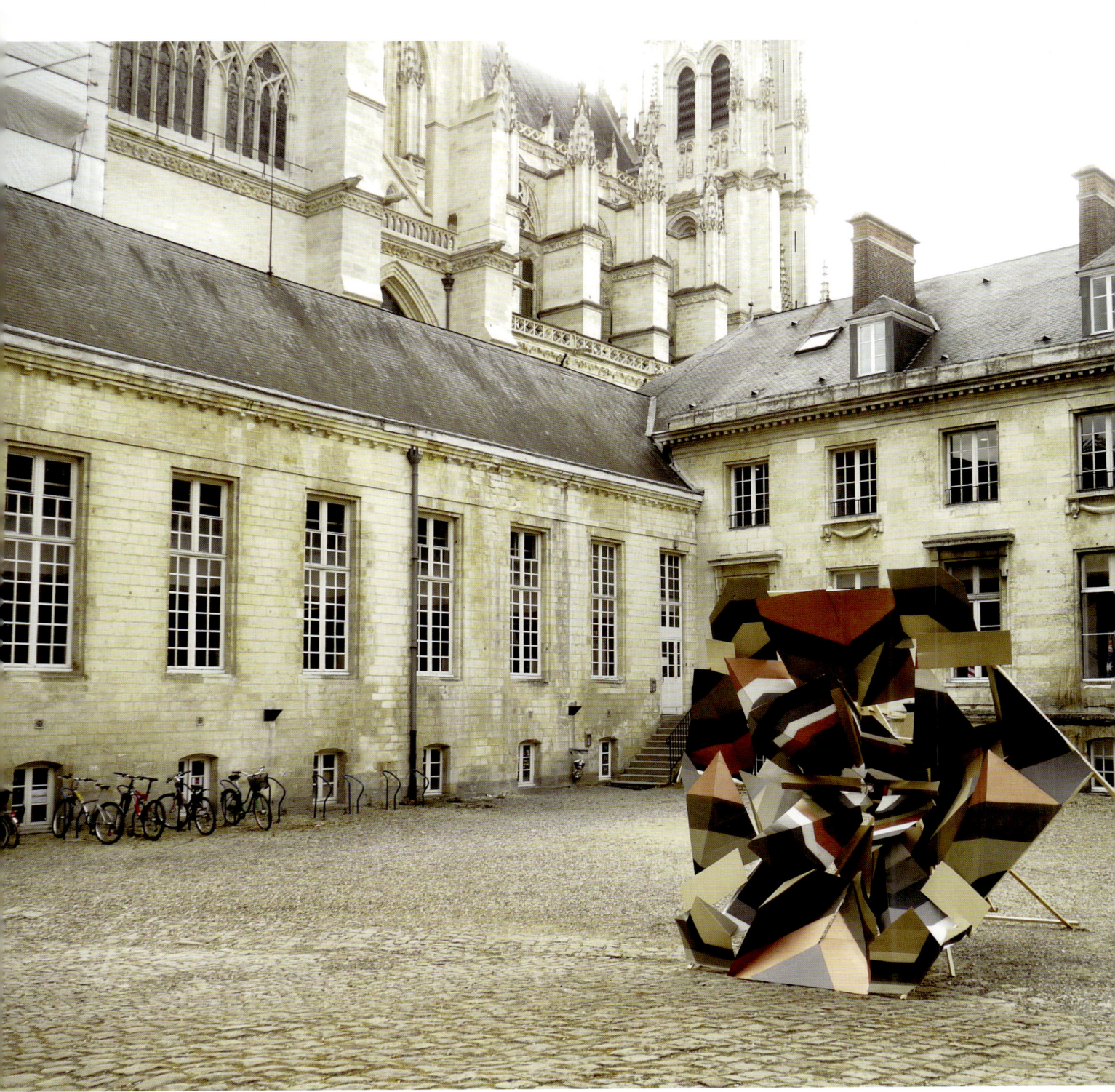

8. **Amiens**

For the celebration of 50 partnership between the Citys Amiens and Dortmund i was invited to do several comissioned pieces throughout the City in the north of France.
Materials: Cardboard, Wood, Tape and Paint.

Artist: Clemens Behr
Country: Germany

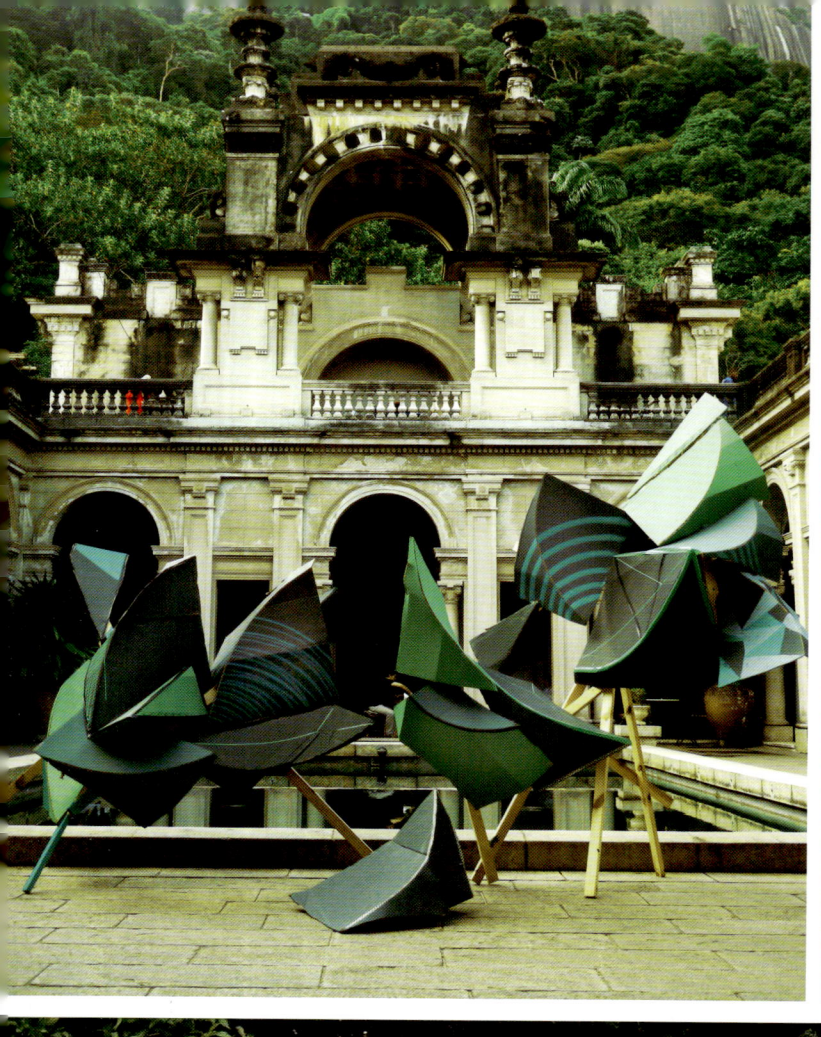
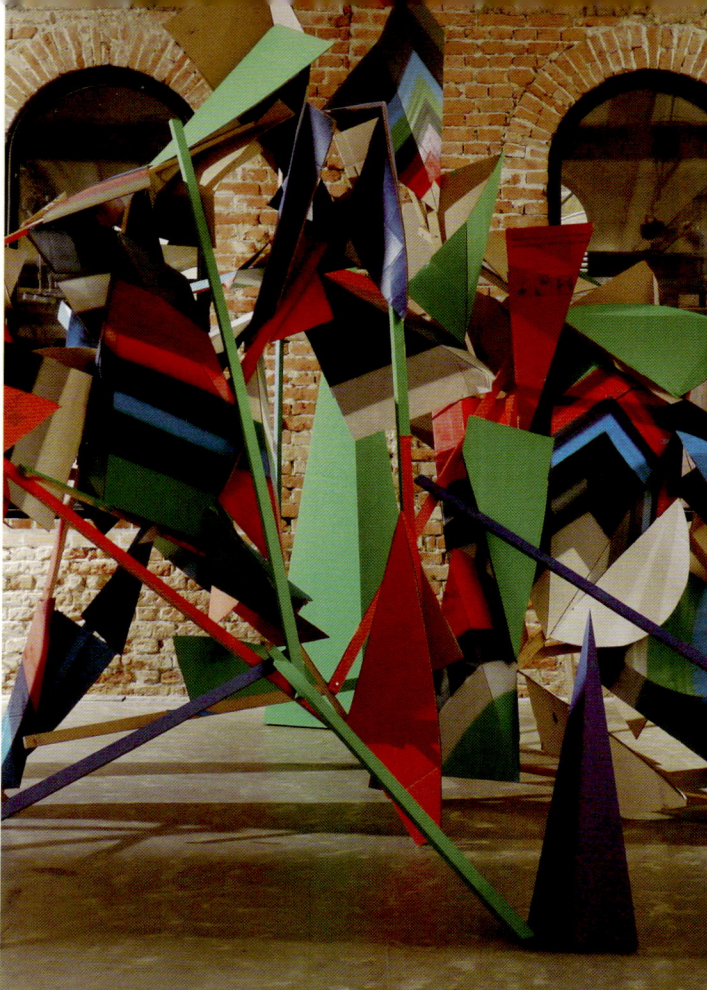

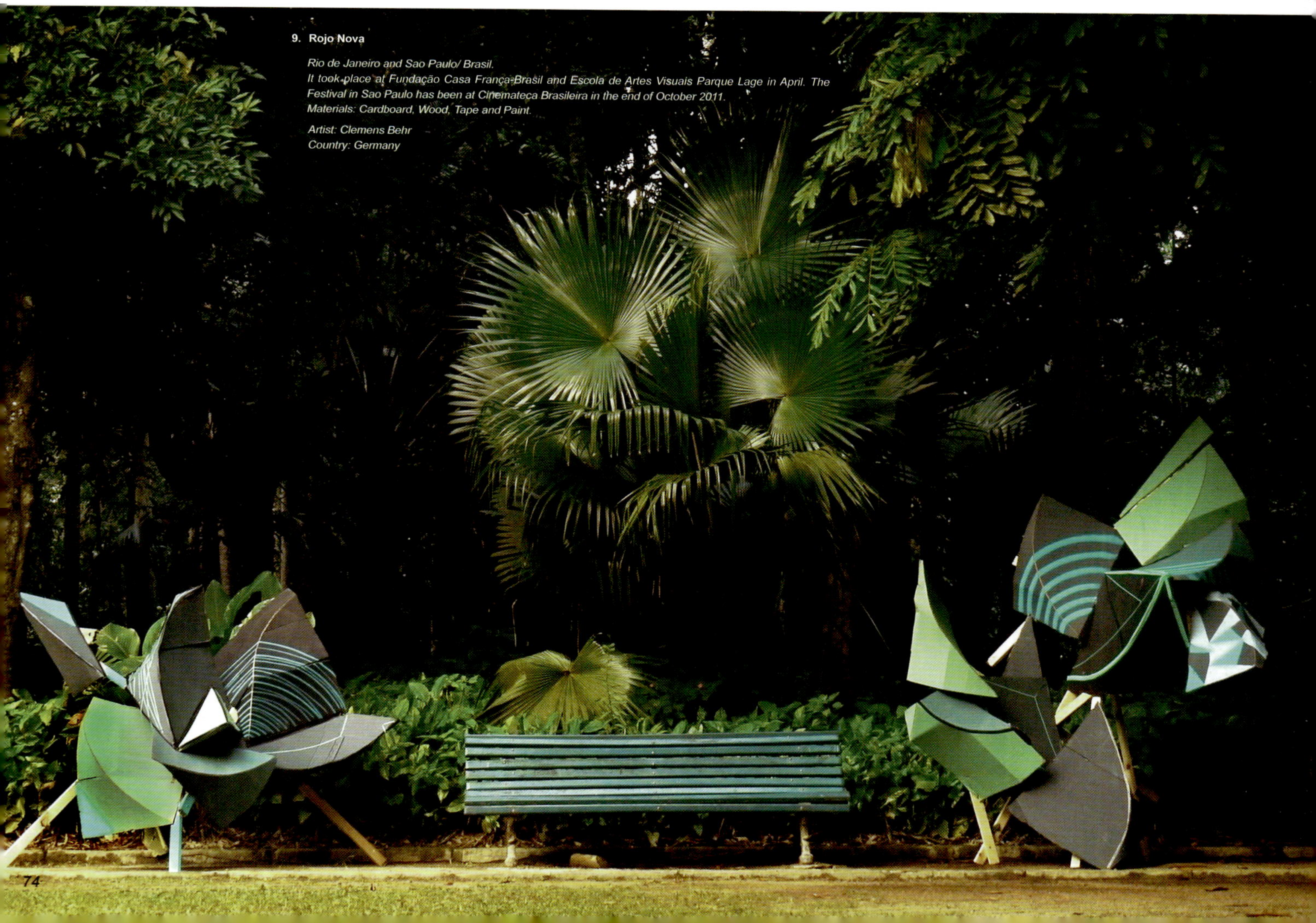

9. Rojo Nova

Rio de Janeiro and Sao Paulo/ Brasil.
It took place at Fundação Casa França-Brasil and Escola de Artes Visuais Parque Lage in April. The Festival in Sao Paulo has been at Cinemateca Brasileira in the end of October 2011.
Materials: Cardboard, Wood, Tape and Paint.

Artist: Clemens Behr
Country: Germany

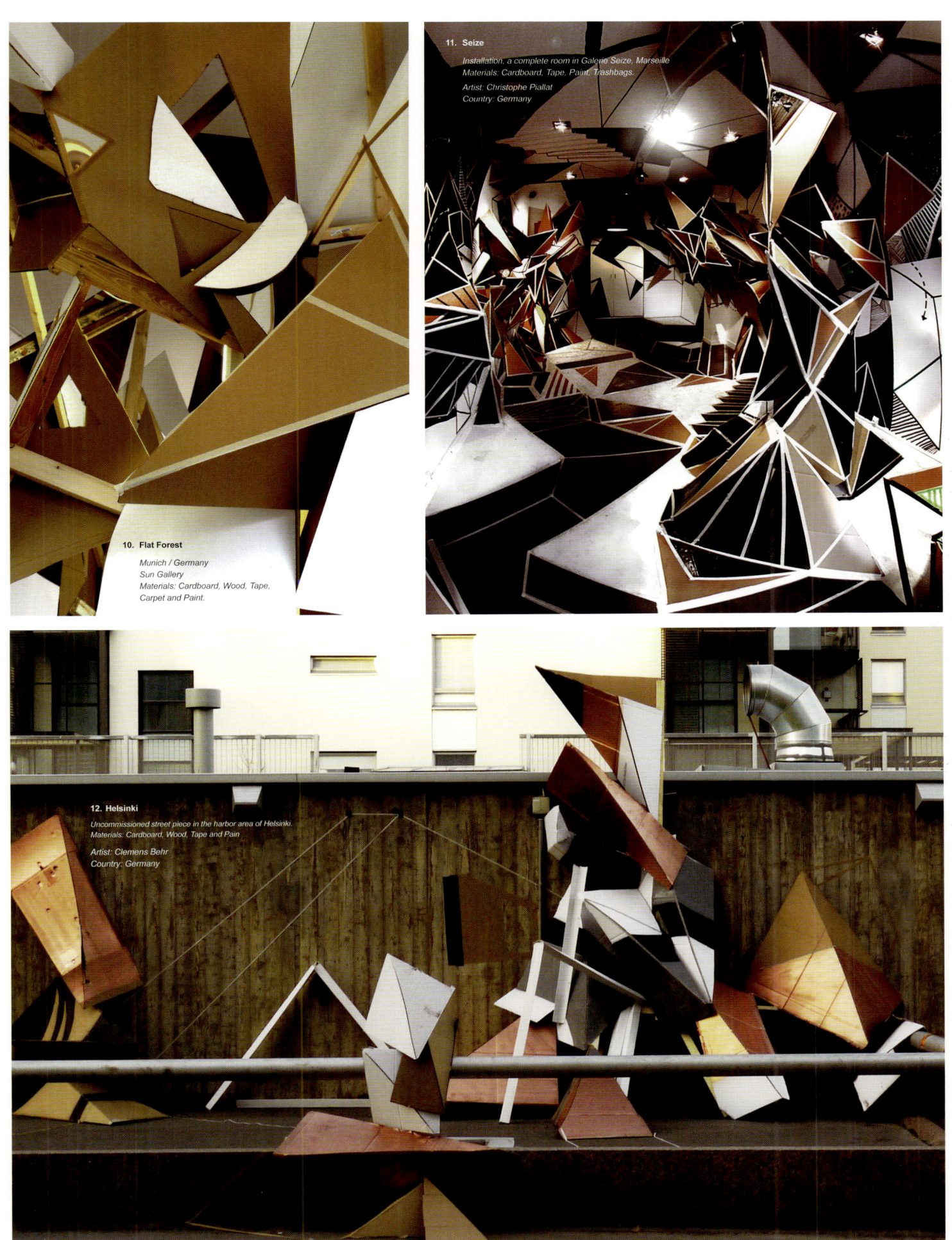

10. Flat Forest

Munich / Germany
Sun Gallery
Materials: Cardboard, Wood, Tape, Carpet and Paint.

11. Seize

Installation, a complete room in Galerie Seize, Marseille
Materials: Cardboard, Tape, Paint, Trashbags.

Artist: Christophe Piallat
Country: Germany

12. Helsinki

Uncommissioned street piece in the harbor area of Helsinki.
Materials: Cardboard, Wood, Tape and Pain

Artist: Clemens Behr
Country: Germany

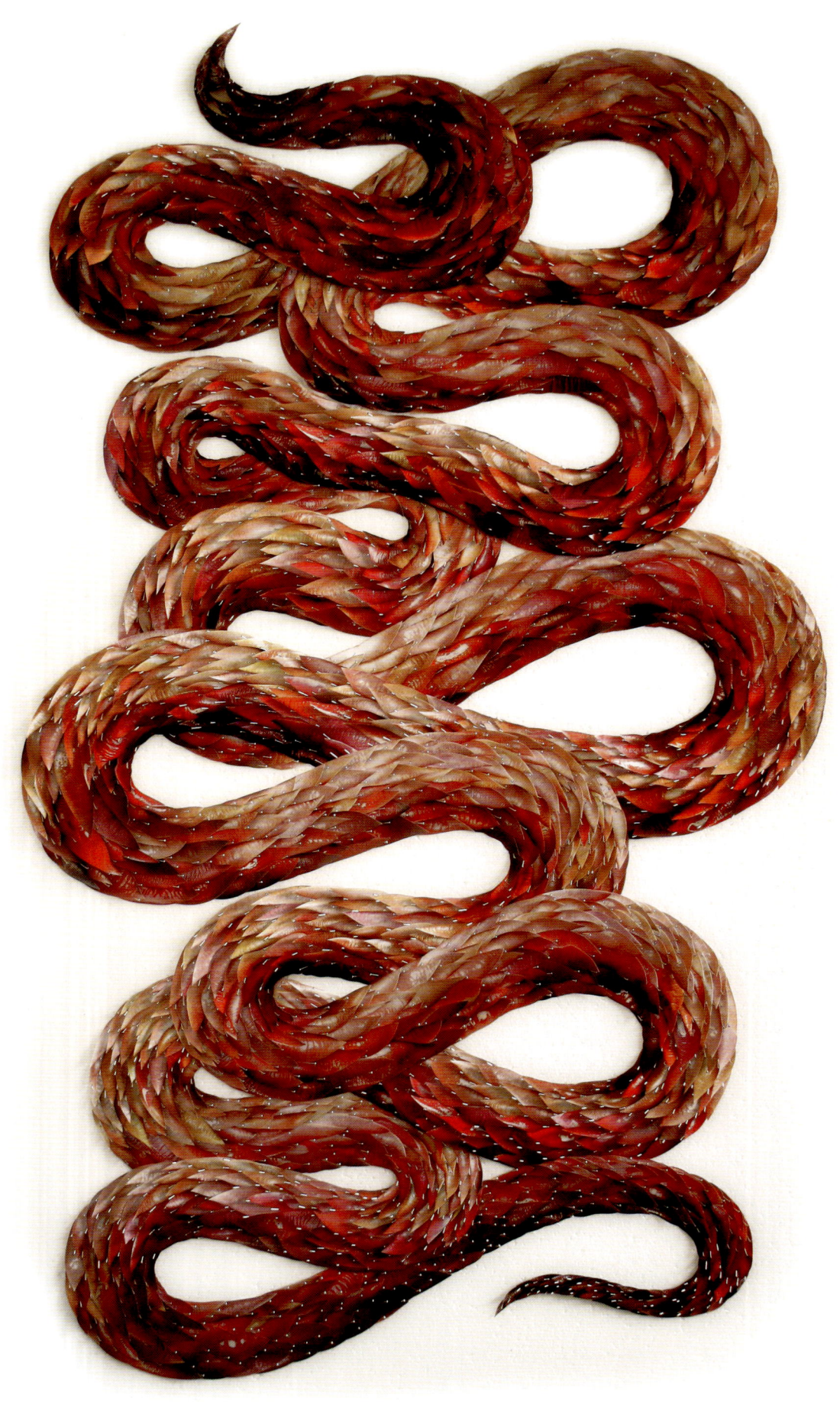

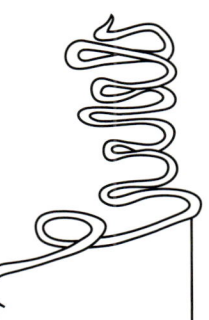

1. *22 footer*
2. *Born Again*
3. *Superstar Cluster*
4. *For Gucci*
5. *Misha Barton For Bebe*
6. *Person of The Year*
7. *Posh + Becks*
8. *Swarm*
9. *Tail*

---David Adey

1. **22 footer**
Materials/Process: Images of lips from fashion magazines are cut and assembled with pins on a foam panel.
Dimensions: 27 x 46 inches
Artist: David Adey Country: USA
Gallery/Dealer: Scott White Contemporary Art, La Jolla, CA

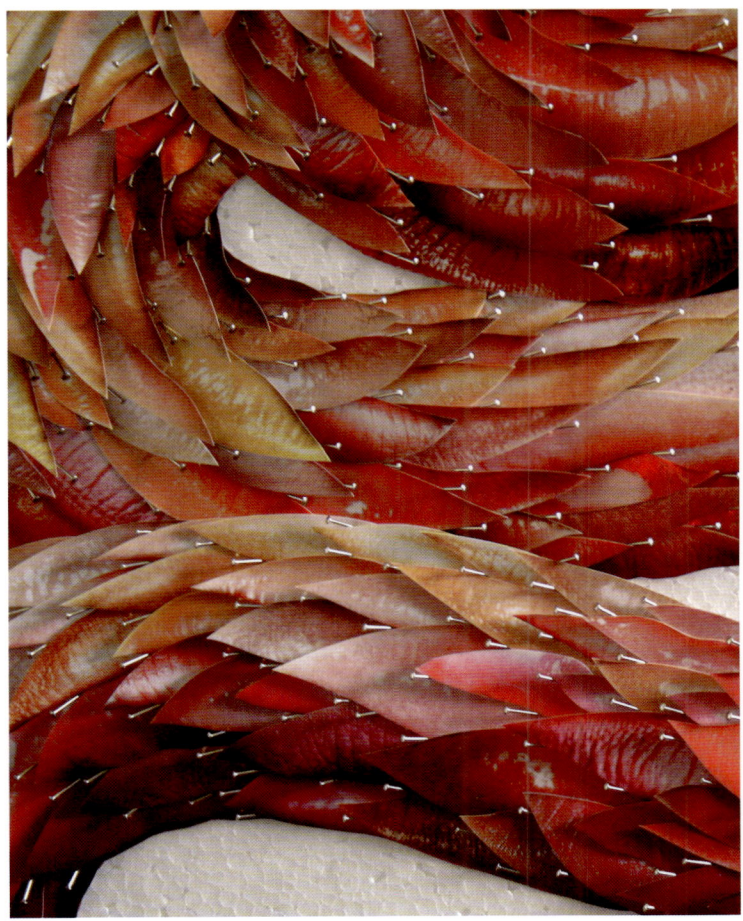

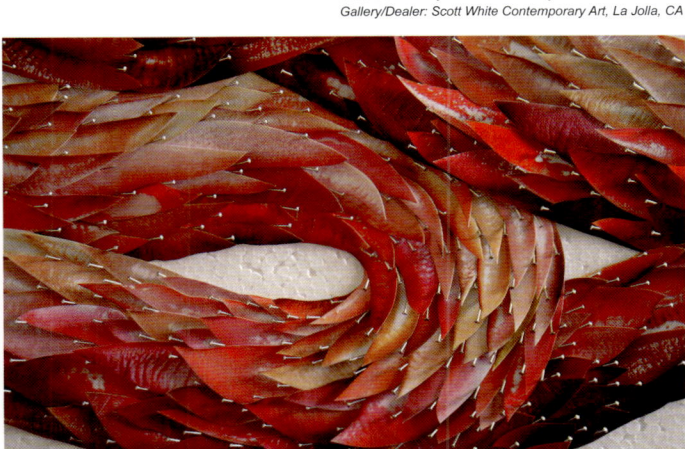

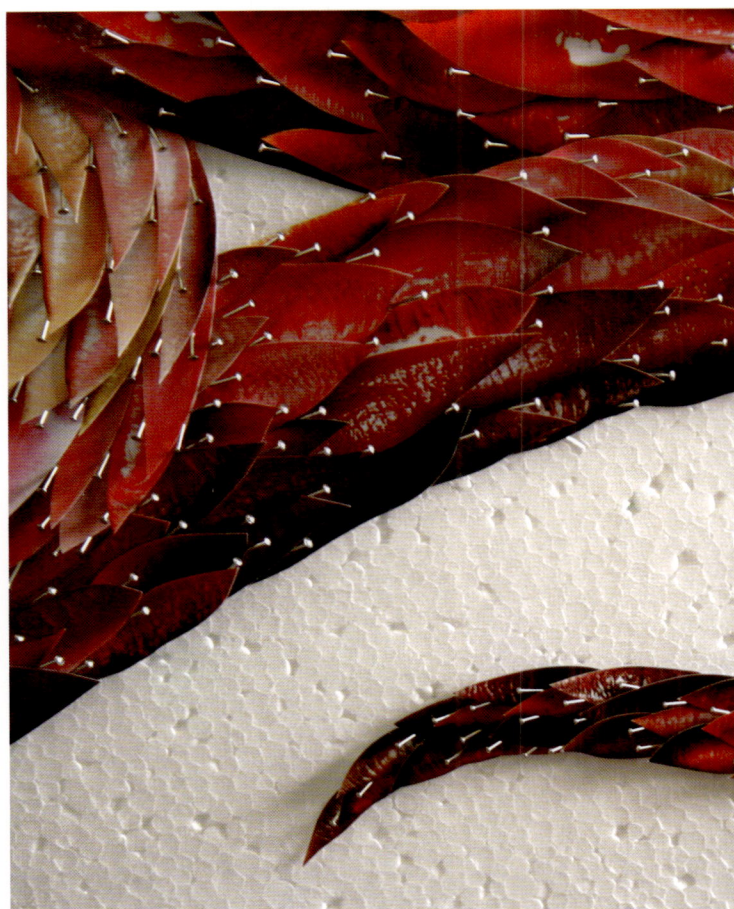

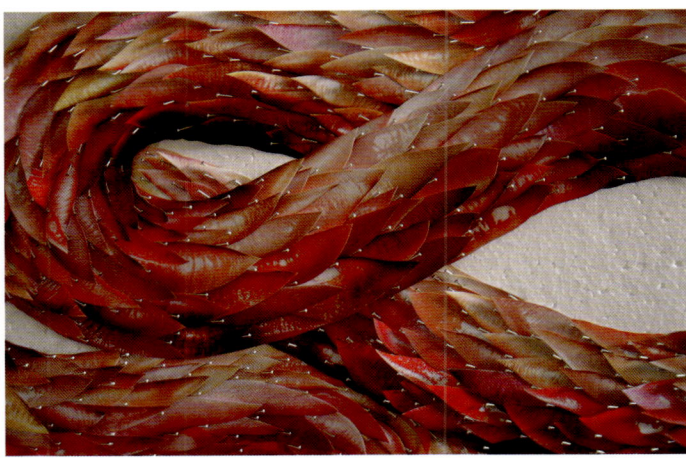

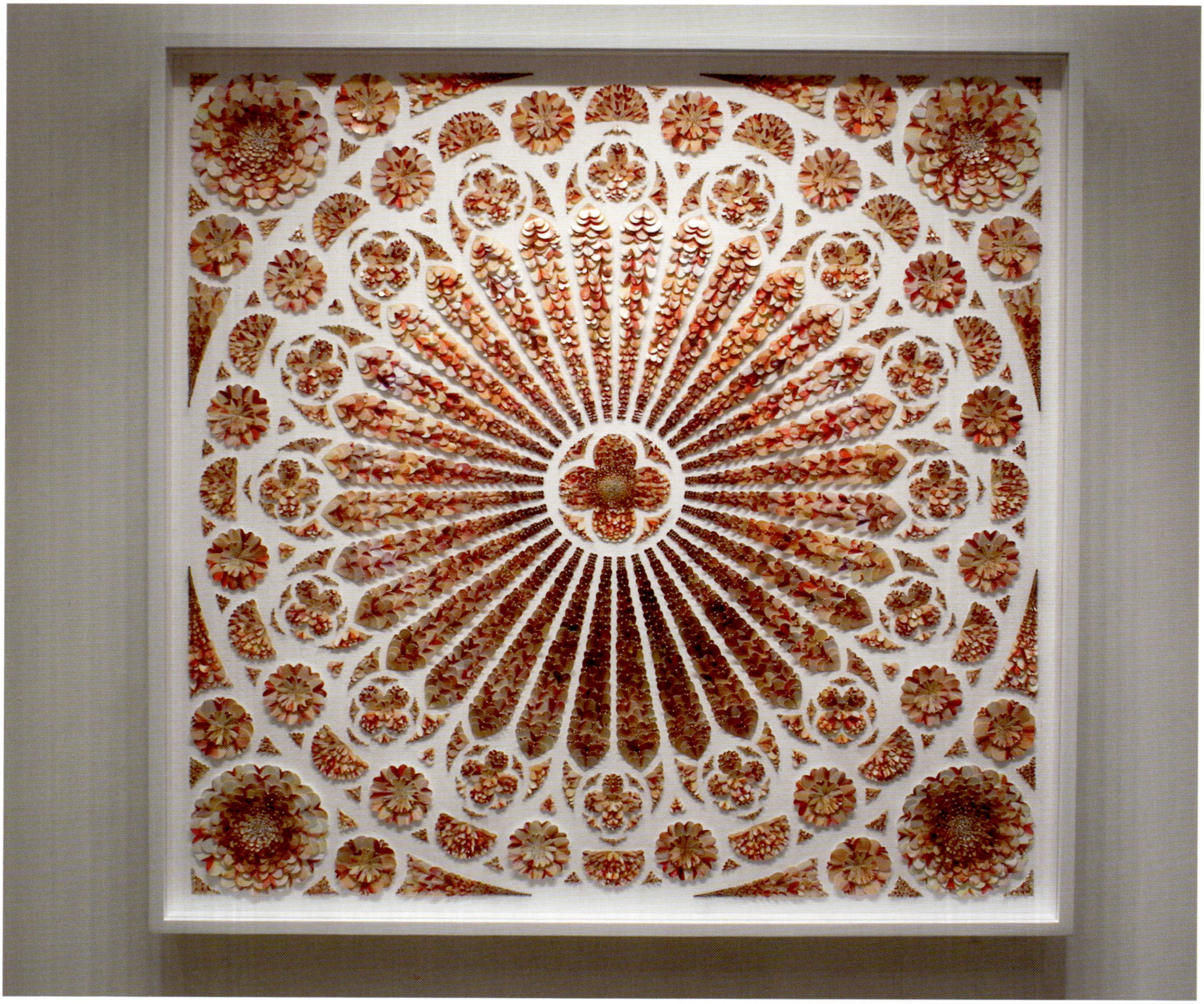

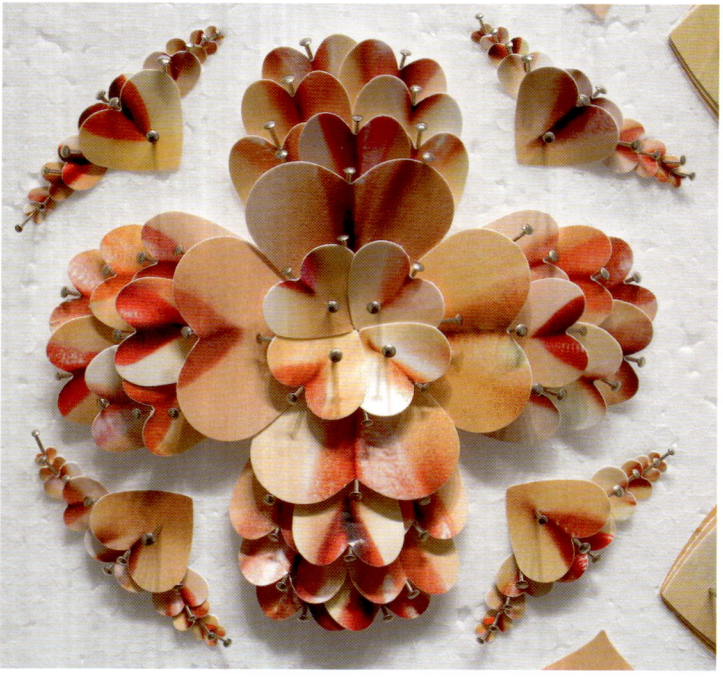
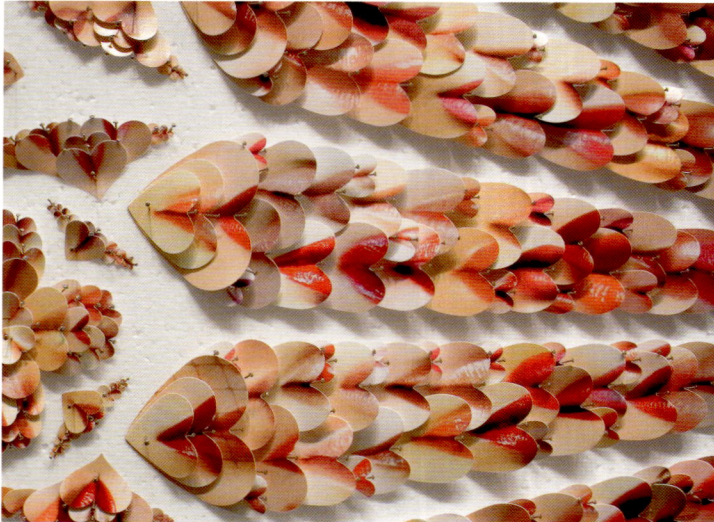

2. Born Again

Materials/Process: Images of lips from fashion magazines are cut using an assortment of heart-shaped craft punches and assembled with pins on a foam panel.
Dimensions: 48 x 48 inches
Artist: David Adey   Country: USA
Gallery/Dealer: Scott White Contemporary Art, La Jolla, CA

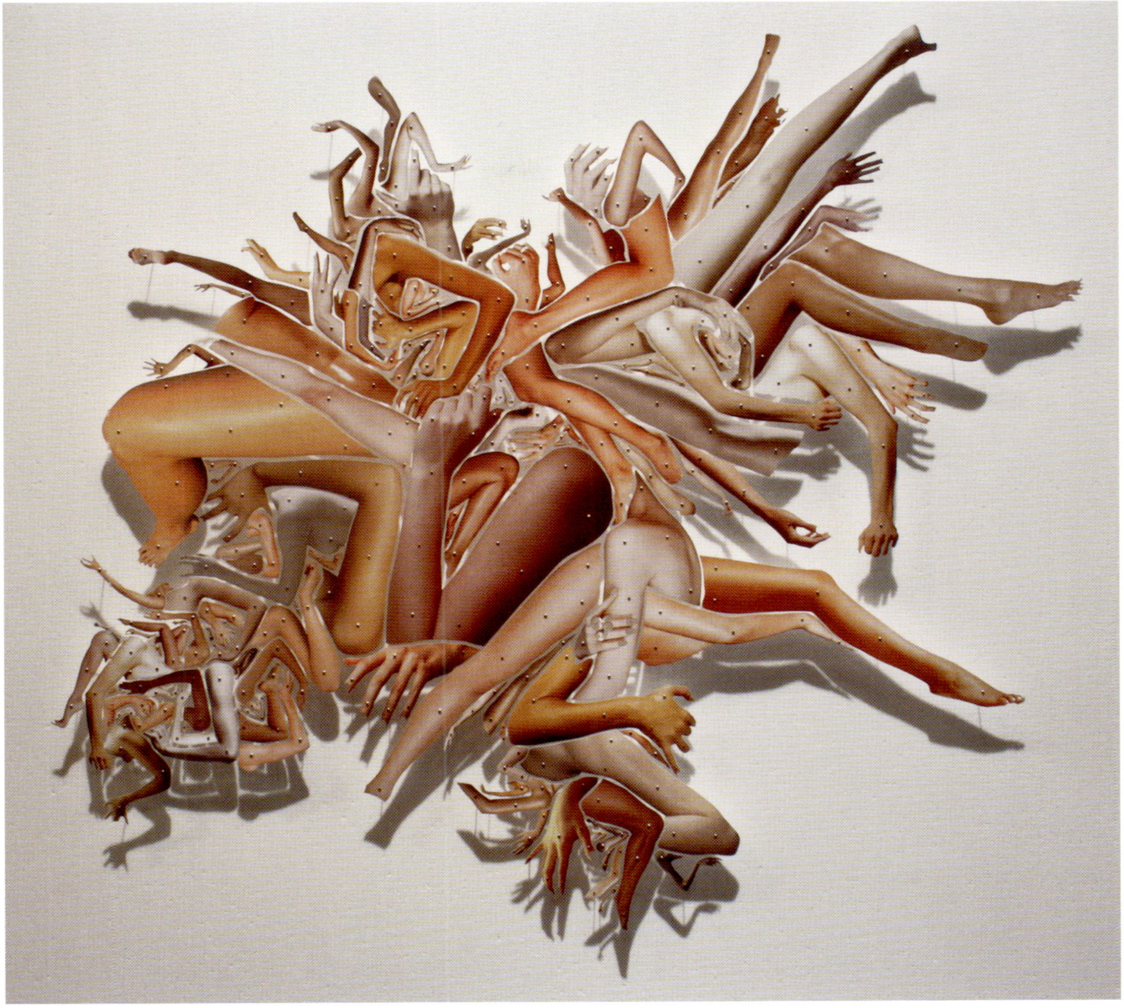

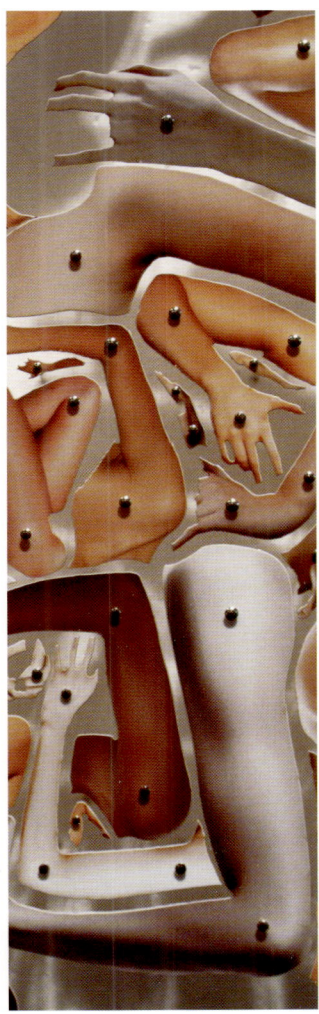
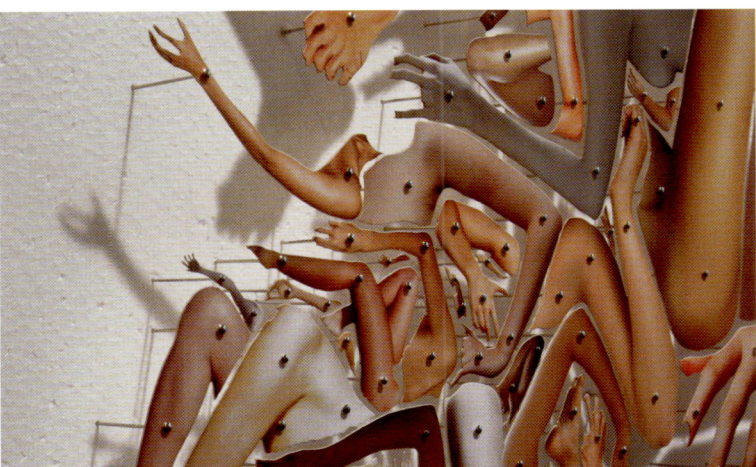
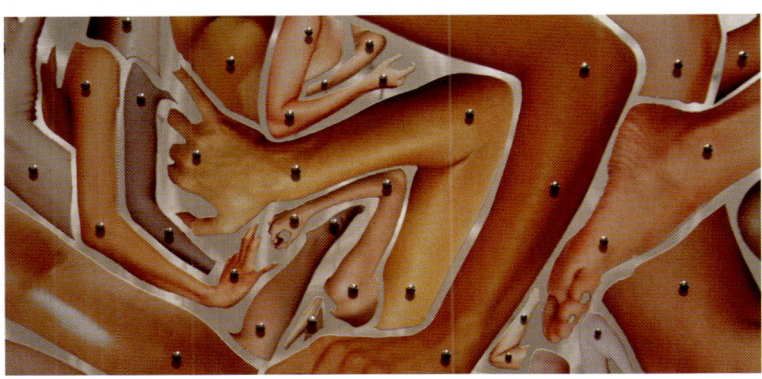
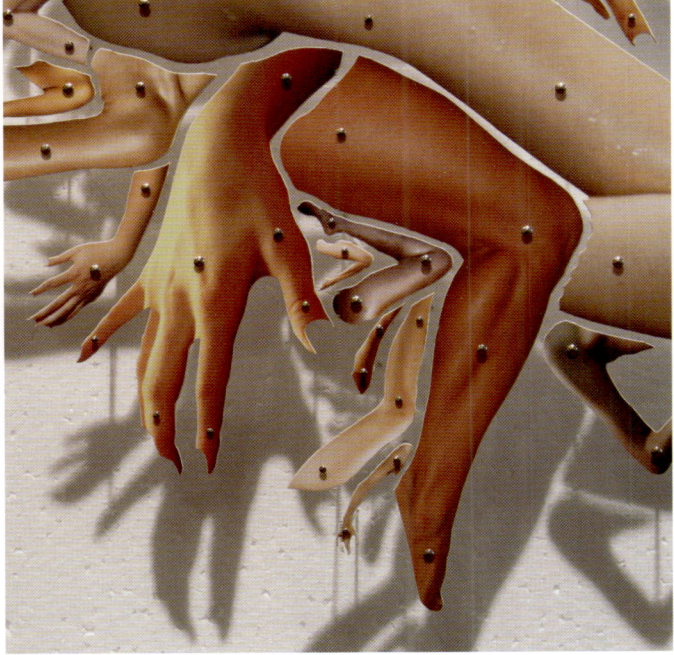

3. **Superstar Cluster**

Materials: Digital images, laser-cut digital print, pins, foam panel
Description: Fashion and celebrity images are collected from various online sources via Google image search. Digital prints are laser-cut and pinned to a foam panel.
Dimensions: 35 x 35 x 3 1/2 inches
Artist: David Adey   Country: USA
Gallery/Dealer: Scott White Contemporary Art, La Jolla, CA

4. For Gucci

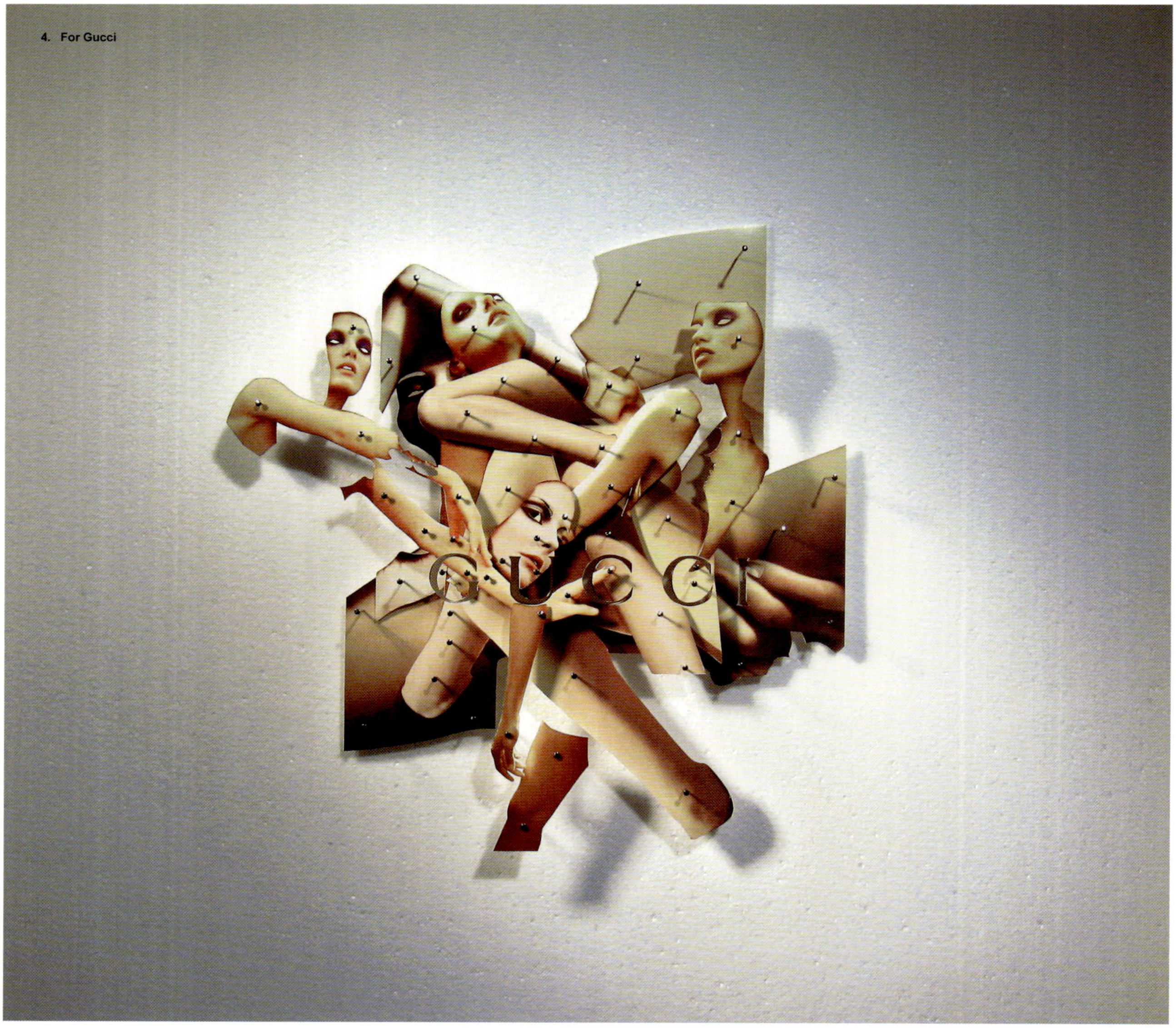

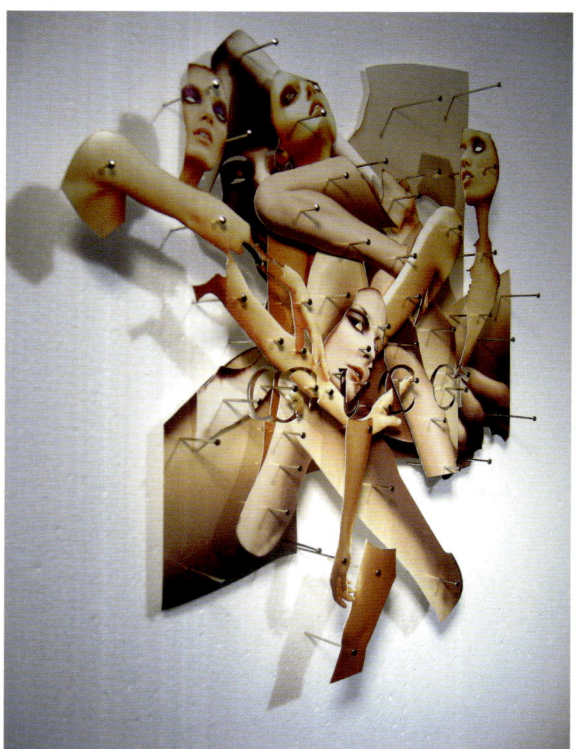
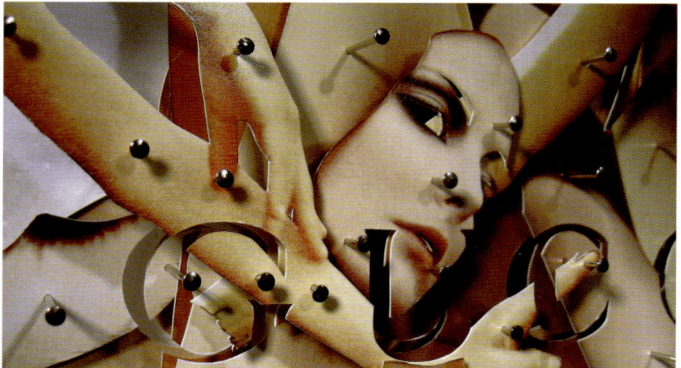
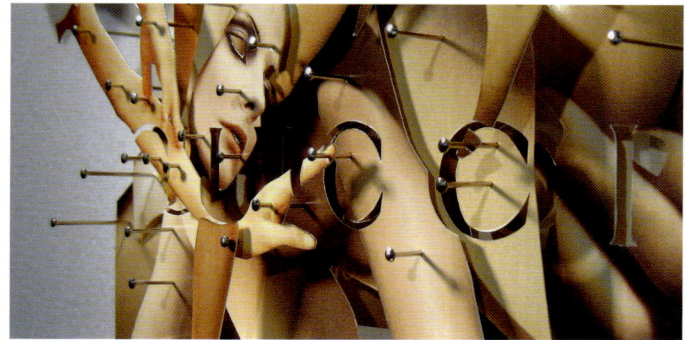

4. For Gucci

Materials/Process: A series of Gucci ads are layered with logos aligned. Only the areas of skin which touch the logo are extracted from each ad. The extracted skin is reassembled in layers with pins on a foam panel, creating a complete logo in negative space.
Dimensions: 24 x 24 inches
Artist: David Adey   Country: USA
Gallery/Dealer: Scott White Contemporary Art, La Jolla, CA.

5. Misha Barton For Bebe

Materials/Process: Skin is isolated and extracted from a Bebe bus-shelter poster with a collection of craft-punches. The deconstructed image is re-assembled with pins on a foam panel.
Dimensions: 68 x 47.5 x 3.25 inches
Artist: David Adey   Country: USA
Gallery/Dealer: Scott White Contemporary Art, La Jolla, CA

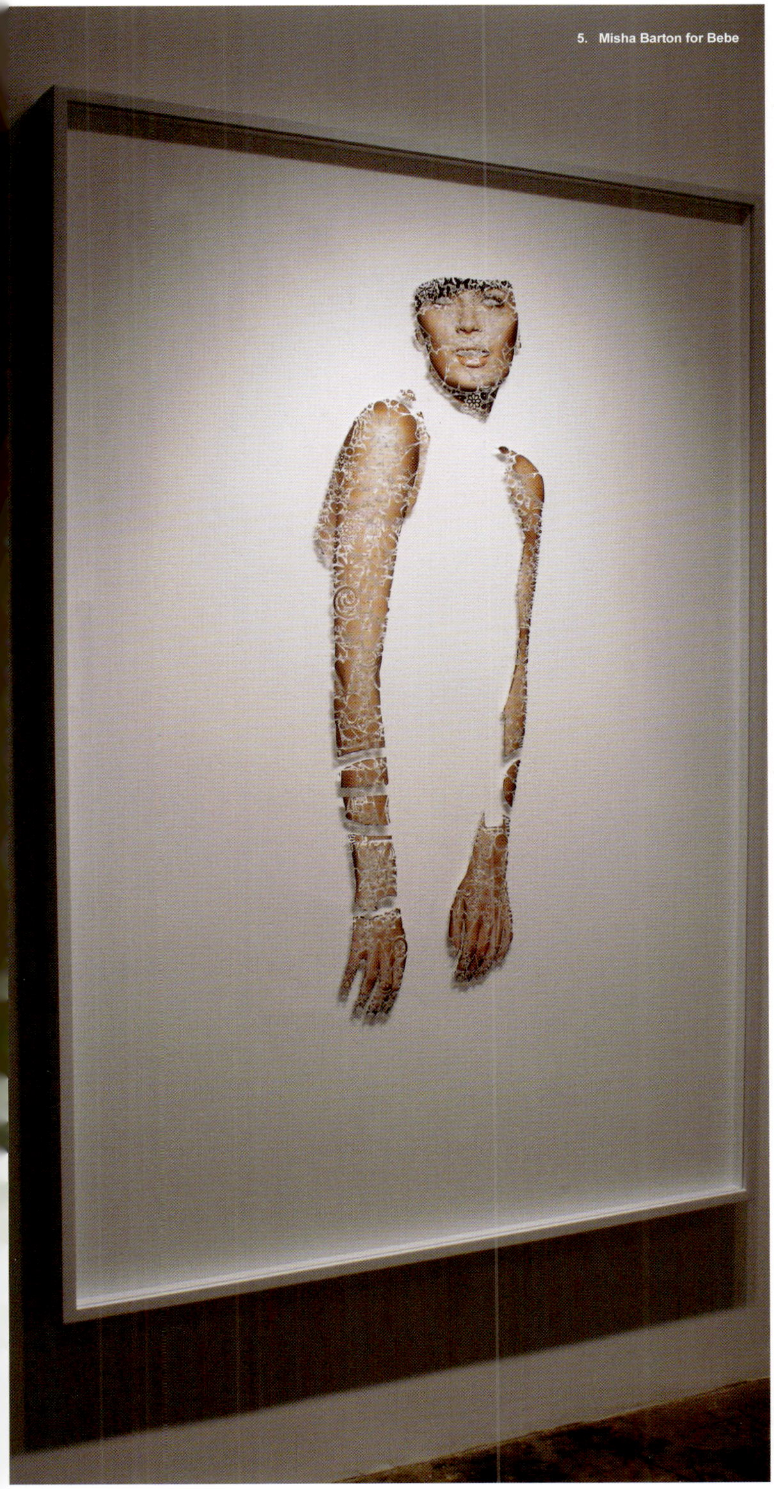

5. Misha Barton for Bebe

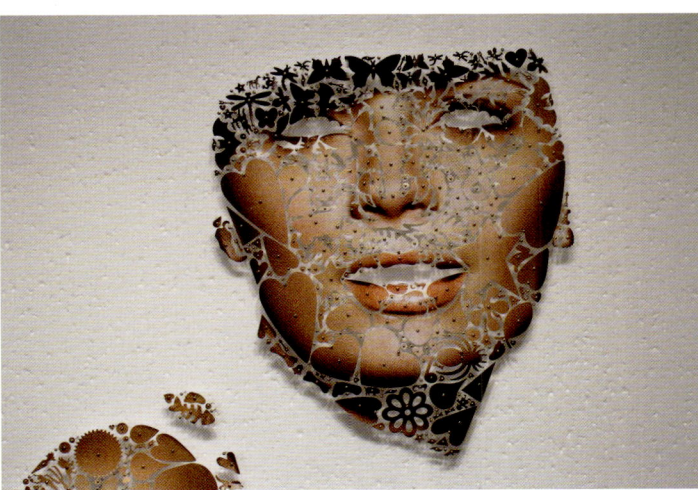
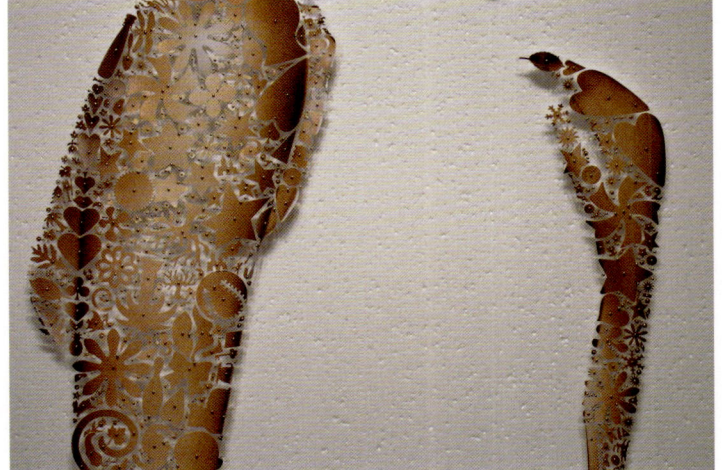
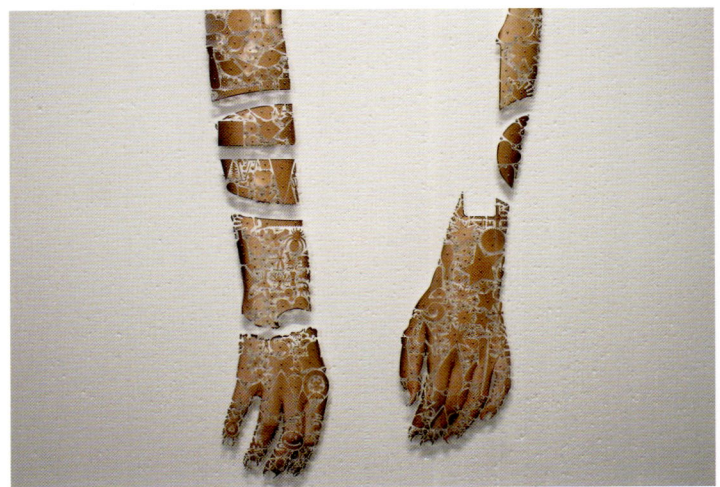

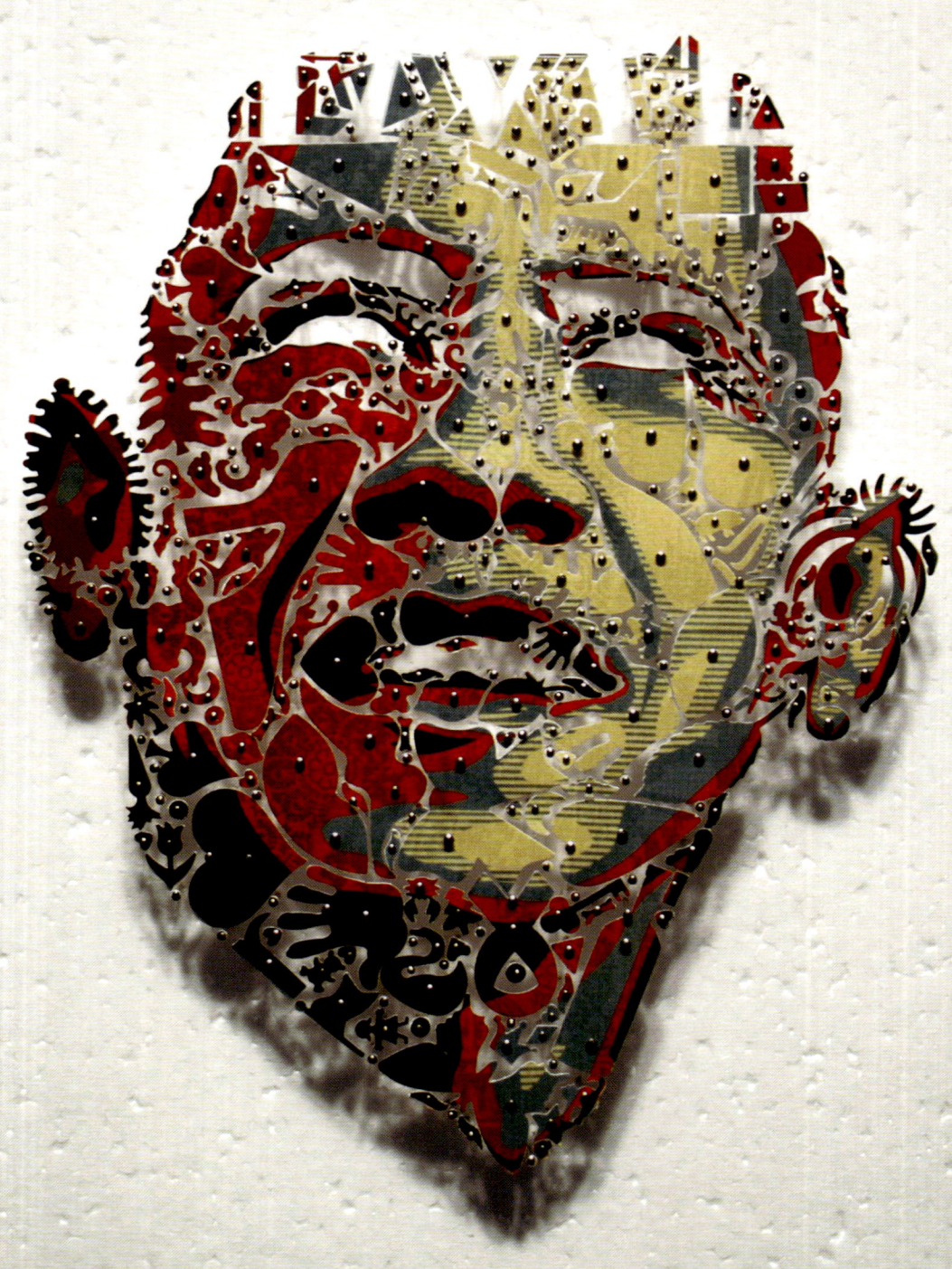

6. Person of The Year

Materials/Process: Time Magazine's Person of the Year cover, featuring Shepard Fairey's illustration of Barack Obama. Illustrated skin is extracted with a variety of craft-punches. The deconstructed image is re-assembled with pins on a foam panel.
Dimensions: 24 x 18 inches
Artist: David Adey Country: USA
Gallery/Dealer: Scott White Contemporary Art, La Jolla, CA

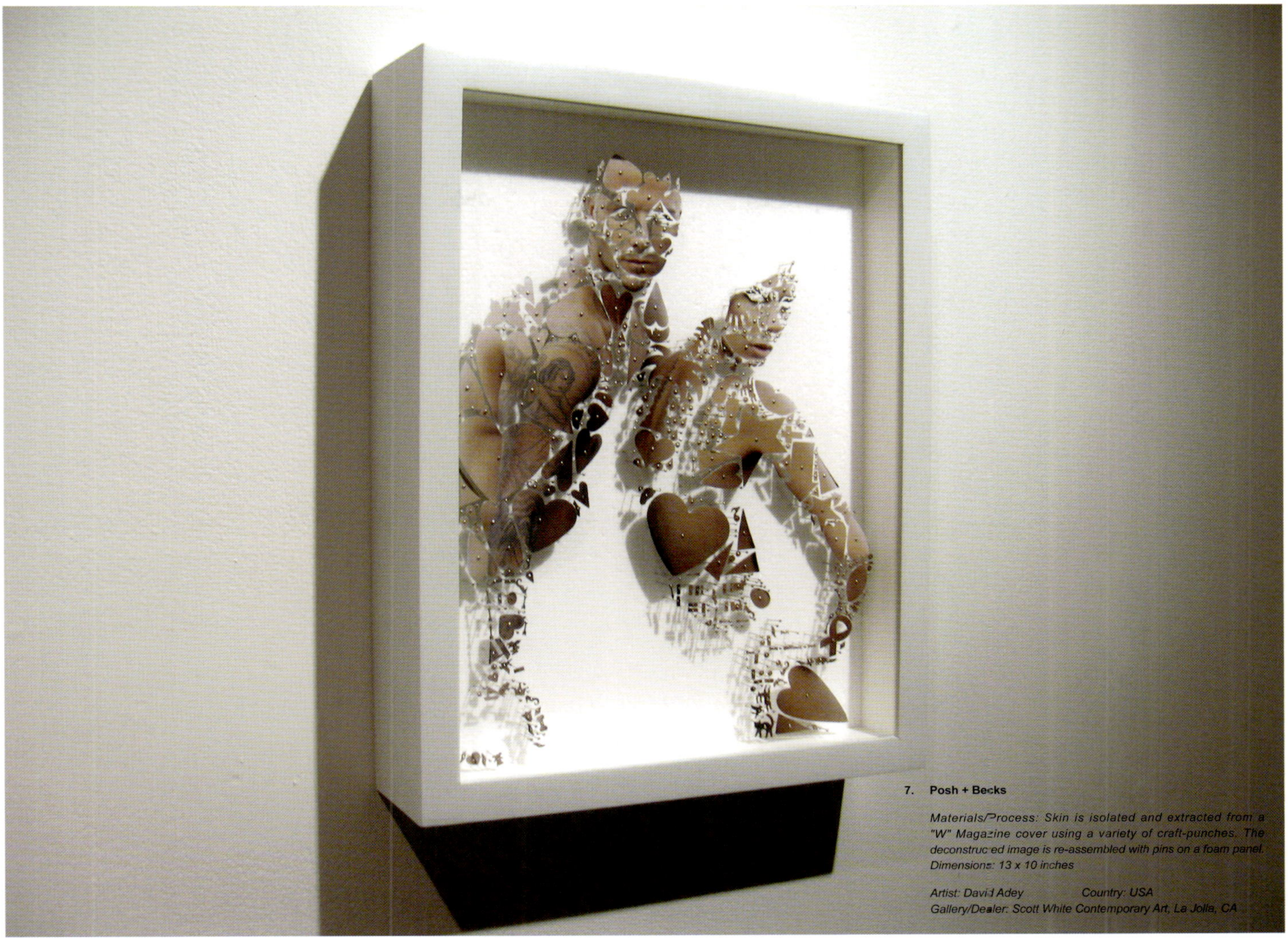

7. **Posh + Becks**

Materials/Process: Skin is isolated and extracted from a "W" Magazine cover using a variety of craft-punches. The deconstructed image is re-assembled with pins on a foam panel. Dimensions: 13 x 10 inches

Artist: David Adey *Country:* USA
Gallery/Dealer: Scott White Contemporary Art, La Jolla, CA

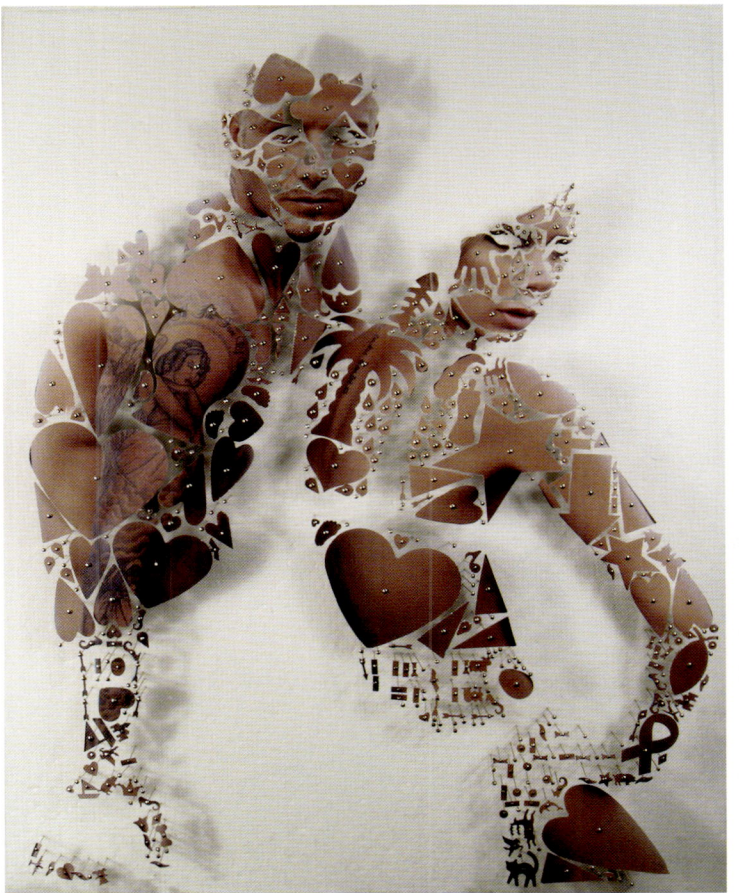
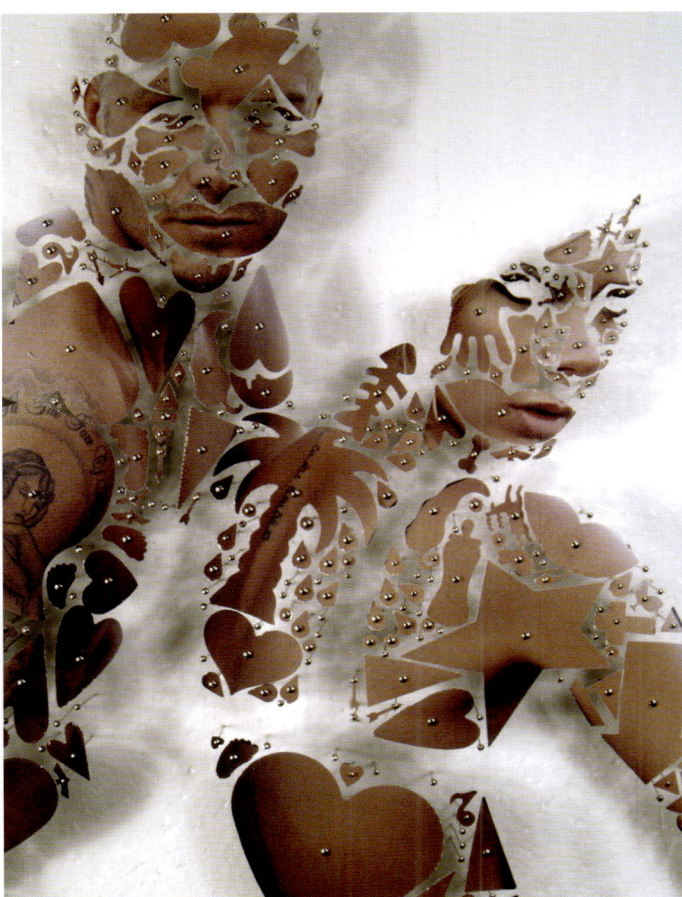

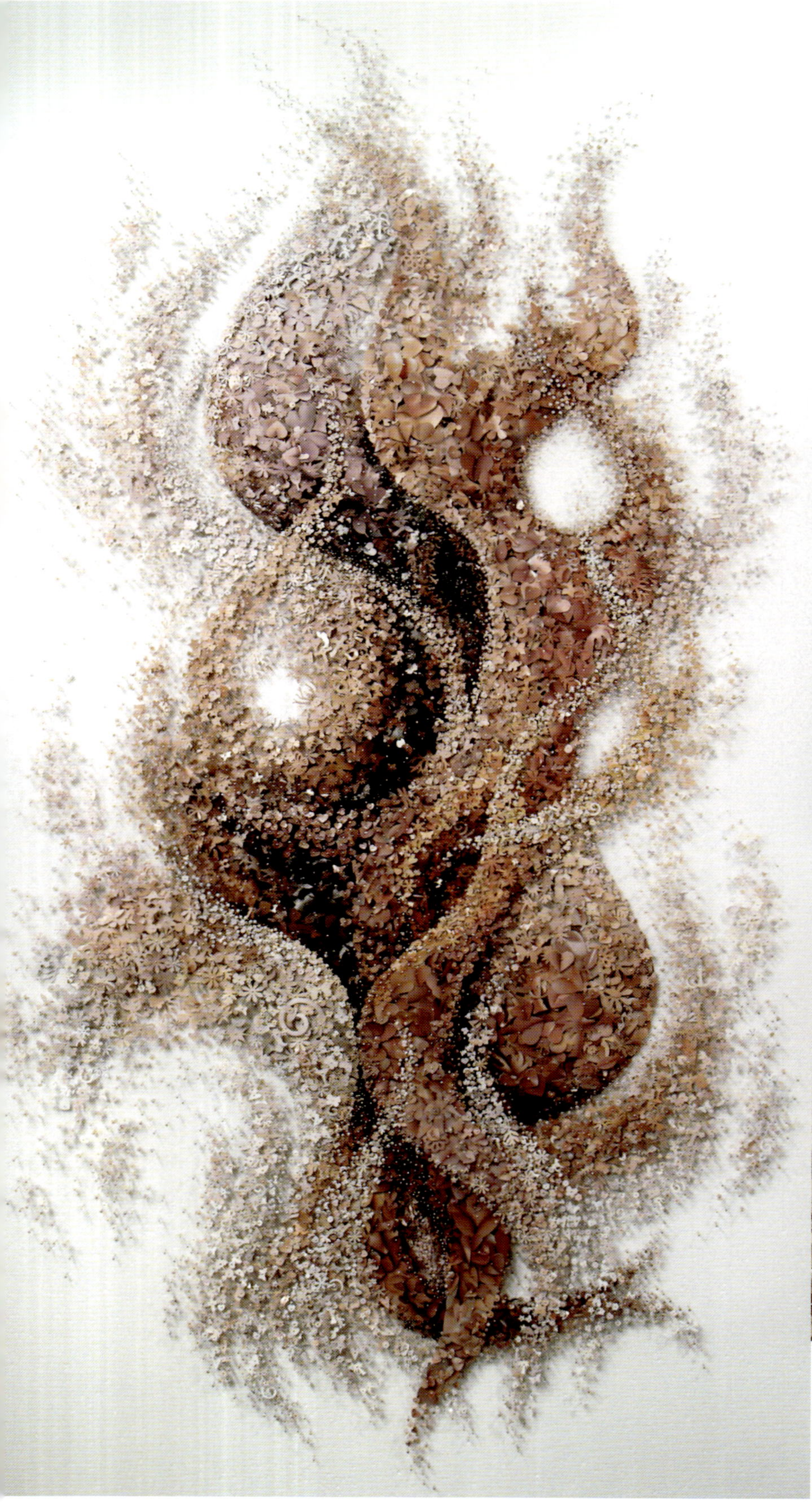

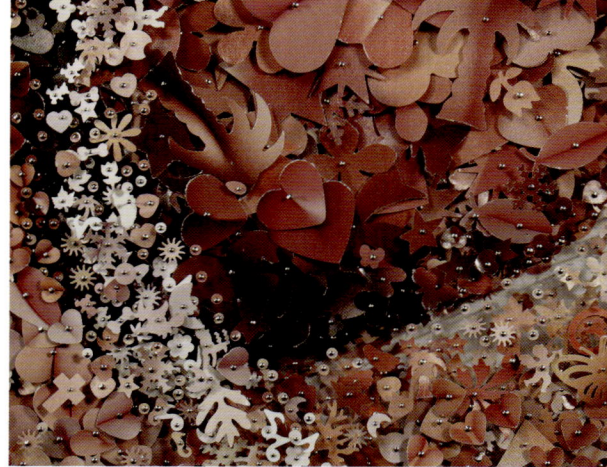
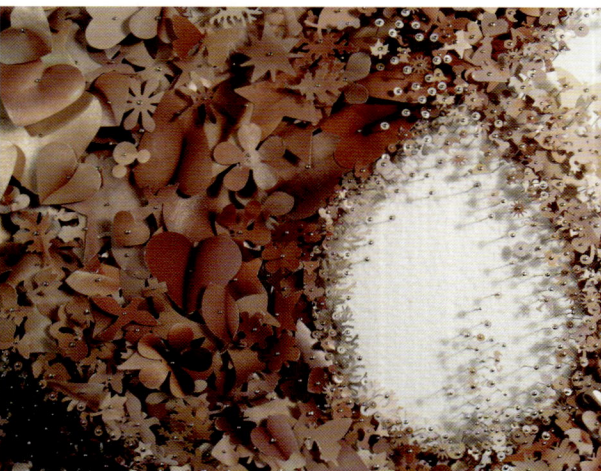
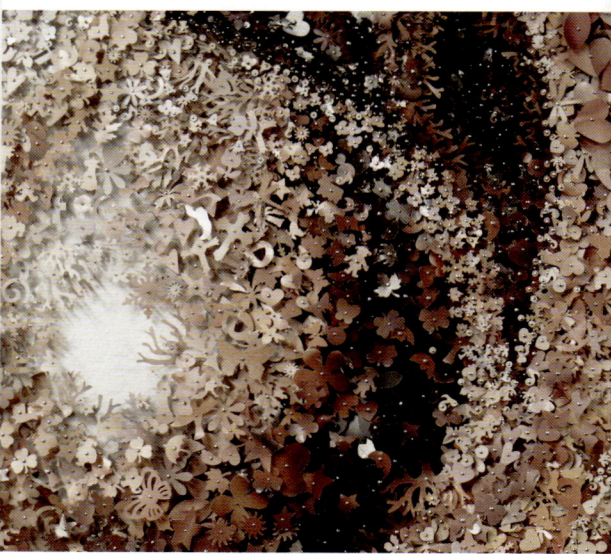

8. Swarm

Materials/Process: Skin is extracted from various fashion magazine ads using a collection of craft punches. Pieces are assembled with pins on a foam panel.
Dimensions: 65 x 40 inches

Artist: David AdeyCountry: USA
Gallery/Dealer: Scott White Contemporary Art, La Jolla, CA

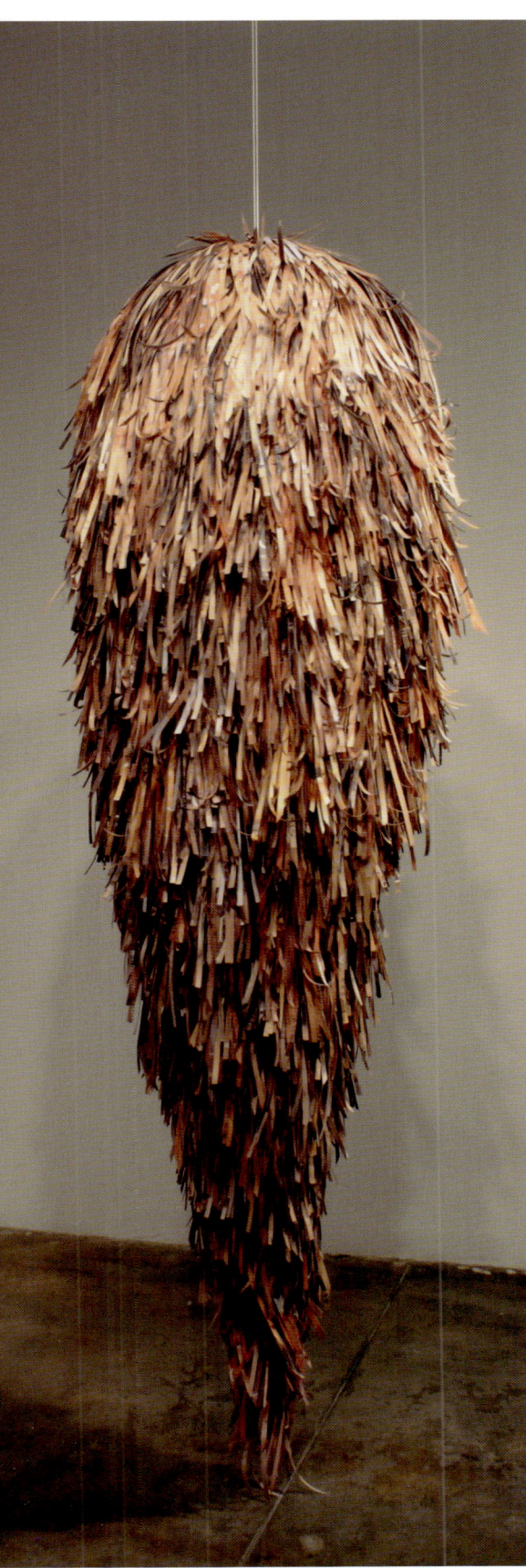

9. Tail

Materials/Process: Fashion magazine ads run through a paper shredder.
Dimensions: 5 feet, 10 inches (height)

Artist: David Adey   Country: USA
Gallery/Dealer: Scott White Contemporary Art, La Jolla, CA

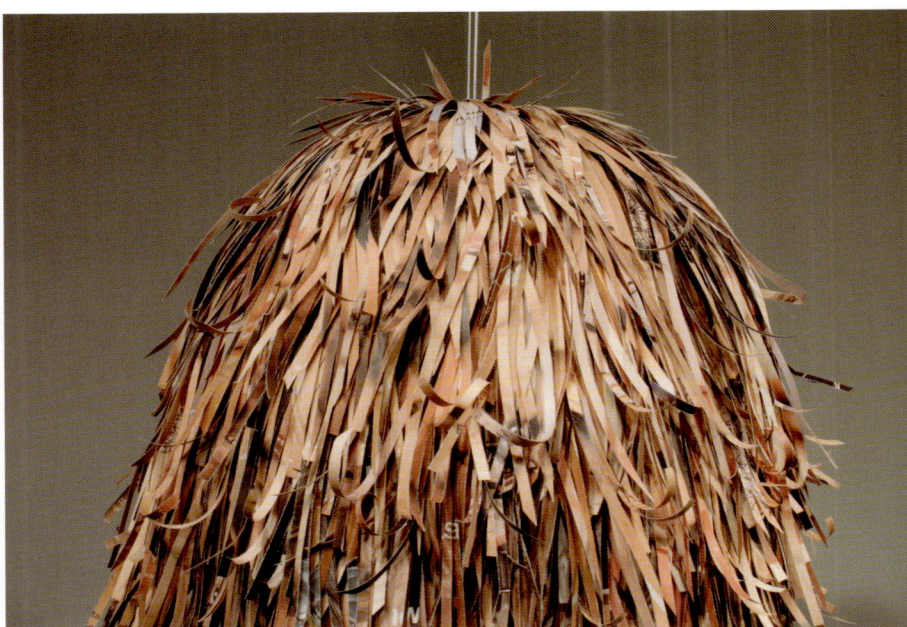

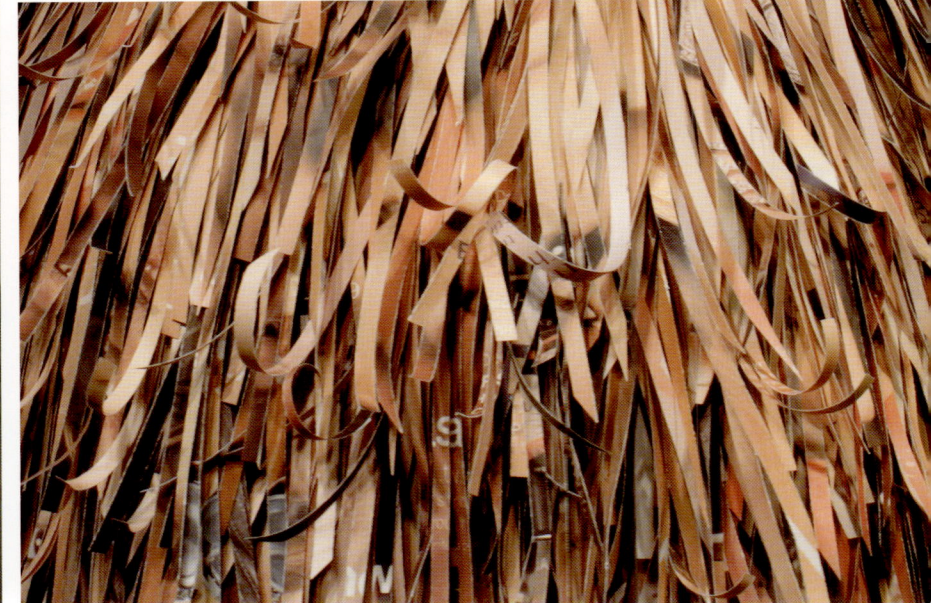

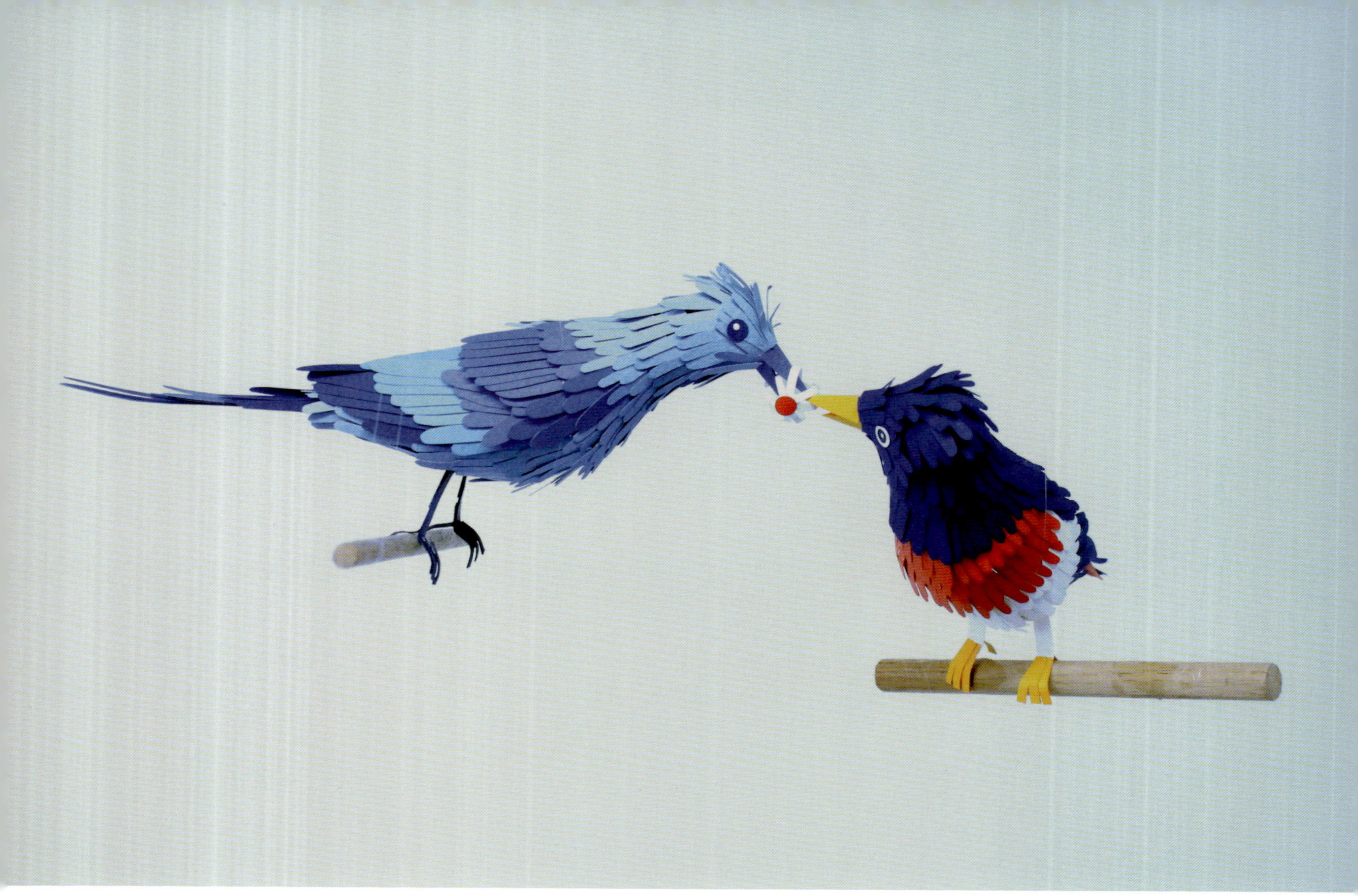

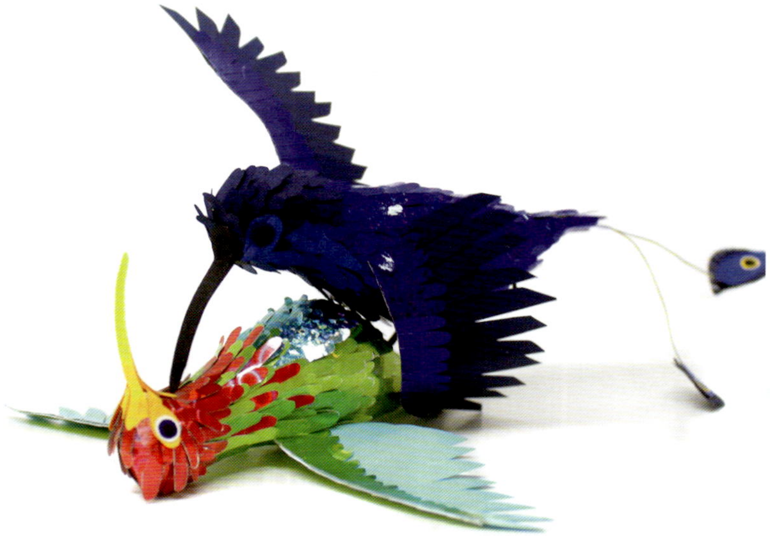

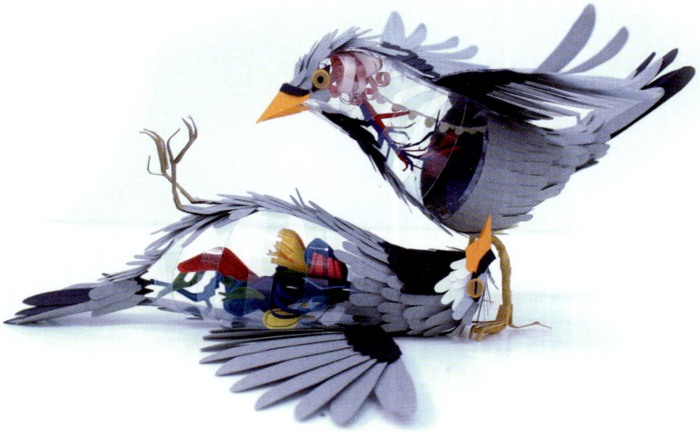

Paper Bird Sculpture

Serie of works made in paper hand-cut and assembled piece by piece with detail over a paper structure.

---Diana Beltran Herrera

Artist: Diana Beltran Herrera
Country: Colombia
Photographer: Diana Beltran Herrera

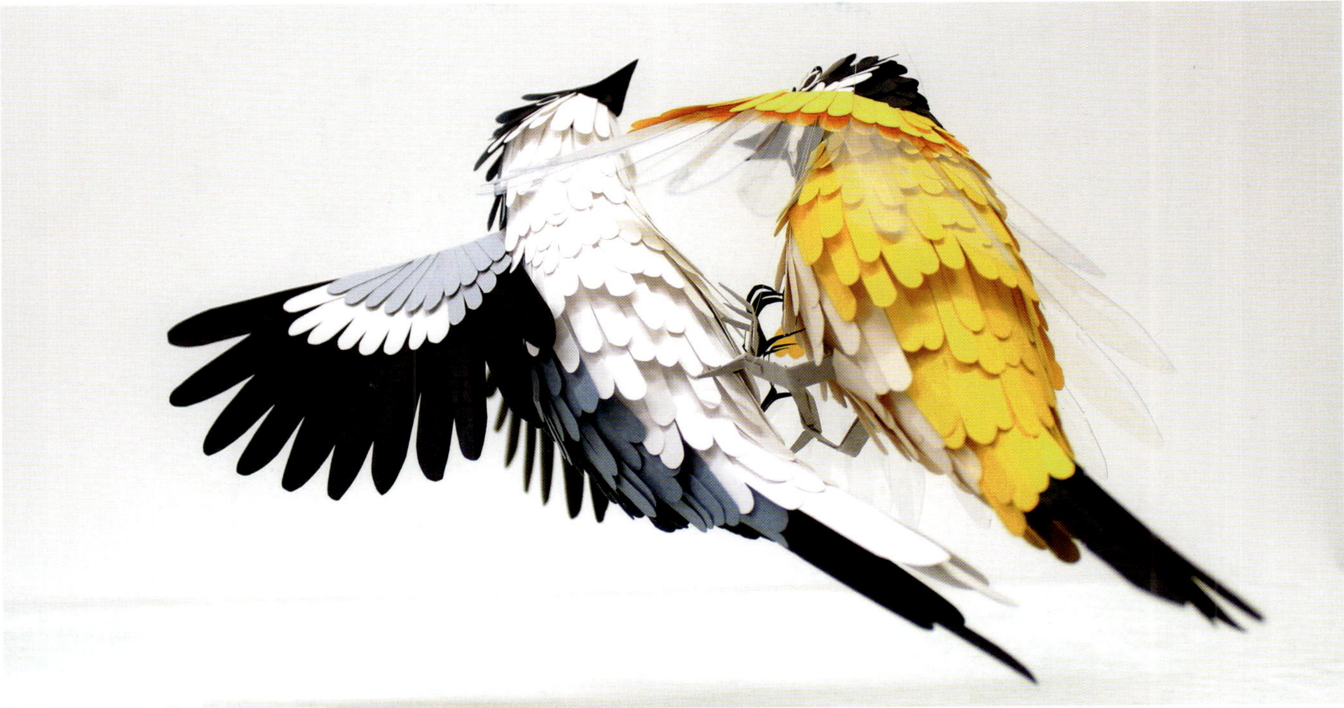

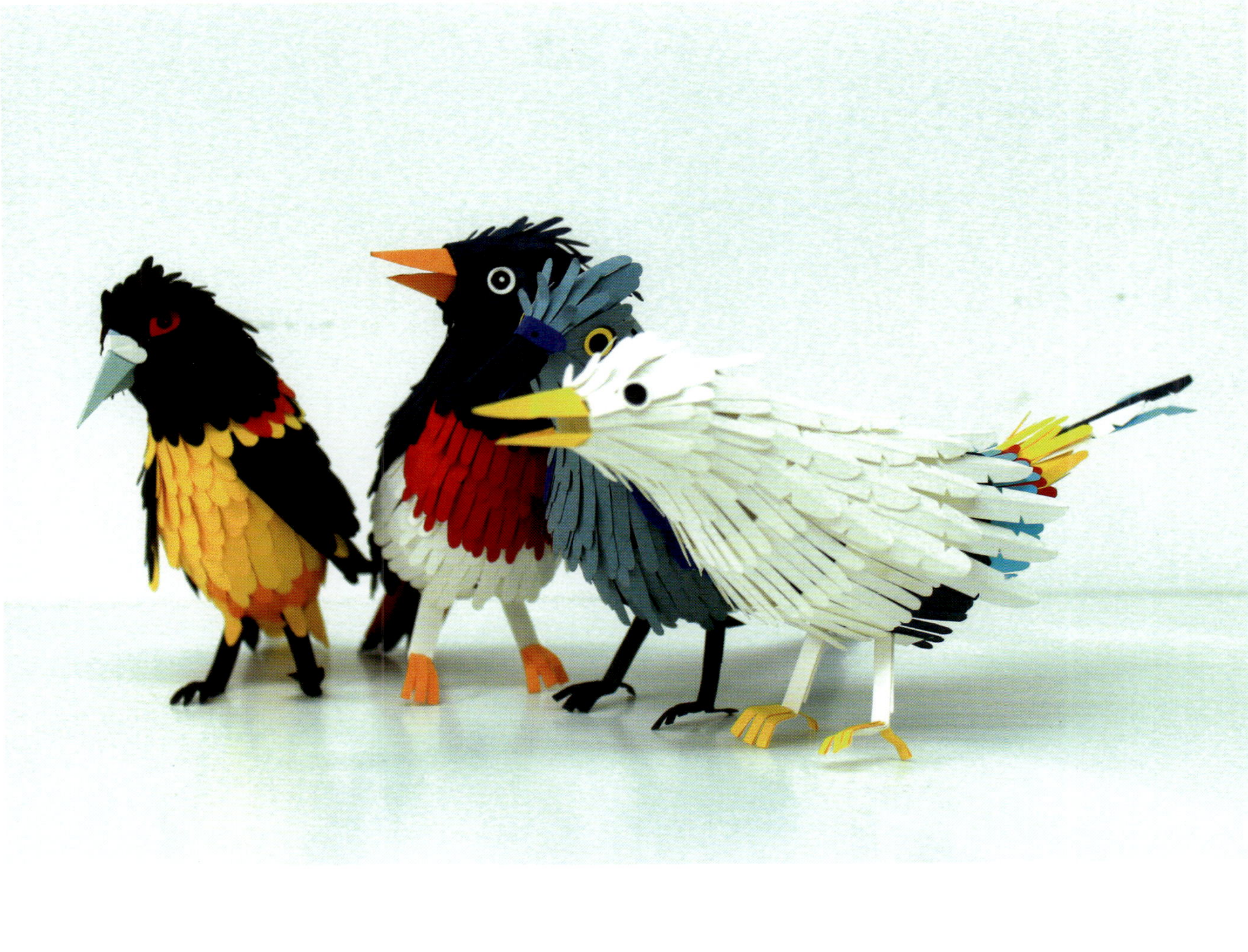

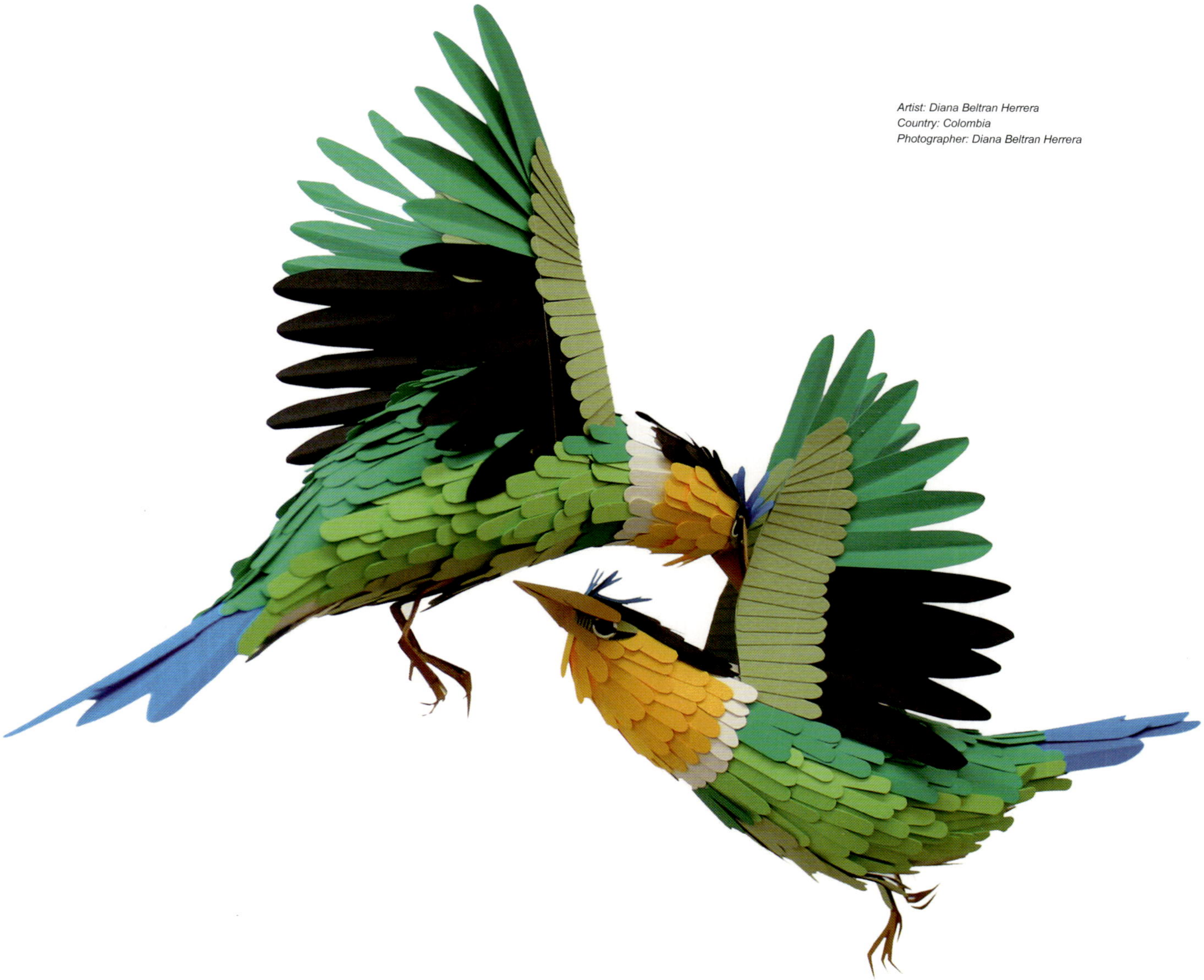

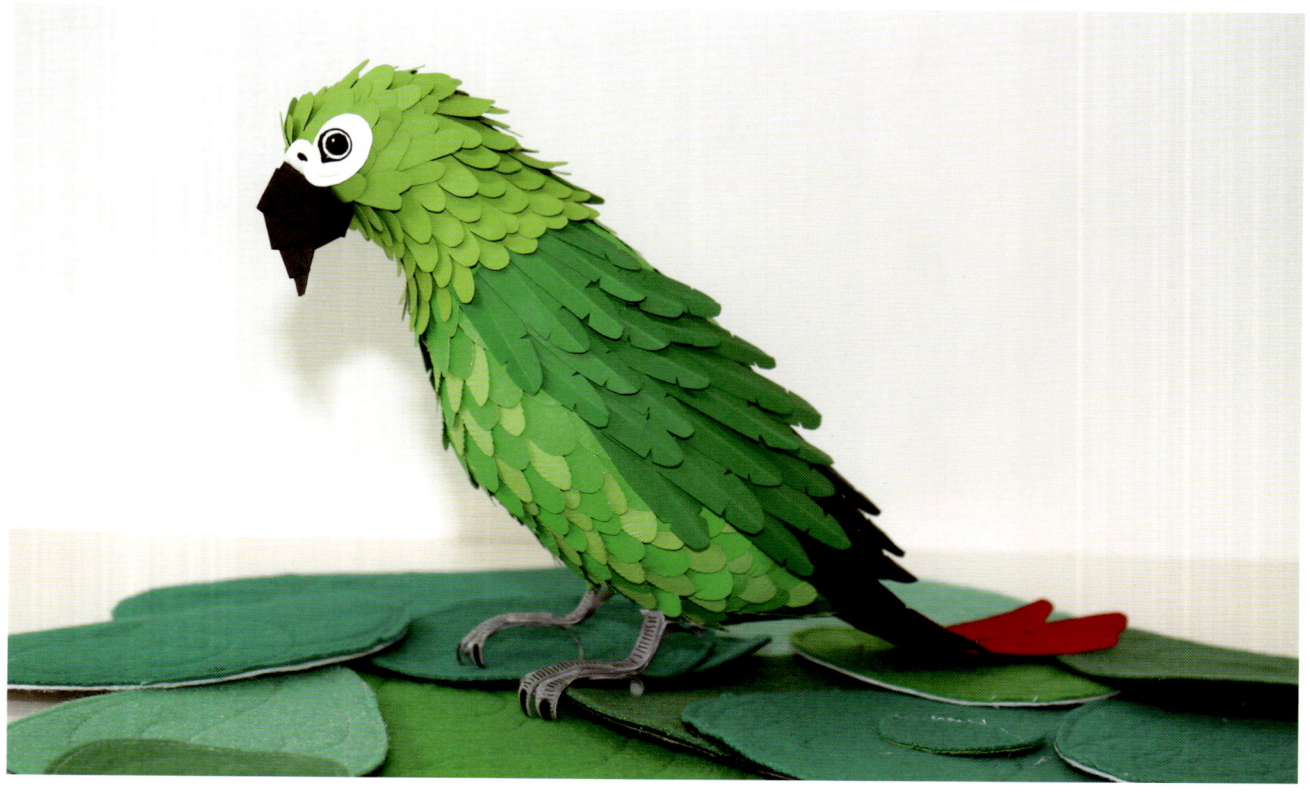

Artist: Diana Beltran Herrera
Country: Colombia
Photographer: Diana Beltran Herrera

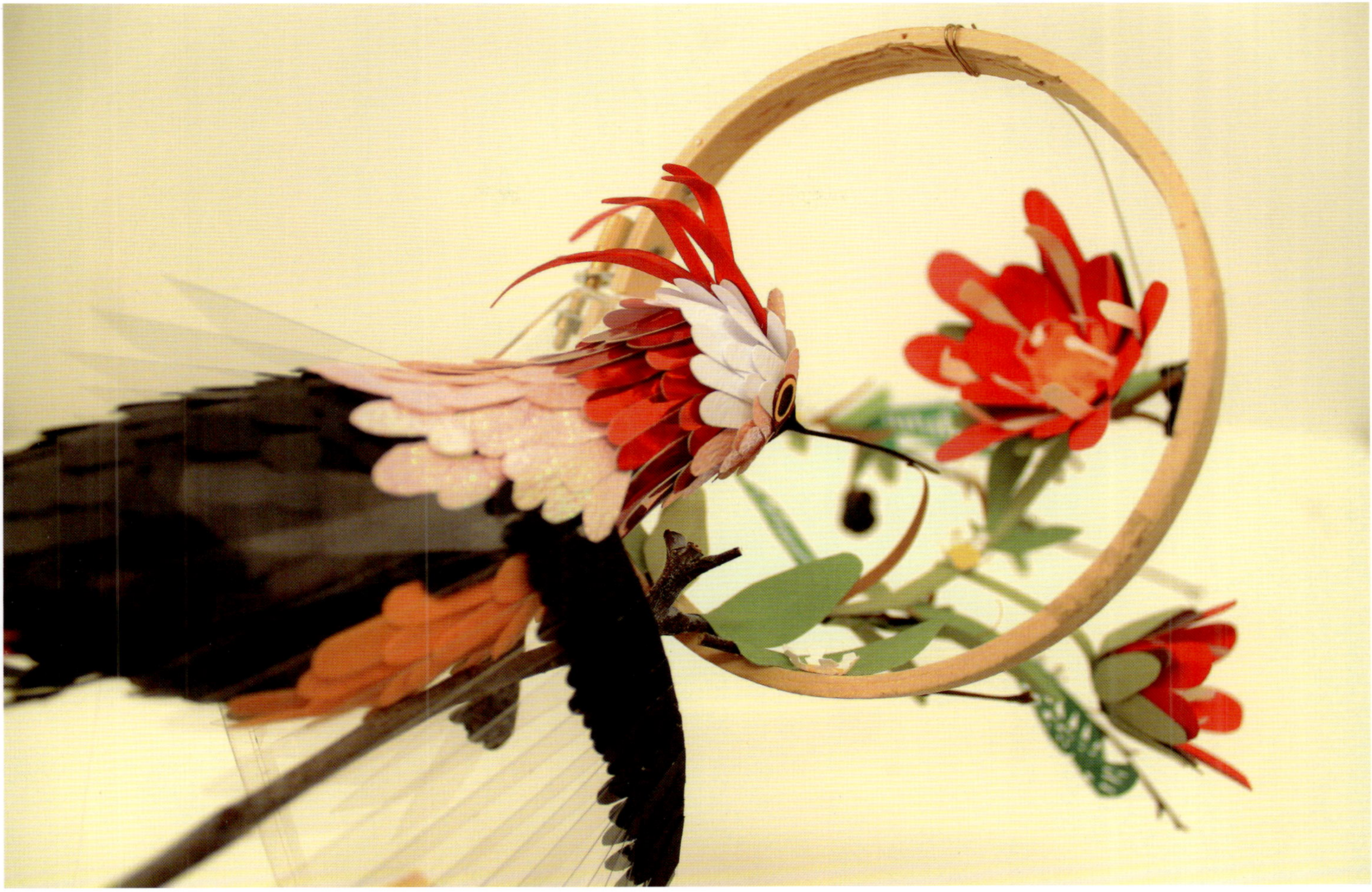

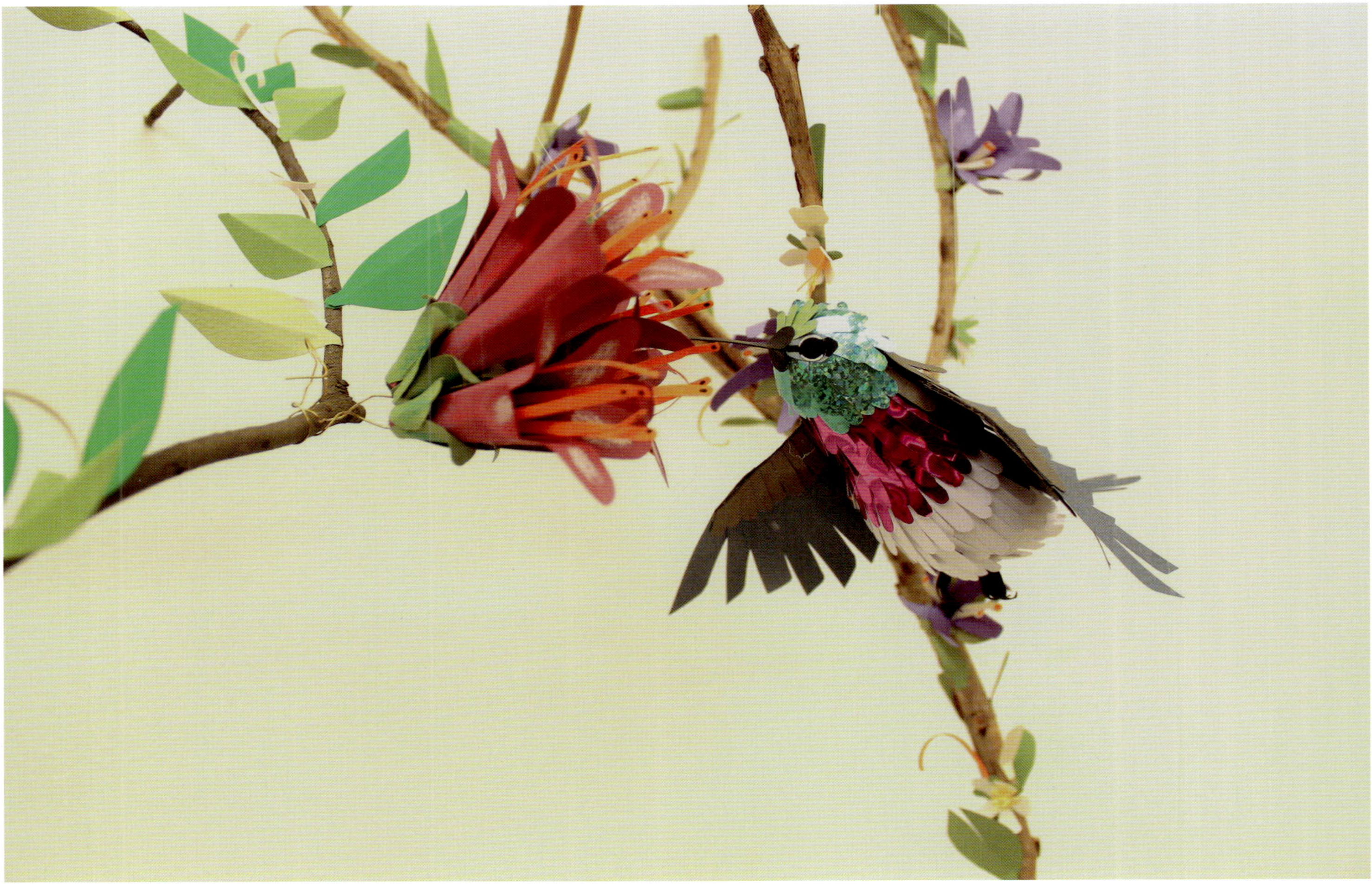

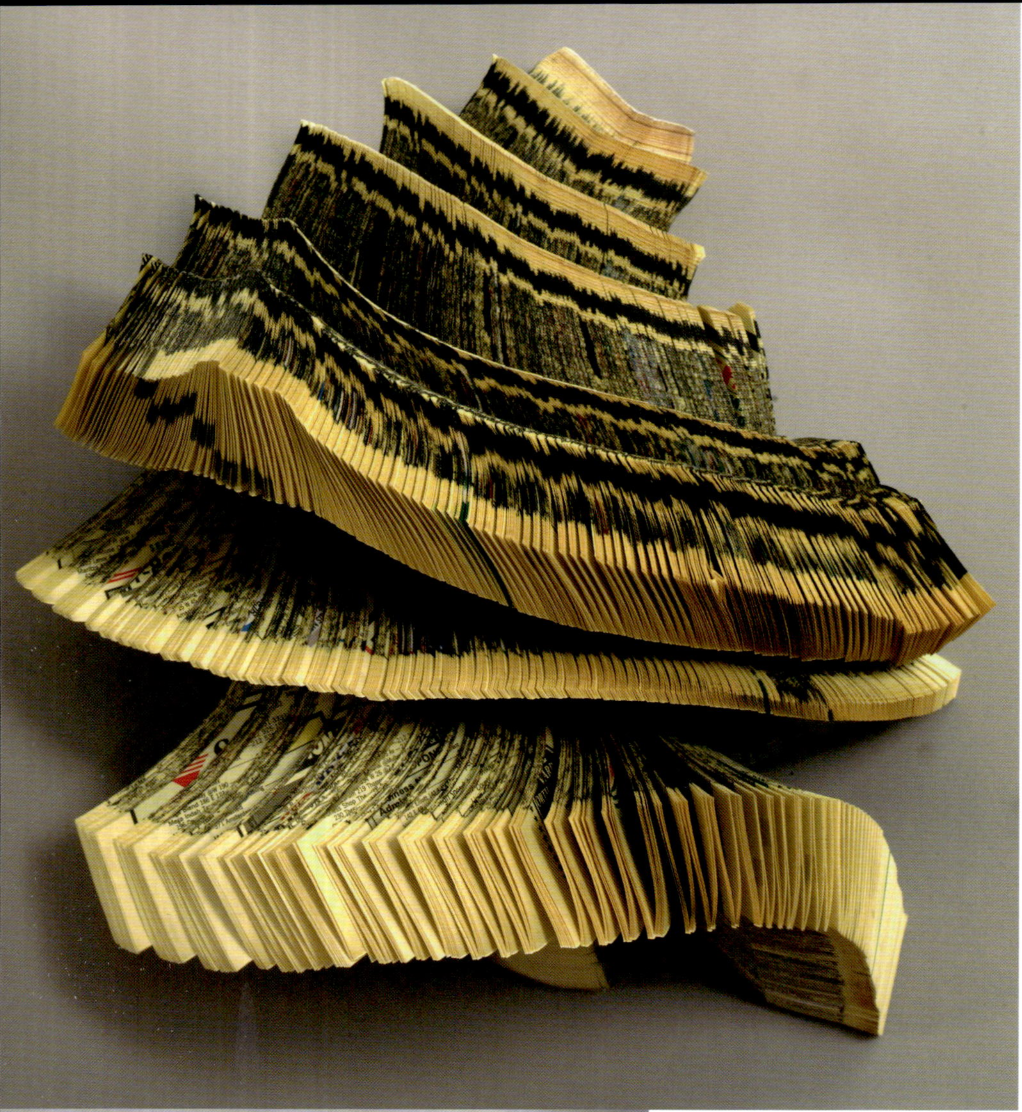

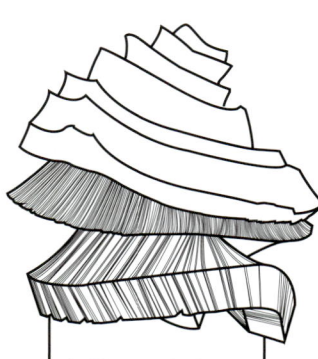

1. **Disaster Series: Twister**
2. **Erosion #19: Eroding Continents**
3. **The Many Lives of Miss Chatelaine**
4. **The Silent Question**
5. **Masked Vocabulary**
6. **Dis/connecting Old Glory**
7. **Vector**
8. **Tract: Ryder Univ.**

---Doug Beube

1. **Disaster Series: Twister**

   14 x 15 x 5 in.
   Altered phone book

   Artist: Doug Beube   Country: Canada

Selective parts of a New York City yellow phone book, with thousands of business names are cut away. Sections of the text block and the spine of the book are removed making it flexible allowing the pages to be manipulated into different forms. Mounted on the wall, the book appears to be floating across a vertical plane, as if a photograph of a bird caught it off balance flying in a storm, a wizard's hat, even a hurricane or 'twister,' spinning out of control. The deep cuts in the book reveals striations of black ink for the print and white bands for the columns on the pages transforming them into a soft fabric.

Pulled into a fixed position, the book appears to be stressed, reminiscent of circus contortionists that morph their bodies into seemingly impossible positions or toys that transform themselves into fantastic architectural shapes. Sometimes words get 'twisted,' either intentionally spoken to deceive or by misunderstanding their meanings. As a metaphor for human communication and speech, what is said does not always produce its intended result.

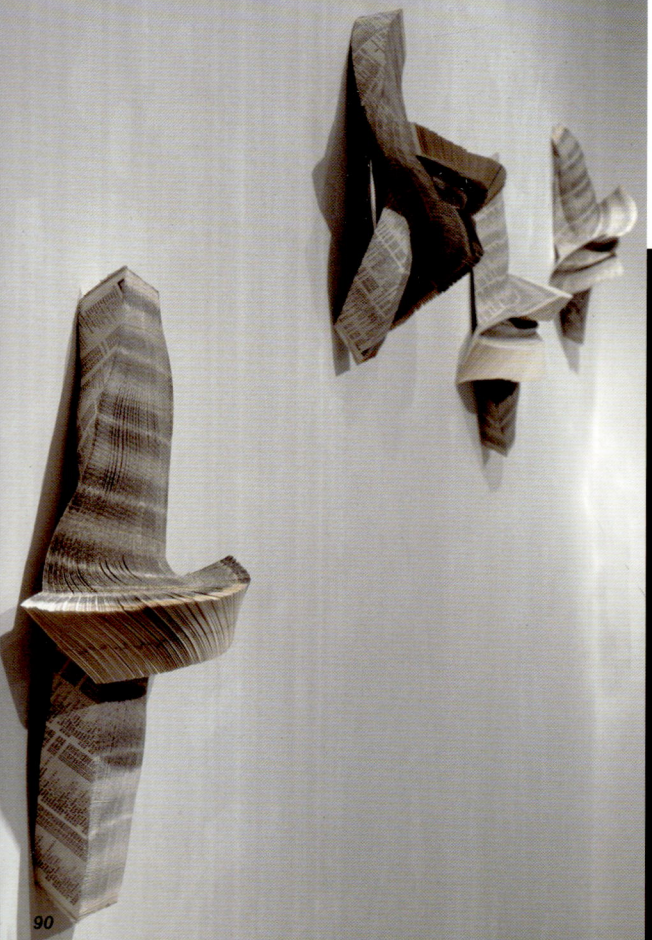

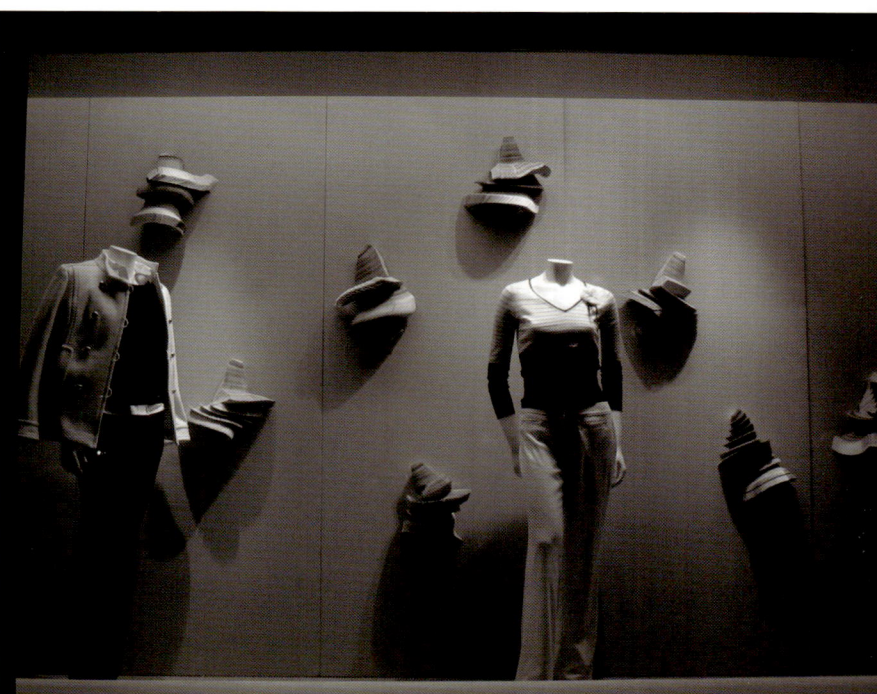

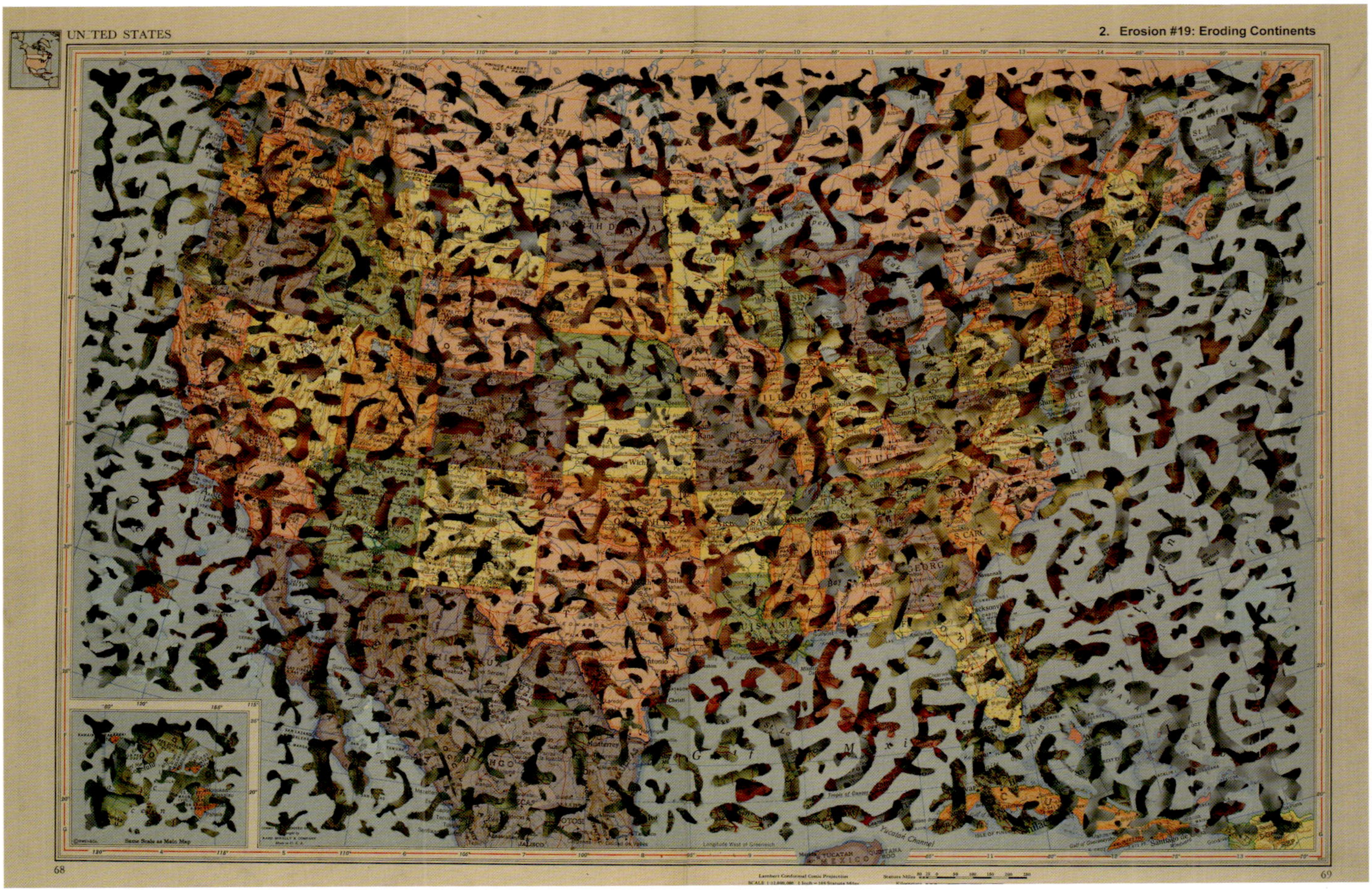

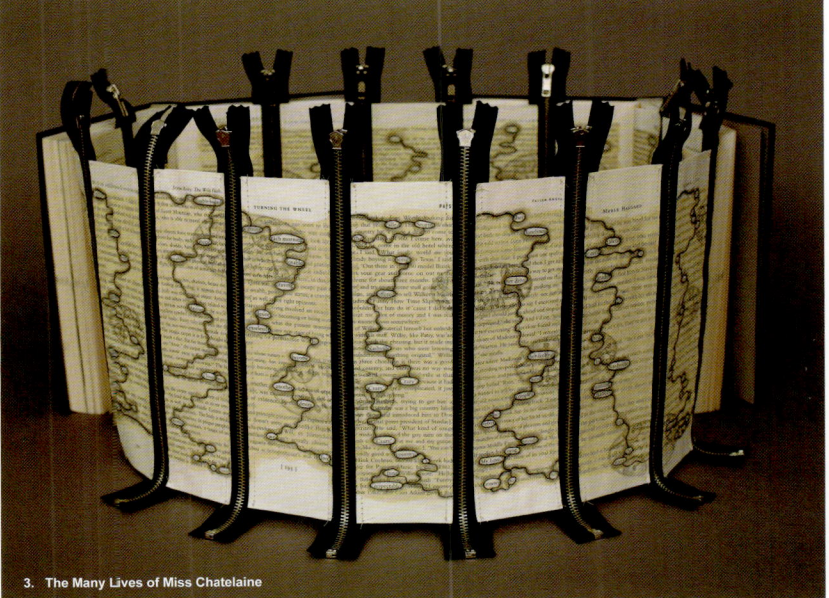

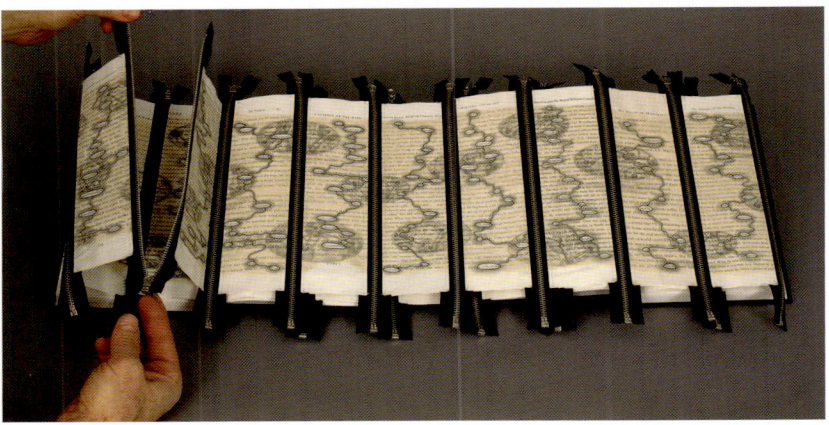

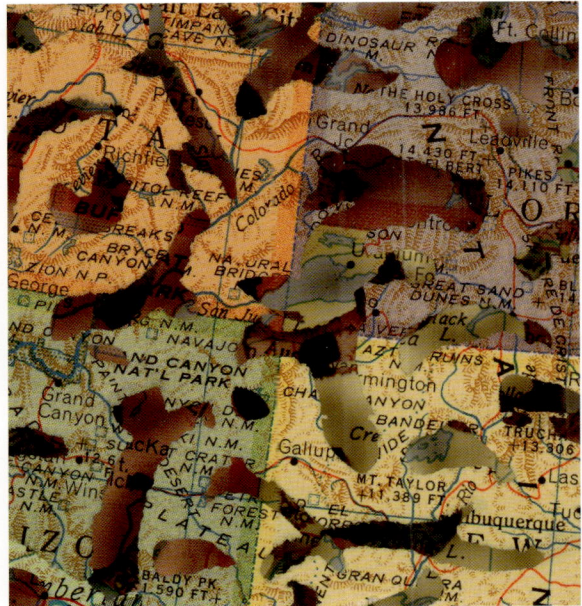

2. **Erosion #19: Eroding Continents**
13 x 20 x 2 in. collage
Altered atlas, collage, foam core.

This piece appears to be a worm-eaten map of the United States and parts of North America. At a closer look, the viewer sees that below this surface is another ravaged continent and, barely visible below that, another, and so forth, including each of the major continents. Quarter-inch spacers separate the layers of disfigured continental maps, giving them a sense of depth as if they are relief maps or aerial views of some terrain on Google Maps.

3. **The Many Lives of Miss Chatelaine**
9 1/2 x 7 1/4 x 2 in. (closed); 9 1/2 x 60 x 2 in. (open)
Altered books, collage, sculpture, acrylic, ink, thread, paper, zippers

The piece itself incorporates my interests in mixed media, collage, sculpture, drawing, written text, and cut paper, all stitched together with zippers that lend the object its great flexibility. The composite portrait both figuratively and literally unfolds. Thus the book can be read as either a flat or three-dimensional piece of artwork. When all the pages are zipped the book can stand upright in a circle and be read from any direction. When turned on its side with all the pages zipped, a concertina or accordion perspective configuration is apparent. When one of the middle pages is unzipped, the circle is broken and the book can lie level on a plane flat showing the full span of the pages end to end.

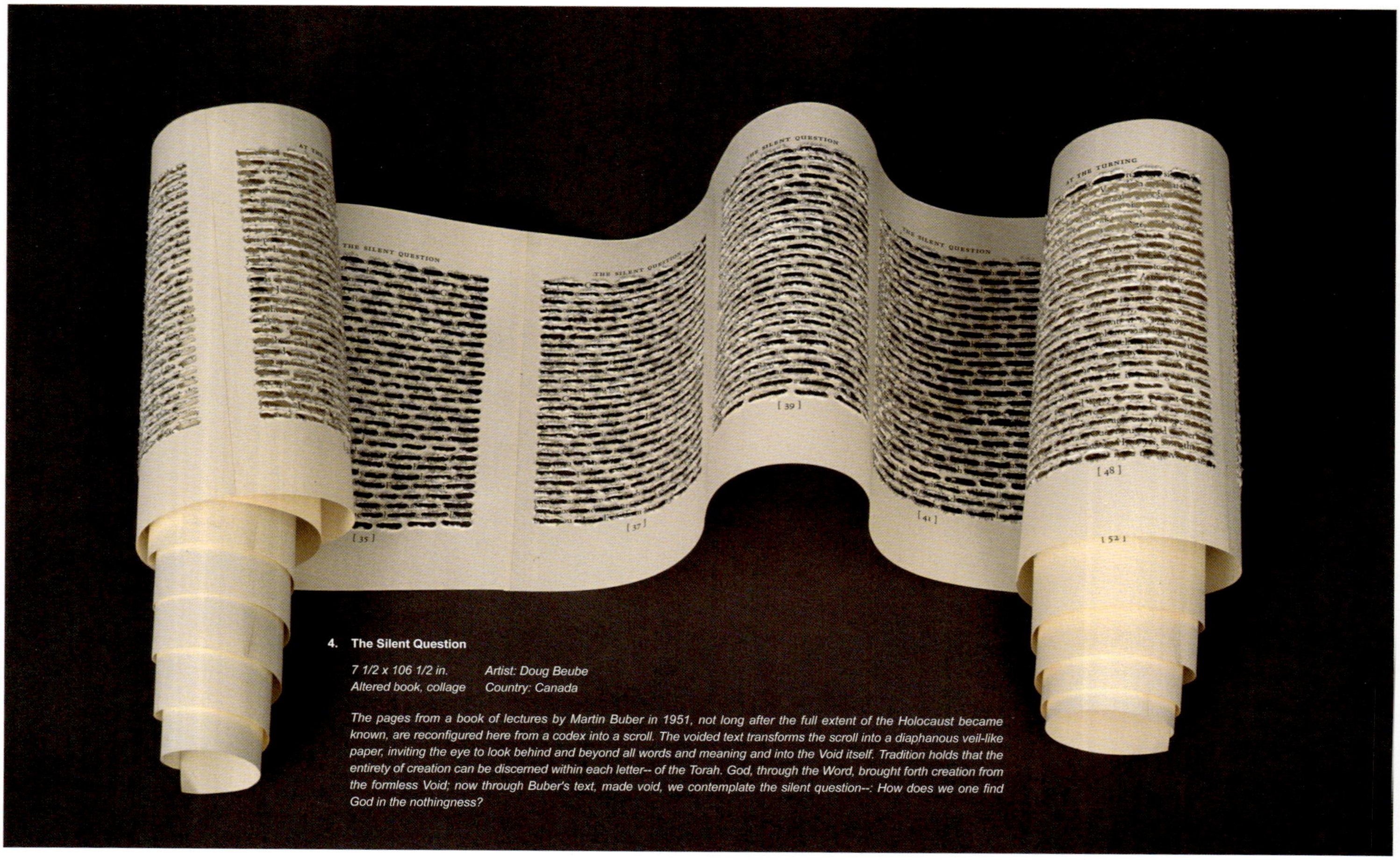

4. The Silent Question

7 1/2 x 106 1/2 in. Artist: Doug Beube
Altered book, collage Country: Canada

The pages from a book of lectures by Martin Buber in 1951, not long after the full extent of the Holocaust became known, are reconfigured here from a codex into a scroll. The voided text transforms the scroll into a diaphanous veil-like paper, inviting the eye to look behind and beyond all words and meaning and into the Void itself. Tradition holds that the entirety of creation can be discerned within each letter-- of the Torah. God, through the Word, brought forth creation from the formless Void; now through Buber's text, made void, we contemplate the silent question--: How does we one find God in the nothingness?

5. Masked Vocabulary

19 1/2 x 6 1/4 x 5 3/4 in.
Altered dictionary and book, metal, marble, wood

Masked Vocabulary is a dictionary that is transformed into a mask. It can be used to either hide or reveal feelings, depending upon intention. We can either use words to communicate poetically and educate others, speak hateful and prejudicial phrases or hide our true intentions depending how whether we are connected to the words and vocabulary we use.

Artist: Doug Beube Country: Canada

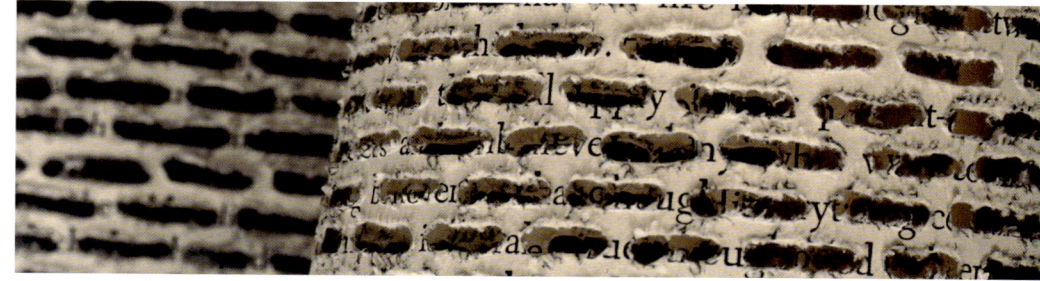

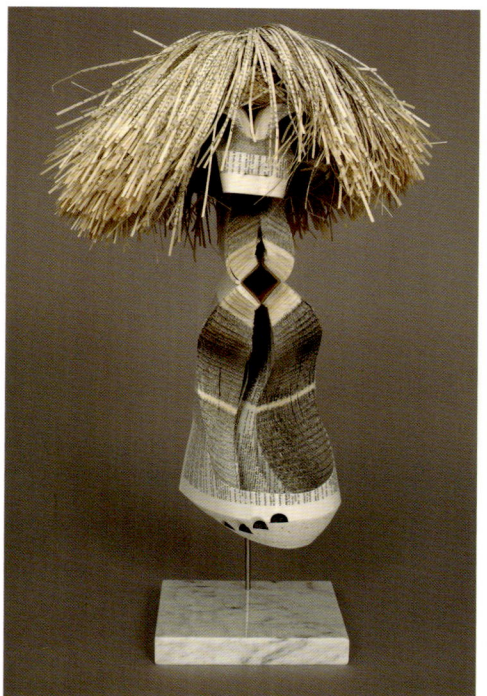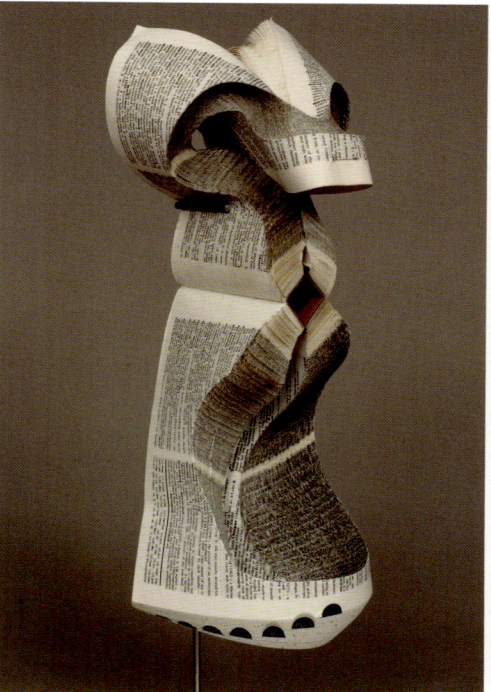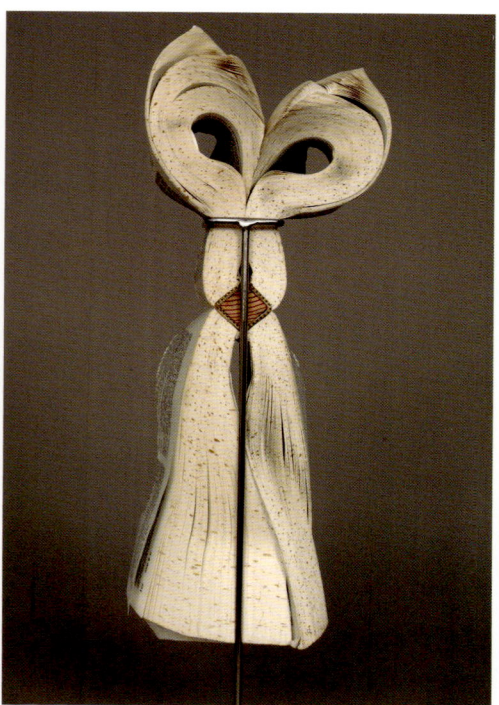

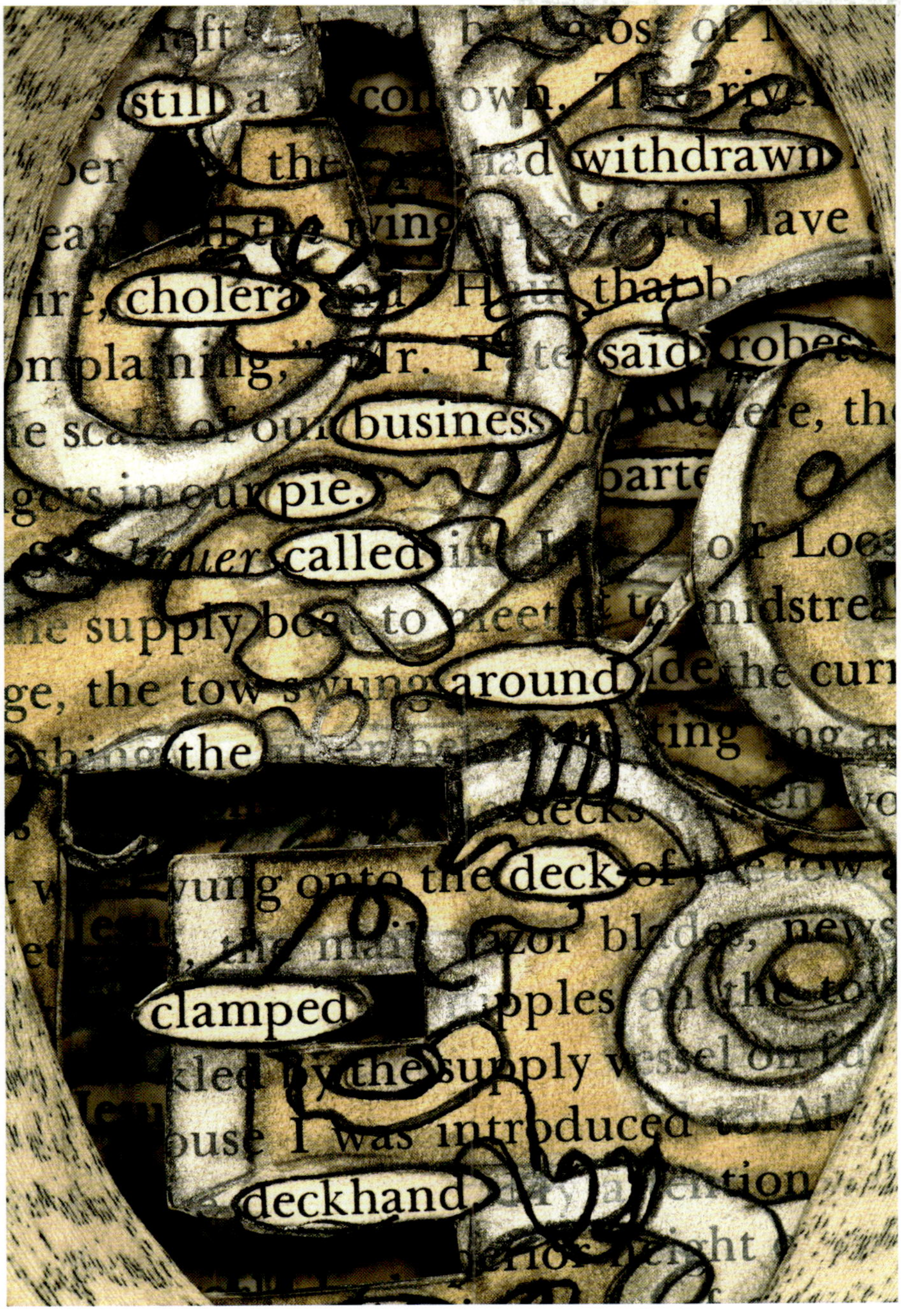

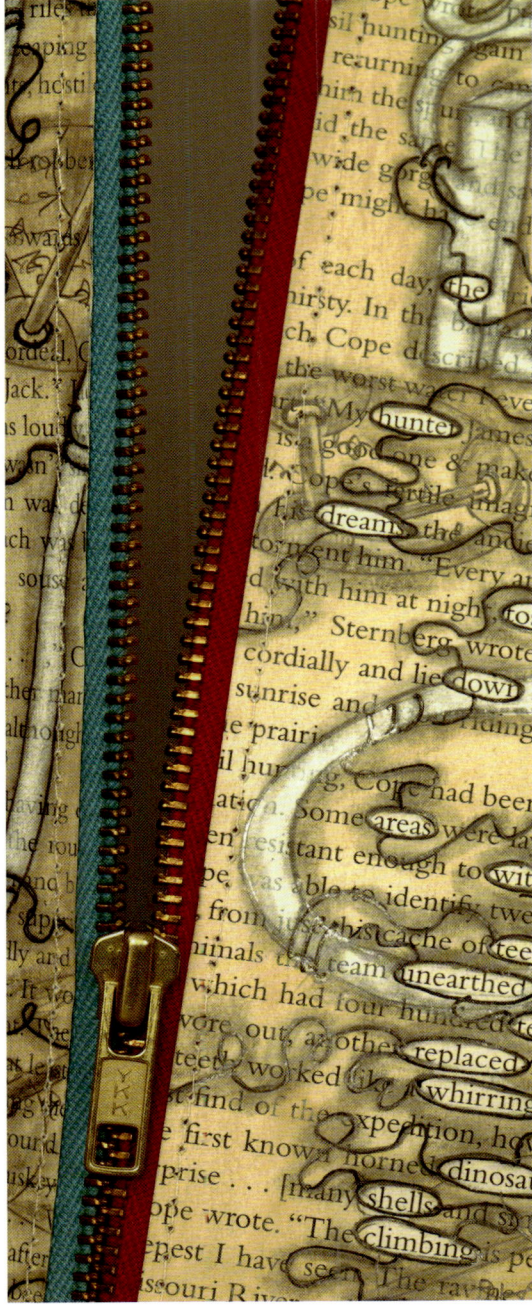

6. Disconnecting Old Glory

12 x 26 x 11 in.
Altered book, collage, gouache, ink, graphite, dyed zippers.

The piece itself incorporates my interests in mixed media, collage, sculpture, drawing, written text, and cut paper, all stitched together with colored zippers that lend the object its great flexibility. The book can be read as either a flat or three-dimensional piece of artwork. When all the pages are zipped the book can stand upright and be read from any direction. When turned on its side with all the pages zipped, a concertina or accordion configuration is apparent.

Artist: Doug Beube
Country: Canada

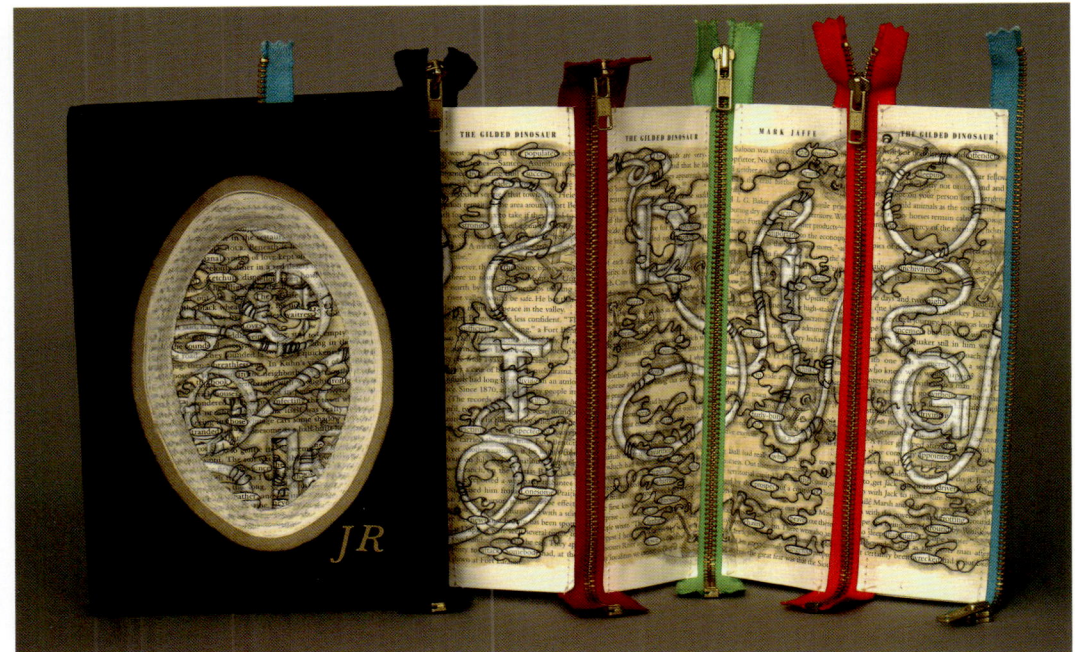

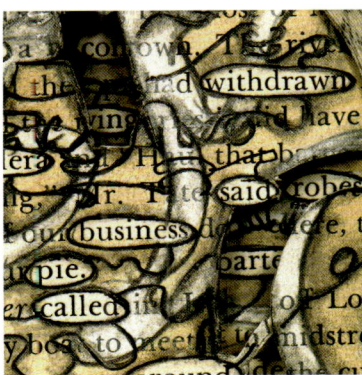

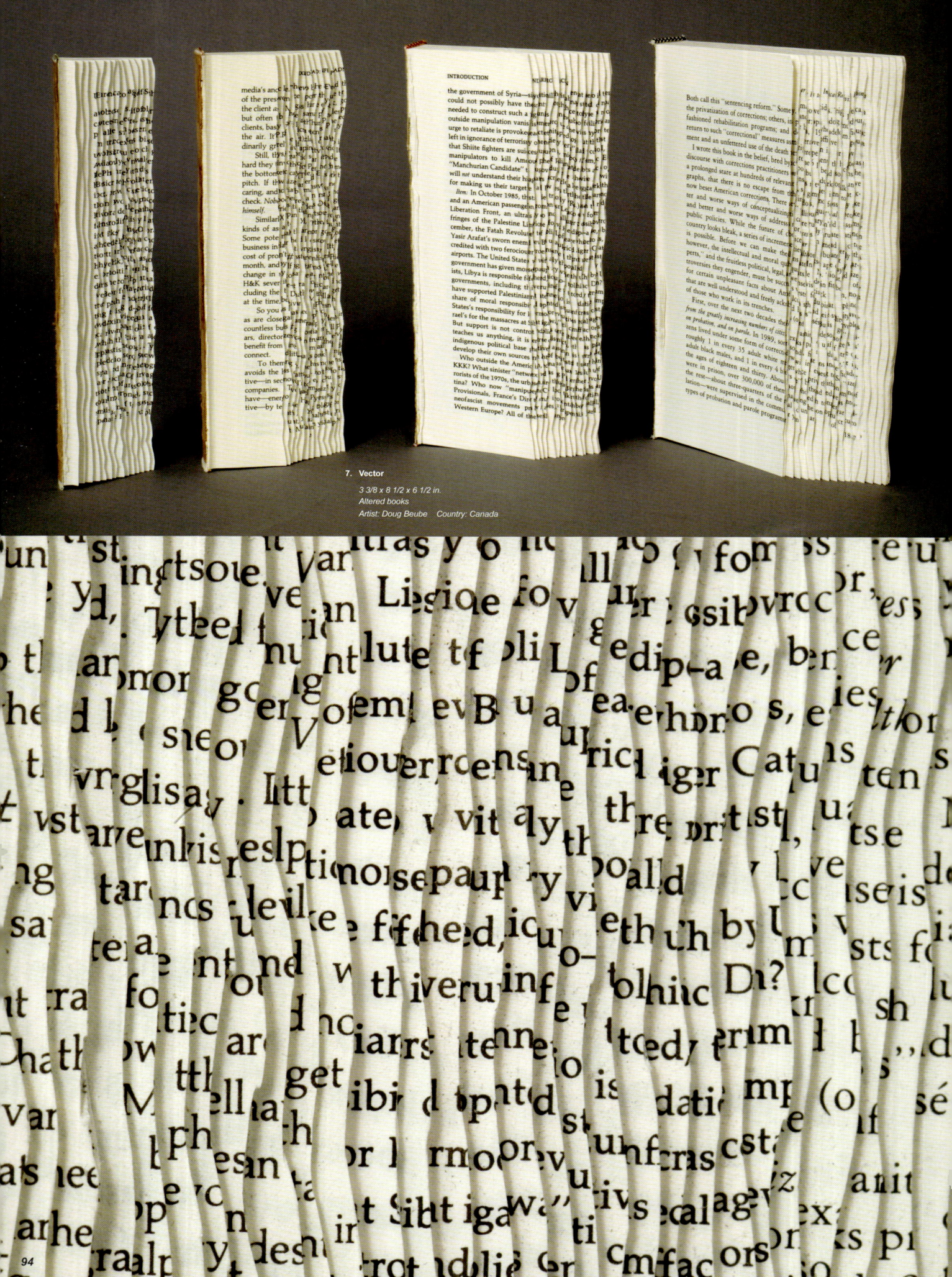

7. *Vector*
3 3/8 x 8 1/2 x 6 1/2 in.
Altered books
Artist: Doug Beube   Country: Canada

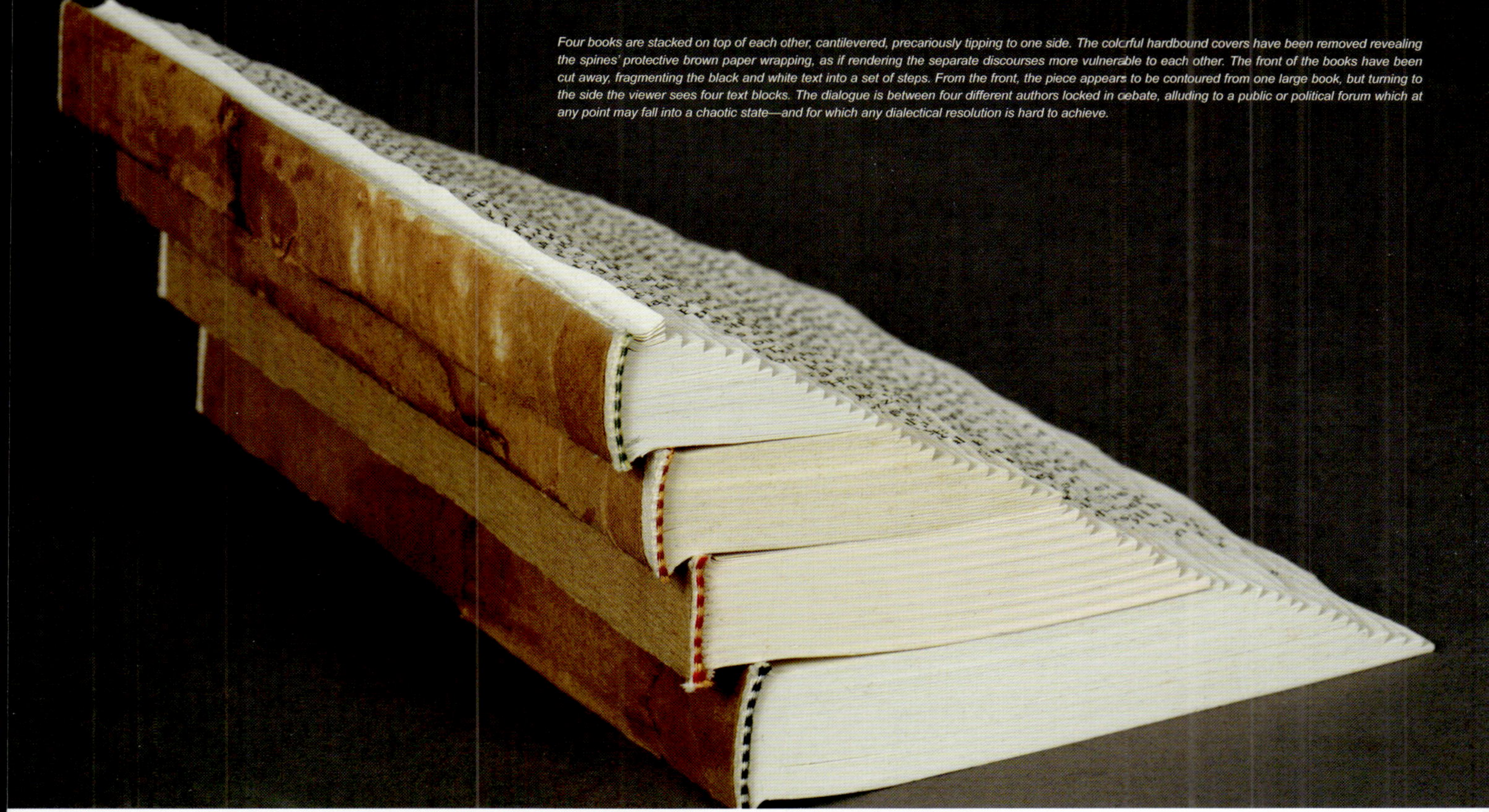

Four books are stacked on top of each other, cantilevered, precariously tipping to one side. The colorful hardbound covers have been removed revealing the spines' protective brown paper wrapping, as if rendering the separate discourses more vulnerable to each other. The front of the books have been cut away, fragmenting the black and white text into a set of steps. From the front, the piece appears to be contoured from one large book, but turning to the side the viewer sees four text blocks. The dialogue is between four different authors locked in debate, alluding to a public or political forum which at any point may fall into a chaotic state—and for which any dialectical resolution is hard to achieve.

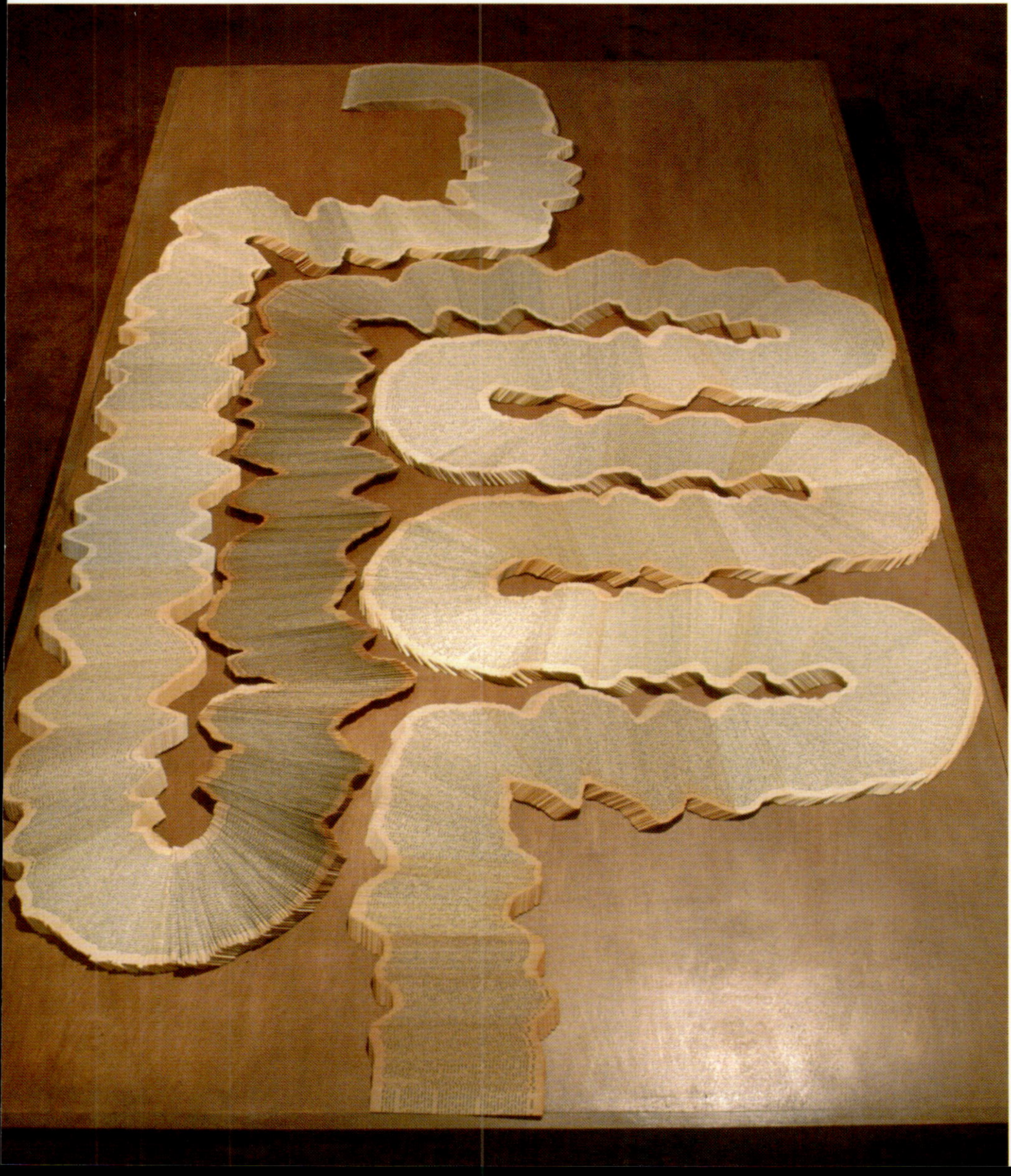

8. **Tract: Ryder Univ.**

   $4 \times 8 \times 1/2$ ft.
   Fifty romance and mystery novels.

   Tract uses approximately fifty soft cover books sliced into one inch strips. The installation cascades across the floor like an organic river or EEG wave, and is comprised of acid brown romance novels and pulp fiction paperbacks. Gravity holds the pages together in their fragile formation.

   Artist: Doug Beube   Country: Canada

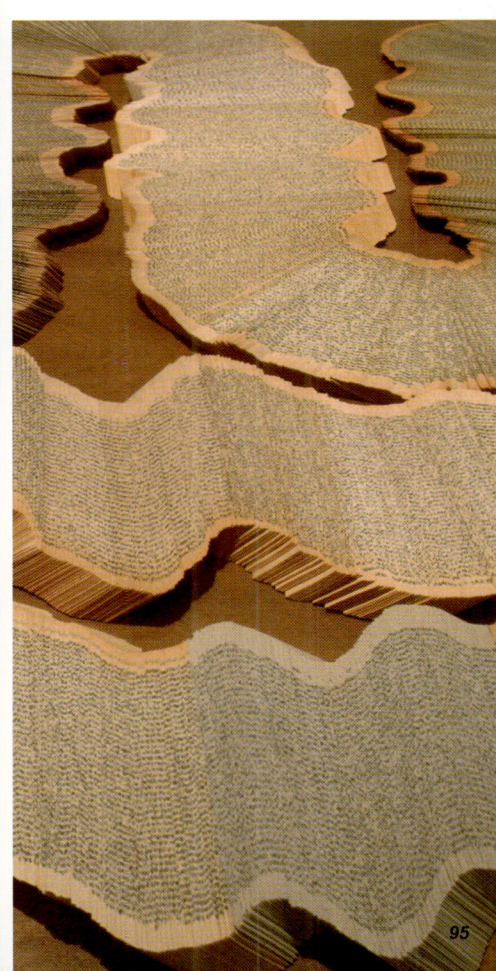

1. **Brown's Bible**
Carved Bible, ribbon, lamp. 10,5 x 3,5 x 12,5 inches.
Artist: Guy Laramée   Country: Canada

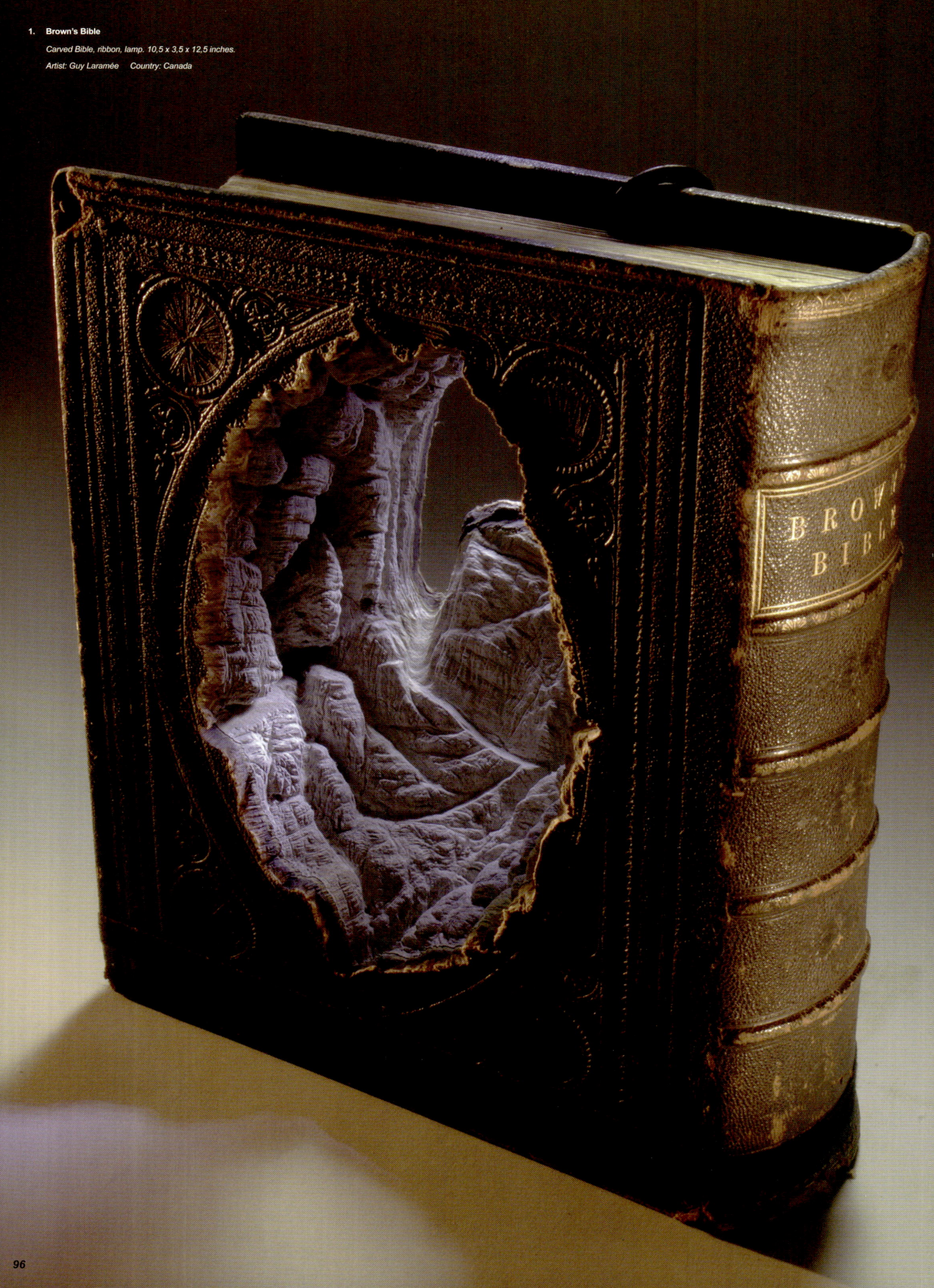

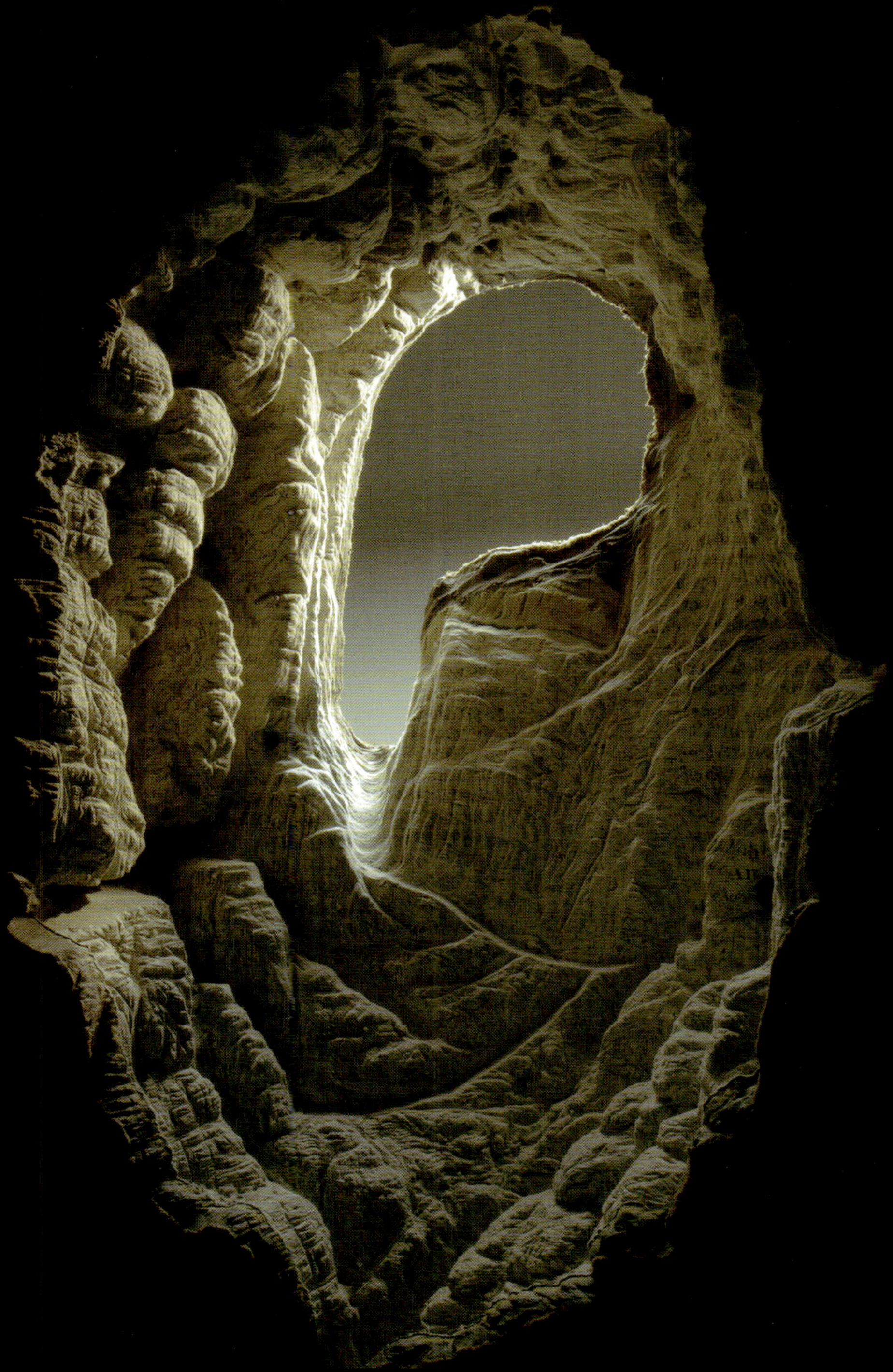

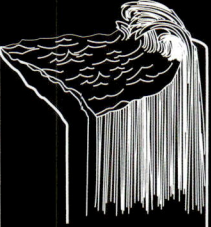

1. Brown's Bible
2. El Mor Por Las Montaña Nos Cura
3. Grand Larousse
4. Chinese Dictionary
5. Mountains
6. Larousse Methodical
7. In Advance of a Broken Land
8. Great Wave
9. The Web

—Guy Laramée

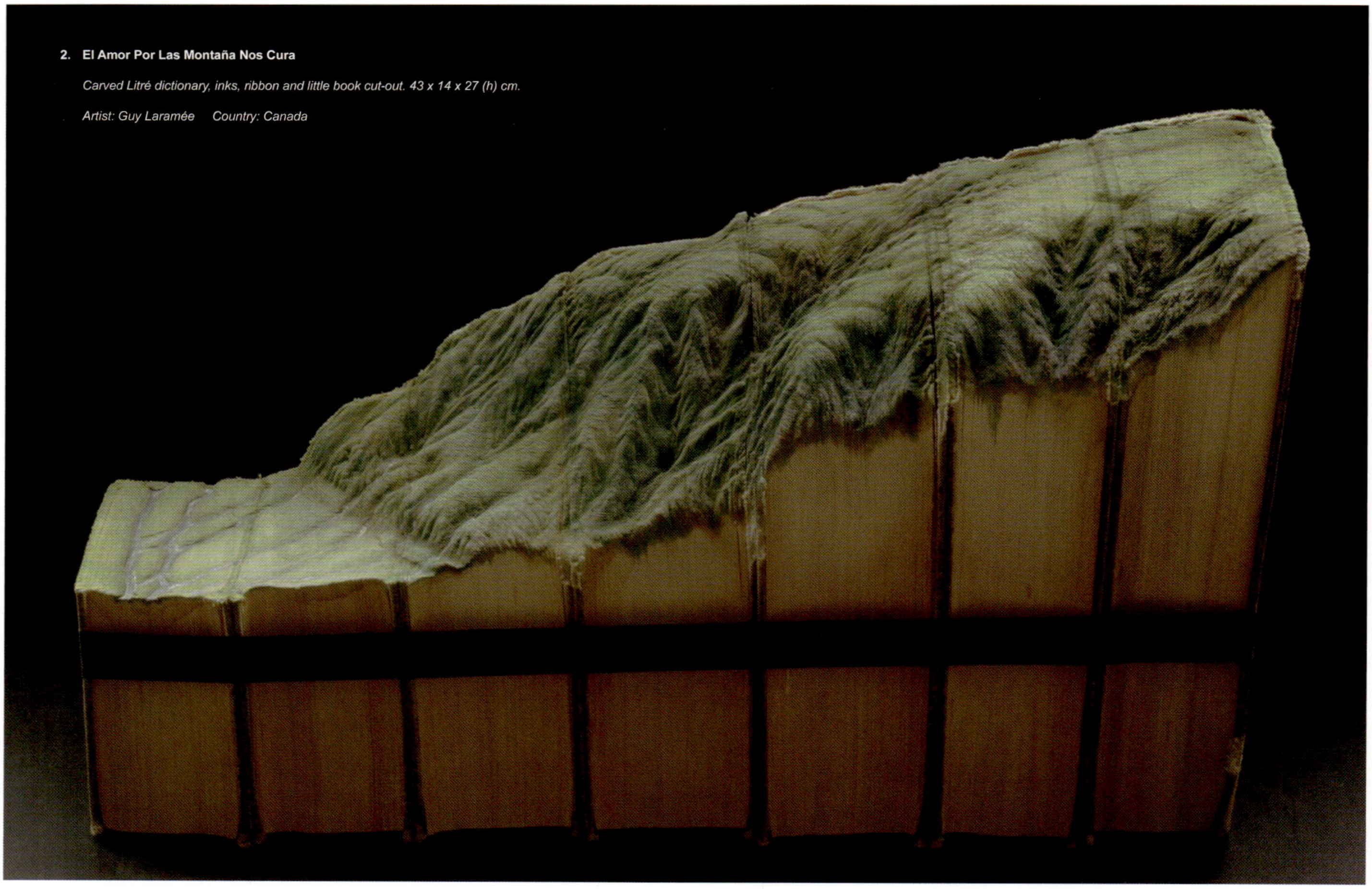

2. **El Amor Por Las Montaña Nos Cura**

Carved Litré dictionary, inks, ribbon and little book cut-out. 43 x 14 x 27 (h) cm.

Artist: Guy Laramée   Country: Canada

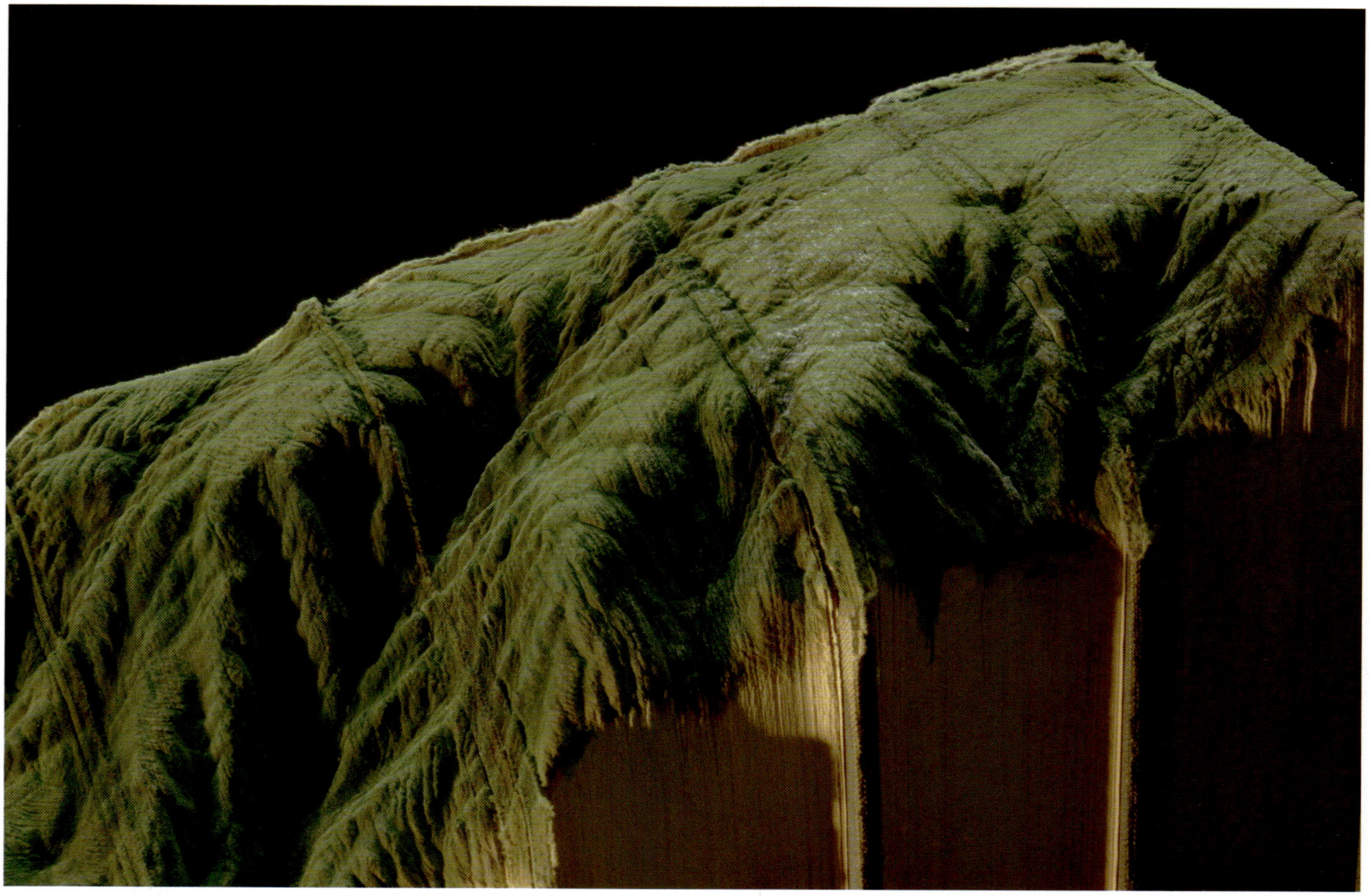

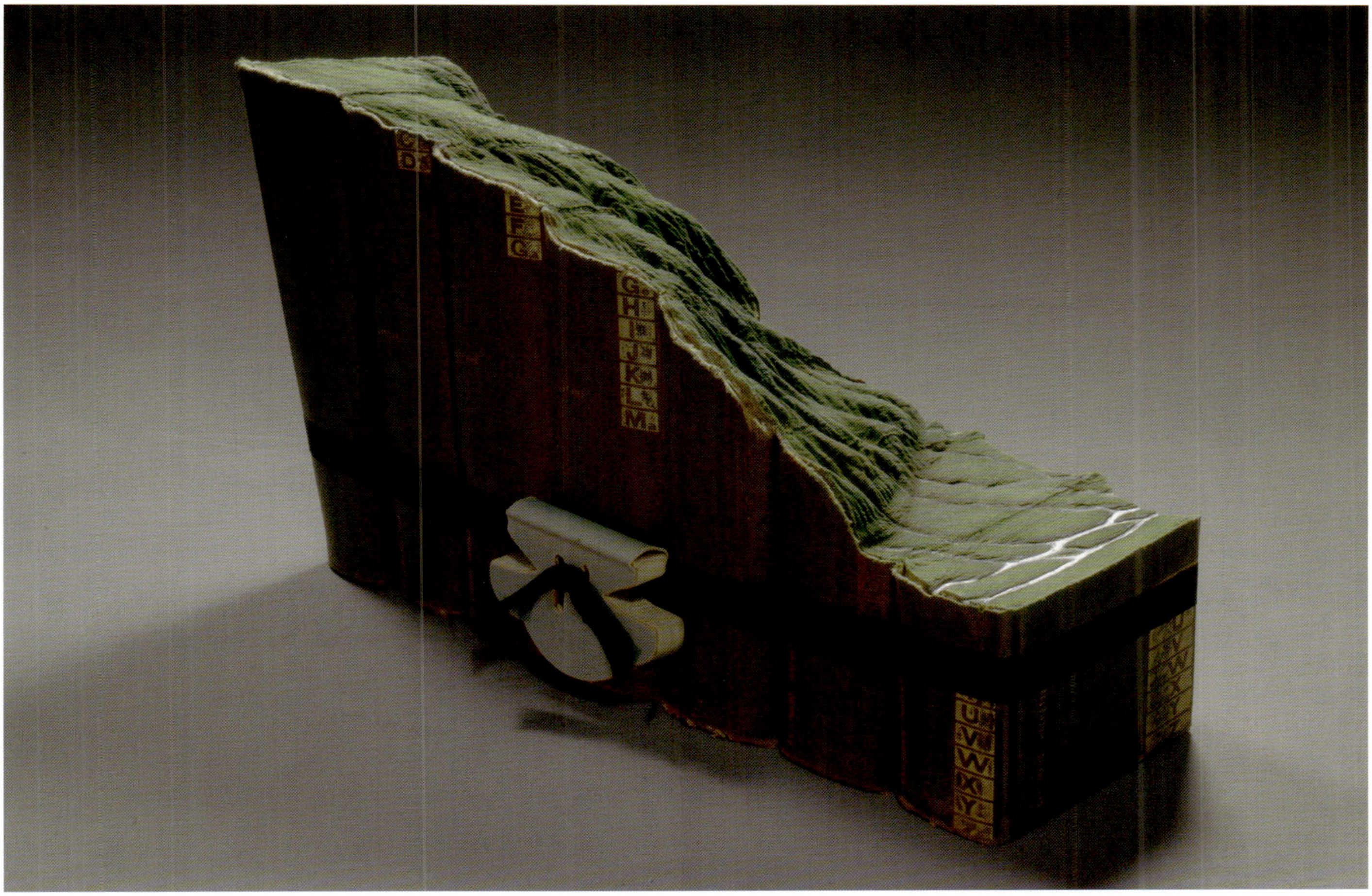

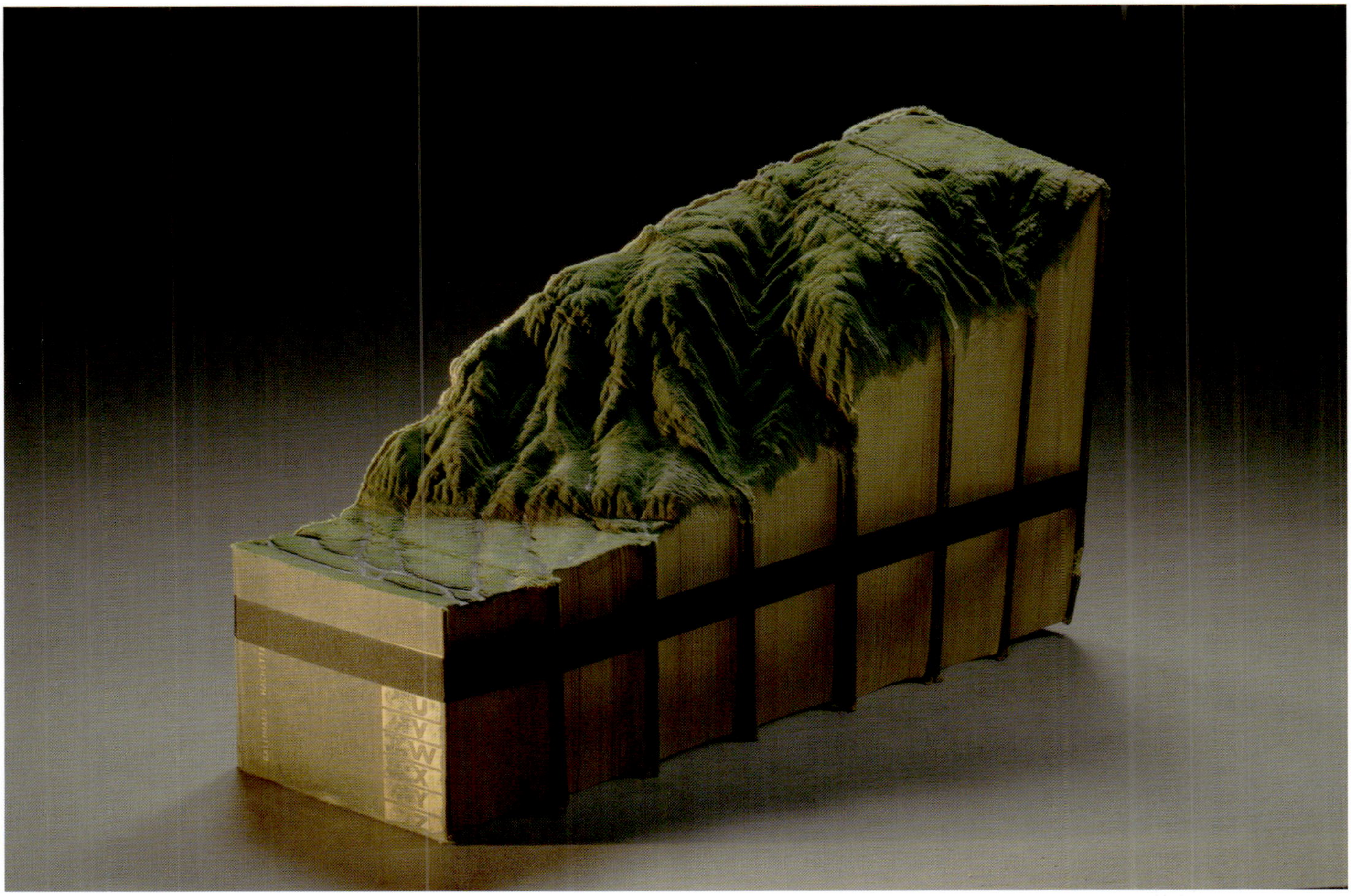

99

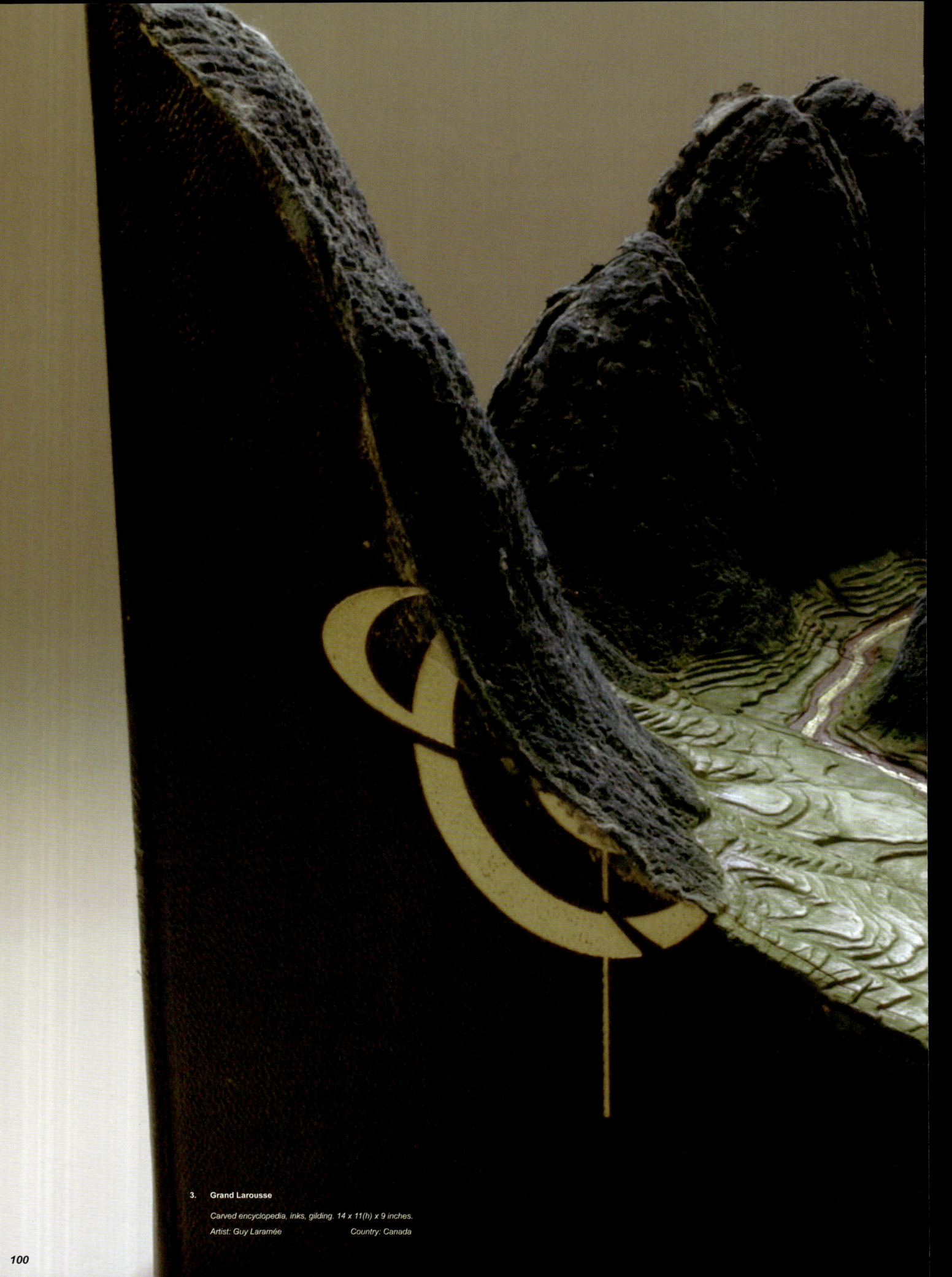

3. **Grand Larousse**
Carved encyclopedia, inks, gilding. 14 x 11(h) x 9 inches.
Artist: Guy Laramée Country: Canada

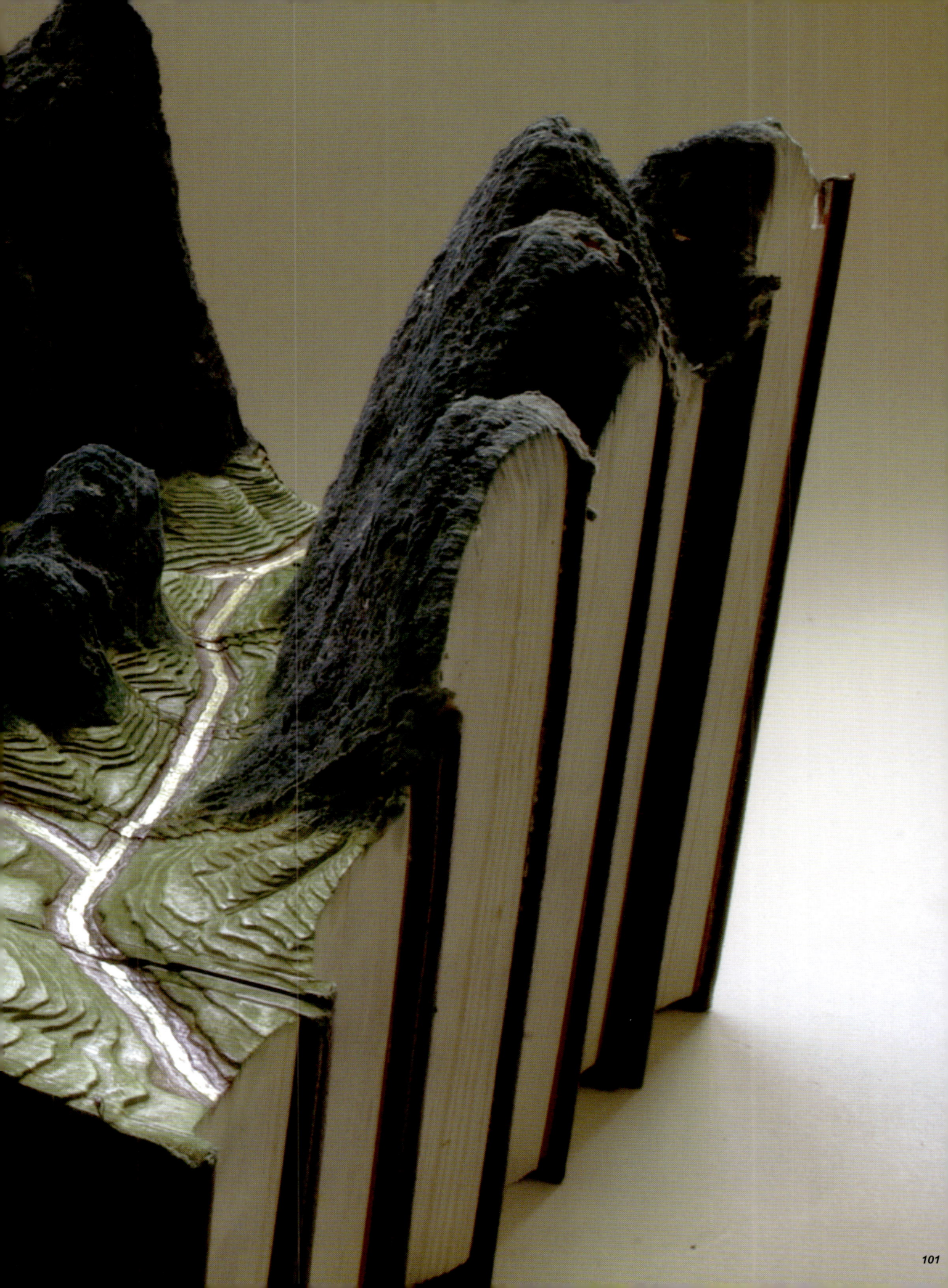

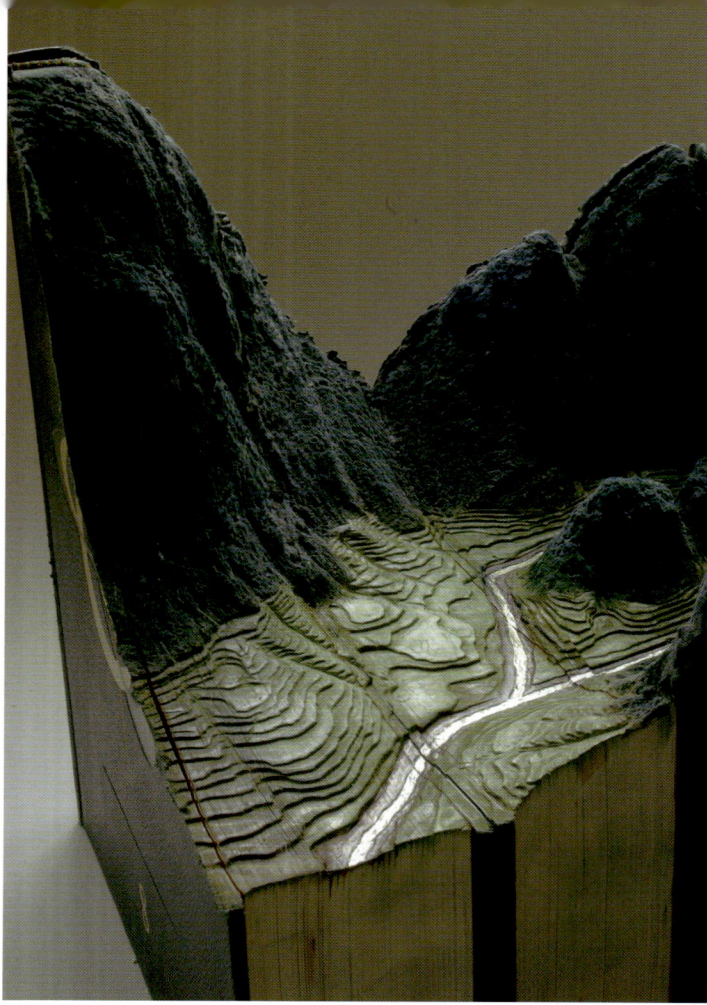

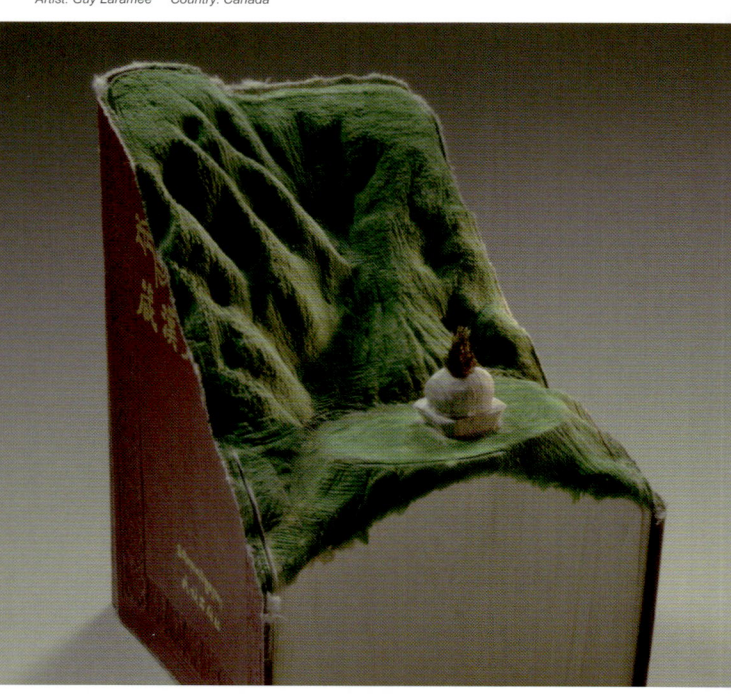

4. Chinese Dictionary - Tibetan
Carved book, 9.75 x 6.75 x 3 inches.
Artist: Guy Laramée   Country: Canada

4. Chinese Dictionary

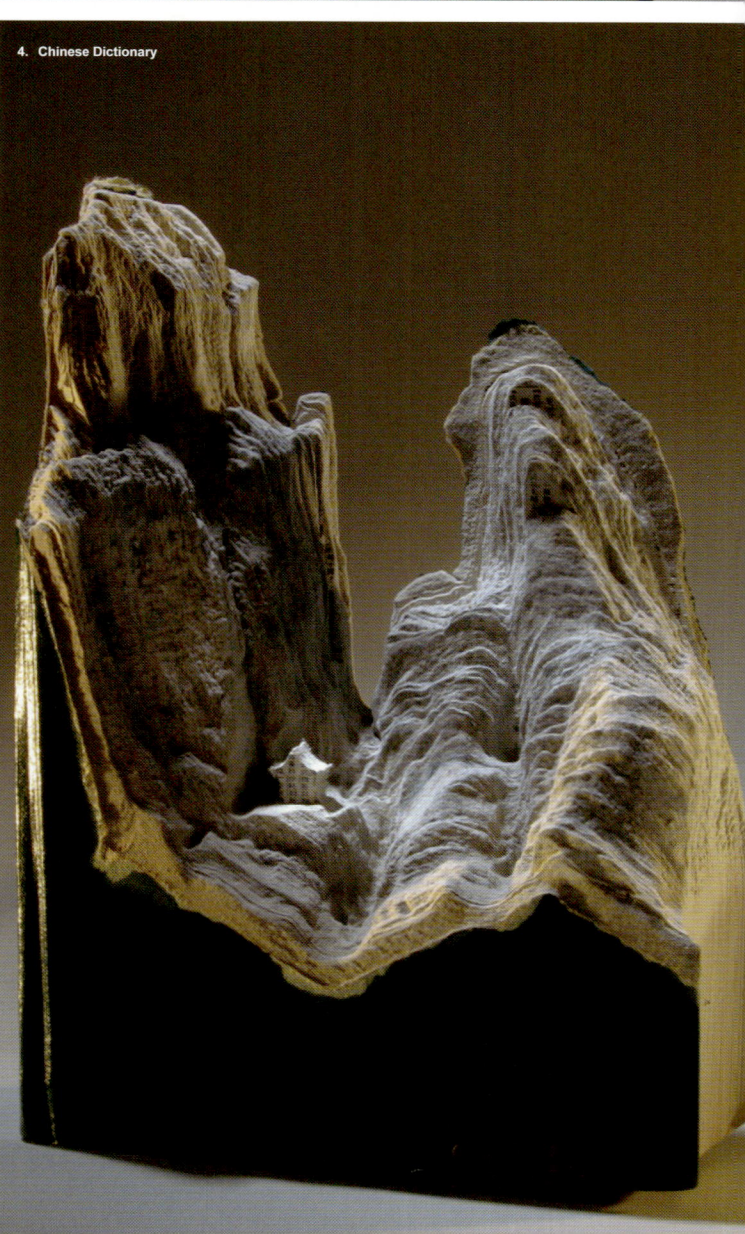

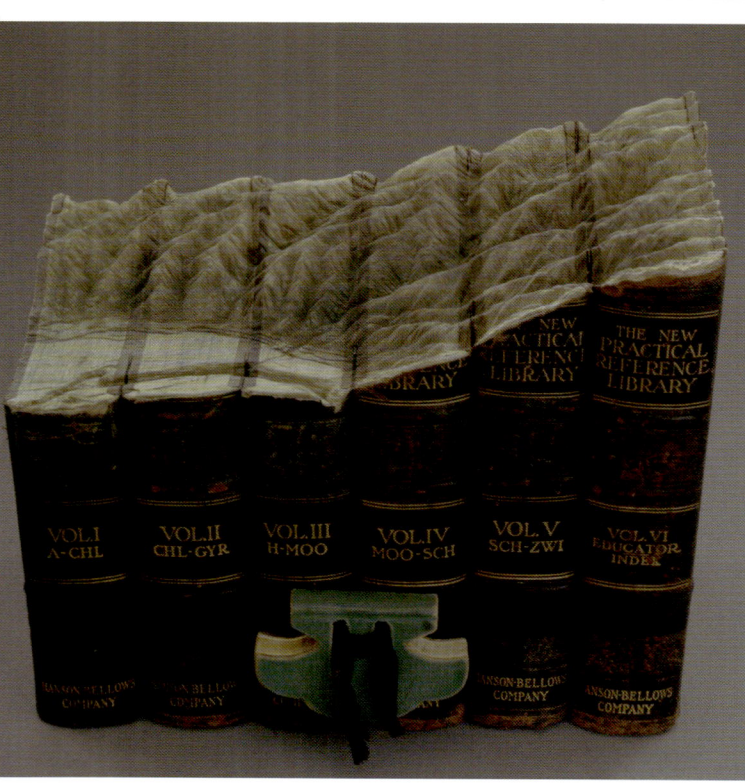

5. Mountains
Carved books (The New Practical Reference Library), inks, ribbon and cutout book. 11 x 6,5 x 10 inches.
Artist: Guy Laramée   Country: Canada

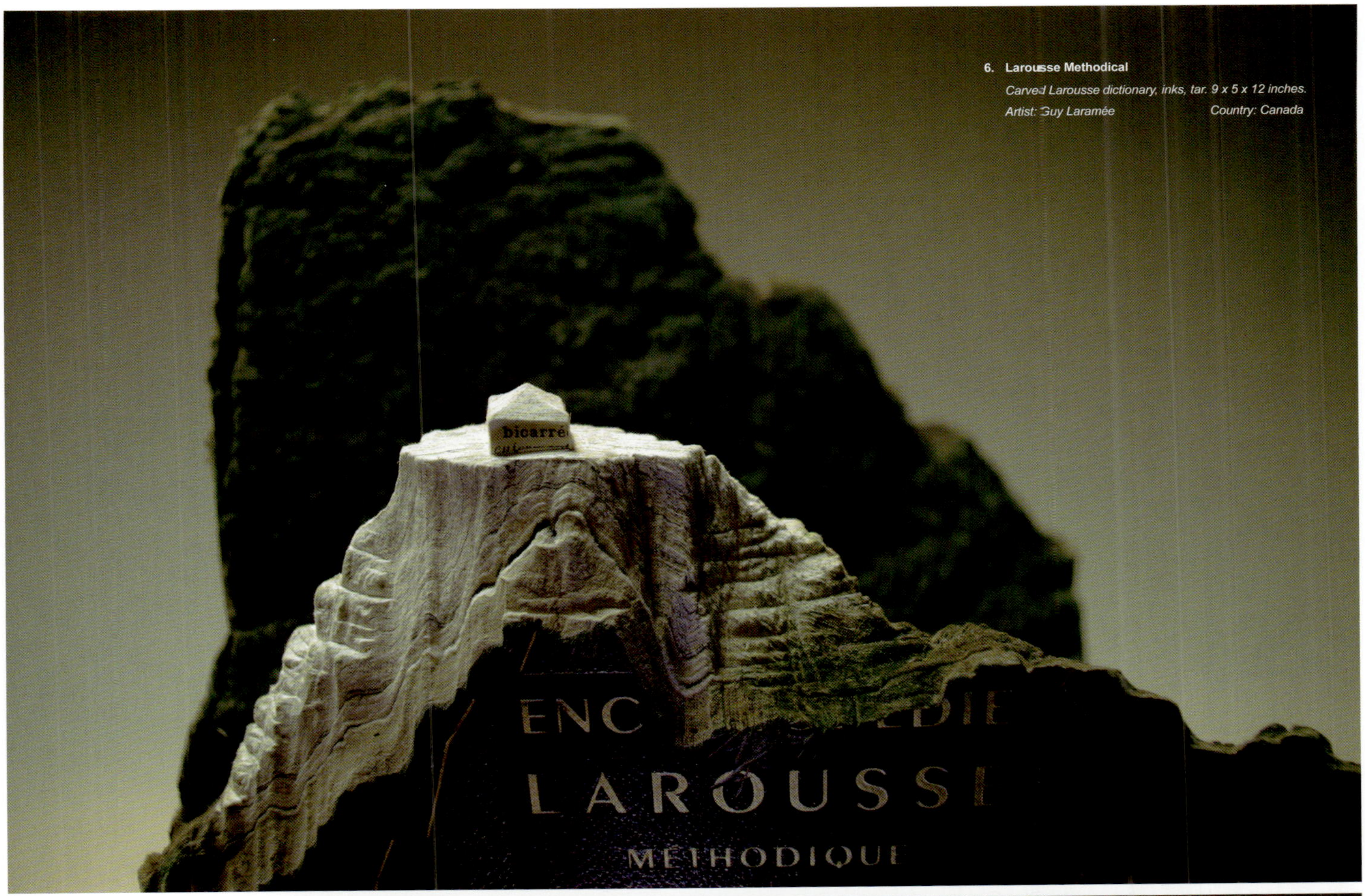

6. **Larousse Methodical**
Carved Larousse dictionary, inks, tar. 9 x 5 x 12 inches.
Artist: Guy Laramée   Country: Canada

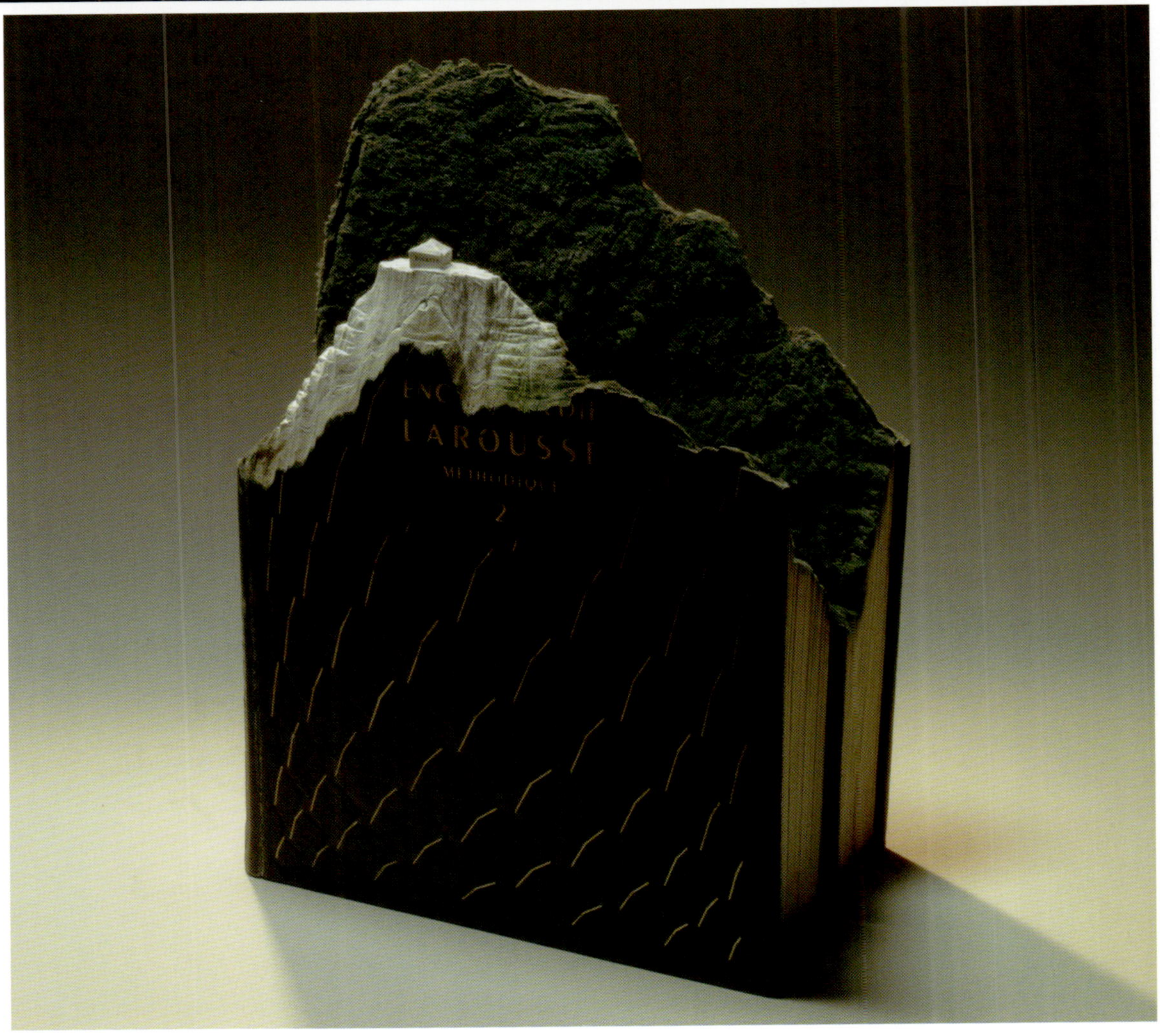

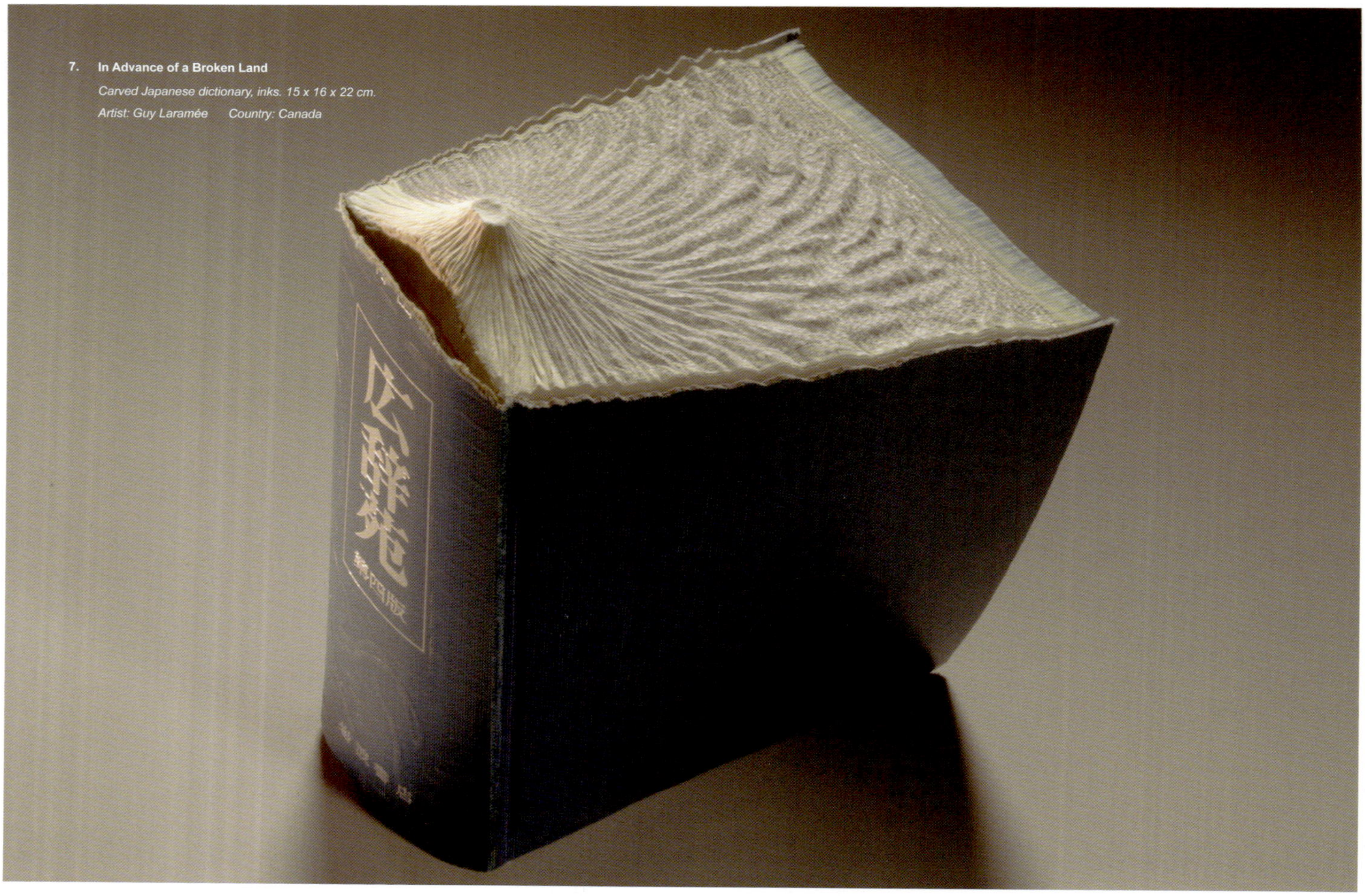

7. **In Advance of a Broken Land**
Carved Japanese dictionary, inks. 15 x 16 x 22 cm.
Artist: Guy Laramée   Country: Canada

8. **Great Wave**
Carved book (Biblical references), inks. 19 x 15 x 23 cm.
Artist: Guy Laramée   Country: Canada

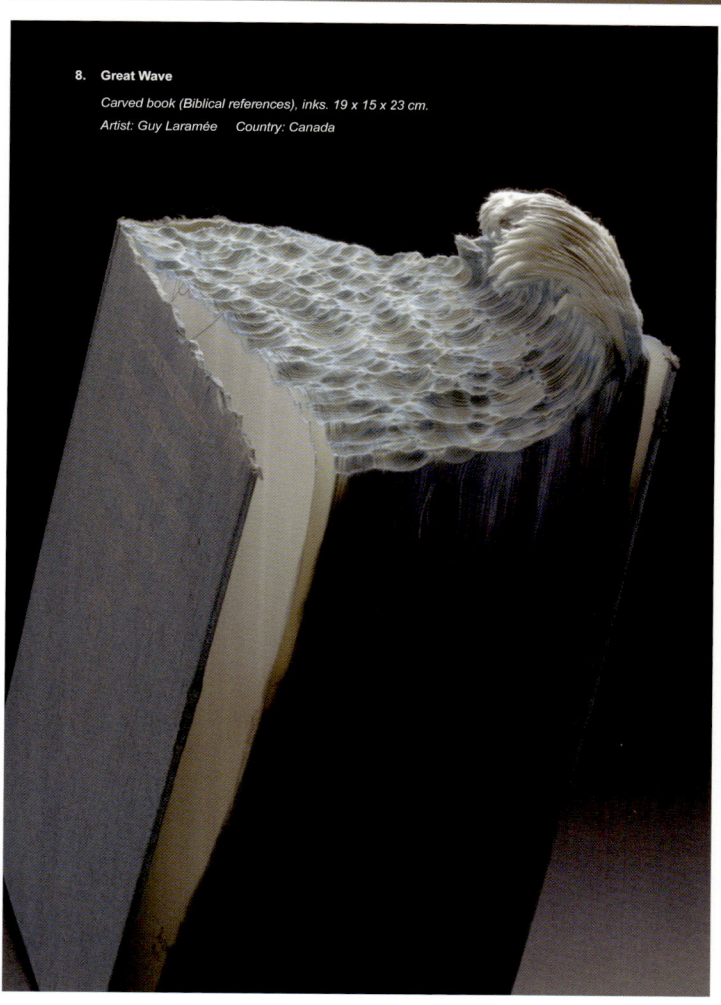

7. **In Advance of a Broken Land**

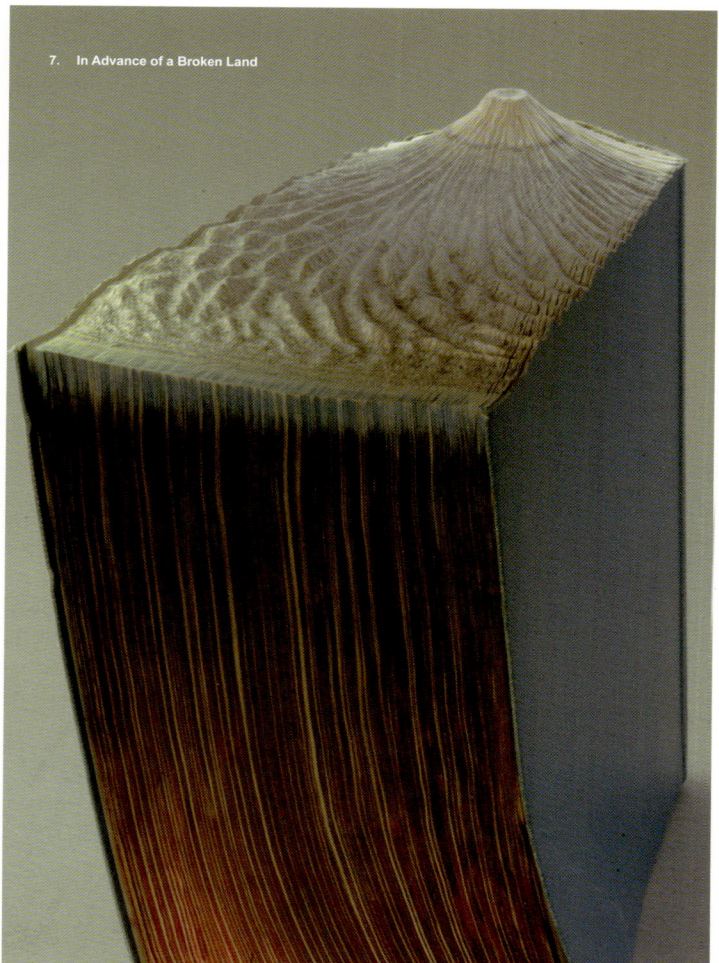

5. MOUNTAINS

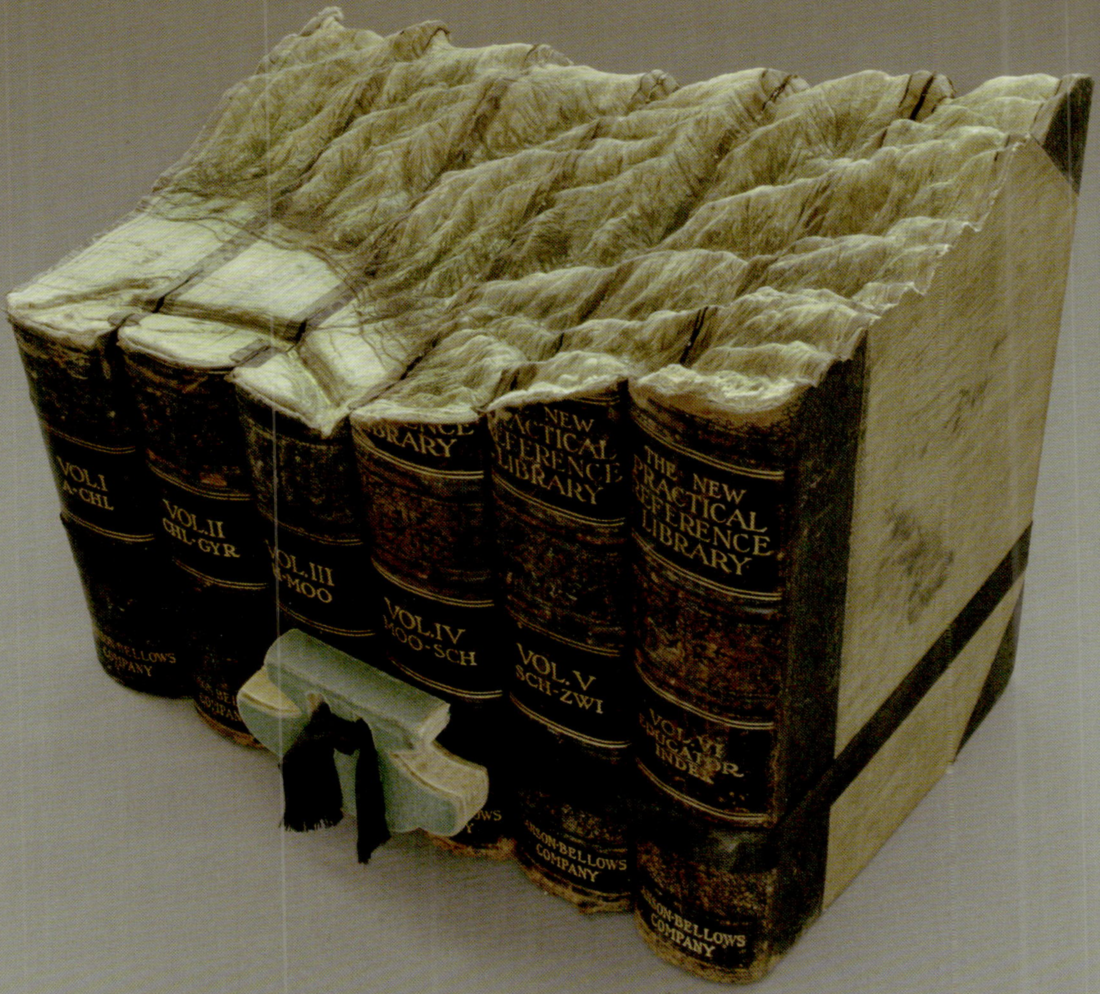

9. **The Web**
Carved dictionary (The Webster Encyclopedic Dictionary of English Language), tints, paint (covers), copper holder. 11,5 x 9 x 23 inches.
Artist: Guy Laramée   Country: Canada

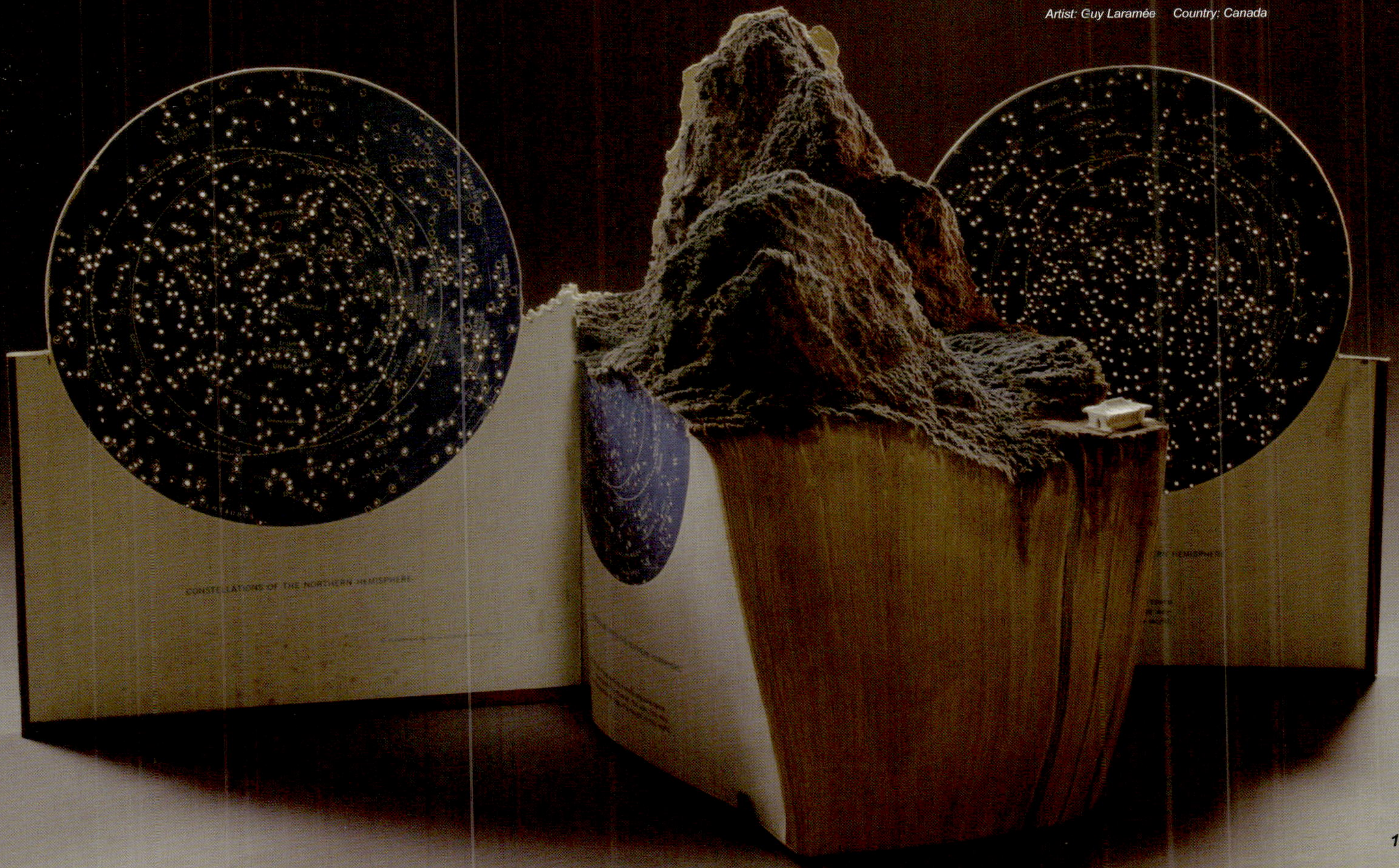

105

1. **Eternal Lotus - Musical Score**

I've created this piece based on the musical scores of the song which was specially made by my friend for my artworks.

Artist: Hina Aoyama
Country: Japan
Photographer: Christophe Jacquemet

2. **Sakura Chandelier**

I spent five hours a day and it took two months to complete this piece.

Artist: Hina Aoyama
Country: Japan
Photographer: Christophe Jacquemet

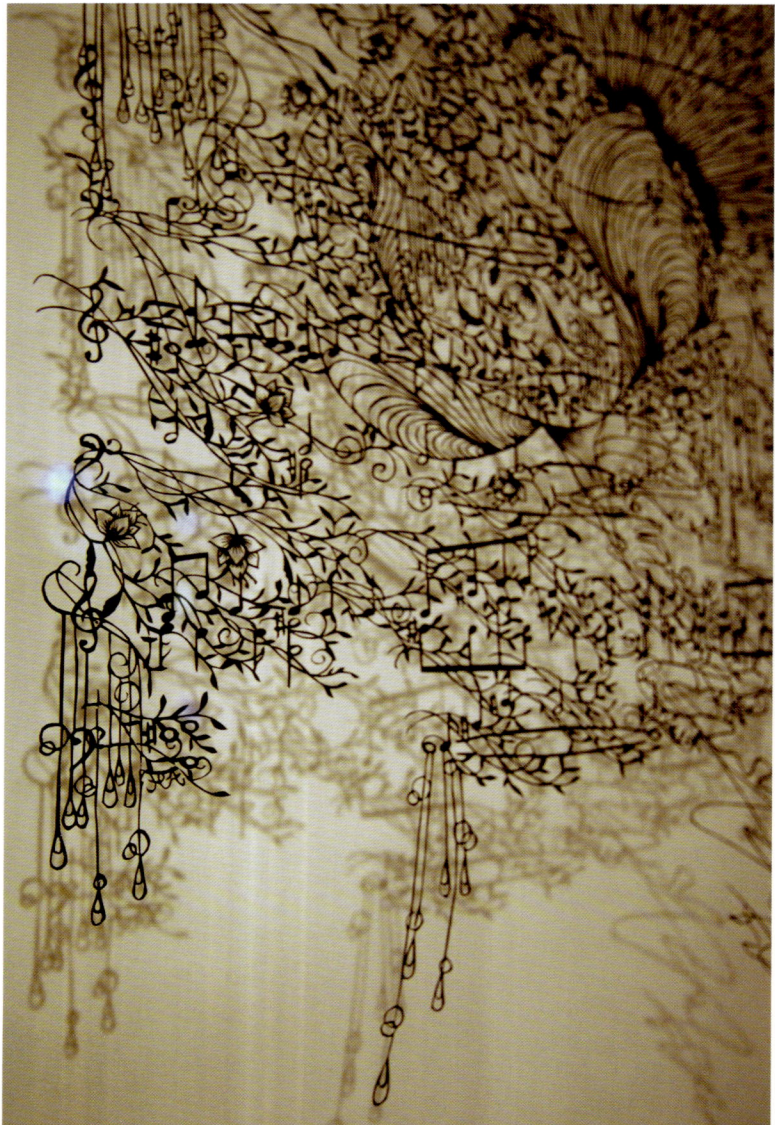
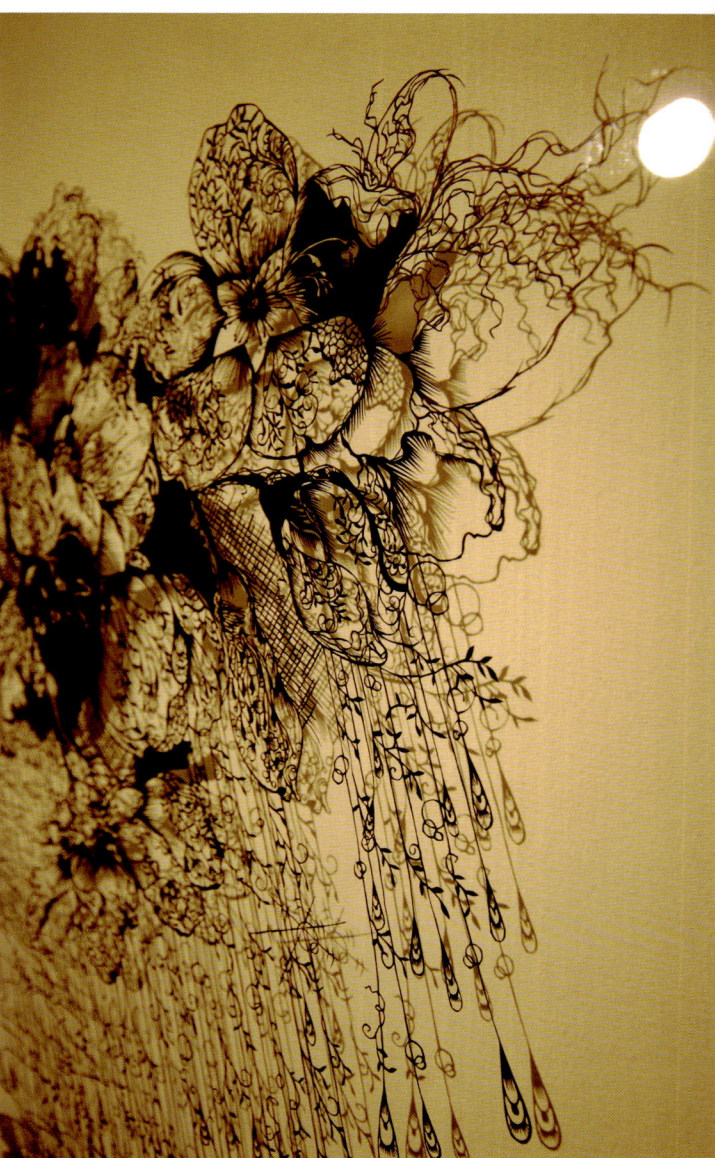
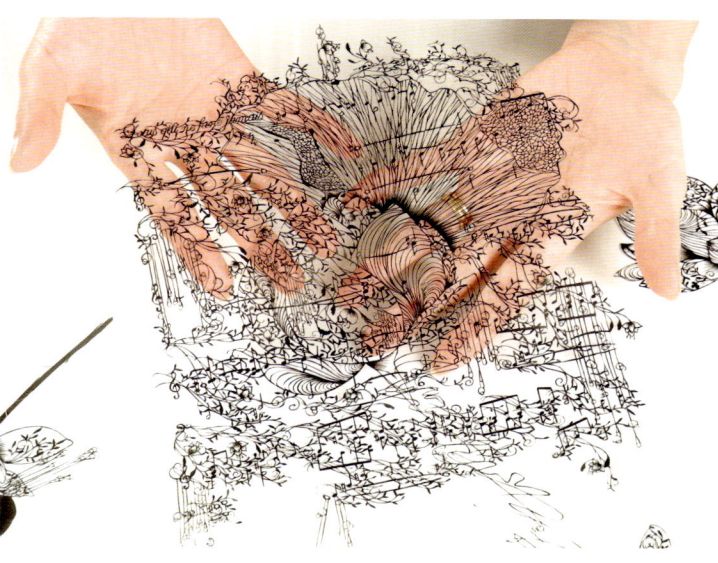
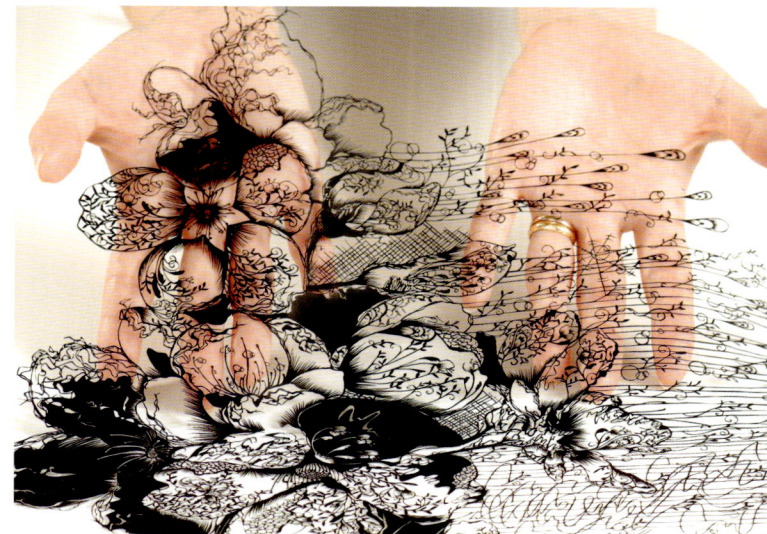

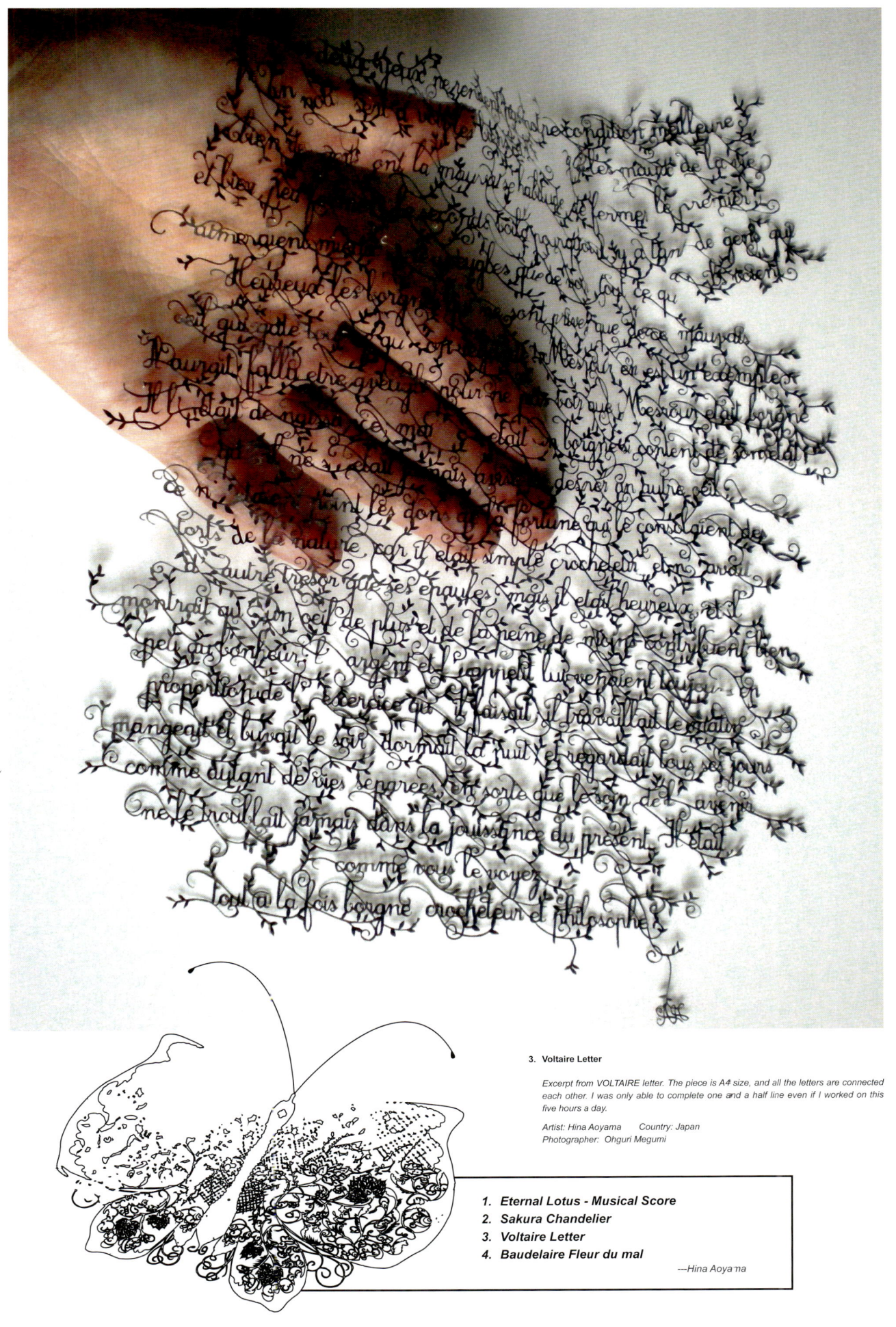

3. Voltaire Letter

Excerpt from VOLTAIRE letter. The piece is A4 size, and all the letters are connected each other. I was only able to complete one and a half line even if I worked on this five hours a day.

Artist: Hina Aoyama   Country: Japan
Photographer: Ohguri Megumi

1. **Eternal Lotus - Musical Score**
2. **Sakura Chandelier**
3. **Voltaire Letter**
4. **Baudelaire Fleur du mal**

---Hina Aoyama

4. Baudelaire Fleur du mal

Excerpt from the poem of Baudelaire [Fleur du mal]

Artist: Hina Aoyama
Photographer: Hiramatsu Ikuo

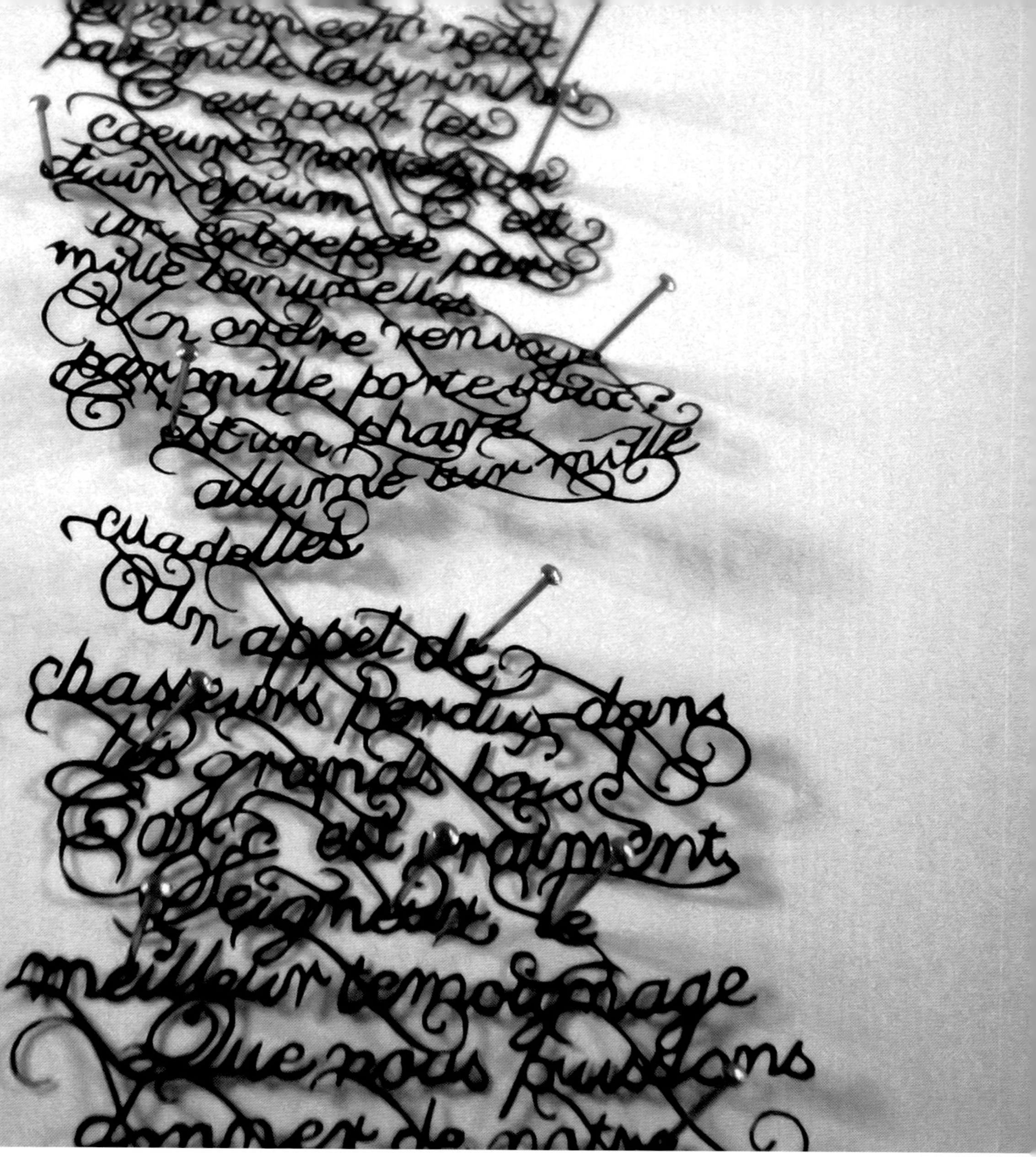

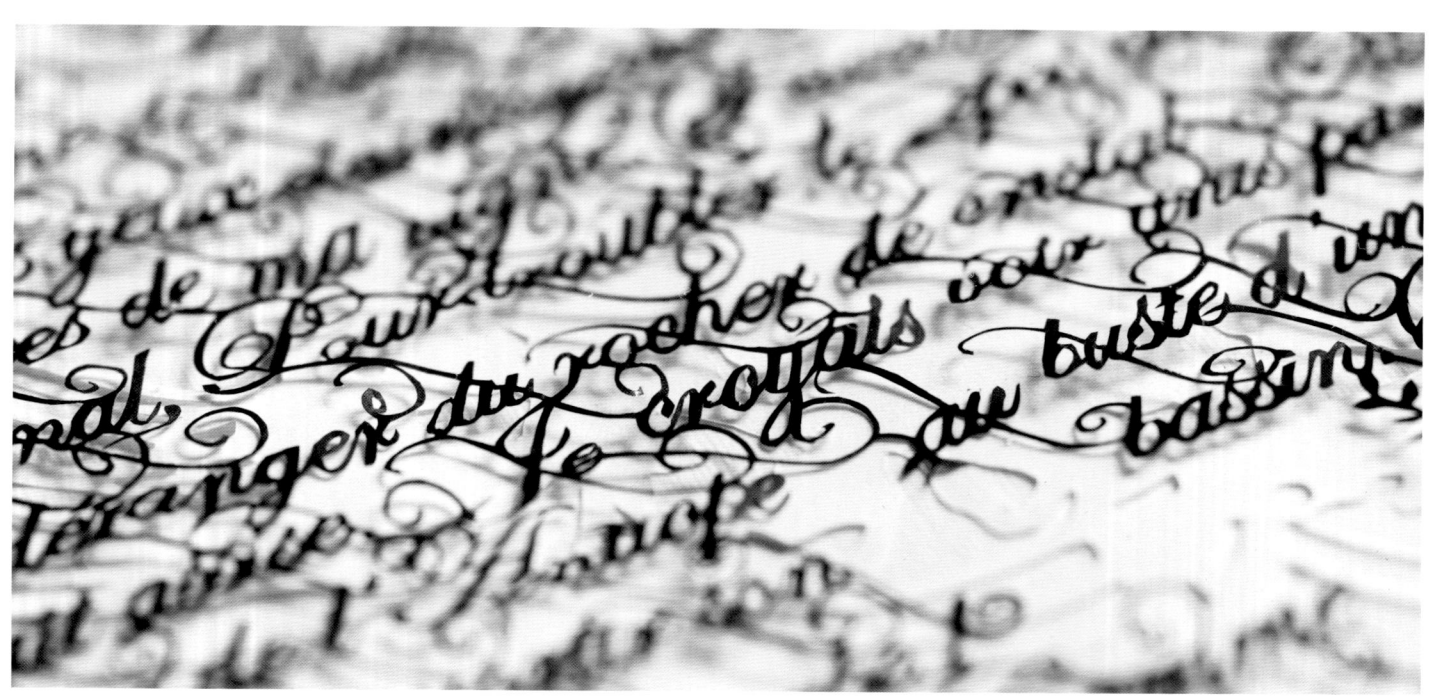

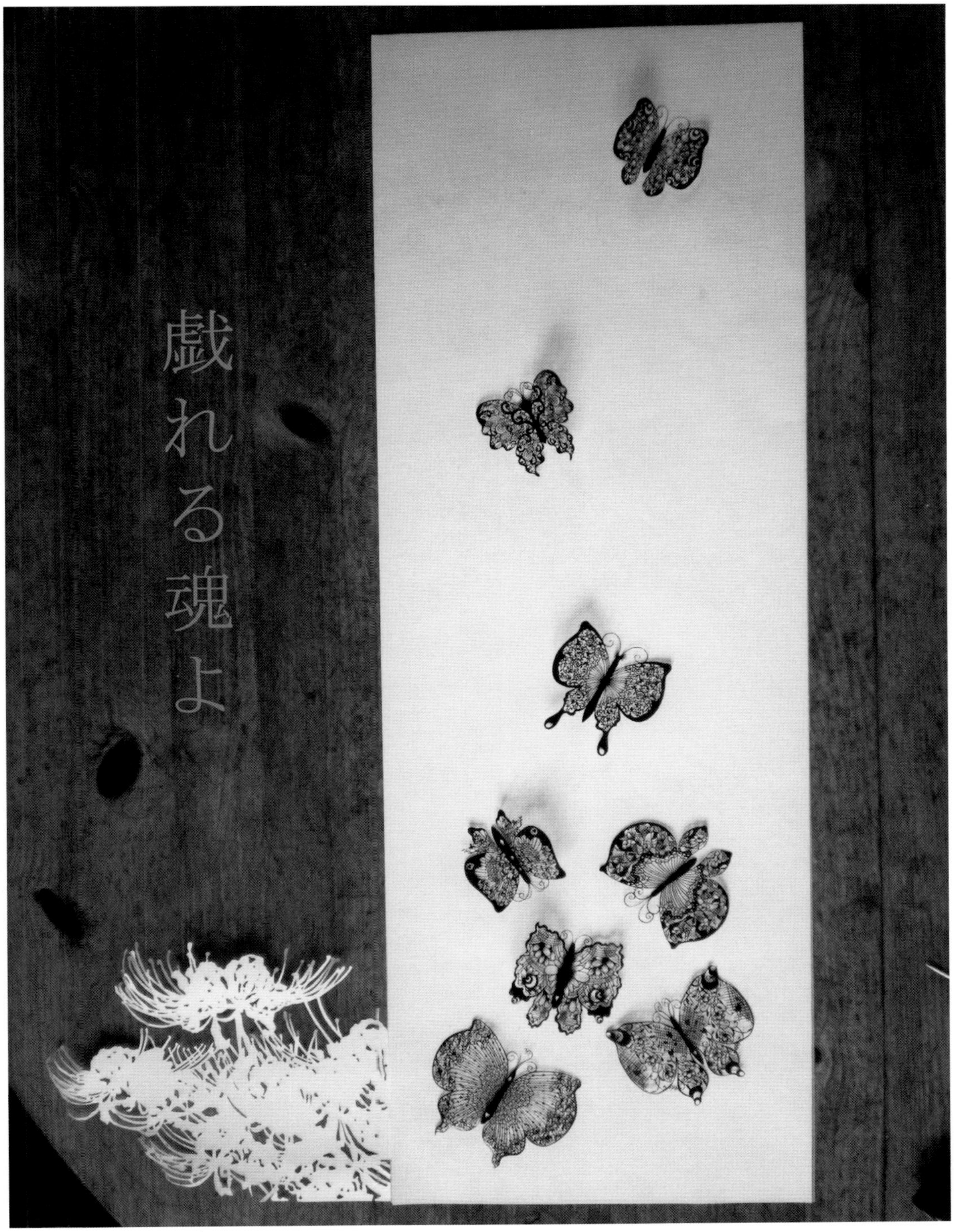

戯れる魂よ

4. Baudelaire Fleur du mal

Butterflies inspired by the poem of Baudelaire [Fleur du mal]

Artist: Hina Aoyama
Photographer: Hiramatsu Ikuo

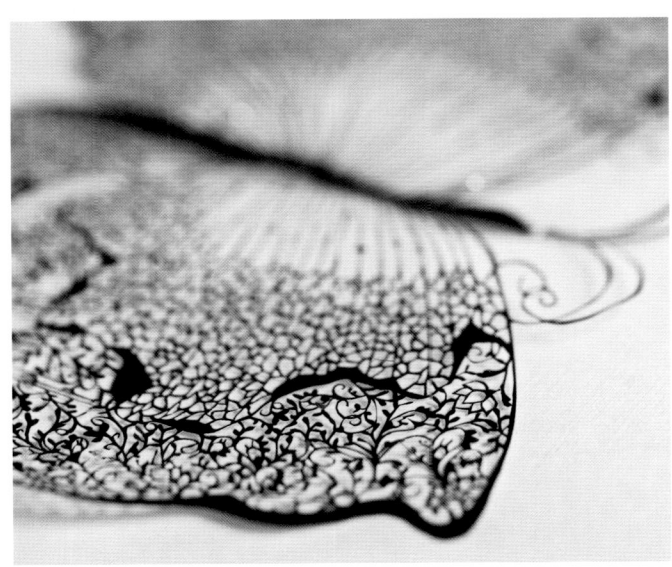
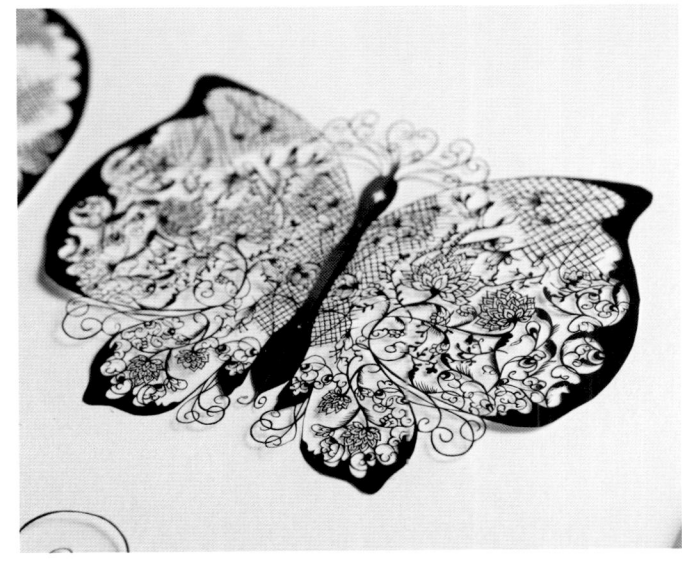

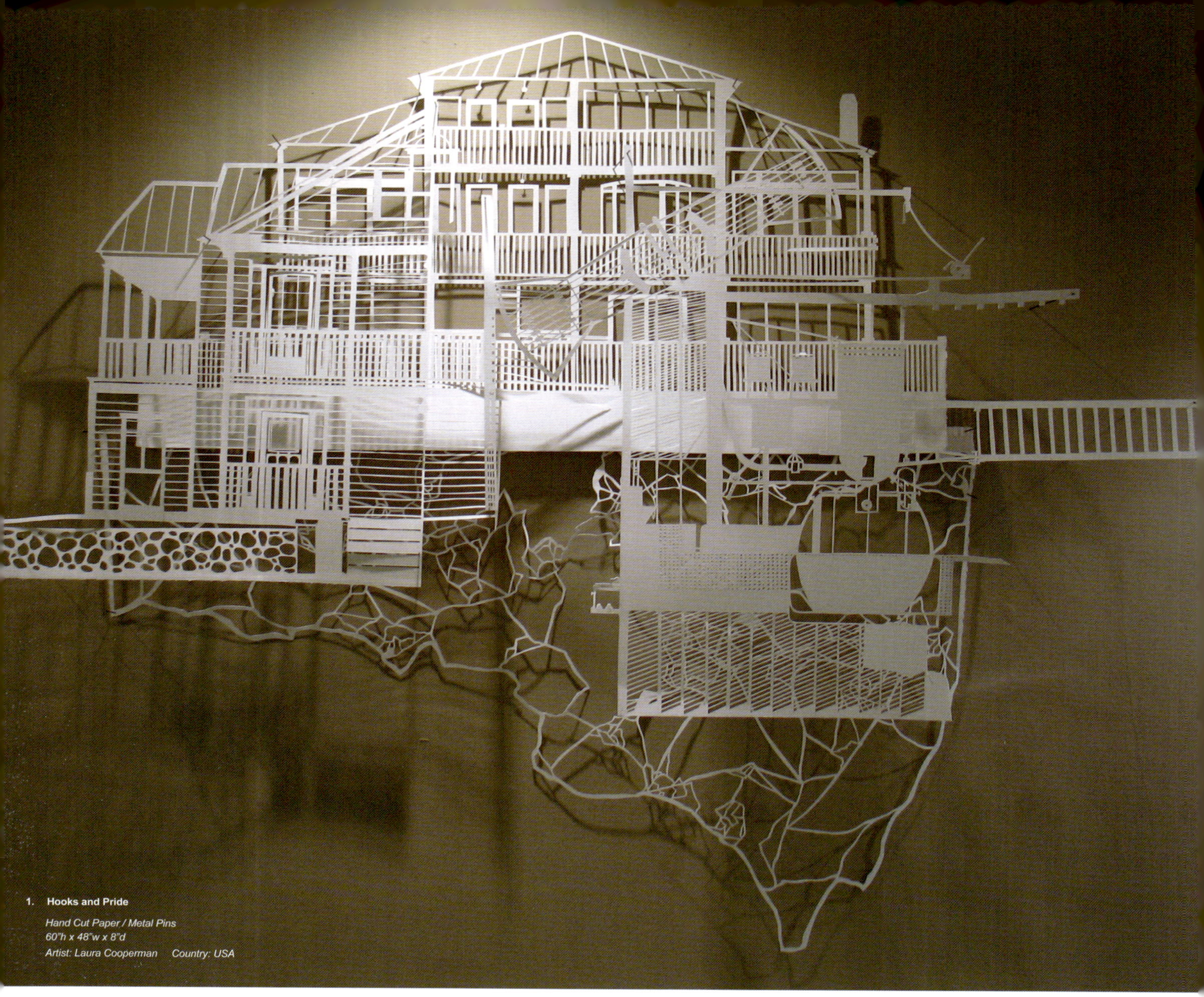

1. **Hooks and Pride**
Hand Cut Paper / Metal Pins
60"h x 48"w x 8"d
Artist: Laura Cooperman   Country: USA

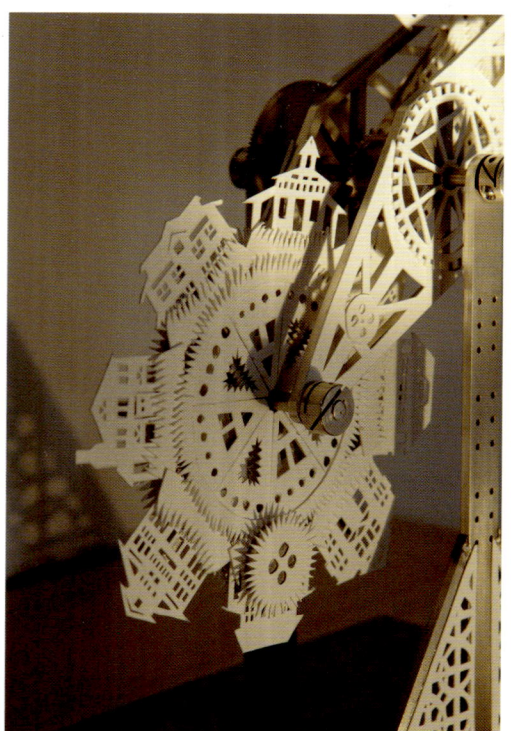

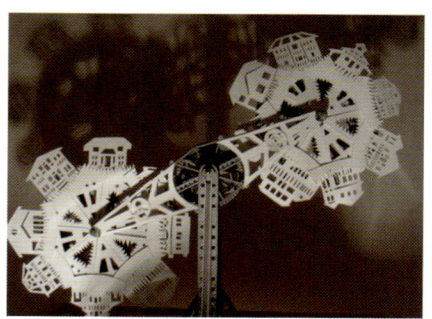

2. **Drill**
Hand Cut Paper / Metal / Wood
22"h x 15"w x 14"d
Artist: Laura Cooperman   Country: USA

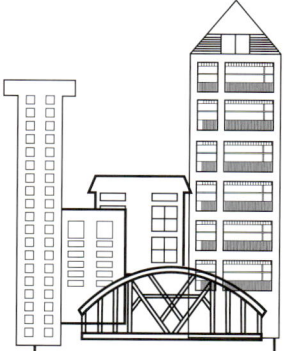

1. Hooks and Pride
2. Drill
3. SUPERvision I
4. SUPERvision II
5. Installation No Where But Up
6. Detail Pole to Pole
7. Detail Calm Corridors
8. Two for One
9. Detail Shifting Planes

---Laura Cooperman

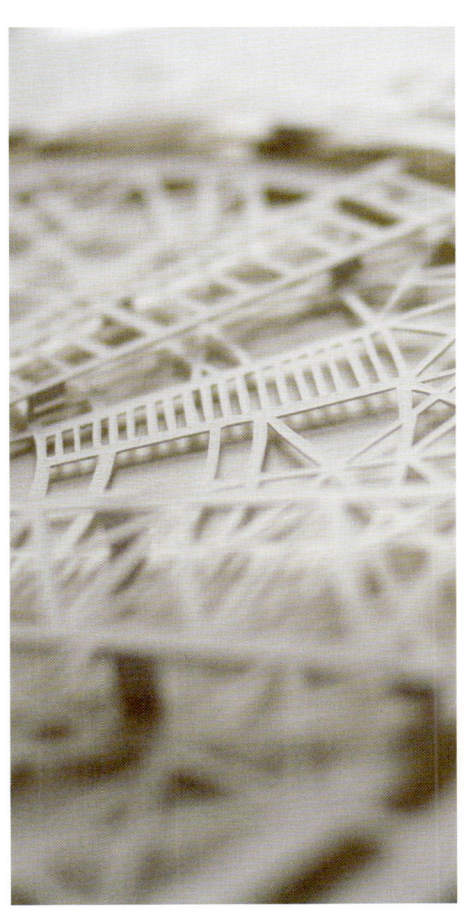
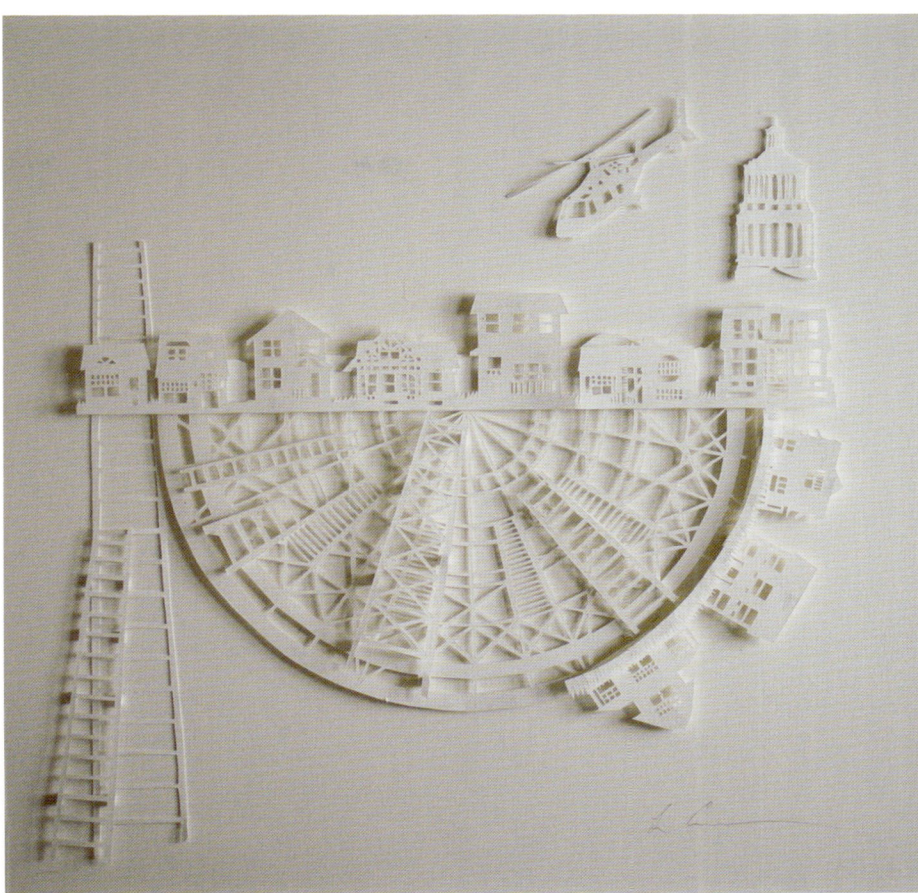

3. **SUPERvision I**
   Hand Cut Paper
   24"h x 24"w
   Artist: Laura Cooperman
   Country: USA

4. **SUPERvision II**
   hand cut paper
   24"h x 24"w
   Artist: Laura Cooperman
   Country: USA

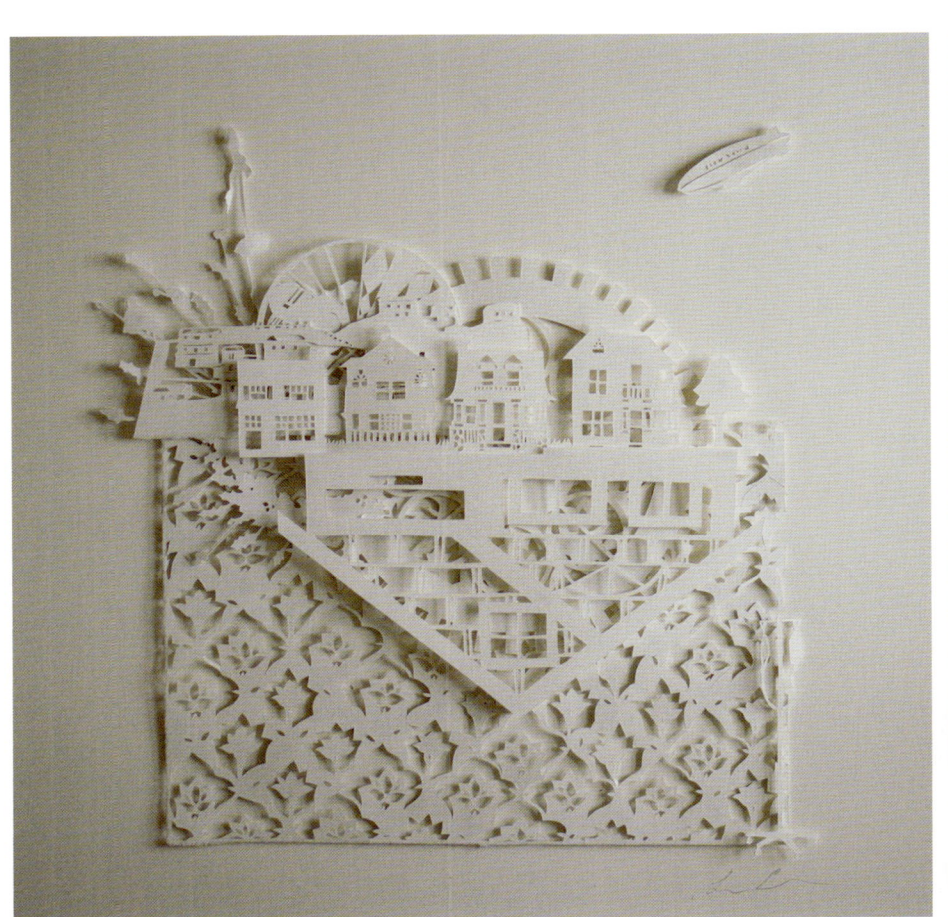
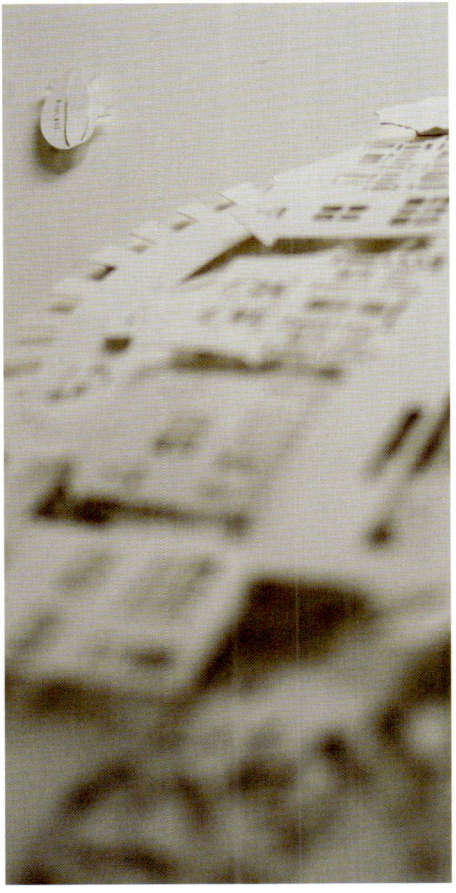

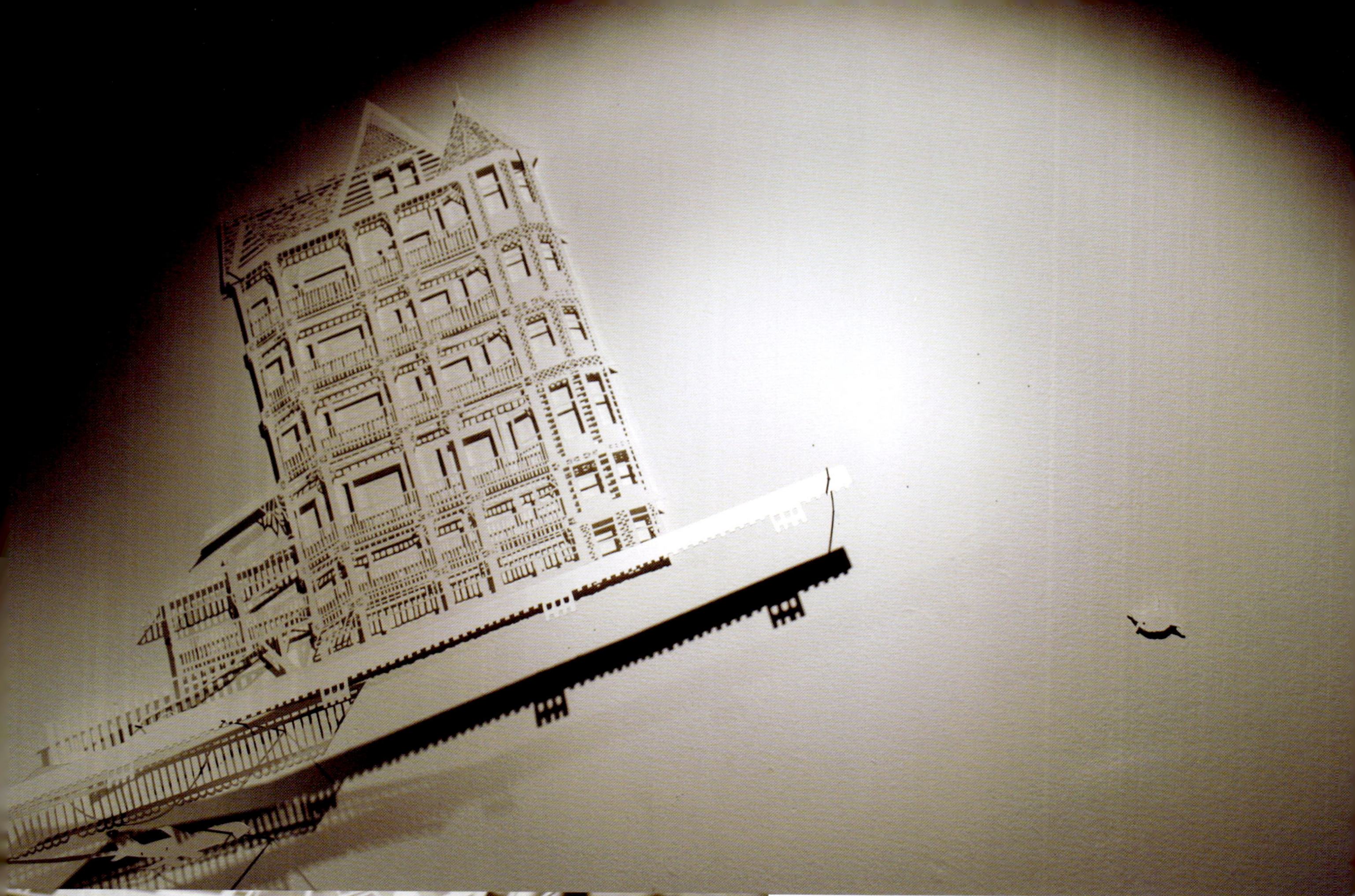

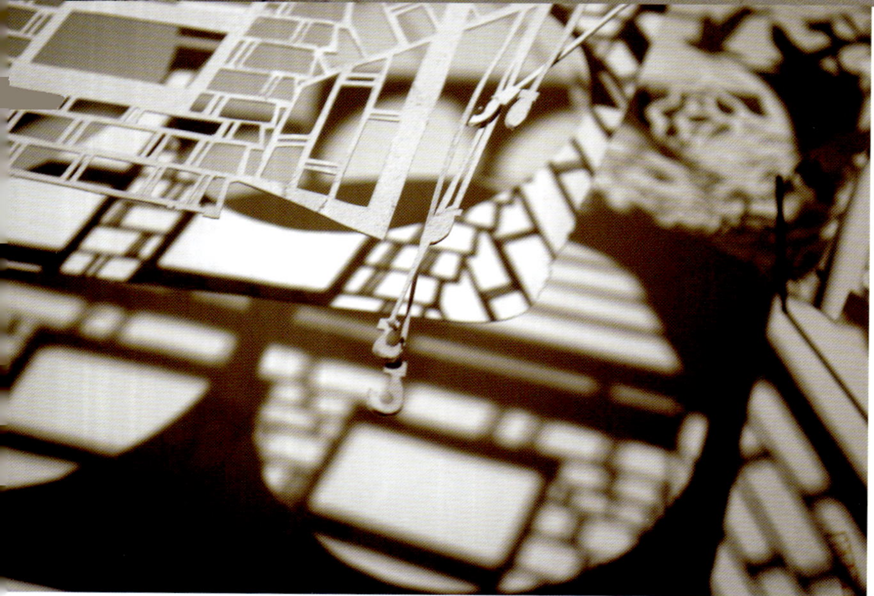

5. **Installation No Where But Up**

   Hand Cut Paper / Metal Pins
   8'h x 24'w x 2'd

   Artist: Laura Cooperman
   Country: USA

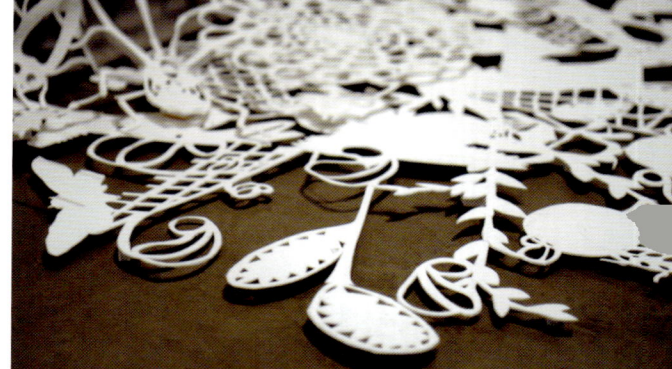

8. **Two for One**
Hand Cut Paper 16"h x 24"w
Artist: Laura Cooperman
Country: USA

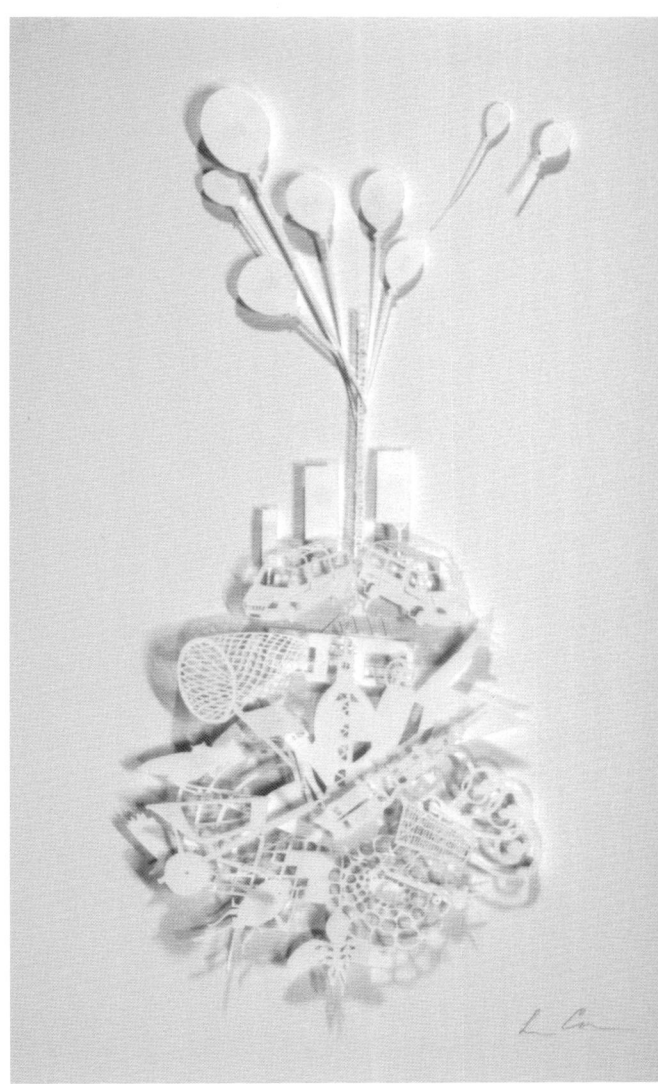

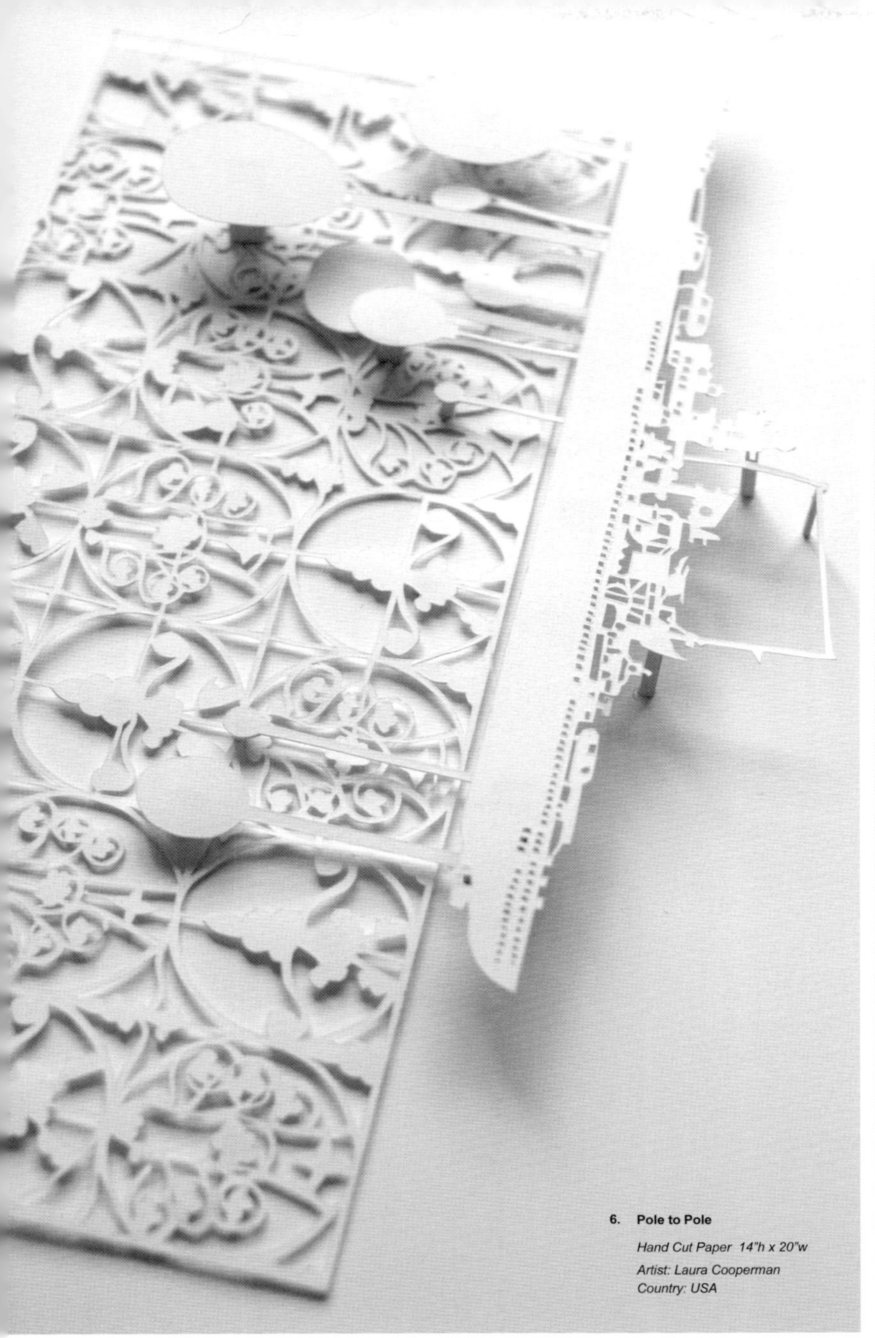

6. **Pole to Pole**
Hand Cut Paper 14"h x 20"w
Artist: Laura Cooperman
Country: USA

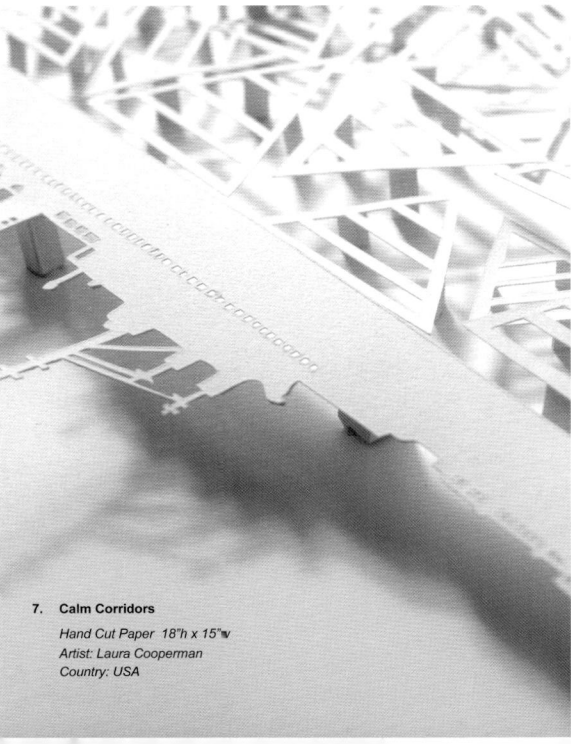

7. **Calm Corridors**
Hand Cut Paper 18"h x 15"w
Artist: Laura Cooperman
Country: USA

8. **Two for One**

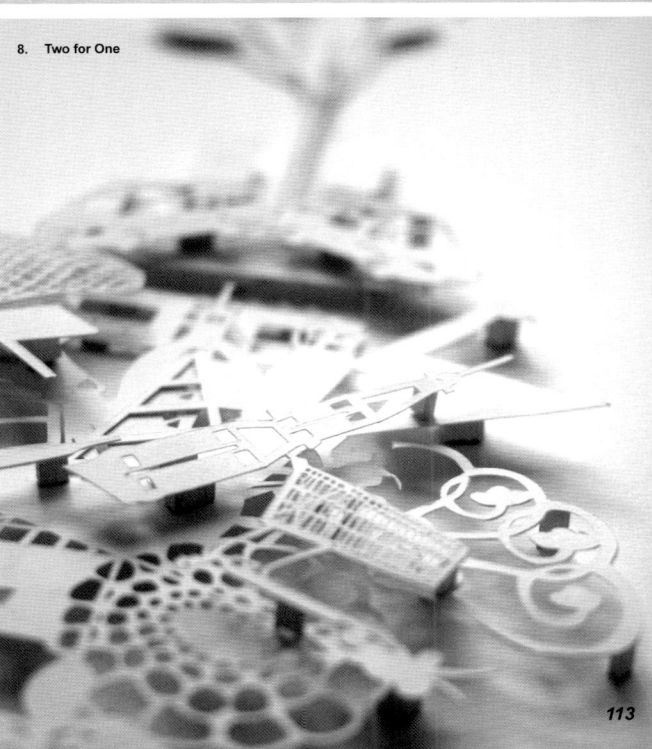

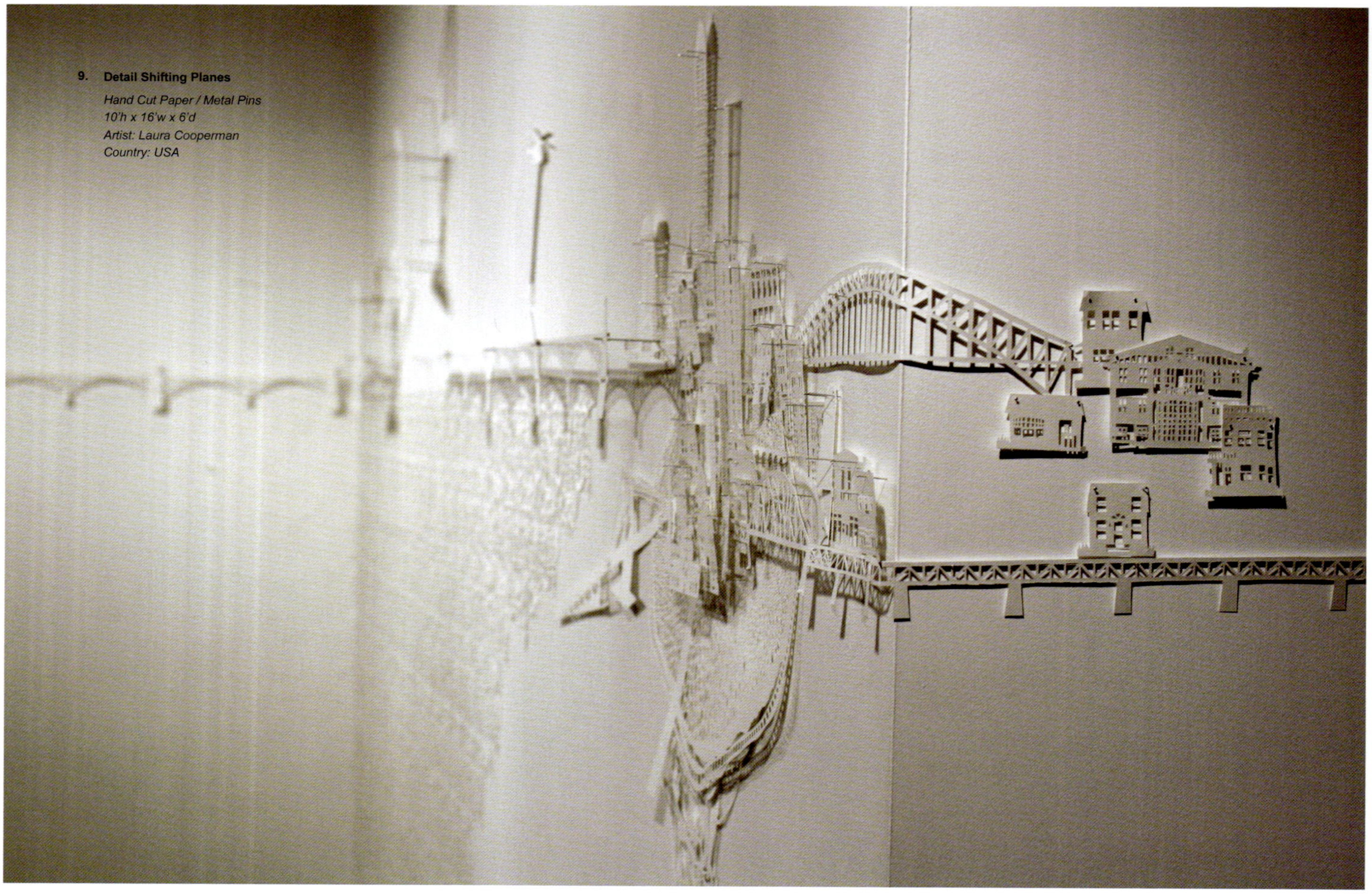

9. **Detail Shifting Planes**
   Hand Cut Paper / Metal Pins
   10'h x 16'w x 6'd
   Artist: Laura Cooperman
   Country: USA

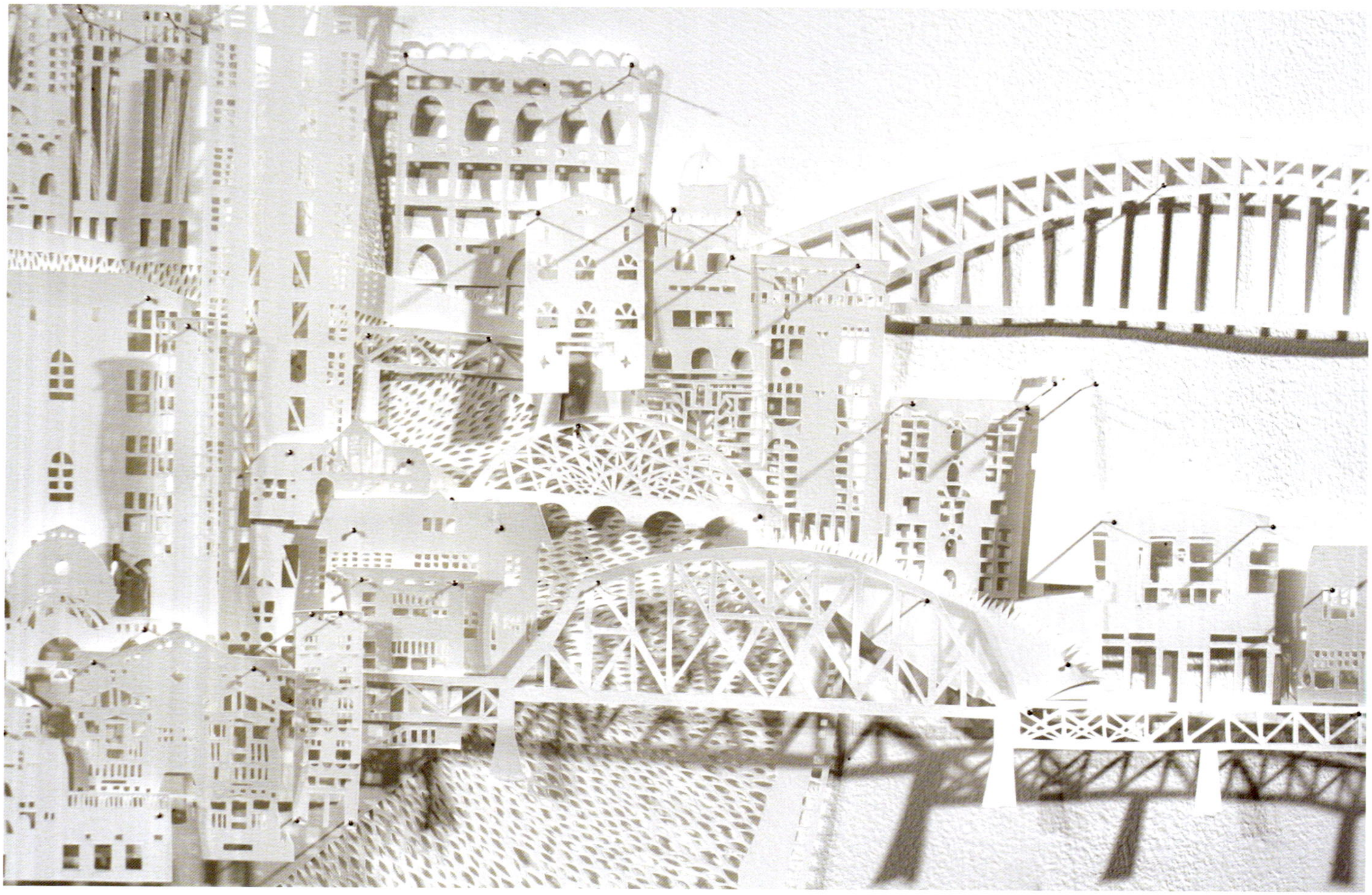

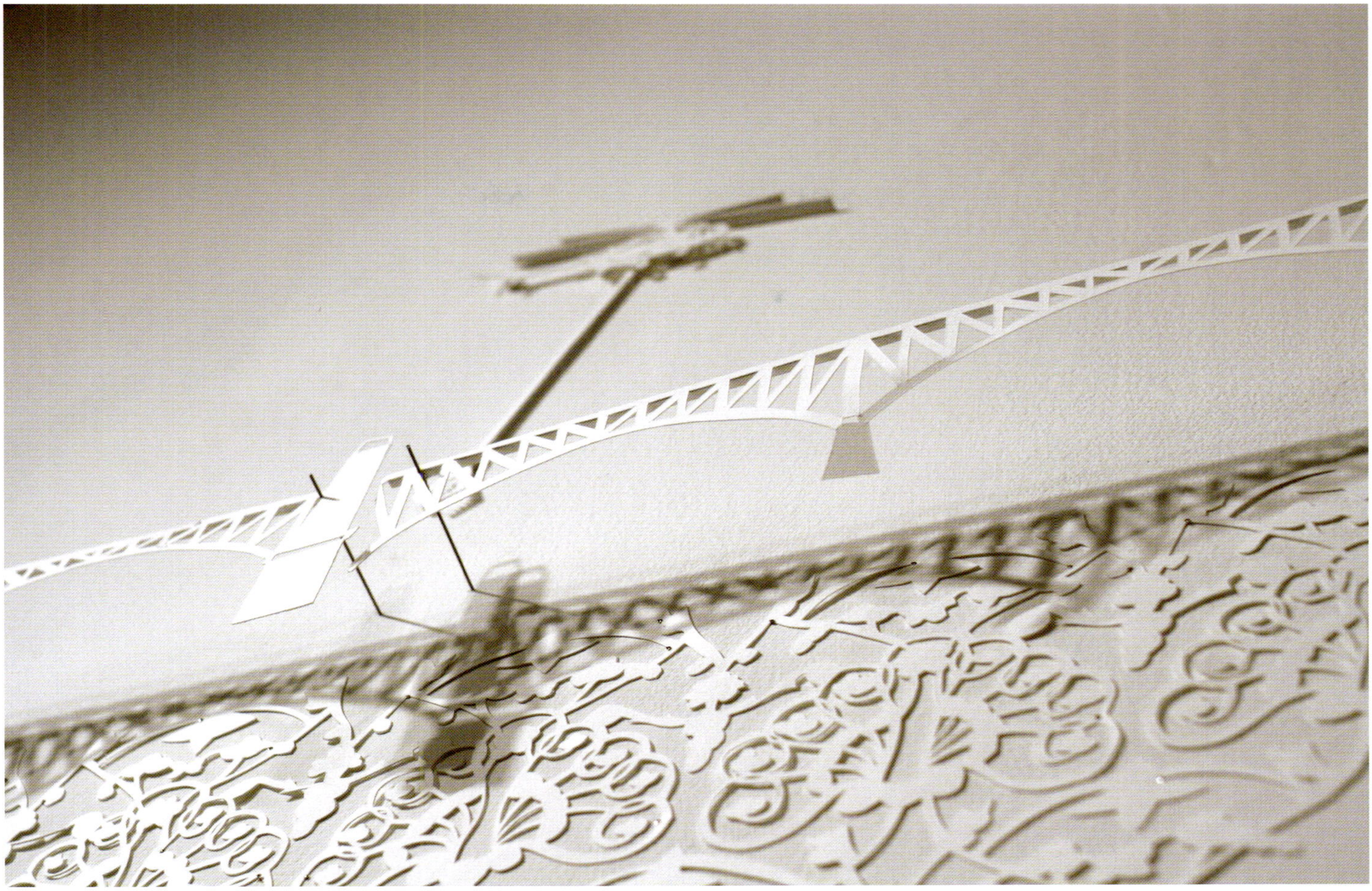

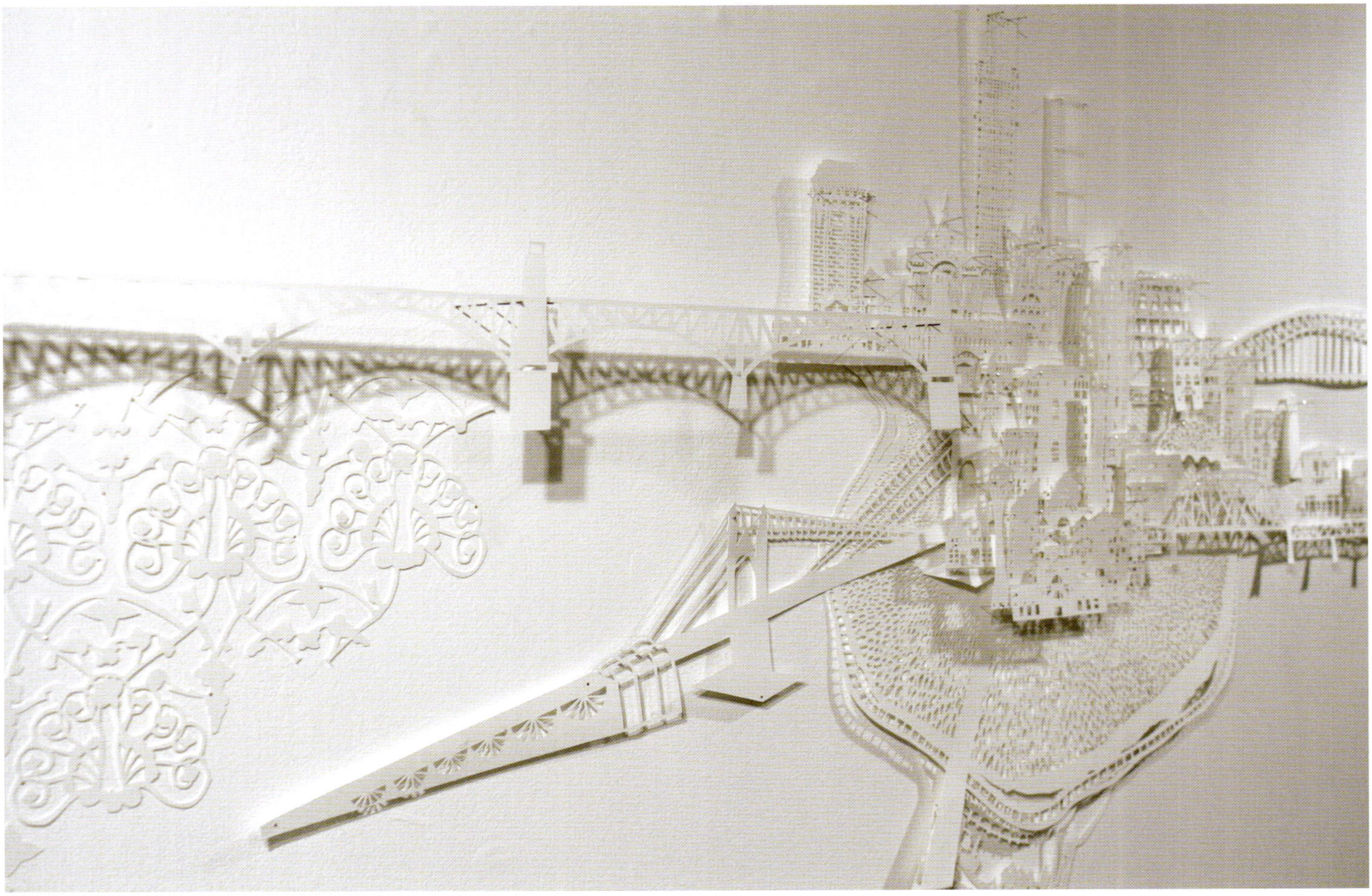

115

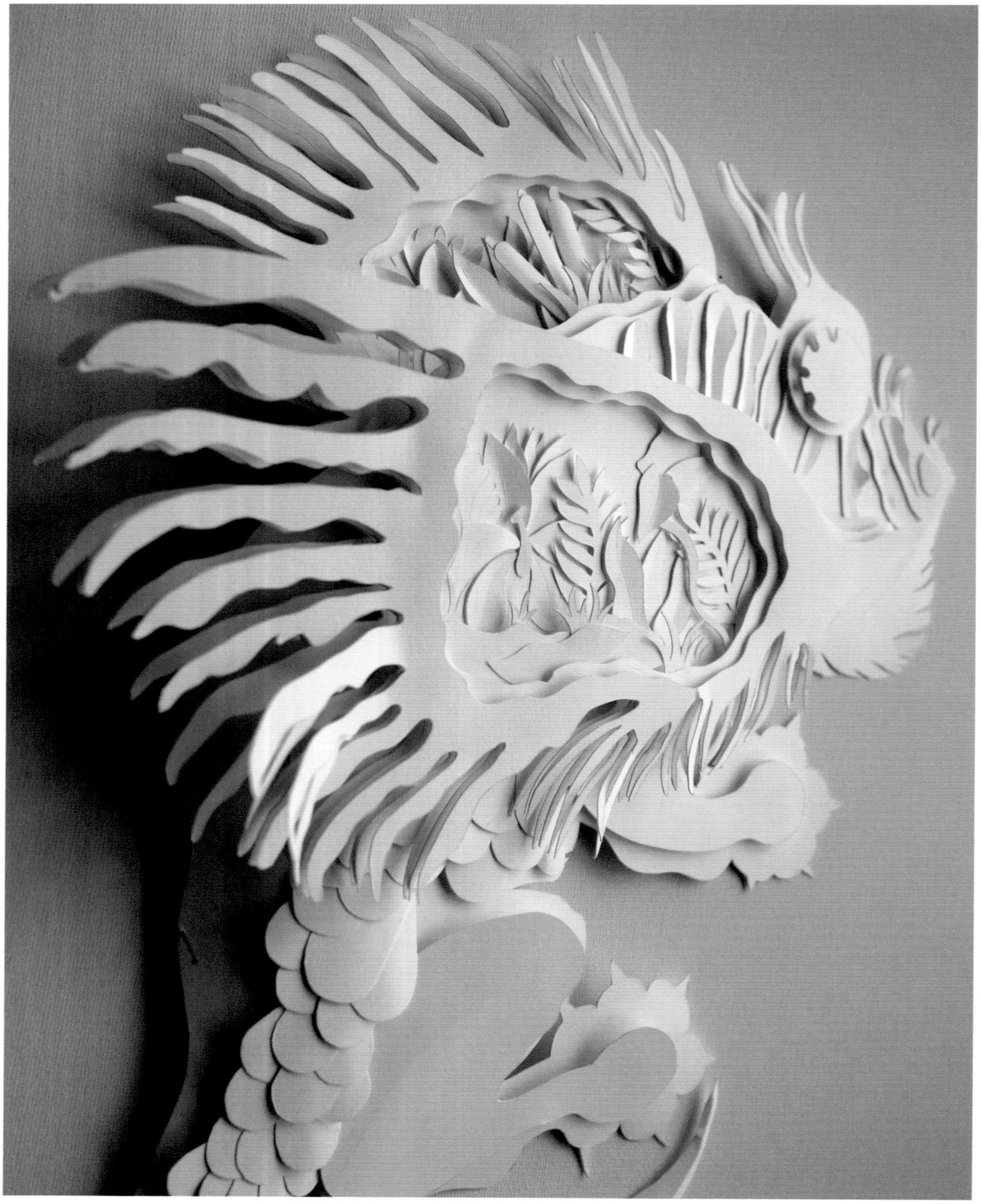

1. **Space of fantasies**

   Space of Fantasies is a model based on my imagination about the hybrids of different animals and plants.

   Artist: Lee Huey Ming
   Country: Malaysia
   Photographer: Lee Huey Ming

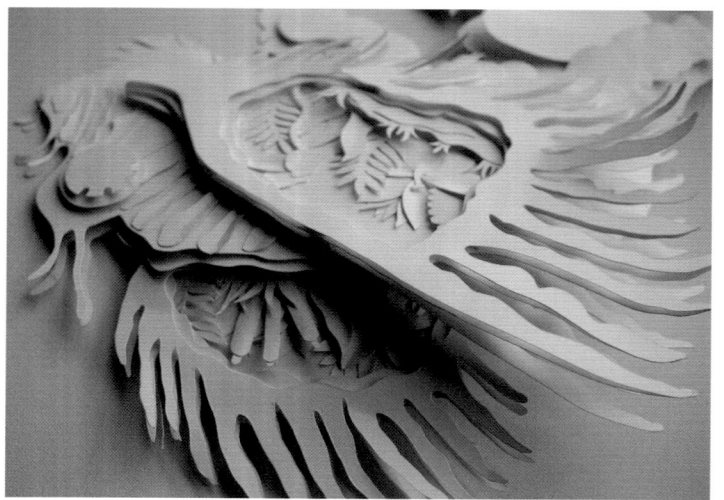
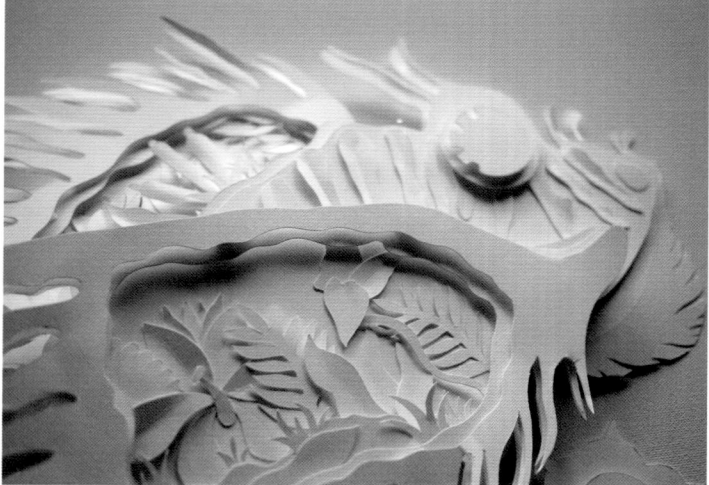

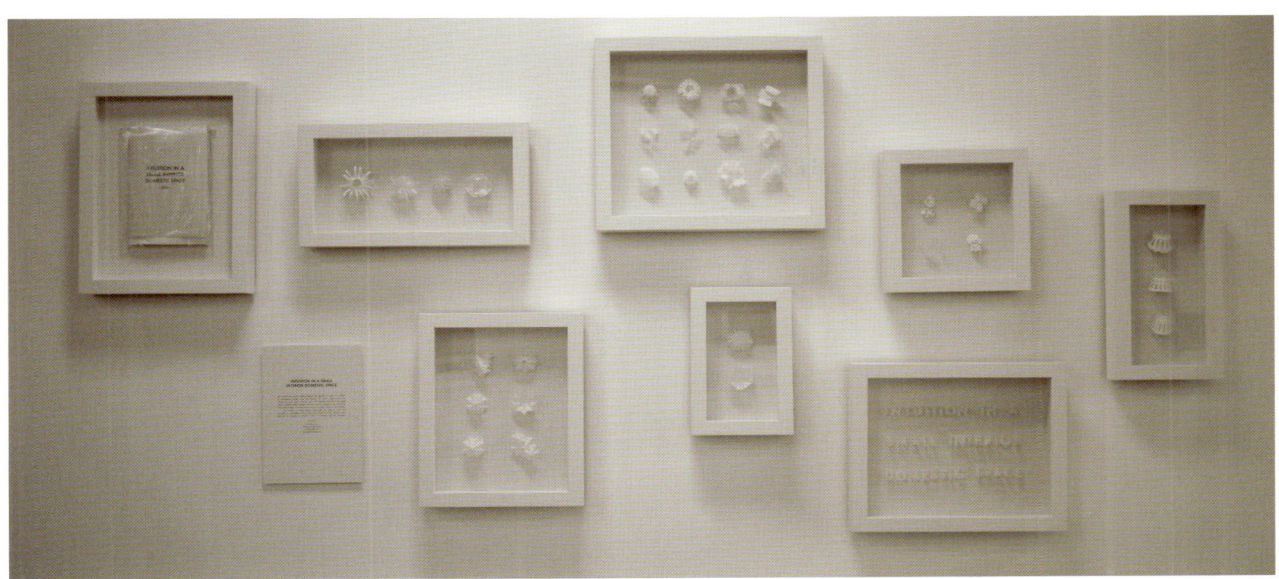

2. Intuition in a small interior domestic space

This practice-led research project explores the potential of paper as a medium to communicate complex ideas and emotions. Through this exploration I will employ the notion of water as a conceptual lens through which I will consider ideas related to the small domestic space. The project work will not set out to overtly represent water but will be used as a way to imaginatively retreat from and respond to the small domestic space. Through these conceptual strategies I intend to test the way paper can be manipulated and question if it is able to communicate the subtle and complicated ideas which underpin this research.

Artist: Lee Huey Ming
Country: Malaysia
Photographer: Lee Huey Ming

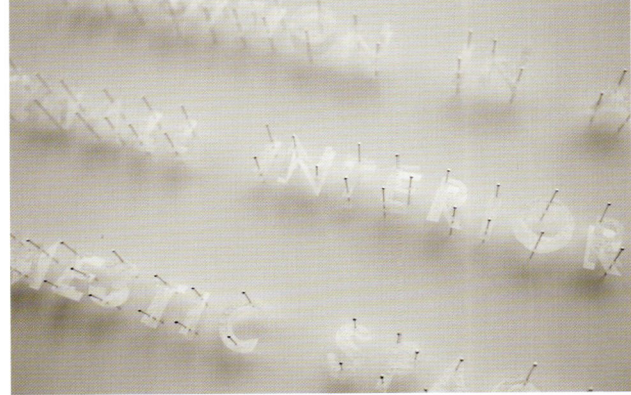

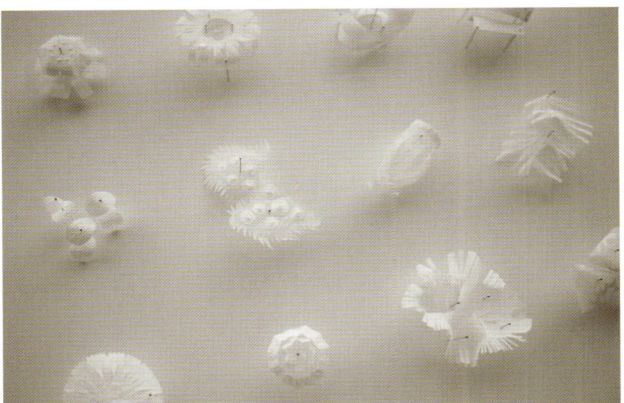

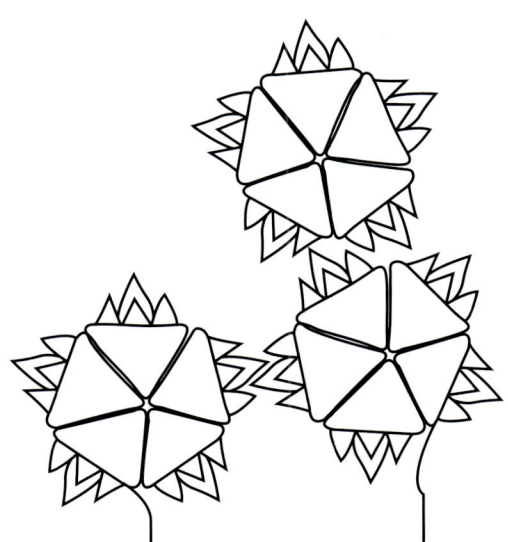

1. **Space of fantasies**
2. **Intuition in a small interior domestic space**
3. **Noticing the unnoticed**

---Lee Huey Ming

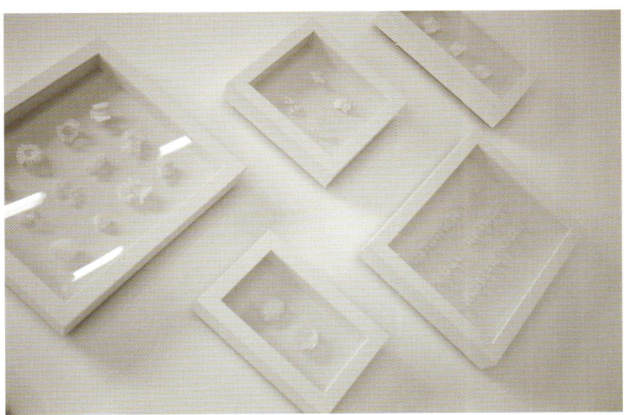

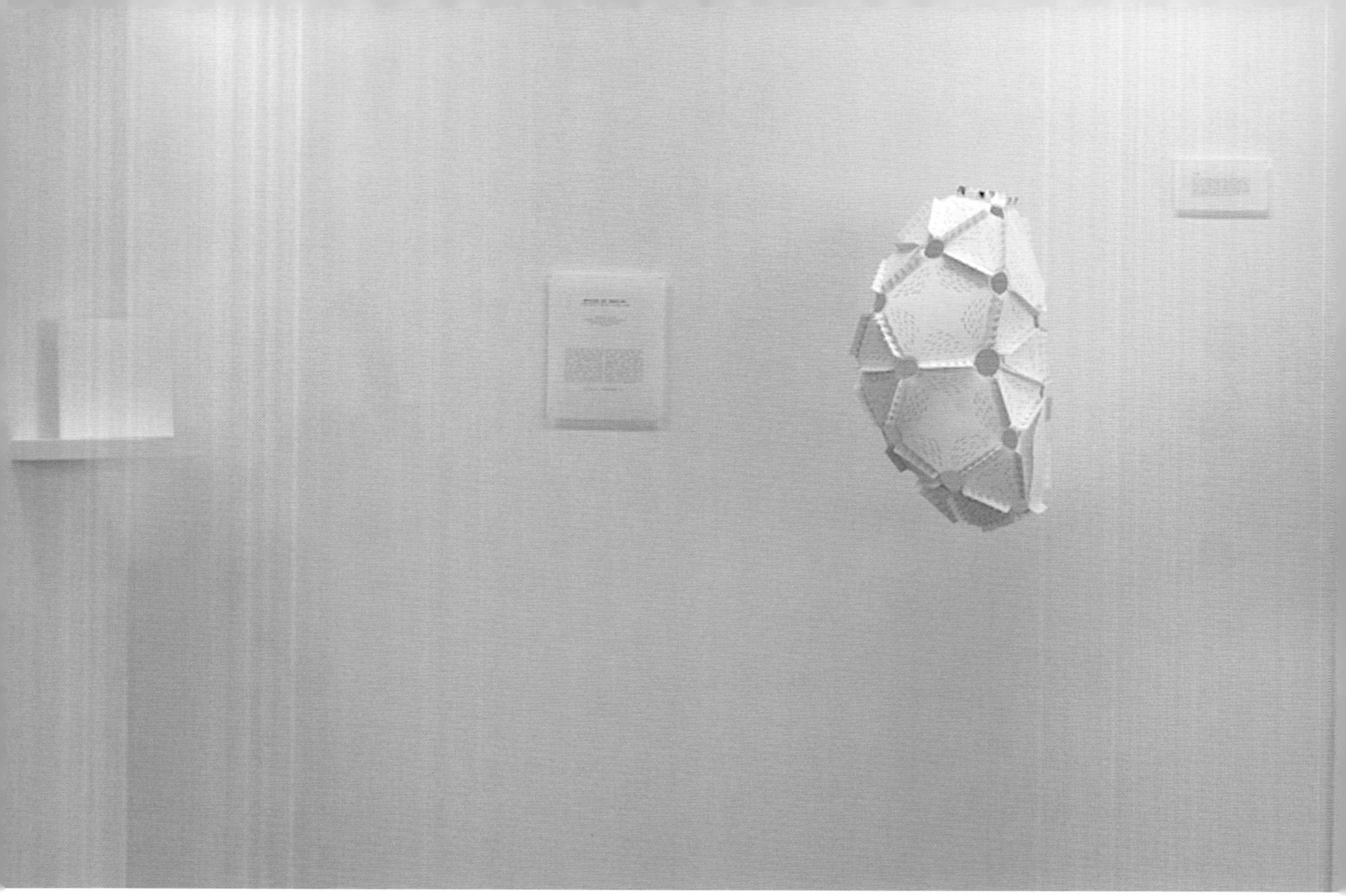

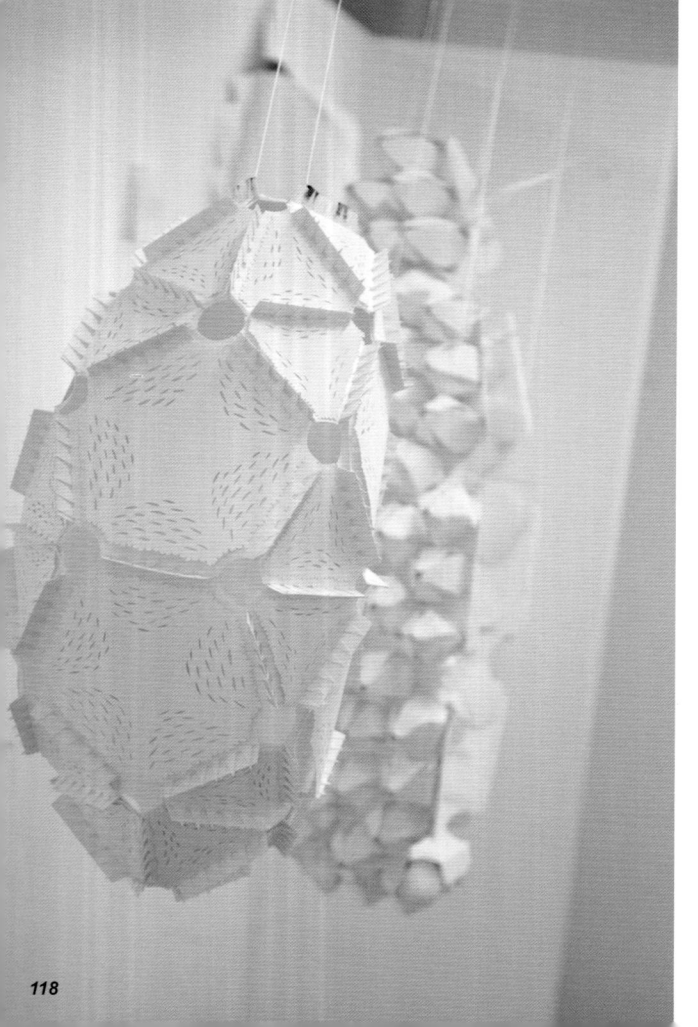
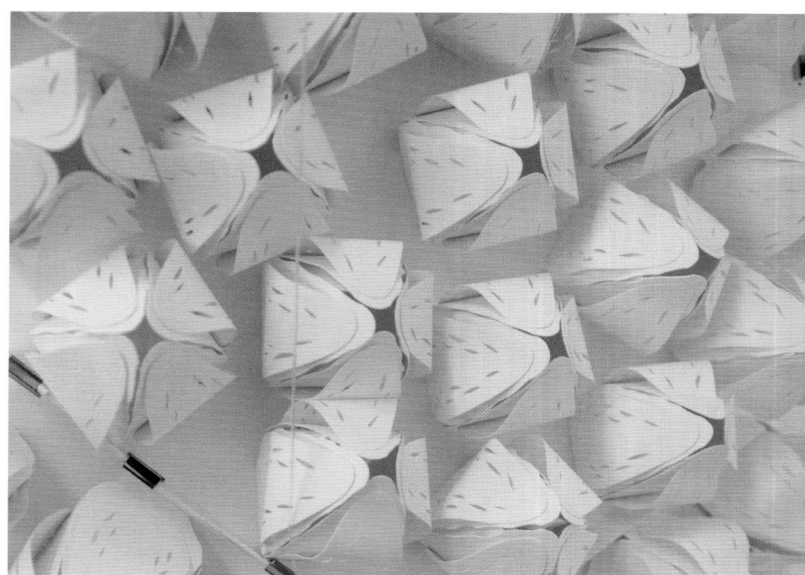

3. **Noticing the unnoticed**

Noticing the unnoticed is a narrative based on allergies that I have as a child. In this project I translate the subjective experience of three allergies that were significant in my growing up: asthma, eczema and sinusitis problems.

Artist: Lee Huey Ming
Country: Malaysia
Photographer: Ivan Liang

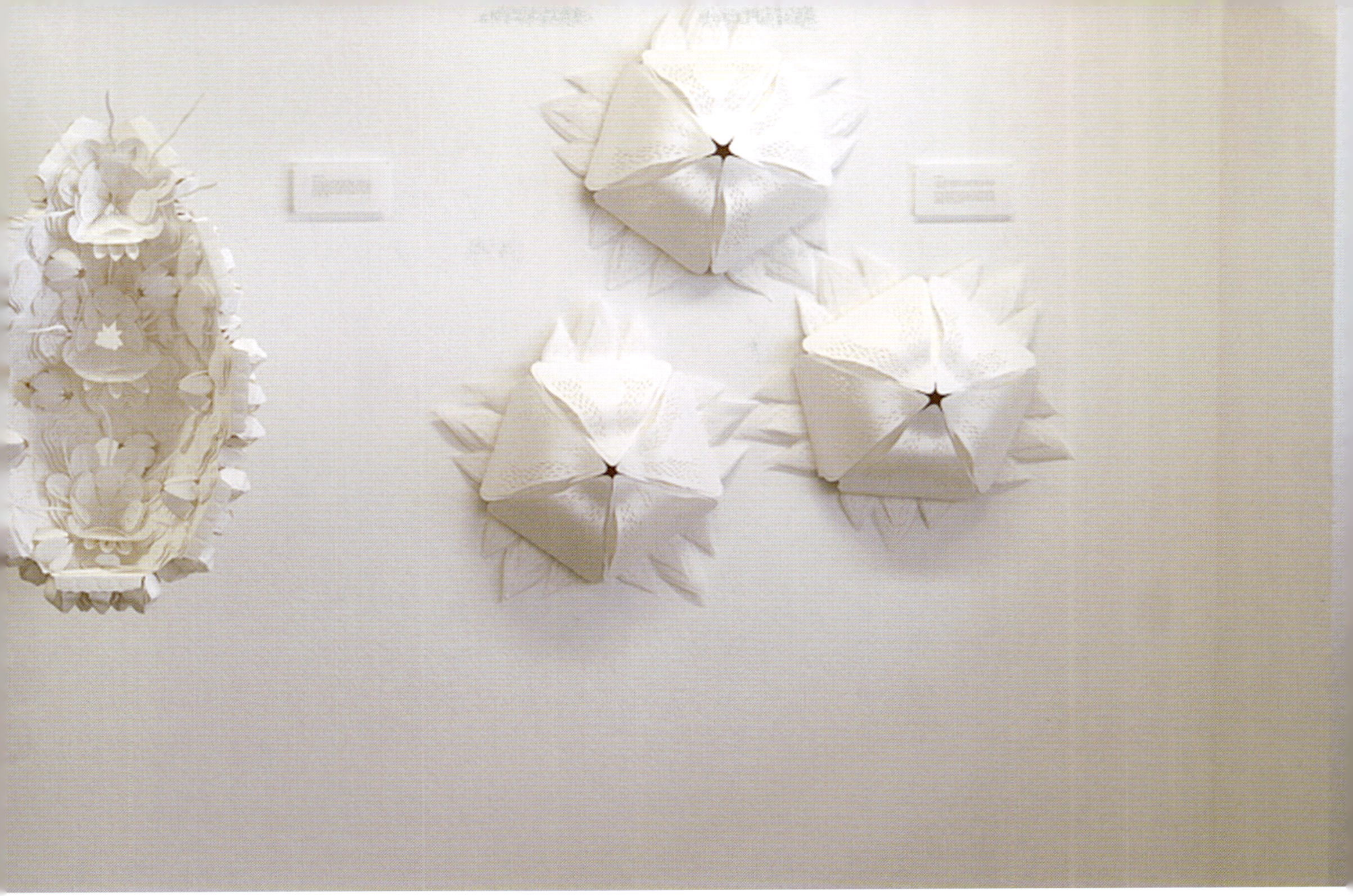

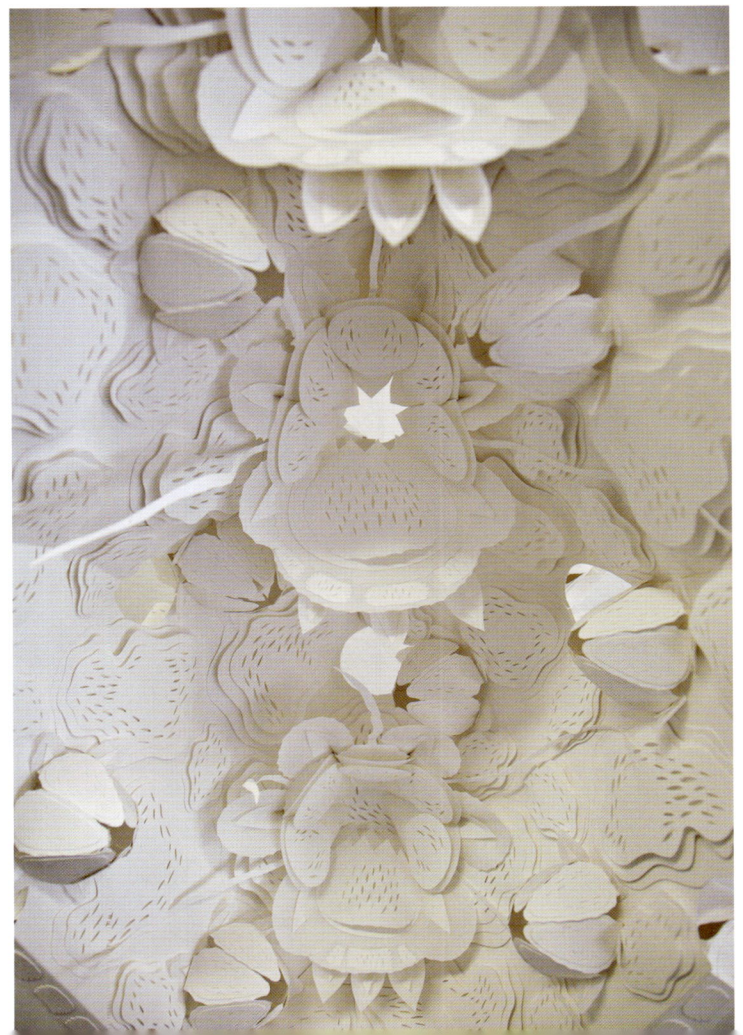
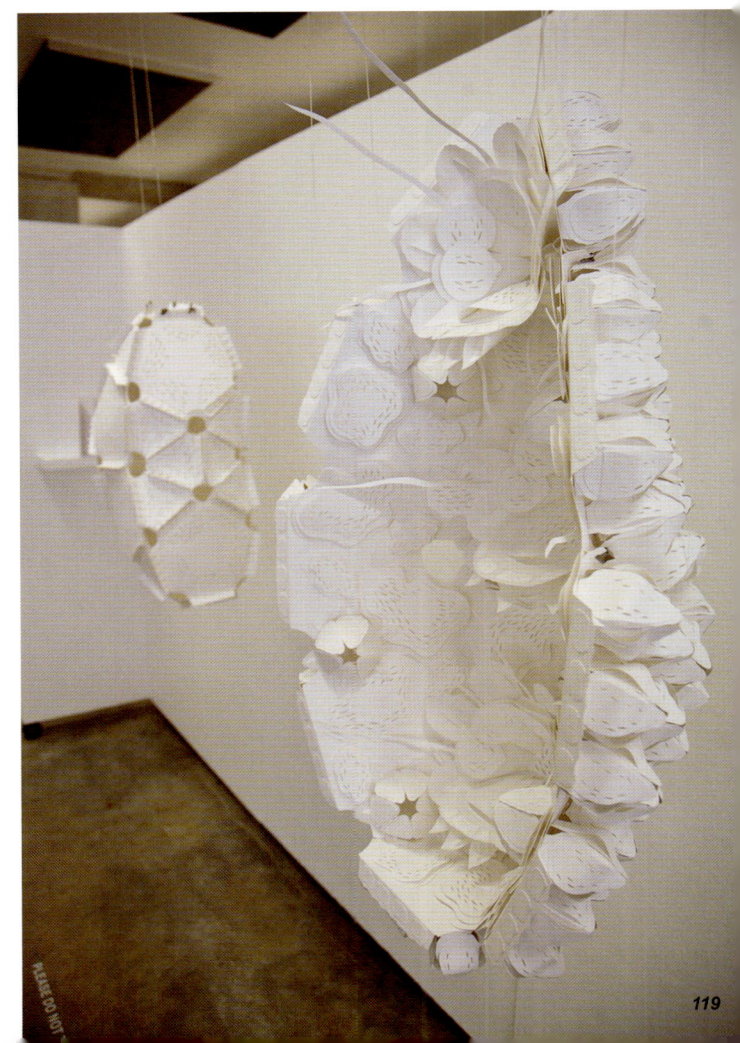

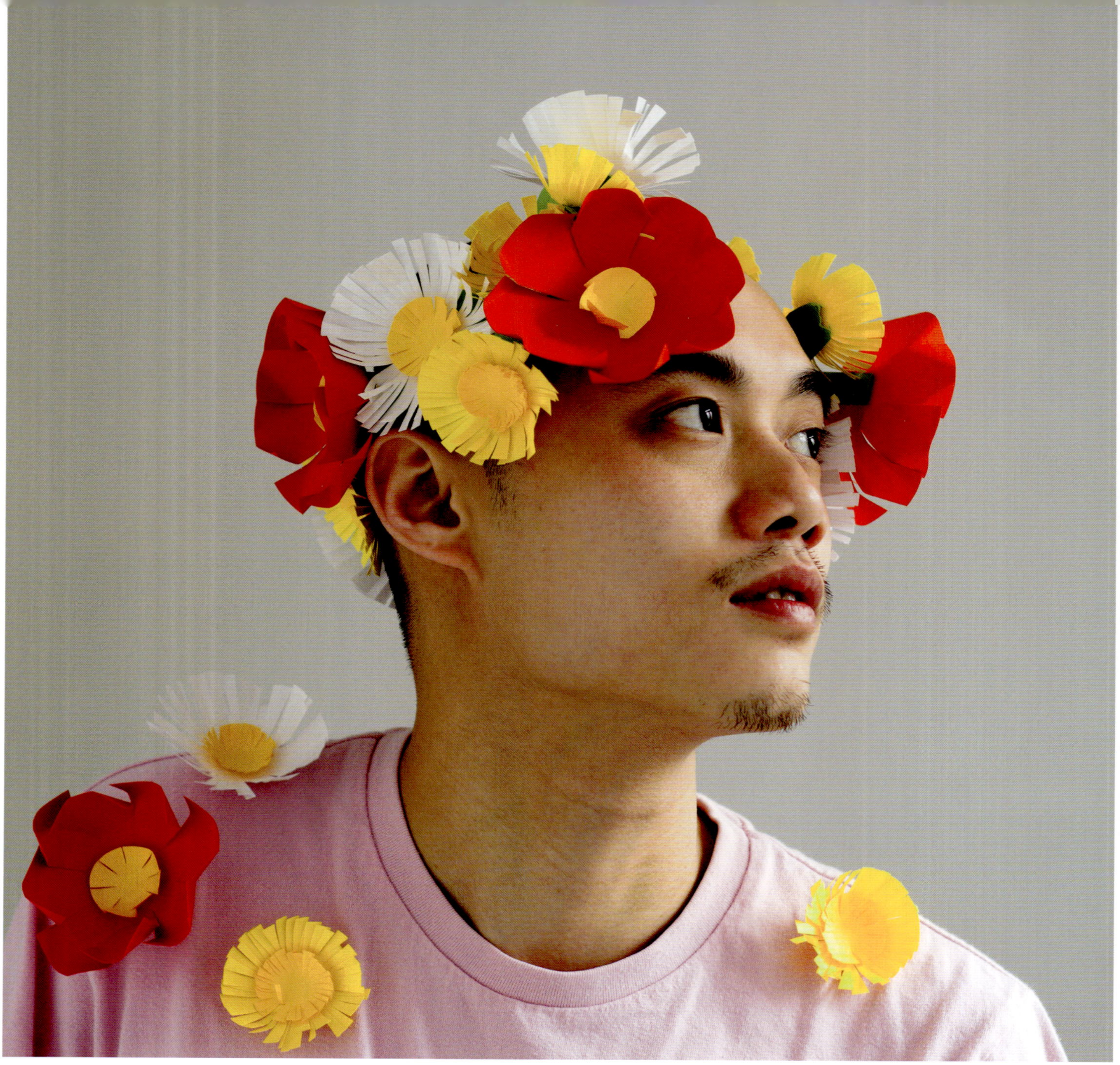

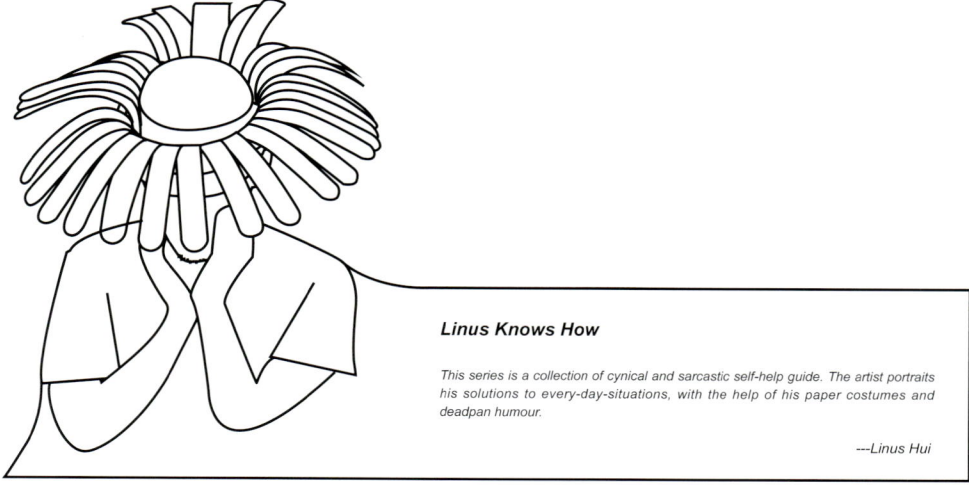

Linus Knows How

This series is a collection of cynical and sarcastic self-help guide. The artist portraits his solutions to every-day-situations, with the help of his paper costumes and deadpan humour.

---Linus Hui

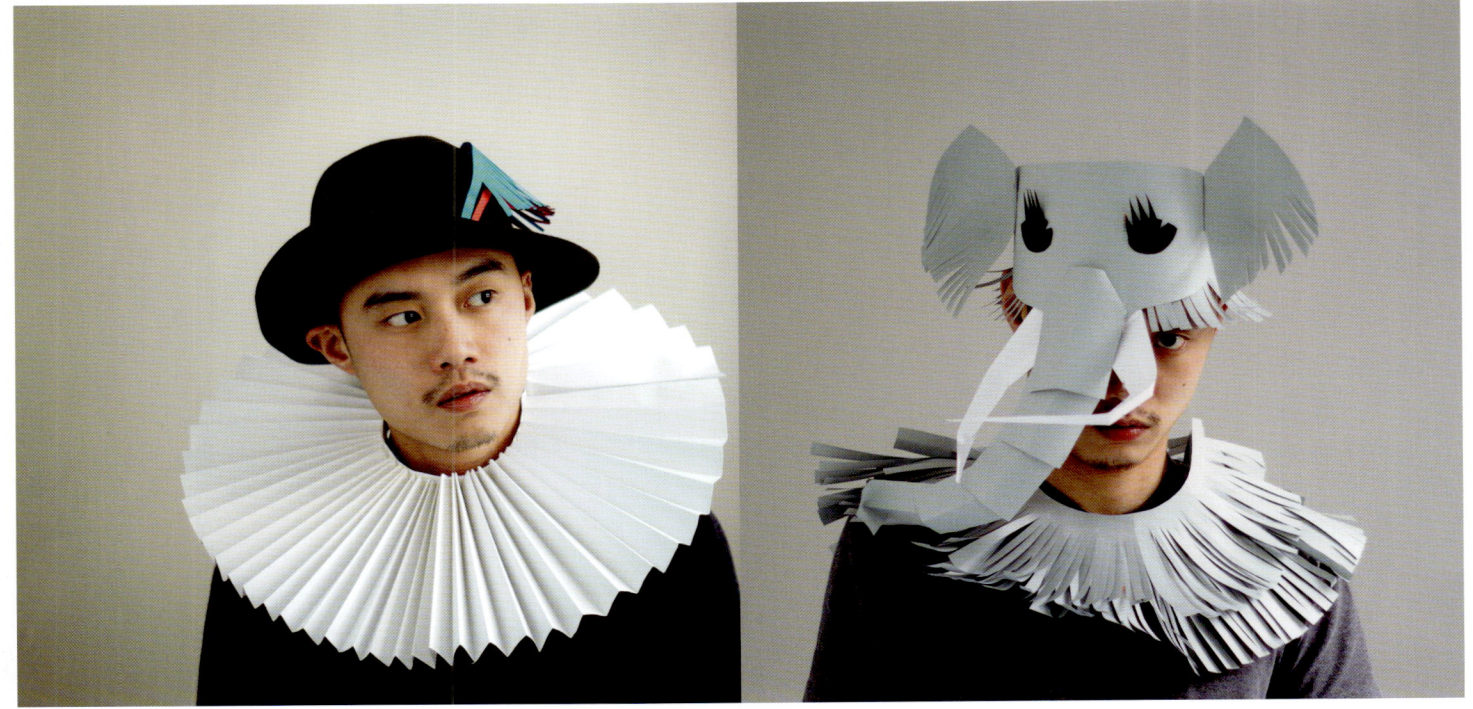
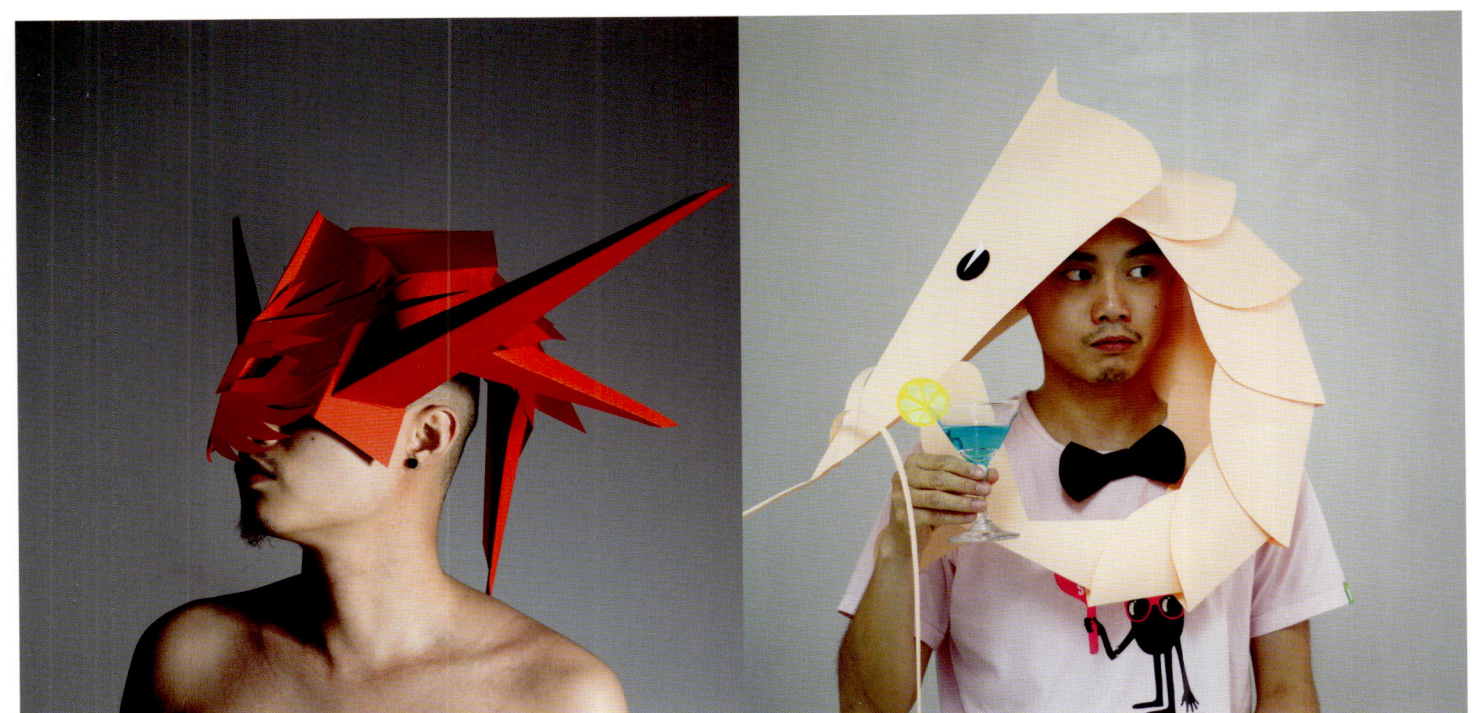

Artist: Linus Hui
Country: Hong Kong, China
Photographer: Linus Hui

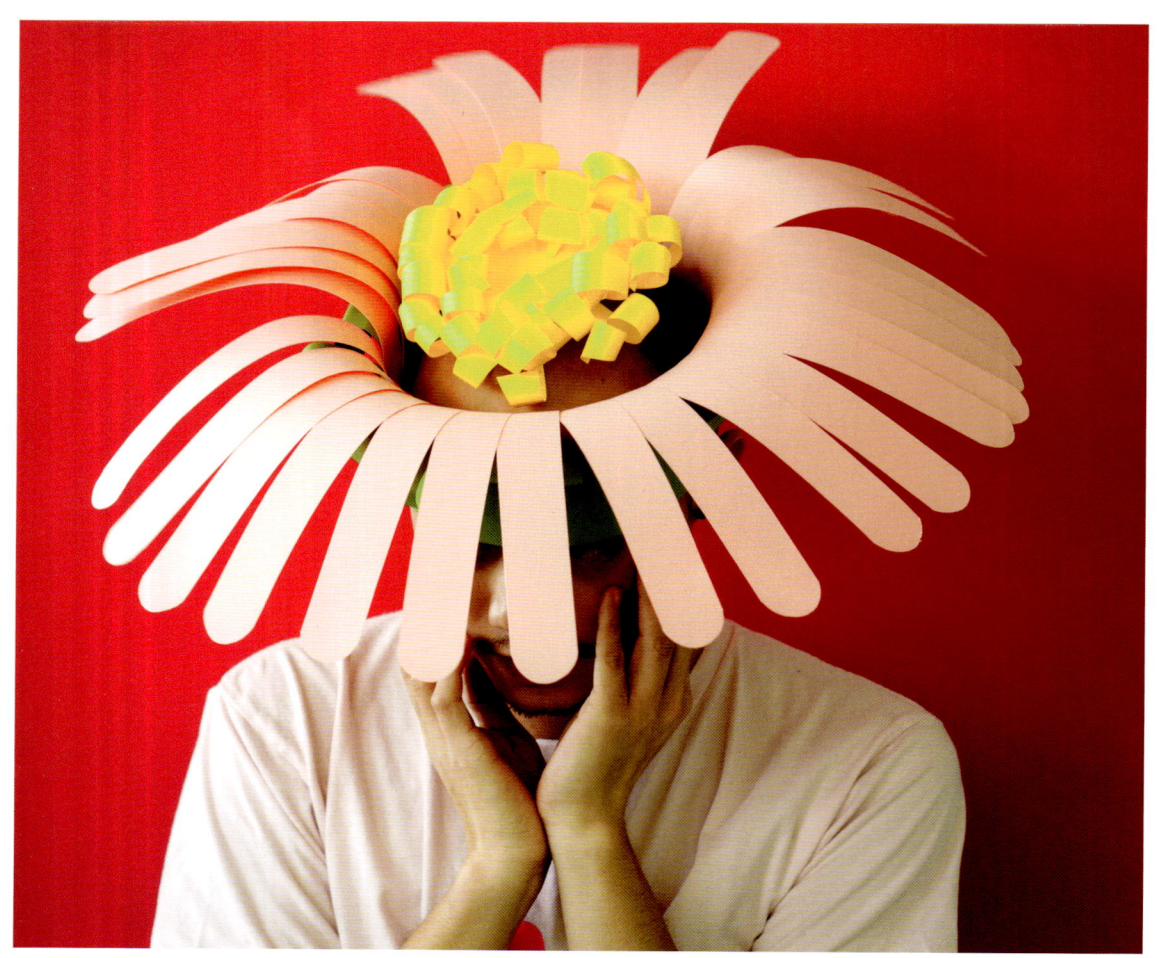
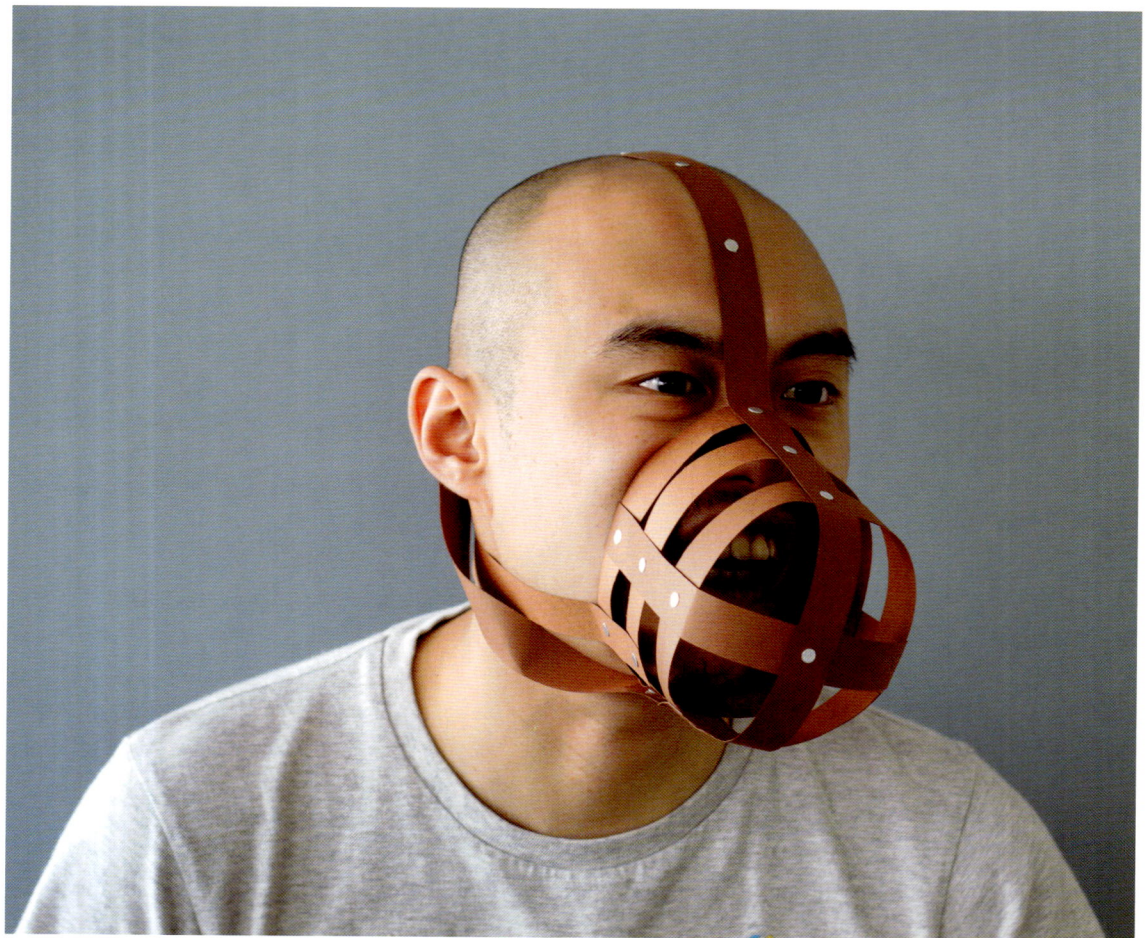

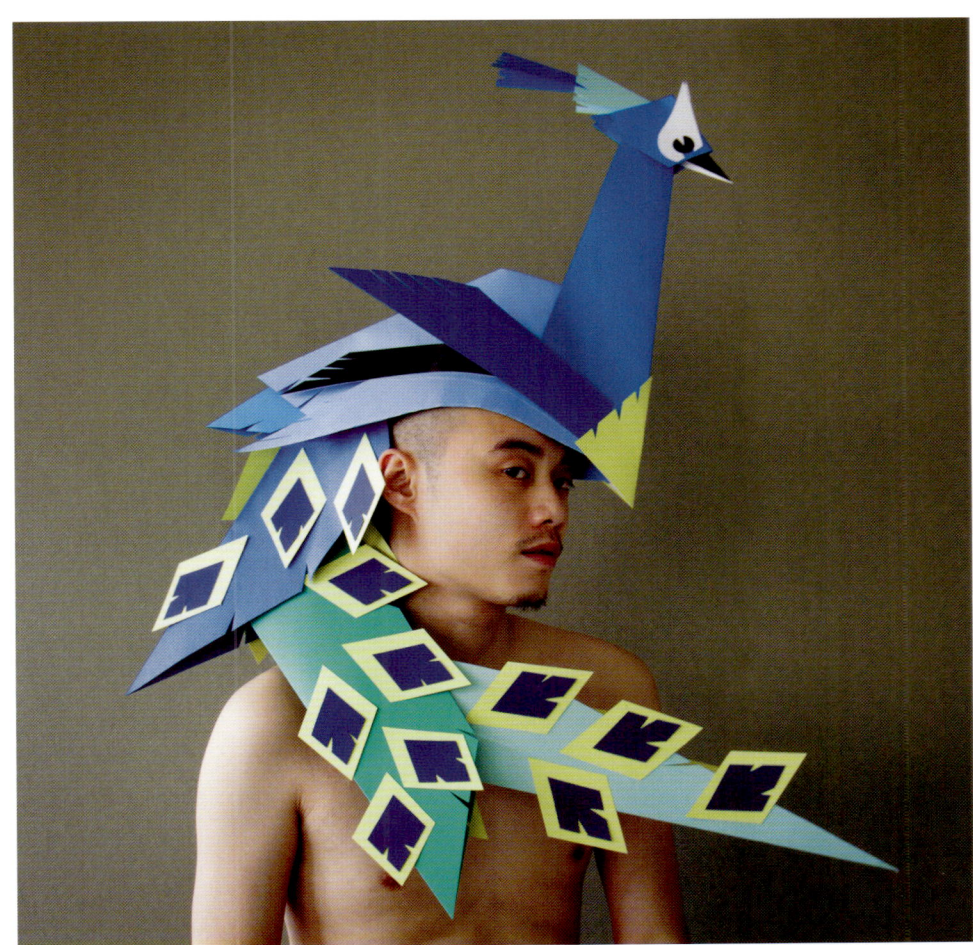

Artist: Linus Hui
Country: Hong Kong, China
Photographer: Linus Hui

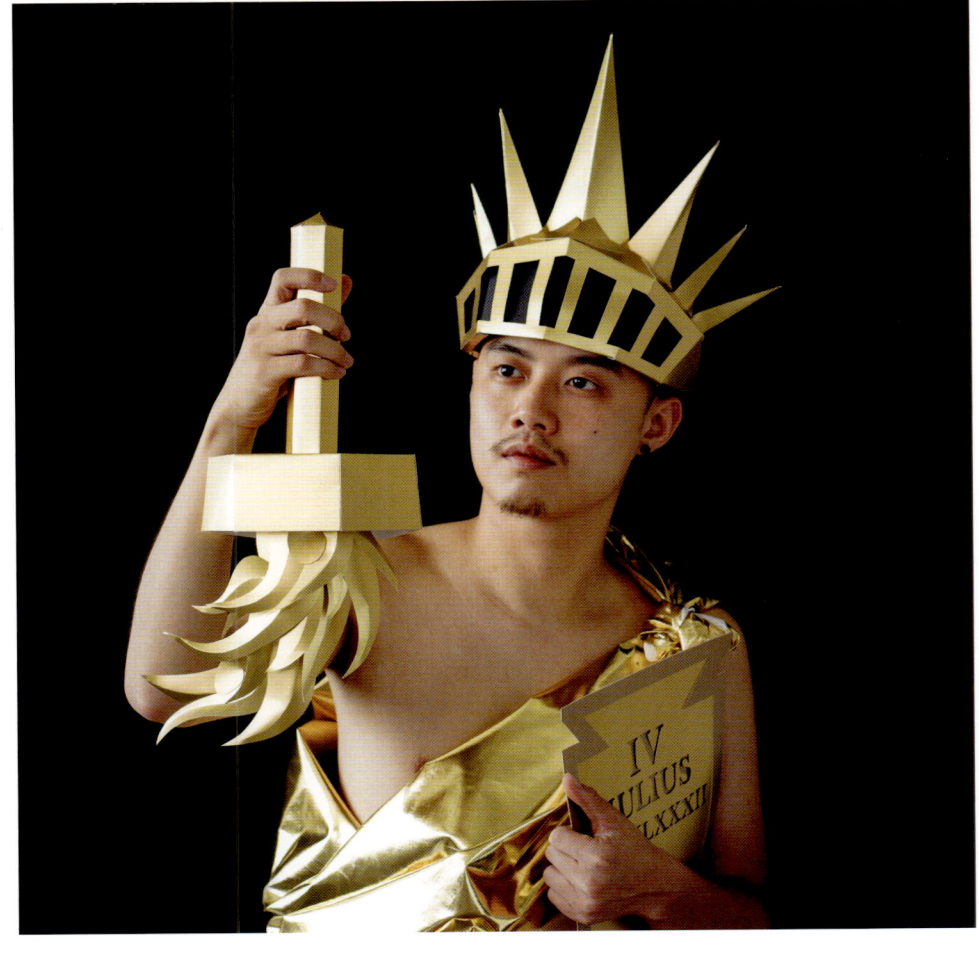

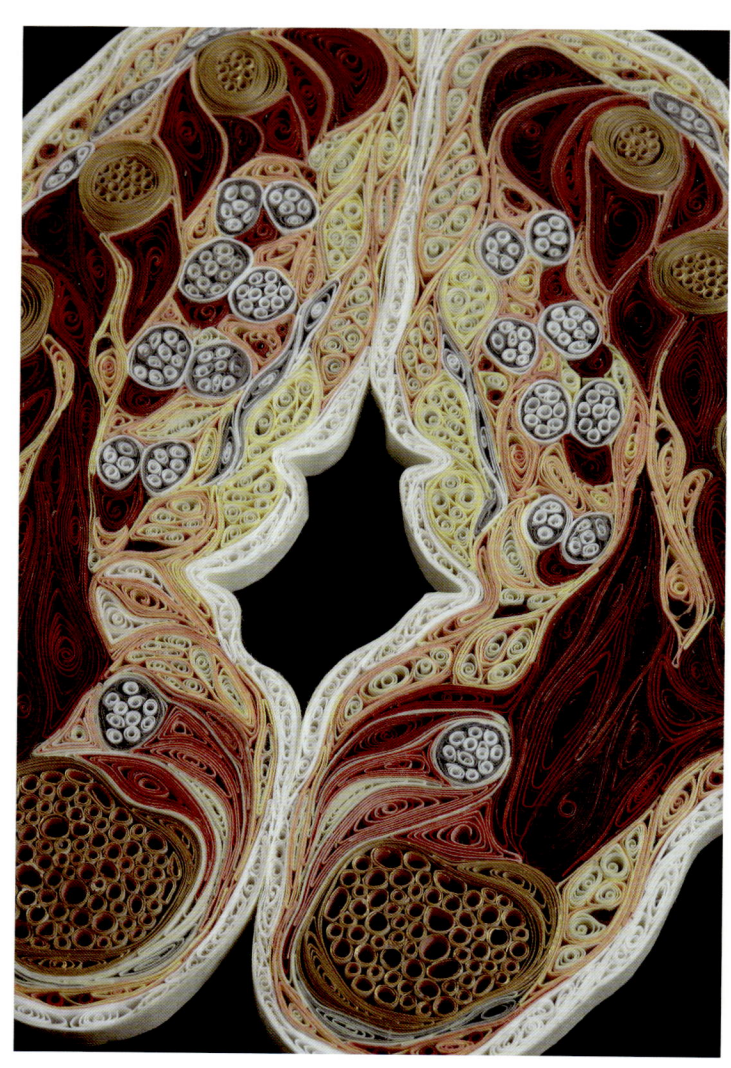
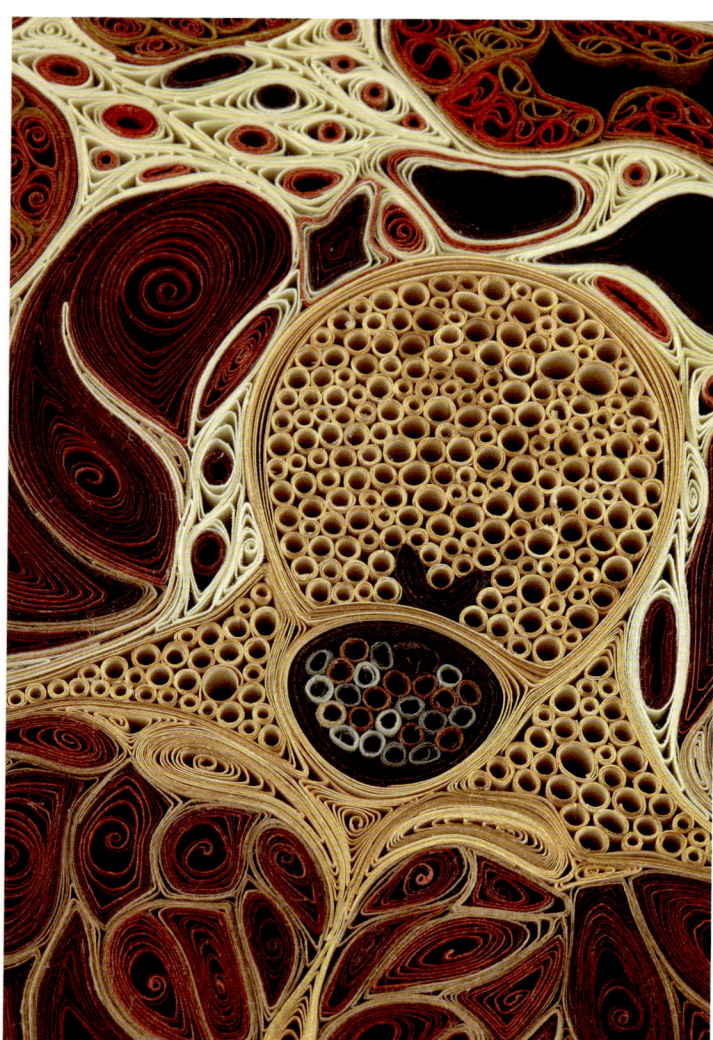

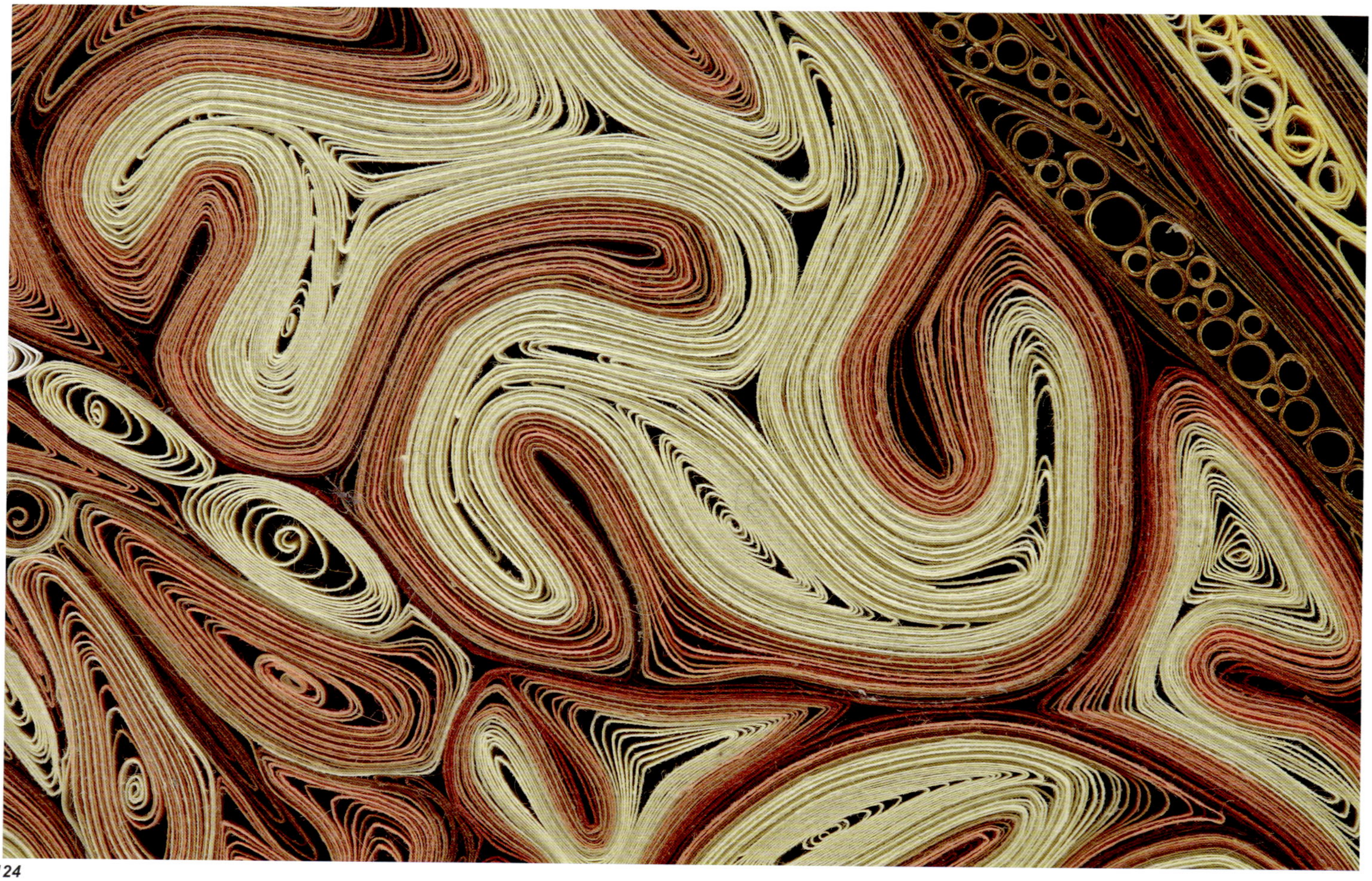

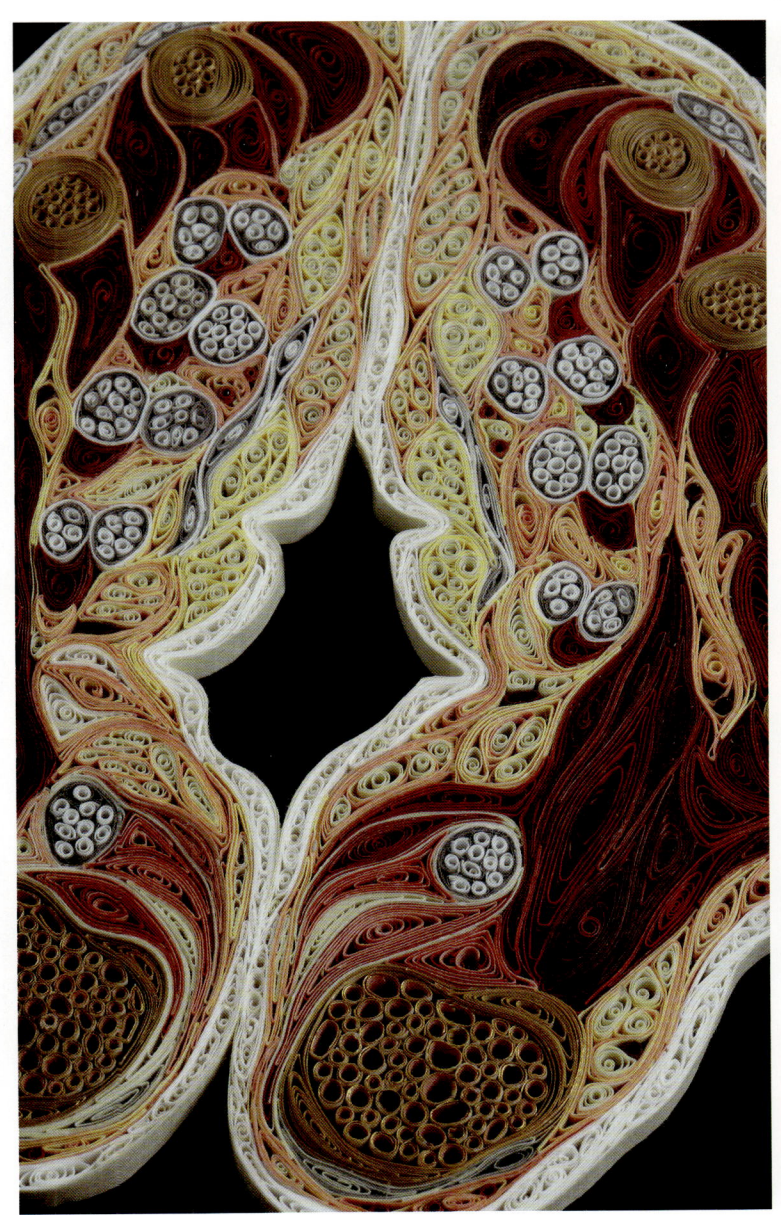
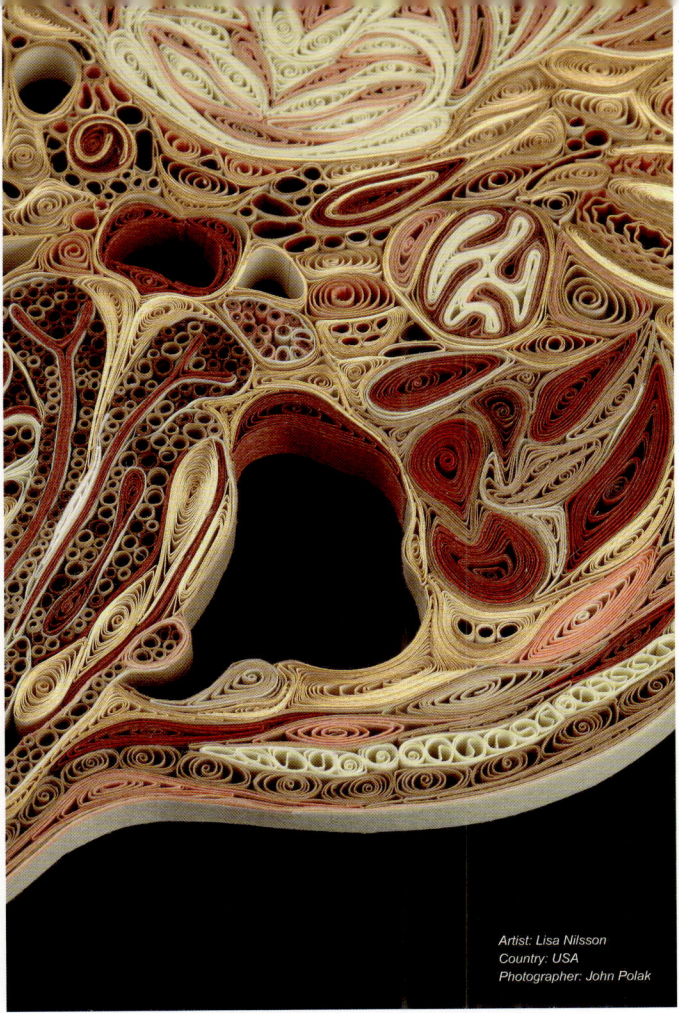

Artist: Lisa Nilsson
Country: USA
Photographer: John Polak

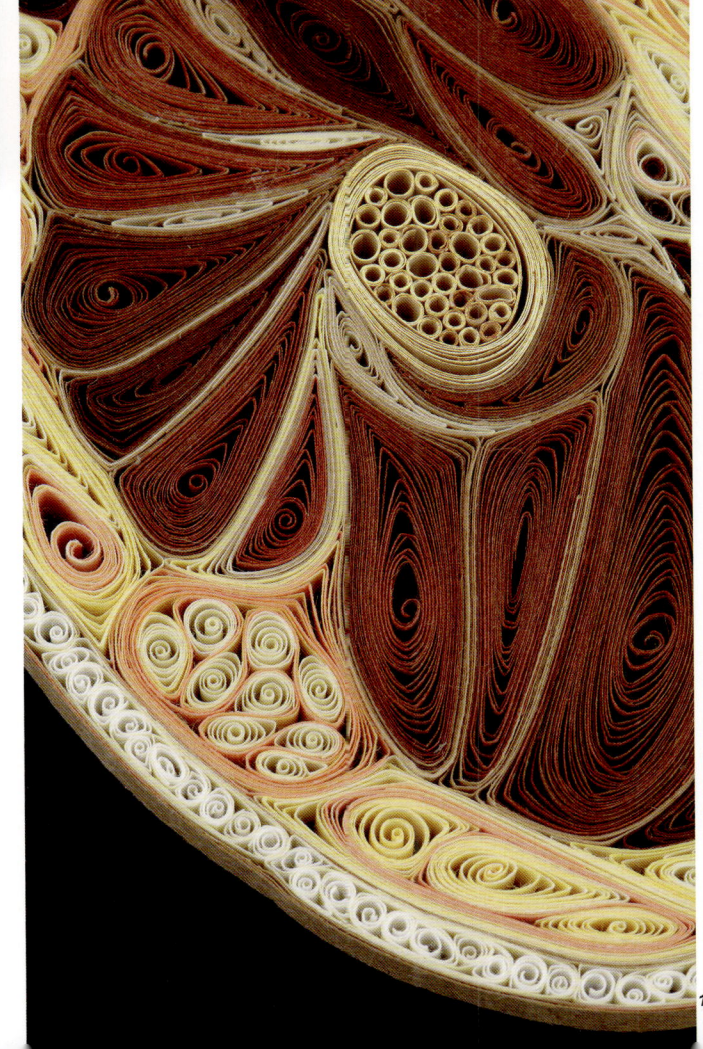

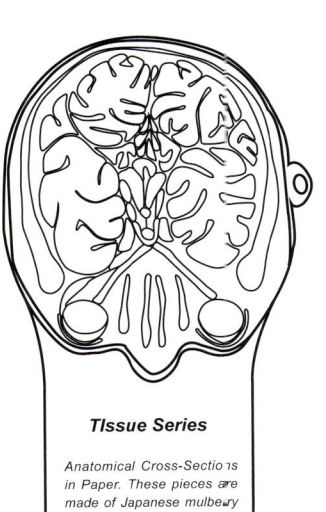

Tissue Series

Anatomical Cross-Sections in Paper. These pieces are made of Japanese mulberry paper and the gilded edges of old books. They are constructed by a centuries old paper craft called quilling or paper filigree.

---Lisa Nilsson

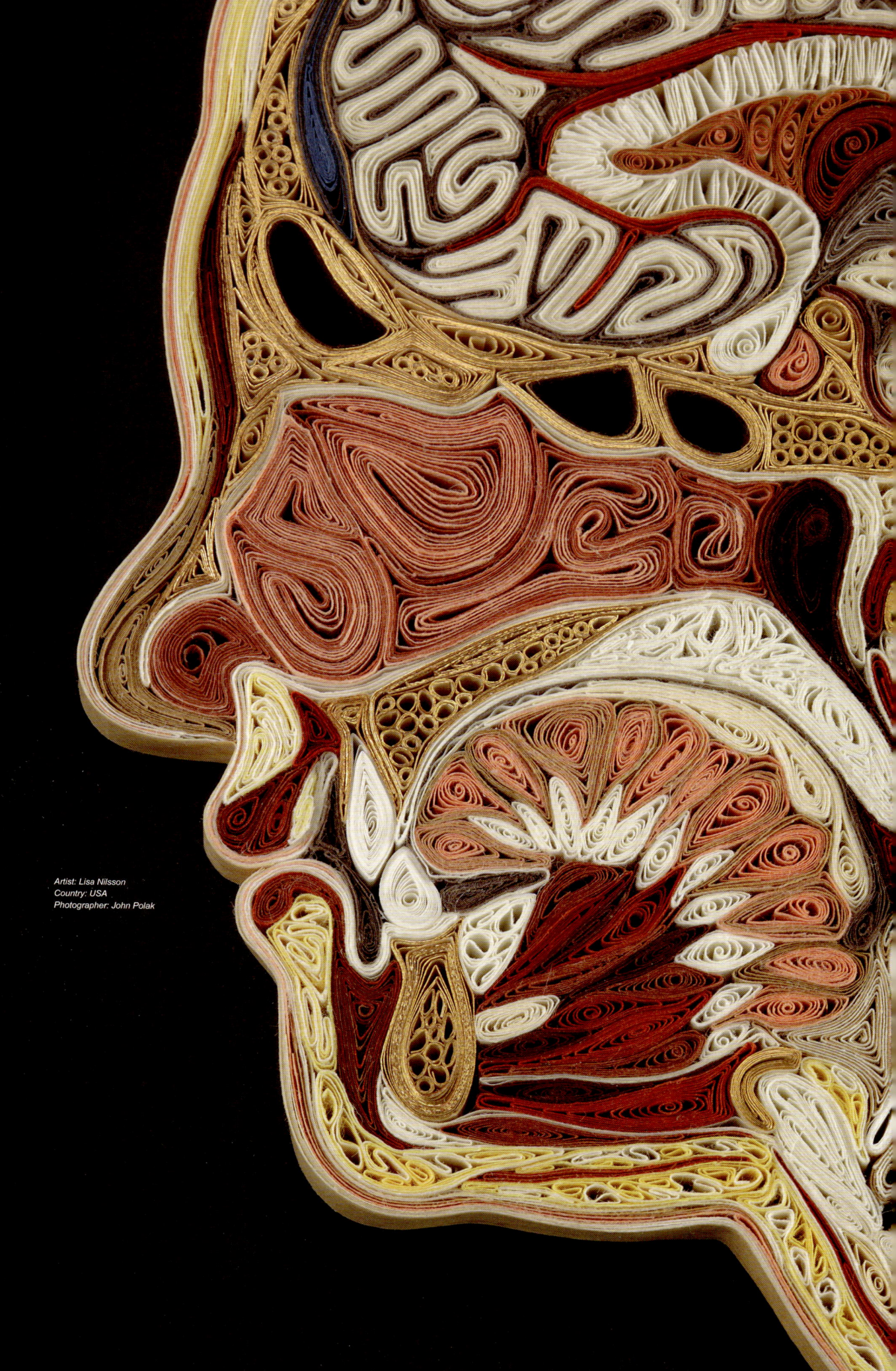

Artist: Lisa Nilsson
Country: USA
Photographer: John Polak

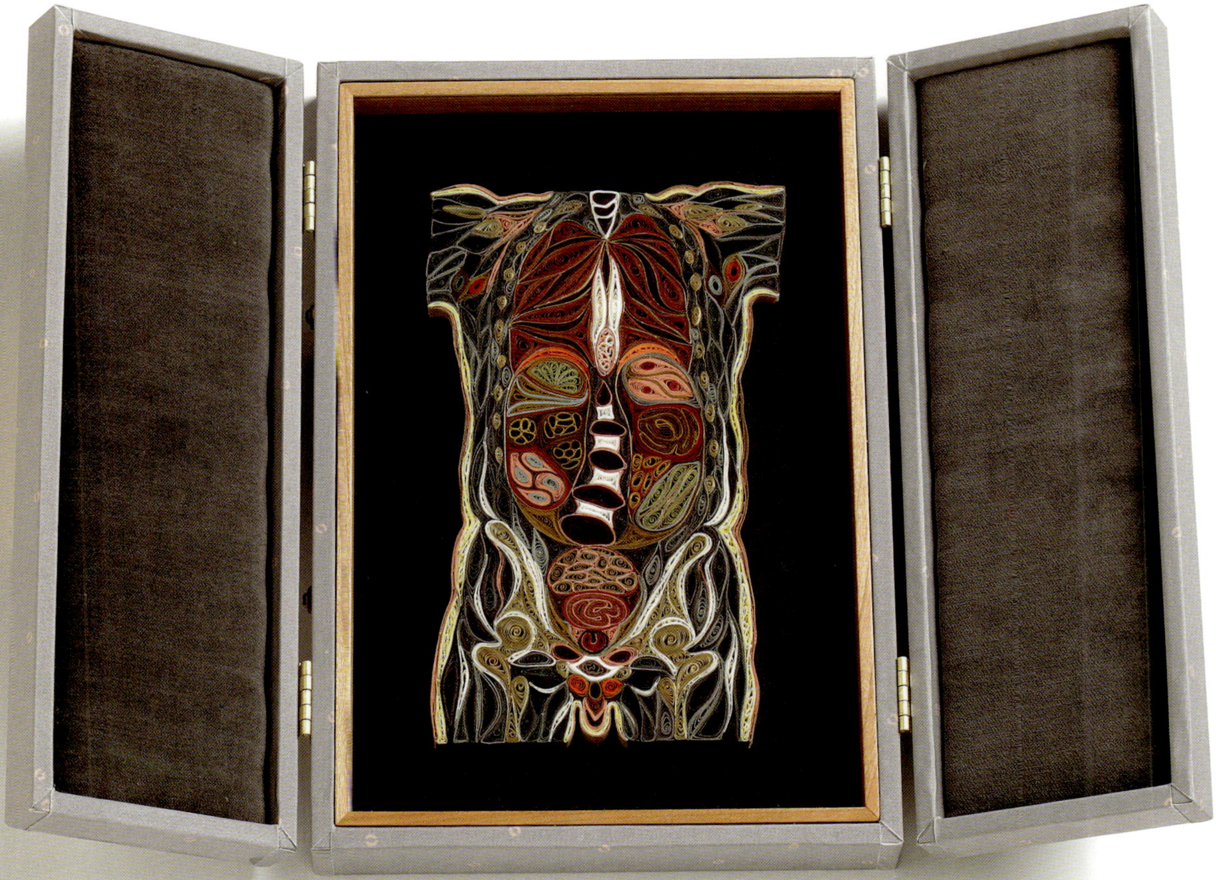

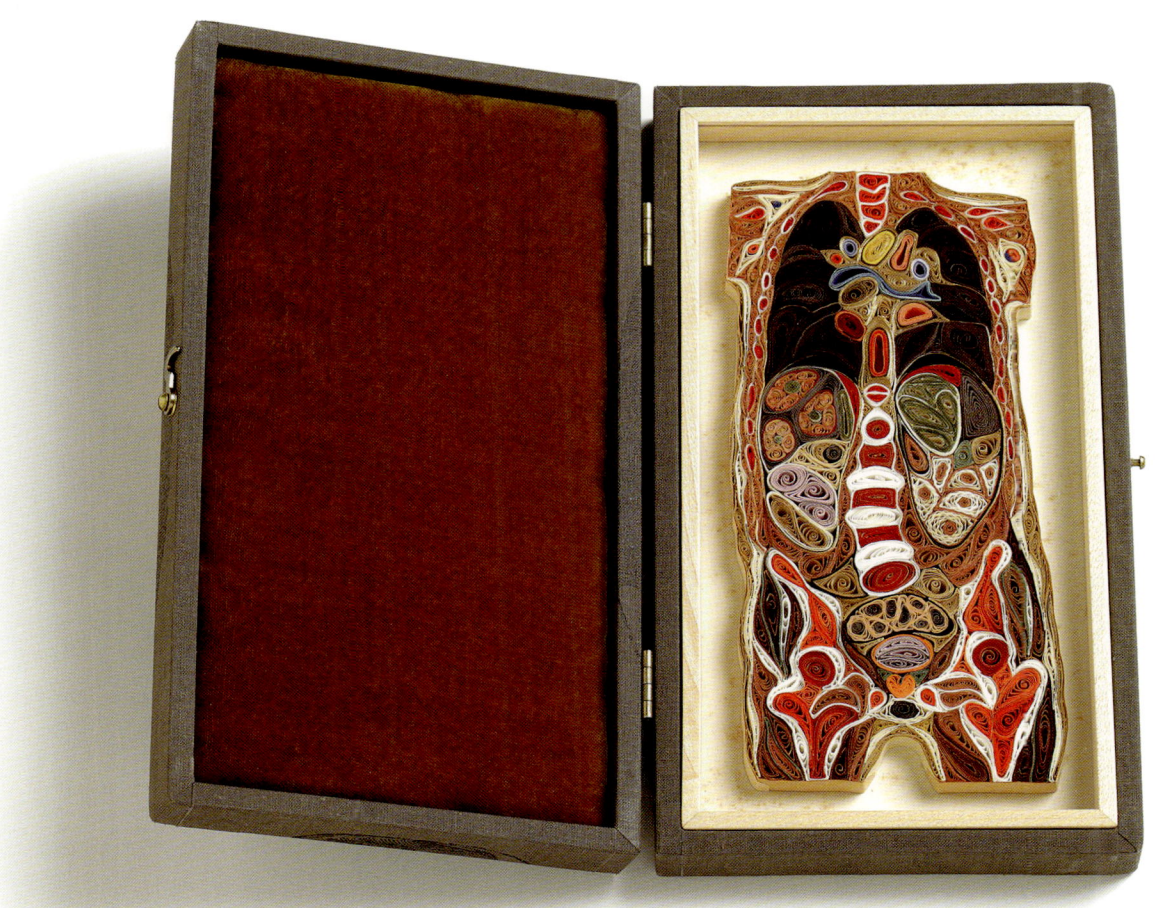

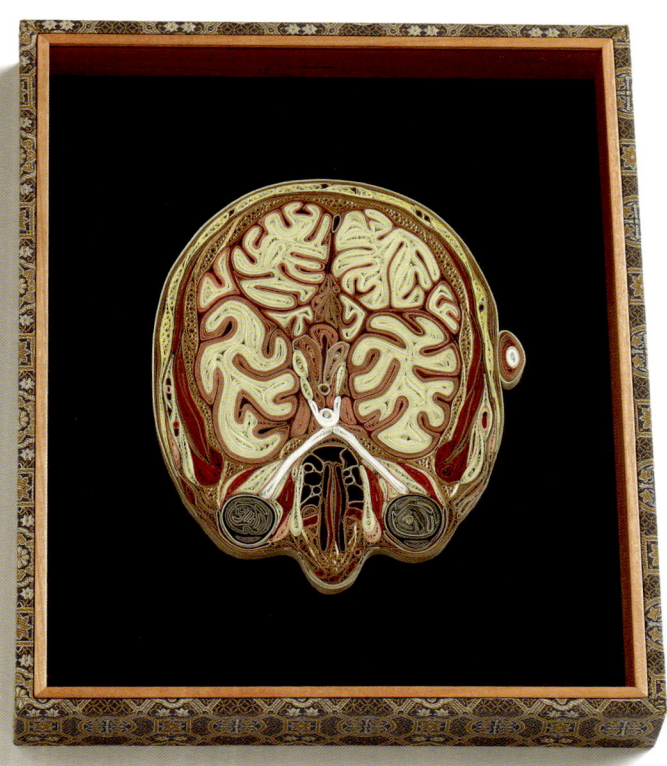
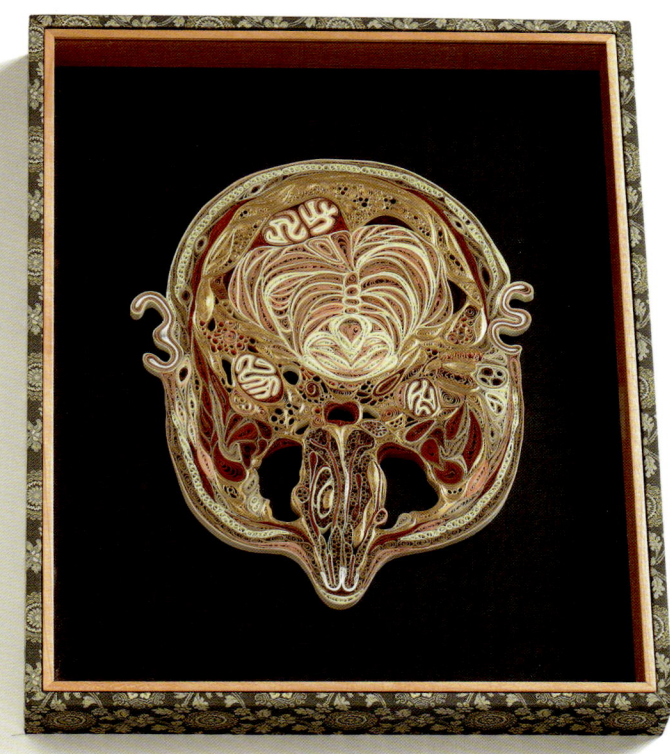
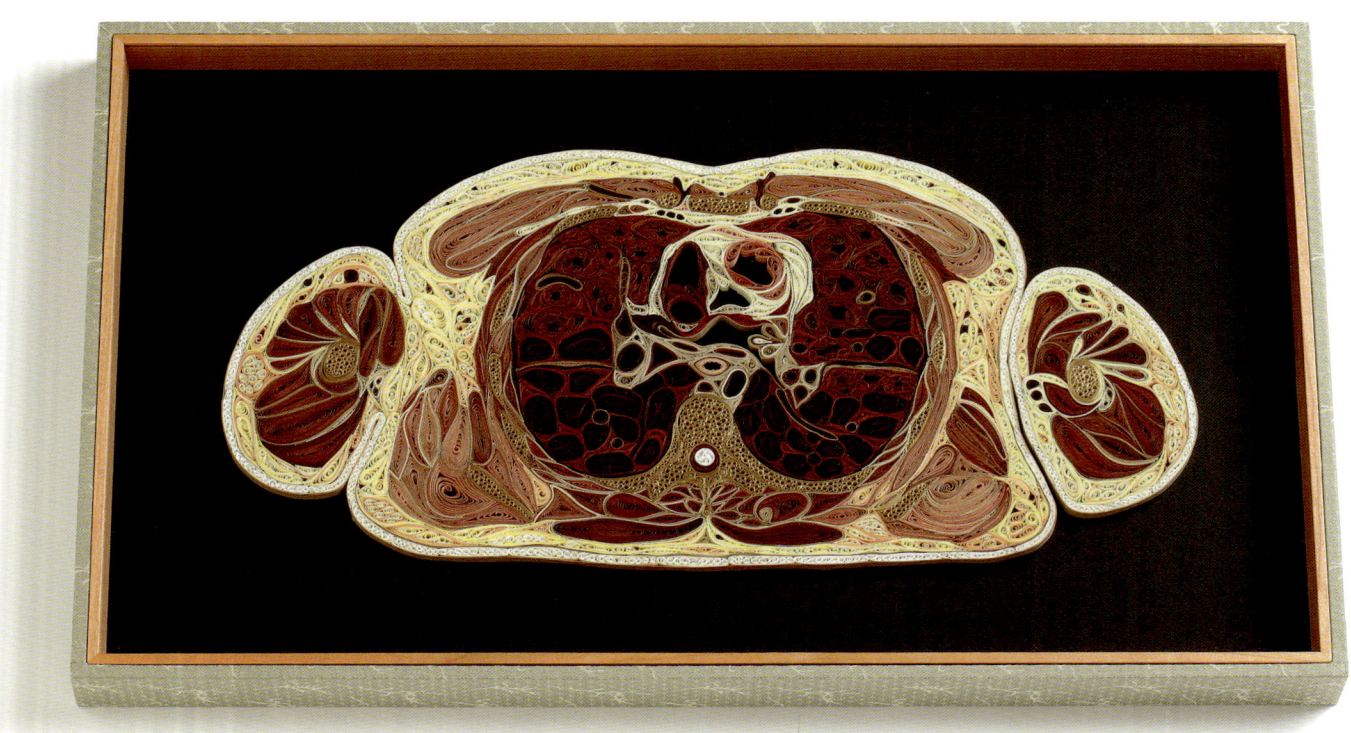

Artist: Lisa Nilsson
Country: USA
Photographer: John Polak

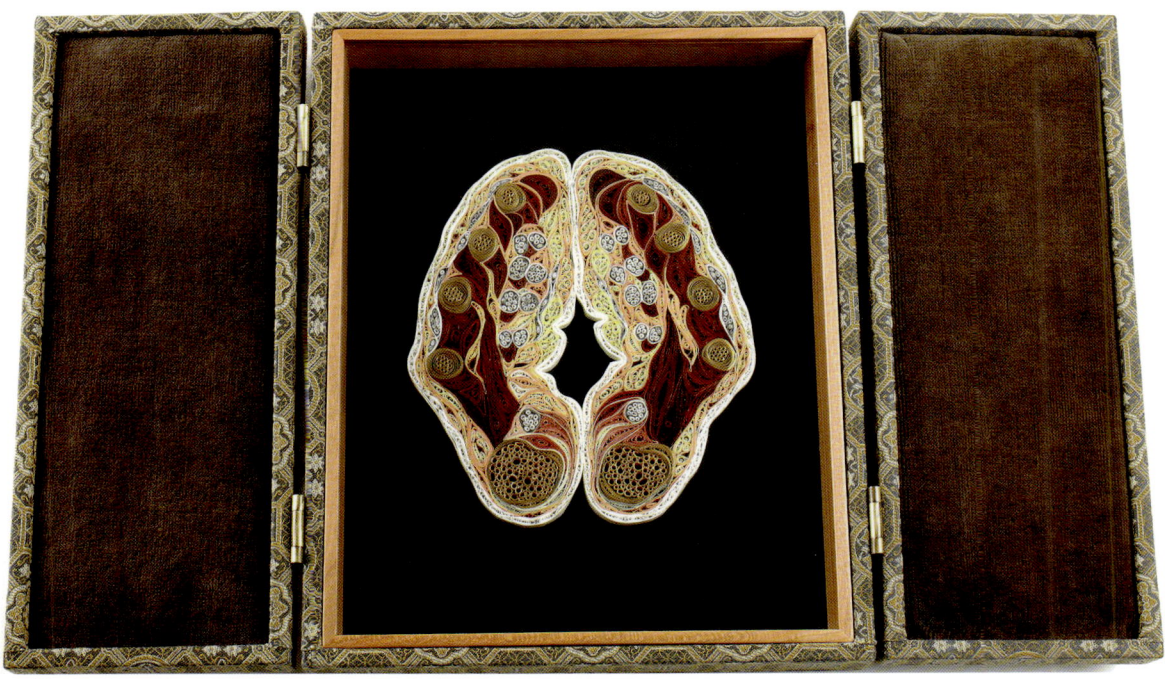

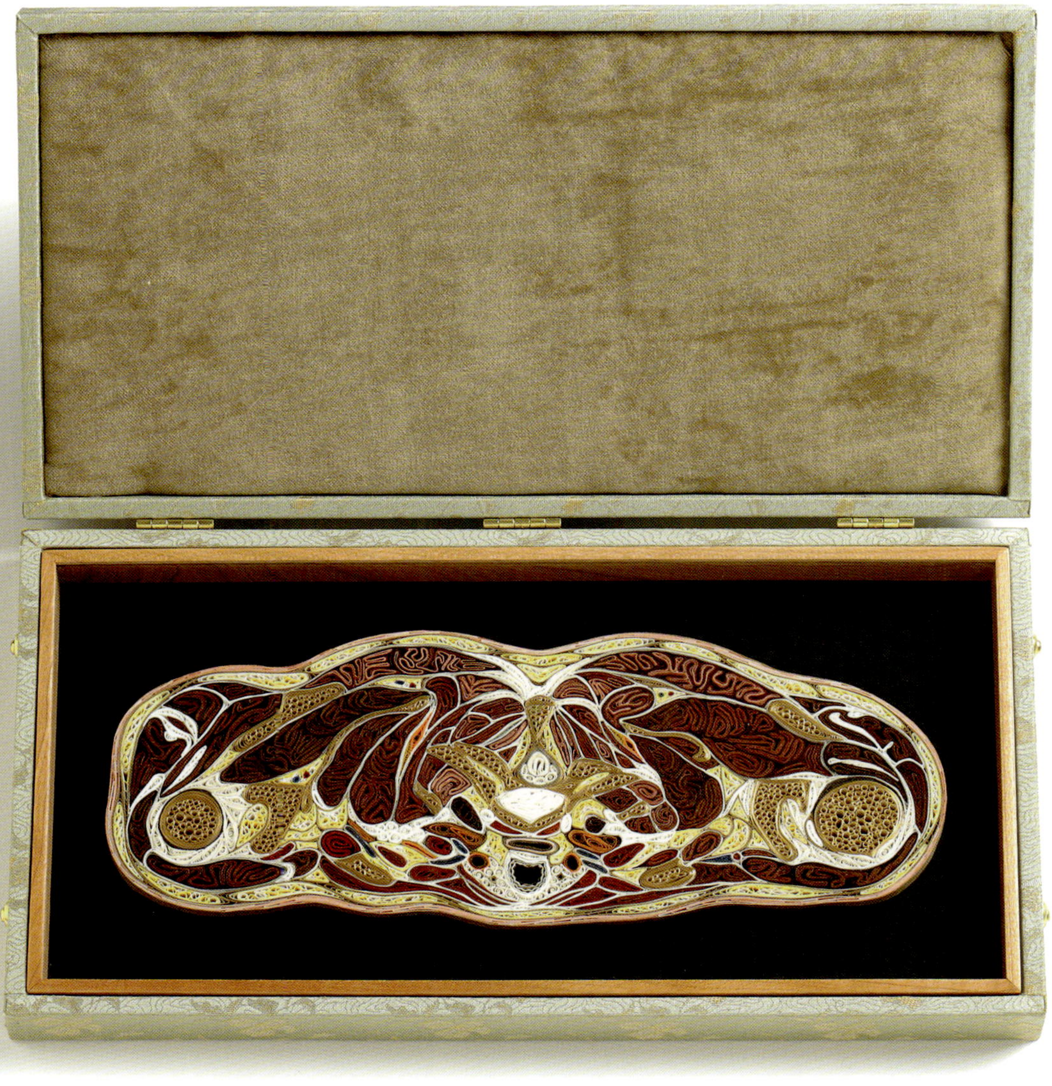

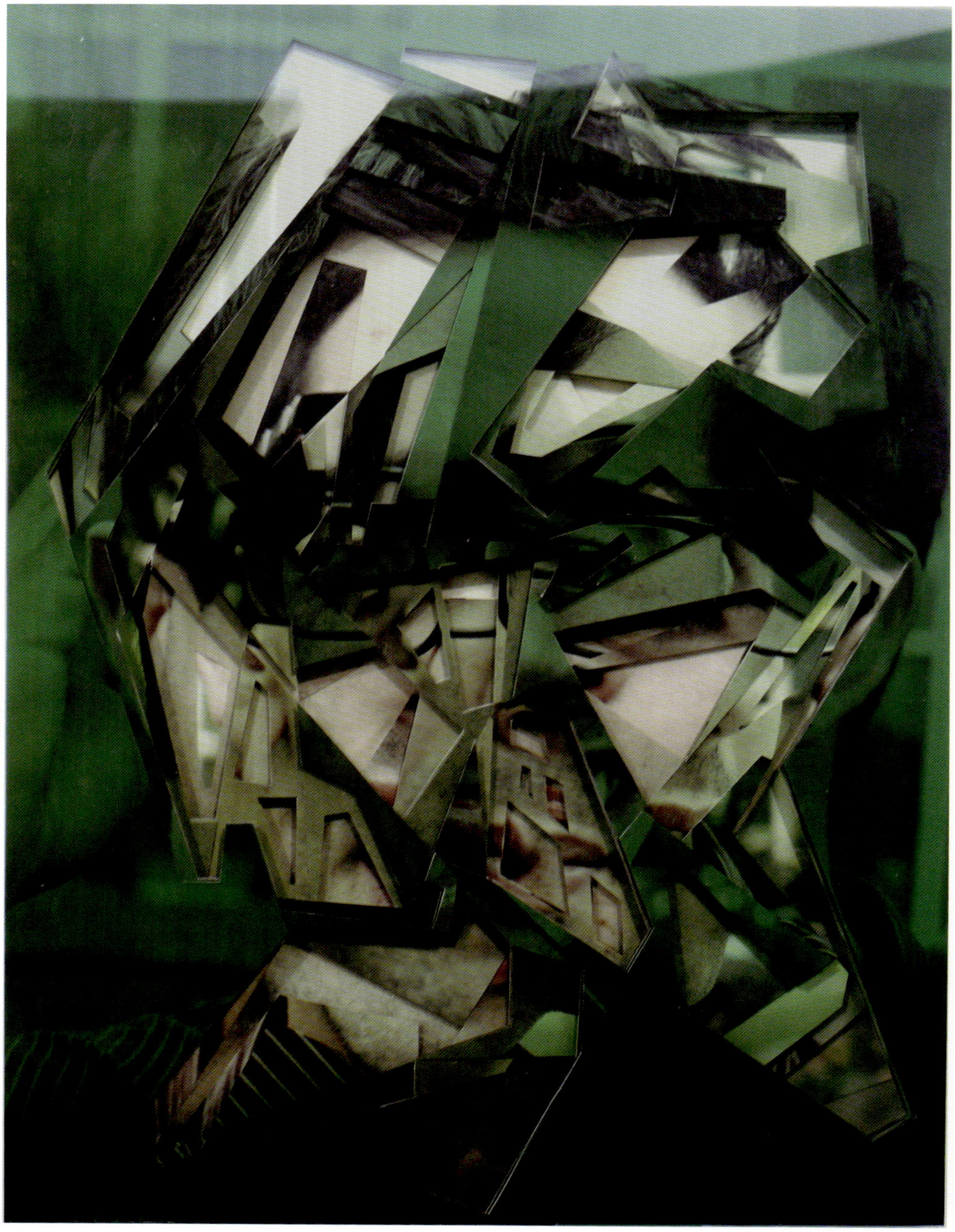

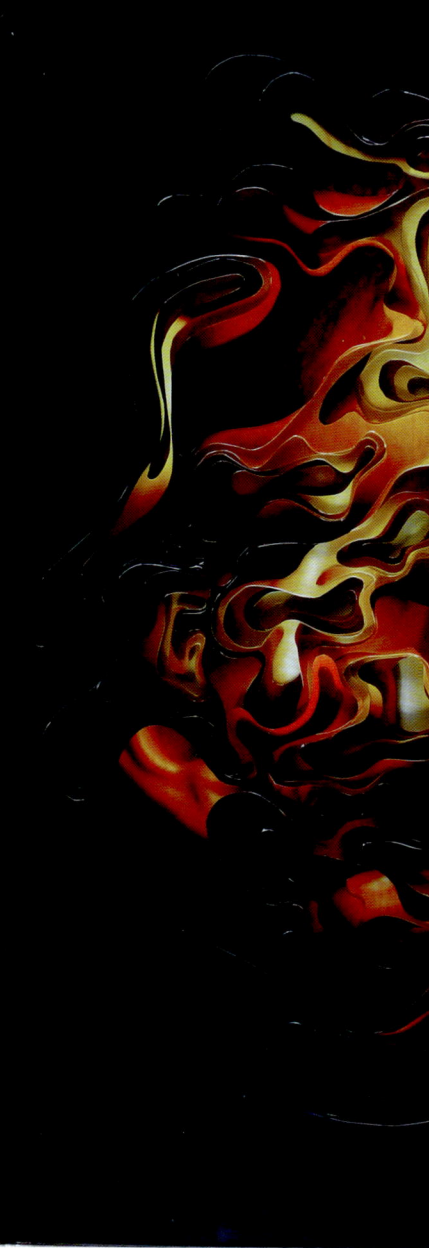

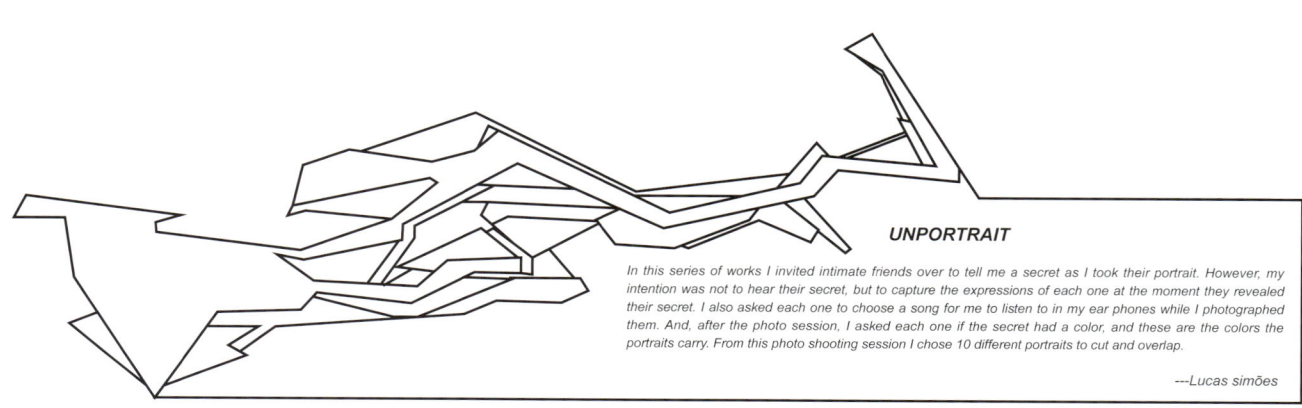

UNPORTRAIT

In this series of works I invited intimate friends over to tell me a secret as I took their portrait. However, my intention was not to hear their secret, but to capture the expressions of each one at the moment they revealed their secret. I also asked each one to choose a song for me to listen to in my ear phones while I photographed them. And, after the photo session, I asked each one if the secret had a color, and these are the colors the portraits carry. From this photo shooting session I chose 10 different portraits to cut and overlap.

---Lucas simões

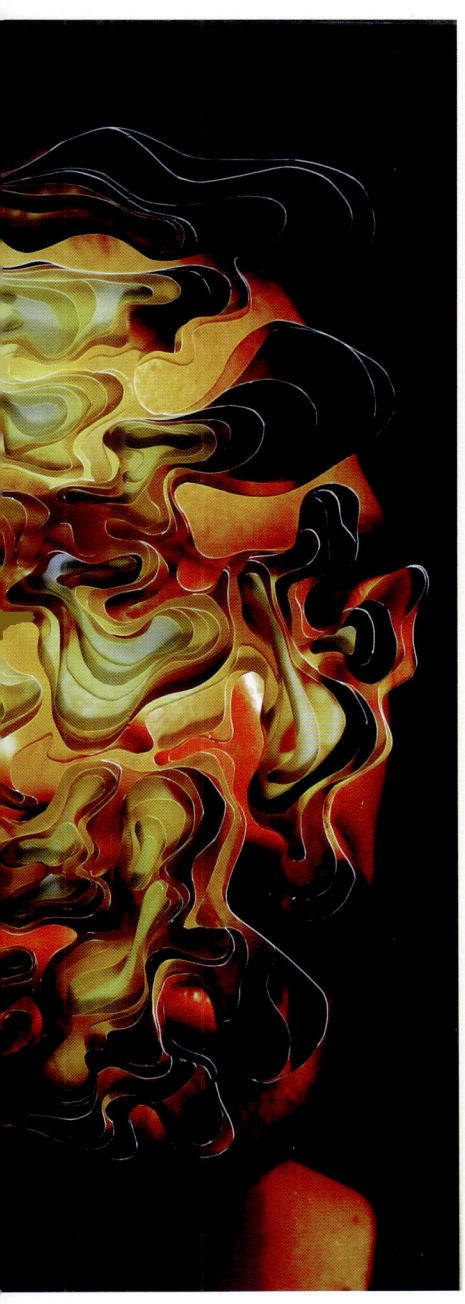

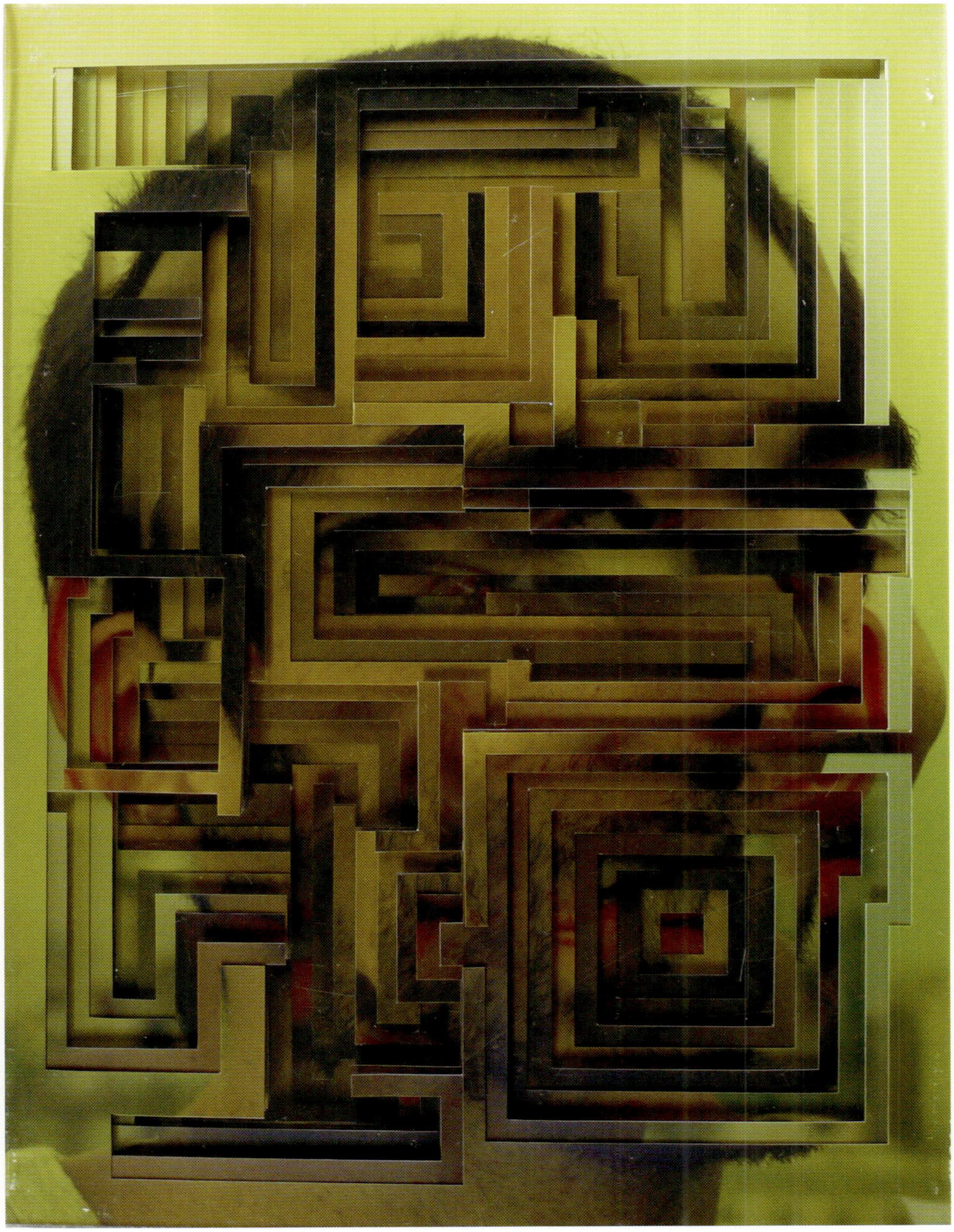

UNPORTRAIT

Artist: Lucas simões
Country: Brasil
Photographer: Lucas simões
Assistant: Ana Lucia Pacheco

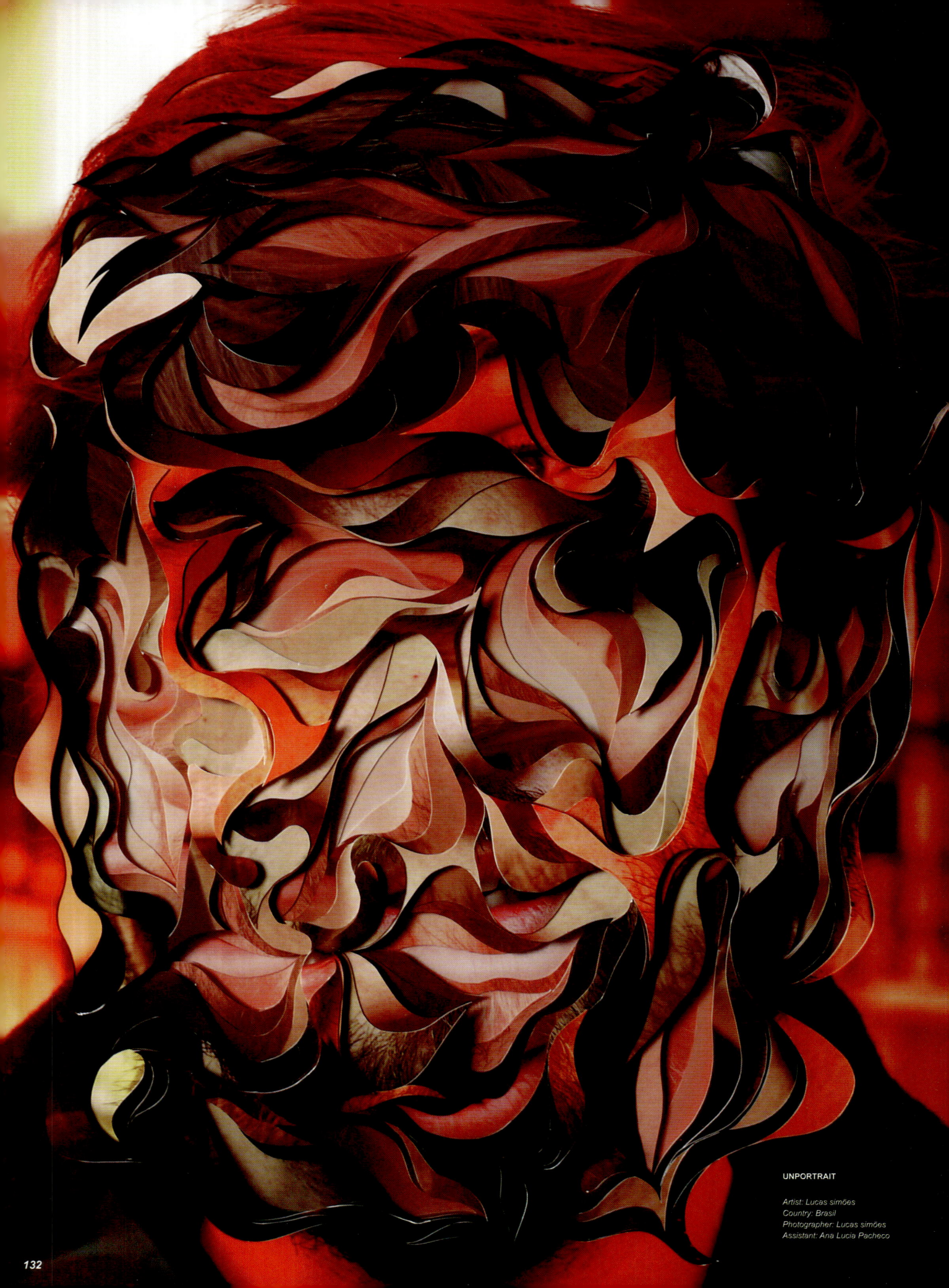

UNPORTRAIT

Artist: Lucas simões
Country: Brasil
Photographer: Lucas simões
Assistant: Ana Lucia Pacheco

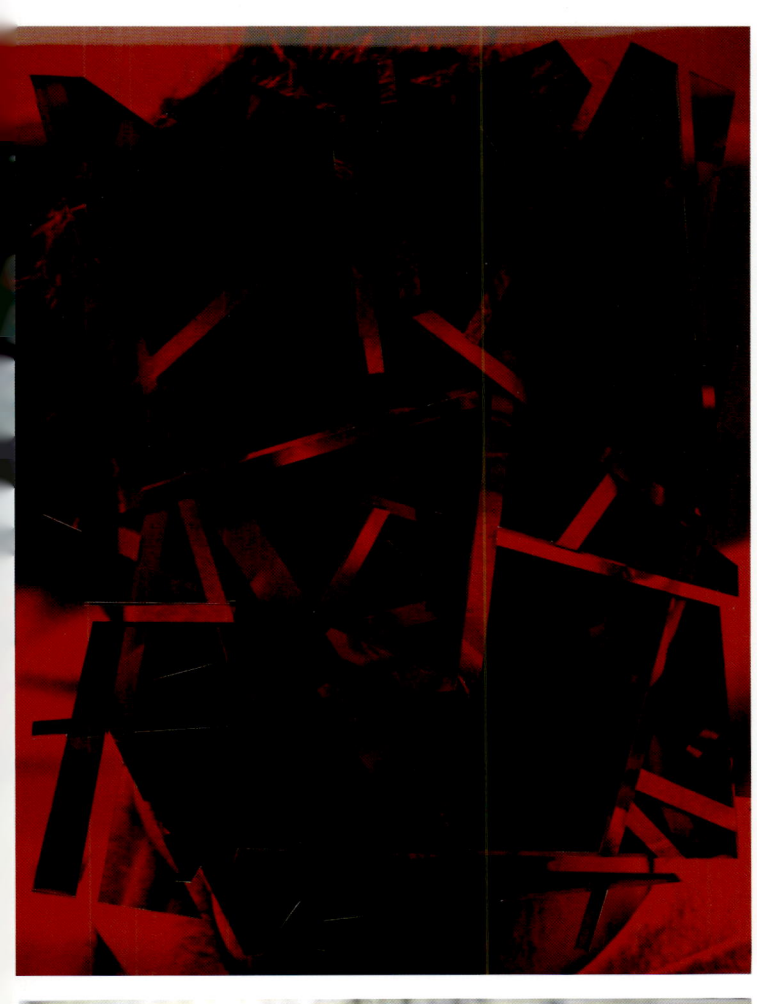
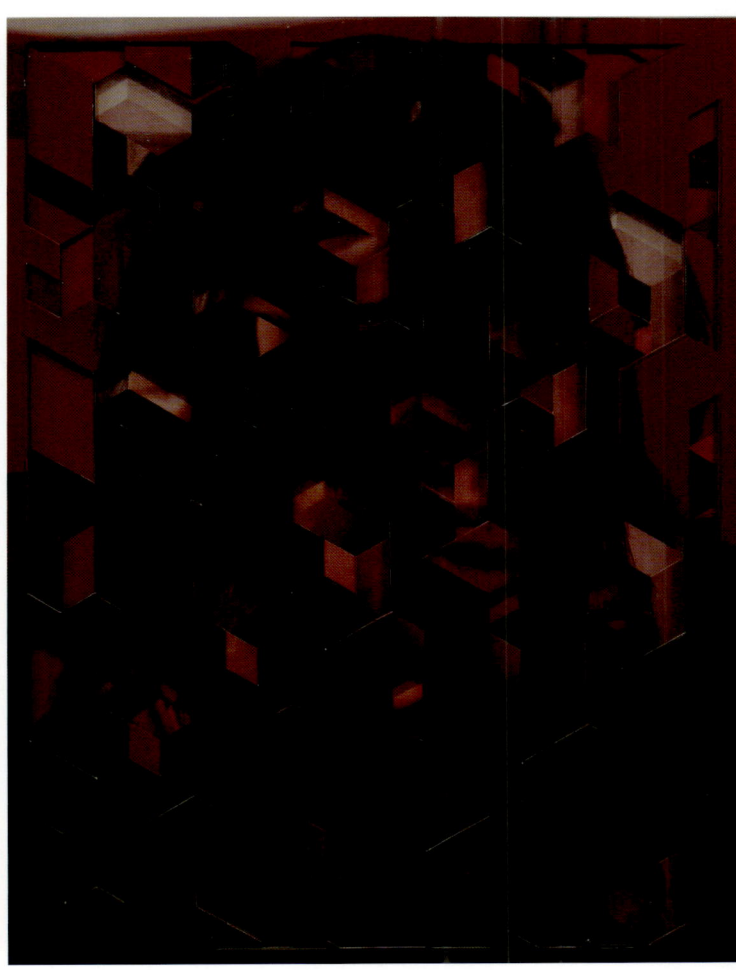
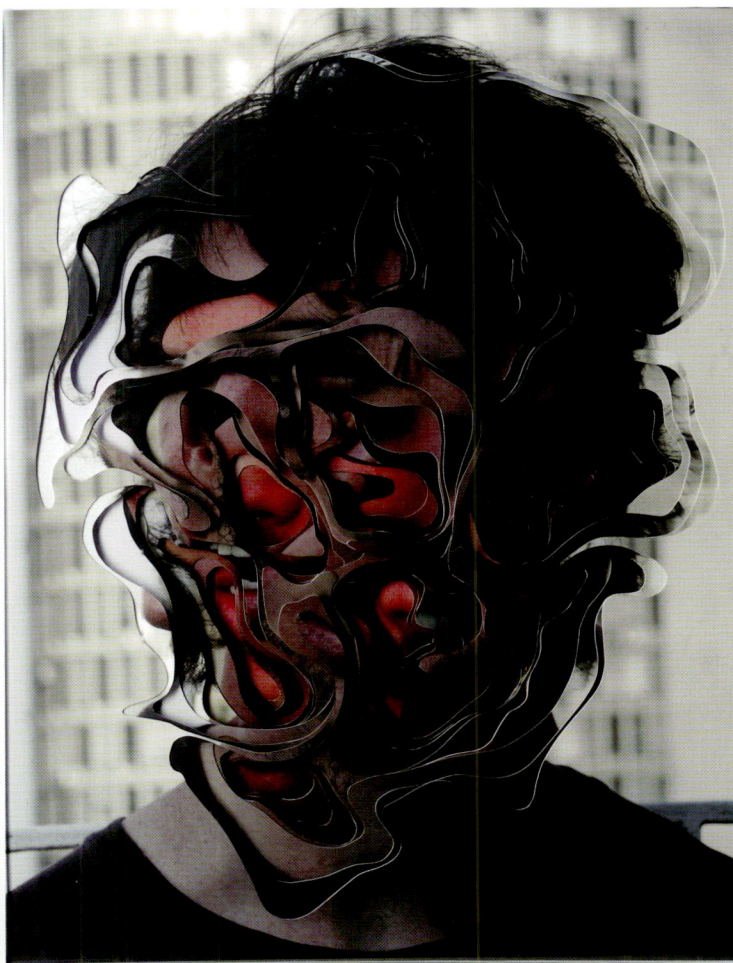
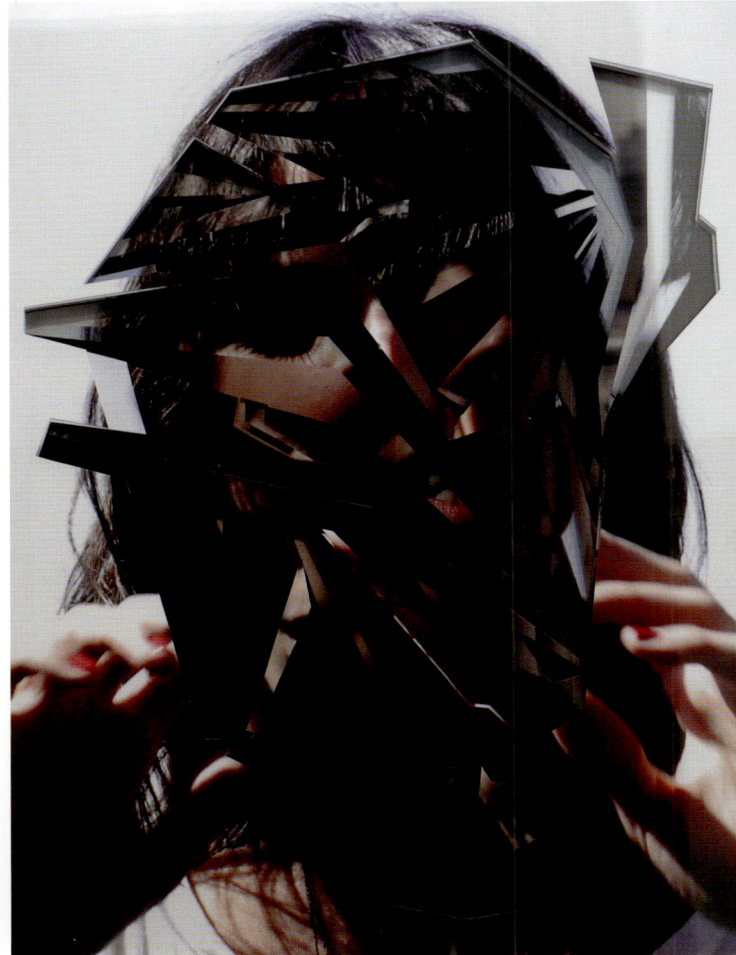

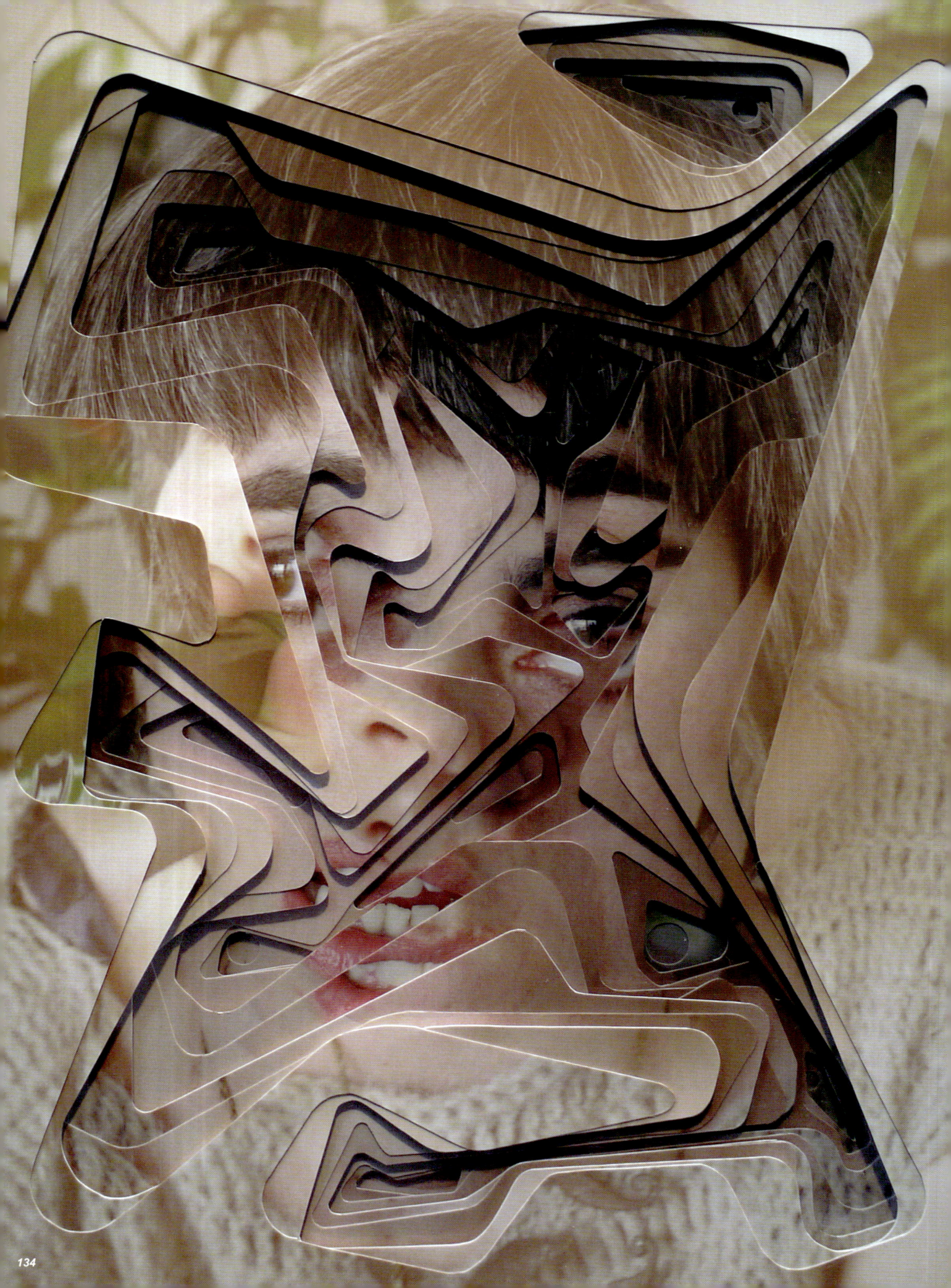

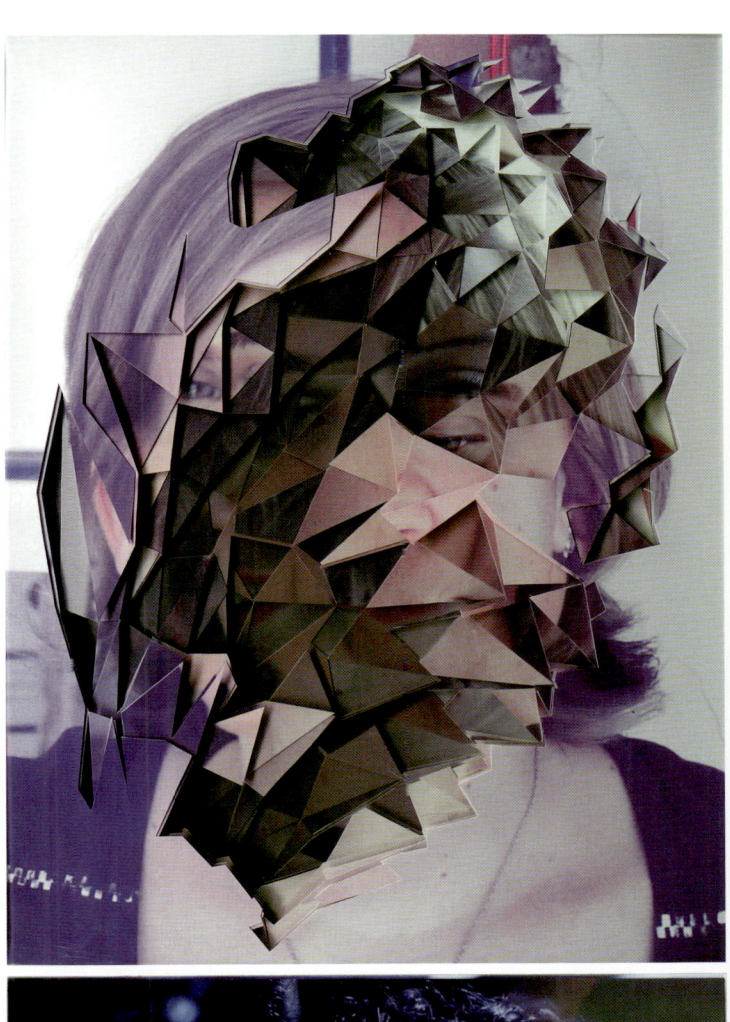

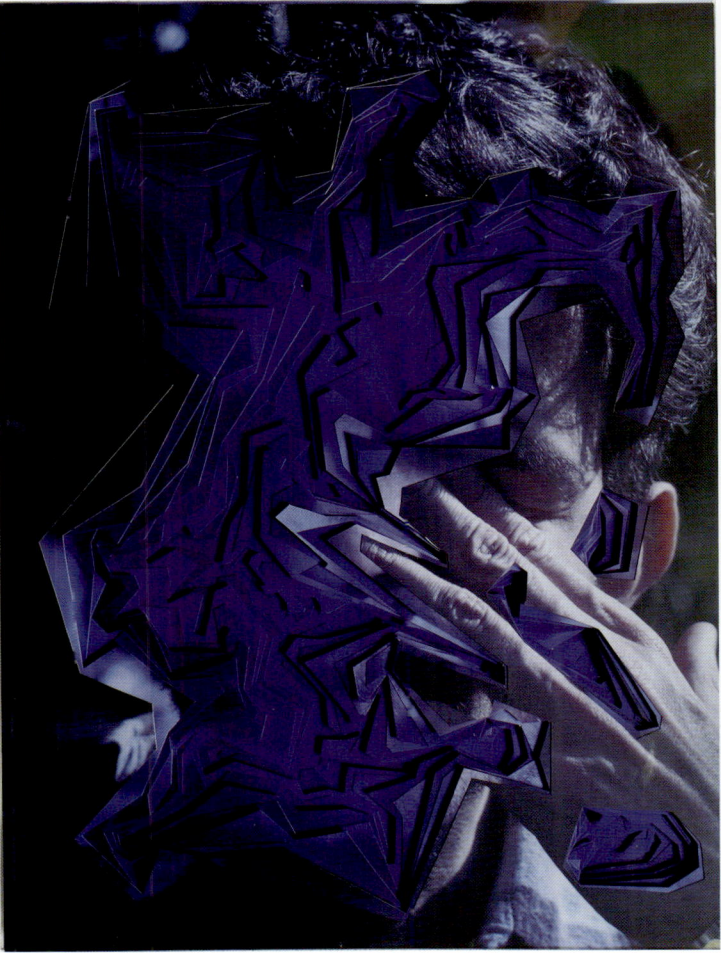

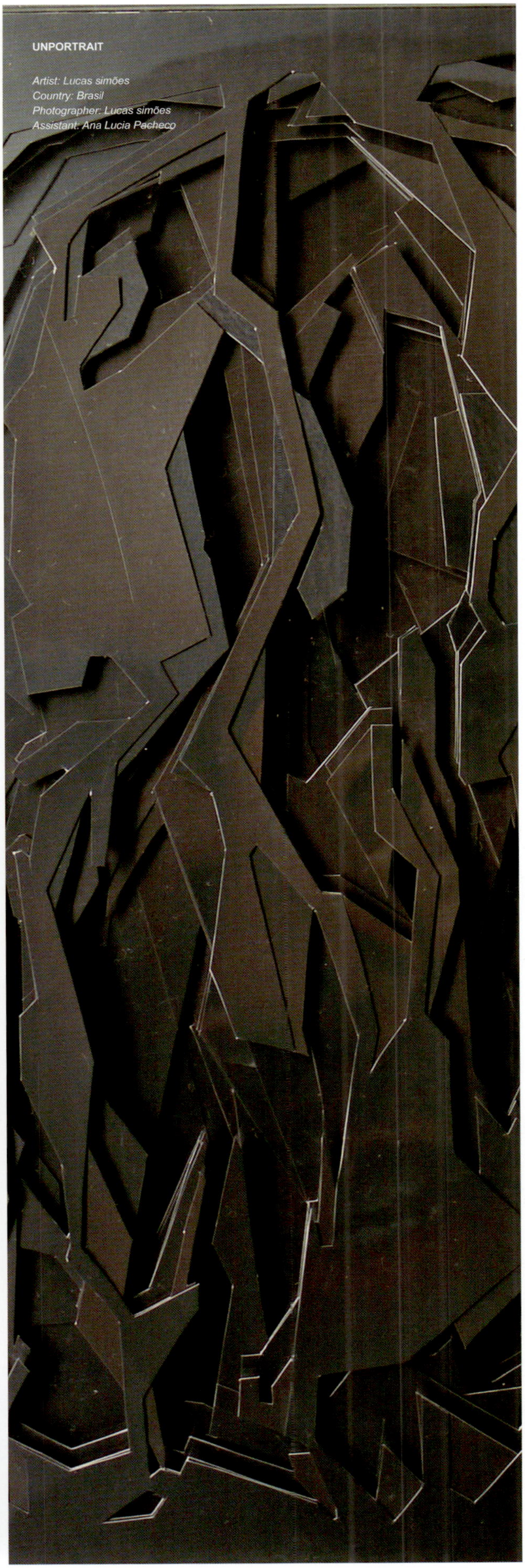

UNPORTRAIT

Artist: Lucas simões
Country: Brasil
Photographer: Lucas simões
Assistant: Ana Lucia Pacheco

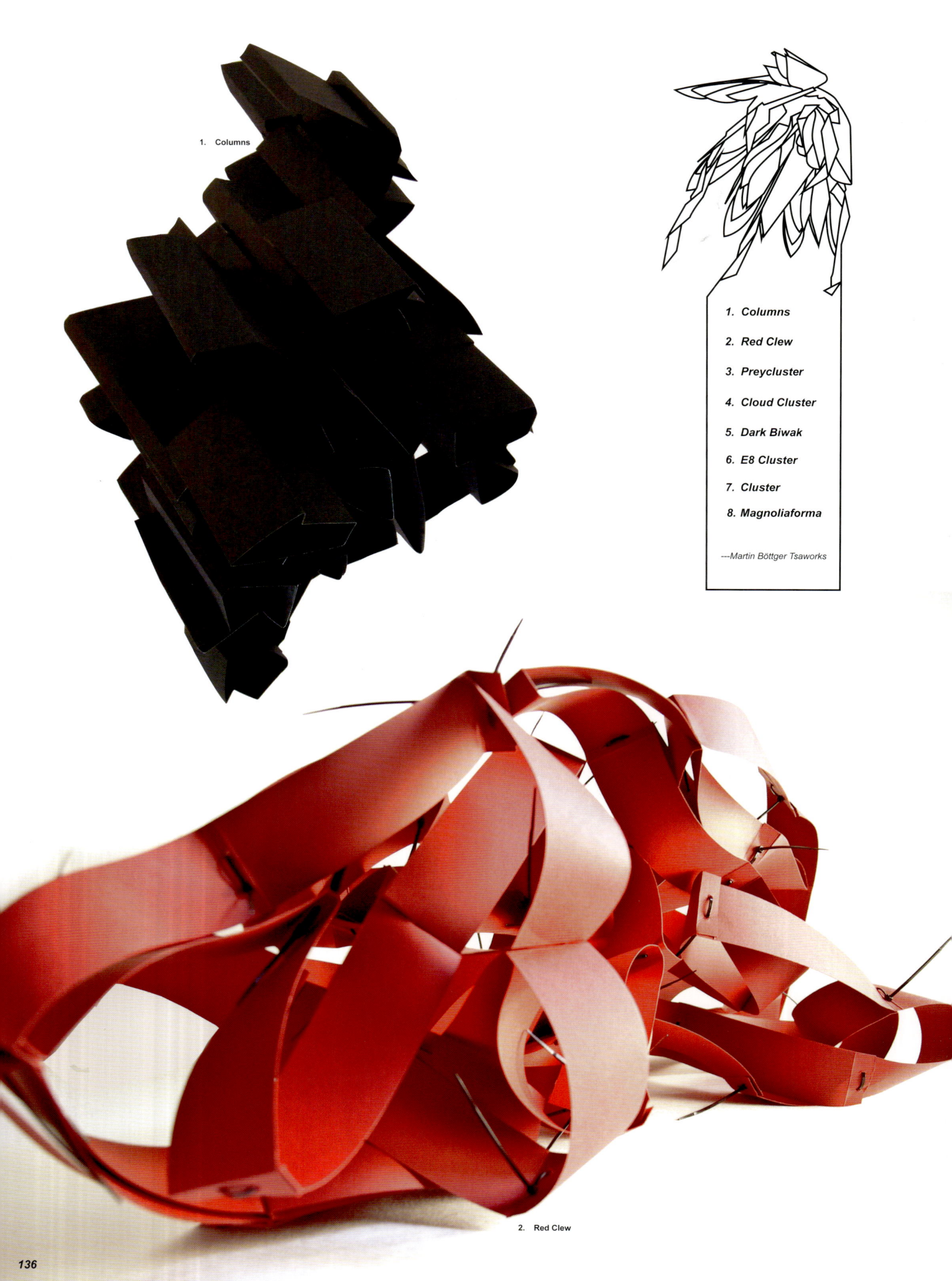

1. Columns
2. Red Clew
3. Preycluster
4. Cloud Cluster
5. Dark Biwak
6. E8 Cluster
7. Cluster
8. Magnoliaforma

---Martin Böttger Tsaworks

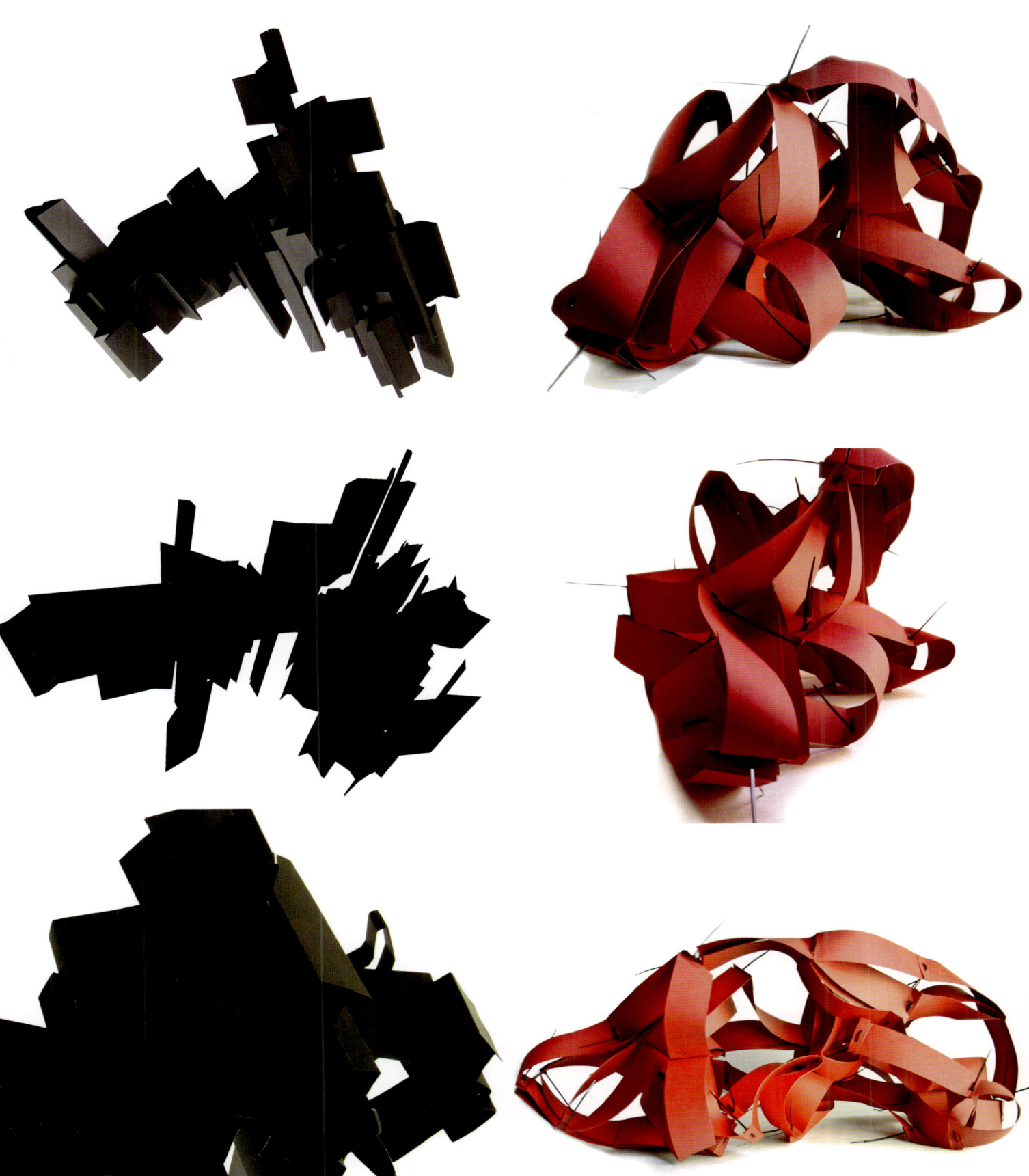

1. Columns

Columns is an exploration of stones in ireland. Size: 90x 60x 90 cm / Material: Cardboard

Artist: Martin Böttger TSAWORKS
Country: Germany
Photographer: Martin Böttger

2. Red Clew

Red Clew is an soft tranformable shape made with paper and cable clips. Size: 70x30x30 cm

Artist: Martin Böttger TSAWORKS
Country: Germany
Photographer: Martin Böttger

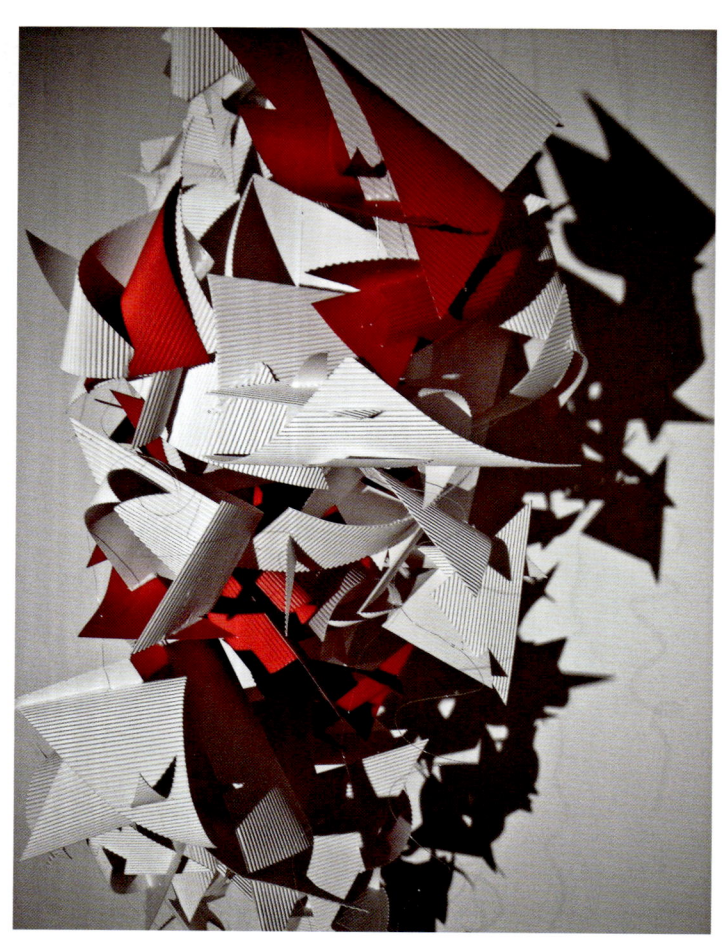
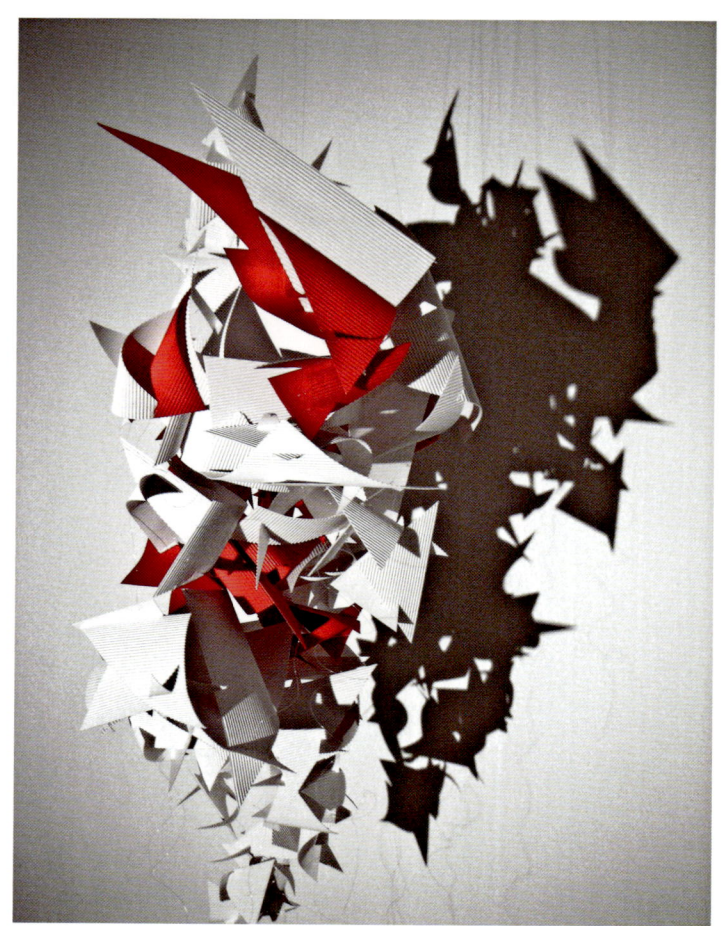

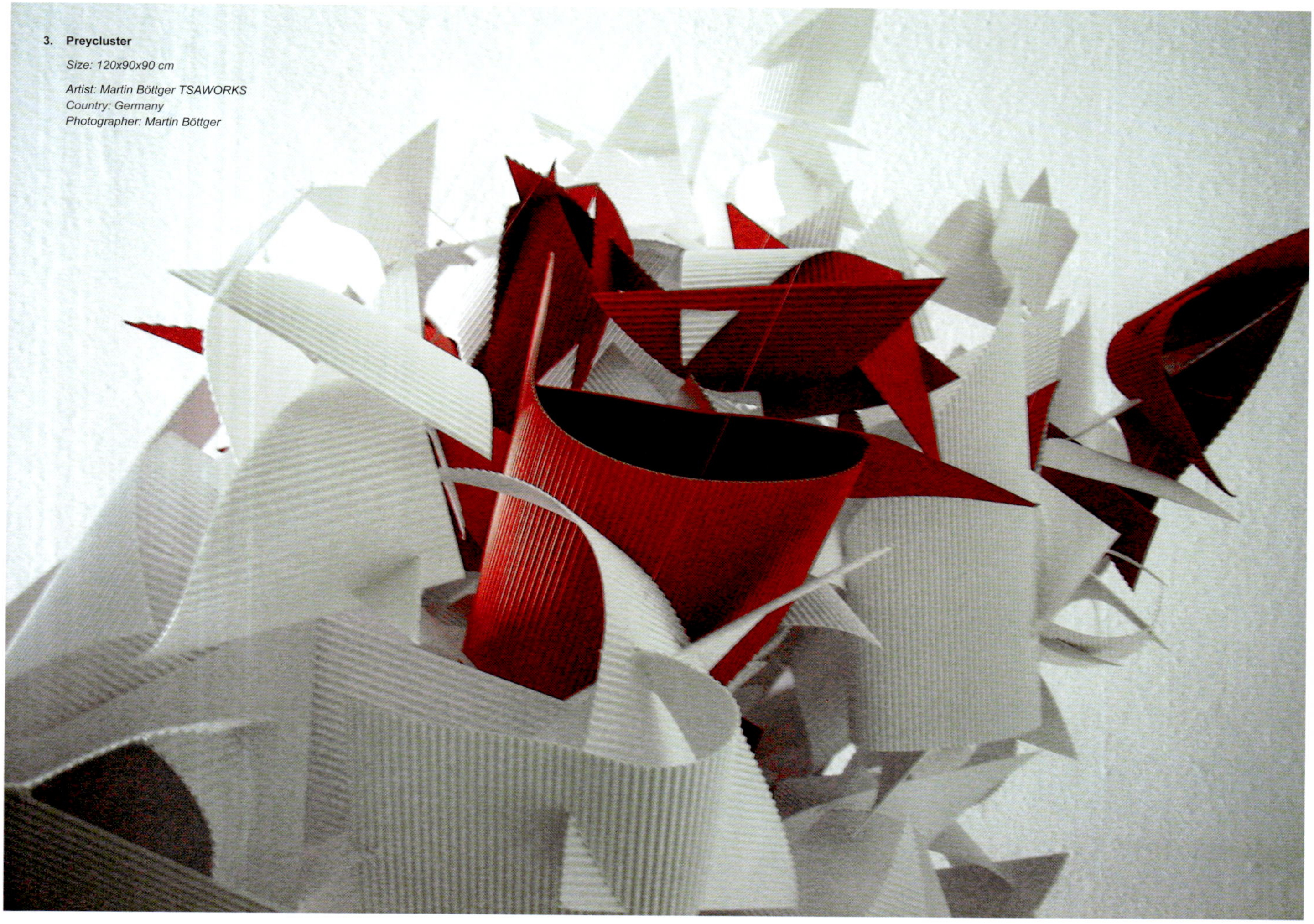

3. **Preycluster**
Size: 120x90x90 cm

Artist: Martin Böttger TSAWORKS
Country: Germany
Photographer: Martin Böttger

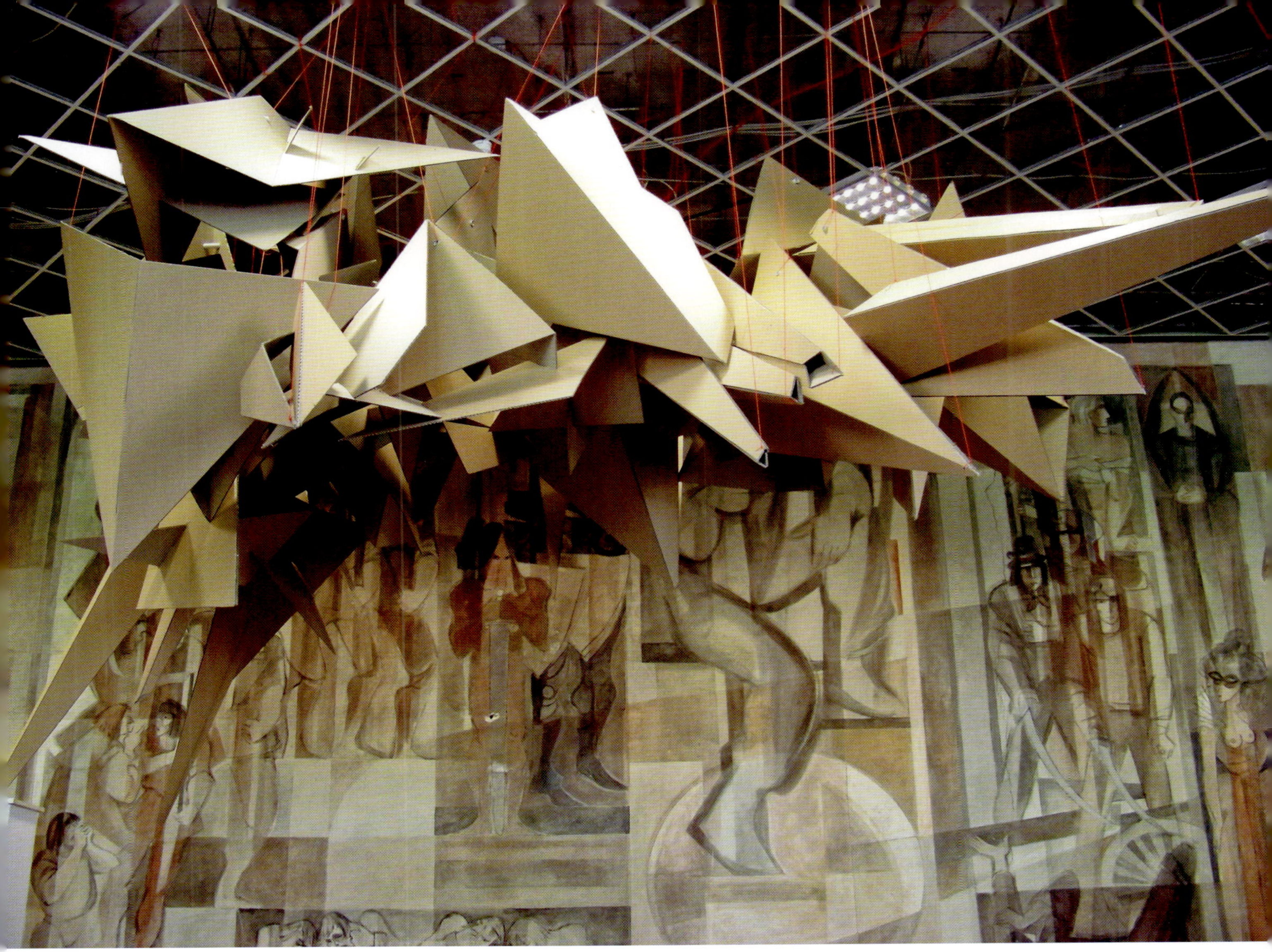

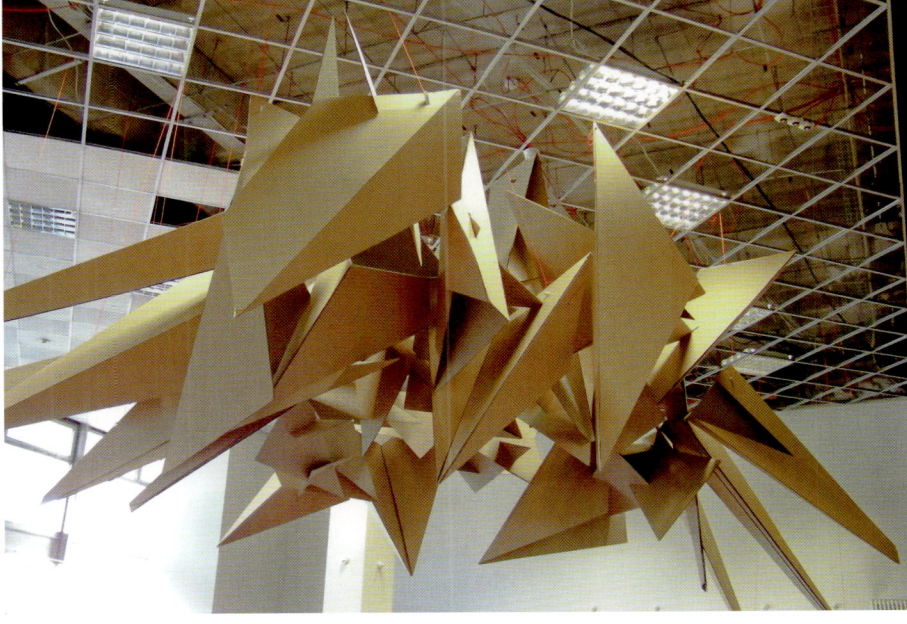
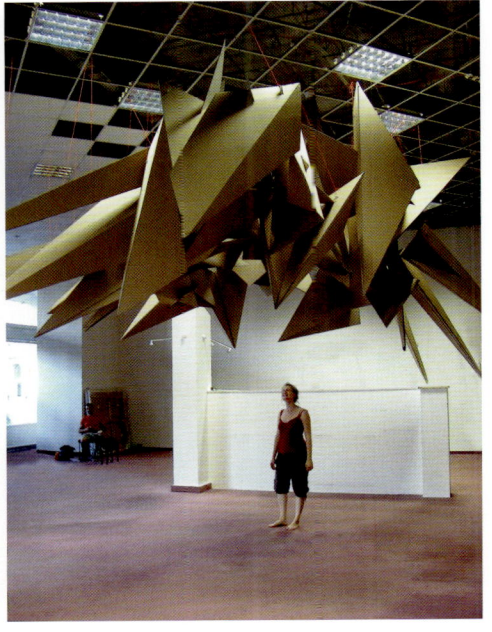

4. Cloud Cluster

The structure is based on triangle-shapes in different variations, the construction was shown at the Localize Festival in Potsdam in the entrance hall of the "Stadt- und Landesbibliothek".
Size : 6 x 3 x 3 meters / Material : Cardboard

Artist: Martin Böttger TSAWORKS
Country: Germany
Photographer: Martin Böttger

5. Dark Biwak (Uferhallen Berlin)

*Final Degree work in Visual Communication and New Media at the School of Art and Design Kassel.
I realized the Installation at the Uferstudios Berlin.*

Size: 5 x 12 x 5 meters / Materials: Cardboard / Wood

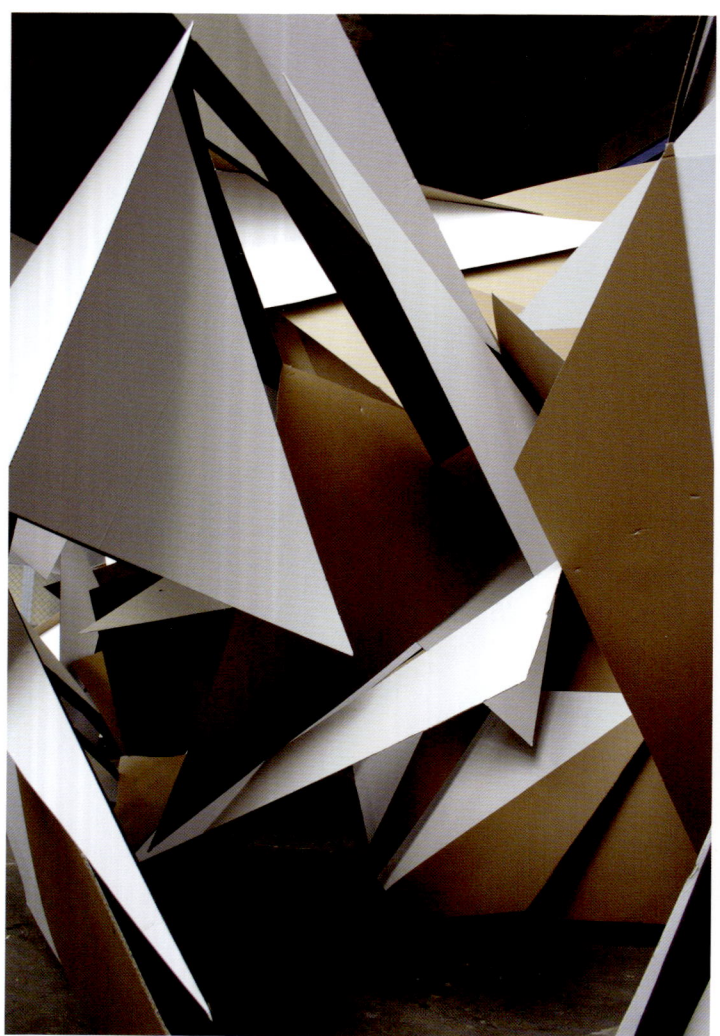
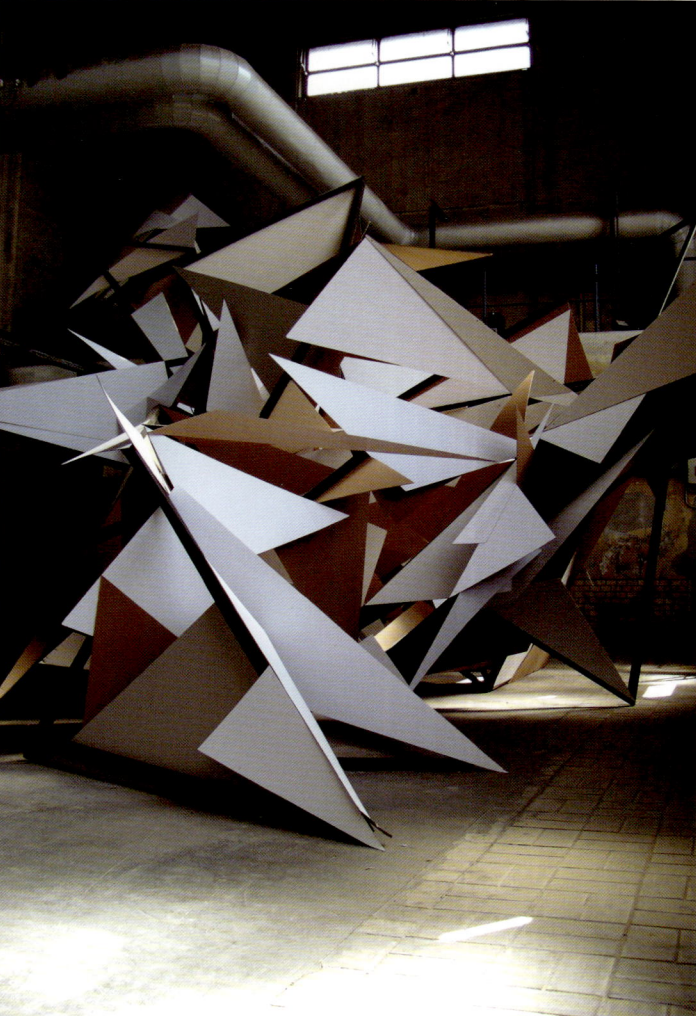

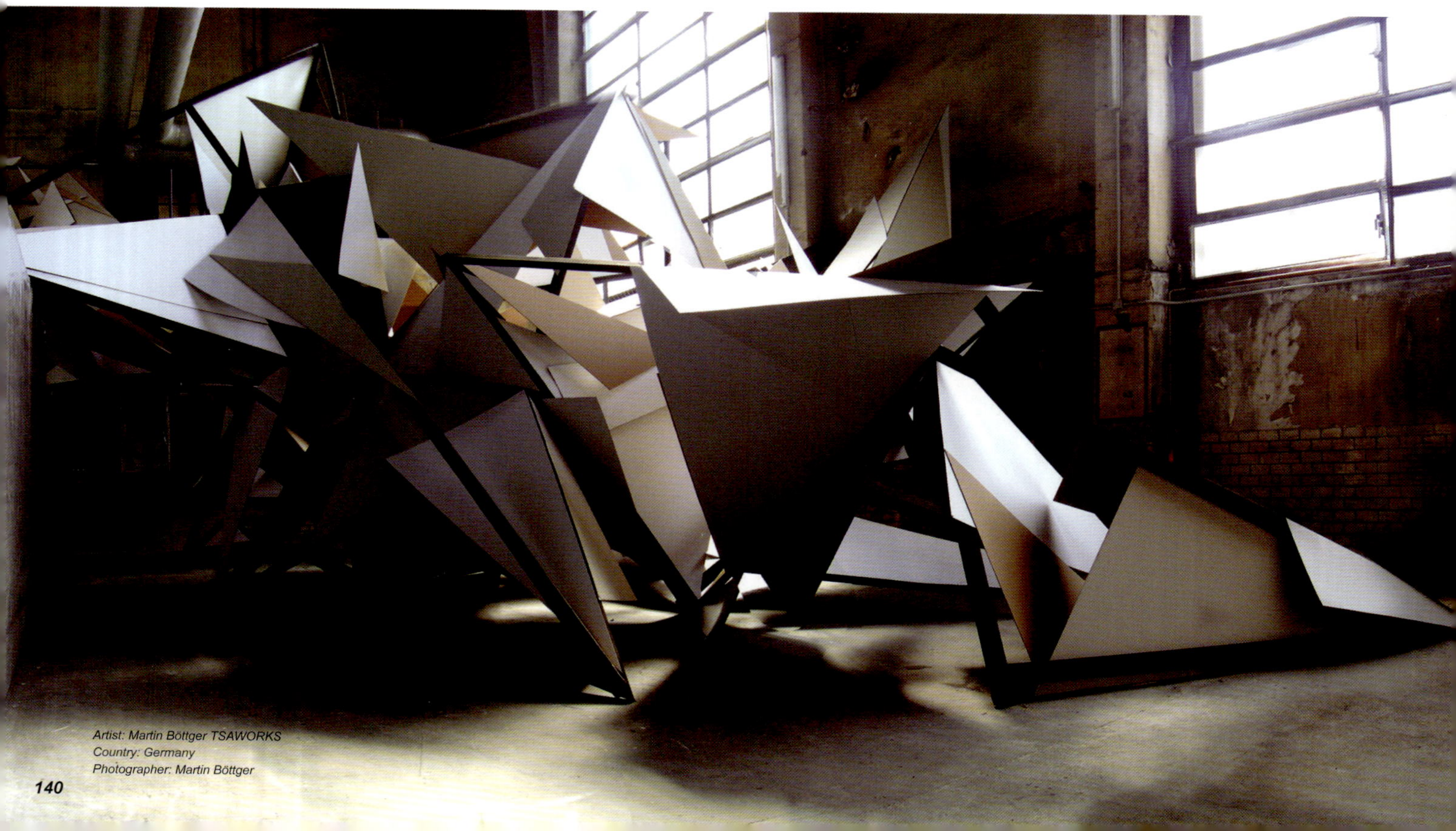

Artist: Martin Böttger TSAWORKS
Country: Germany
Photographer: Martin Böttger

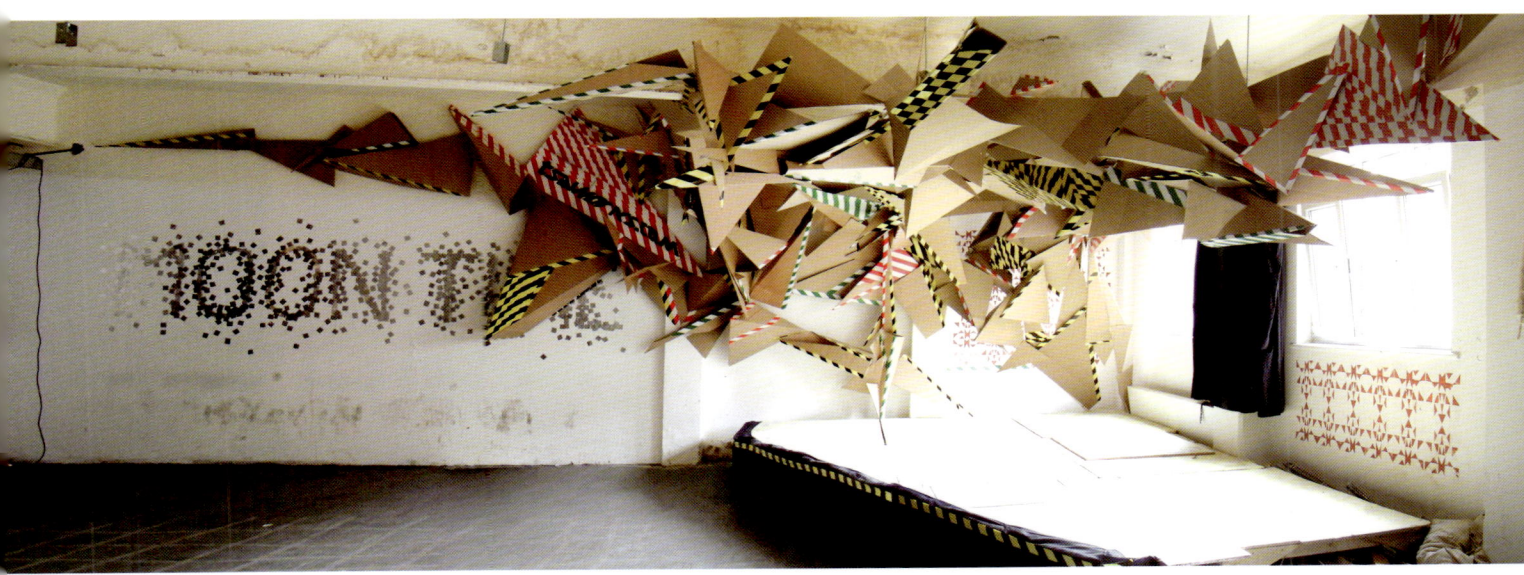

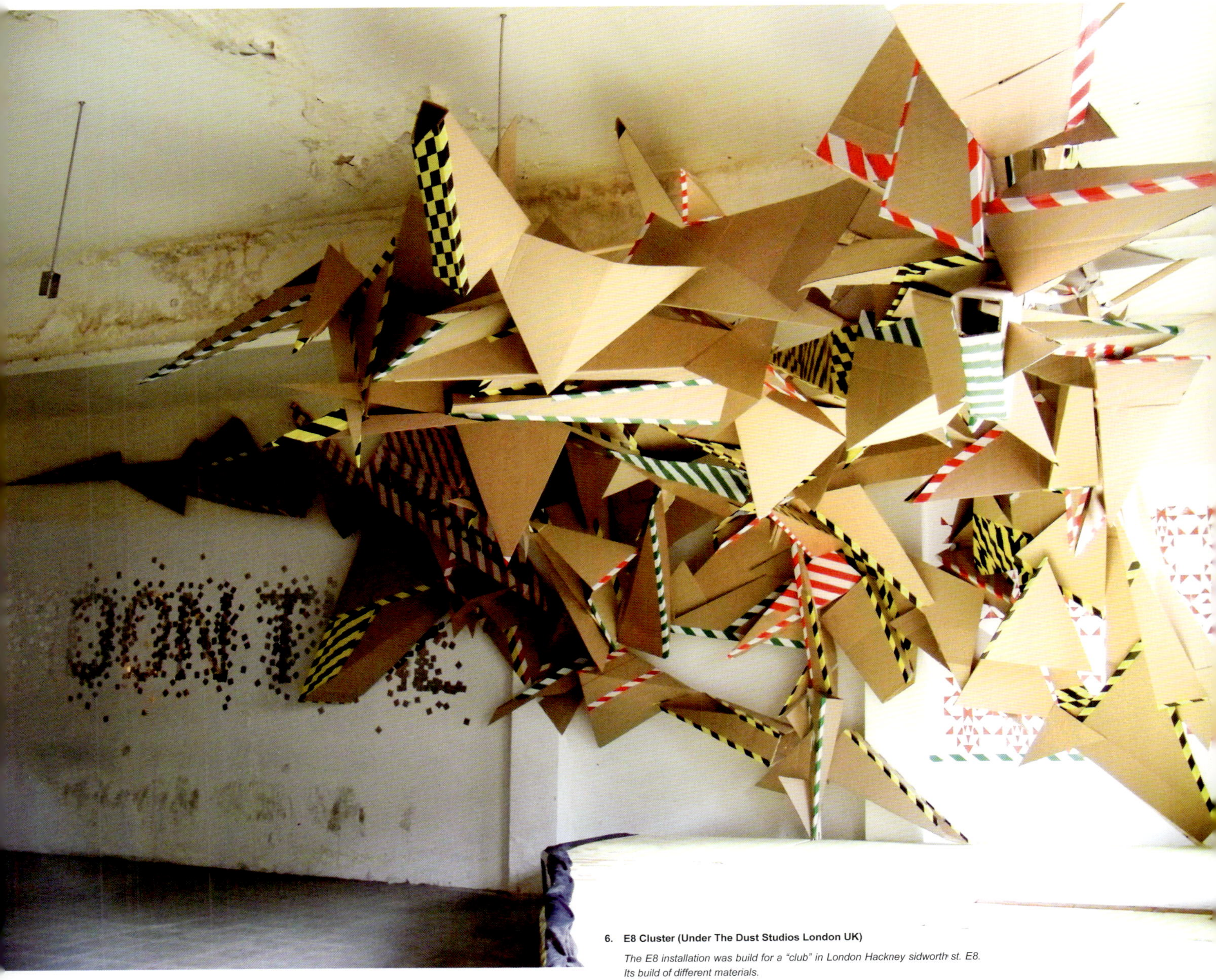

6. E8 Cluster (Under The Dust Studios London UK)

The E8 installation was build for a "club" in London Hackney sidworth st. E8.
Its build of different materials.

Size: 16 x 3 x 4 meters / Materials: Cardboard / Wood Sticks / Tape

Artist: Martin Böttger TSAWORKS
Country: Germany
Photographer: Martin Böttger

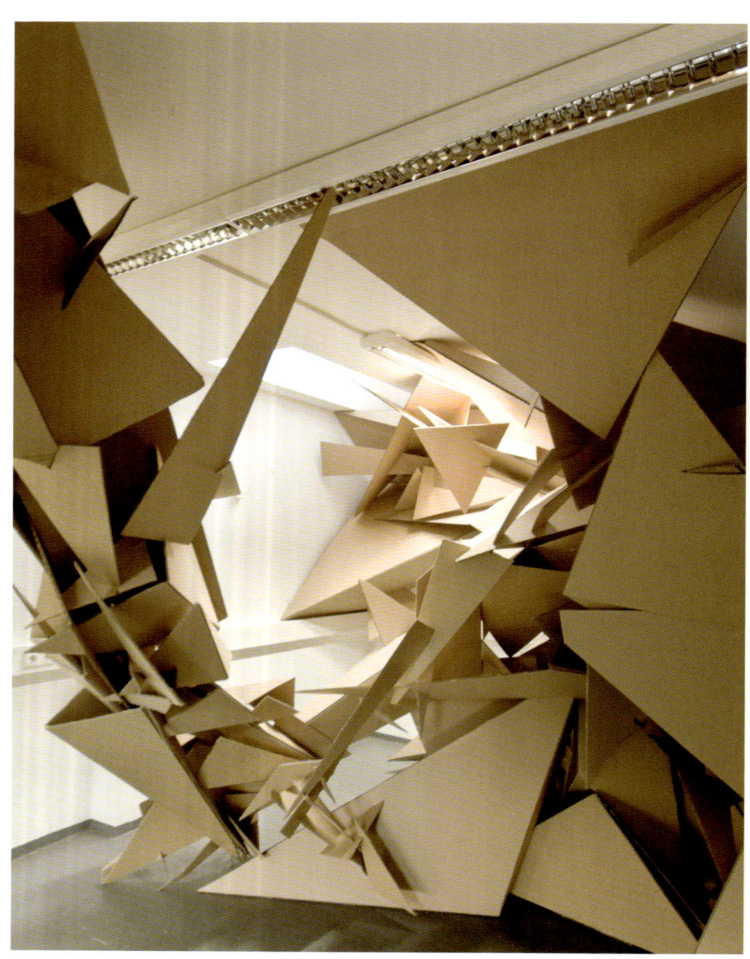
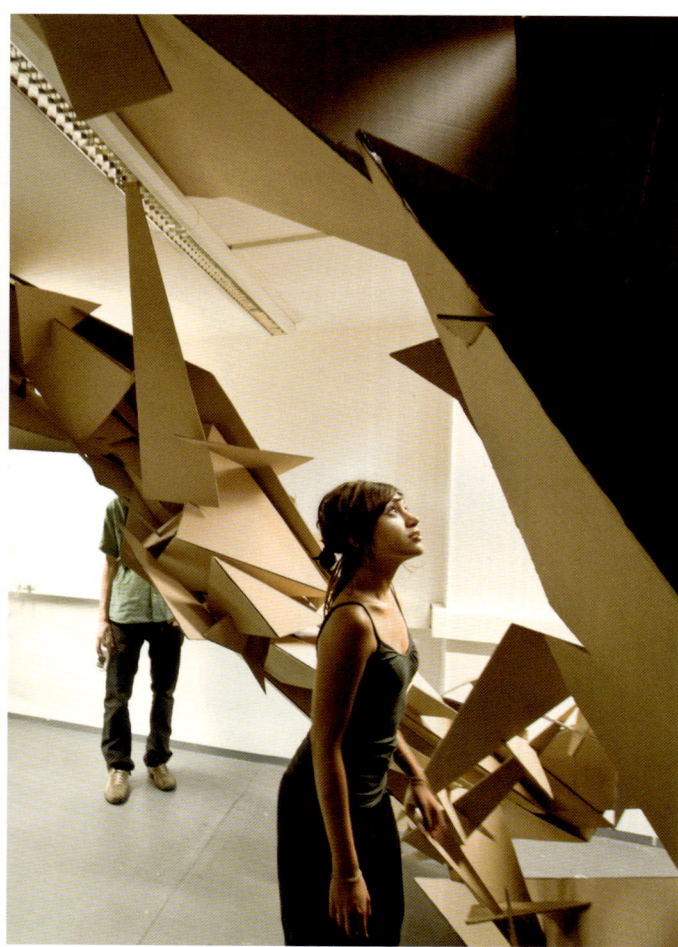

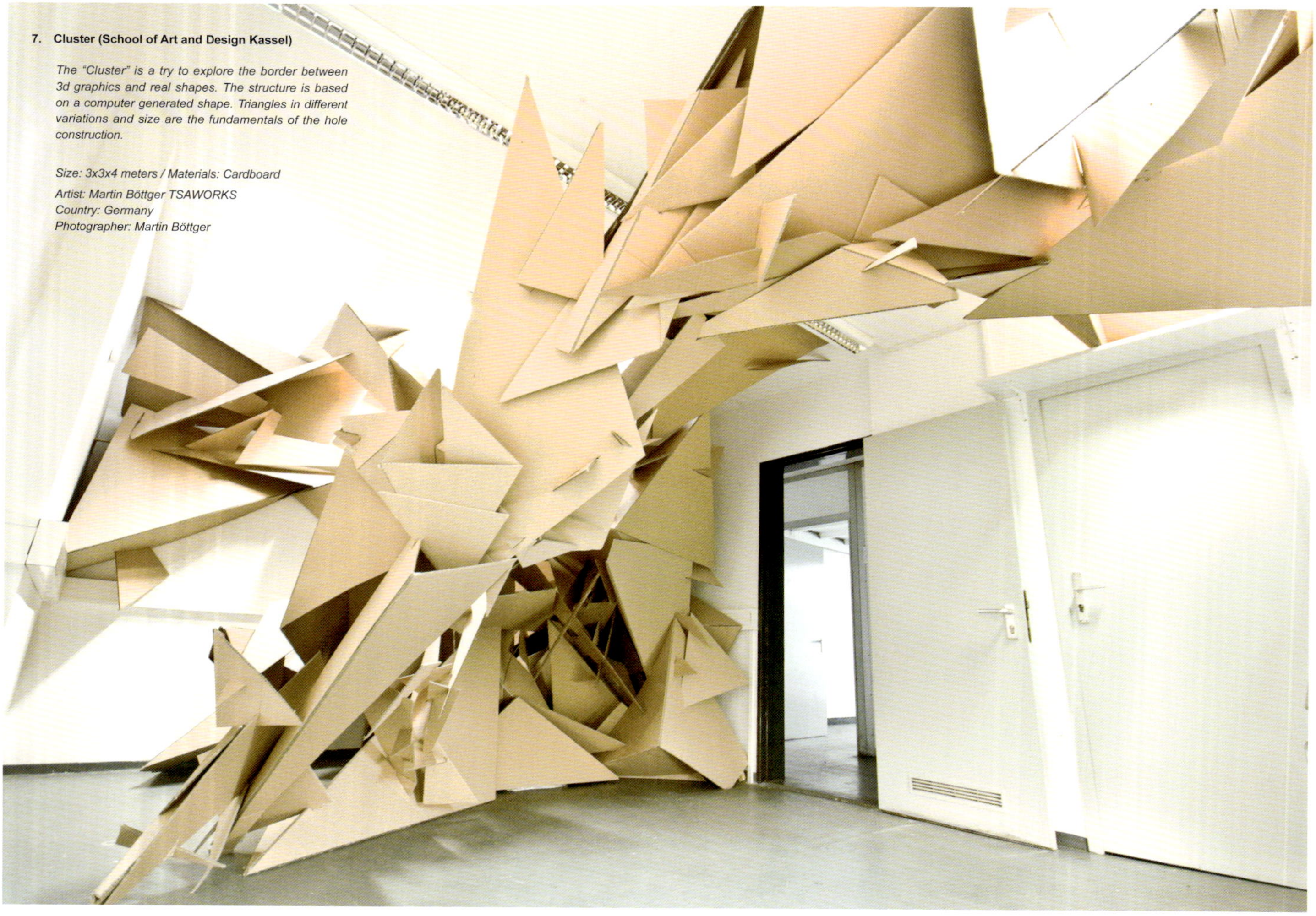

7. Cluster (School of Art and Design Kassel)

The "Cluster" is a try to explore the border between 3d graphics and real shapes. The structure is based on a computer generated shape. Triangles in different variations and size are the fundamentals of the hole construction.

Size: 3x3x4 meters / Materials: Cardboard
Artist: Martin Böttger TSAWORKS
Country: Germany
Photographer: Martin Böttger

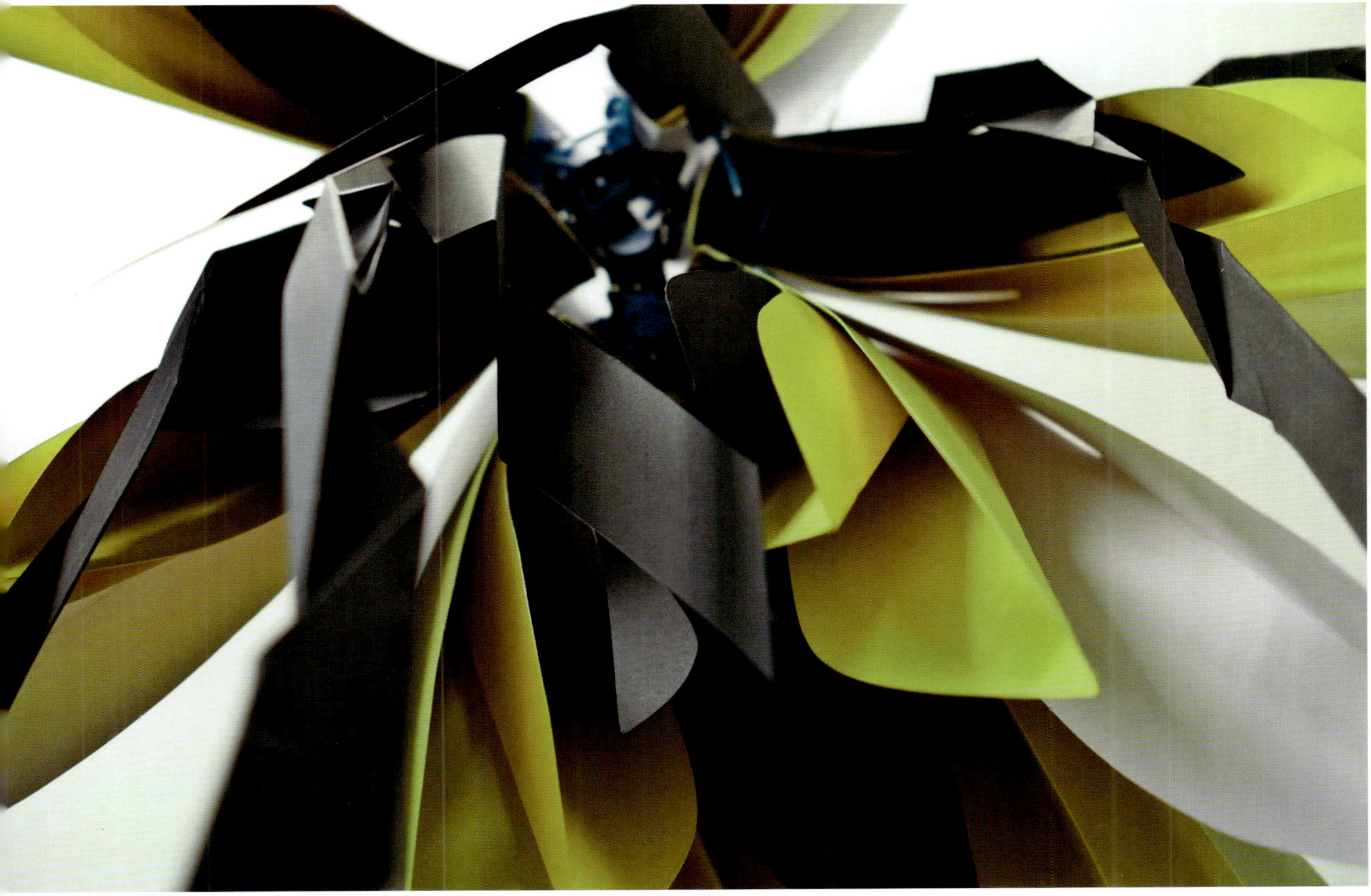

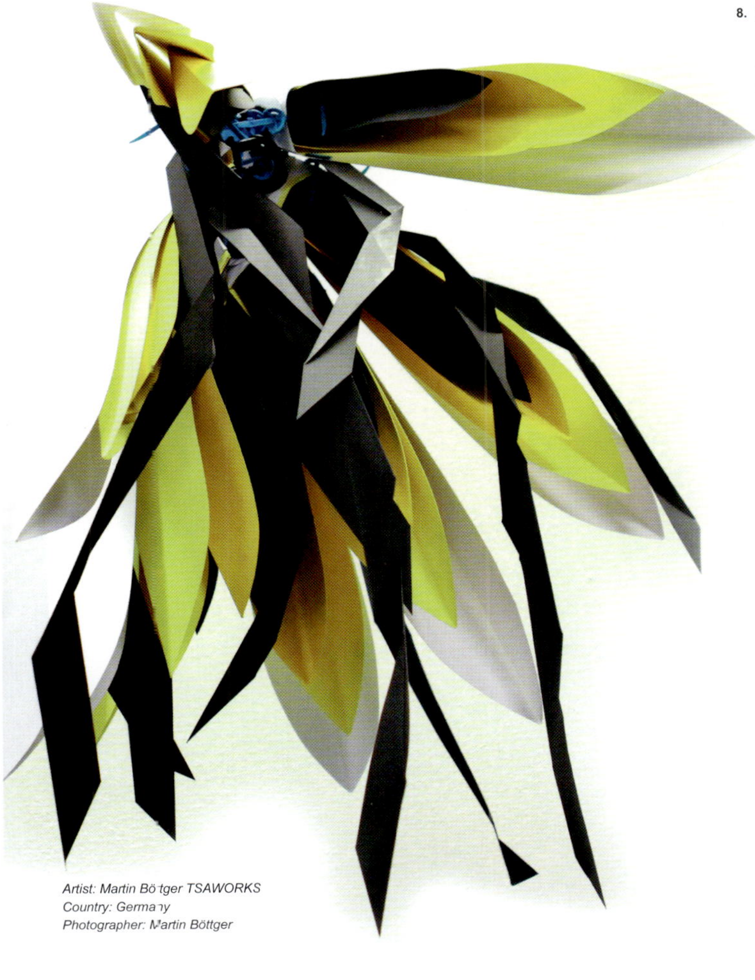

8. Magnoliaforma

"Magnoliaforma" is a project in collaboration with MAKEDO "a set of connectors for creating thinks form the stuff around you".

Size: 0.90 m x 0.90 m x 0.70 m
Materials: Colored Cards / Makedo Kit

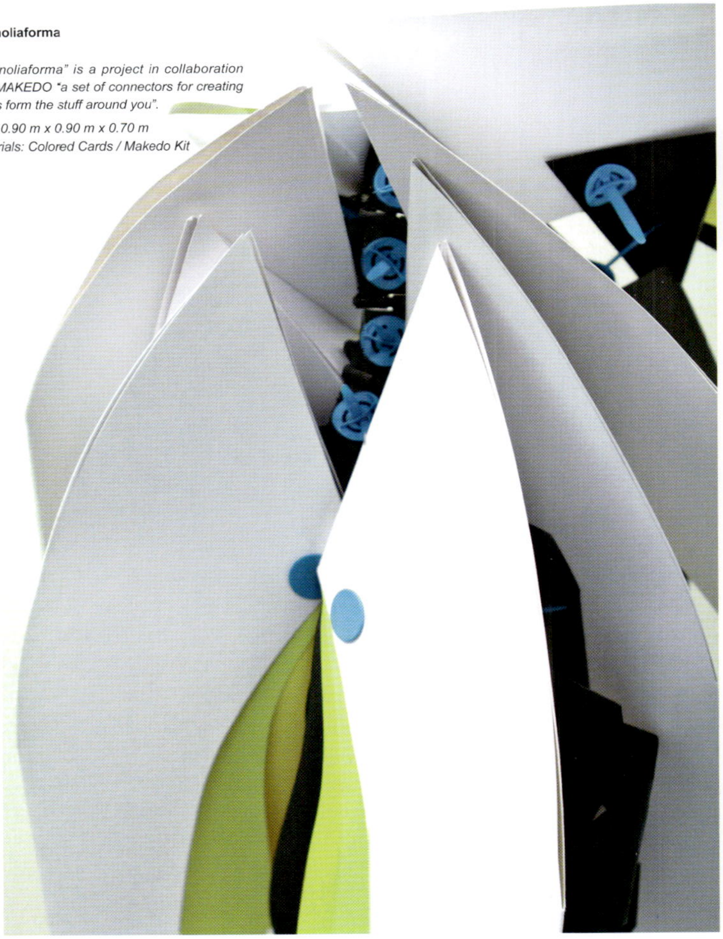

Artist: Martin Böttger TSAWORKS
Country: Germany
Photographer: Martin Böttger

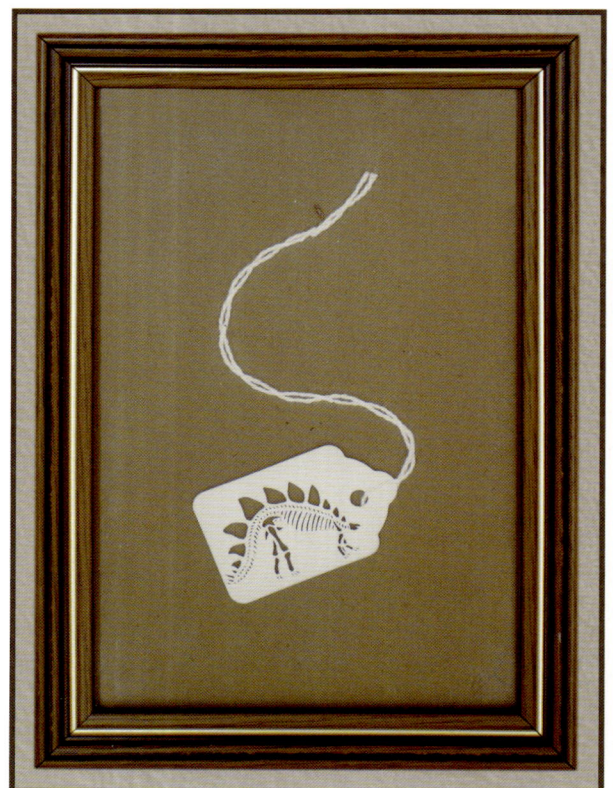
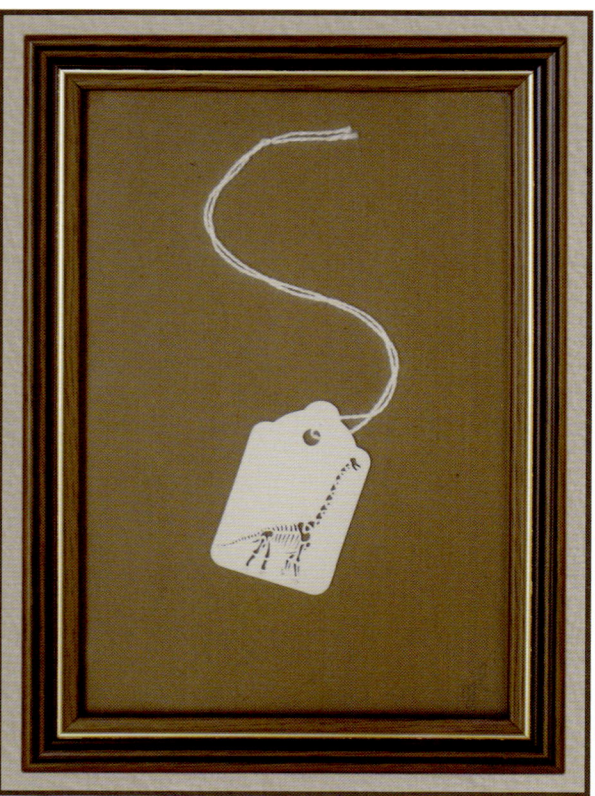

1. **Dinosaur Tags**
   Set of 4 Dinosaur tags features Stegosaurus ~ Tyrannosaurus Rex ~ Brachiosaurus ~ Spinosaurus. Each tag is approximately 25x40mm
   Artist: Michael Lomax   Country: UK

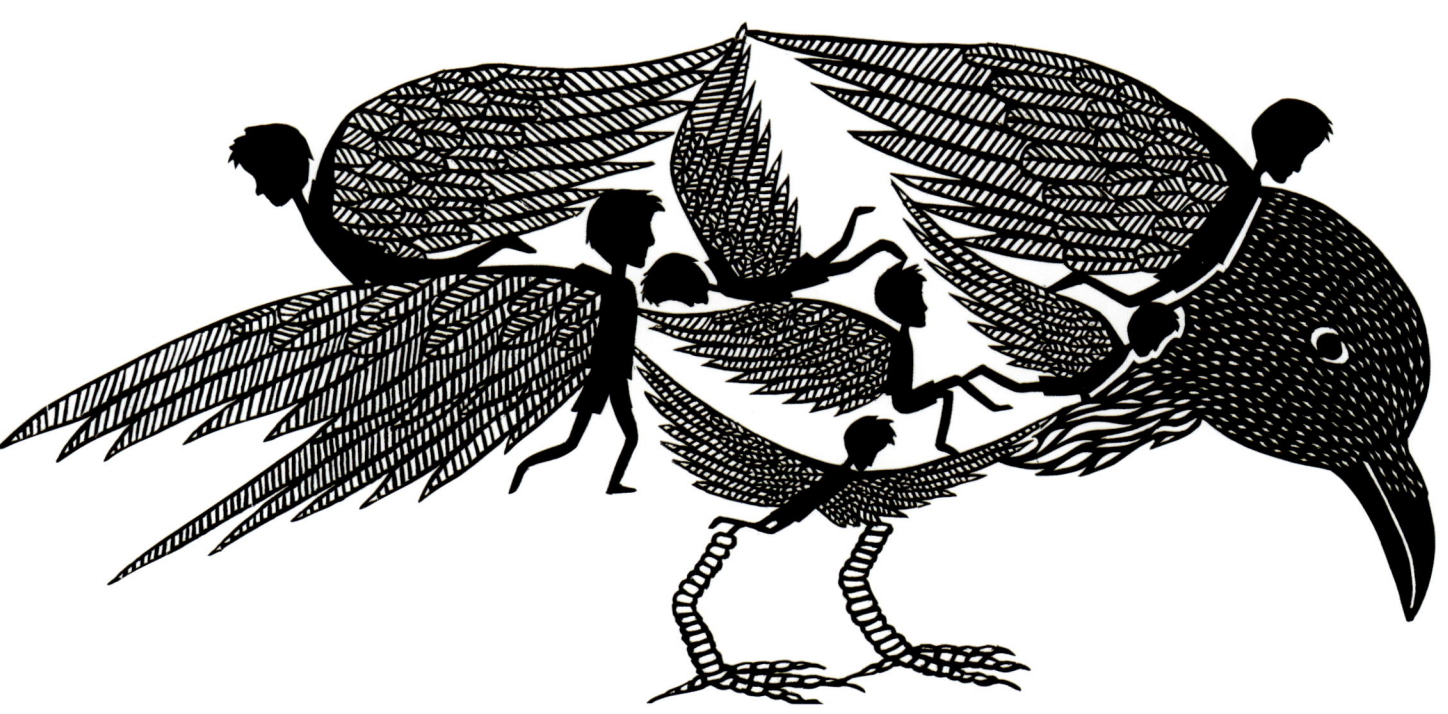

2. **The Seven Ravens**
   The Seven Ravens is an A5 papercut based on the Brothers Grimm fairytale of the same name. The final papercut is framed between 2 panes of glass without a background.
   Artist: Michael Lomax   Country: UK

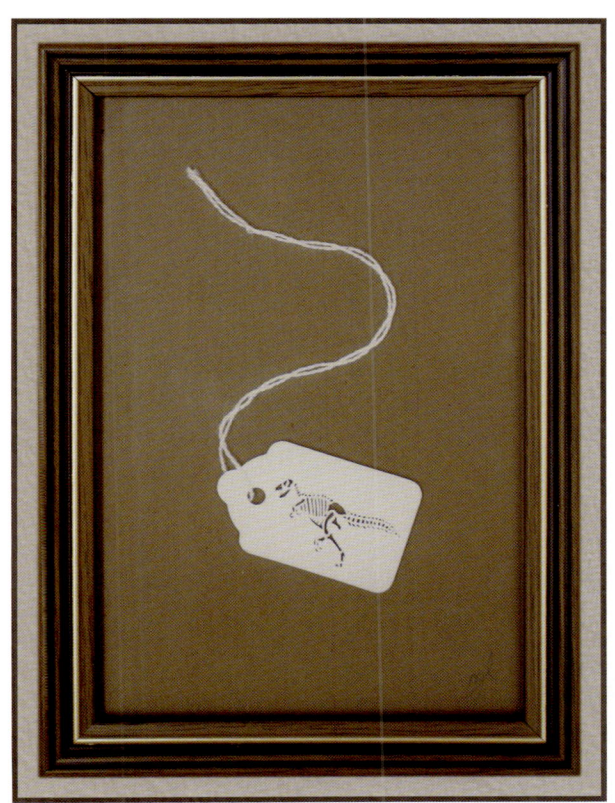
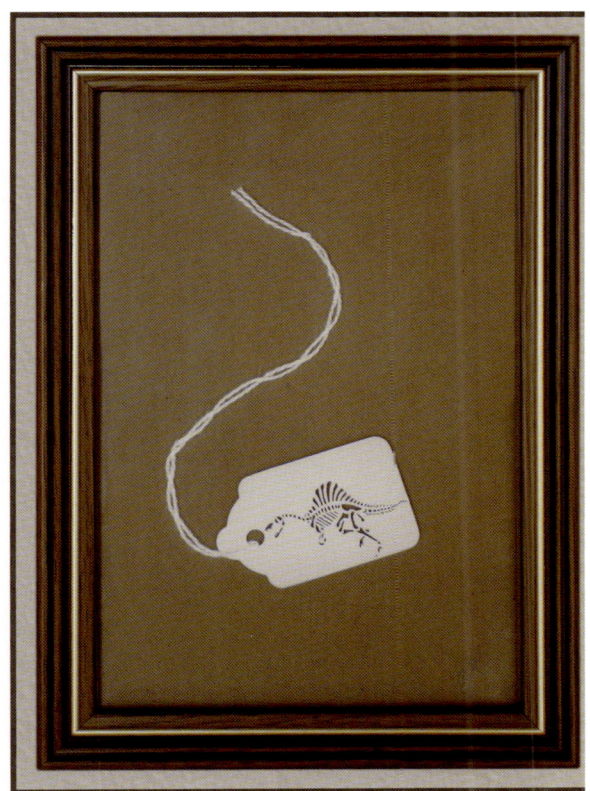
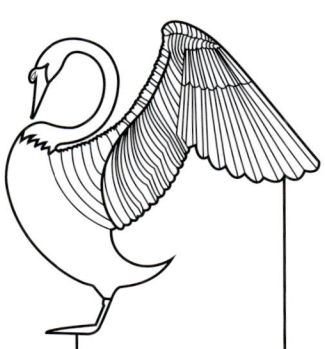

1. Dinosaur Tags
2. The Seven Ravens
3. Butterflies
4. Blodeuwedd
5. White Swan
6. Hans Christian Andersen's The Most Incredible Thing

---Michael Lomax

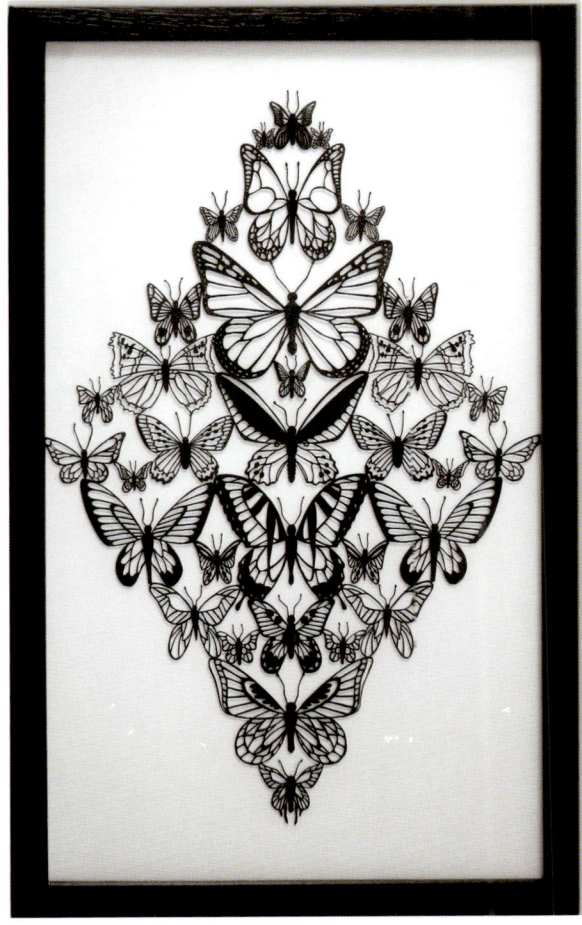

3. **Butterflies** Artist: Michael Lomax
Papercut Country: UK

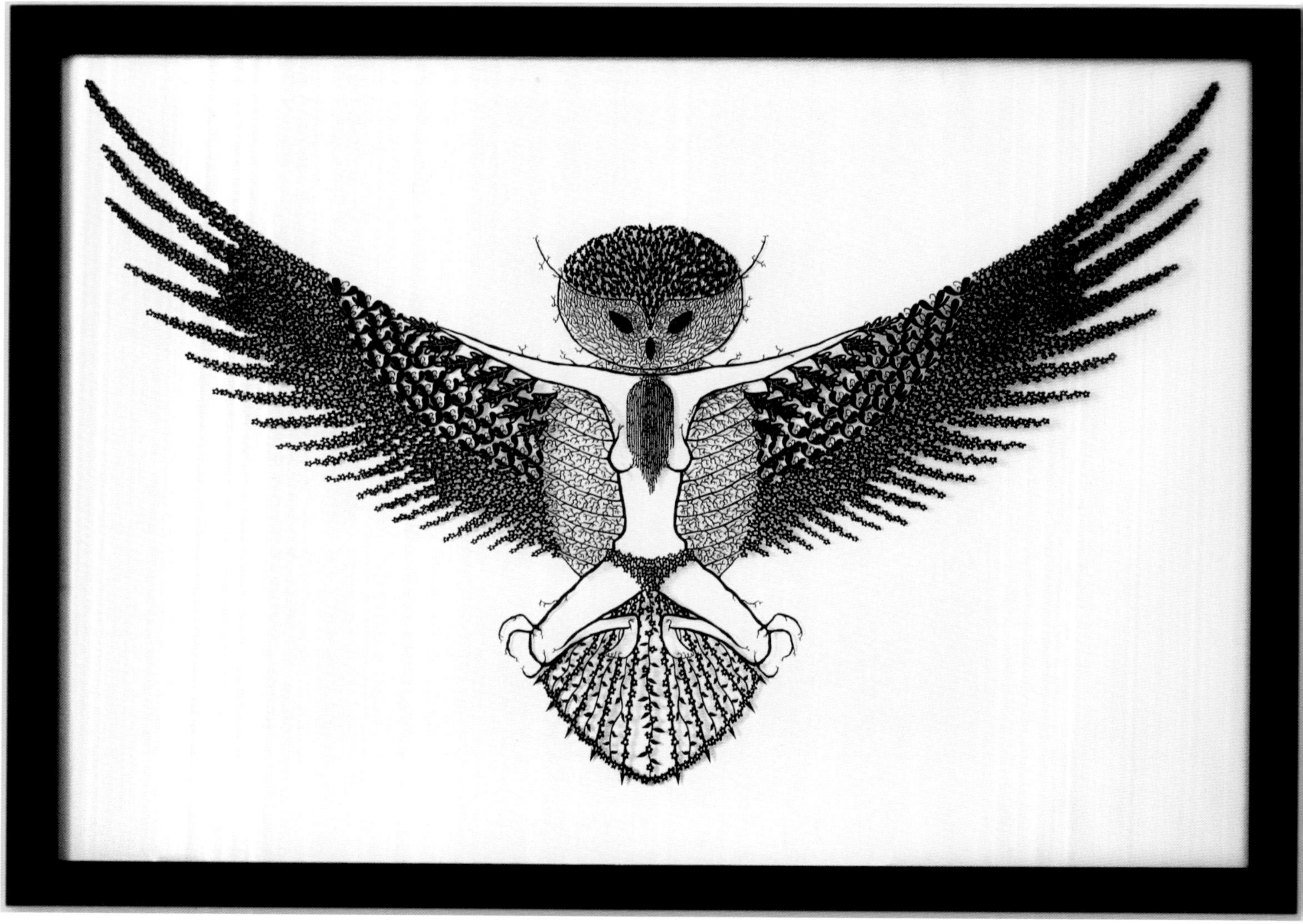

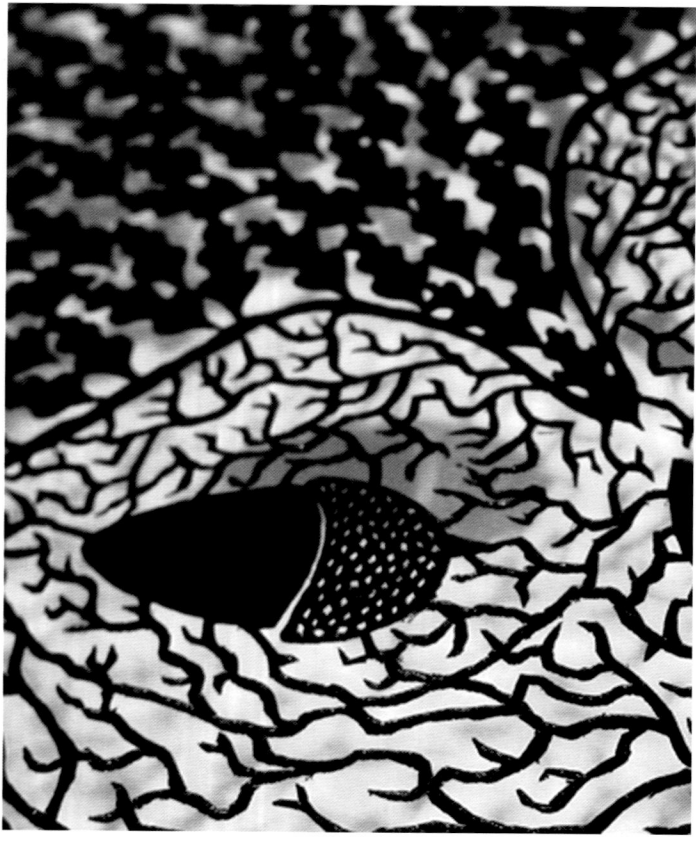
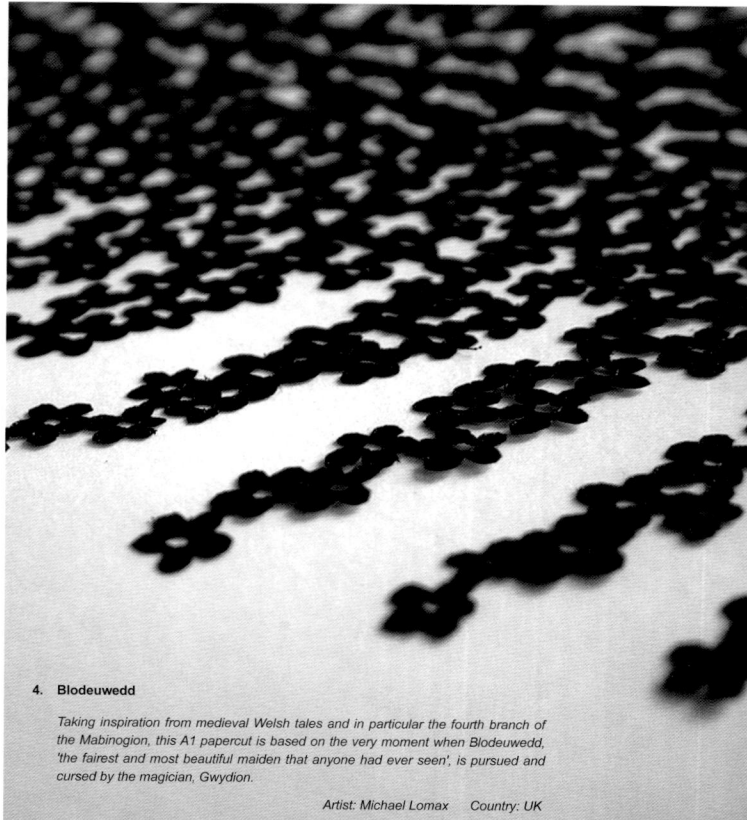

4. Blodeuwedd

Taking inspiration from medieval Welsh tales and in particular the fourth branch of the Mabinogion, this A1 papercut is based on the very moment when Blodeuwedd, 'the fairest and most beautiful maiden that anyone had ever seen', is pursued and cursed by the magician, Gwydion.

Artist: Michael Lomax   Country: UK

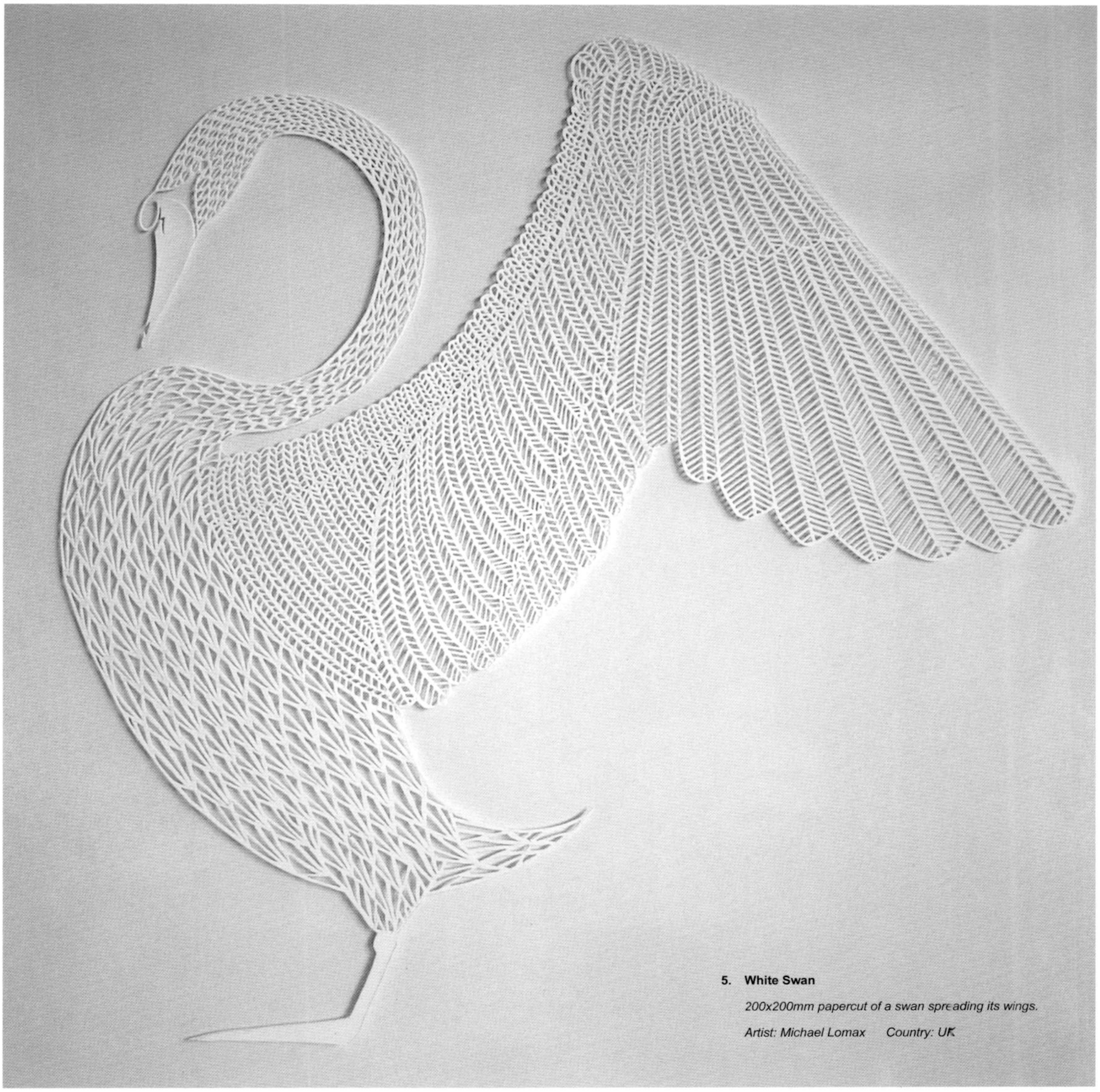

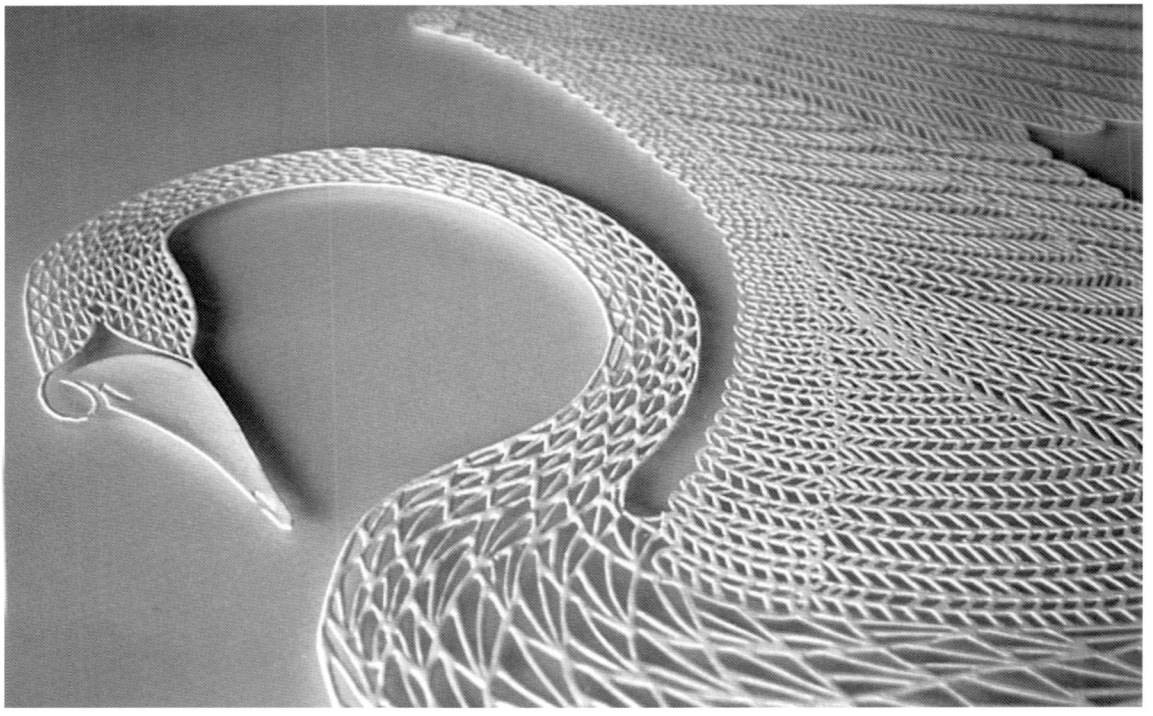

5. **White Swan**

   200x200mm papercut of a swan spreading its wings.
   Artist: Michael Lomax   Country: UK

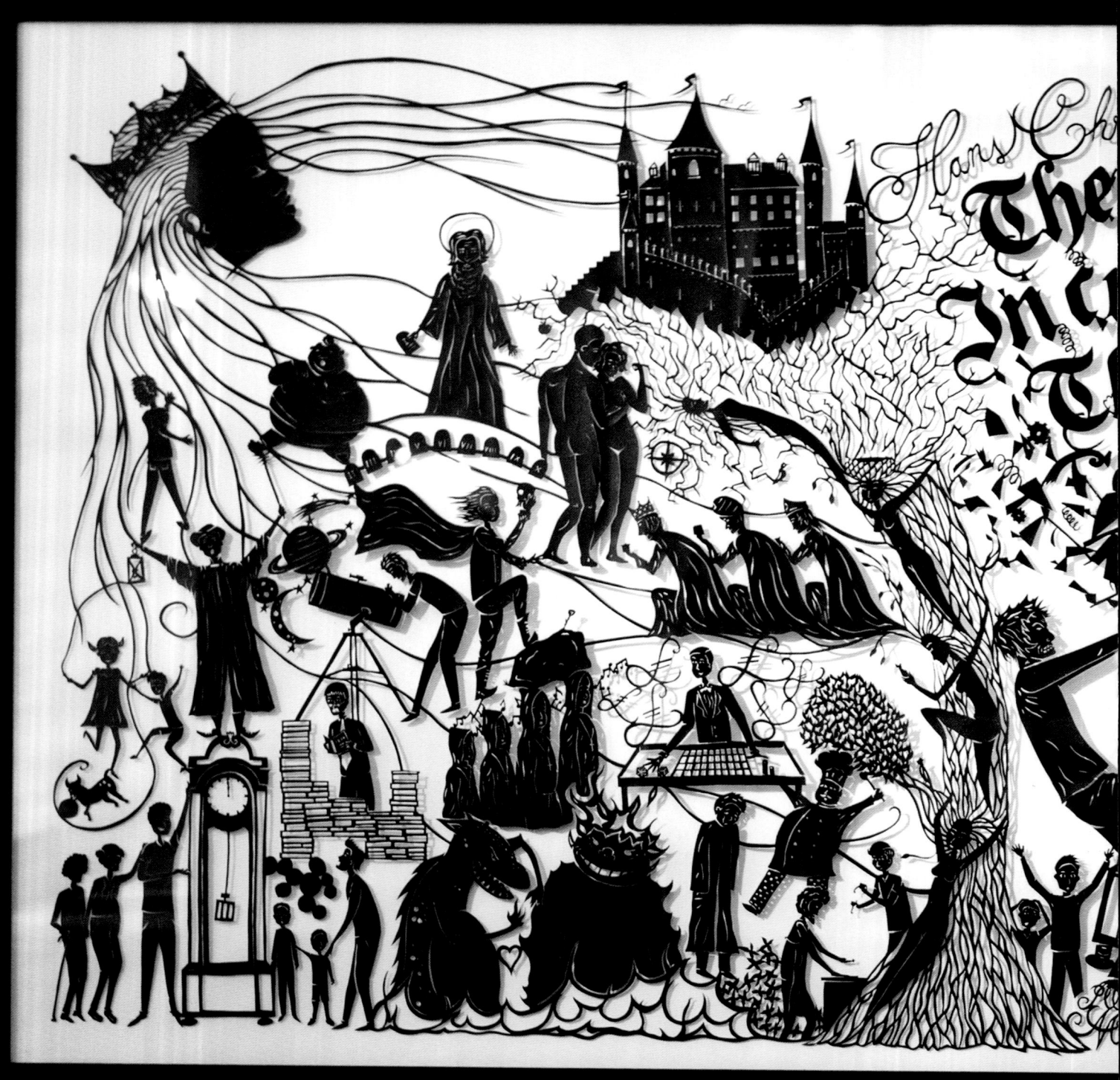

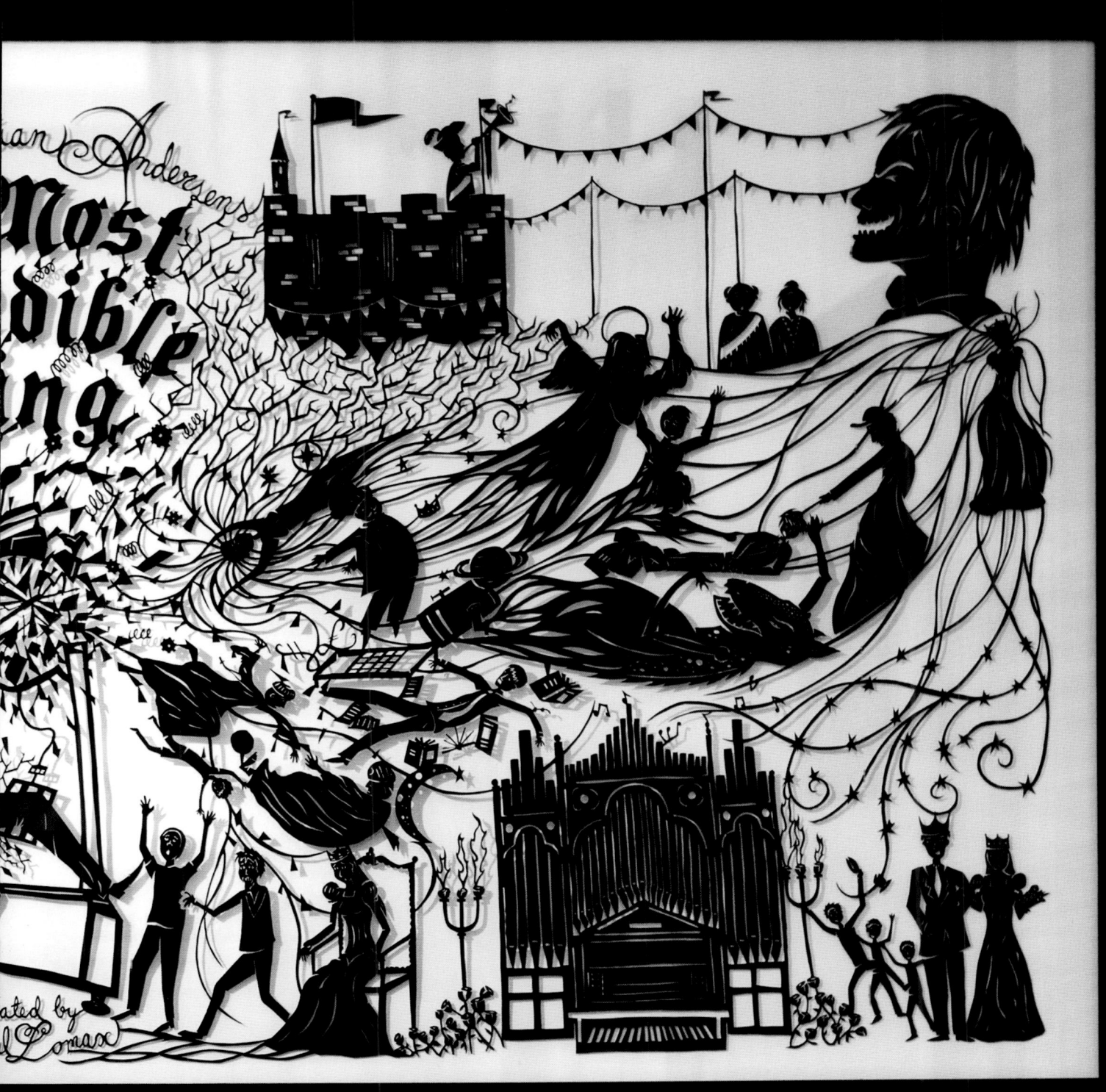

6. **Hans Christian Andersen's The Most Incredible Thing**

   1782x846mm papercut illustrating Hans Christian Andersen fairytale The Most Incredible Thing.

   Artist: Michael Lomax
   Country: UK

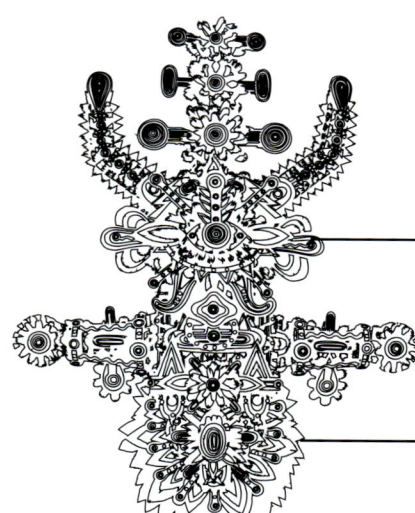

1. Chromasouls
2. Power Tower
3. Ostensorium
4. Home Tree
5. Exotic Matter
6. Awaken and Free What Has Been Asleep
7. Power Shapes

---*Michael Velliquette*

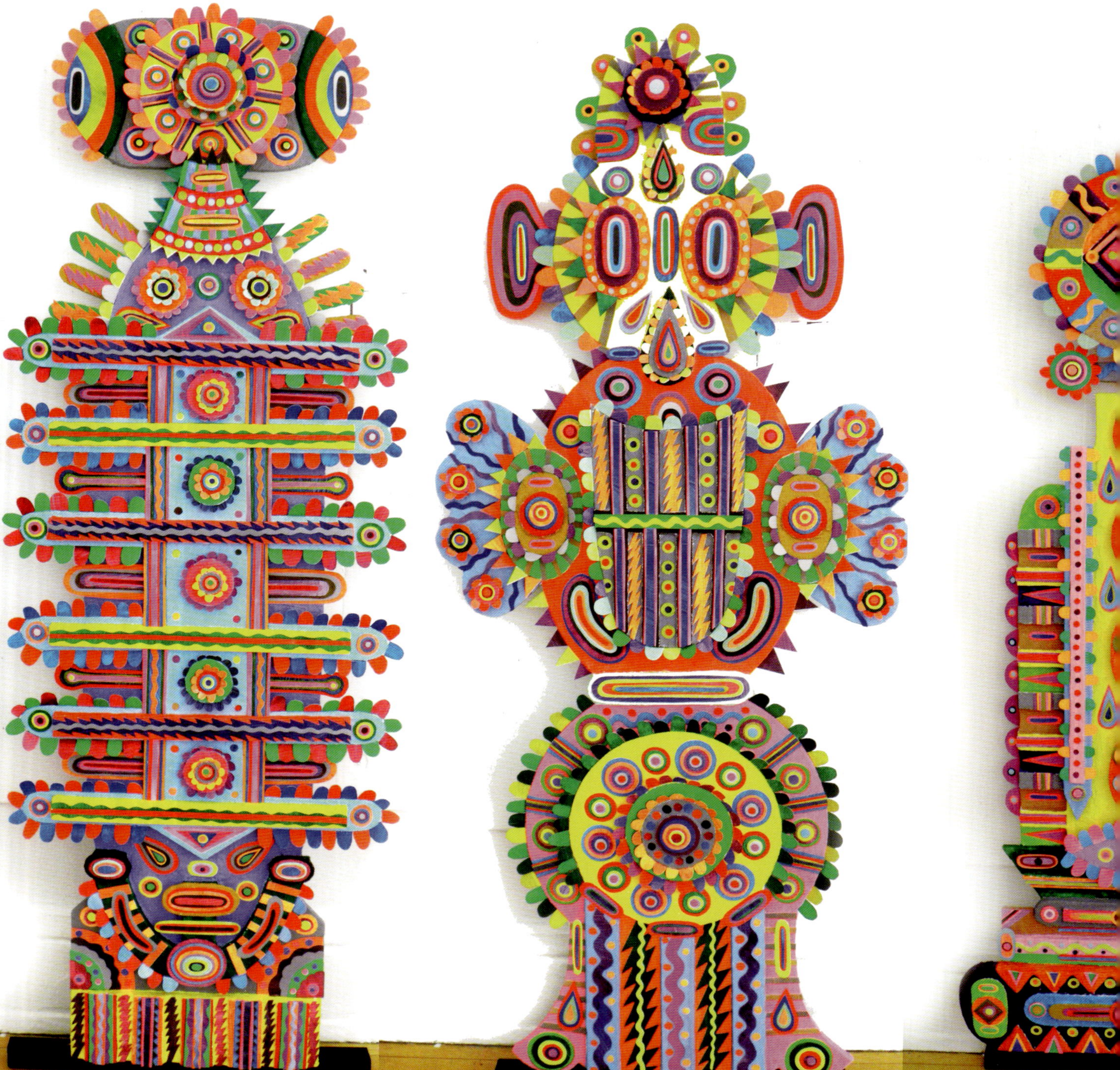

1. **Chromasouls**

   Chromasouls are a series of foam, paint, and paper sculptures that represent good luck talismans. Each figure is approximately 70 x 24 x 3 inches (178 x 61 x 7.6 cm)

   Artist: Michael Velliquette
   Country: USA
   Photographer: Michael Velliquette

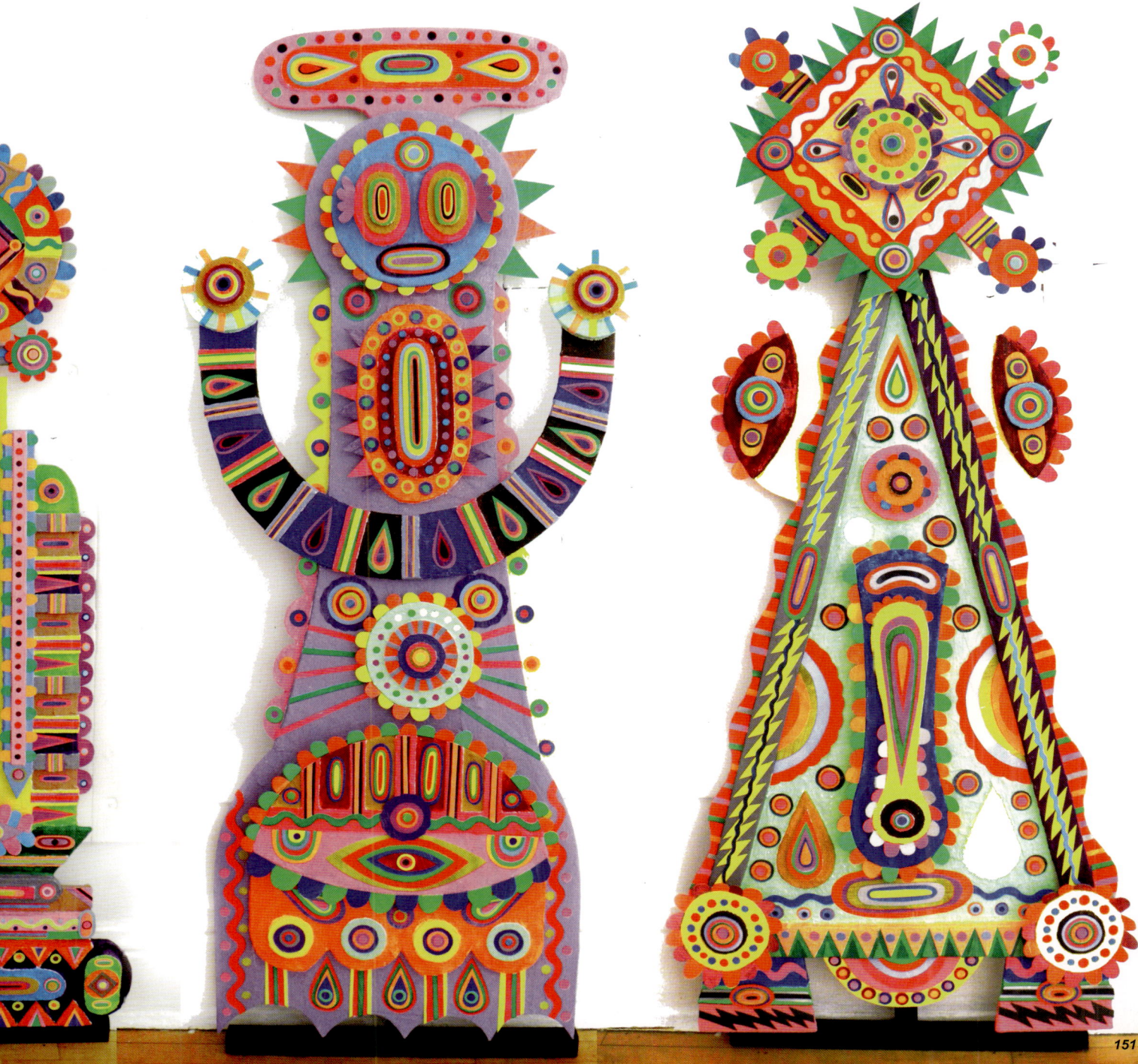

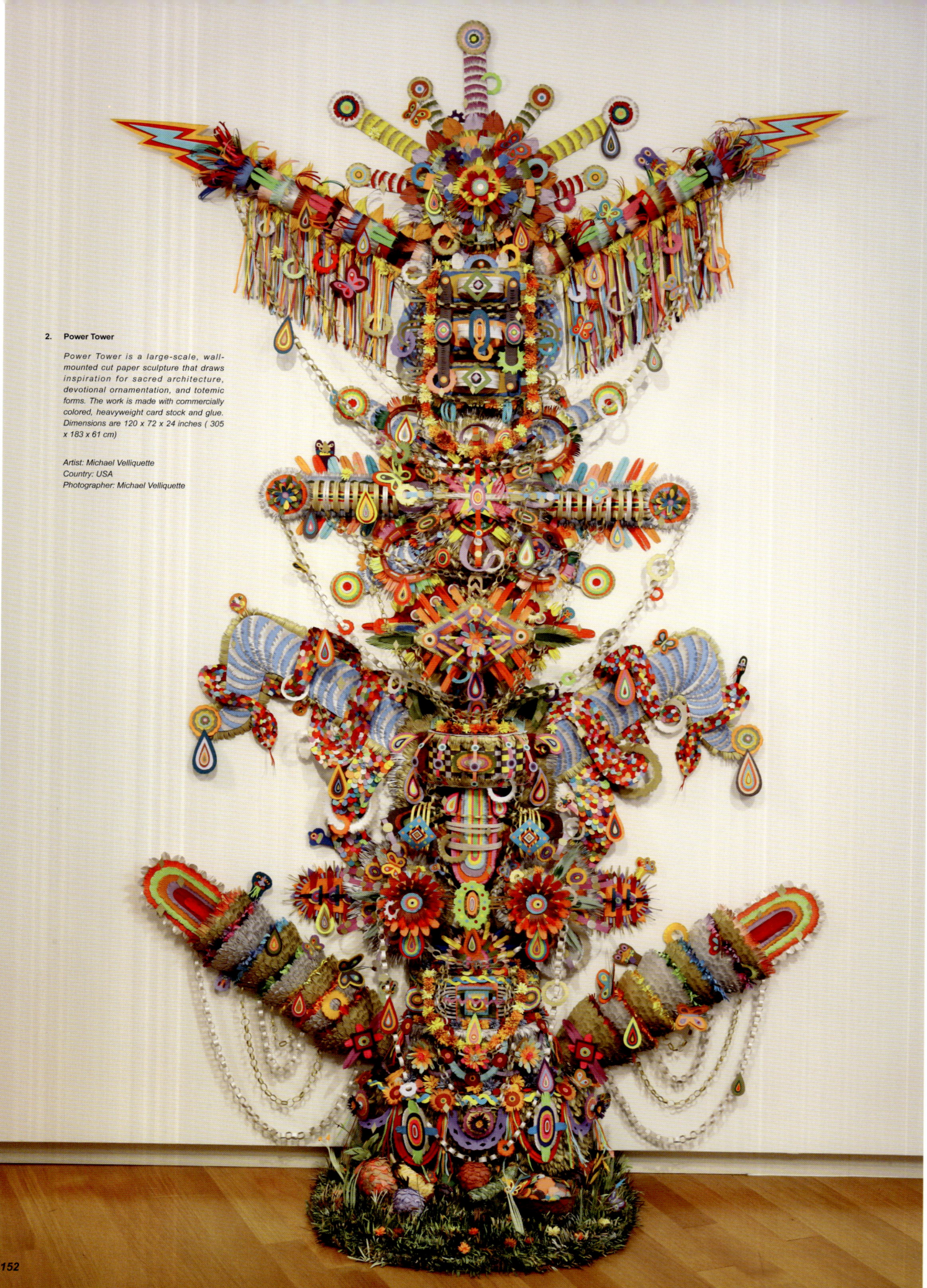

2. **Power Tower**

   Power Tower is a large-scale, wall-mounted cut paper sculpture that draws inspiration for sacred architecture, devotional ornamentation, and totemic forms. The work is made with commercially colored, heavyweight card stock and glue. Dimensions are 120 x 72 x 24 inches (305 x 183 x 61 cm)

   Artist: Michael Velliquette
   Country: USA
   Photographer: Michael Velliquette

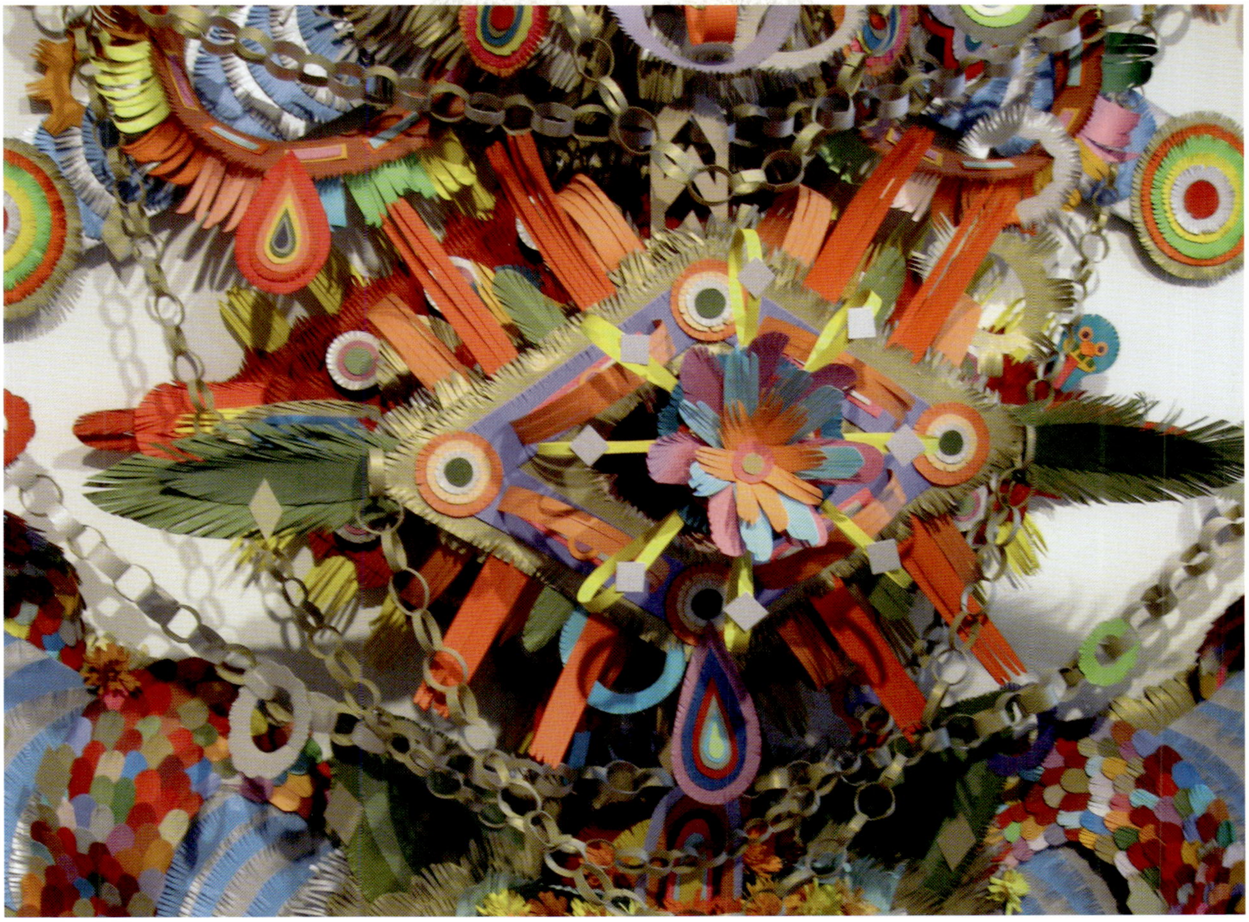

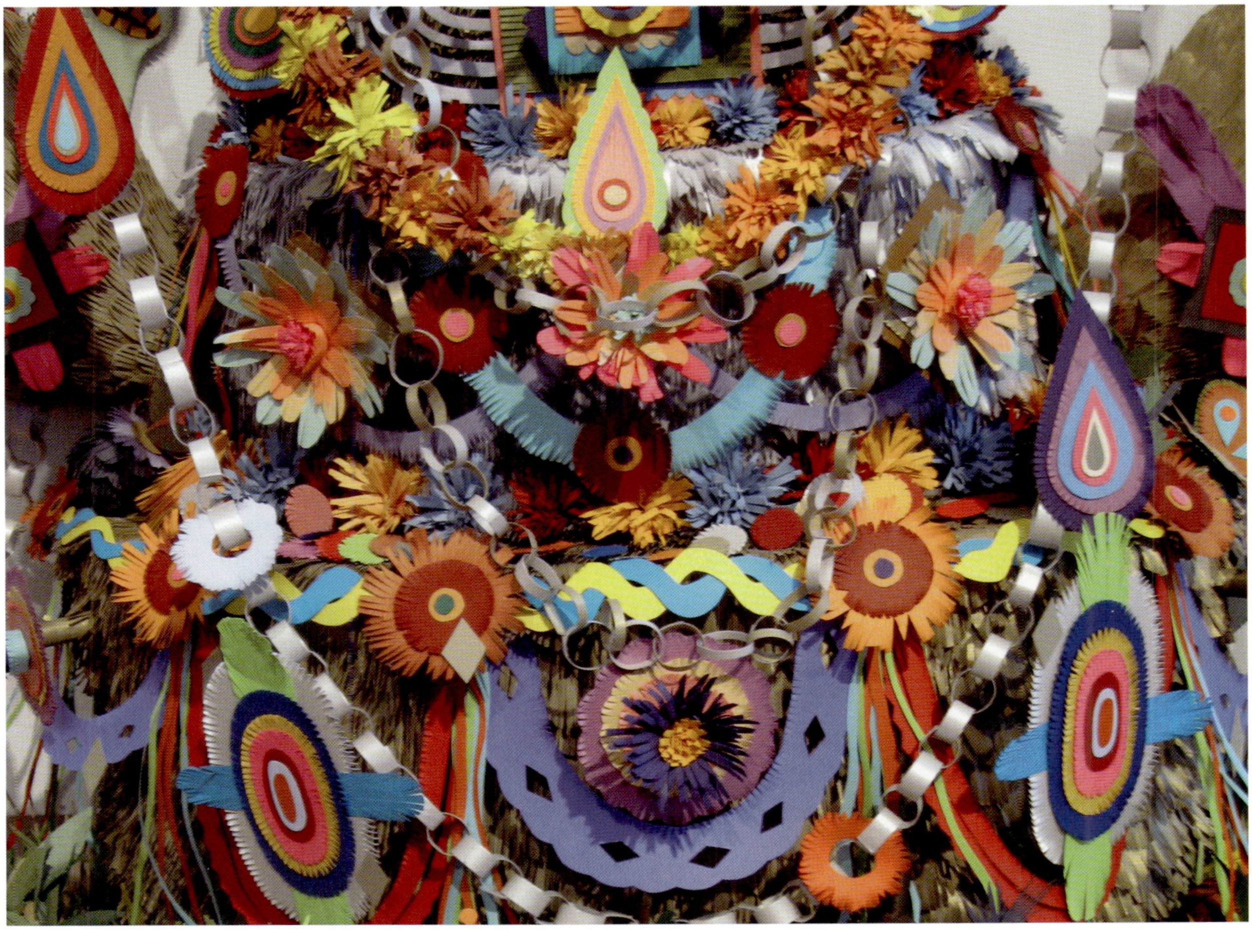

3. Ostensorium

(Ostensorium 1 / Ostensorium 2)

Ostensorium 1
Paper, acrylic, foam, glue
26" x 16" x 3"

Ostensorium 2
Paper, acrylic, foam, glue
24" x 14" x 3"

Artist: Michael Velliquette
Country: USA
Photographer: Michael Velliquette

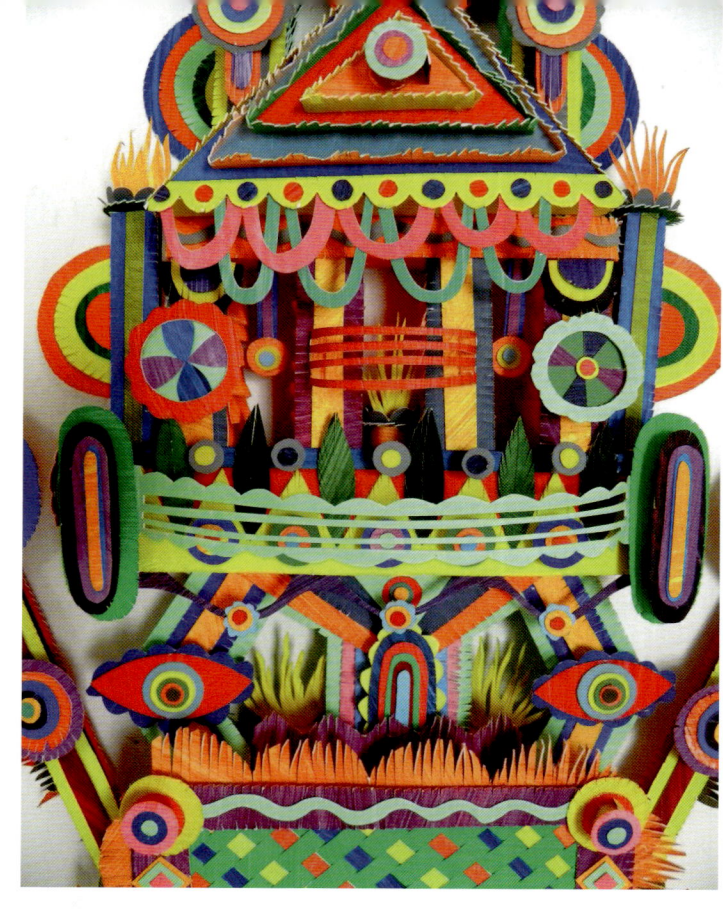
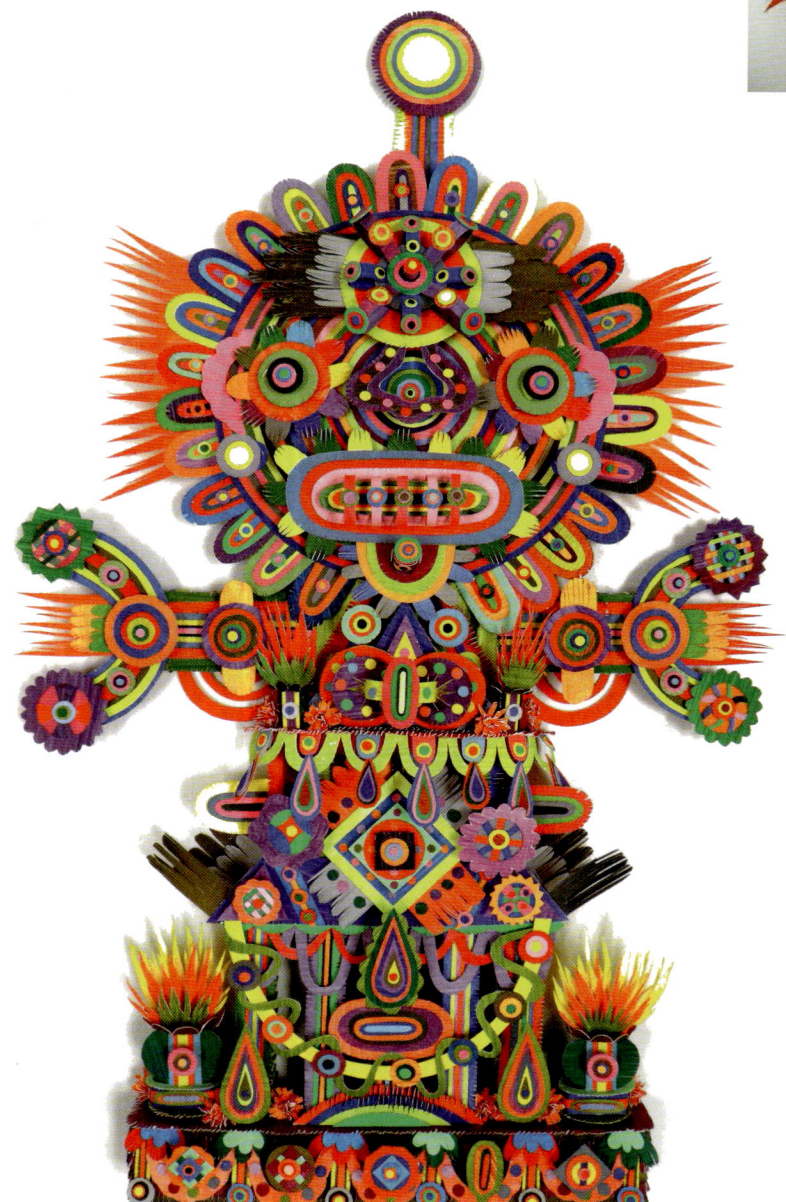
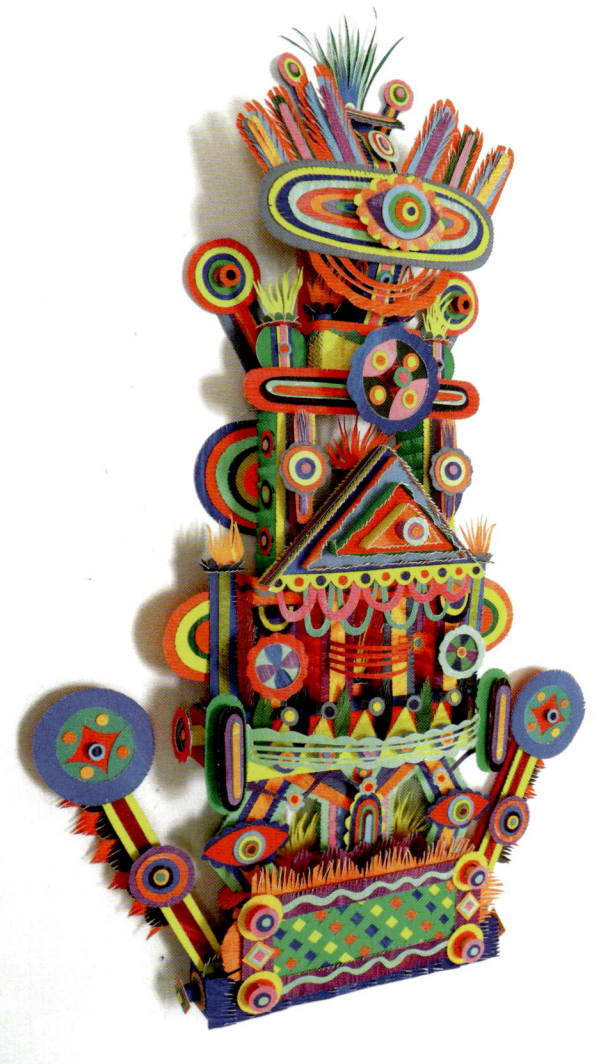

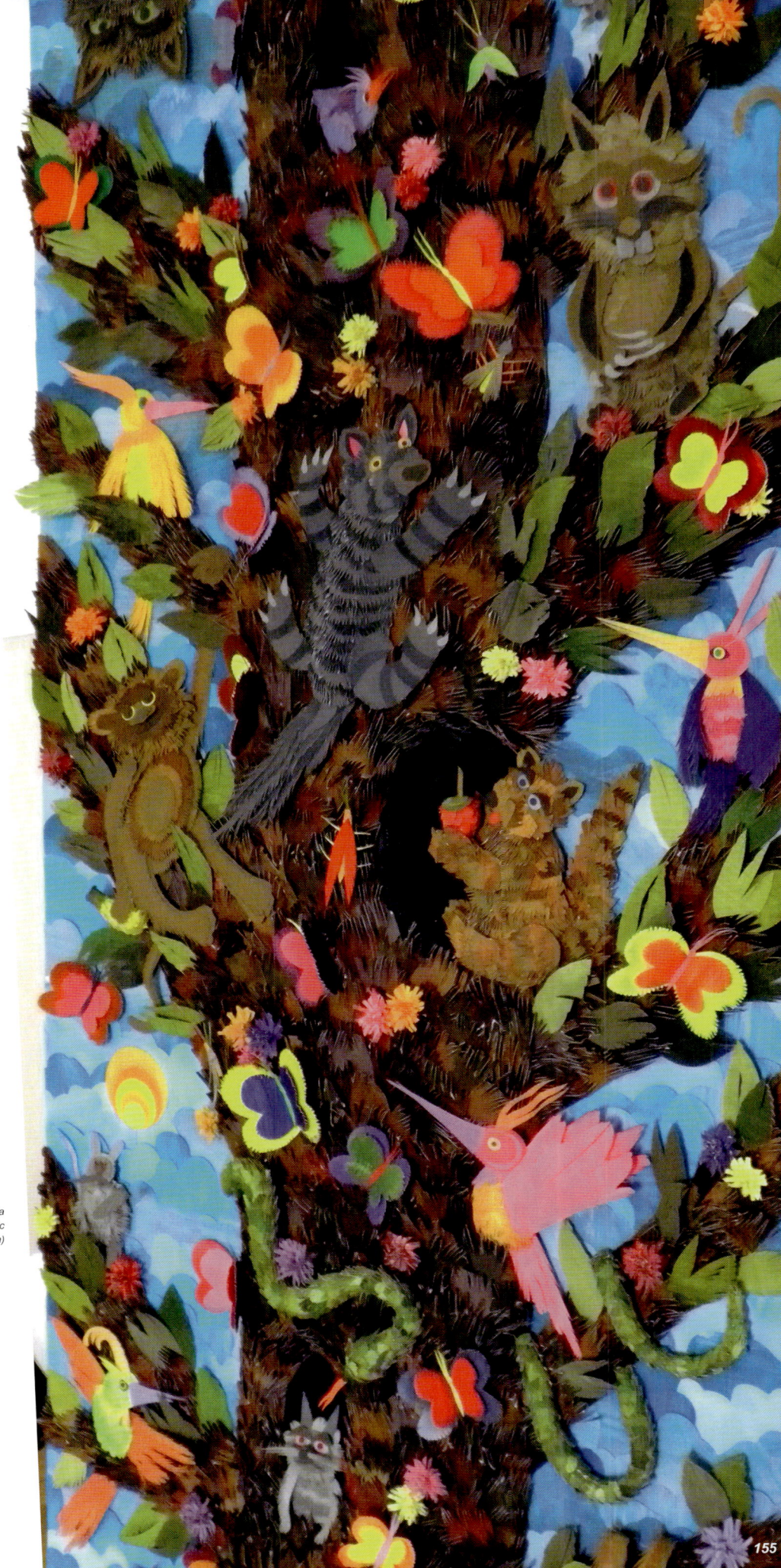

4. **Home Tree**

Home Tree is a narrative vignette of a large tree that is host to a plethora of animal friends. The work is made with paper, acrylic and glue. Dimensions are 60 x 36 x 3 inches (152 x 91 x 7.62 cm)

Artist: Michael Velliquette
Country: USA
Photographer: Michael Velliquette

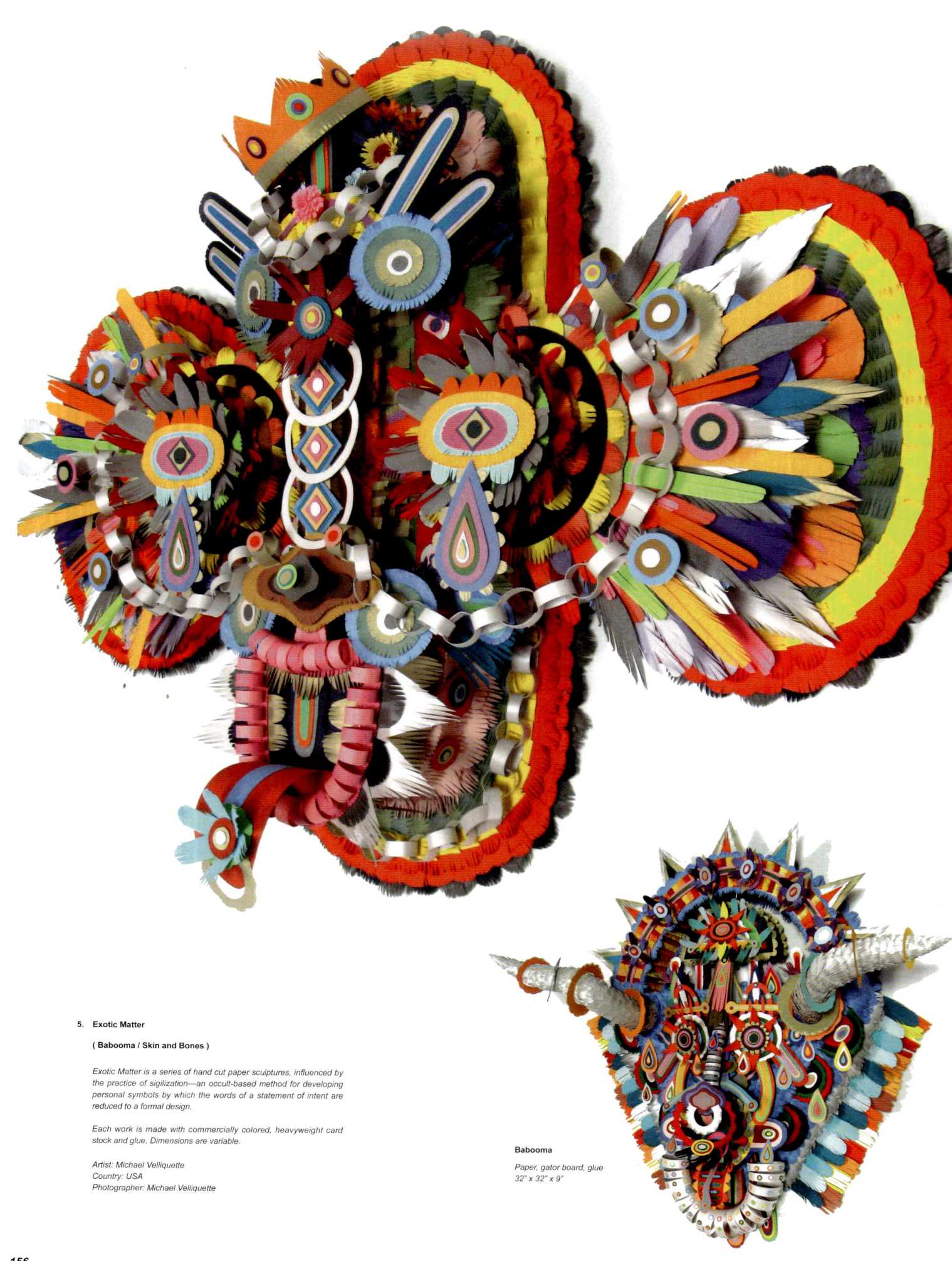

5. **Exotic Matter**

   (Babooma / Skin and Bones)

   Exotic Matter is a series of hand cut paper sculptures, influenced by the practice of sigilization—an occult-based method for developing personal symbols by which the words of a statement of intent are reduced to a formal design.

   Each work is made with commercially colored, heavyweight card stock and glue. Dimensions are variable.

   Artist: Michael Velliquette
   Country: USA
   Photographer: Michael Velliquette

Babooma

Paper, gator board, glue
32" x 32" x 9"

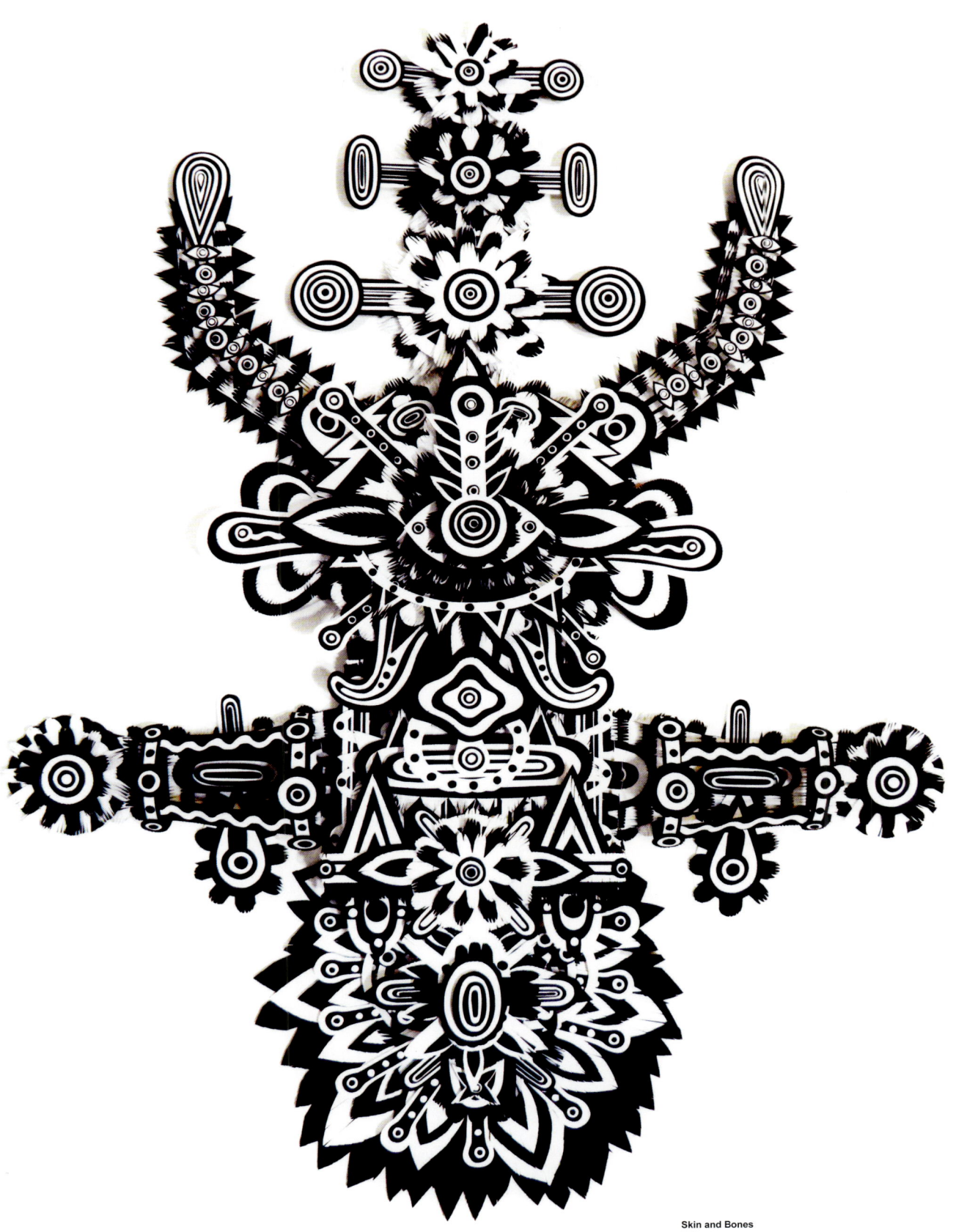

Skin and Bones

Paper, gator board, glue
41" x 32" x 6"

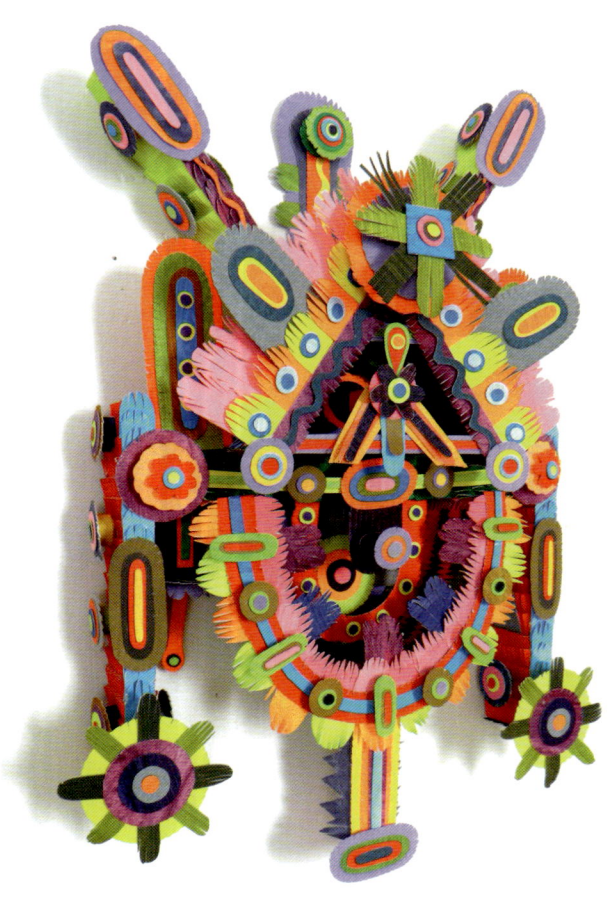

Lil' Orphist *Paper, gator board, acrylic, glue*   13.5" x 10" x 3"

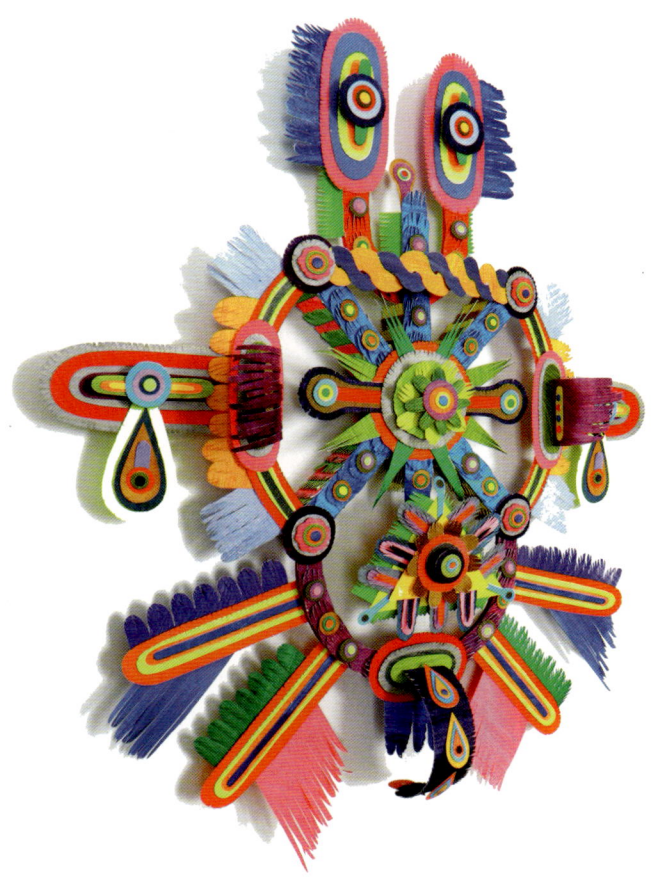

Simhasana *Paper, gator board, acrylic, glue*   20.5 x 16.5 x 2

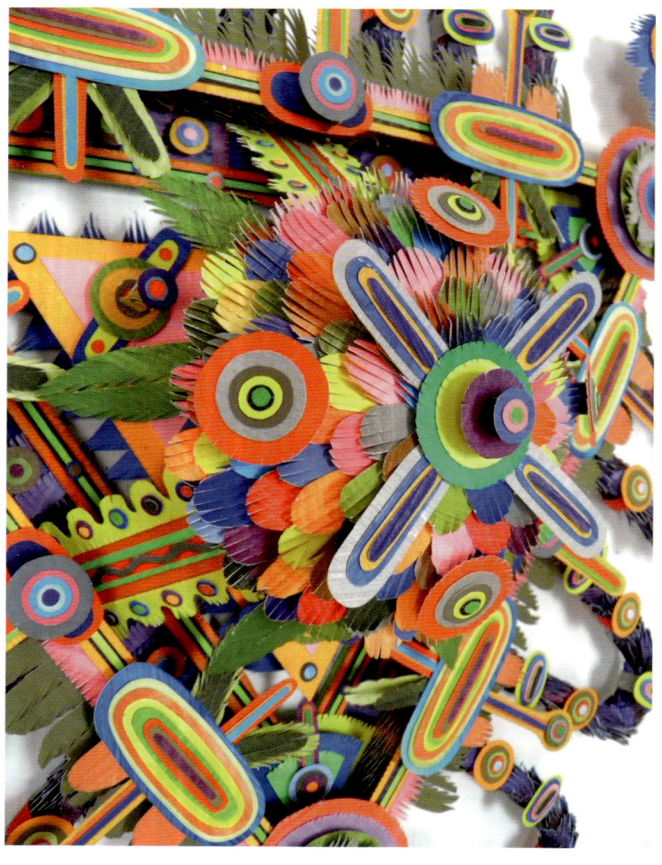

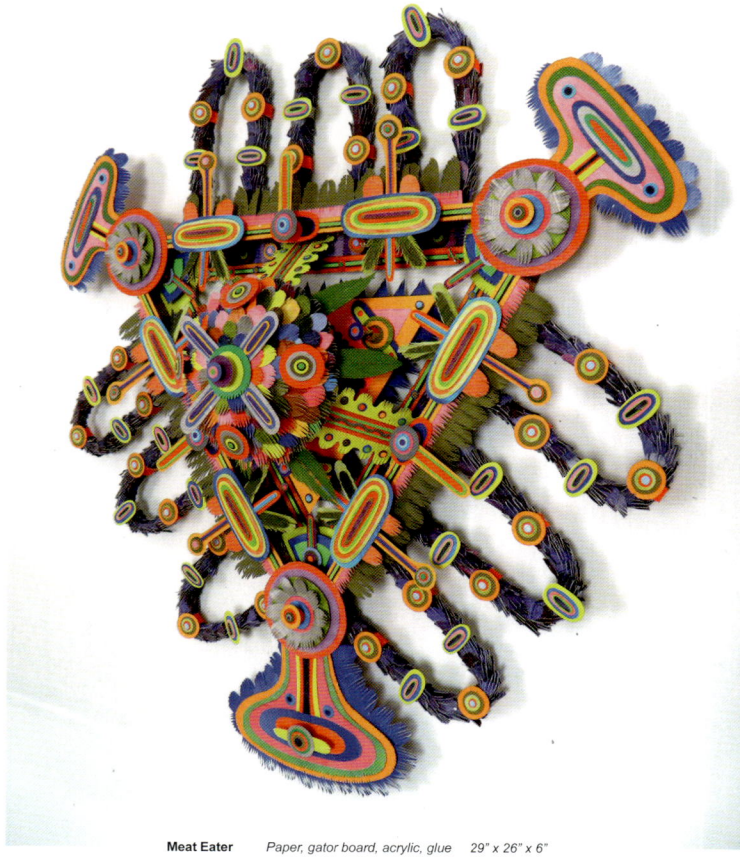

Meat Eater *Paper, gator board, acrylic, glue*   29" x 26" x 6"

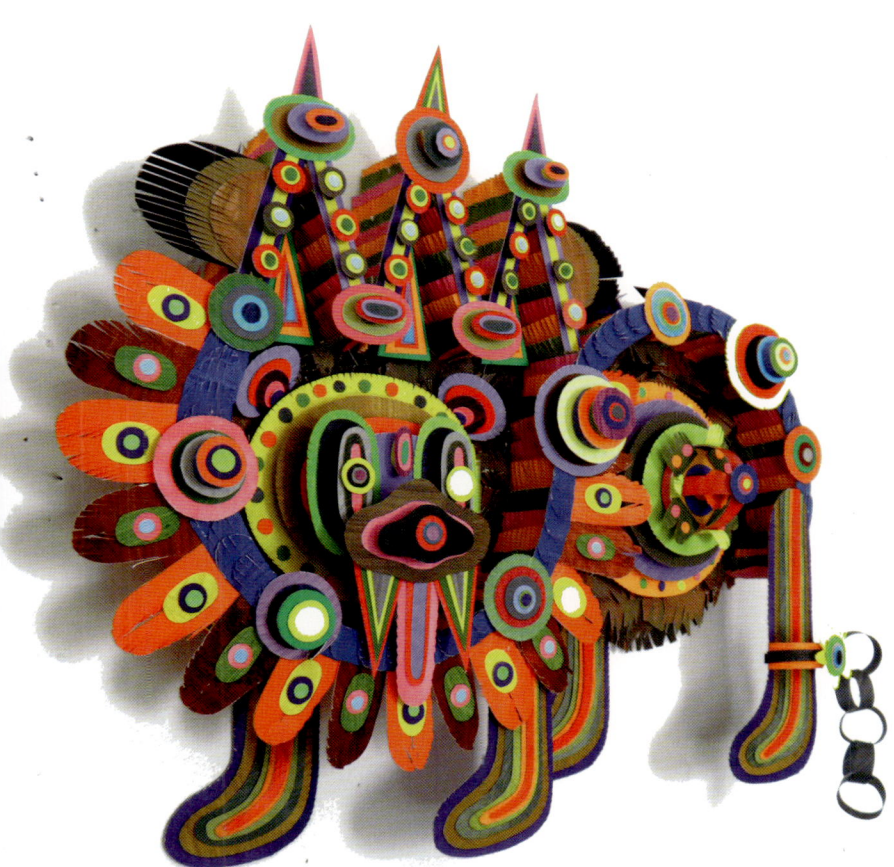

6. **Awaken and Free What Has Been Asleep**
   (Lil'Orphist / Simhasana / Beast Unbound / Meat Eater)

Awaken and Free What Has Been Asleep is a series of hand cut paper sculptures, influenced by the practice of sigilization—an occult-based method for developing personal symbols by which the words of a statement of intent are reduced to a formal design.

Each work is made paper, acrylic, and glue. Dimensions are variable.

Artist: Michael Velliquette
Country: USA
Photographer: Michael Velliquette

7. **Power Shapes**
   (Diamond / Insight)

Power Shapes are a series of hand cut paper sculptures that explore sacred architecture and three-dimensional mandalas. Each work is made with commercially colored, heavyweight card stock and glue. Each work is approximately 14 x 14 x 4 inches (35.5 x 35.5 x 2.54 cm)

Artist: Michael Velliquette
Country: USA
Photographer: Michael Velliquette

Beast Unbound   Paper, gator board, acrylic, glue   14.5" x 15.5" x 3.5"

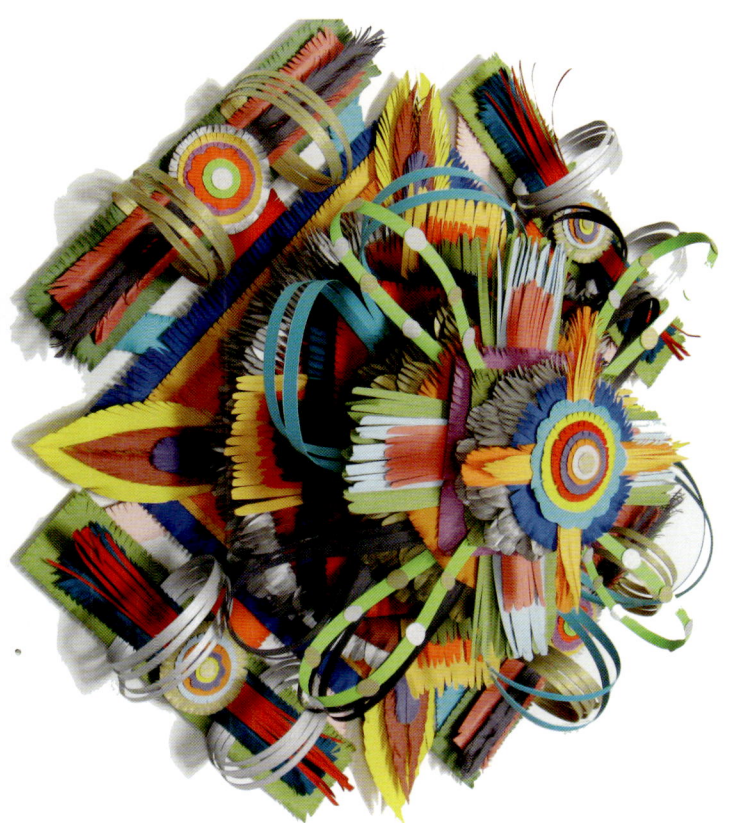

Diamond (Rumination)   Paper, gator board, glue   14" x 14" x 6"

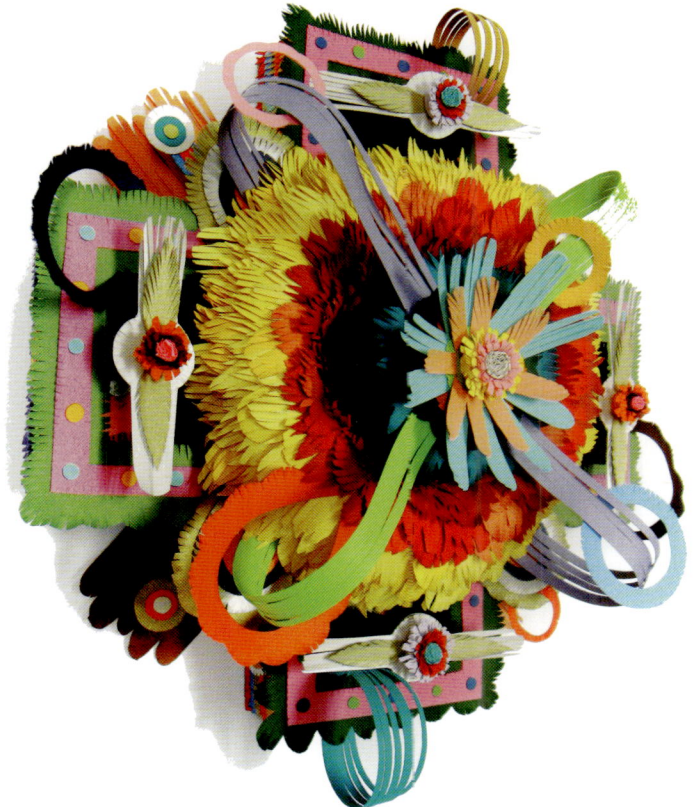

Insight   Paper, gator board, glue   14" x 14" x 6"

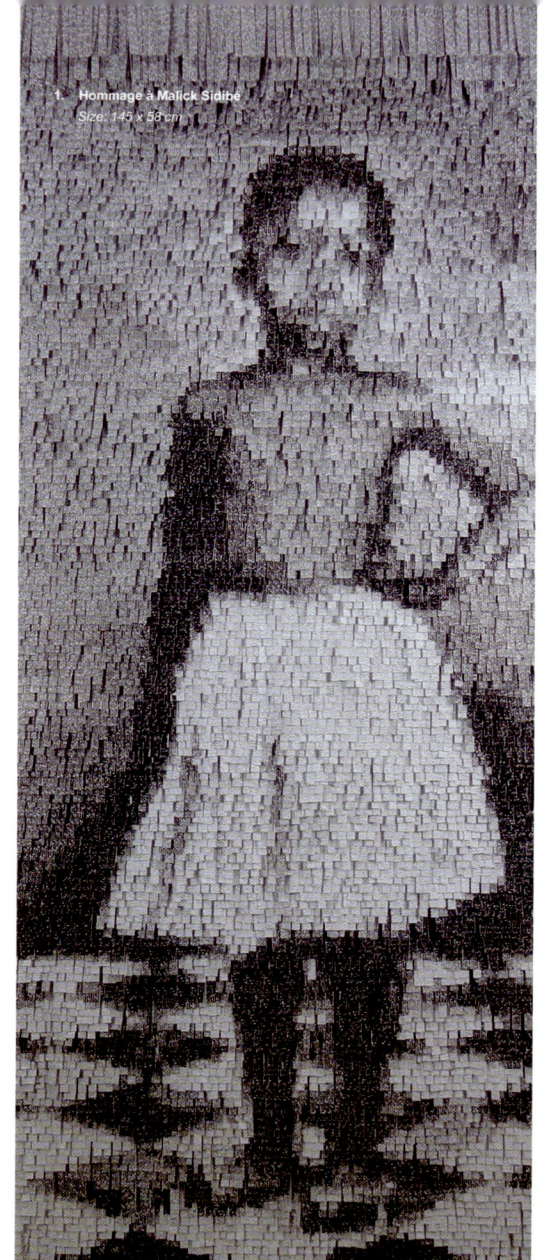

1. **Hommage à Malick Sidibé**
Size: 145 x 53 cm

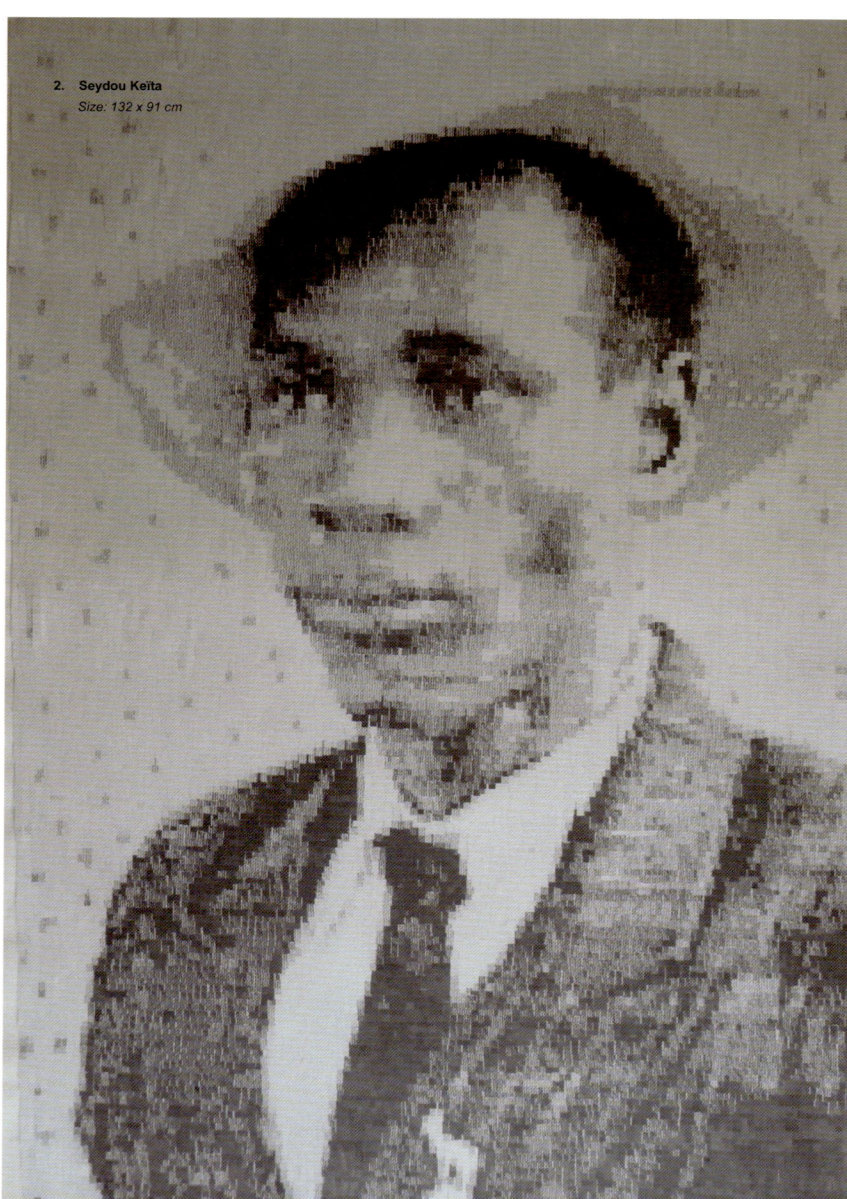

2. **Seydou Keïta**
Size: 132 x 91 cm

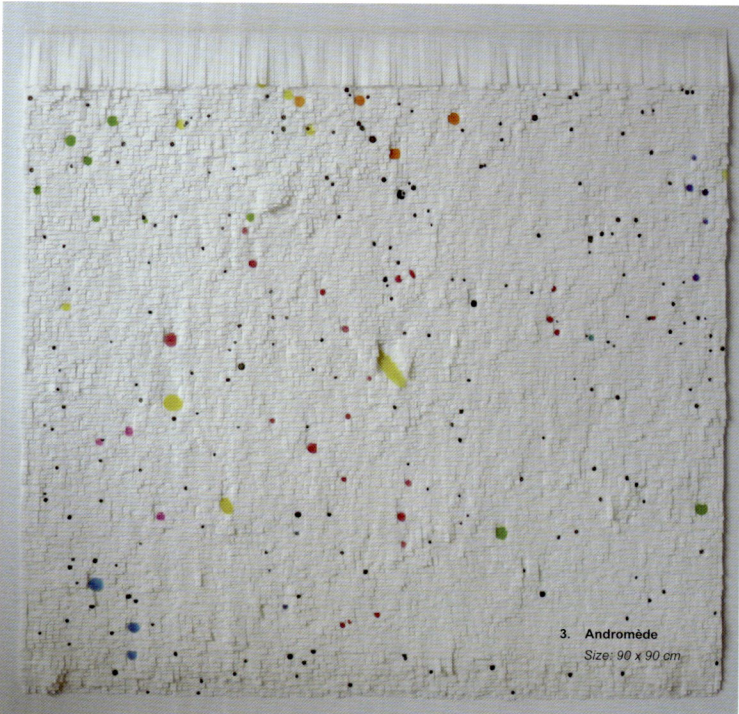

3. **Andromède**
Size: 90 x 90 cm

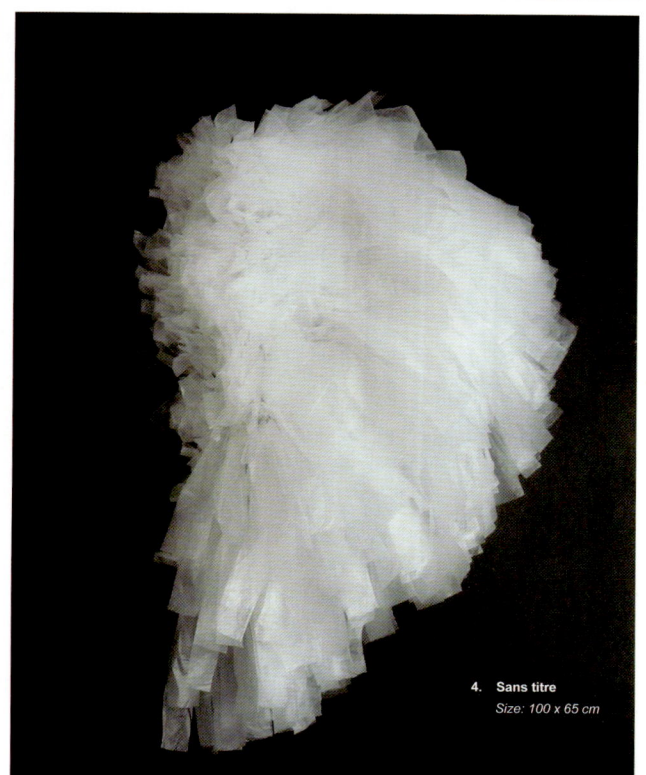

4. **Sans titre**
Size: 100 x 65 cm

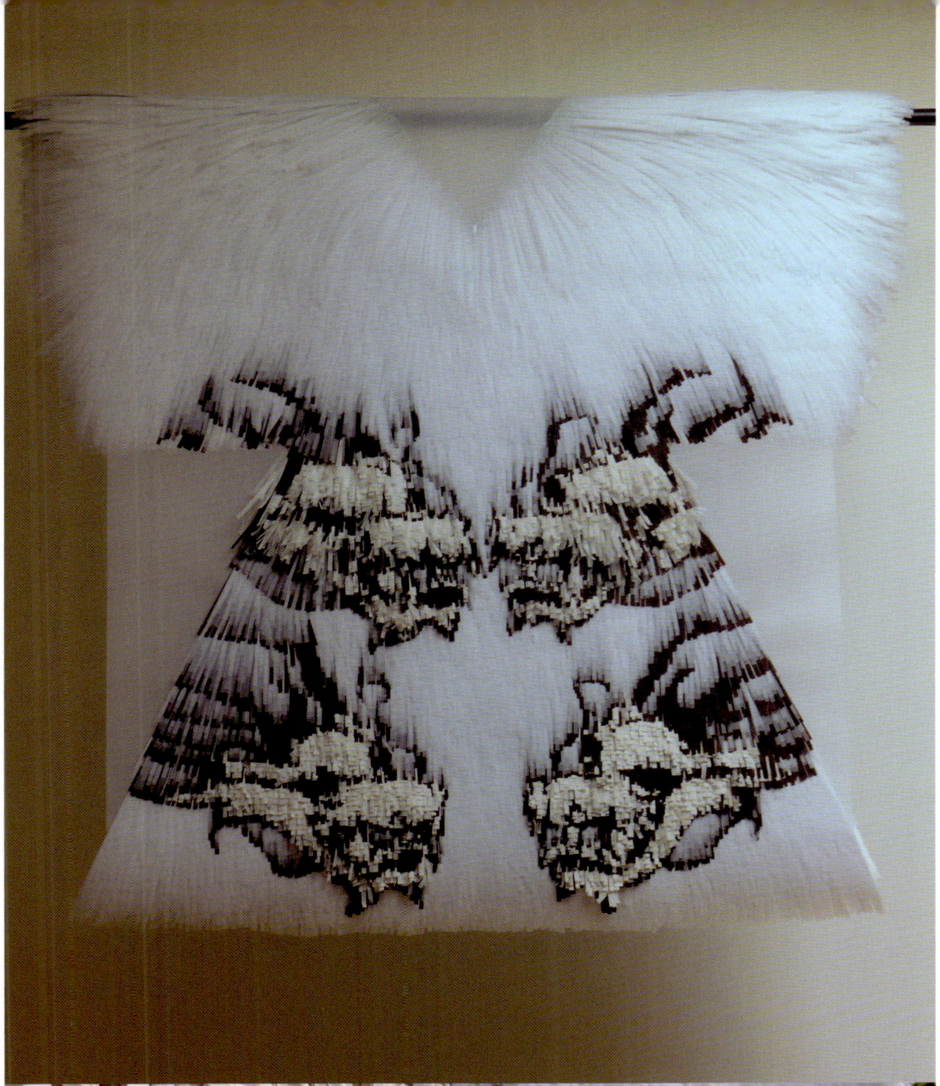

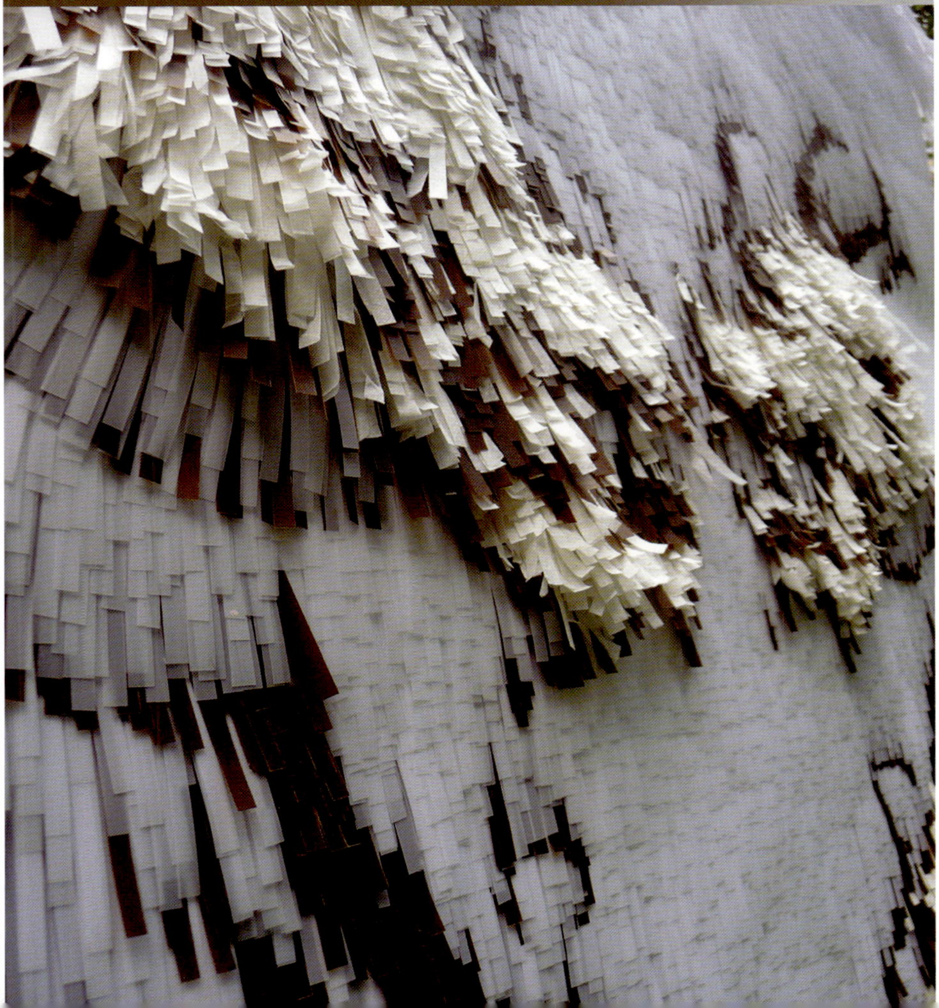

5. **Kabuki**
Size: 35 x 85 cm

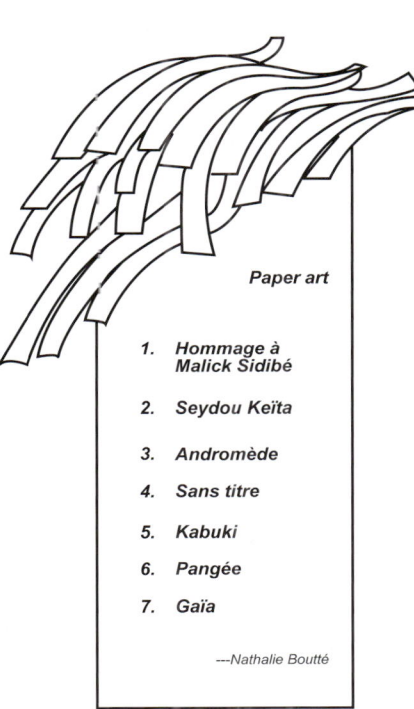

Paper art

1. Hommage à Malick Sidibé
2. Seydou Keïta
3. Andromède
4. Sans titre
5. Kabuki
6. Pangée
7. Gaïa

---Nathalie Boutté

Nathalie Boutté cuts long narrow strips of paper that she patiently assembles from recycled tissue paper and discarded novels, one by one thus creating a feather effect with constantly evolves. She uses colour and grey as well as tracing paper to create an even more varied effect. The strips are densely layered like thatch on a roof, exposing just the tips that act like pixels toから lager images.

Artist: Nathalie Boutté
Country: France

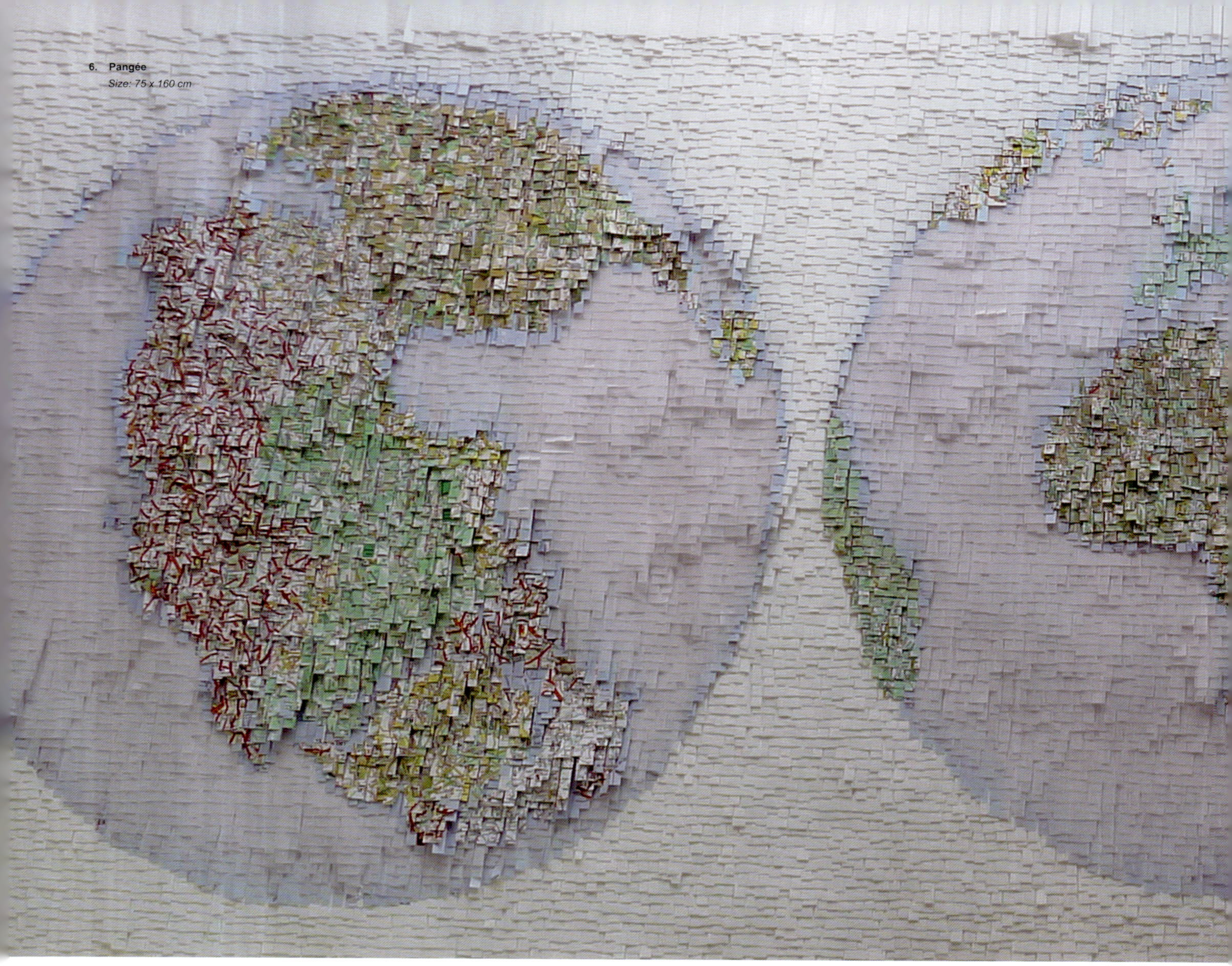

6. Pangée
Size: 75 x 160 cm

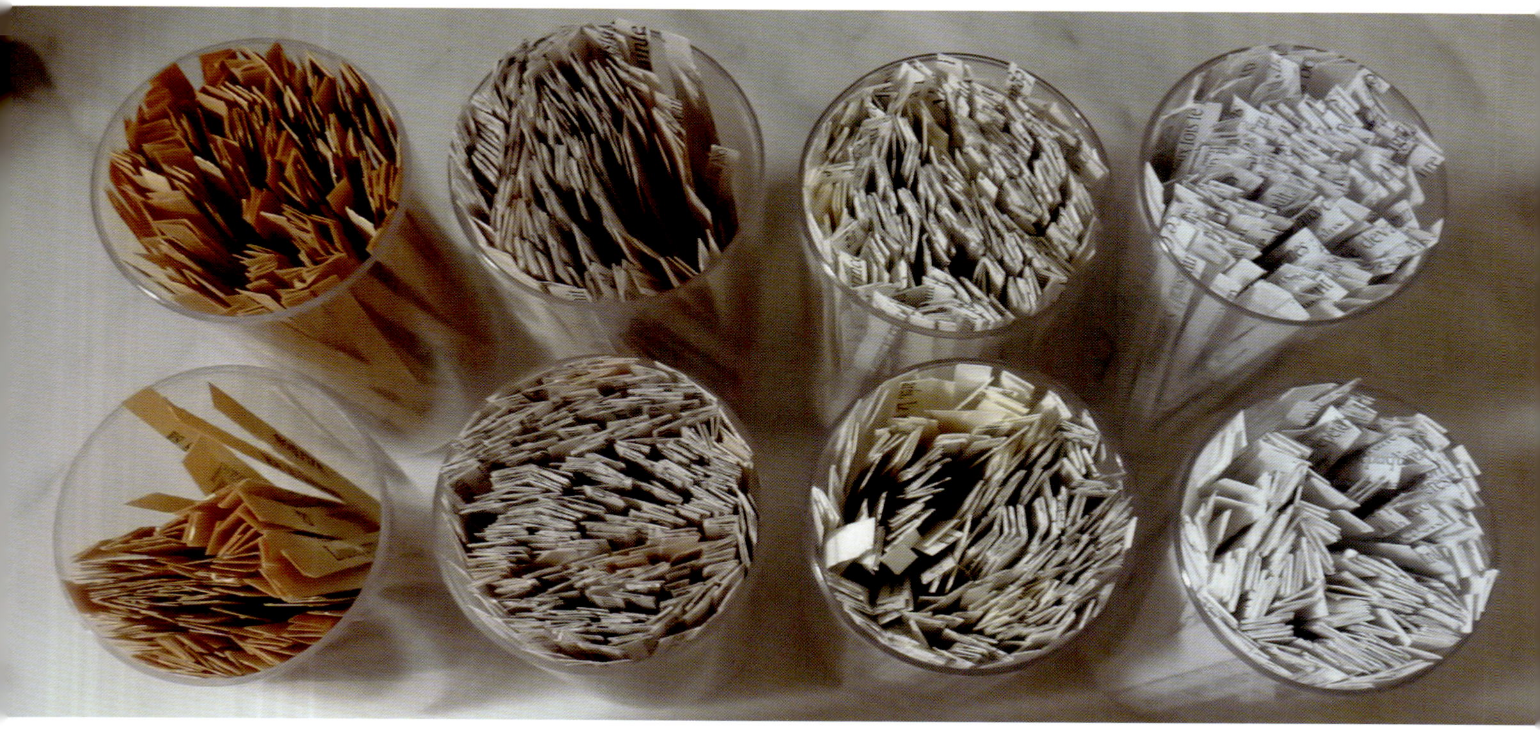

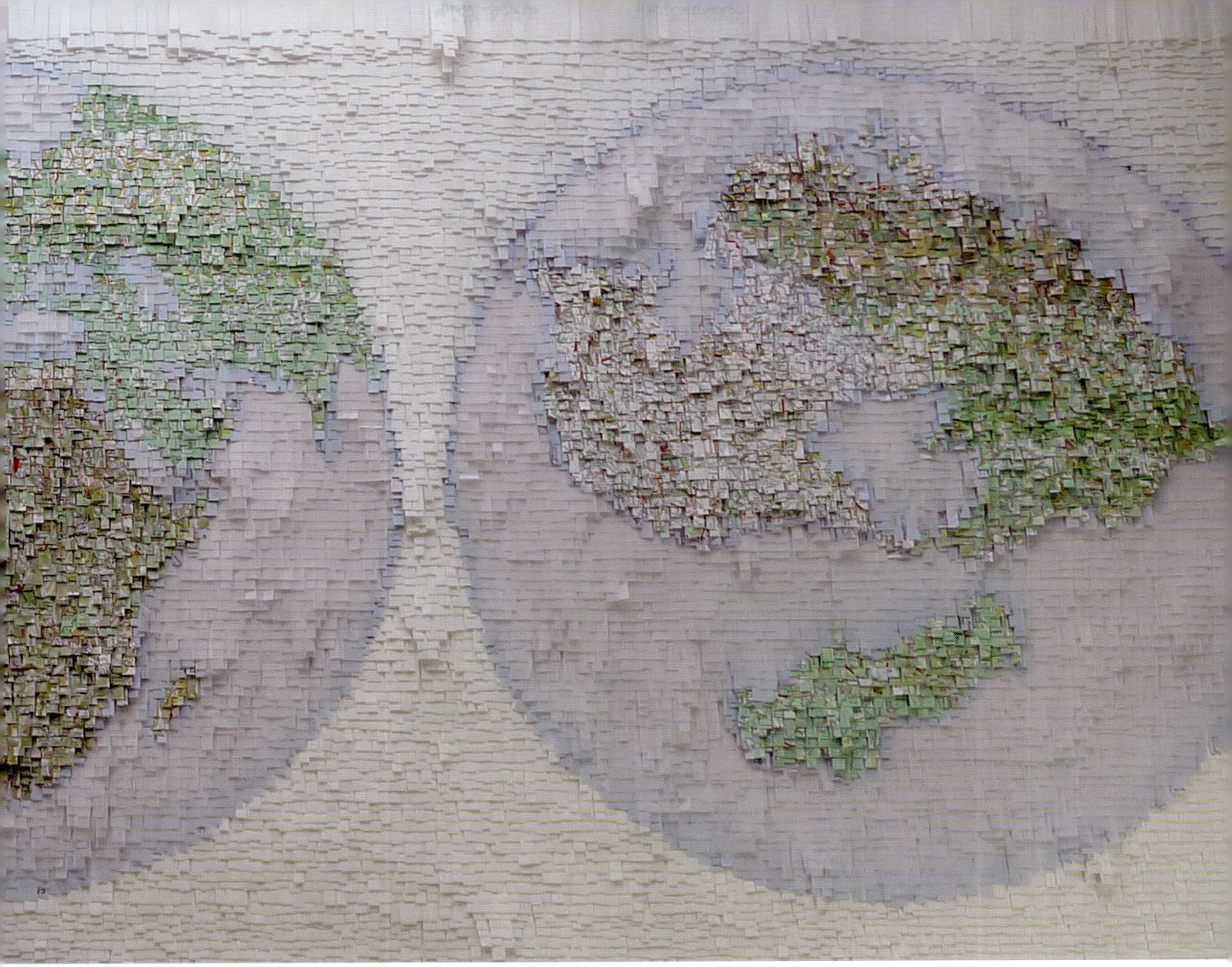

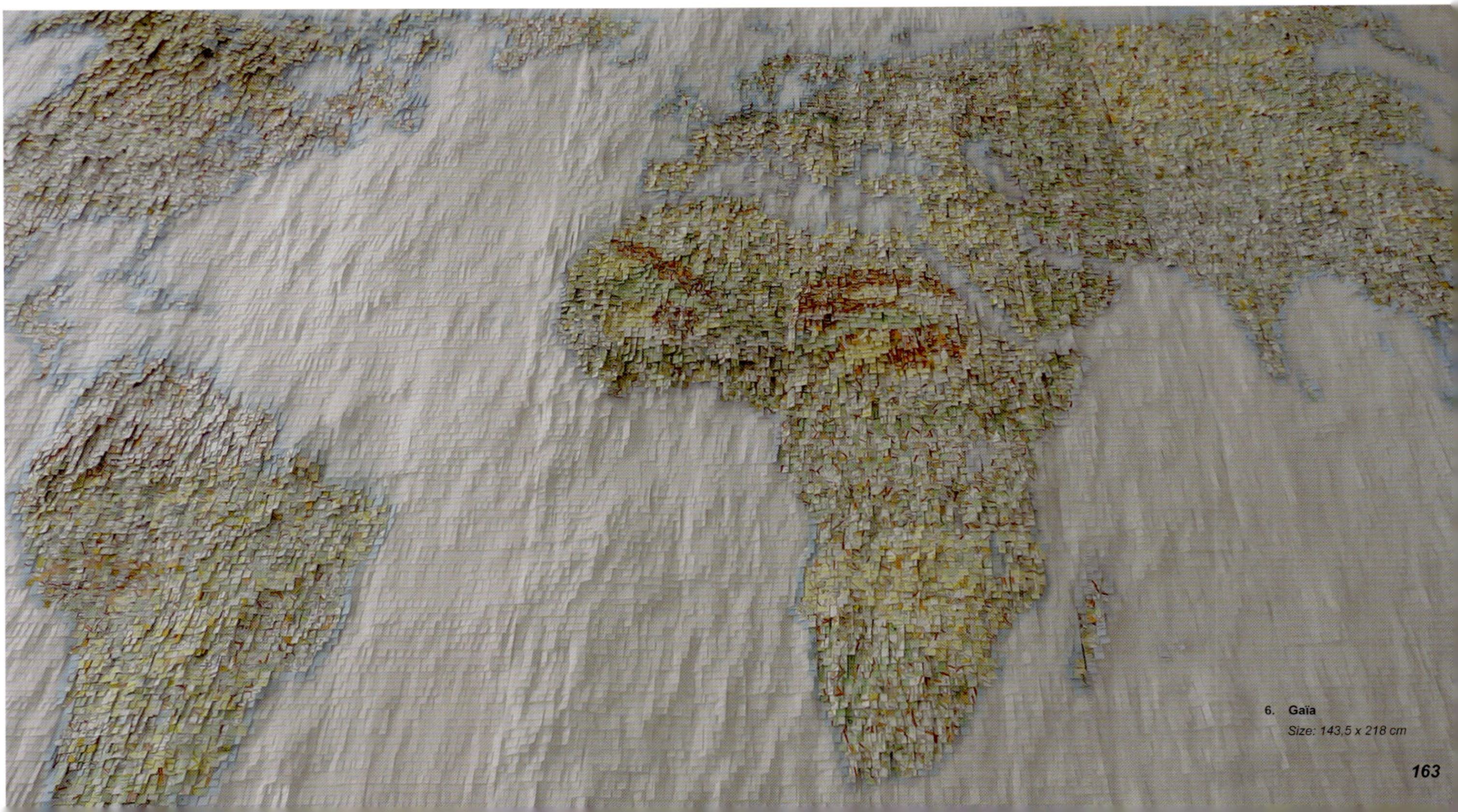

6. Gaïa
   Size: 143,5 x 218 cm

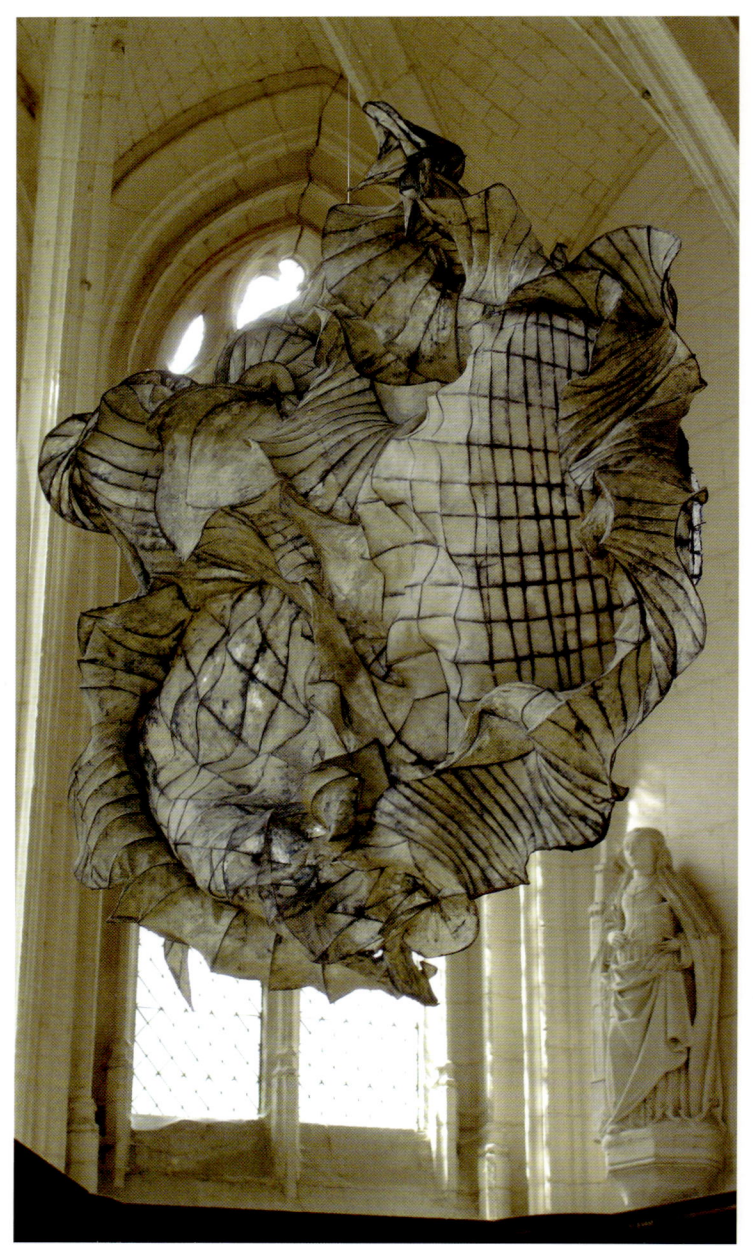
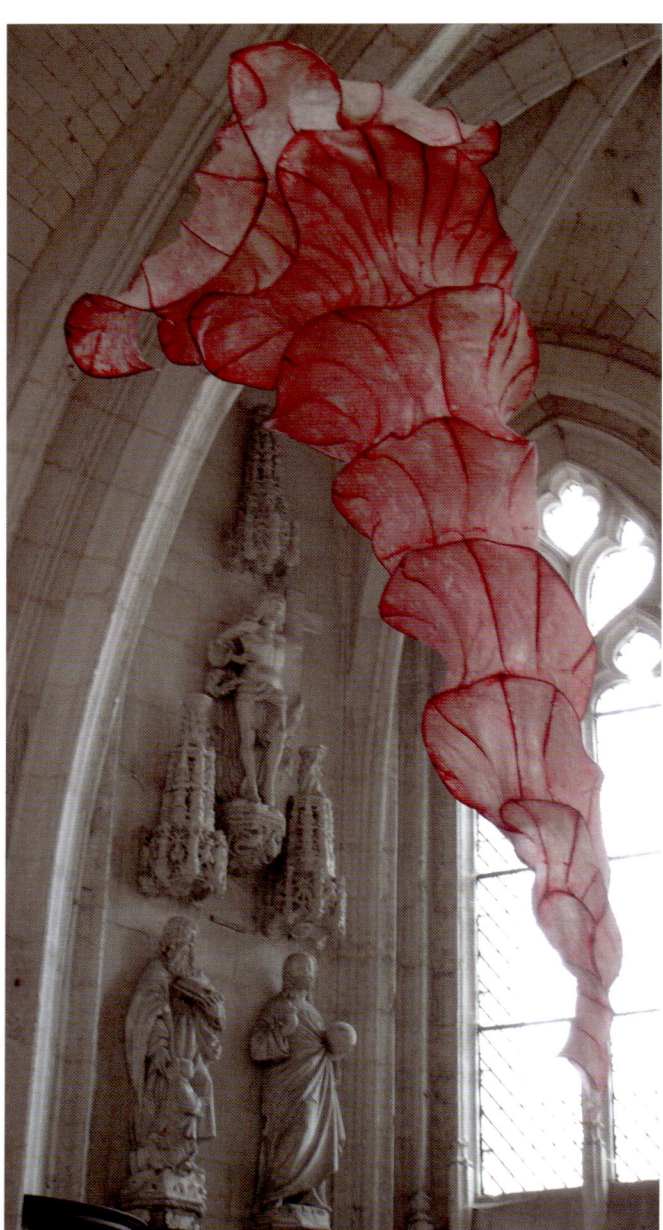
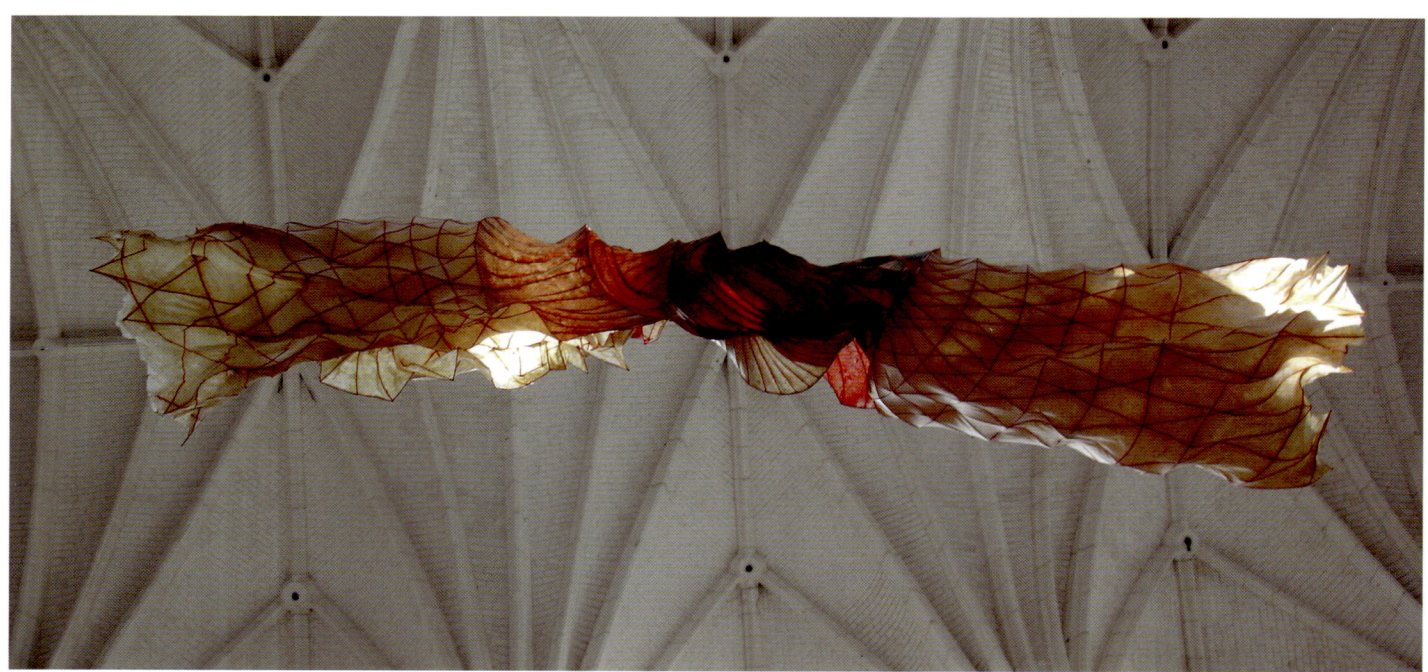

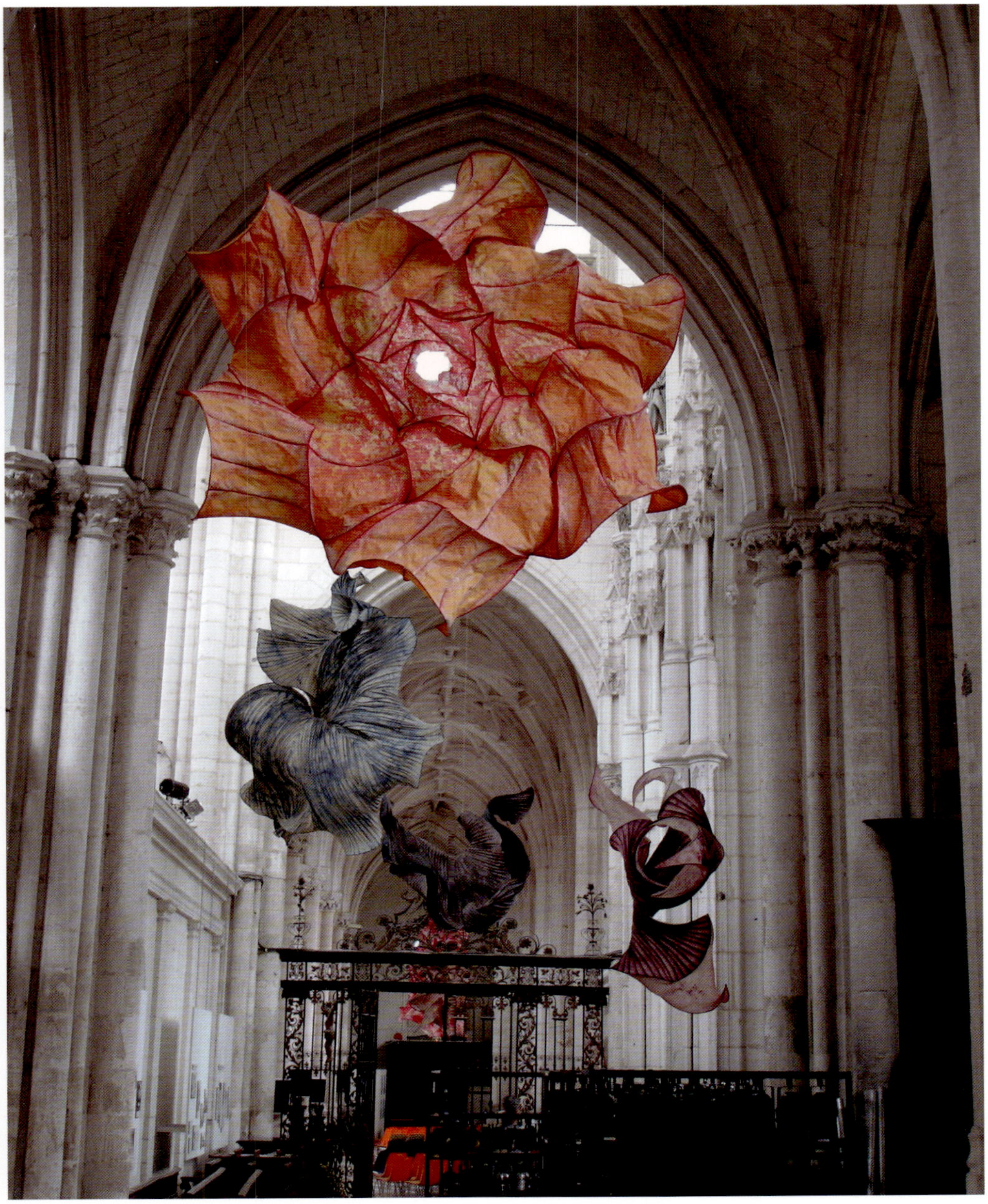

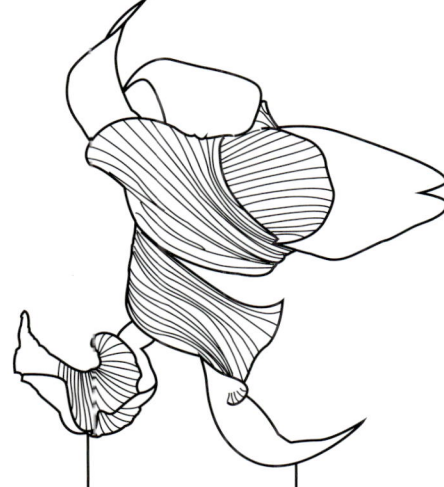

Exhibition in the Abbey of Saint Riquier, Somme, France

The surroundings of the Flamboyant Gothic Abbey from the early Middle Ages formed the most spectacular background for my paper sculptures.

The architecture of the Gothic Abbey with alll its ribs and arches resounded in my work. The light in all its open spaces created by stain glass windows showed the transparence of my work. The lightness of my paper sculptures made them softly turn and move on the air streams of the singing public.

---Peter Gentenaar

Artist: Peter Gentenaar
Country: Holland
Client: La commune de Saint-Riquier (France)
Photographer: P.Gentenaar

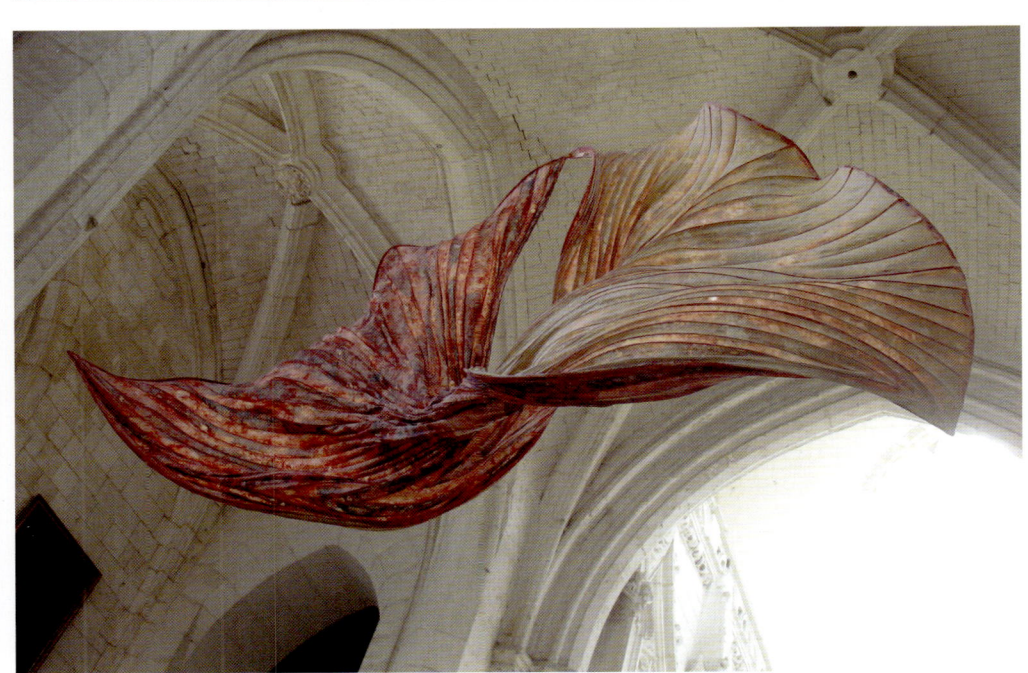

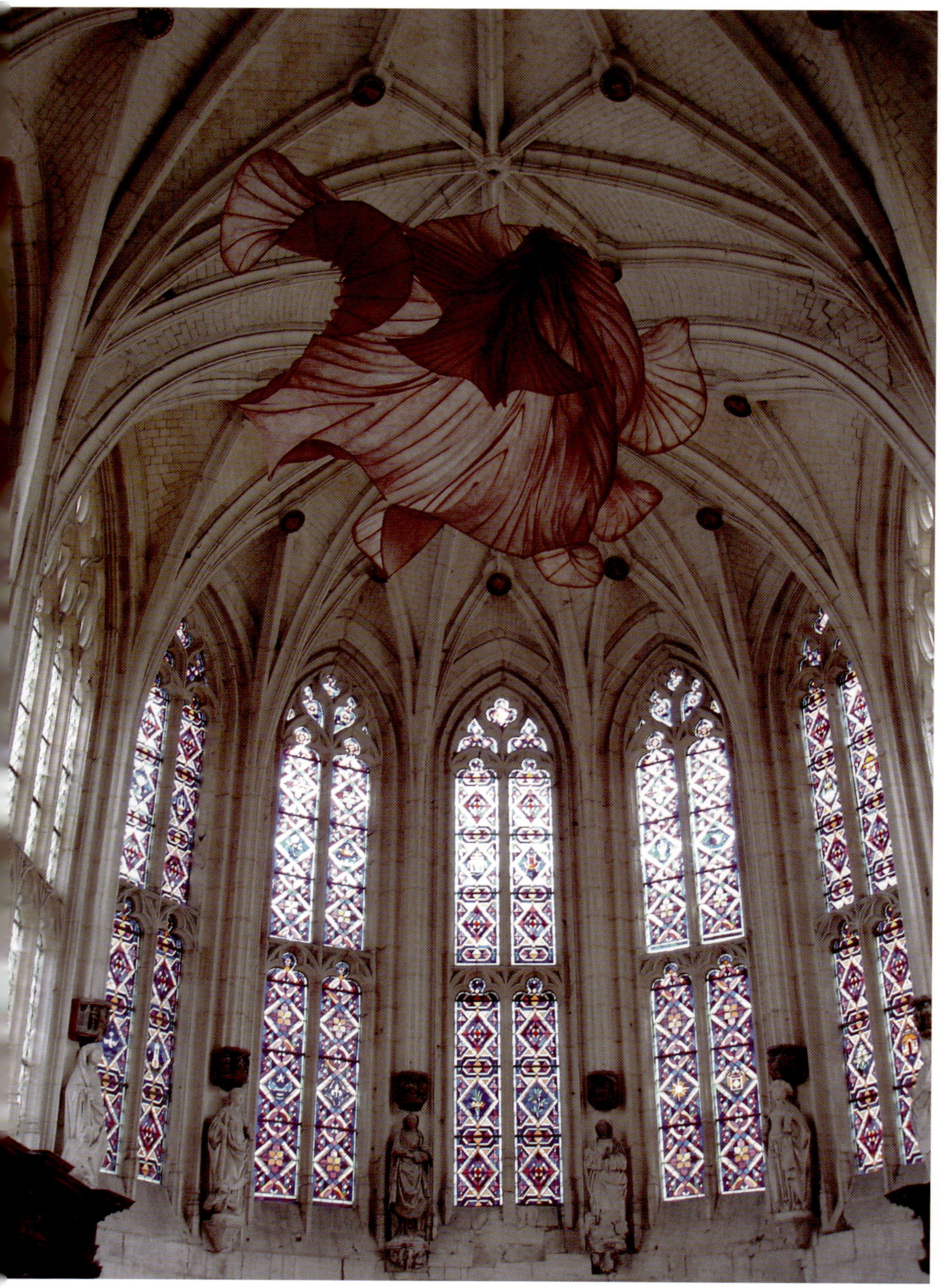

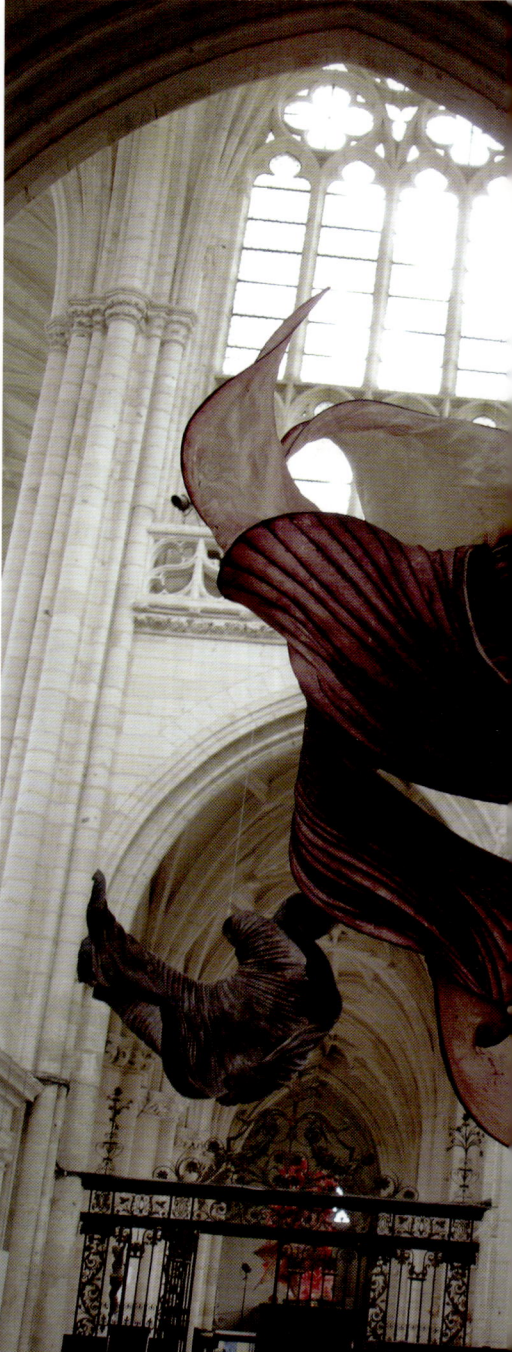

Artist: Peter Gentenaar
Country: Holland
Client: La commune de Saint-Riquier (France)
Photographer: P.Gentenaar

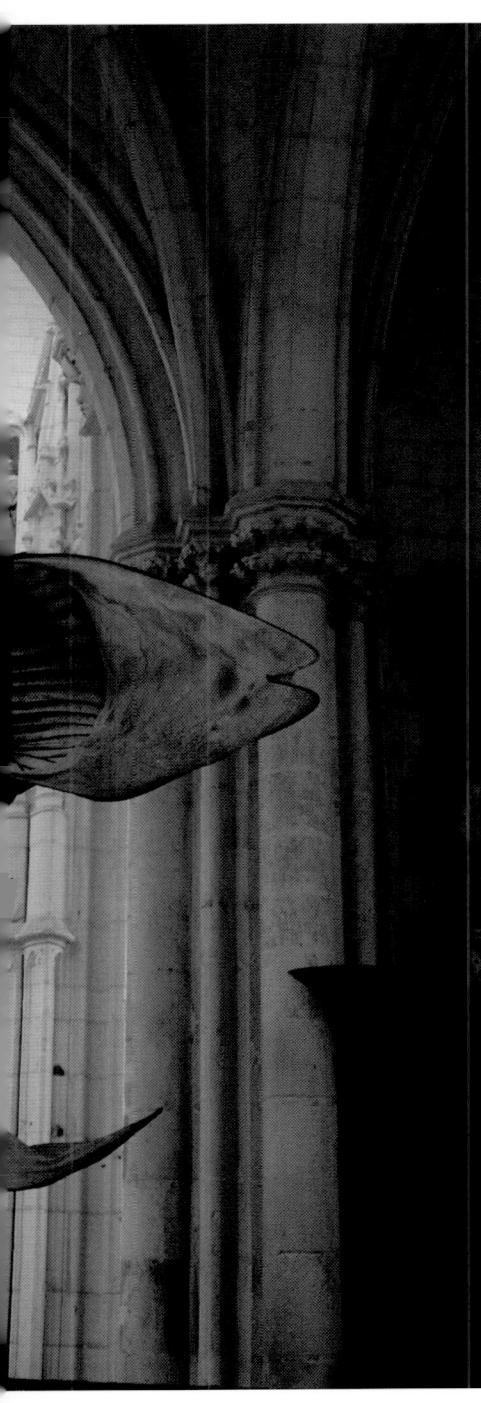

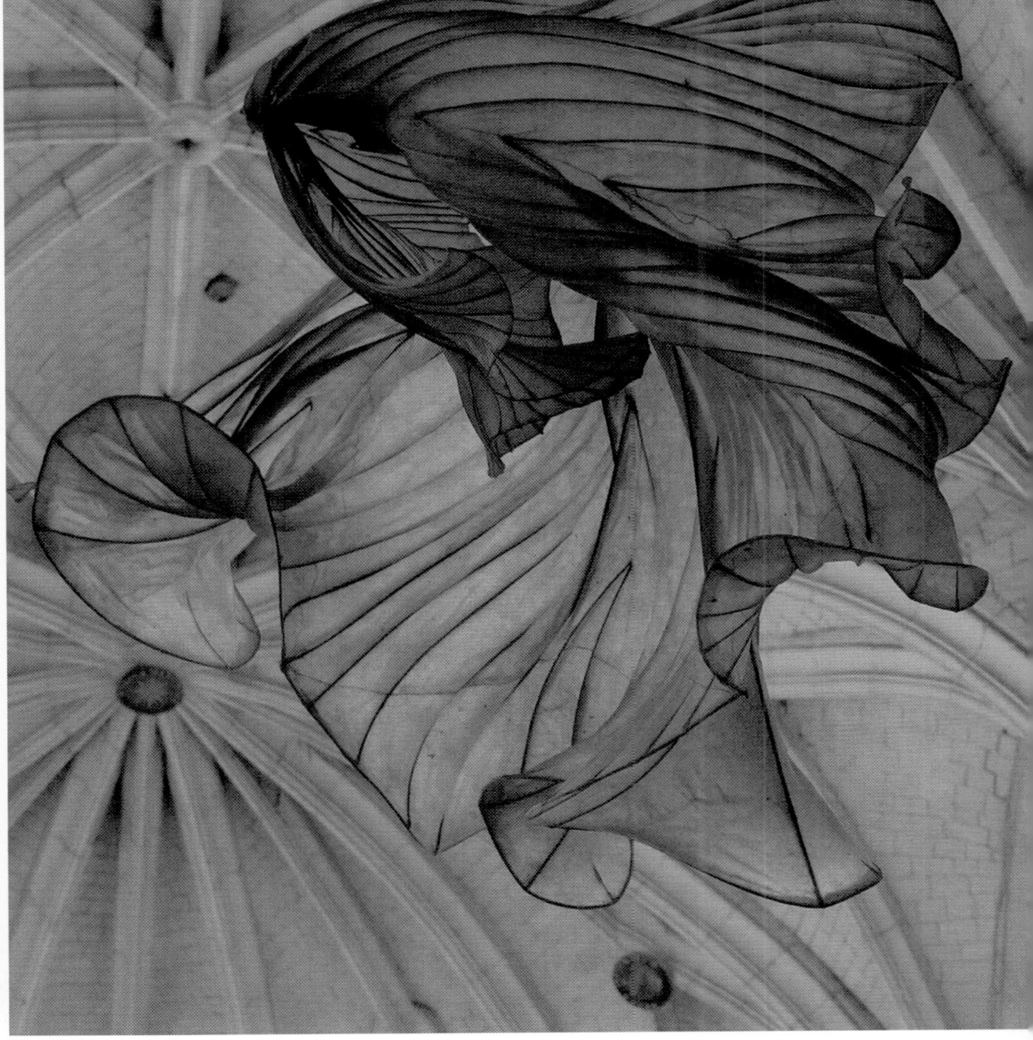

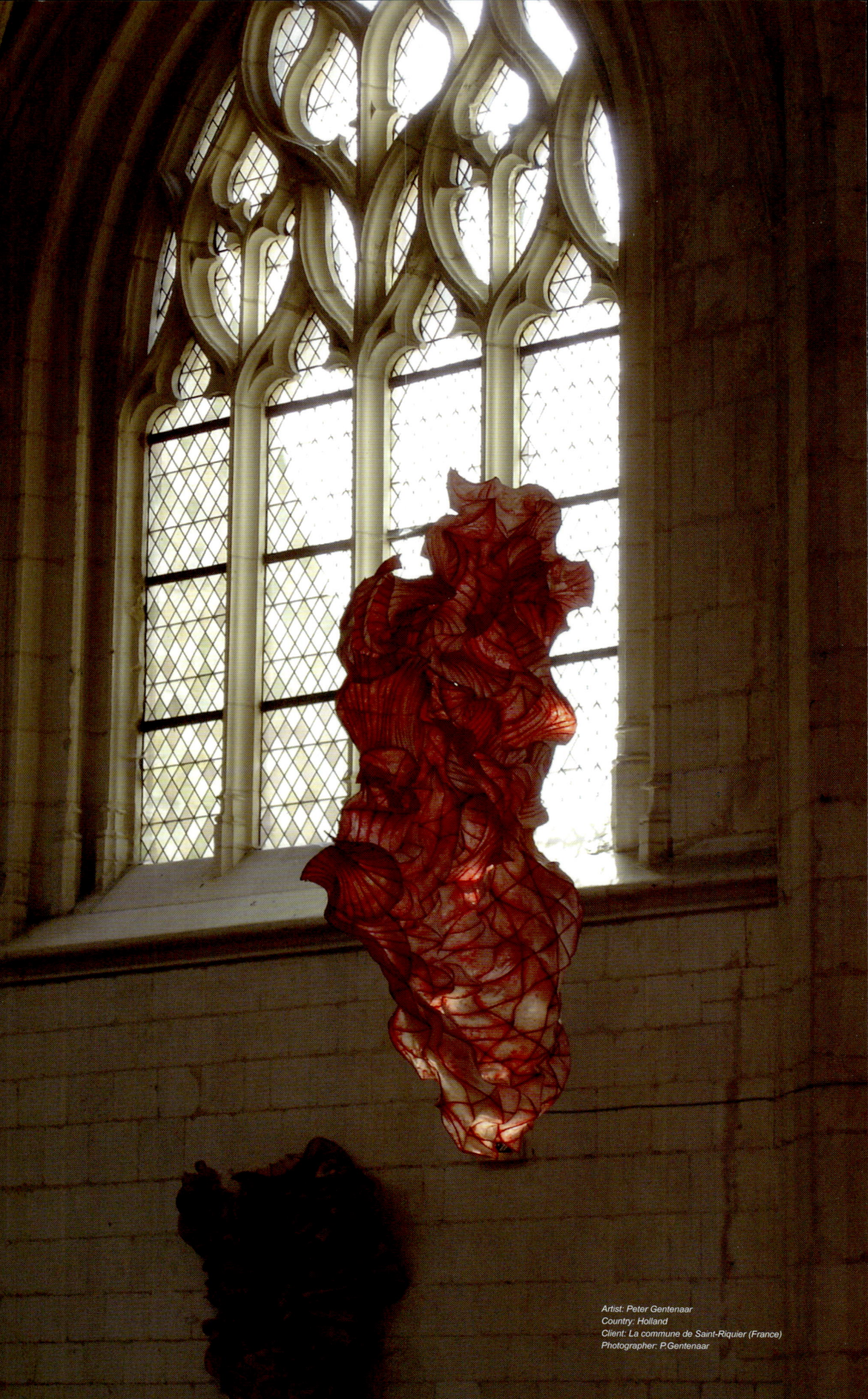

Artist: Peter Gentenaar
Country: Holland
Client: La commune de Saint-Riquier (France)
Photographer: P.Gentenaar

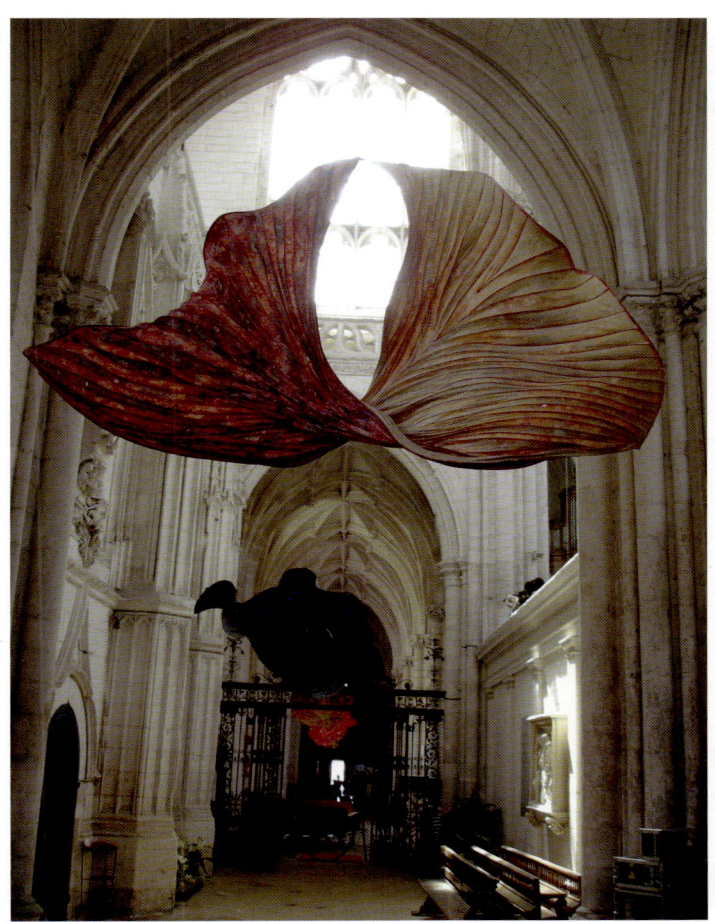
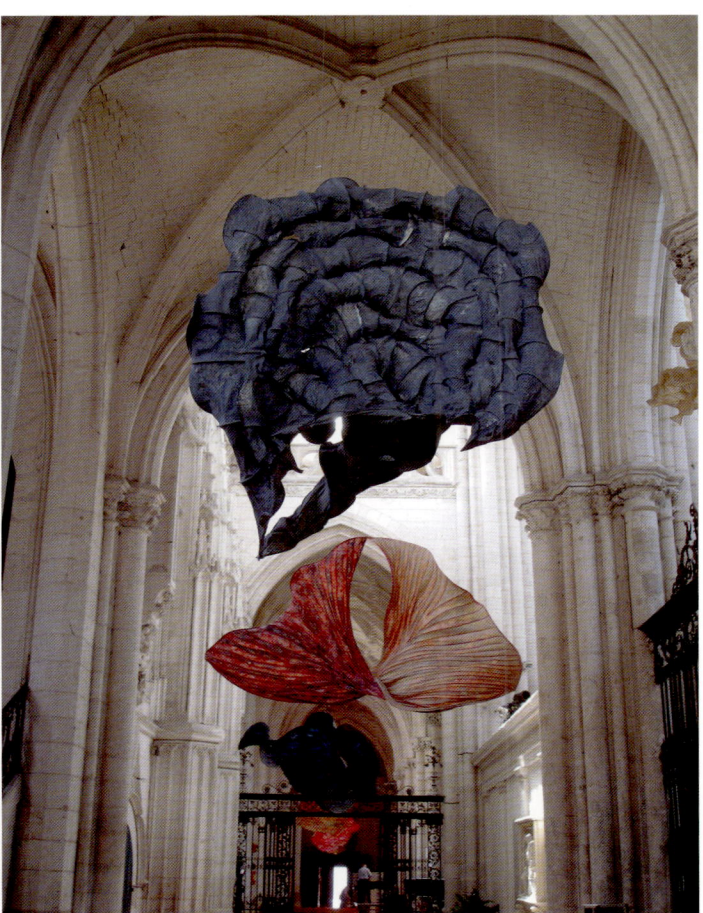

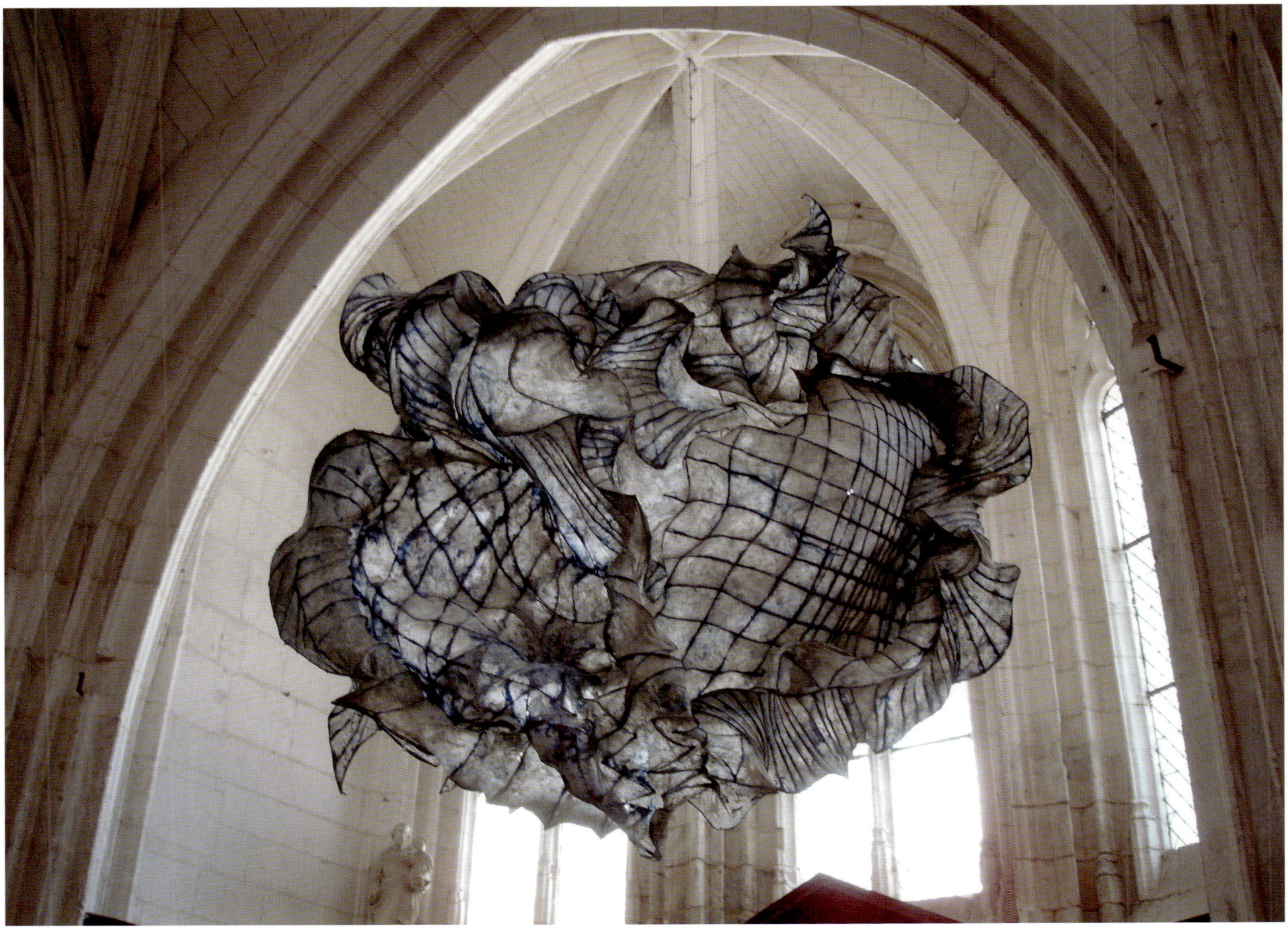

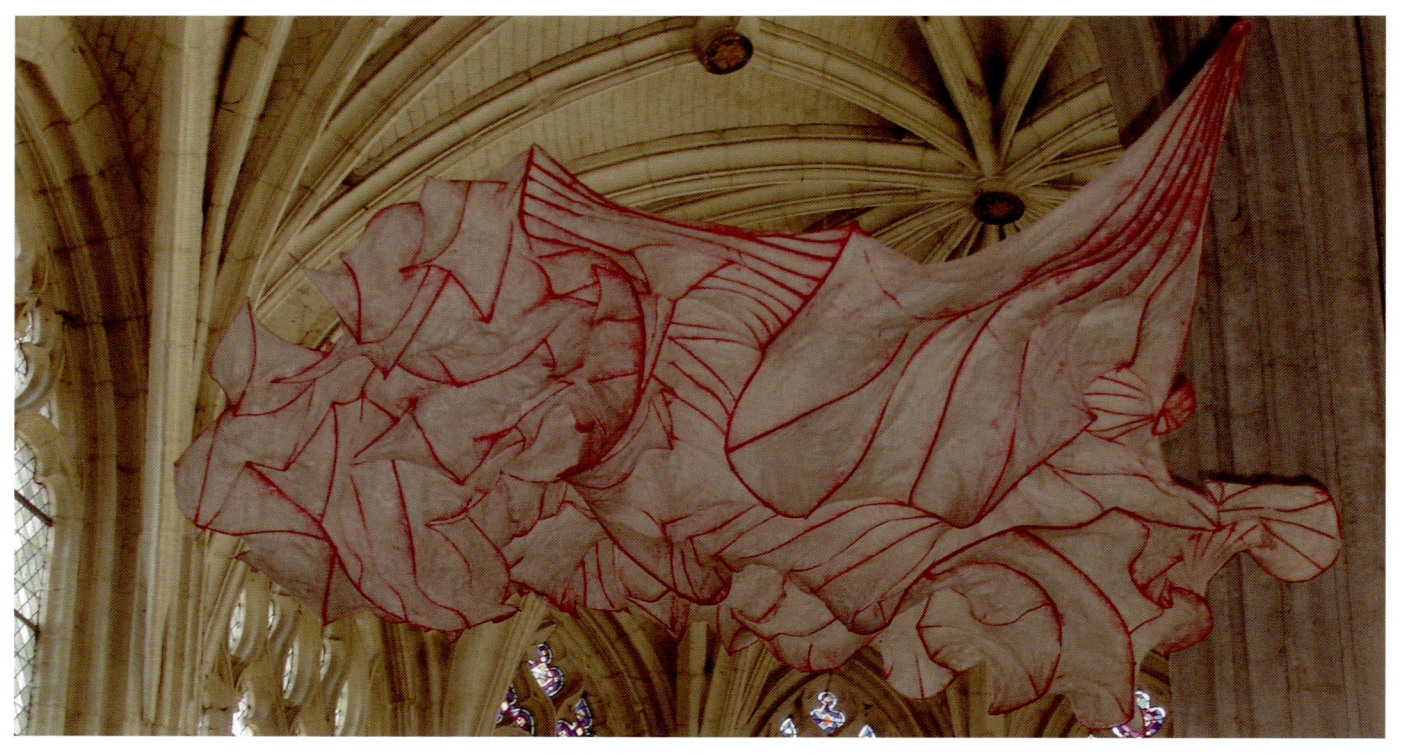

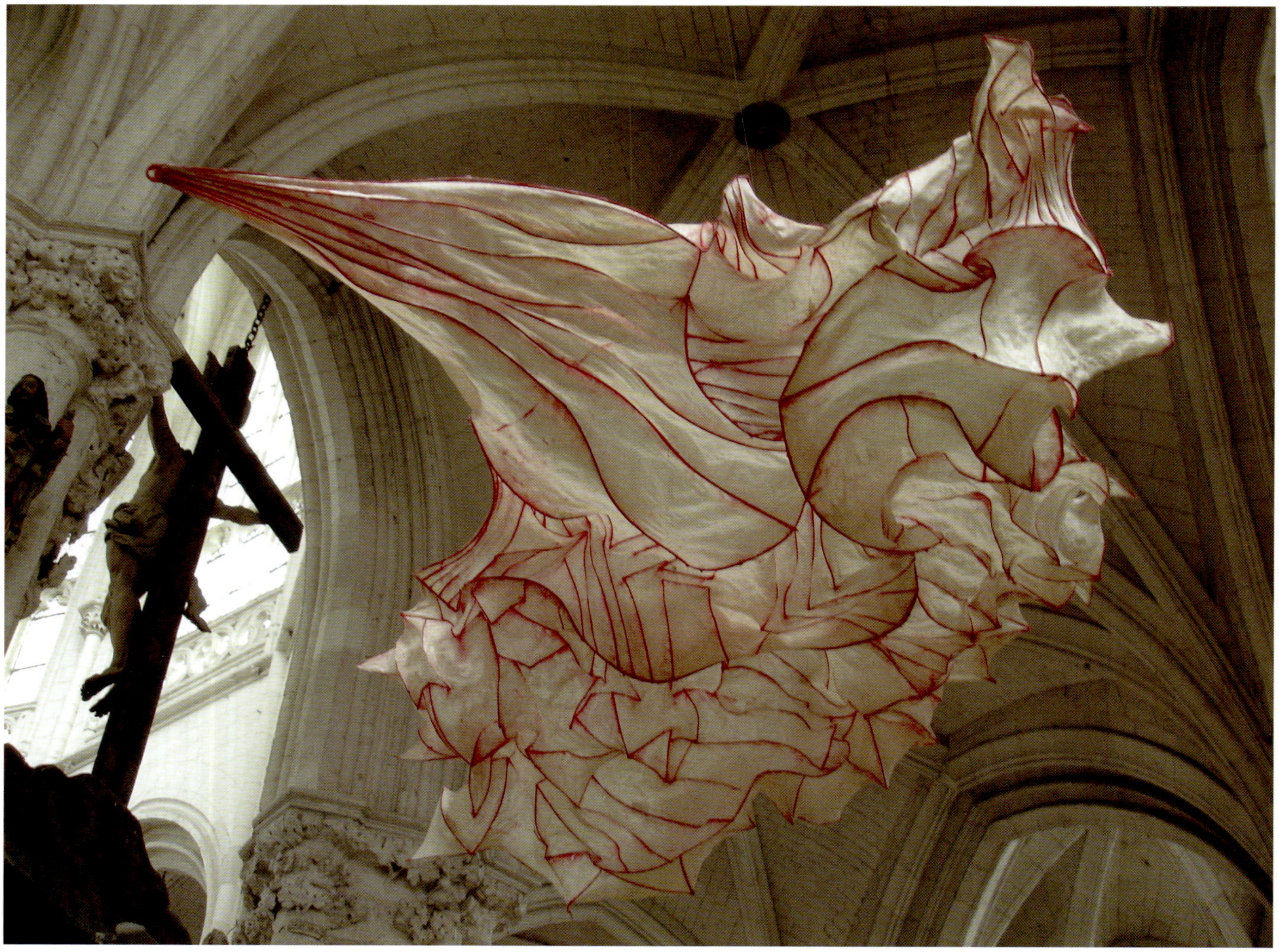

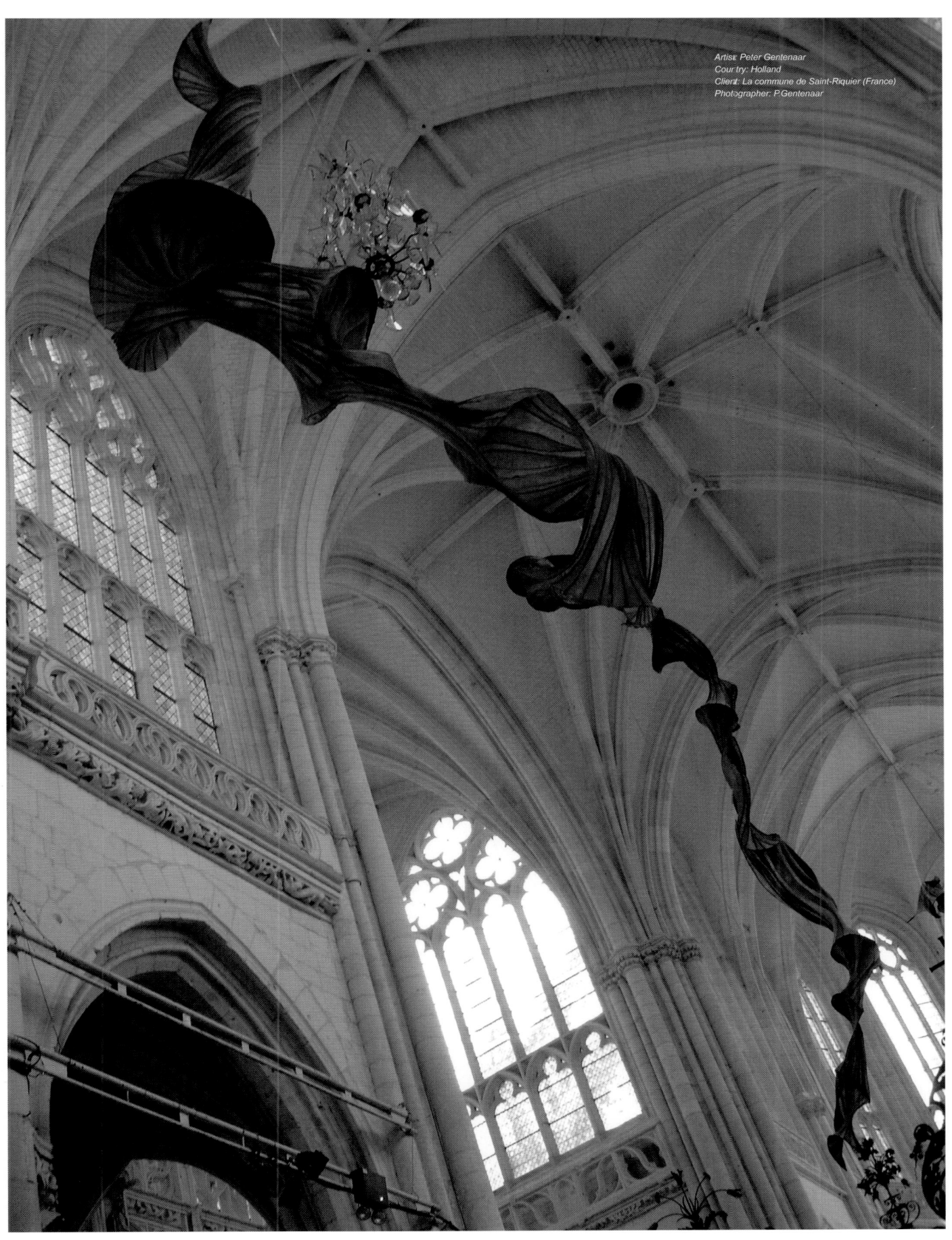

Artist: Peter Gentenaar
Country: Holland
Client: La commune de Saint-Riquier (France)
Photographer: P.Gentenaar

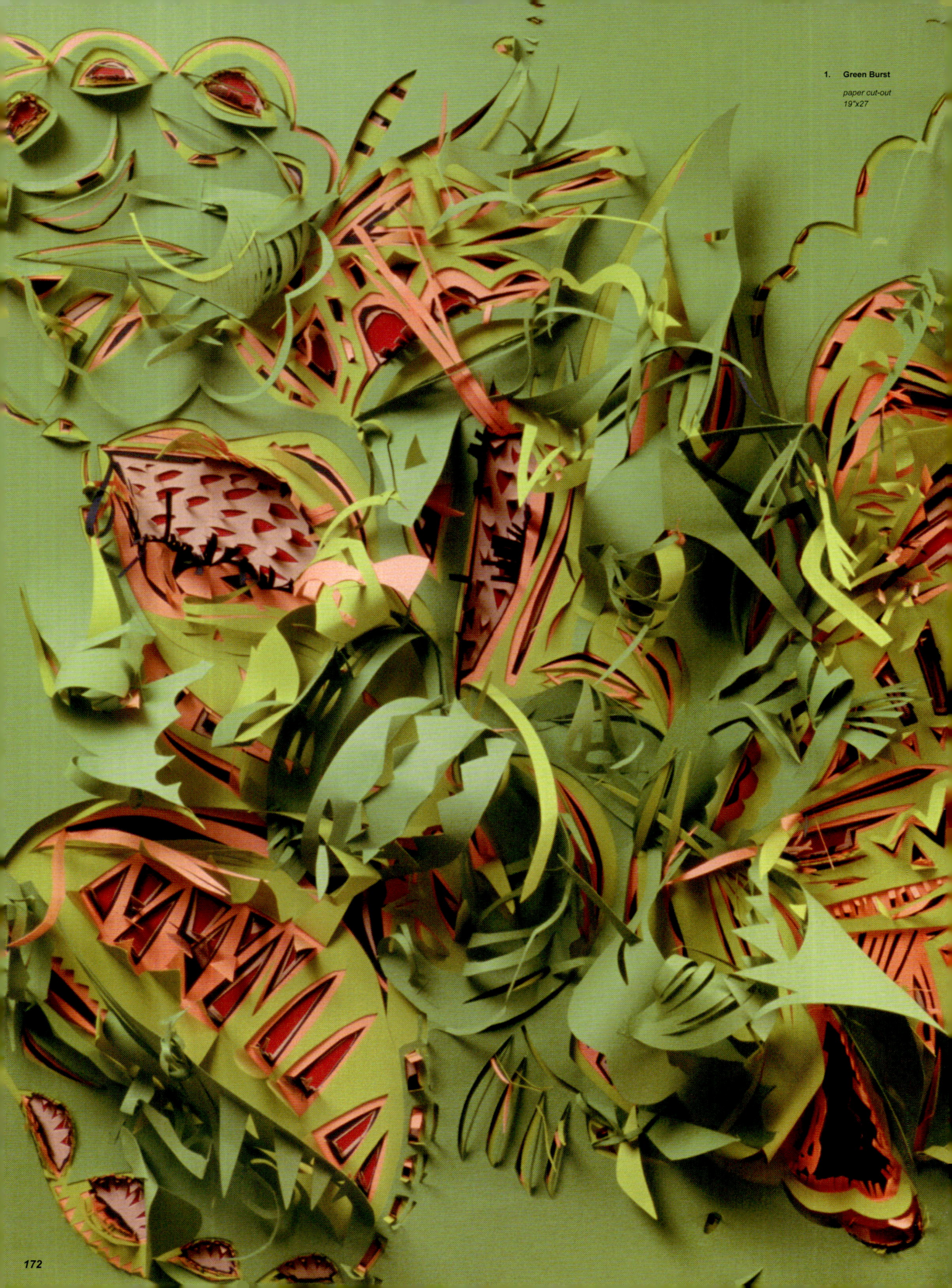

1. **Green Burst**
paper cut-out
19"x27

2. Natura

colored pencil, cut-out, collage
21" x 20"

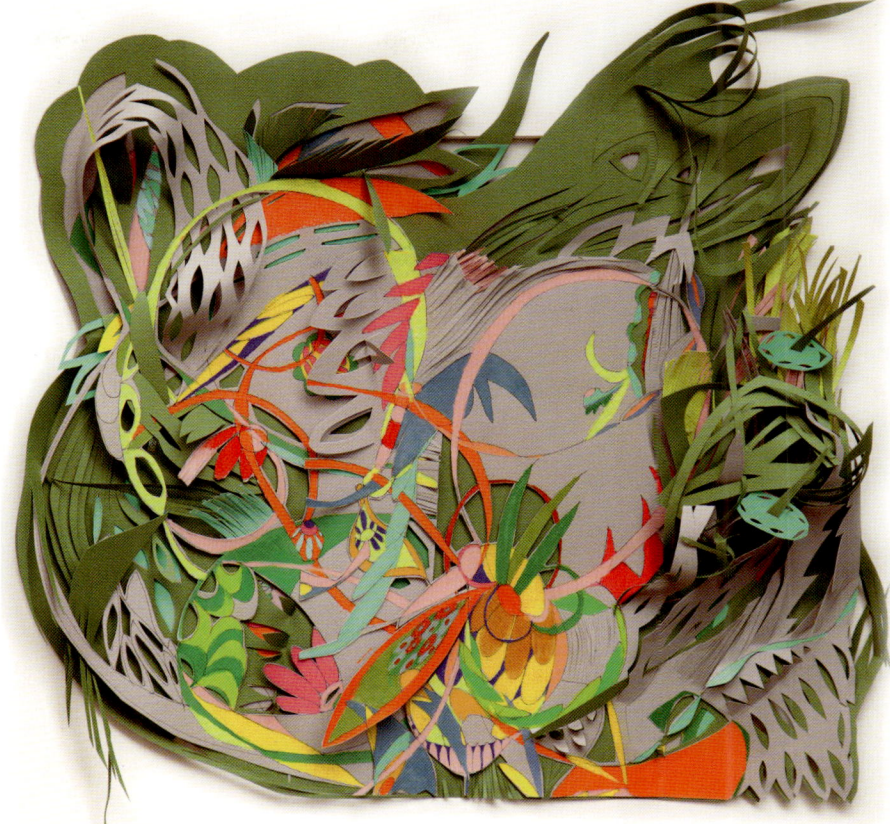

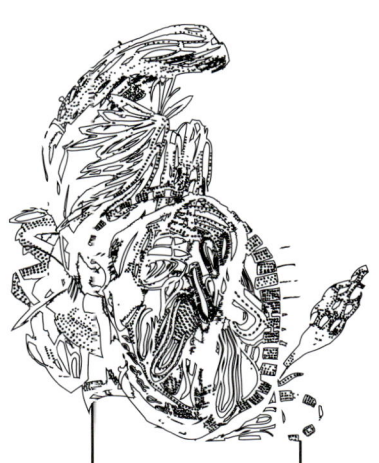

In Bloom, Natural Precision

1. Green Burst
2. Natura
3. Navy Wonder
4. Vision Pure
5. Physis
6. Combustible Rose
7. The Weekend
8. Andrade
9. Human Nature
10. Bonnefoy

---Simone Lourenço

3. Navy Wonder

paper cut-out
19"x27"

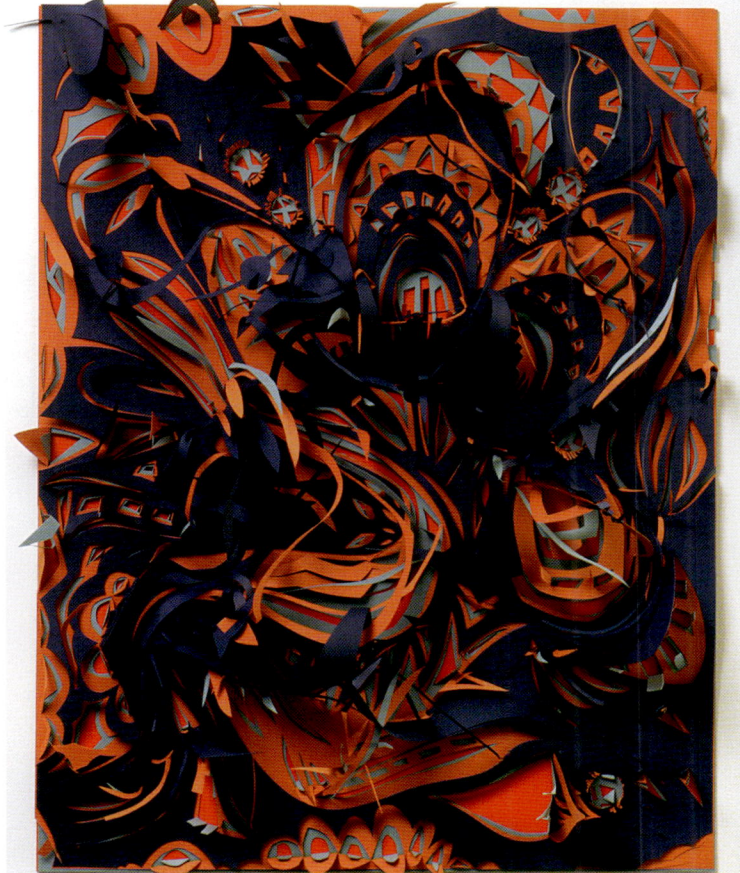

I have always held a fascination with the plant kingdom and patterns in nature. My intent is to capture the movement of growth and infiniteness in plant and animal life. I create space and naturalistic elements in the 2-D cut-outs by carving and weaving multi-layers of paper into shapes, excising parts to build on line and detail. When using markers, I allow the marks made from previous drawings to impress the direction of what will be next.

Botany books reference my work in the anatomy of plants along with flower arranging for elegant balance and composition. Above all, nature itself, cyclical in beauty and ever changing inform these works.

Artist: Simone Lourenço
Country: USA
Galleries: Overtones, Los Angeles, CA; Vincent Price Art Museum, Los Angeles, CA; Space on White, New York, NY.

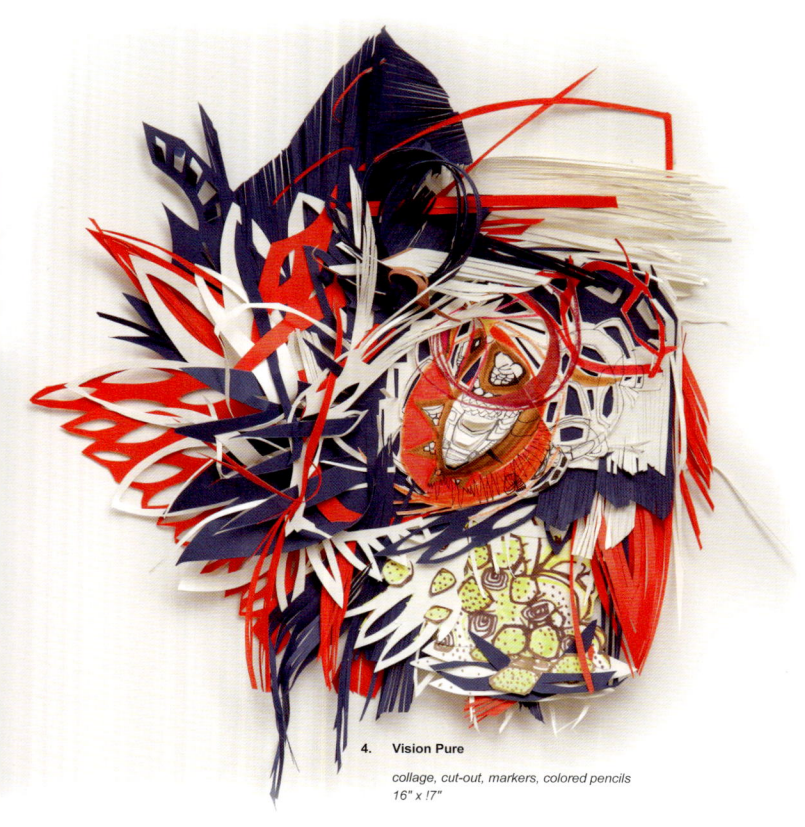

4. **Vision Pure**
collage, cut-out, markers, colored pencils
16" x 17"

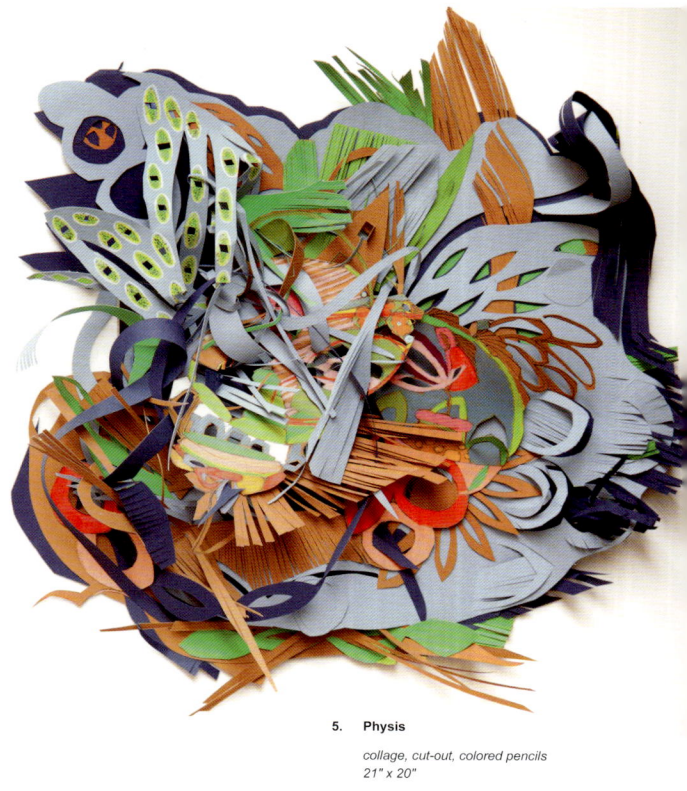

5. **Physis**
collage, cut-out, colored pencils
21" x 20"

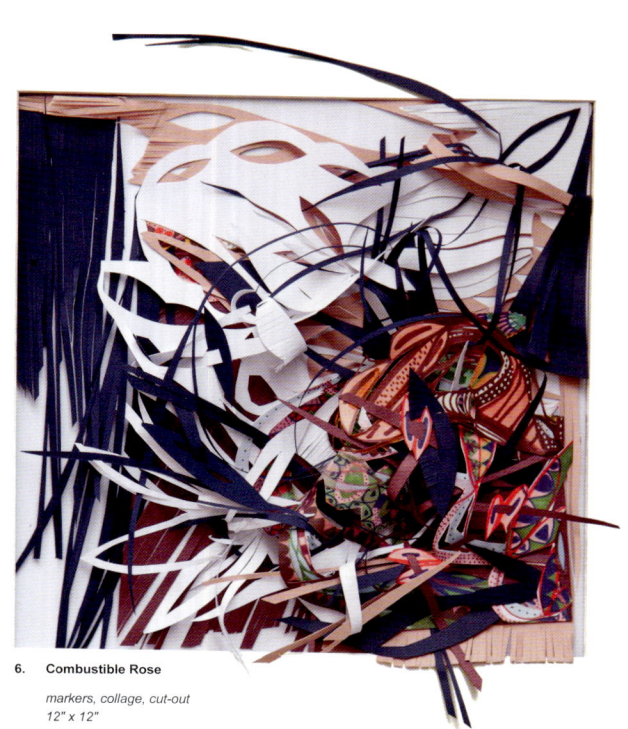

6. **Combustible Rose**
markers, collage, cut-out
12" x 12"

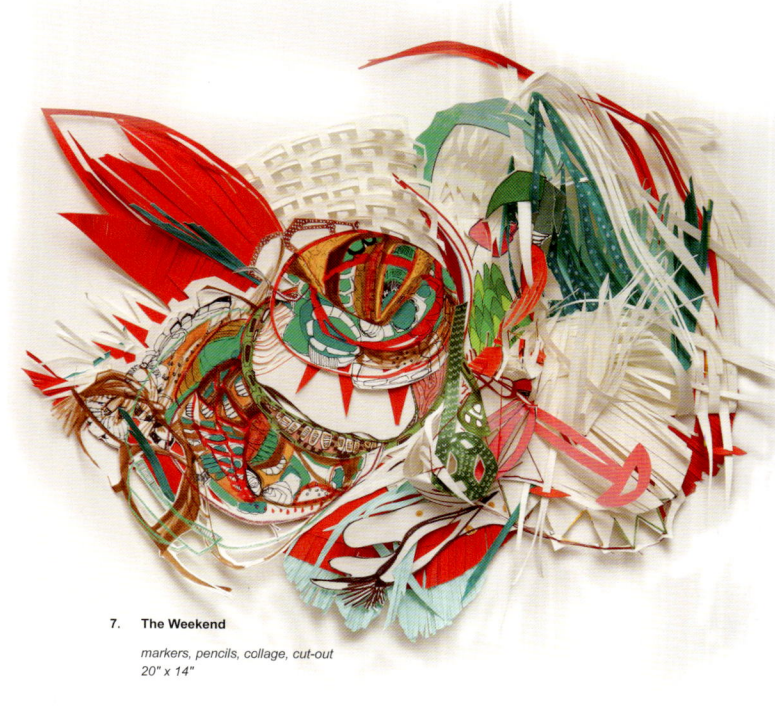

7. **The Weekend**
markers, pencils, collage, cut-out
20" x 14"

8. Andrade

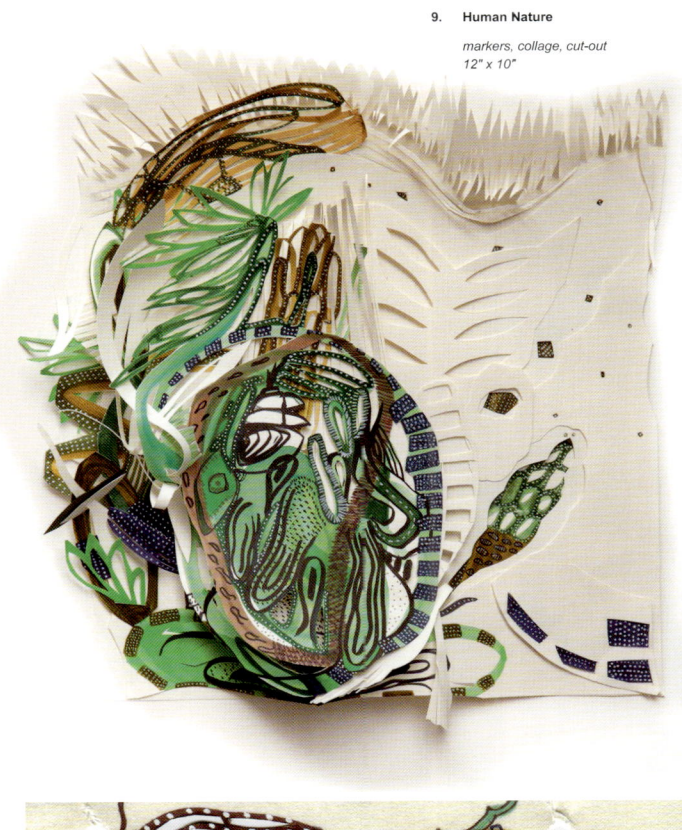

9. **Human Nature**
markers, collage, cut-out
12" x 10"

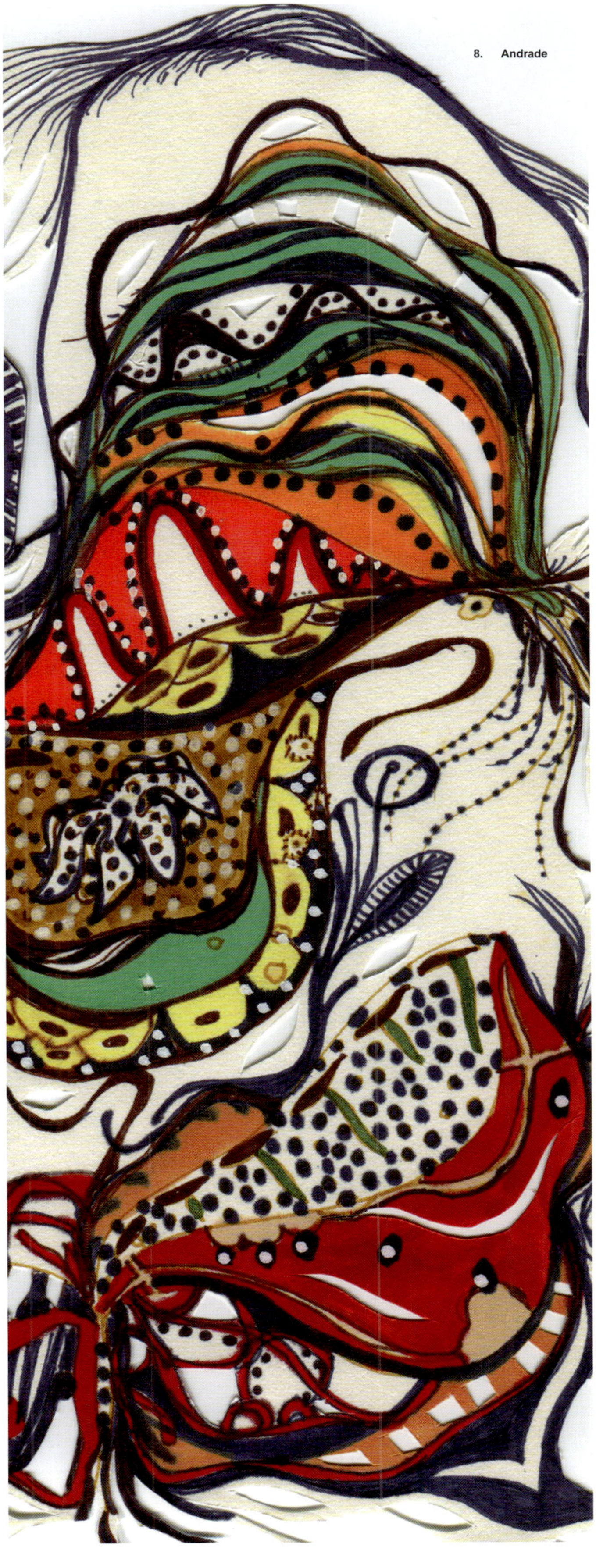

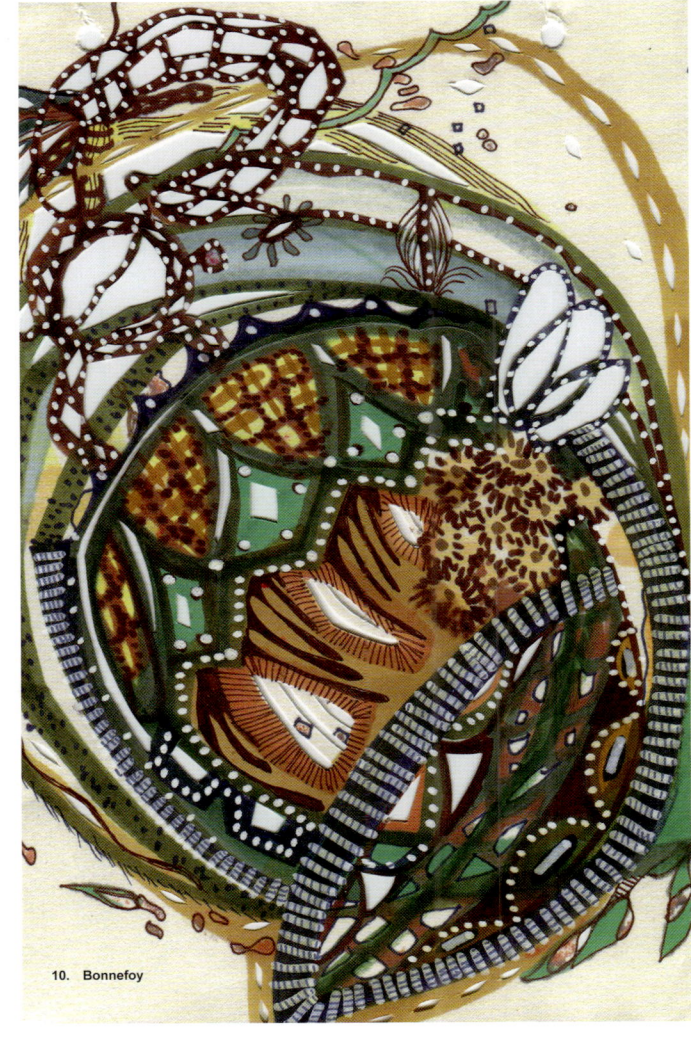

10. Bonnefoy

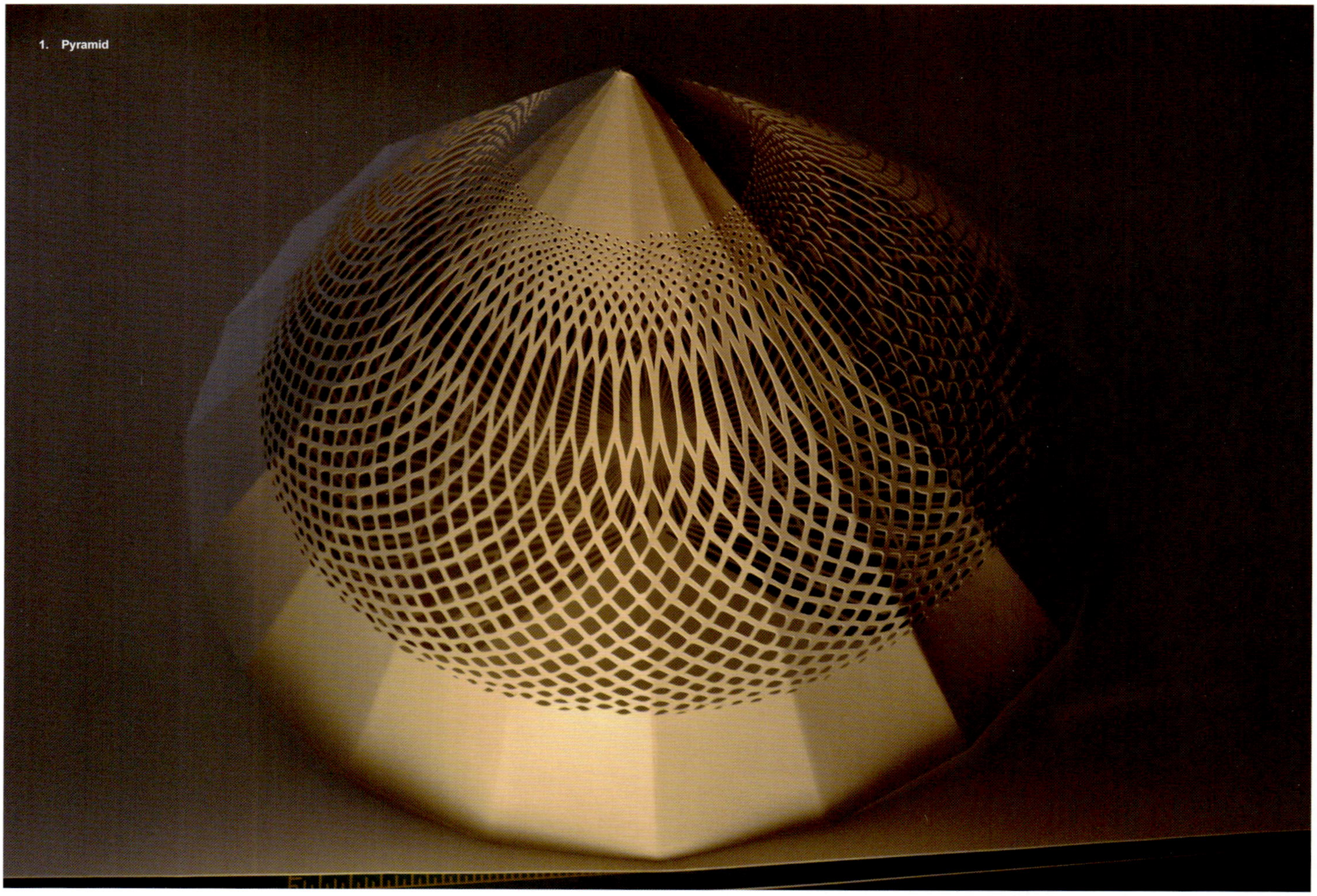

1. Pyramid

2. Polyhedral

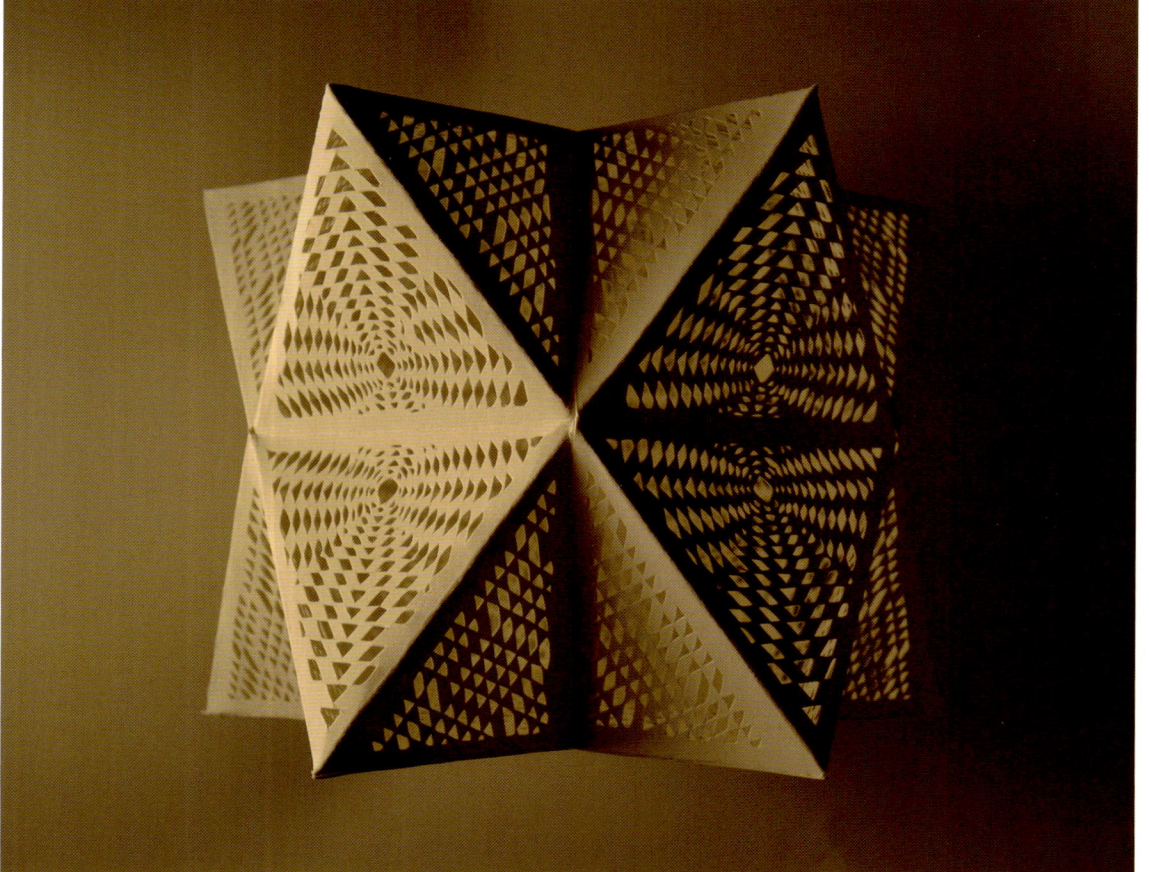

Hand cut paper: Intricate geometrical patterns are cut, layered and folded into three-dimensional works. Light-play and shadows interact with the form at times creating a magic-eye effect. Breaking up the information but still retaining it's geometrical organization. The themes reflect mutiplicity, fragility and synchrony in nature.

Artist: Tahiti Pehrson
Country: U.S.A
Photographer: Tahiti Pehrson

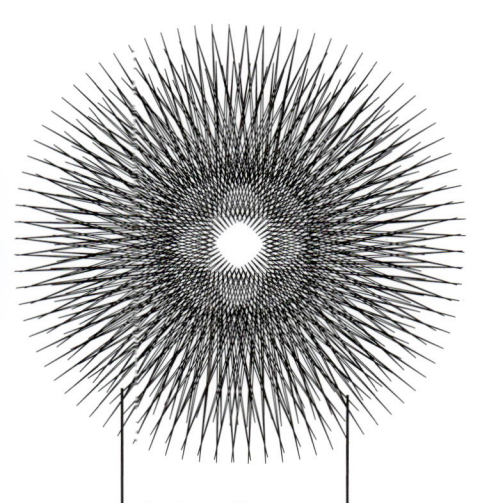

1. Pyramid
2. Polyhedral
3. Hexagrammic Prism
4. Dark Energy Dark
5. Genesis
6. Sea of Love
7. Ascending Spiral
8. Blue
9. Orange Crush

---Tahiti Pehrson

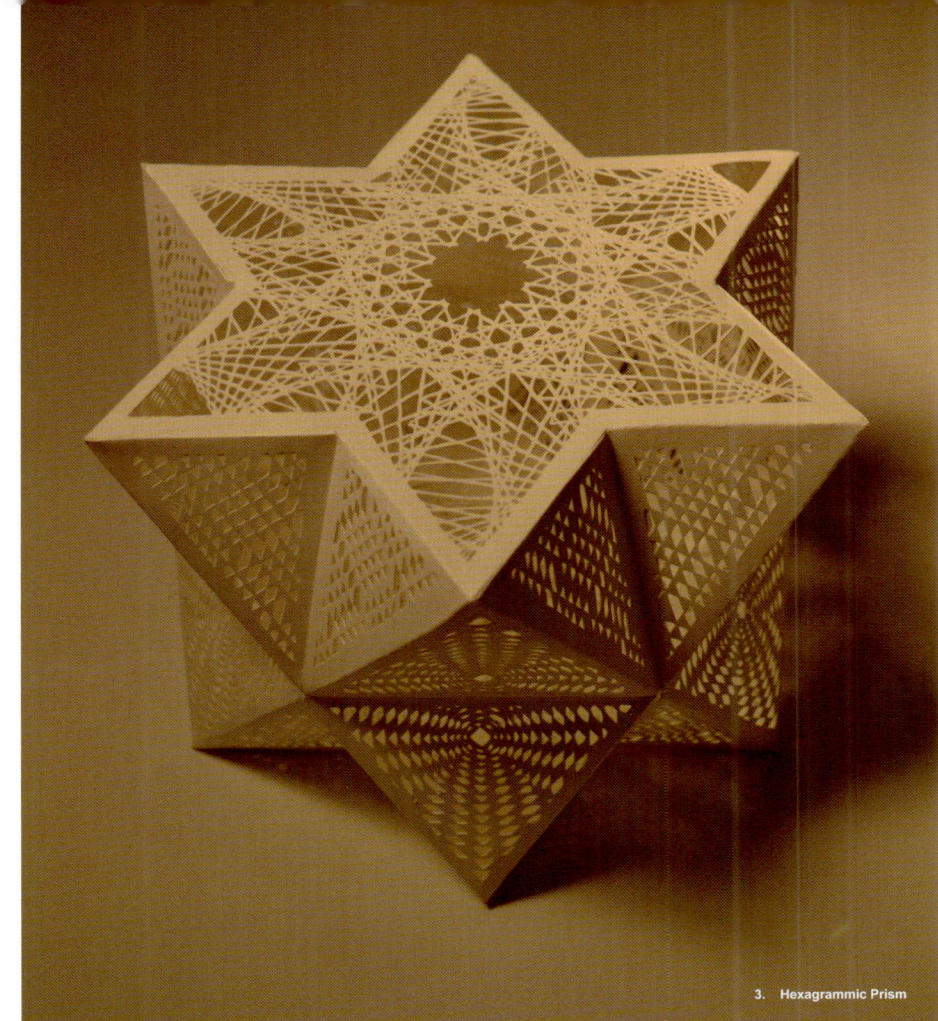

3. Hexagrammic Prism

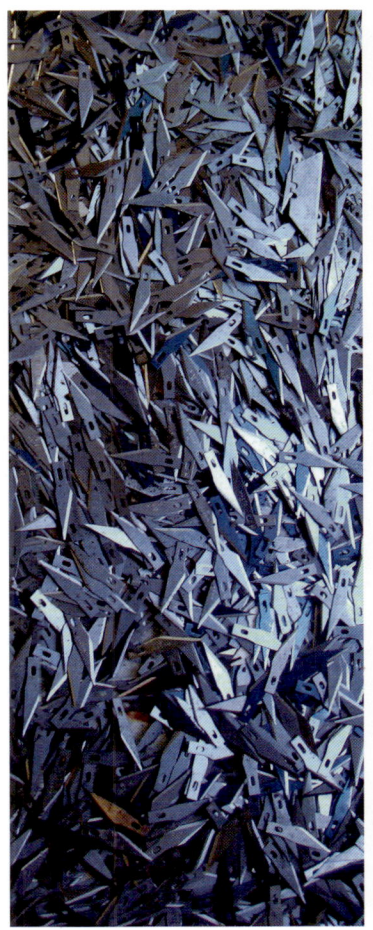

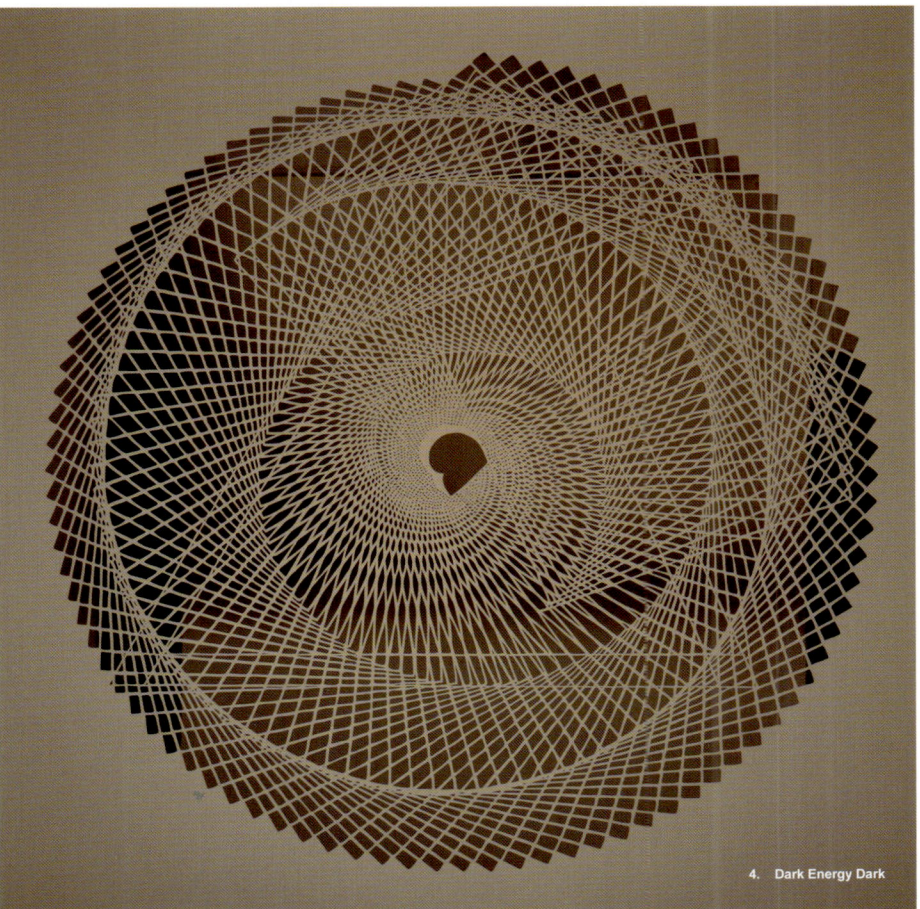

4. Dark Energy Dark

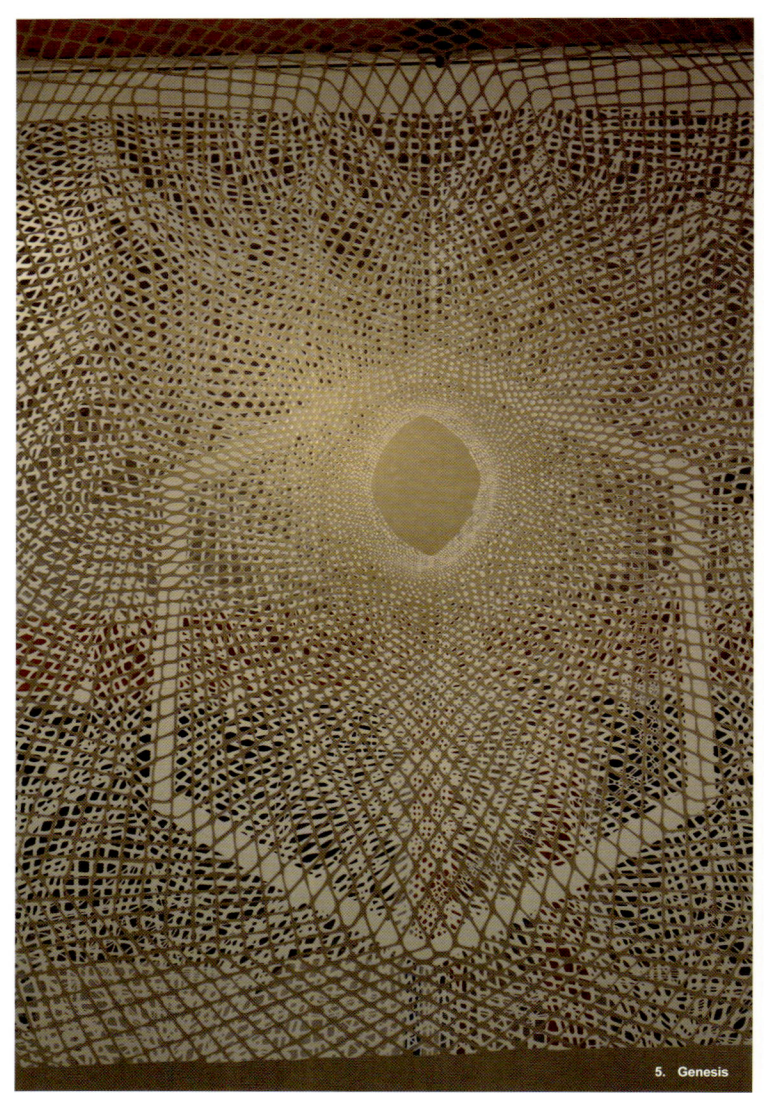

5. Genesis

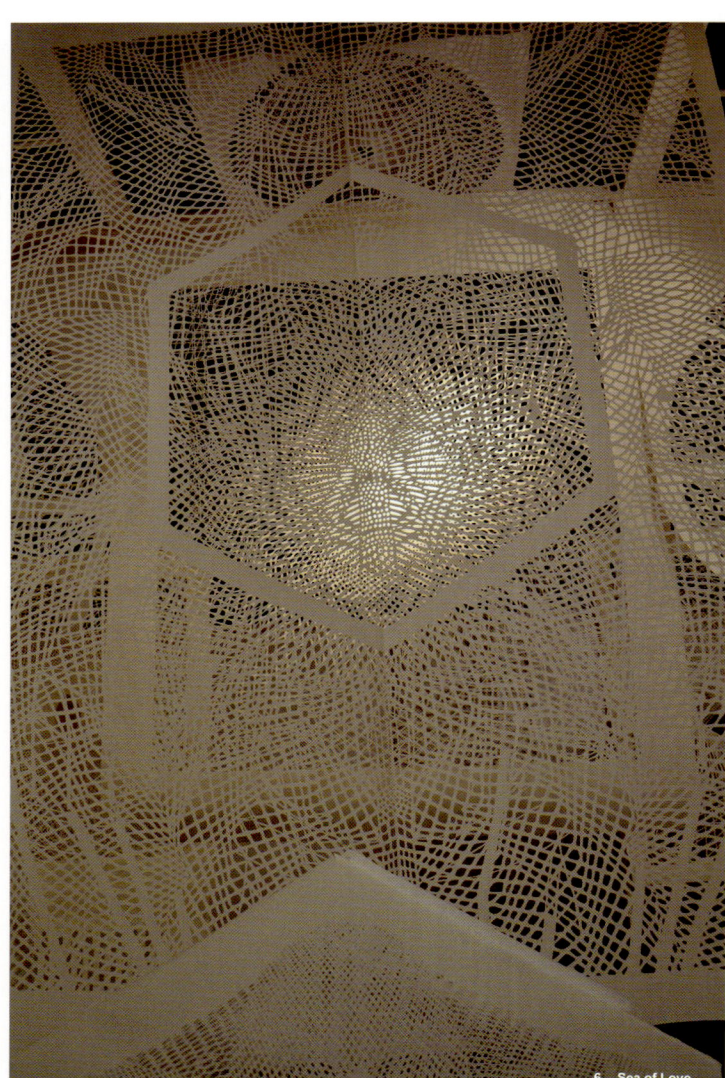

6. Sea of Love

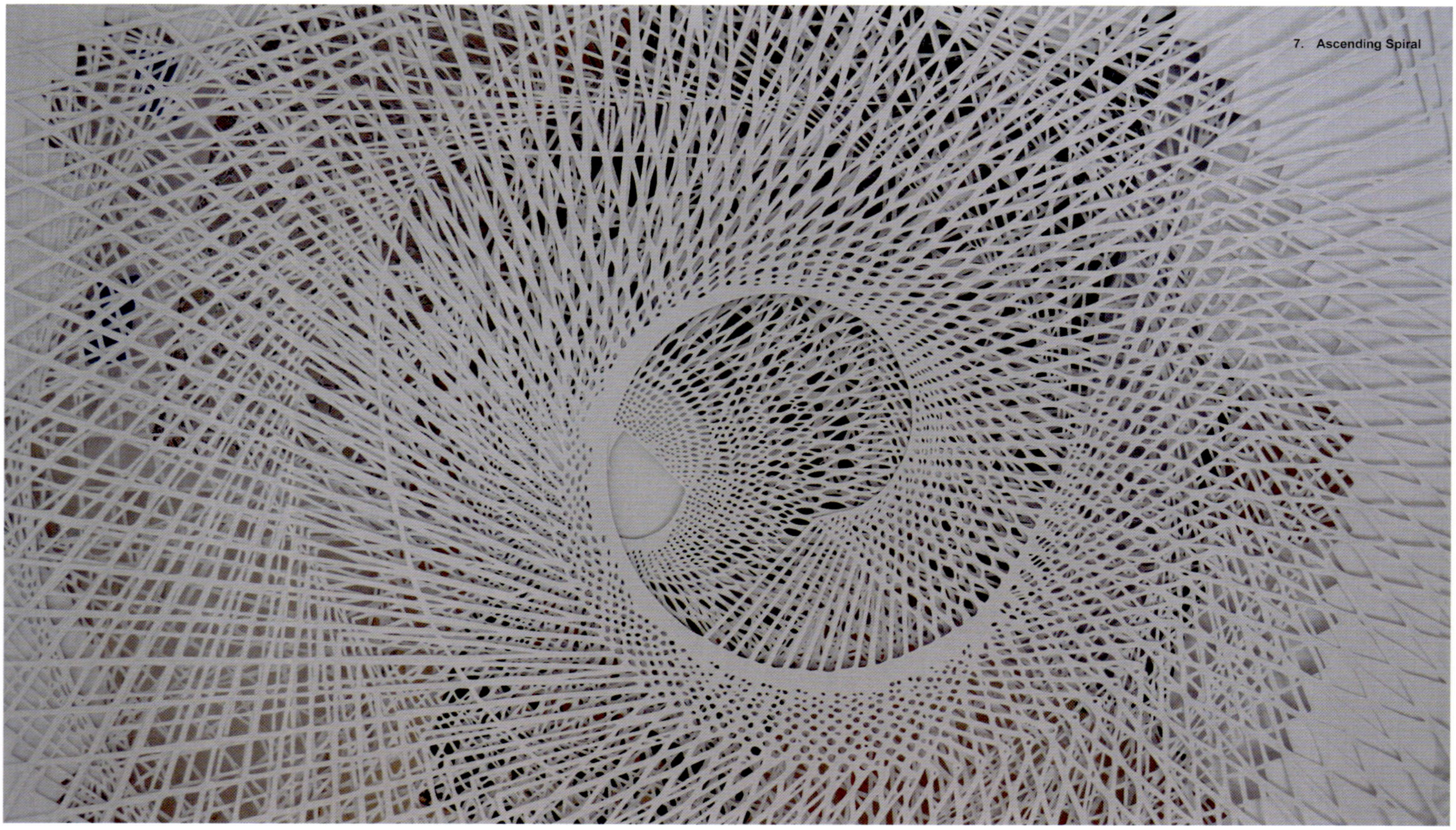

7. Ascending Spiral

8. Blue

9. Orange Crush

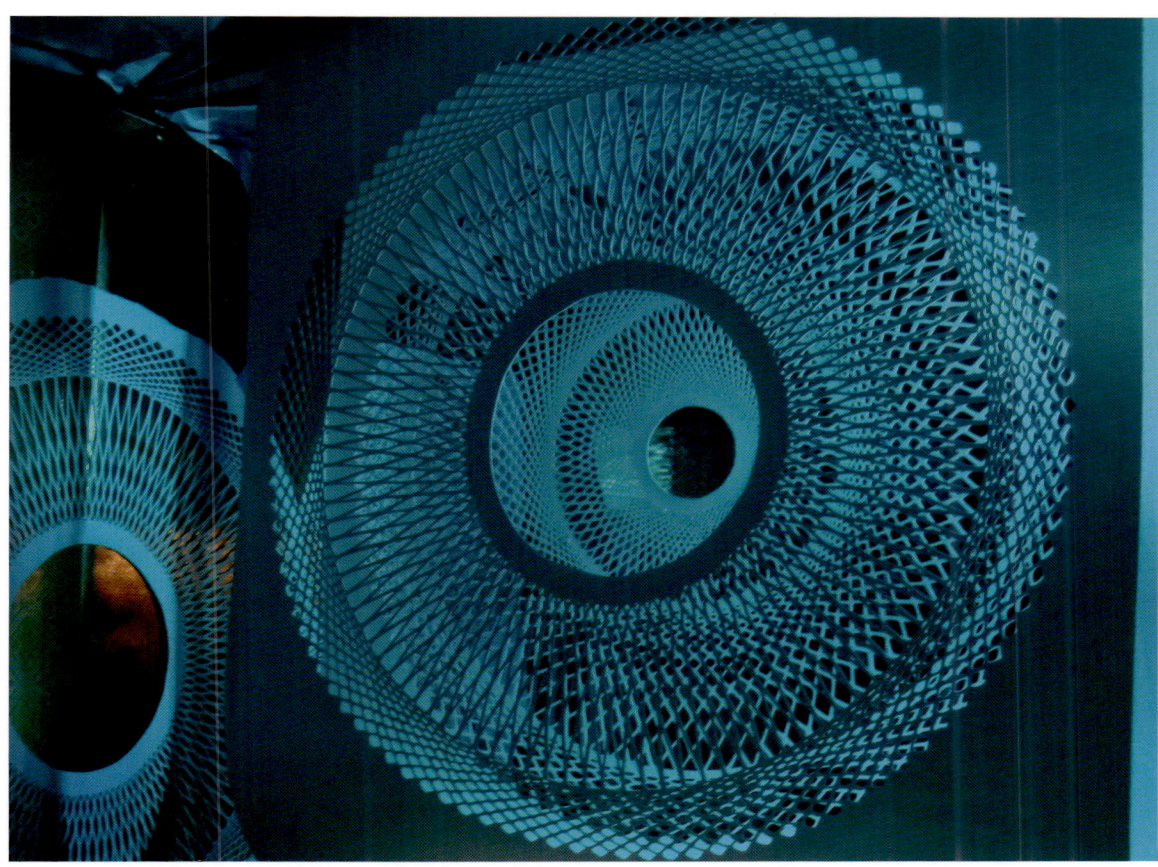

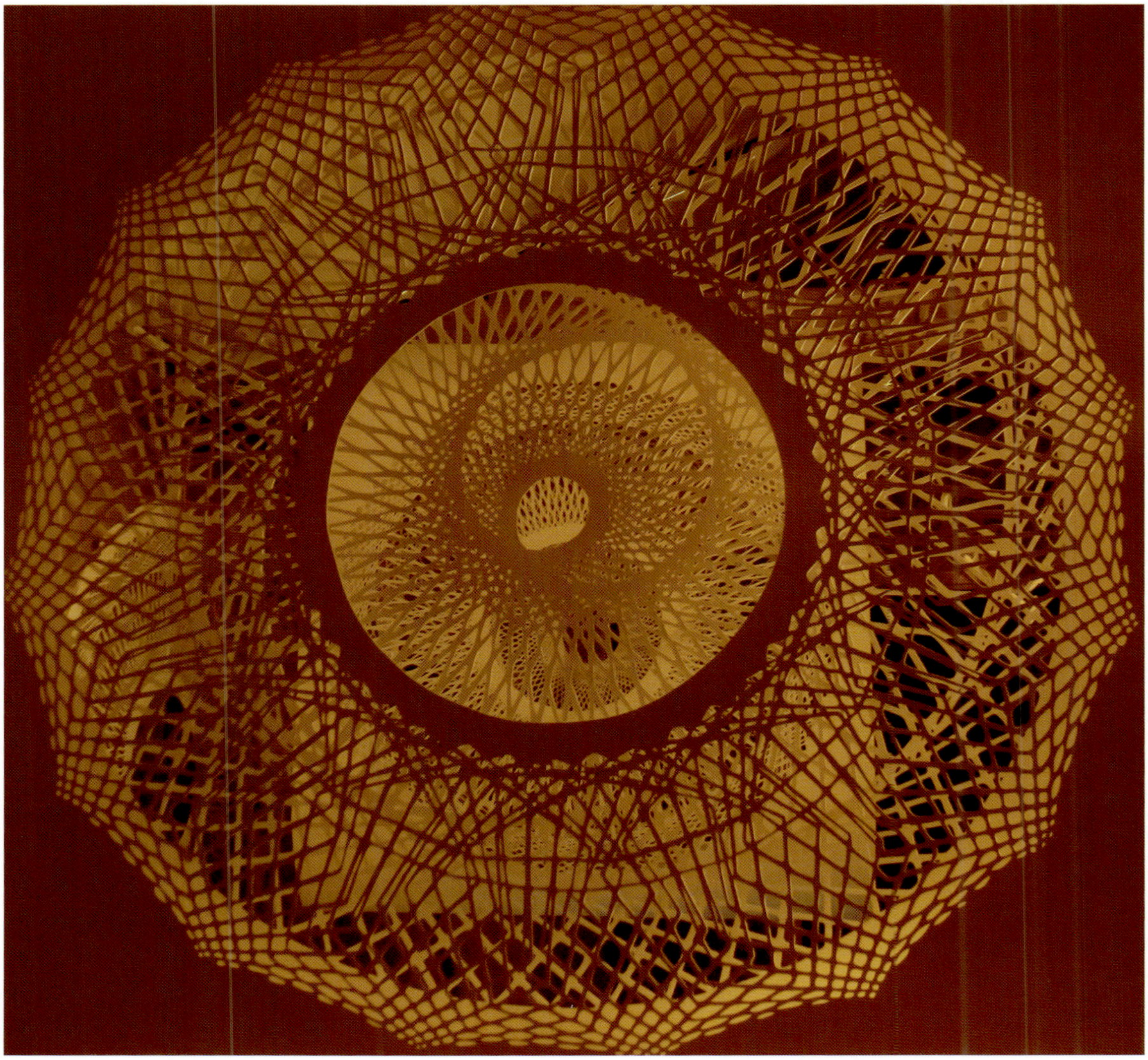

Artist: Tahiti Pehrson
Country: U.S.A
Photographer: Tahiti Pehrson

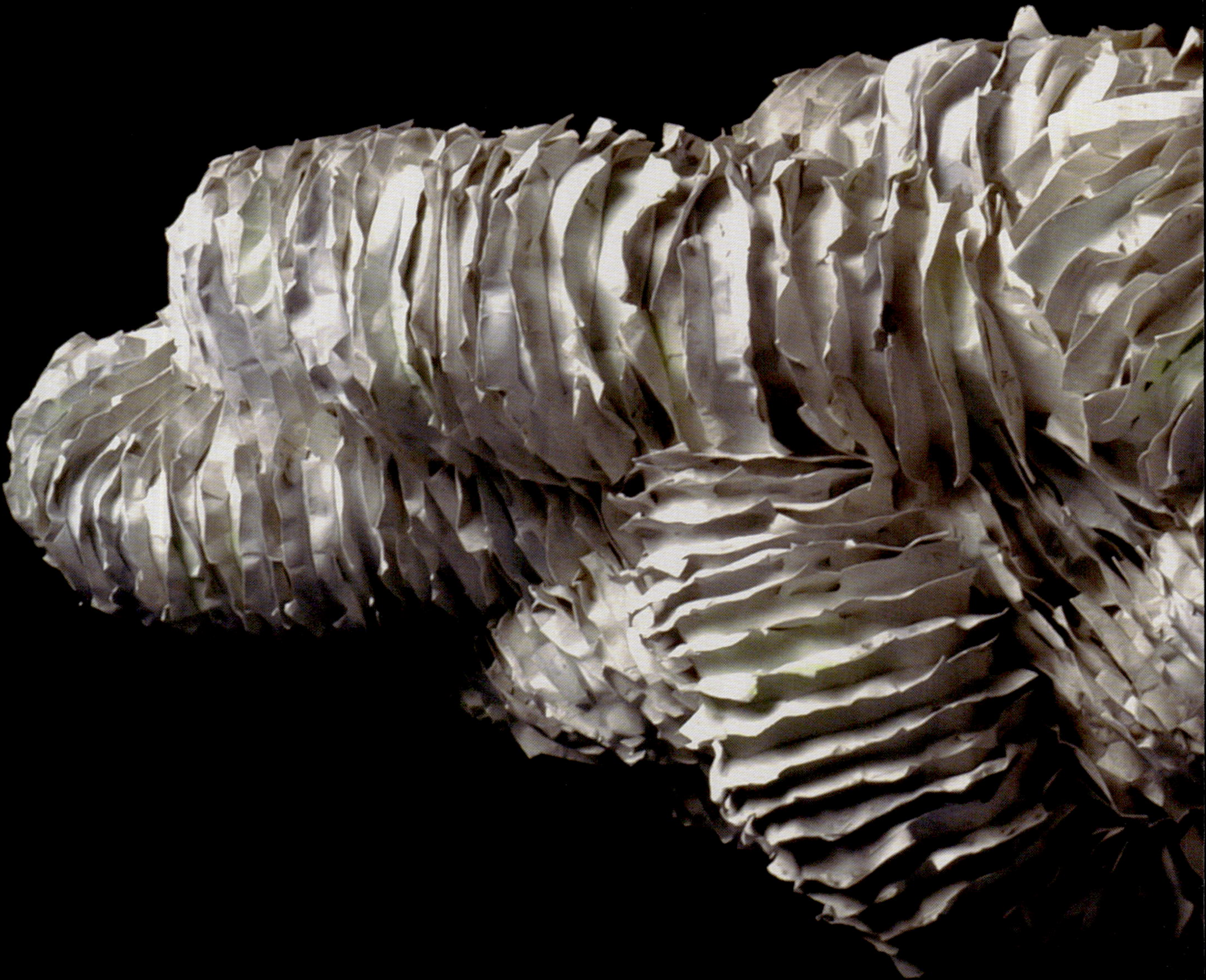

1. **Cloud 1**

Size: 29 x 27 x 70 cm
Material: Old Newspaper
It is a white raincloud,- a kind cloud, nourishing with its content.
It is peaceful and calm.

Artist: Valérie Buess
Country: Germany
Photographer: Michael Gleim

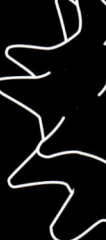

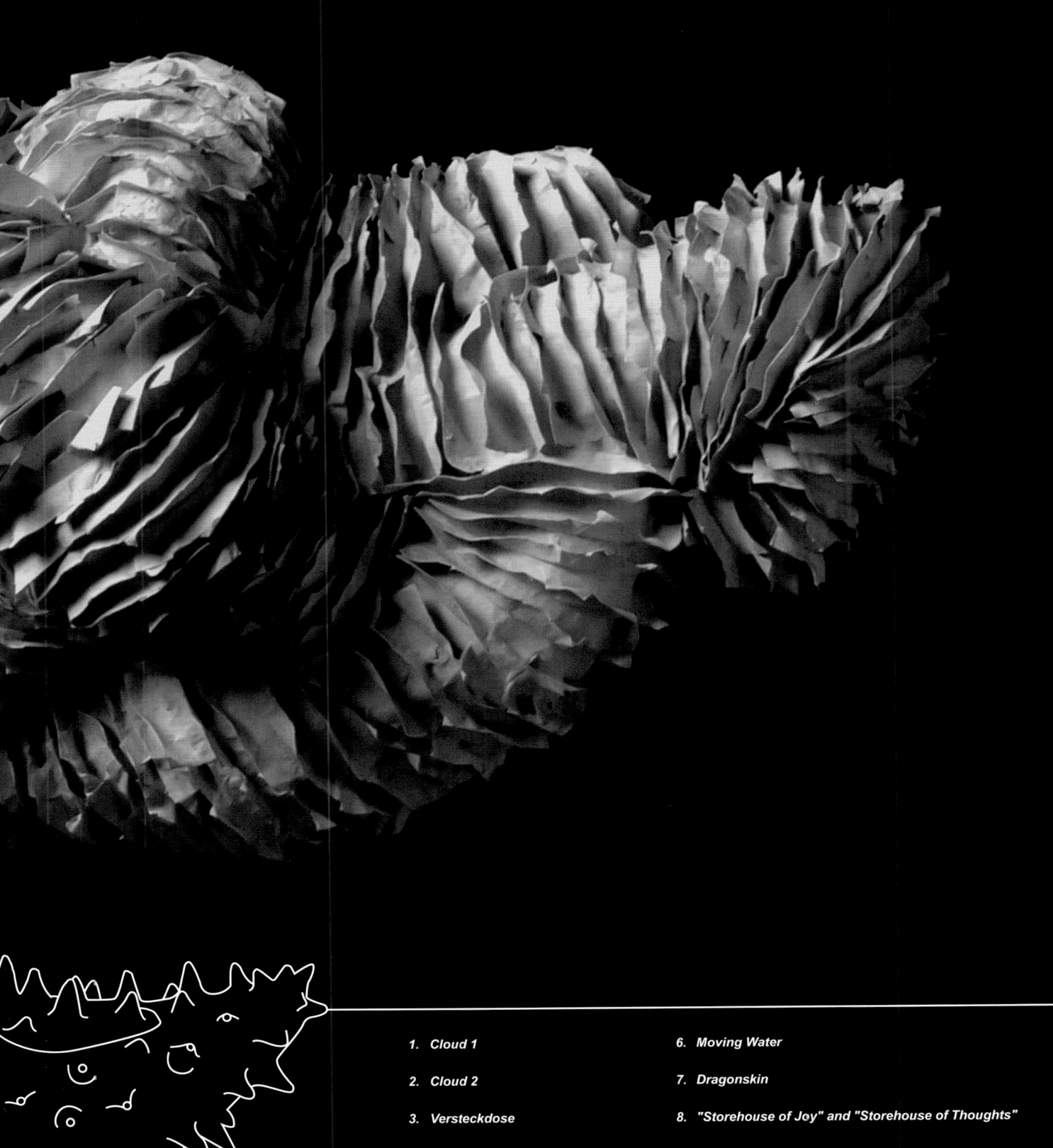

1. Cloud 1
2. Cloud 2
3. Versteckdose
4. Warm Skin
5. Where Thoughts Arise
6. Moving Water
7. Dragonskin
8. "Storehouse of Joy" and "Storehouse of Thoughts"
9. Krausen
10. Catch It !

---Valérie Buess

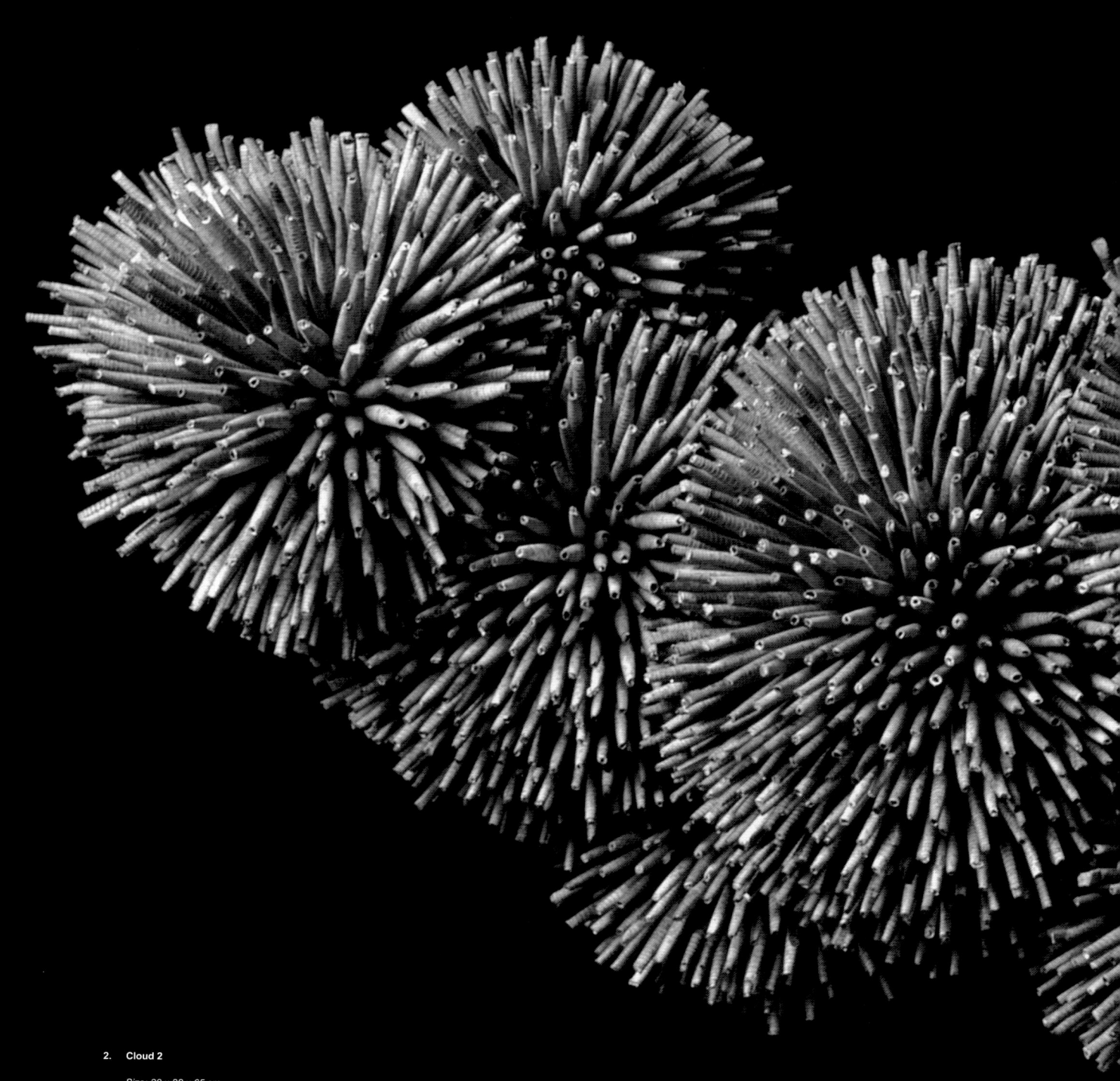

2. **Cloud 2**

Size: 30 x 28 x 65 cm
Material: Car Insurance Application Forms
It is a dark scary cloud,- it could creat a loud thunderstorm.
It protects itself,- not possible to be touched.

Artist: Valérie Buess
Country: Germany
Photographer: Michael Gleim

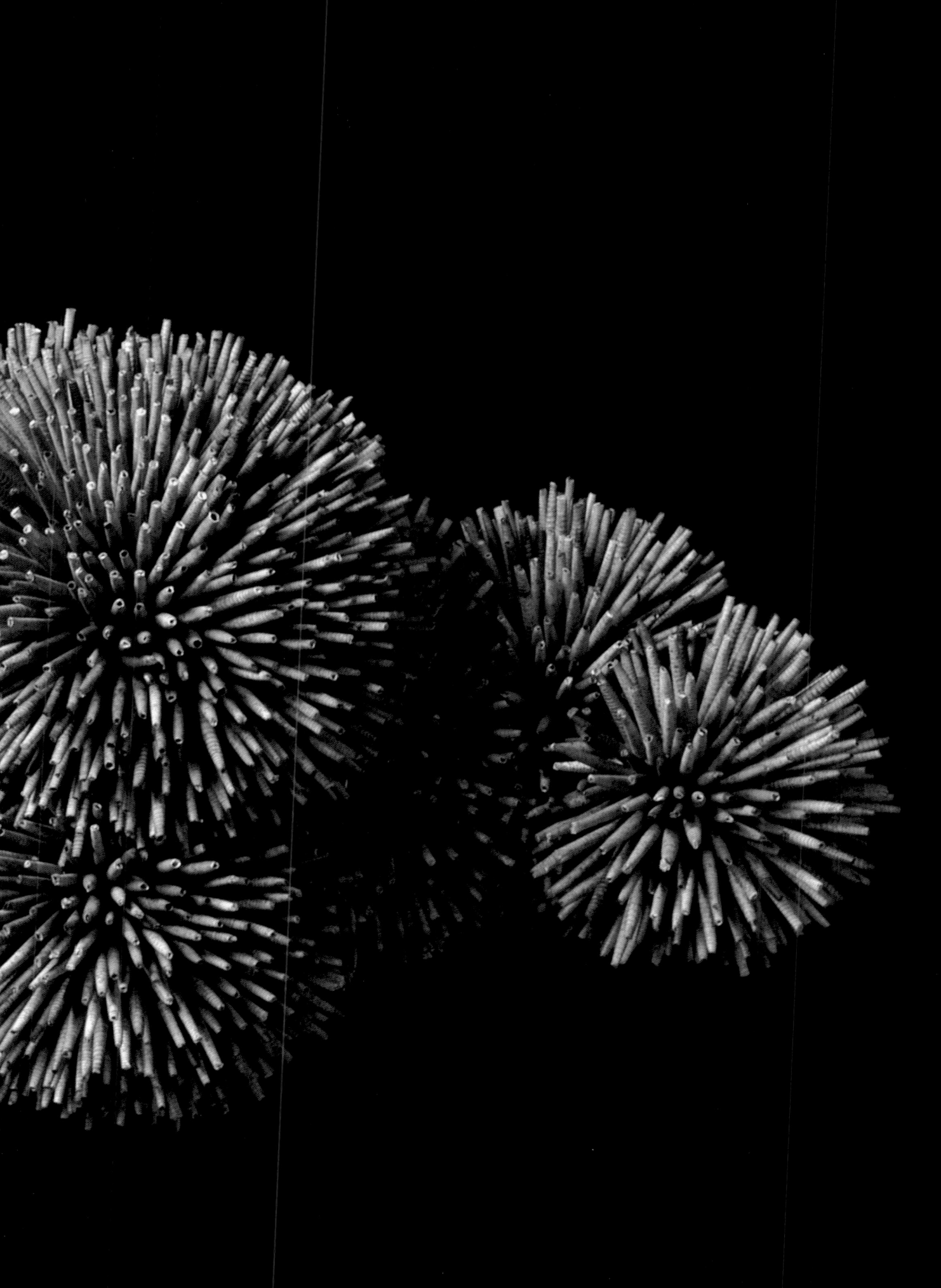

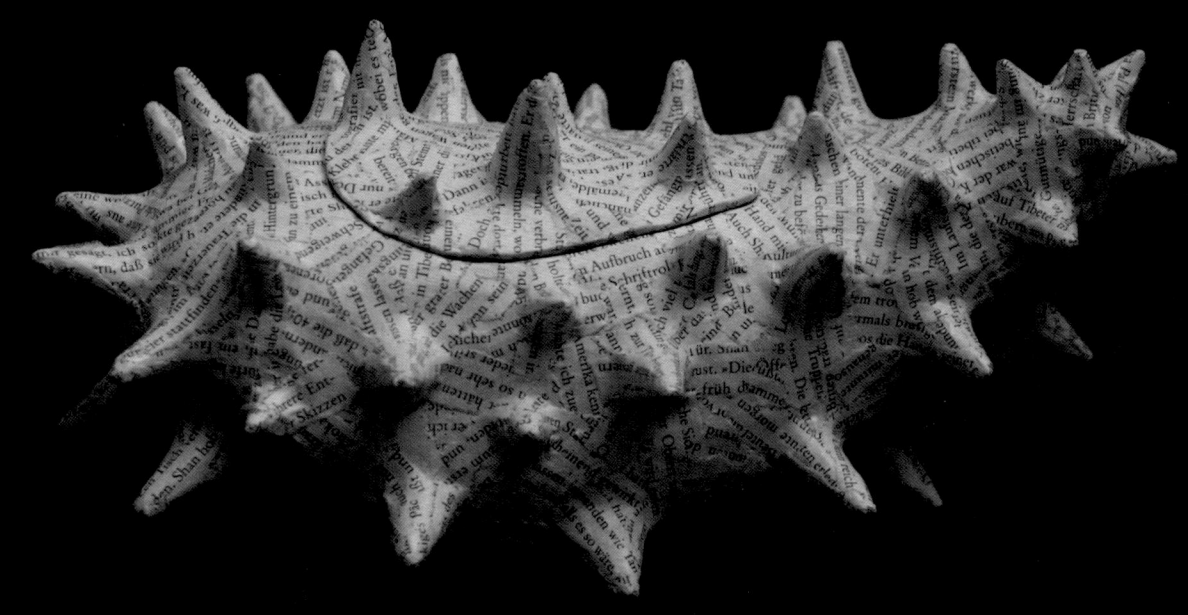

3. **Versteckdose**

   Size: 26 x 16 x 16 cm
   Material: Newspaper, Old Paperback

   Artist: Valérie Buess
   Country: Germany
   Photographer: Valérie Buess

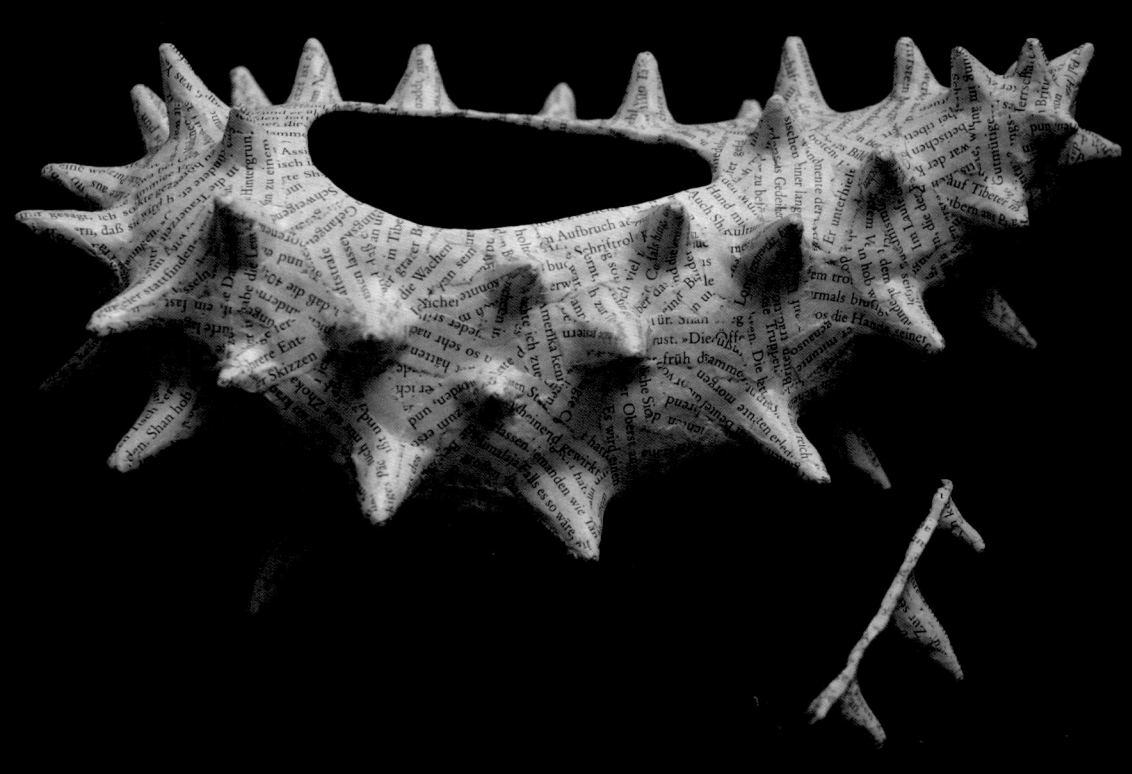
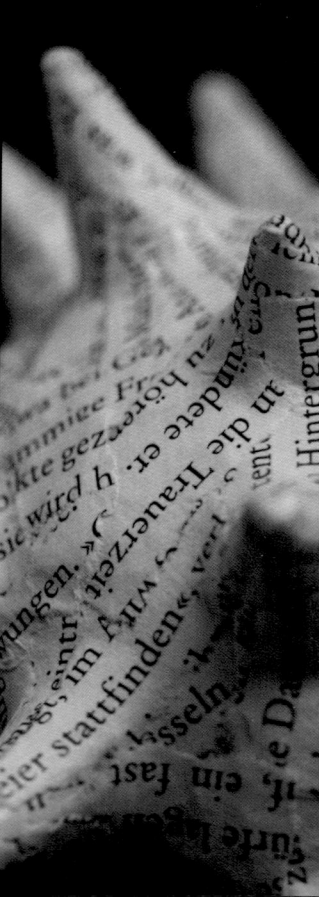

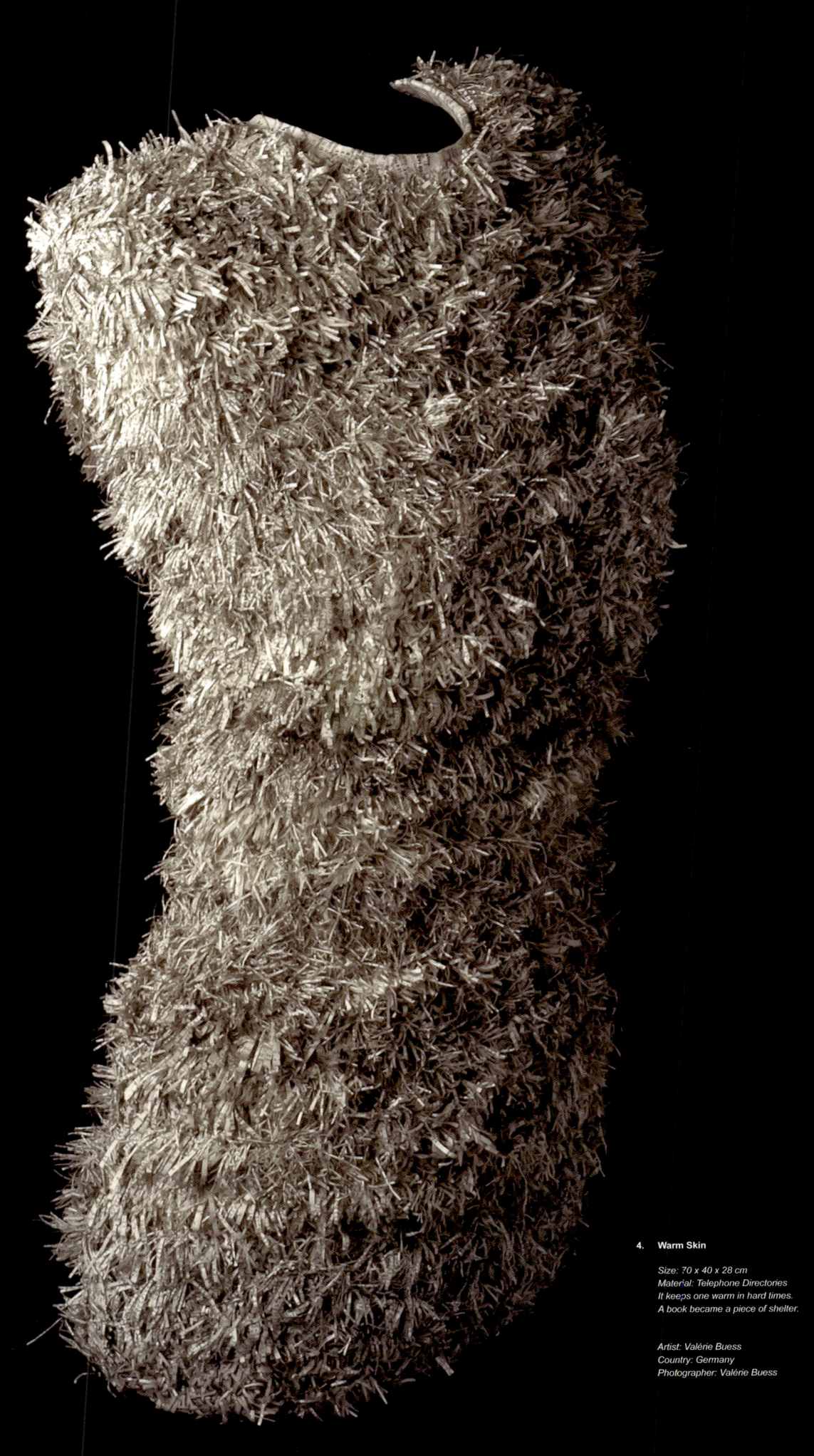

4. Warm Skin

Size: 70 x 40 x 28 cm
Material: Telephone Directories
It keeps one warm in hard times.
A book became a piece of shelter.

Artist: Valérie Buess
Country: Germany
Photographer: Valérie Buess

5. **Where Thoughts Arise**

Size: 14 x 14 x 11 cm
Material: Old Paperback

Artist: Valérie Buess
Country: Germany
Photographer: Valérie Buess

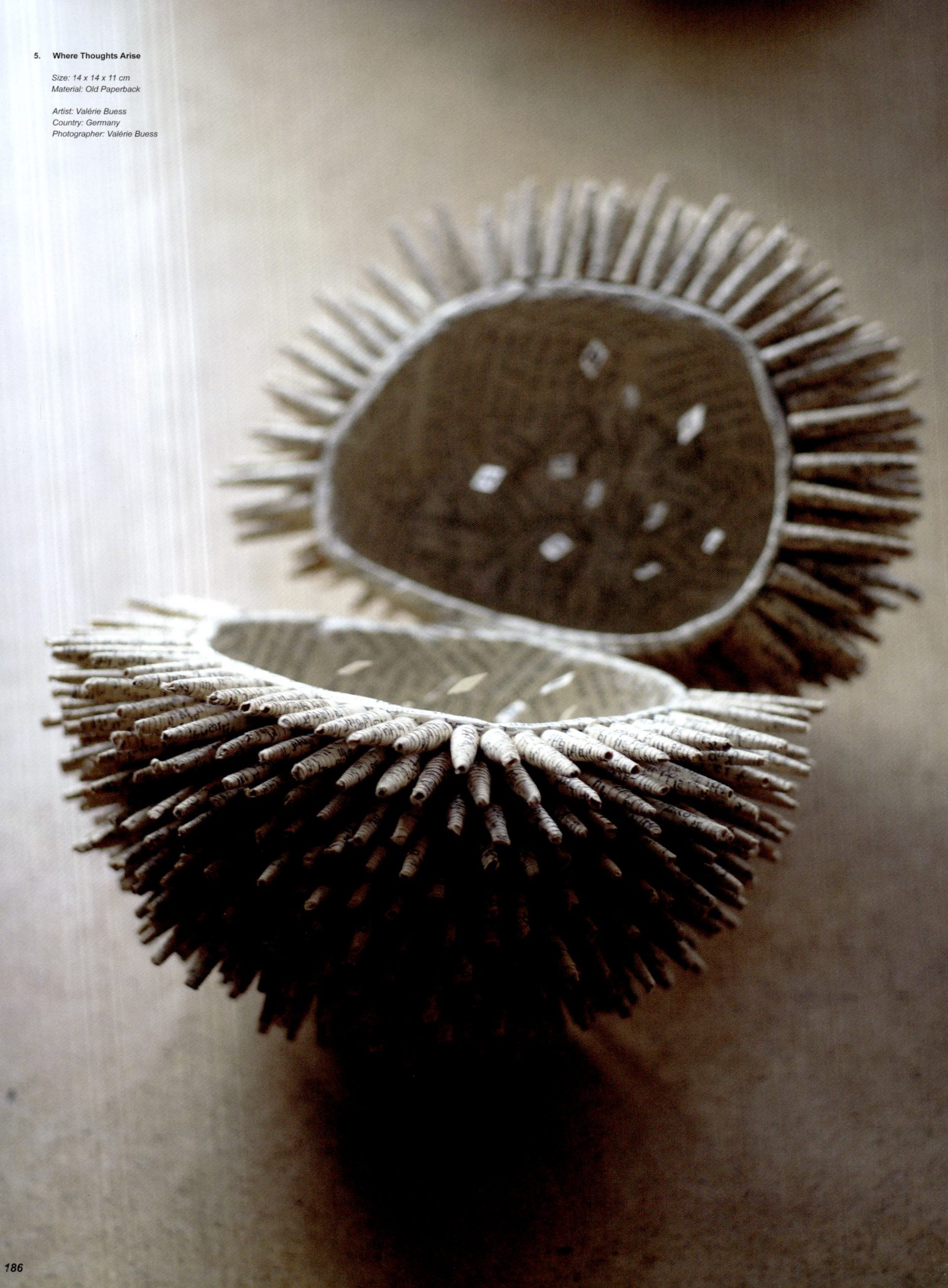

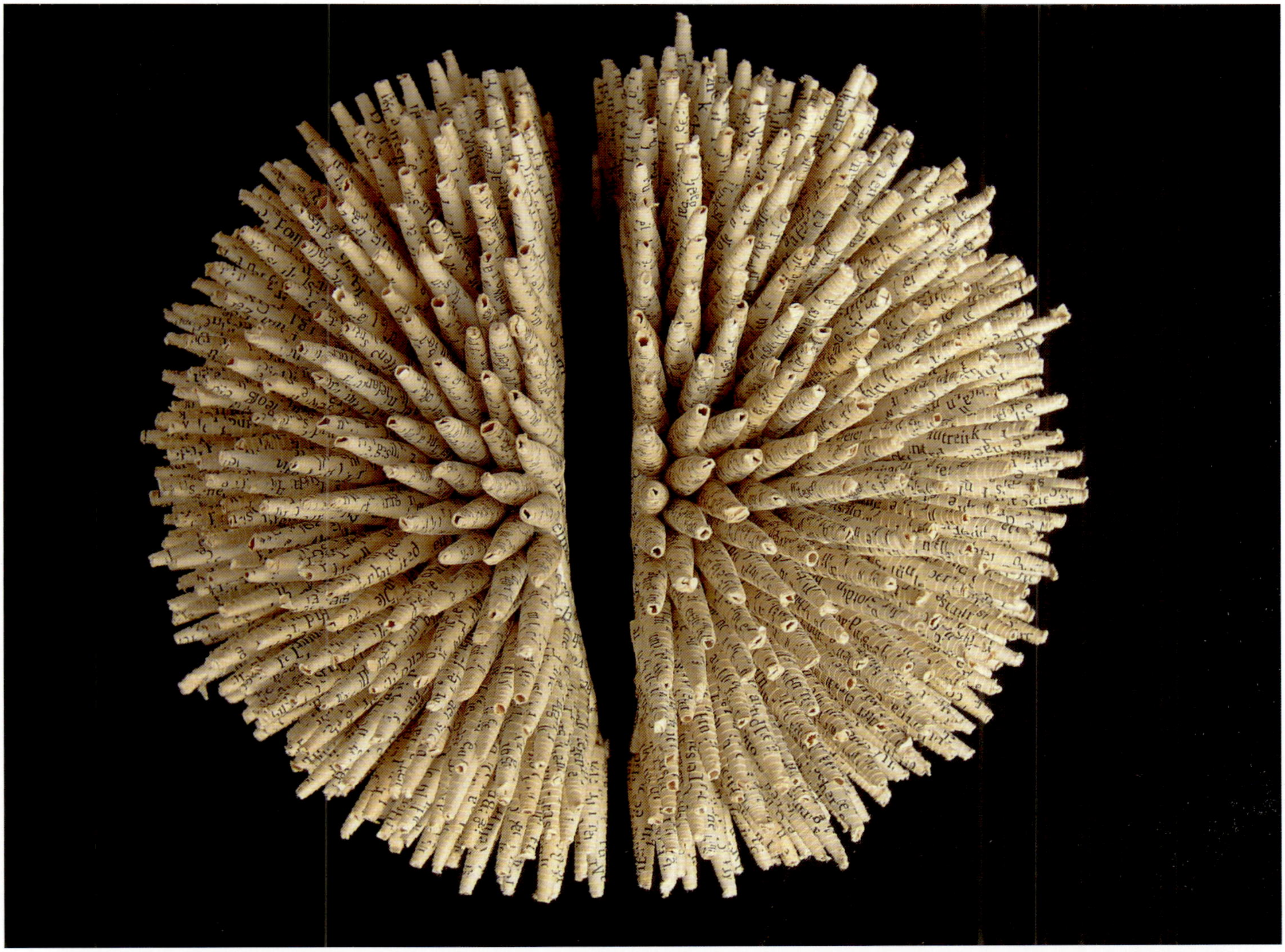

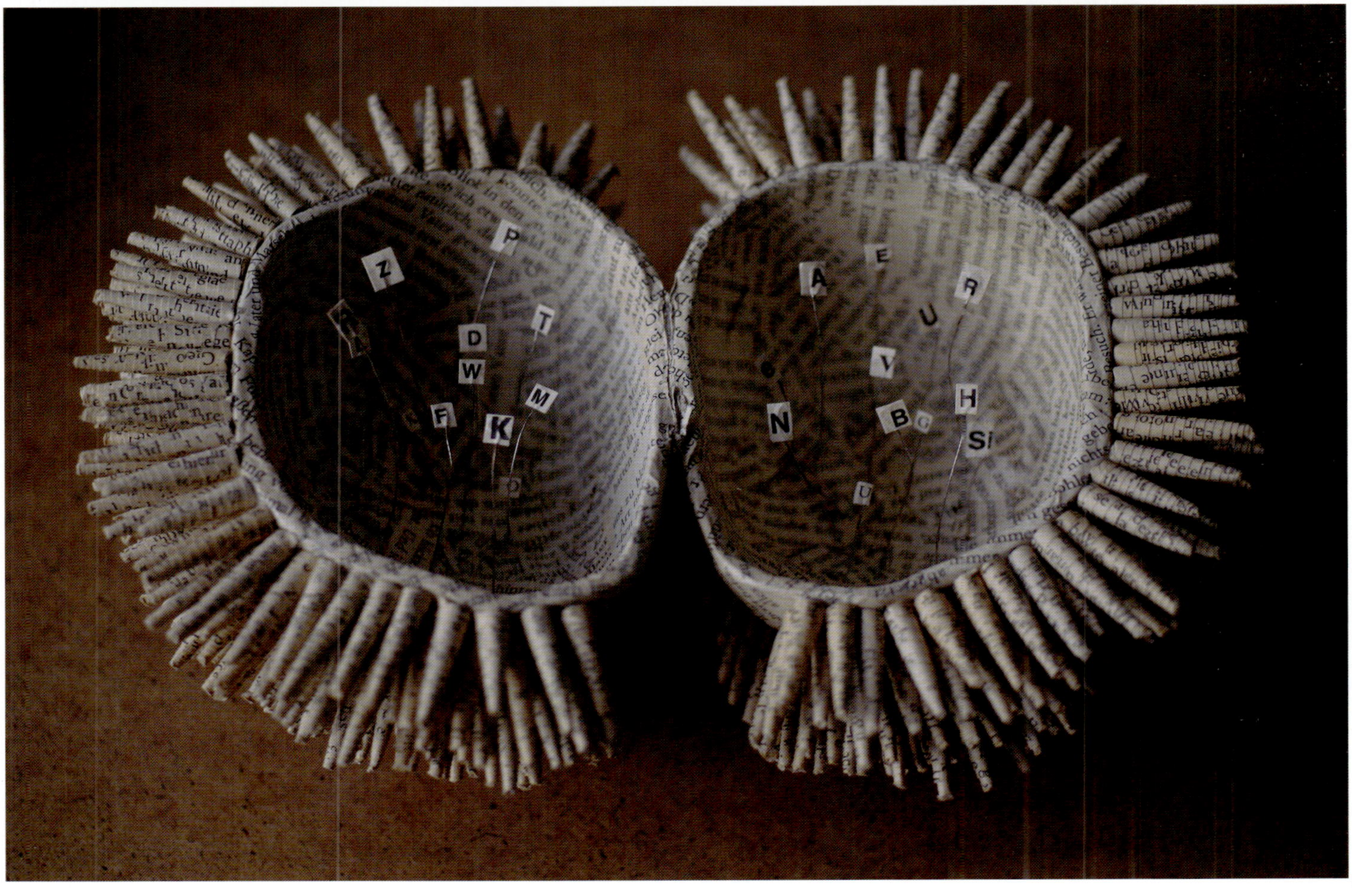

187

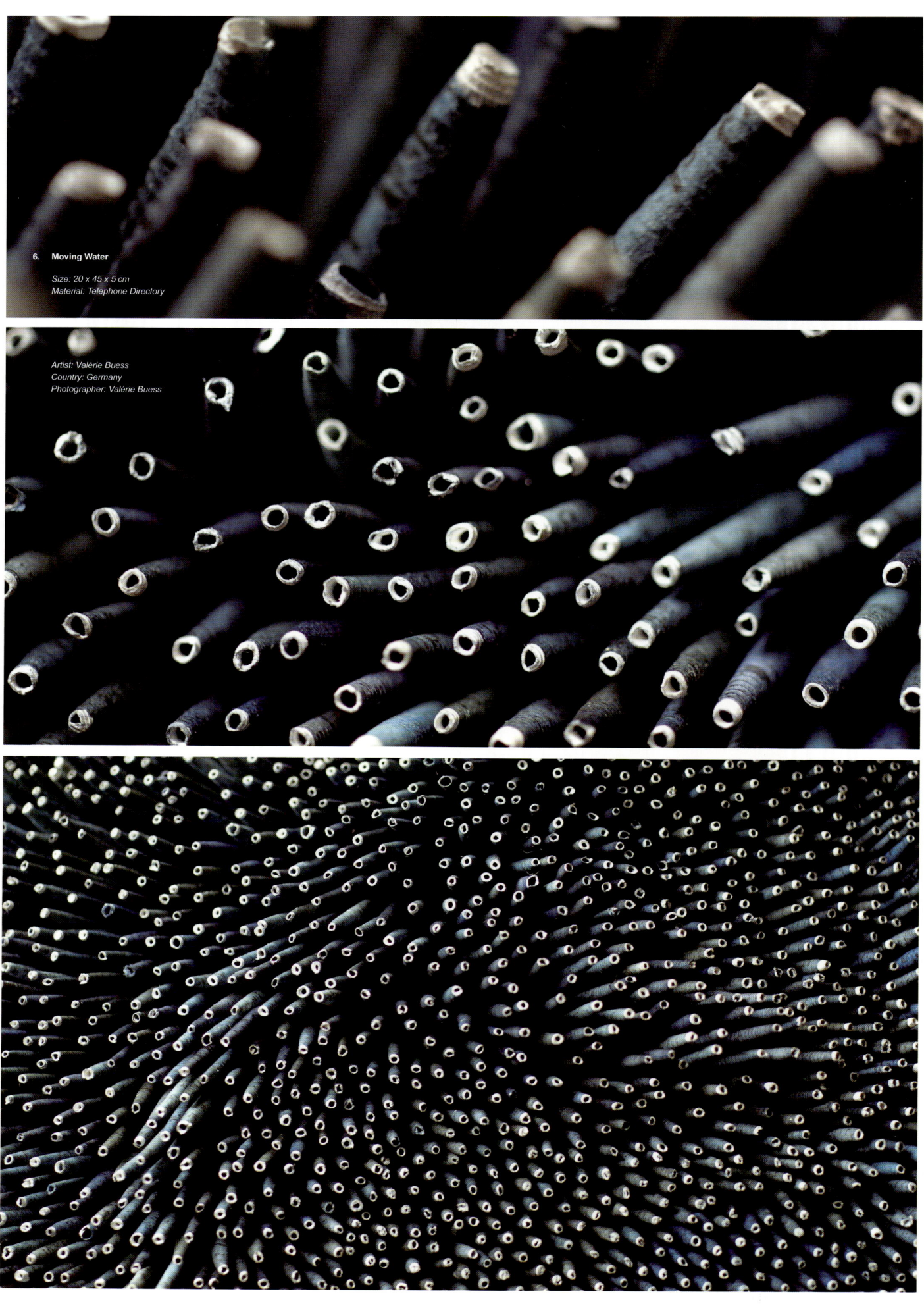

6. Moving Water

Size: 20 x 45 x 5 cm
Material: Telephone Directory

Artist: Valérie Buess
Country: Germany
Photographer: Valérie Buess

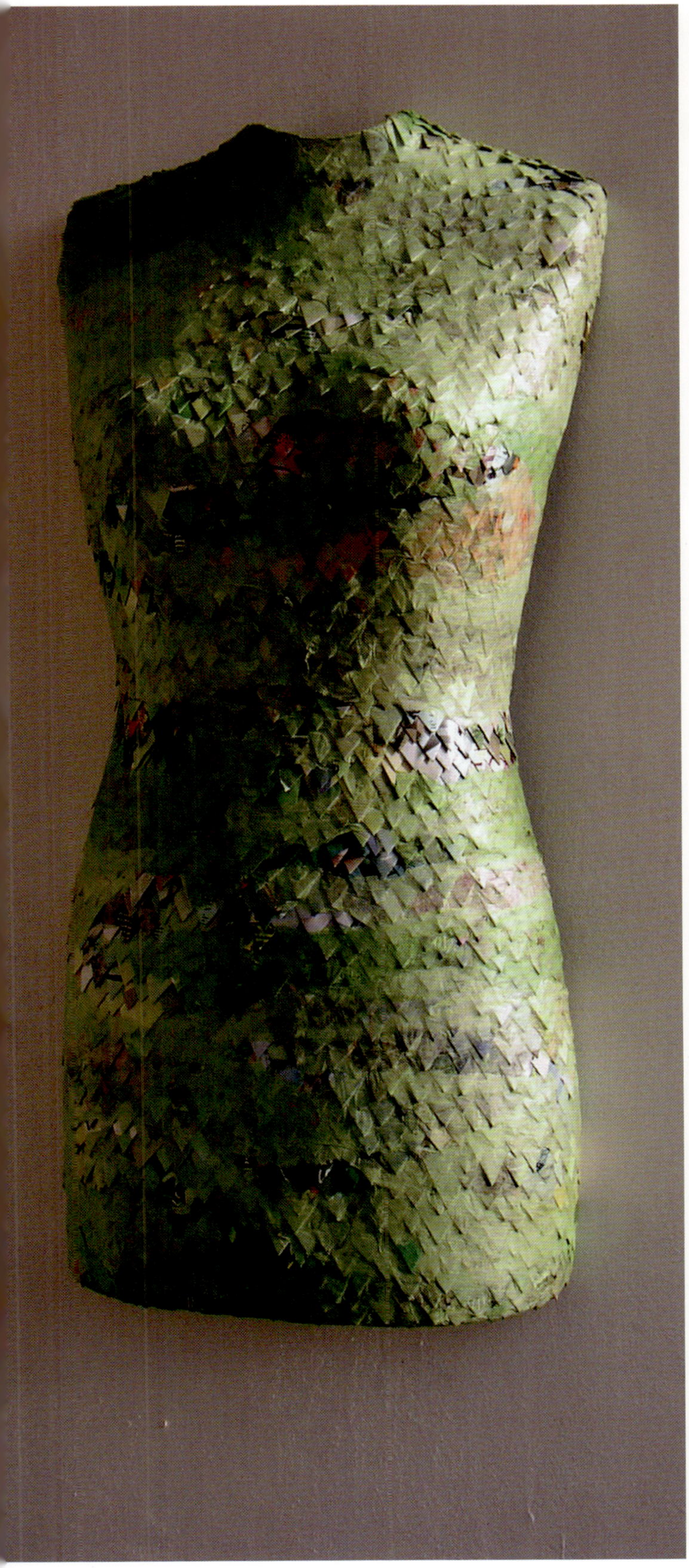

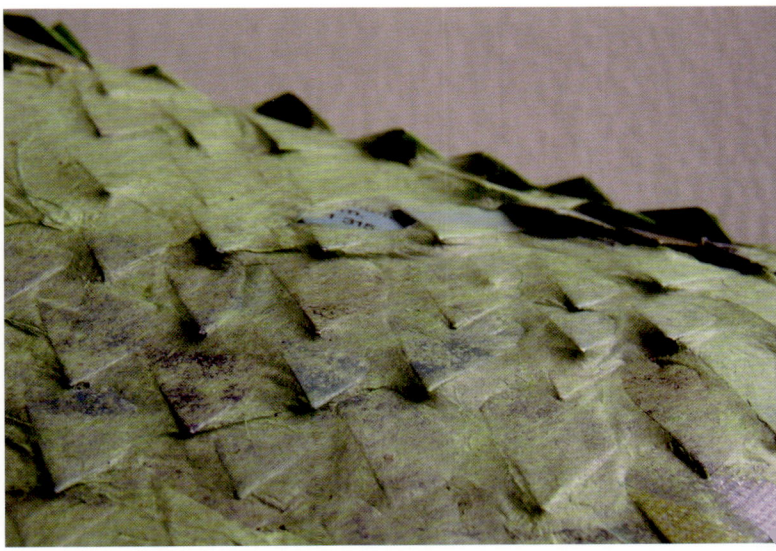
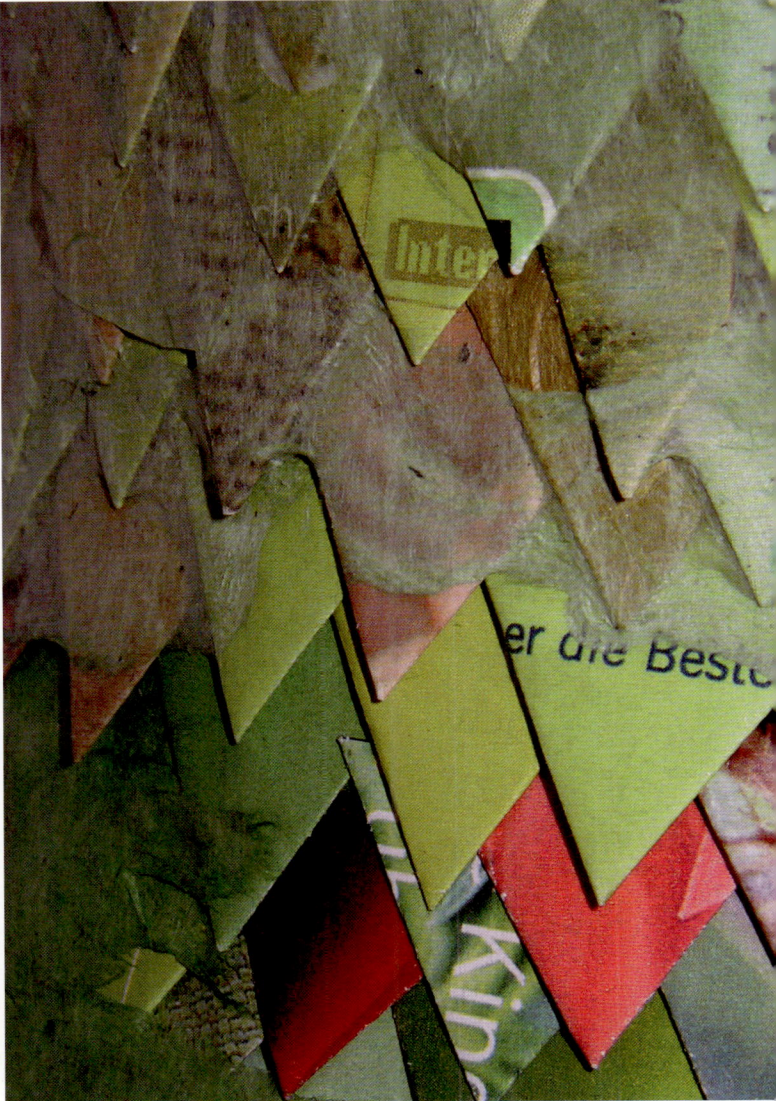

7. Dragonskin

Size: 75 x 35 x 20 cm
Material: Newspaper, Magazines, Handmade Nepalese Paper

Artist: Valérie Buess
Country: Germany
Photographer: Valérie Buess

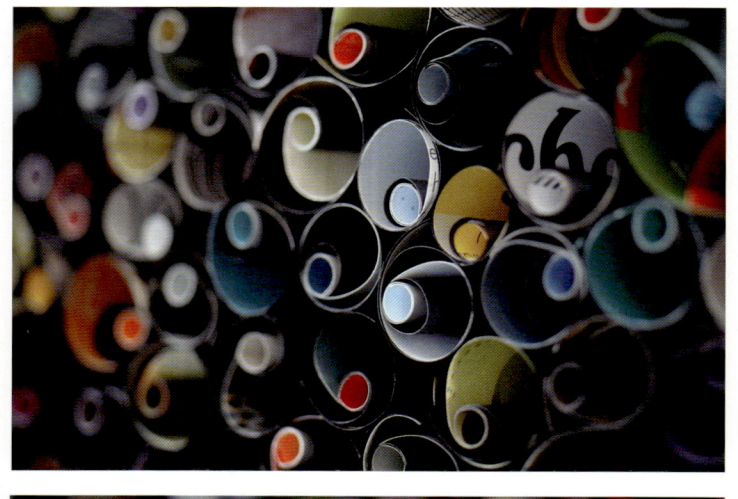
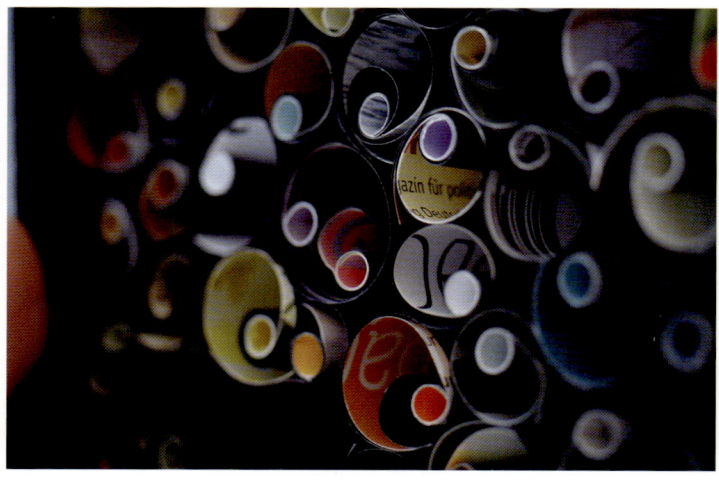
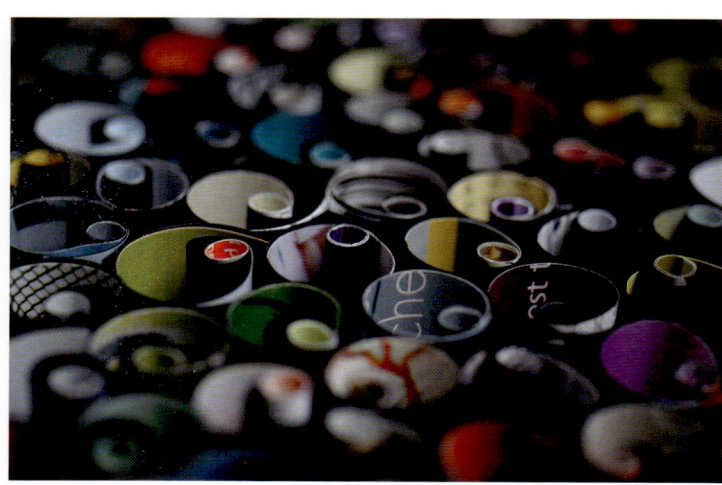
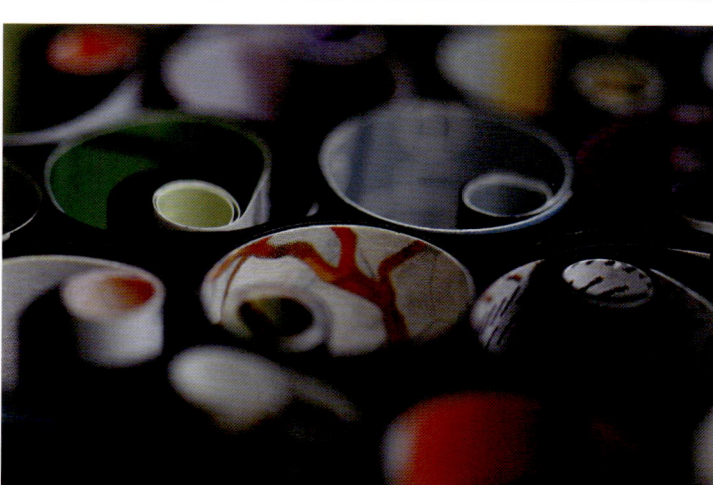

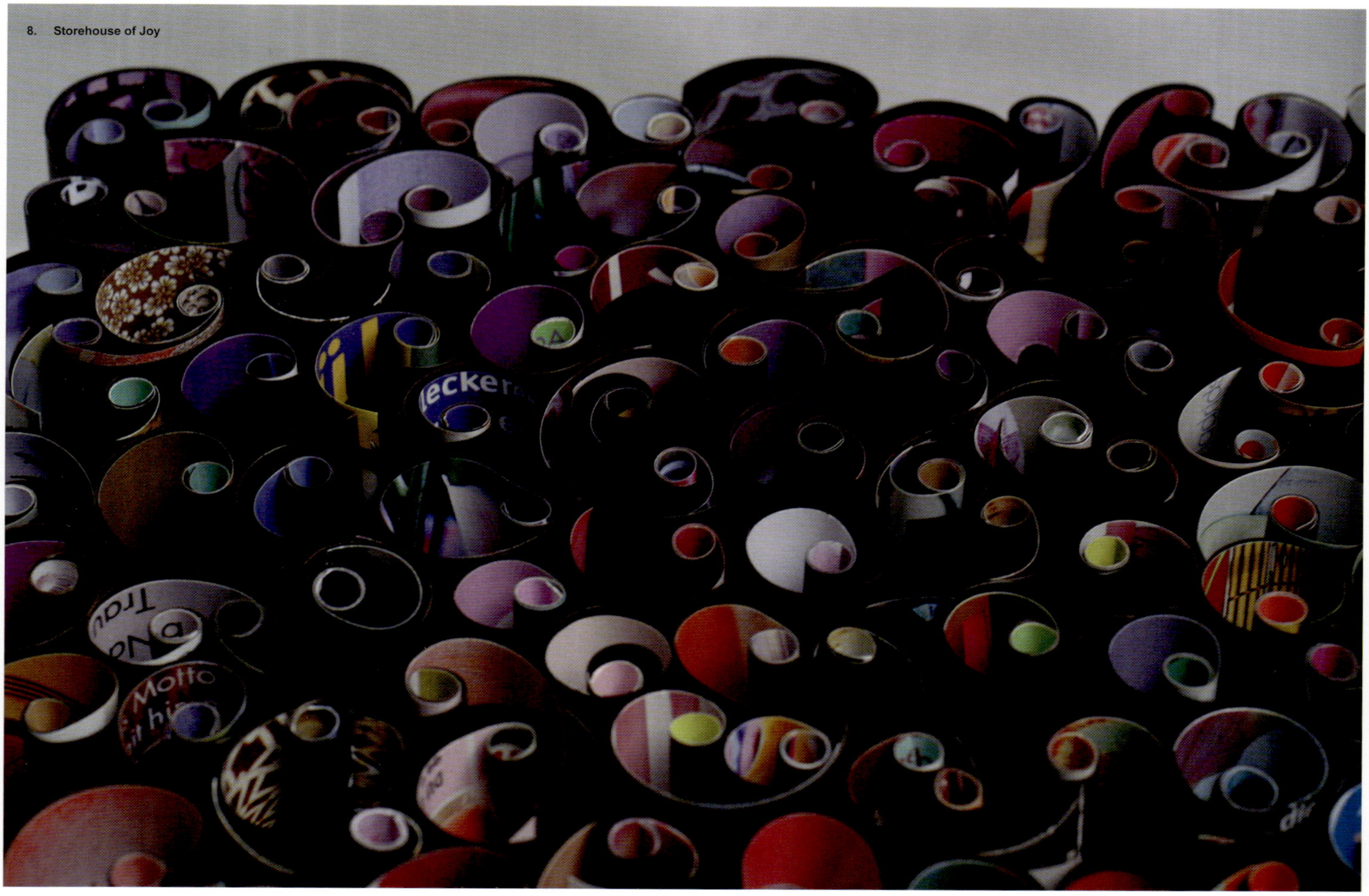

8. Storehouse of Joy

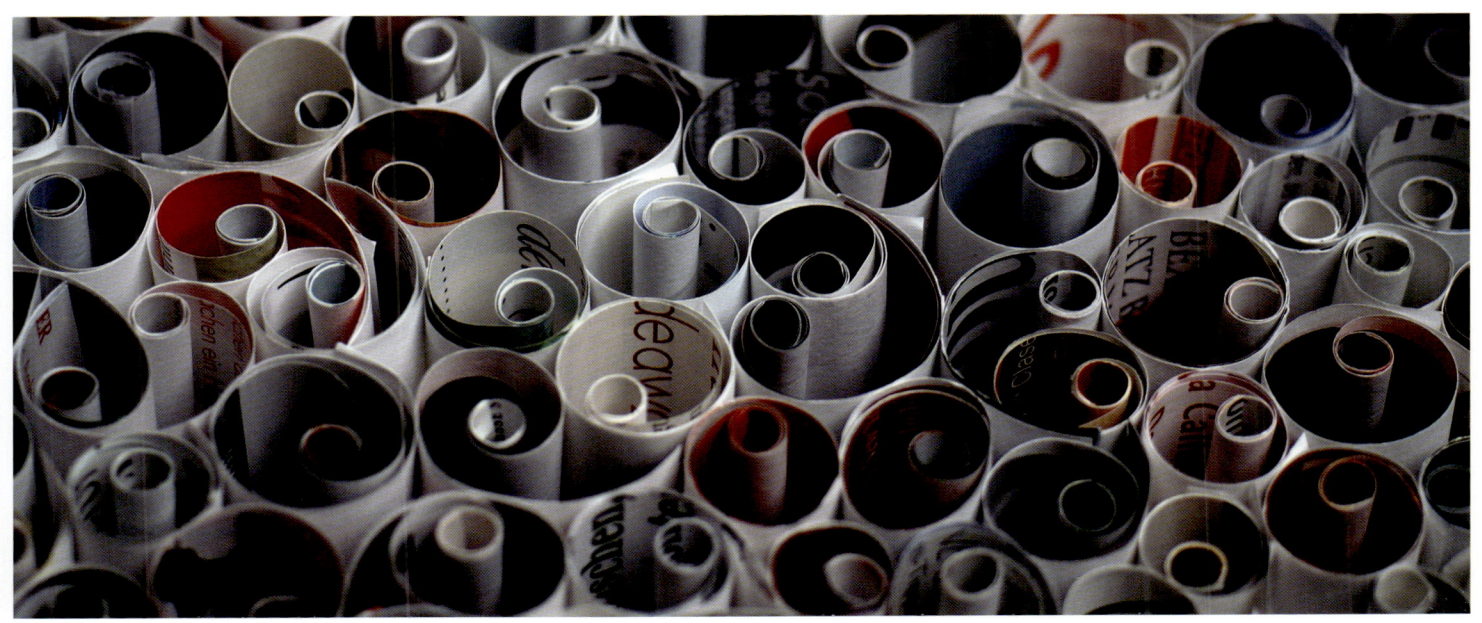

8. Storehouse of Thoughts

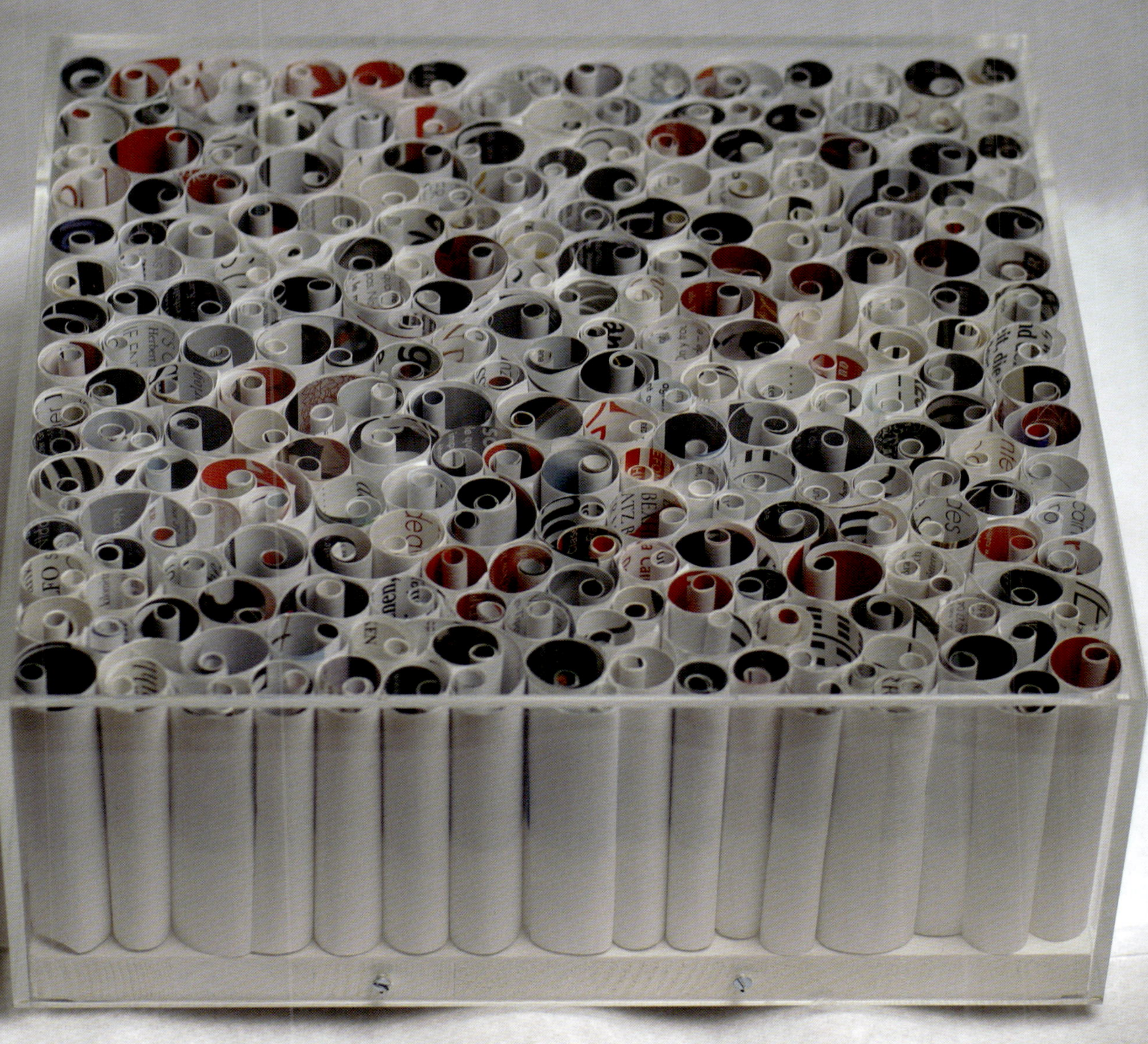

Size: 25.5 x 25.5 x 10.5 cm
Material: Od Magazines, Drawing/Writing Paper

Artist: Valérie Buess
Country: Germany
Photographer: Valérie Buess

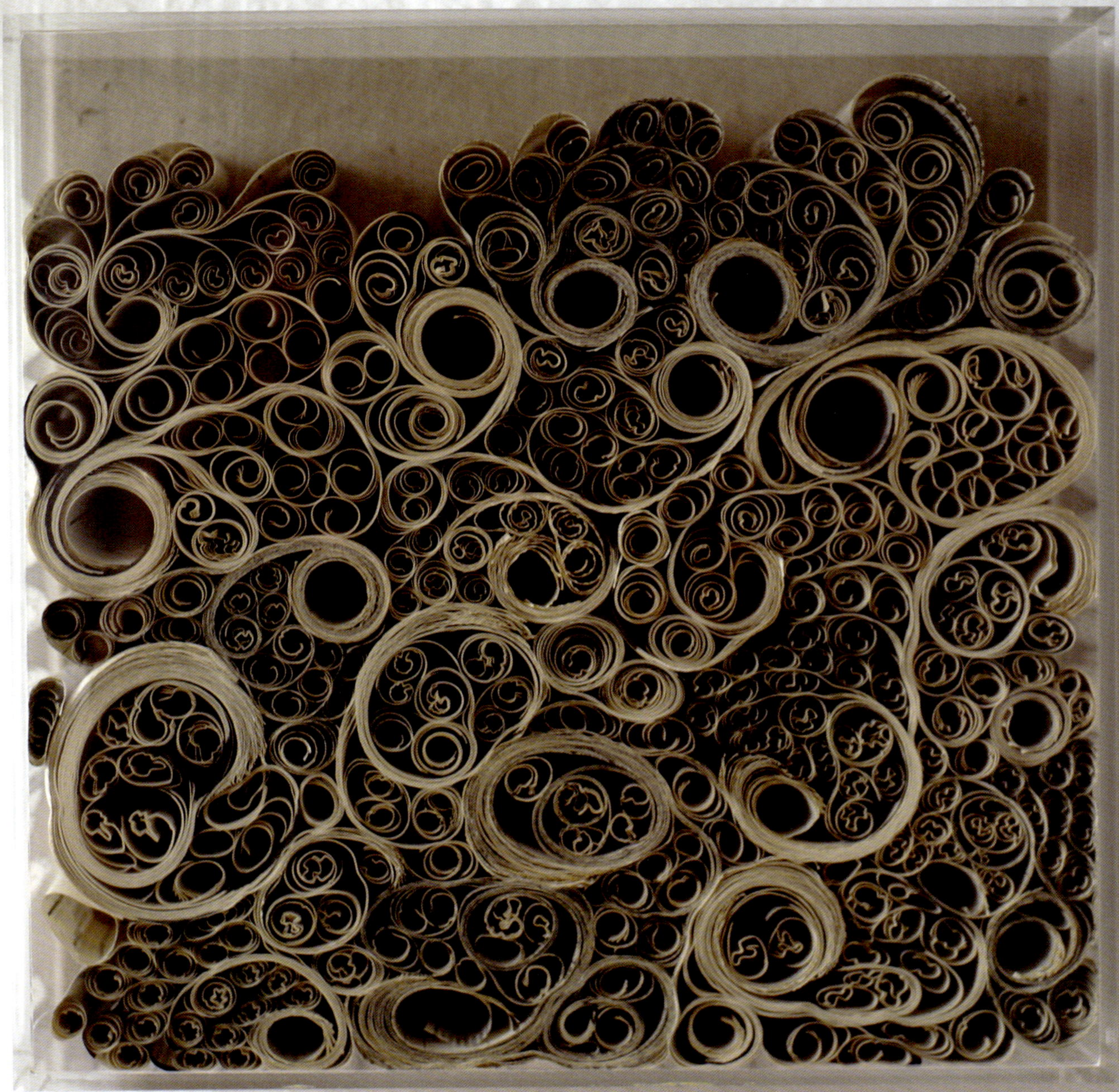

9. Krausen
Size: 25.5 x 25.5 x 10.5 cm
Material: Old Train Timetables
Artist: Valérie Buess
Country: Germany
Photographer: Valérie Buess

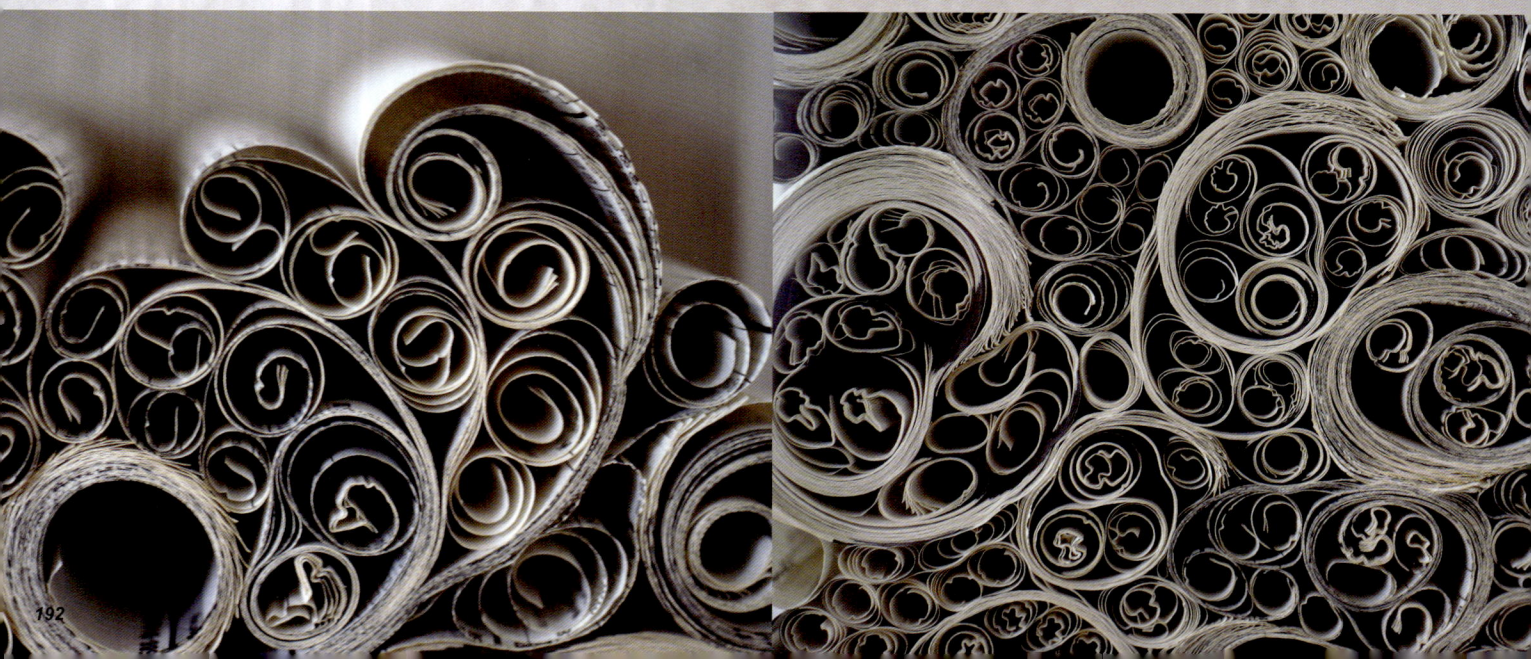

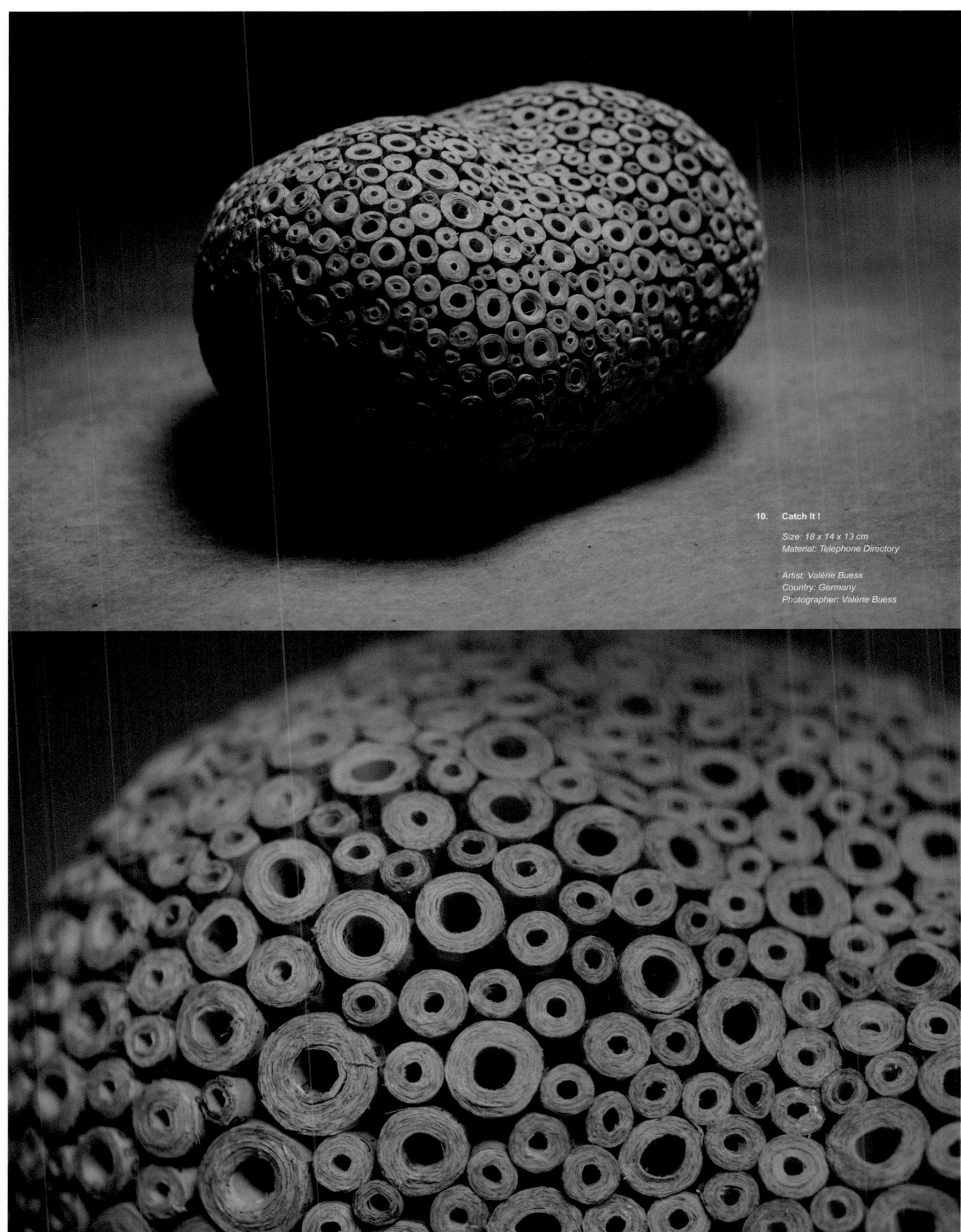

10. **Catch It !**

Size: 18 x 14 x 13 cm
Material: Telephone Directory

Artist: Valérie Buess
Country: Germany
Photographer: Valérie Buess

1. **Euphoria**

Installation, Paper Cut | 183 x 488 x 366 cm

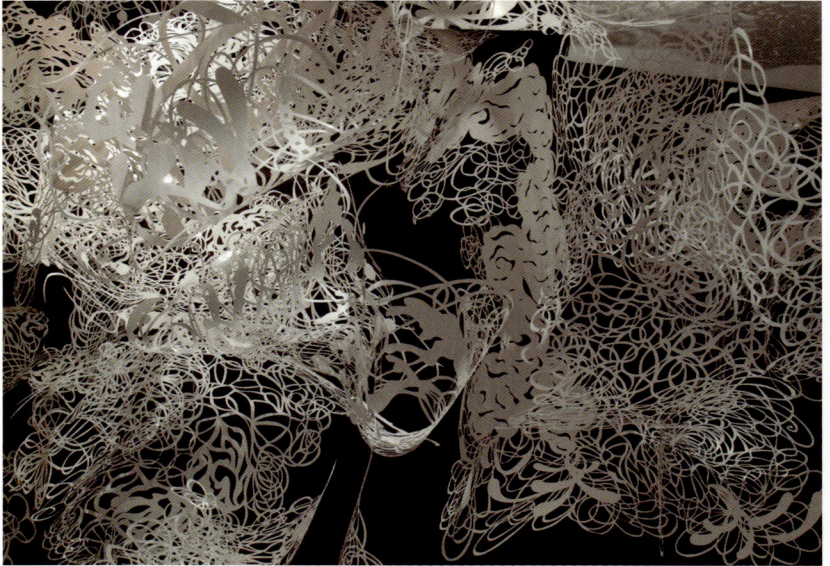
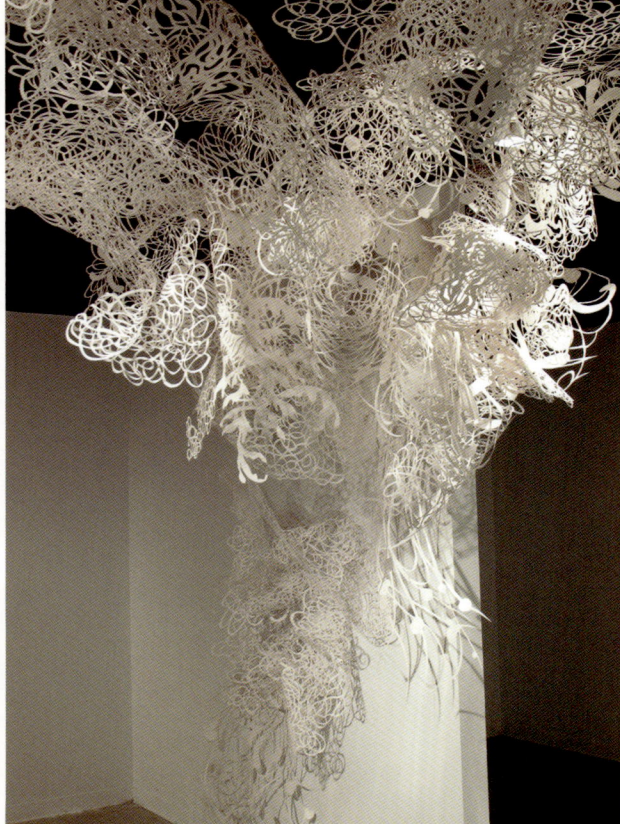
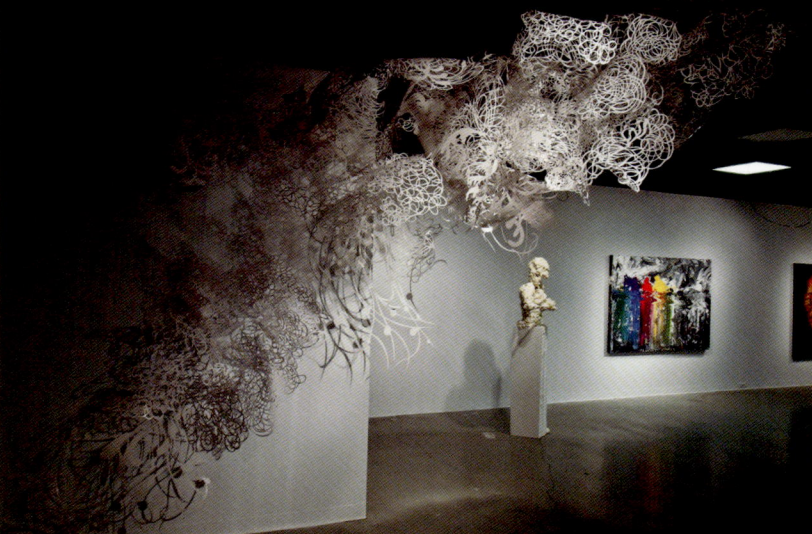
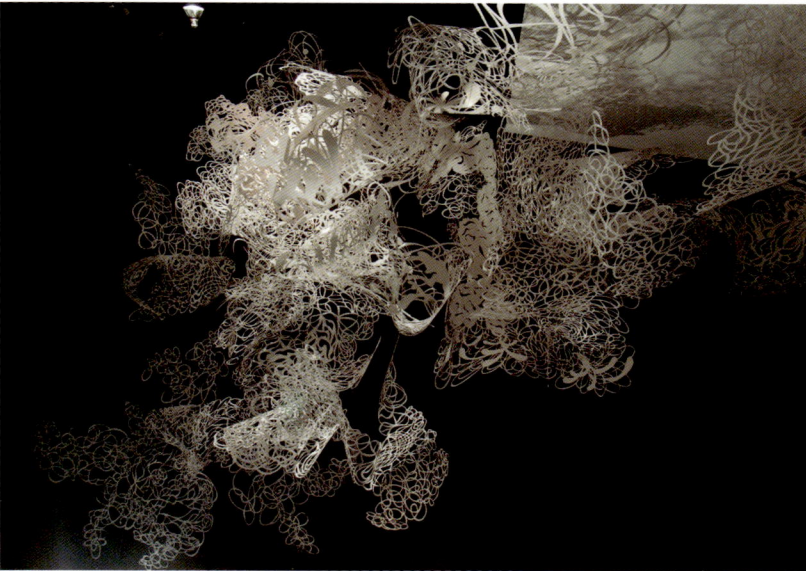
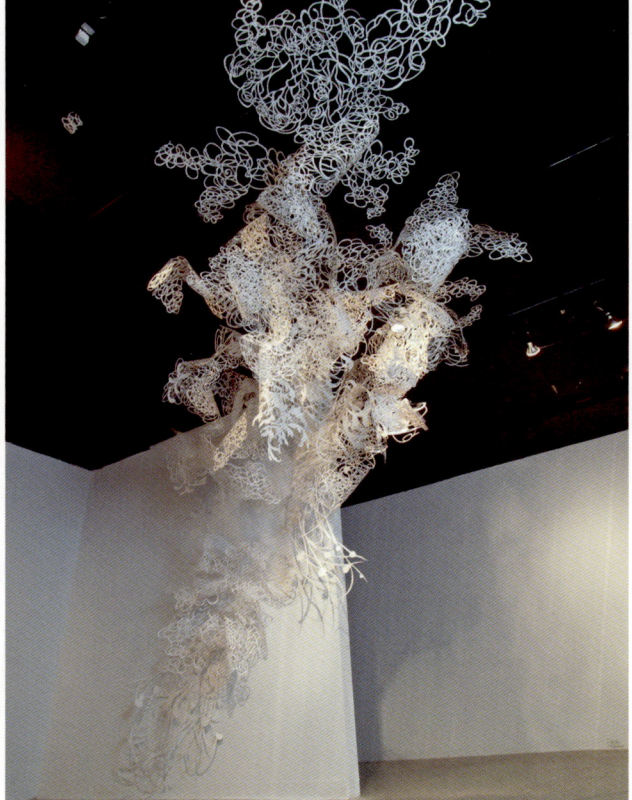

Artist: Vanessa Alarie
Country: Canada
Photographer: Vanessa Alarie / Mathieu Normandin

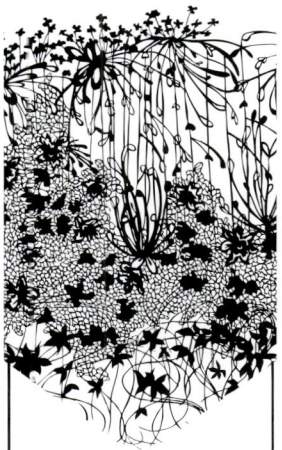

1. *Euphoria*
2. *Euphoria v.2*
3. *Explorations*
4. *Florilège*
5. *Vertige*
6. *InTempsPérie*
7. *Dentelles*

Sensual fusion of forces of this world, euphoria detail, symbiosis patterns exploding gently in a universe that defy the space-time. All these shapes cut from paper, all these gaps through which pass the light ensure the continuation of the journey: that of the eye, heart and mind. Spaces for silence and contemplation.

---Vanessa Alarie

2. Euphoria v.2
Installation, Paper Cut | 183 x 488 x 366 cm

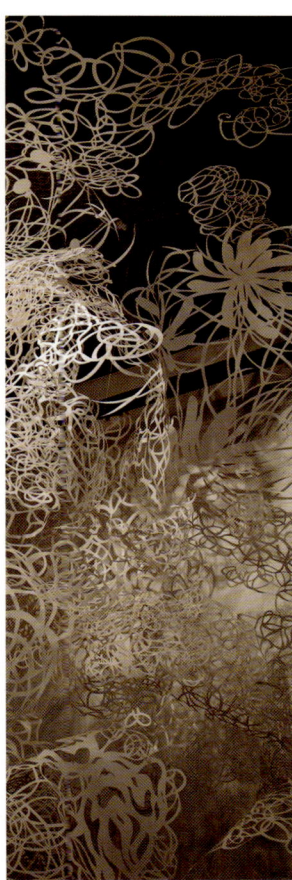
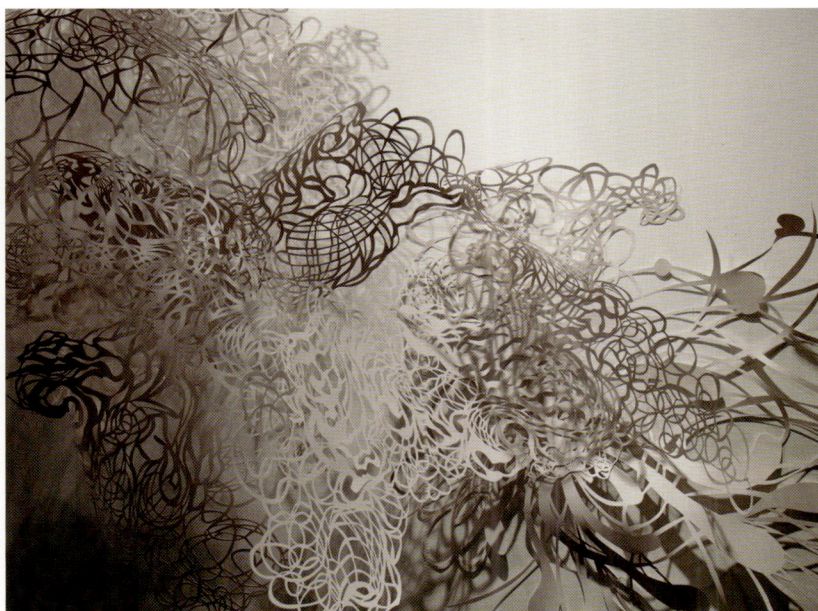
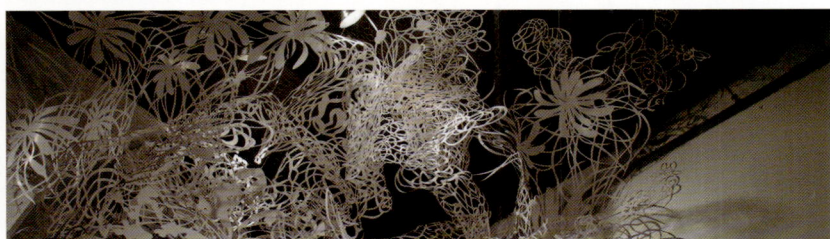
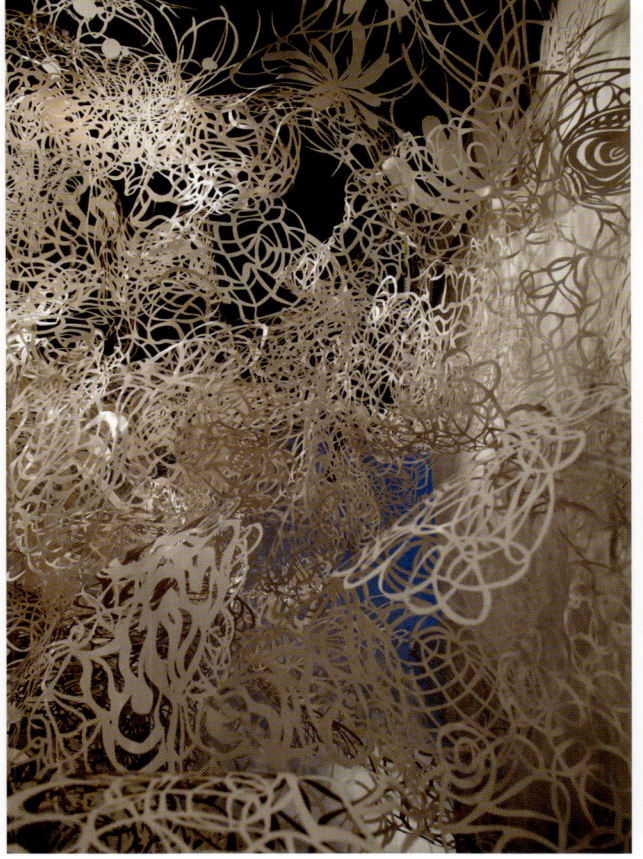
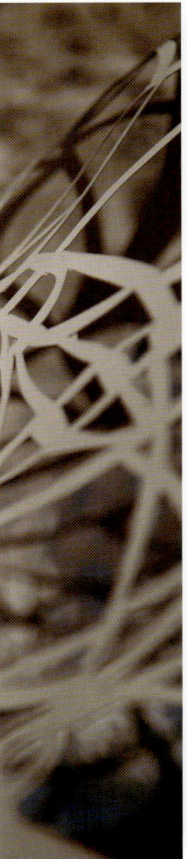
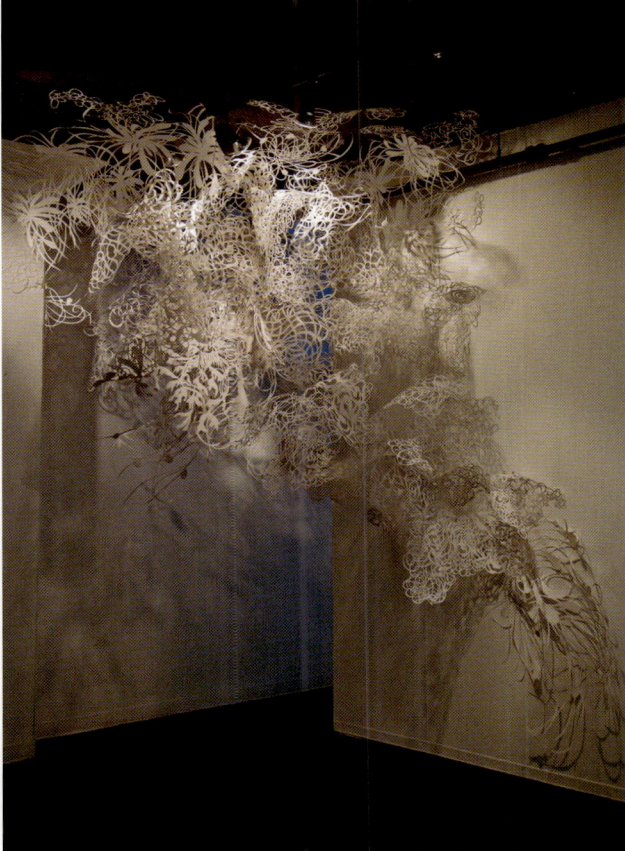

Artist: Vanessa Alarie
Country: Canada
Photographer: Mathieu Normandin

3. Explorations

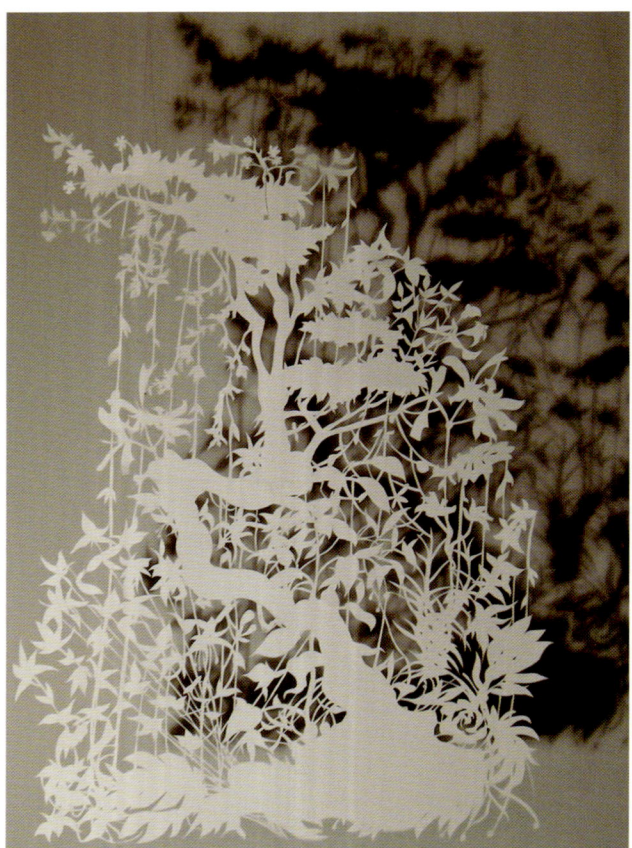
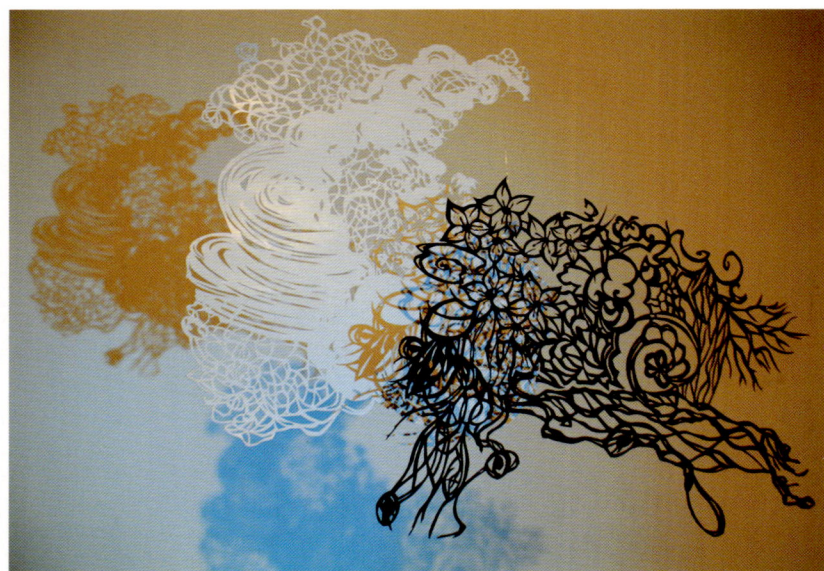
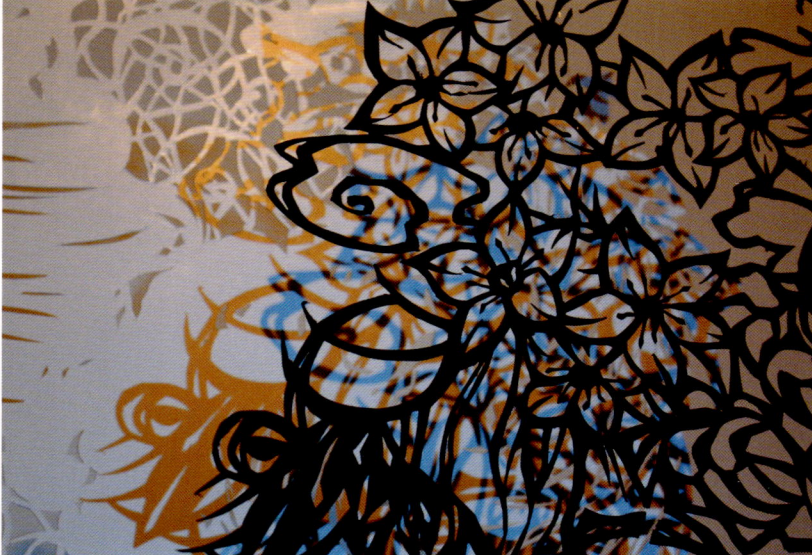
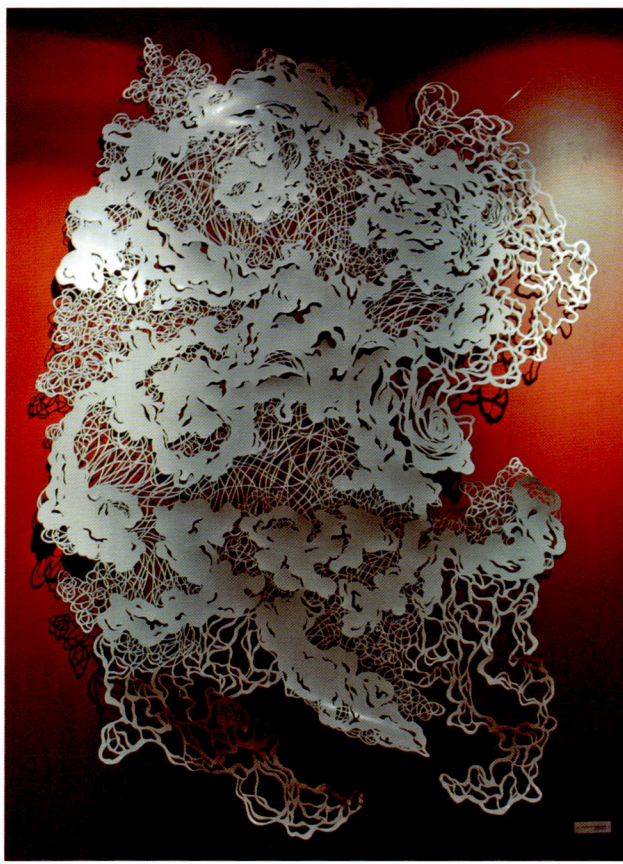
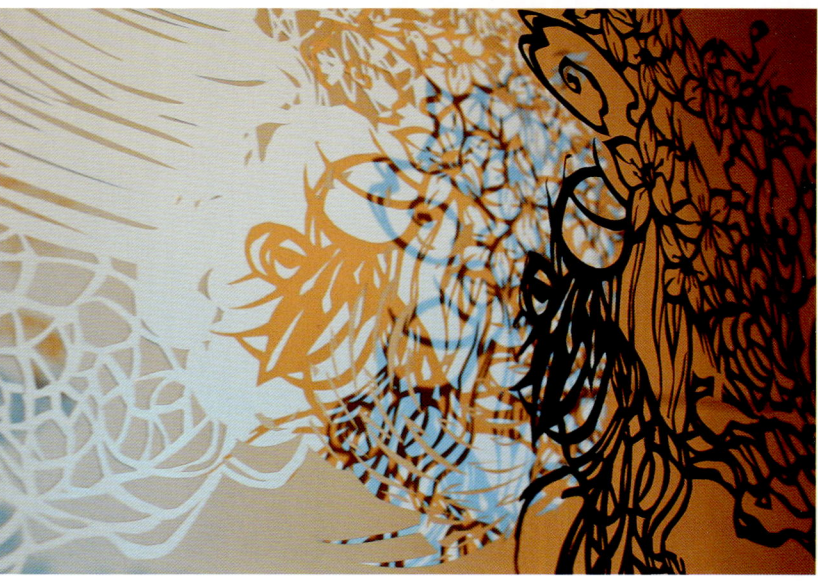

Artist: Vanessa Alarie
Country: Canada
Photographer: Vanessa Alarie / Mathieu Normandin

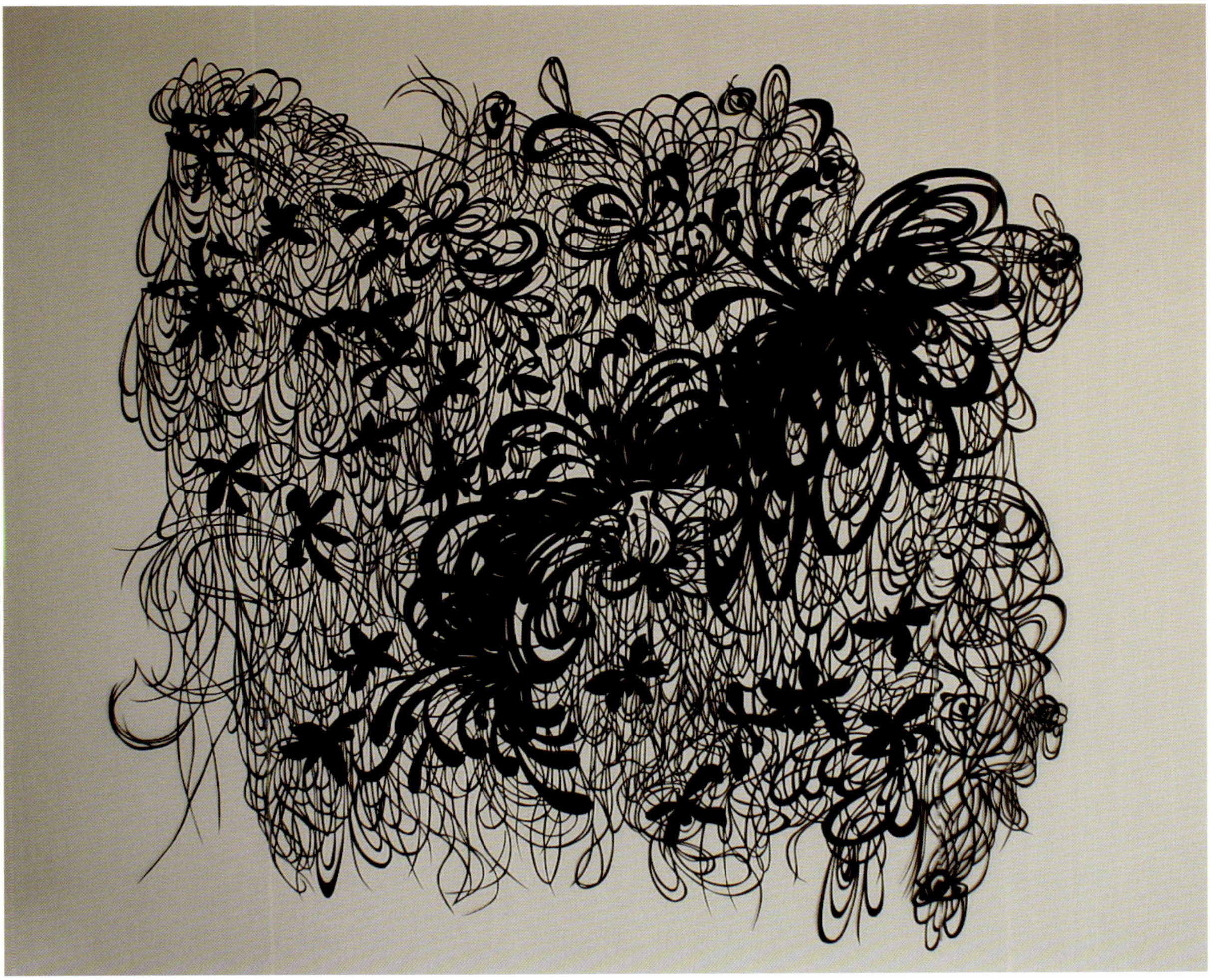

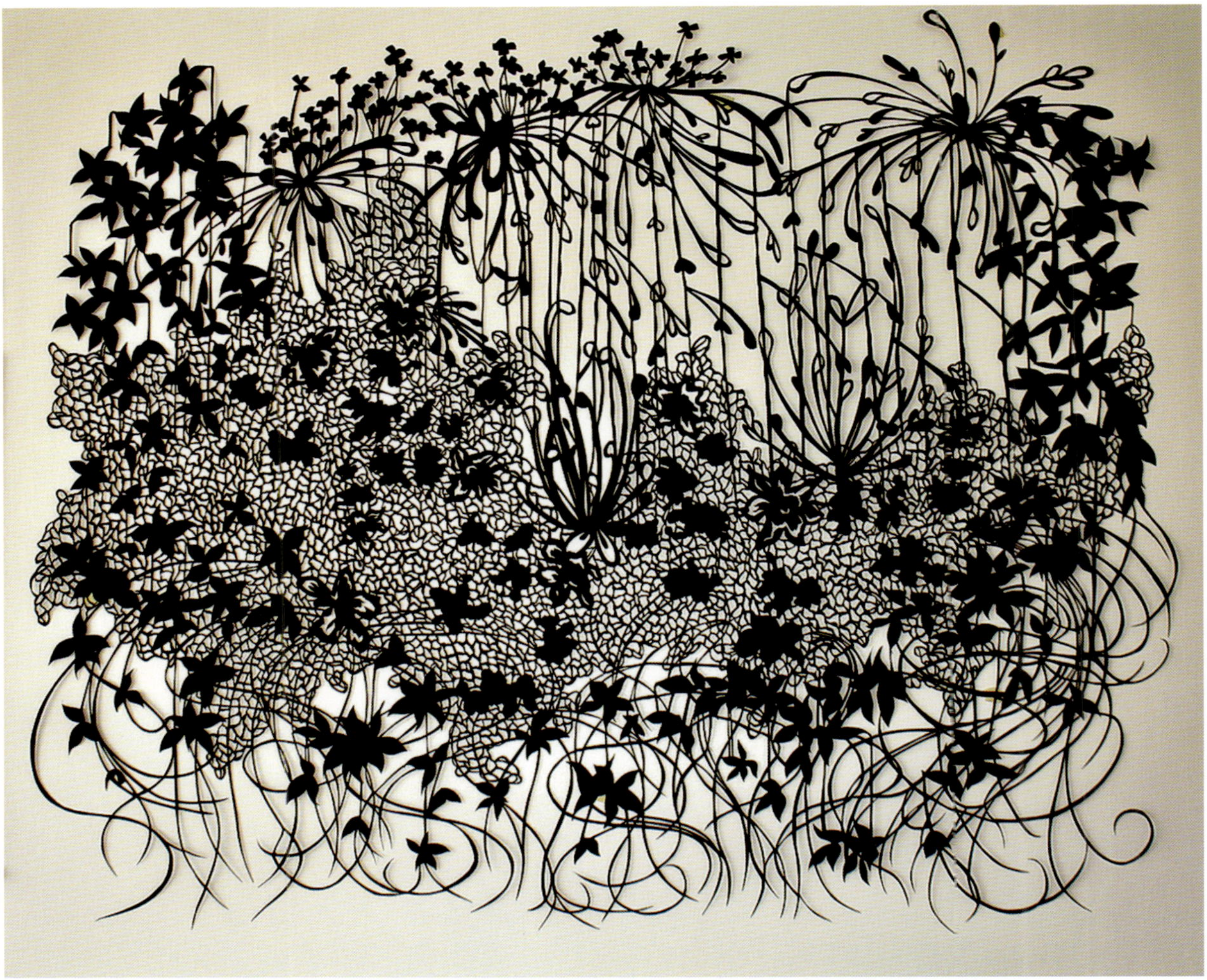

4. Florilège

Paper Cut | 150 x 180 cm

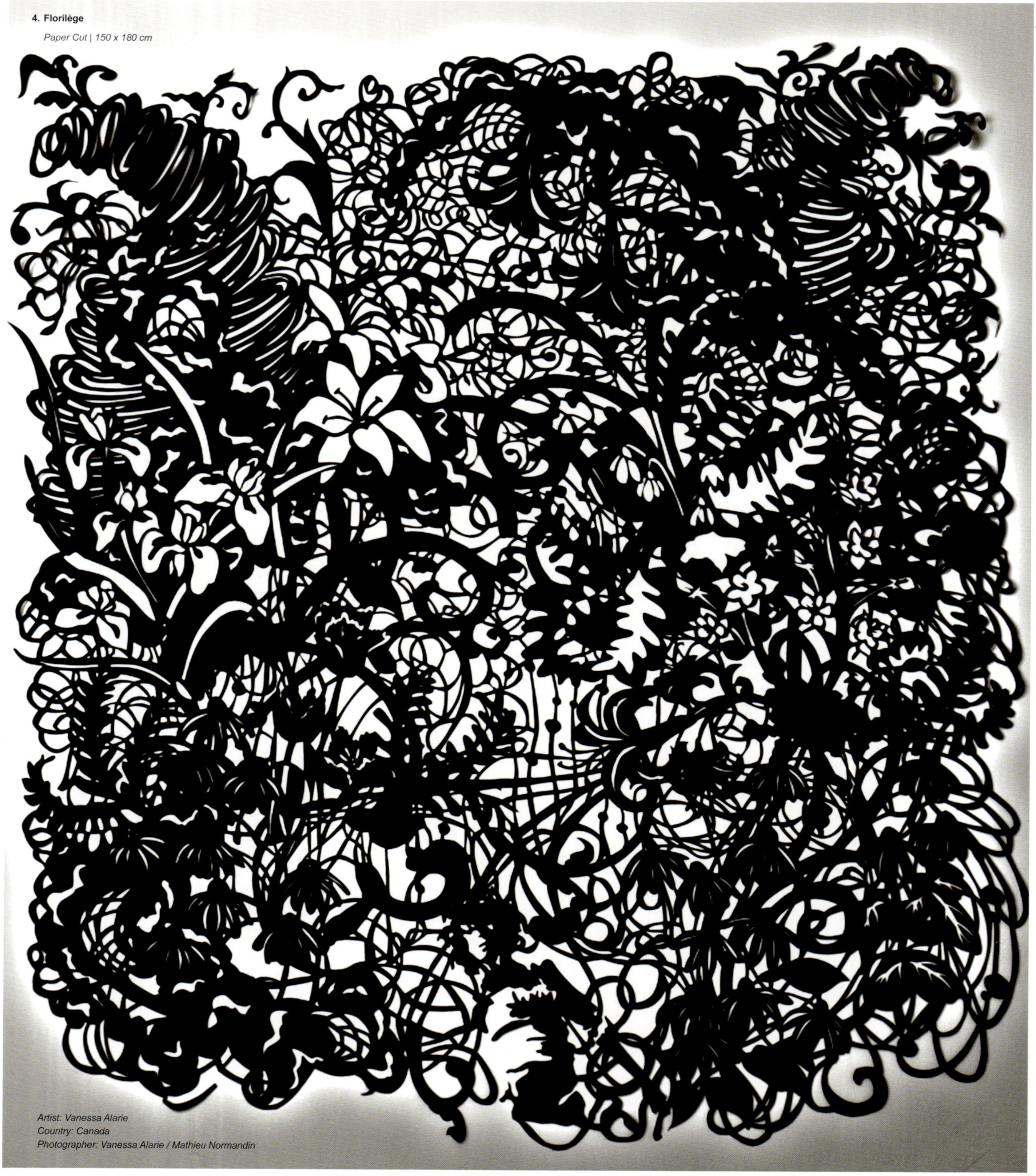

Artist: Vanessa Alarie
Country: Canada
Photographer: Vanessa Alarie / Mathieu Normandin

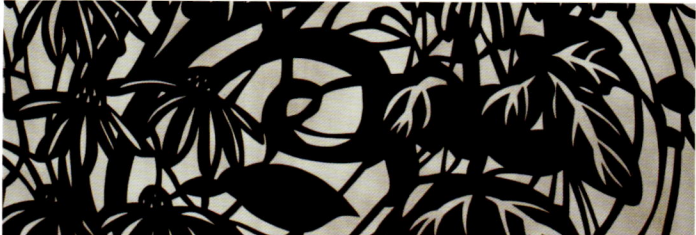
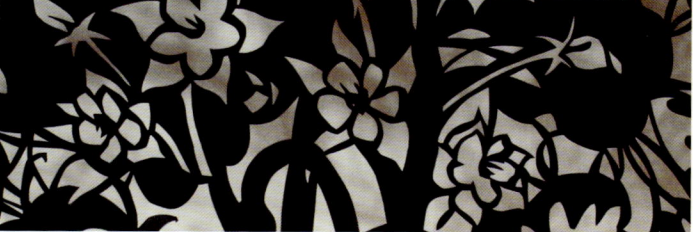

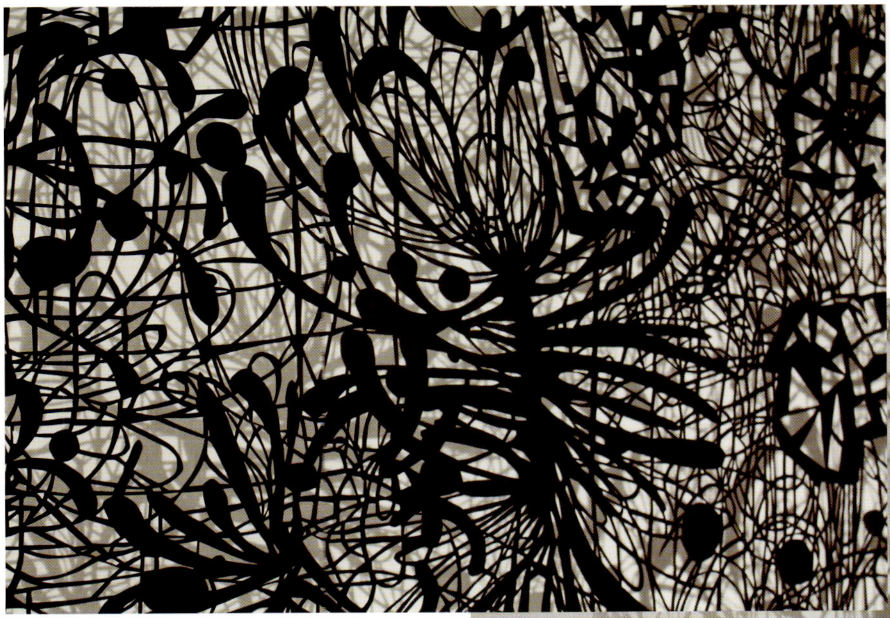

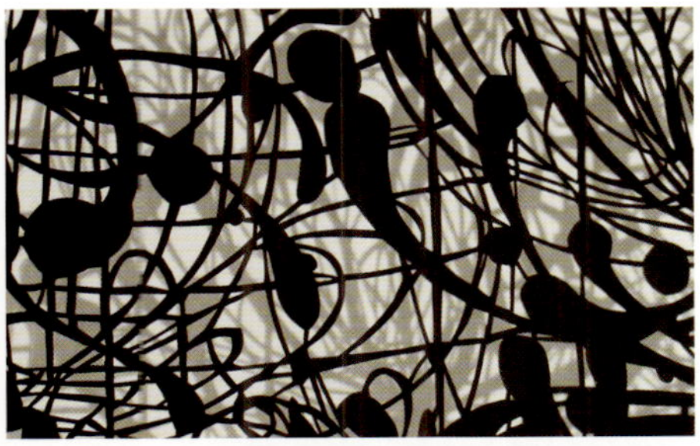

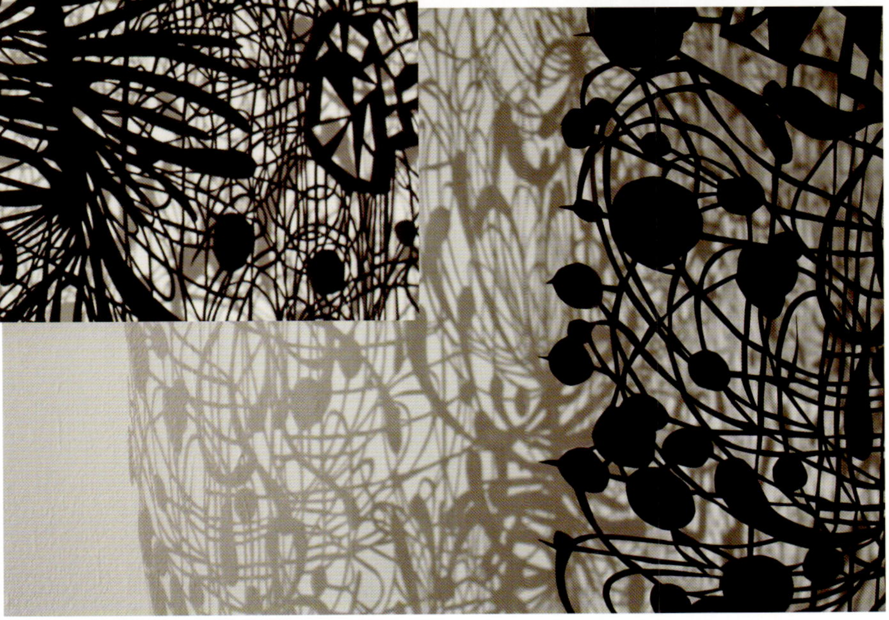

5. **Vertige**

Paper Cut | 253 x 148 cm

Artist: Vanessa Alarie
Country: Canada
Photographer: Vanessa Alarie / Mathieu Normandin

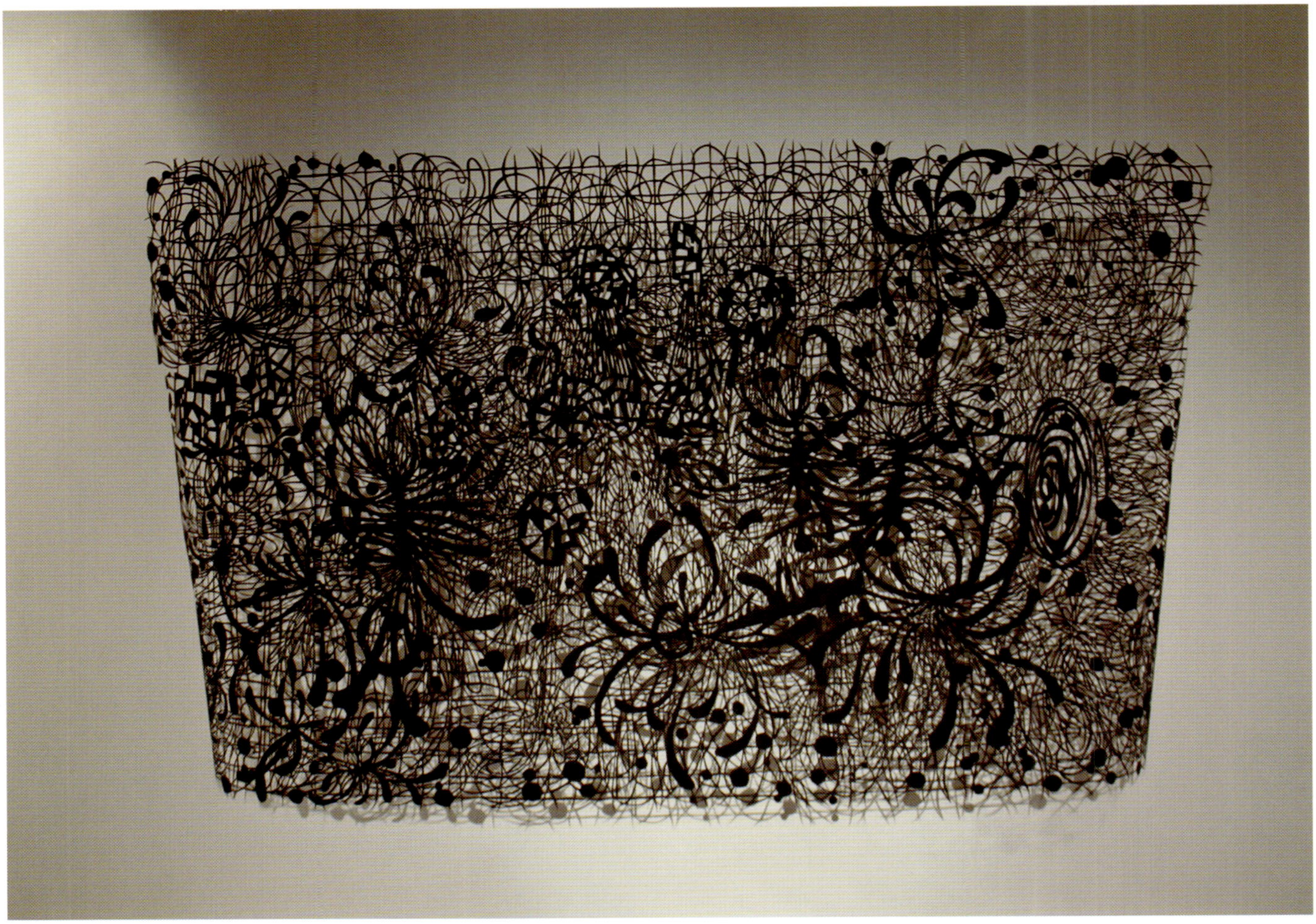

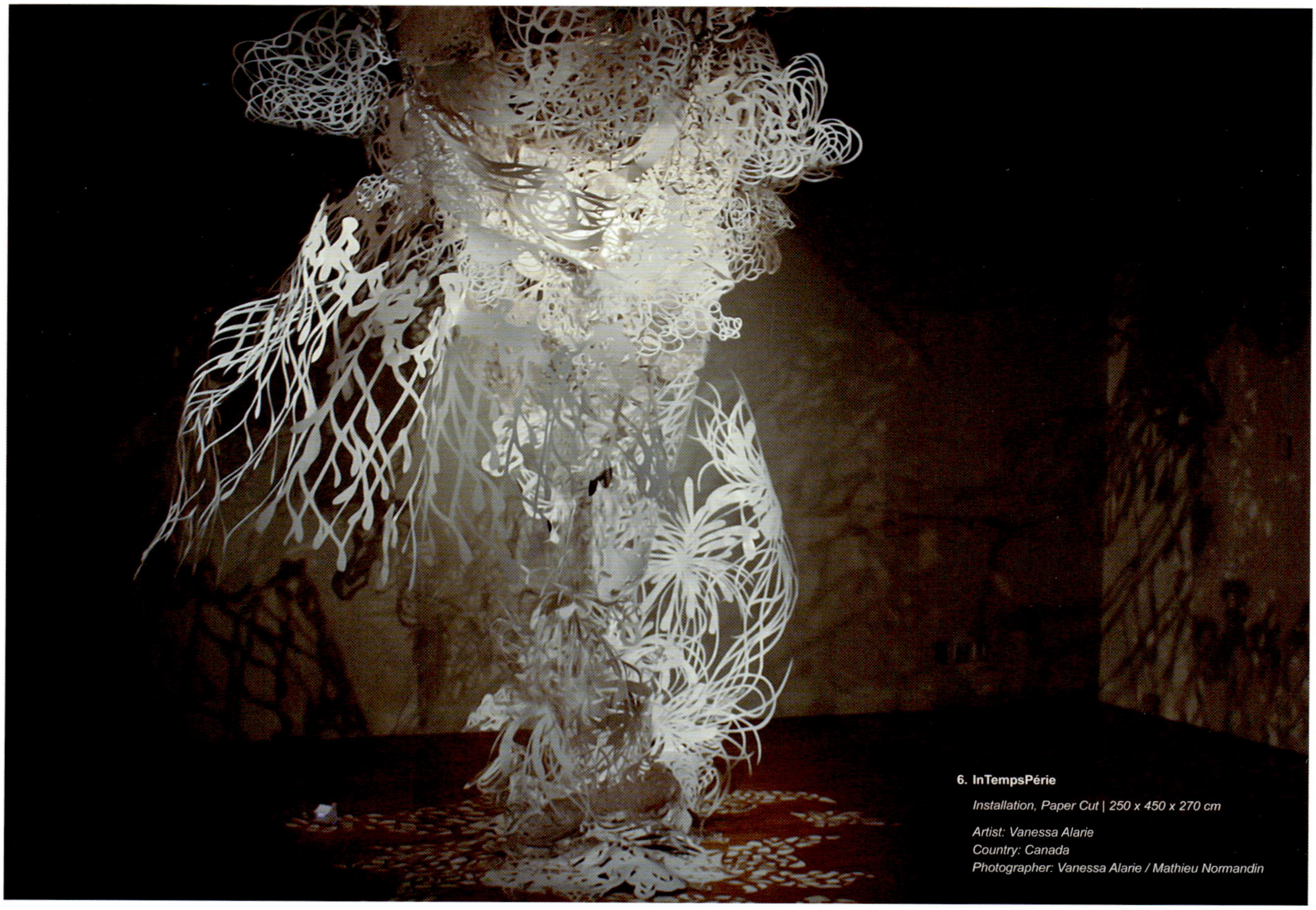

6. InTempsPérie

Installation, Paper Cut | 250 x 450 x 270 cm

Artist: Vanessa Alarie
Country: Canada
Photographer: Vanessa Alarie / Mathieu Normandin

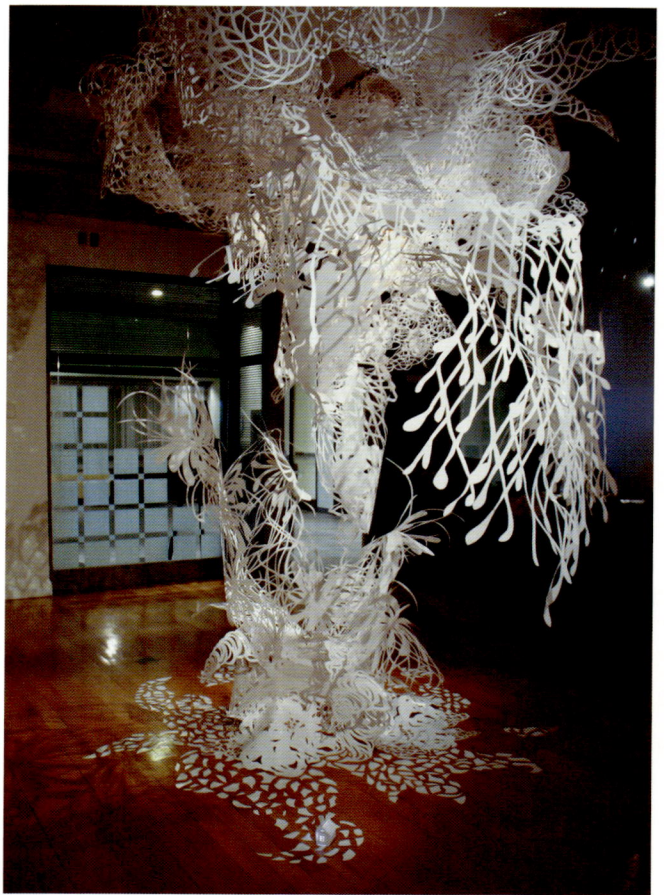
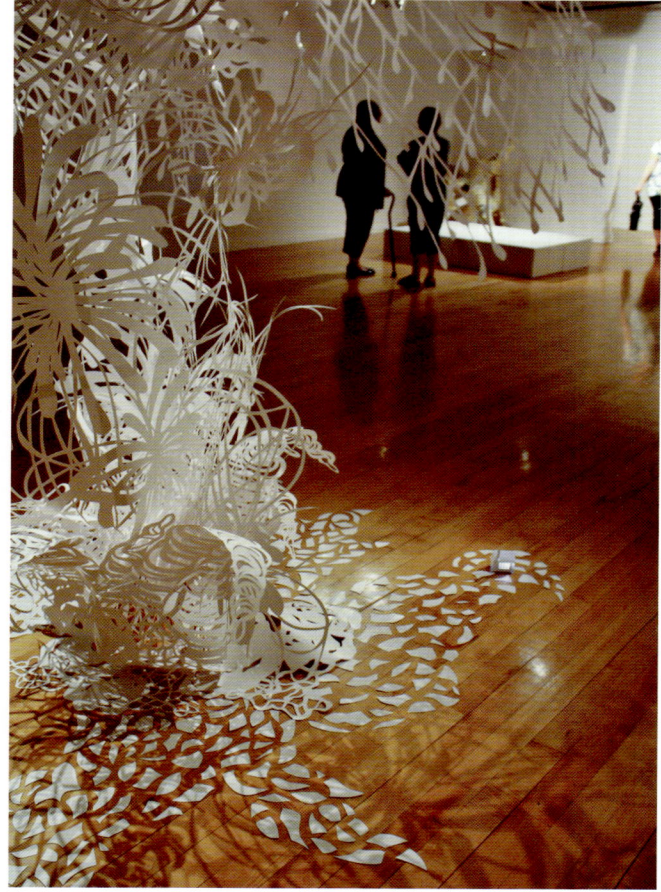

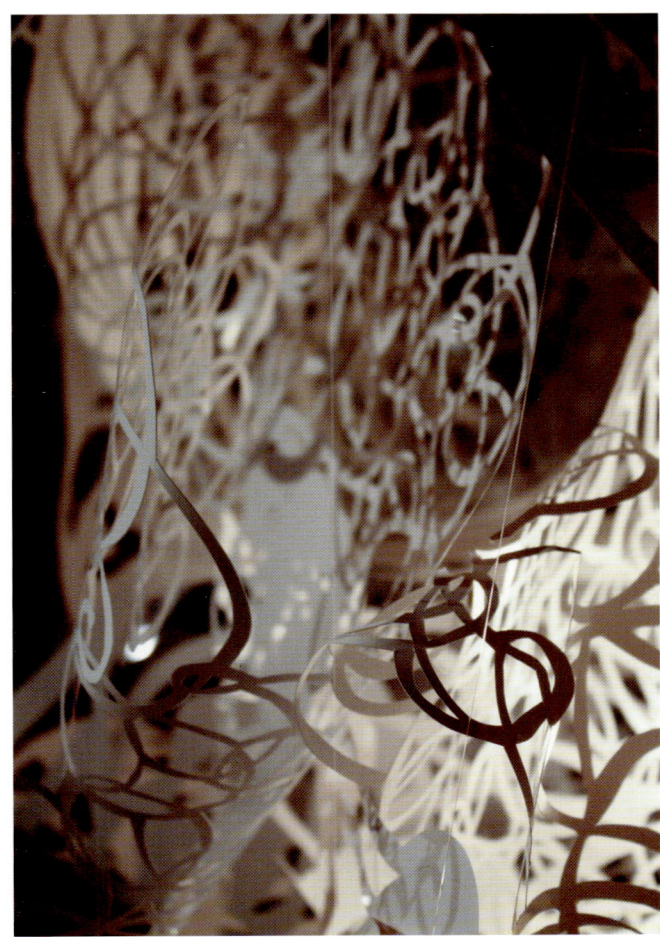
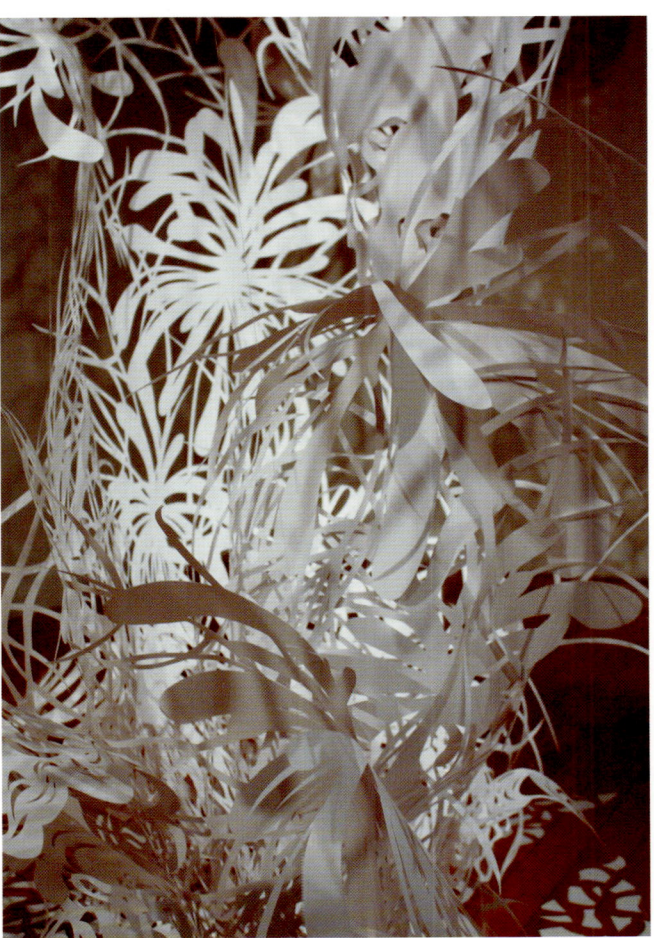

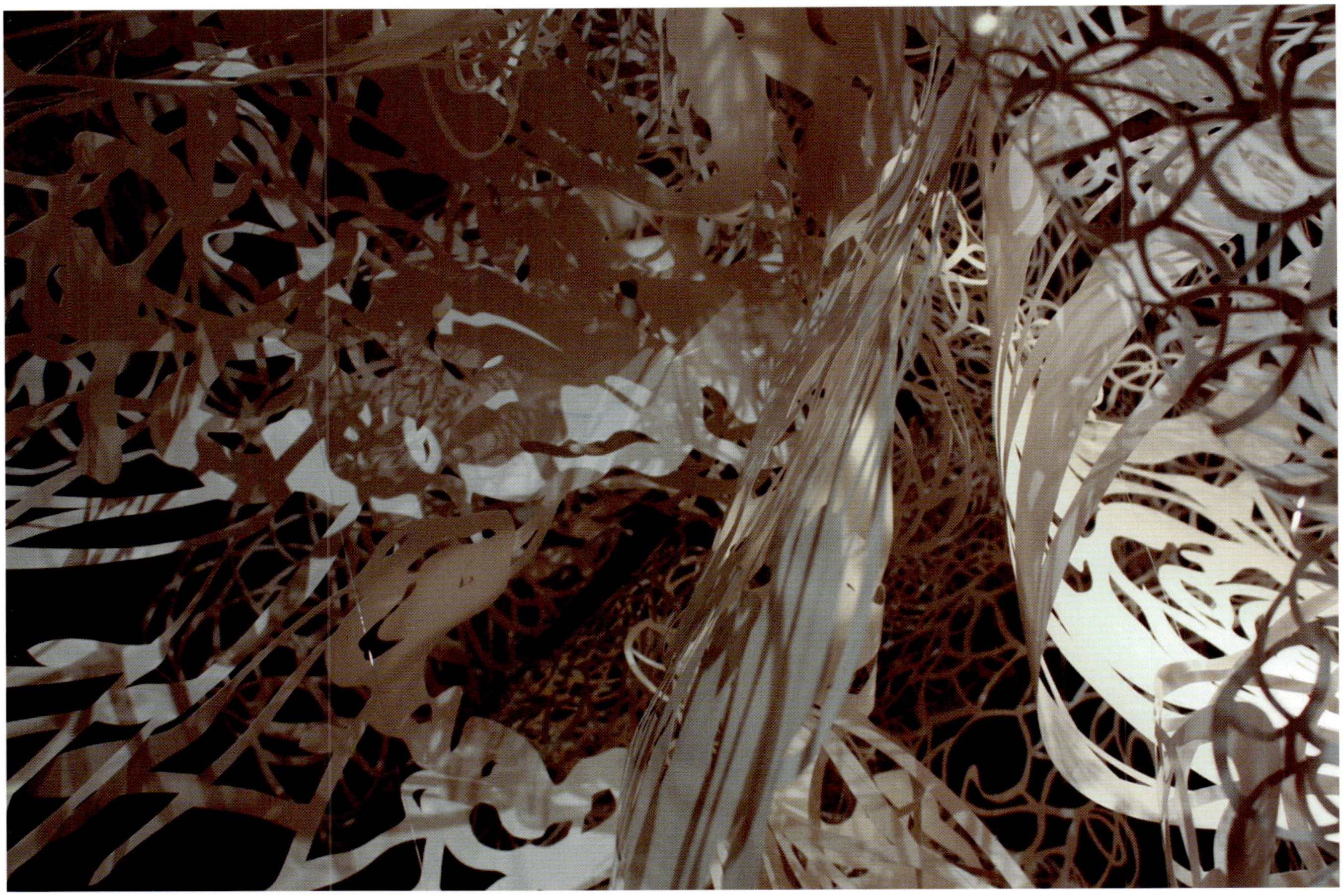

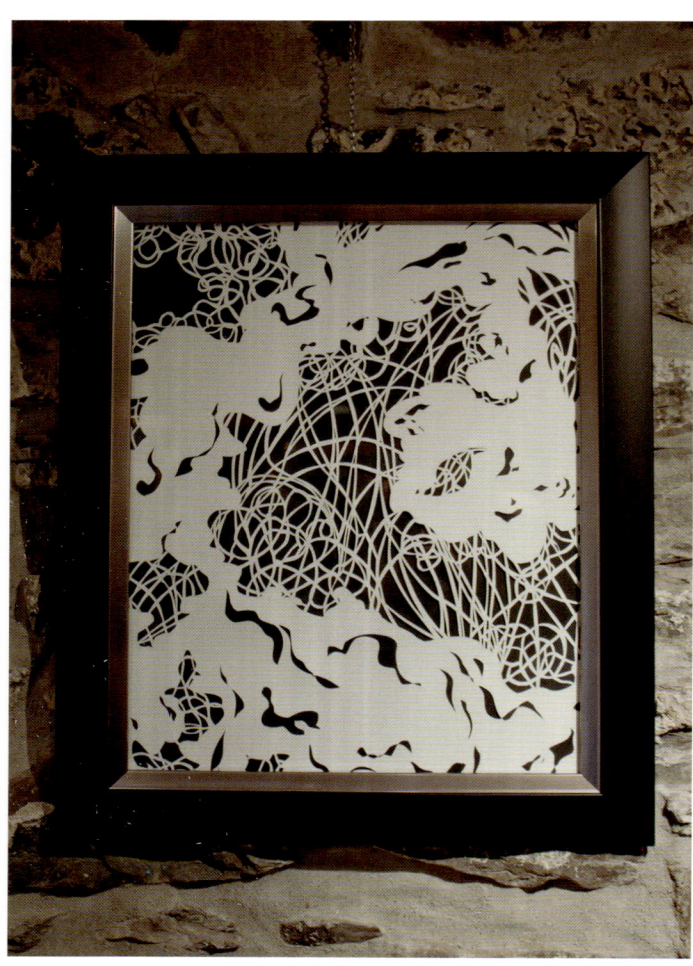
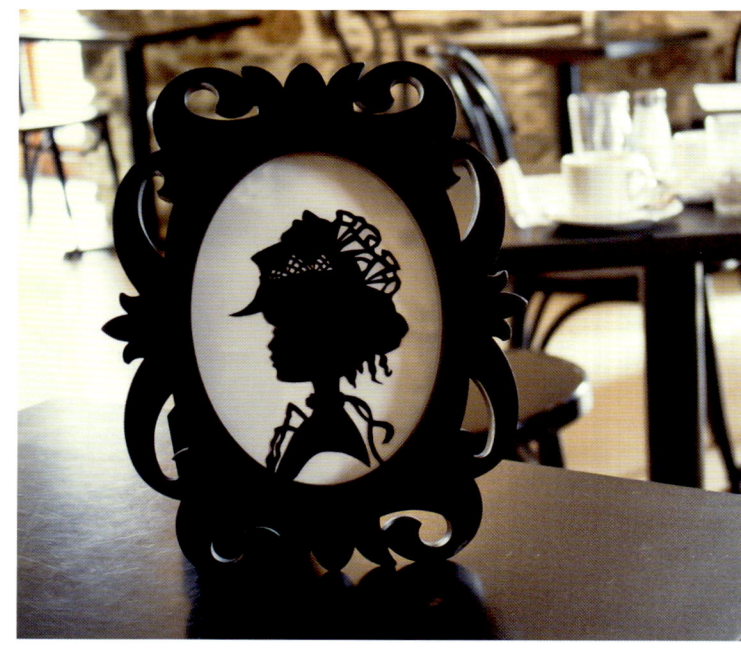
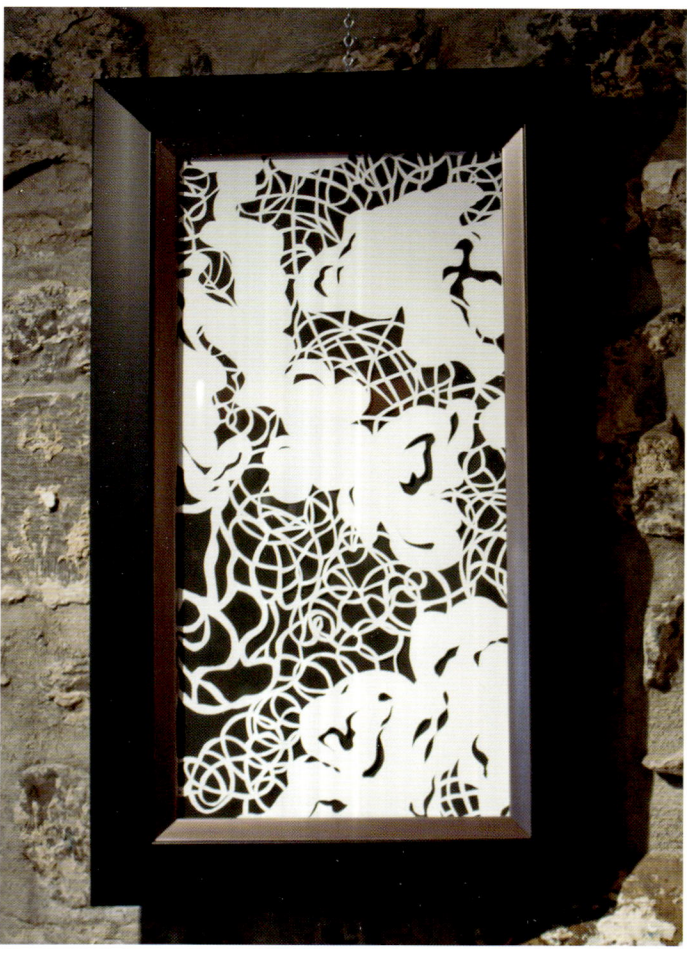
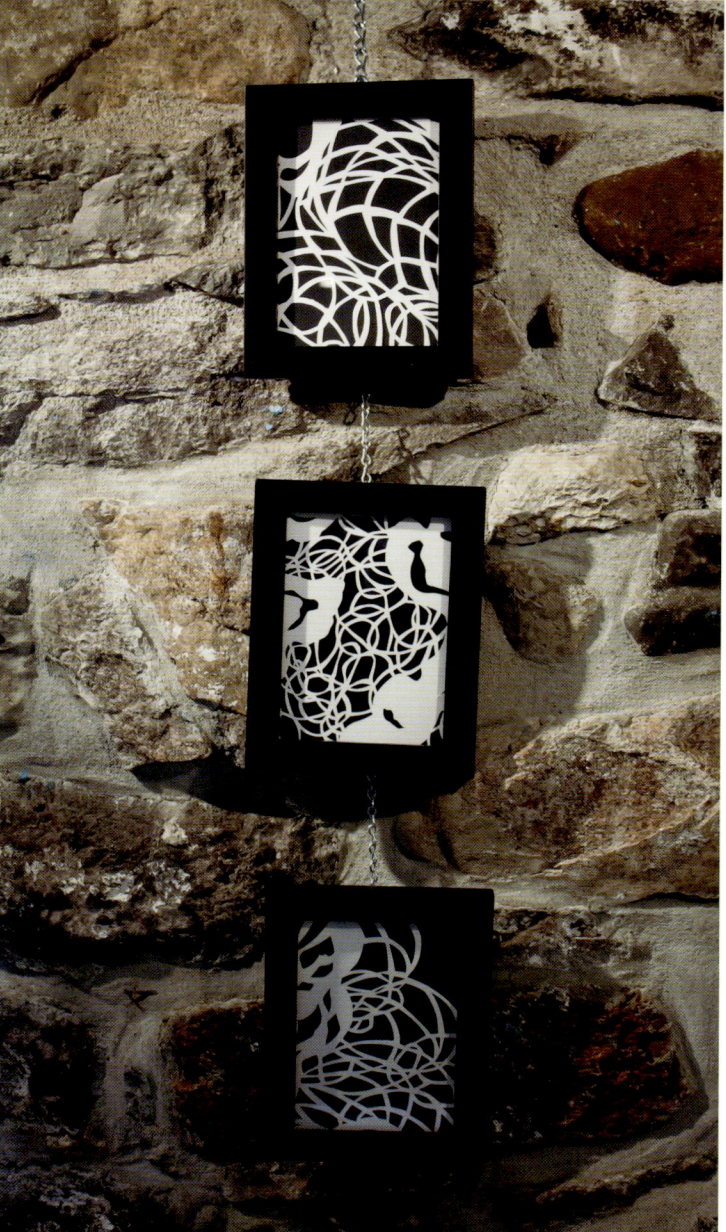

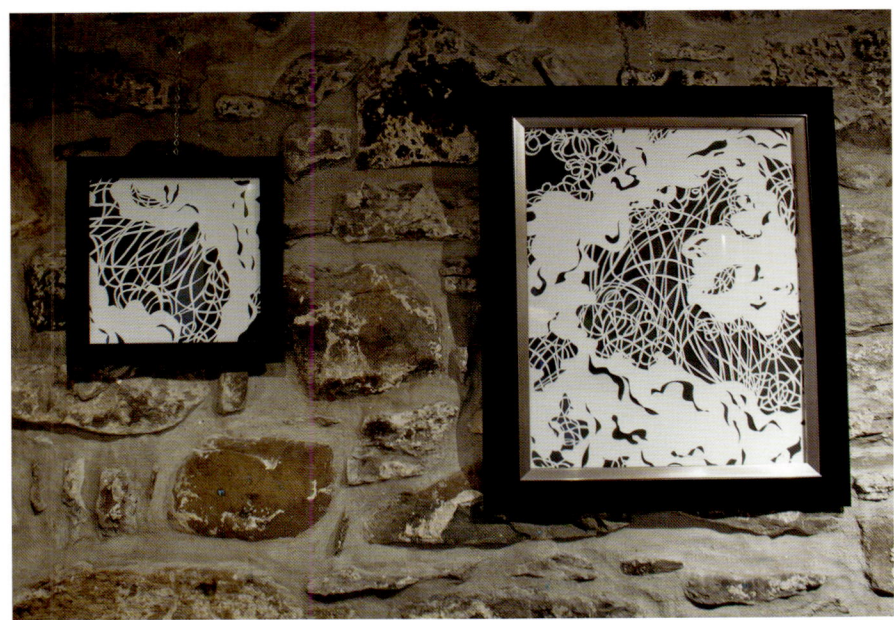

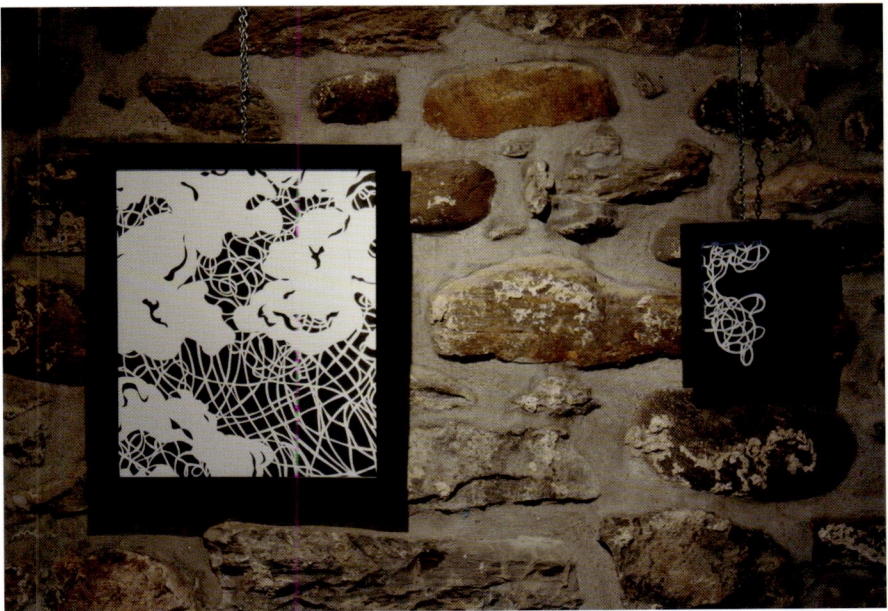

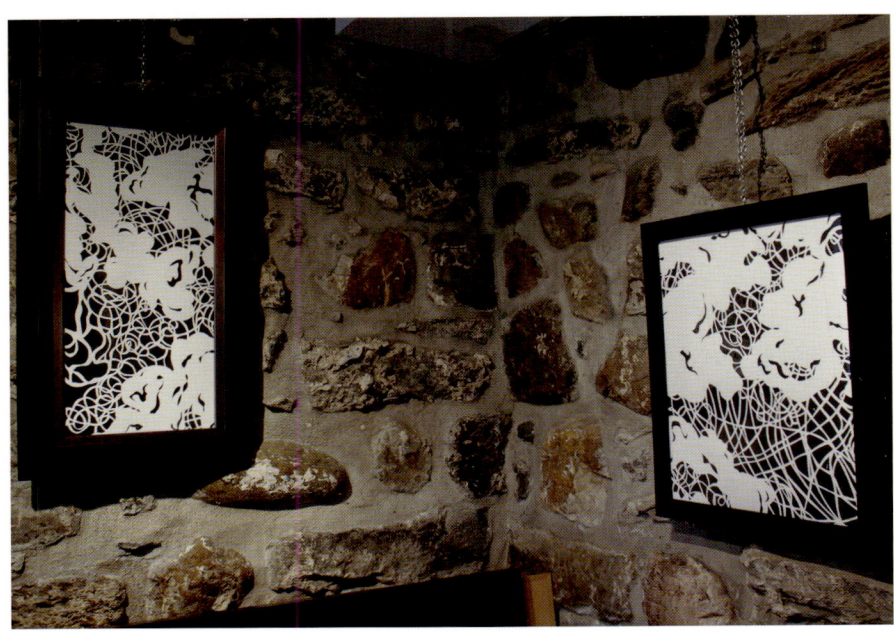

5. Dentelles

Exposition solo, Paper Cut

Paper laces and drawings in space, these works explore the relation between the ambiguity of the visual field and the contemplative state.
The symbiosis of geometric and organic patterns generate an imaginative universe that invite us to instrospection and to the meditative state that live within the artist when she creates them. These works are a poetic comment on our life, our rythm and our wolrd constantly changing and evolving. Detail euphoria, these patterns grow gently in the universe that was defined by the artist: the frames and our eyes.

Artist: Vanessa Alarie
Country: Canada
Photographer: Mathieu Normandin

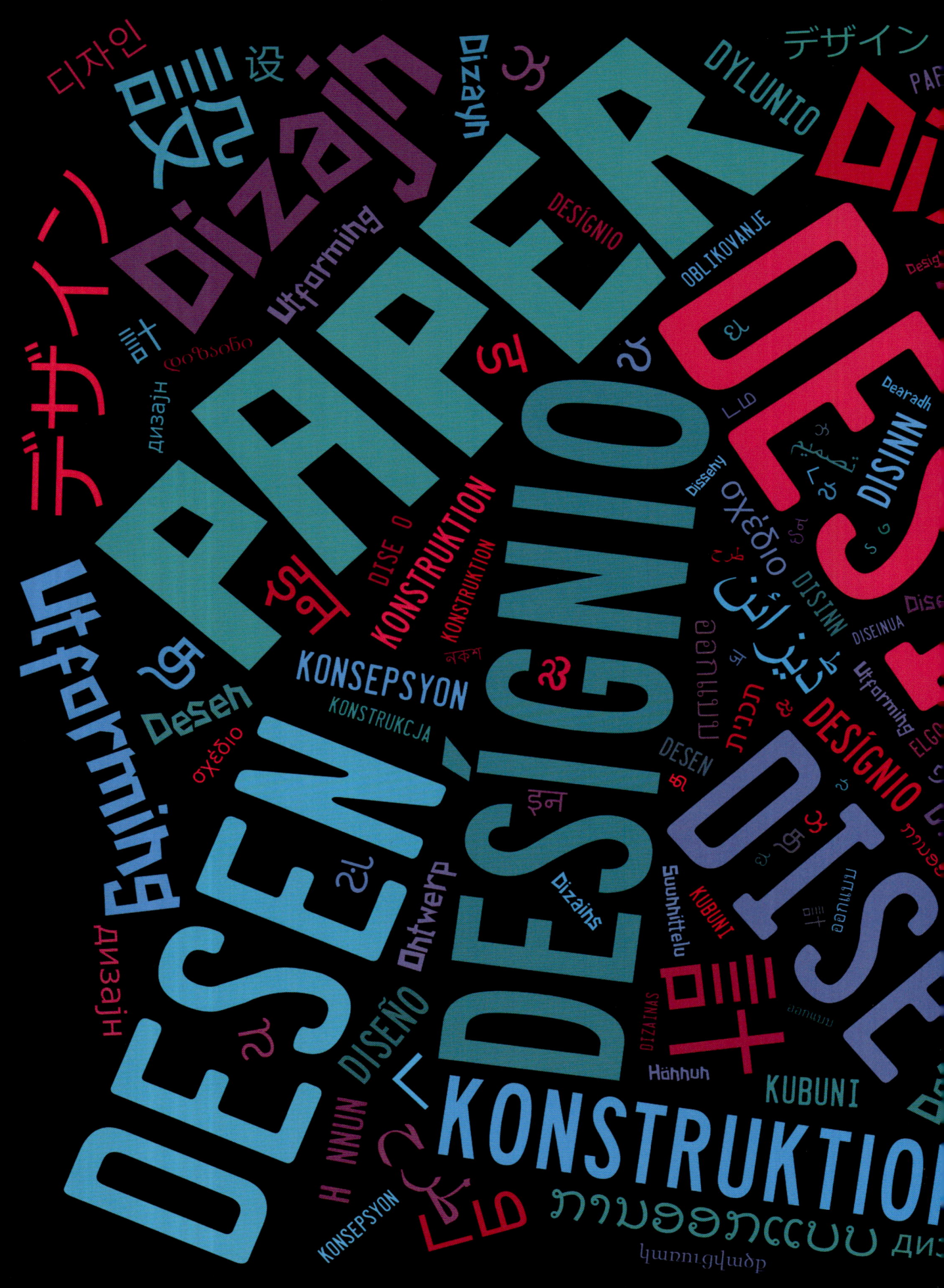

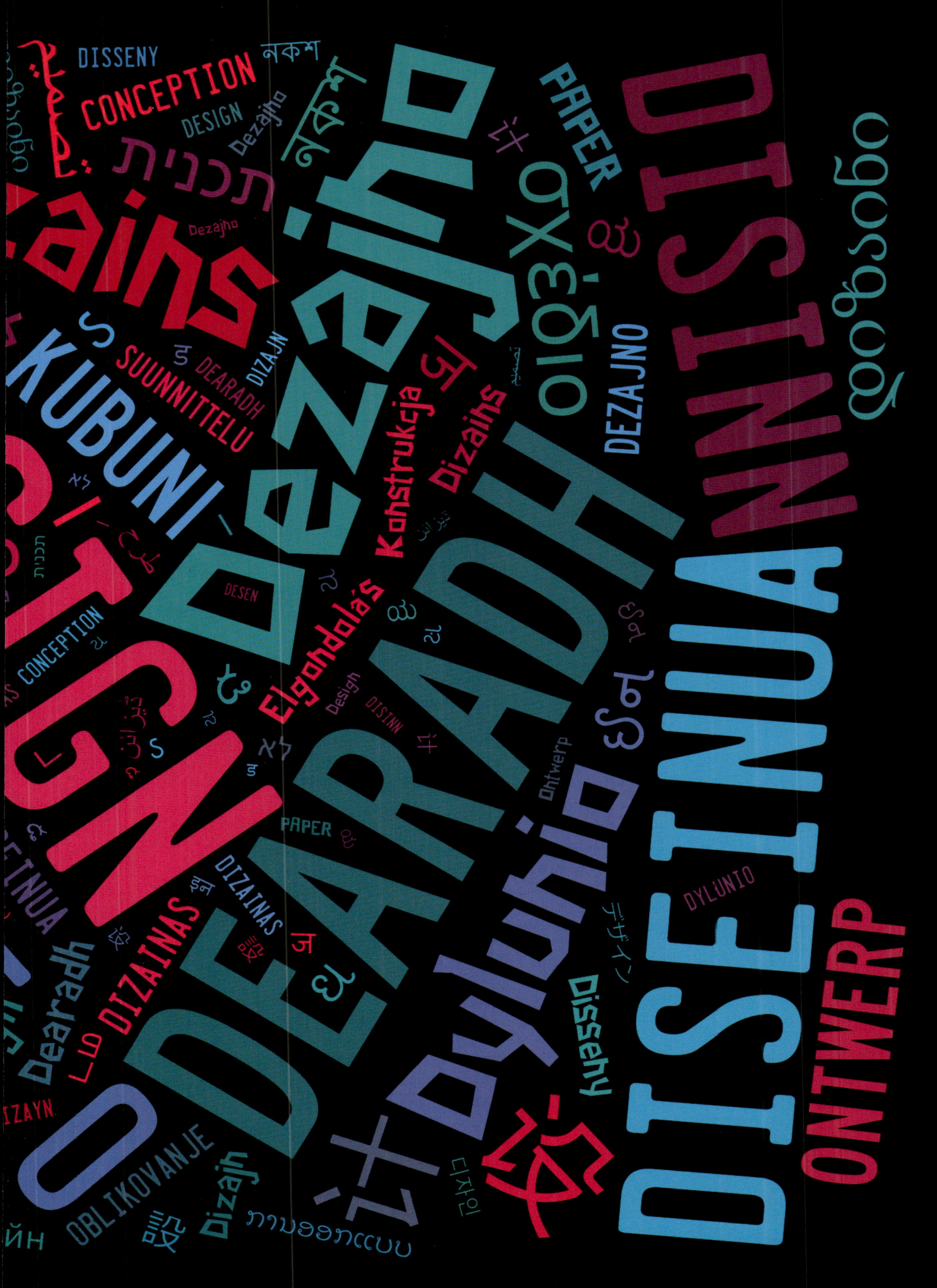

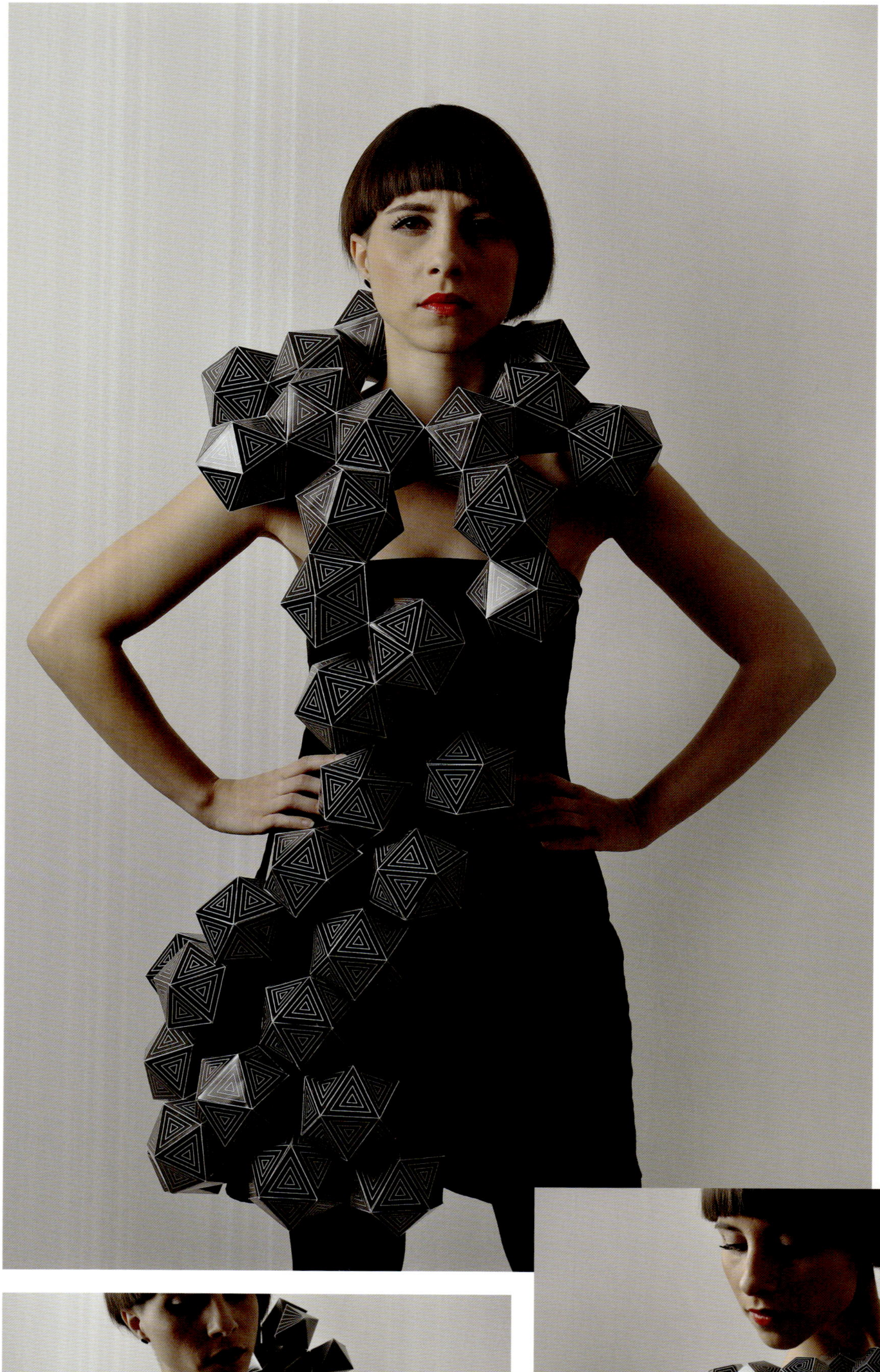

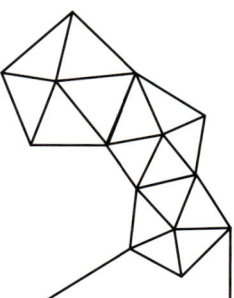

Plato's Collection

"Geometry existed before the creation" - Plato

The main inspiration for the Plato's Collection is located in Platonic solids. The collection consists of five unique dresses/costumes handcrafted from a combination of textiles and paper.

This project examines the concept of geometrically arranged and structured space in relation to the human body. It is the most appropriate to call it a study of perception and contrast, and study of relation between artificial and organic, amorphous and geometric. Each of the five Platonic solids is a basic building element for making dresses. Simplicity of form and use of black and white print patterns on rigid paper emphasize the sculptural collection, its attitude toward the body and overall expression in space. Therefore, Plato's collection does not fit into the category of everyday fashion and can be considered as a stage costume, and is intended for stage performances, fashion editorials and other special purposes.

---Amila Hrustic

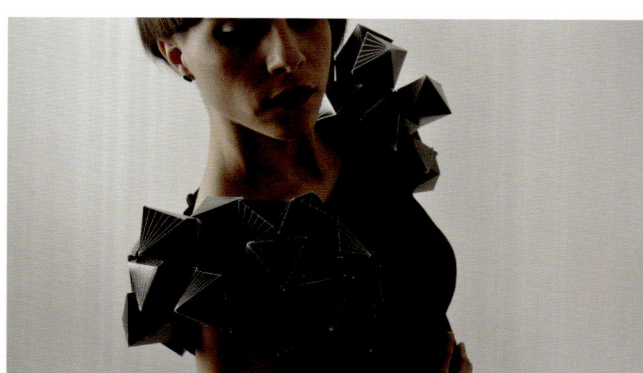

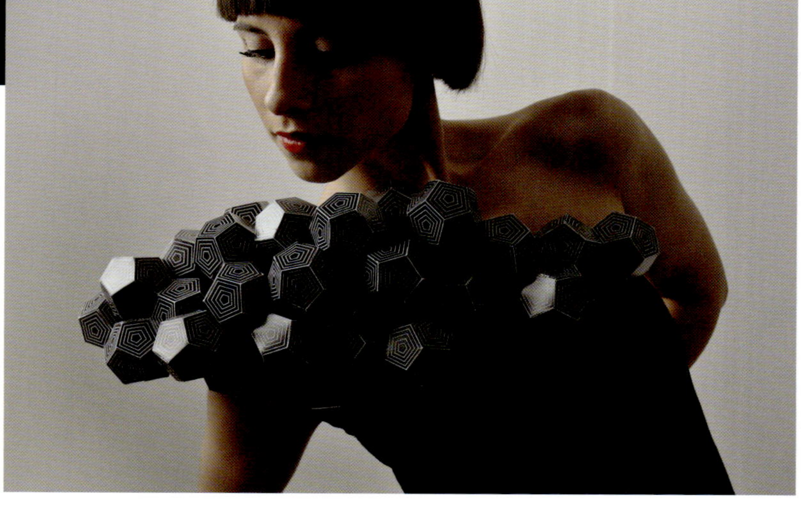

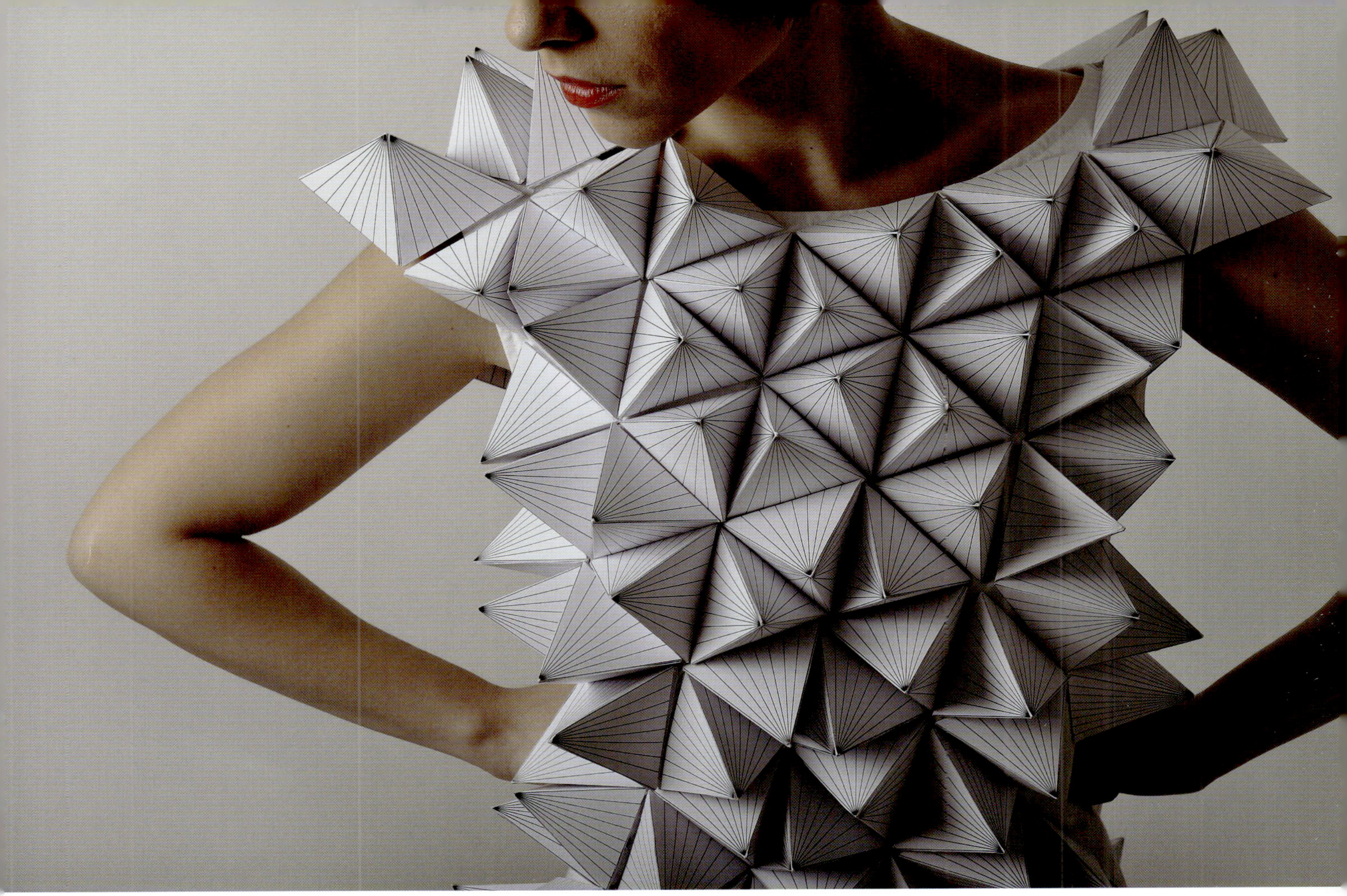

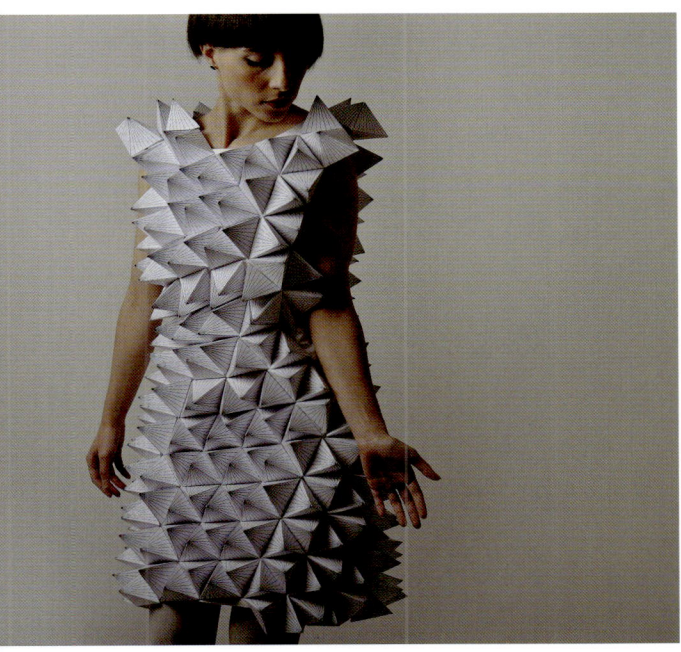

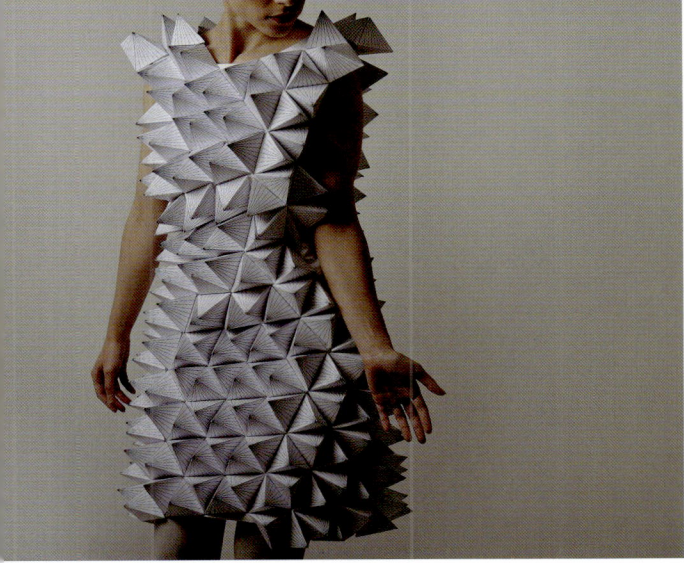

Designer: Amila Hrustic
Country: Bosnia and Herzegovina
Creative Director: Amila Hrustic
Photographer: Irfan Redzovic

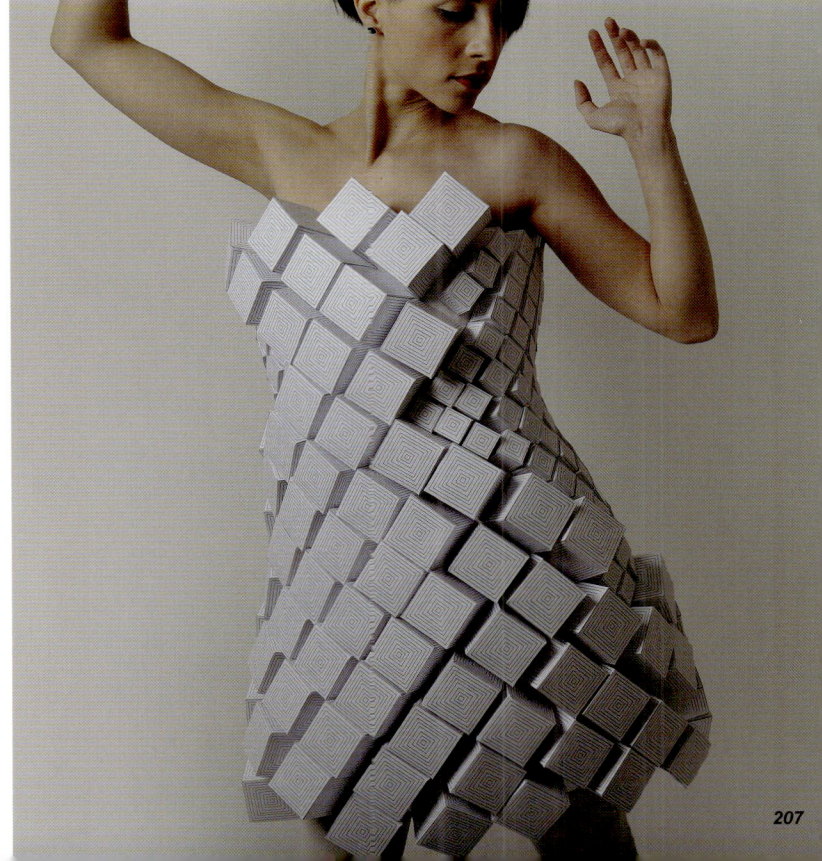

Plato, the great Greek philosopher, studied what we now call "Platonic solids". No one knows who first described the shapes of these bodies, perhaps early Pythagoreans, but some, including Euclid, say that it was a close friend of Plato's Theaetetus.

There are only five Platonic solids: tetrahedron, cube, octahedron, dodecahedron and icosahedron.

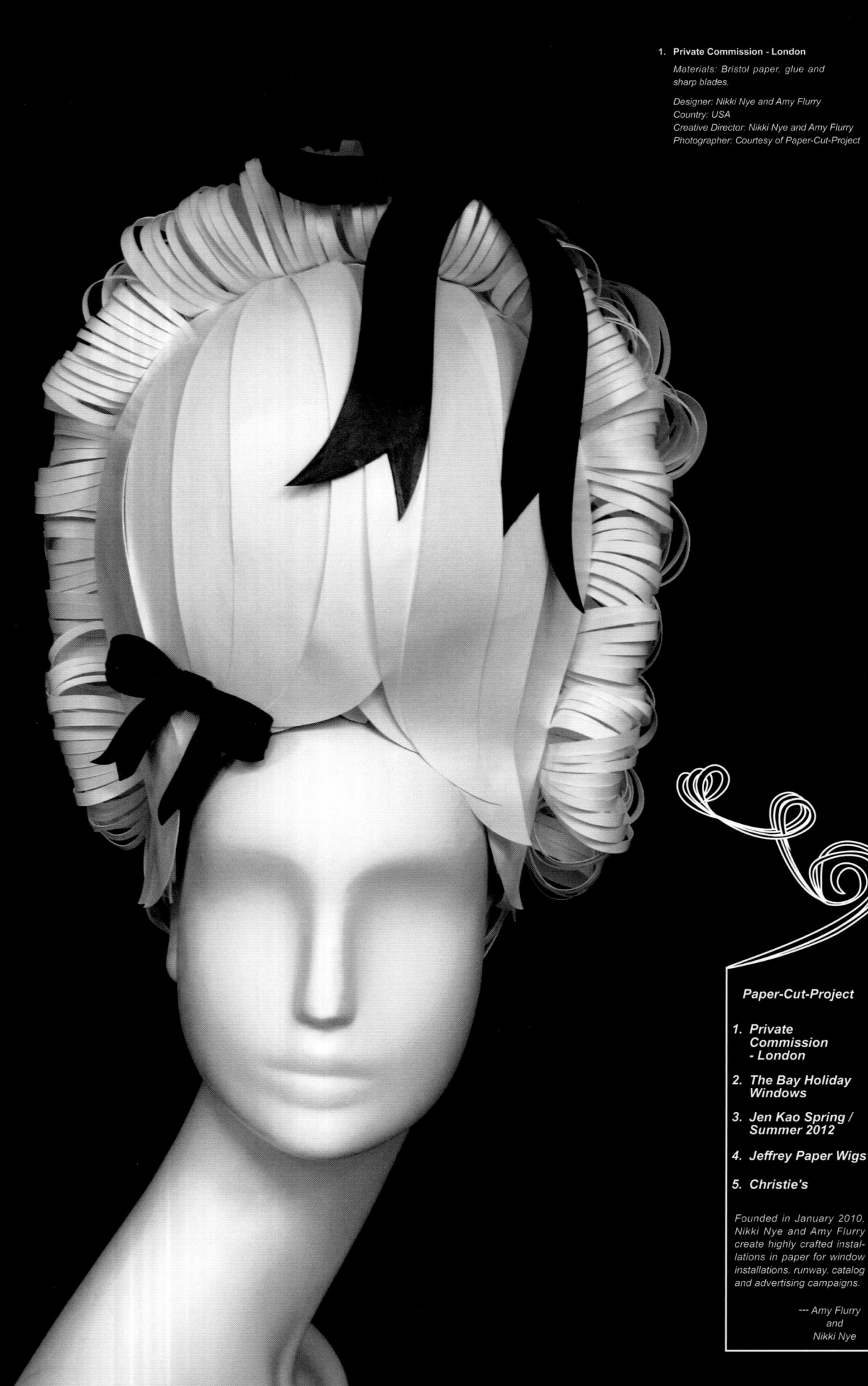

1. **Private Commission - London**

   Materials: Bristol paper, glue and sharp blades.

   Designer: Nikki Nye and Amy Flurry
   Country: USA
   Creative Director: Nikki Nye and Amy Flurry
   Photographer: Courtesy of Paper-Cut-Project

   Paper-Cut-Project

   1. **Private Commission - London**
   2. **The Bay Holiday Windows**
   3. **Jen Kao Spring / Summer 2012**
   4. **Jeffrey Paper Wigs**
   5. **Christie's**

   Founded in January 2010, Nikki Nye and Amy Flurry create highly crafted installations in paper for window installations, runway, catalog and advertising campaigns.

   --- Amy Flurry and Nikki Nye

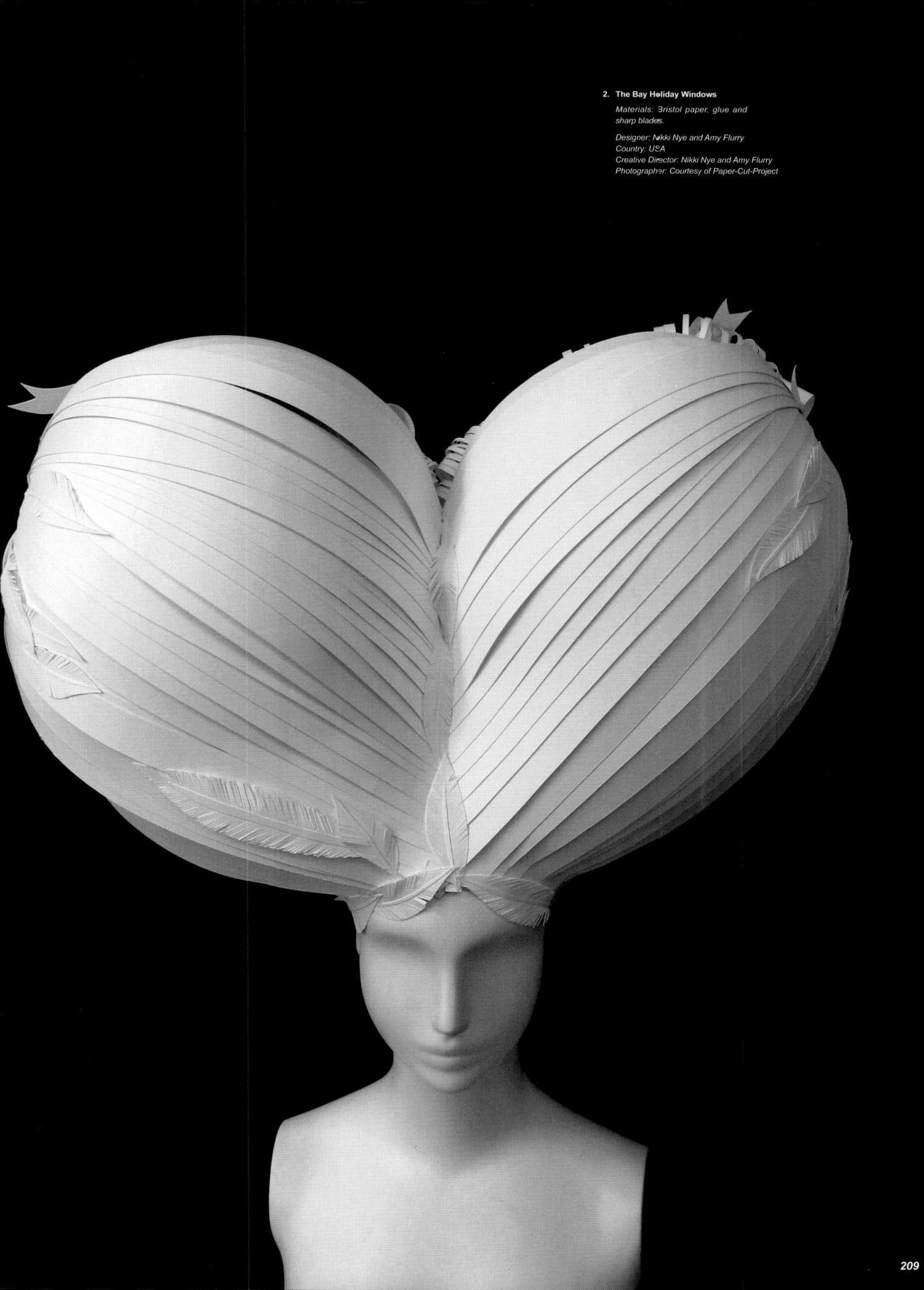

2. **The Bay Holiday Windows**

Materials: Bristol paper, glue and sharp blades.

Designer: Nikki Nye and Amy Flurry
Country: USA
Creative Director: Nikki Nye and Amy Flurry
Photographer: Courtesy of Paper-Cut-Project

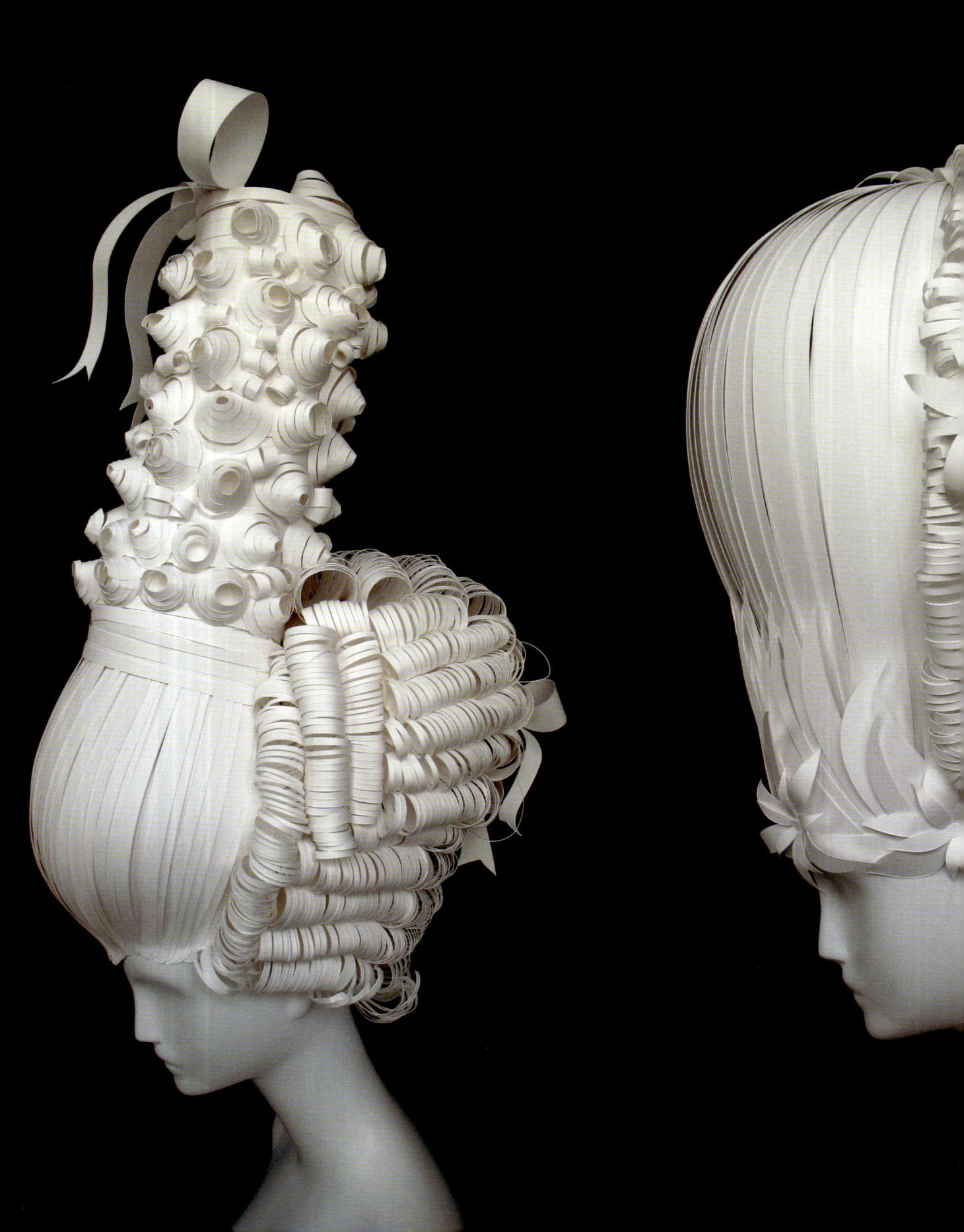

2. **The Bay Holiday Windows**

Materials: Bristol paper, glue and sharp blades.

Designer: Nikki Nye and Amy Flurry
Country: USA
Creative Director: Nikki Nye and Amy Flurry
Photographer: Courtesy of Paper-Cut-Project

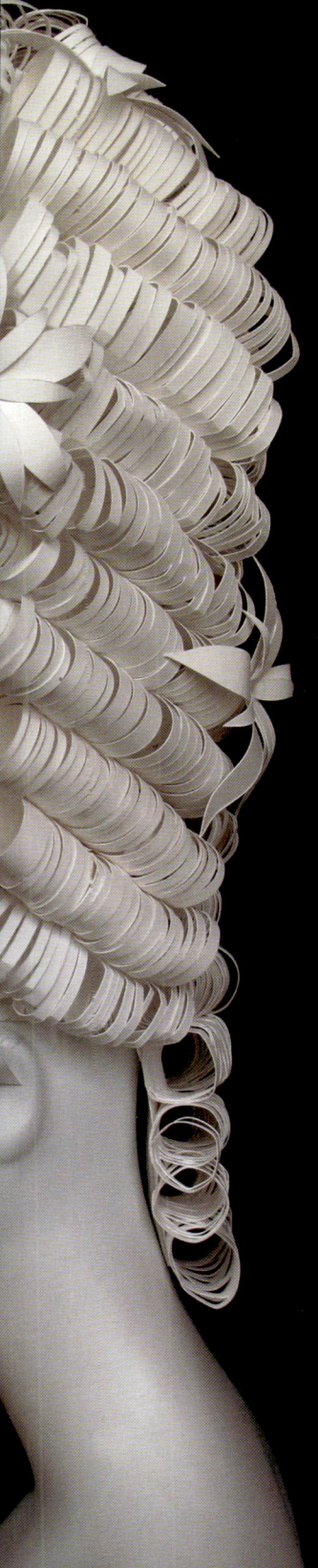

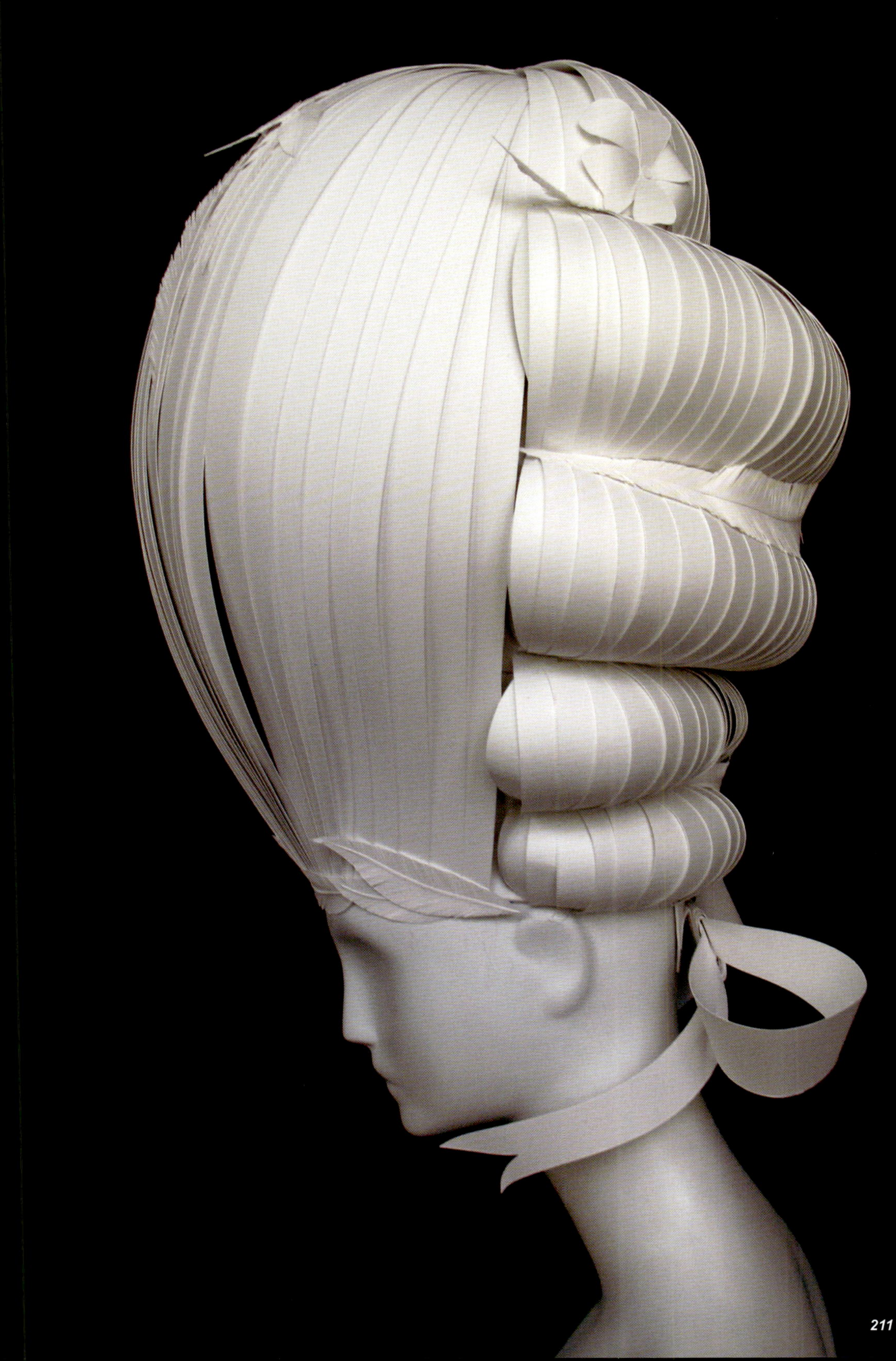

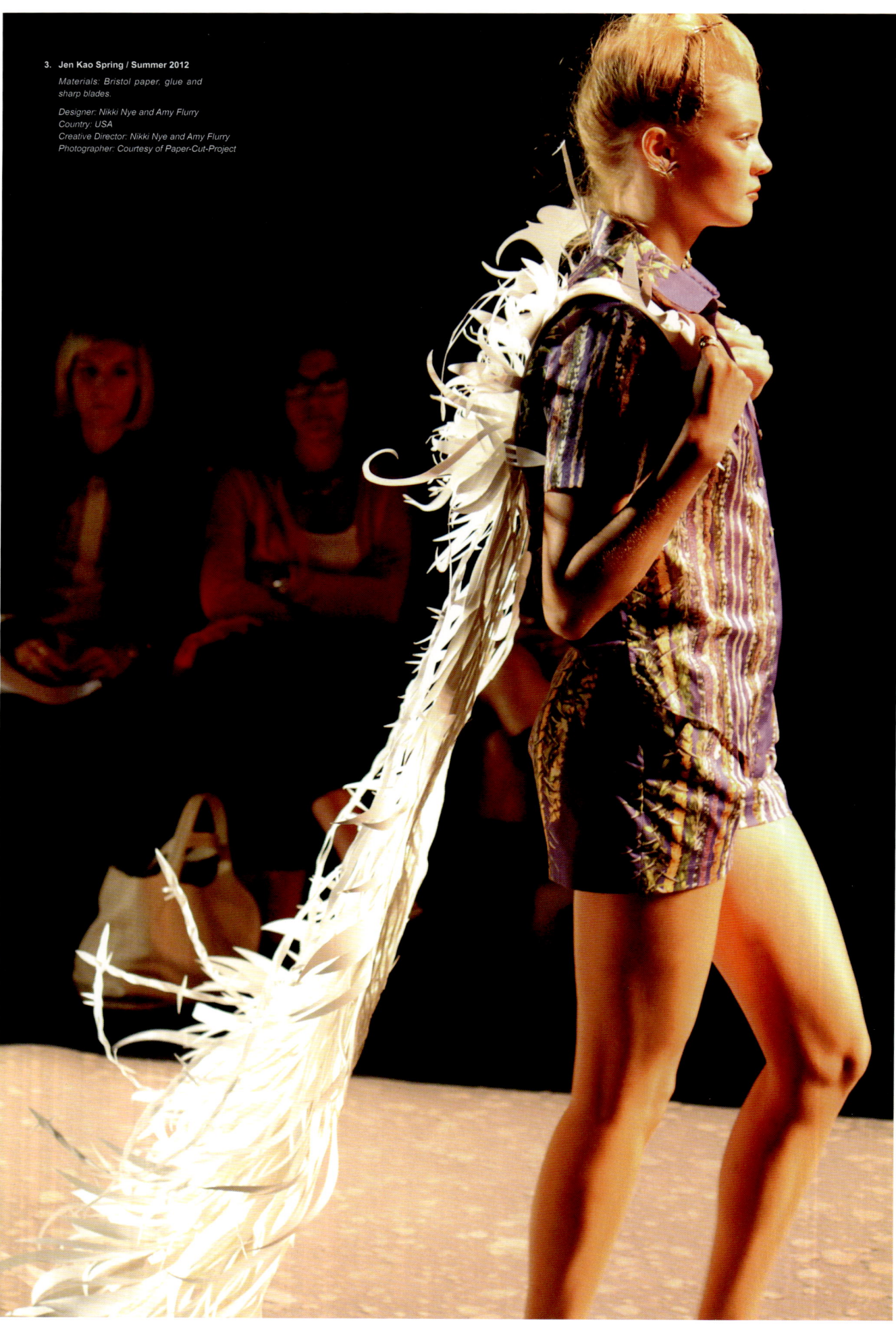

3. Jen Kao Spring / Summer 2012

Materials: Bristol paper, glue and sharp blades.

Designer: Nikki Nye and Amy Flurry
Country: USA
Creative Director: Nikki Nye and Amy Flurry
Photographer: Courtesy of Paper-Cut-Project

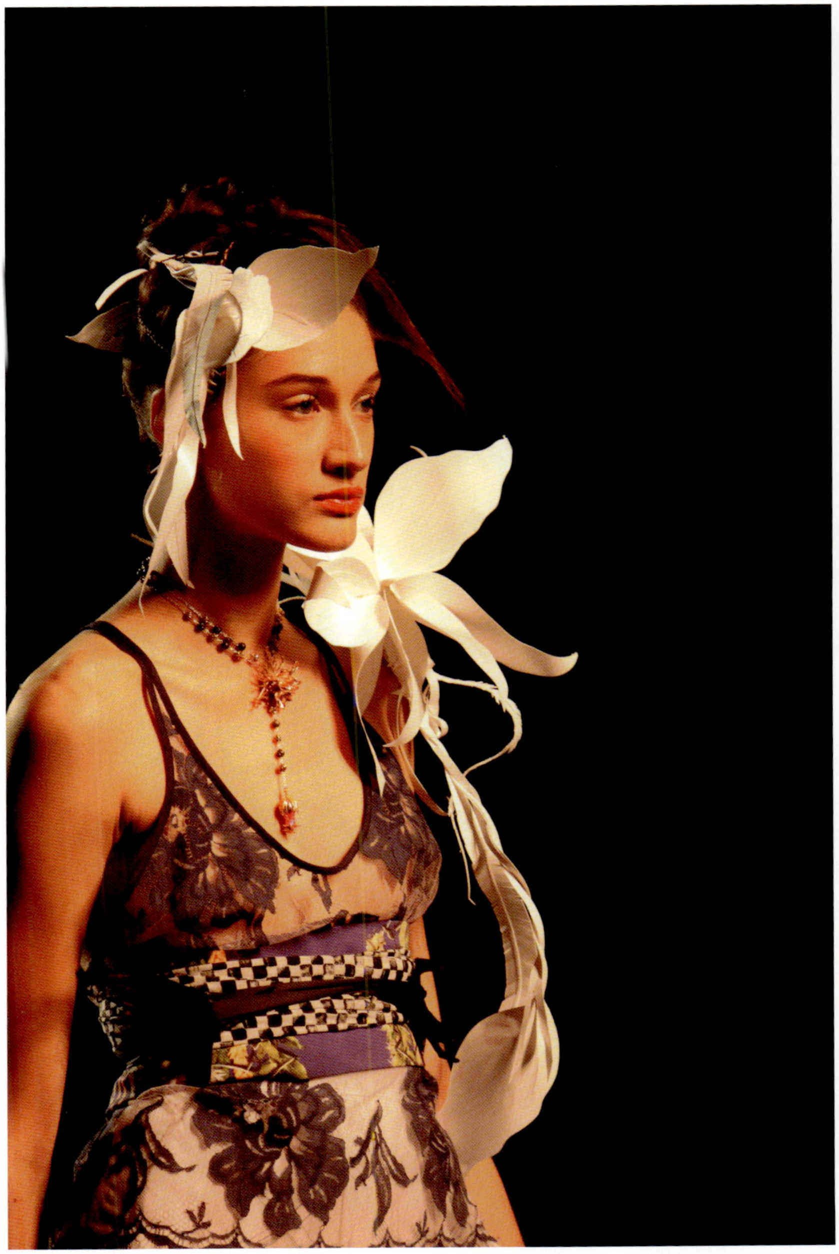

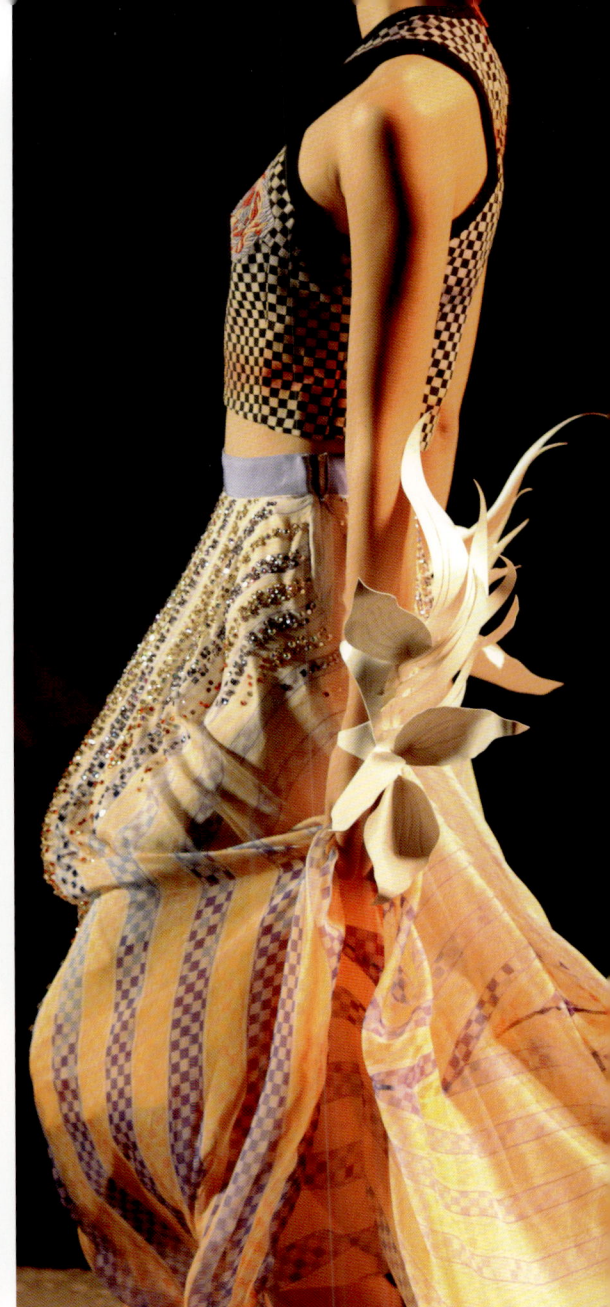
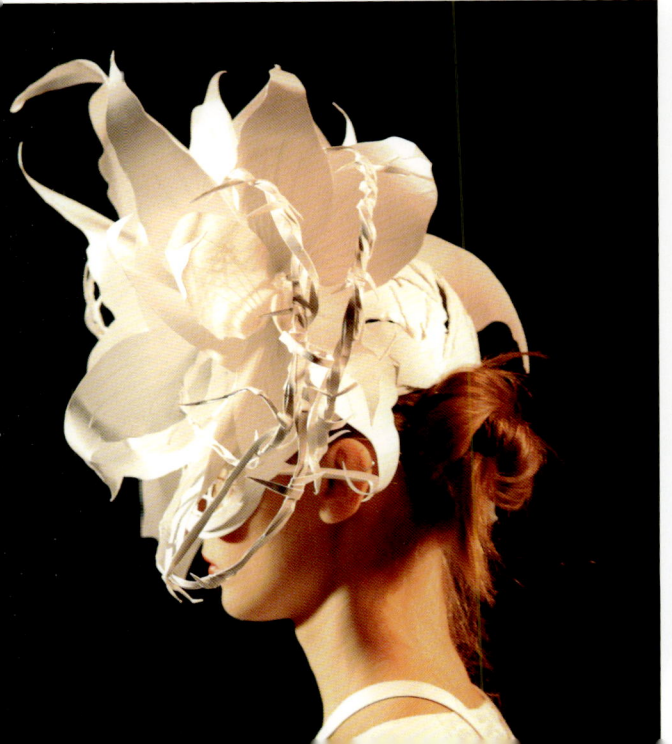
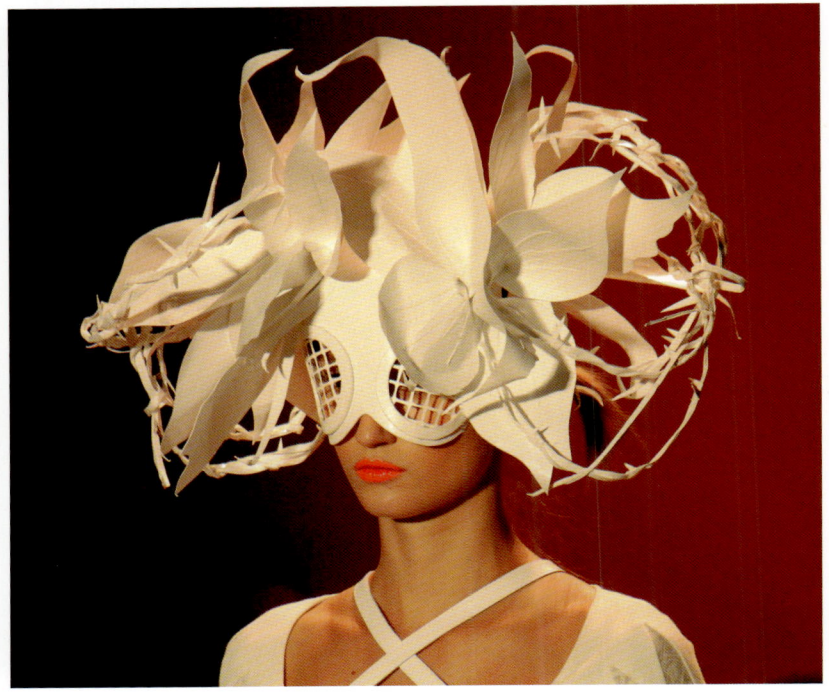

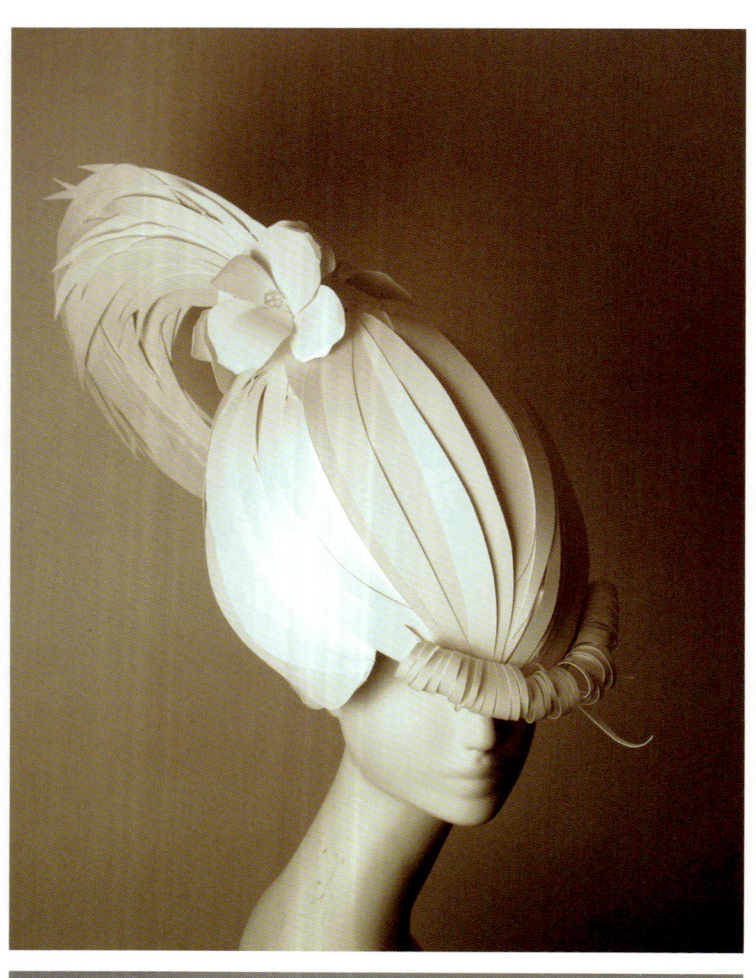

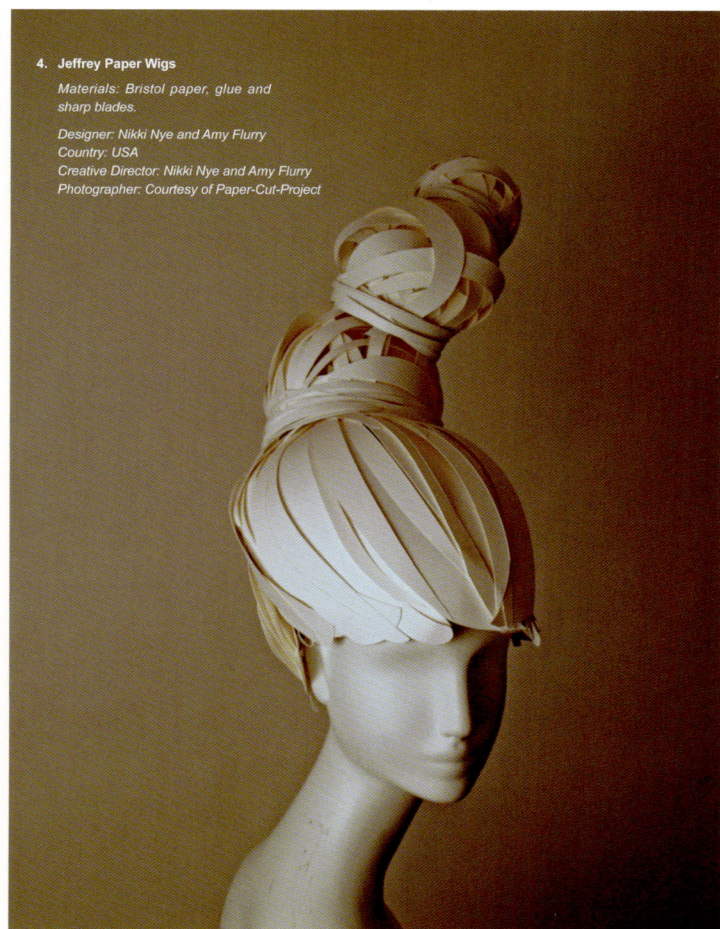

4. Jeffrey Paper Wigs

Materials: Bristol paper, glue and sharp blades.

Designer: Nikki Nye and Amy Flurry
Country: USA
Creative Director: Nikki Nye and Amy Flurry
Photographer: Courtesy of Paper-Cut-Project

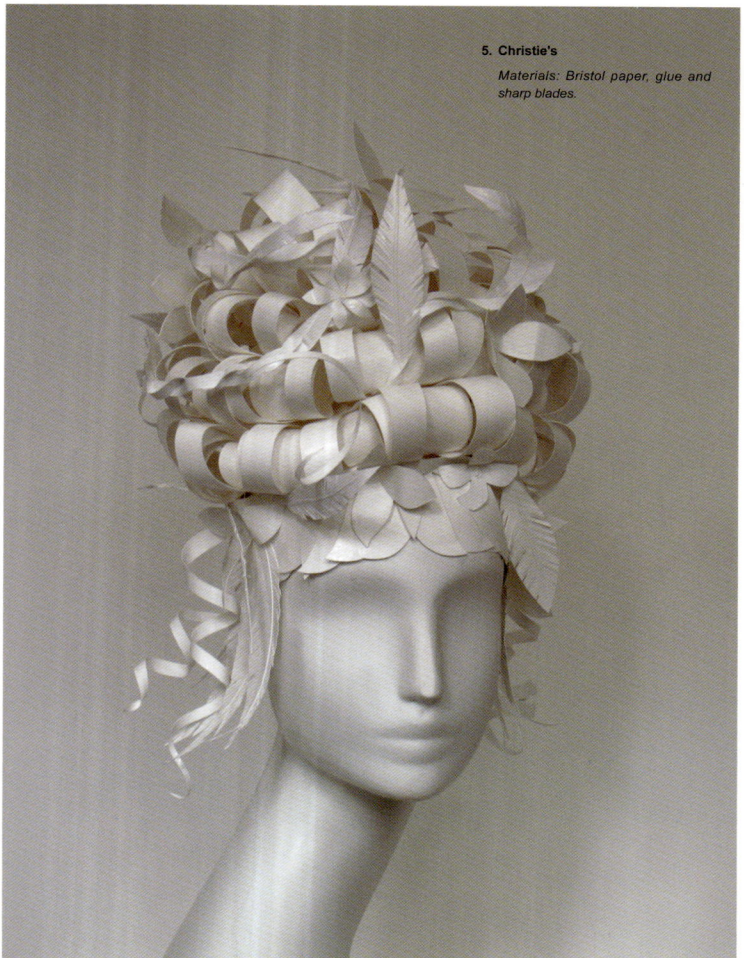

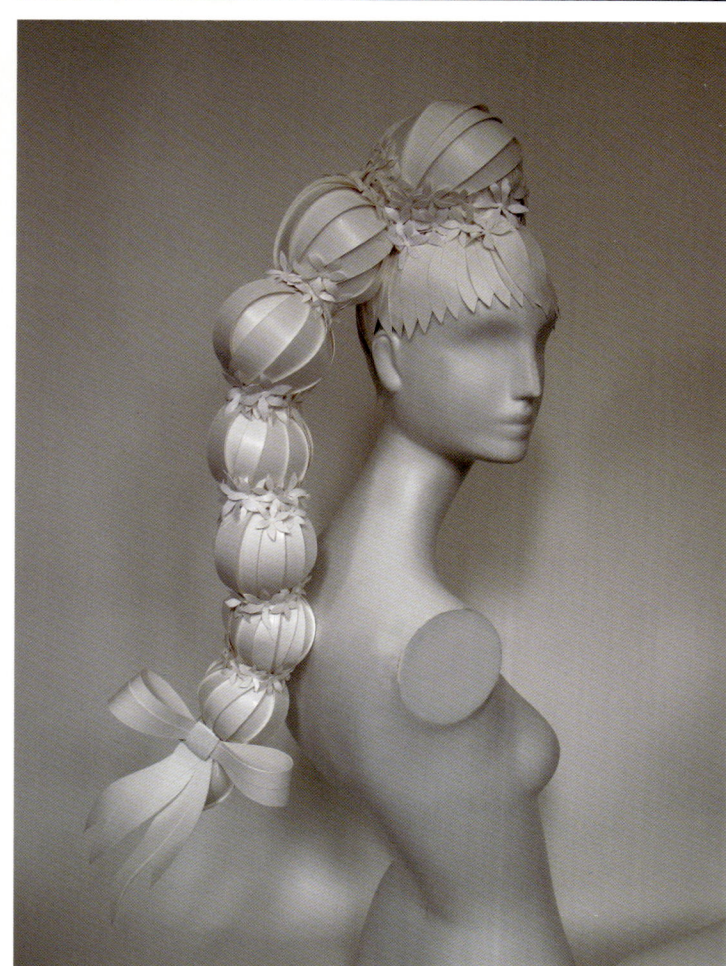

5. Christie's

Materials: Bristol paper, glue and sharp blades.

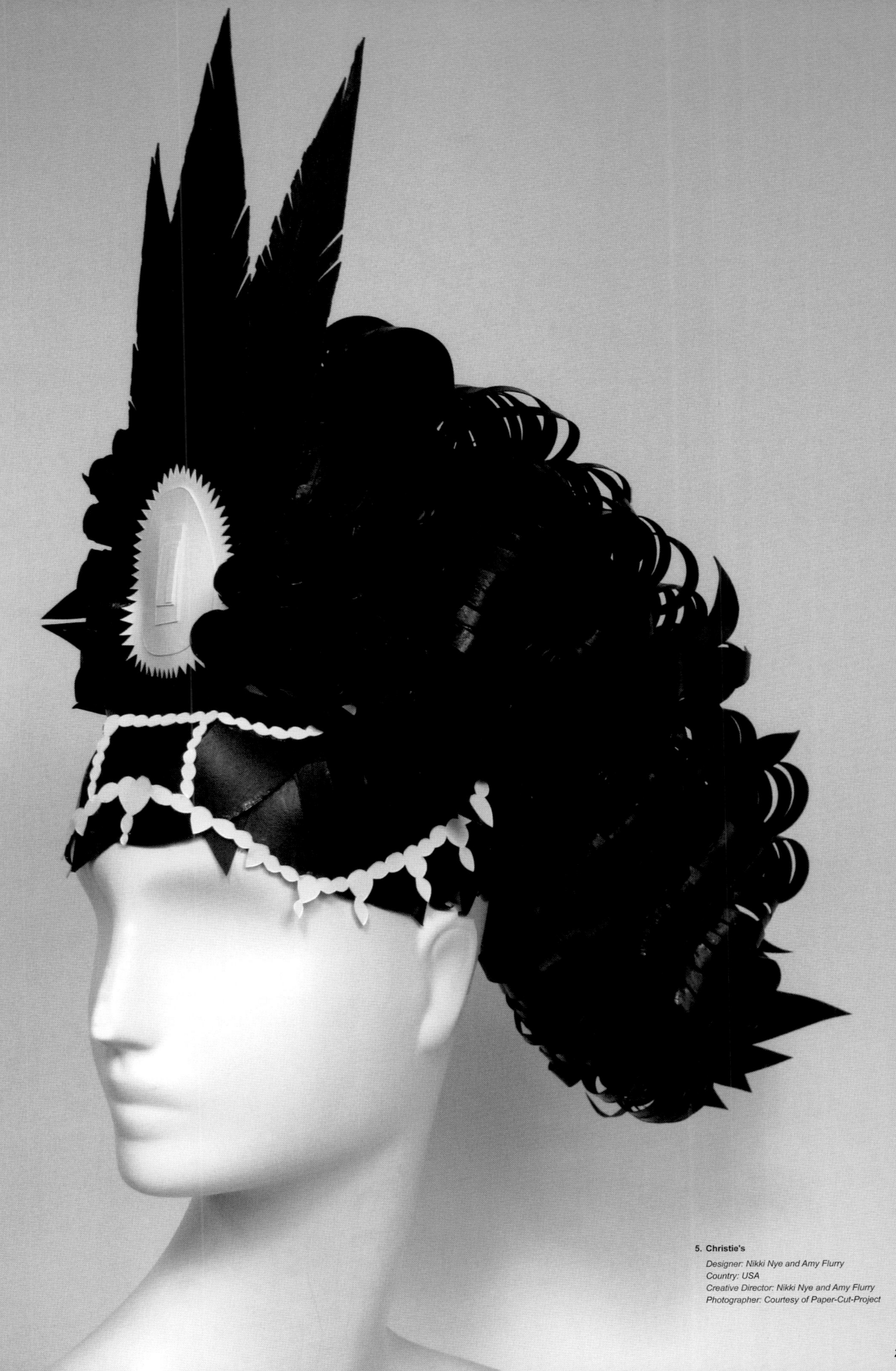

5. Christie's
Designer: Nikki Nye and Amy Flurry
Country: USA
Creative Director: Nikki Nye and Amy Flurry
Photographer: Courtesy of Paper-Cut-Project

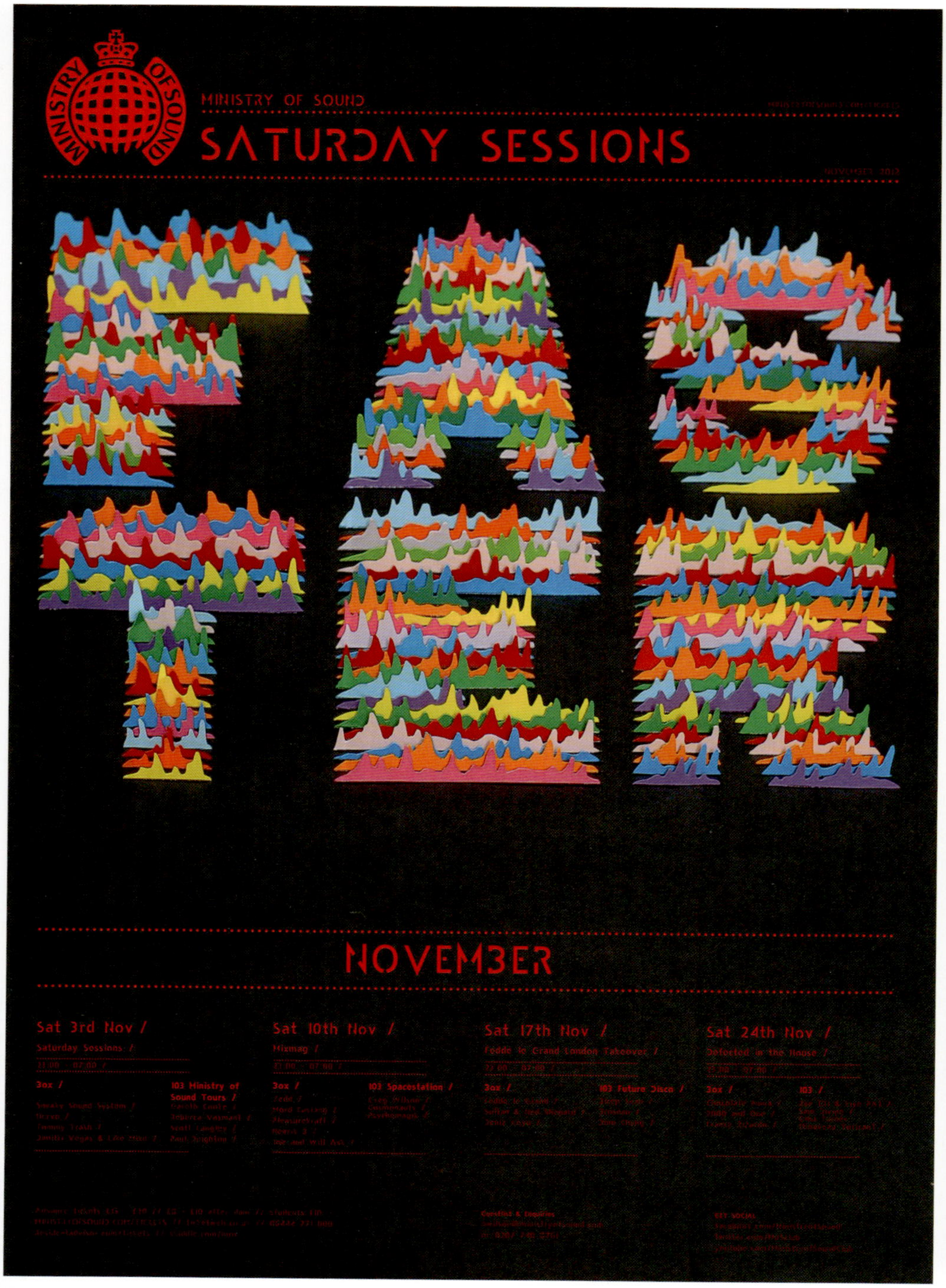

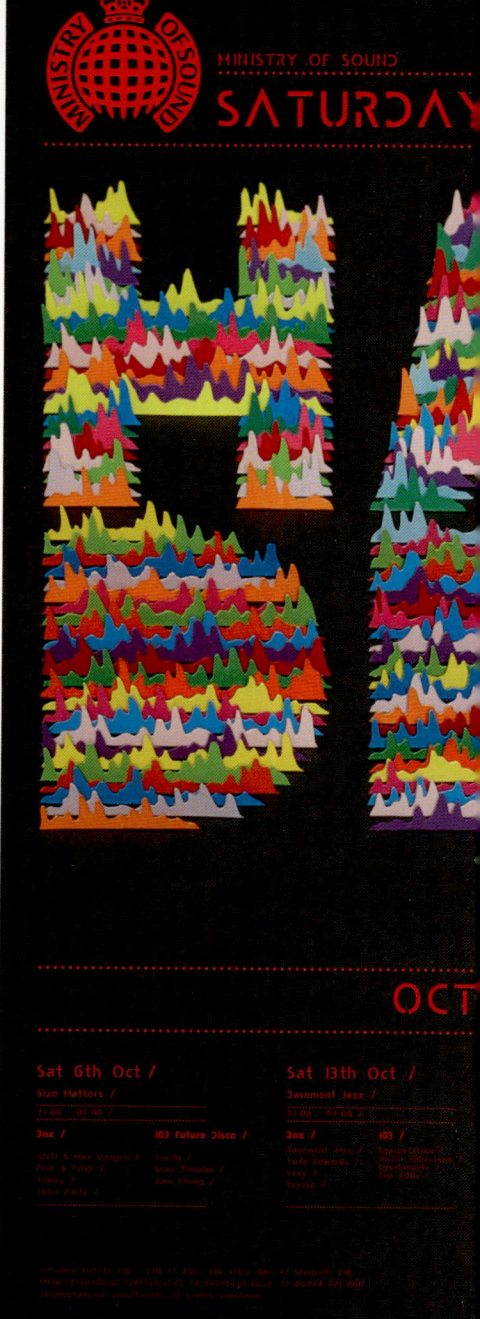
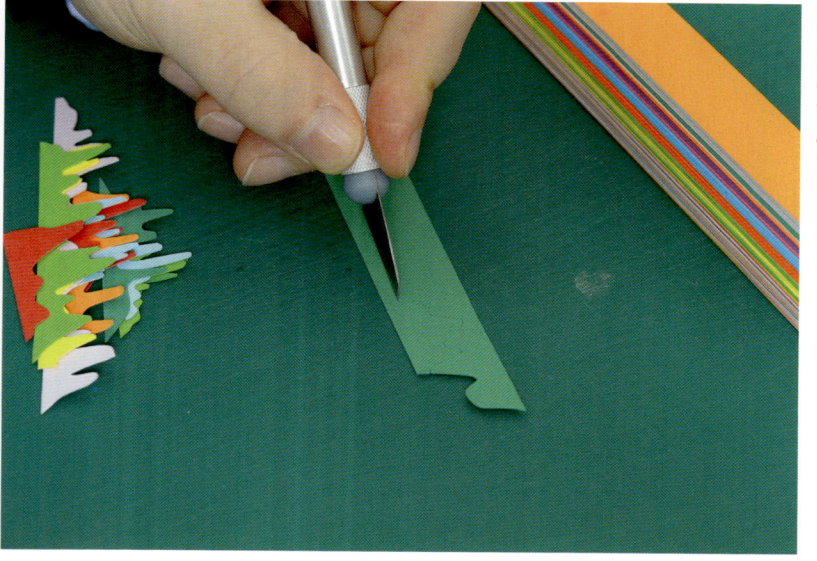

The project captures the atmosphere of a Saturday Sessions set. The letterforms are constructed of an accumulation of sound waves derived from the sound and energy of a set as a whole i.e. the DJ, the crowd and even the person your dancing with.

Designer: Andrew Bradford
Country: UK
Client: Ministry of Sound
Photographer: Andrew Bradford

Ministry of Sound - Saturday Sessions

---Andrew Bradford

This project was created in response to the brief set by Studio Output on behalf of the Ministry of Sound, Saturday Sessions, for the A & A D competition.

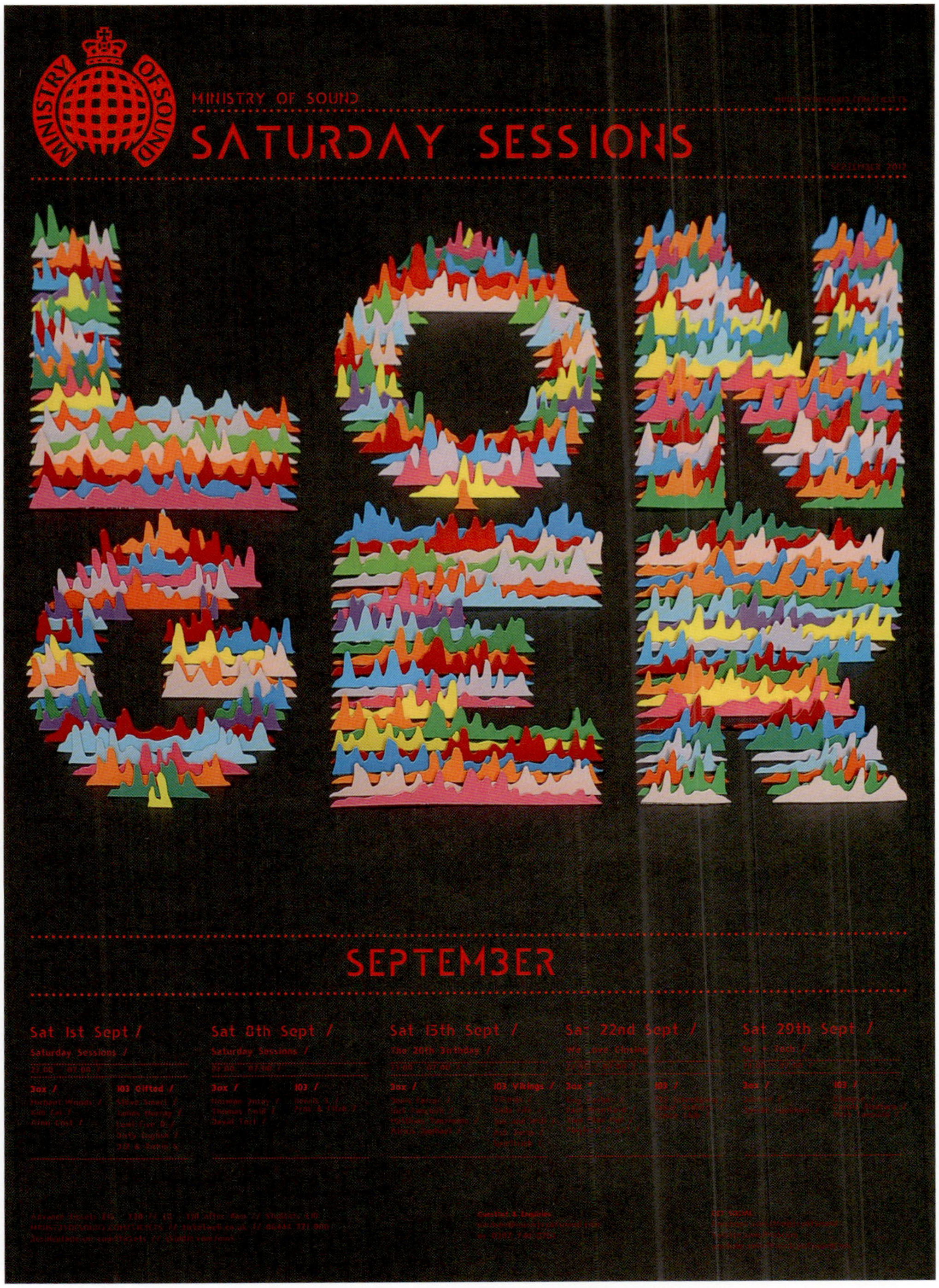

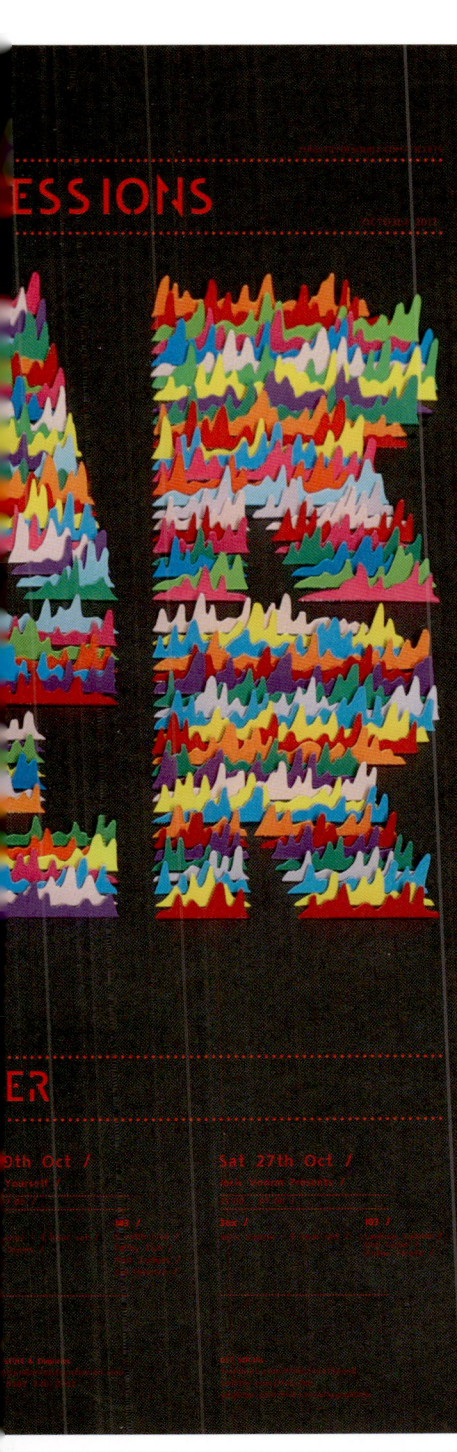
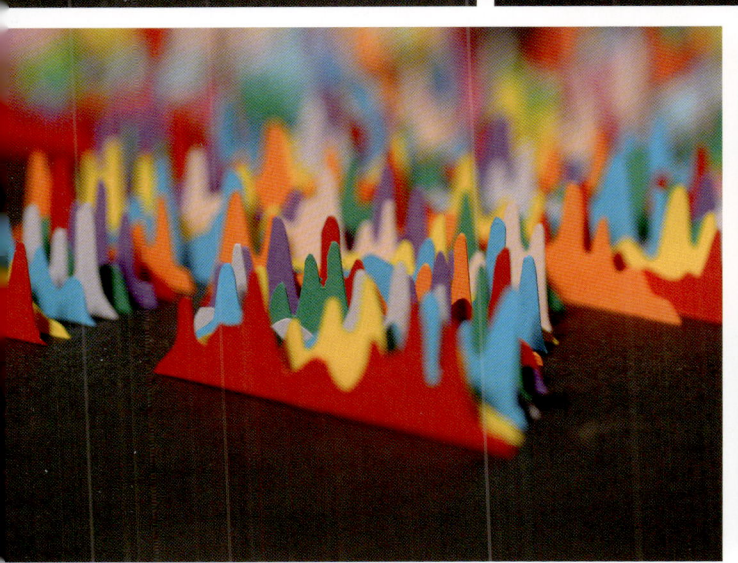
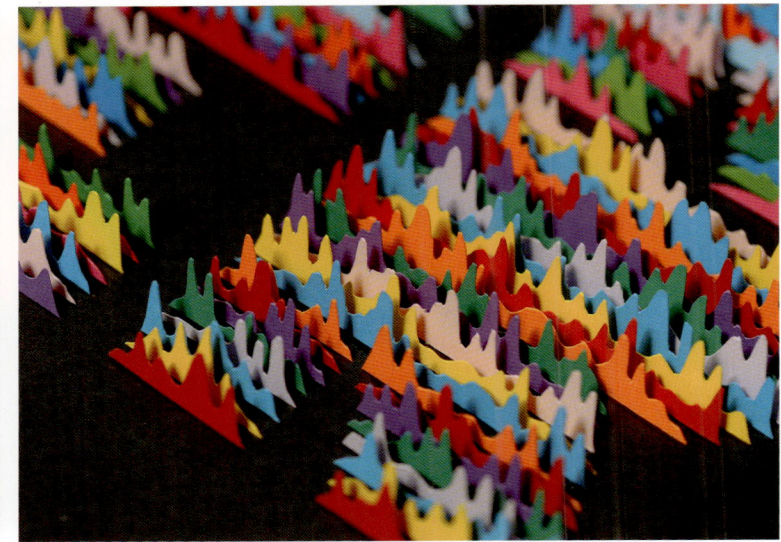

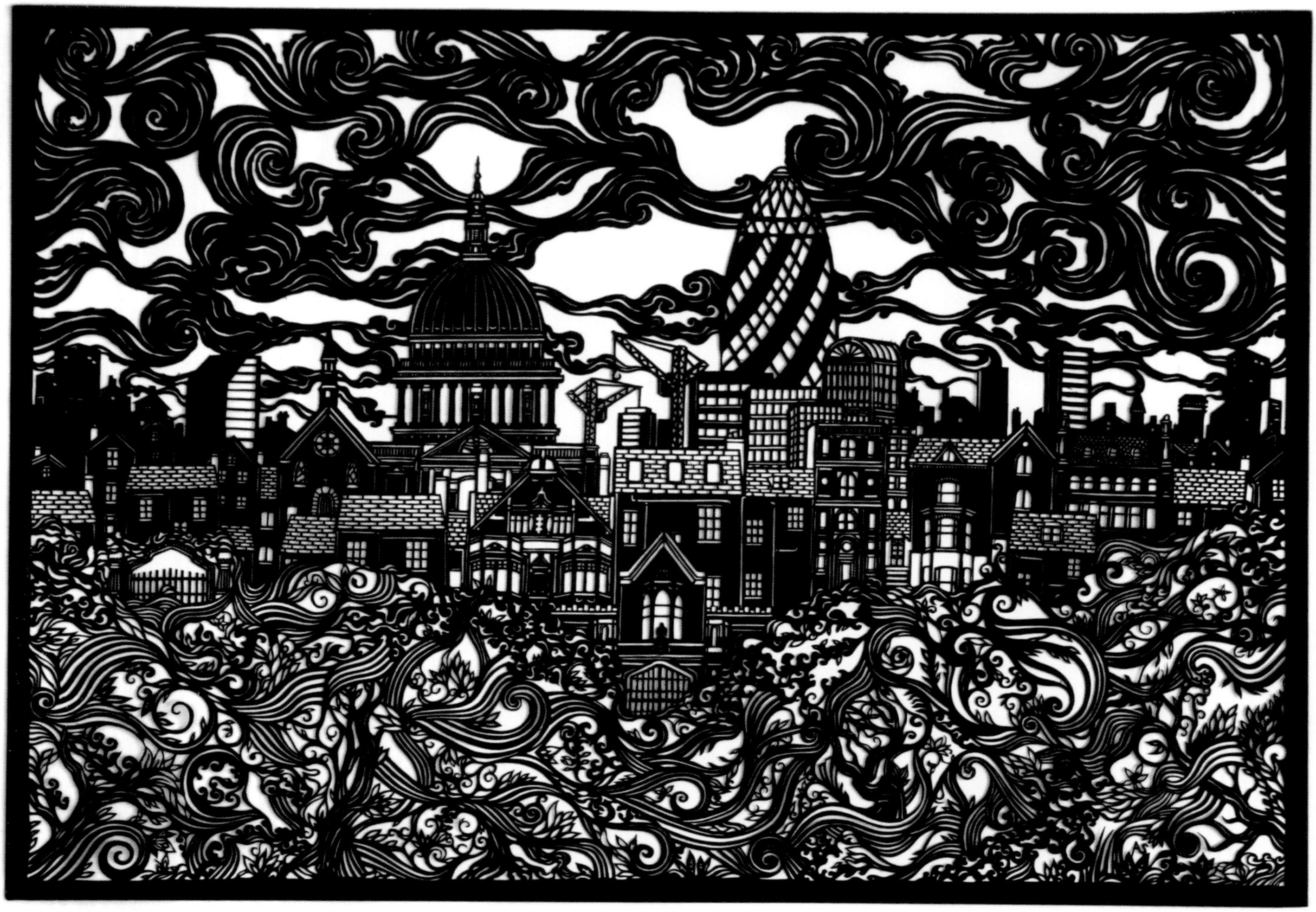

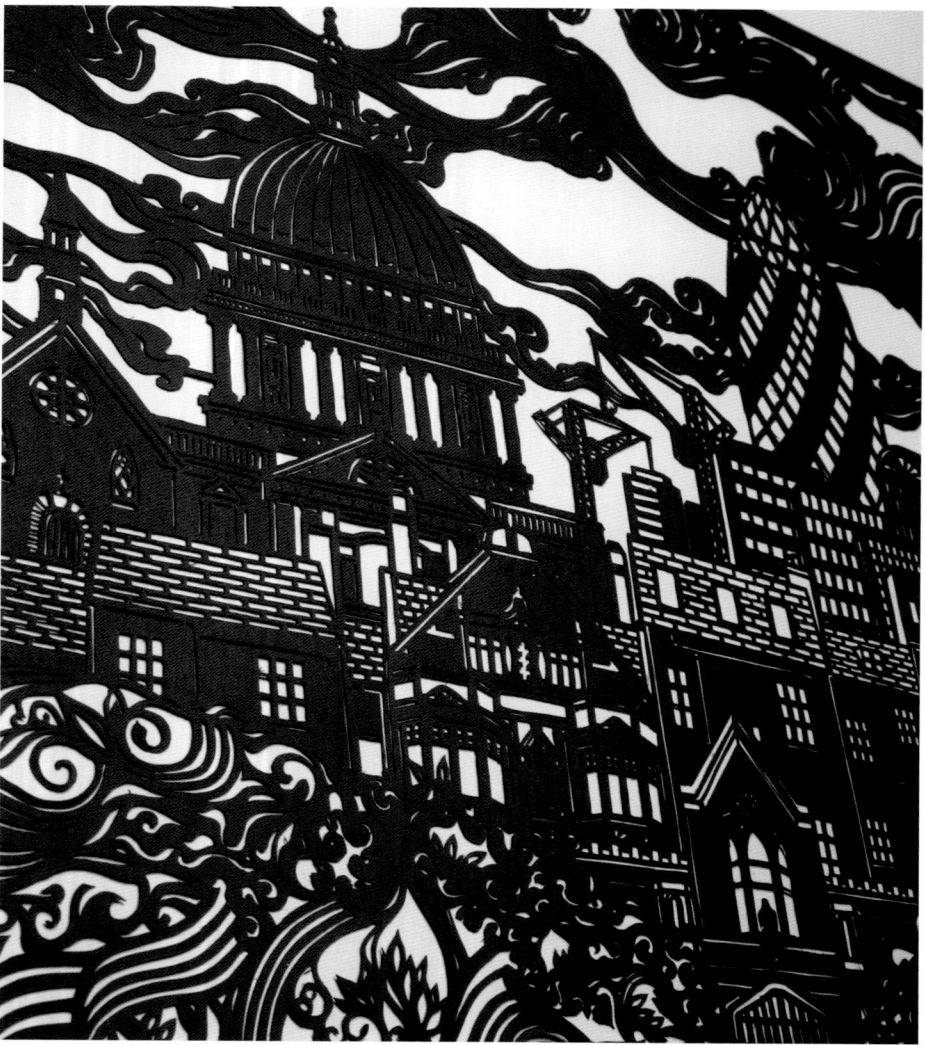

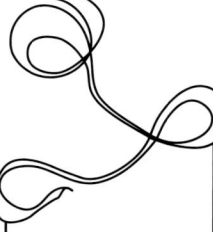

1. 'London Cityscape' Commission

2. Dust Clouds In The Eagle Nebula

3. 'African Weaver Bird' Commission

4. Bird on Branch Commission

5. Hermés Paper Sculptures

6. 'Ice Caverns' Oriel Mostyn Gallery

7. They Loved What They Found

8. Queen Victoria's Mourning Dress Installation

9. Queen Victoria's Wedding Dress Installation

---Andy Singleton

1. 'London Cityscape' Commission

A privately commissioned paper cut work of Londons famous skyline. Hand cut paper, 160gsm

Designer: Andy Singleton
Country: UK
Photographer: Nicholas Singleton

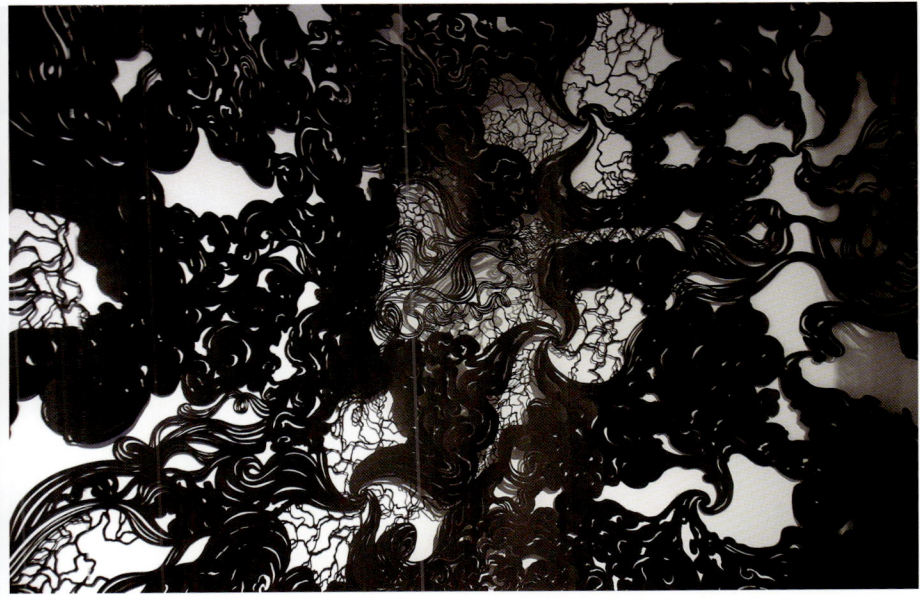
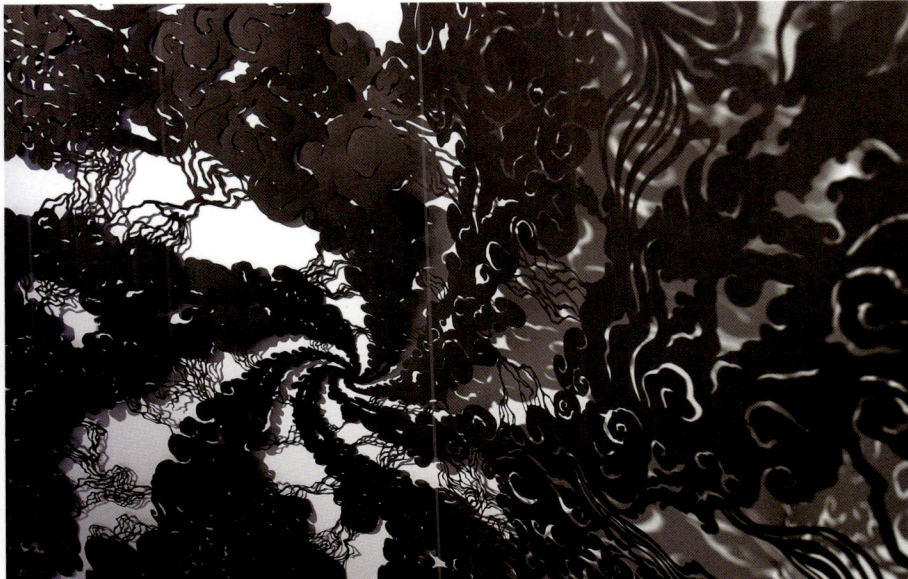
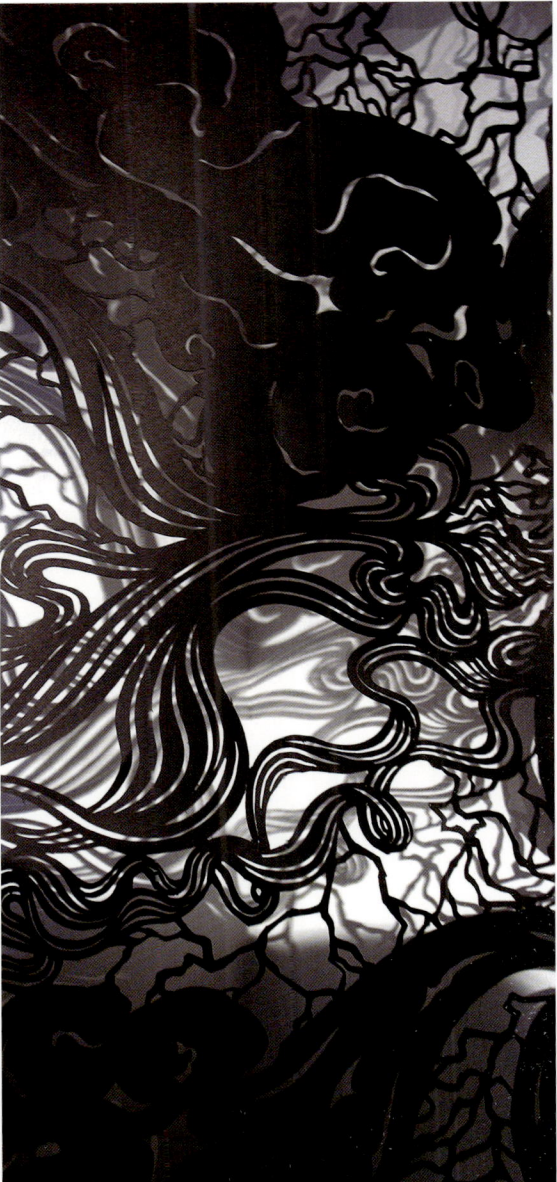

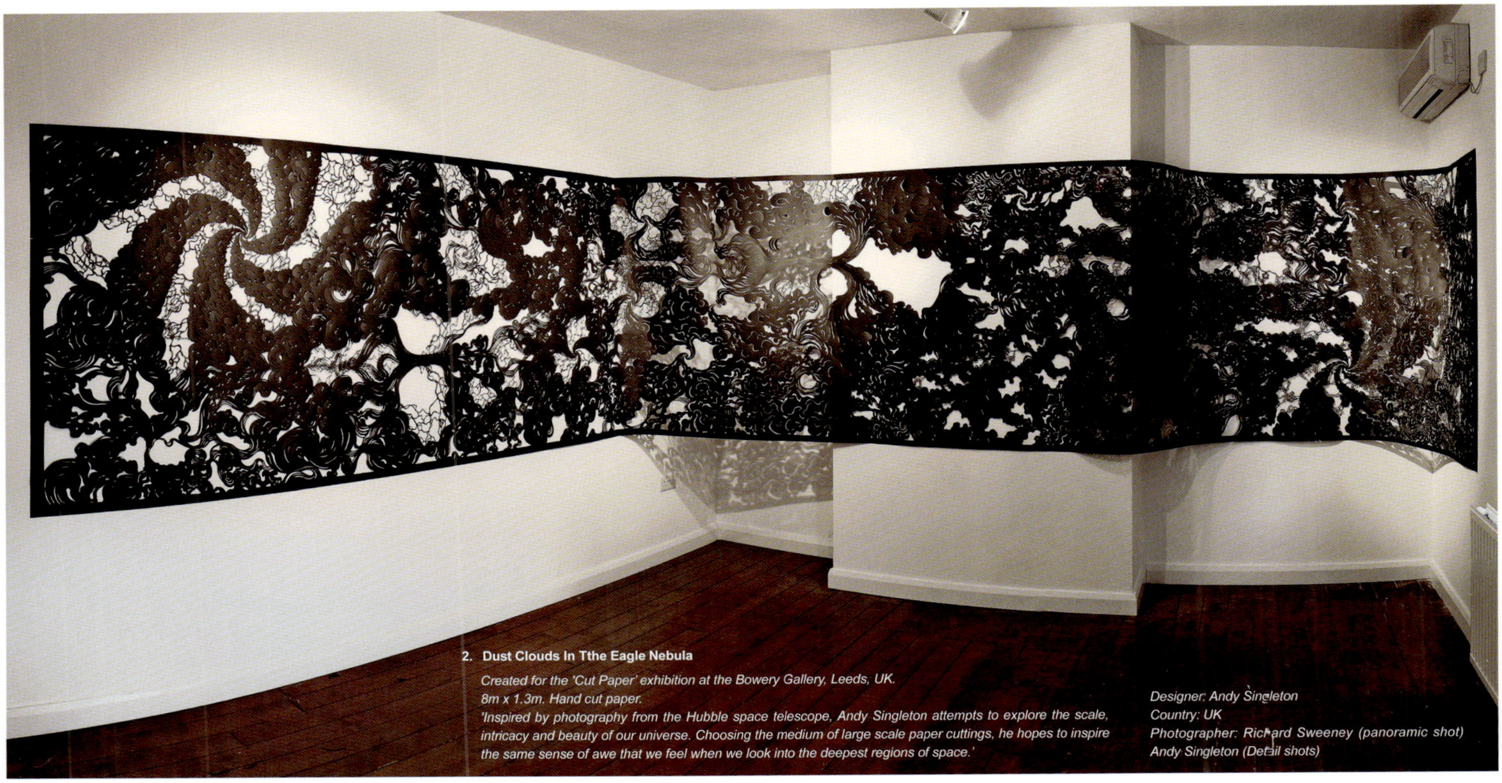

2. Dust Clouds In The Eagle Nebula

Created for the 'Cut Paper' exhibition at the Bowery Gallery, Leeds, UK.
8m x 1.3m. Hand cut paper.

'Inspired by photography from the Hubble space telescope, Andy Singleton attempts to explore the scale, intricacy and beauty of our universe. Choosing the medium of large scale paper cuttings, he hopes to inspire the same sense of awe that we feel when we look into the deepest regions of space.'

Designer: Andy Singleton
Country: UK
Photographer: Richard Sweeney (panoramic shot)
Andy Singleton (Detail shots)

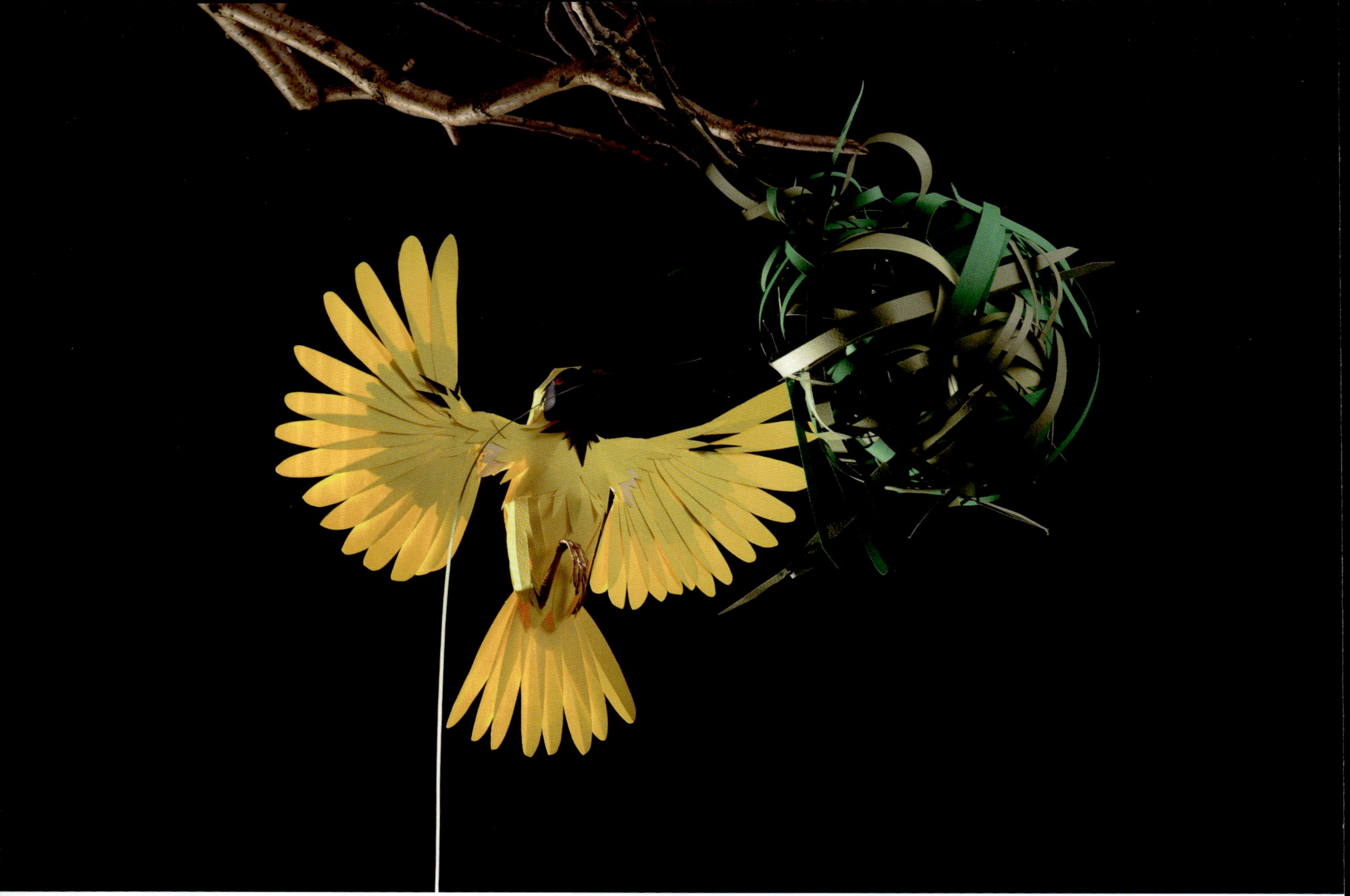

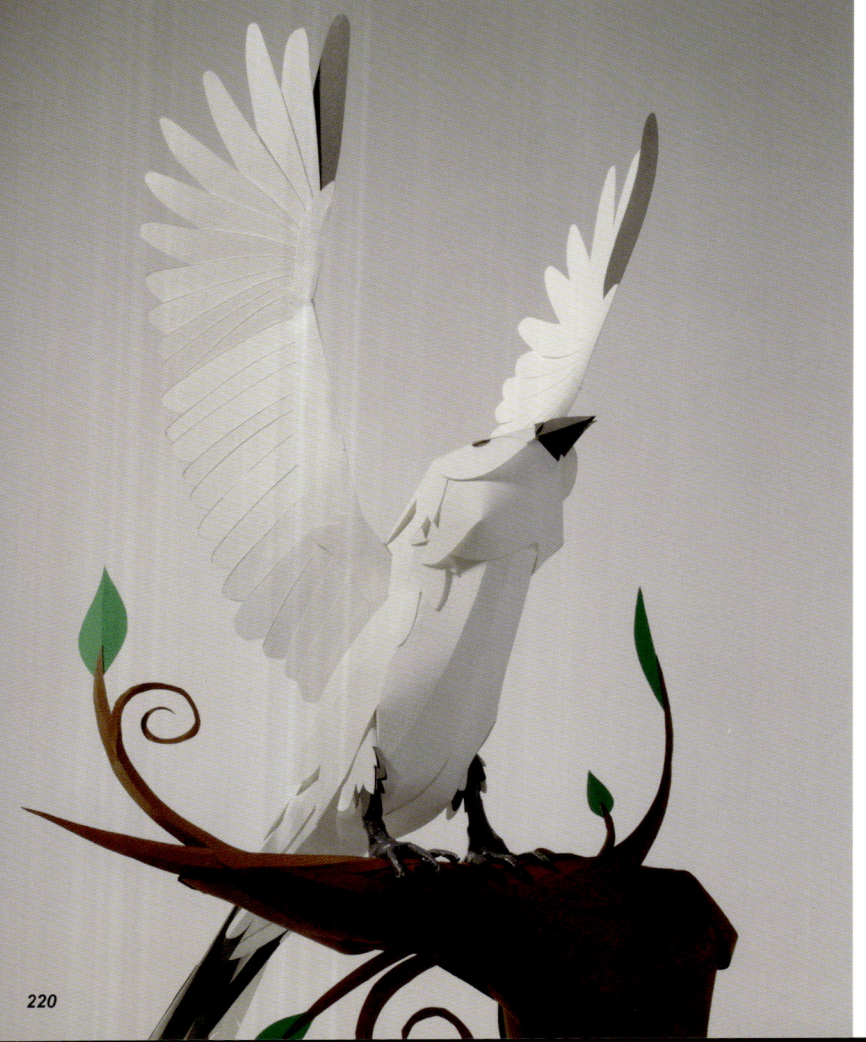

3. **'African Weaver Bird' Commission**

   The piece was Commission by DDB Australia with a brief to create a 3D paper model of an African Weaver bird from an exisiting photograph. The piece was hand cut, scored and folded from 160gsm paper

   Designer: Andy Singleton
   Country: UK
   Design Agency: DDB Australia
   Creative Director: Michael Ashton
   Photographer: Andy Singleton

4. **Bird on Branch Commission**

   The piece was Commission by by designers Seifried and Mack to create this paper bird on branch piece inspired by taxidermy birds. The piece was used as part of the decor of a new library the designers had created the interior for.

   Designer: Andy Singleton
   Country: UK
   Design Agency: Seifried and Mack (Germany)
   Creative Director: Felix Severin Mack
   Photographer: Andy Singleton

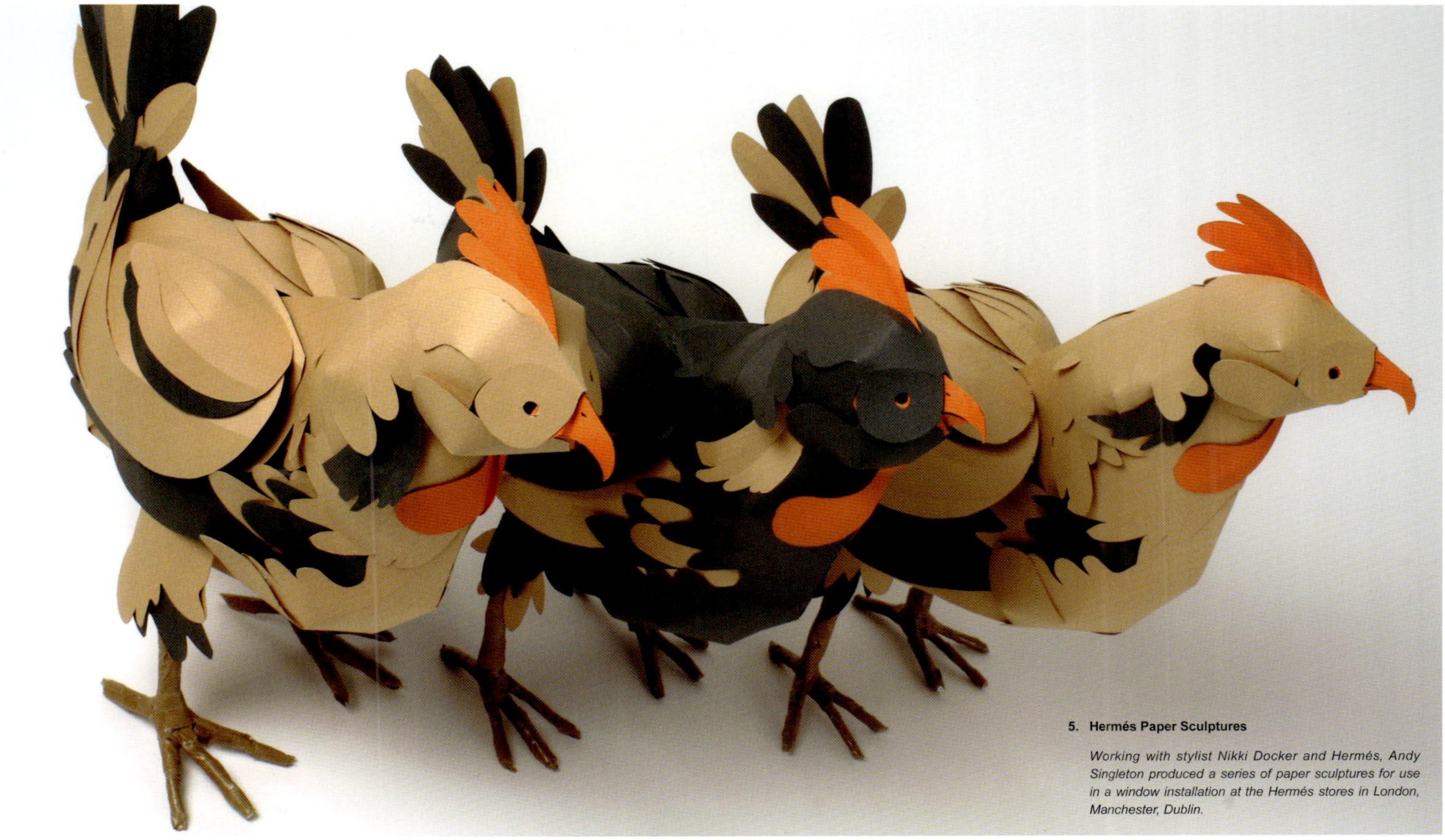

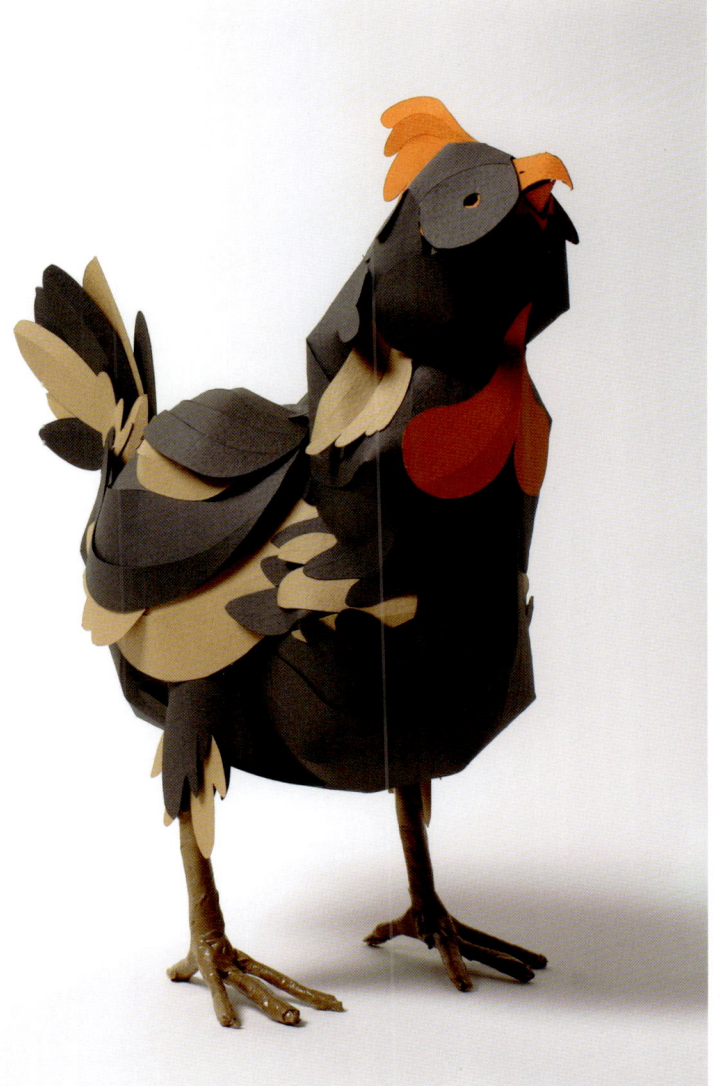

5. Hermés Paper Sculptures

Working with stylist Nikki Docker and Hermés, Andy Singleton produced a series of paper sculptures for use in a window installation at the Hermés stores in London, Manchester, Dublin.

Designer: Andy Singleton
Country: UK
Creative Director: Nikki Docker
Client: Hermés
Photographer: Andy Singleton

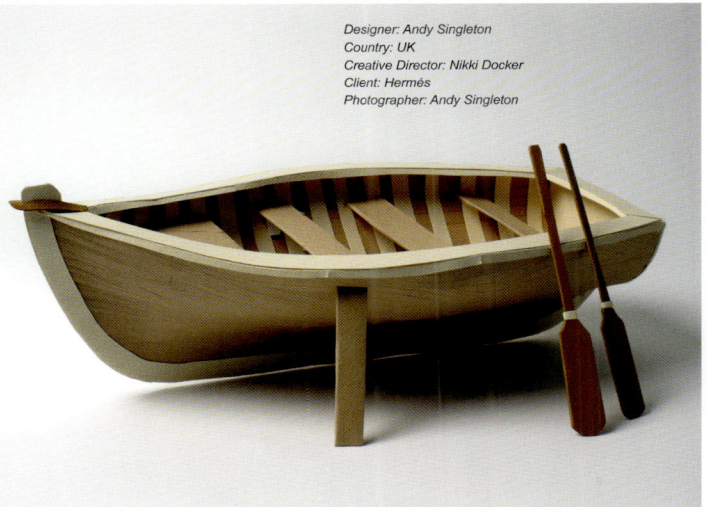

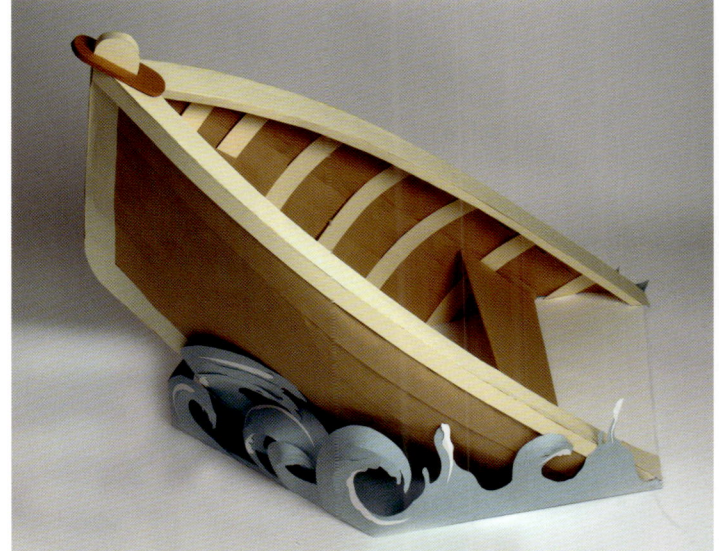

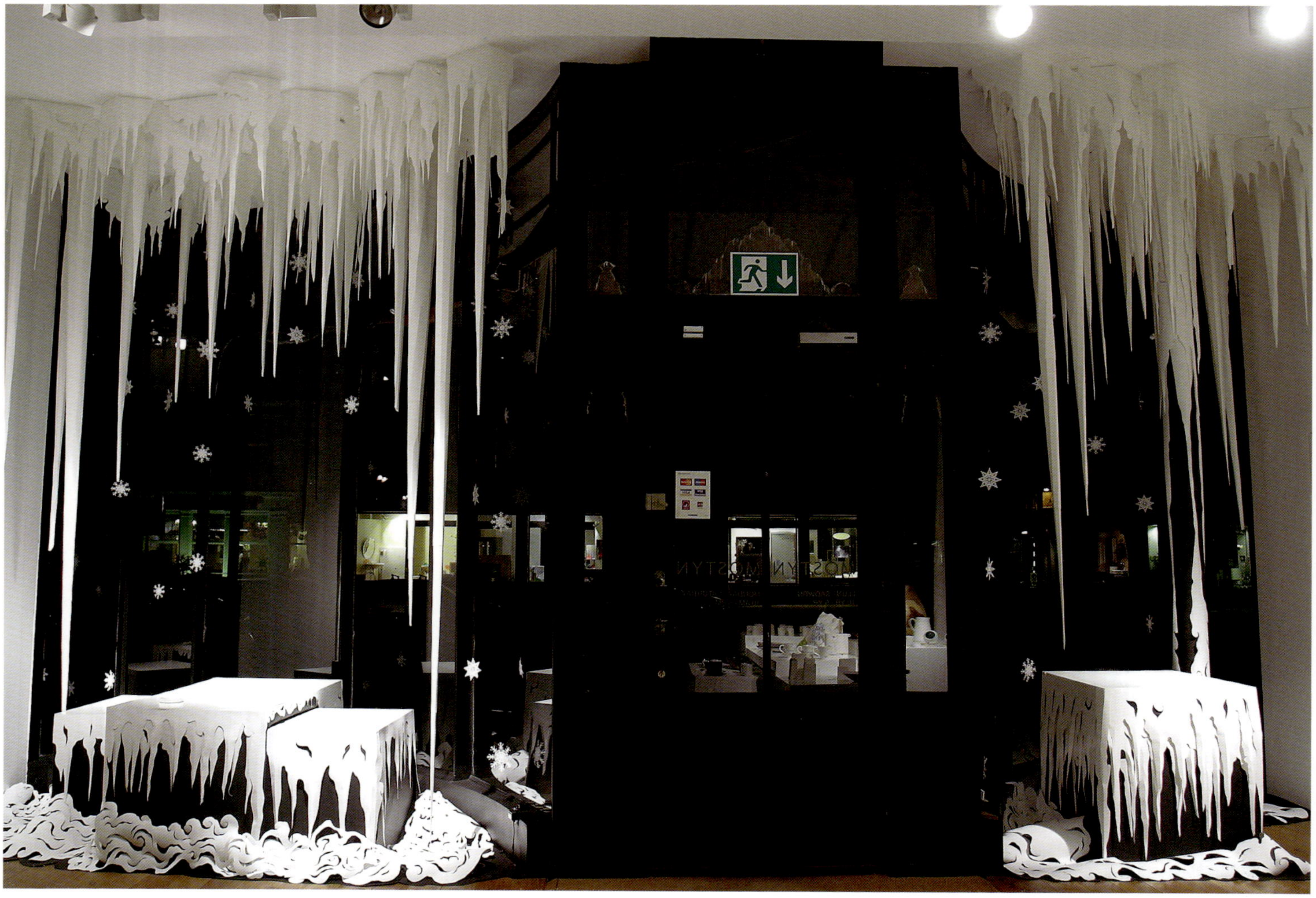

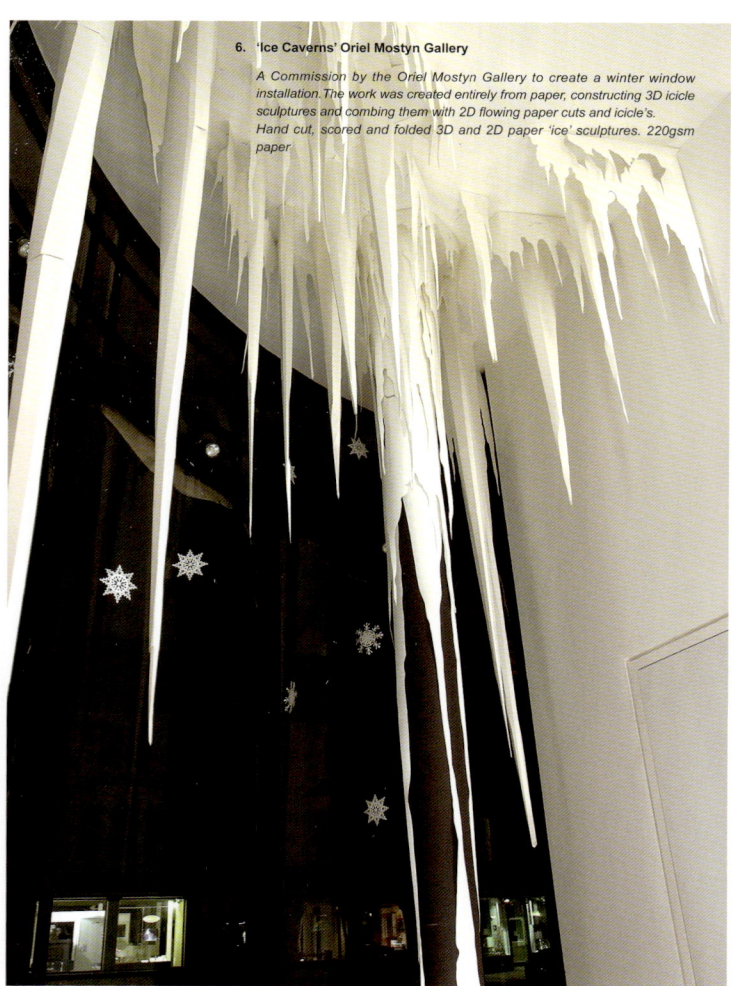

6. 'Ice Caverns' Oriel Mostyn Gallery

A Commission by the Oriel Mostyn Gallery to create a winter window installation. The work was created entirely from paper, constructing 3D icicle sculptures and combing them with 2D flowing paper cuts and icicle's. Hand cut, scored and folded 3D and 2D paper 'ice' sculptures. 220gsm paper

Designer: Andy Singleton
Country: UK (Wales)
Client: Oriel Mostyn Gallery
Photographer: Nicholas Singleton

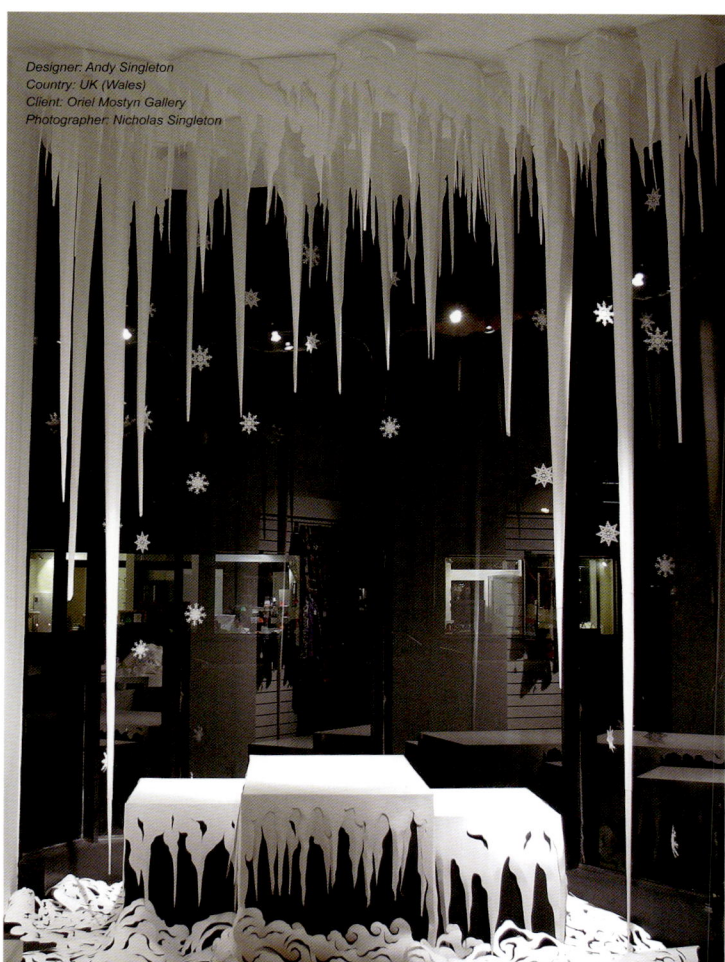

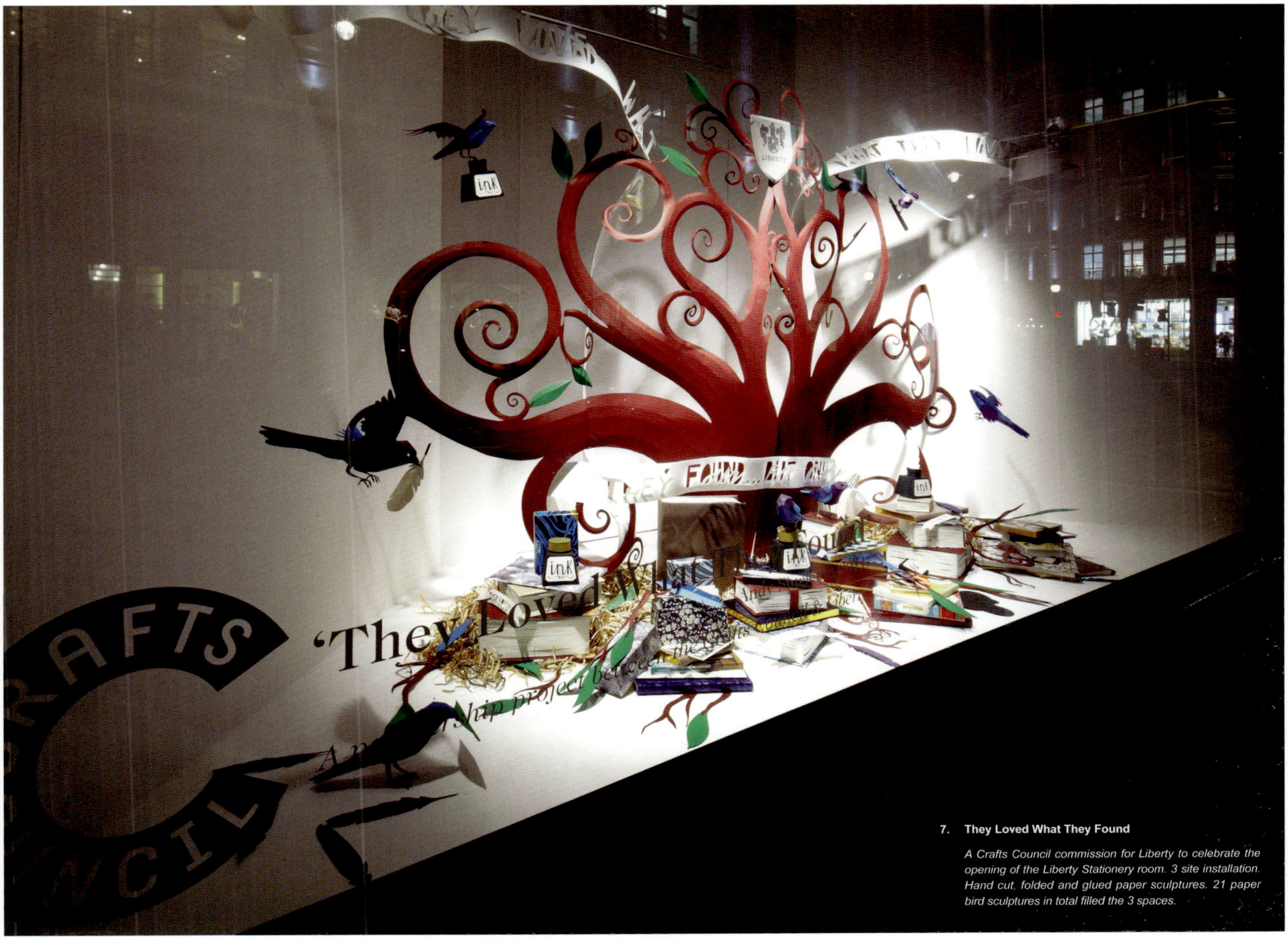

7. **They Loved What They Found**

A Crafts Council commission for Liberty to celebrate the opening of the Liberty Stationery room. 3 site installation. Hand cut, folded and glued paper sculptures. 21 paper bird sculptures in total filled the 3 spaces.

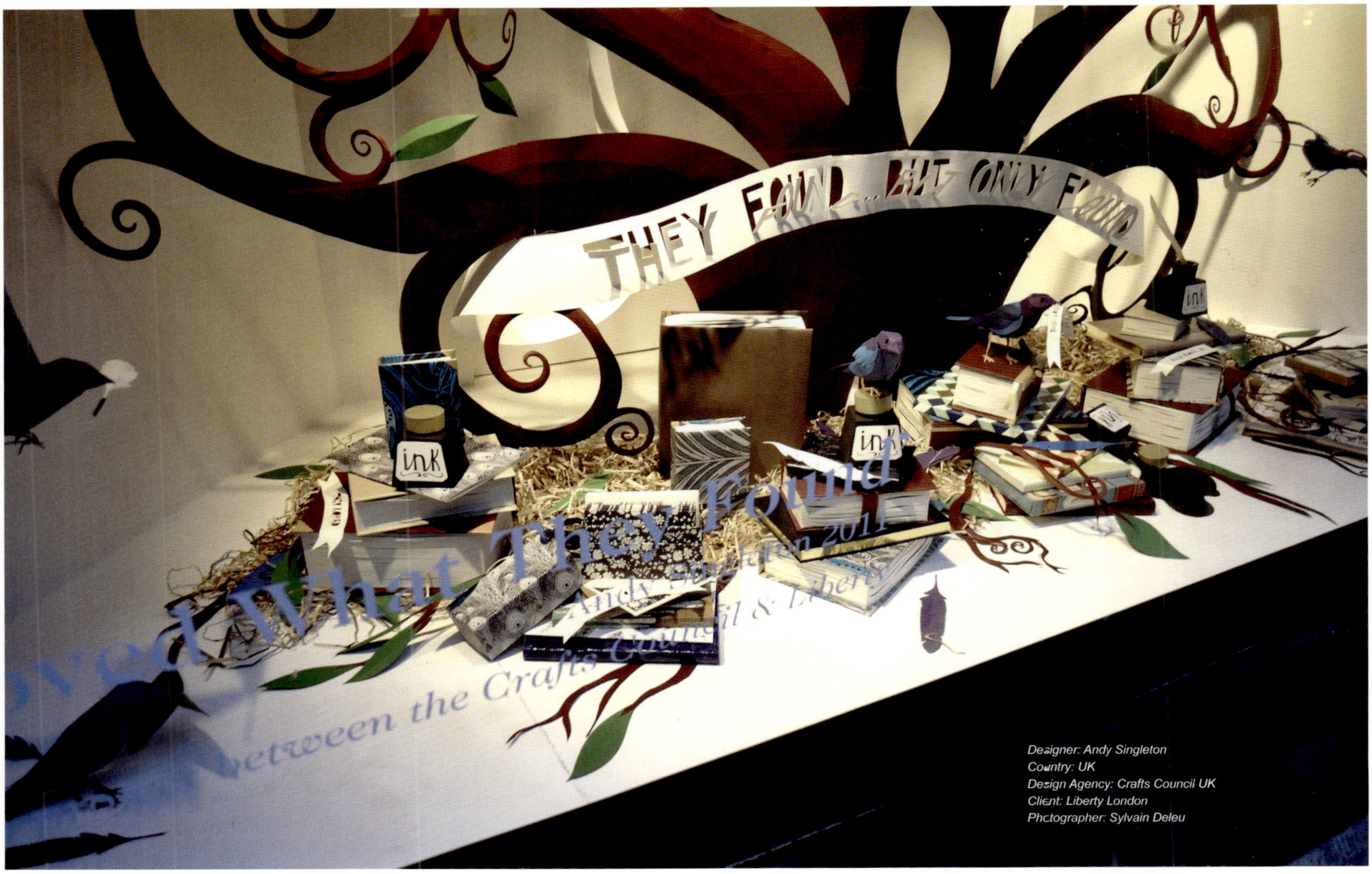

Designer: Andy Singleton
Country: UK
Design Agency: Crafts Council UK
Client: Liberty London
Photographer: Sylvain Deleu

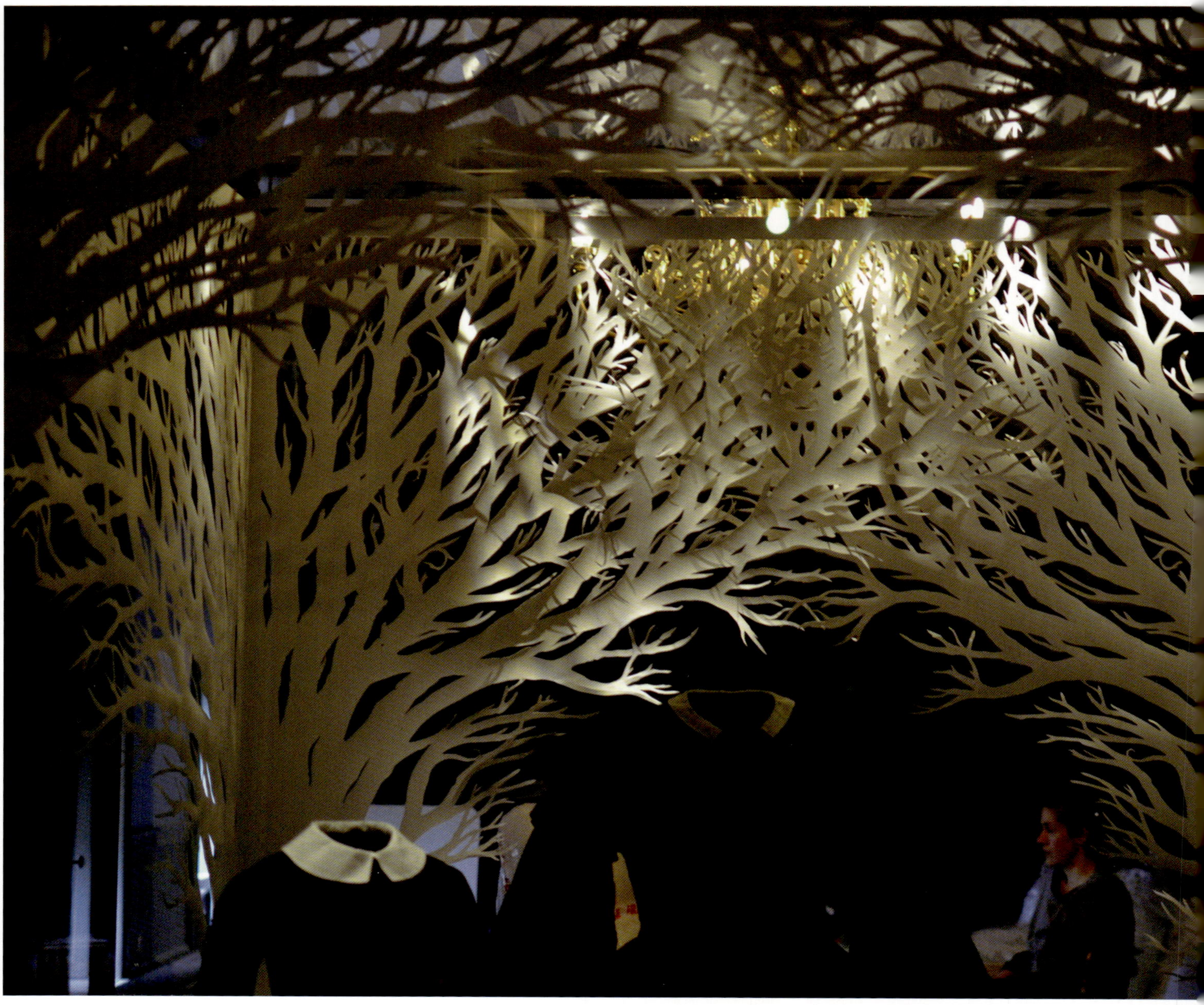

8. Queen Victoria's Mourning Dress Installation

Andy Singleton was commissioned by Kensington Palace to create a paper installation to be housed inside a cabinet with Queen Victoria's original Mouring dress, along with clothing worn by princess Beatrice and prince Leopold at Albert's, Victorias husbands, Funeral. The work is part of the 'Victoria Revealed' Exhibition. The work is made up of hand cut 2D paper trees, inspired by Victorian mourning cards. There are also fallen decaying paper leaves scattered inside the case.

Designer: Andy Singleton
Country: UK
Creative Director: Deirdre Murphy
Client: Kensington Palace
Photographer: Andy Singleton

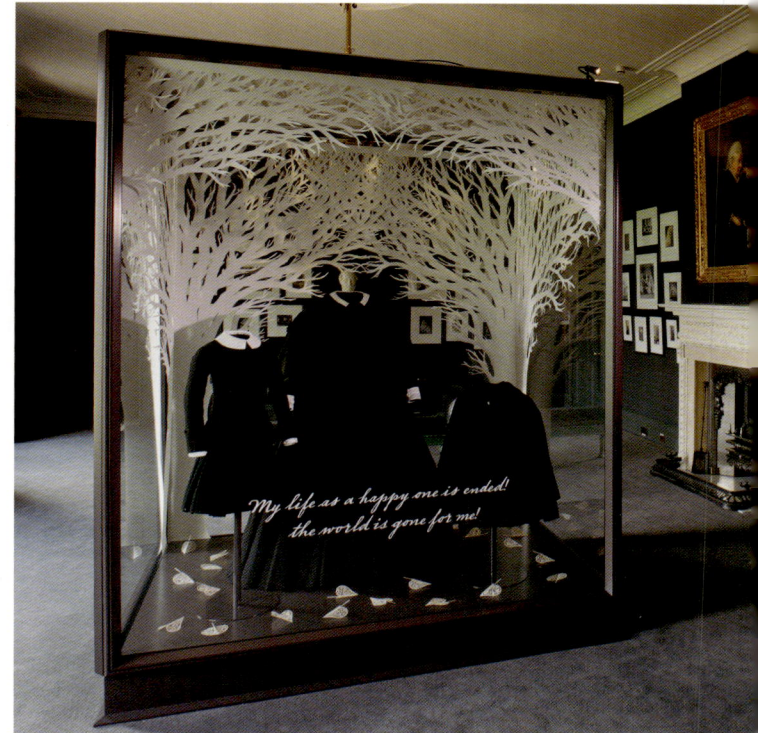

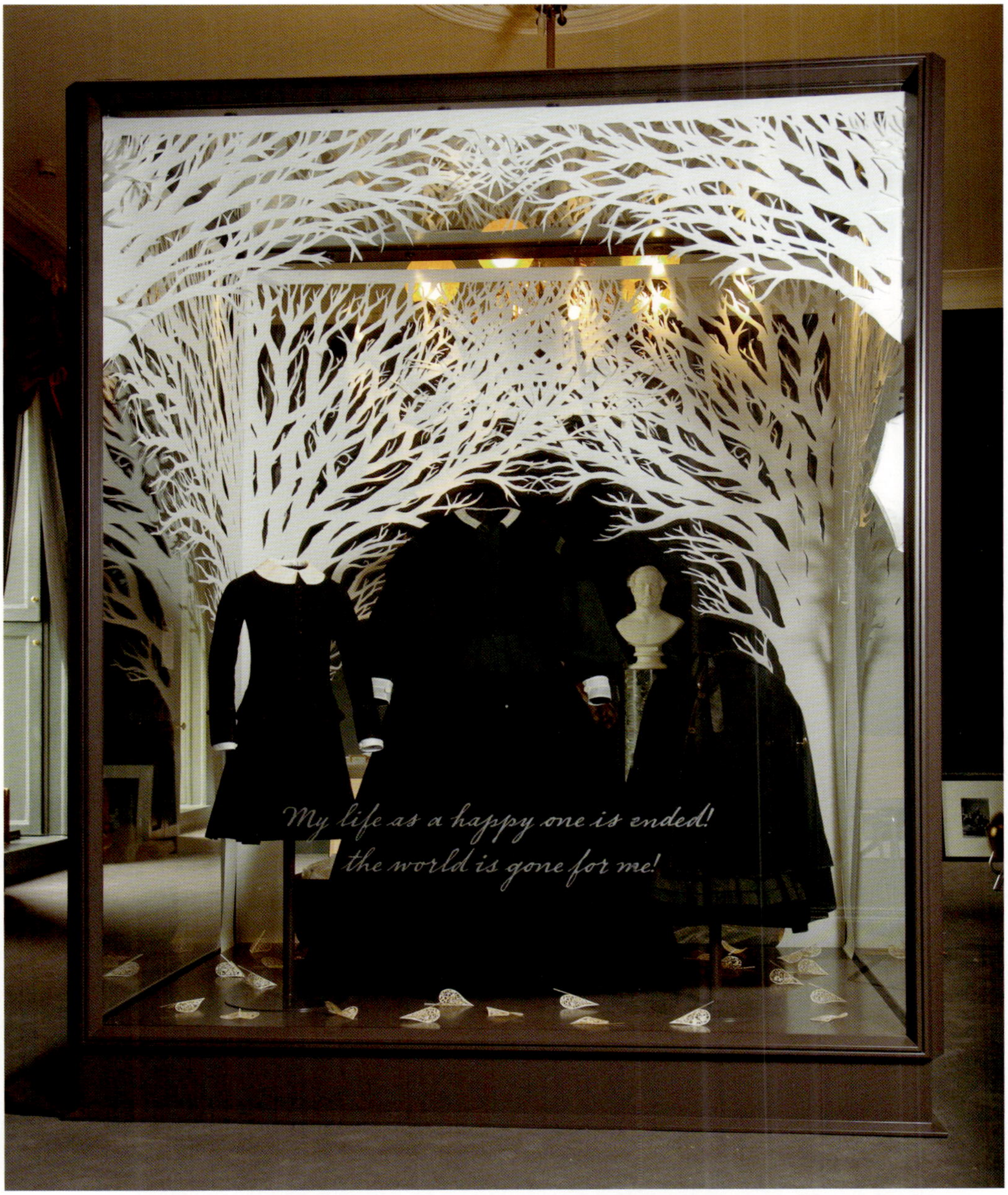

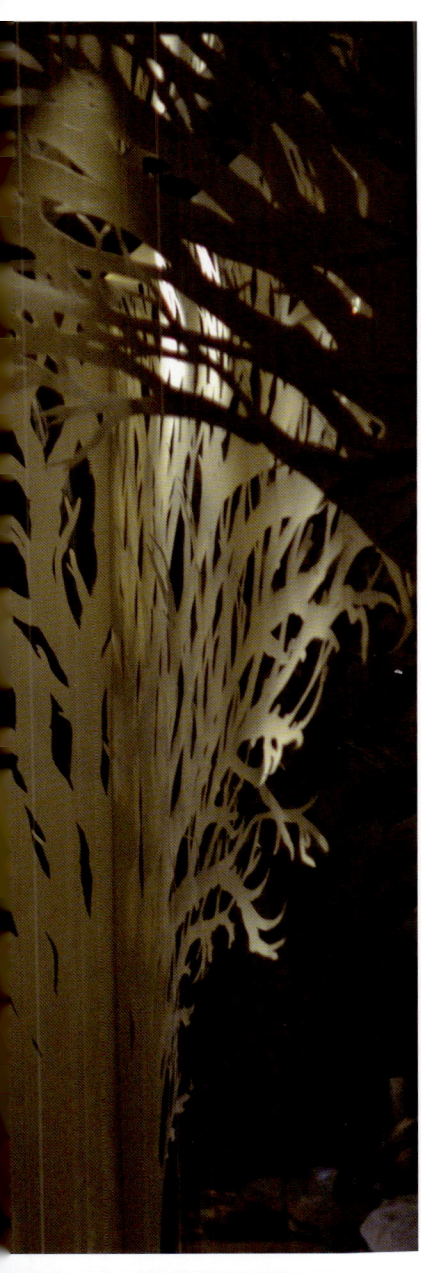
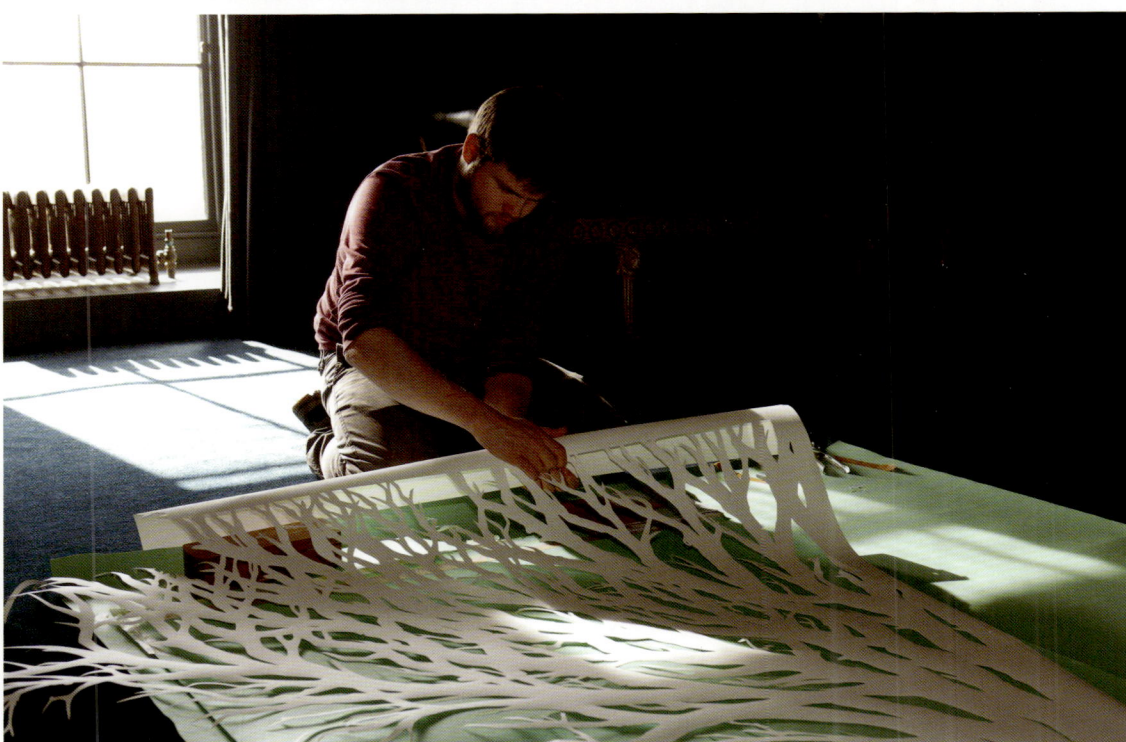
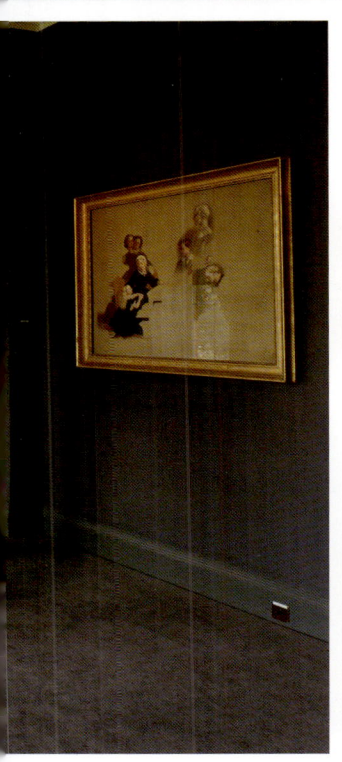

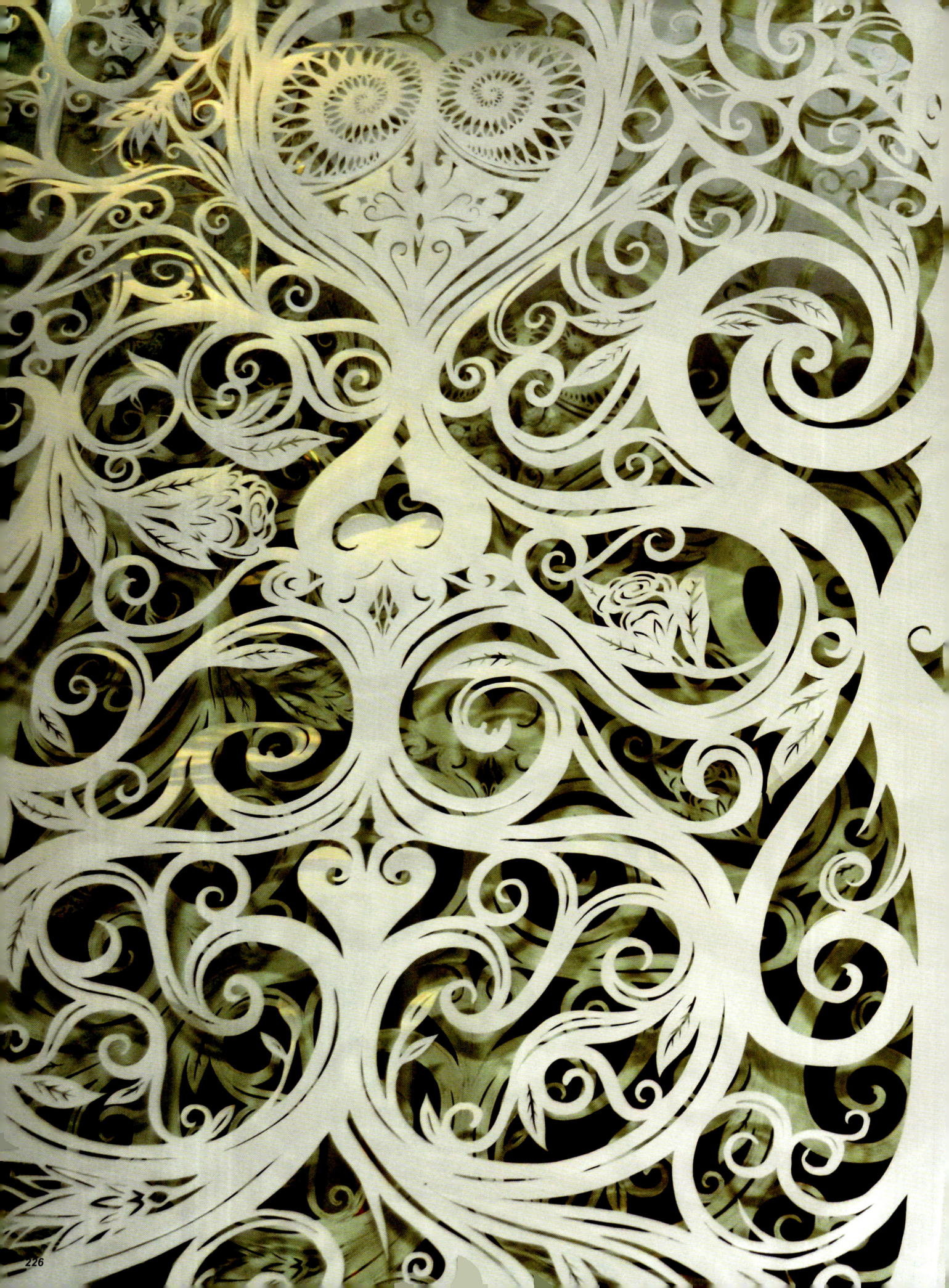

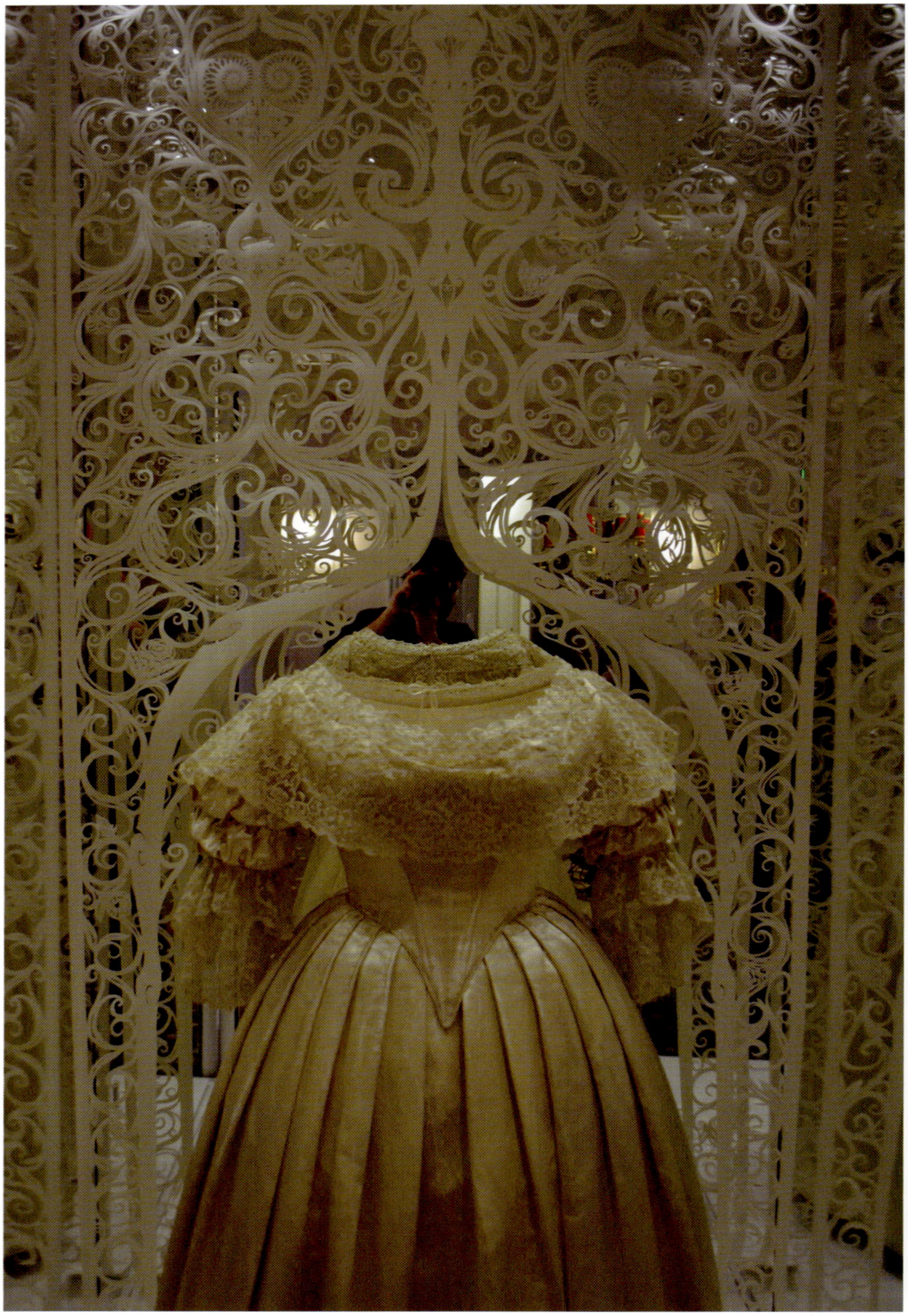

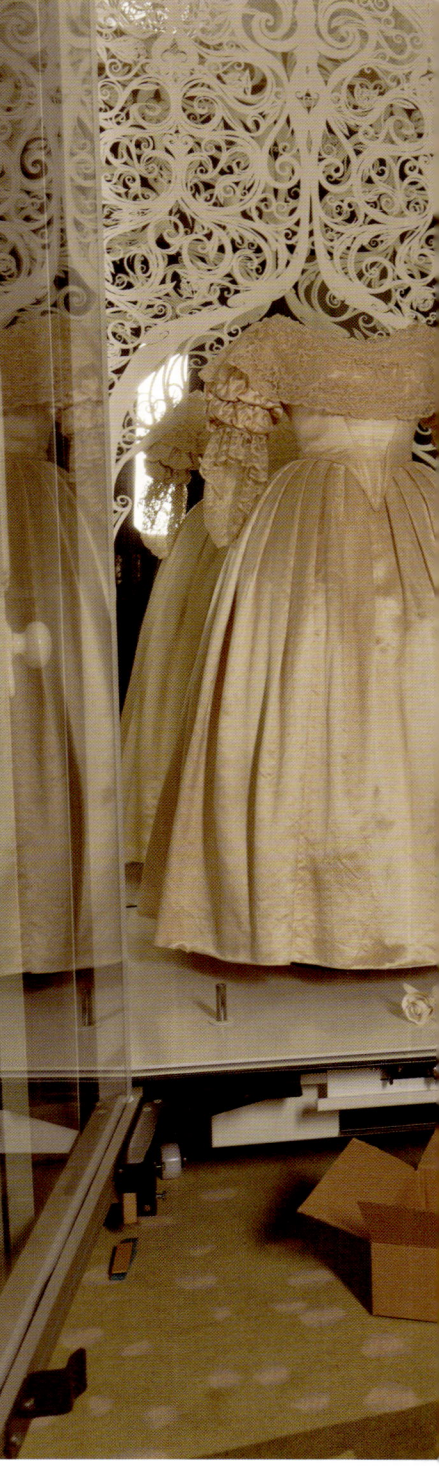

9. Queen Victoria's Wedding Dress Installation

Andy Singleton was commissioned by Kensington Palace to create a paper installation to be housed inside a cabinet with Queen Victoria's orginal wedding dress as part of the 'Victoria Revealed' Exhibition. The work is a 2D hand cut paper panel, inspired by the lace patterns on the original dress, suspended in the cabinet. There are also three 3D paper roses and hundreds of paper petals scatered around the wedding dress.

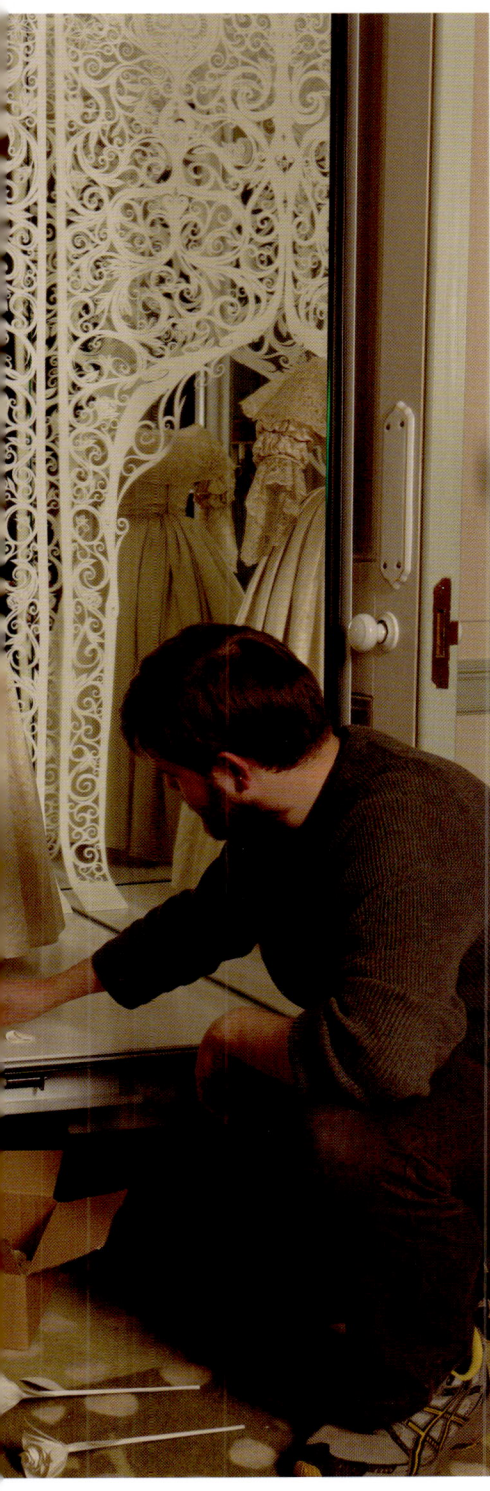

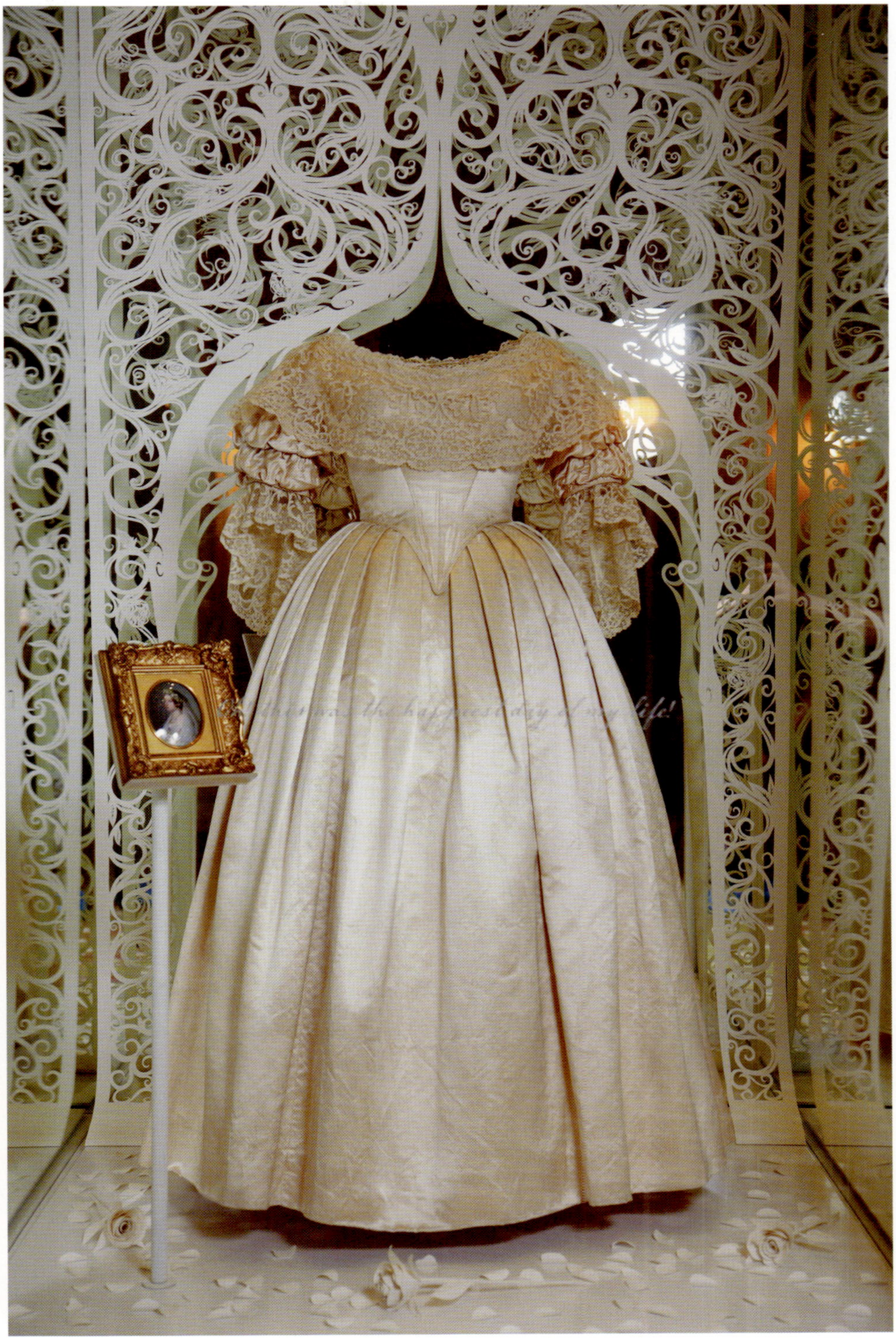

Designer: Andy Singleton
Country: UK
Creative Director: Deirdre Murphy
Client: Kensington Palace
Photographer: Andy Singleton

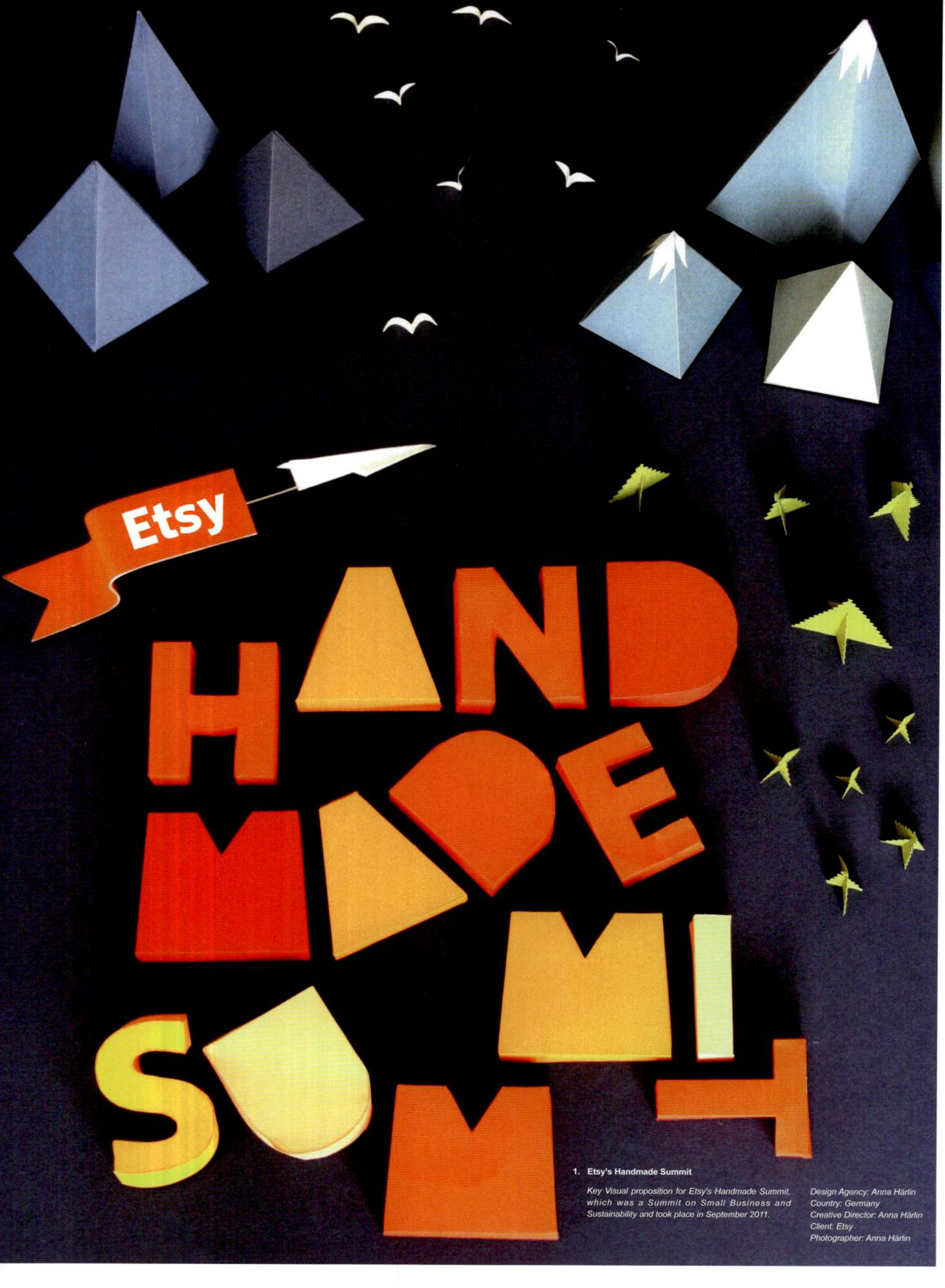

1. **Etsy's Handmade Summit**

Key Visual proposition for Etsy's Handmade Summit, which was a Summit on Small Business and Sustainability and took place in September 2011.

Design Agency: Anna Härlin
Country: Germany
Creative Director: Anna Härlin
Client: Etsy
Photographer: Anna Härlin

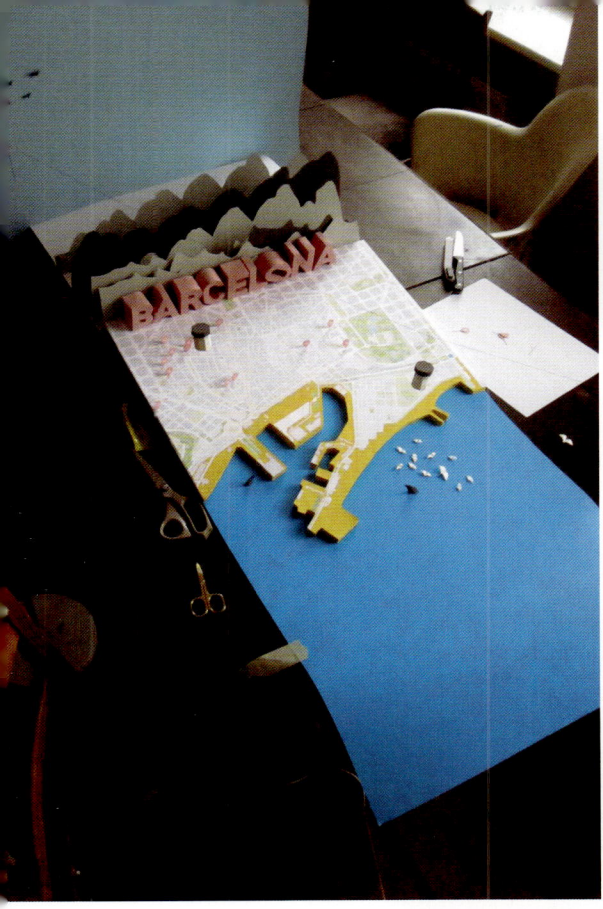
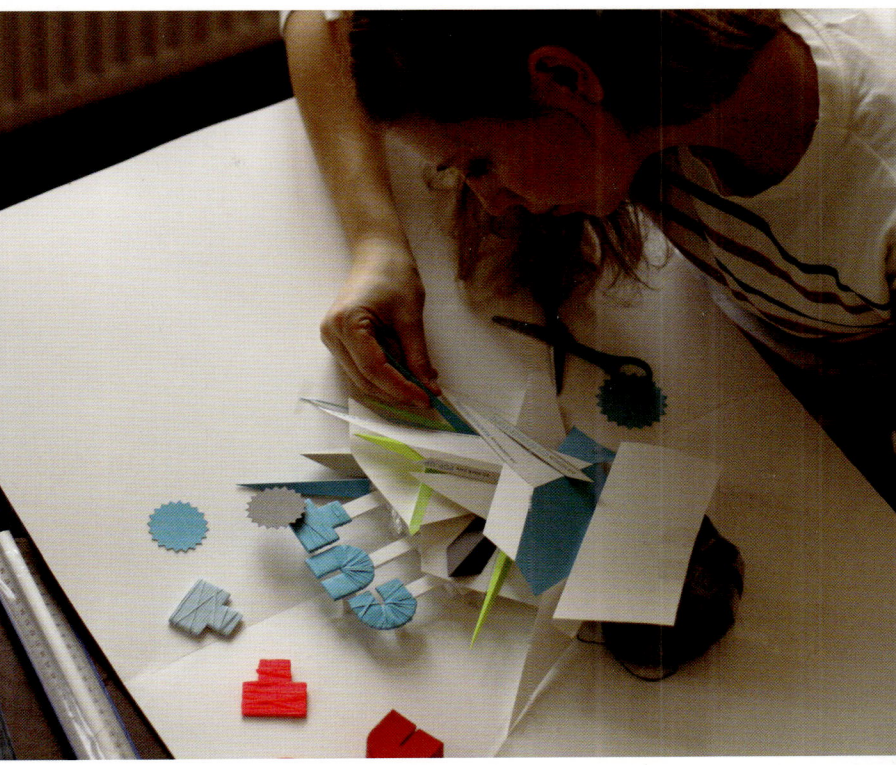
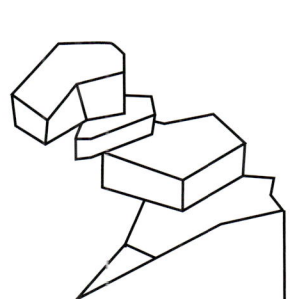
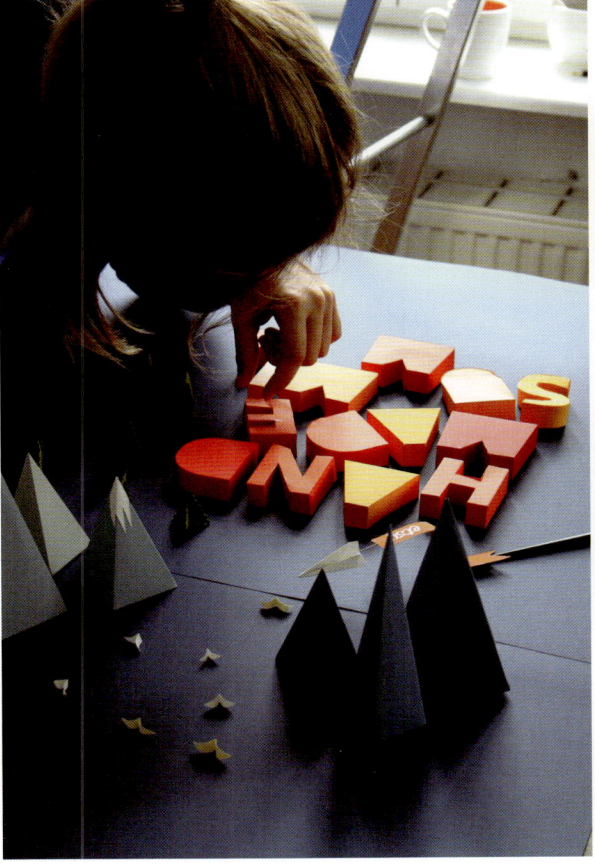
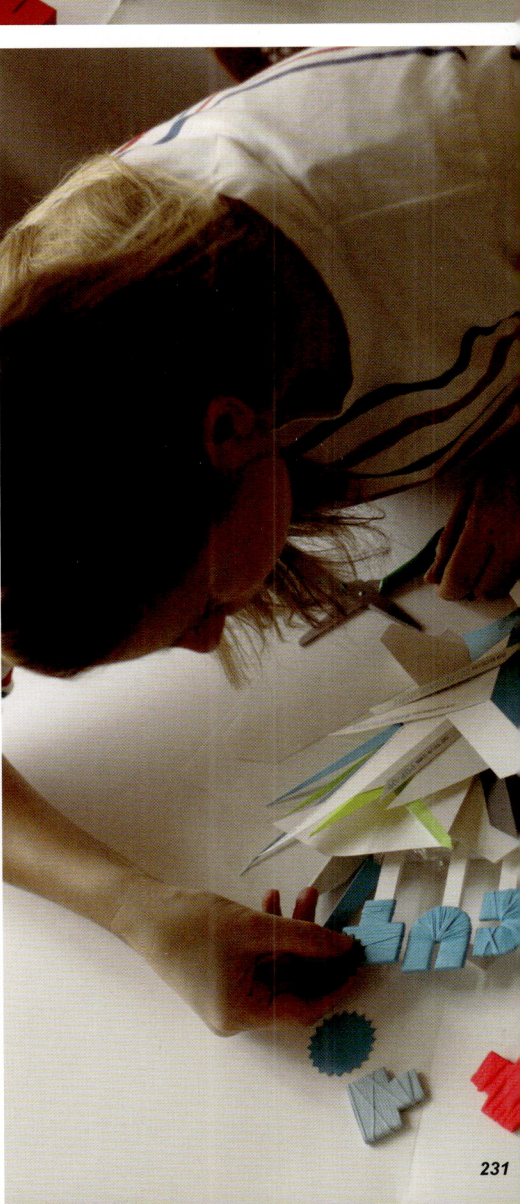

1. Etsy's Handmade Summit
2. Barcelona City
3. Cut Magazine Cover

---Anna Härlin

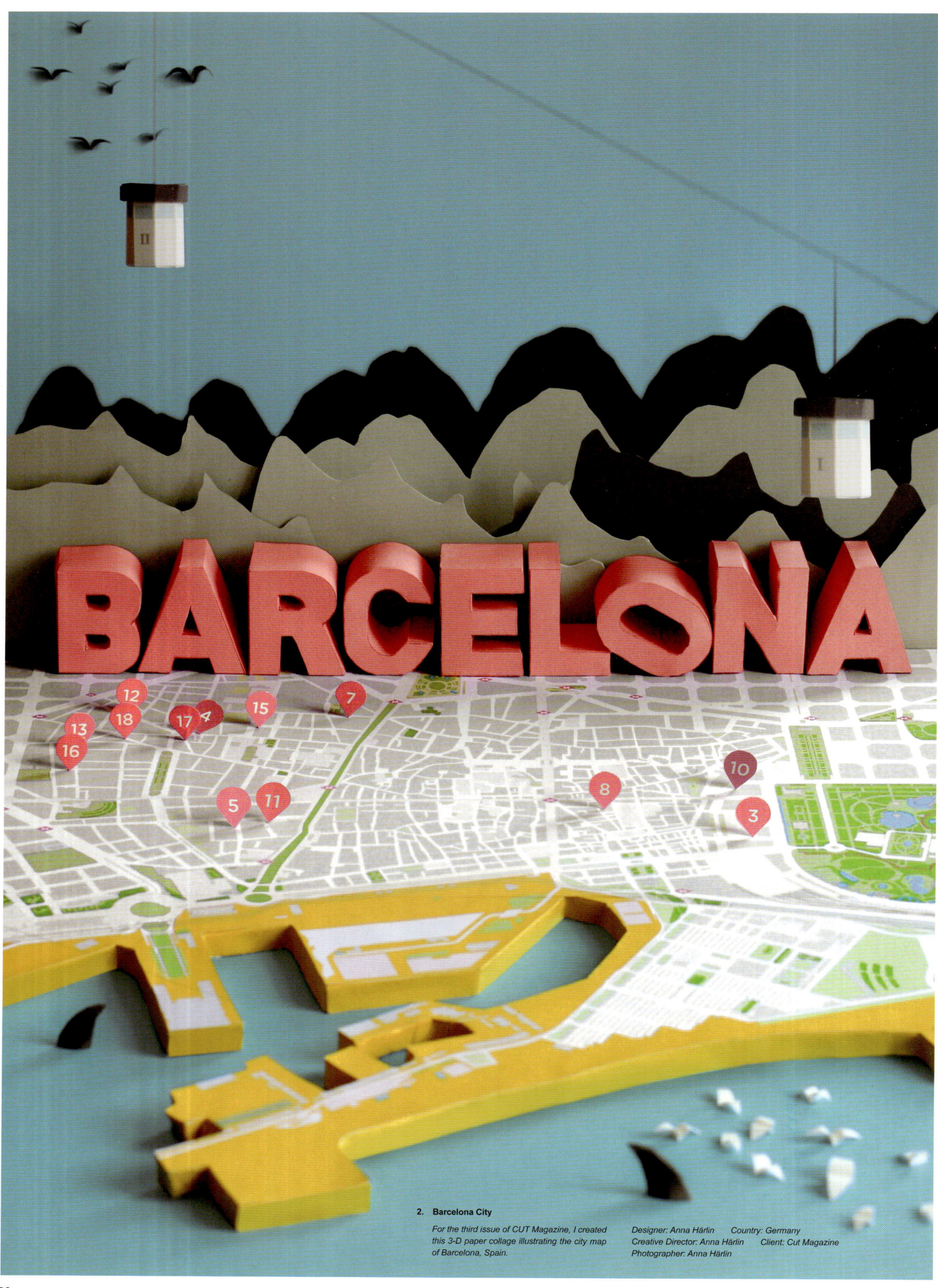

2. Barcelona City

For the third issue of CUT Magazine, I created this 3-D paper collage illustrating the city map of Barcelona, Spain.

Designer: Anna Härlin
Creative Director: Anna Härlin
Photographer: Anna Härlin
Country: Germany
Client: Cut Magazine

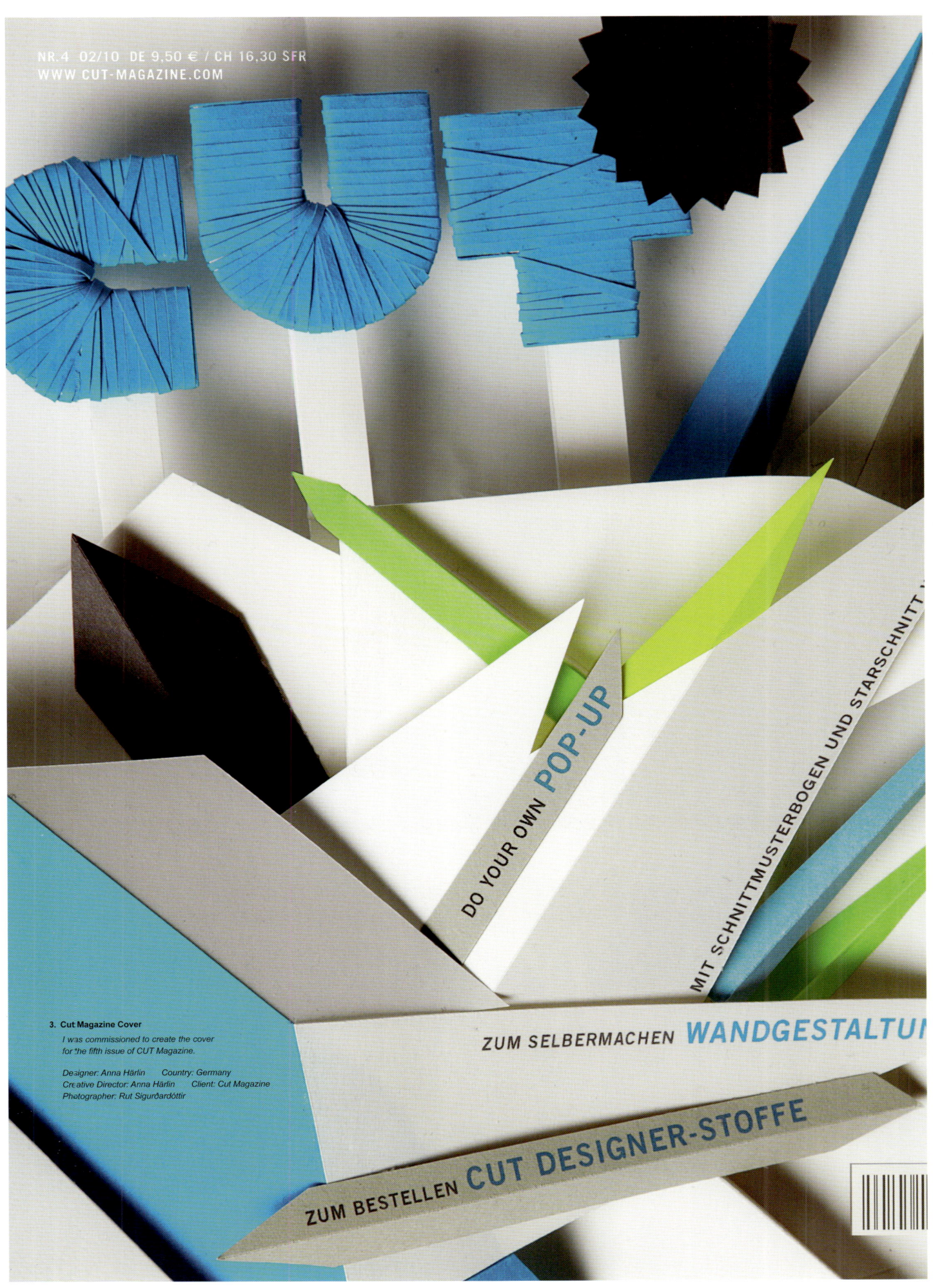

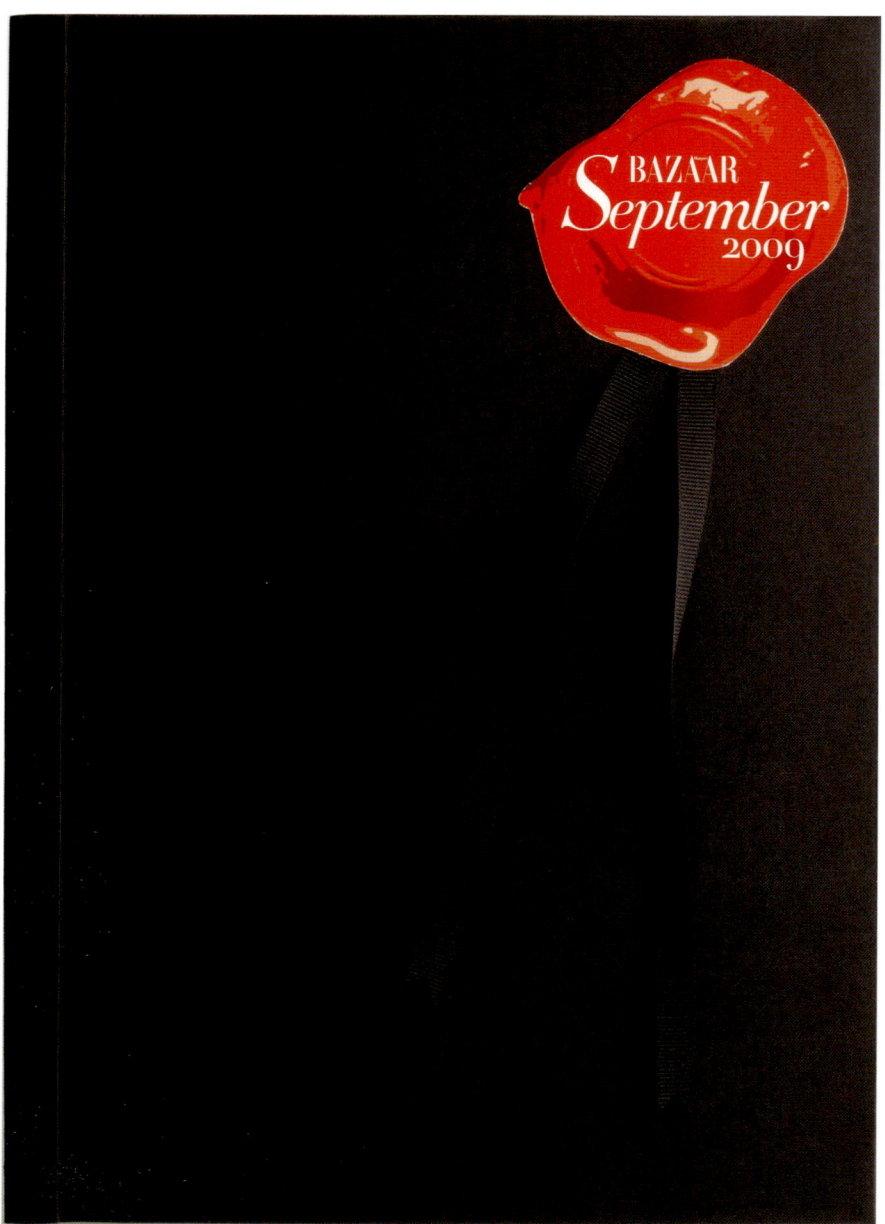

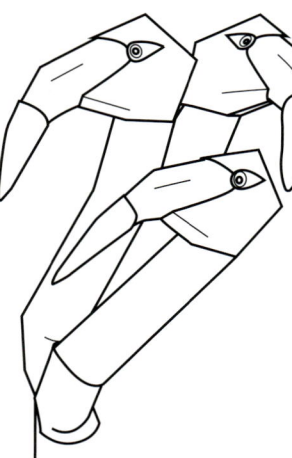

1. Harpers Bazaar Pop-up
2. Desktop Magazine
3. Flamingos
4. Hermès Windows
5. Kylie Minogue: The Goddess Edition
6. Mandalay Flowers
7. Mardi Gras Poster
8. Master Card Poster
9. Opera House Open Day poster
10. Oyster Magazine
11. The Paper Attic
12. Parklife Poster
13. Victorian Insects (Spider + Stag beetle)

---Benja Harney

1. Harpers Bazaar Pop-up

Description: A promotional pop-up book to help the editor of Harpers sell advertising space in the September issue of the magazine.

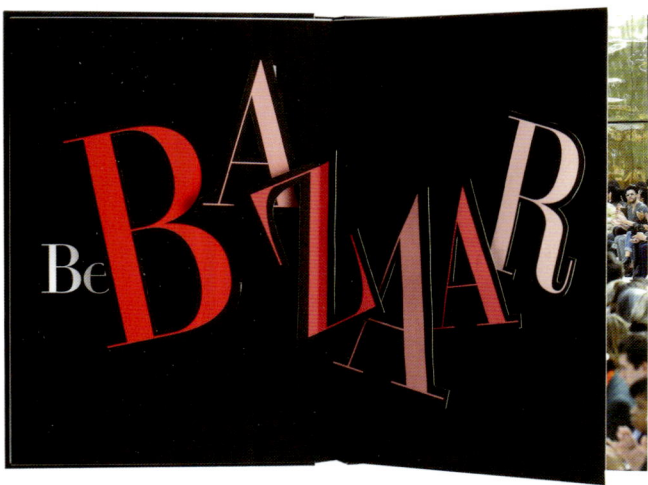

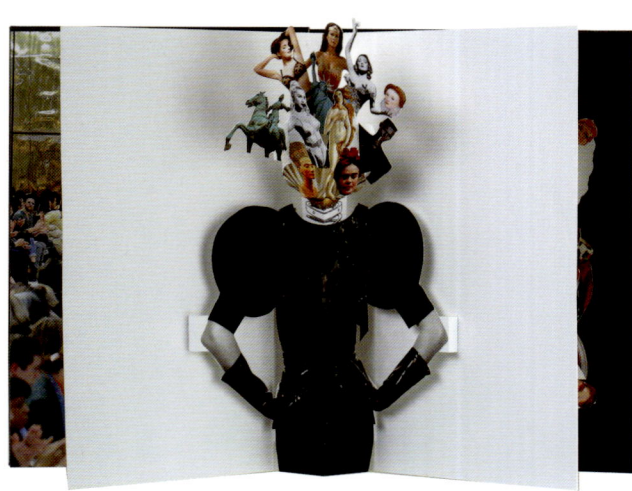

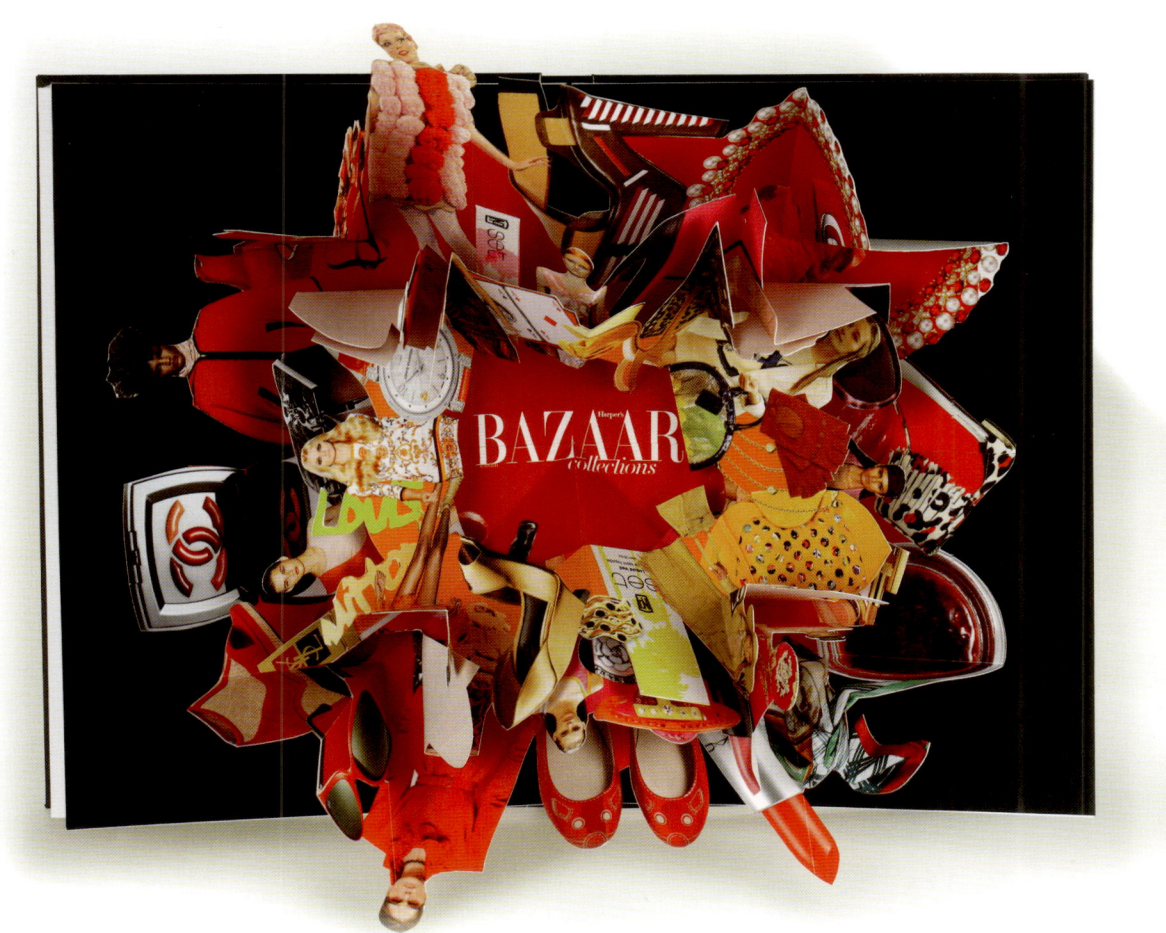

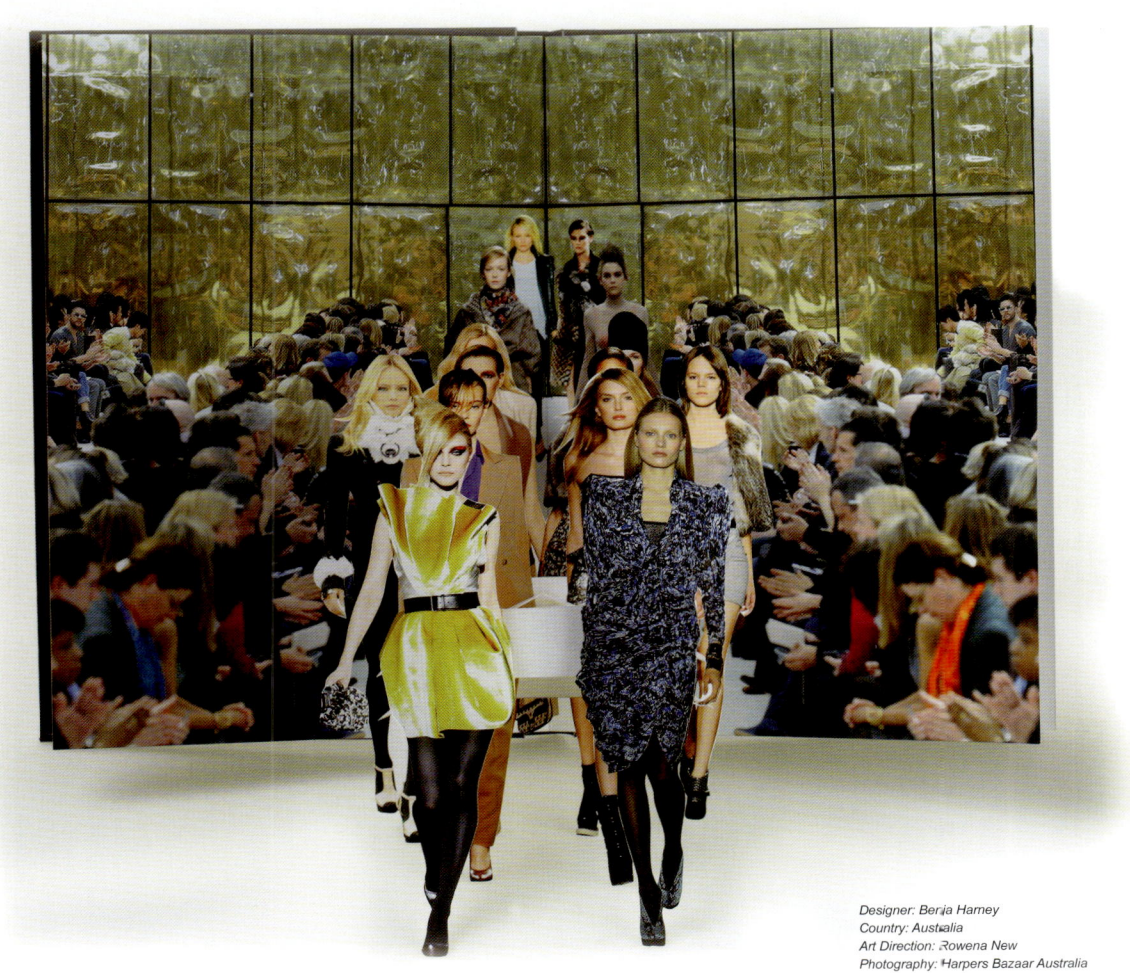

Designer: Berja Harney
Country: Australia
Art Direction: Rowena New
Photography: Harpers Bazaar Australia

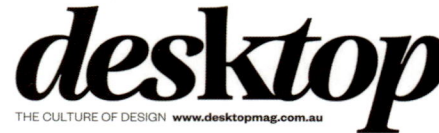
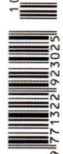

2. Desktop Magazine

Description: A commission for the cover of Desktop magazine.
Designer: Benja Harney
Country: Australia
Photography: Tong and Danny

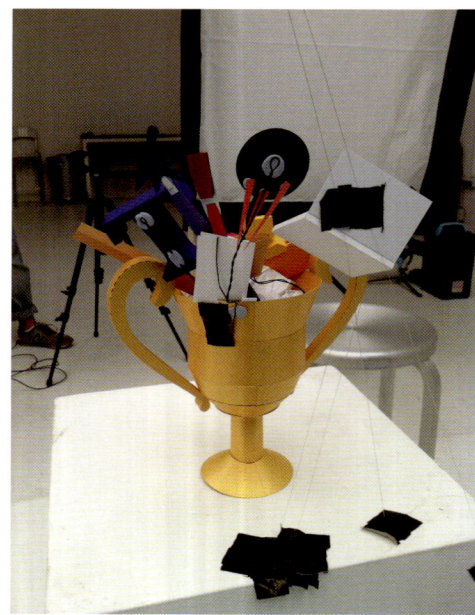
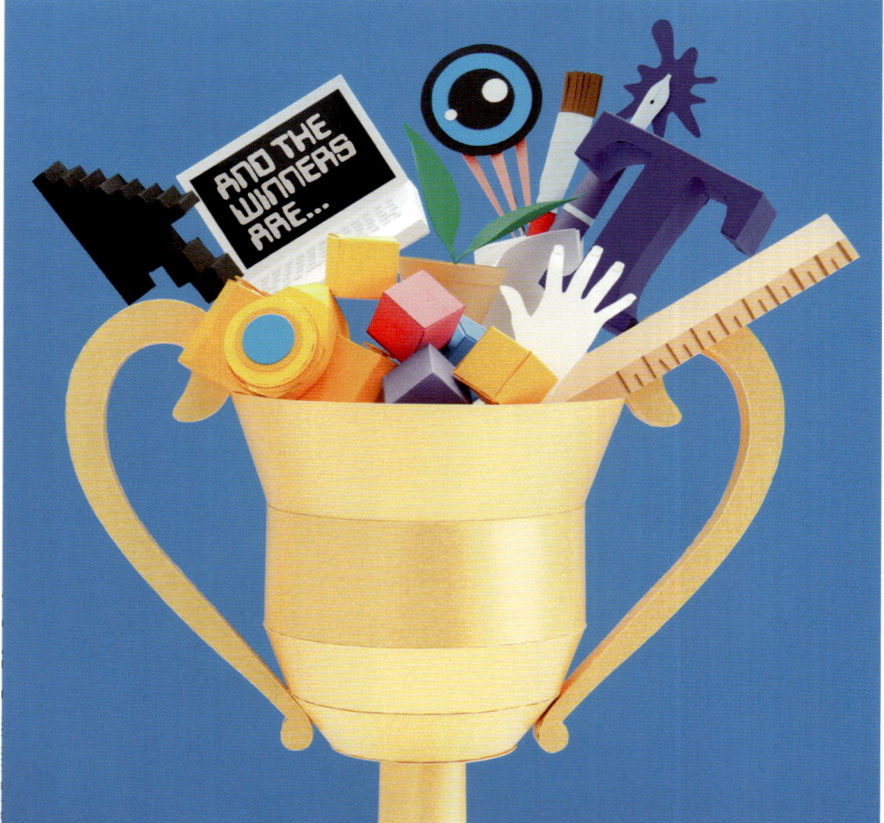
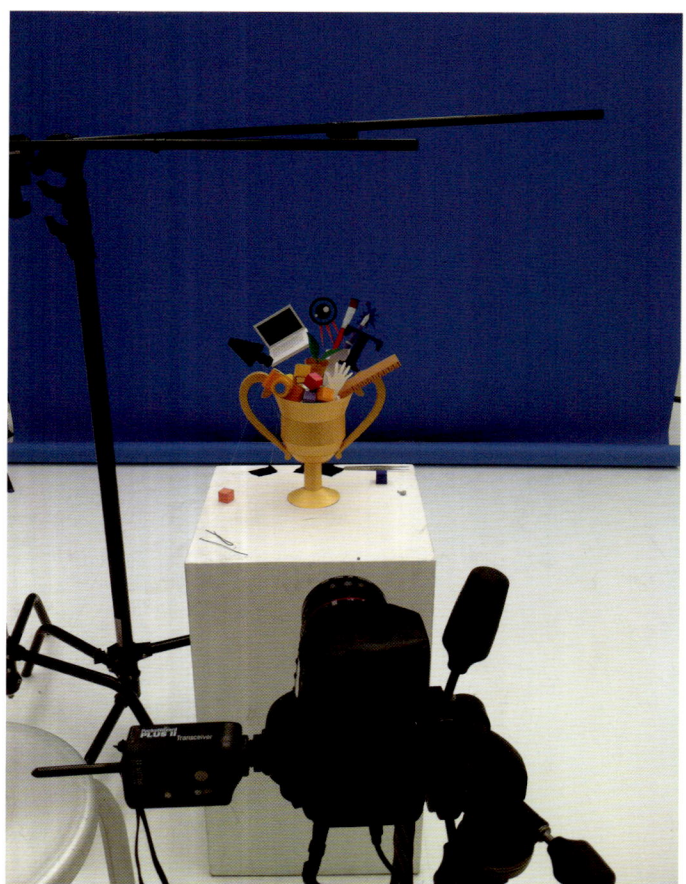
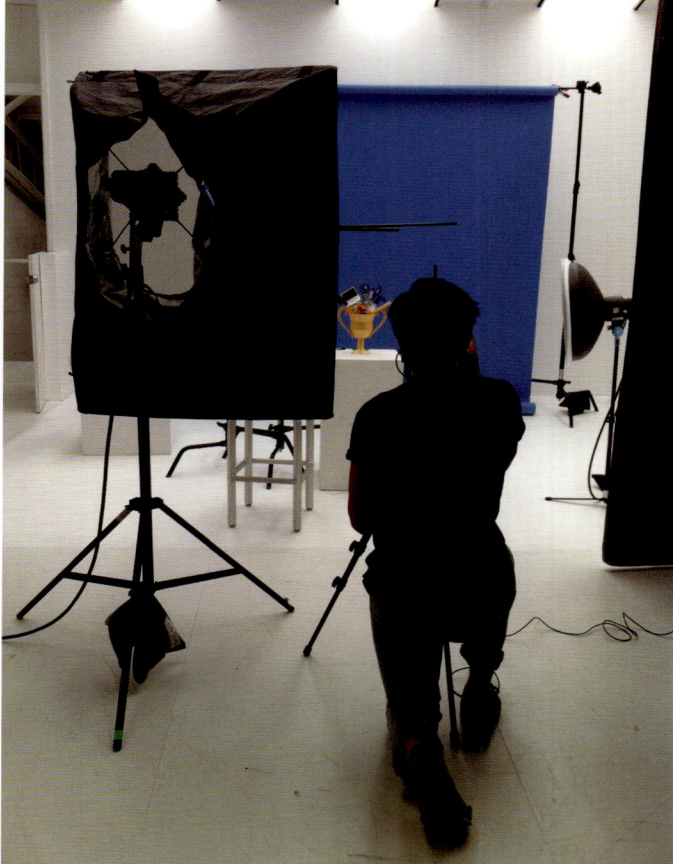

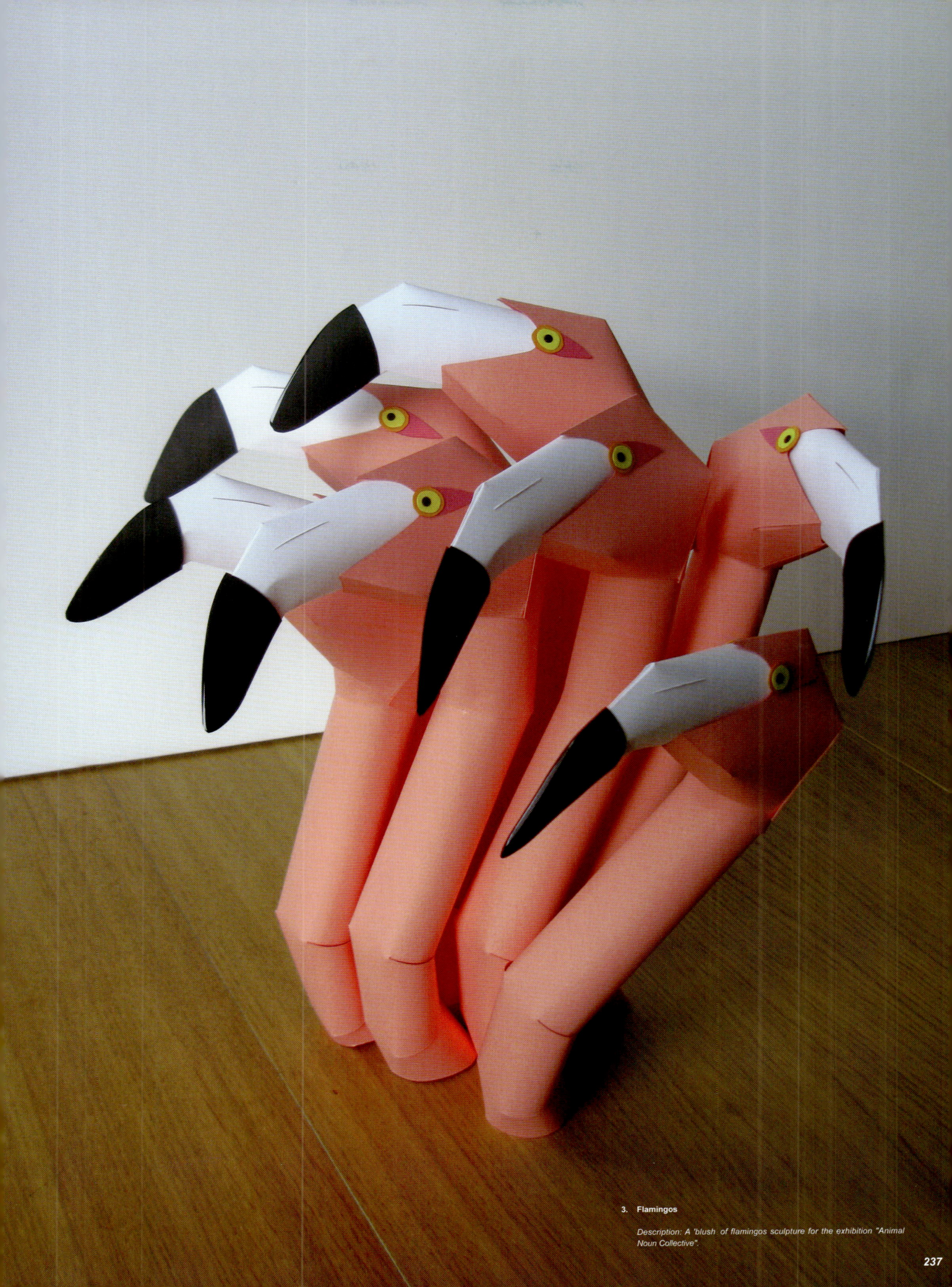

3. Flamingos

Description: A 'blush' of flamingos sculpture for the exhibition "Animal Noun Collective".

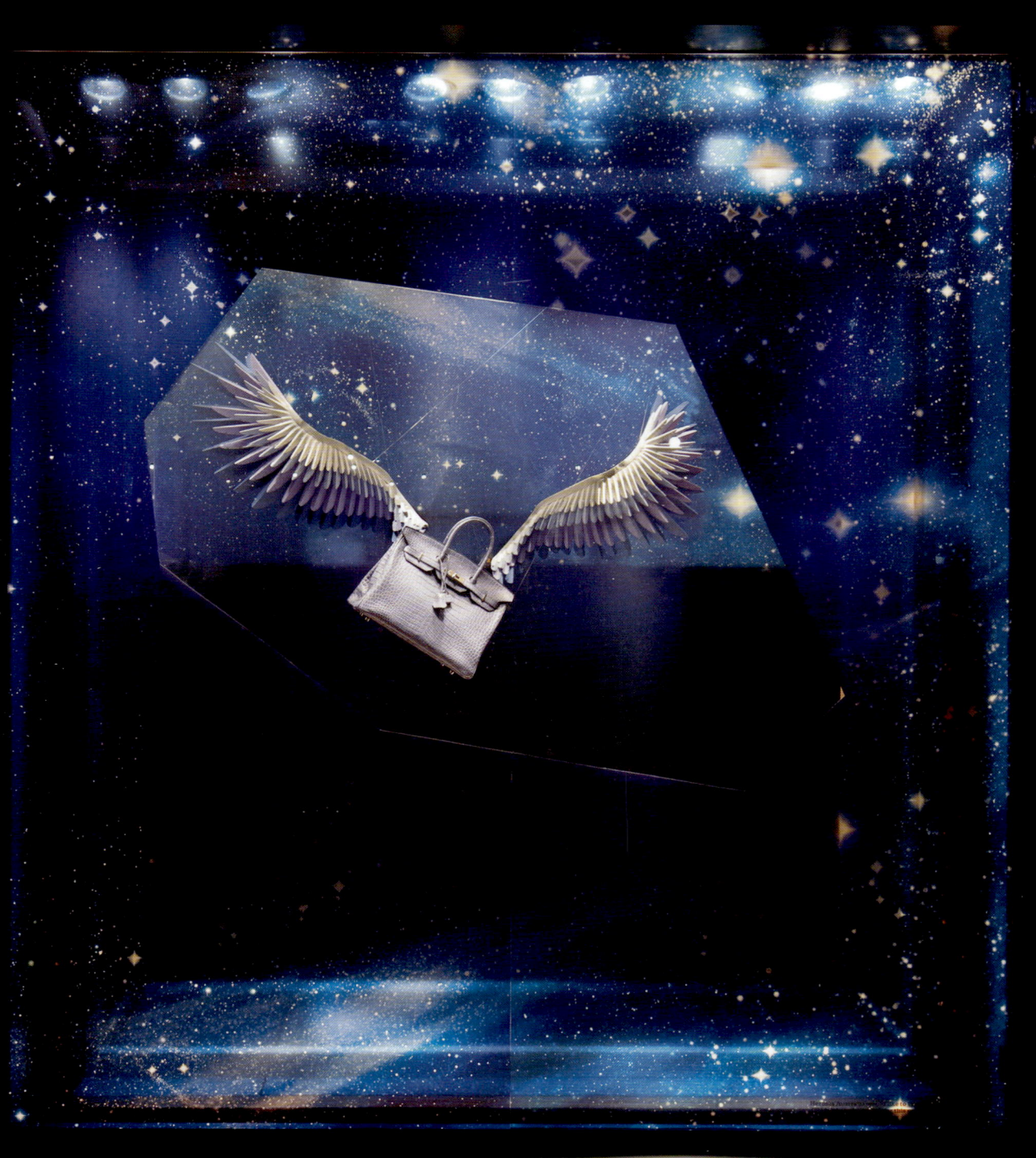

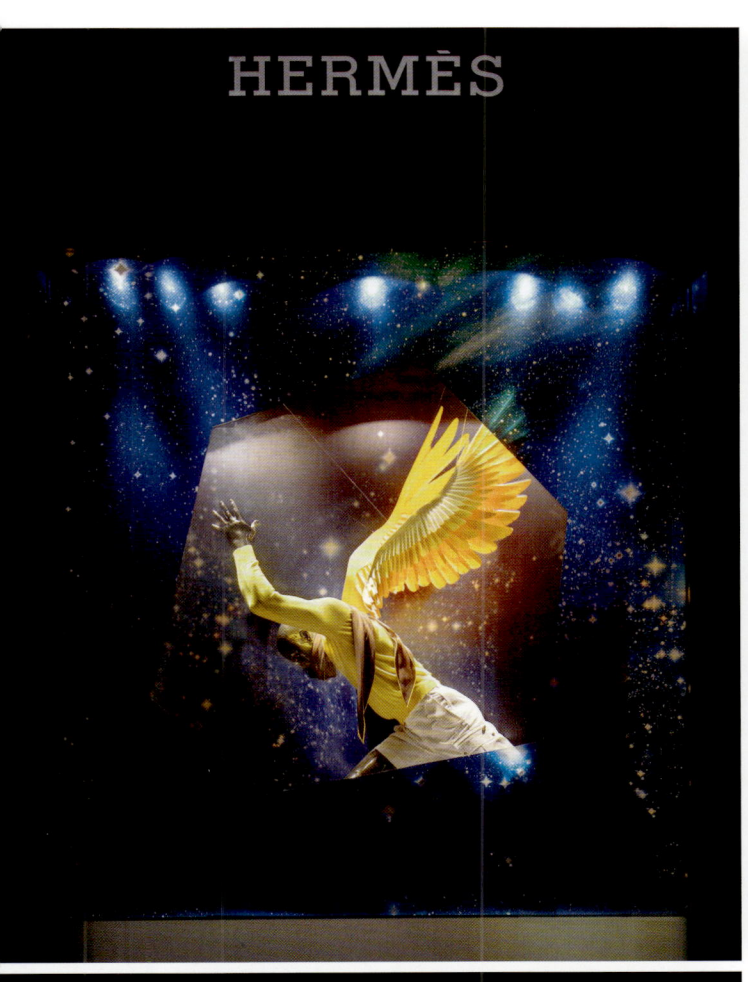
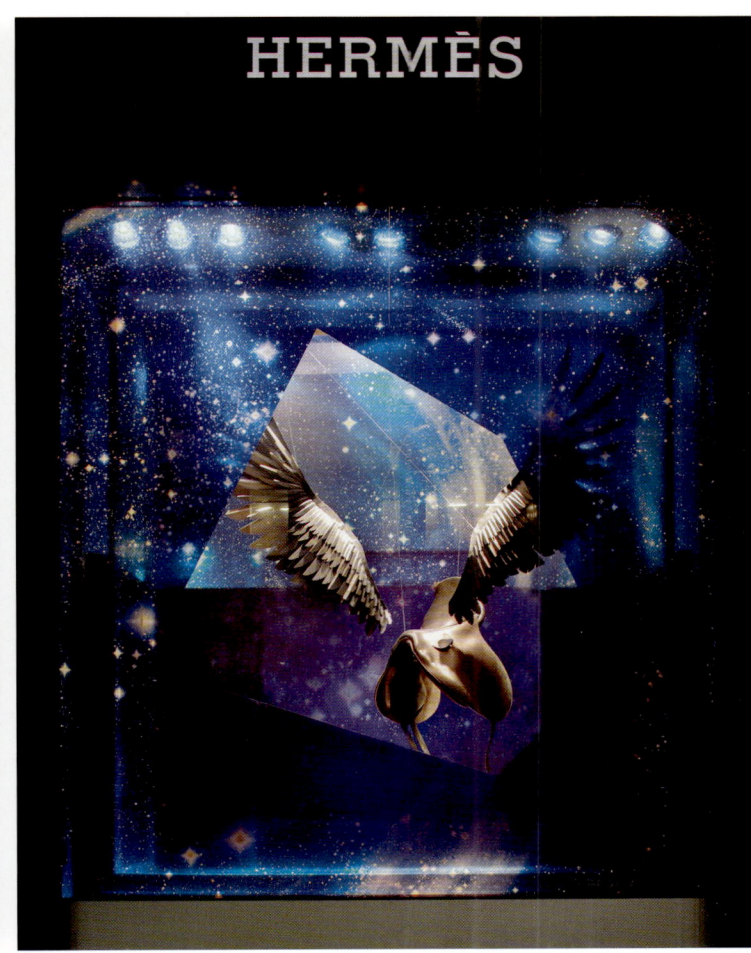
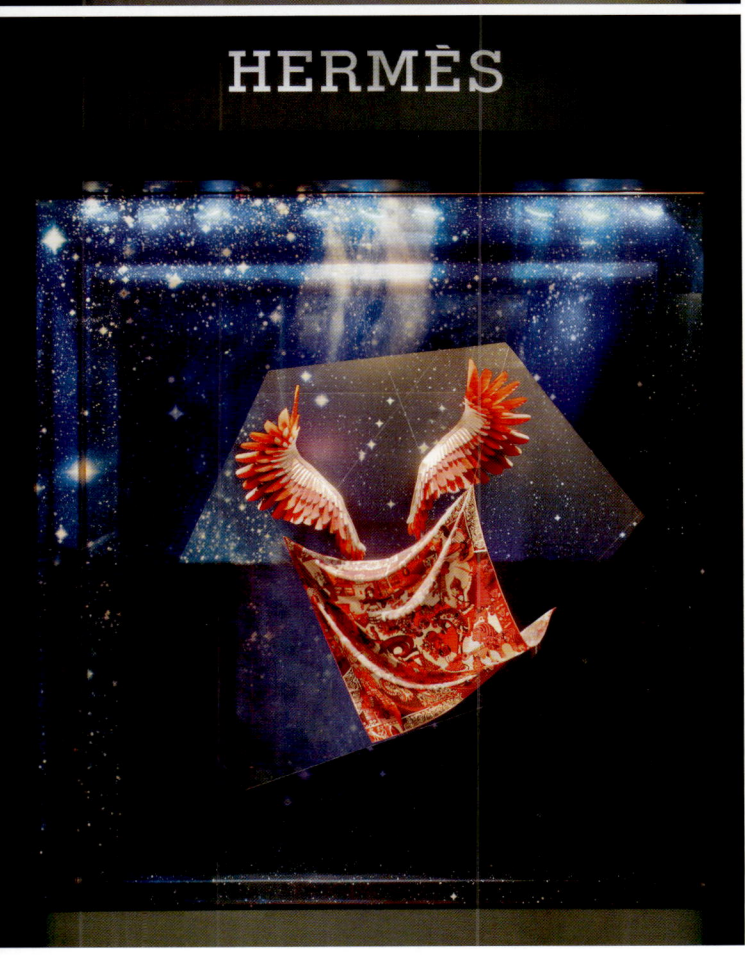

4. Hermès Windows

Description: A window display for the Christmas season at the Sydney Hermès store. 7 pairs of wings comprising 1000s of hand cut feathers.

Designer: Benja Harney
Country: Australia
Art Direction: Chen Lu
Photography: Murray Fredericks

Designer: Benja Harney
Country: Australia
Art Direction: Aaron Palajda / Kero Luangrath

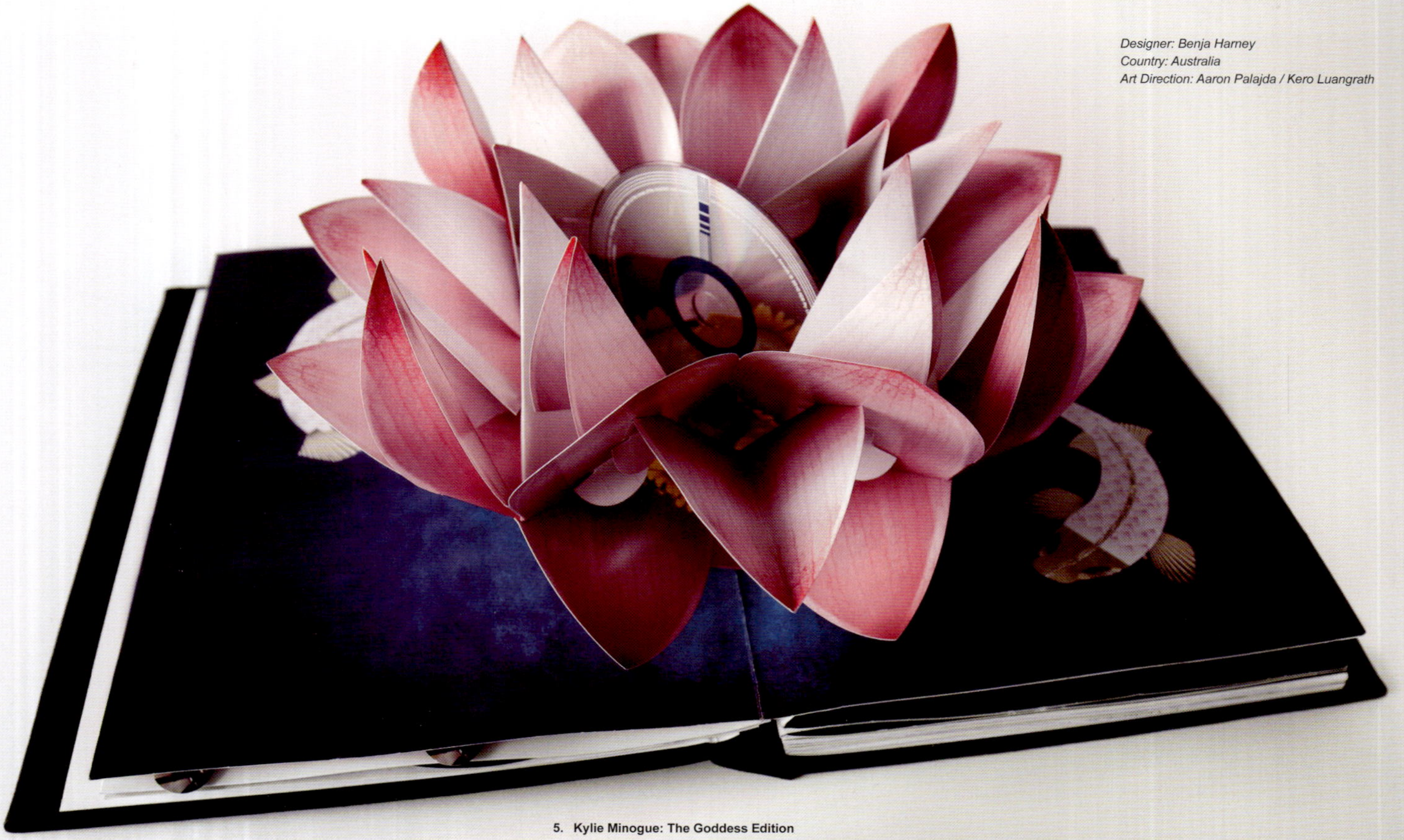

5. **Kylie Minogue: The Goddess Edition**
Description: A limited edition pop-up book created to celebrate Kylie Minogue's Aphrodite world tour and house her CD entitled "Aphrodite". Published by Warner Music Australia.

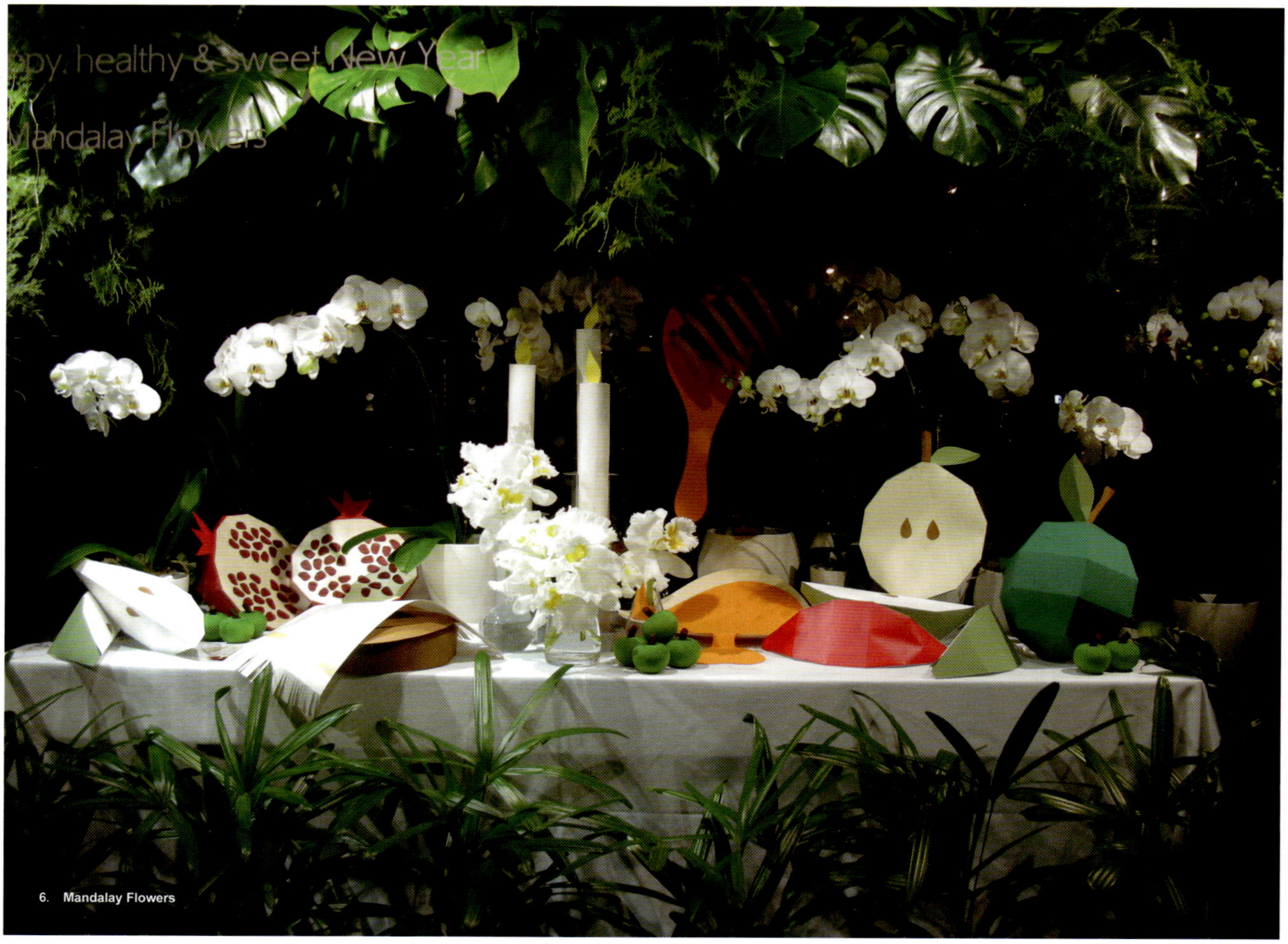

6. **Mandalay Flowers**

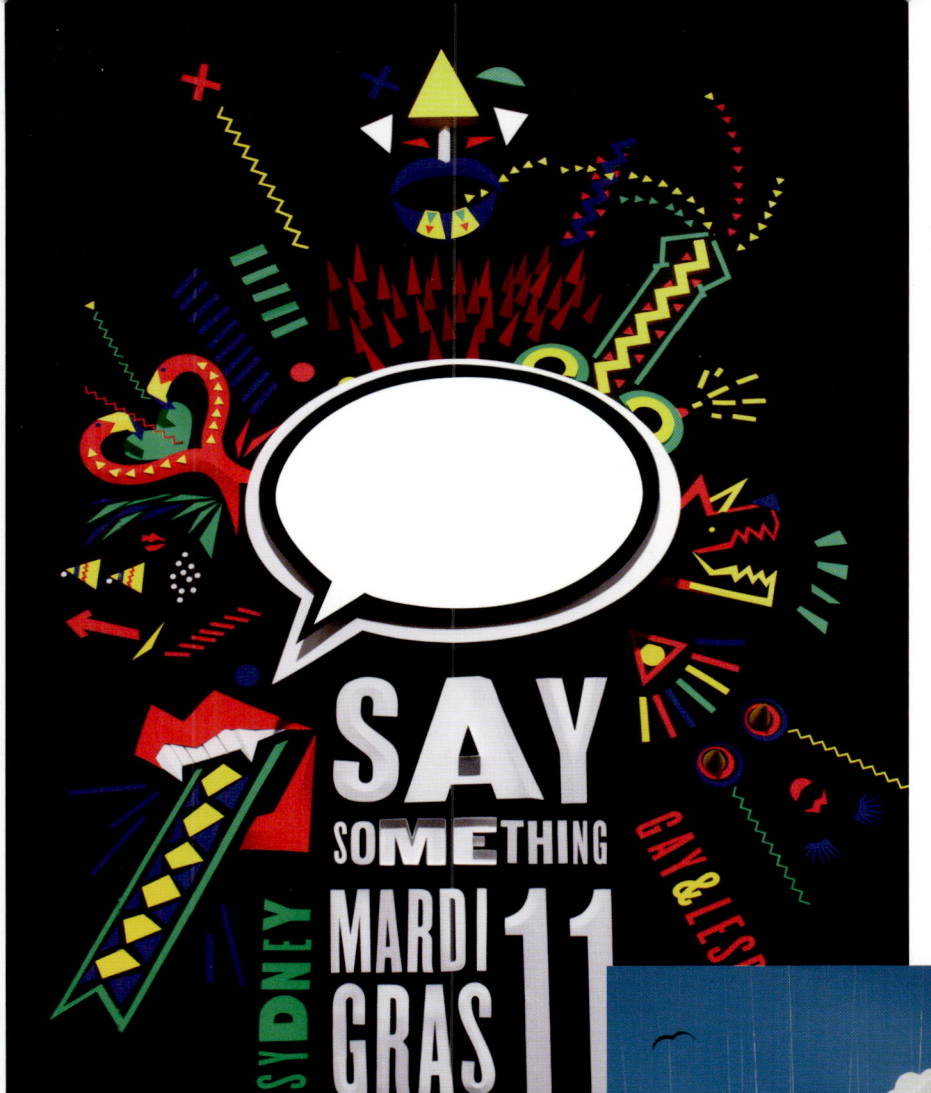

7. Mardi Gras Poster

Description: Branding and collateral design for the Sydney Mardi Gras parade and campaign.

Designer: Benja Harney
Country: Australia
Art Direction: Técha Noble

8. Master Card Poster

Designer: Benja Harney
Country: Australia

6. Mandalay Flowers

Description: A window installation for a local florist.
Designer: Benja Harney
Country: Australia
Photography: Credit not needed

8. Master Card Poster

Description: A poster for the MasterCard 'Priceless Gigs' campaign host by the band Birds of Tokyo.

Designer: Benja Harney
Country: Australia
Art Direction: Pat Armstrong / Shelby Craig

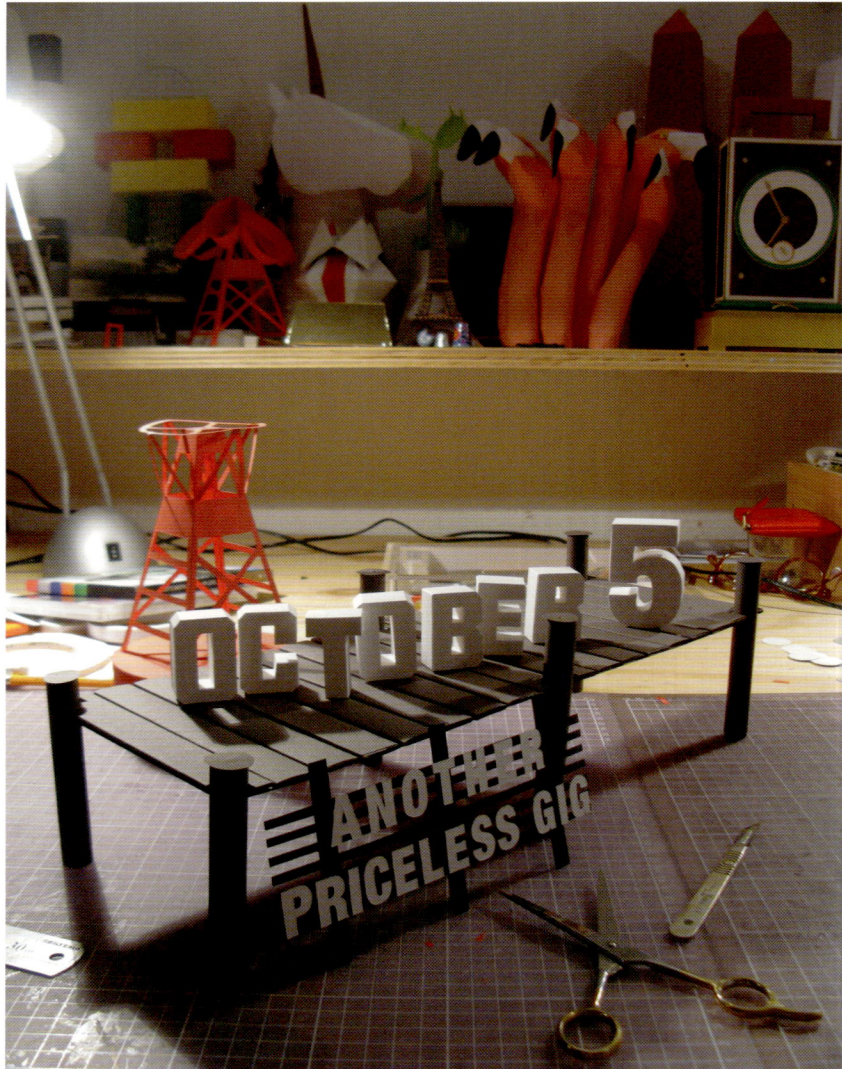

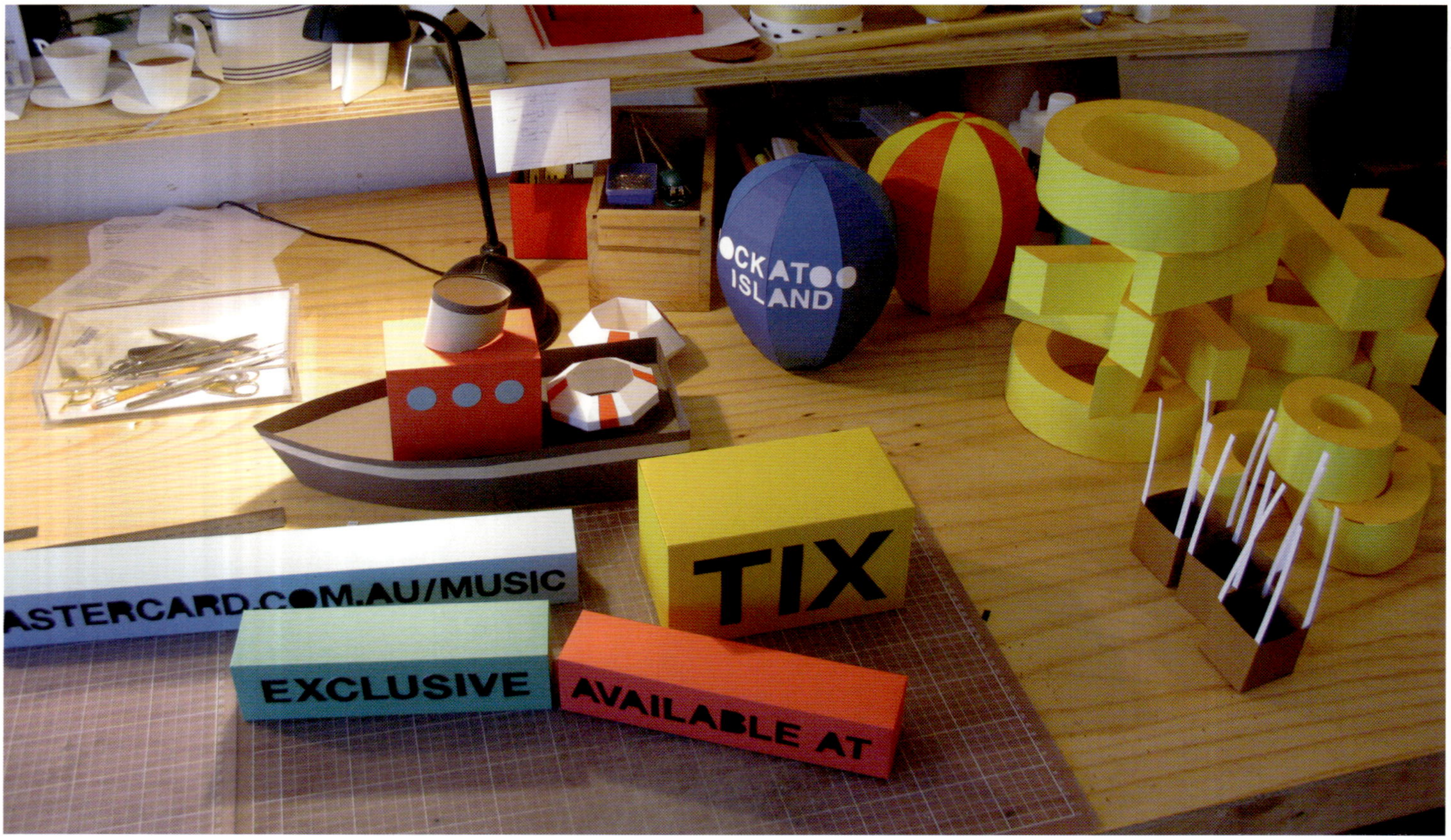

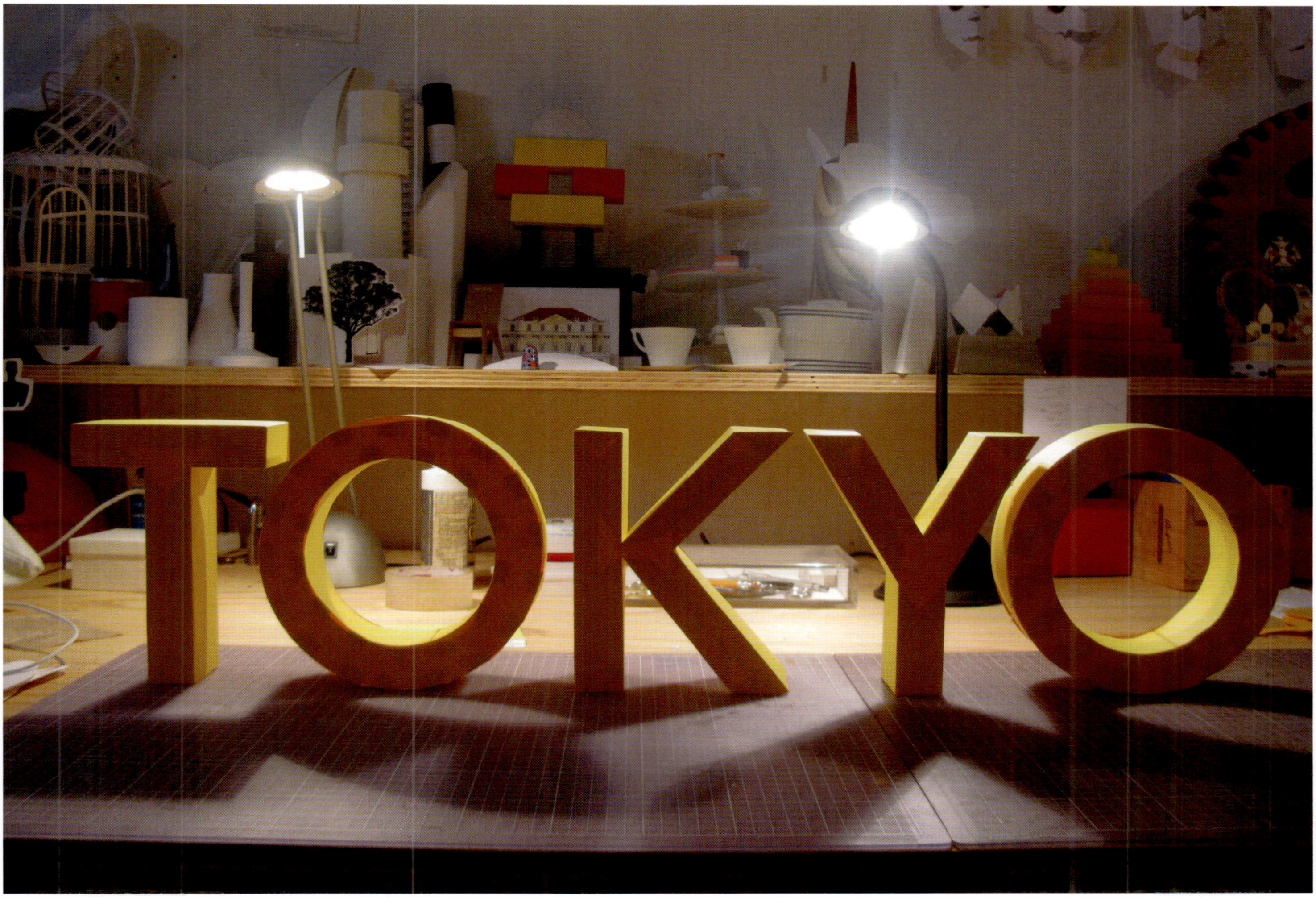

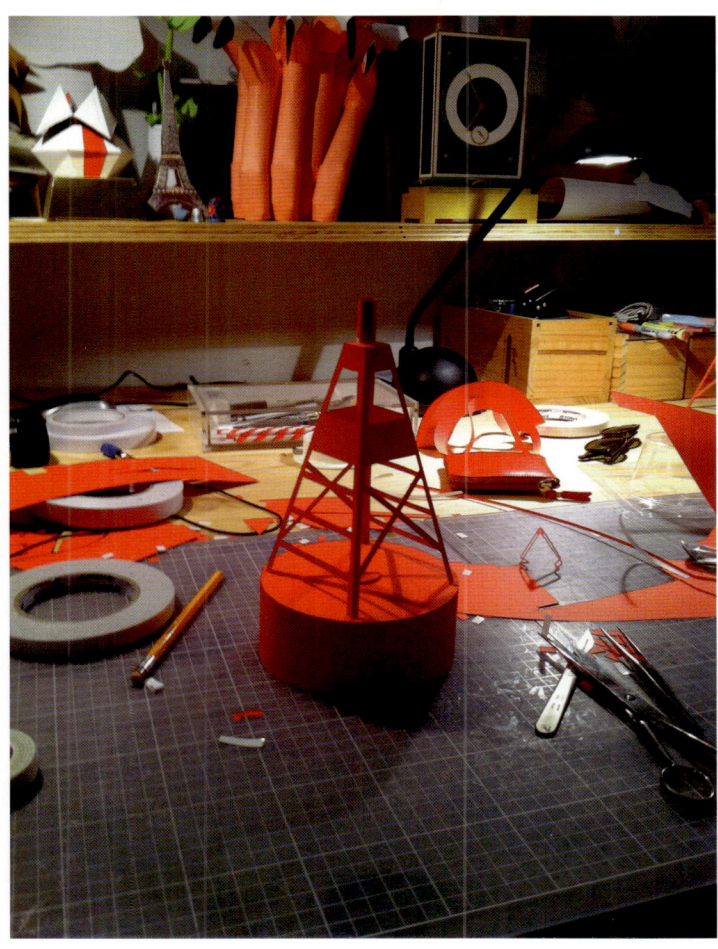
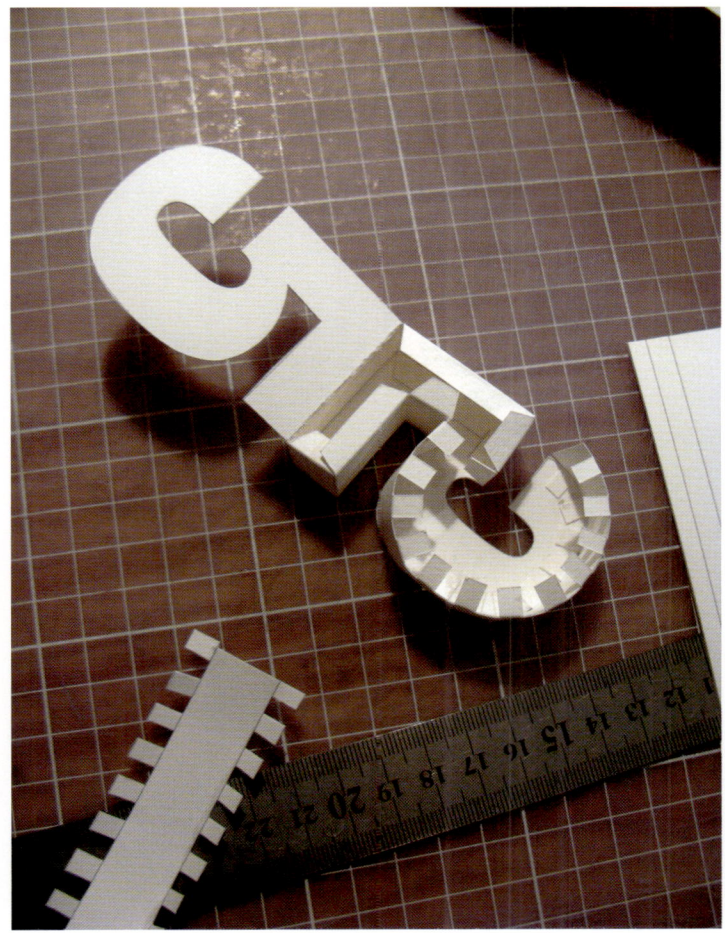

9. Opera House Open Day poster

Description: A poster for Sydney Opera House Open Day.

Designer: Benja Harney
Country: Australia

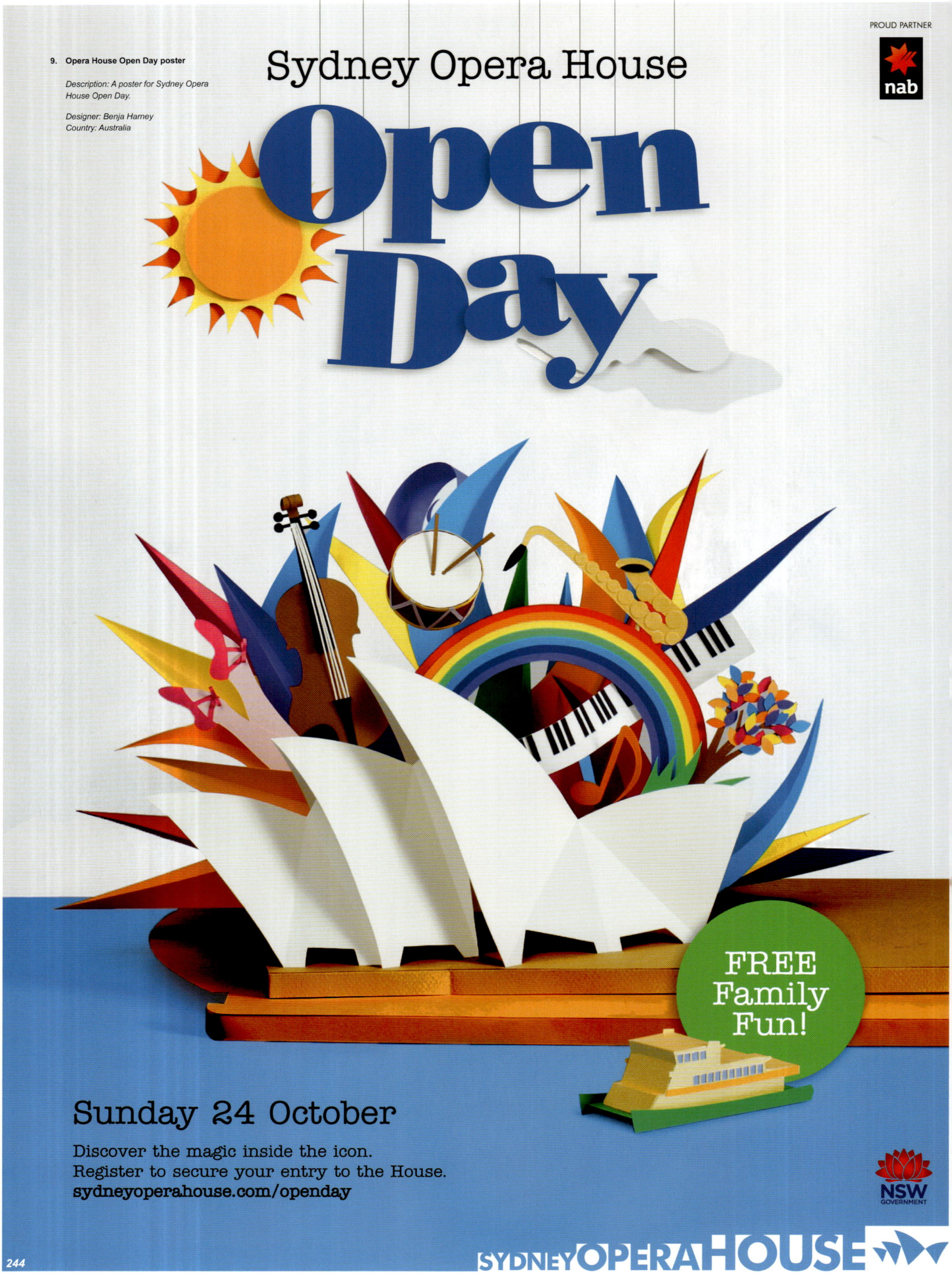

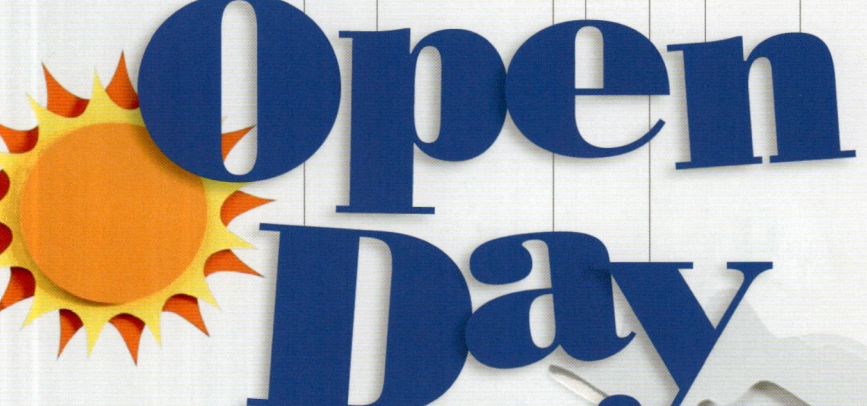

10. Oyster Magazine

Description: A bespoke creation for Oyster Magazine's 100th issue. 100 ascending coloured prisms based on the theme of the issue - "dreams".

Designer: Benja Harney
Country: Australia

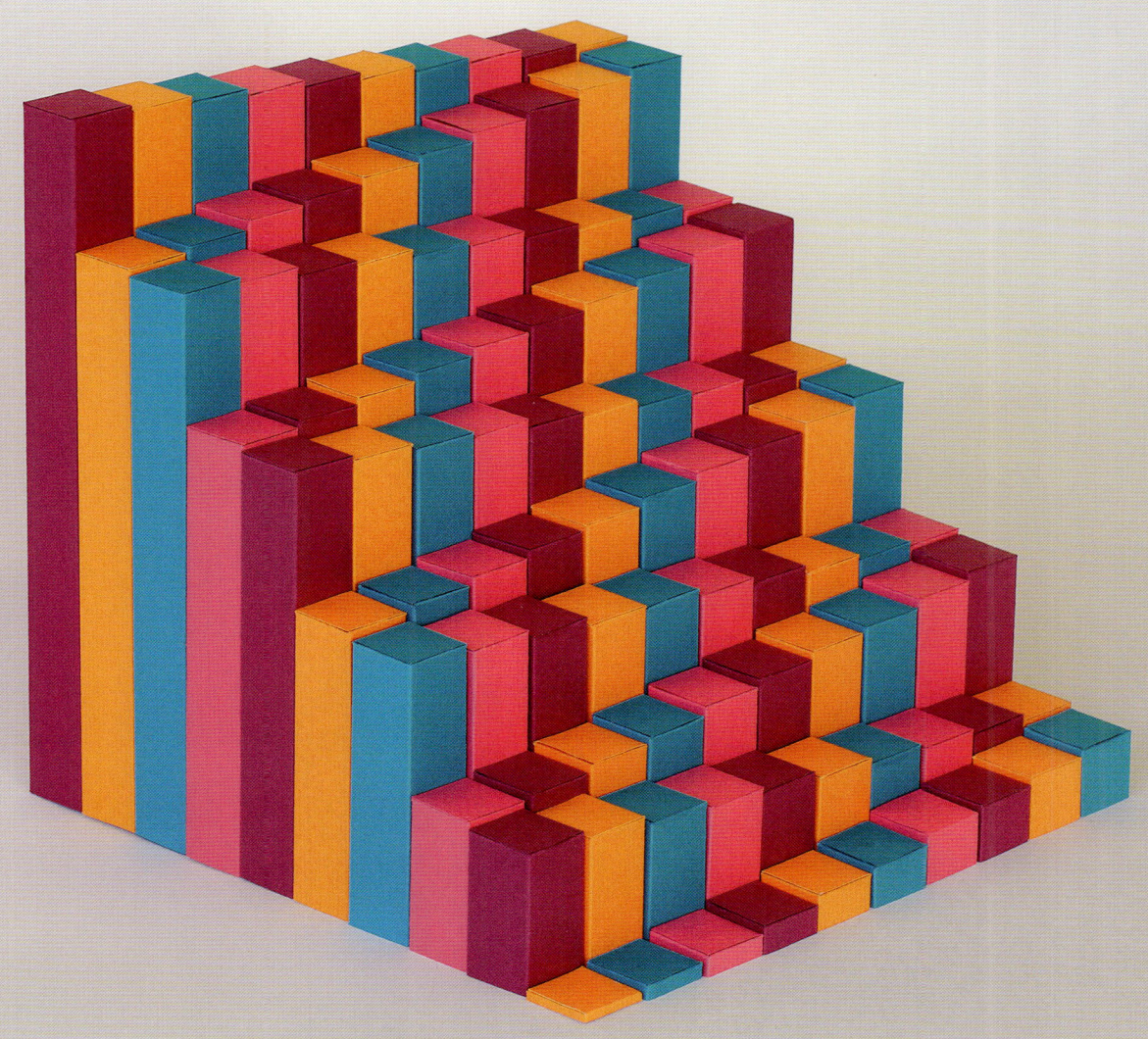

11. The Paper Attic

Clock and Ice Skates sculptures created for my first solo exhibition "The Paper Attic".
Designer: Benja Harney
Country: Australia

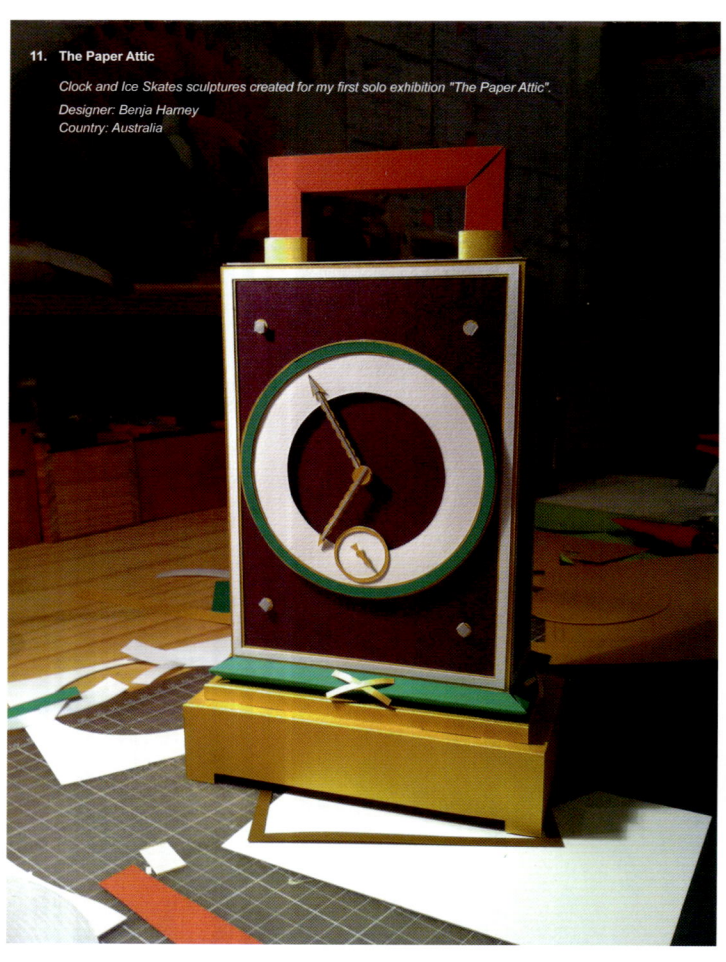
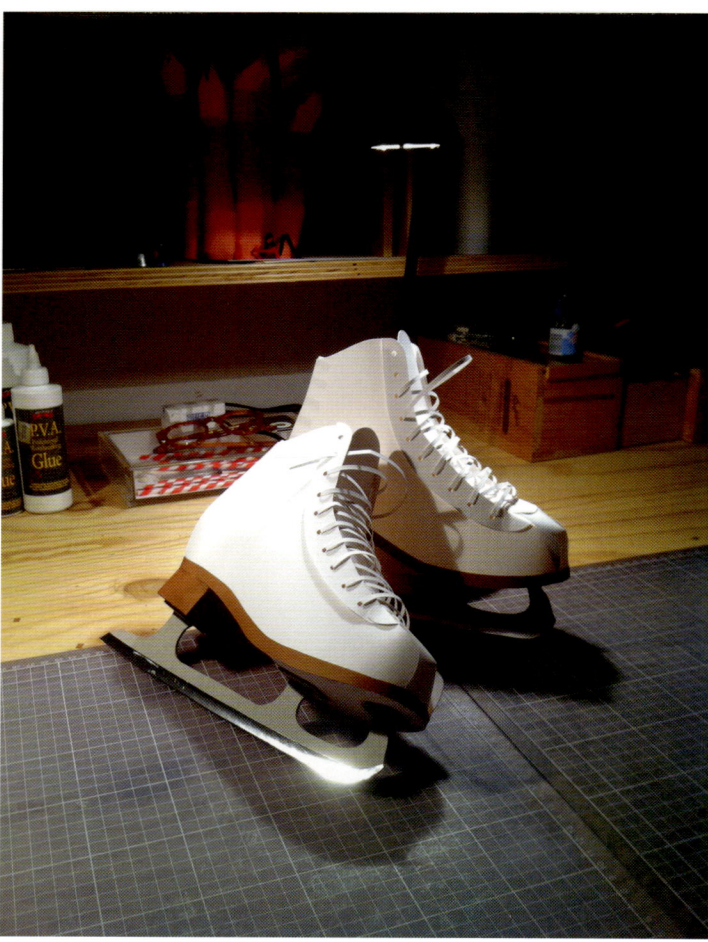

12. Parklife Poster

Description: Branding and collateral design for the Parklife Music Festival and campaign.
Designer: Benja Harney   Country: Australia
Art Direction and Photography: Briton Smith / Vissukamma Ratsaphong

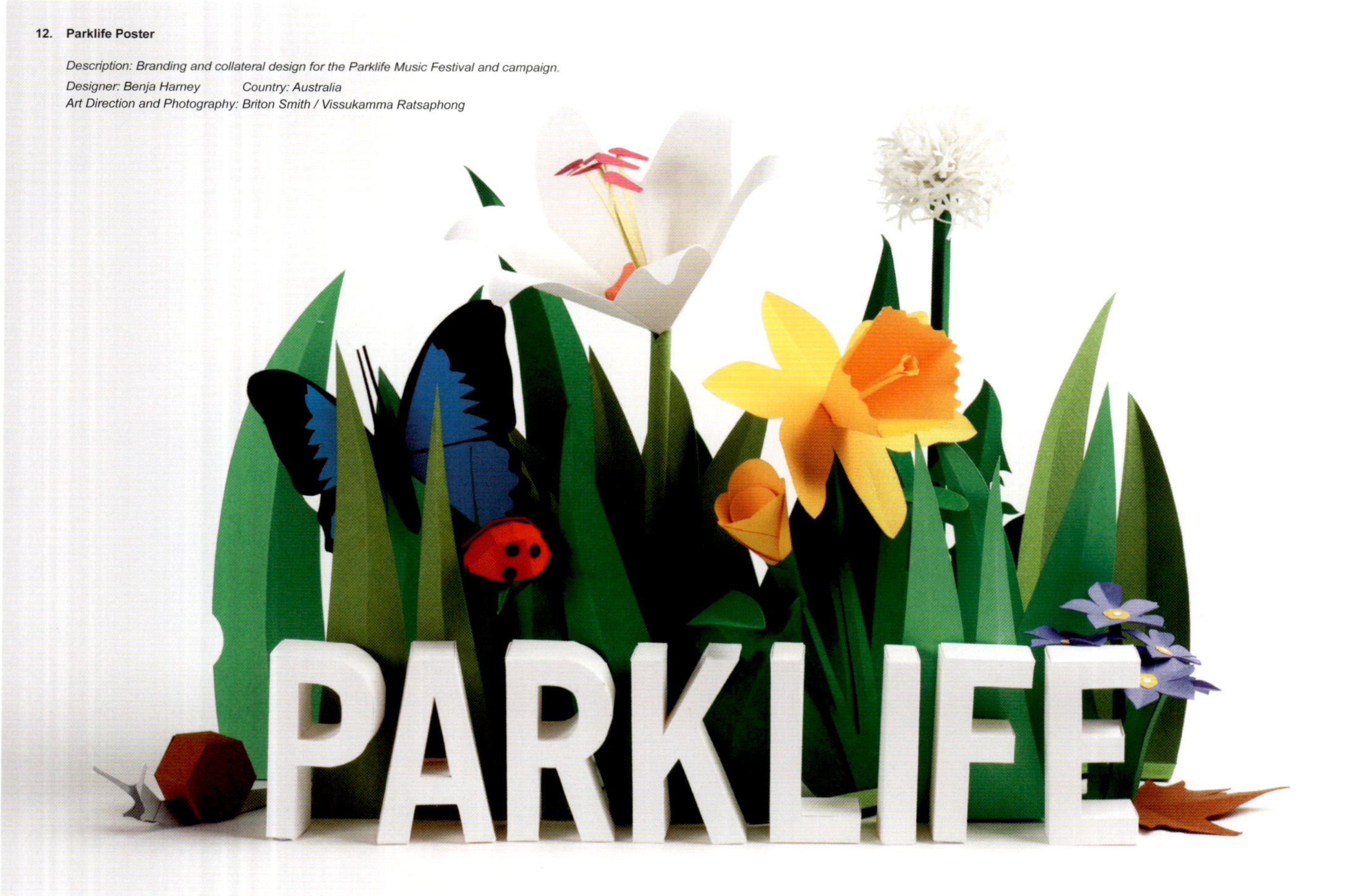

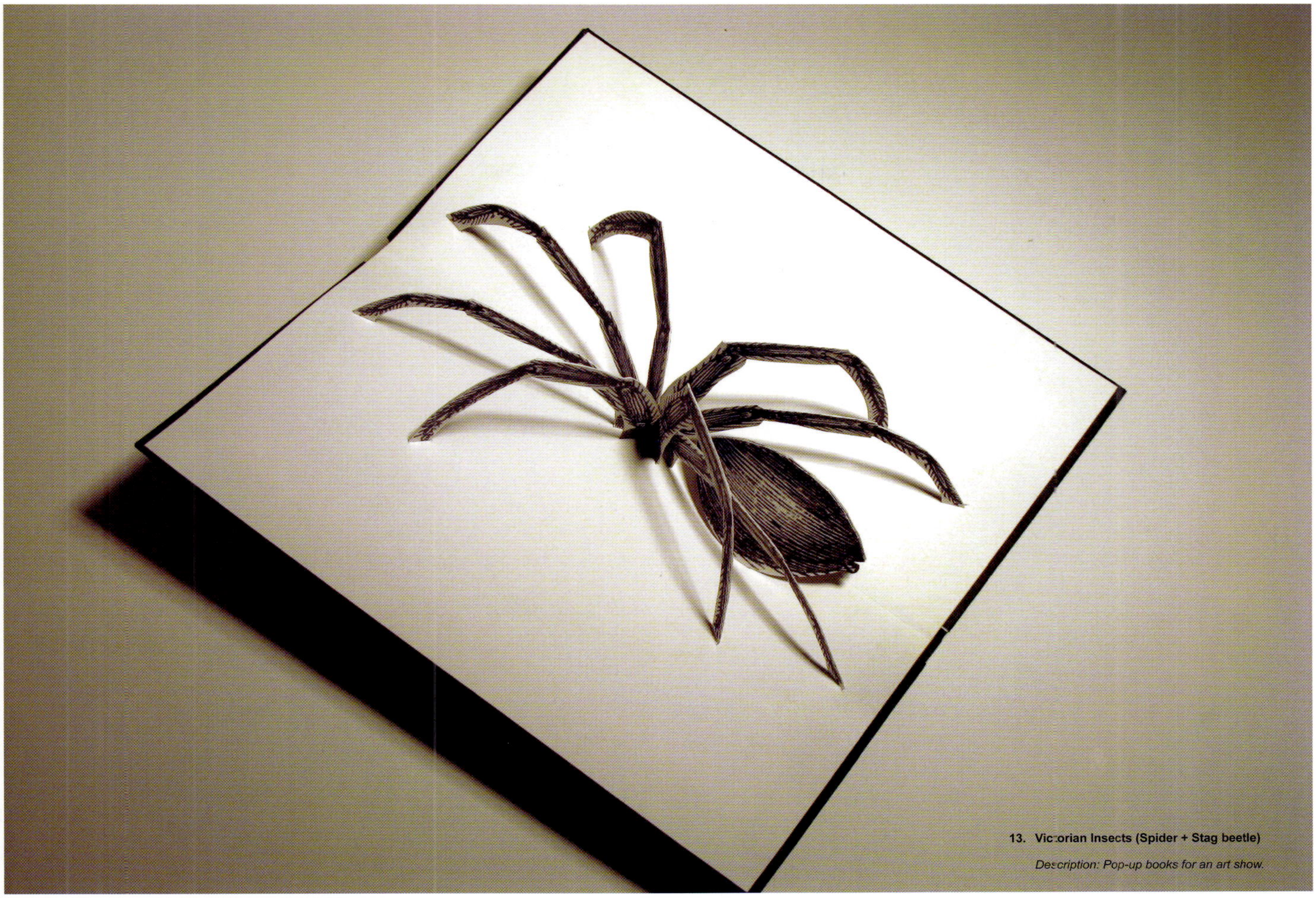

13. Victorian Insects (Spider + Stag beetle)
Description: Pop-up books for an art show.

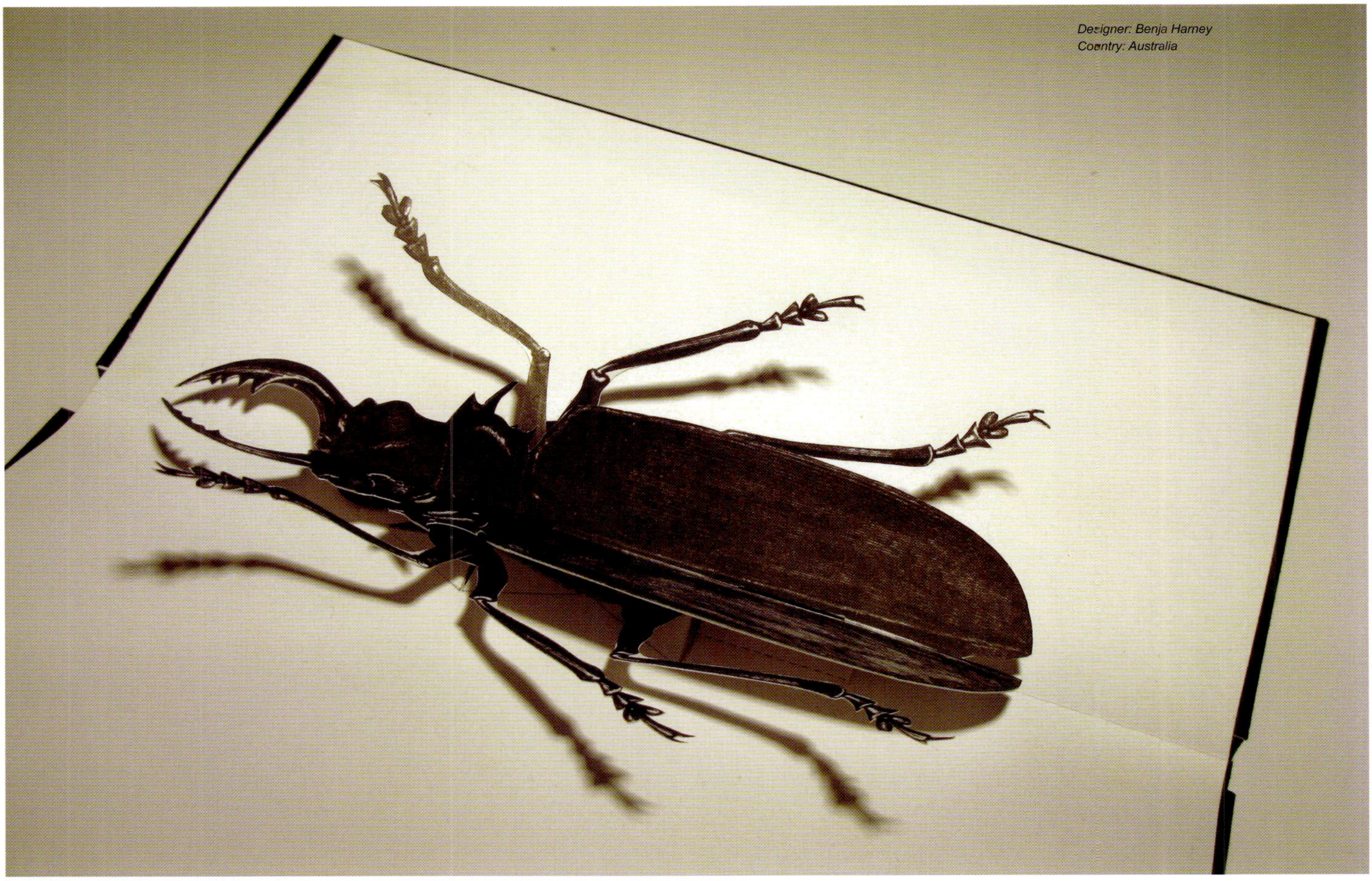

Designer: Benja Harney
Country: Australia

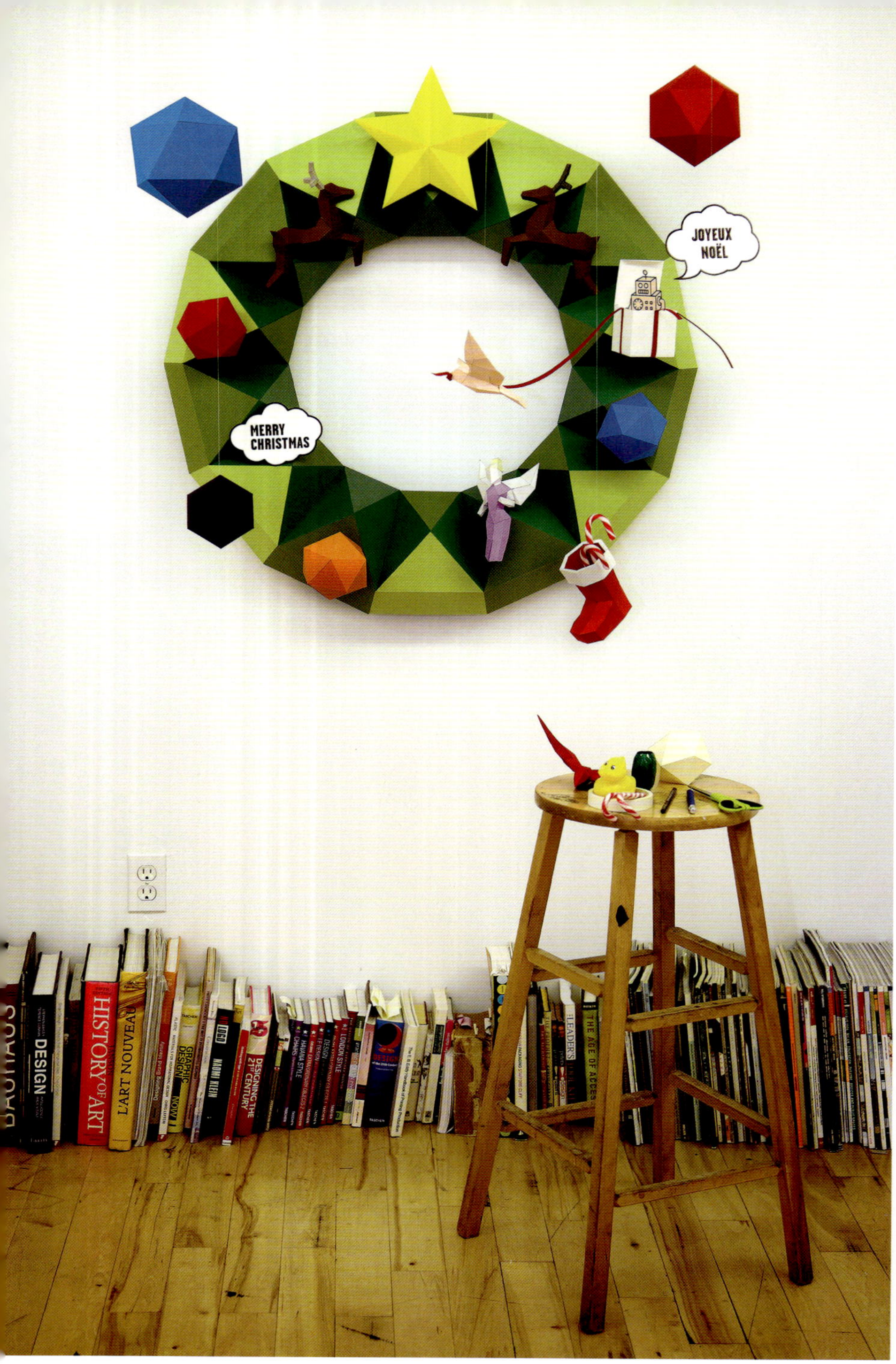

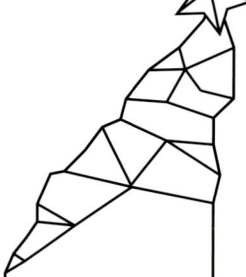

1. **Chrsitmas Wreath**

    This unique Christmas wreath was created as a greeting card, to send wishes to family, friends and colleagues. It was conceived digitally in 3d, and then handcrafted into a paper sculpture.

    --- Kyosuke Nishida
    Brian Li Sui Fong
    Dominic Liu

2. **Still Life Comes Alive**

    This piece was created and exhibited during the Concordia University Design program's end of year exhibition in 2010, in Montréal Canada.

    --- Kyosuke Nishida
    Brian Li Sui Fong
    Sean Yendrys
    Dominic Liu
    Stefan Spec
    Duc Tran

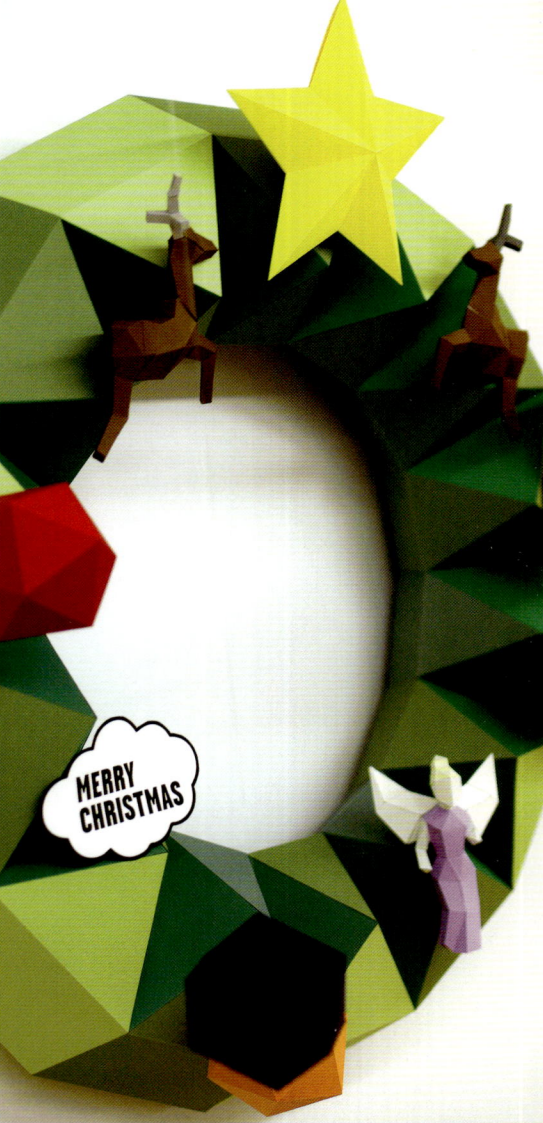

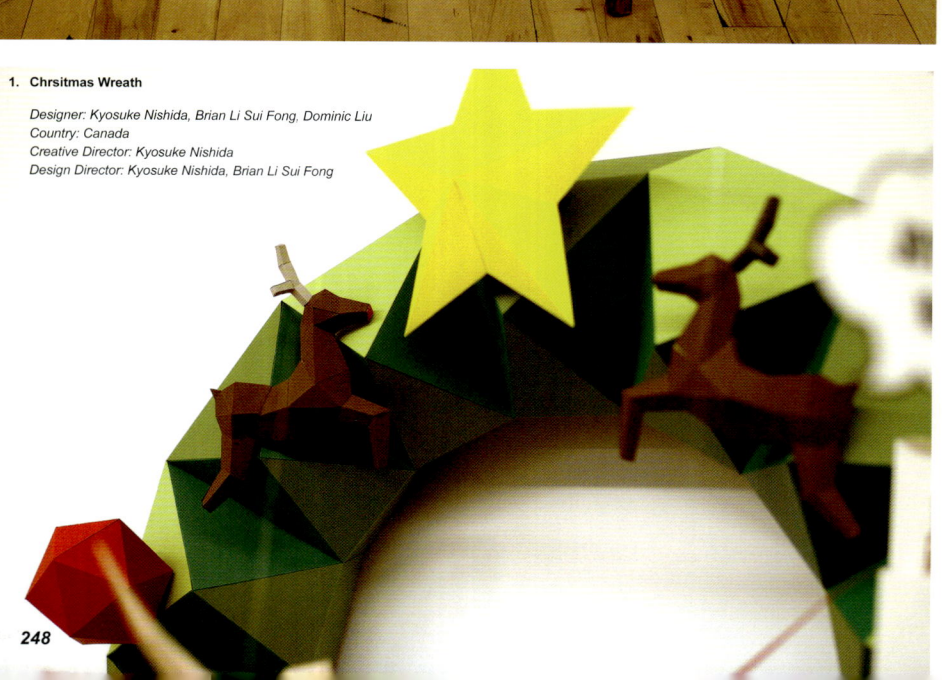

1. **Chrsitmas Wreath**

Designer: Kyosuke Nishida, Brian Li Sui Fong, Dominic Liu
Country: Canada
Creative Director: Kyosuke Nishida
Design Director: Kyosuke Nishida, Brian Li Sui Fong

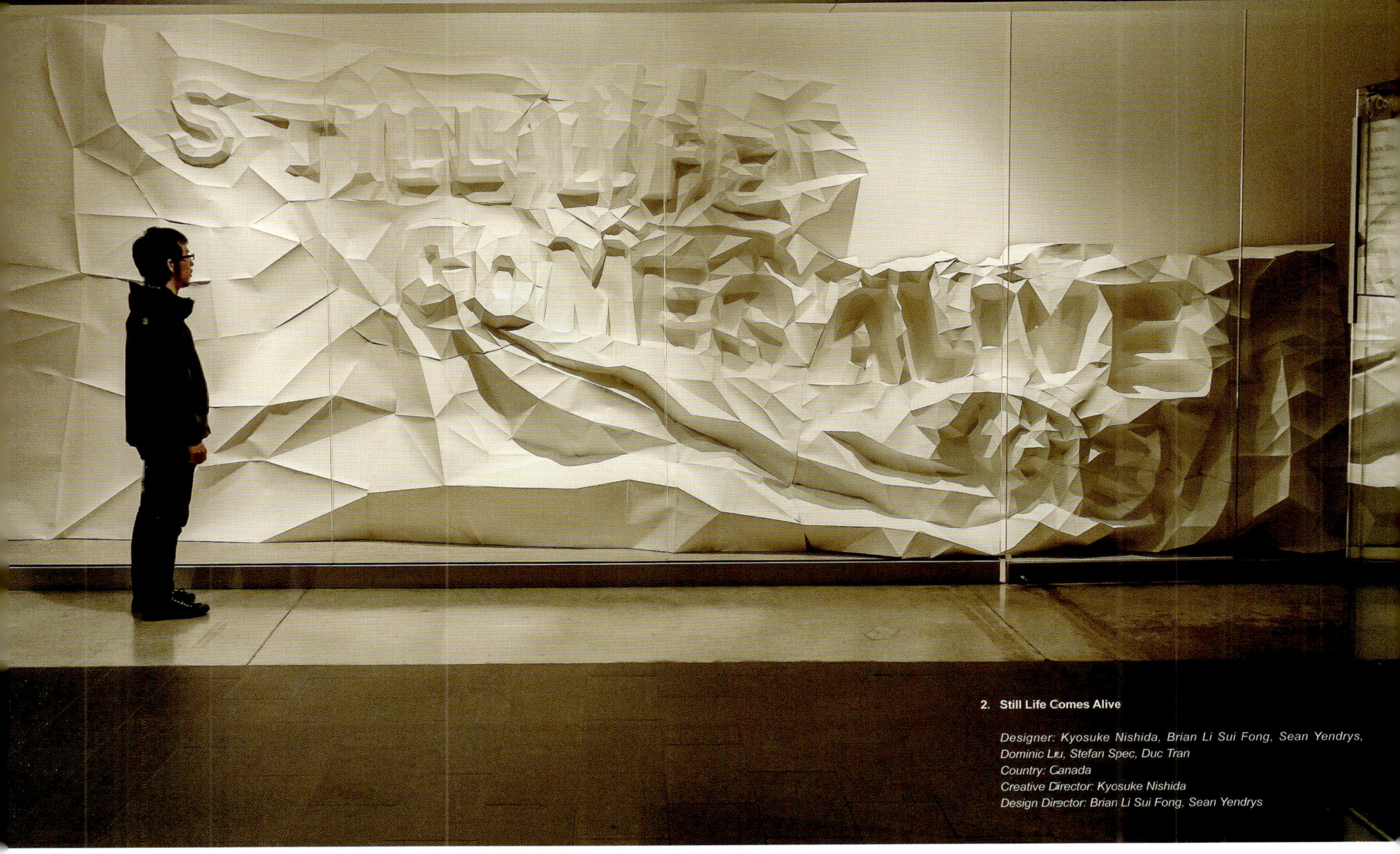

2. Still Life Comes Alive

Designer: Kyosuke Nishida, Brian Li Sui Fong, Sean Yendrys, Dominic Liu, Stefan Spec, Duc Tran
Country: Canada
Creative Director: Kyosuke Nishida
Design Director: Brian Li Sui Fong, Sean Yendrys

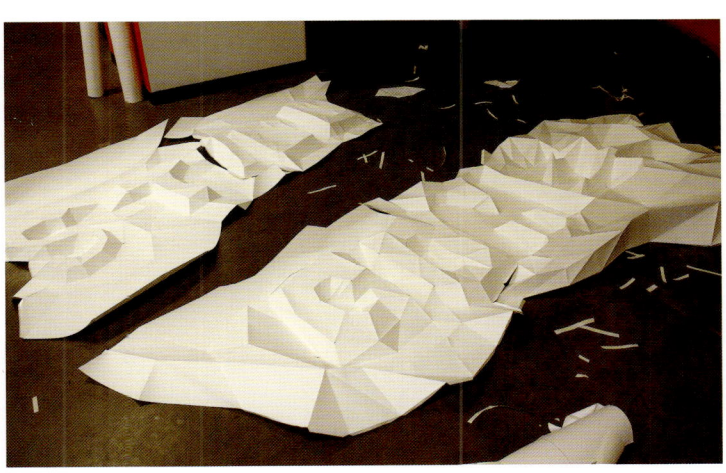
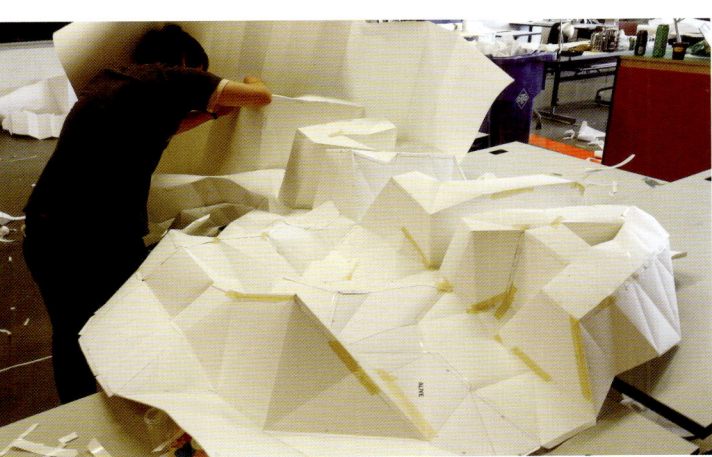
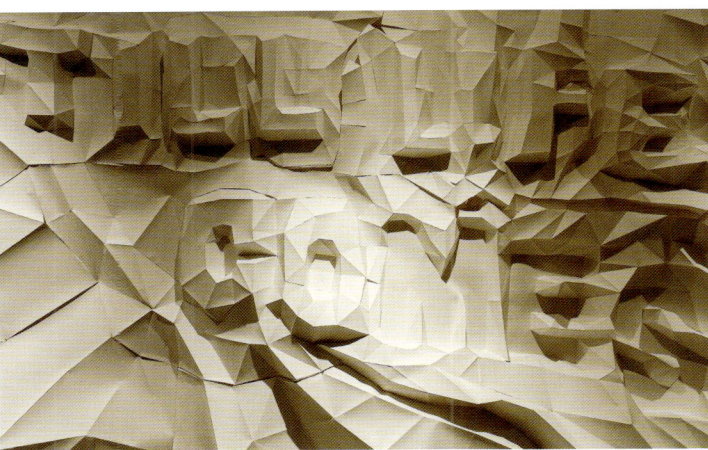
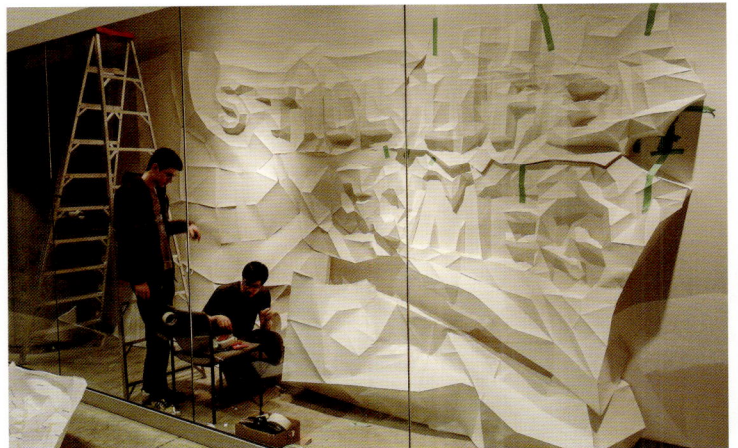

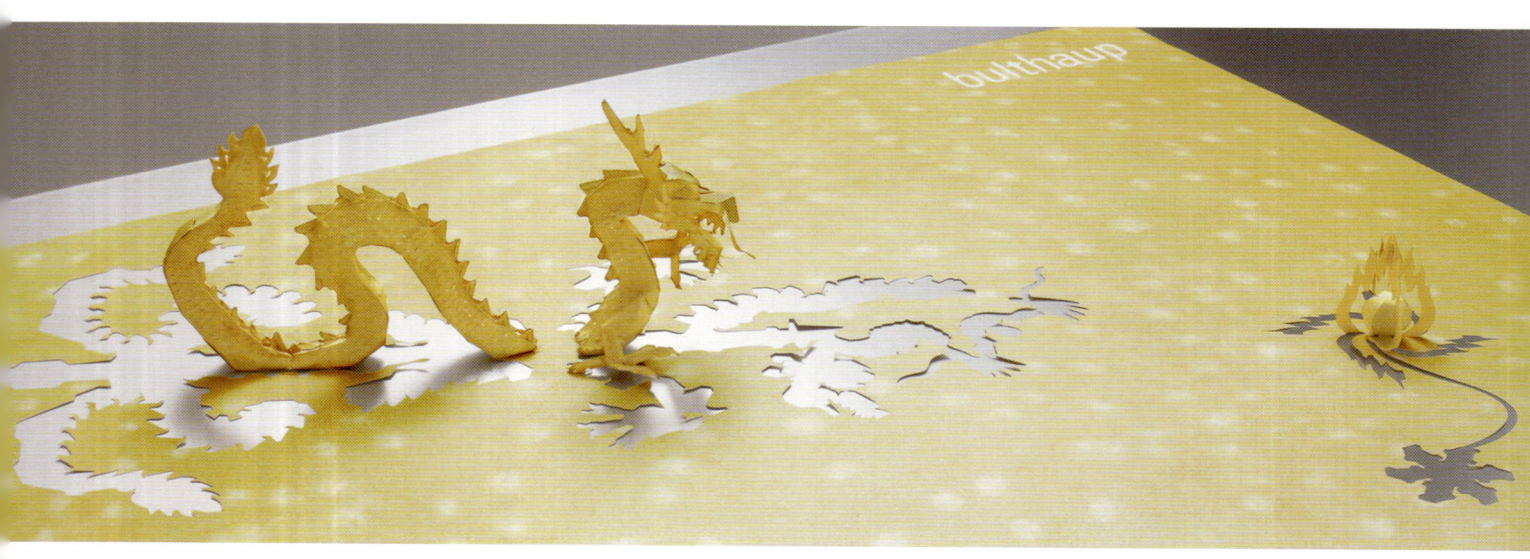

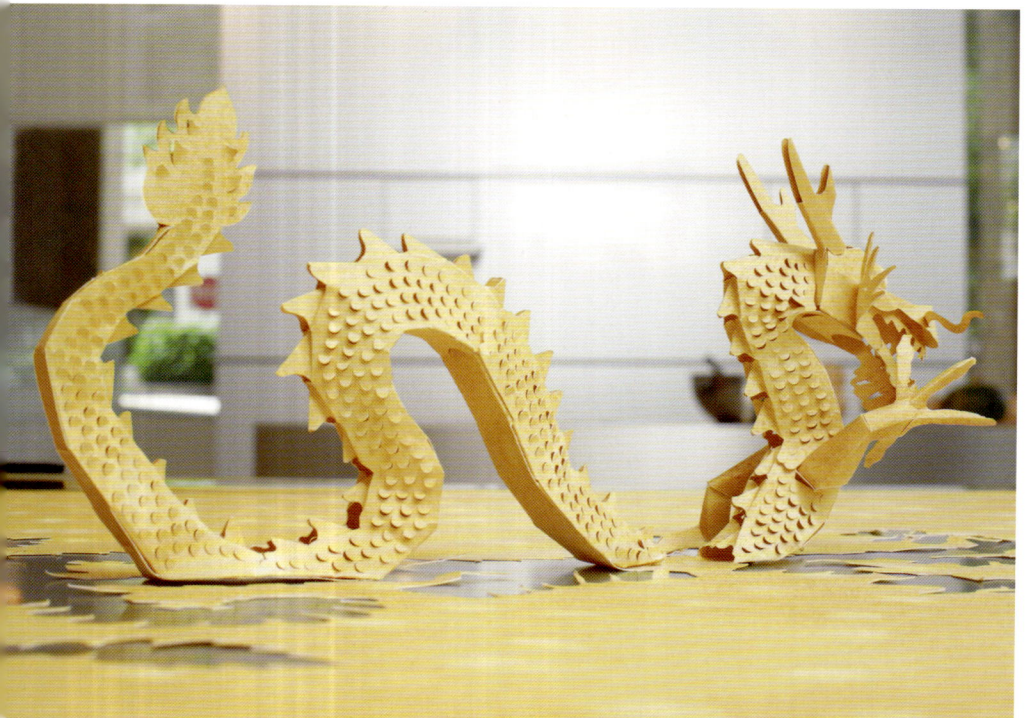

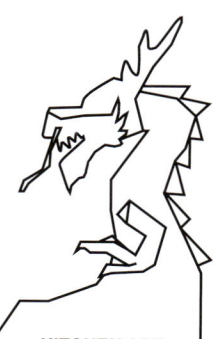

KITCHEN ART

By exhibiting a series of intricate art, Potato Koi, Cucumber Crane & Pear Dragon, in the showroom, bulthaup demonstrates how the precision of their knives elevates everyday food preparation to a whole new level of artistry.

---Chan Hwee Chong

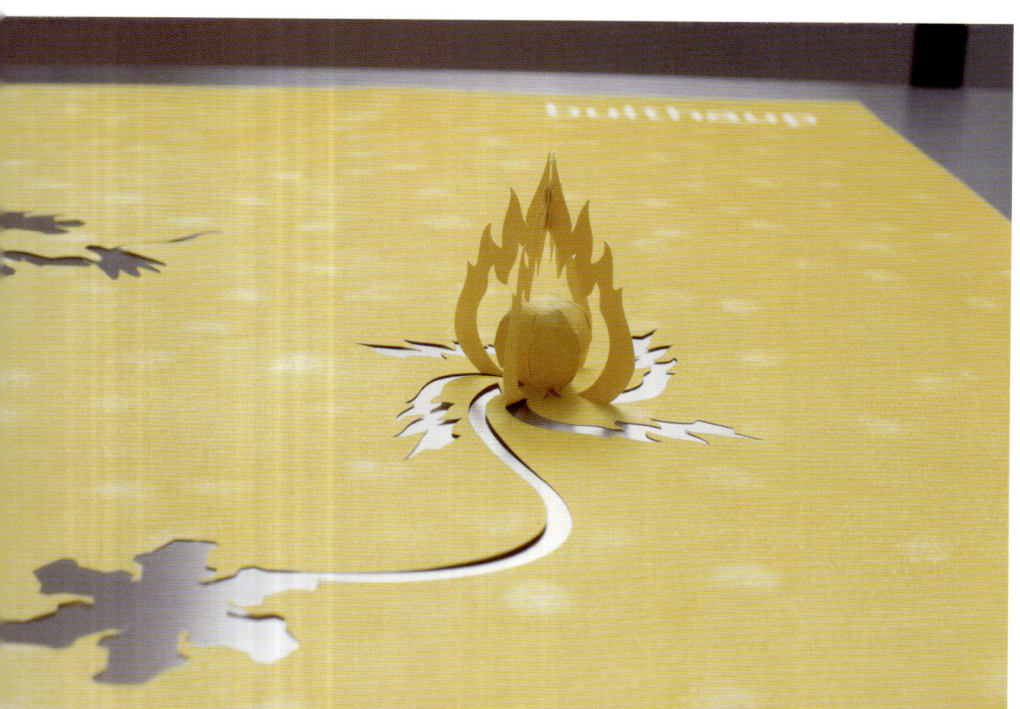

Design Agency: Ogilvy & Mather
Country: Singapore
Executive Creative Director: Todd McCracken
Creative Director: Eric Yeo
Art Director: Kat Tan, Chan Hwee Chong
Client: Bulthaup
Photographer: Teo Chai Guan
Copywriter: Serene Loong
Paper Sculptor: Rei

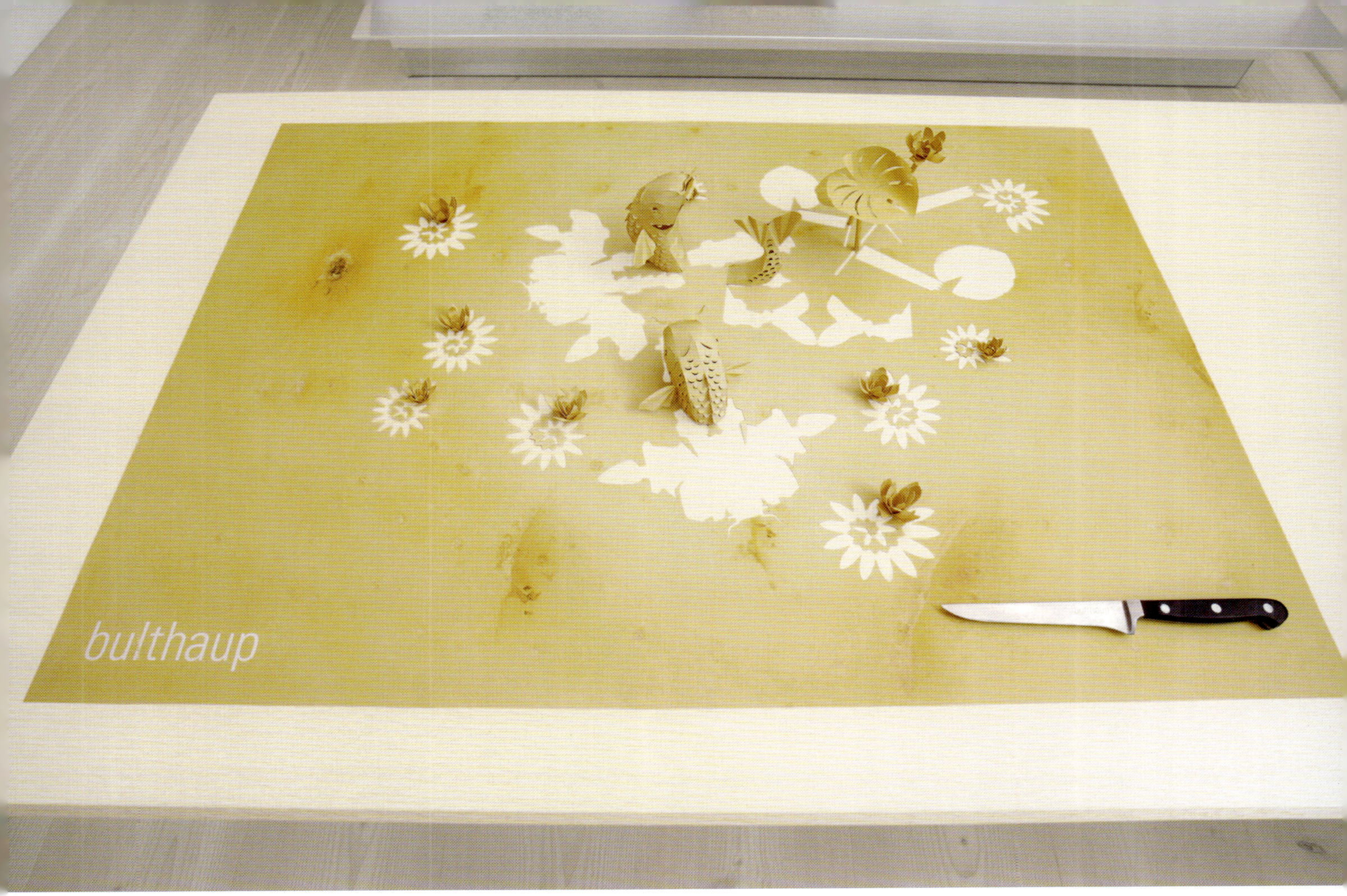

bulthaup

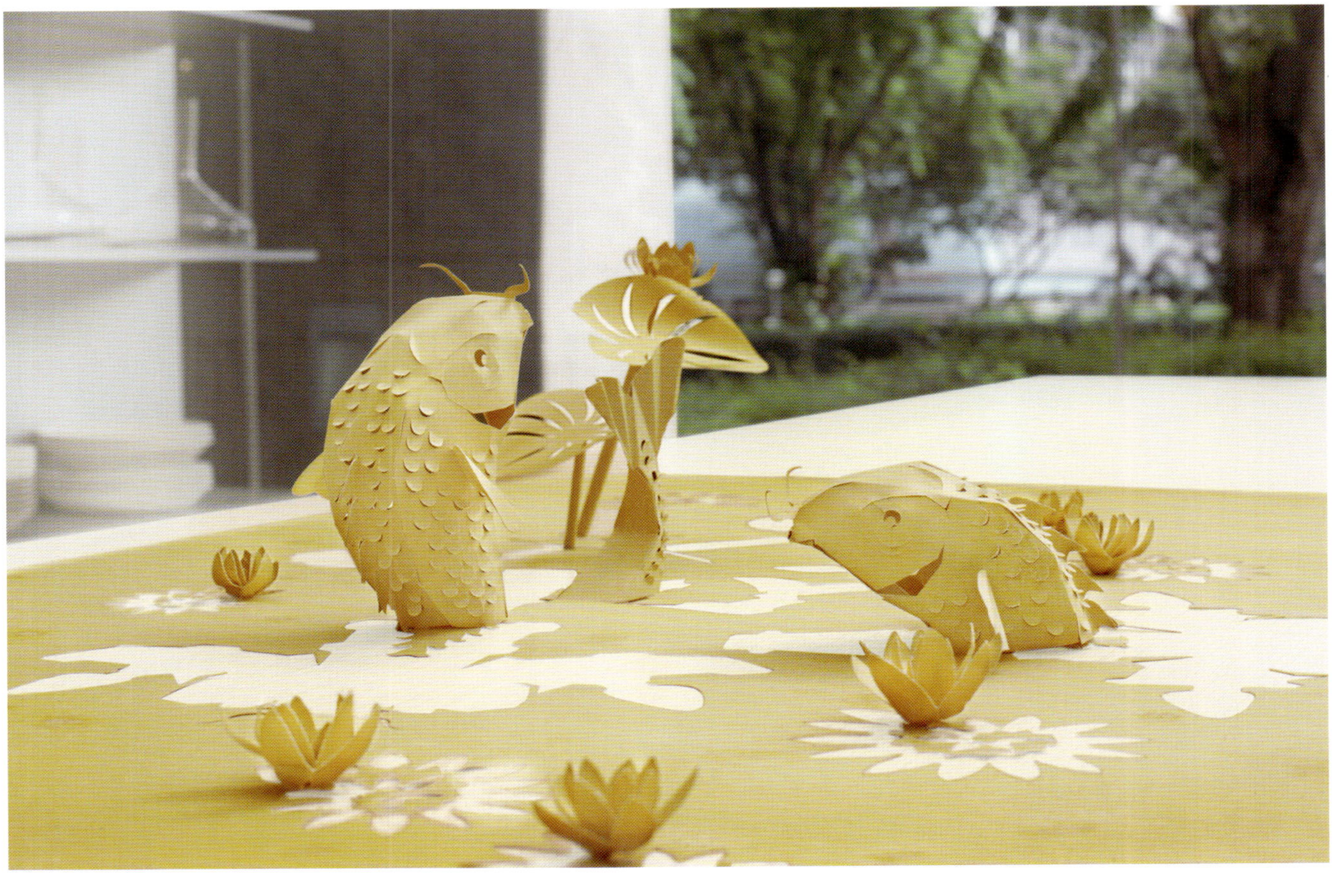

Design Agency: Ogilvy & Mather
Country: Singapore
Executive Creative Director: Todd McCracken
Creative Director: Eric Yeo
Art Director: Kat Tan, Chan Hwee Chong
Client: Bulthaup
Photographer: Teo Chai Guan
Copywriter: Serene Loong
Paper Sculptor: Rei

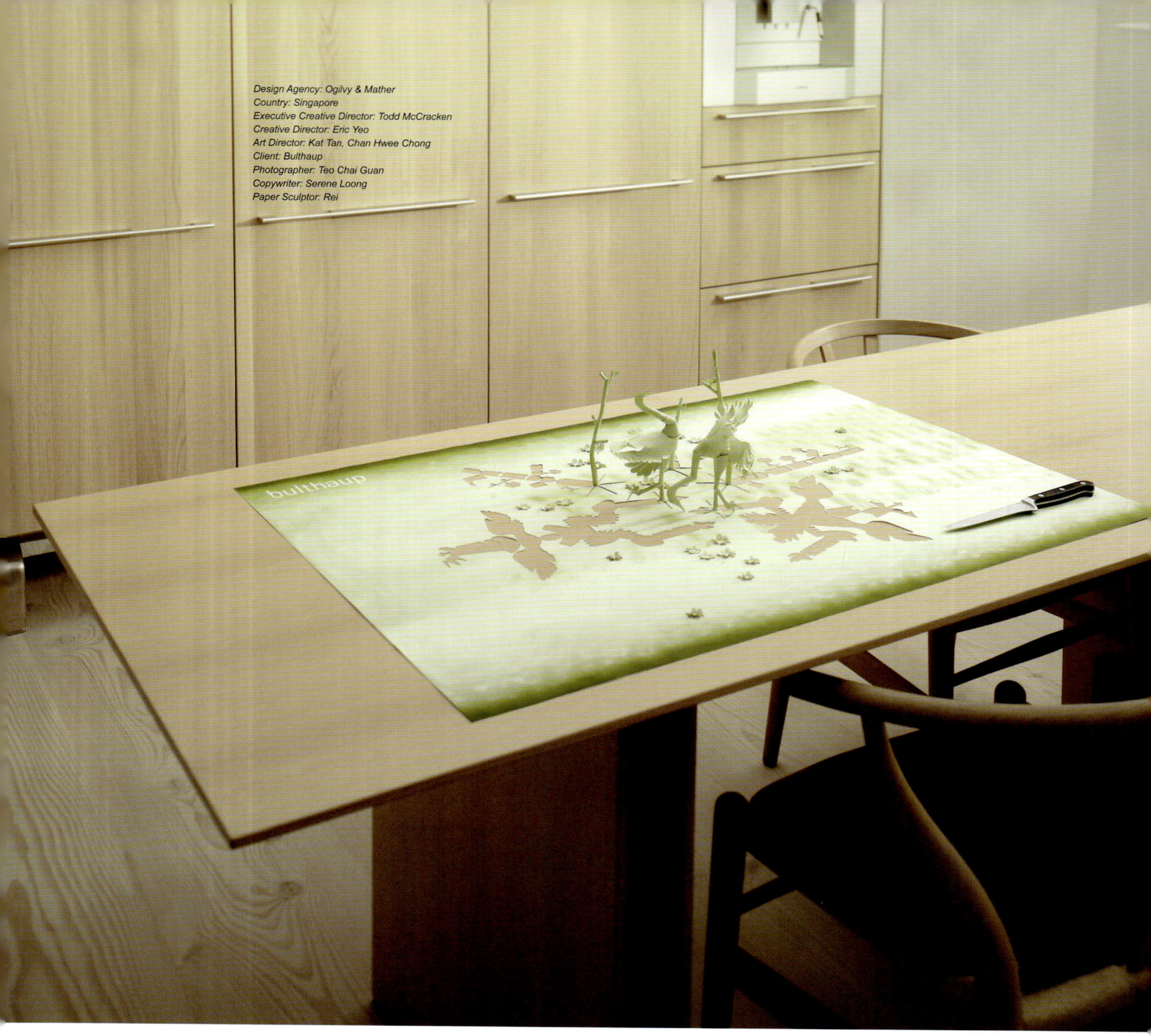

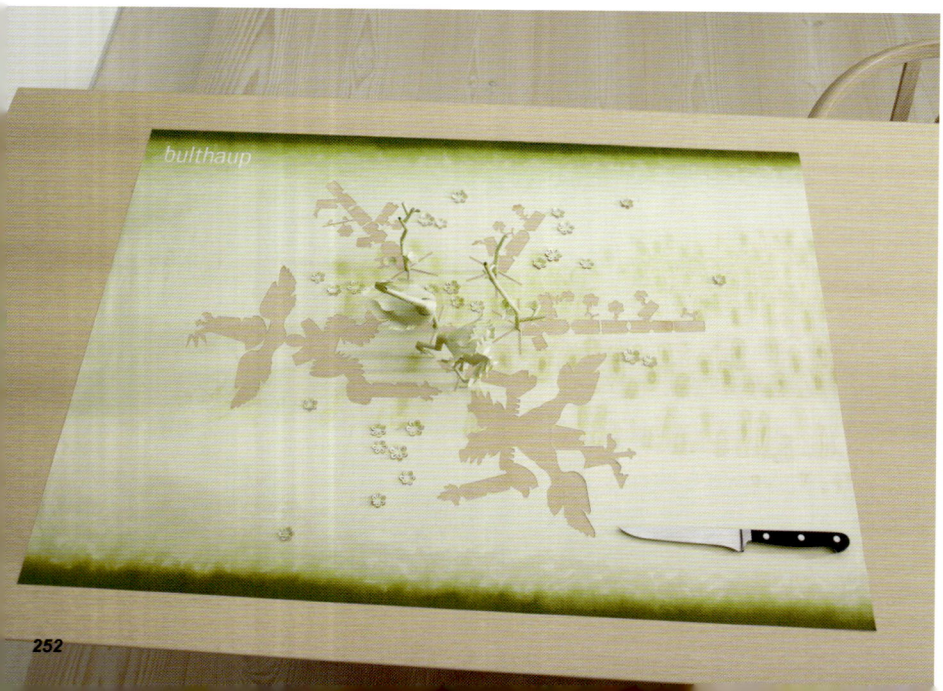
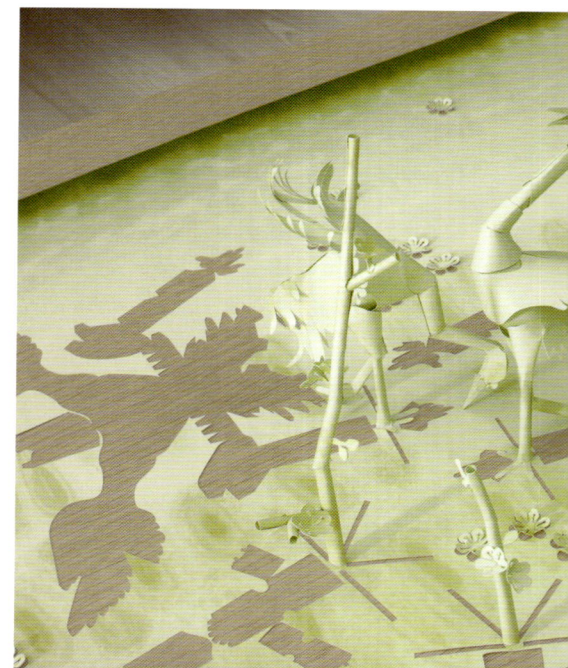

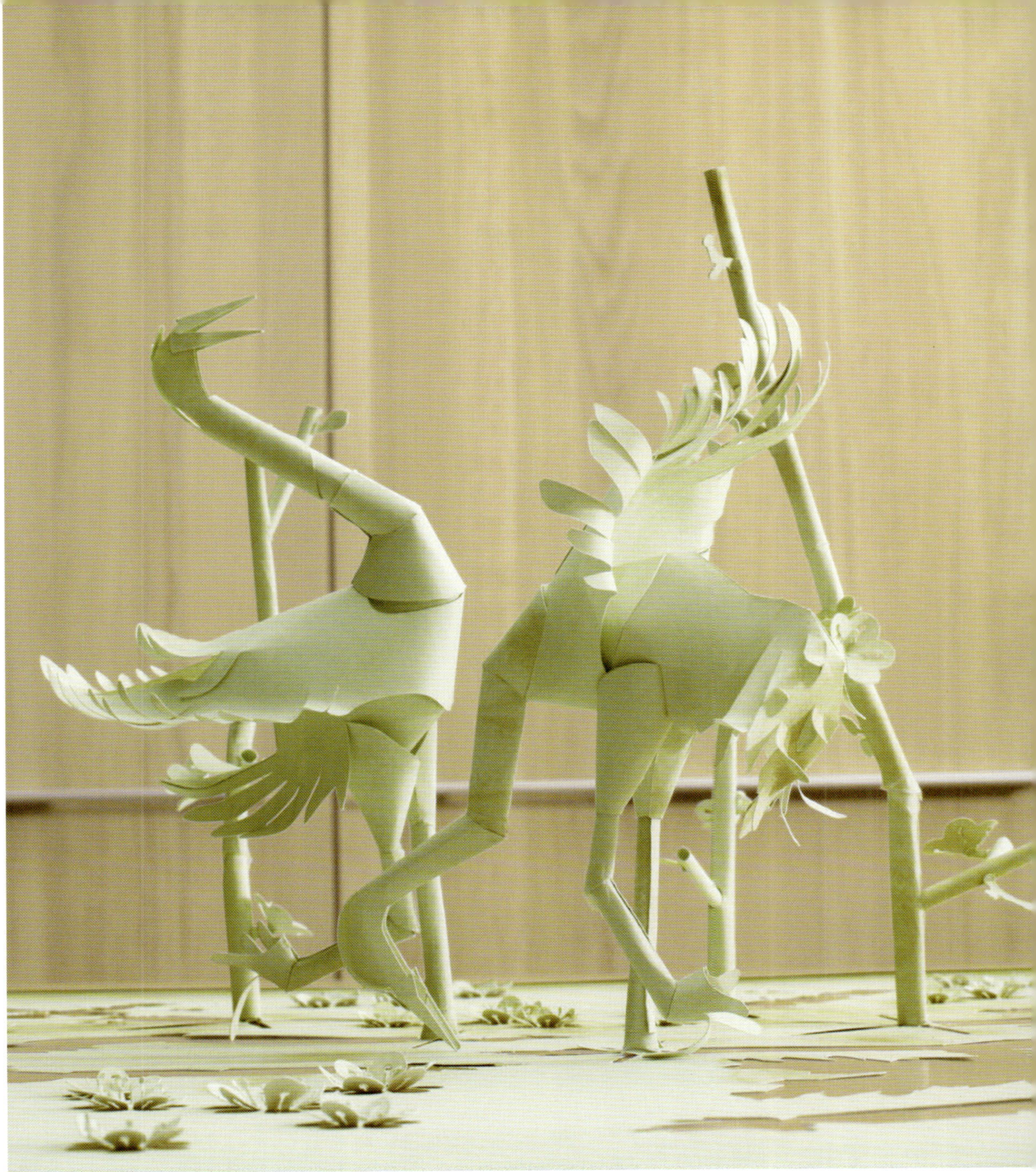

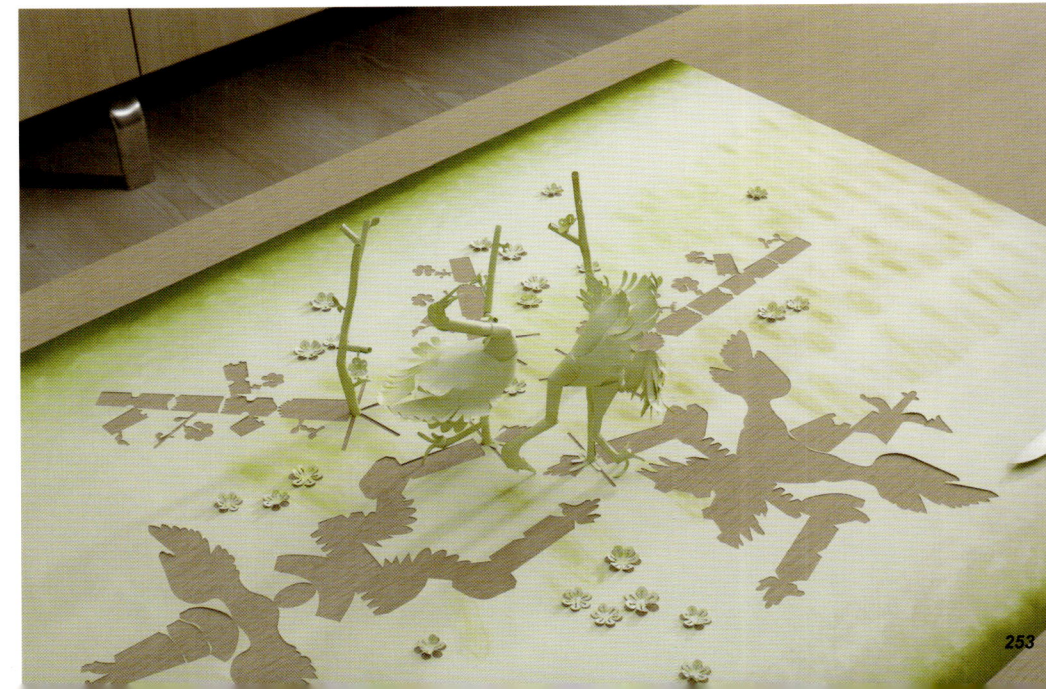
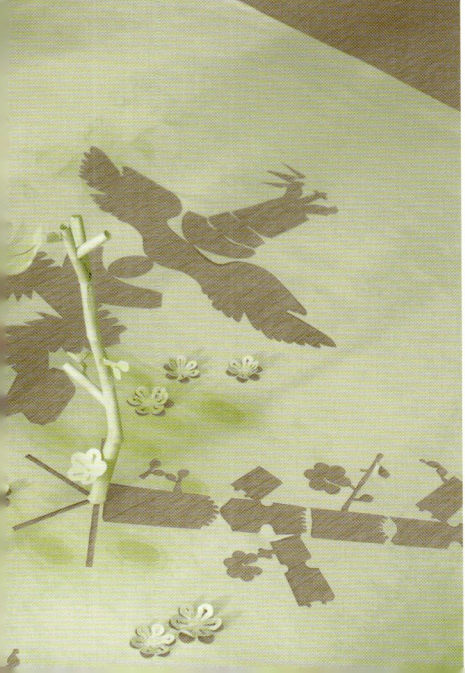

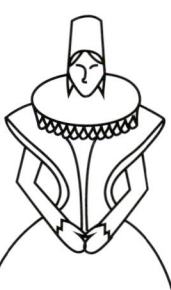

Dame di Cartone / Cardboard Ladies

Between two – and three-dimensional perception, a gallery of nine unique portraits ranging from Cubism to 17th Century and Fifties-era. Neither paper dolls nor real women: just pensive, emerging figures.

---Christian Tagliavini

Designer: Christian Tagliavini
Country: Switzerland
Photographer: Christian Tagliavini

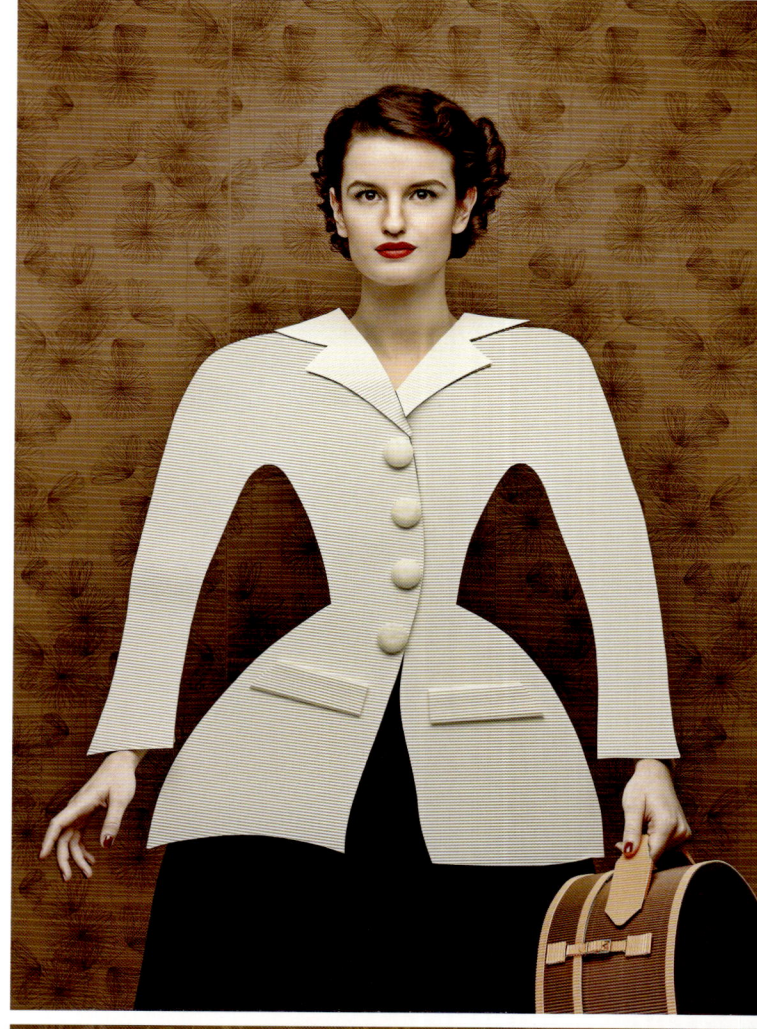

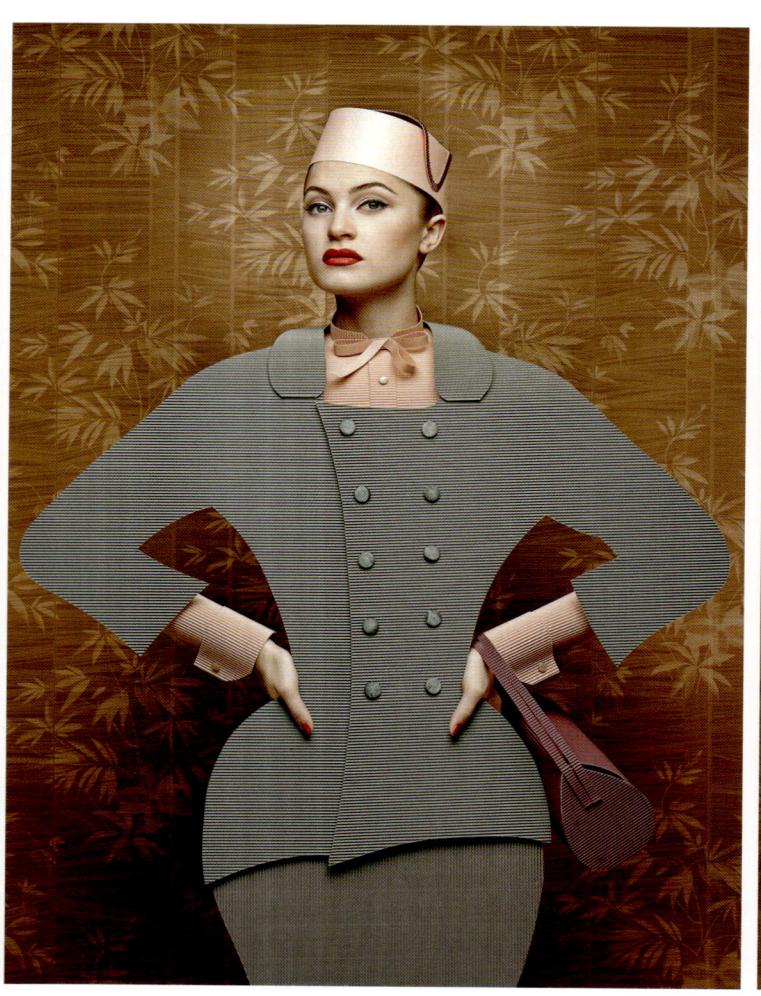

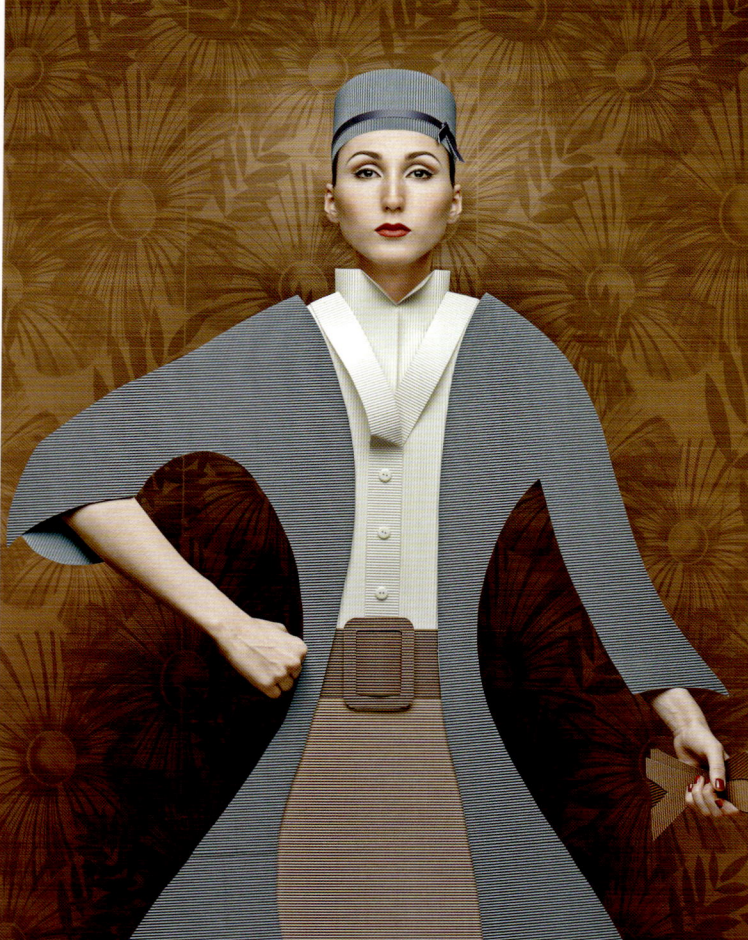

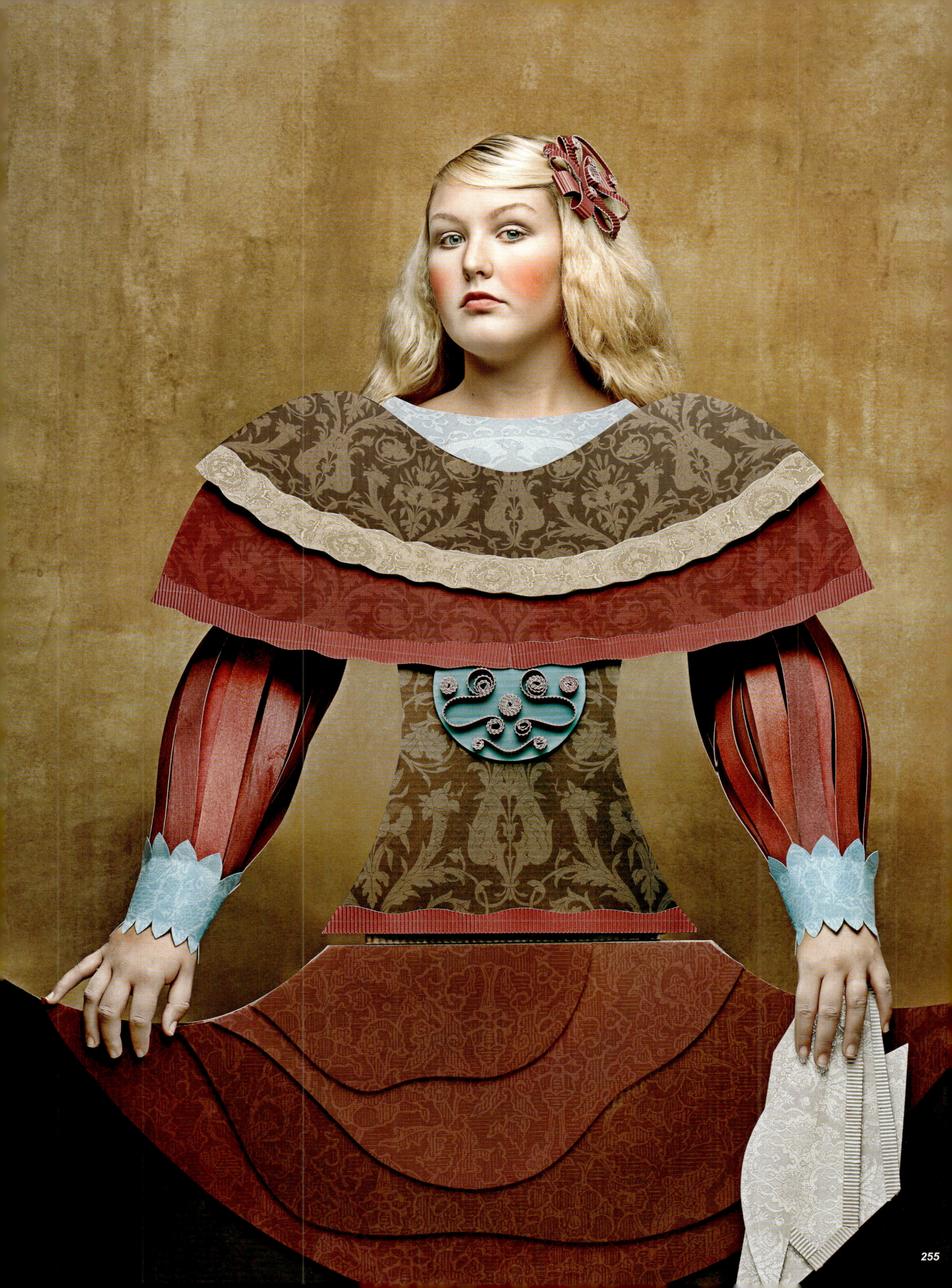

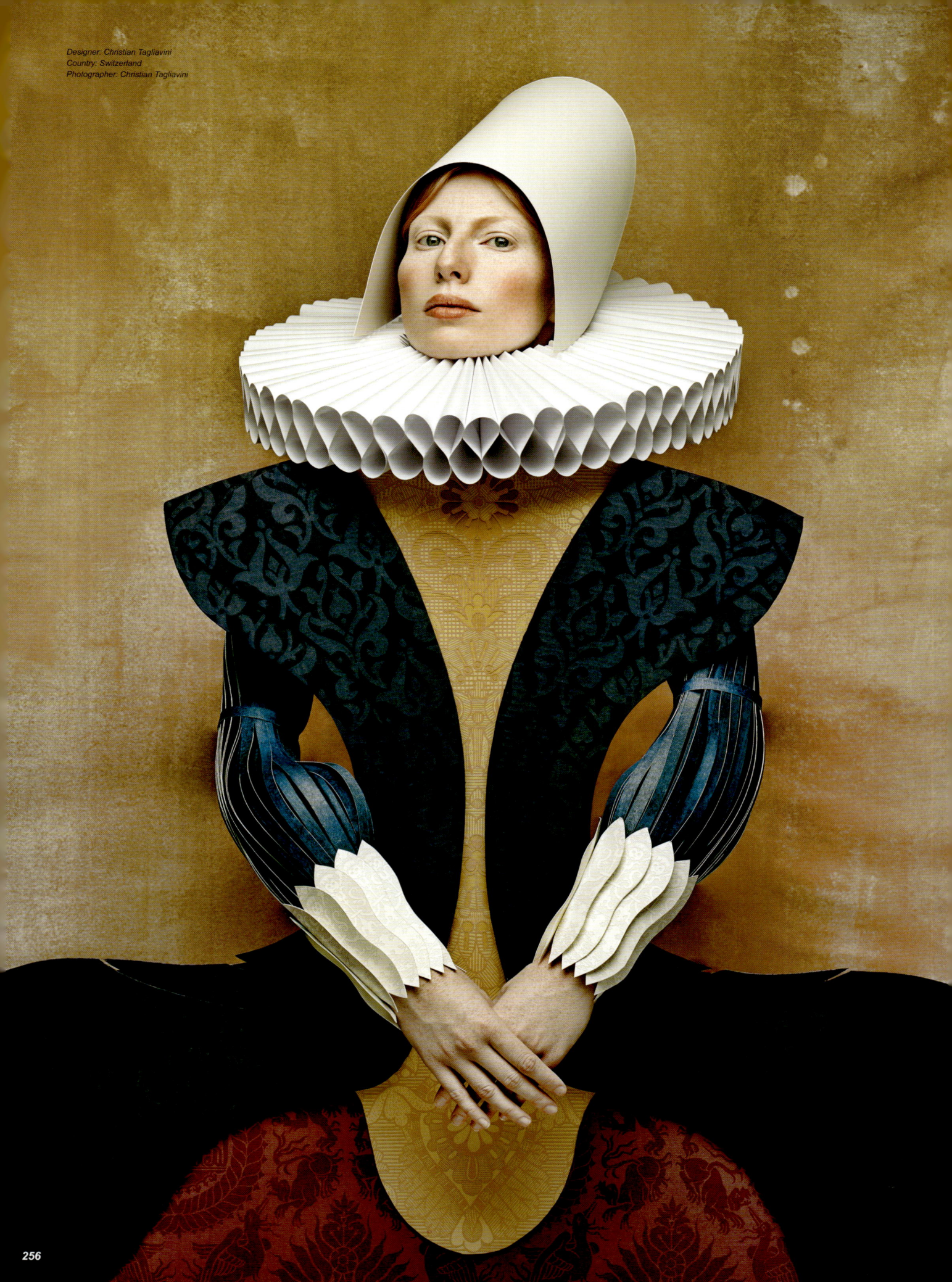

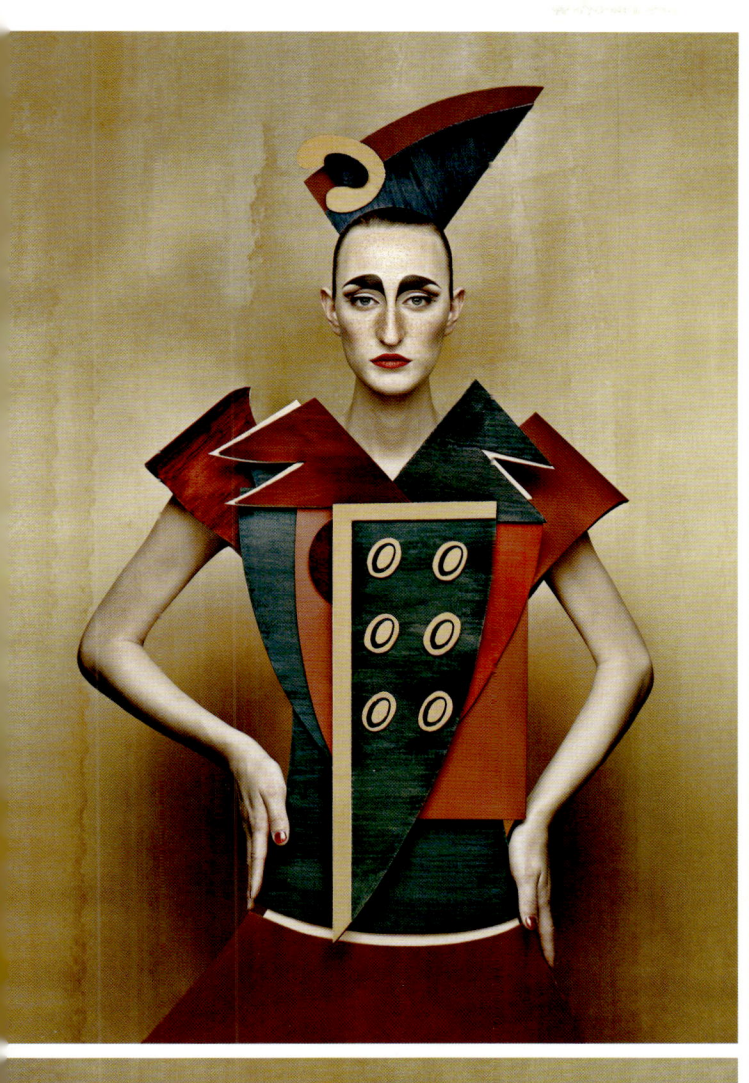
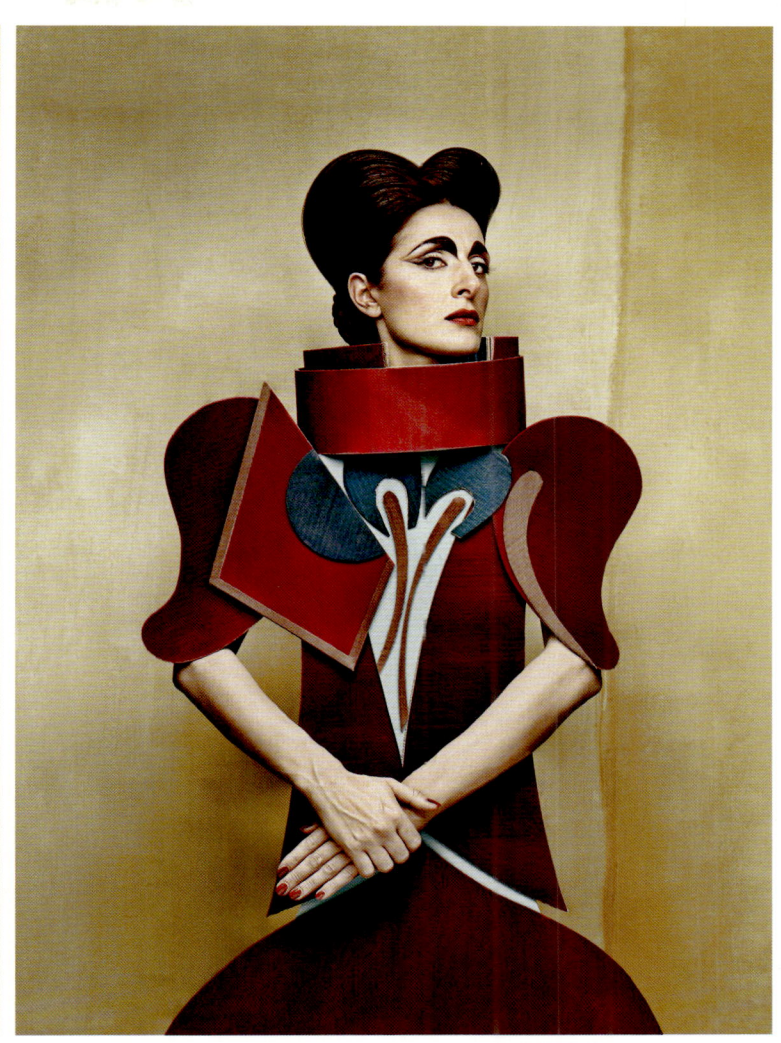
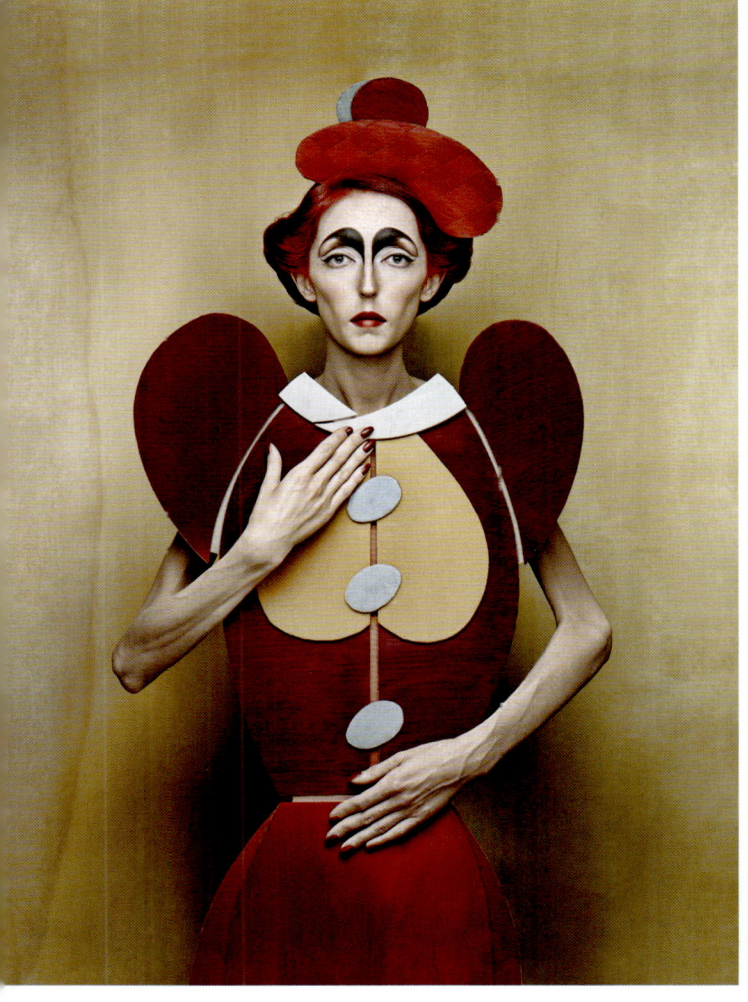
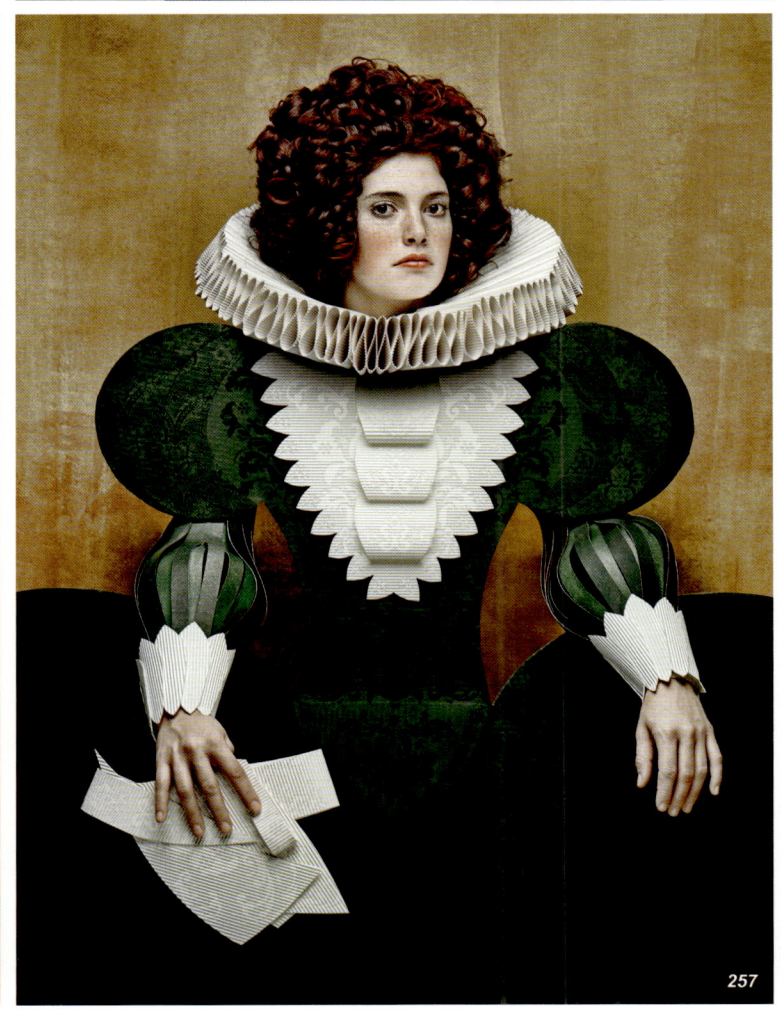

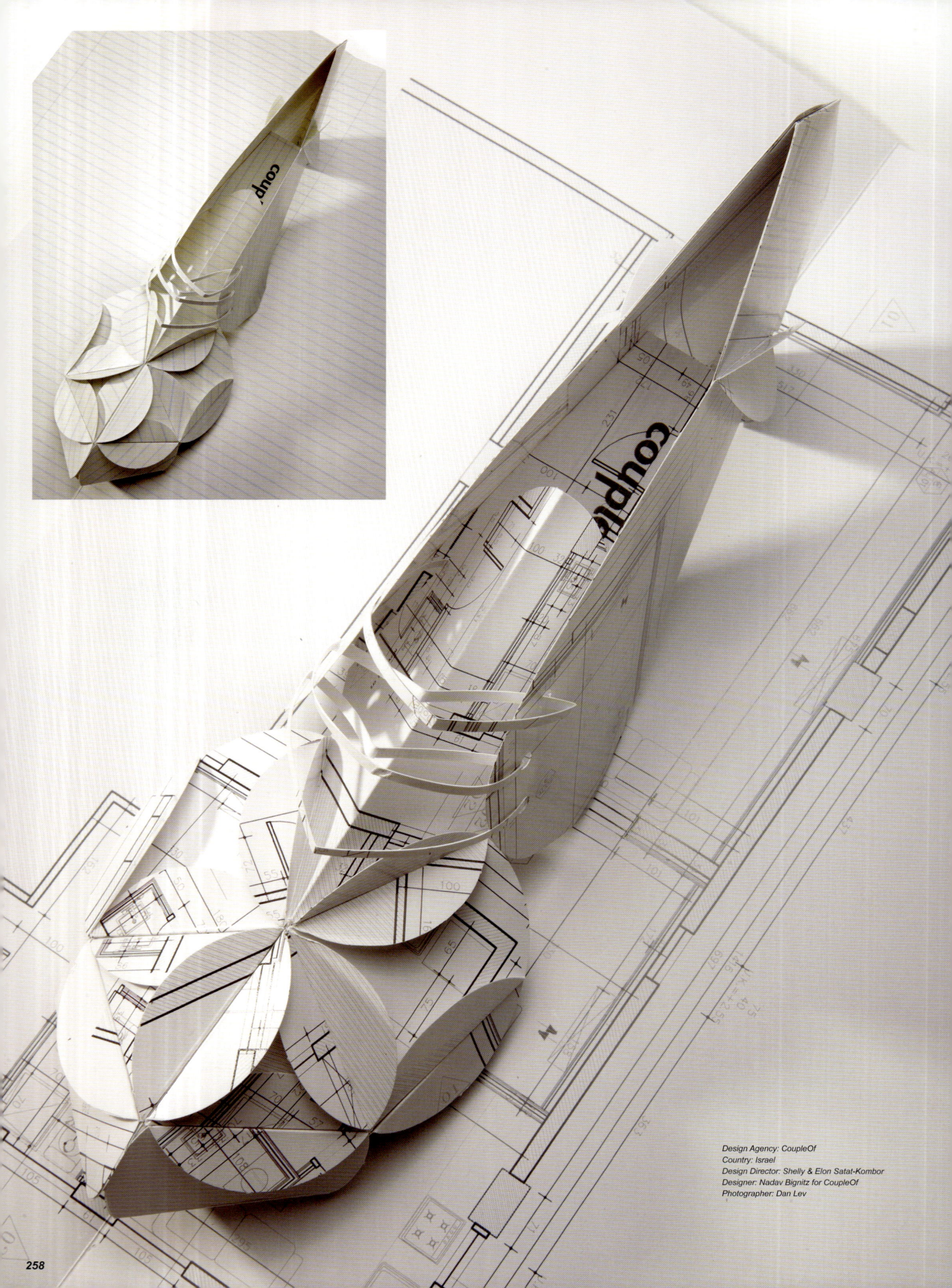

Design Agency: CoupleOf
Country: Israel
Design Director: Shelly & Elon Satat-Kombor
Designer: Nadav Bignitz for CoupleOf
Photographer: Dan Lev

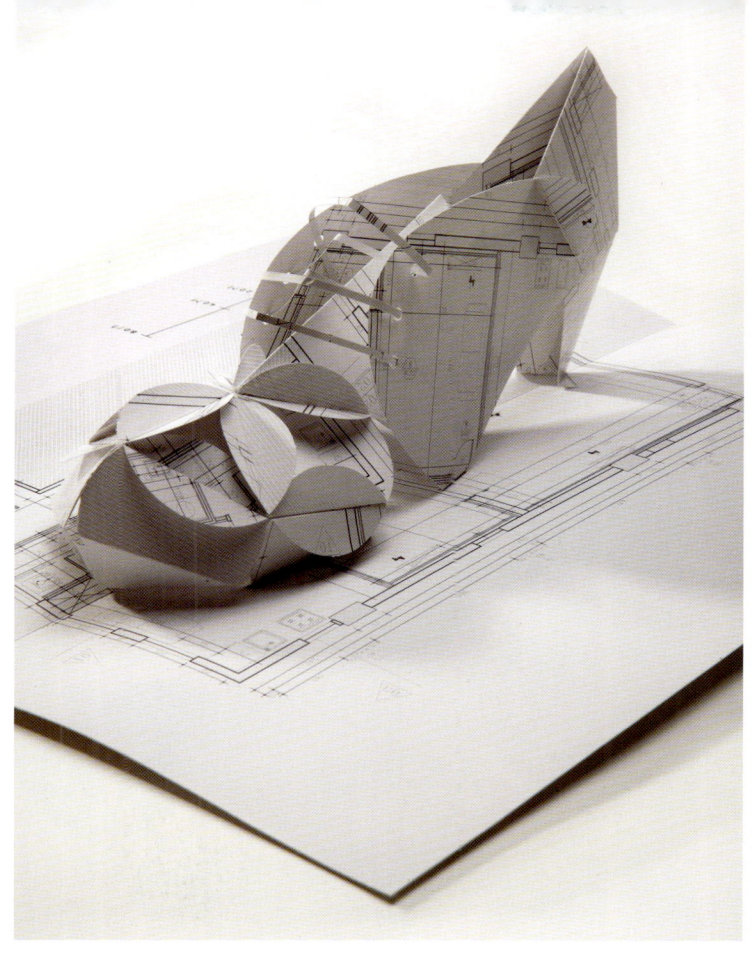
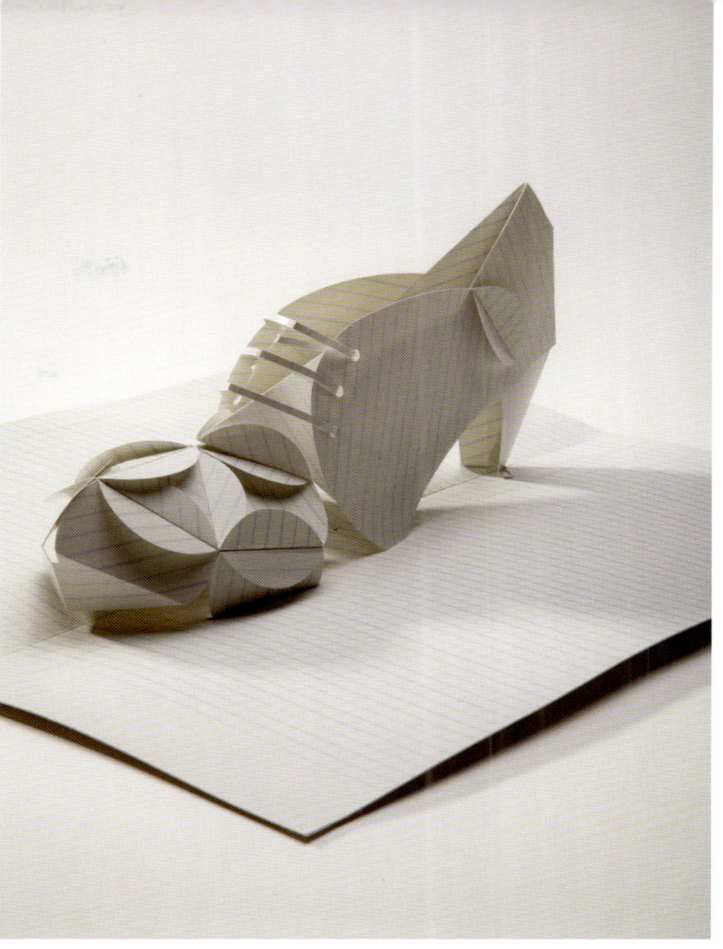
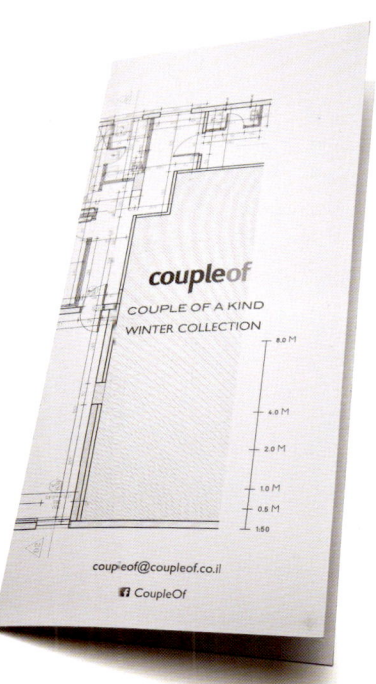
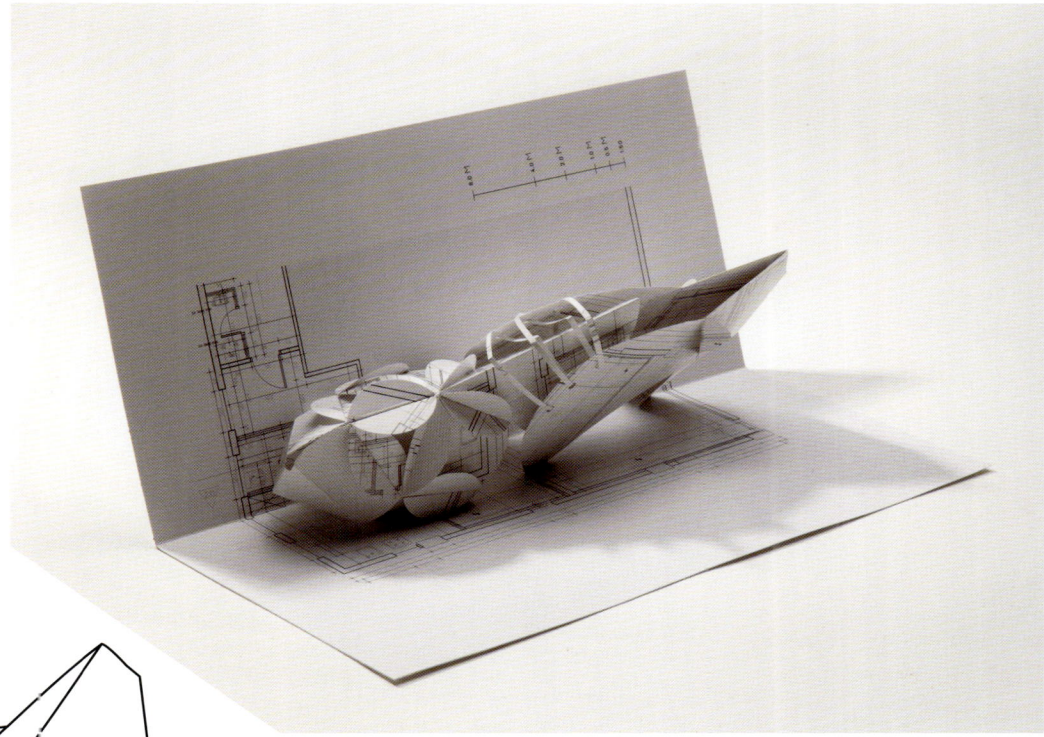

Pop Up Lily Shoe

CoupleOf, the Israeli based shoe brand, continues its dialog with different art disciplines.
This season, next to the brands shoe collection, you can find real size paper works by Nadav Bignitz; Architect and part of art group 'Team etc'.
Nadav created his Pop-Up version, paper folds opening into the CoupleOf 'Lily' laced shoe.
The technique of creating a paper Pop-Up is the opposite of traditional leather shoemaking. The flat paper is engineered in a complex pattern, becoming a surprising Pop-Up 3 dimensional shoe.
In the series three graphics; one is a typical school notebook, the second is an architectural plan, and the third is the desirable red shoe on the familiar Israeli sesame floor.

---CoupleOf

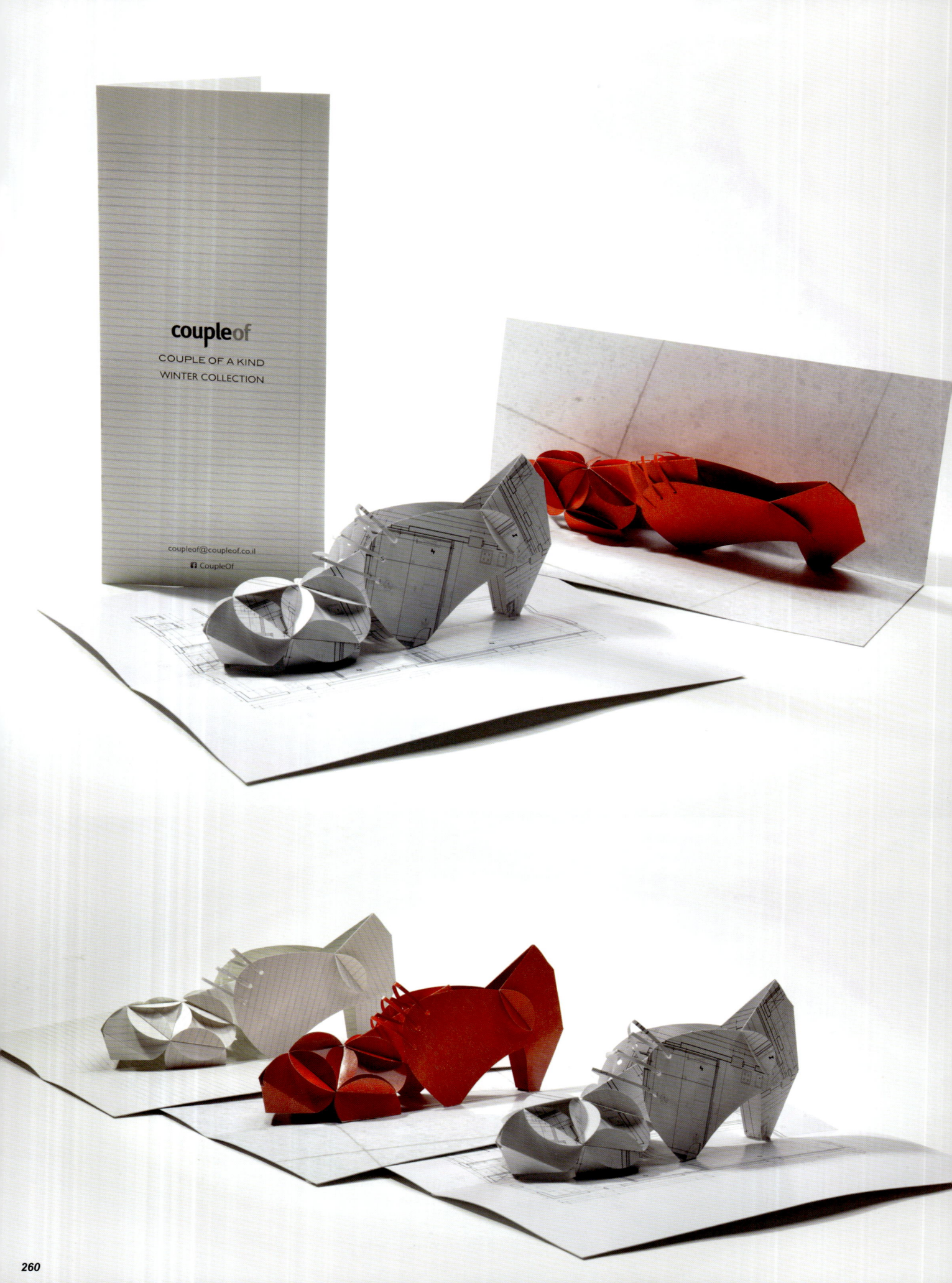

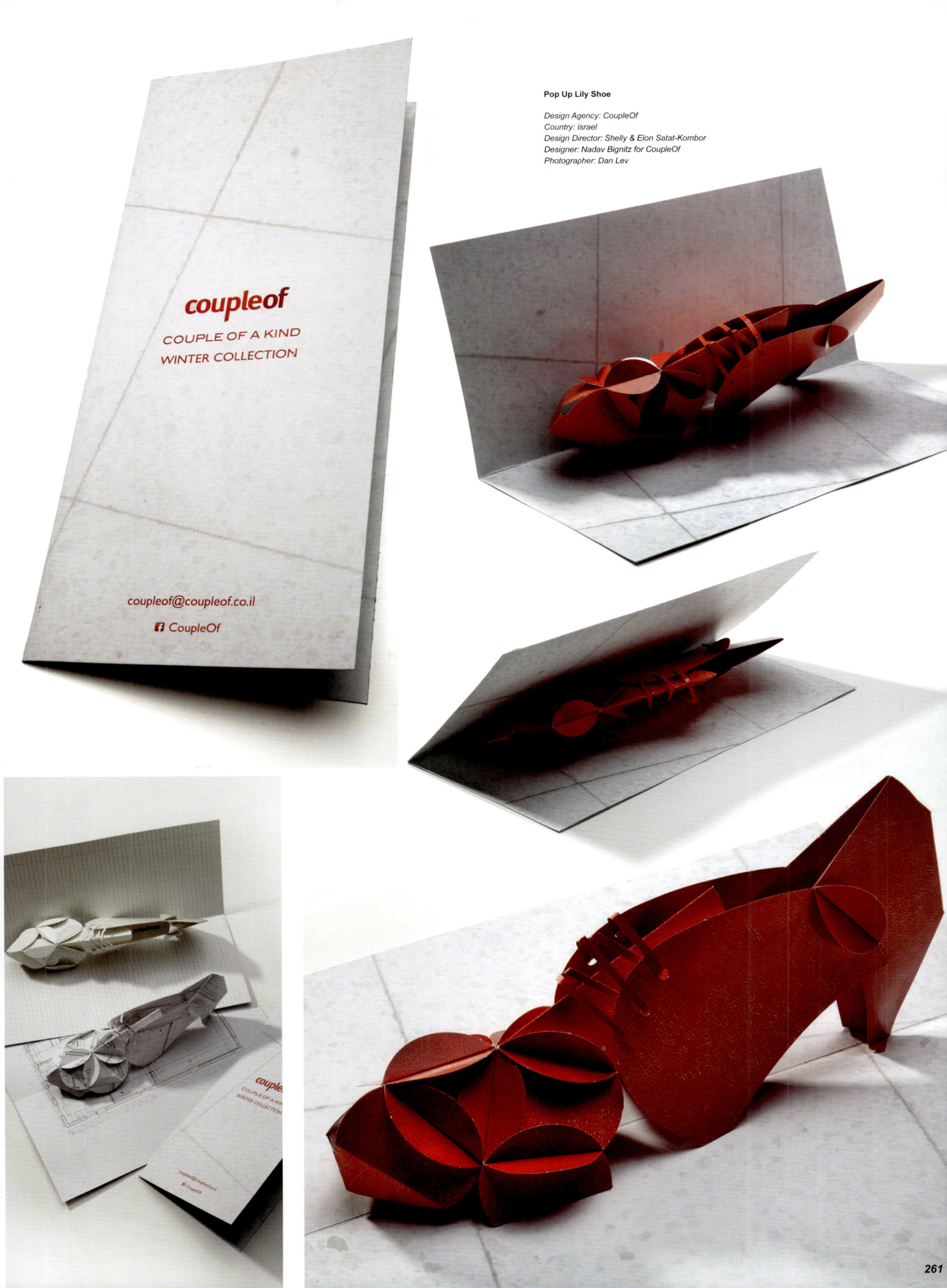

Pop Up Lily Shoe

Design Agency: CoupleOf
Country: Israel
Design Director: Shelly & Elon Satat-Kombor
Designer: Nadav Bignitz for CoupleOf
Photographer: Dan Lev

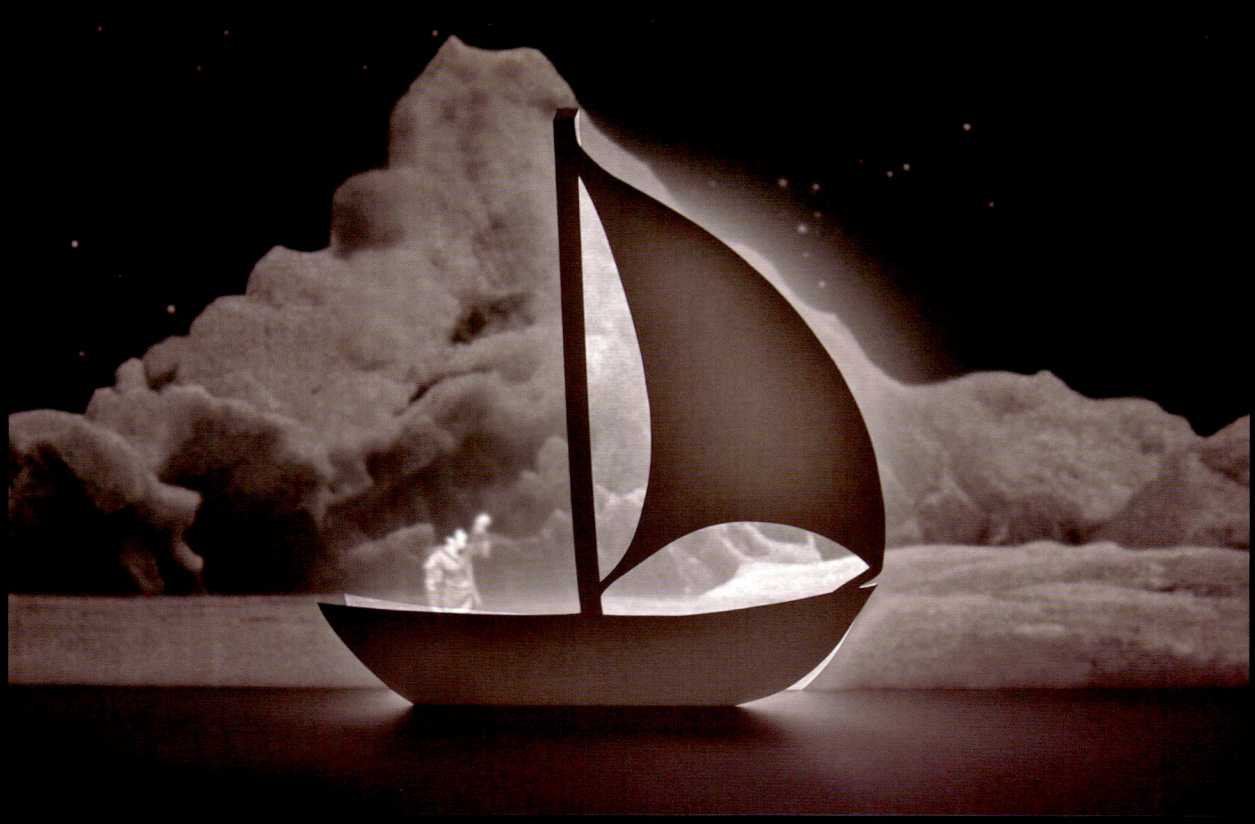

1. **The Icebook**

   Designer: Davy & Kristin McGuire
   Country: UK
   Photographer: Davy and Kristin McGuire

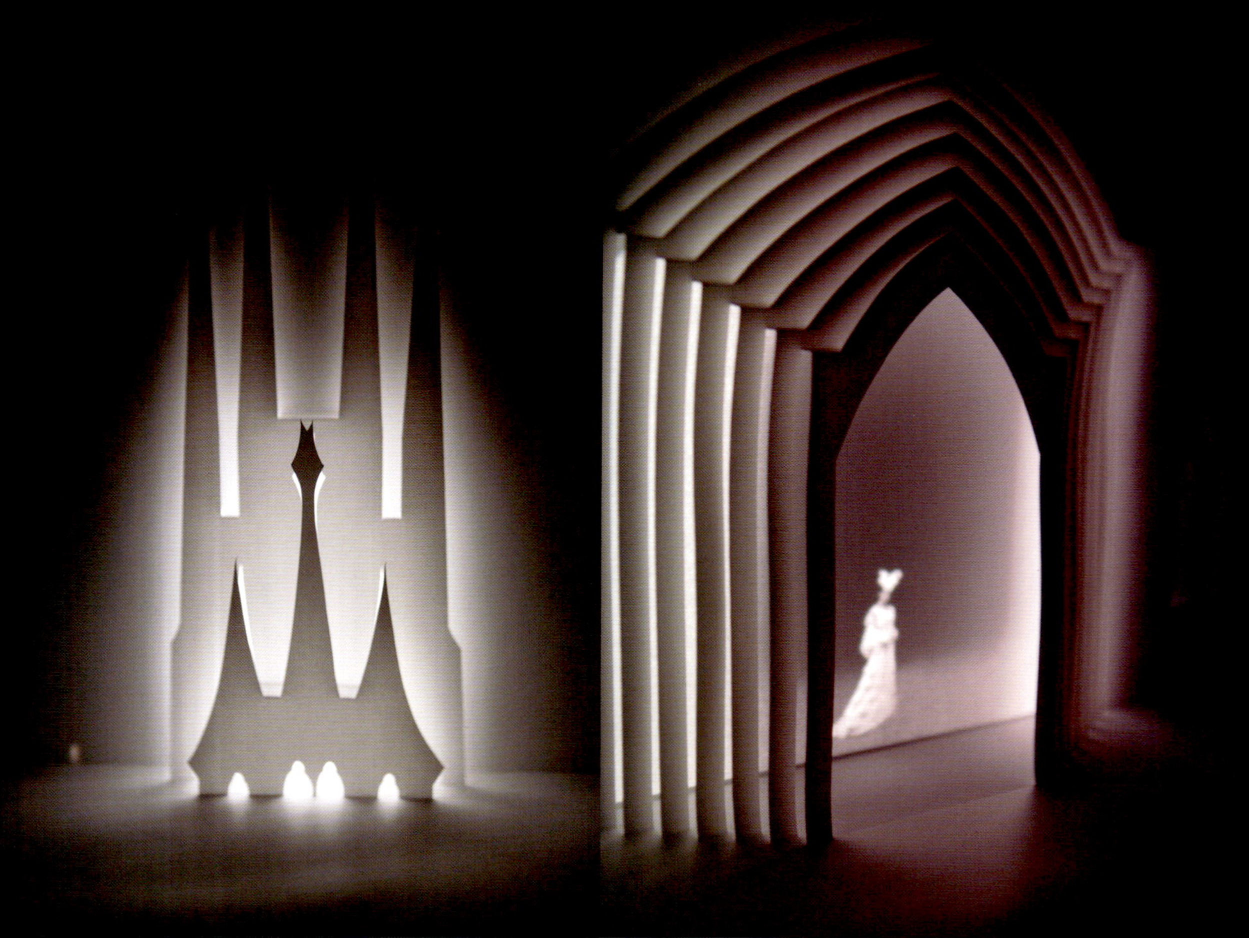

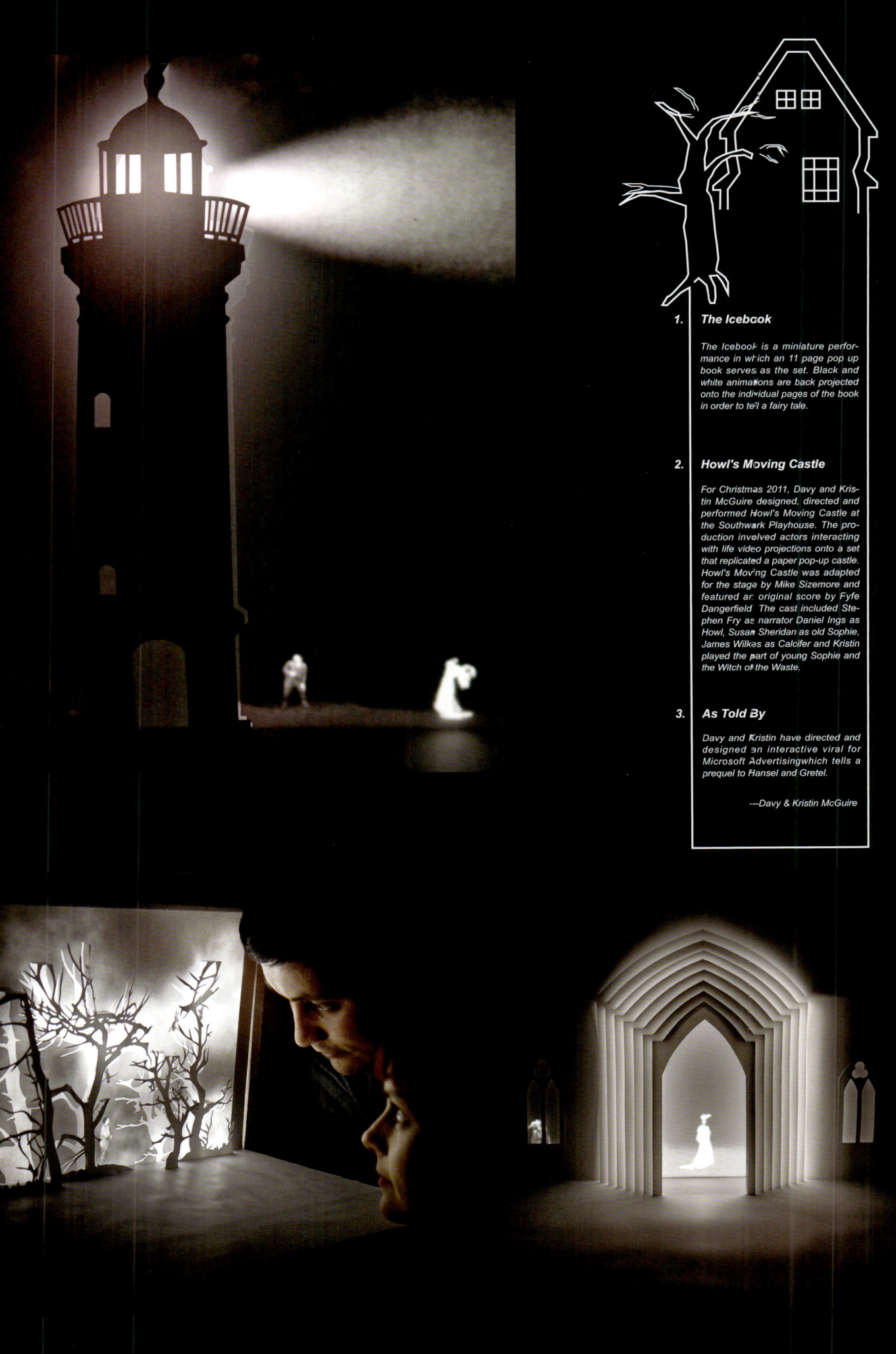

1. **The Icebook**

   The Icebook is a miniature performance in which an 11 page pop up book serves as the set. Black and white animations are back projected onto the individual pages of the book in order to tell a fairy tale.

2. **Howl's Moving Castle**

   For Christmas 2011, Davy and Kristin McGuire designed, directed and performed Howl's Moving Castle at the Southwark Playhouse. The production involved actors interacting with life video projections onto a set that replicated a paper pop-up castle. Howl's Moving Castle was adapted for the stage by Mike Sizemore and featured an original score by Fyfe Dangerfield. The cast included Stephen Fry as narrator, Daniel Ings as Howl, Susan Sheridan as old Sophie, James Wilkes as Calcifer and Kristin played the part of young Sophie and the Witch of the Waste.

3. **As Told By**

   Davy and Kristin have directed and designed an interactive viral for Microsoft Advertising which tells a prequel to Hansel and Gretel.

   ---Davy & Kristin McGuire

2. **Howl's Moving Castle**

Designer: Davy & Kristin McGuire
Country: UK
Client: Southwark Playhouse
Photographer: Davy and Kristin McGuire

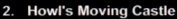

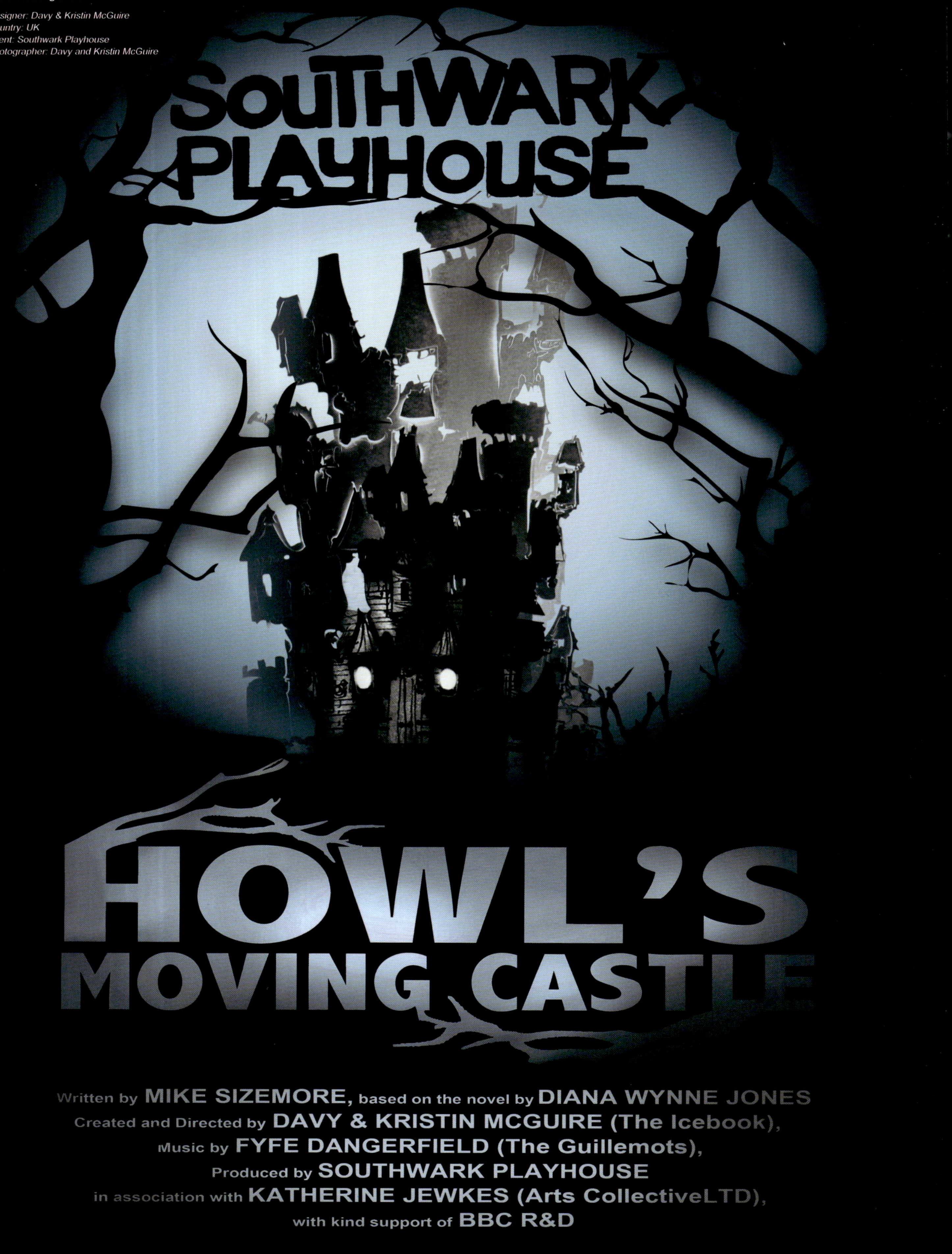

Written by MIKE SIZEMORE, based on the novel by DIANA WYNNE JONES
Created and Directed by DAVY & KRISTIN McGUIRE (The Icebook),
Music by FYFE DANGERFIELD (The Guillemots),
Produced by SOUTHWARK PLAYHOUSE
in association with KATHERINE JEWKES (Arts CollectiveLTD),
with kind support of BBC R&D

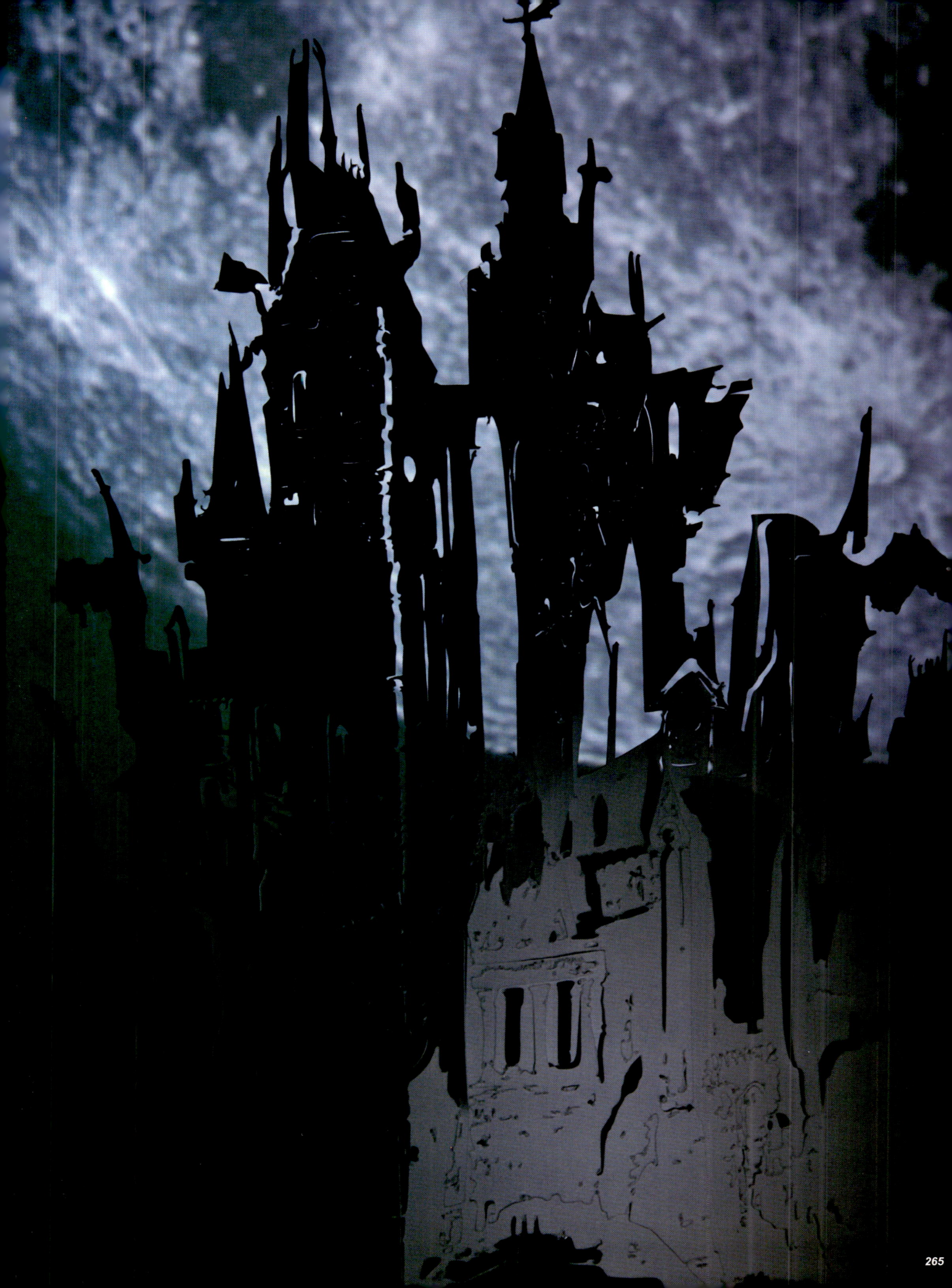

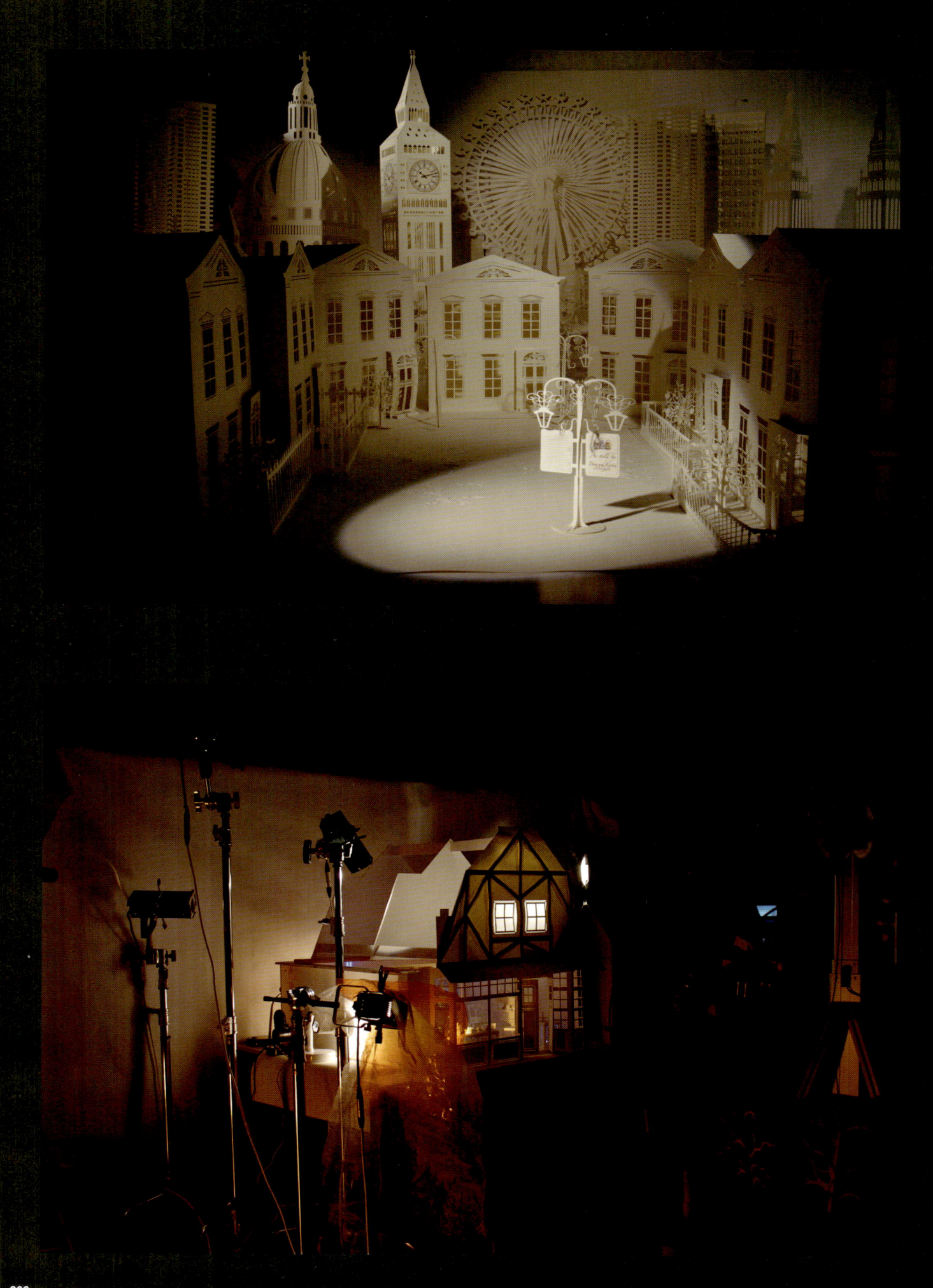

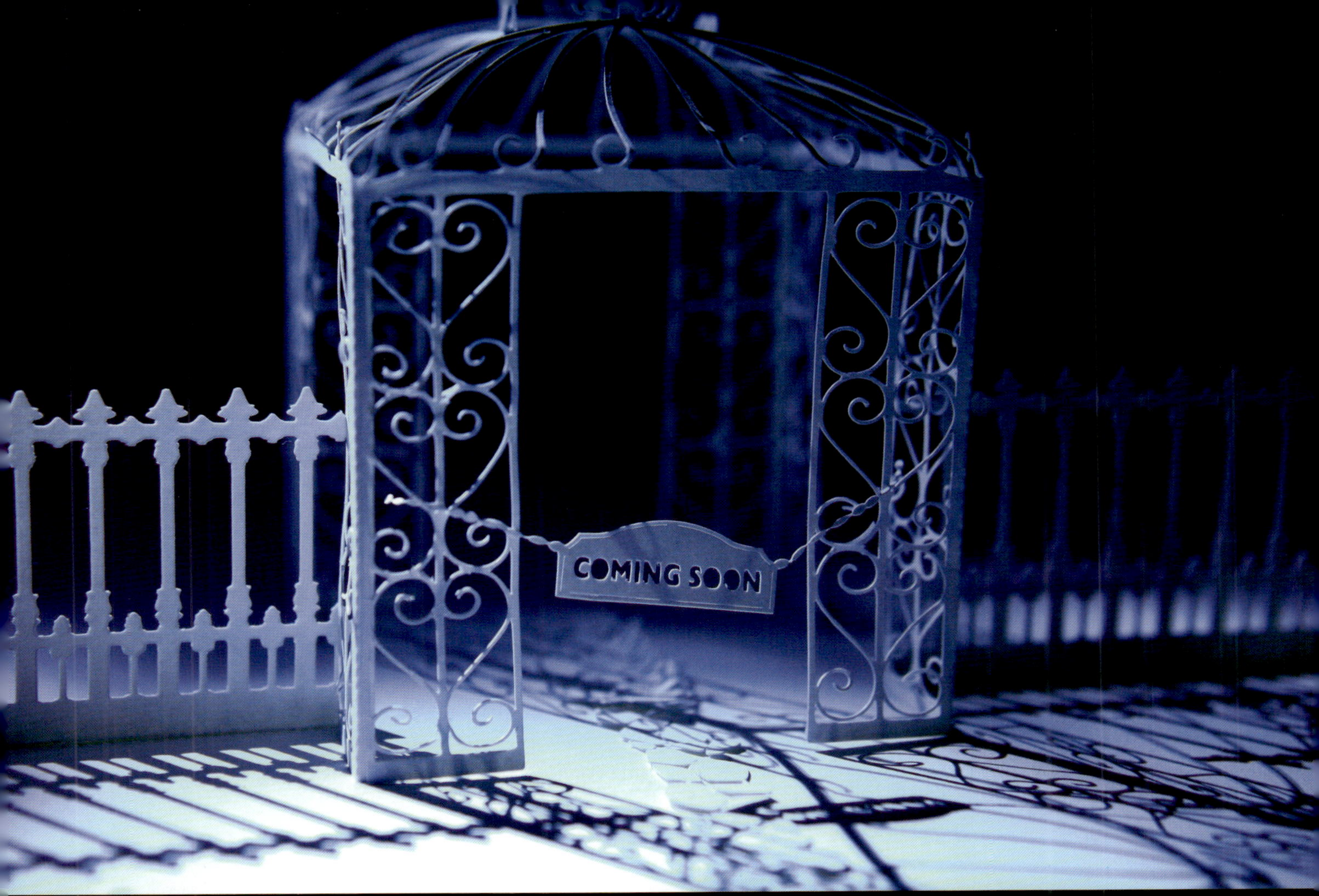

3. **As Told By**

Designer: Davy & Kristin McGuire
Country: UK
Client: Microsoft Advertising
Photographer: Davy and Kristin McGuire

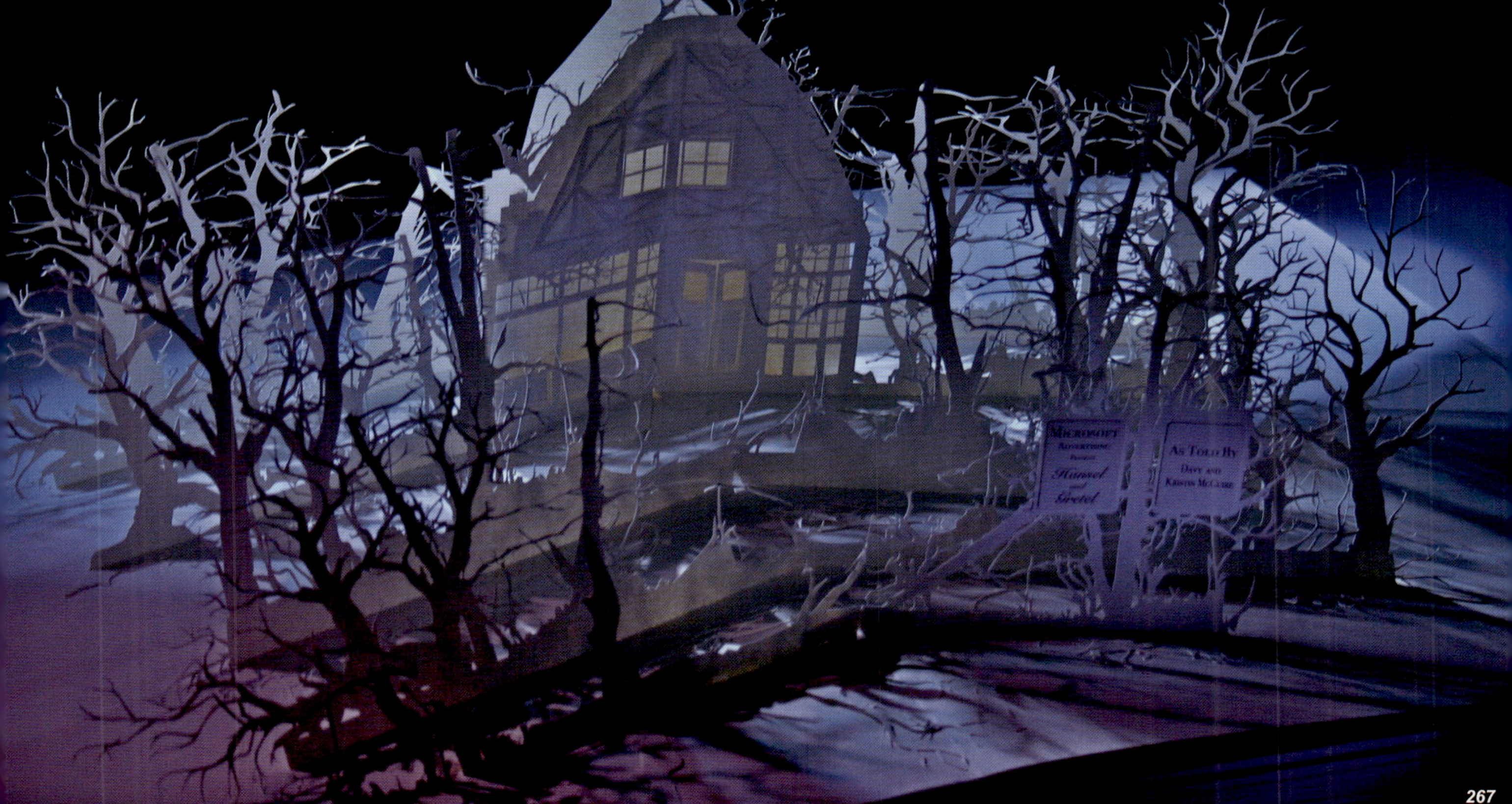

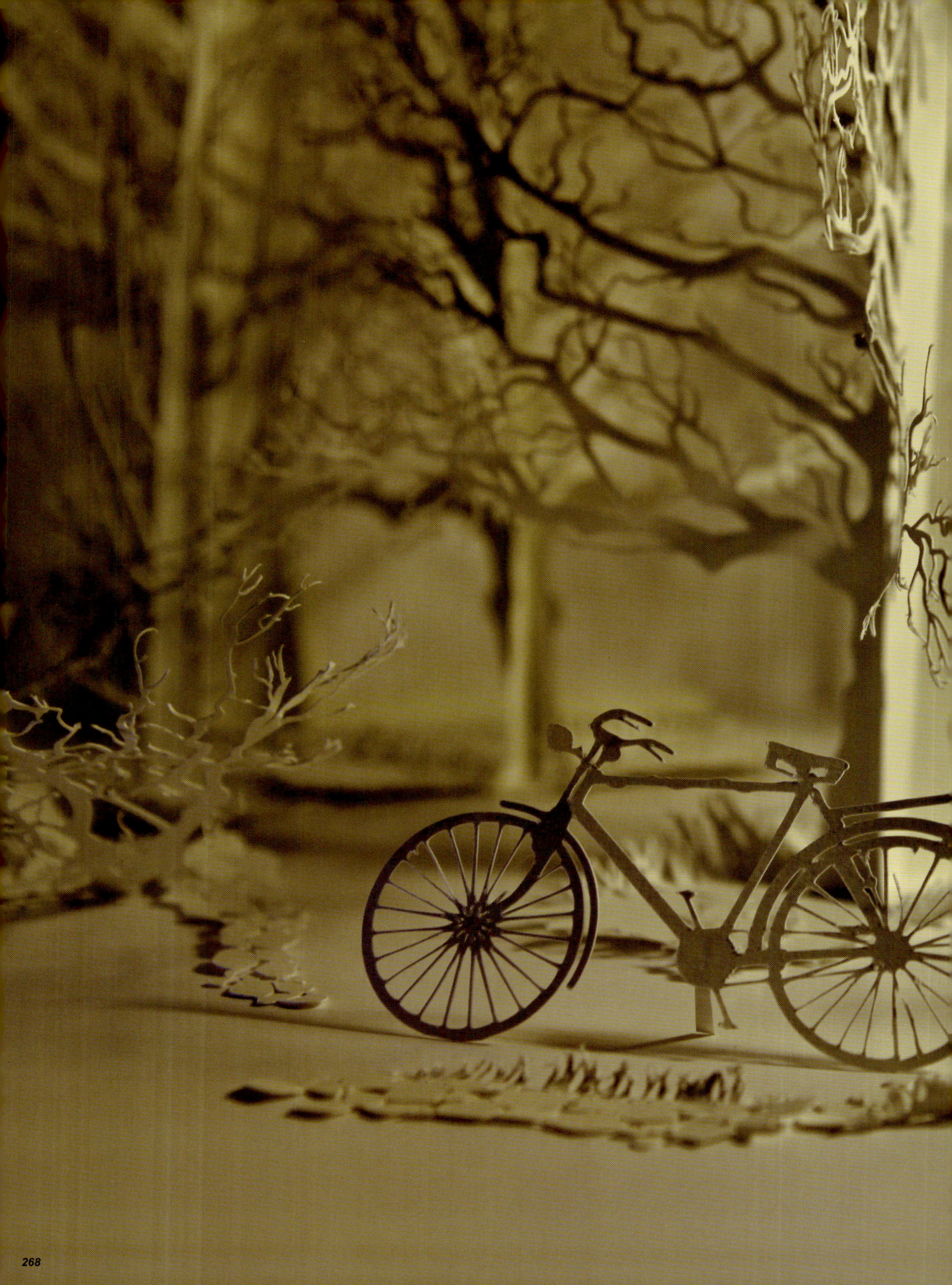

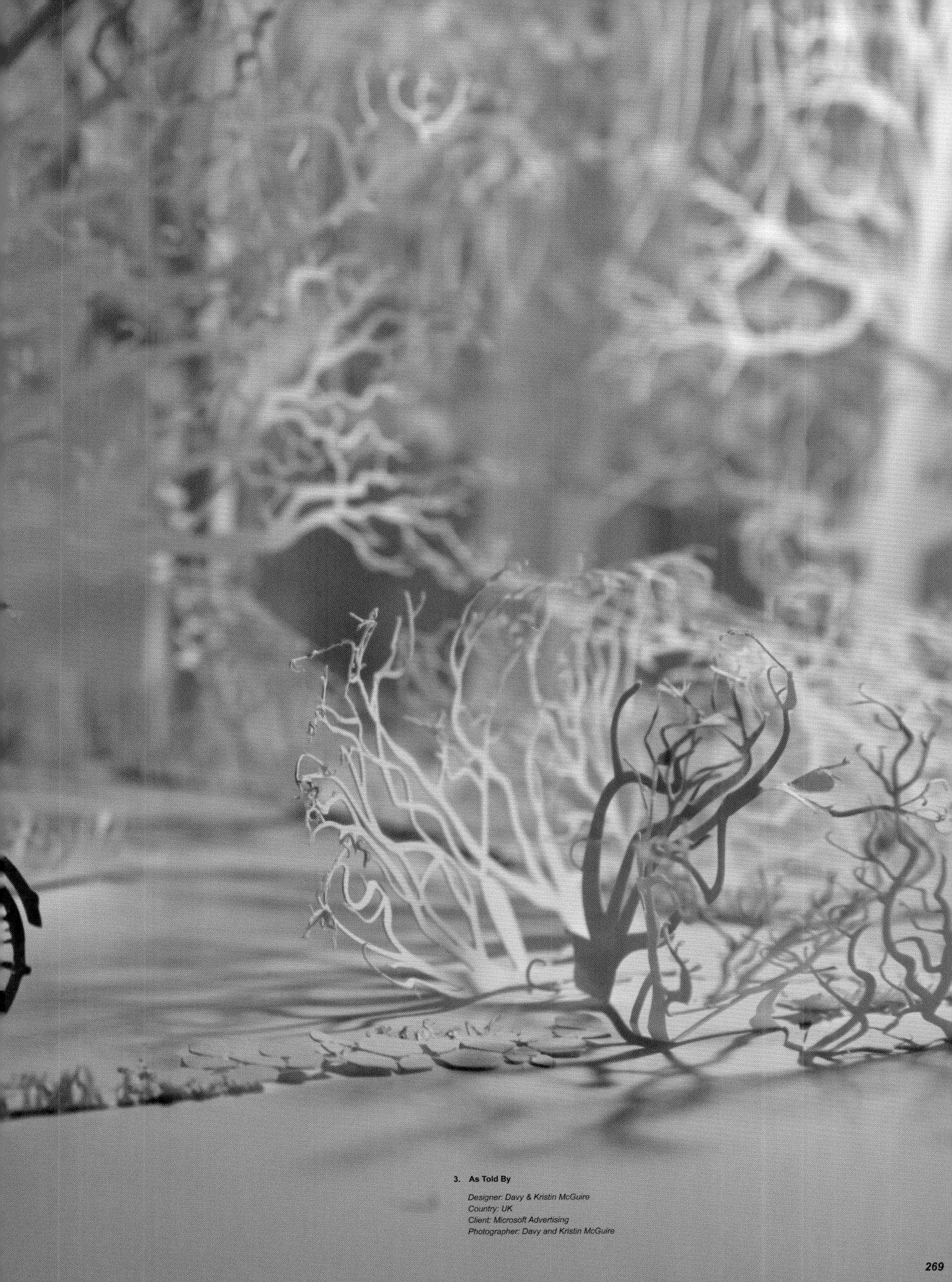

3. As Told By

Designer: Davy & Kristin McGuire
Country: UK
Client: Microsoft Advertising
Photographer: Davy and Kristin McGuire

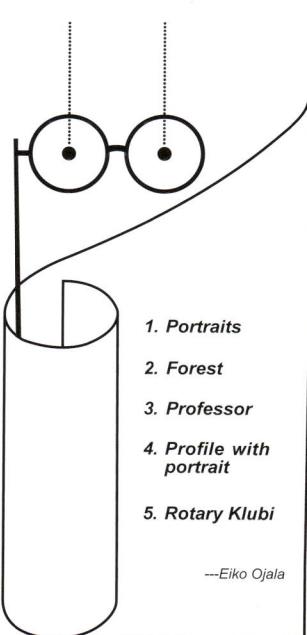

1. Portraits
2. Forest
3. Professor
4. Profile with portrait
5. Rotary Klubi

---Eiko Ojala

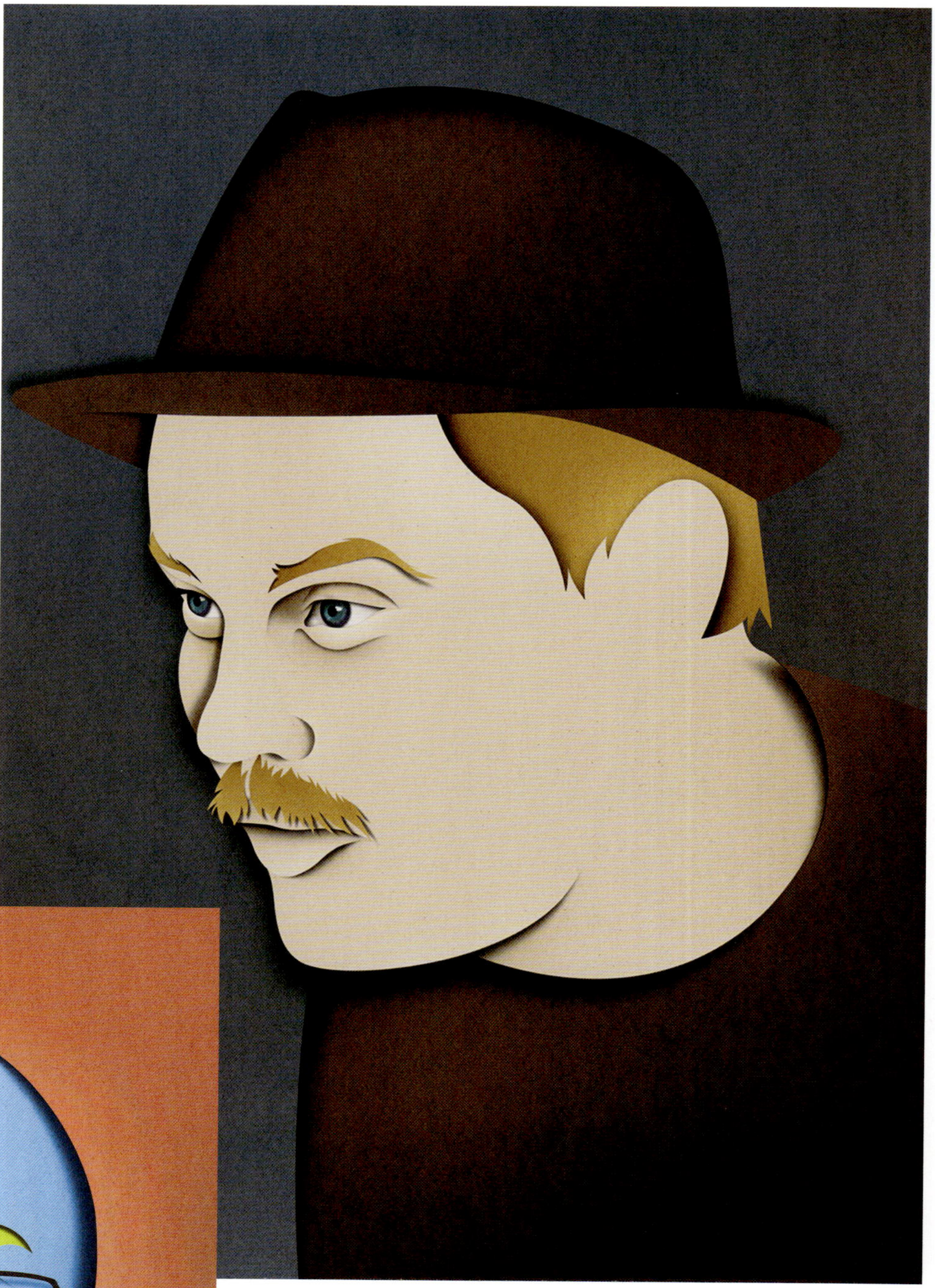

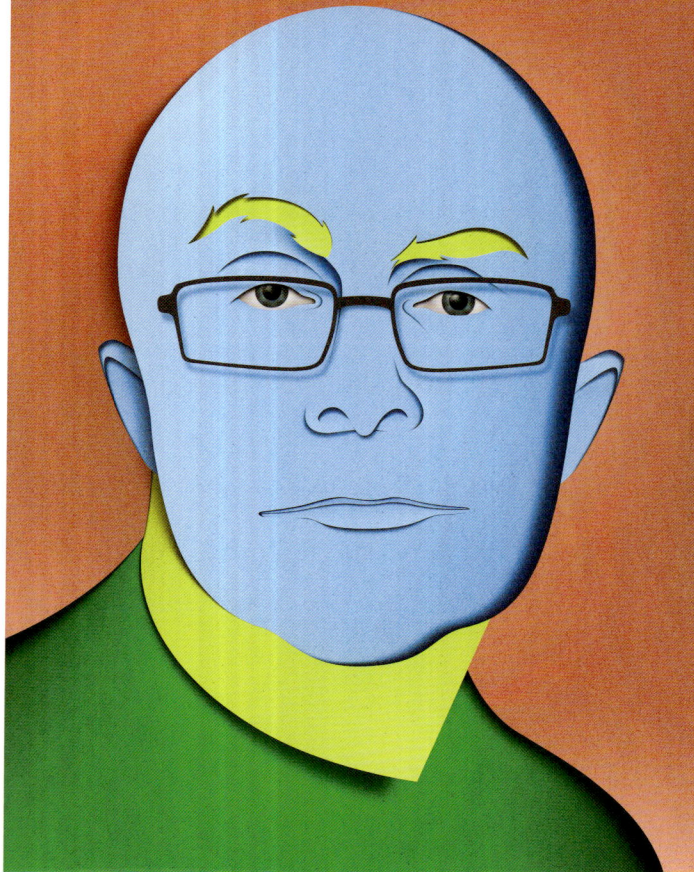

1. **Portraits**

   Portrait series for monthly magazine "Anne & Stiil" about famous Estonian persons.

   Designer: Eiko Ojala
   Country: Estonia
   Creative Director: Eiko Ojala
   Client: Anne & Stiil

Designer: Eiko Ojala
Country: Estonia
Creative Director: Eiko Ojala
Client: Anne & Stiil

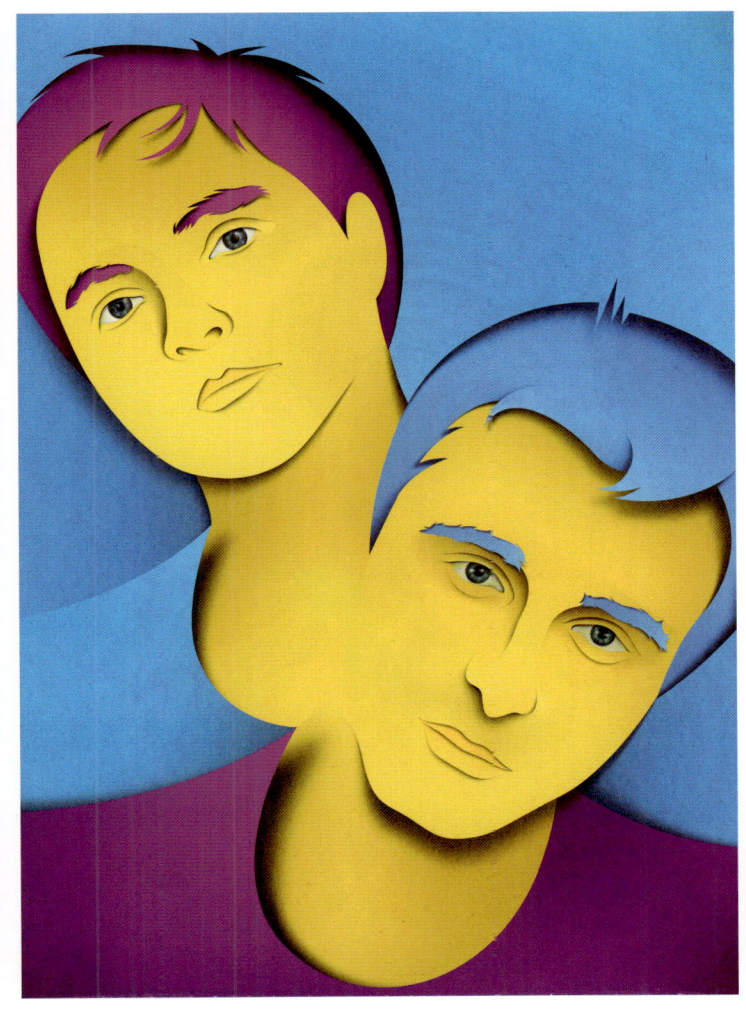
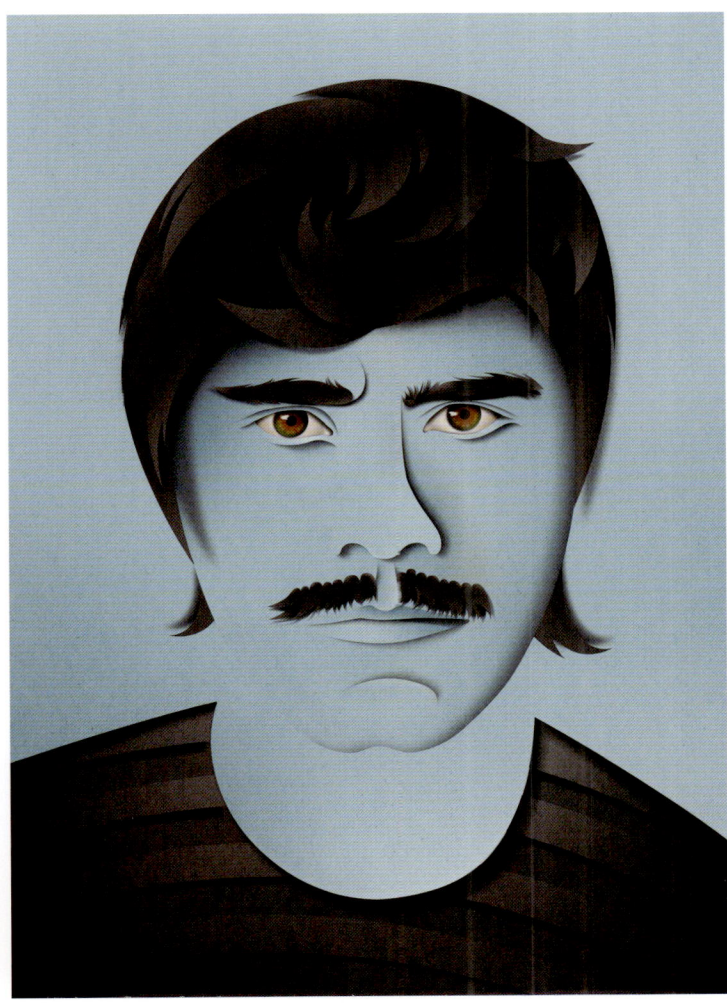

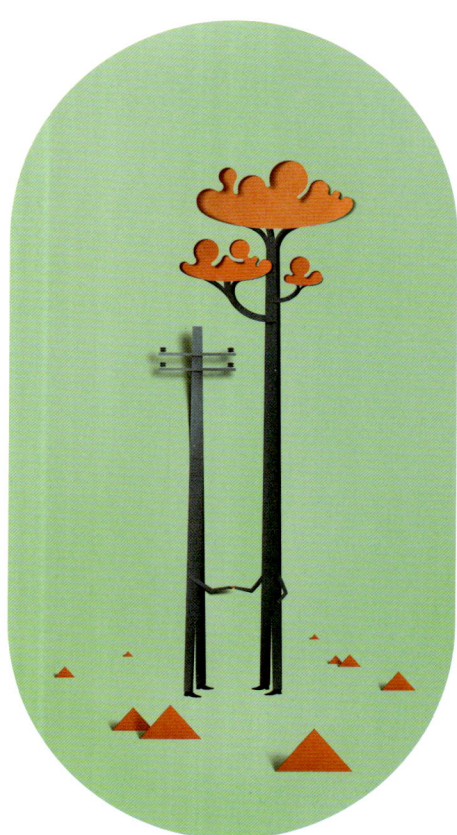
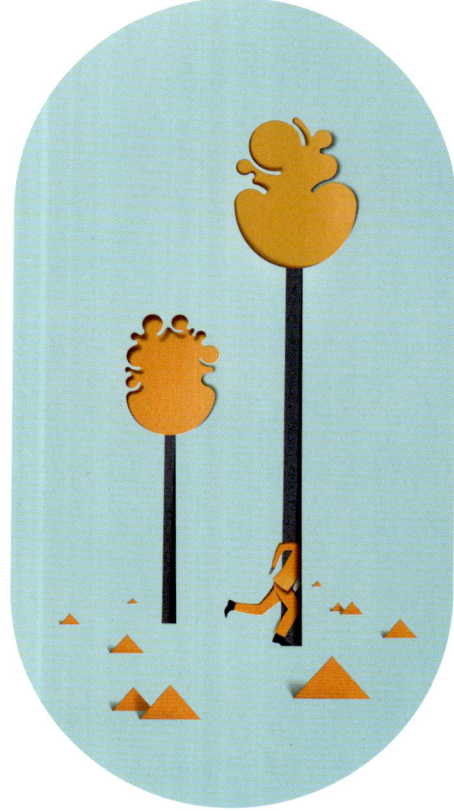
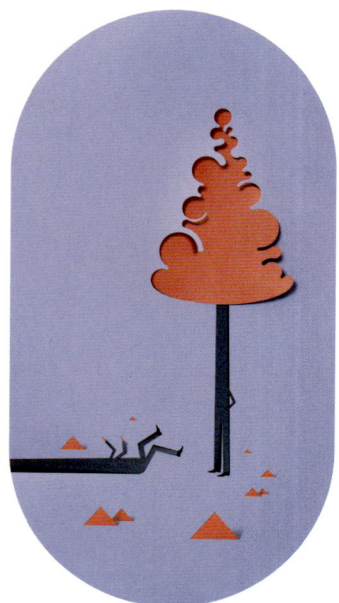
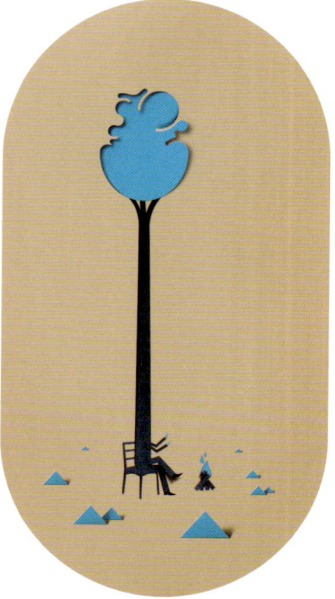
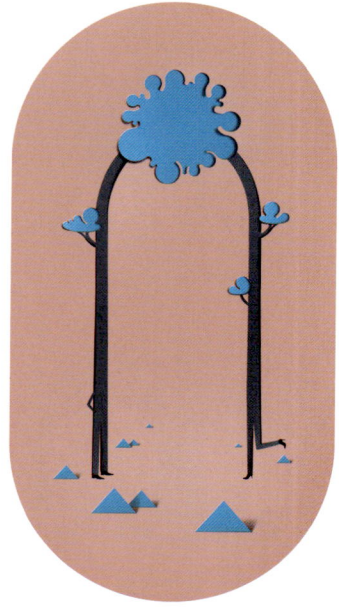

2. **Forest**

Personal illustration series for solo exhibition "Teine Lõige" ("Second Cut").

Designer: Eiko Ojala
Country: Estonia
Creative Director: Eiko Ojala

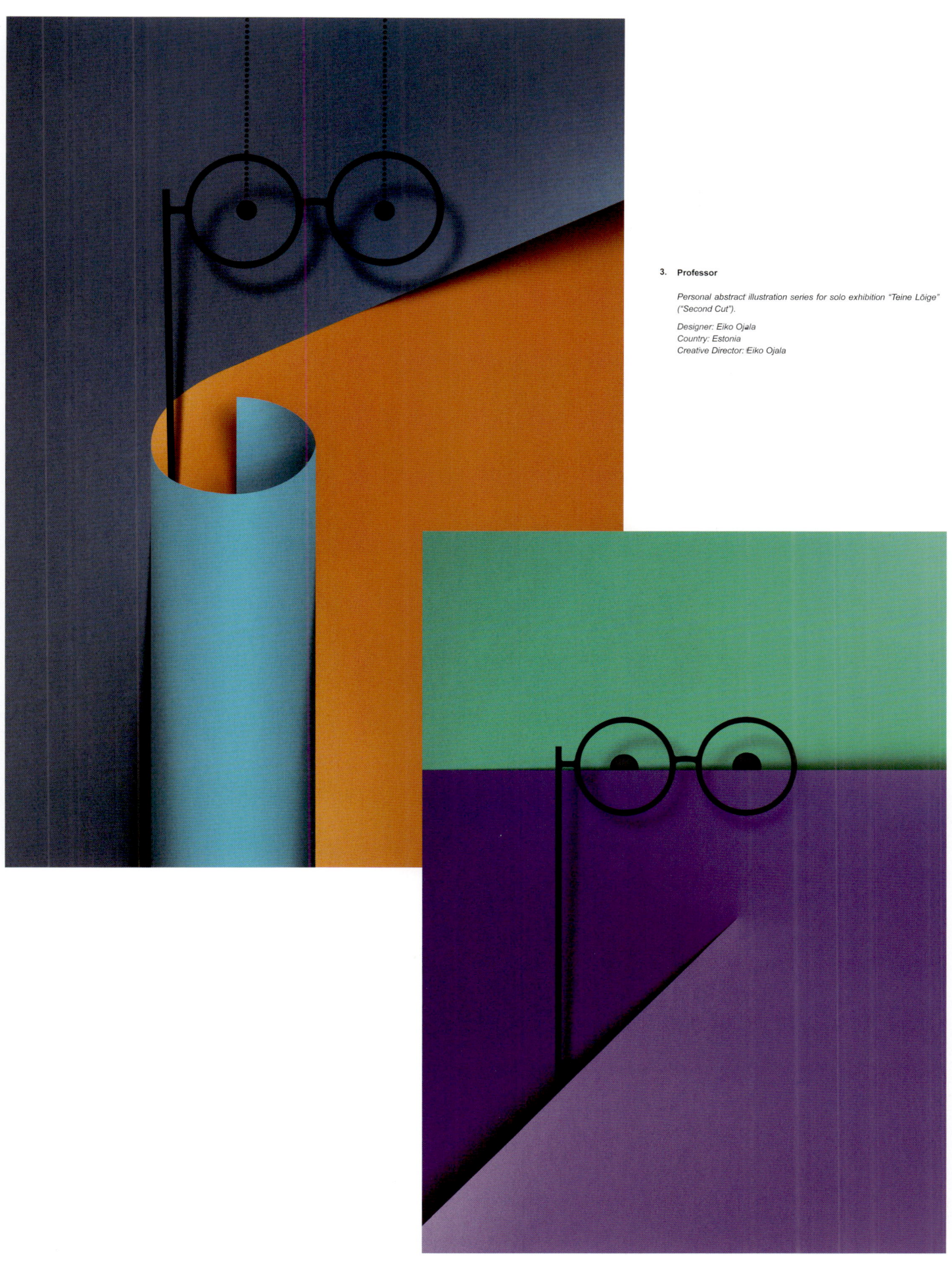

3. **Professor**

Personal abstract illustration series for solo exhibition "Teine Lõige" ("Second Cut").

Designer: Eiko Ojala
Country: Estonia
Creative Director: Eiko Ojala

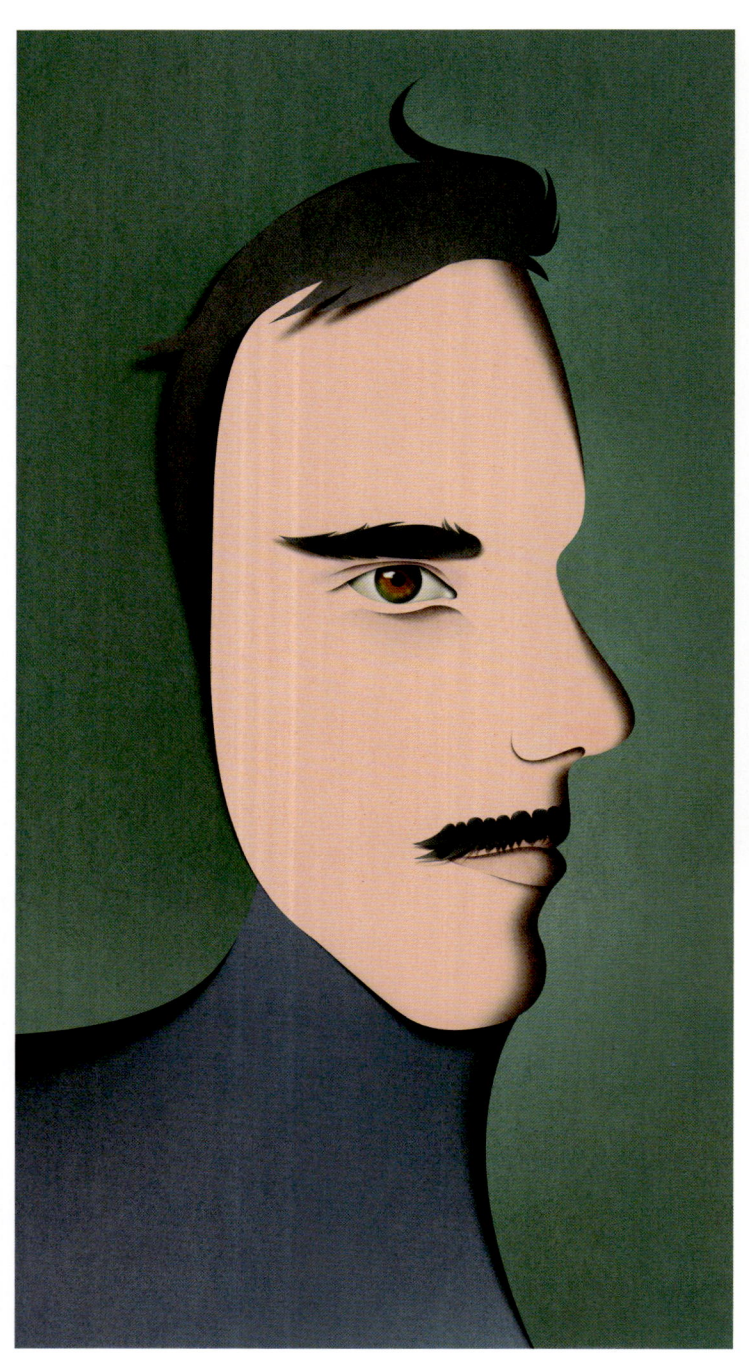
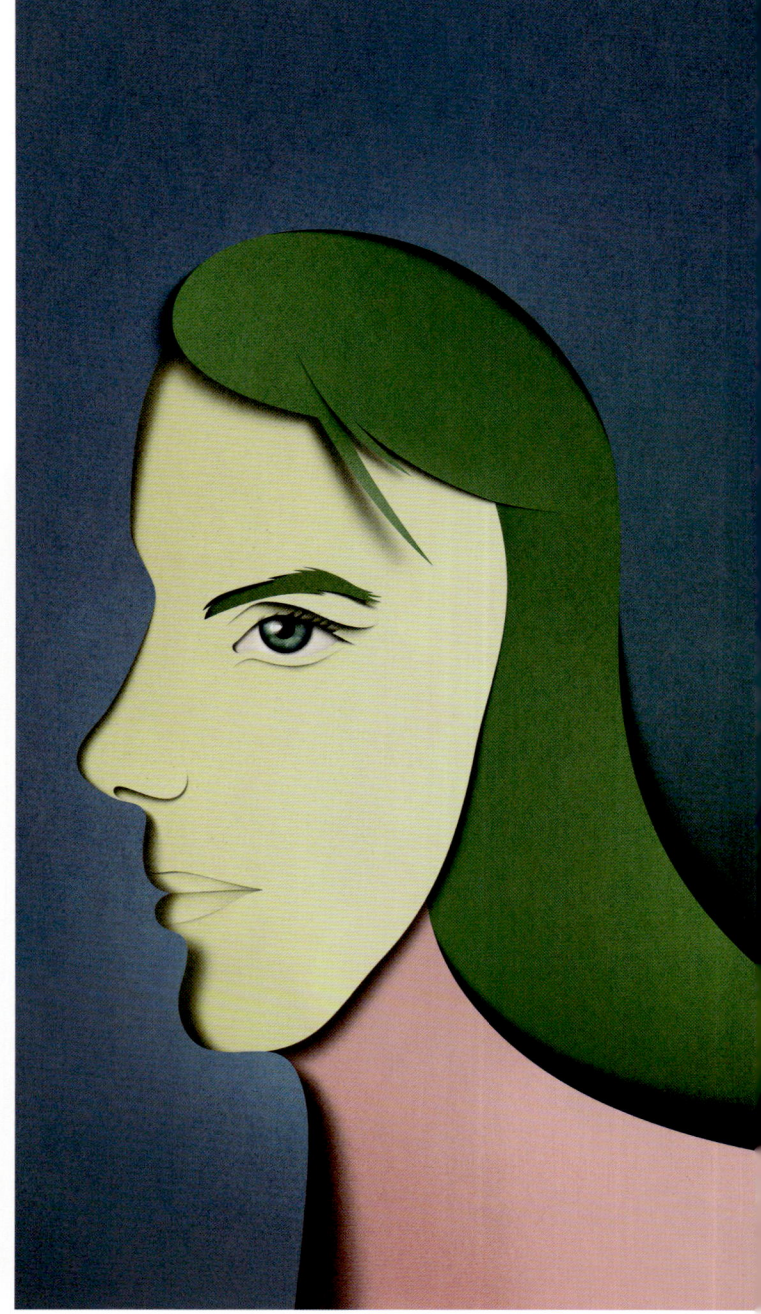

4. **Profile With Portrait**

Personal abstract illustration series for solo exhibition "Teine Lõige" ("Second Cut").

Designer: Eiko Ojala
Country: Estonia
Creative Director: Eiko Ojala

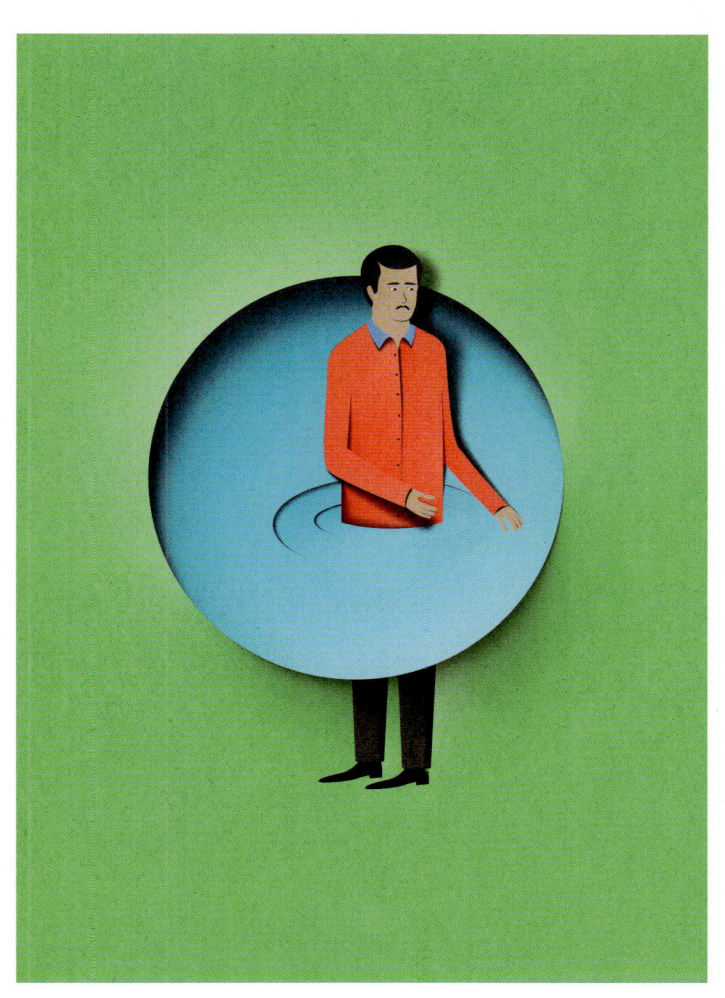
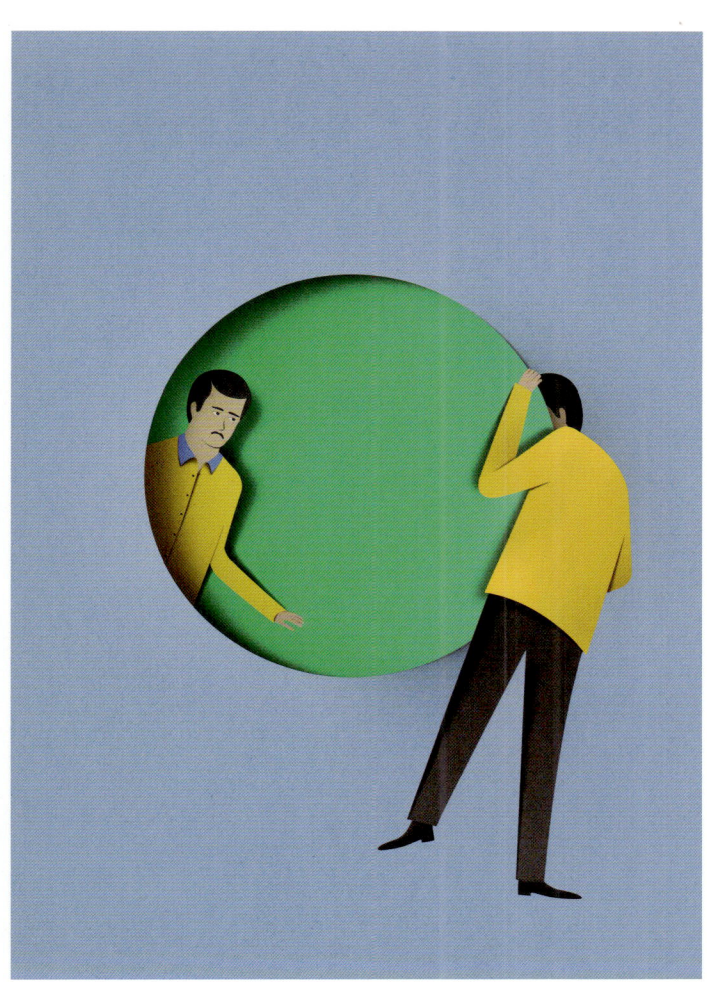
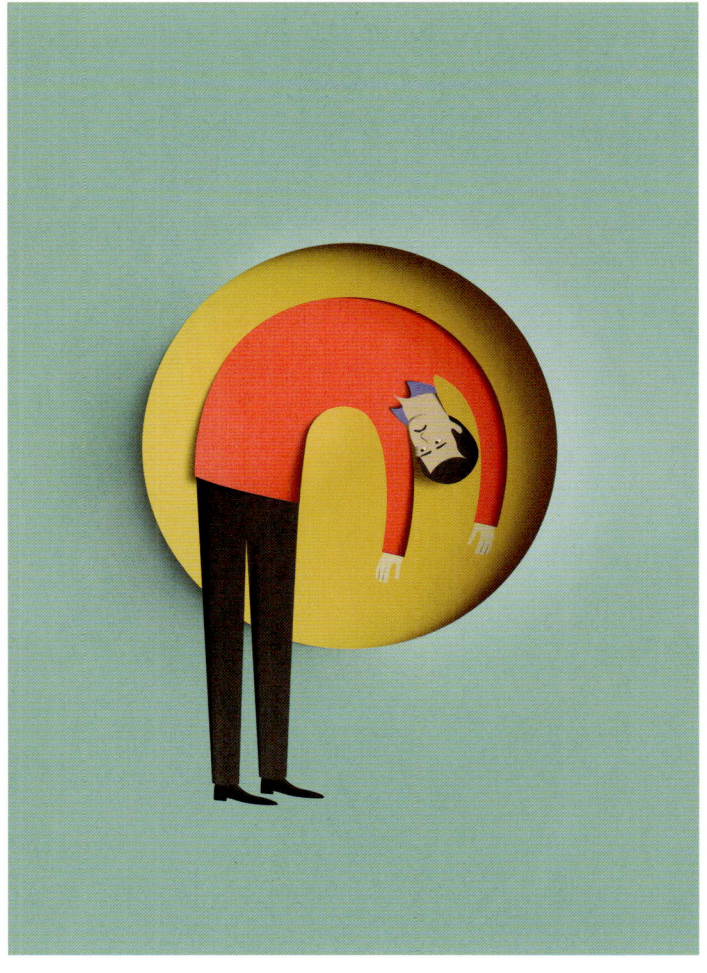
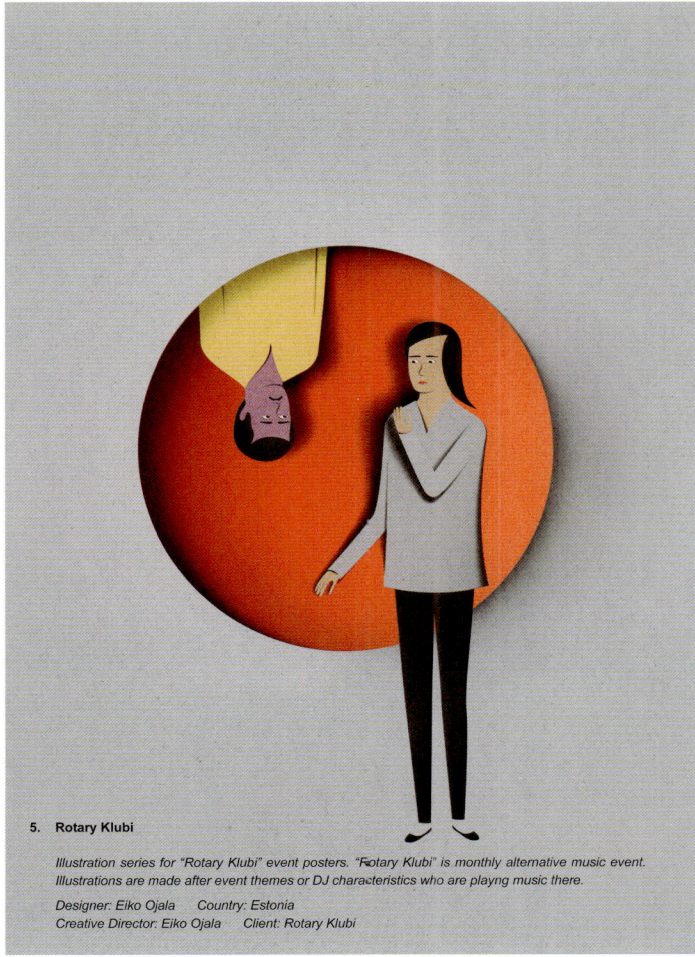

5. Rotary Klubi

Illustration series for "Rotary Klubi" event posters. "Rotary Klubi" is monthly alternative music event. Illustrations are made after event themes or DJ characteristics who are playng music there.

Designer: Eiko Ojala   Country: Estonia
Creative Director: Eiko Ojala   Client: Rotary Klubi

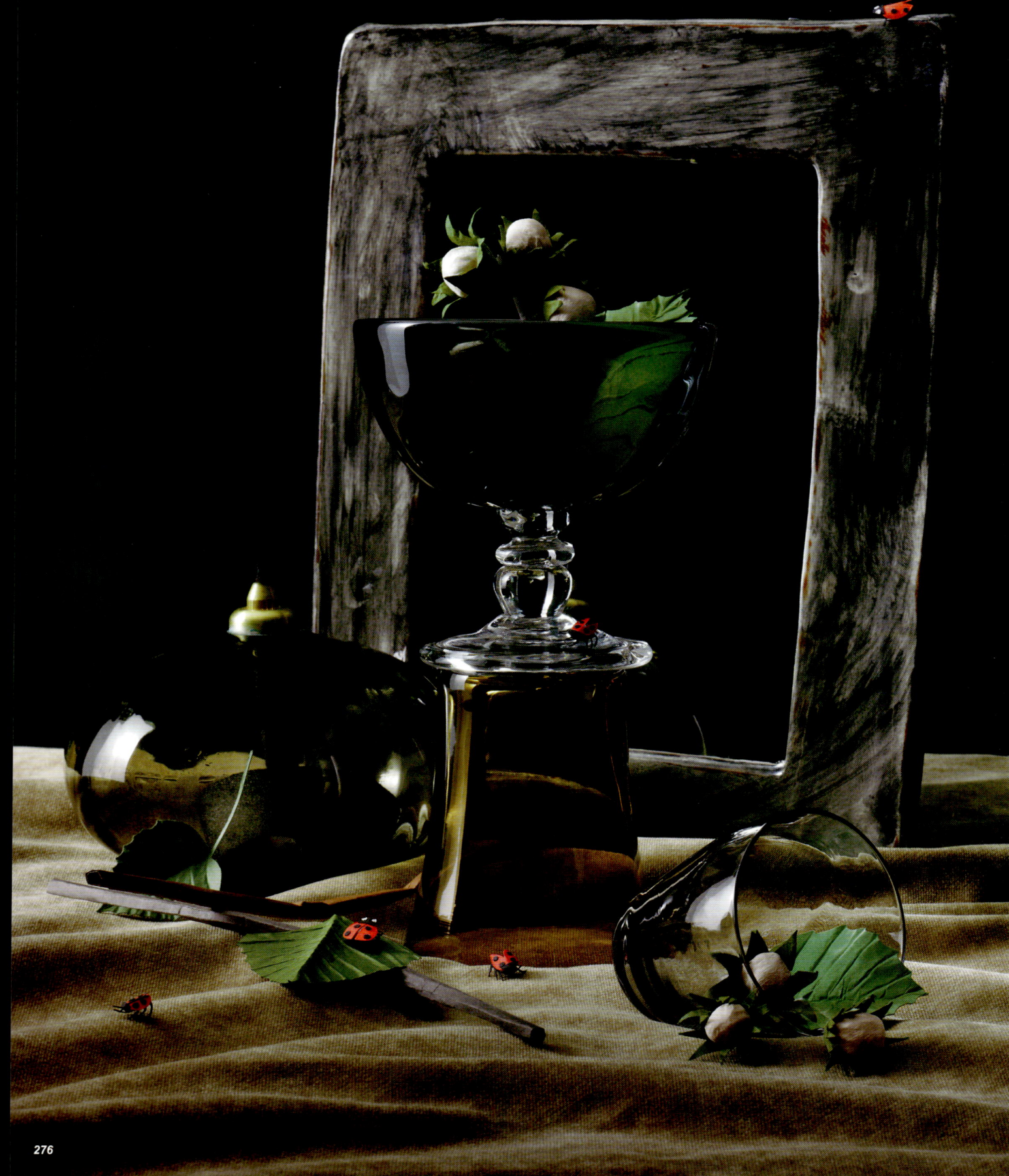

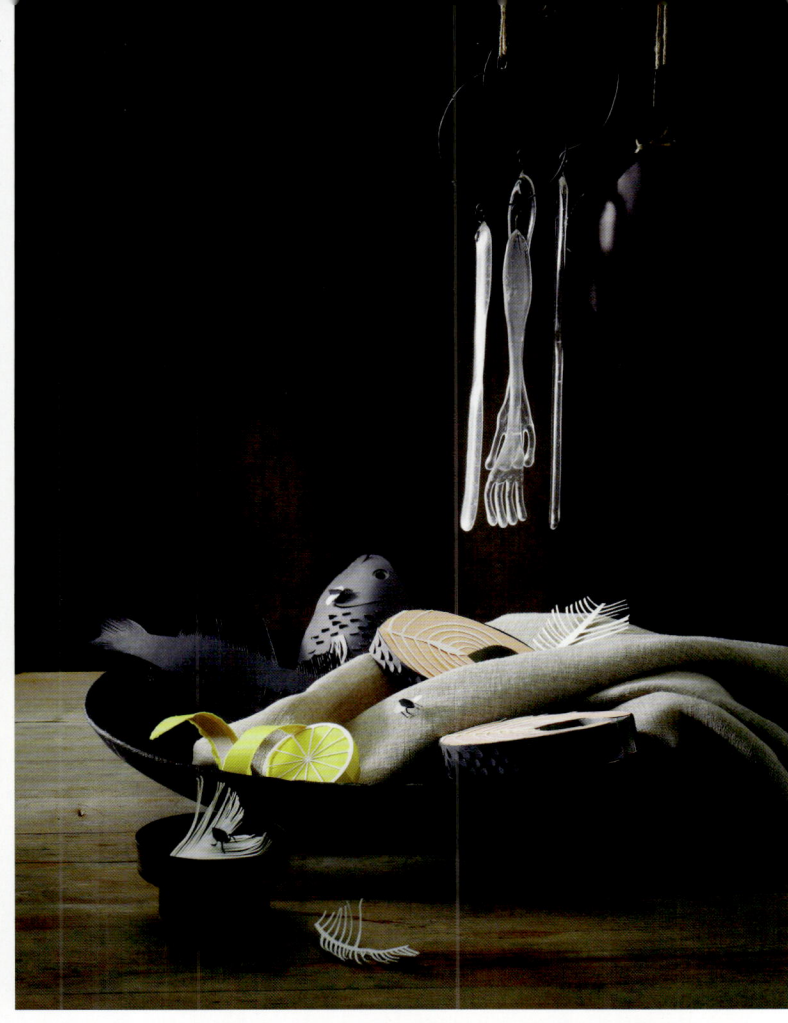

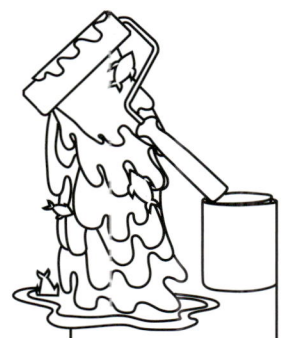

1. Smaklöst
2. Orchid
3. Peonies
4. Dessert
5. Main Course
6. Starter
7. Fish
8. Boats
9. Tilly & Gul
10. Graduates Insurance
11. Shortcut

---Fideli Sundqvist

1. **Smaklöst**

We have done an interpretation of the classic still life. Still life usually depicts natural and manmade objects, in our pictures the natural objects has been replaced with folded paper. The pieces are almost weightless and lack the qualities that the original has, taste, smell, nourishment and so on. We want the eye to stop for a second and recognize that something is different but at the same time we want the pictures to be as timeless and beautiful as the 16th century paintings that we have been inspired by.

Designer / Papercut artist: Fideli Sundqvist
Country: Sweden
Creative Director: Fideli Sundqvist / Olivia Jeczmyk / Joanna Lavén
Photographer: Olivia Jeczmyk
Stylist: Joanna Lavén

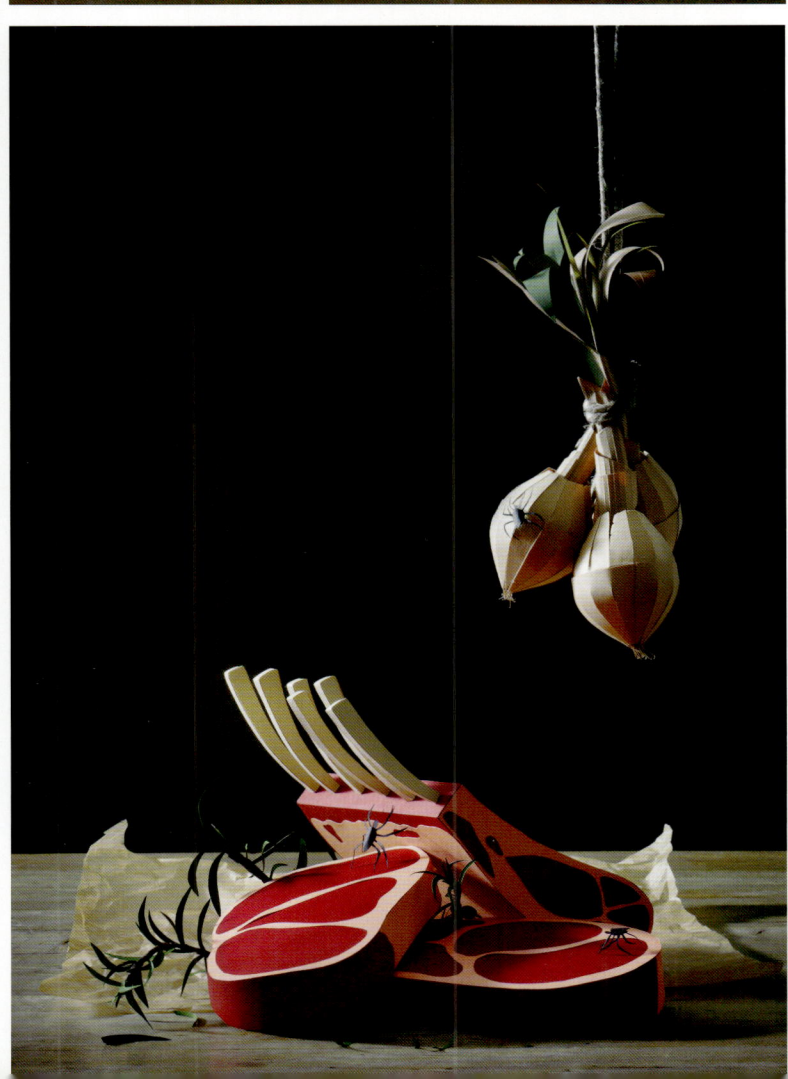

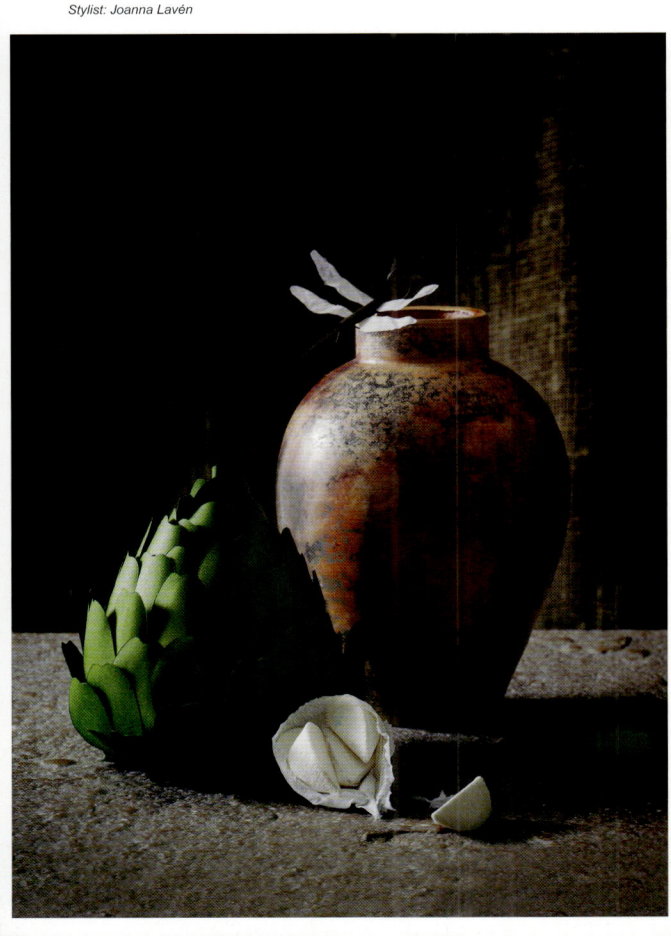

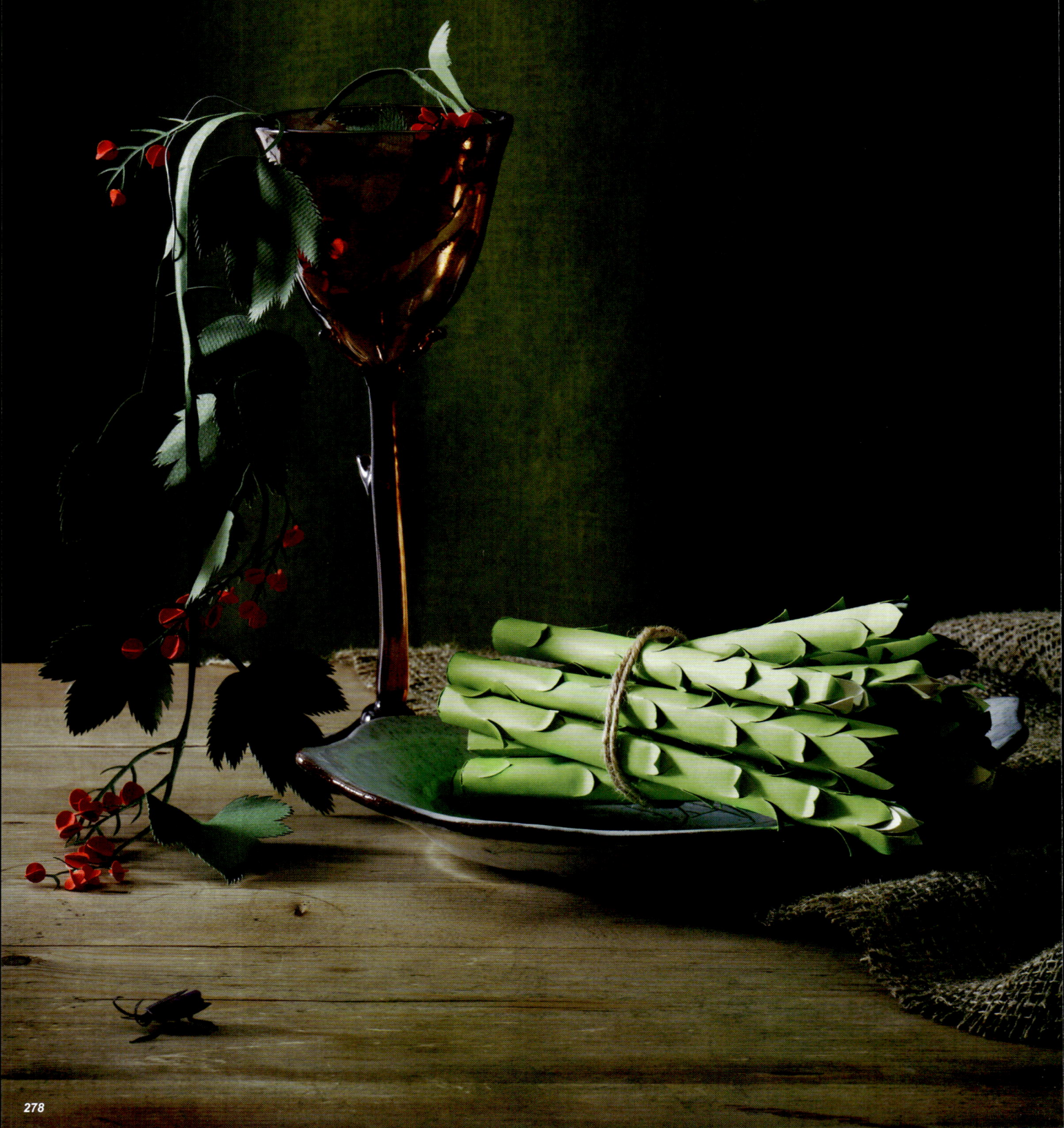

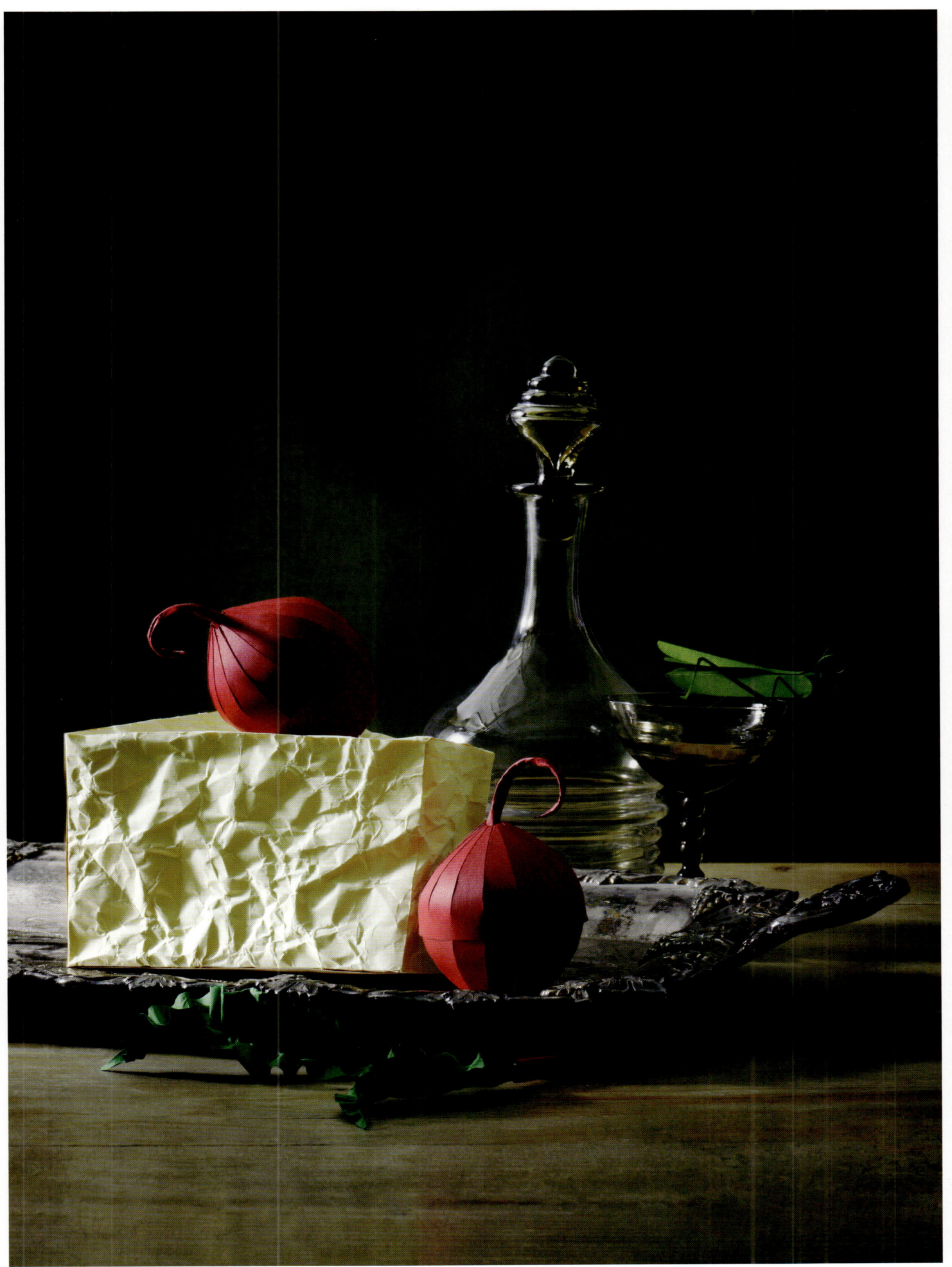

1. **Smaklöst**

   Designer / Papercut artist: Fideli Sundqvist
   Country: Sweden
   Creative Director: Fideli Sundqvist / Olivia Jeczmyk / Joanna Lavén
   Photographer: Olivia Jeczmyk
   Stylist: Joanna Lavén

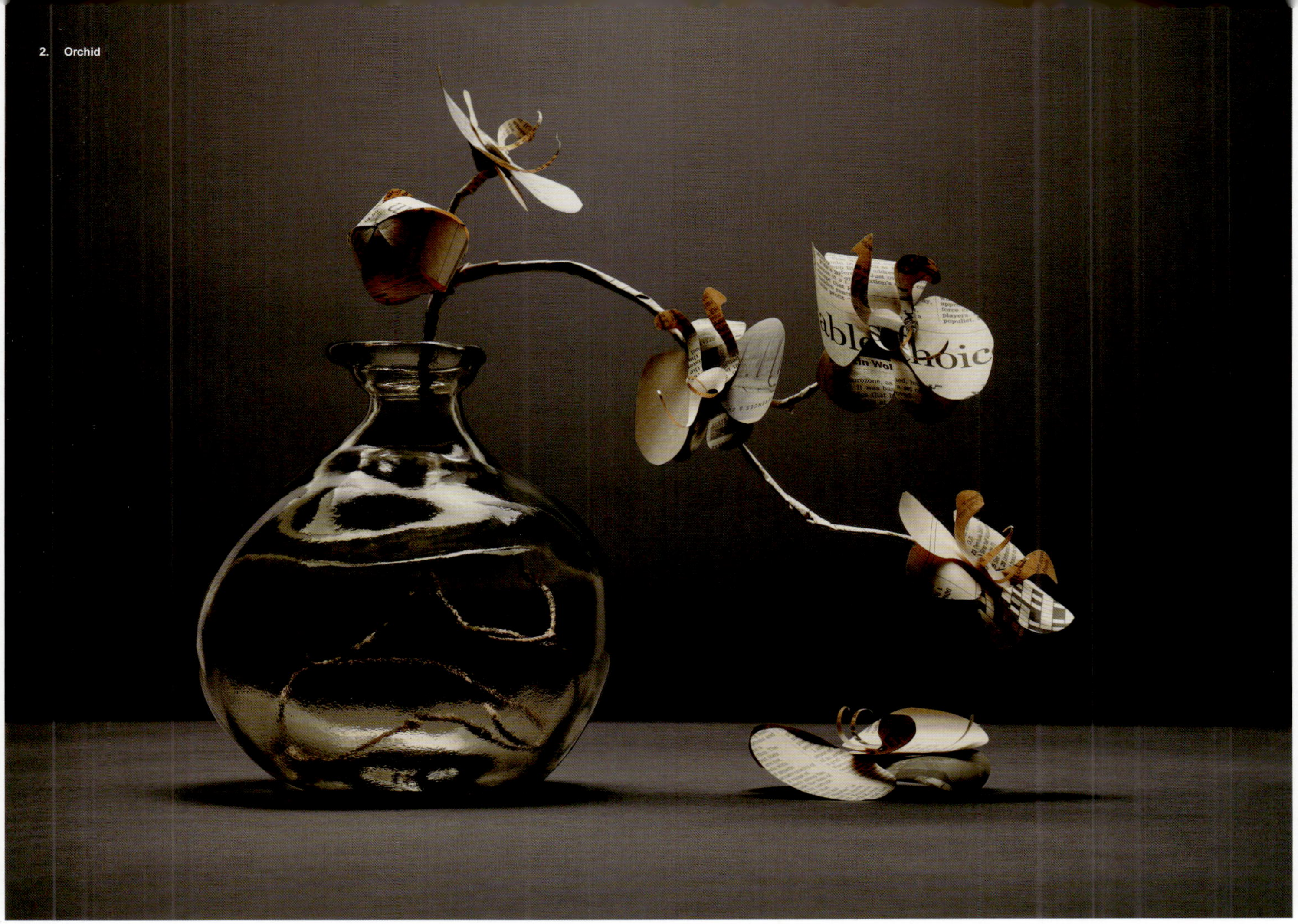

2. Orchid

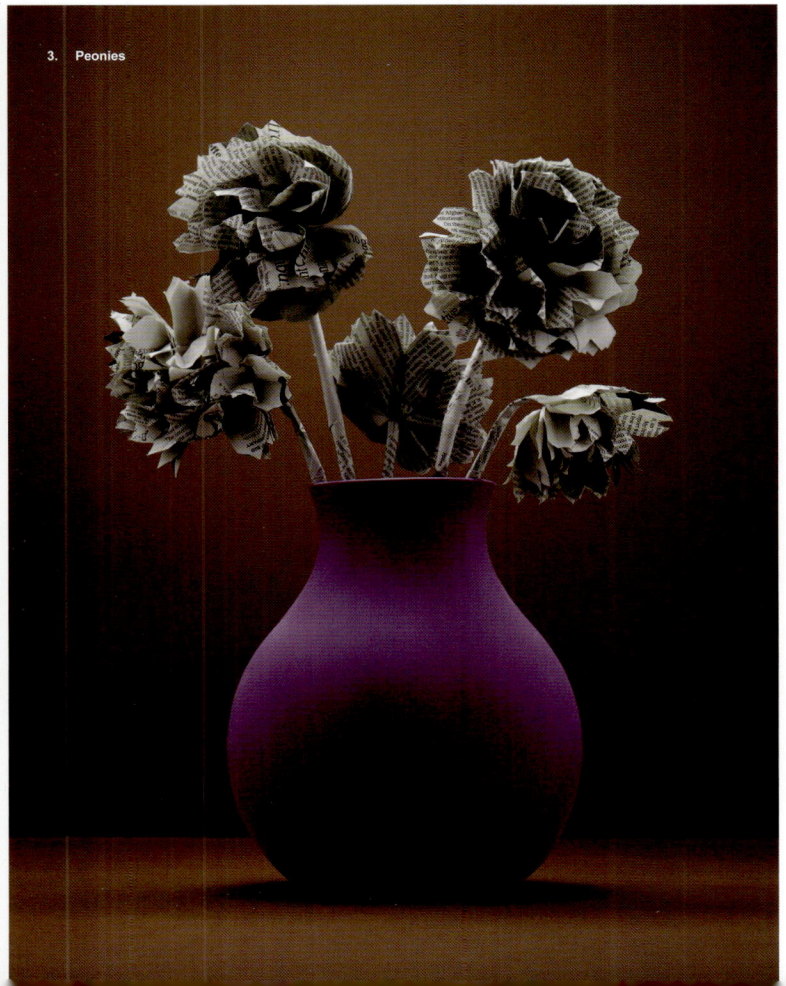

3. Peonies

2. Orchid
Own project, flowers folded in newspaper.

3. Peonies
Own project, flowers folded in newspaper.

Designer / Papercut artist: Fideli Sundqvist
Country: Sweden
Creative Director: Olivia Jeczmyk / Fideli Sundqvist
Photographer: Olivia Jeczmyk

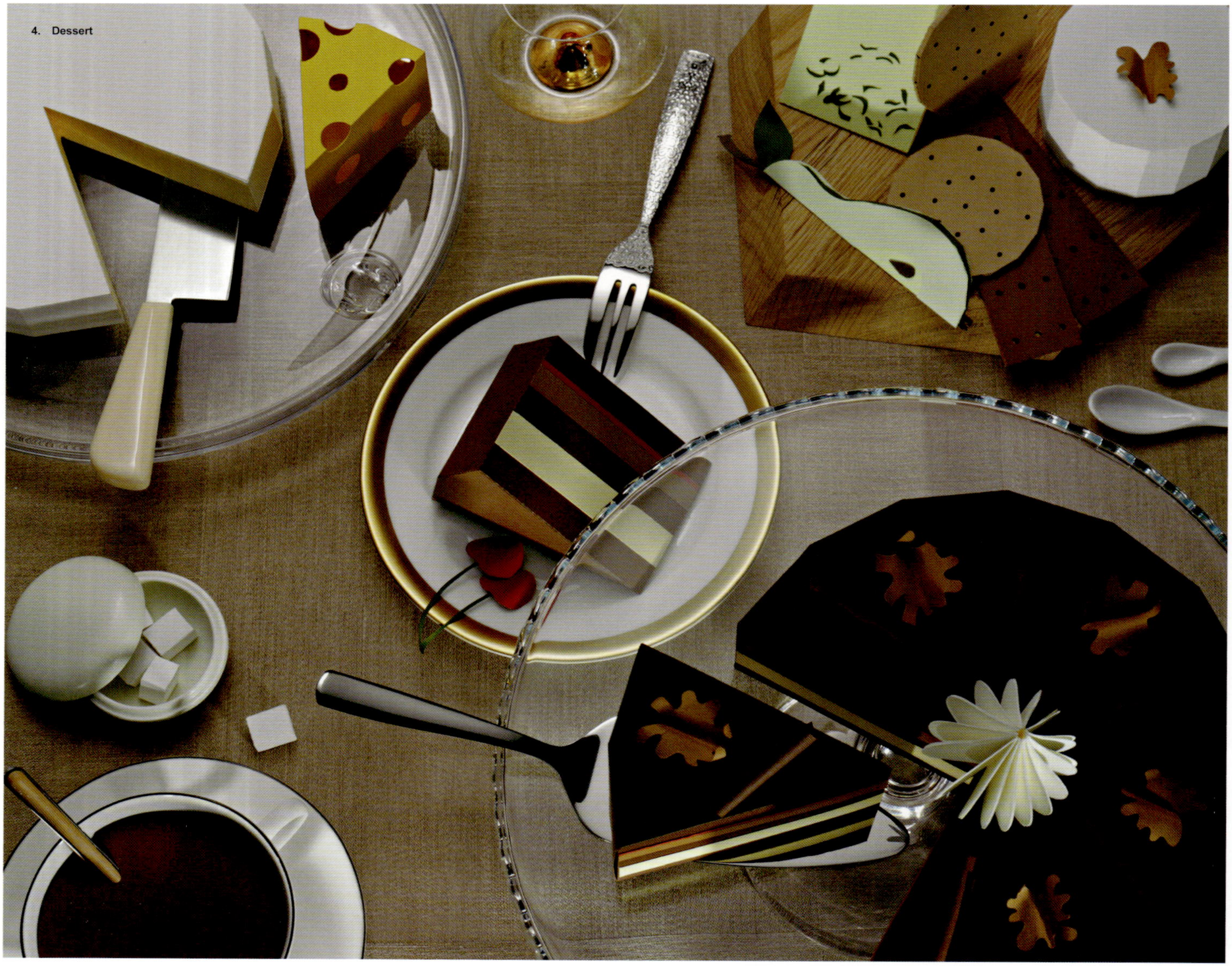

4. Dessert

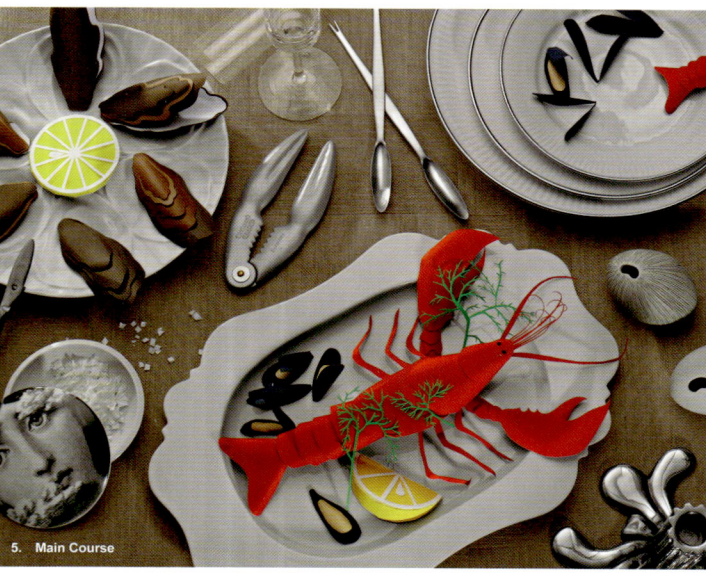

5. Main Course

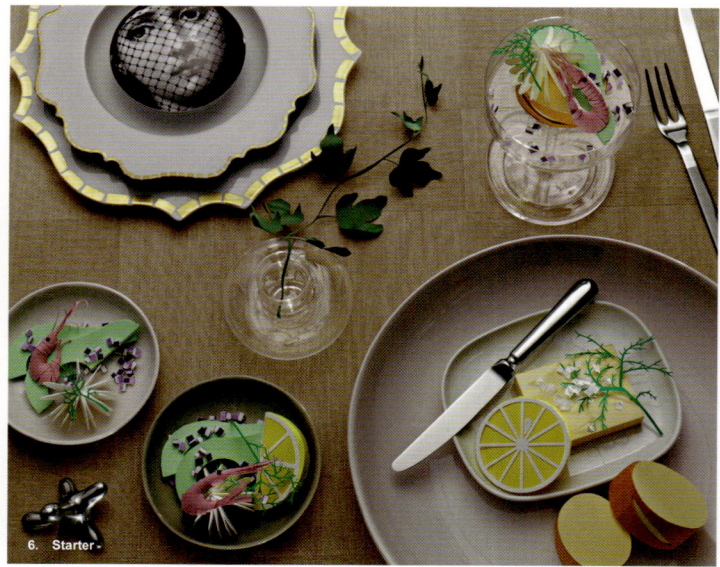

6. Starter

4. **Dessert**
The dessert in a three-course buffet, folded in paper.

5. **Main Course**
The main course in a three-course buffet, folded in paper.

6. **Starter**
The starter in a three-course buffet, folded in paper.

Designer / Papercut artist: Fideli Sundqvist
Country: Sweden
Creative Director: Saša Antić / Olivia Jeczmyk / Fideli Sundqvist
Client: PLAZA magazine
Photographer: Olivia Jeczmyk
Stylist: Saša Antić

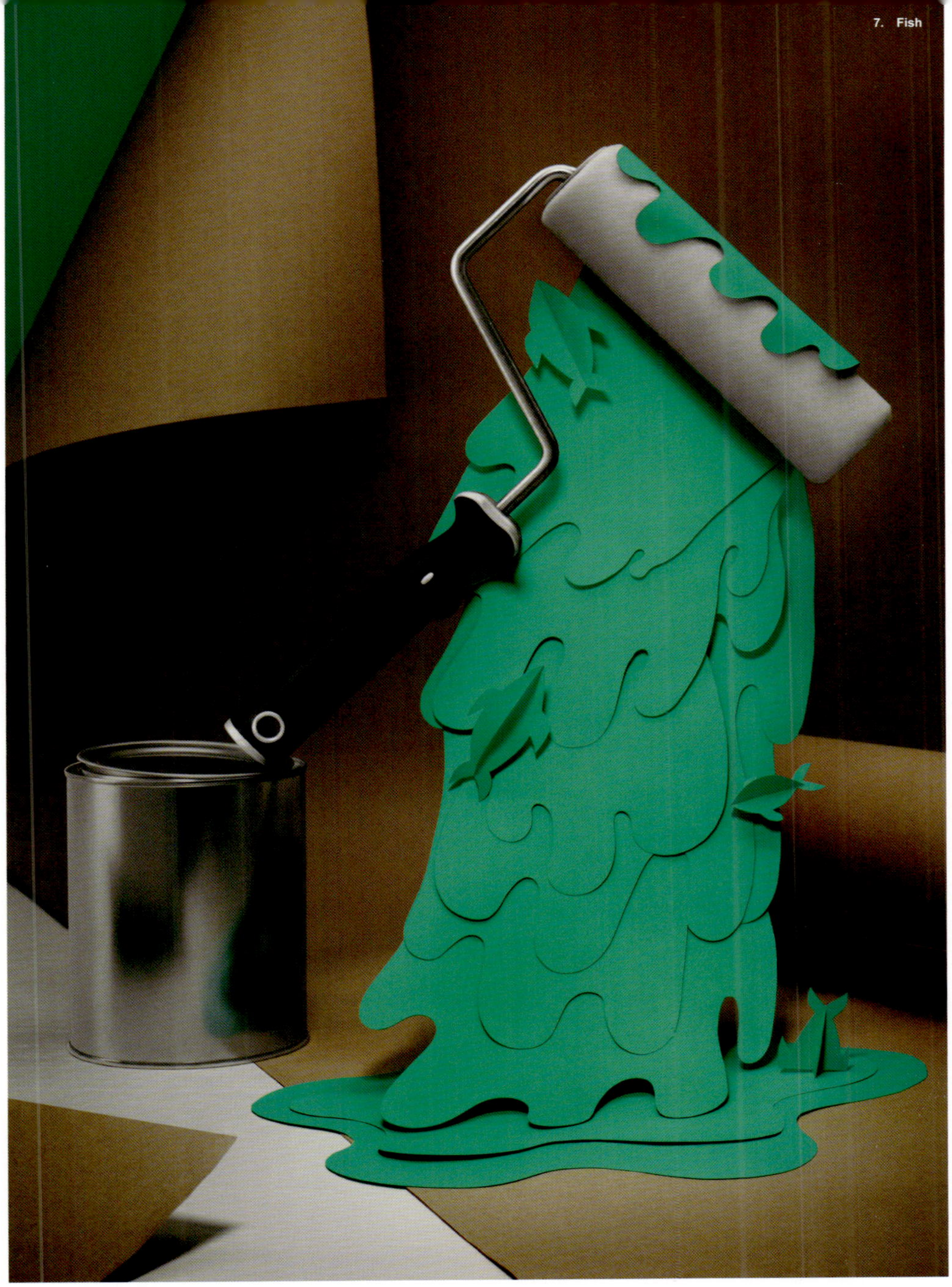

7. **Fish**
Own project, color and splashes.

8. **Boats**
Own project, color and splashes.

Designer / Papercut artist: Fideli Sundqvist
Country: Sweden
Creative Director: Olivia Jeczmyk / Fideli Sundqvist
Photographer: Olivia Jeczmyk

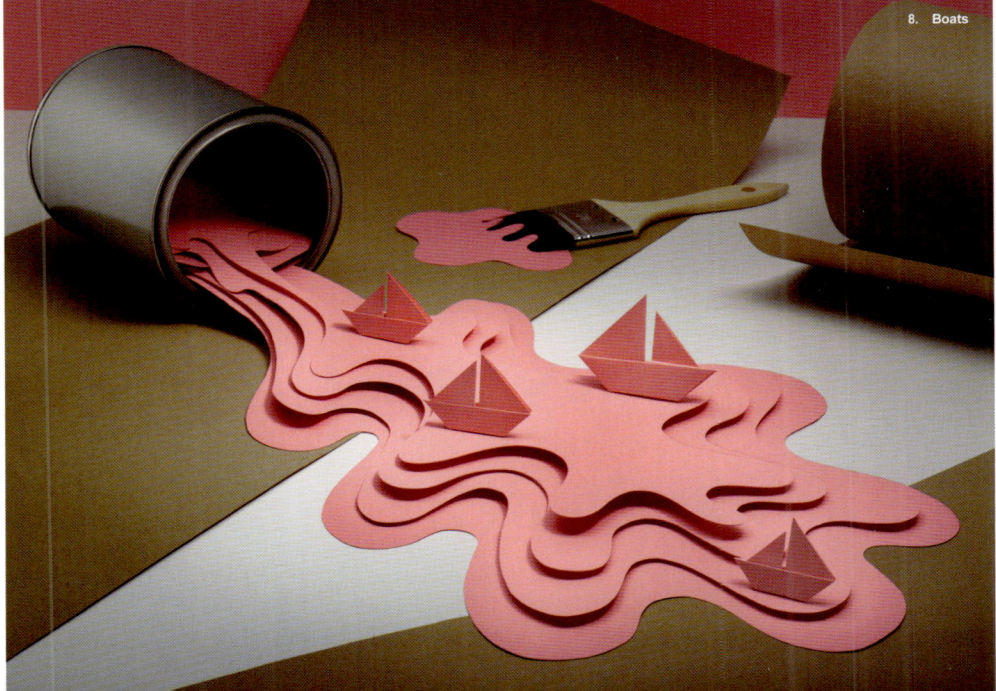

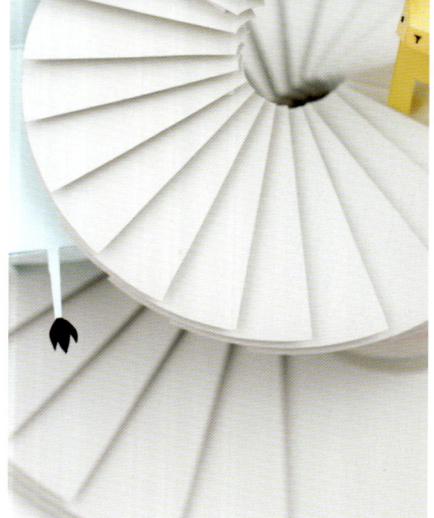
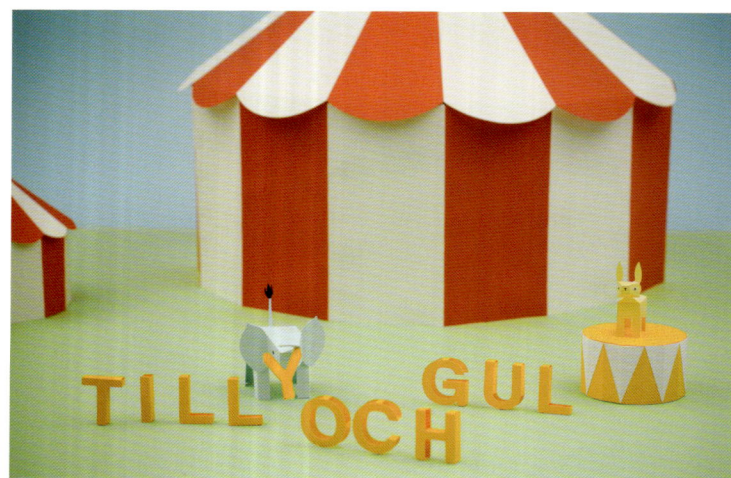
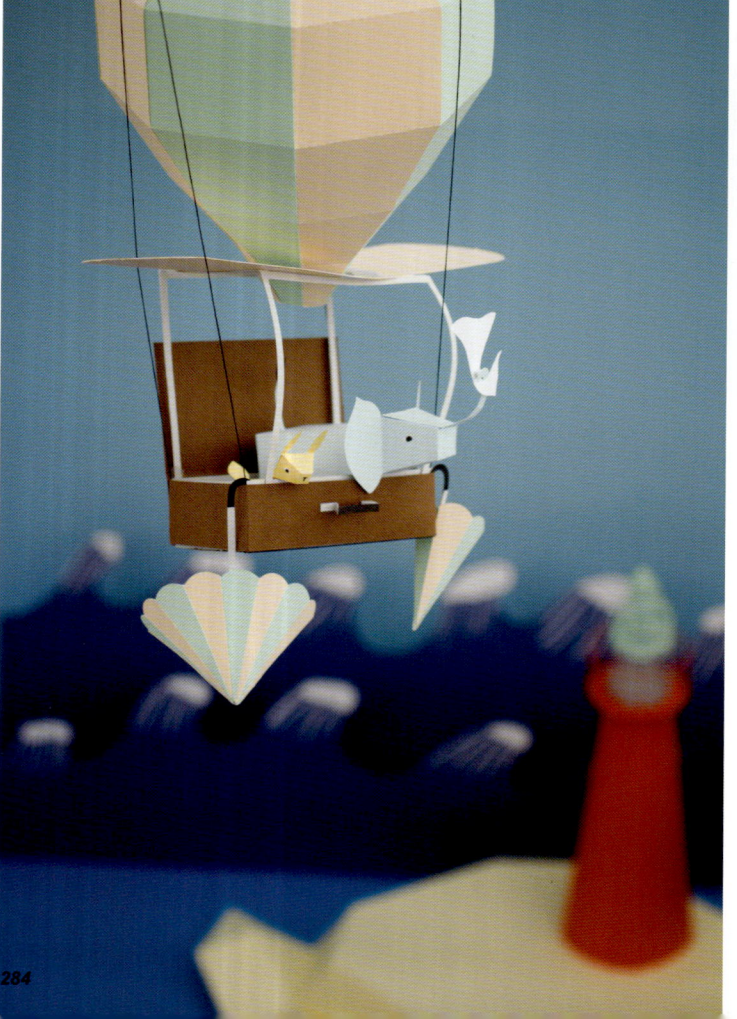
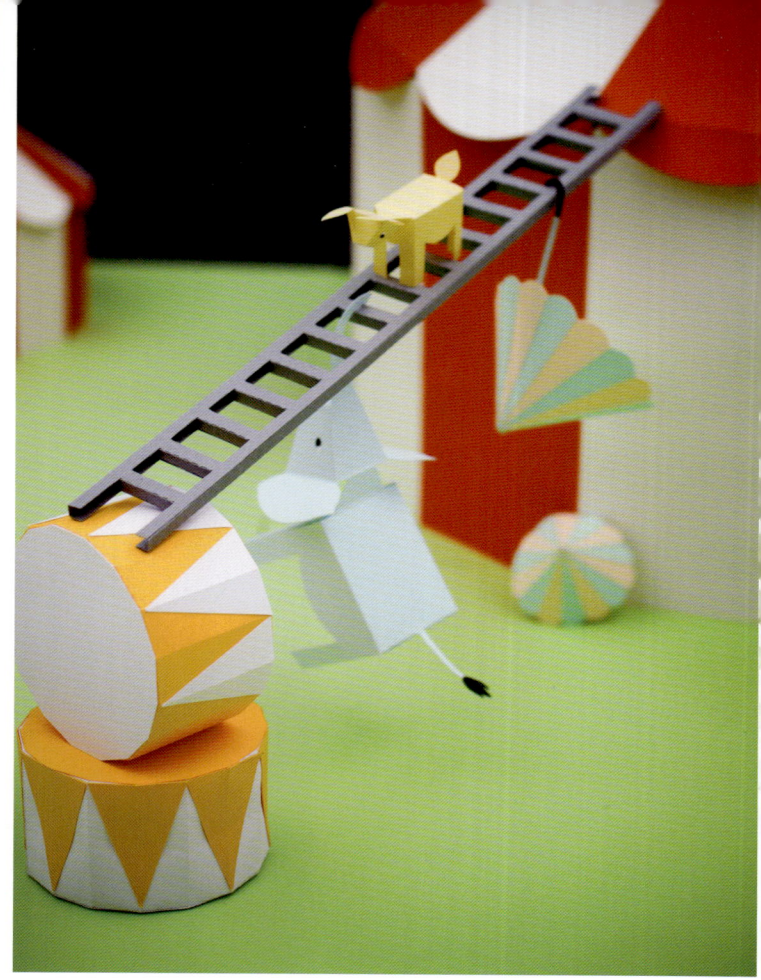
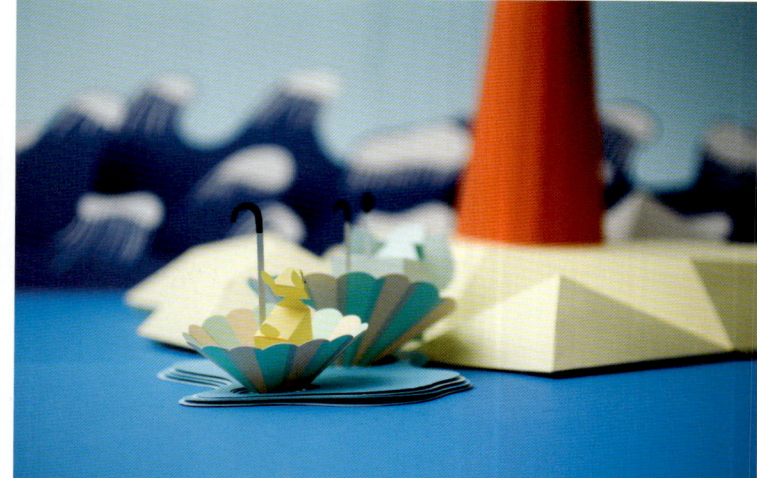

9. **Tilly & Gul**

"Tilly & Gul" is a three-dimensional picture story built from paper. It's about two small friends and their adventures on the sea.

Designer / Papercut artist: Fideli Sundqvist
Country: Sweden
Creative Director: Fideli Sundqvist
Photographer: Fideli Sundqvist

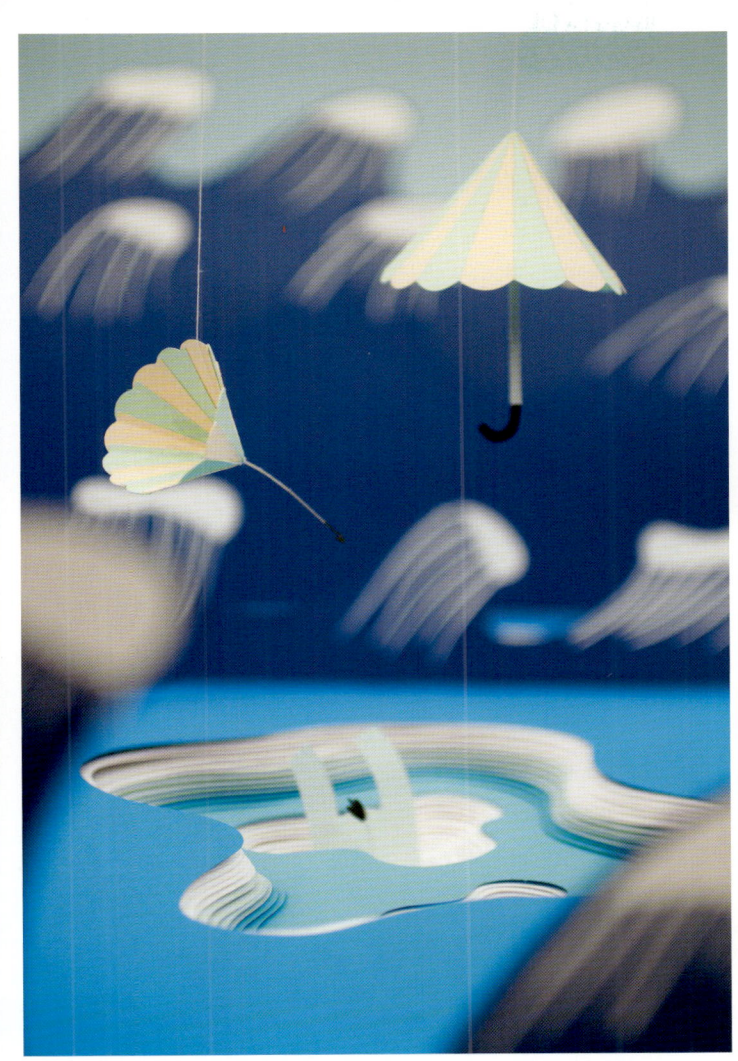
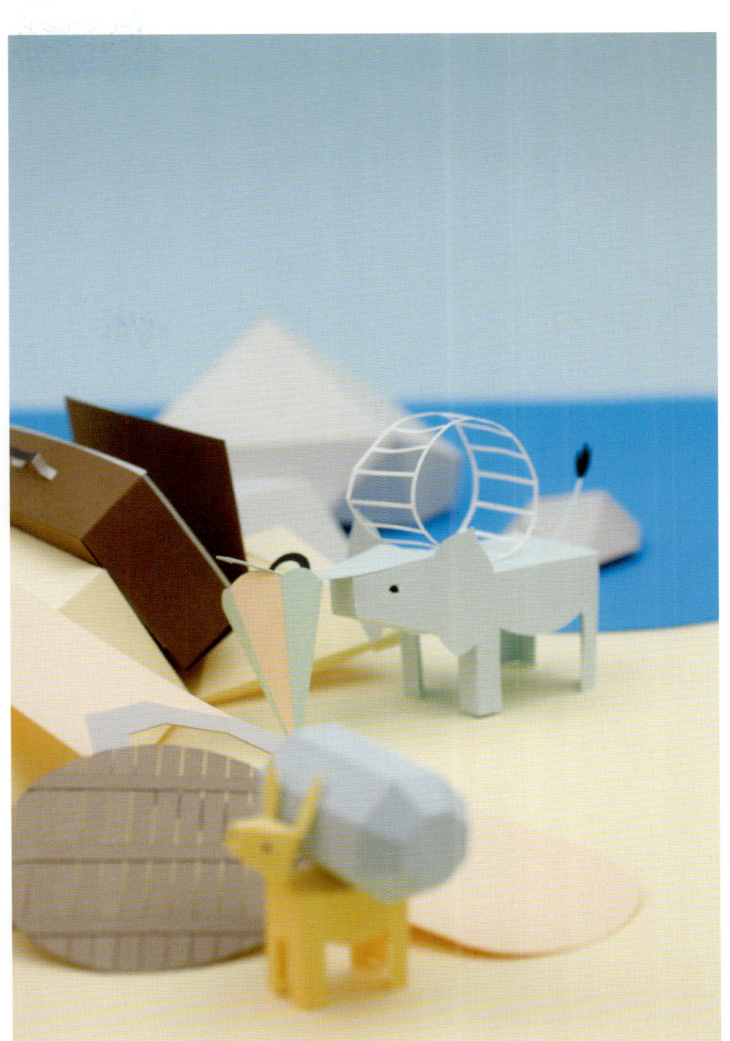

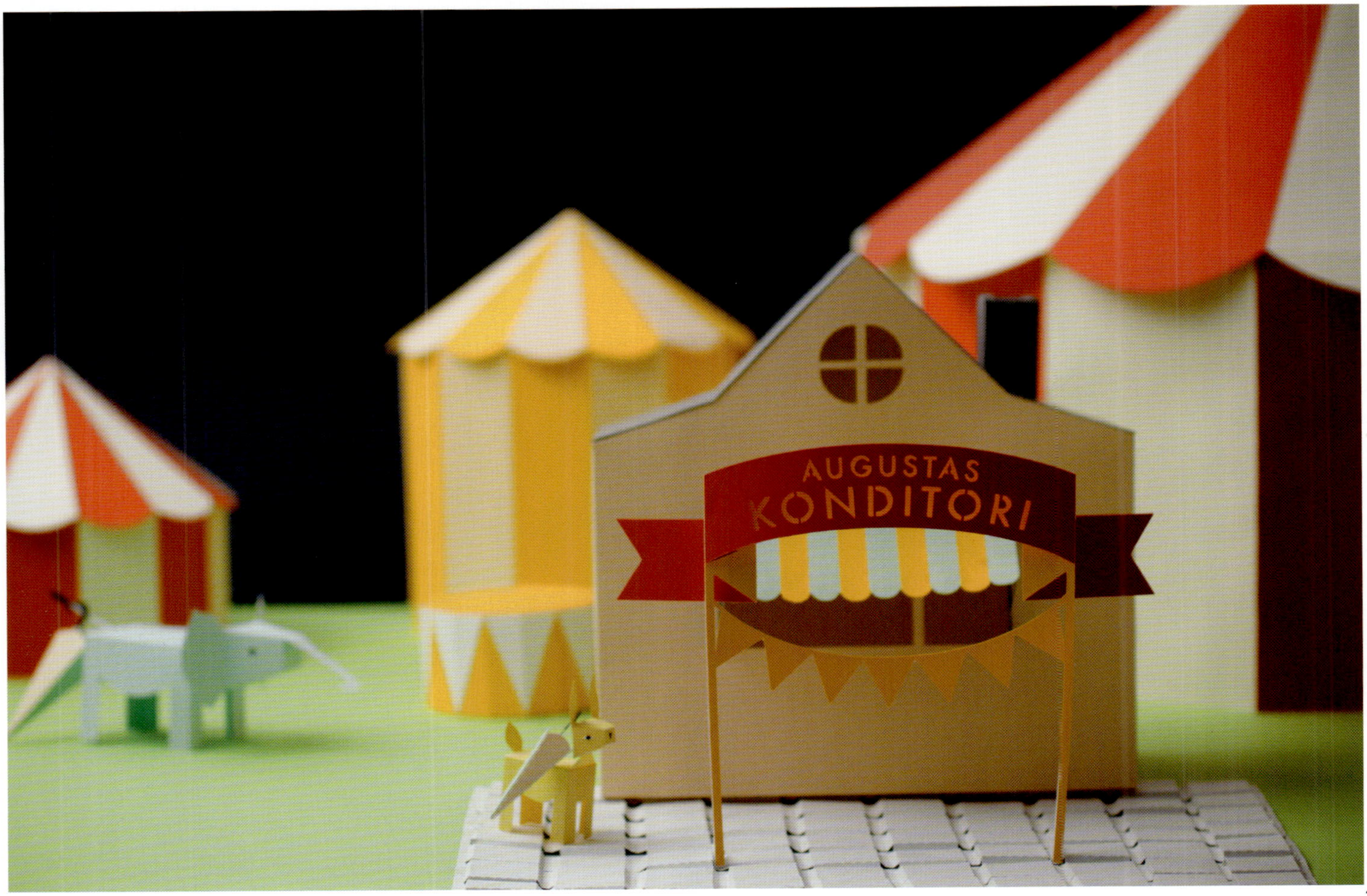

285

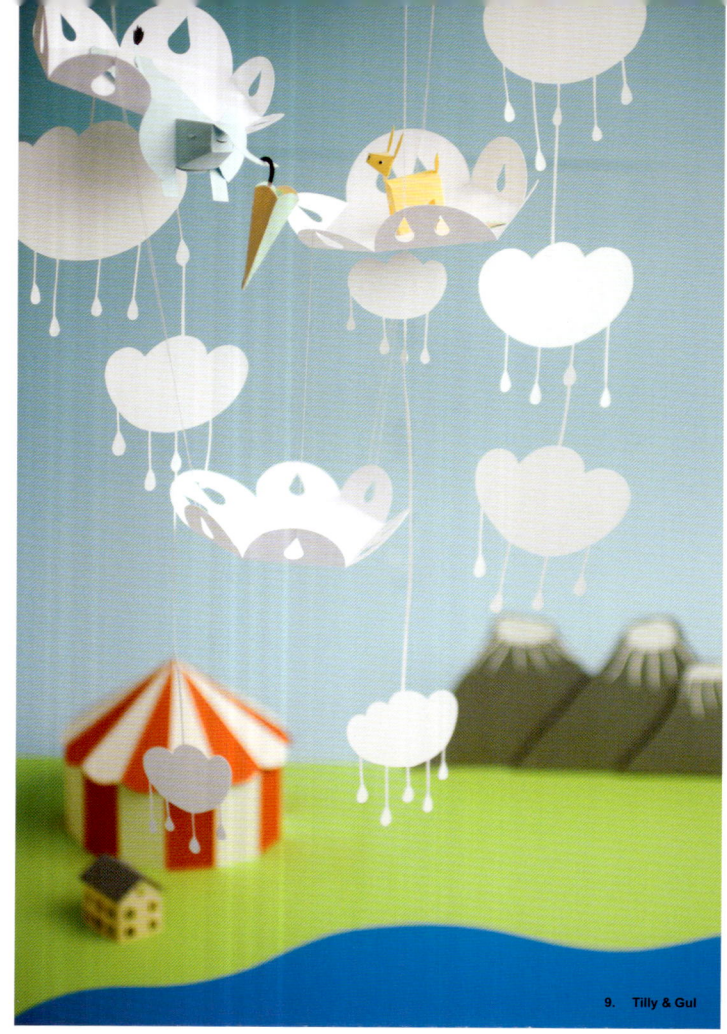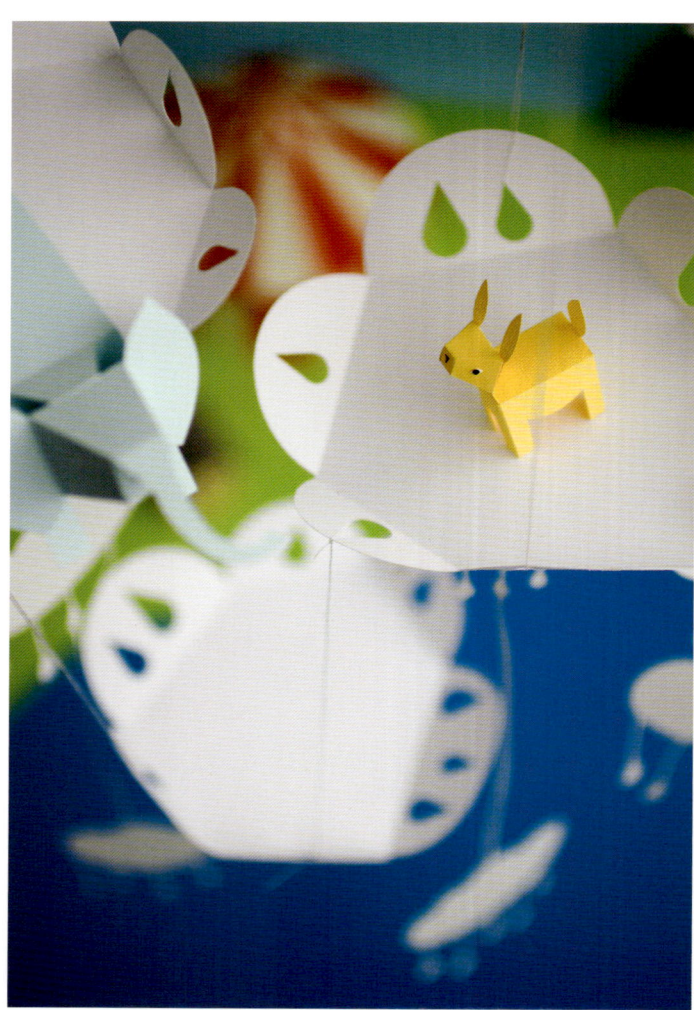

9. Tilly & Gul

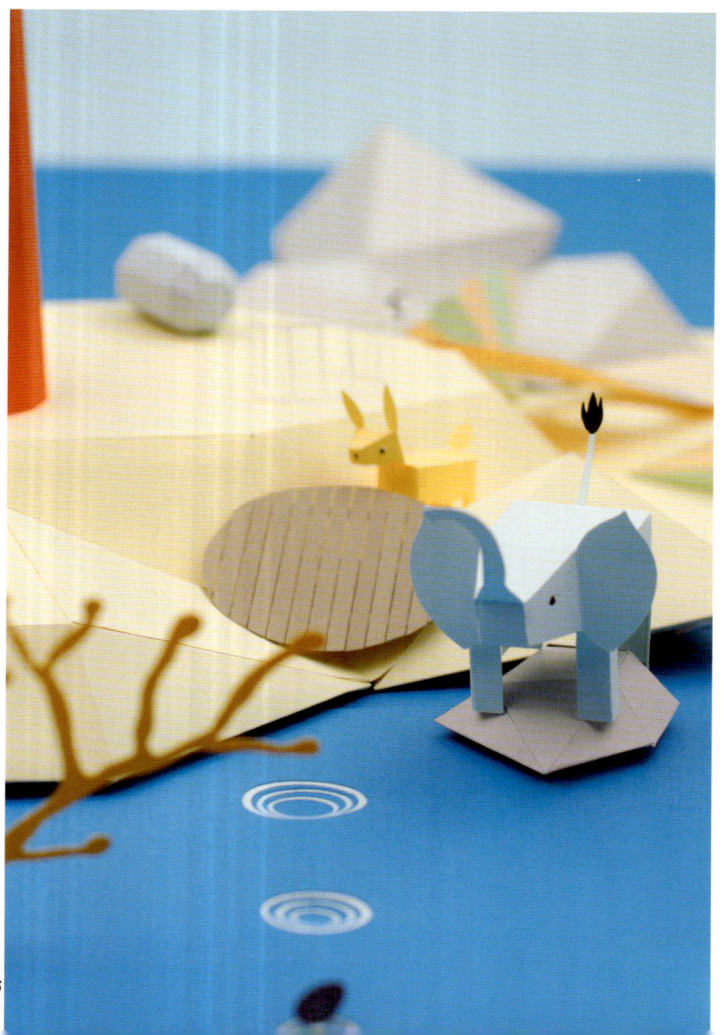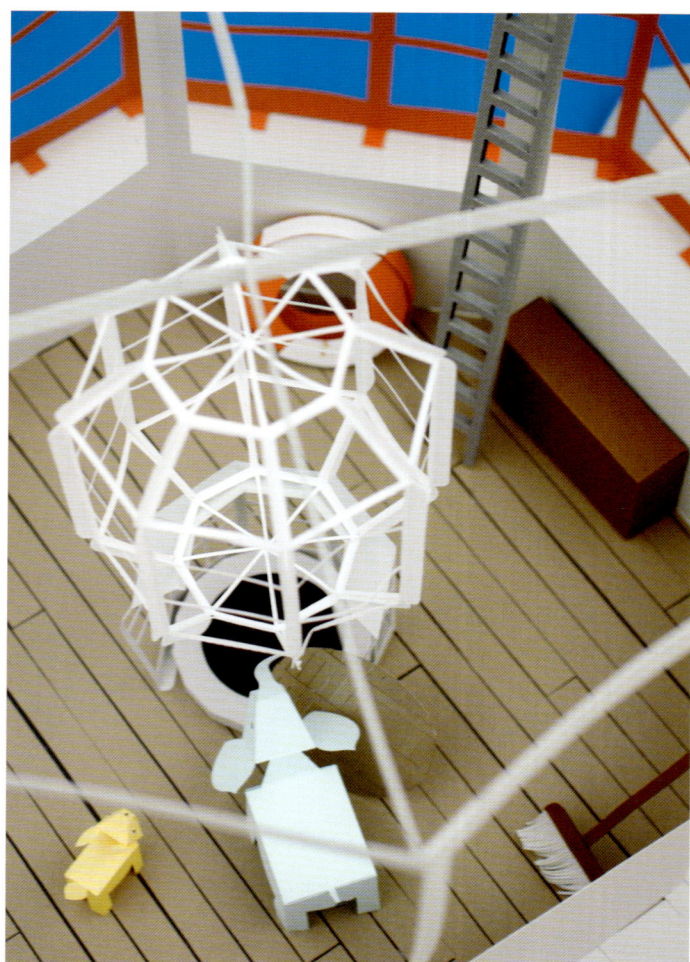

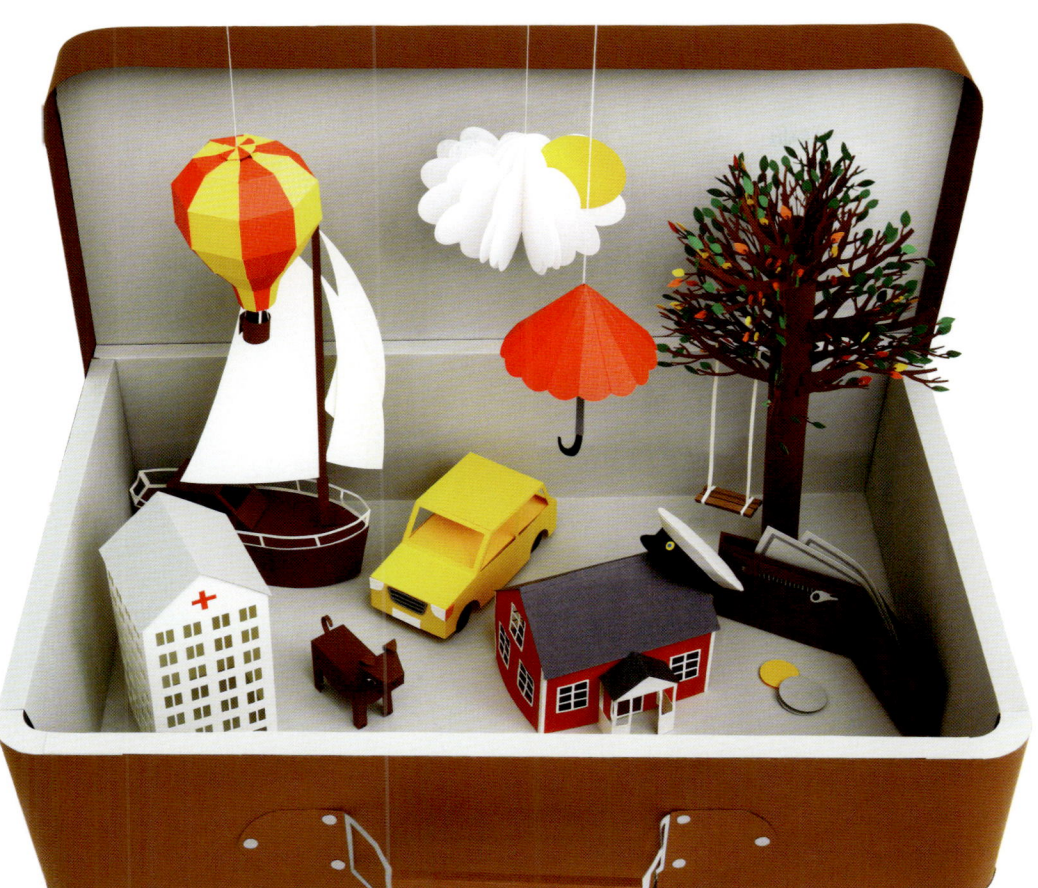

10. Akademikerförsäkring / Graduates Insurance

Any insurance type is a separate figure built in paper.
These can together then build up into a small world.

Designer / Papercut artist: Fideli Sundqvist
Country: Sweden
Creative Director: Jörgen Jörälv / Niklas Ackerstedt (AD)
Design Director: FamiljenPangea / Joanna Lavén / Fideli Sundqvist

11. Shortcut

One interpretation of the contents of the magazine "Shortcut".

Designer / Papercut artist: Fideli Sundqvist
Country: Sweden
Creative Director / AD: Johan Sundqvist
Photographer: Jezzica Sunmo

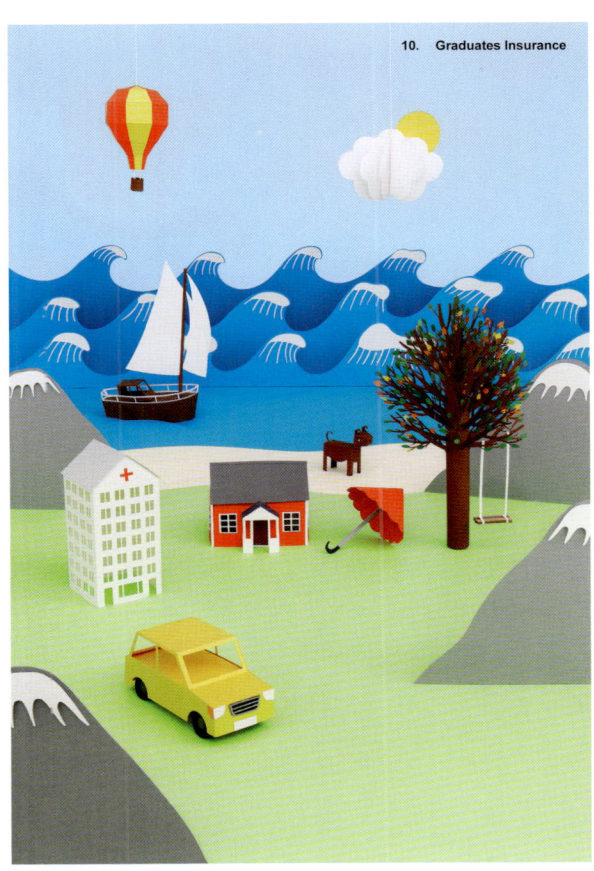

10. Graduates Insurance

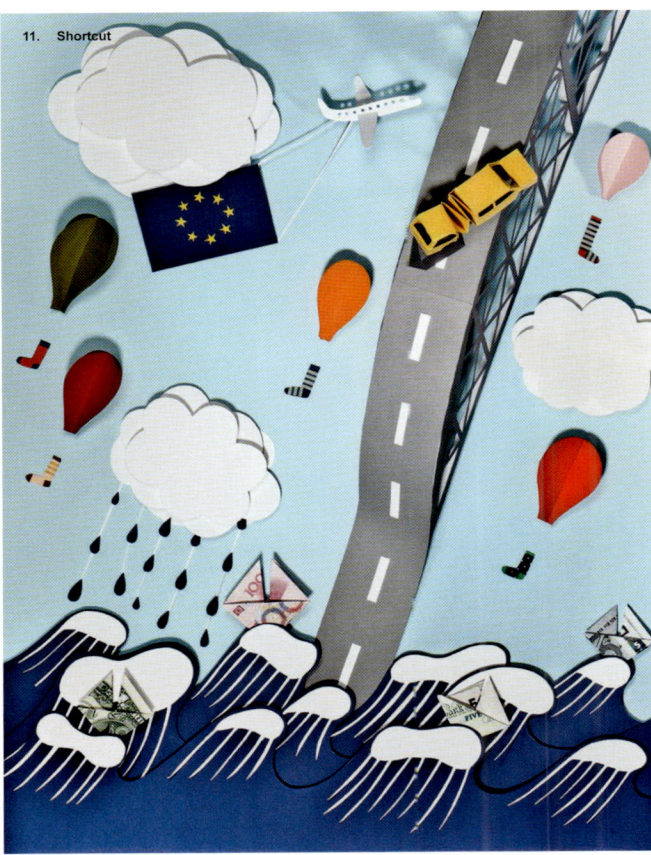

11. Shortcut

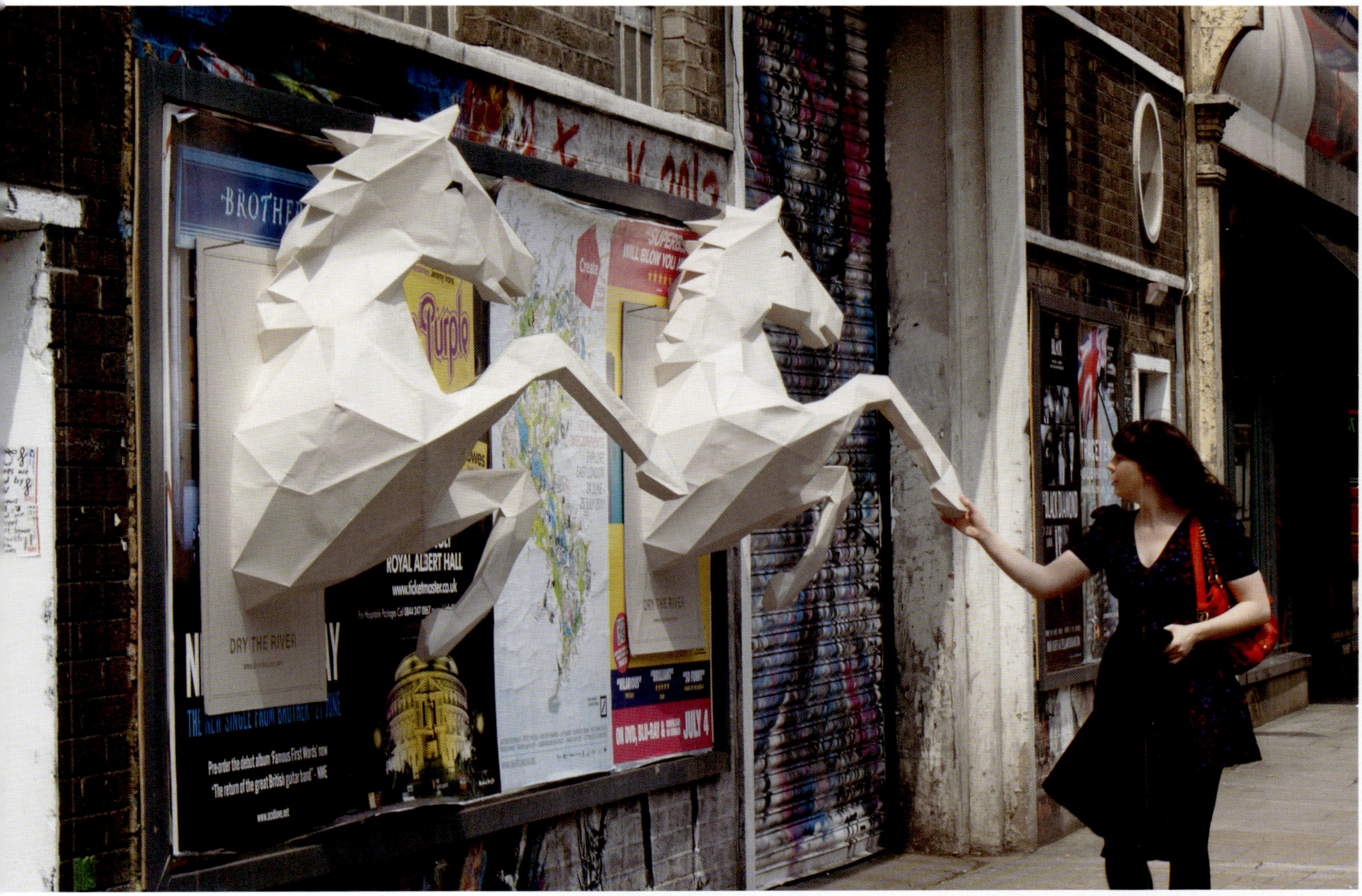

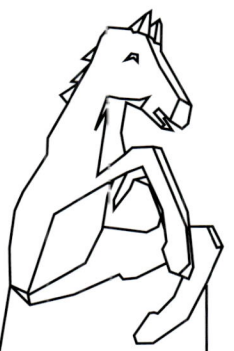

Dry the River Horse's – a 3D papercraft poster project

We created these huge paper-craft posters for the new RCA signing Dry the River. FOAM intern Xavier Barrade designed the 3D horses in Google Sketch Up before Printing out all of the component parts and assembling them by hand. The flat "base" for each poser was a screen printed by Bob Wight Pop in East London. Each poster took around 35 hours to complete.

---FOAM Agency

Once they were built we hung them around London with the help of a hammer and some rusty nails. Director Ricky Stanton made us a charming short film showing passers'-by reacting to the posters. We achieved great coverage in the art, design, creative and music press, and the Dry the River official video shot up from 10,000 views to 256,000 views as a result of the publicity caused by the campaign.

Design Agency: FOAM Agency
Country: UK
Designer: Xavier Barrade
Creative Director: Phil Clandillon & Steve Milbourne
Client: RCA Label Group (UK)Ltd
Photographer: Ricky Stanton

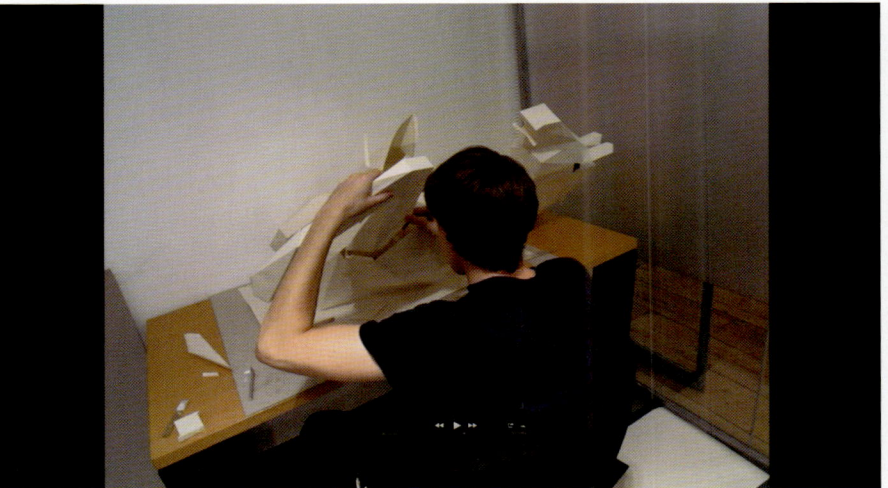

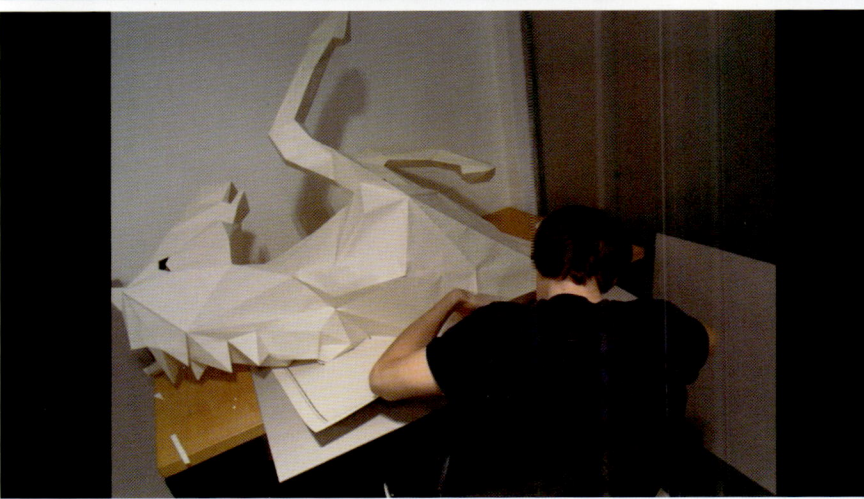

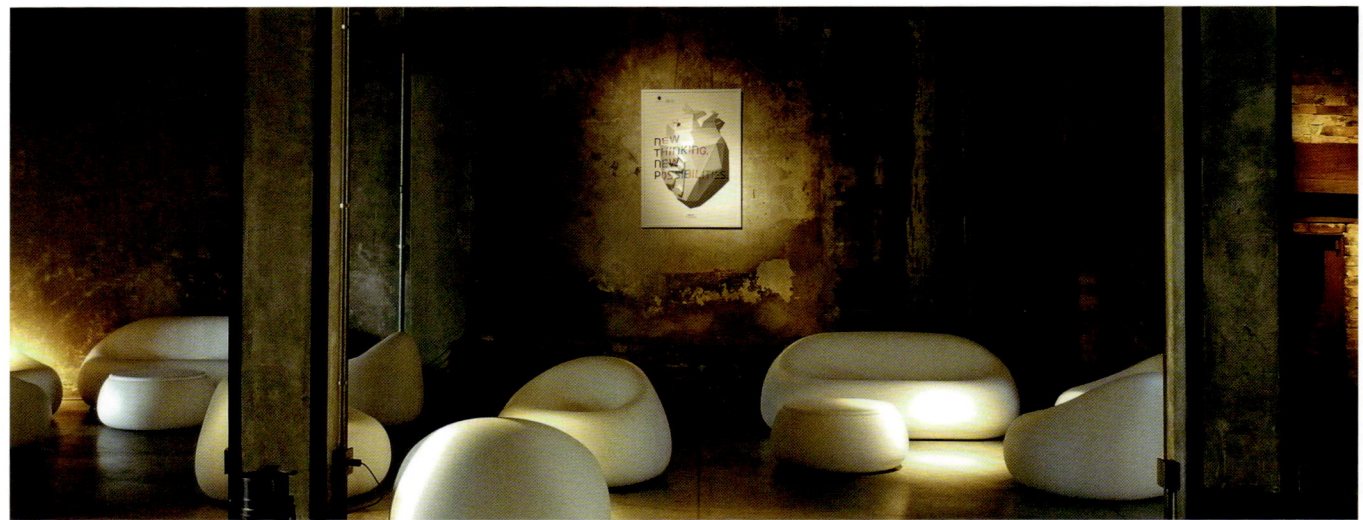

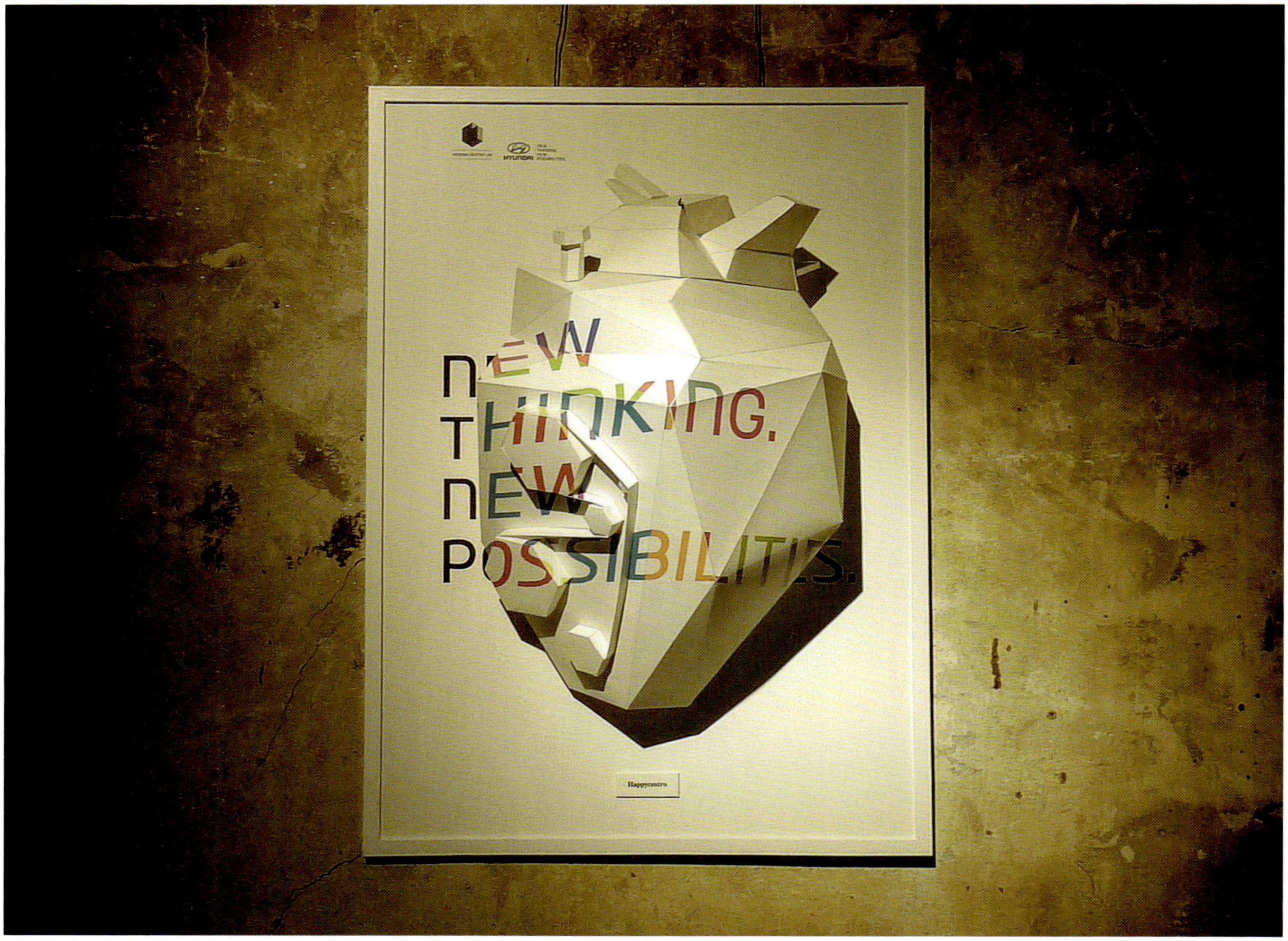

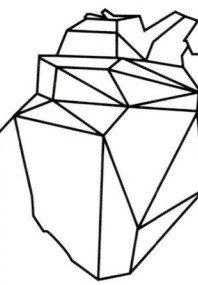

1. Cuore Motore – Hyundai. New Thinking. New Possibilities

Hyundai, on the occasion of Milano Design Week 2012, announced a prize-on-call to produce a poster whose theme to be interpreted is "New Thinking, New Possibilities".
It has been both the starting and ending point of our approach: We decided to interpret the concept to the deepest, starting by breaking the one and only rule: do not modify the pay-off visual. Our "New Thinking" dealt with walking the untreaded path. The unexpected hides new possibilities to be discovered, and we followed that direction just by changing point of view.
That's why we decided to look at the sentence not only as a sequence of words, but as a typographic object too, whose appearance could be manipulated without loosing its meaning.
There's one and only point of view from which the poster reads the correct sentence, while slightly shifting aside the trick is unveiled: the typography lays upon the multifaceted paper object underneath, being split to spread over faces that build the heart/engine up.
Technlogy, technique, machine – Love, Passion, Man.
Forever elements of a unique universe, the first being generated from the other's creativity.
Many issues are telling ourselves about the need that tech development get closer to human needs and his environment. They are more and more the pivot of every new project that's why a small human thrones over the symbol of his own huge creative power.

---Happycentro

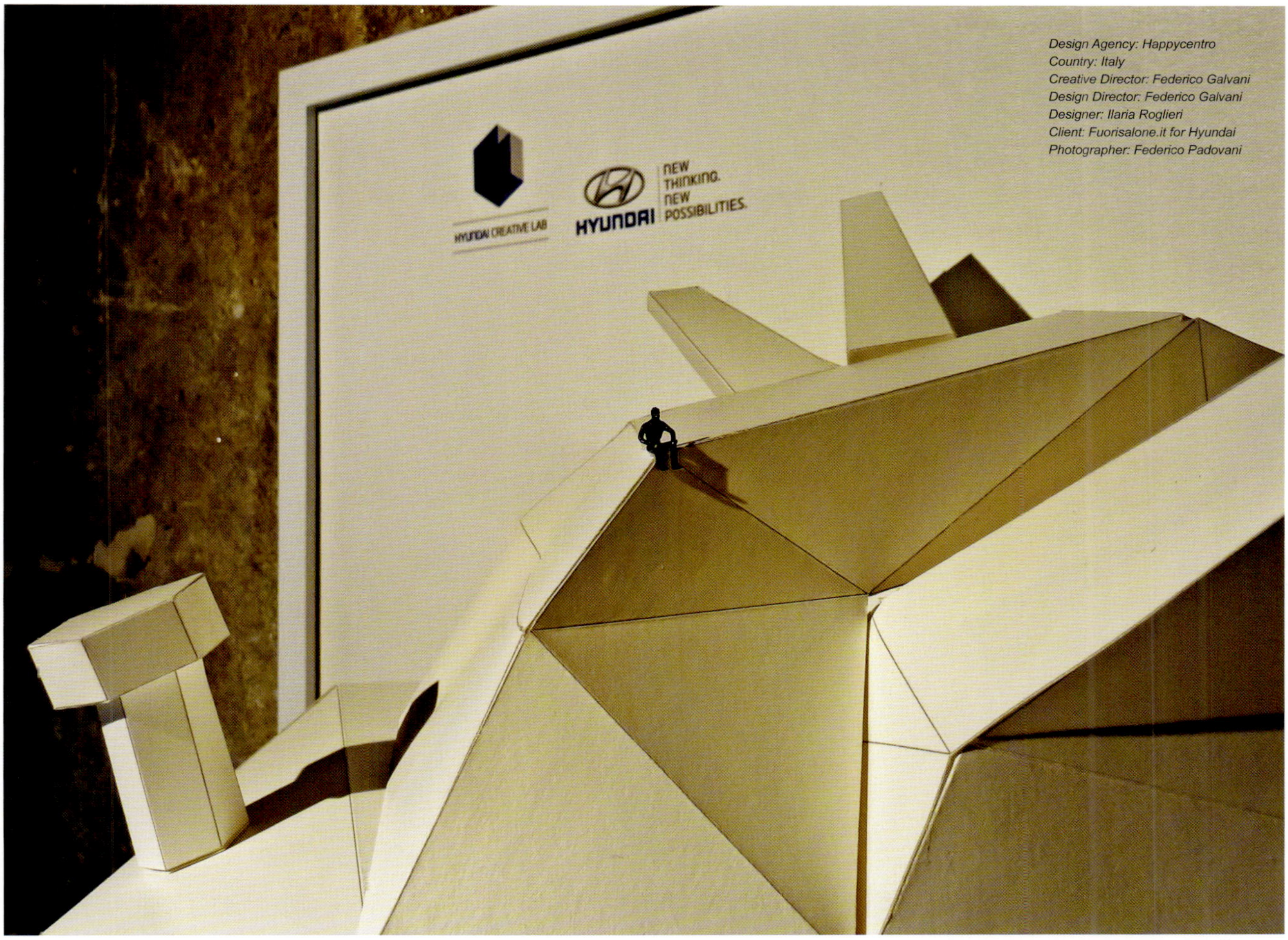

Design Agency: Happycentro
Country: Italy
Creative Director: Federico Galvani
Design Director: Federico Galvani
Designer: Ilaria Roglieri
Client: Fuorisalone.it for Hyundai
Photographer: Federico Padovani

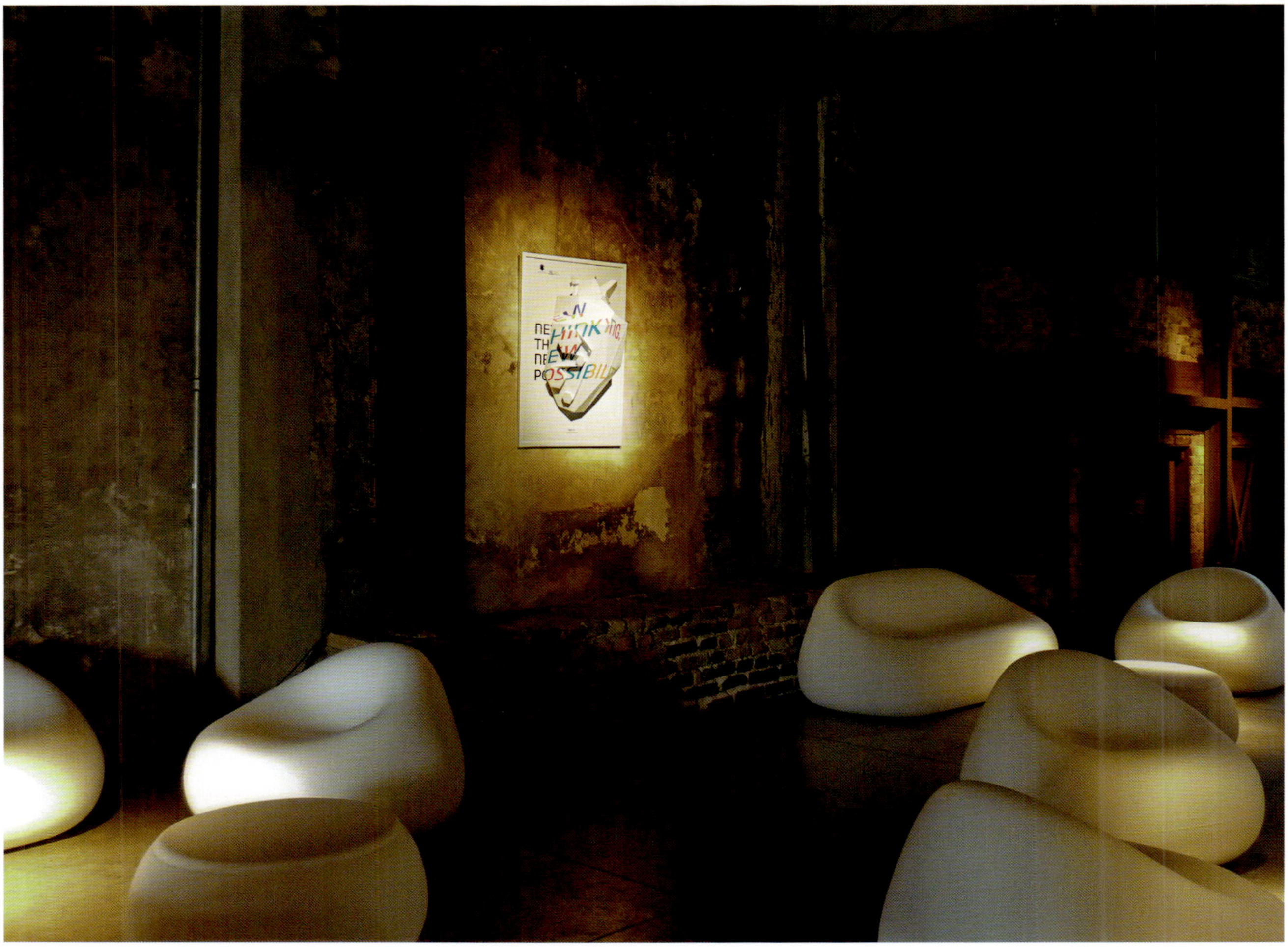

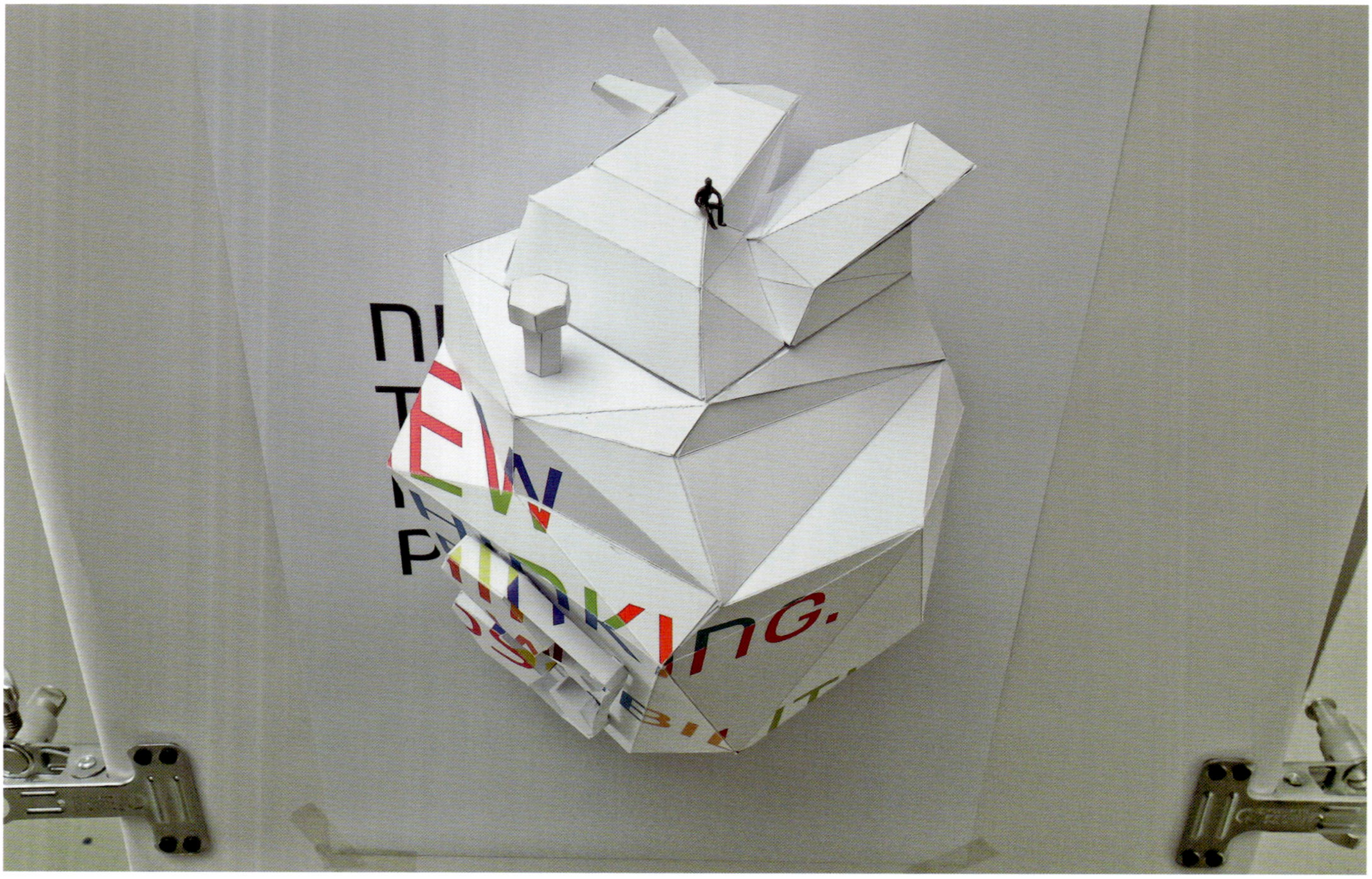

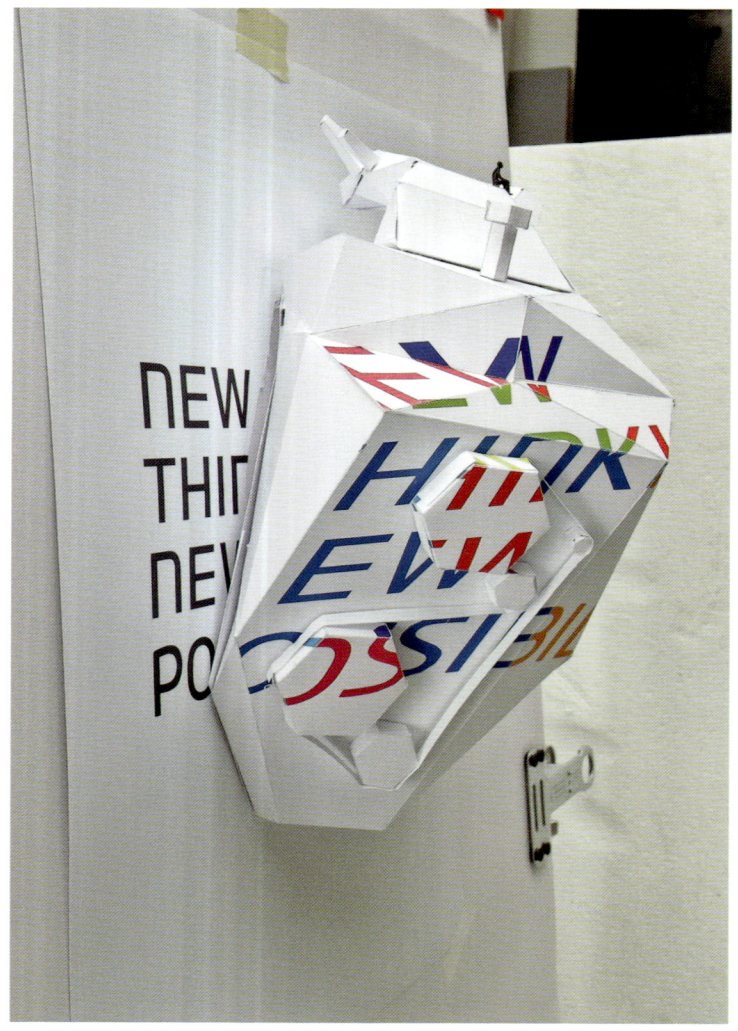
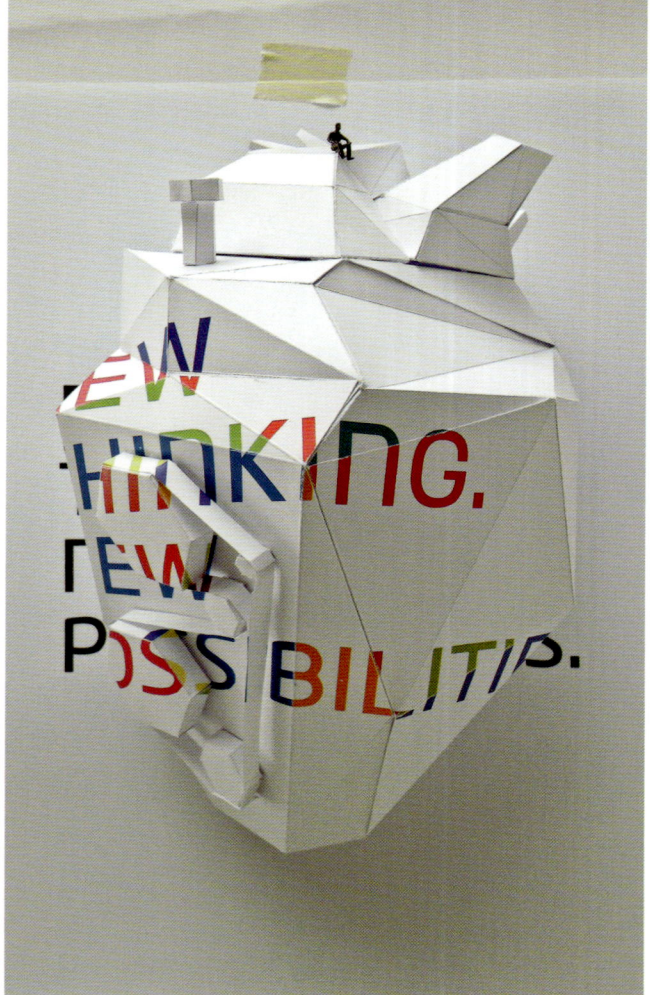

1. *Cuore Motore – Hyundai. New Thinking. New Possibilities*

Design Agency: Happycentro
Country: Italy
Creative Director: Federico Galvani
Design Director: Federico Galvani
Designer: Ilaria Roglieri
Client: Fuorisalone.it for Hyundai
Photographer: Federico Padovani

 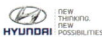

HYUNDAI IX 35

SCALA 1:10

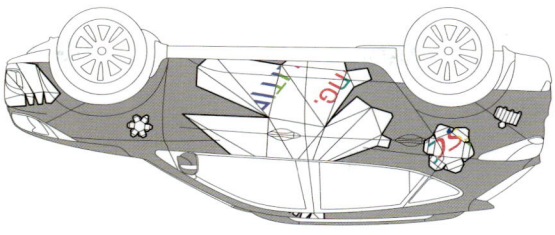

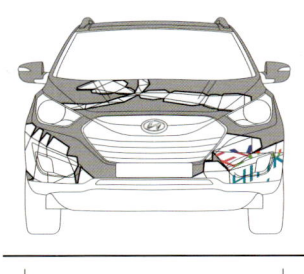 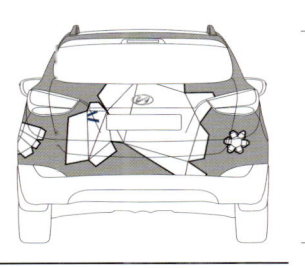

1.820   880   2.640   890   1.592
4.410
1.670

HYUNDAI IX 35

FOTO

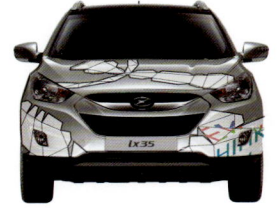 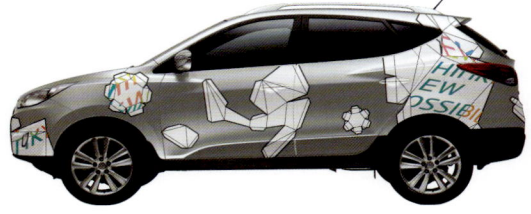 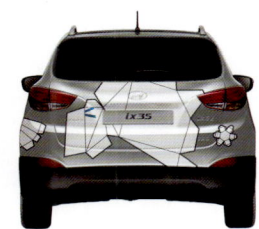

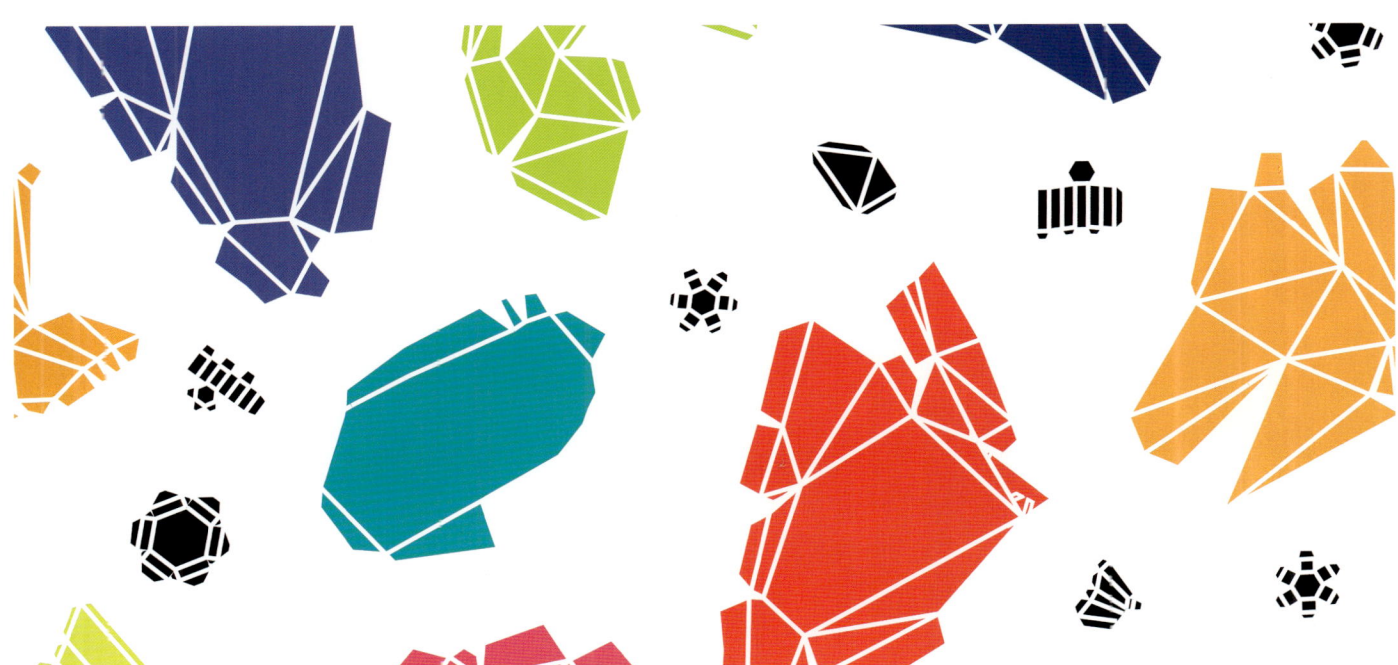

2. **Paper Objects**

This is a selfpromotional project. We really like the crafting feeling, the paper surfaces and the mix of the process ink. We love the culture of origami and with this project we personally tried to reinterpret the forms that arise from the paper. These are abstract forms and in the background you can see their structure. The light coming through the window and so it is a natural light, a daylight.

Design Agency: Happycentro
Country: Italy
Creative Director: Federico Galvani
Client: Self Commisioned

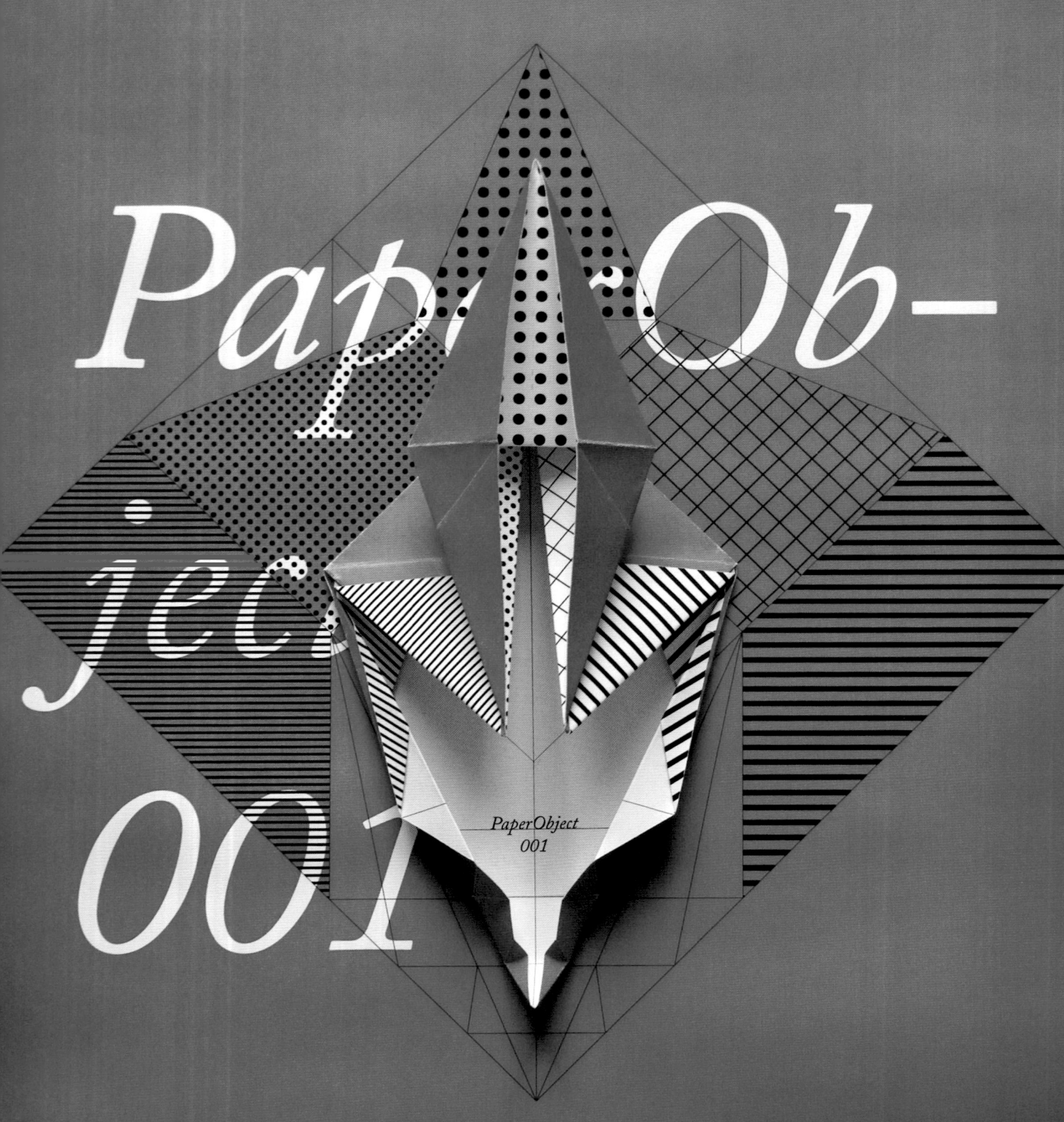

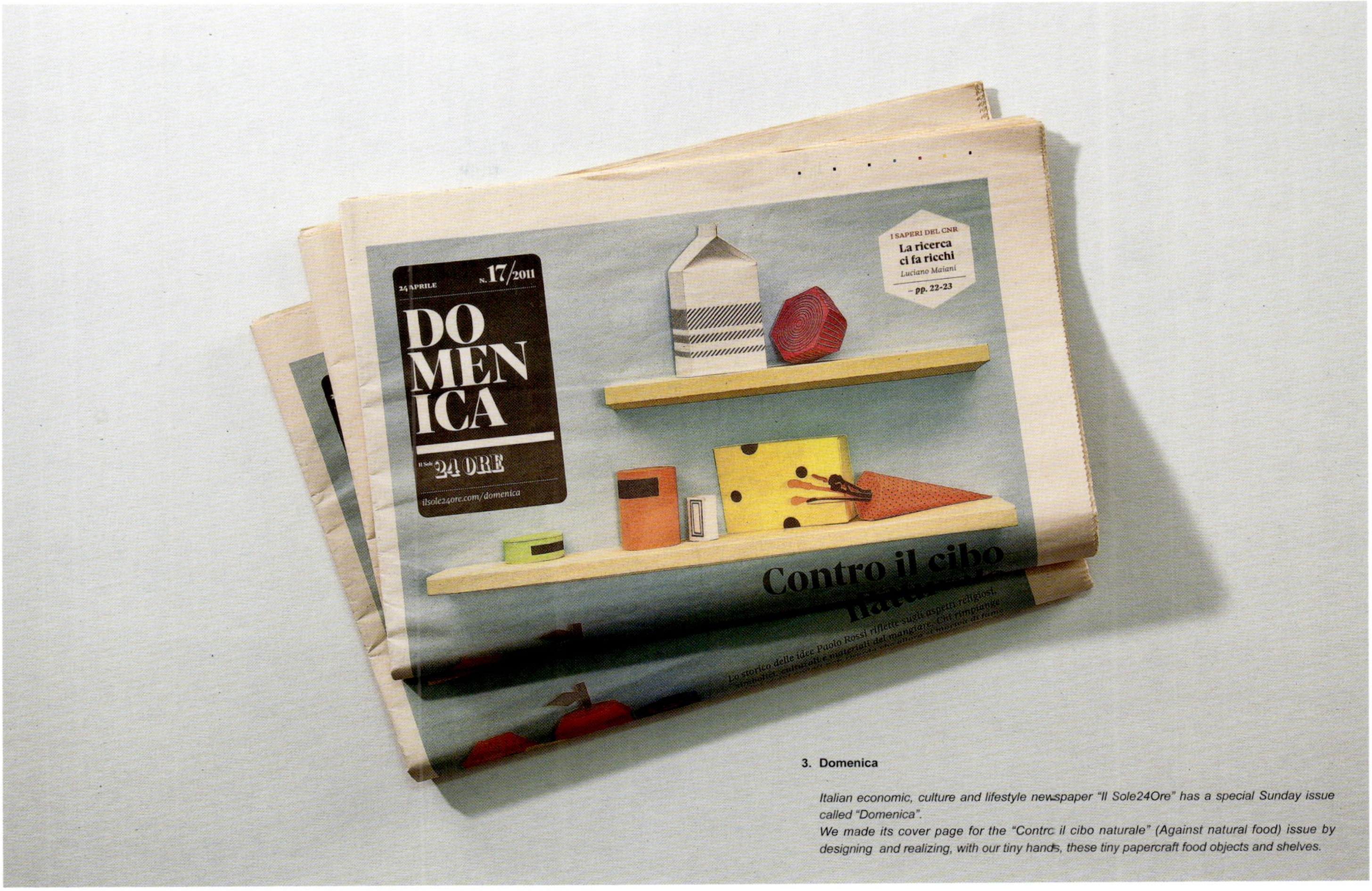

3. Domenica

Italian economic, culture and lifestyle newspaper "Il Sole24Ore" has a special Sunday issue called "Domenica".
We made its cover page for the "Contro il cibo naturale" (Against natural food) issue by designing and realizing, with our tiny hands, these tiny papercraft food objects and shelves.

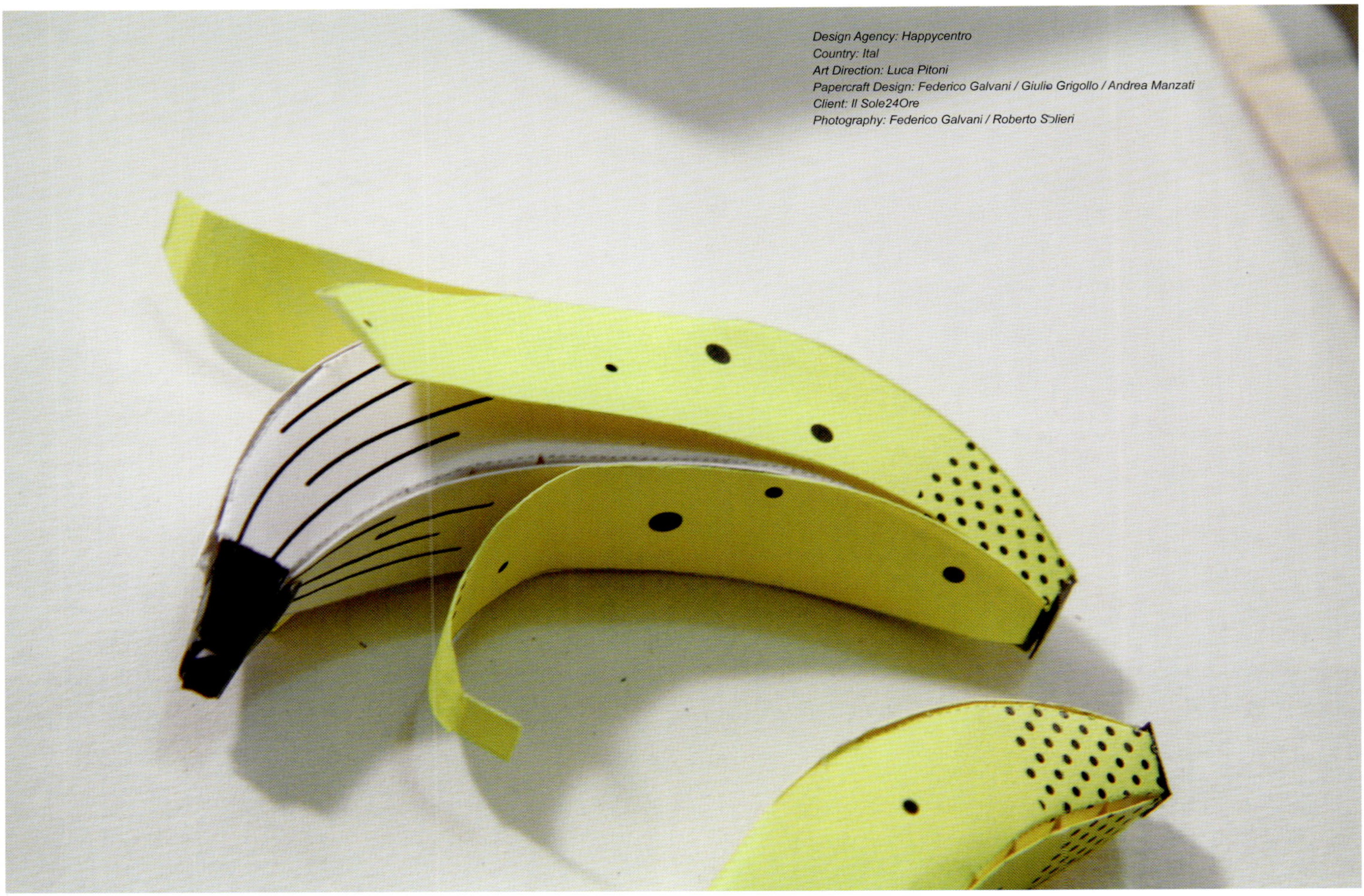

Design Agency: Happycentro
Country: Ital
Art Direction: Luca Pitoni
Papercraft Design: Federico Galvani / Giulie Grigollo / Andrea Manzati
Client: Il Sole24Ore
Photography: Federico Galvani / Roberto Solieri

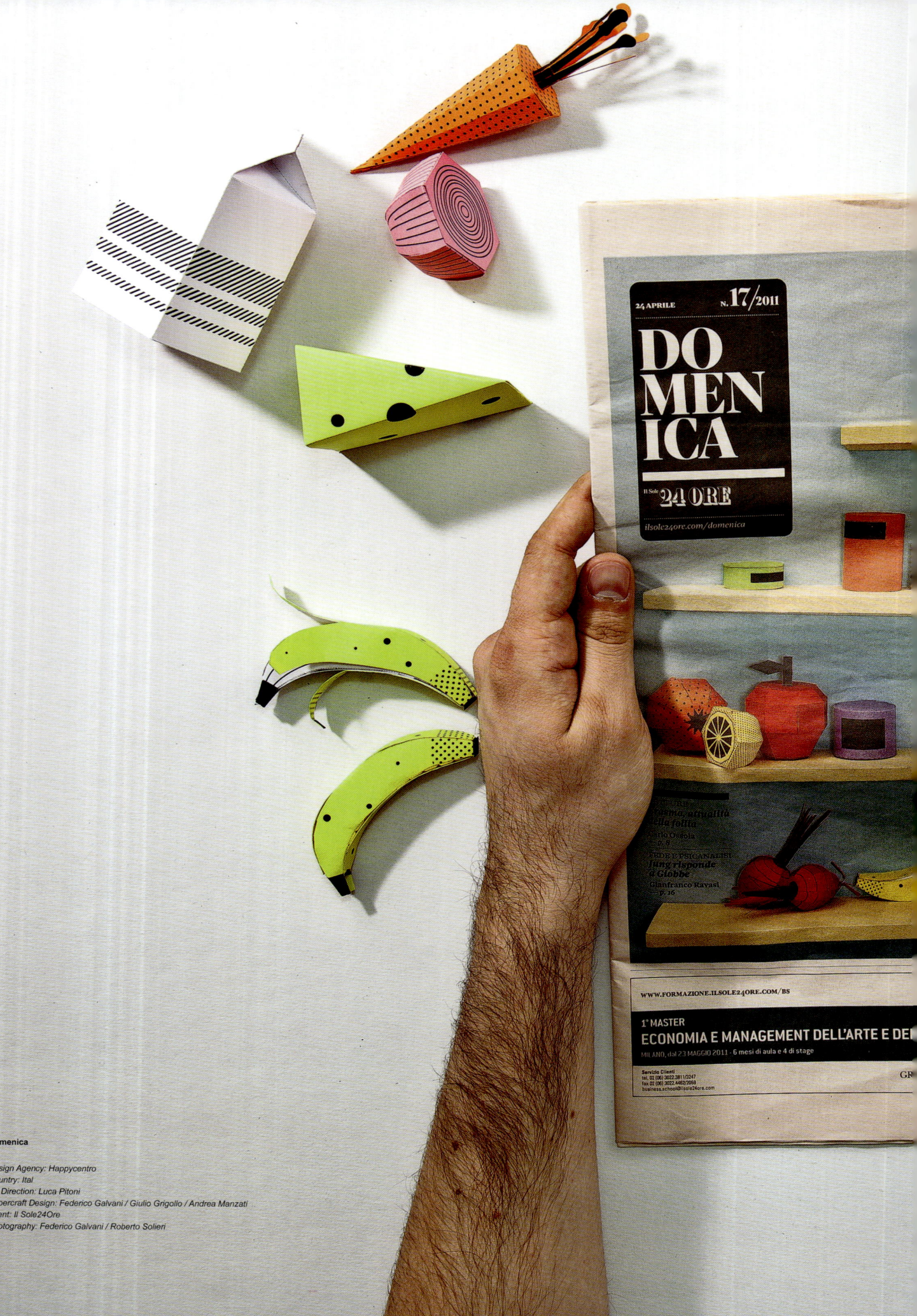

3. Domenica

Design Agency: Happycentro
Country: Ital
Art Direction: Luca Pitoni
Papercraft Design: Federico Galvani / Giulio Grigollo / Andrea Manzati
Client: Il Sole24Ore
Photography: Federico Galvani / Roberto Solieri

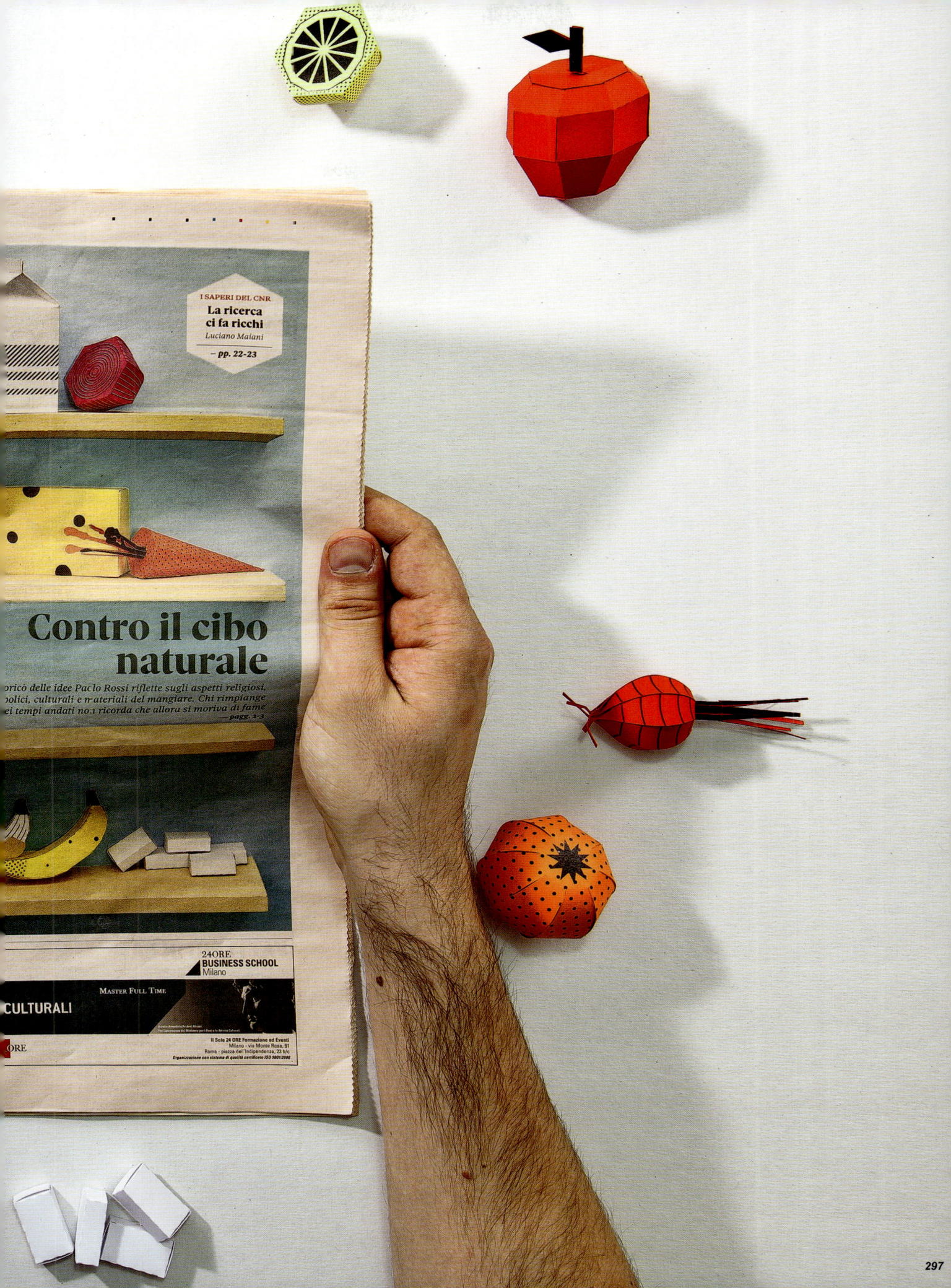

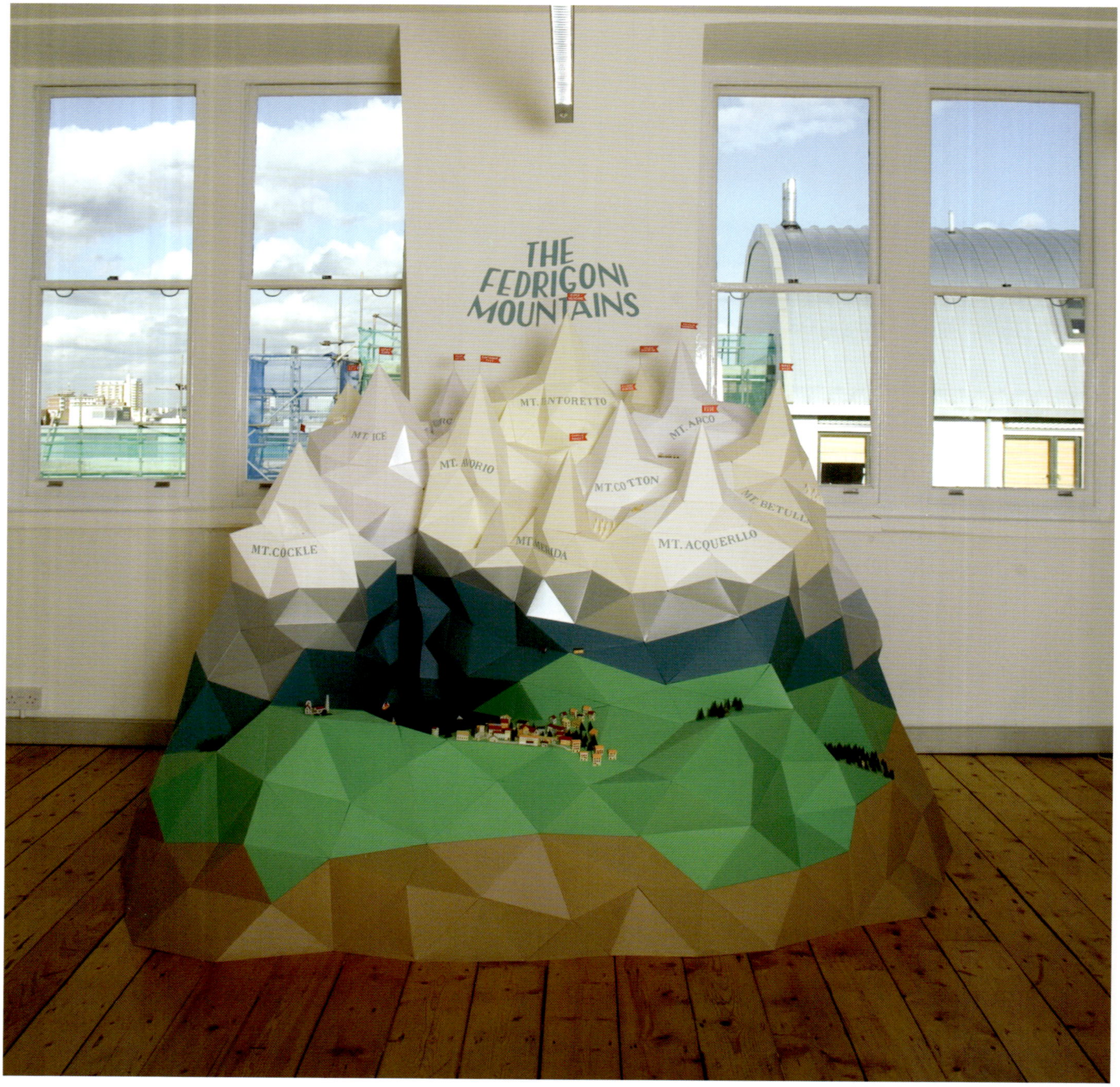

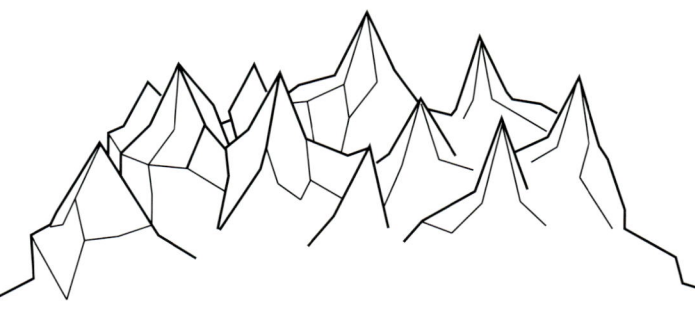

The Fedrigoni Mountains

The Paper Company, Fedrigoni invited me to create an installation to show off their range of papers in their London showroom. Fedrigoni's Paper Mill is located near Verona, Italy, and surrounded by the Dolomite Mountains. This inspired me to make a mountain range, around which I build little paper scenes like a mountain village, monster footprints, and a crashed aeroplane. It took me about 3 weeks, and literally mountains of paper to make, with the help of graphic designer Alex Ostrowski. I named each mountain peak after the names of the white papers. Twelve intrepid illustrators were invited to visualise an imaginary exploration of the paper slopes, resulting in an exhibition of their discoveries.

---Hattie Newman

Designer: Hattie Newman
Country: UK
Client: Fedrigoni
Photographer: Guy Archard

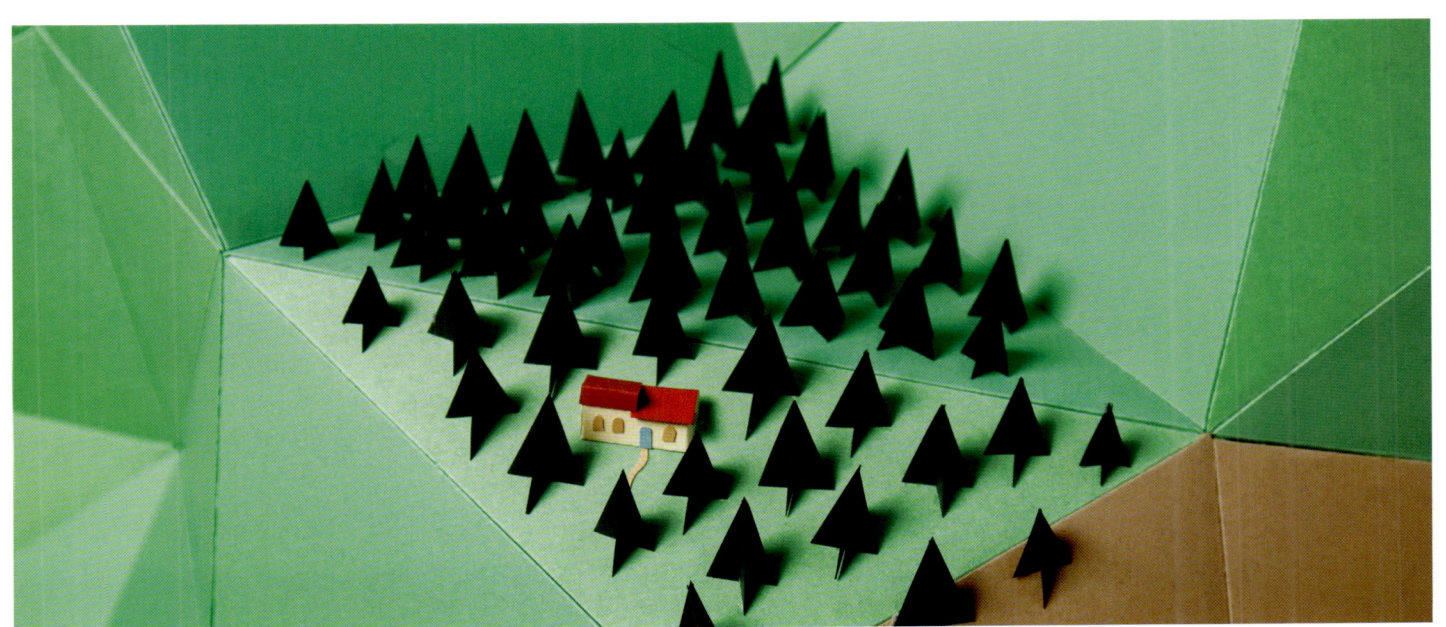
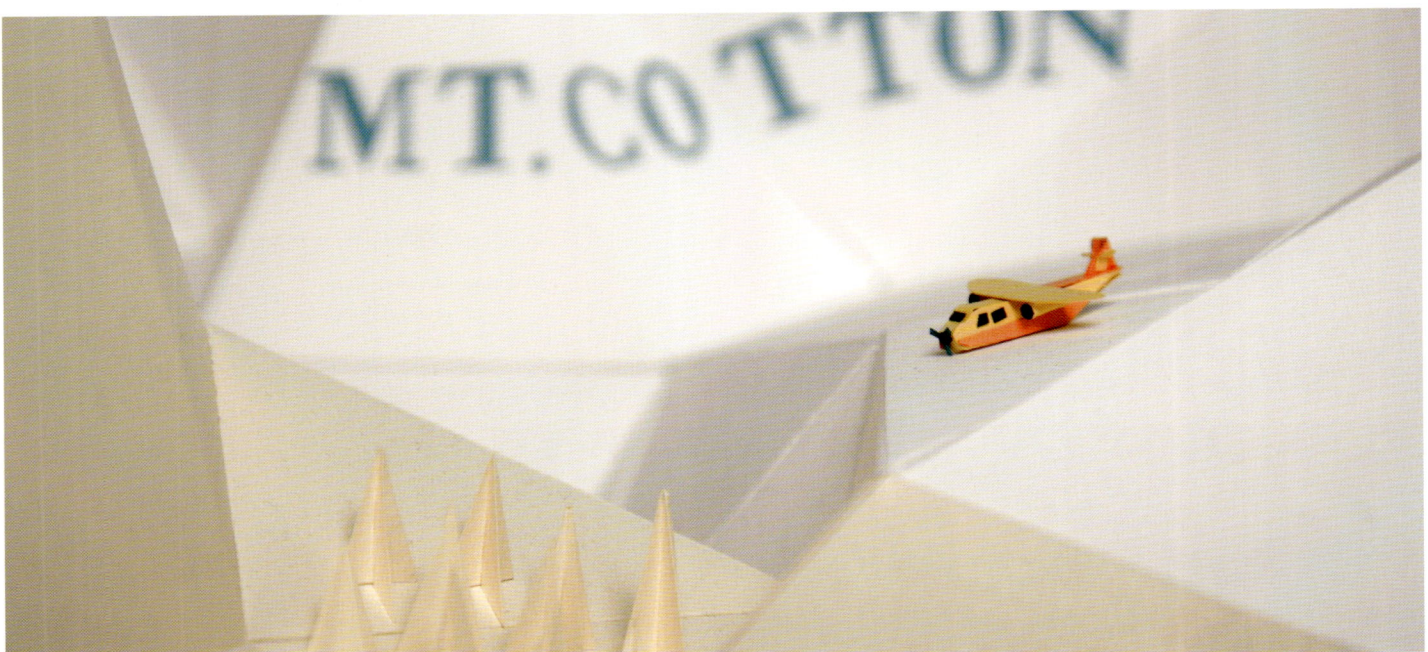
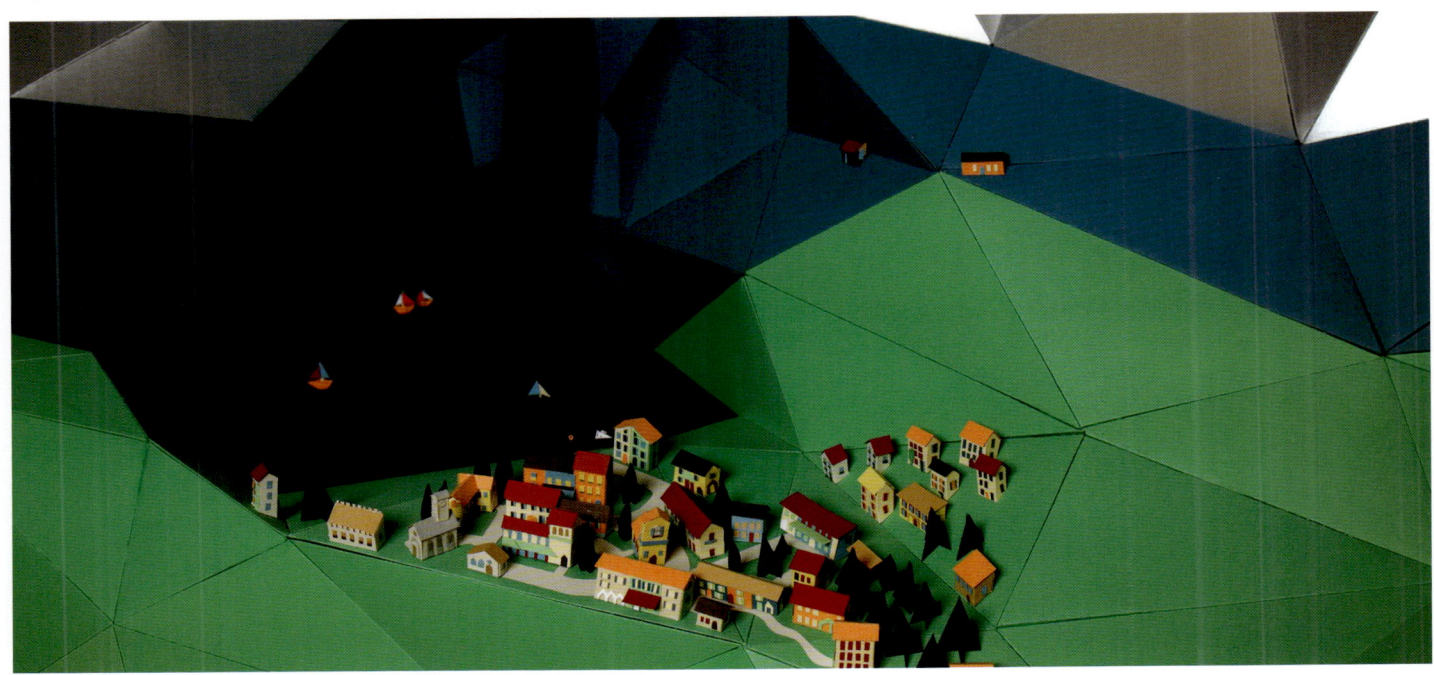

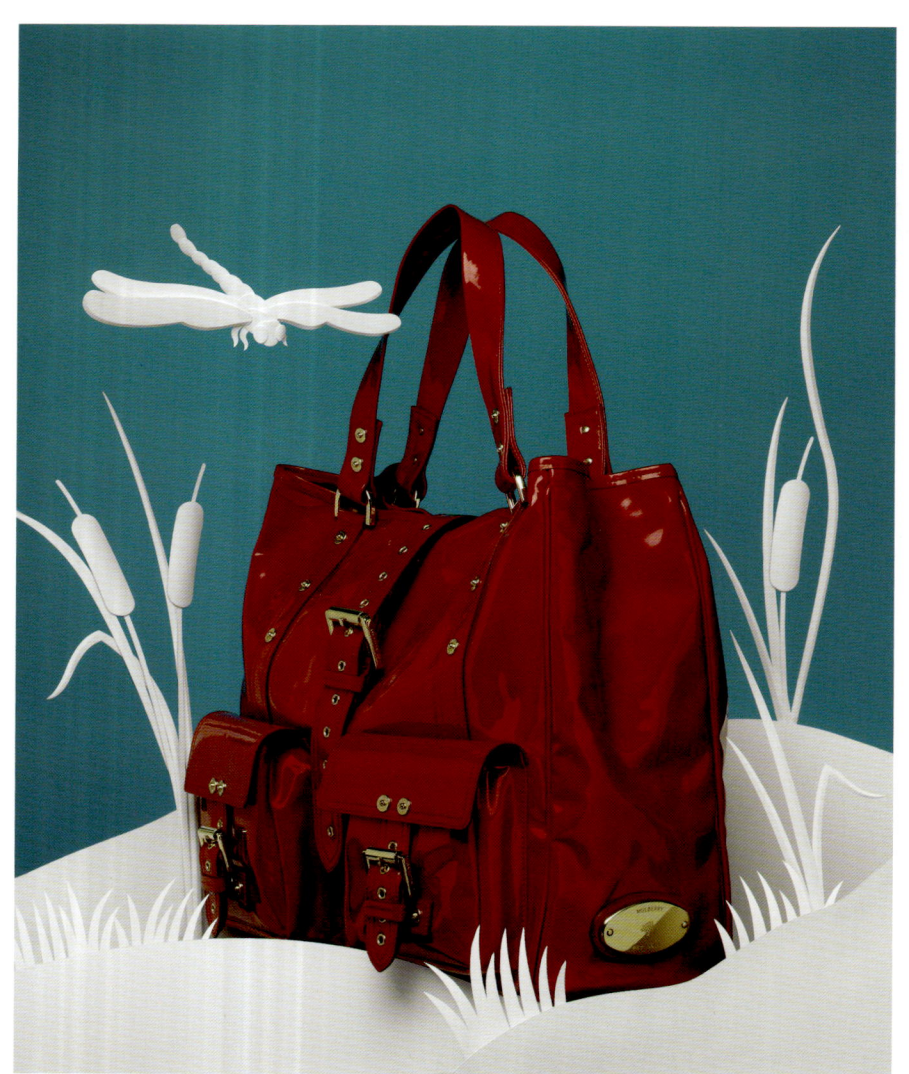
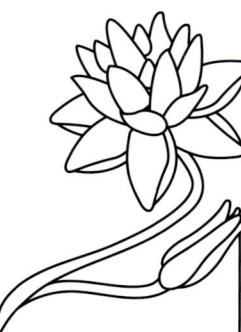

1. Bloomi's Spring
2. Galerie Lafayette
3. Hearts On Fire, The World's Most Perfectly Cut Diamond
4. Knorr Alfredo and Cheddar Pasta Saucesa
5. Secret Stone / Best Kept Secret
6. La Grande Epicerie
7. Polo Ralph Lauren Dragon
8. Peninsula Shanghai Hotel Dragon
9. Peninsula Chicago Hotel Dragon

---Jeff Nishinaka

1. Bloomingdale's Spring Catalog

Designer: Jeff Nishinaka   Country: USA
Design Agency: Bloomingdale's Creative Services
Creative Director: Amy Hansen
Client: Bloomingdale's (USA)
Photographer: Bela Borsodi

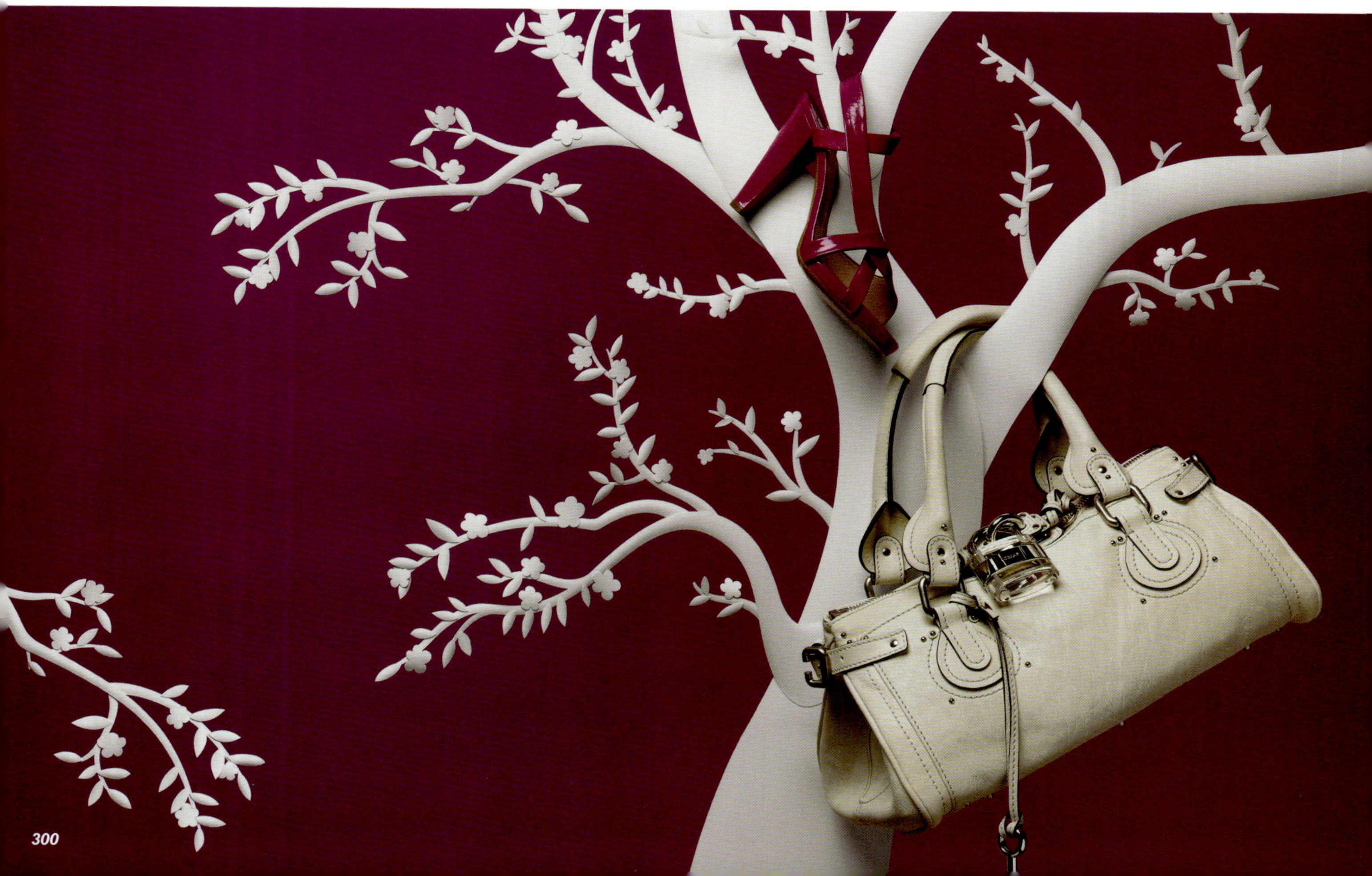

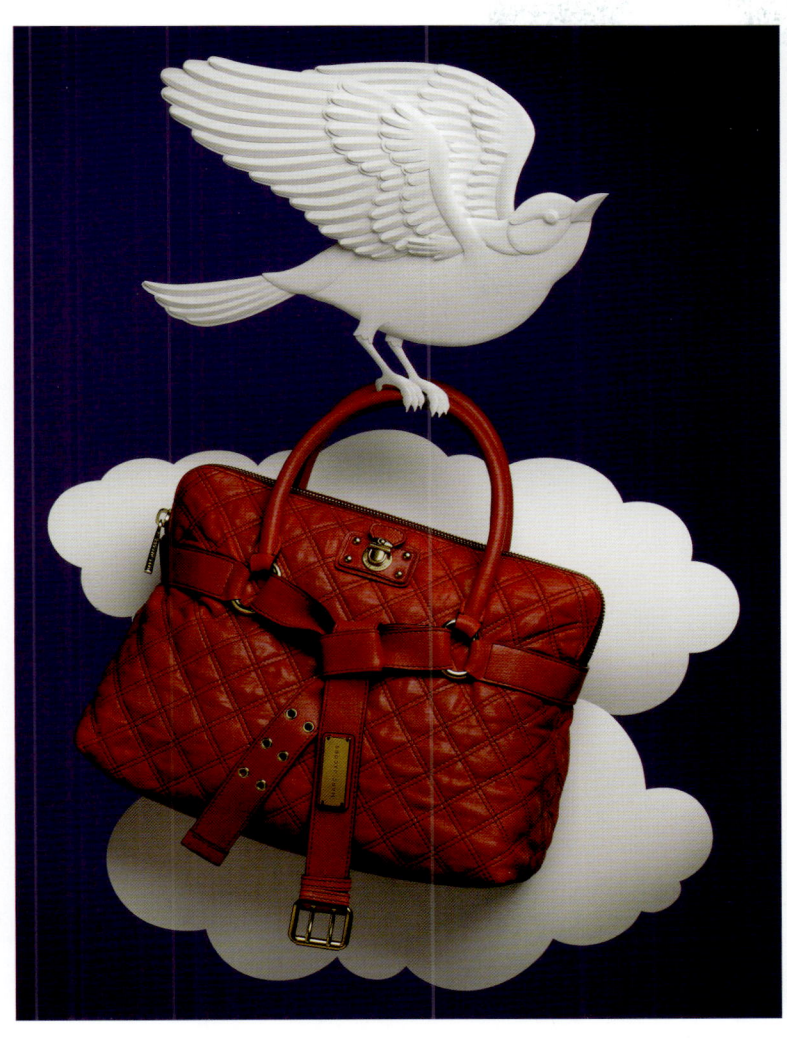
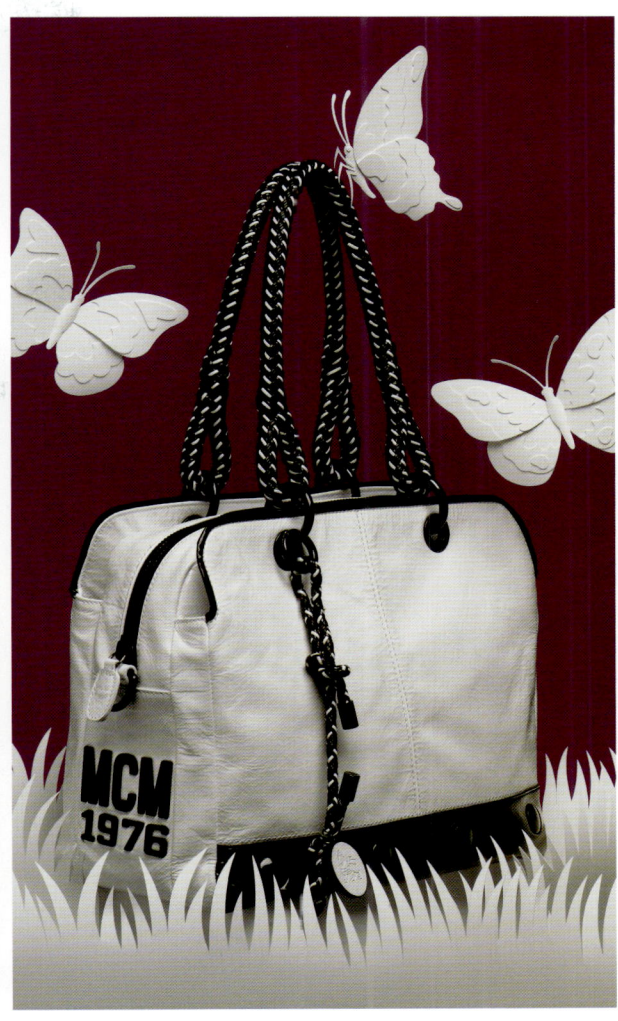
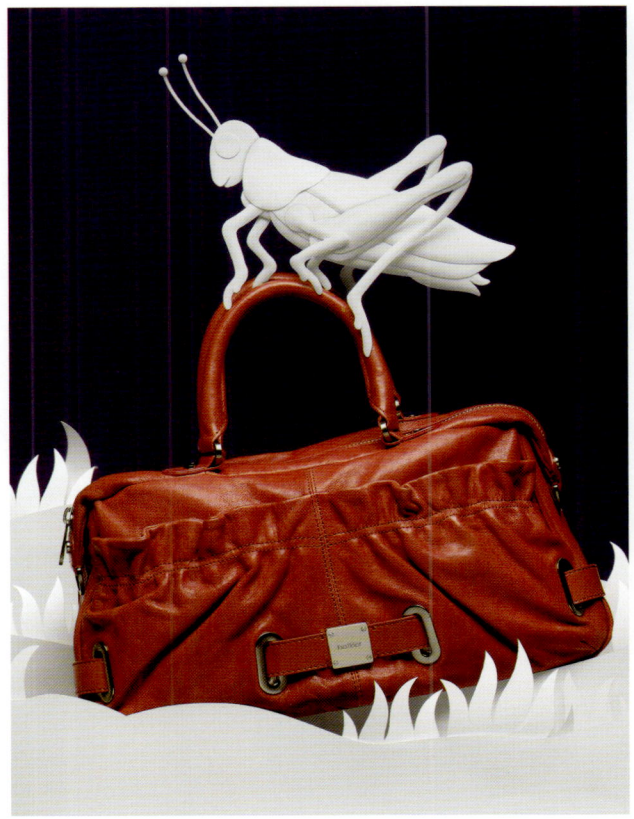
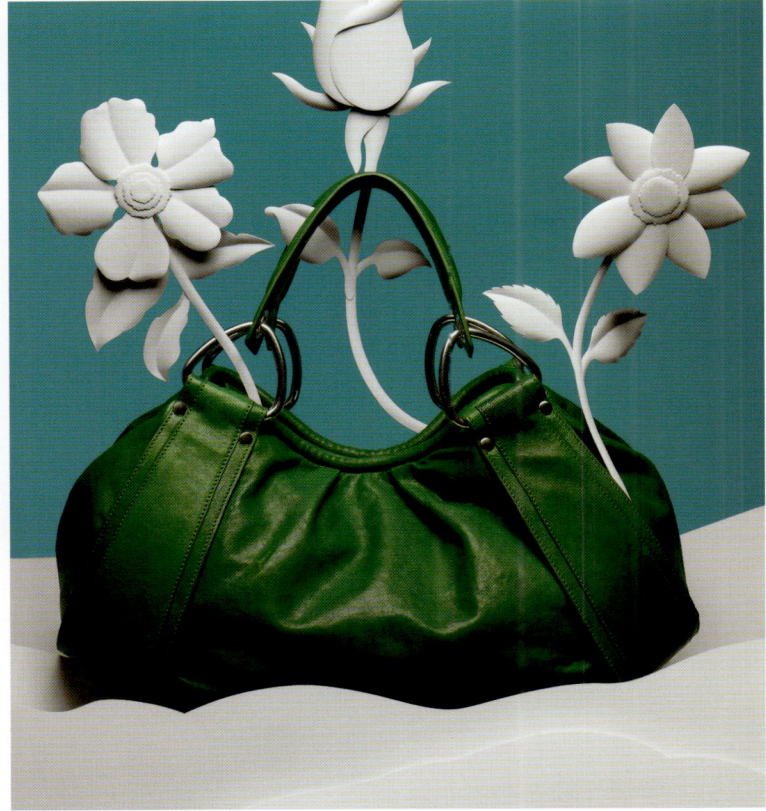

1. Bloomingdale's Spring Catalog

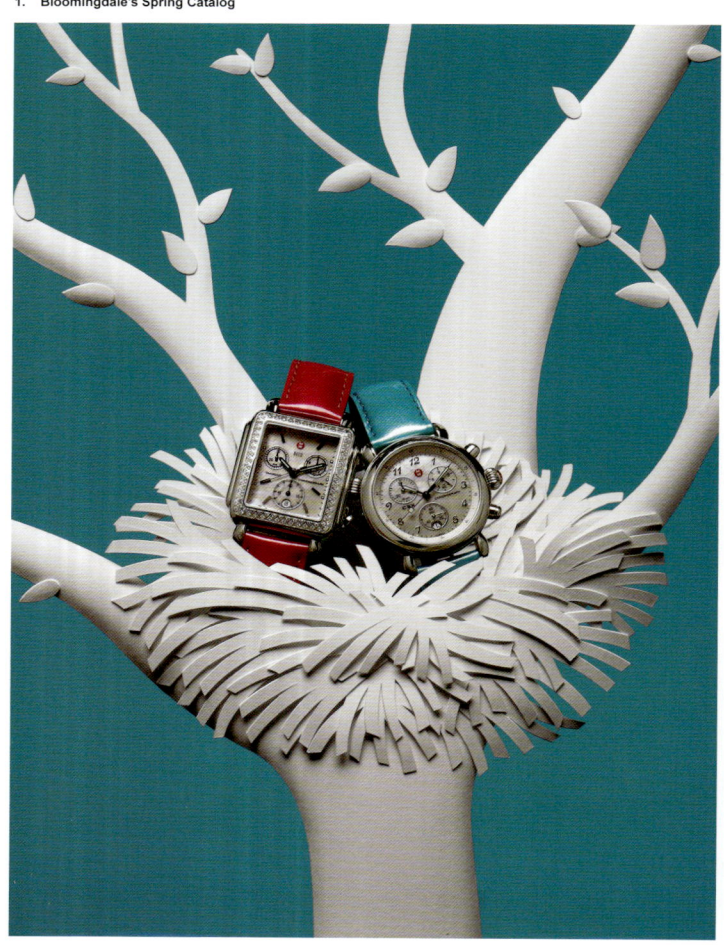
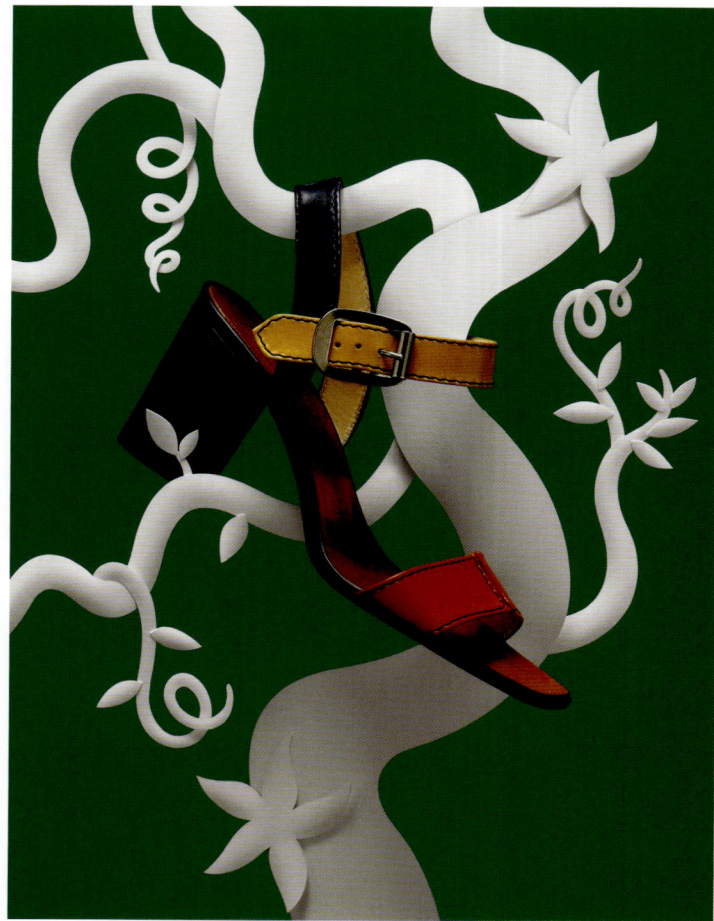
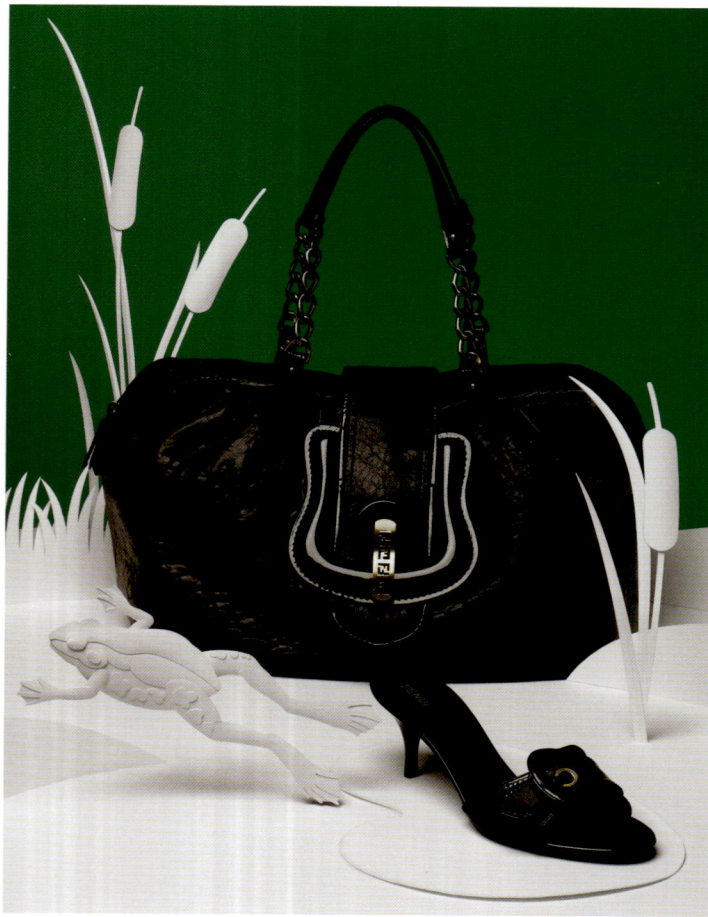
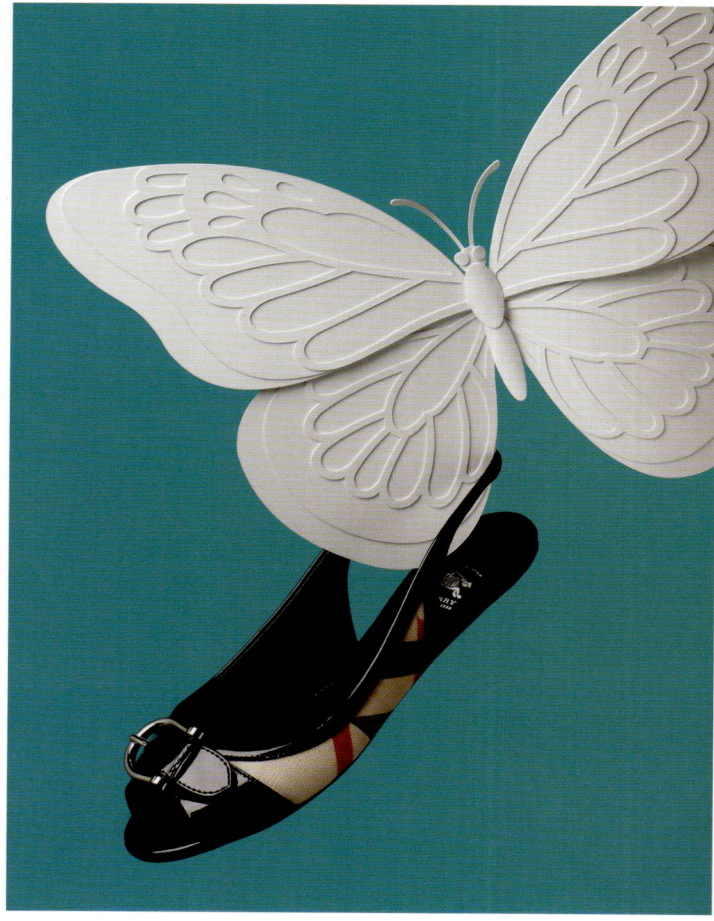

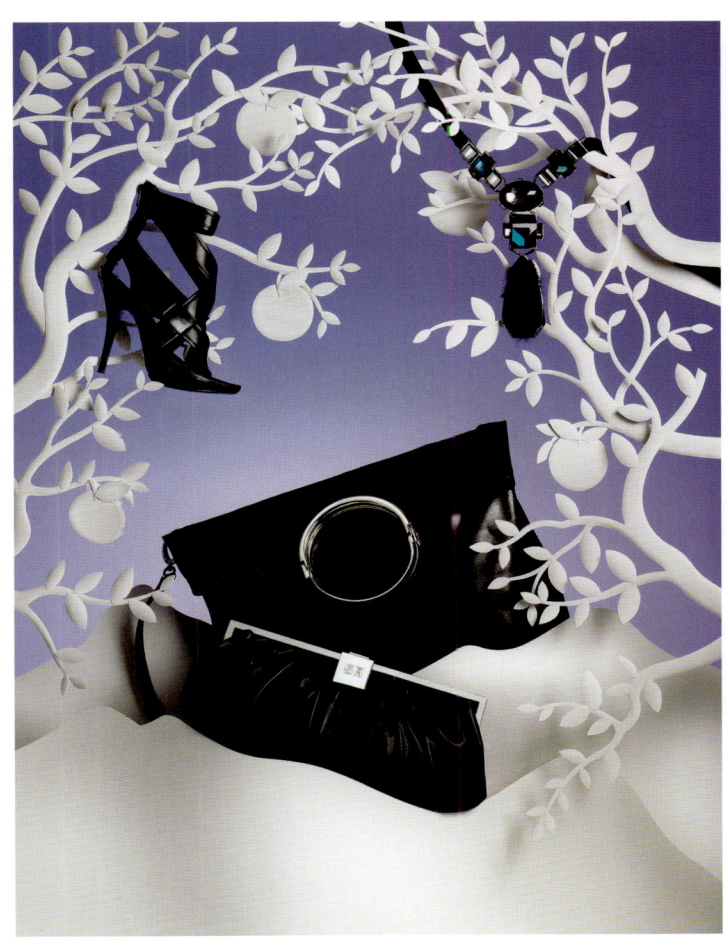
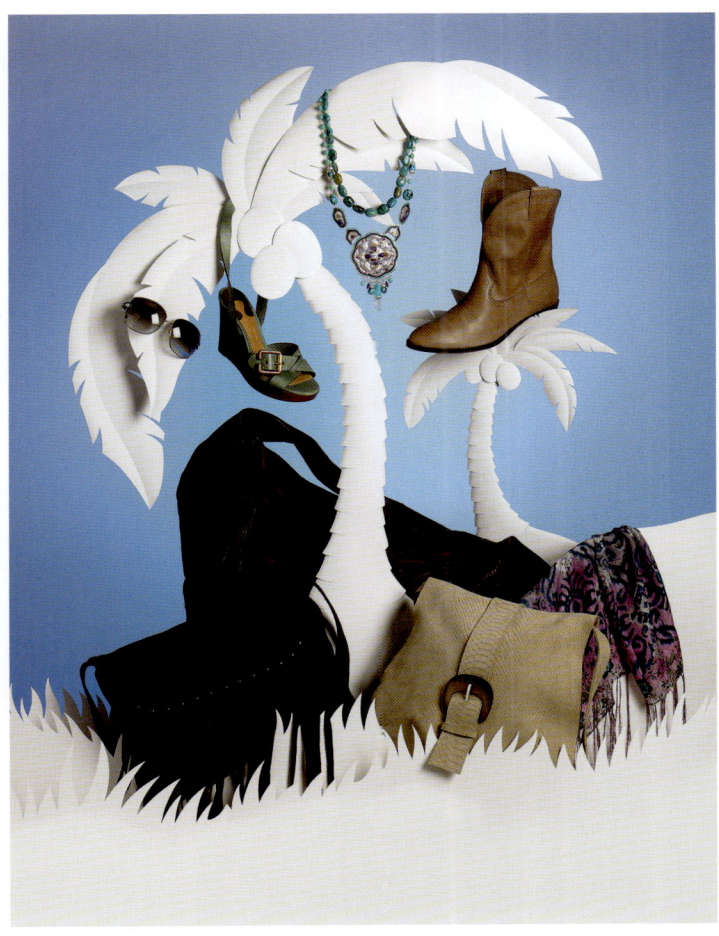
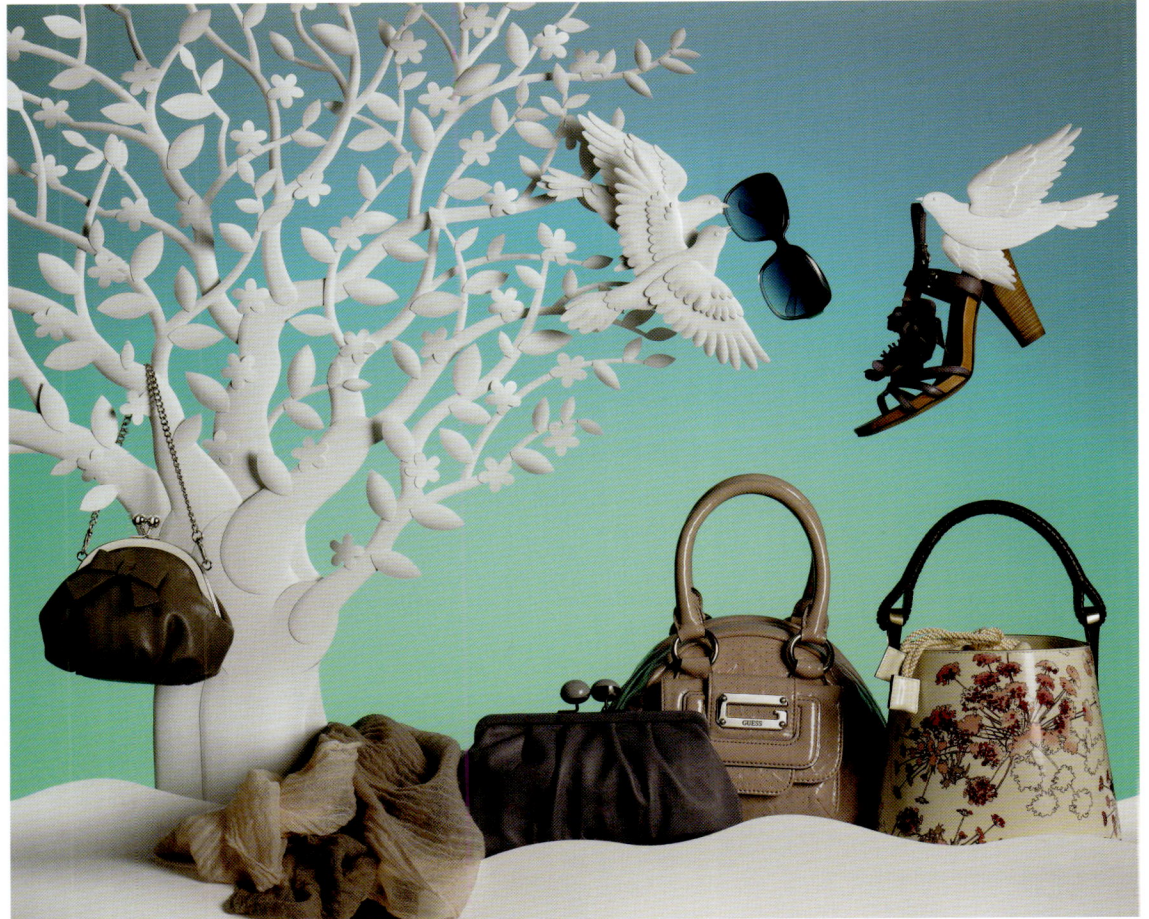

2. Galerie Lafayette Spring Catalog

Designer: Jeff Nishinaka
Country: USA
Design Agency: Galerie Lafayette
Creative Director: Laetitia
Client: Galerie Lafayette (France)
Photographer: Bela Borsodi

2. Galerie Lafayette Spring Catalog

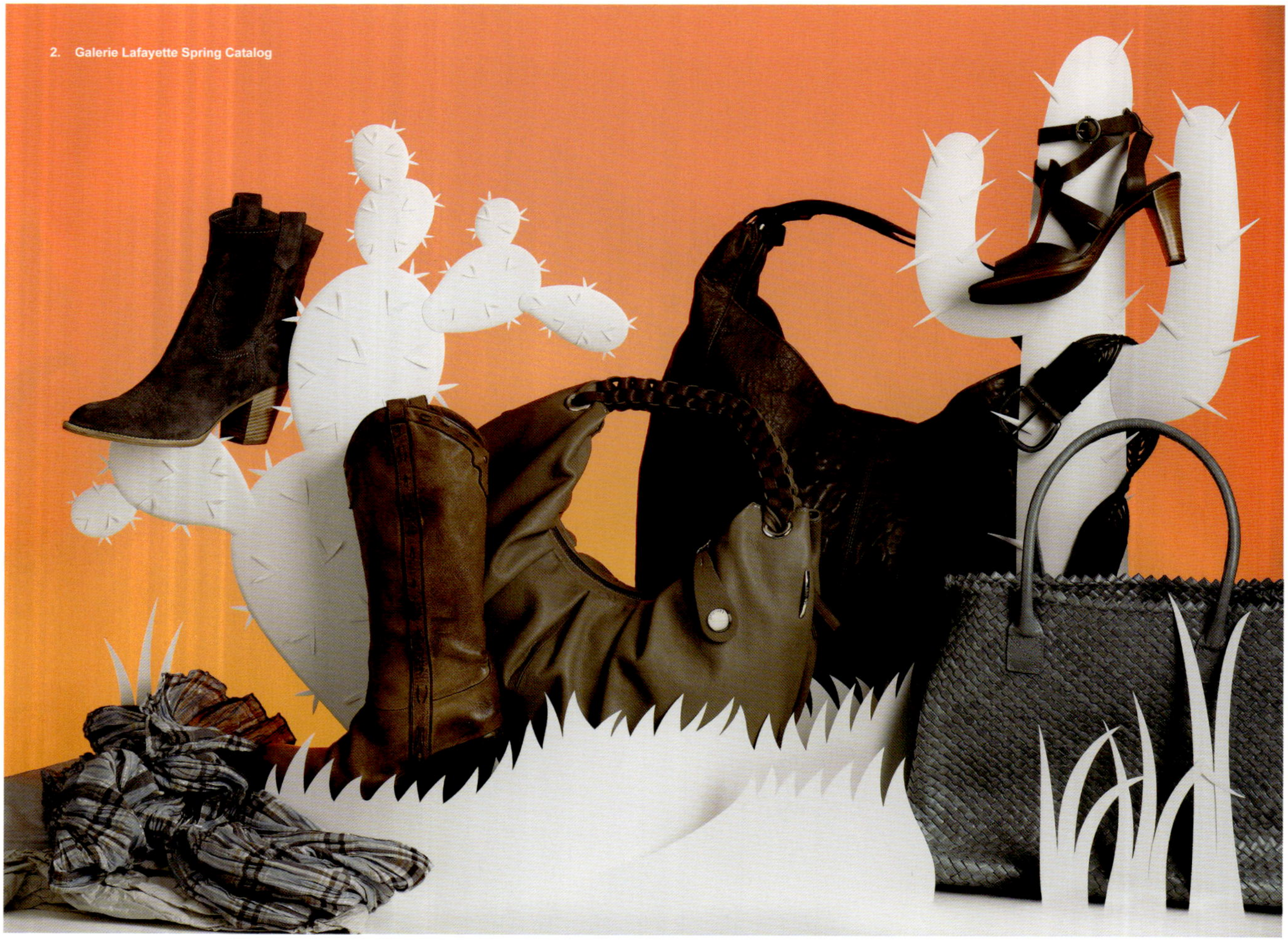

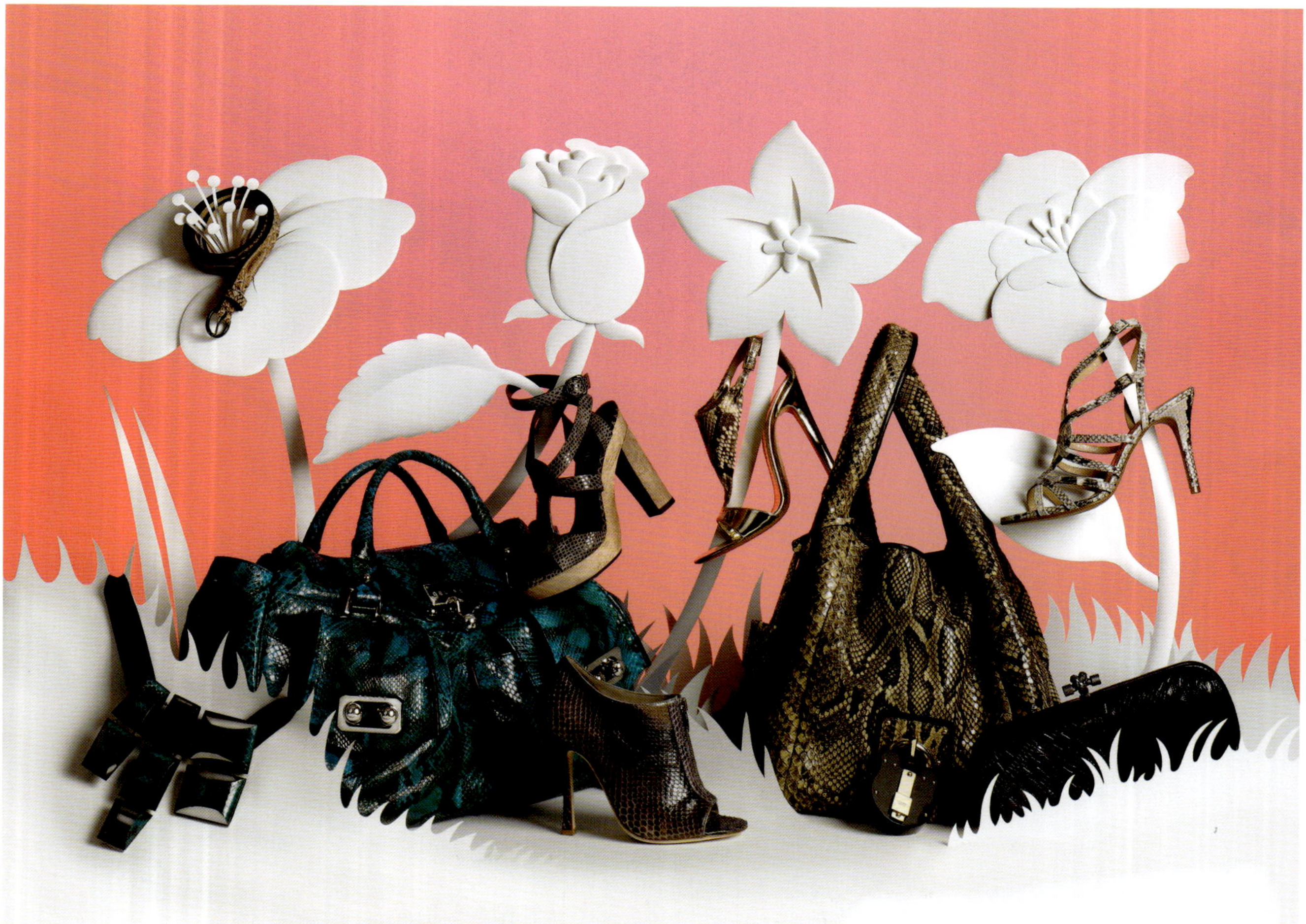

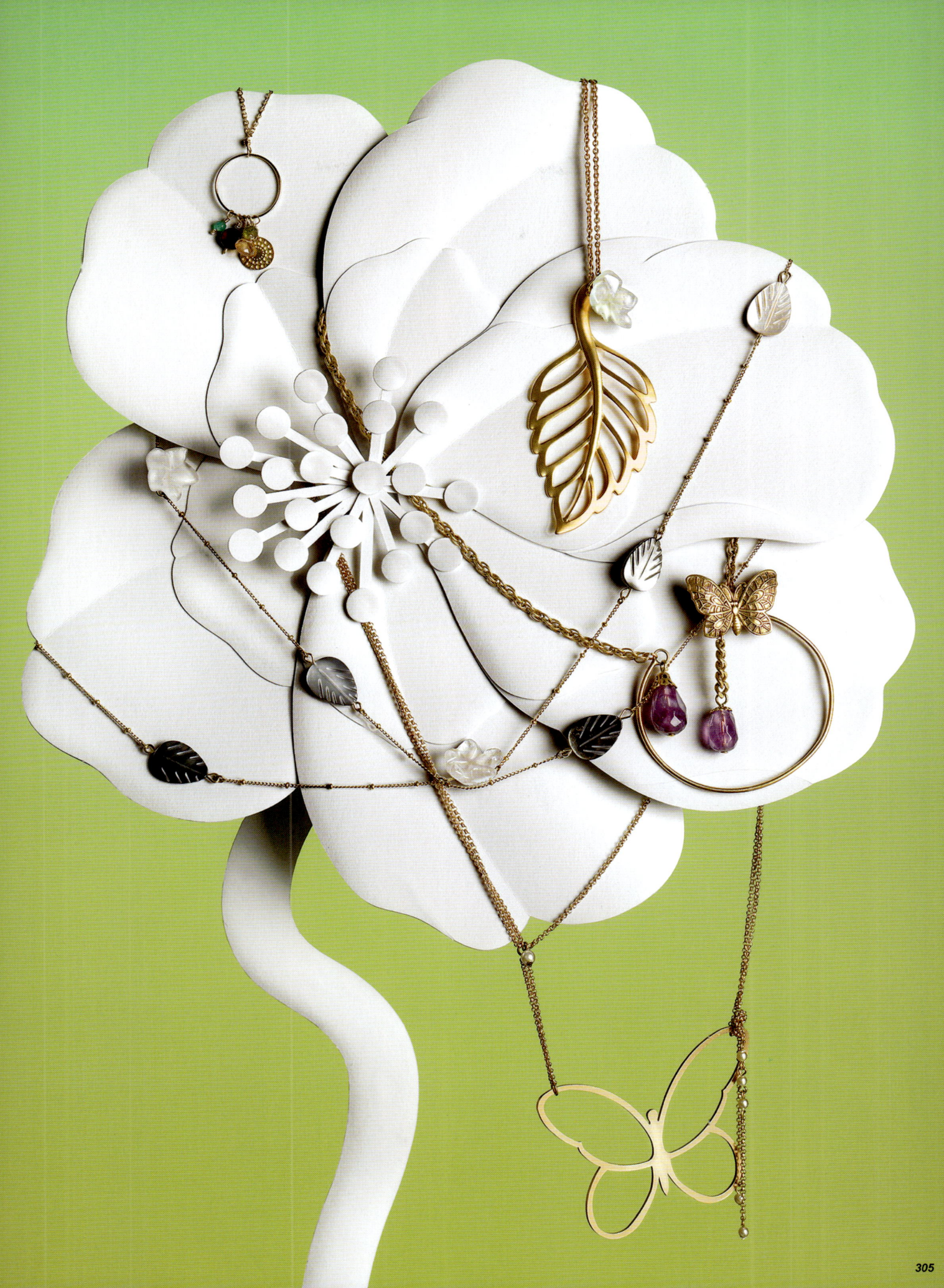

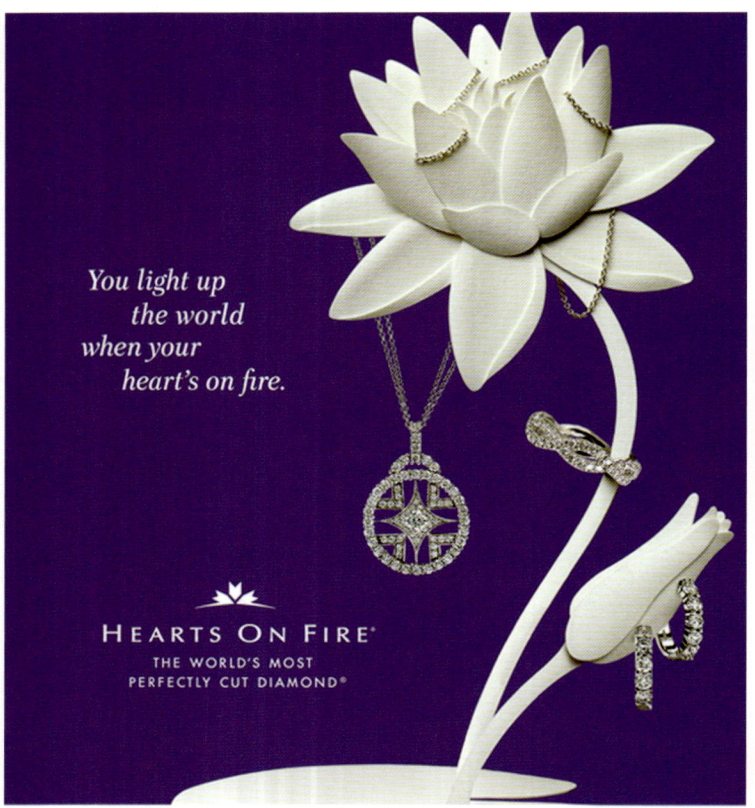
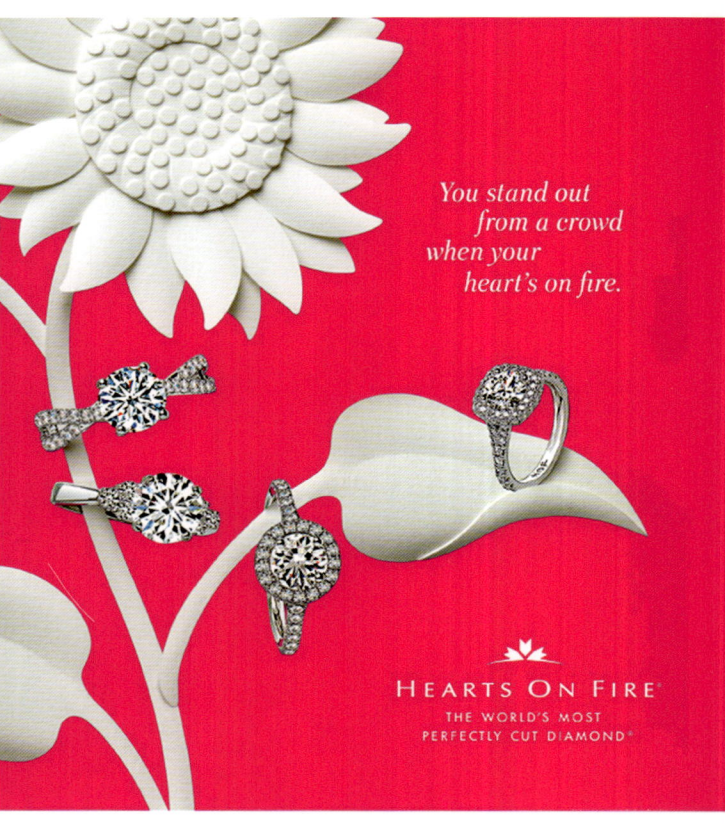

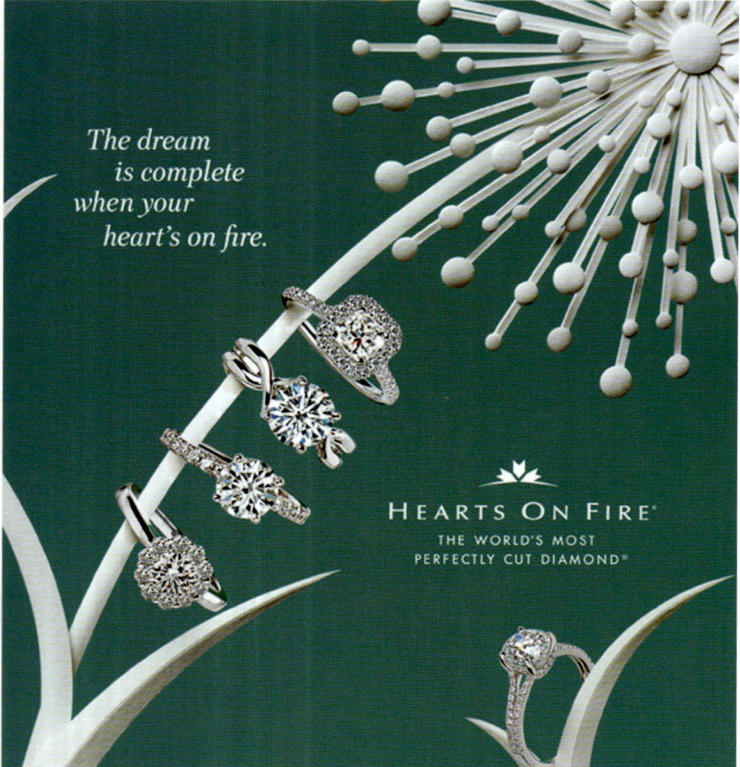

3. Hearts On Fire, The World's Most Perfectly Cut Diamond

Hearts On Fire, magazine advertisement appeared in Elle, Marie Claire, and Harper's Bazaar.

Designer: Jeff Nishinaka
Country: USA
Design Agency: Hearts On Fire / In-House
Creative Director: Wayne Stott
Marketing Director: Julie Barry
Client: Hearts On Fire (USA)
Photographer: Bela Borsodi

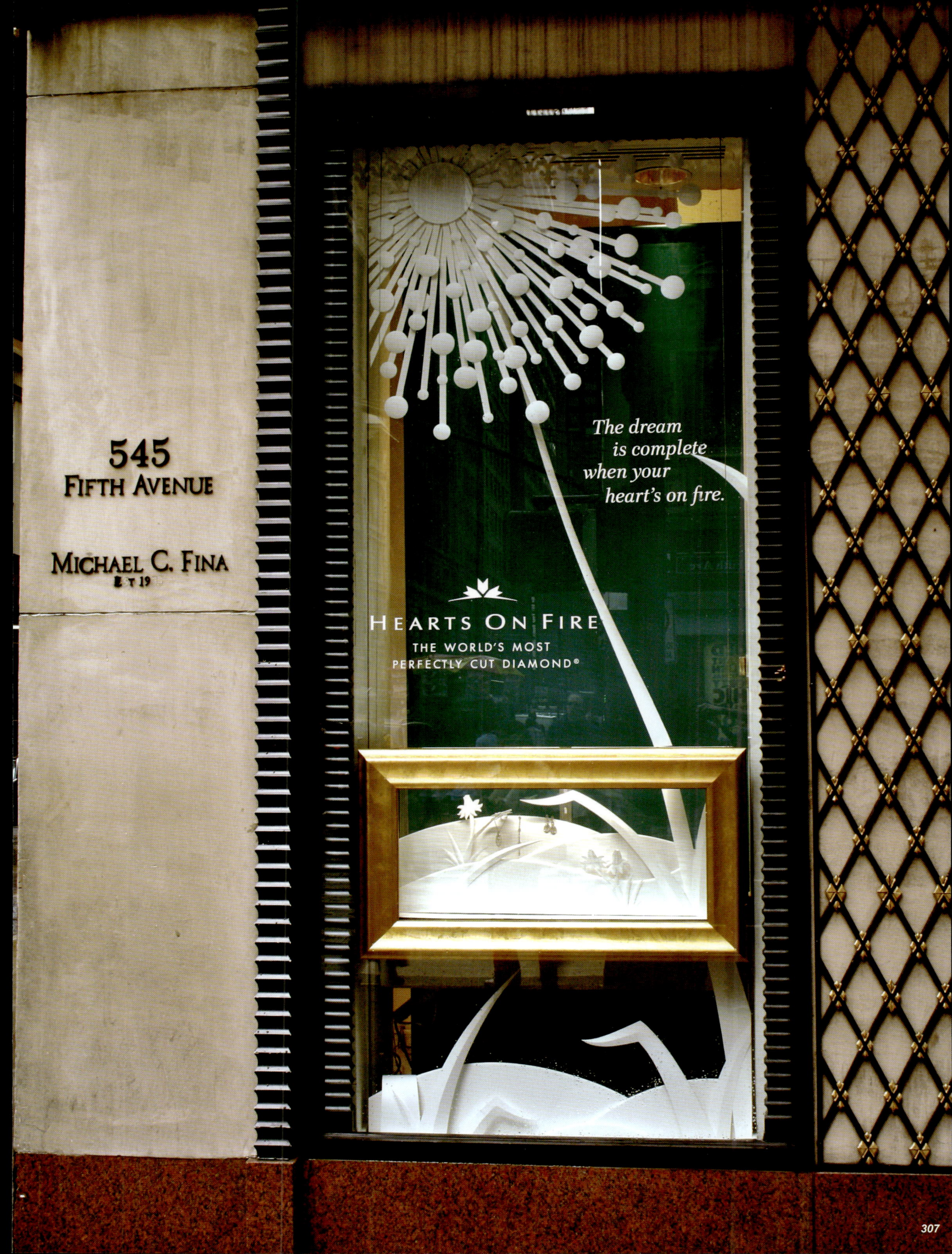

545
Fifth Avenue

Michael C. Fina
Est 19

The dream is complete when your heart's on fire.

Hearts On Fire
THE WORLD'S MOST
PERFECTLY CUT DIAMOND®

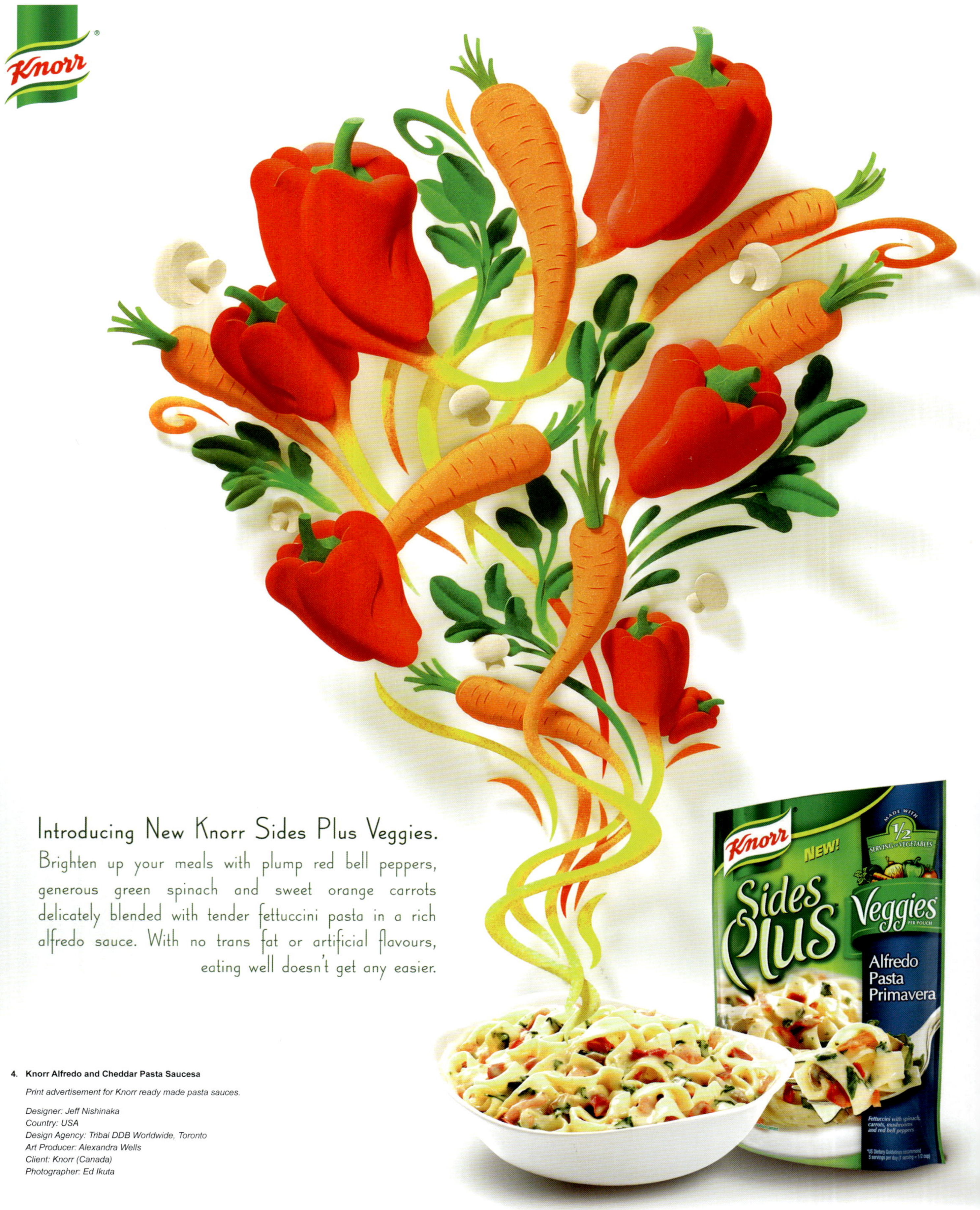

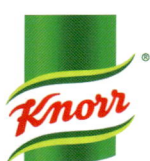

Introducing New Knorr Sides Plus Veggies.
Brighten up your meals with plump red bell peppers, generous green spinach and sweet orange carrots delicately blended with tender fettuccini pasta in a rich alfredo sauce. With no trans fat or artificial flavours, eating well doesn't get any easier.

4. Knorr Alfredo and Cheddar Pasta Saucesa
Print advertisement for Knorr ready made pasta sauces.

Designer: Jeff Nishinaka
Country: USA
Design Agency: Tribal DDB Worldwide, Toronto
Art Producer: Alexandra Wells
Client: Knorr (Canada)
Photographer: Ed Ikuta

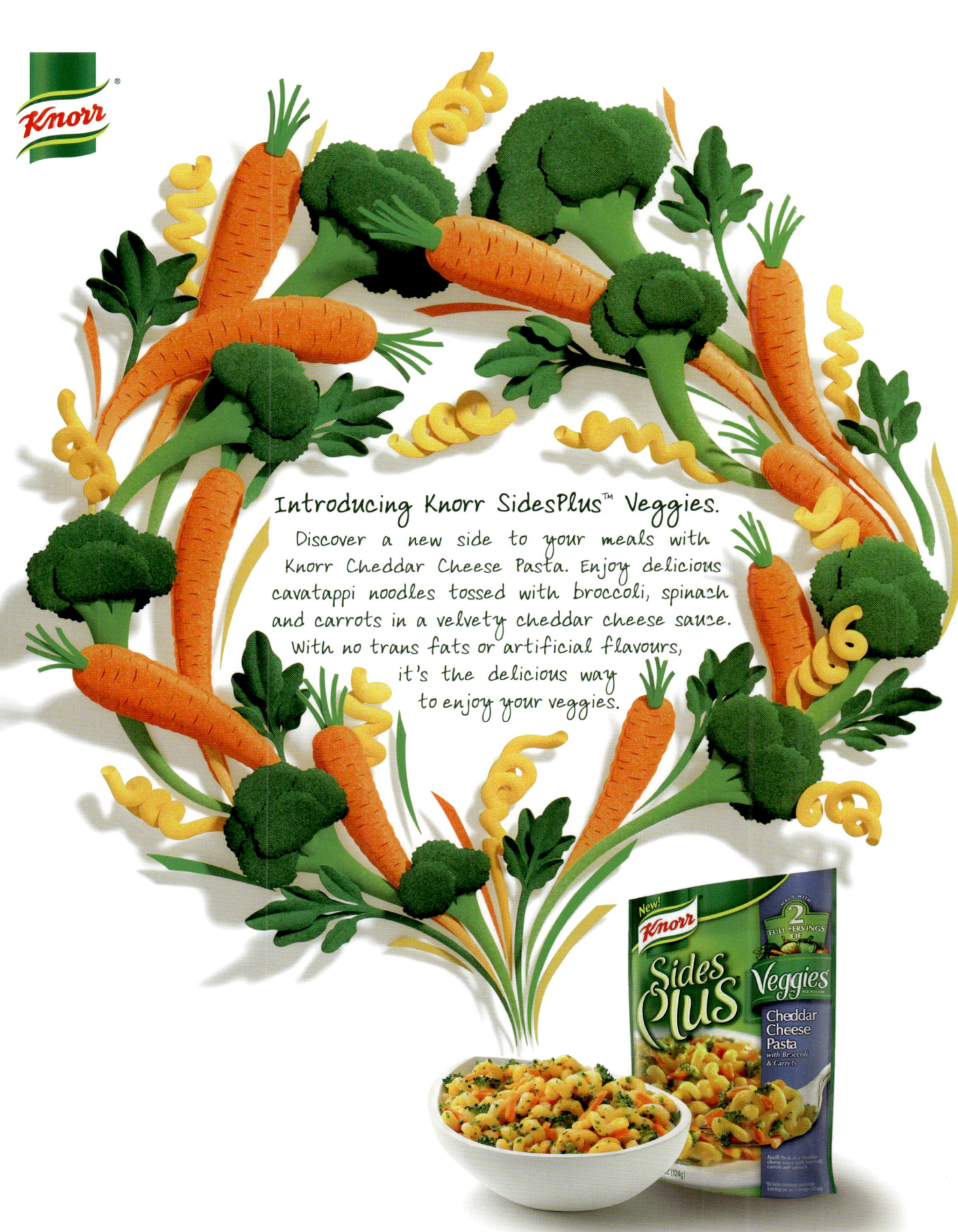

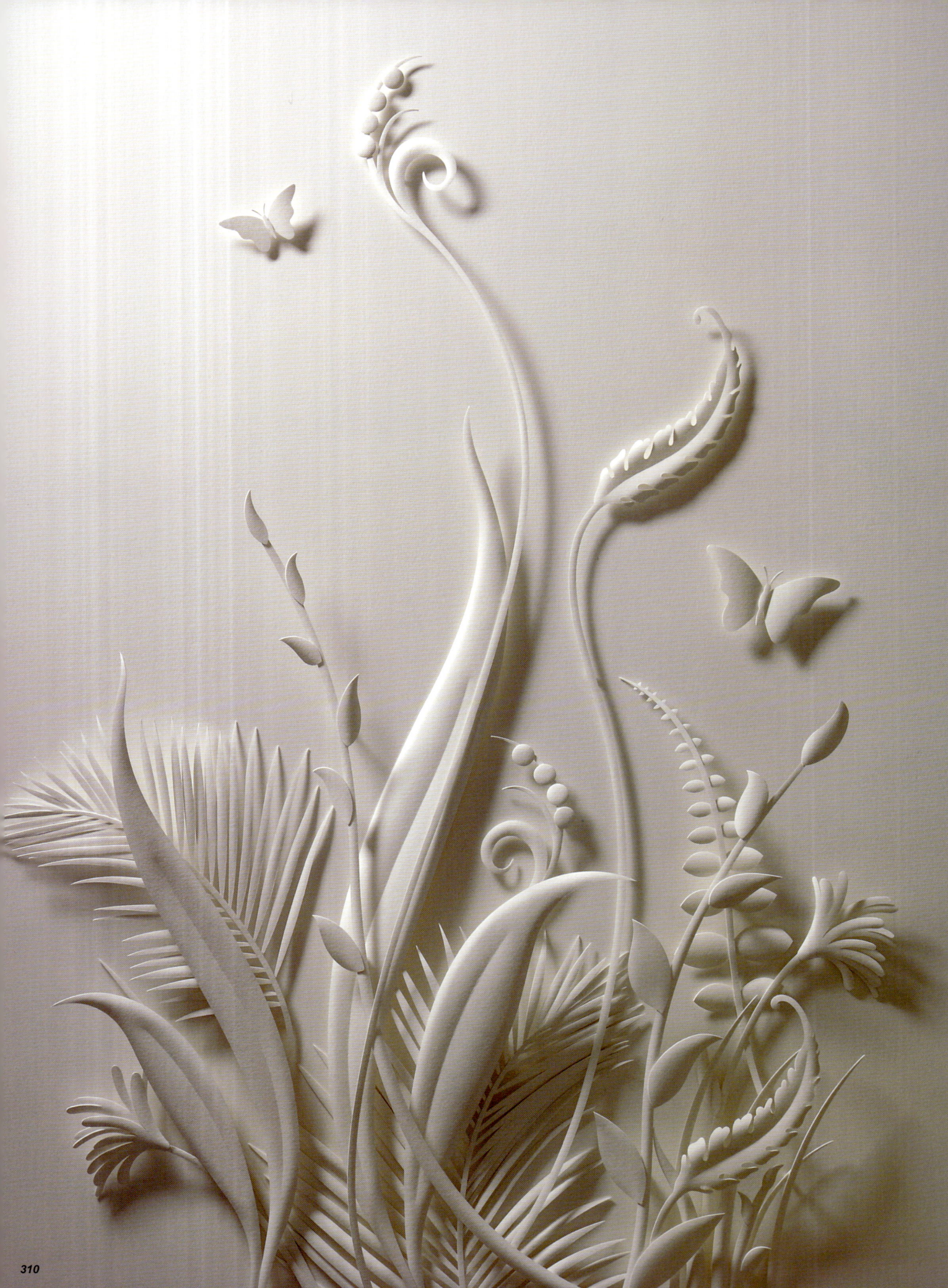

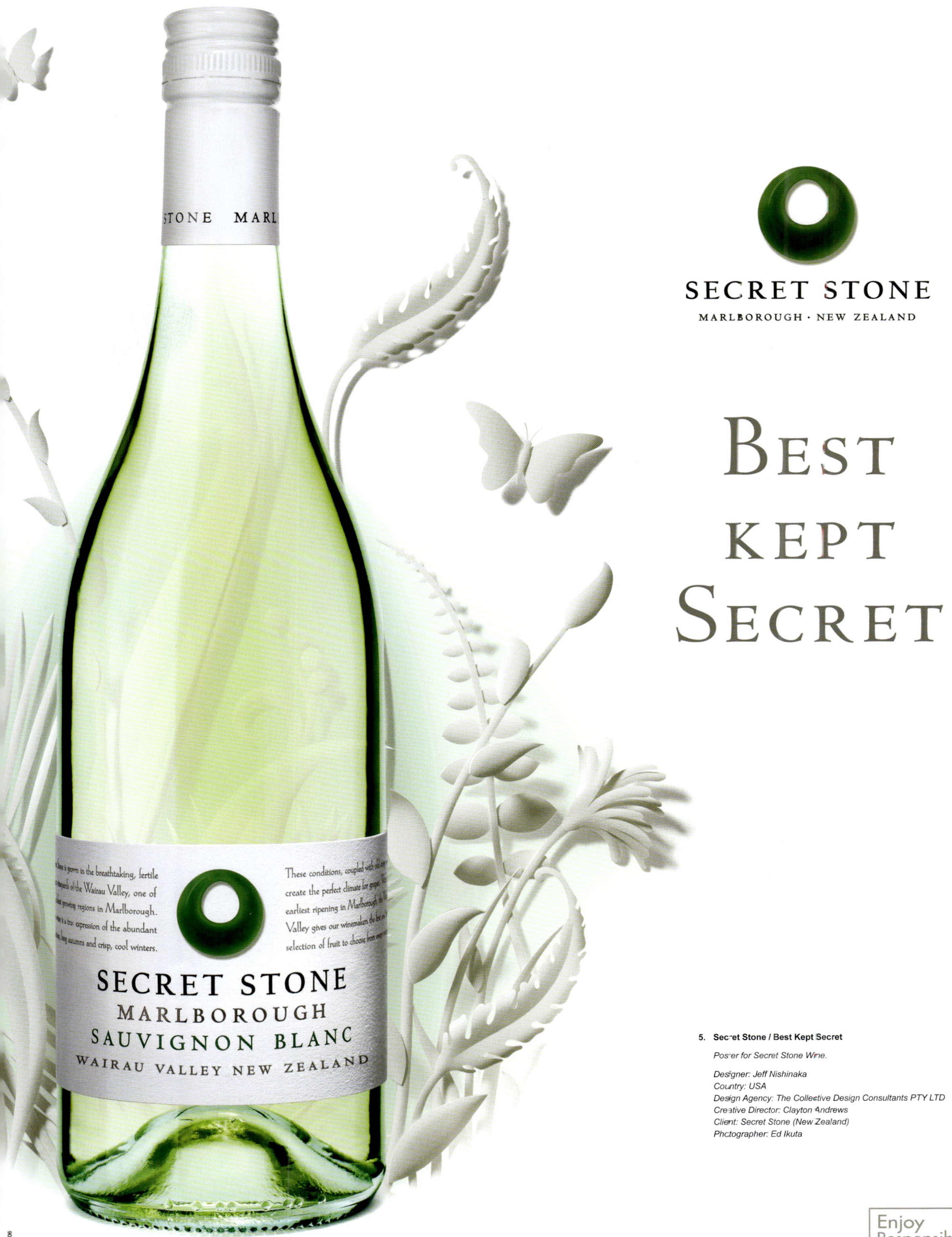

BEST KEPT SECRET

Secret Stone
MARLBOROUGH · NEW ZEALAND

5. **Secret Stone / Best Kept Secret**

Poster for Secret Stone Wine.

Designer: Jeff Nishinaka
Country: USA
Design Agency: The Collective Design Consultants PTY LTD
Creative Director: Clayton Andrews
Client: Secret Stone (New Zealand)
Photographer: Ed Ikuta

Enjoy Responsibly

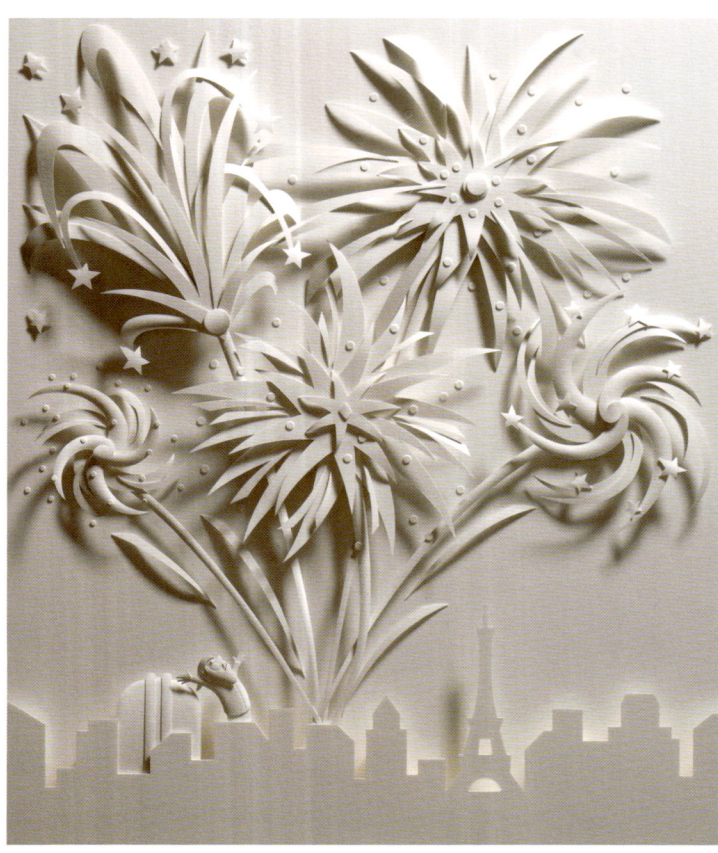
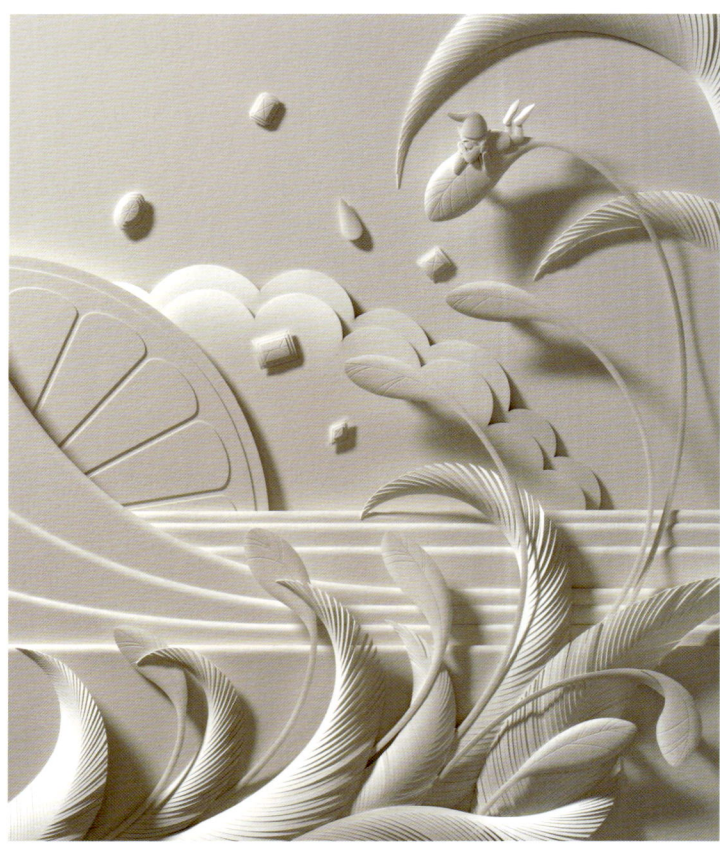
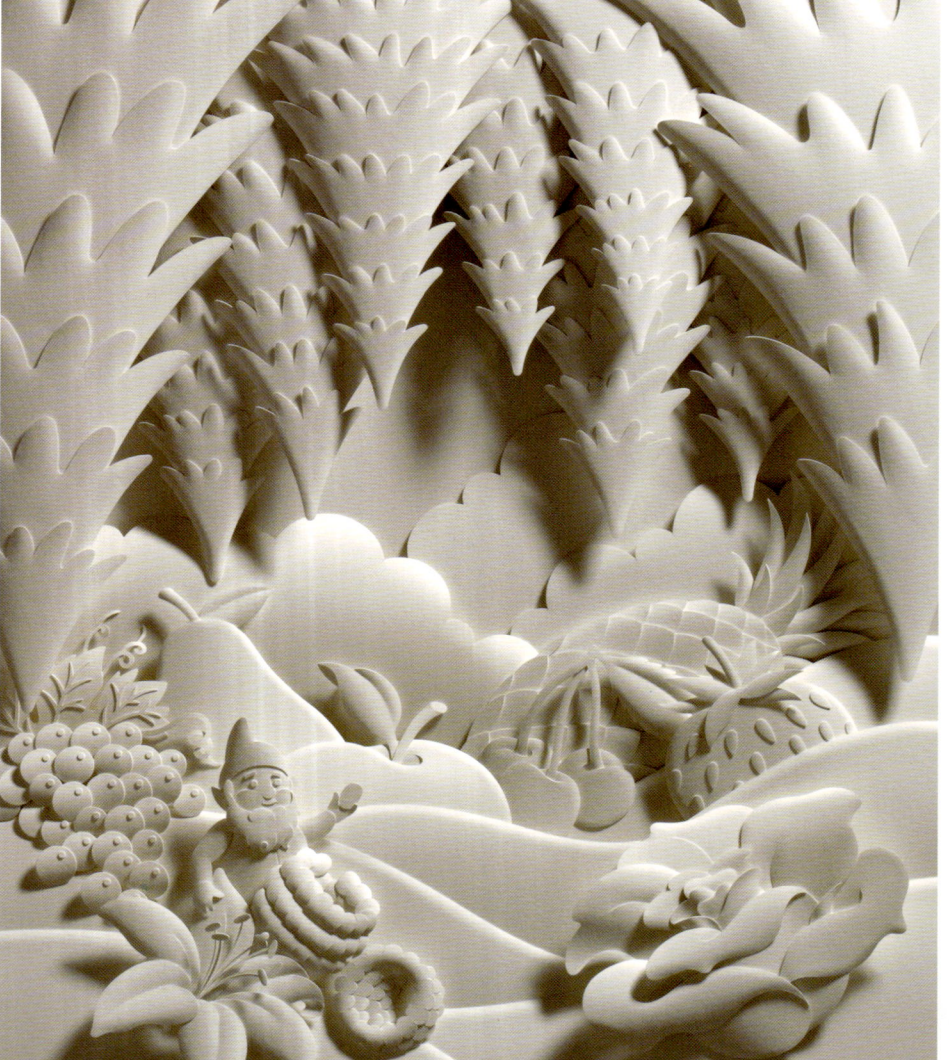

6. **La Grande Epicerie**

   La Grande Epicerie Christmas food catalog and store banner.

   Designer: Jeff Nishinaka
   Country: USA
   Design Agency: Vue sur la Ville
   Creative Director: Anne Barcat
   Client: Bon Marche La Grande Epicerie de Paris (France)
   Photographer: Ed Ikuta

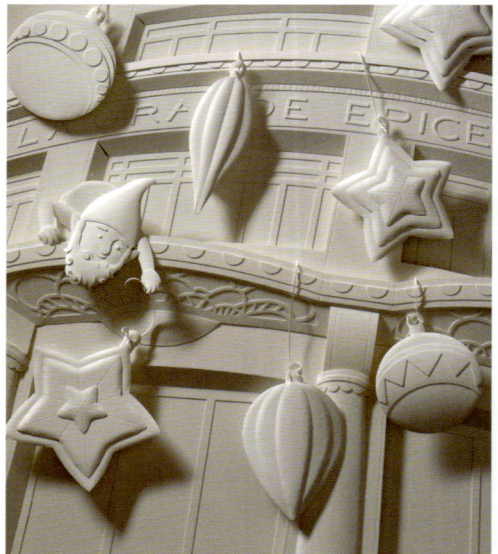

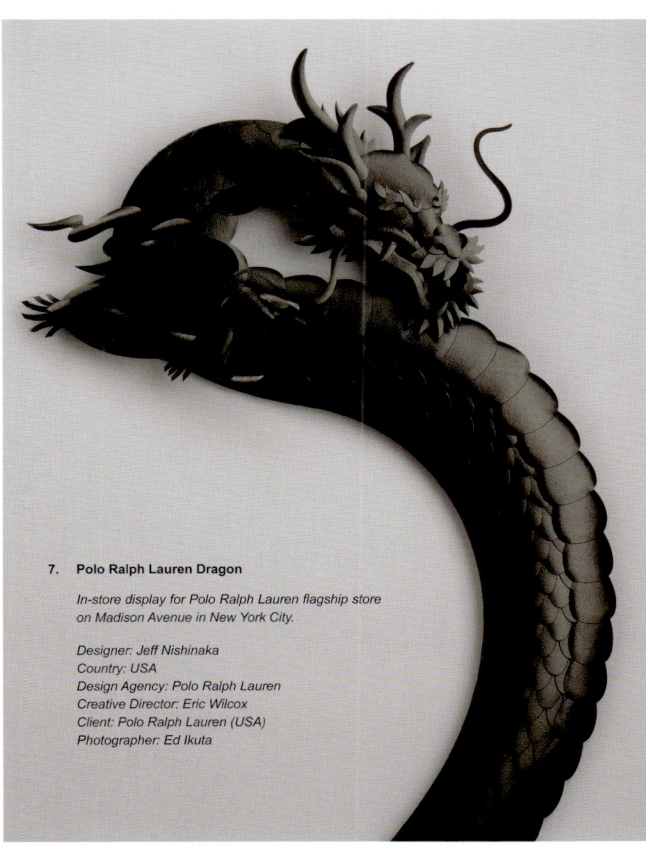
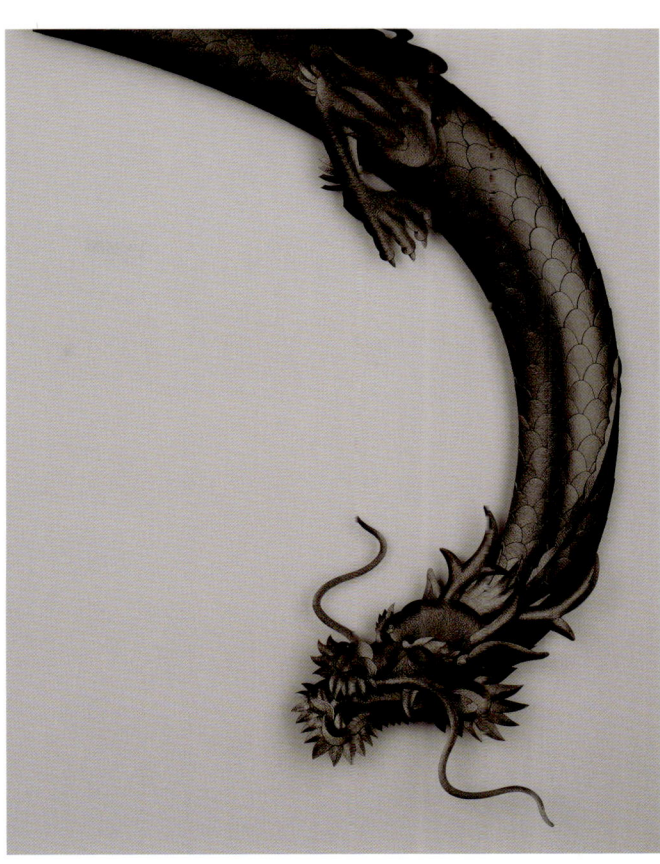

7. Polo Ralph Lauren Dragon

In-store display for Polo Ralph Lauren flagship store on Madison Avenue in New York City.

Designer: Jeff Nishinaka
Country: USA
Design Agency: Polo Ralph Lauren
Creative Director: Eric Wilcox
Client: Polo Ralph Lauren (USA)
Photographer: Ed Ikuta

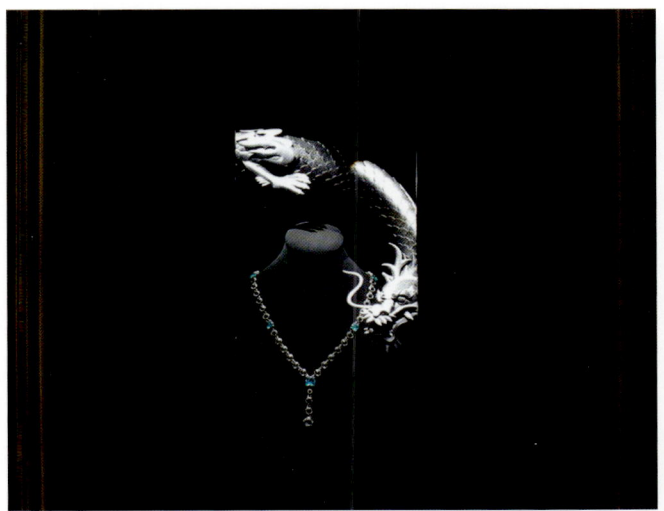
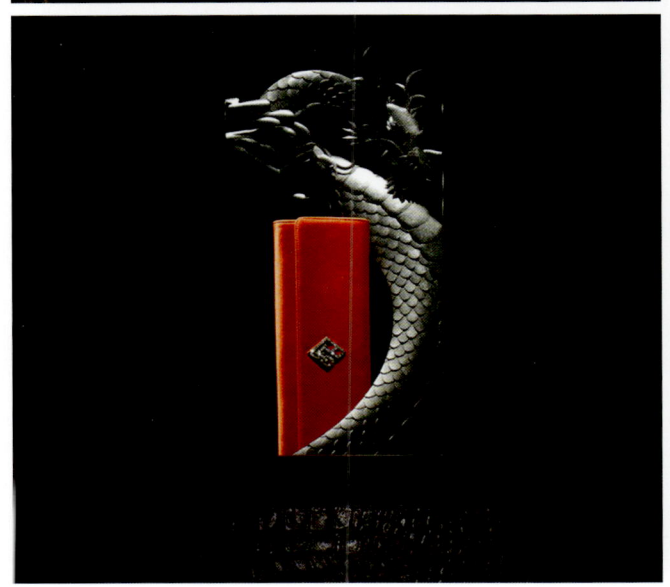

8. Peninsula Shanghai Hotel Dragon

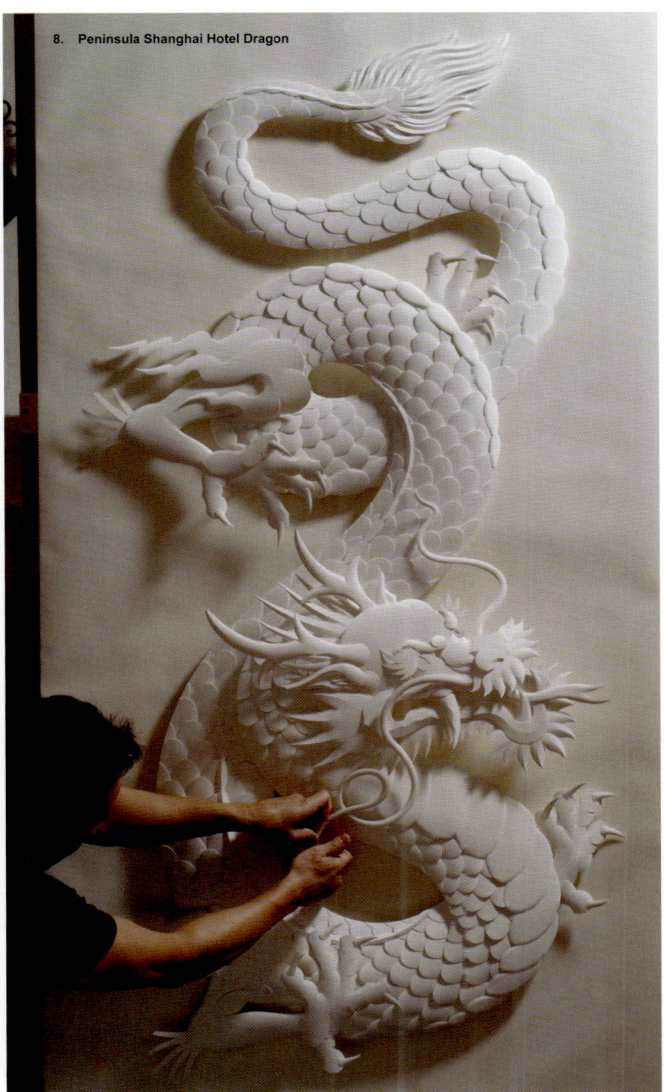

8. Peninsula Shanghai Hotel Dragon

8. **Peninsula Shanghai Hotel Dragon**

   Original art displayed inside the Shanghai Terrace Restaurant.

   Designer: Jeff Nishinaka
   Country: USA
   Design Agency: Sabrina Fung Fine Arts / Hong Kong
   Client: Peninsula Shanghai Hotel Dragon (China)
   Photographer: Ed Ikuta

9. **Peninsula Chicago Hotel Dragon**

   Original art displayed at the entrance to the Yi Long Court Restaurant.

   Designer: Jeff Nishinaka
   Country: USA
   Design Agency: Sabrina Fung Fine Arts / Hong Kong
   Client: Peninsula Chicago Hotel Dragon (USA)
   Photographer: Jeff NIshinaka

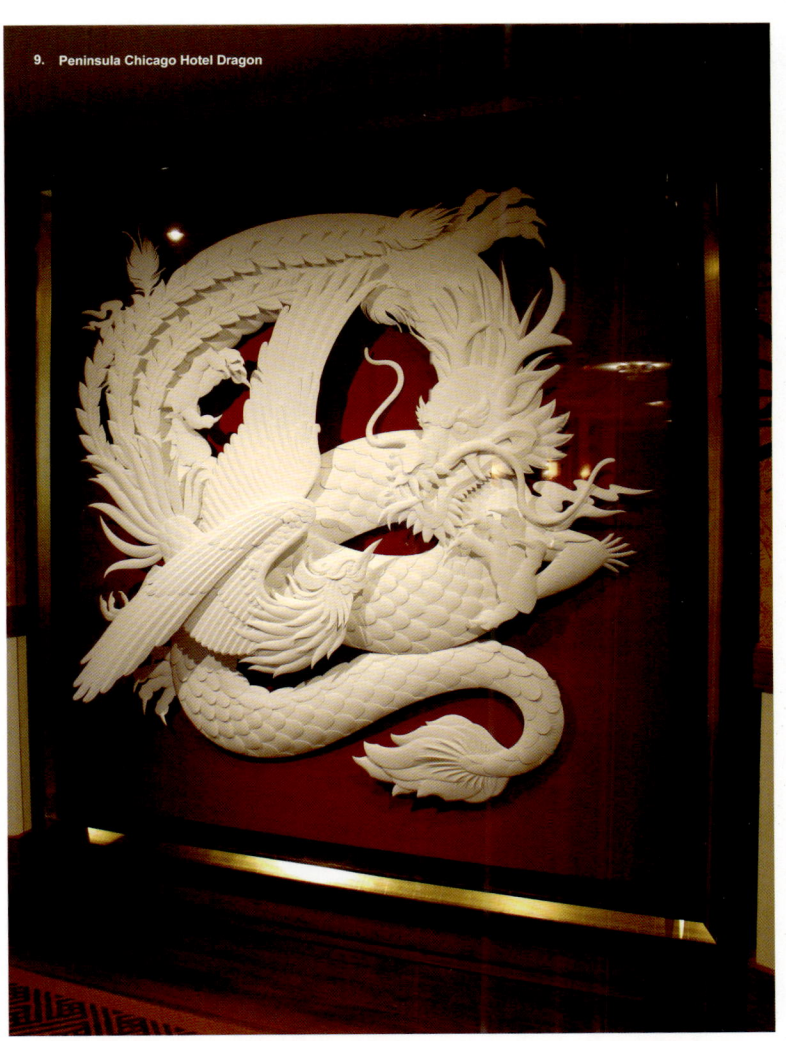

9. Peninsula Chicago Hotel Dragon

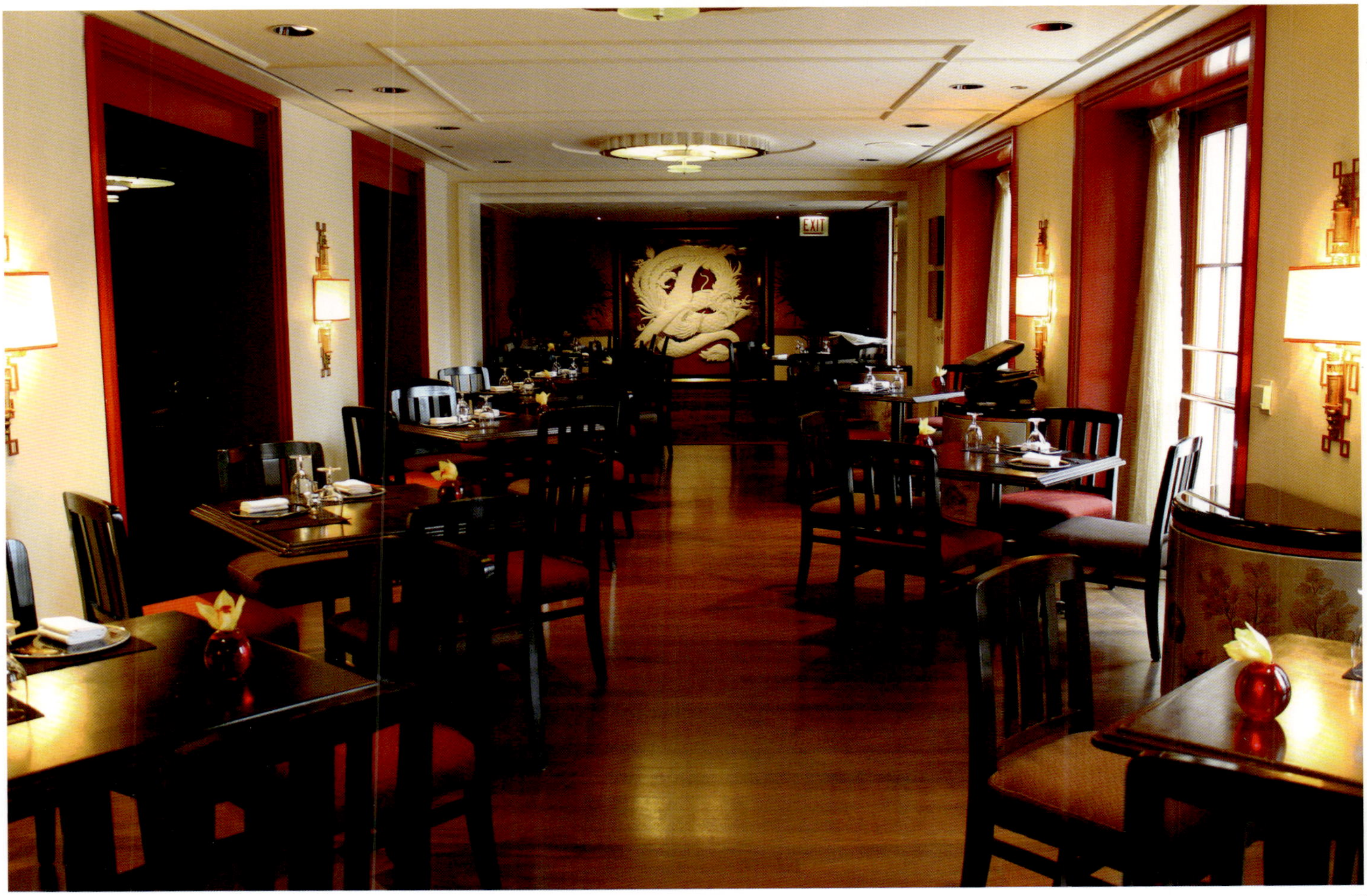

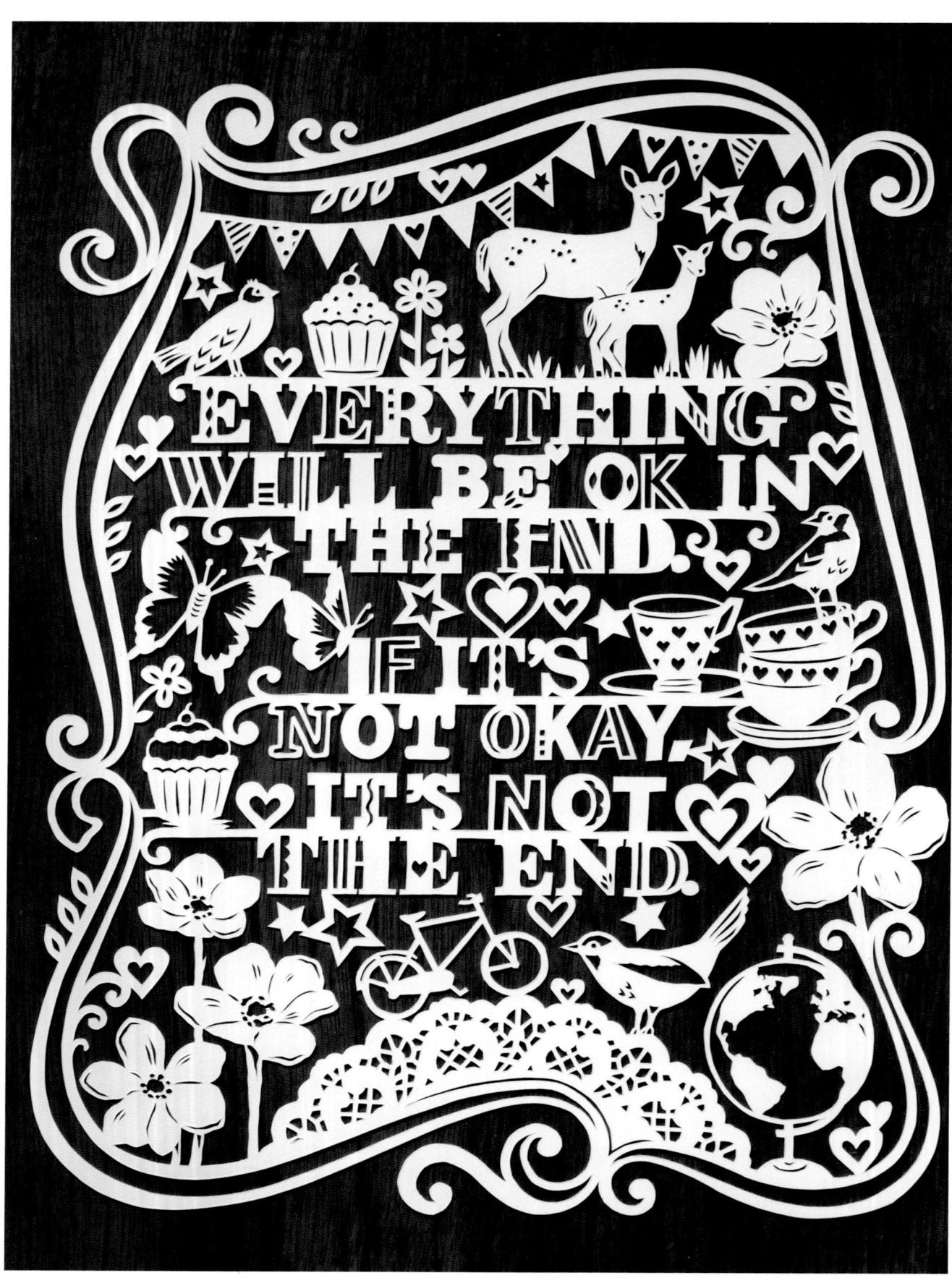

1. **Everything Will Be Ok**

   This was a 21st birthday present from father to his daughter. She chose the phrase and the all the things that made her happy, like cupcakes and butterflies.
   Designer: Julene Harrison   Country: UK   Creative Director: Julene Harrison   Client: Private   Photographer: Julene Harrison

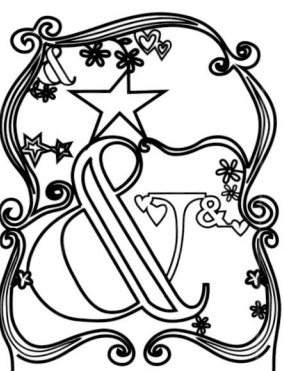

1. Everything Will Be Ok
2. Tornado-Love
3. You Are The Beez Neez
4. Nivea - Pure and Natural
5. Jude, the Blue Terrier
6. Net-A-Porter Advent Calendar
7. My Ampersand
8. Spring Arts Guide
9. The Mostly True Story of Jack
10. Tea Glorious Tea
11. O2 Christmas

---Julene Harrison

Designer: Julene Harrison
Country: UK
Creative Director: Julene Harrison
Client: Private
Photographer: Julene Harrison

2. **Tornado-Love**

This First anniversary celebration paper-cut tells the story of how and where the couple in question met. I love the movement in this piece. I think it was a very windy day indeed!

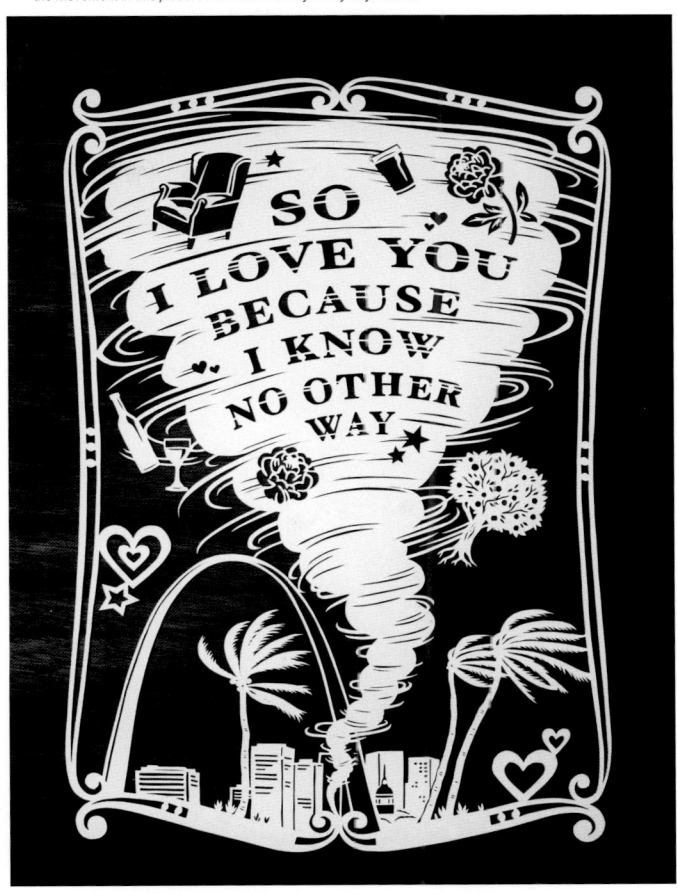

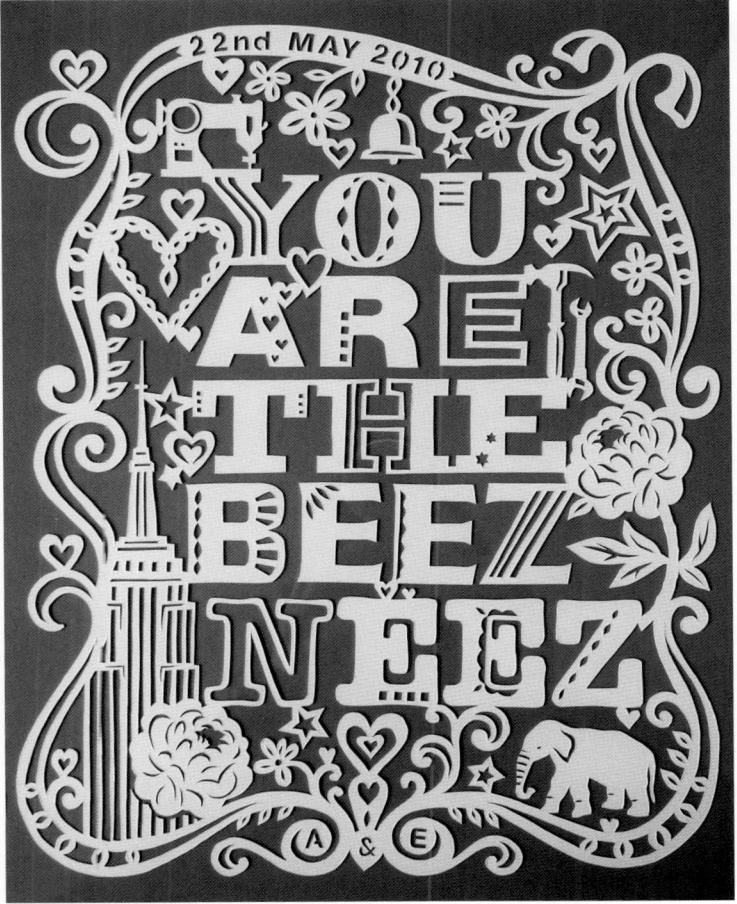

3. **You Are The Beez Neez**

This paper-cut was a wedding gift for a couple who wanted to comemorate their special day. They chose some elements to be included in the design that were special/significant to them inc the Empire State Building an elephant and some peonies.

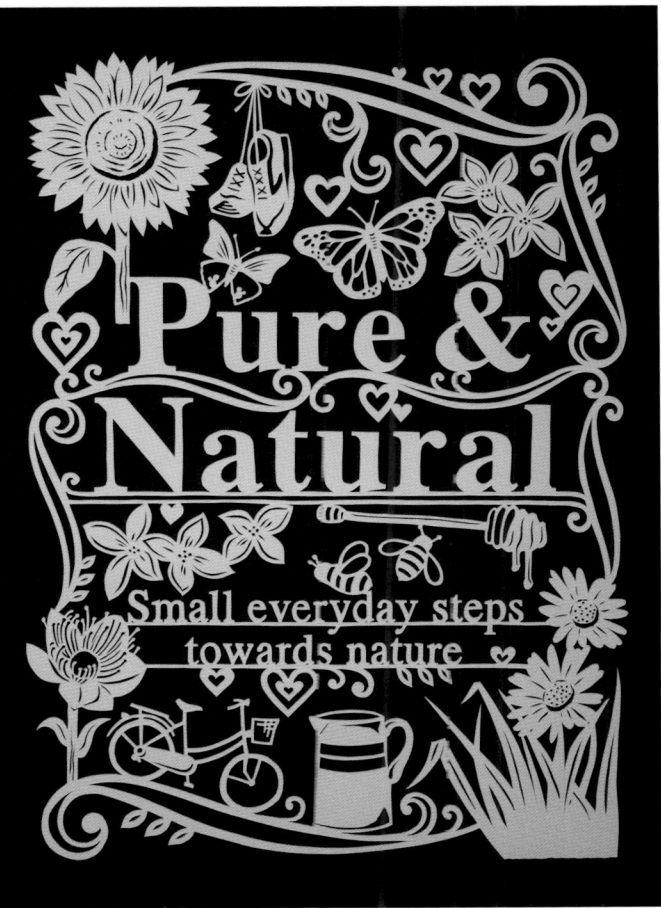

4. **Nivea - Pure and Natural**   Photographer: Glen Milner / Matt Simmonds

Commissioned by the The Telegraph Newspaper this paper-cut was the cover of a Nivea sponsored supplement. The illustration invokes nature, vitality and healthy living.
Designer: Julene Harrison   Country: UK   Design Agency: Central Illustration Agency
Creative Director: Carollyn Vassallo   Client: The Telegraph Newspaper

317

5.

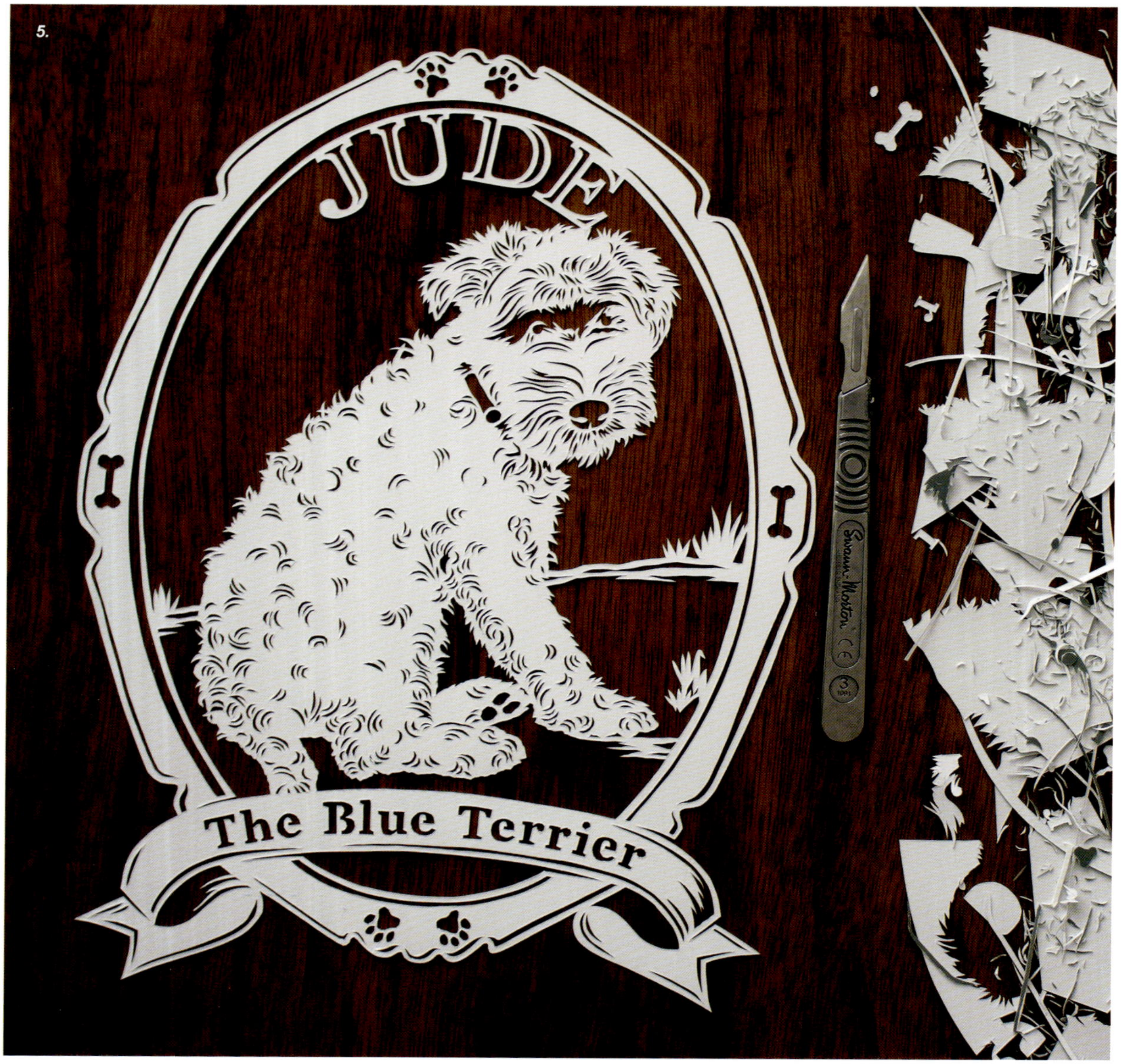

6.

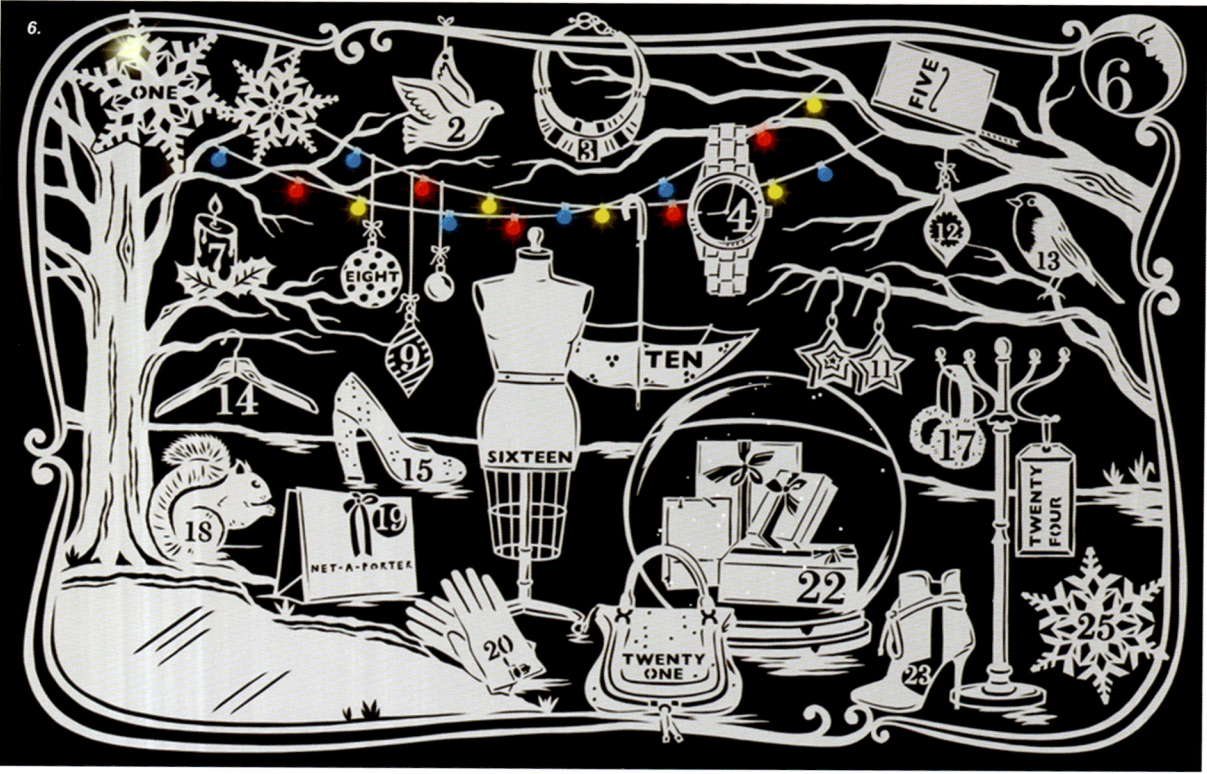

5. **Jude, the Blue Terrier**

Why not have your best friend immortalised in paper? This is a piece of personal/promotional work. I know how much people love their pets!

Designer: Julene Harrison
Country: UK
Creative Director: Julene Harrison
Photographer: Julene Harrison

6. **Net-A-Porter Advent Calendar**

Online advent calendar for fashion retailers – Net-A-Porter.com. On line the string of lights flashed and snow fell in the snow globe. Very festive and pretty. Each day a new motif was unlocked revealing a give-a-way or new exclusive content.

Designer: Julene Harrison
Country: UK
Design Agency: Central Illustration Agency
Creative Director: Denise Shenton
Client: Net-A-Porter
Photographer: Julene Harrison

7. **My Ampersand**

Private Commission. Given by one man to his girlfriend. I don't know what the significance of the ampersand has to their relationship, but Im sure it means something special. I love the blue gradient ground on this piece.

Designer: Julene Harrison
Country: UK
Creative Director: Julene Harrison
Photographer: Julene Harrison

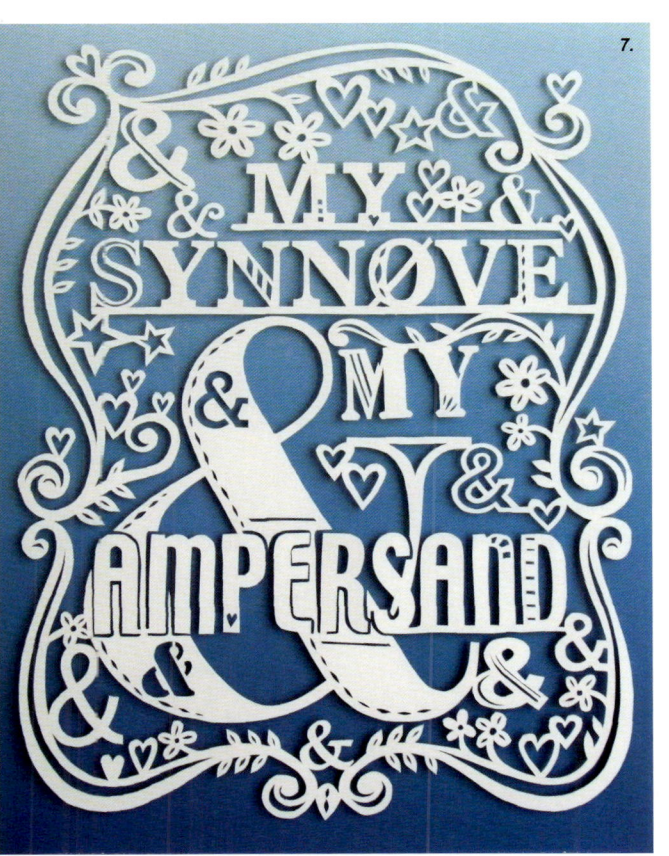

7.

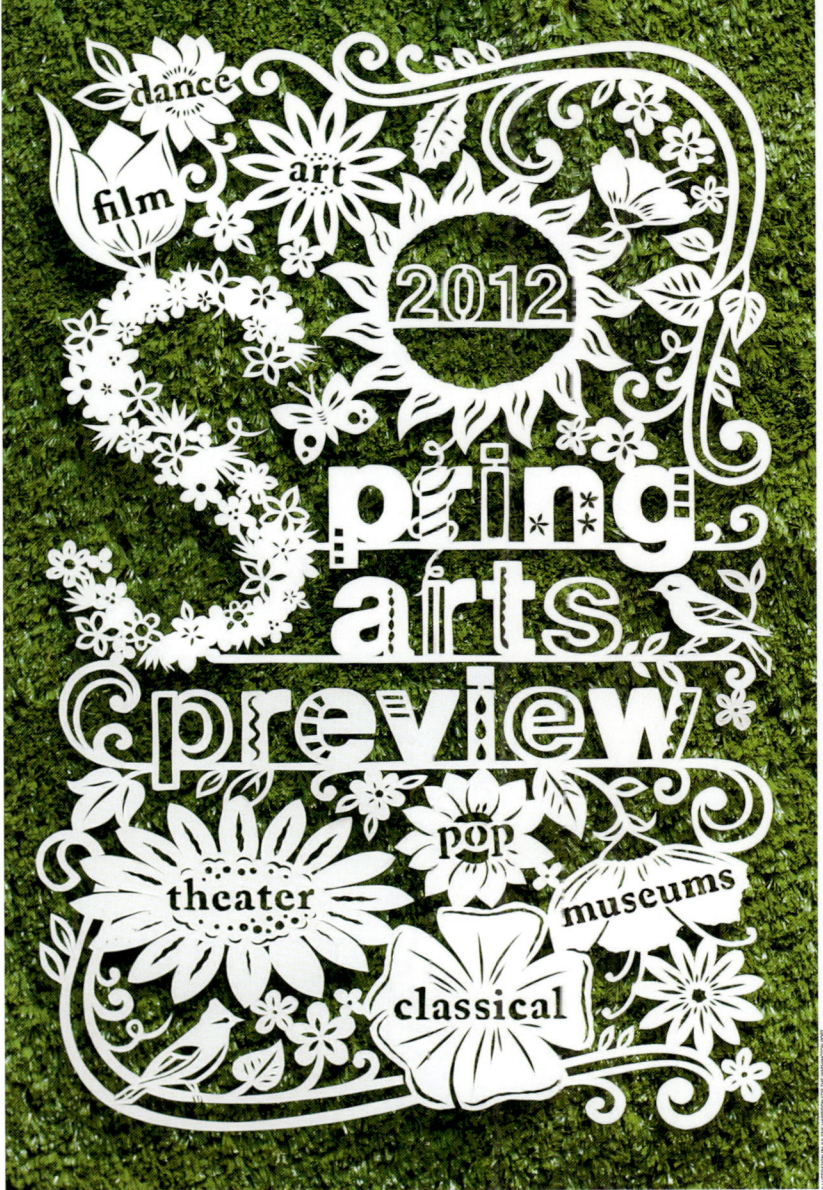

8.

8. **Spring Arts Guide**

2012 Spring Arts Preview for the Washington Post, illustrated with Springflowers/life sprouting out from it.

Designer: Julene Harrison
Country: UK
Design Agency: Bernstein and Andriulli (USA)
Creative Director: Susana Sanchez
Client: Washington Post
Photographer: Julene Harrison

319

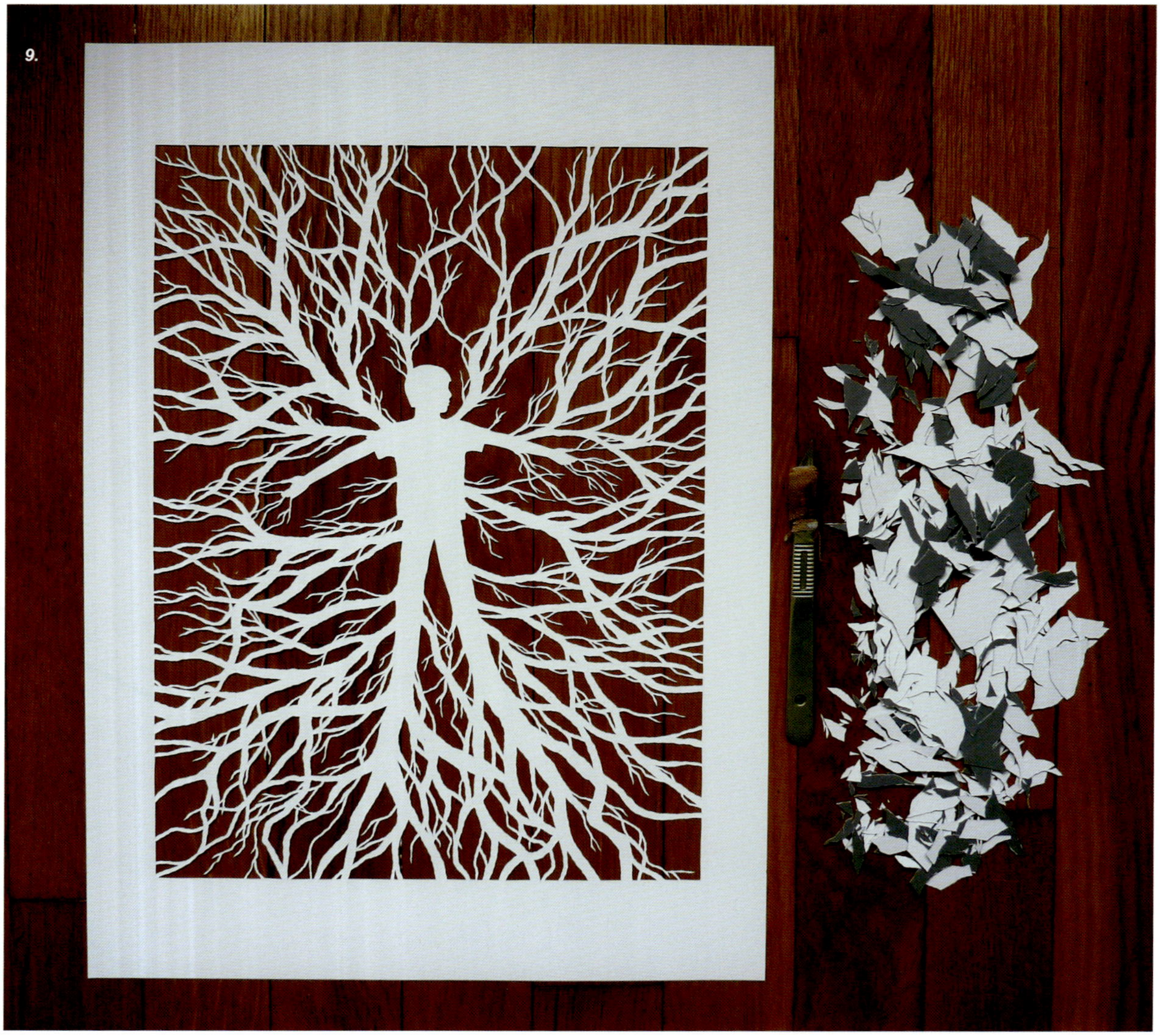

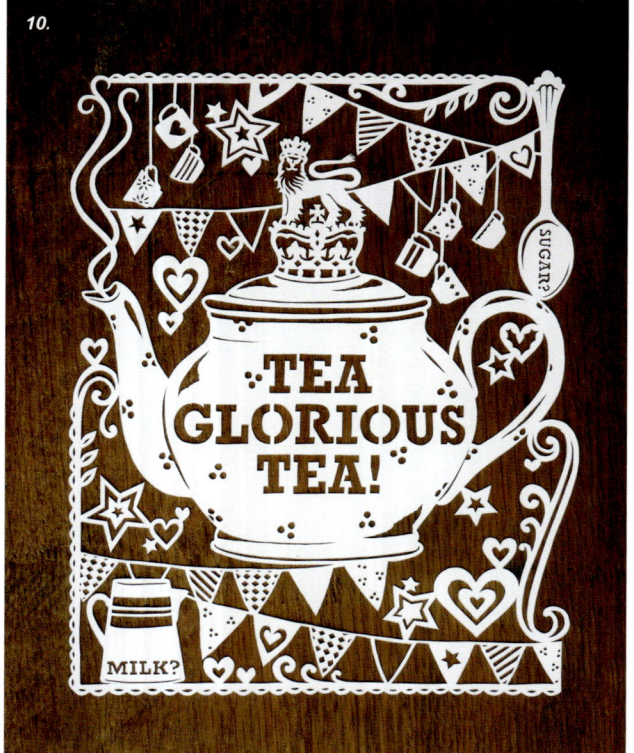

9. The Mostly True Story of Jack

Paper-cut for Book Cover. It's a sort of supernatural story about a boy who should be part of the earth — underground, literally — to keep the spirit balances in check, but he's been brought to the surface to live among normal people, upsetting the natural rhythm of things. The idea for the cover involves Jack being made of fused tree roots, forming him underground with roots coming from all angles.

Designer: Julene Harrison   Country: UK   Creative Director: Ben Mautner
Client: Little, Brown and Company (USA)
Photographer: Julene Harrison

10. Tea Glorious Tea

This is a piece of personal promotional work. With the Royal wedding in 2011, and the Olympics and our Queens 60th jubliee this year, I thought I'd celebrate our nations (and yours') favourite drink. Tea!

Designer: Julene Harrison
Country: UK
Creative Director: Julene Harrison
Photographer: Julene Harrison

11. O2 Christmas

This was such an exciting campaign for me to be involved in. The paper-cuts I worked on were used across the brand for Christmas 2010 — posters, instore literature, online and as window decals. The little yellow duck is their Pay-As-You-Go motif.

Designer: Julene Harrison   Country: UK
Design Agency: VCCP (UK)
Creative Director: Michael Hart / Ben Daly
Client: O2 Telecommunications Company

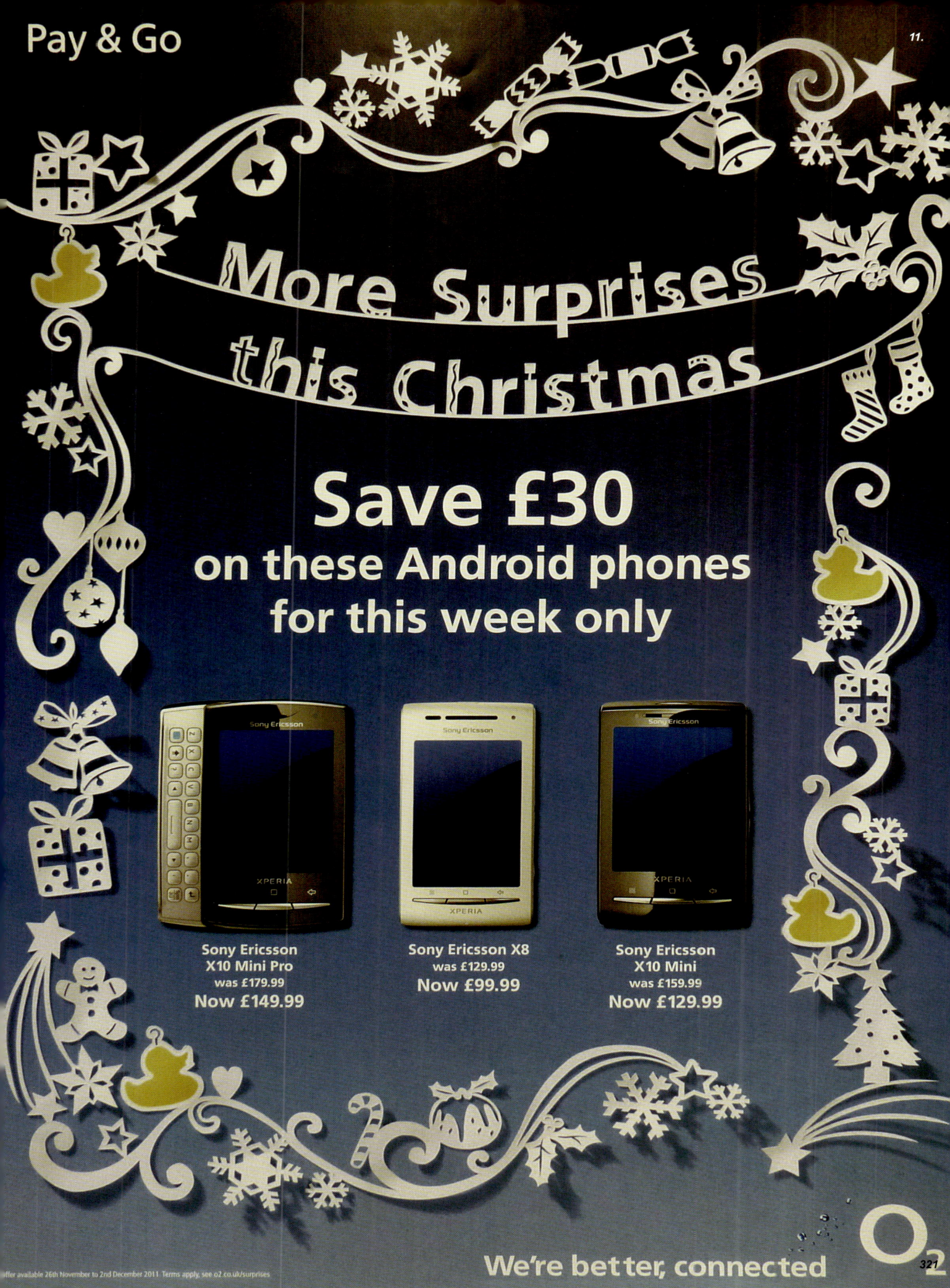

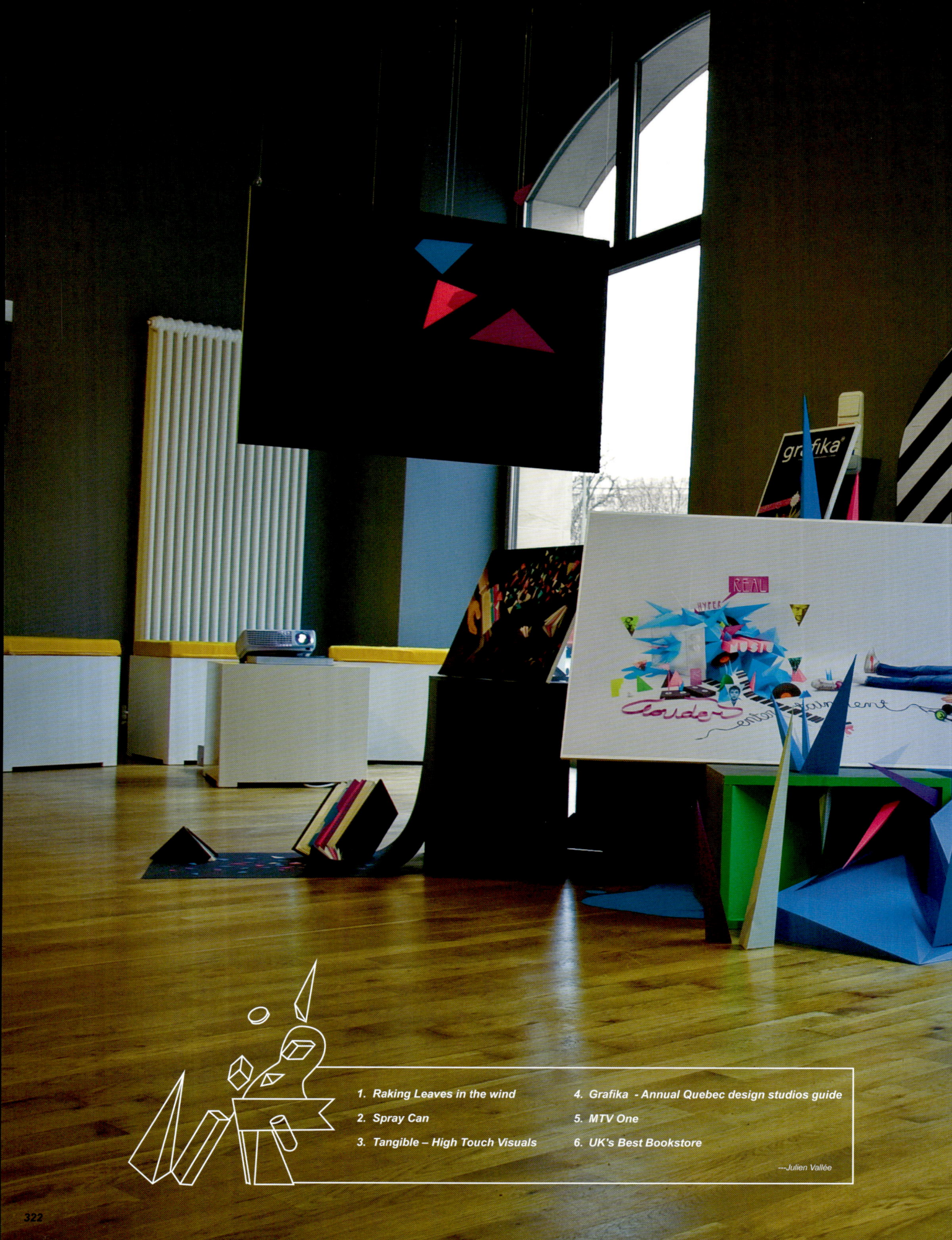

1. Raking Leaves in the wind
2. Spray Can
3. Tangible – High Touch Visuals
4. Grafika - Annual Quebec design studios guide
5. MTV One
6. UK's Best Bookstore

—Julien Vallée

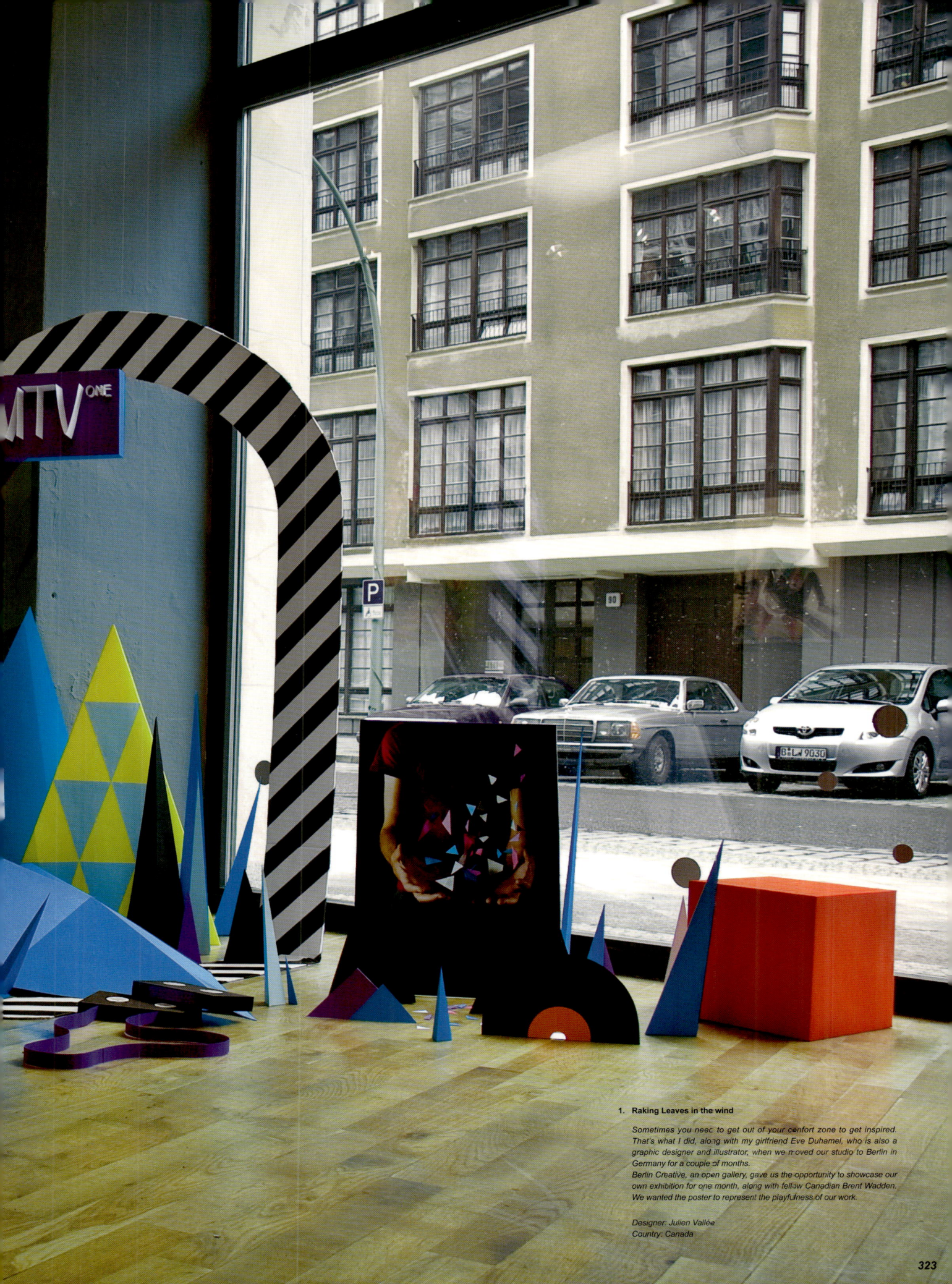

1. Raking Leaves in the wind

Sometimes you need to get out of your comfort zone to get inspired. That's what I did, along with my girlfriend Eve Duhamel, who is also a graphic designer and illustrator, when we moved our studio to Berlin in Germany for a couple of months.
Berlin Creative, an open gallery, gave us the opportunity to showcase our own exhibition for one month, along with fellow Canadian Brent Wadden. We wanted the poster to represent the playfulness of our work.

Designer: Julien Vallée
Country: Canada

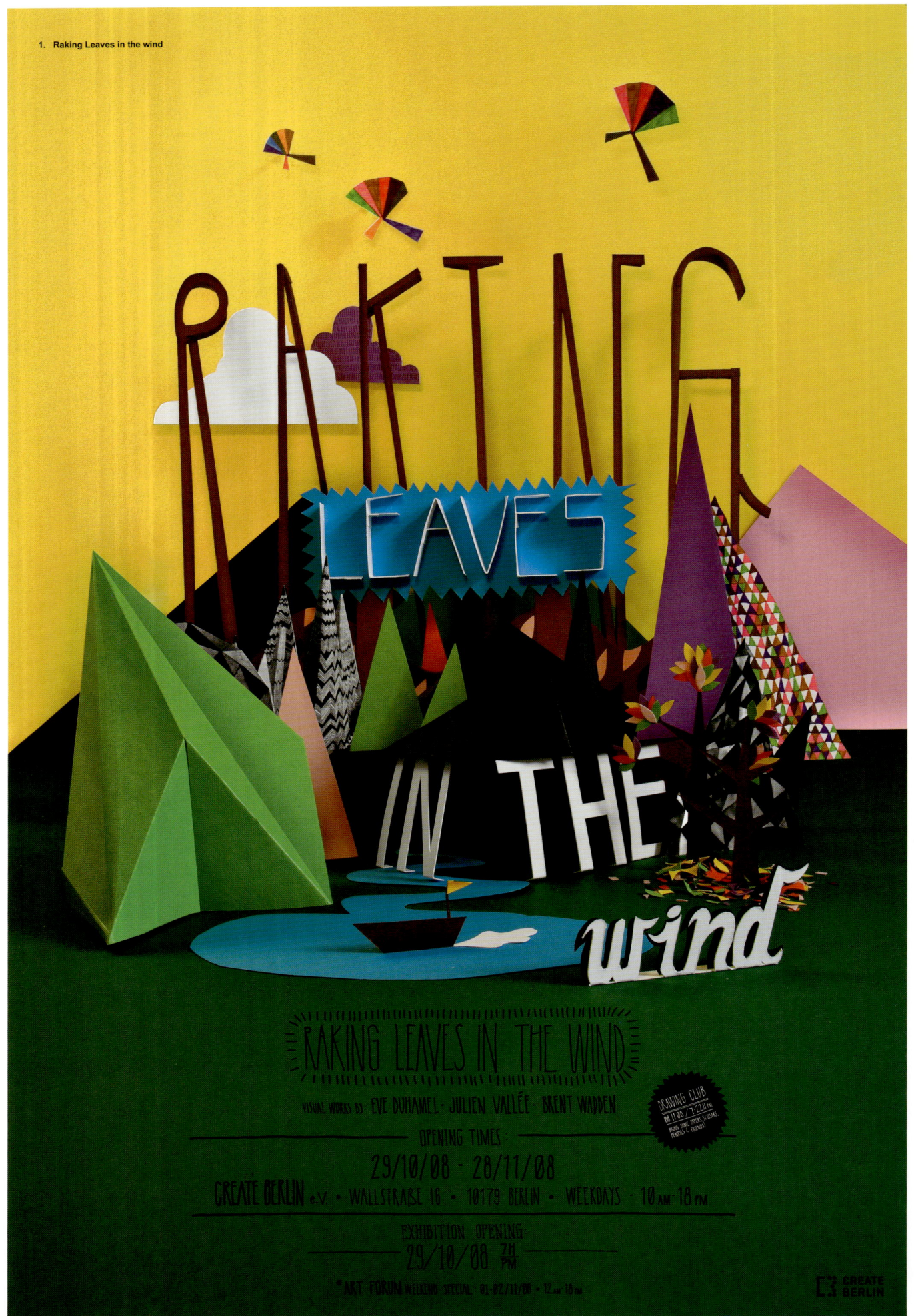

1. Raking Leaves in the wind

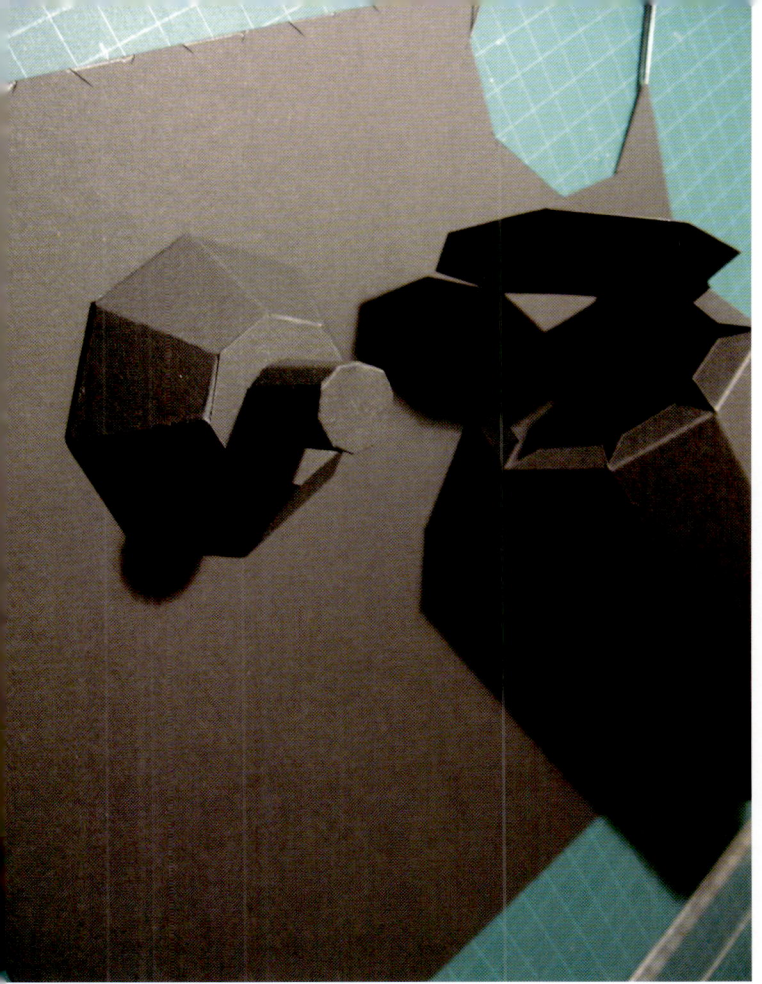

2. Spray Can

Spray Can is a paper sculpture created for the main exhibition of Illustrative Zürich, a leading international festival for contemporary illustration and graphic art.

Country: Canada
Designer: Julien Vallée
Client: Illustrative Zürich

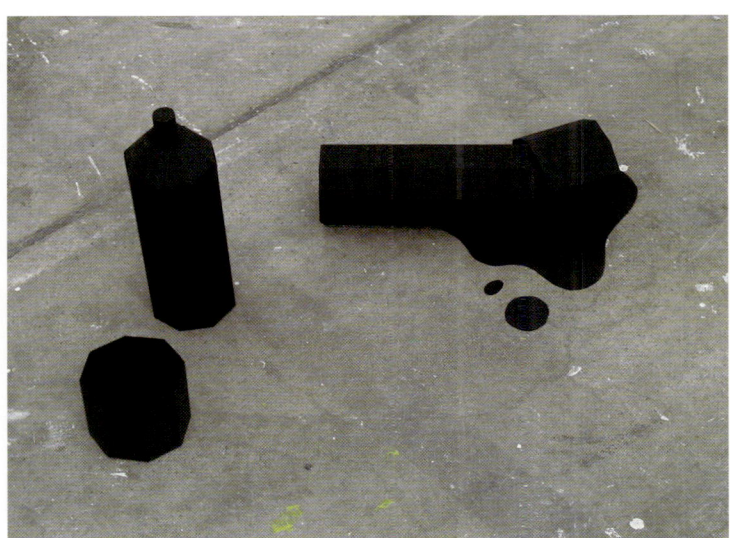

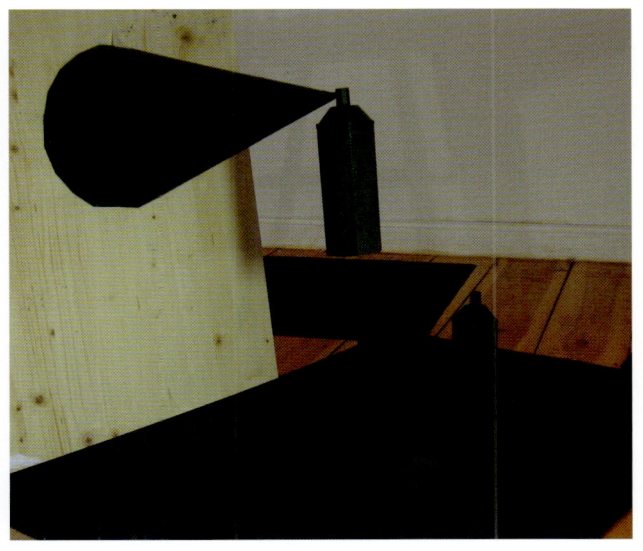

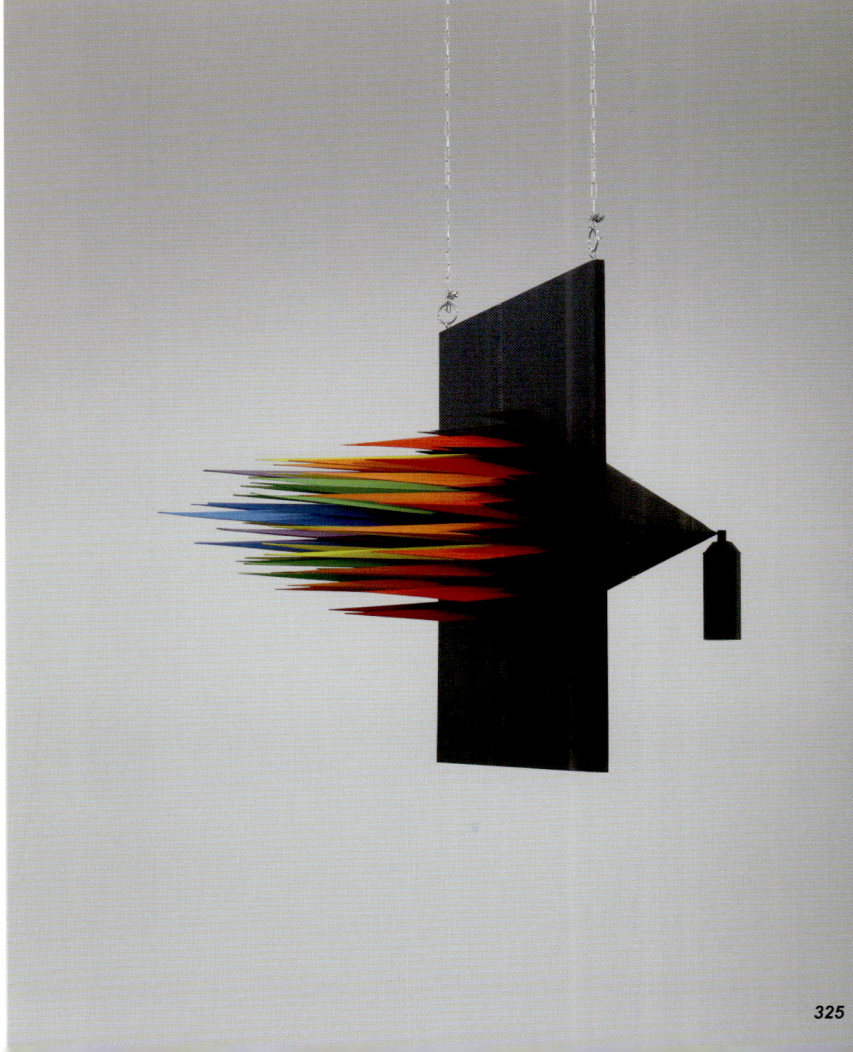

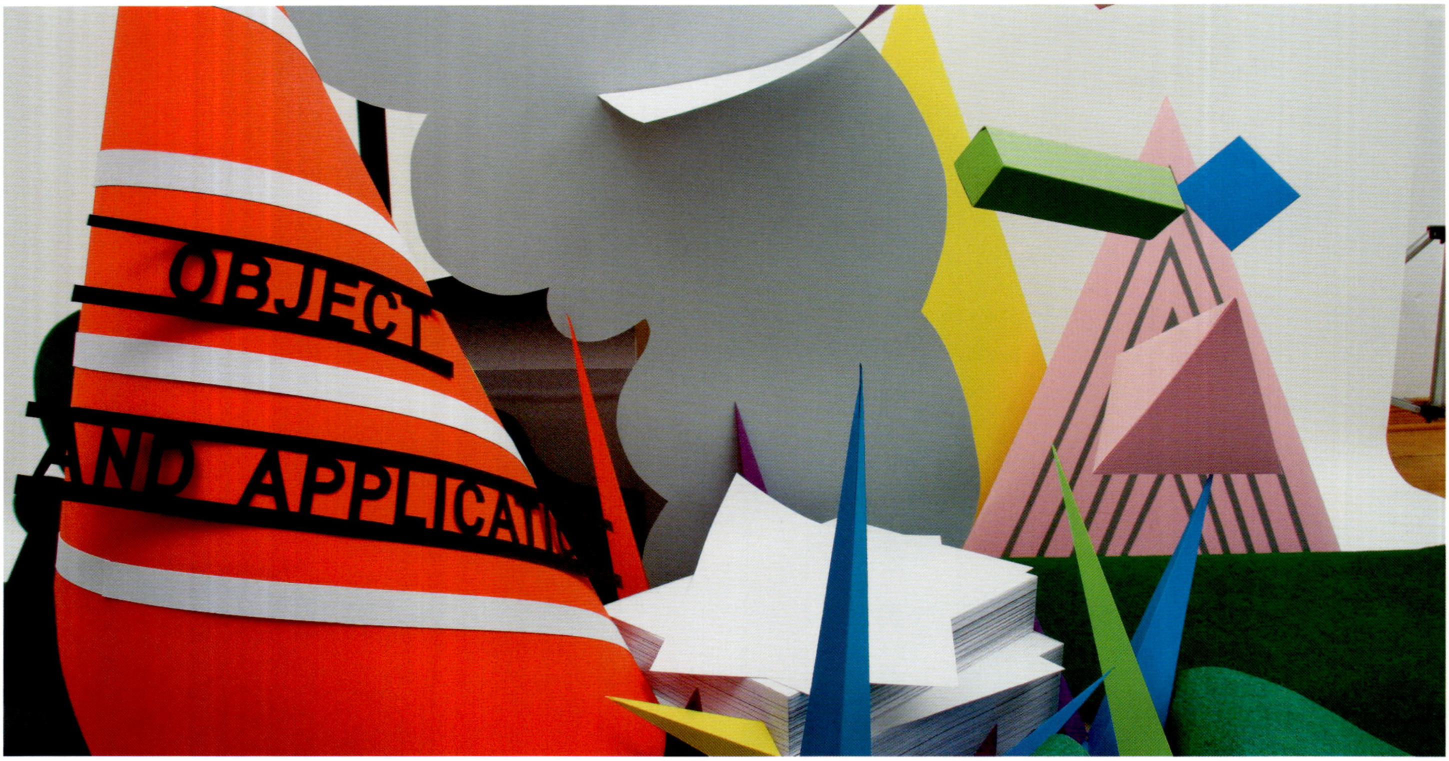

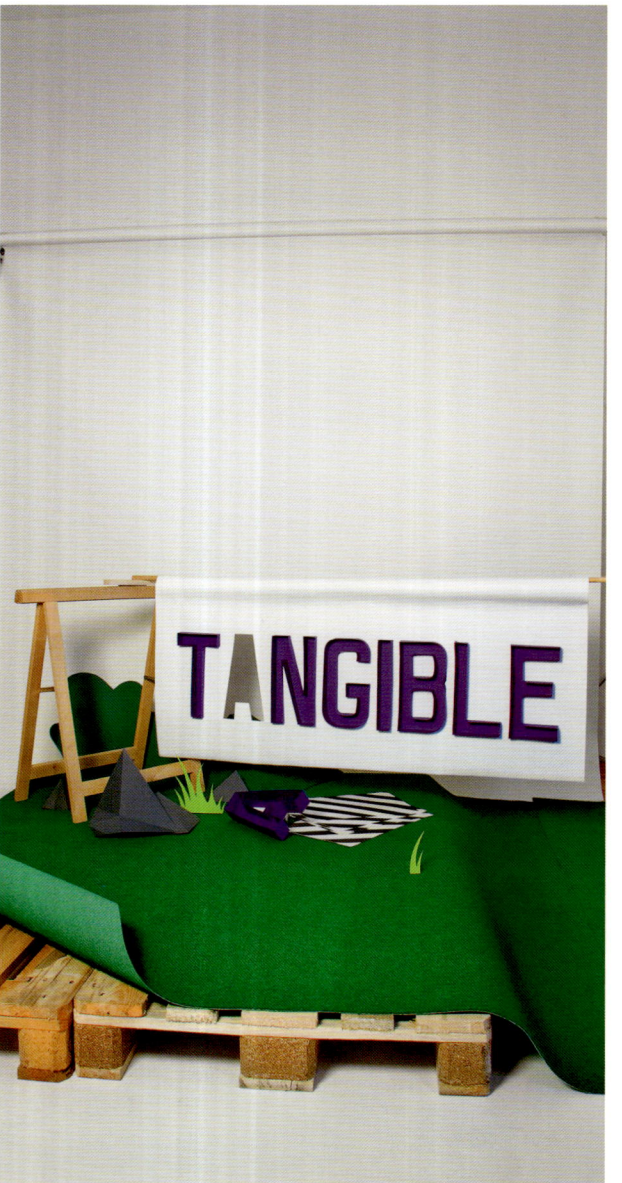
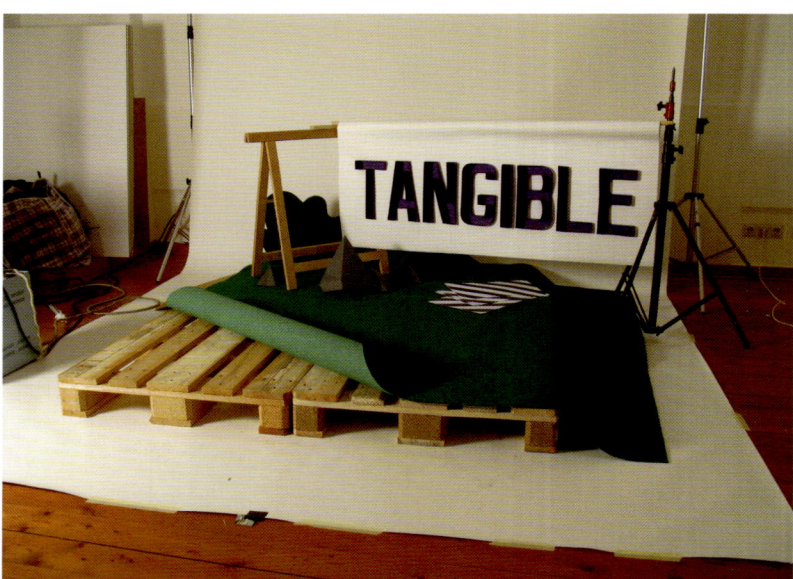
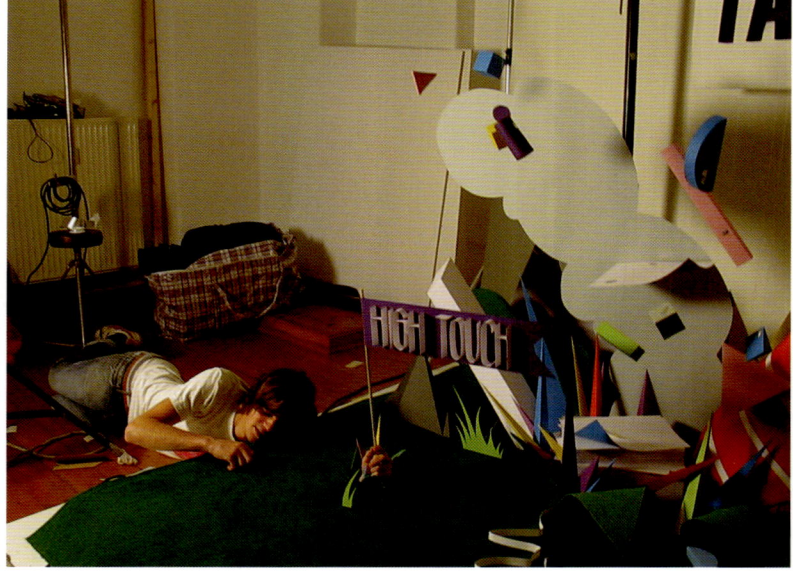

3. Tangible – High Touch Visuals

Gestalten is publisher and creative agency known for their books on a variety of art disciplines an for their ability to anticipate vital trends in visual culture. Tangible is a book that documents how designers are using the stylistic means of graphic design to implement their ideas to three-dimensional design, objects and orchestrated spaces.
For the cover we wanted to celebrate one of our favourite design approaches by creating a human-scale set, busy with details and very playful. Like others today, we try to make the intangible tangible. Manifesting the imaginary into material objects and spaces. Morphing graphic design into

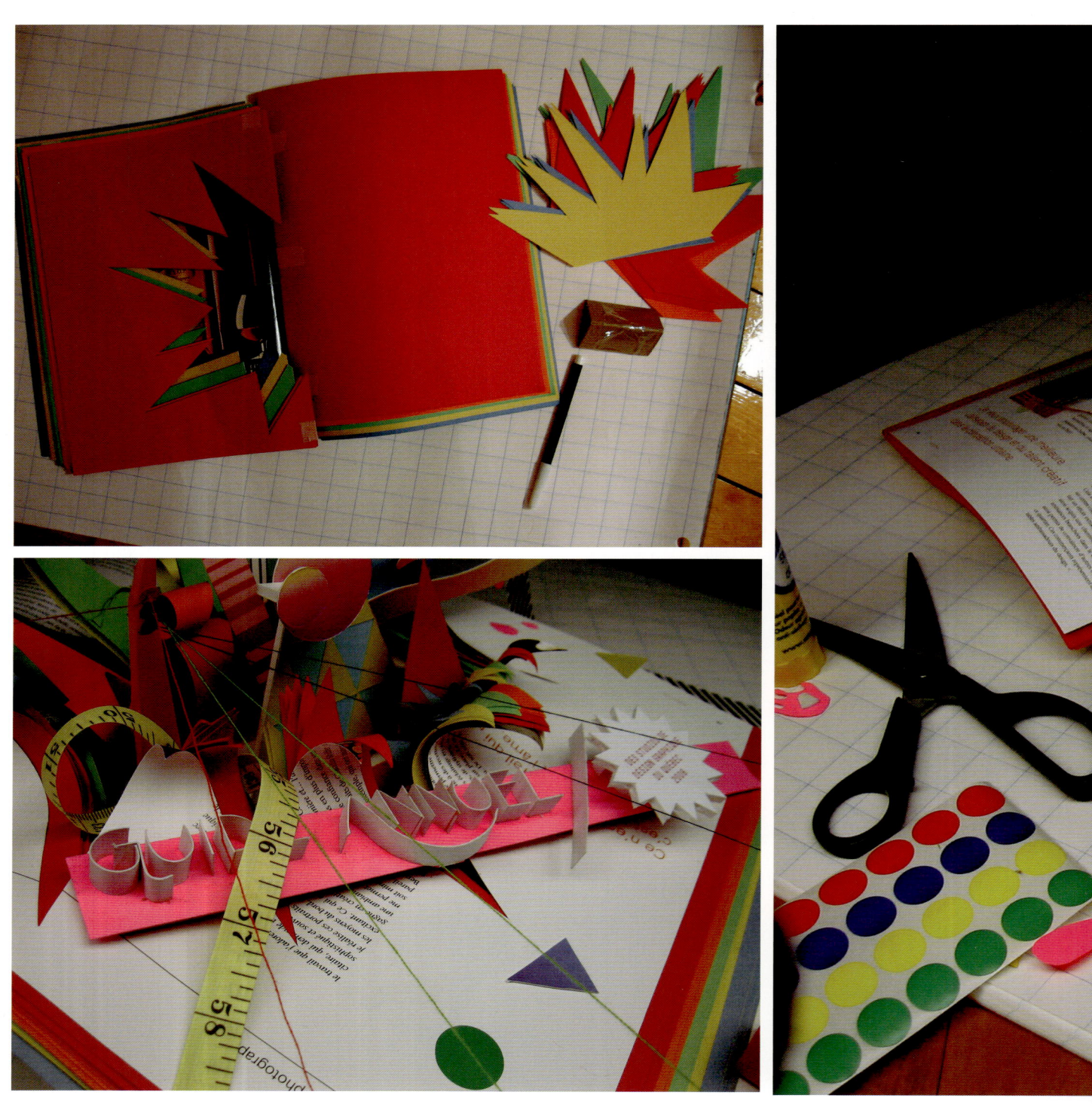

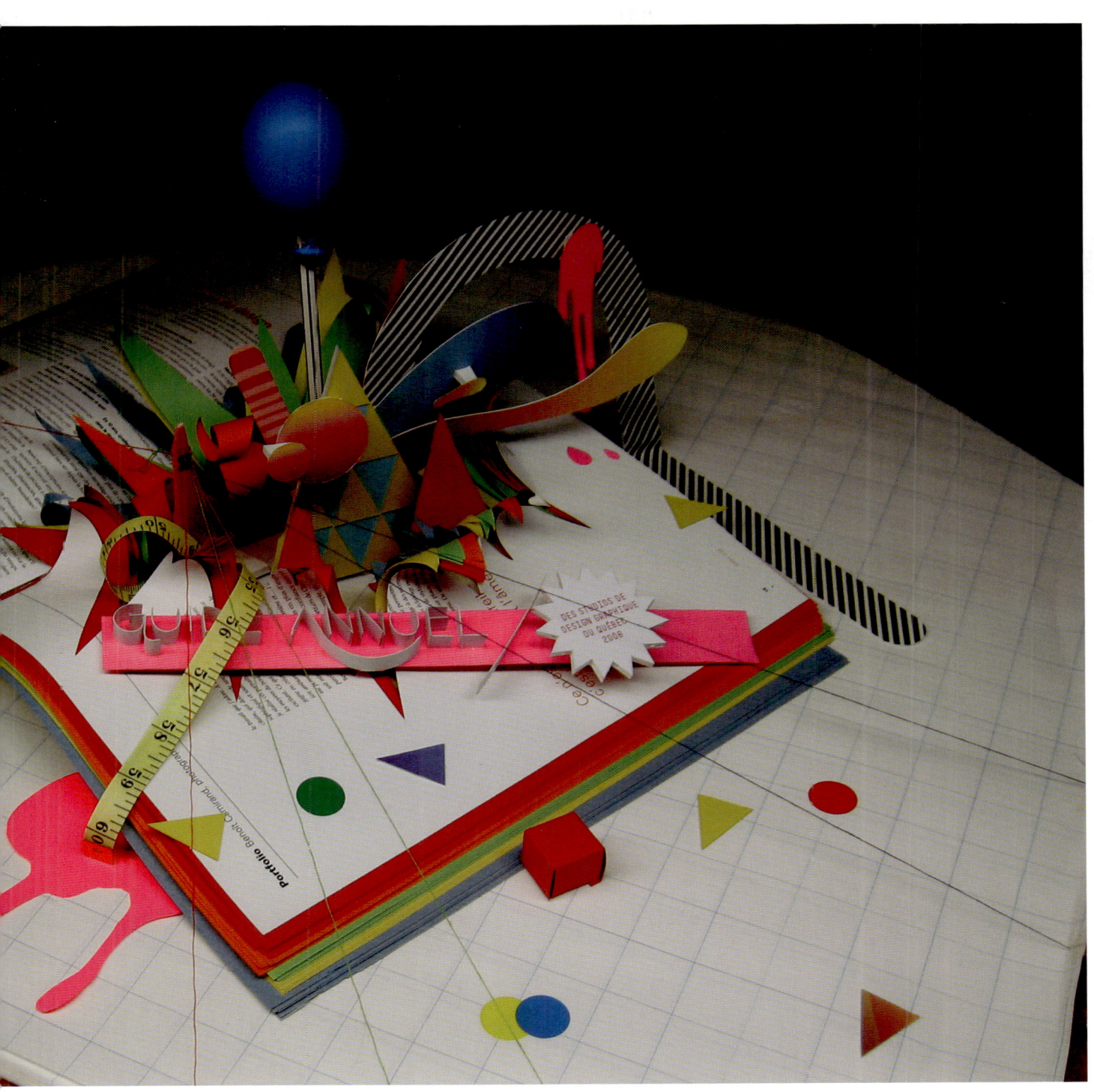

4. Grafika - Annual Quebec design studios guide

Graphika is a magazine and a blog that covers subjects related to graphic design community and the visual communication industry in Quebec. Each year, they publish an issue that lists all the industry professionals of the province, from the simple freelancer to the big time agency. I was asked to do the cover for the issue.

Designer: Julien Vallée
Country: Canada
Client: Gestalten

5. MTV One

The agency DixonBaxi was asked by MTV One to integrate photographs of famous people and make the words hyper-real, music, louder, entertainment and fame part of the picture. That was the brief. The rest was up to us...
The end story is simple: our paper MTV literally blows up in the face of the out-of-frame viewer who has turned it on.

Designer: Julien Vallée Country: Canada
Design Agency: Dixon Baxi (UK)
Client : MTV One
Photographer: Simon Duhamel

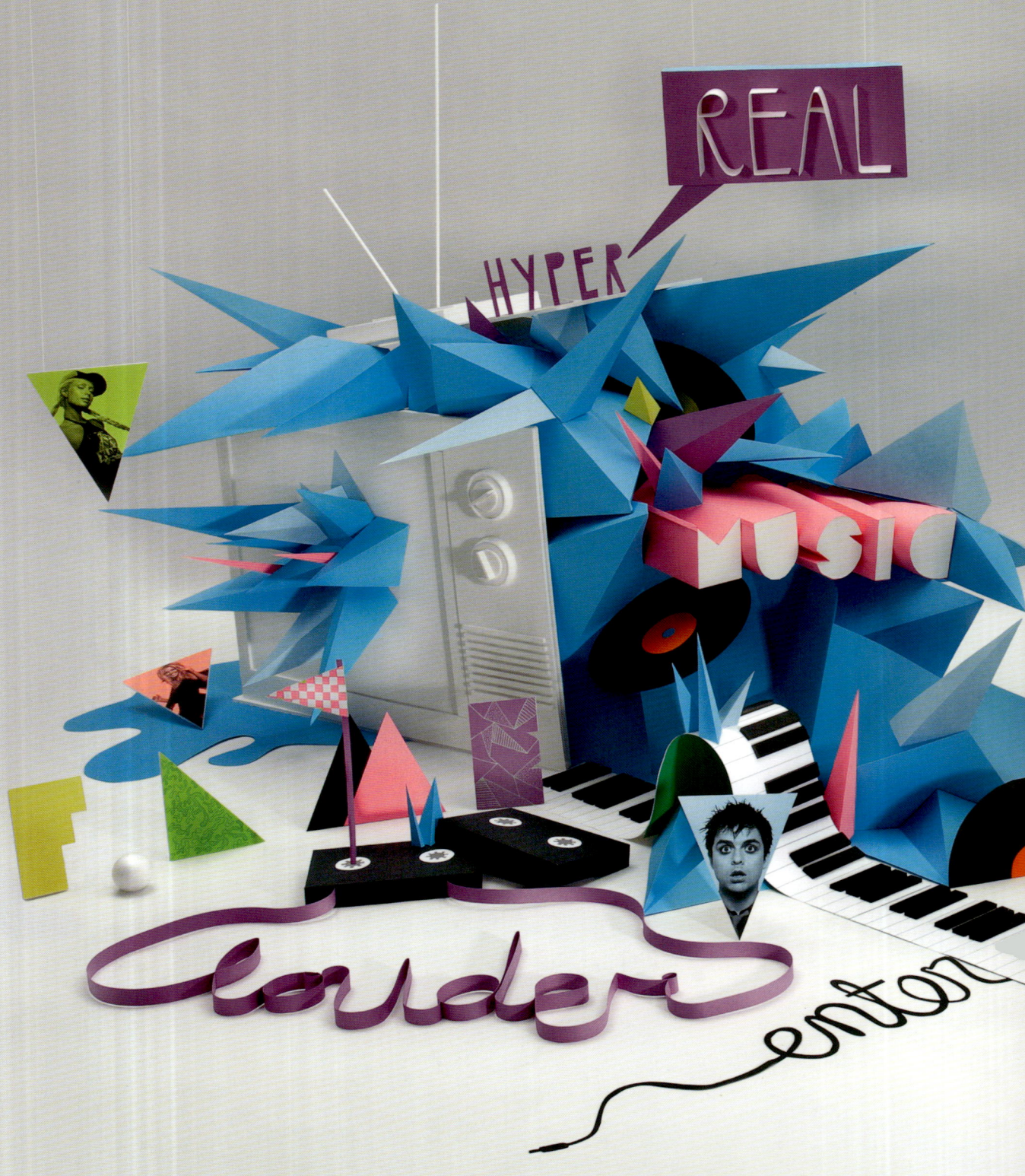

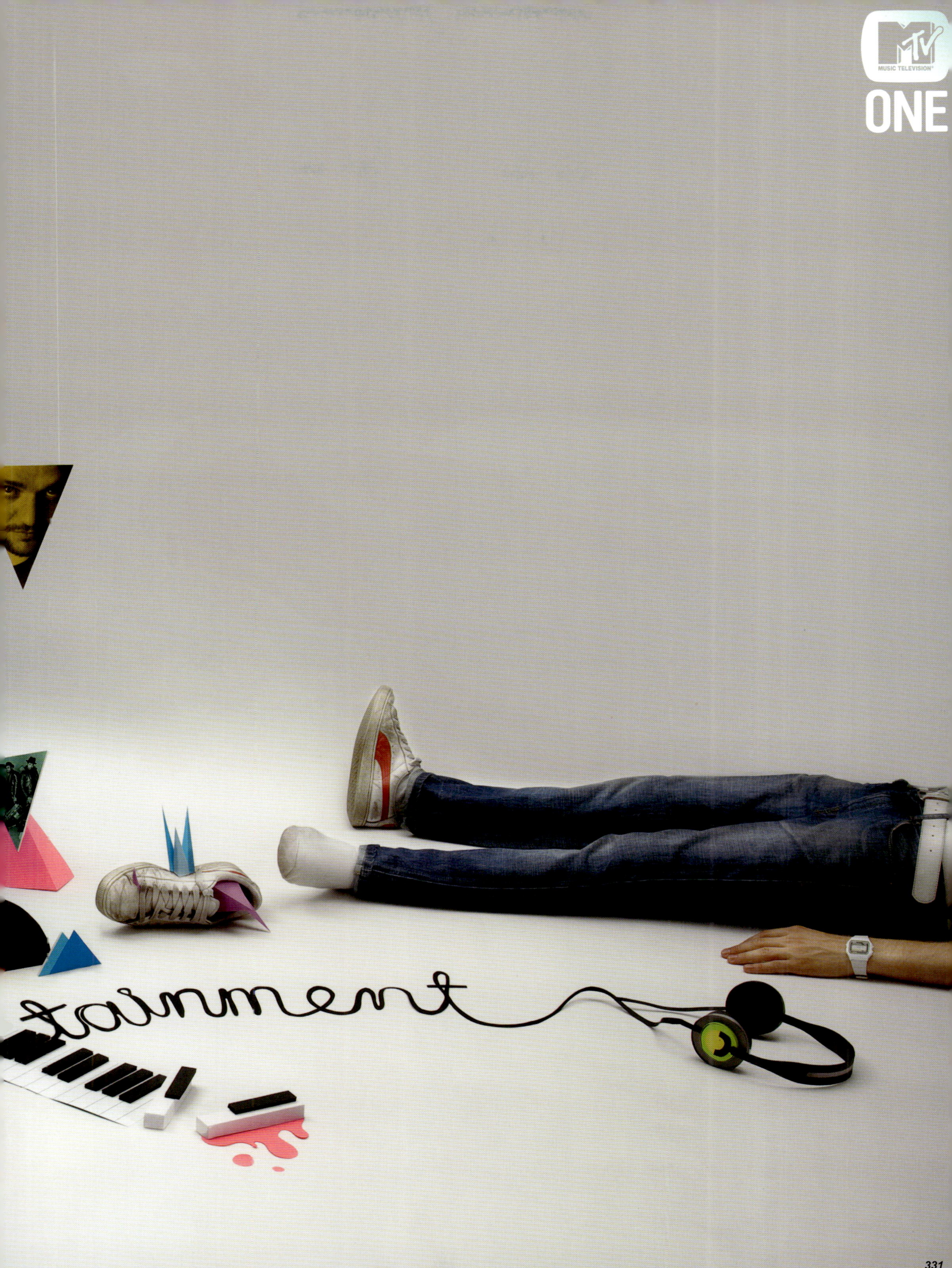

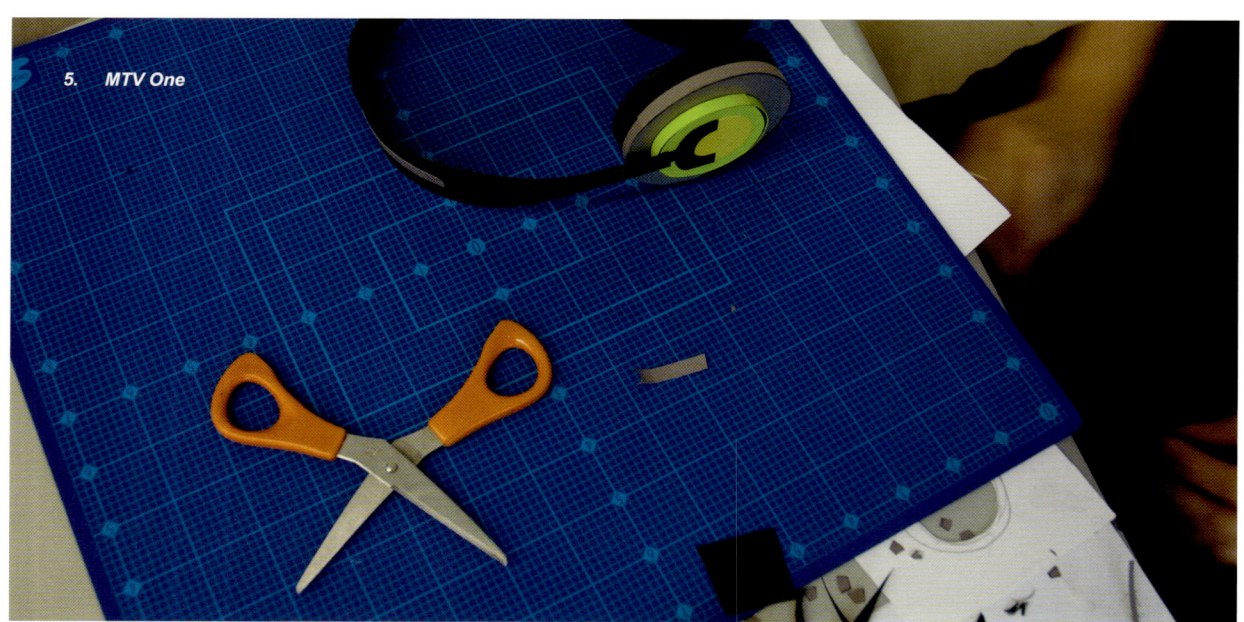

5. MTV One

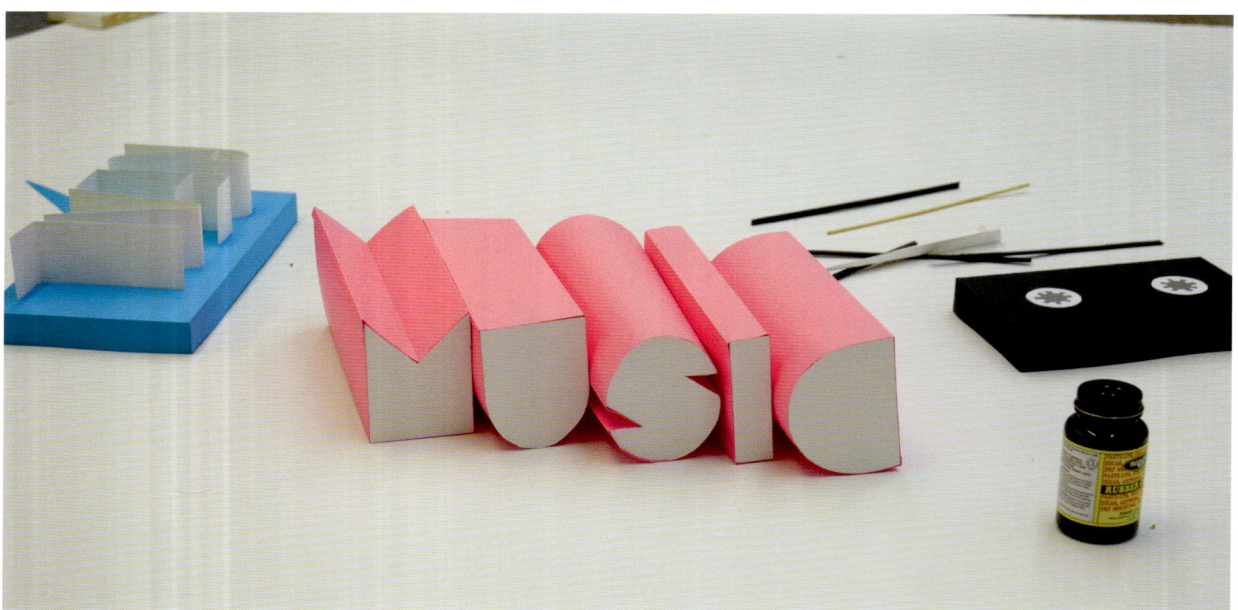

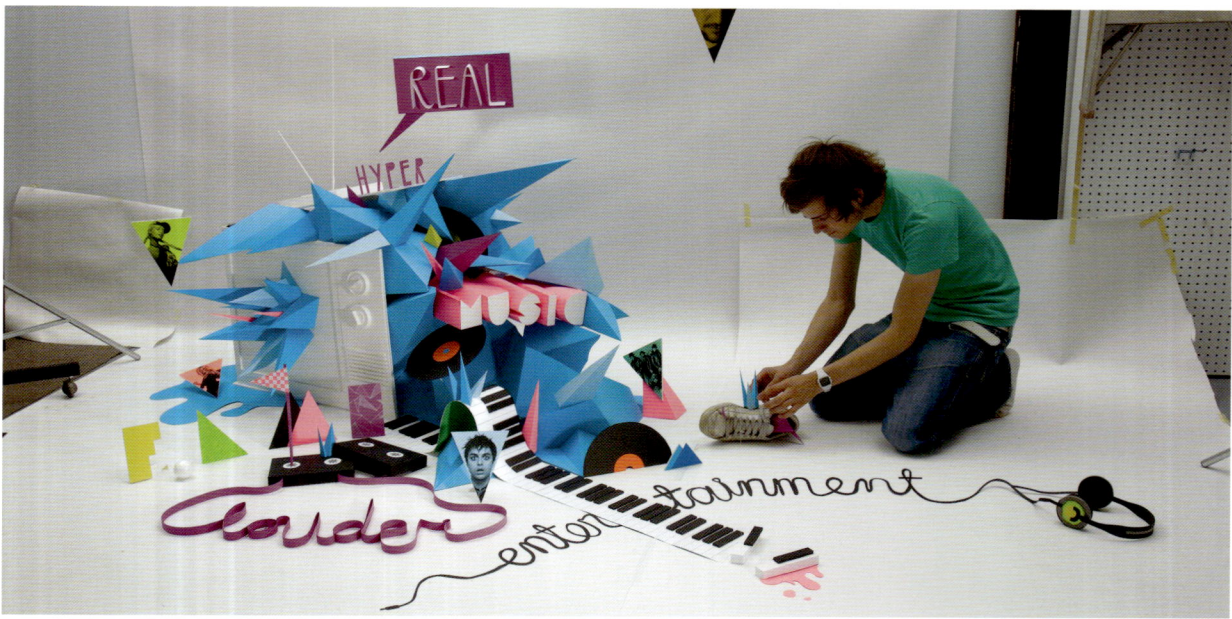

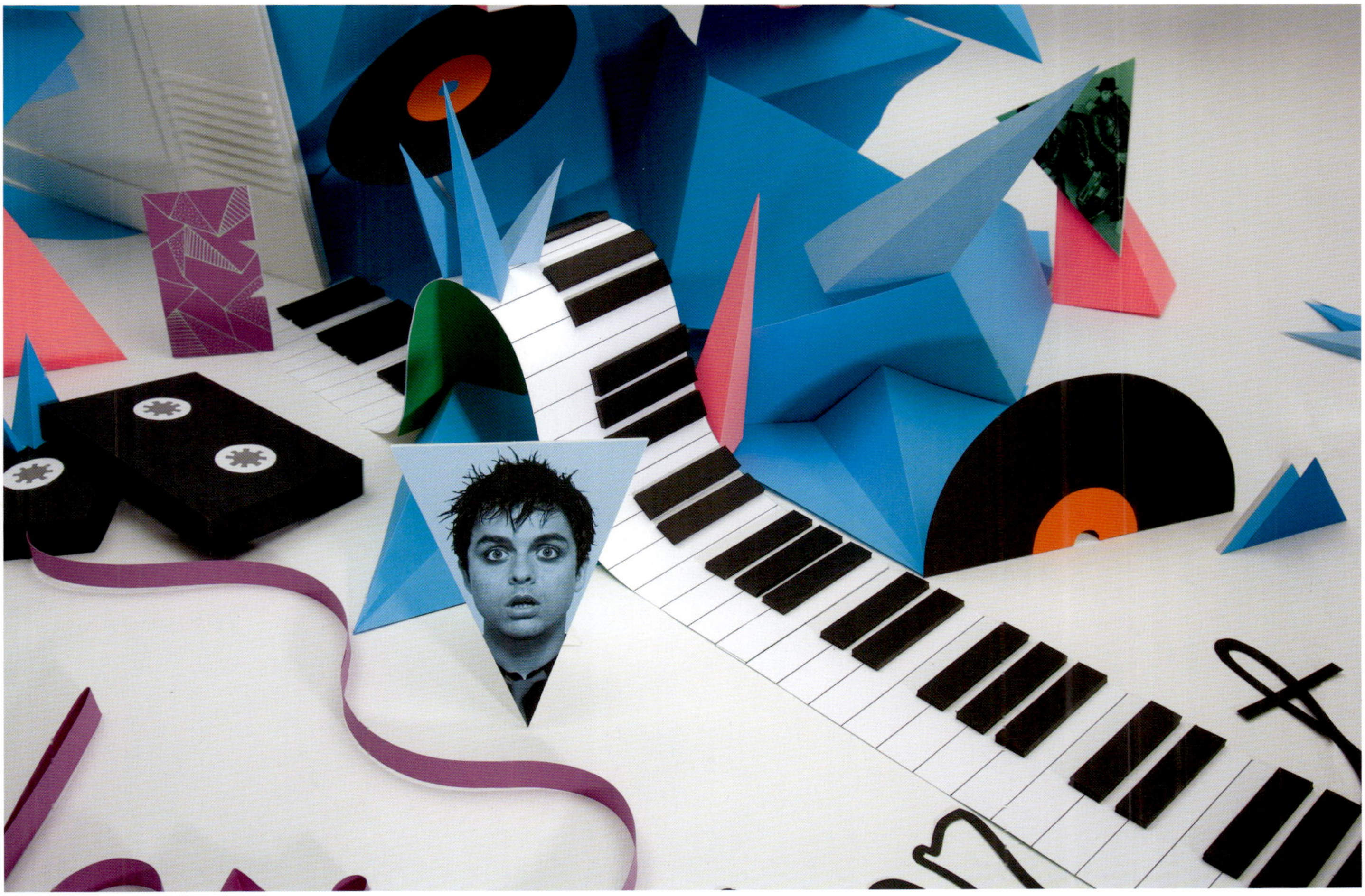

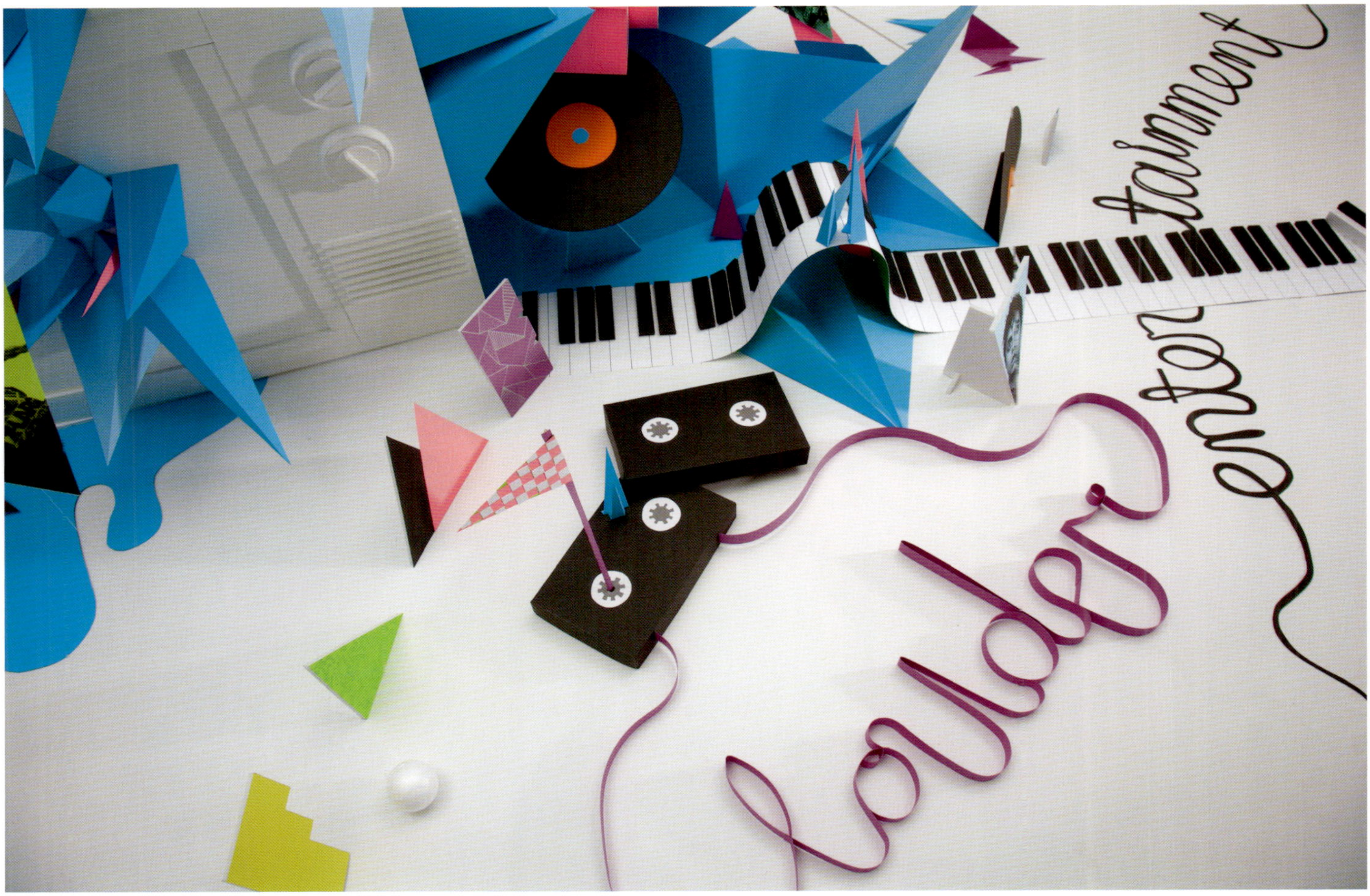

louder entertainment

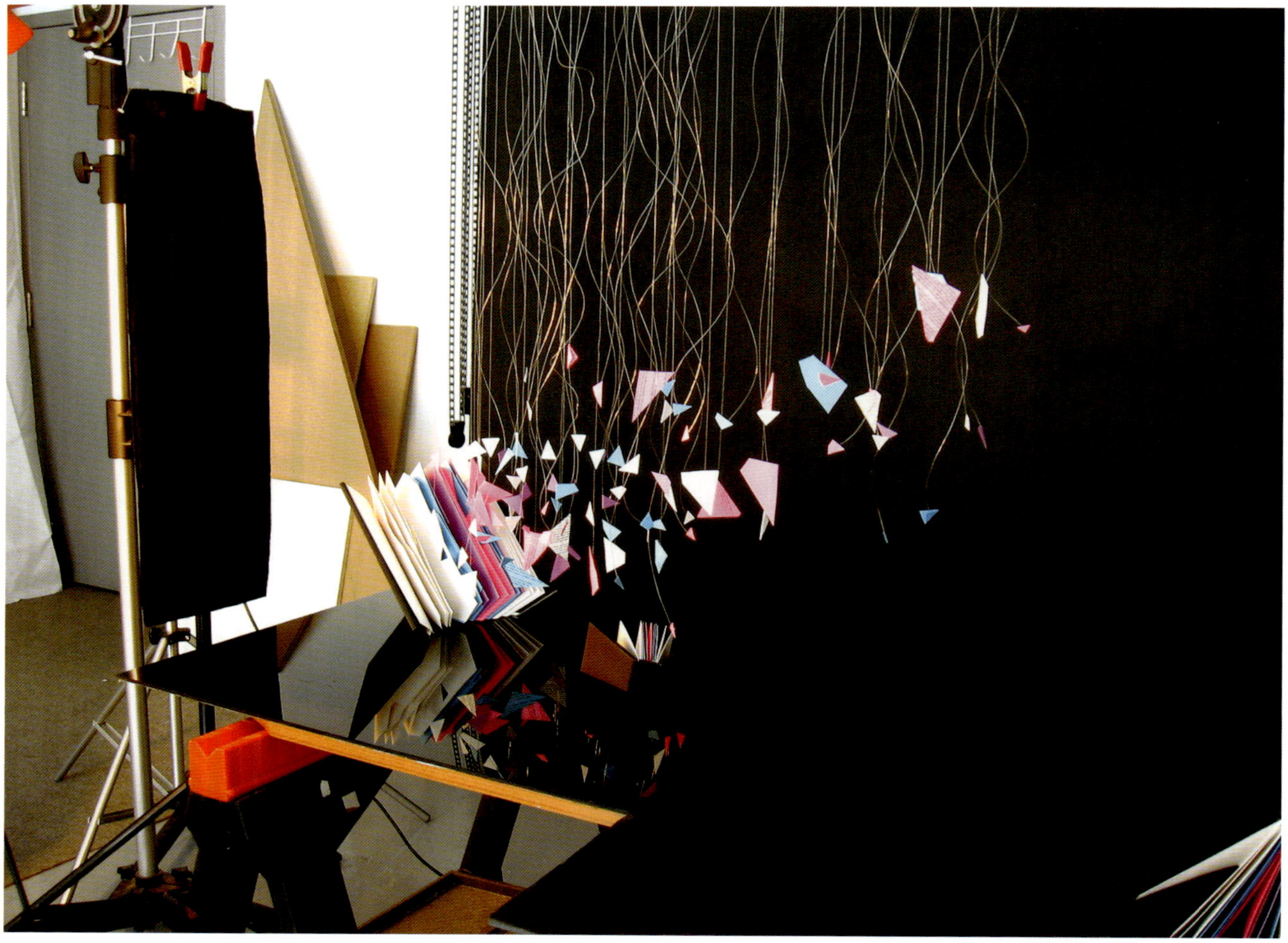

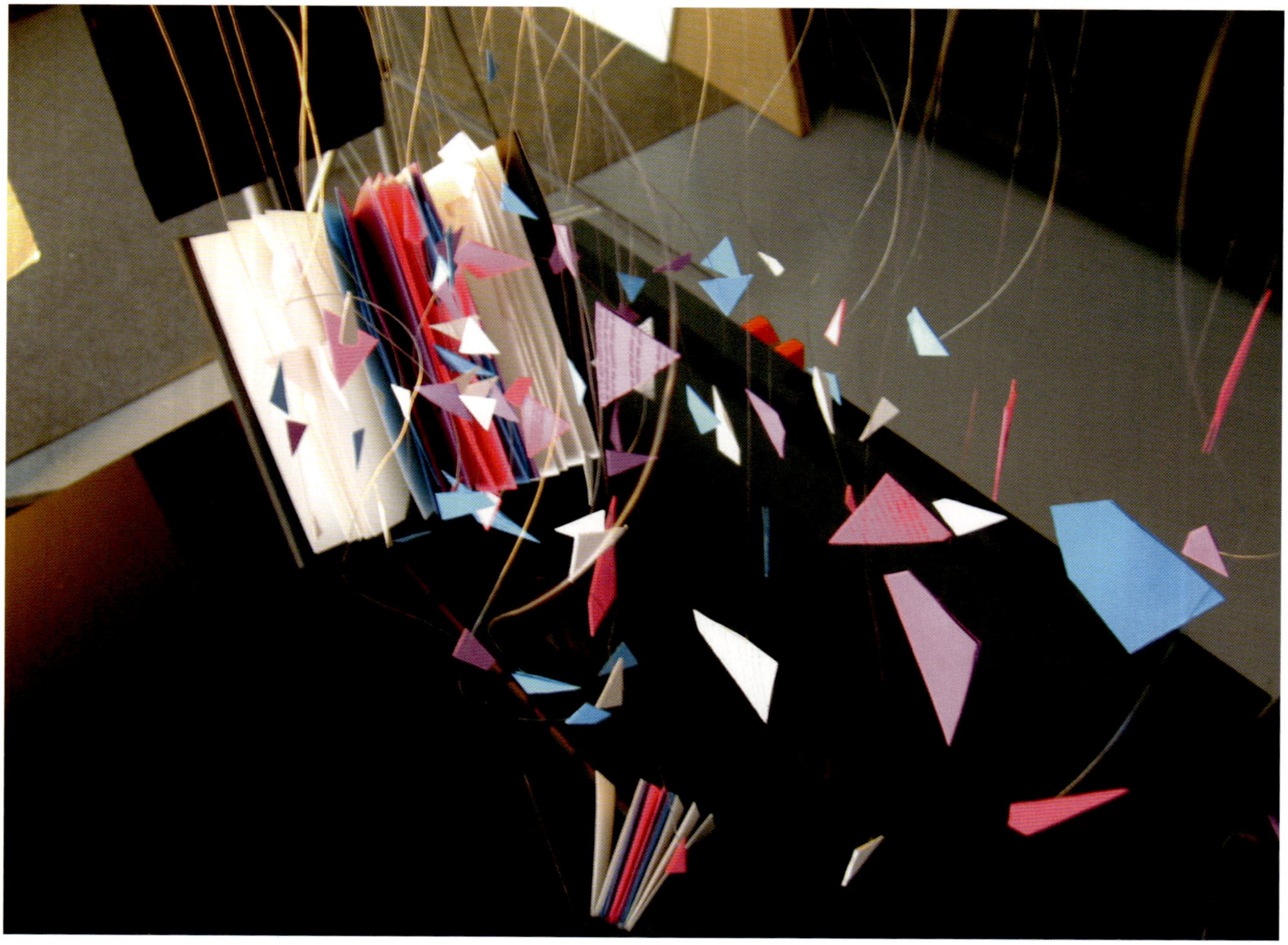

6. UK's Best Bookstore

Elle UK is a British fashion magazine focused on shopping and beauty news. Every year, the magazine features a list of UK's best bookstores.
In a our digital world where books tend to disappear, I was really glad to be commissioned to illustrate this feature. Books have so much to tell; you just need to open the first page to release a story.

Designer: Julien Vallée
Country: Canada
Client : ELLE Decoration UK
Photographer: Simon Duhamel

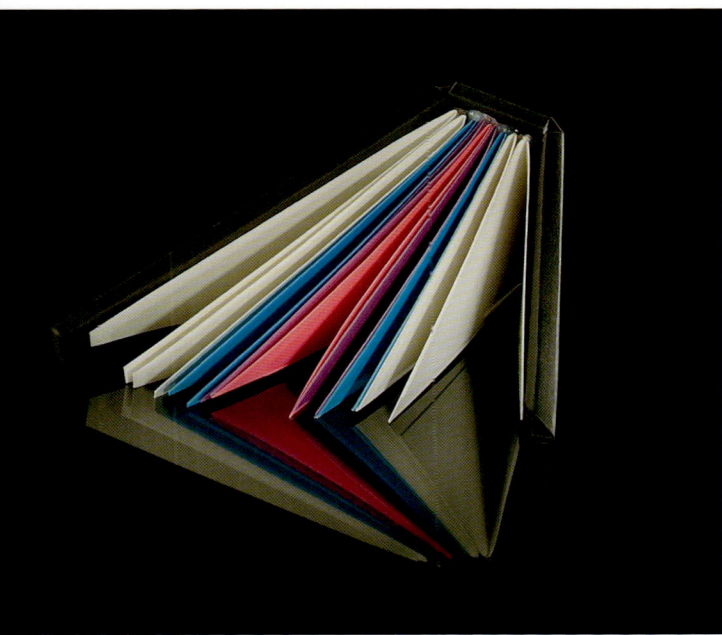
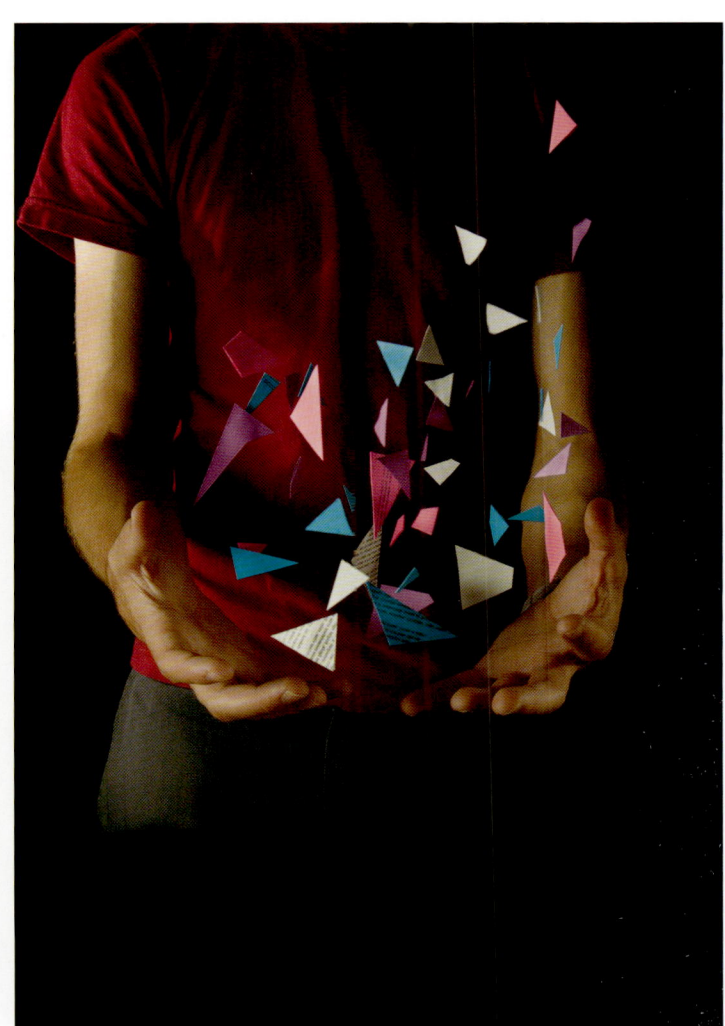

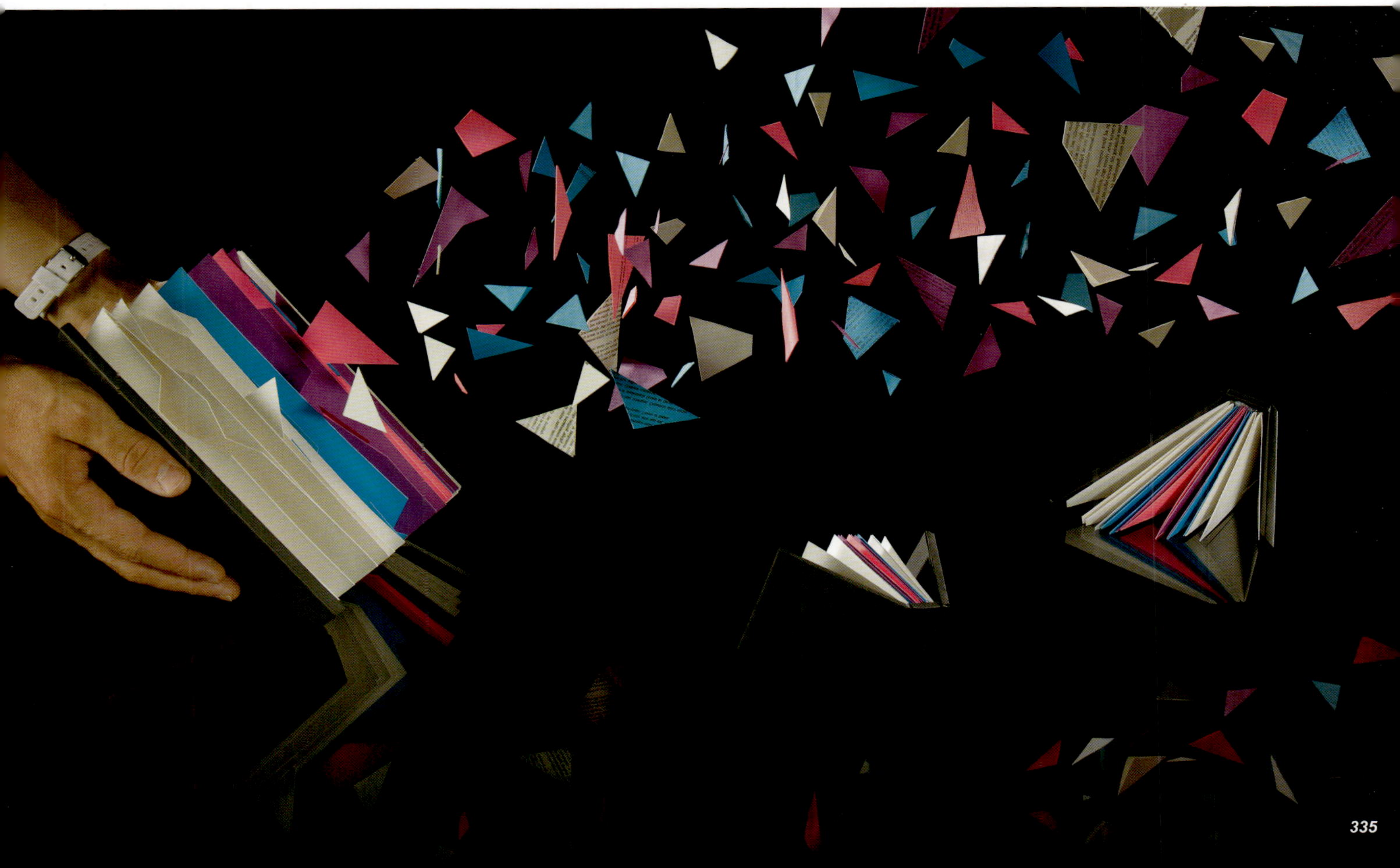

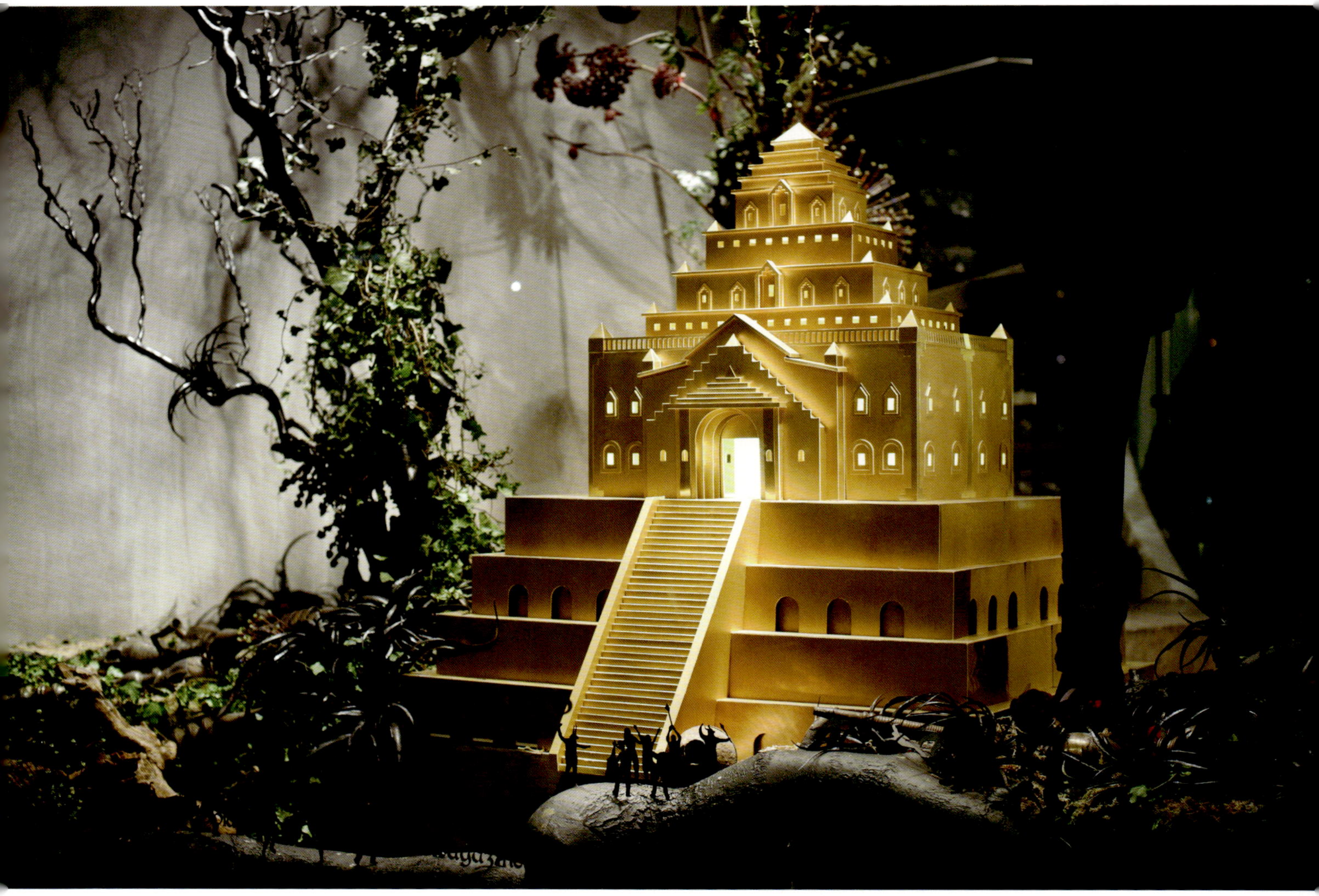

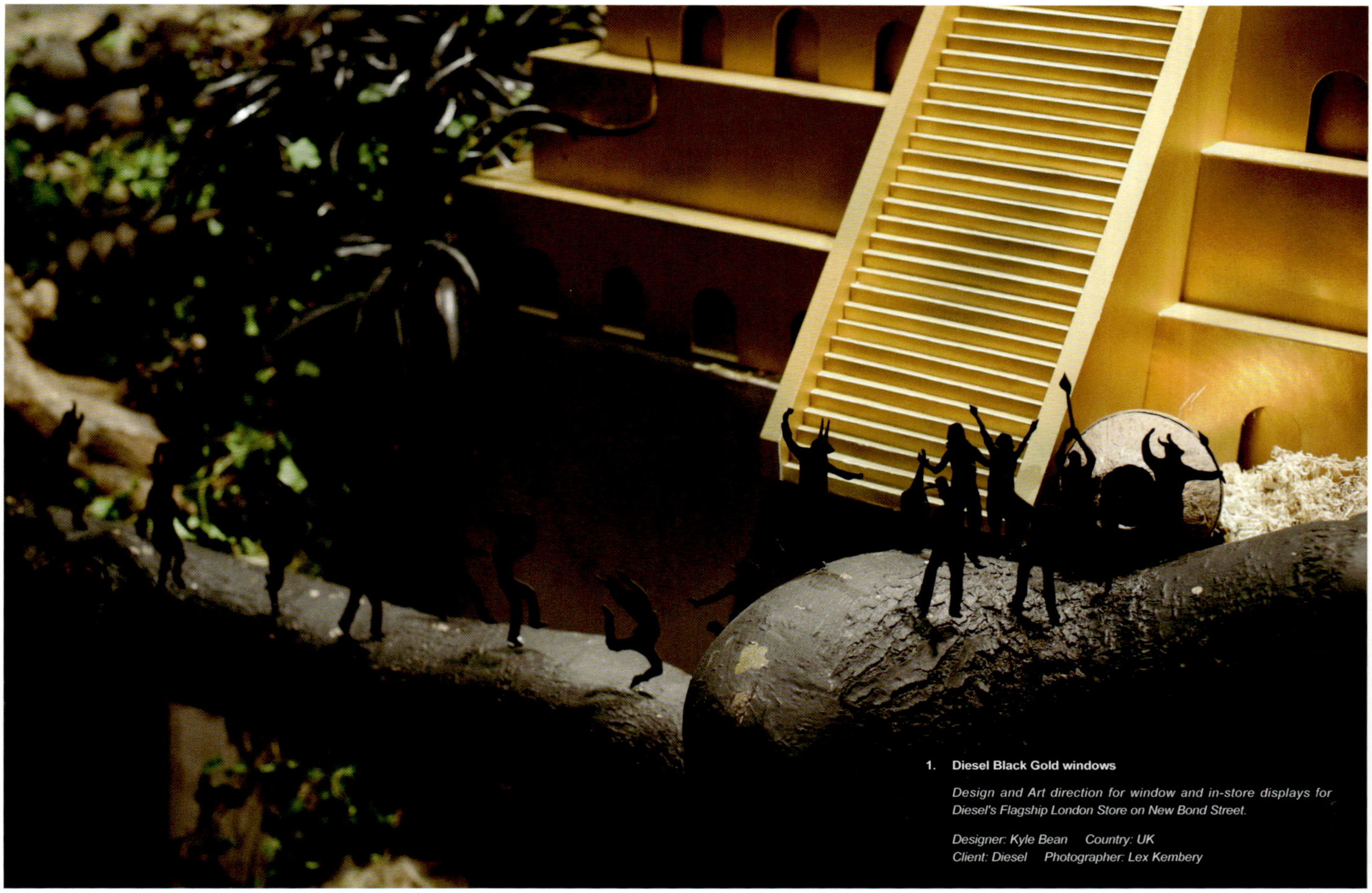

1. **Diesel Black Gold windows**

Design and Art direction for window and in-store displays for Diesel's Flagship London Store on New Bond Street.

Designer: Kyle Bean   Country: UK
Client: Diesel   Photographer: Lex Kembery

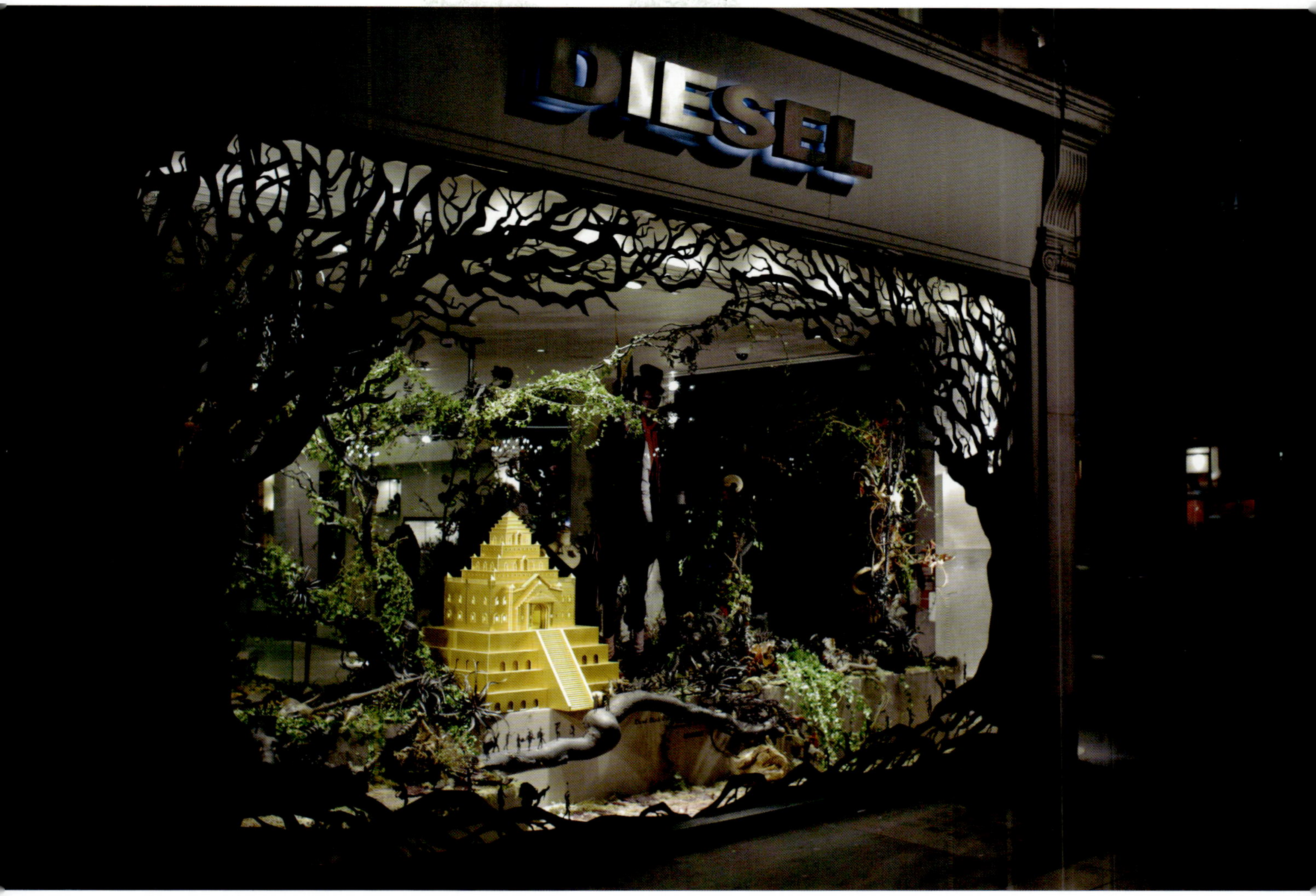

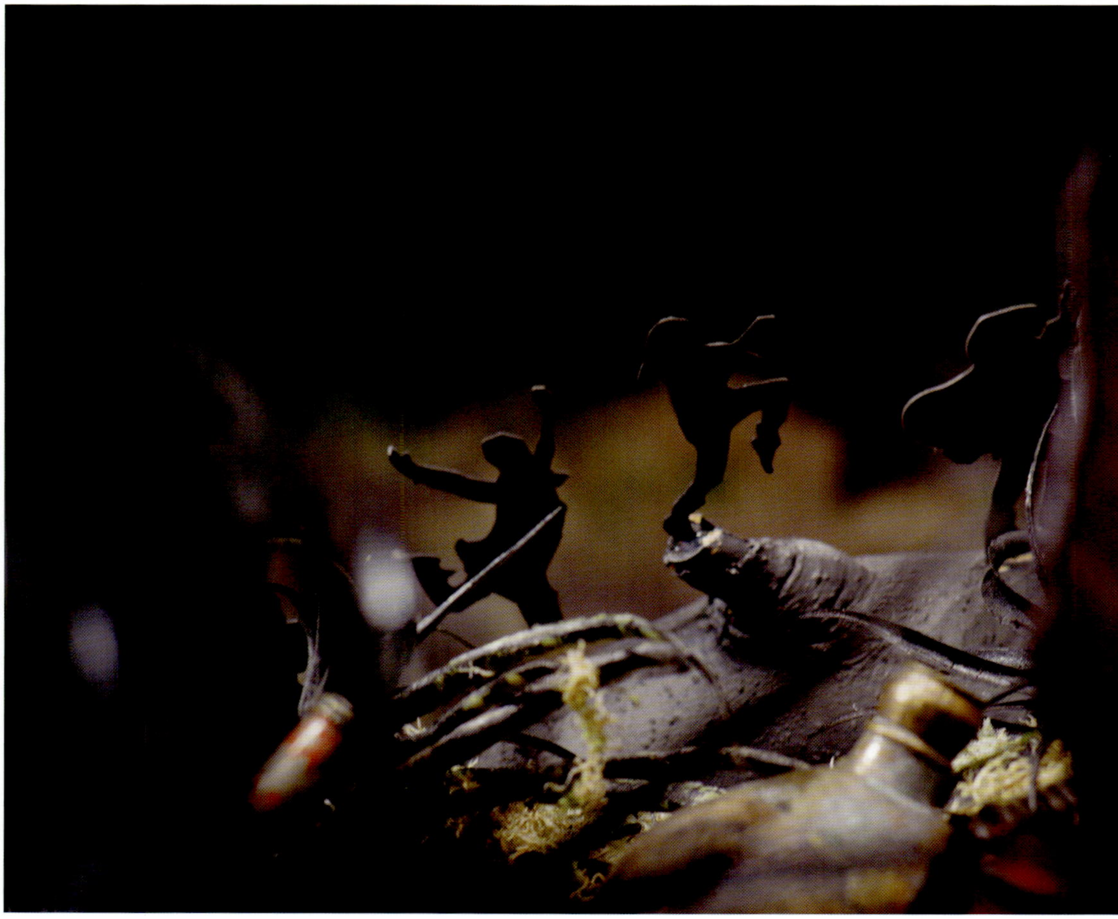

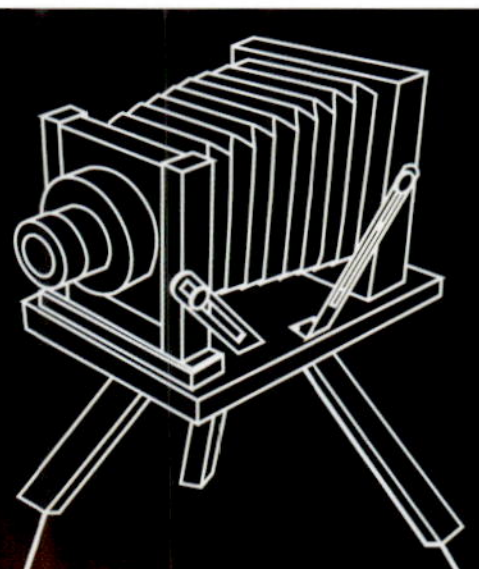

1. Wonderland
2. Milan Preview
3. Hermes
4. Design Museum
5. Communities
6. Louis Vuitton
7. Flower Power
8. Mobile Evolution
9. Paper Plane
10. Upside Down House
11. Mens Health Heart
12. Transformation
13. The Science of Play

----Kyle Bean

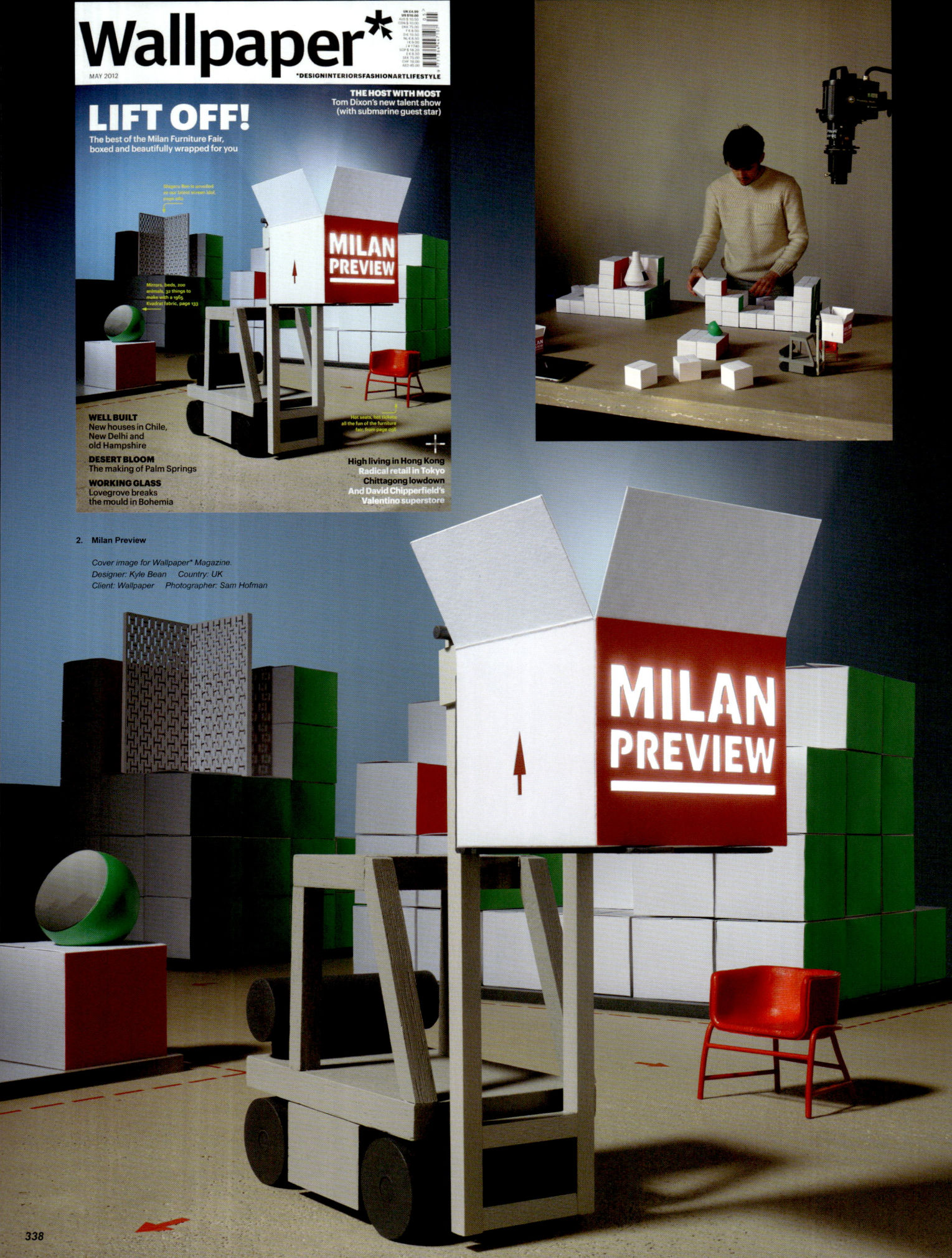

2. Milan Preview

Cover image for Wallpaper* Magazine.
Designer: Kyle Bean   Country: UK
Client: Wallpaper   Photographer: Sam Hofman

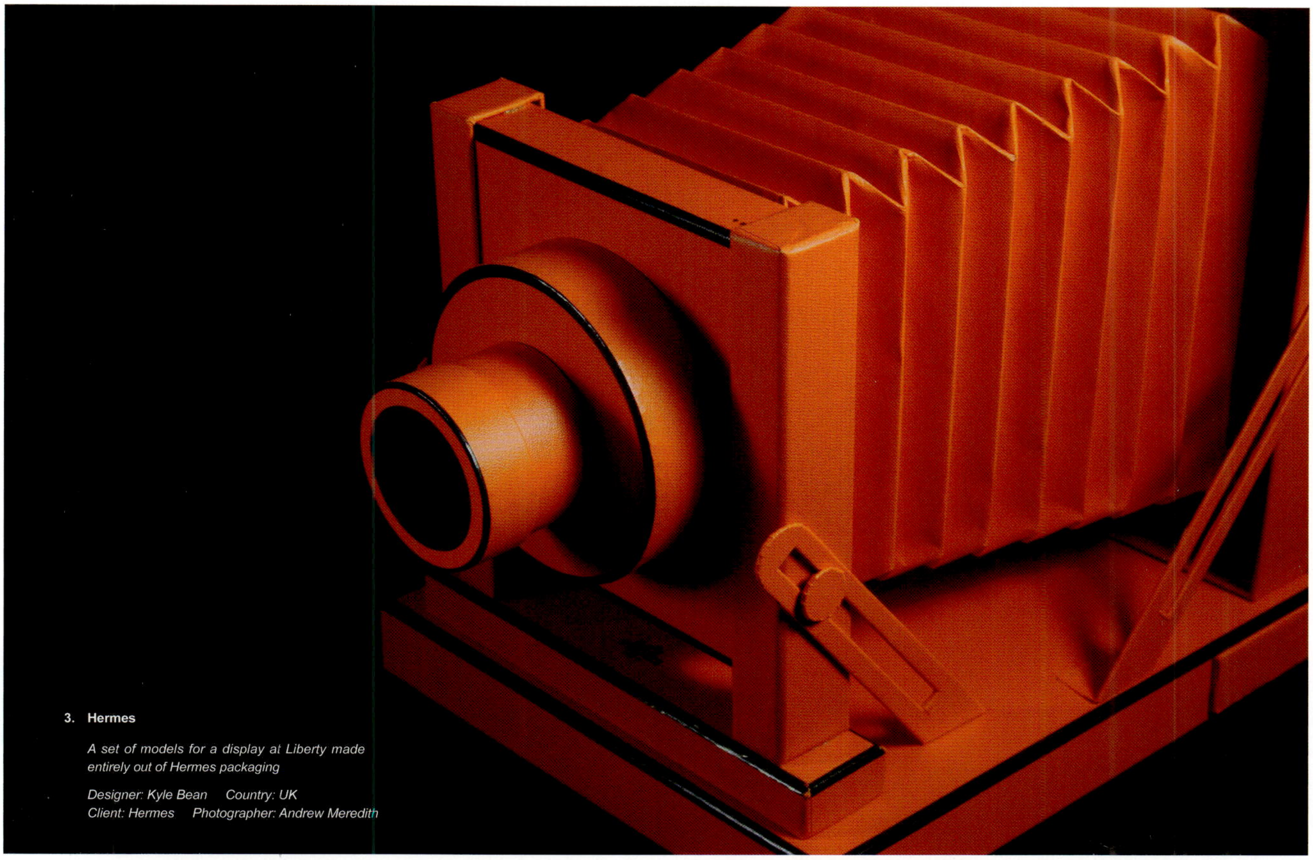

3. **Hermes**

A set of models for a display at Liberty made entirely out of Hermes packaging

Designer: Kyle Bean   Country: UK
Client: Hermes   Photographer: Andrew Meredith

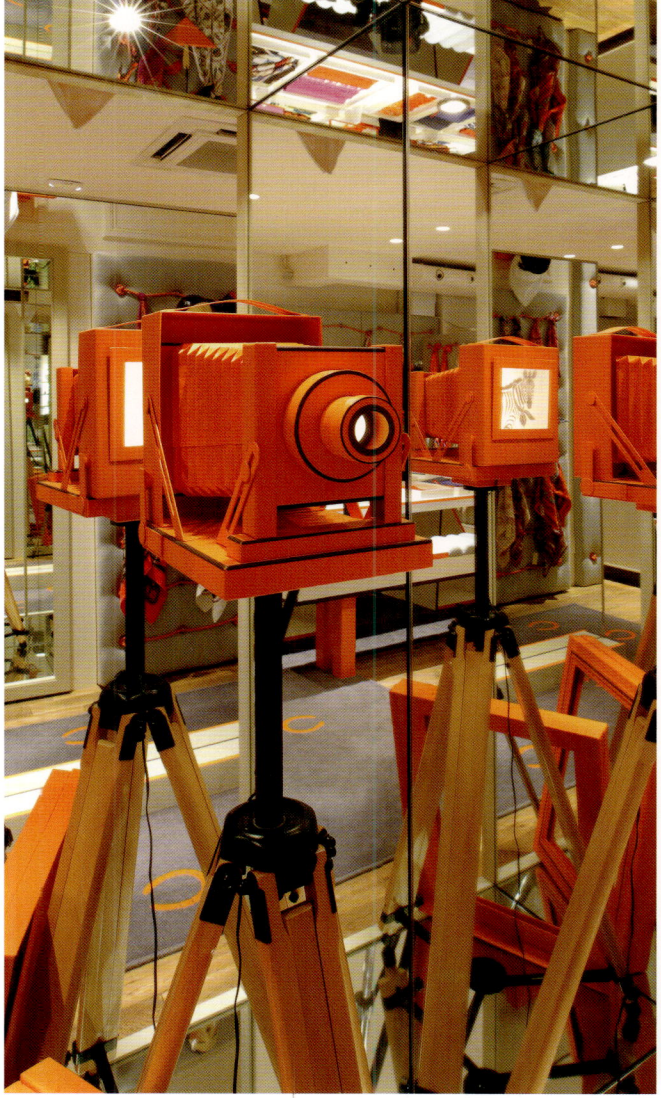
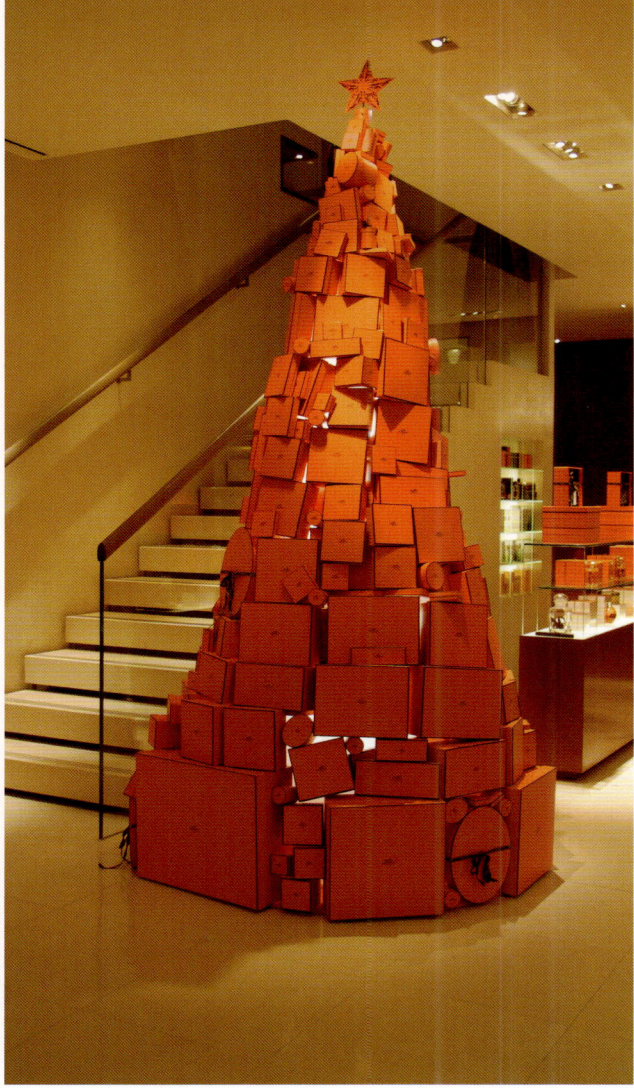

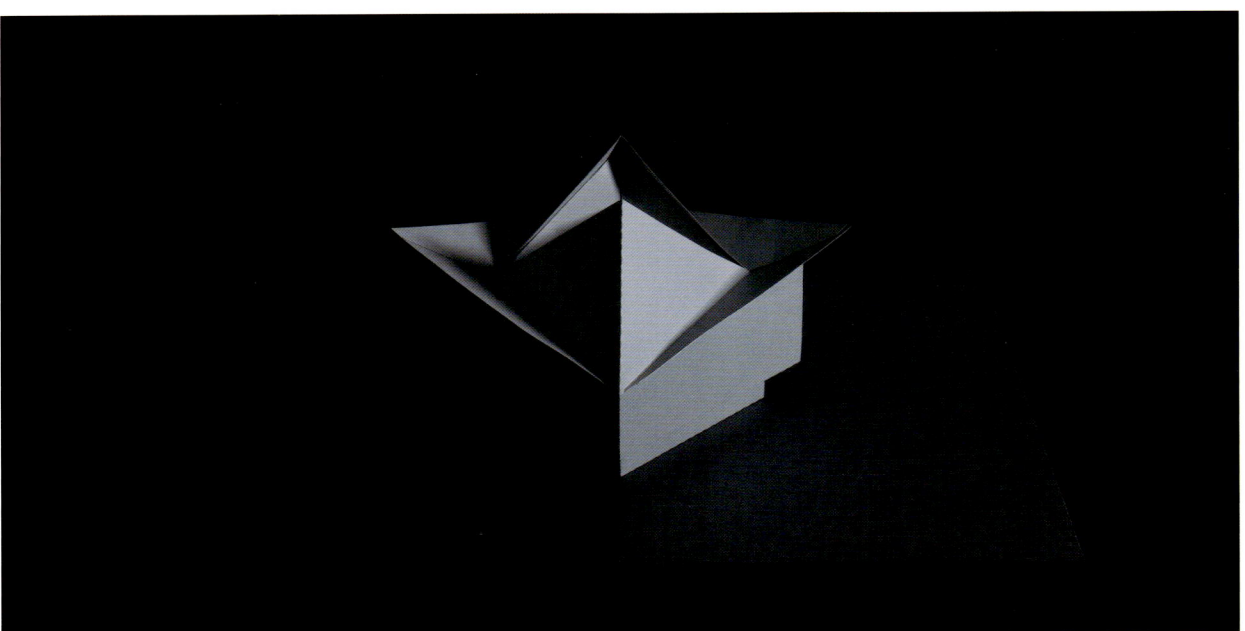
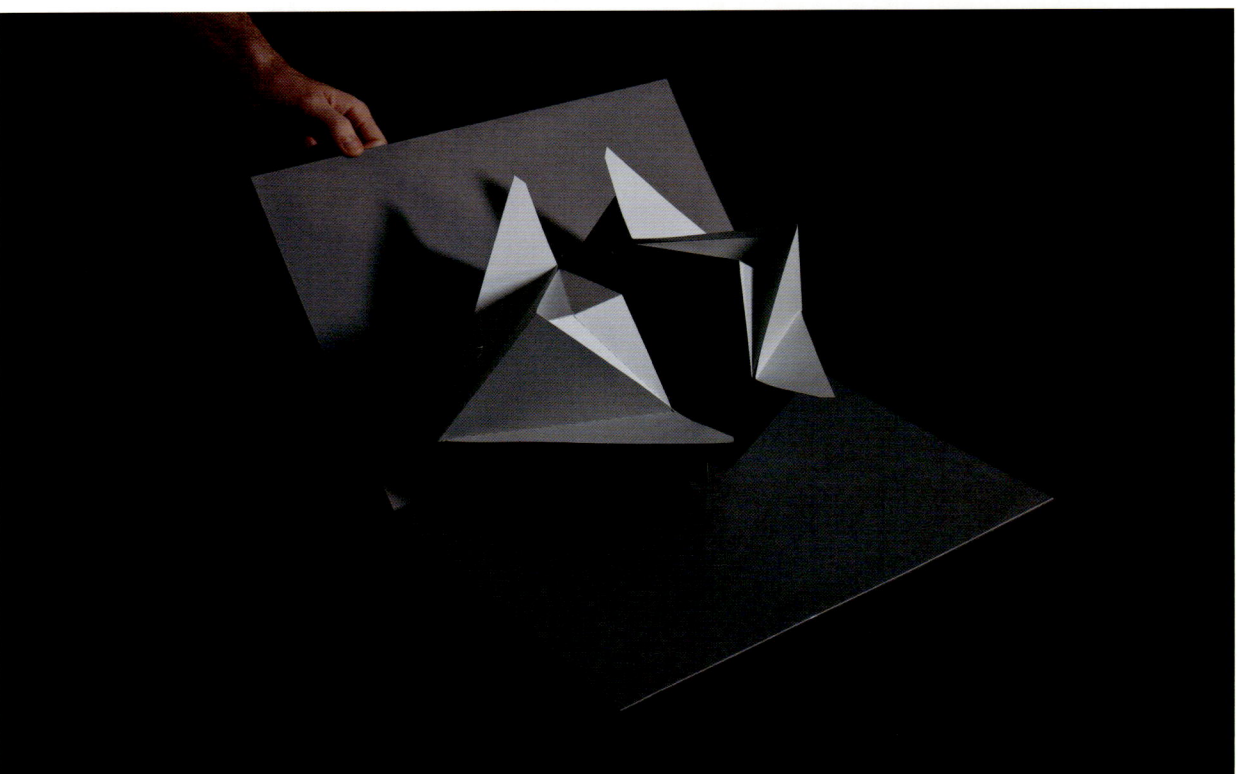

4. **Design Museum Pop-up**

   Card to celebrate the relocatio of the Design Museum to th former Commonwealth Institut in Kensington.

   Designer: Kyle Bean
   Country: UK
   Client: Design Museum

5. **Communities**

   Gatefold cover design for the "communities" issue of Viewpoint magazine.

   Designer: Kyle Bean
   Country: UK
   Client: Viewpoint
   Photographer: Victoria Ling

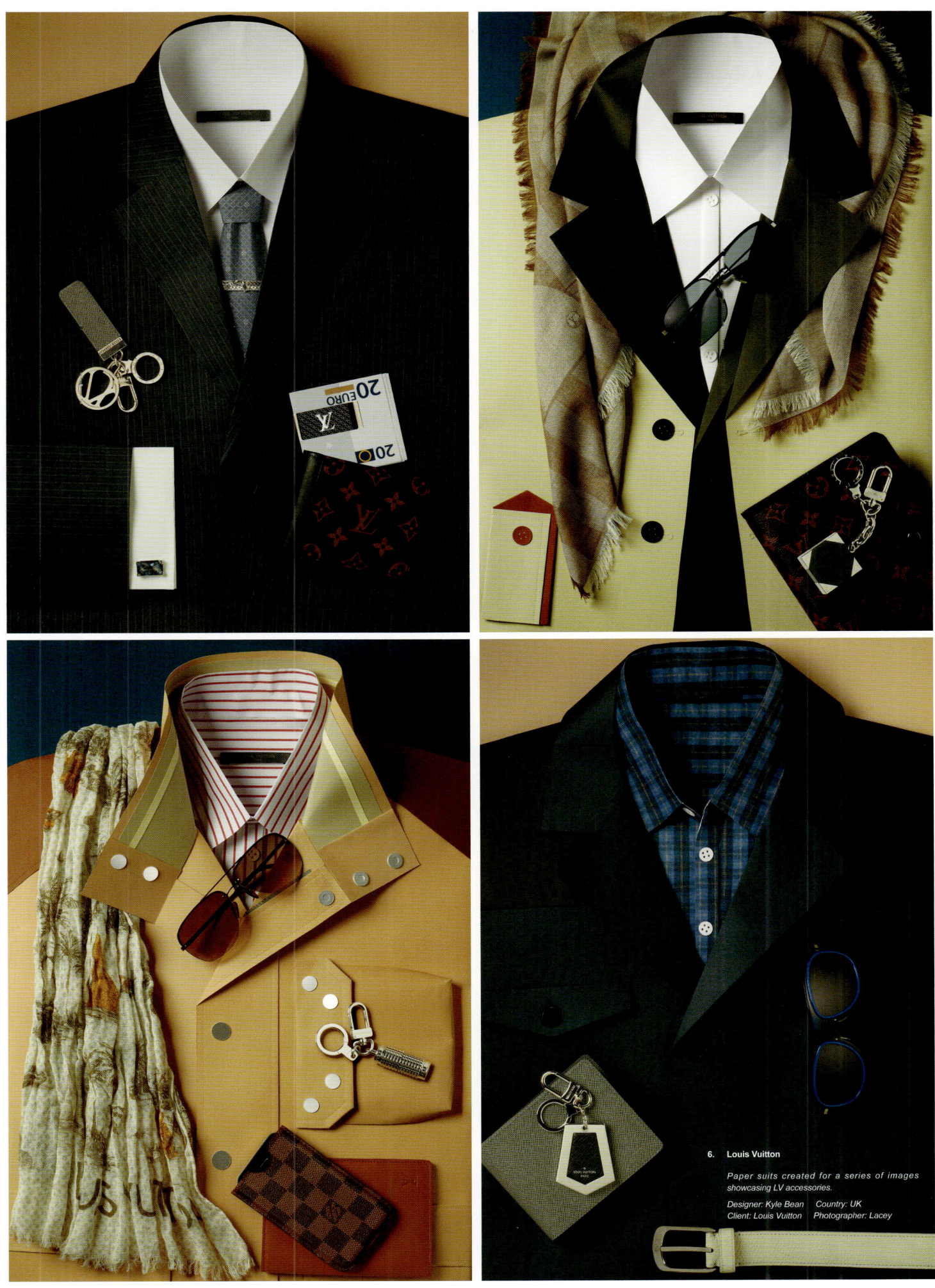

6. Louis Vuitton

Paper suits created for a series of images showcasing LV accessories.

Designer: Kyle Bean Country: UK
Client: Louis Vuitton Photographer: Lacey

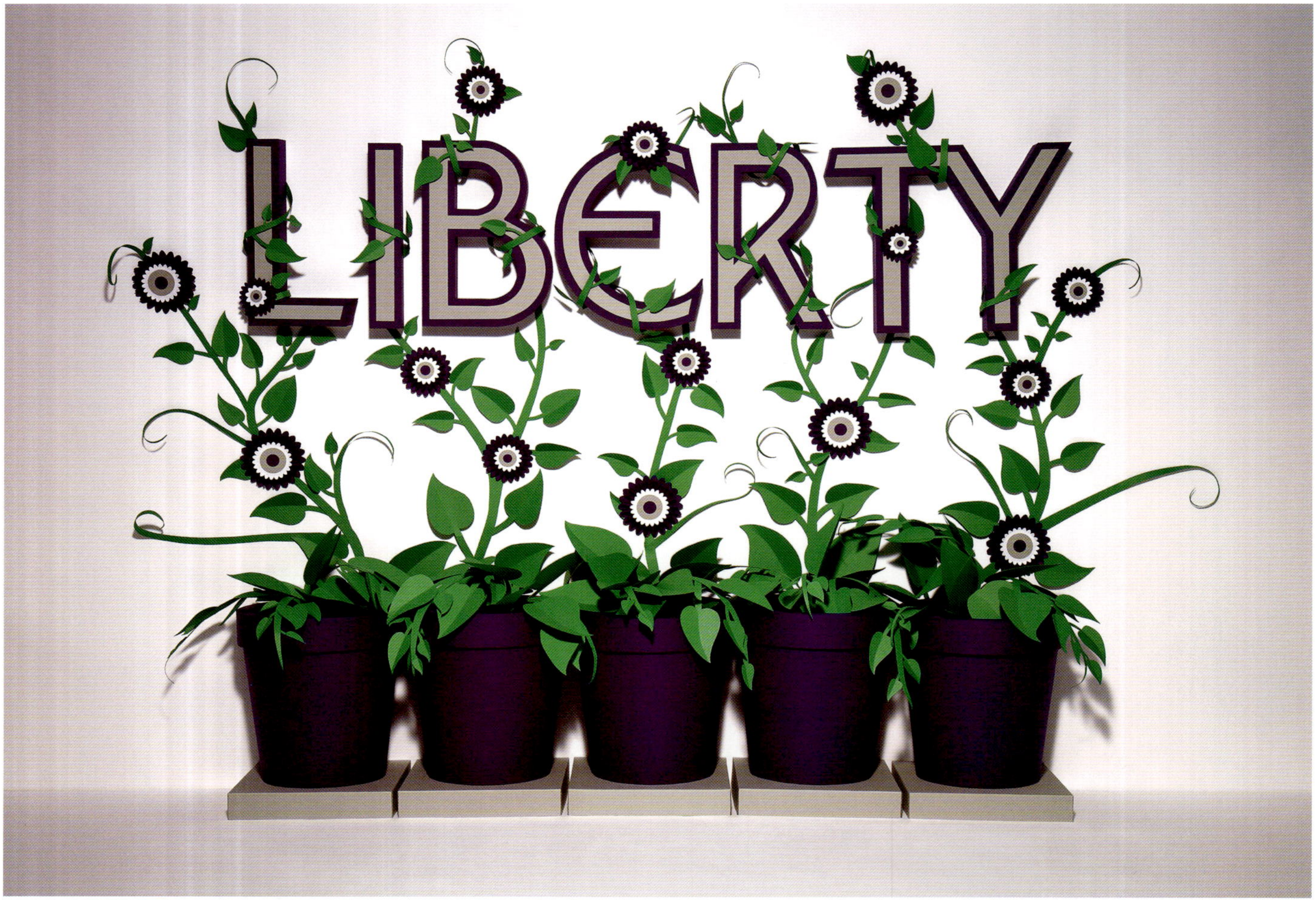

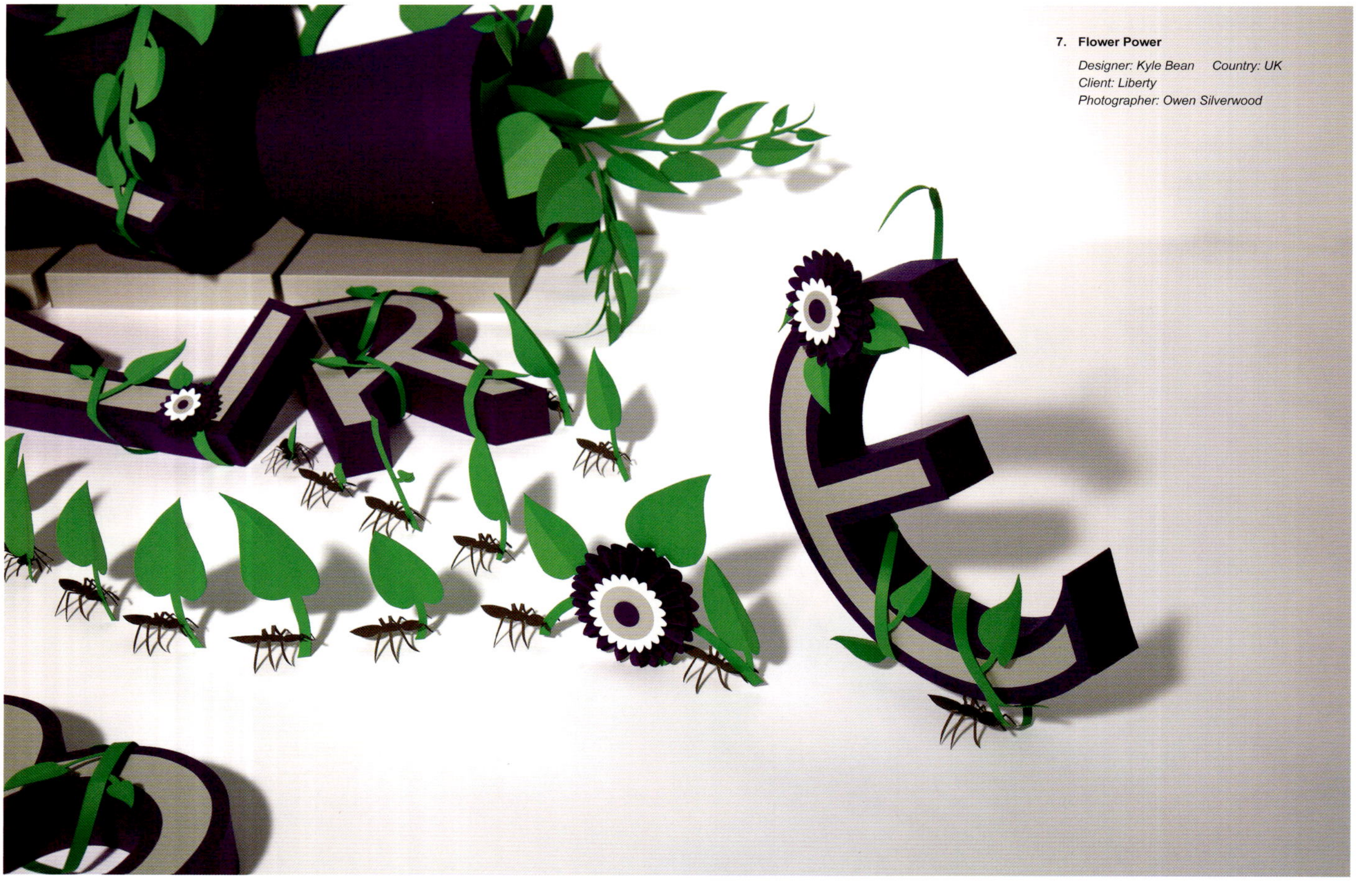

7. **Flower Power**
Designer: Kyle Bean   Country: UK
Client: Liberty
Photographer: Owen Silverwood

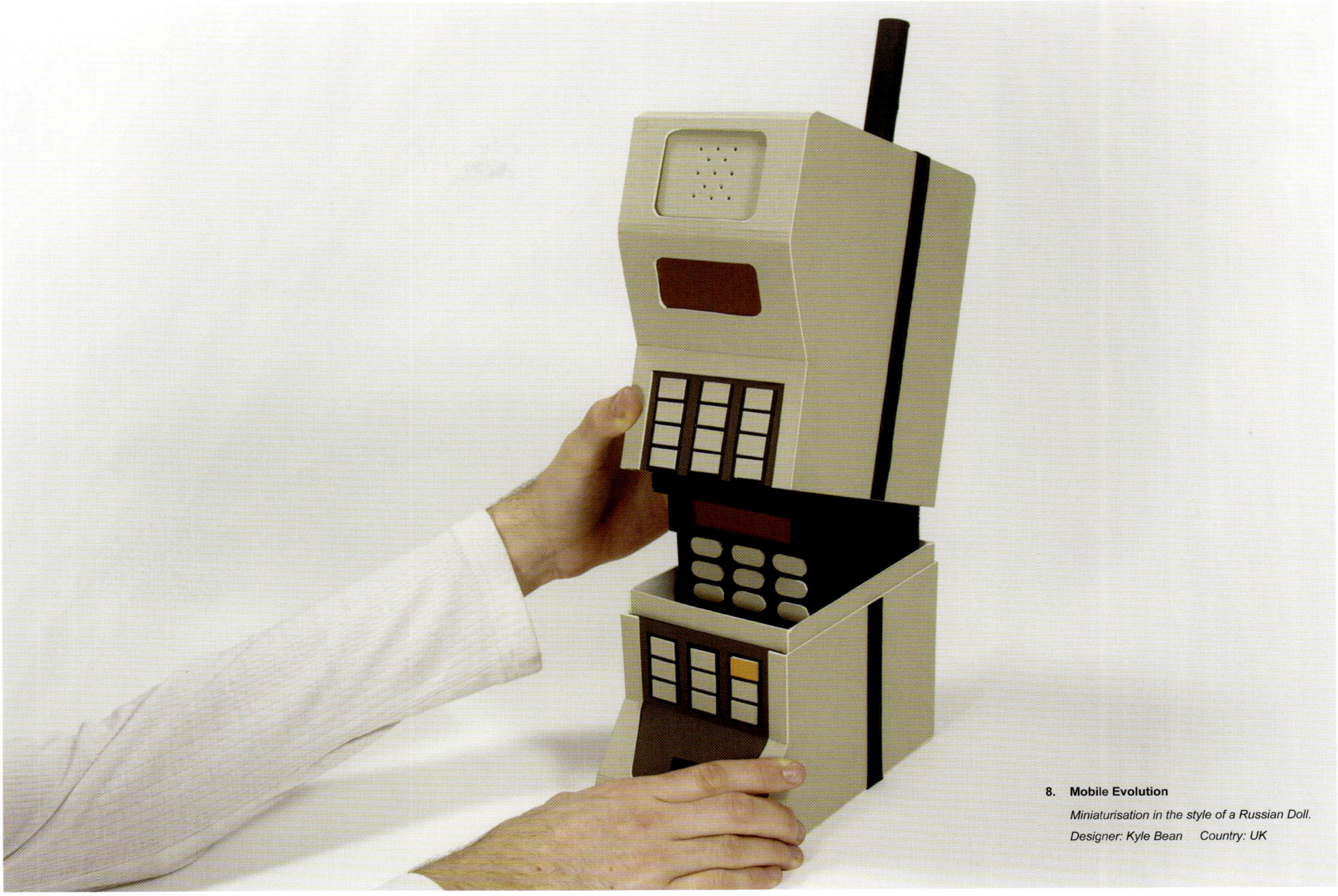

8. Mobile Evolution
Miniaturisation in the style of a Russian Doll.
Designer: Kyle Bean   Country: UK

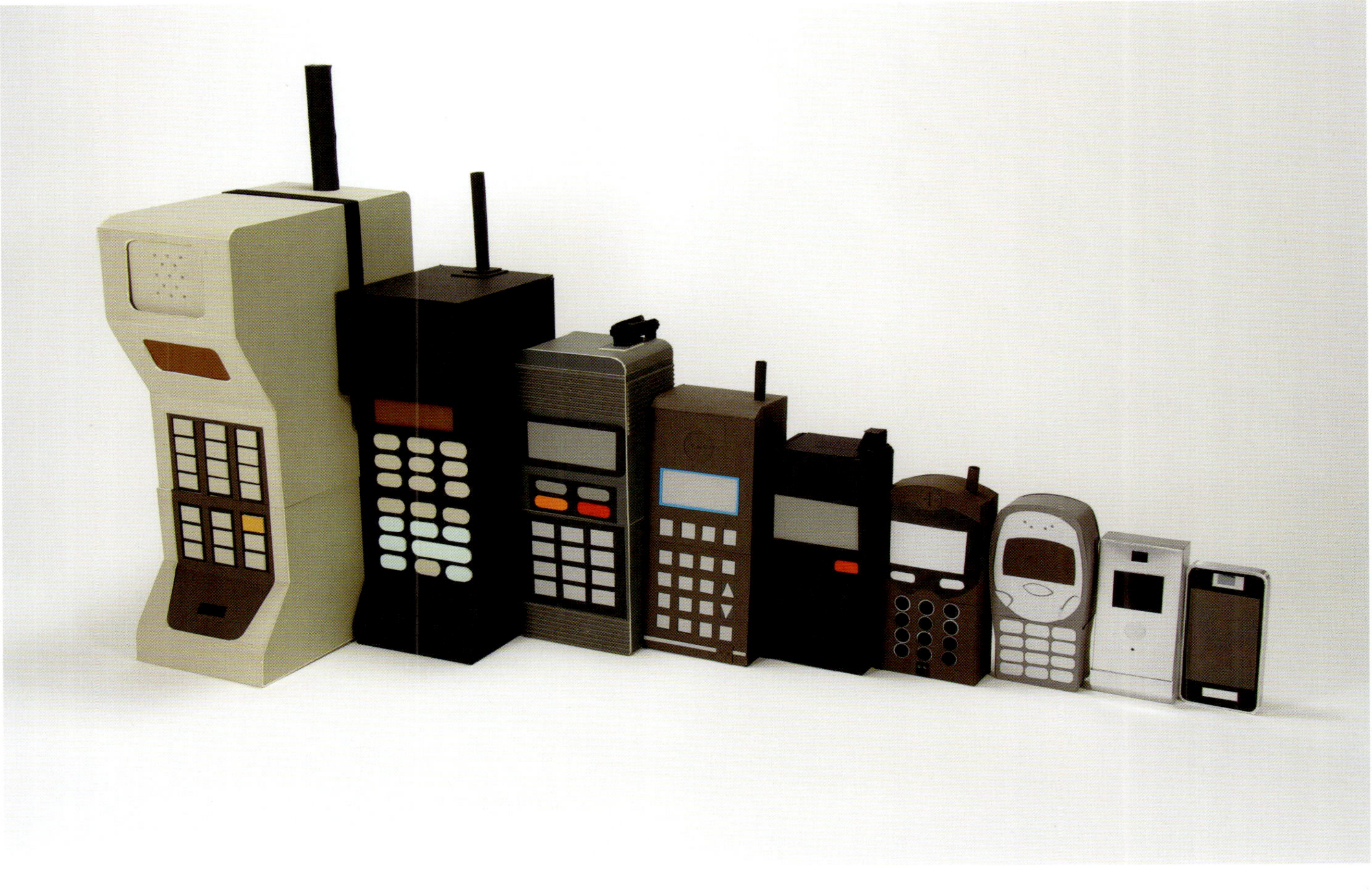

343

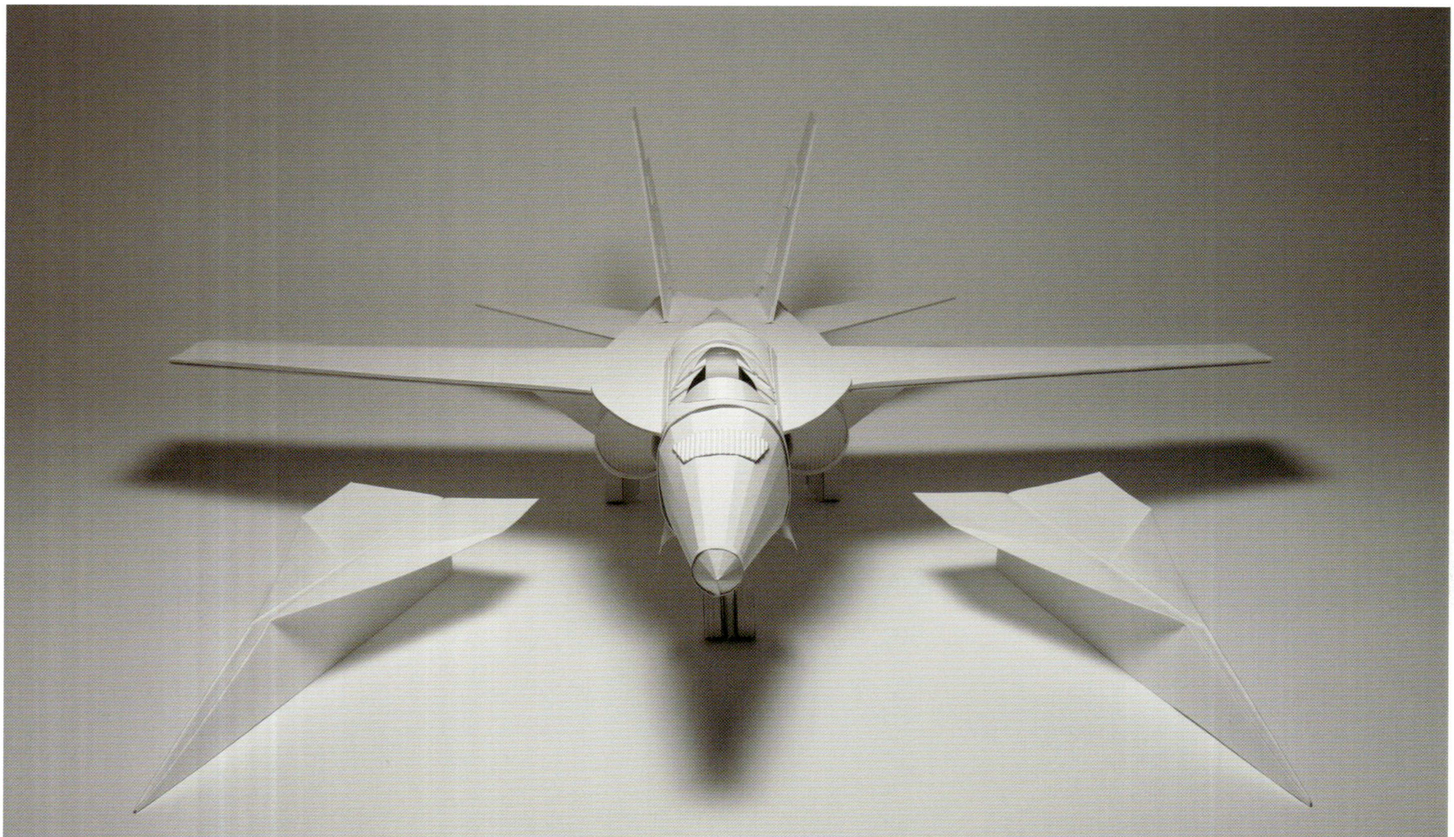

9. Paper Plane
White paper model of a fighter jet alongside traditional paper planes.
Designer: Kyle Bean   Country: UK

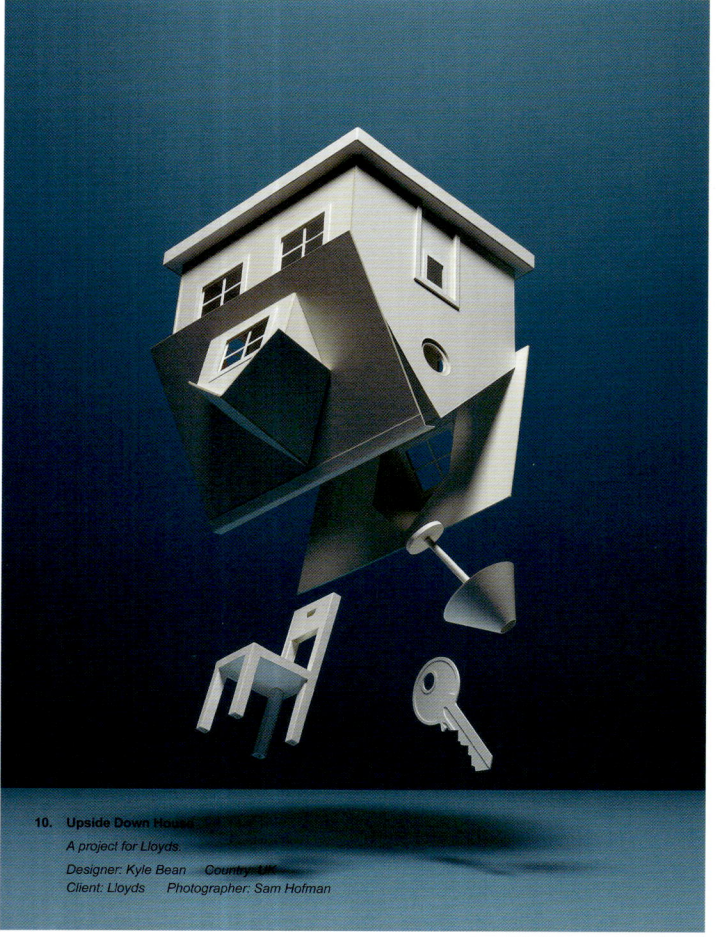

10. Upside Down House
A project for Lloyds.
Designer: Kyle Bean   Country: UK
Client: Lloyds   Photographer: Sam Hofman

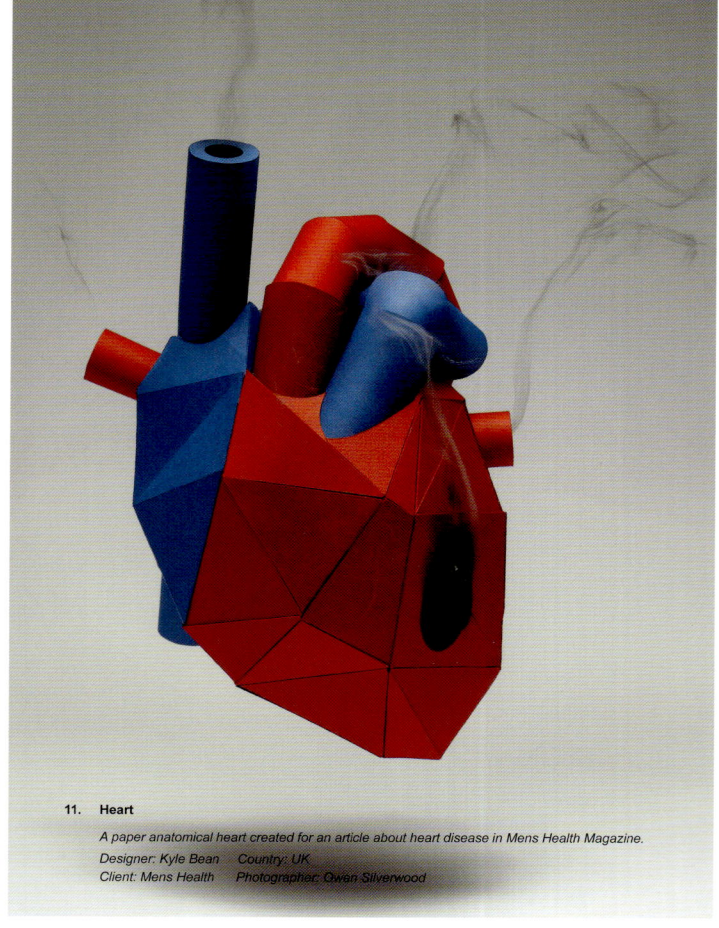

11. Heart
A paper anatomical heart created for an article about heart disease in Mens Health Magazine.
Designer: Kyle Bean   Country: UK
Client: Mens Health   Photographer: Owen Silverwood

11. Transformation Windows

A series of 5 window displays inspired by the law of conservation of mass: "Matter cannot be created or destroyed, only transformed".

Designer: Kyle Bean   Country: UK
Client: Selfridges   Photographer: Mike Dodd / Andrew Meredith

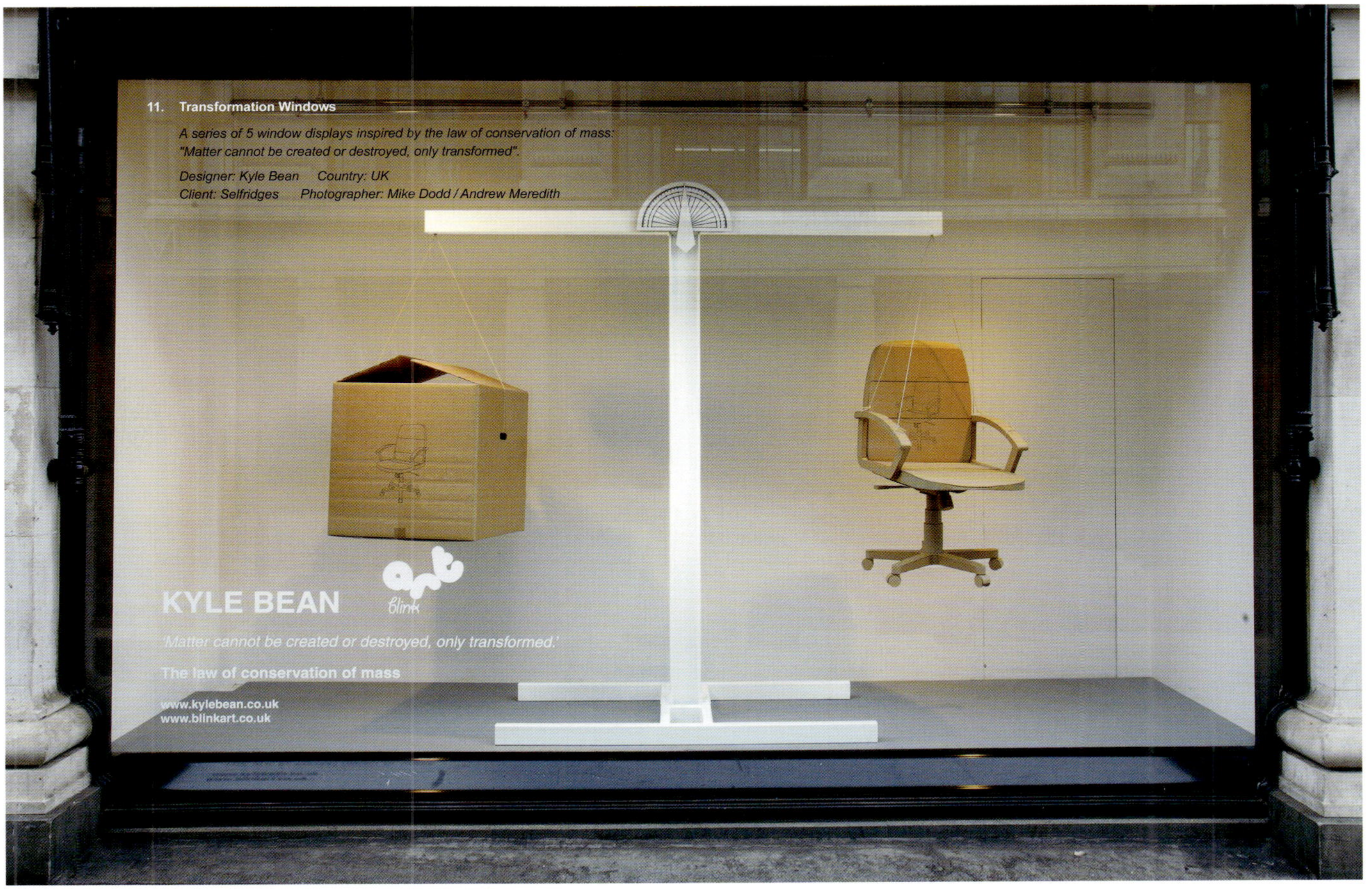

KYLE BEAN

'Matter cannot be created or destroyed, only transformed.'

The law of conservation of mass

www.kylebean.co.uk
www.blinkart.co.uk

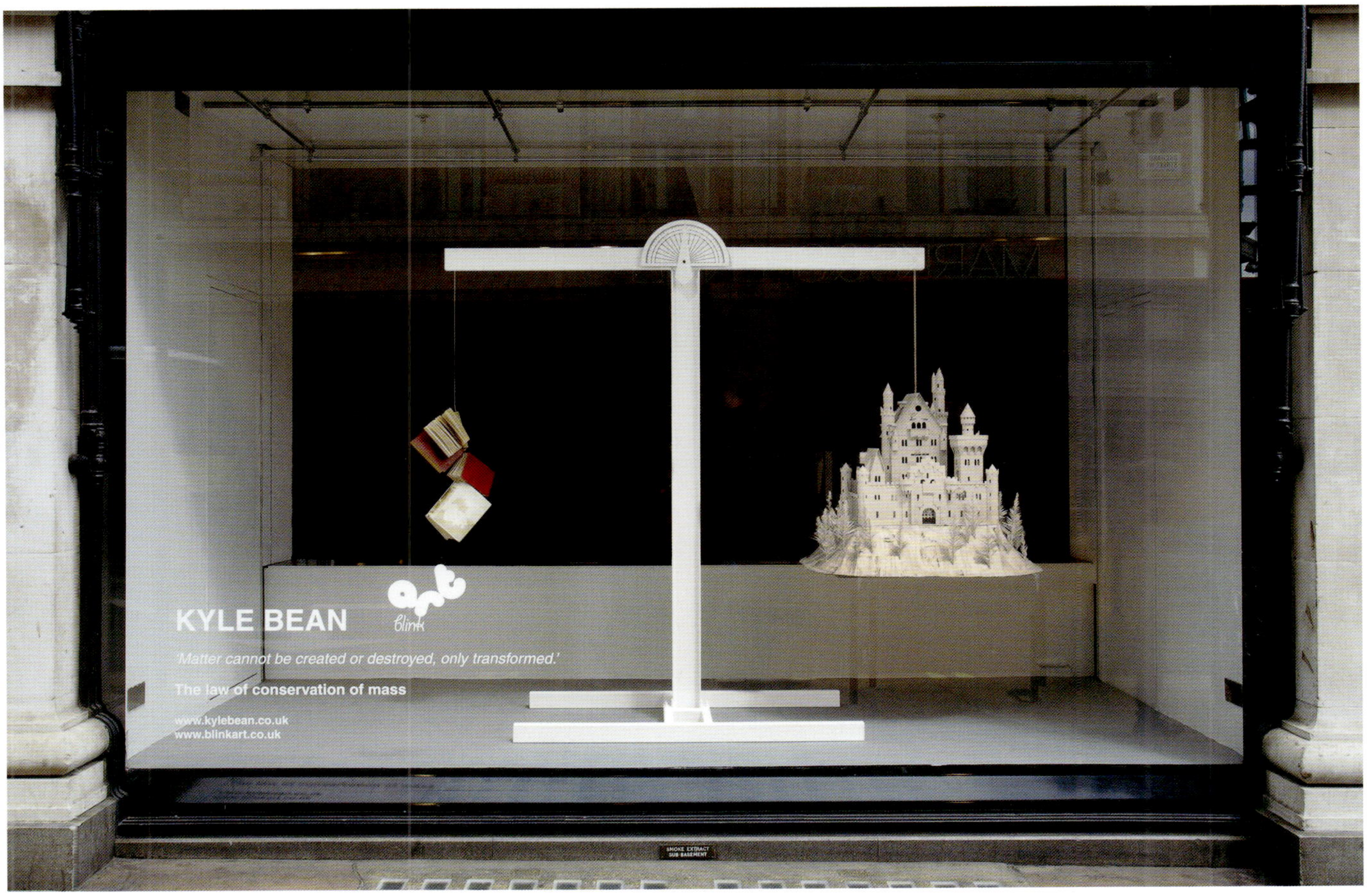

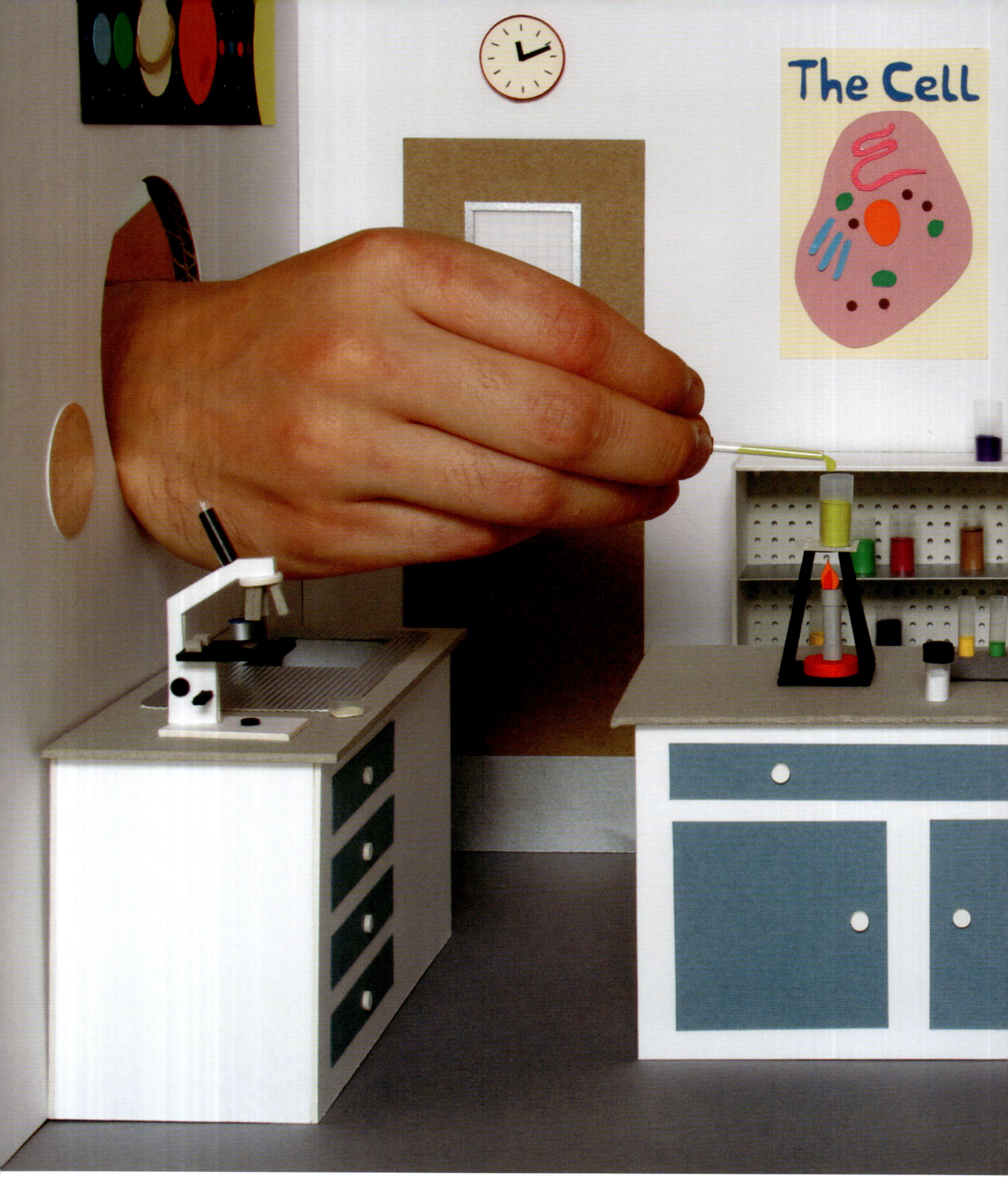

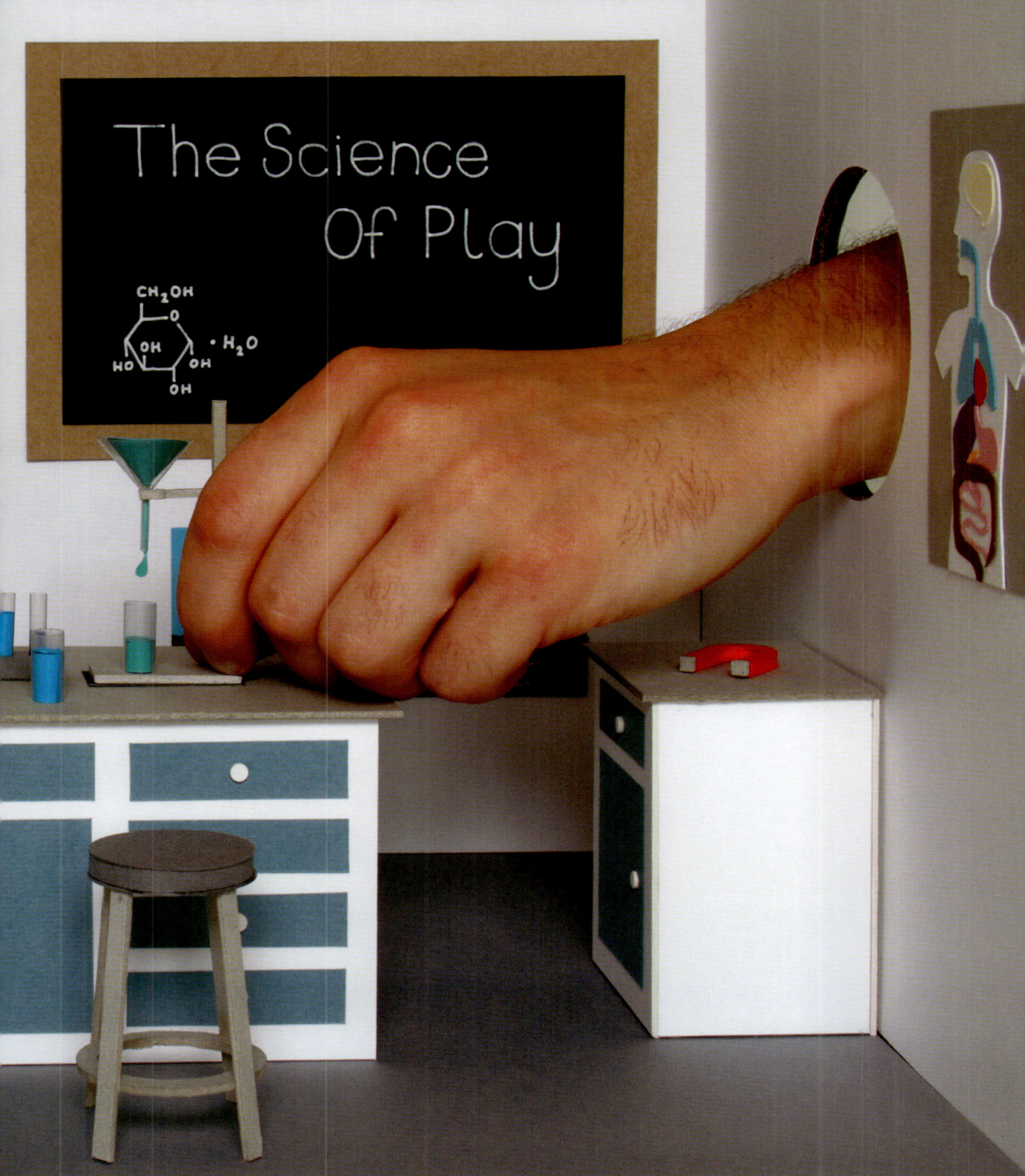

13. The Science of Play
A miniature science laboratory created for Rubbish Magazine.

Designer: Kyle Bean   Country: UK
Client: Rubbish Magazine

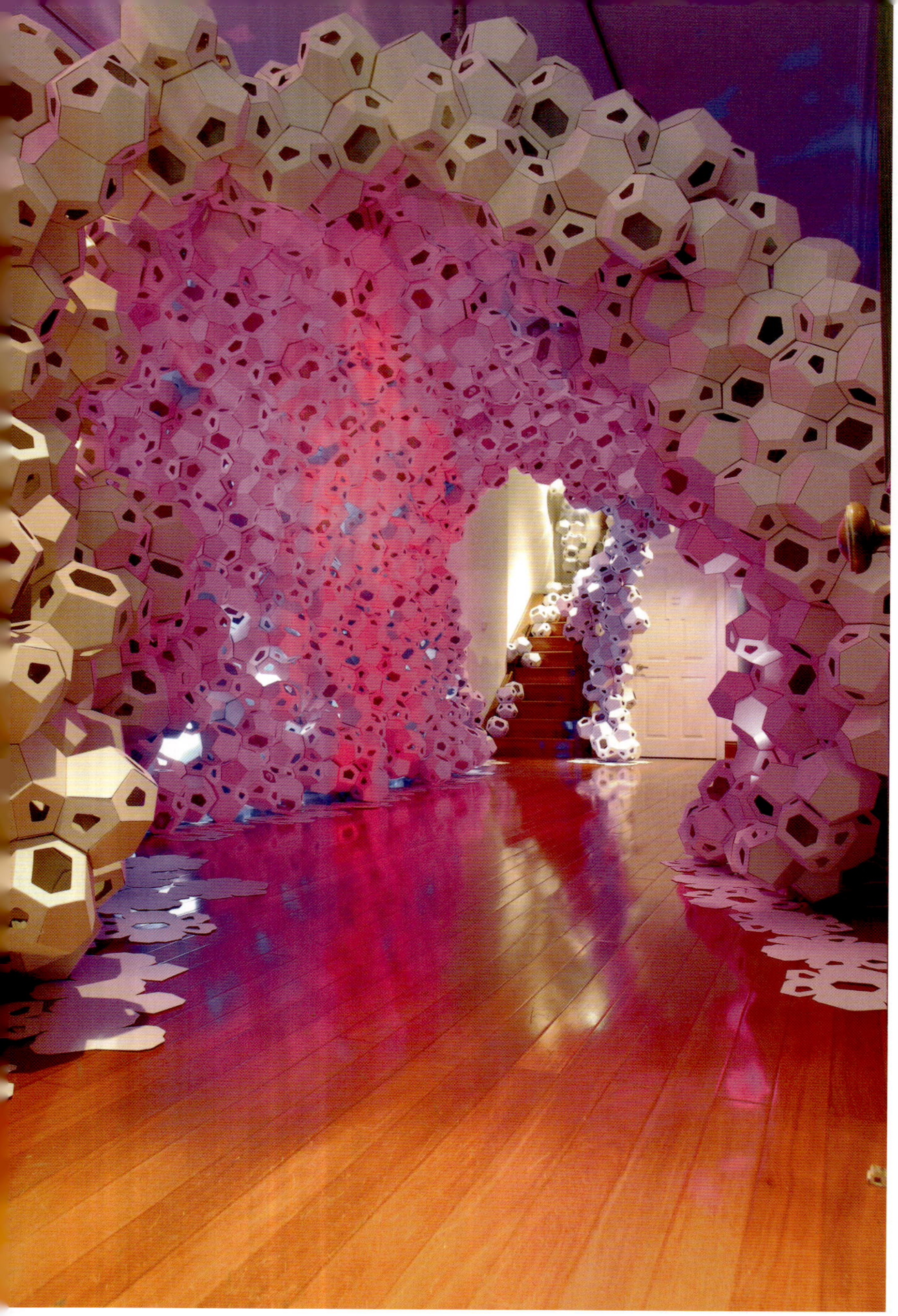

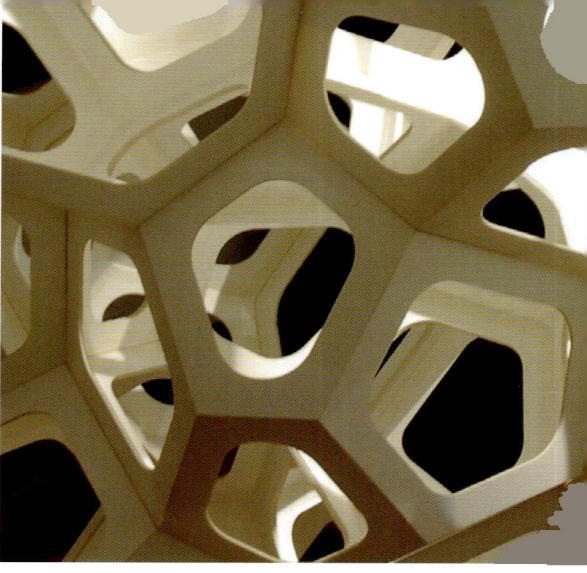

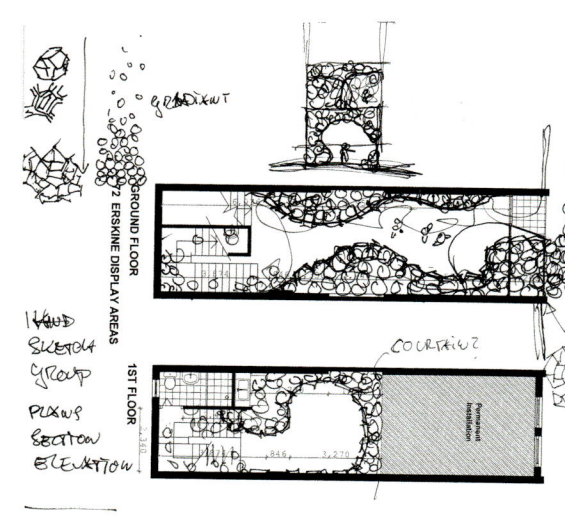

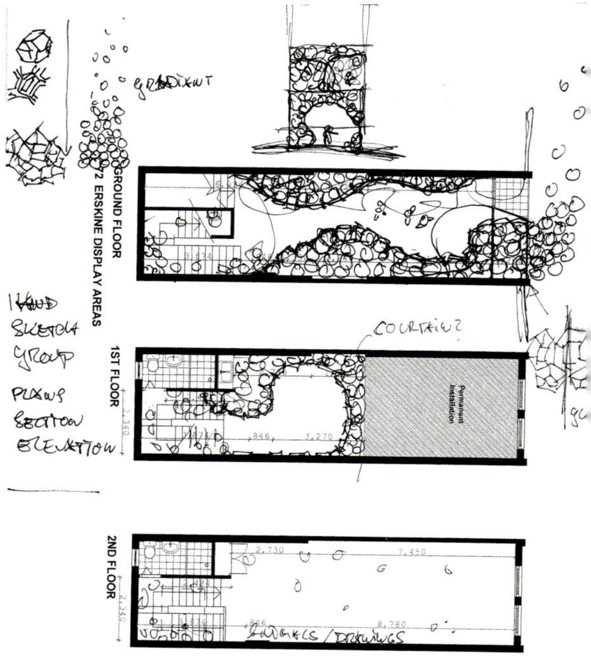

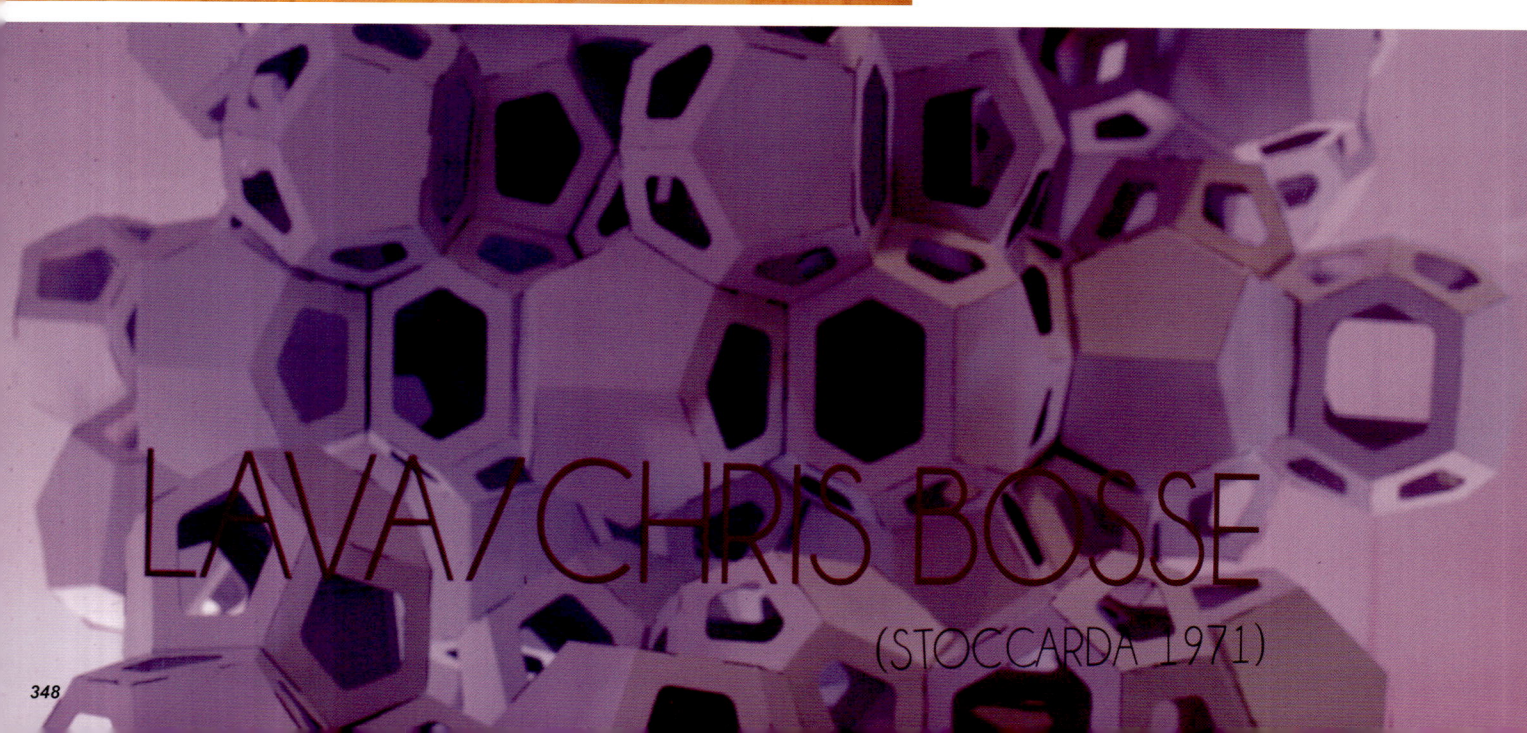

LAVA / CHRIS BOSSE
(STOCCARDA 1971)

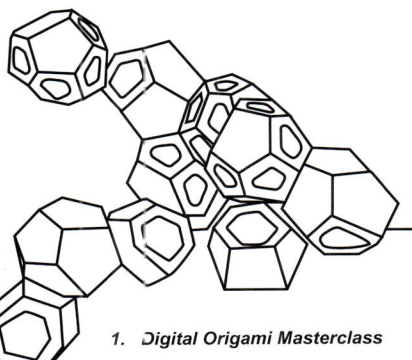

1. **Digital Origami Masterclass**

   Design Agency: LAVA (Laboratory for Visionary Architecture)
   Country: Australia
   Lighting: ERCO (Sydney / Milan)
   Acoustic Installation: Joanne Jakovich
   Client: University of Technology Sydney
   Photographer: LAVA

1. **Digital Origami Masterclass**

   The digital masterclass program at UTS under Anthony Burke invited Chris Bosse to run a highly intensive masterclass.

2. **Vetrine di Natale [Christmas Windows]**

   Laboratory for Visionary Architecture [LAVA] created a window installation for the Famous Italian department store la Rinascente for its Vetrine di Natale [Christmas Windows].

   ---LAVA

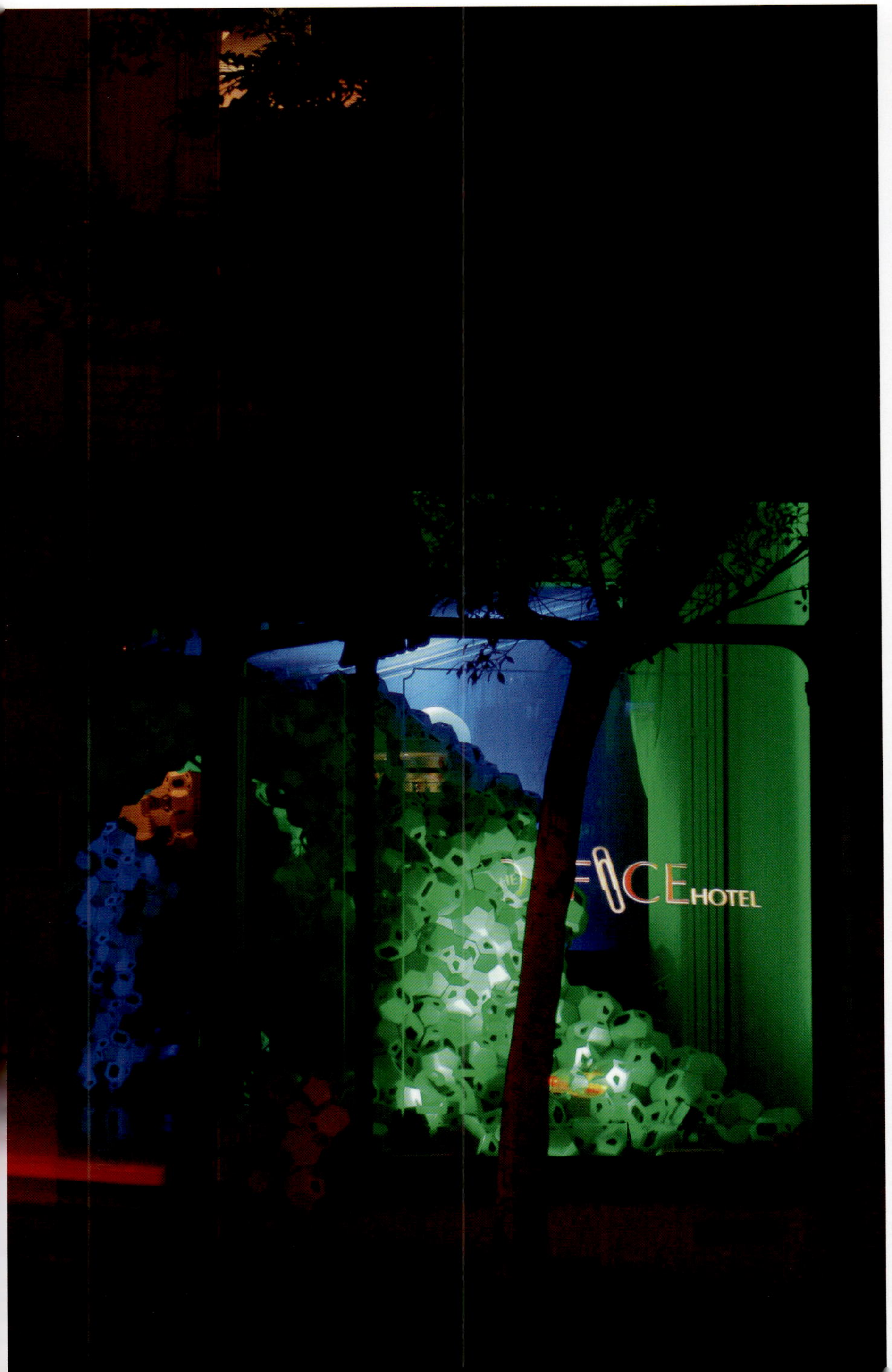

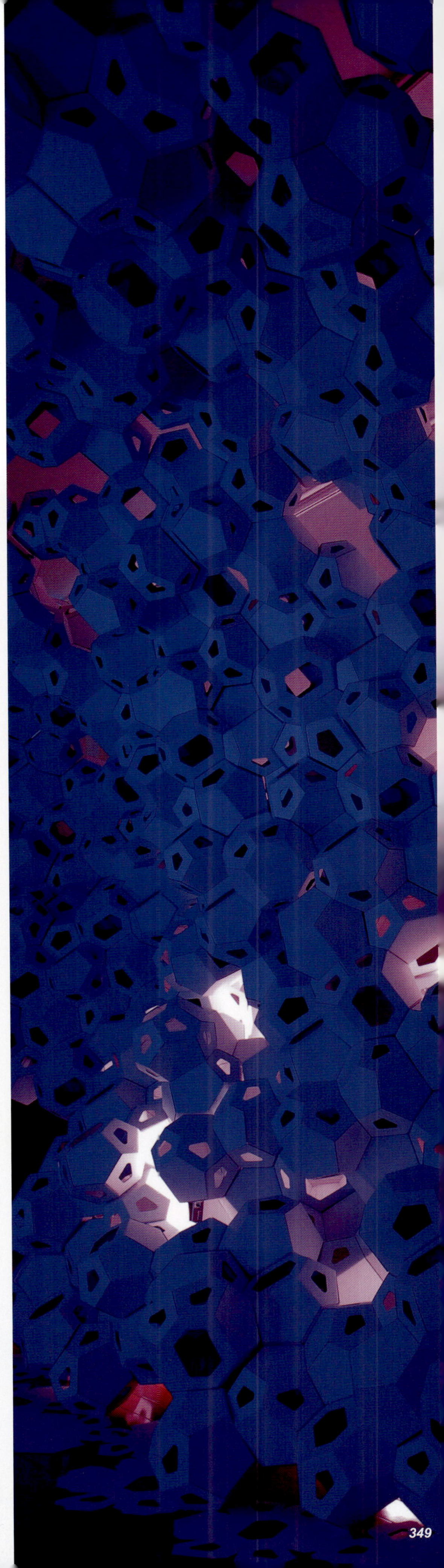

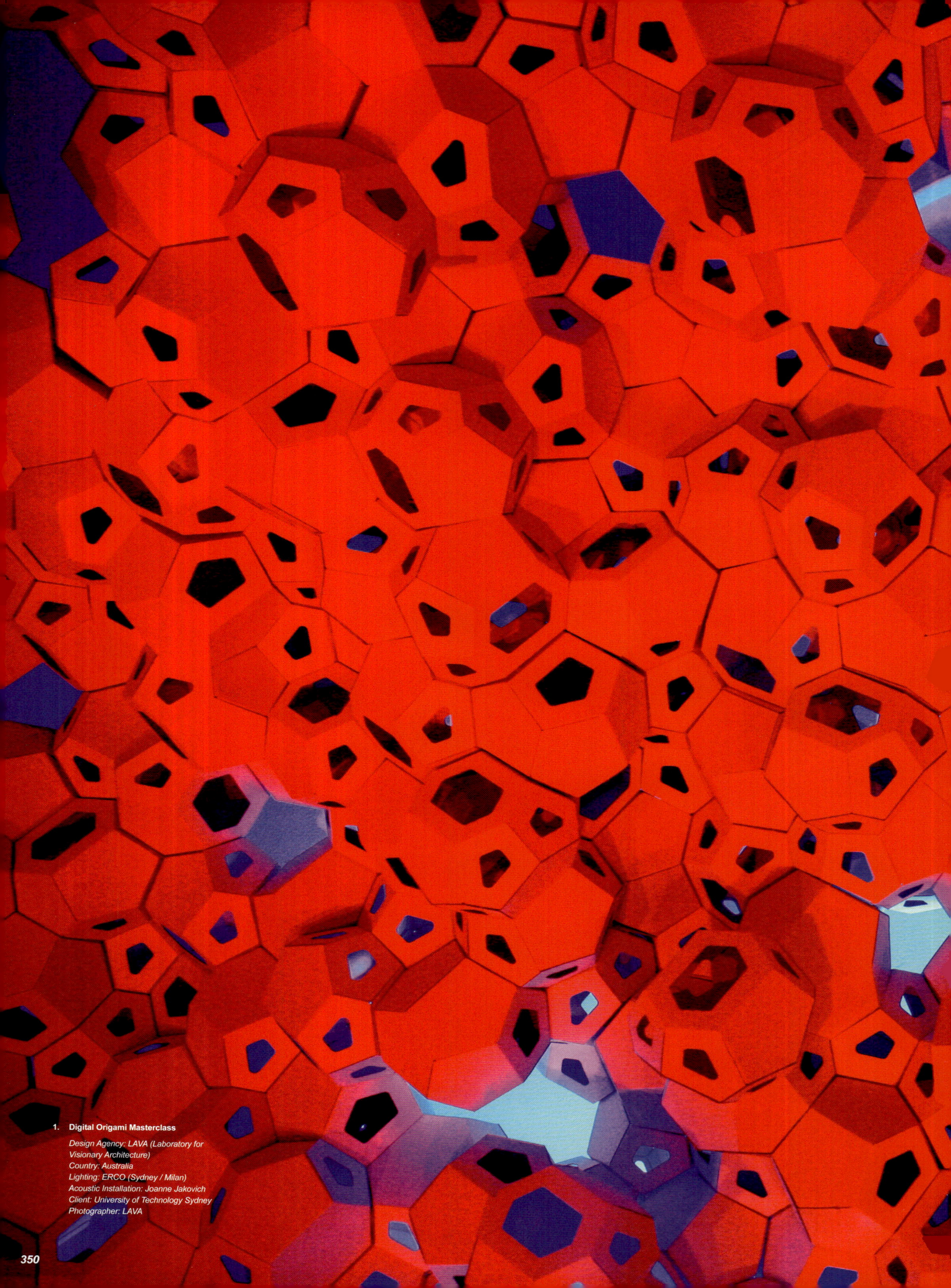

1. **Digital Origami Masterclass**

Design Agency: LAVA (Laboratory for Visionary Architecture)
Country: Australia
Lighting: ERCO (Sydney / Milan)
Acoustic Installation: Joanne Jakovich
Client: University of Technology Sydney
Photographer: LAVA

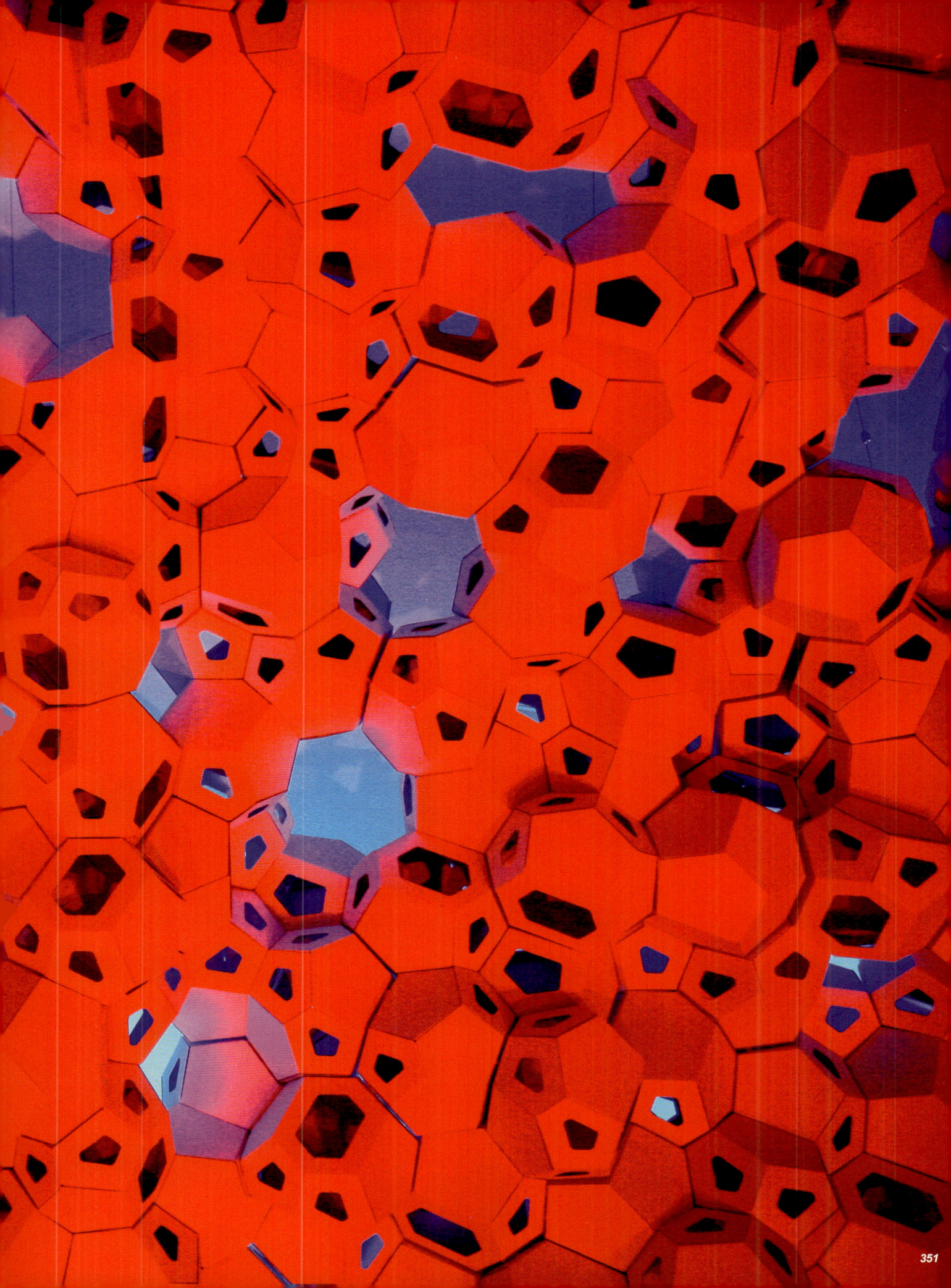

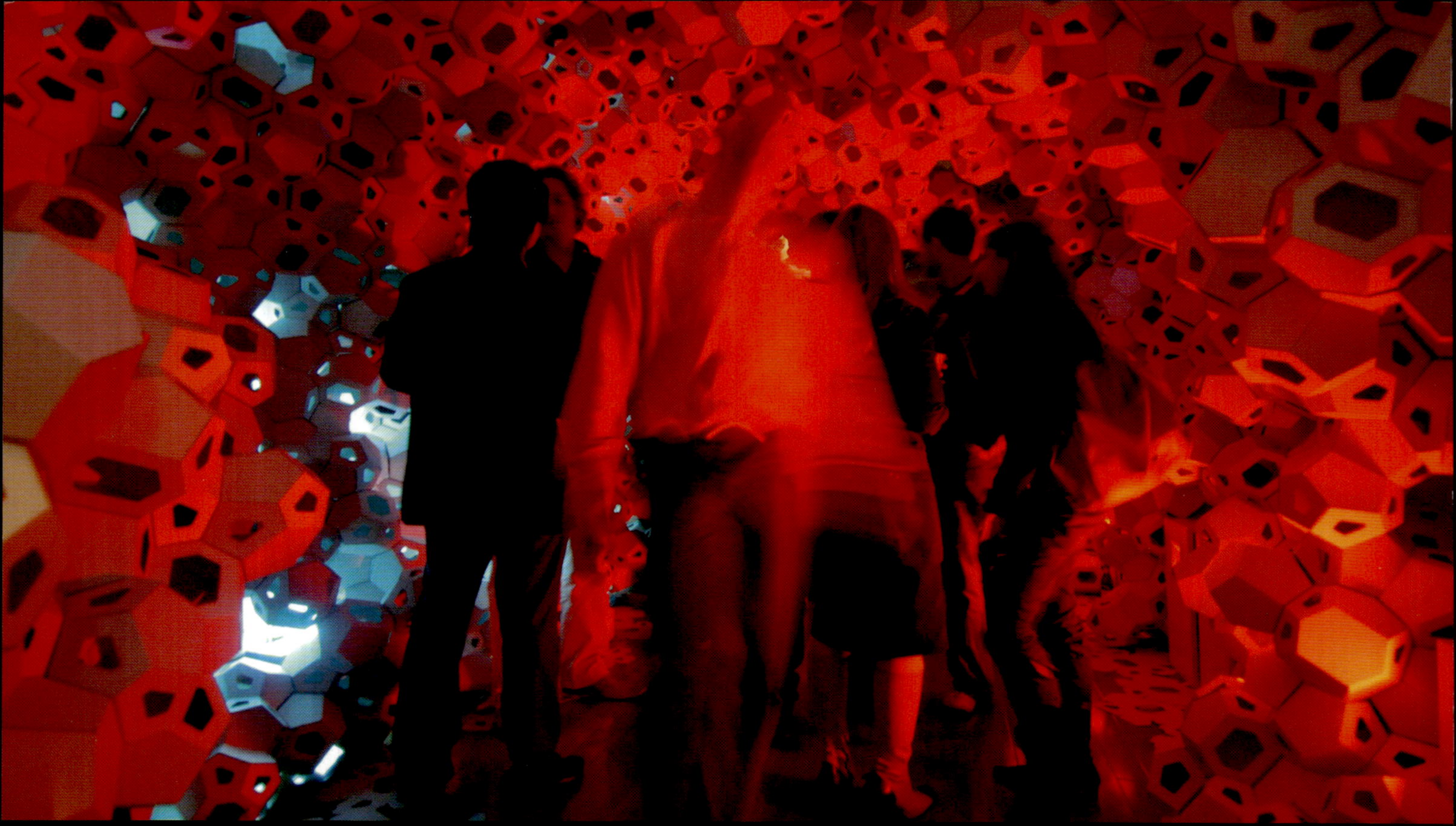

1. **Digital Origami Masterclass**

An ancient Japanese proverb says: "If you meet a person that is able to make many items of different shape by folding up simple sheets of paper, don't think it is trivial, but try to learn."

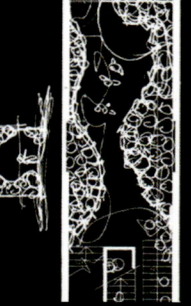 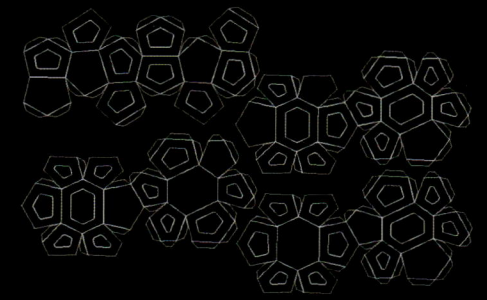 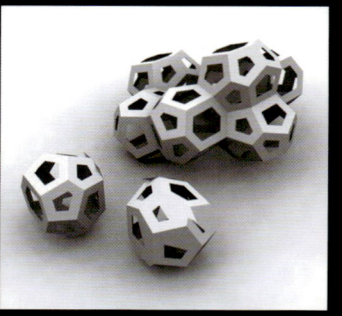 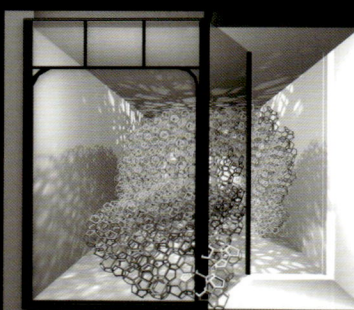

Bosse says: 'The danger of digital creations is the virtual worlds they depend on, or rather the lack of constraints in the virtual if compared to the physical world. Most of the time digital creations end in crazy flythrough computer renderings'. Bosse therefore asked the students to study and research current trends in parametric modeling, digital fabrication and material science and apply this knowledge to a space - filling installation.

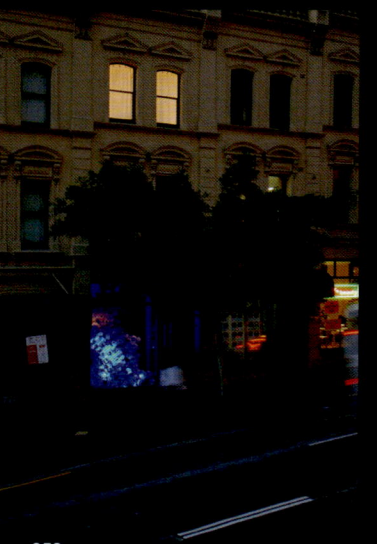 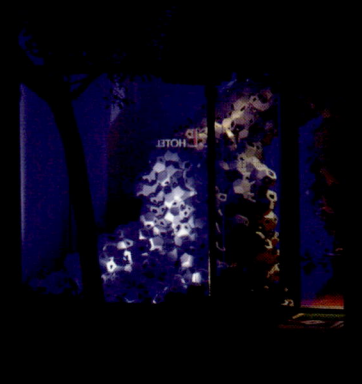 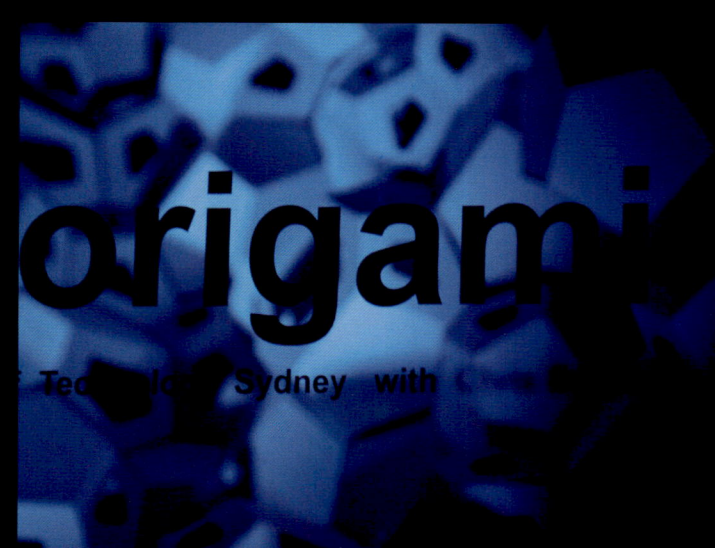

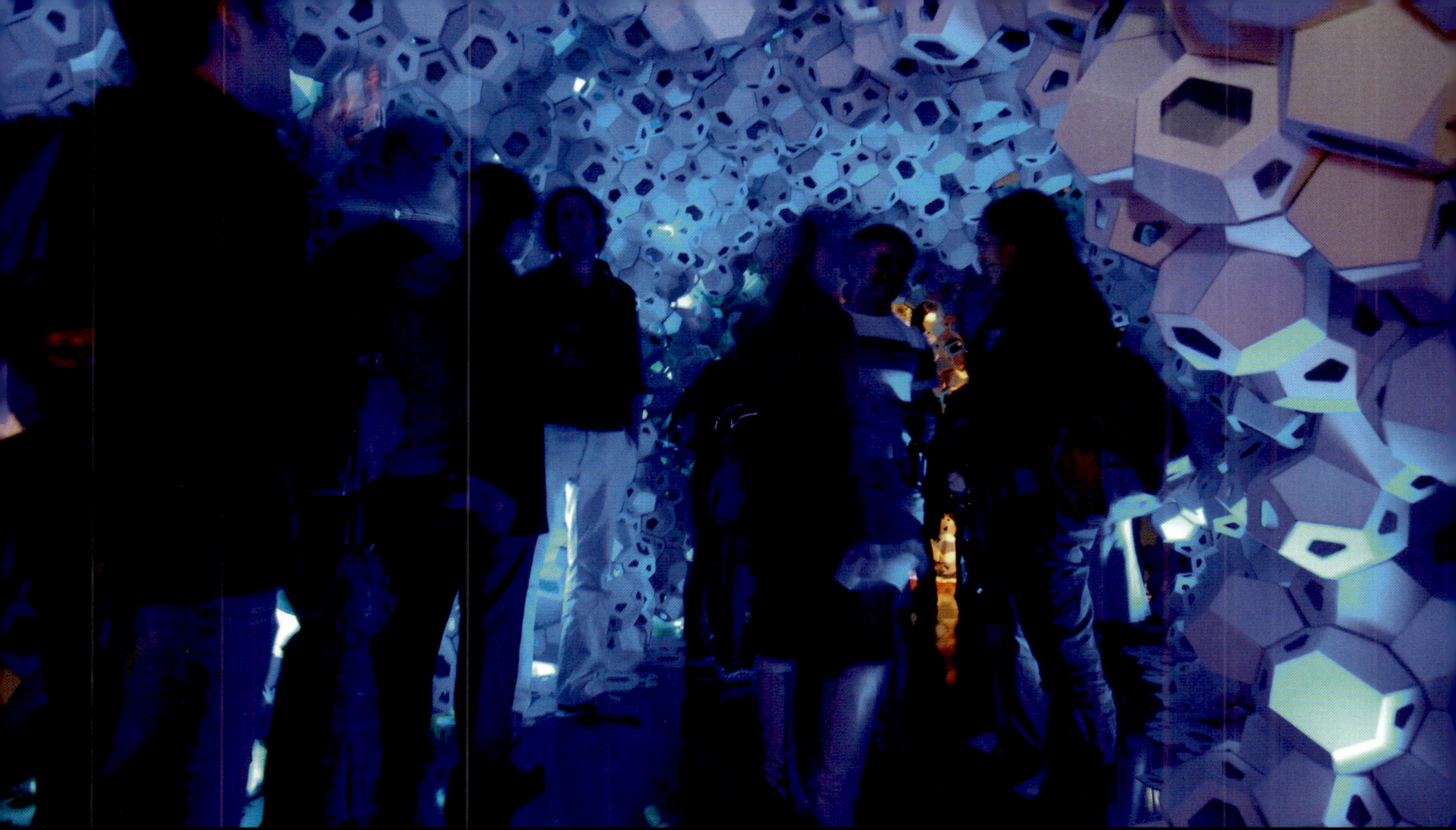

'The aim was to test the fitness of a particular module, copied from nature, to generate architectural space, with the assumption that the intelligence of the smallest unit dictates the intelligence of the overall system. Ecosystems such as reefs act as a metaphor for an architecture where the individual components interact in symbiosis to create an environment.'

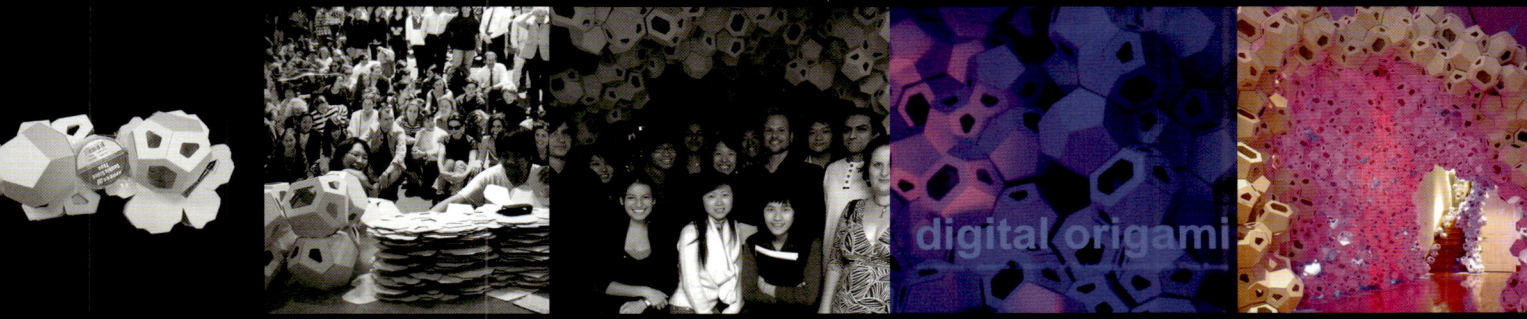

By itself this recognition is an ESD principle that in this instance simplifies the message and visualizes it by creating highly dimensional and sculptural appearance, that plays with space by climbing up walls and arching over to create low, cave - like tunnels. Using 3500 recycled and recyclable cardboard molecules in two different shapes, students explored the intelligence of natural and architectural systems through the smallest elements of design. The students created a mind - blowing reinterpretation of the traditional concept of space. The exhibition incorporated computer controlled luminaries with sophisticated light systems and acoustic Installations by local designer that brought the whole installation to life.

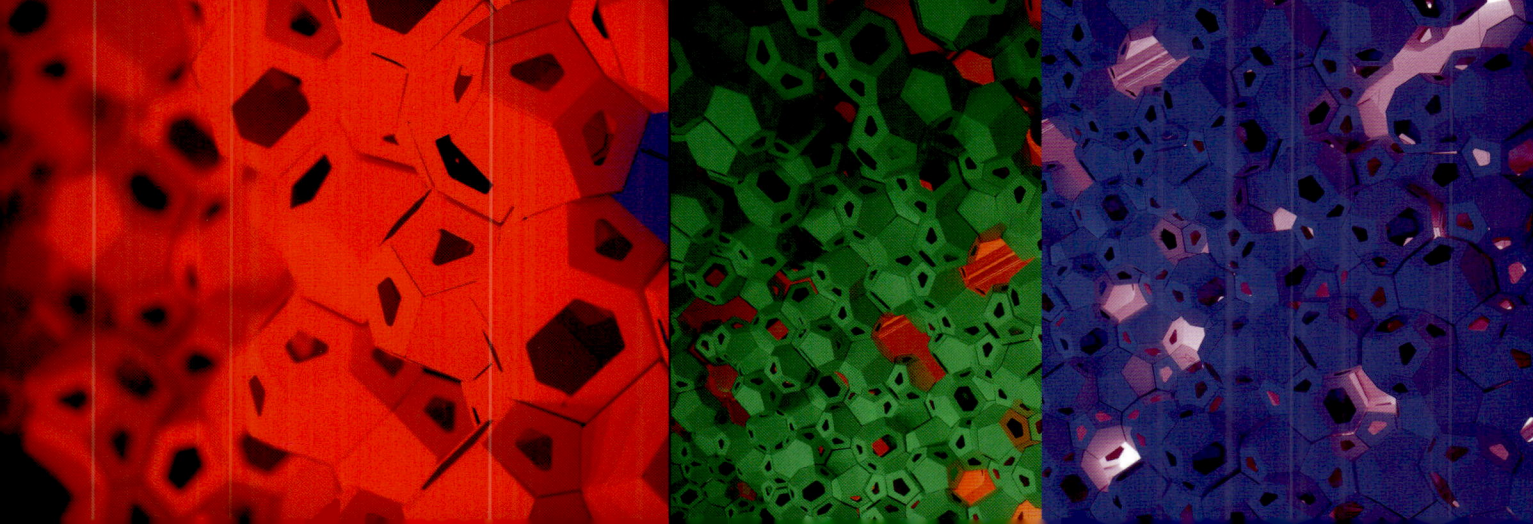

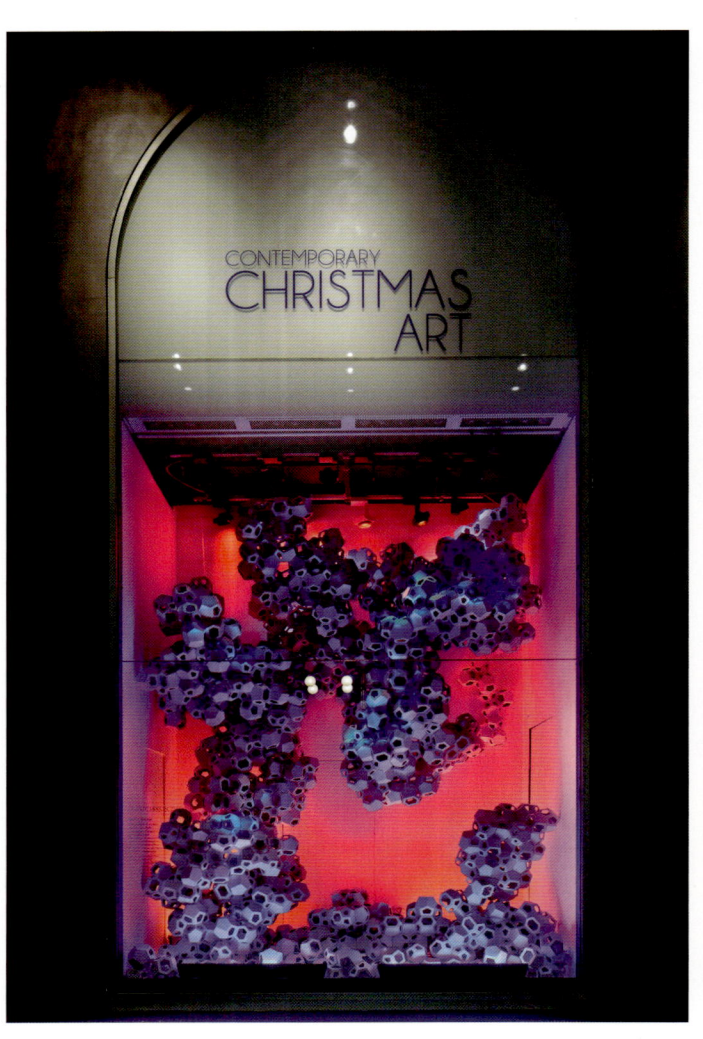
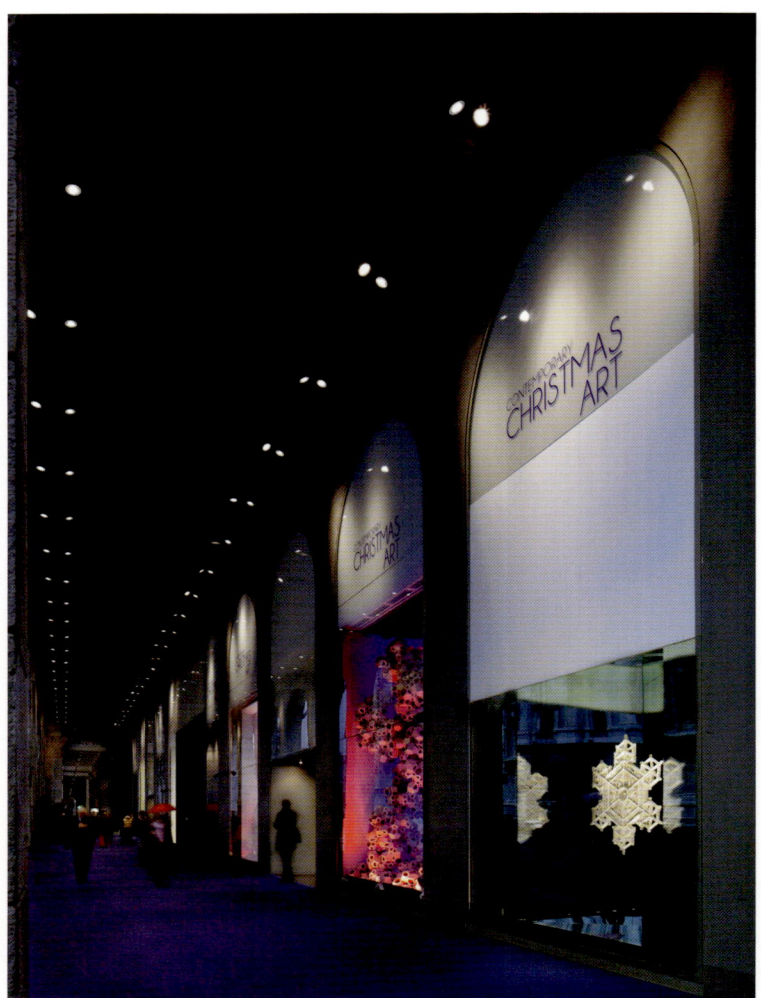

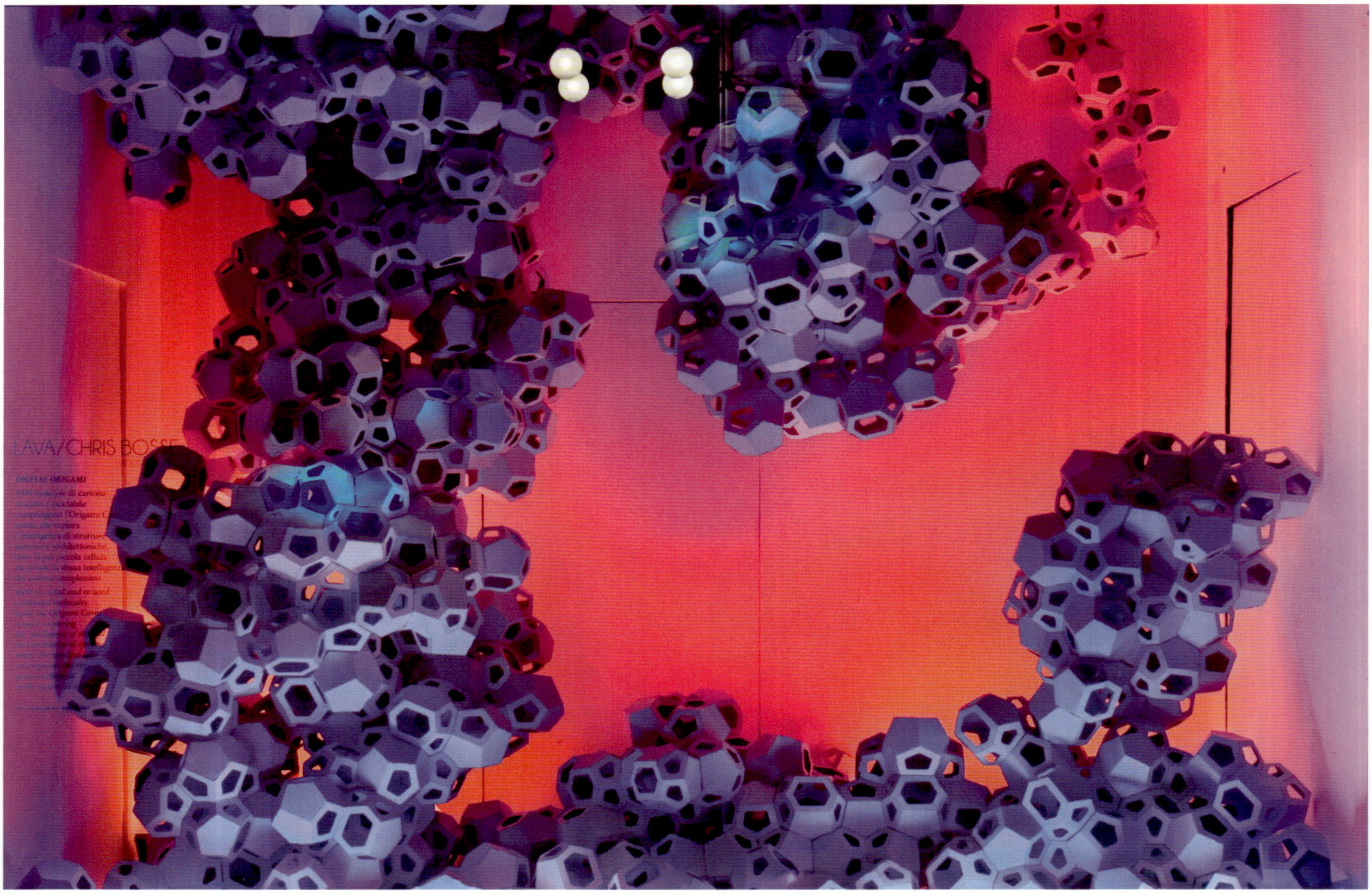

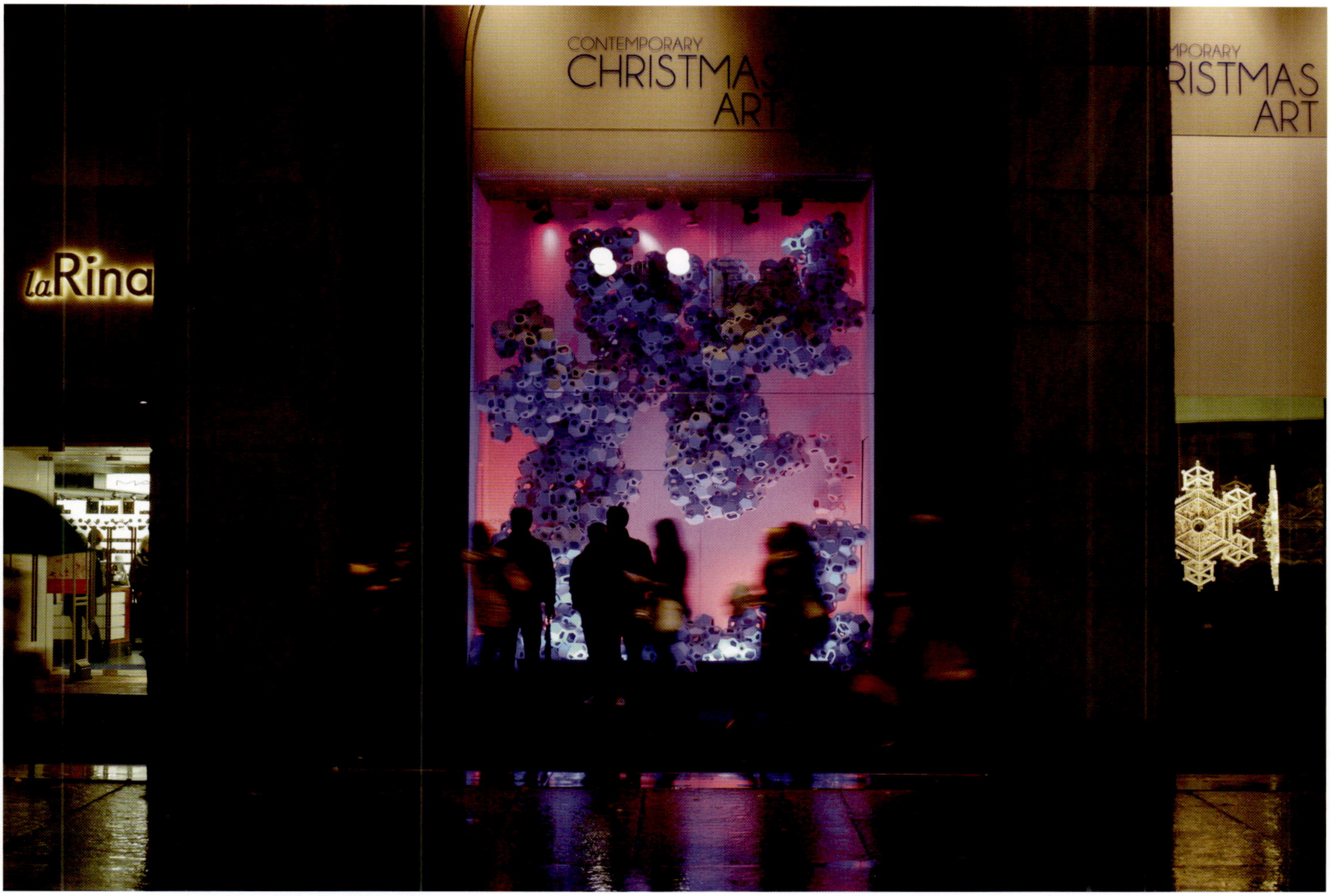

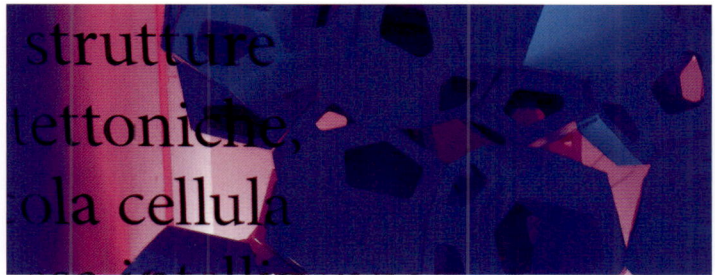

2. Vetrine di Natale [Christmas Windows]

LAVA's origami coral reef used 1500 recycled and recyclable cardboard molecules and explored the intelligence of natural and architectural systems.

The sculpture played with space by climbing up walls and arching over to create coral caves. Based on the geometrical structures of sea foam and corals, the colourful reef came to life through dynamic lighting and sound.

Chris Bosse, director of multinational LAVA, was one of seven designers from around the world to be commissioned to create a window – others were Kirsten Hassenfeld, Gyngy Laky, Andrea Mastrovito, Satsuki Oishi, Richard Sweeney, Margherita Marchioni and Tjep.

The store windows were at la Rinascente at Piazza Duomo, in the centre of Milan, design capital of the world. This was the first time la Rinascente commissioned artists to do Christmas windows.

The installation showed how a particular module, copied from nature, can generate architectural space, and how the intelligence of the smallest unit dictates the intelligence of the overall system.

Ecosystems such as coral reefs act as a metaphor for an architecture where the Individual components interact in symbiosis to create an environment.

Bosse says: "In urban terms, the smallest homes, the spaces they create, the energy they use, the heat and moisture they absorb, multiply into a bigger organizational system, whose sustainability depends on their intelligence".

Current trends in parametric modeling, digital fabrication and material - science were applied to the space - filling installation.

Design Agency: LAVA (Laboratory for Visionary Architecture)
Country: Australia
Art Direction: Independent Ideas
Lighting: ERCO (Sydney / Milan)
Client: La Rinascente (Italy)
Photographer: Filippo Patrese

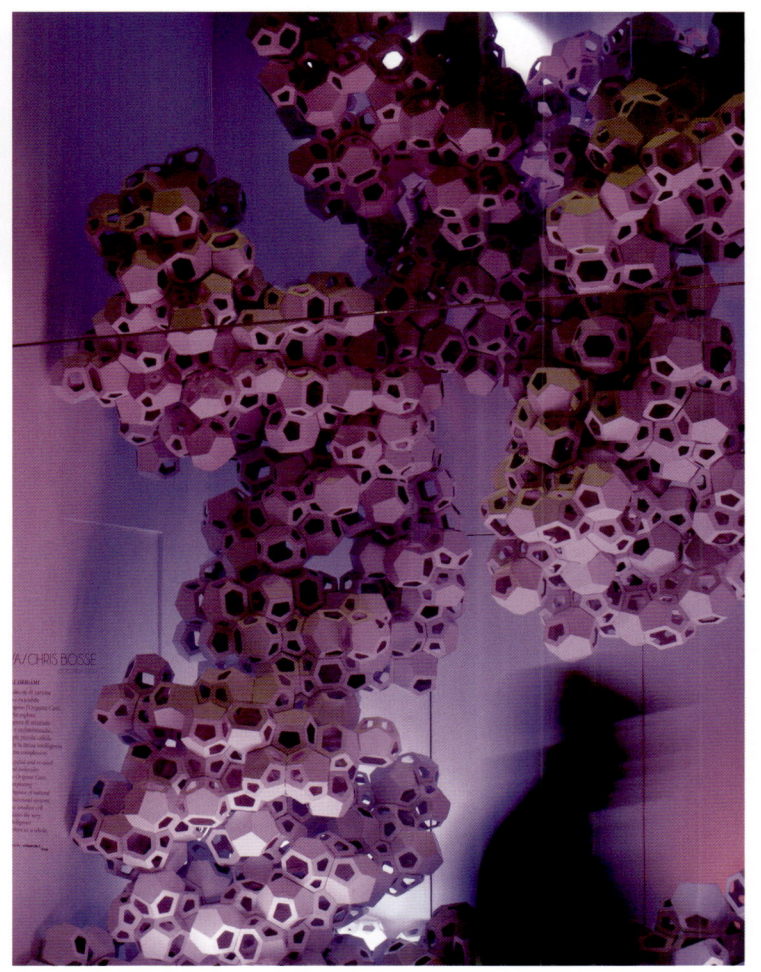

1. Buy Art, Not Drugs!

NO I'M NOT ON ACID 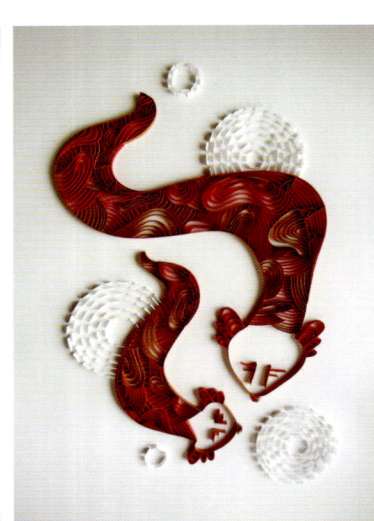 I'M PRETTY SURE I'M NOT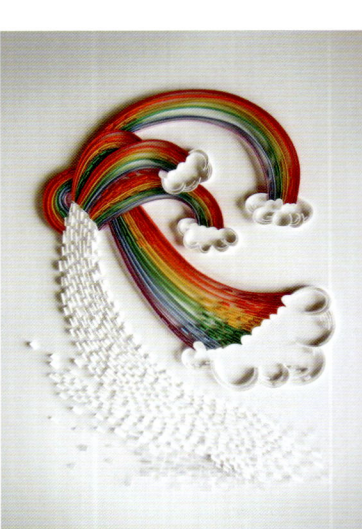

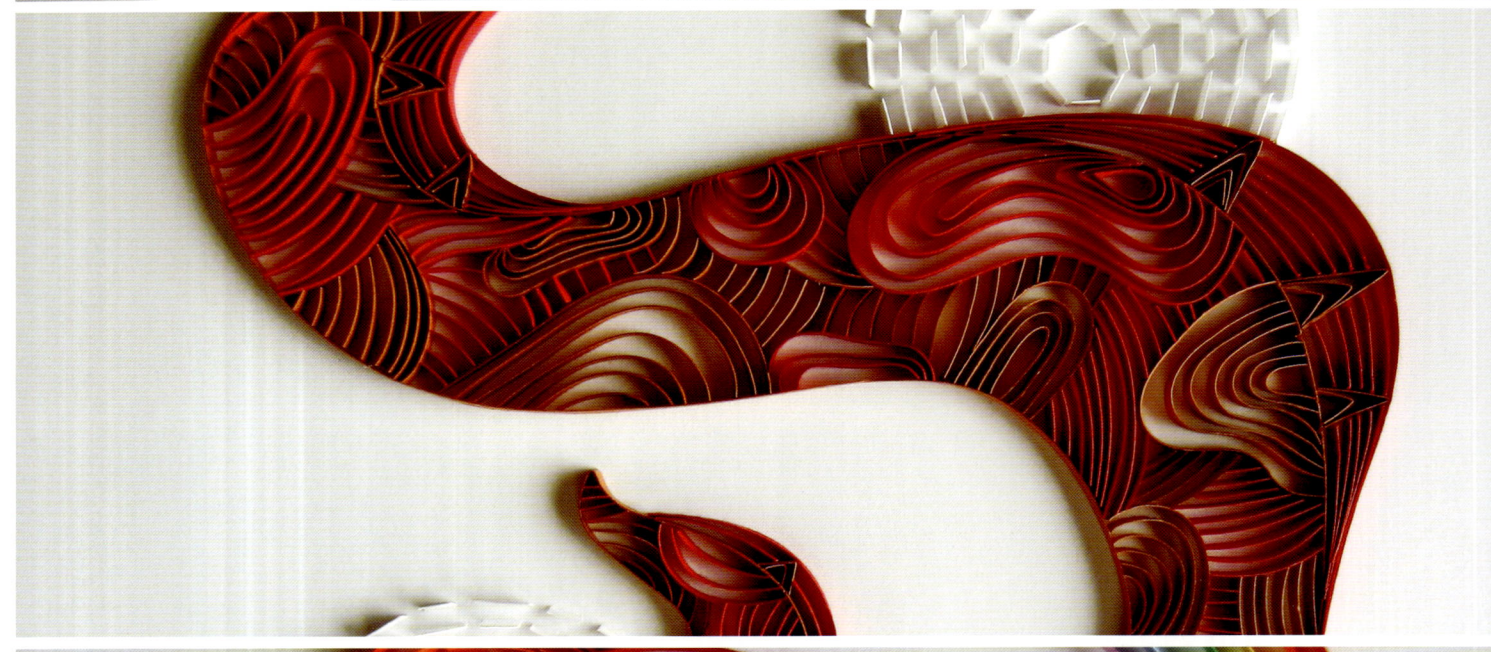

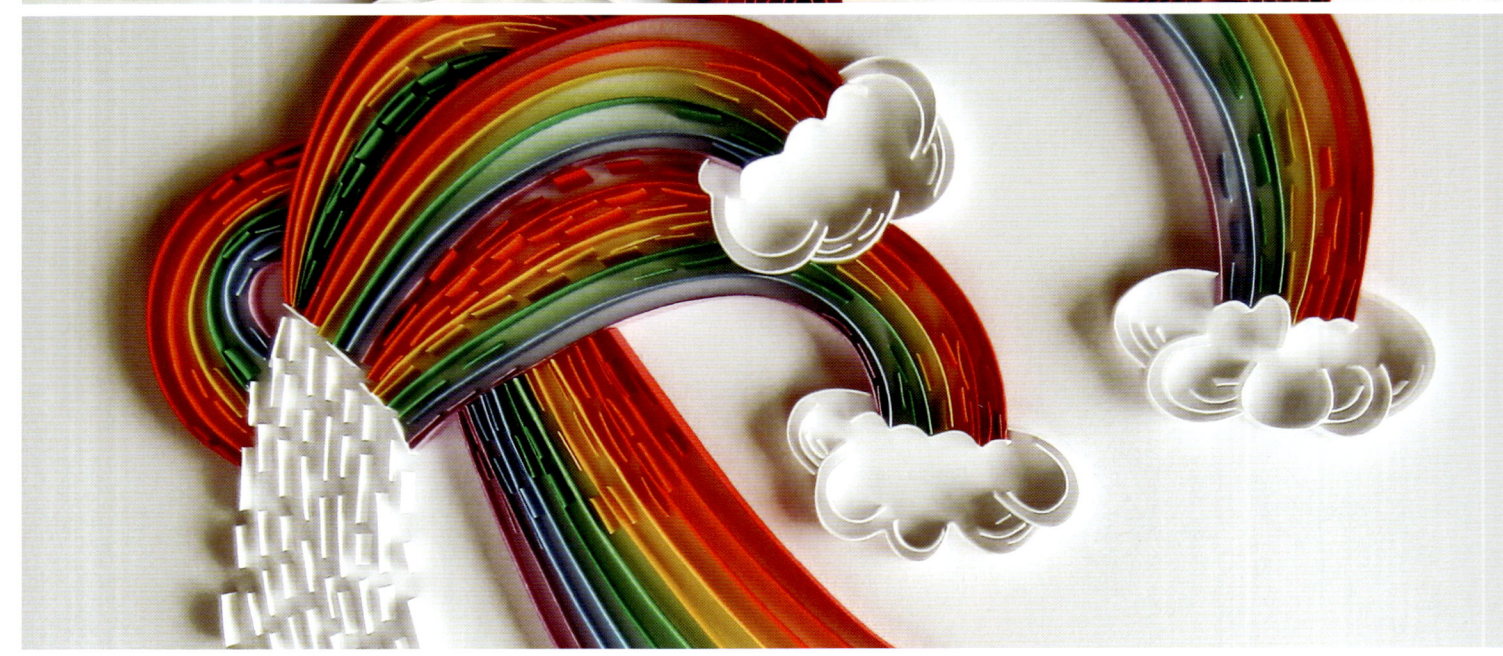

2. Can I Stay?

3. Design Indaba Superstars

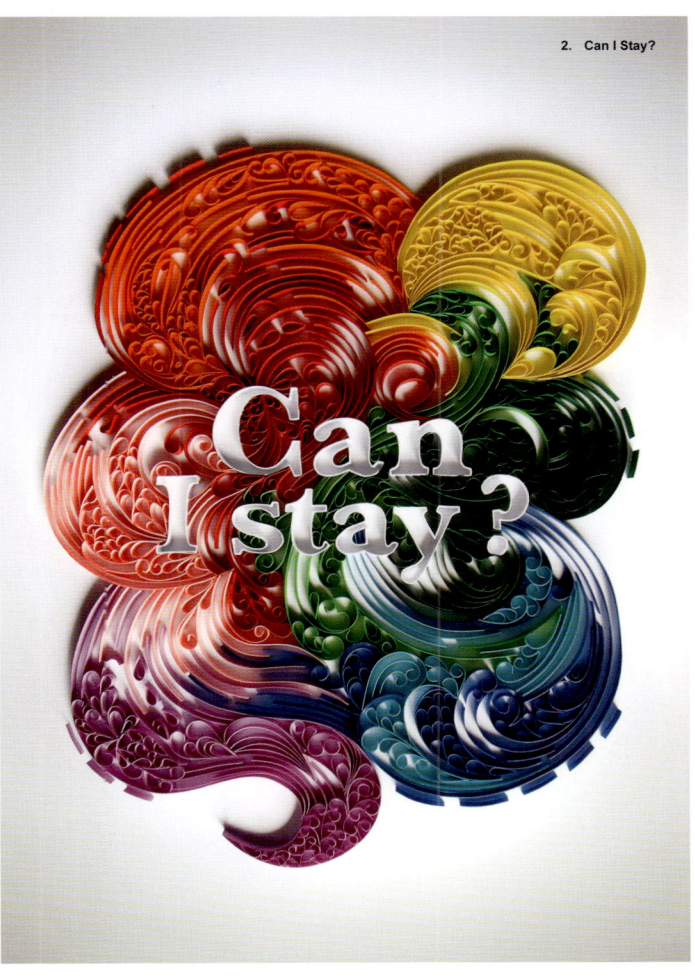
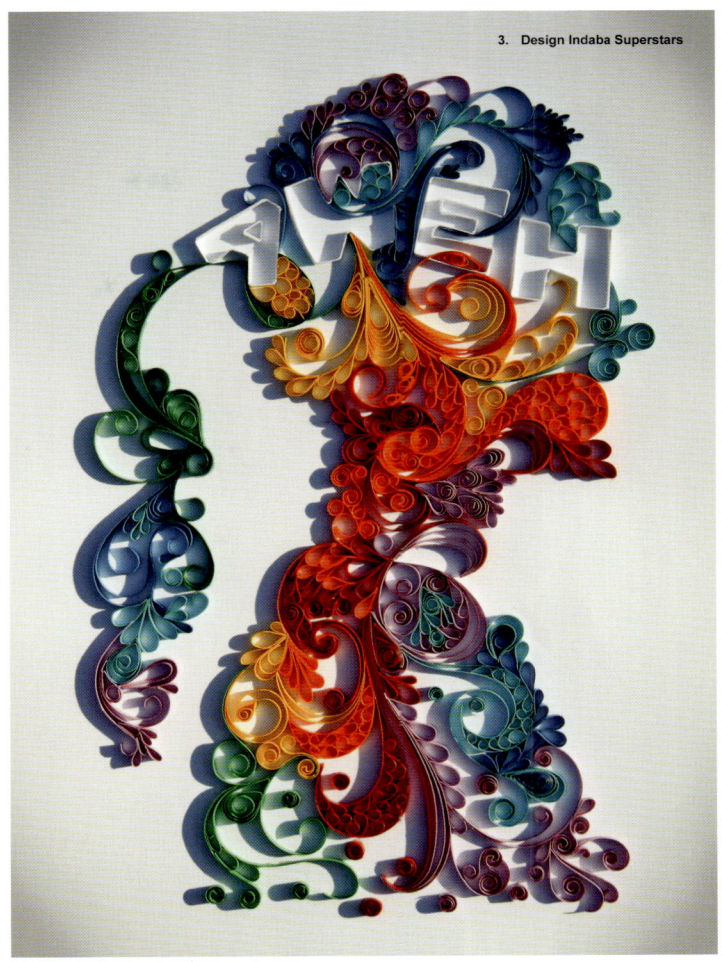

Designer: Lavanya Naidoo
Country: South Africa

4. Vanna – cardboard furniture

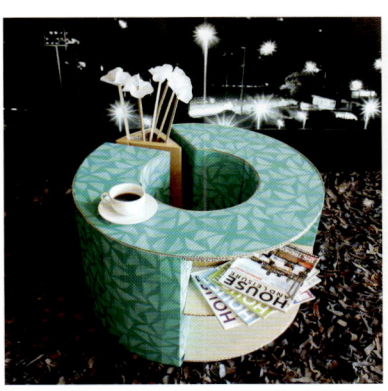
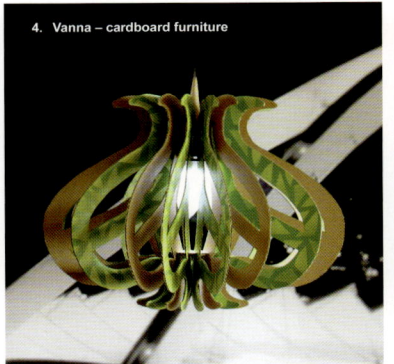
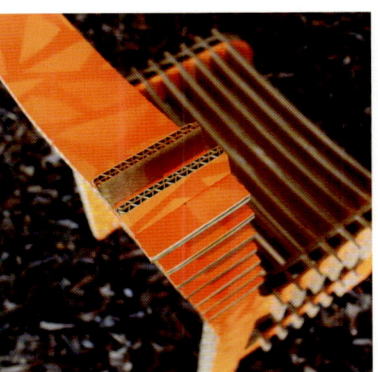

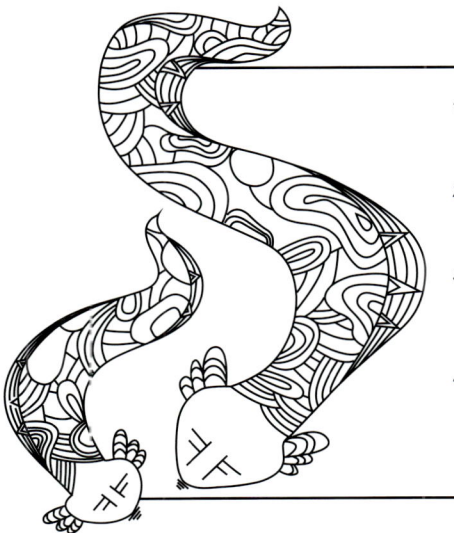

1. **Buy Art, Not Drugs!**
   This series was created for a local exhibition called 'But Art, Not Drugs', hosted in Durban, South Africa. The theme was intended to encourage individuals to spend money on art rather than drugs.

2. **Can I Stay?**
   The concept behind the artwork was to get the receiving agency to make the next move by simply asking the question, 'Can I stay?' The piece itself was initially a very simple outline of a speech bubble, which grew more and more intricate.

3. **Design Indaba Superstars**
   Lavanya's entry was one of her first quilling pieces and included the word 'Aweh!' a colloquial South African exclamation that means something similar to 'that's awesome!' This is accompanied by colourful swirls of intricate detail and painstaking precision. Starting with traditional quilling shapes, she started integrating her own shapes into the piece to create texture and form. This piece took roughly 21 hours to complete and it paid off.

4. **Vanna – cardboard furniture**
   As part of Lavanya's final year BTech degree in Visual Communication she created a brand around cardboard furniture, as there is a market for this in South Africa but no supplier. This entailed creating four collapsible pieces; a chair, coffee table, chandelier and a playful ambient light and developing a fun youthful, yet classy approach to the branding.

   ---Lavanya Naidoo

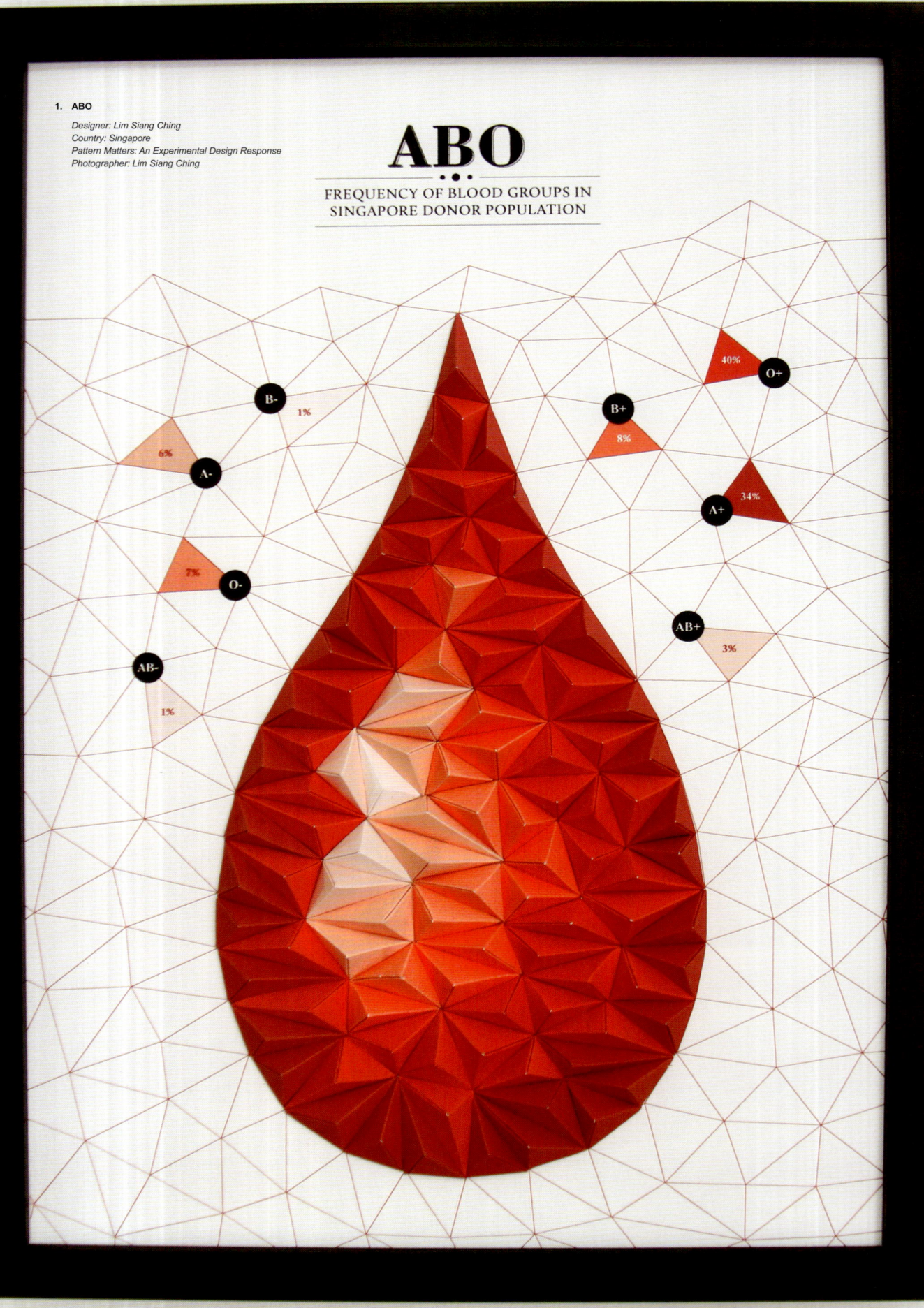

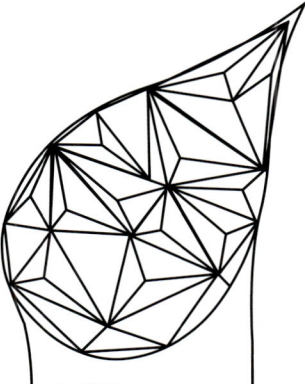

1. **ABO**
2. **DEATH**
3. **ENERGY**

Tangible Paper Infographic

This project inquires on the possibilities to augment the role of a design element – pattern, by looking into explorations of tactility through pattern making. It aims to demonstrate how pattern is an essential element in graphic design; not merely a decorating tool. This experimentation on patterns and its tactile qualities as a visual representation for information is based on three different topics. Since human are naturally drawn to patterns, it could be acquired as a tool to enhance the experience of information by visualizing pattern as a metaphor for information.

---Lim Siang Ching

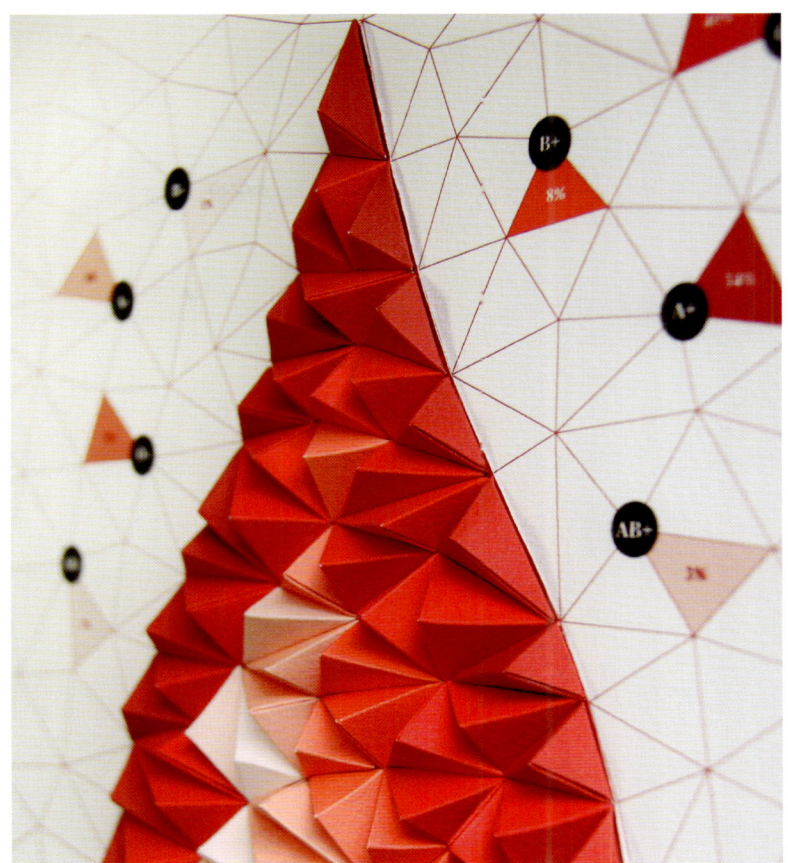

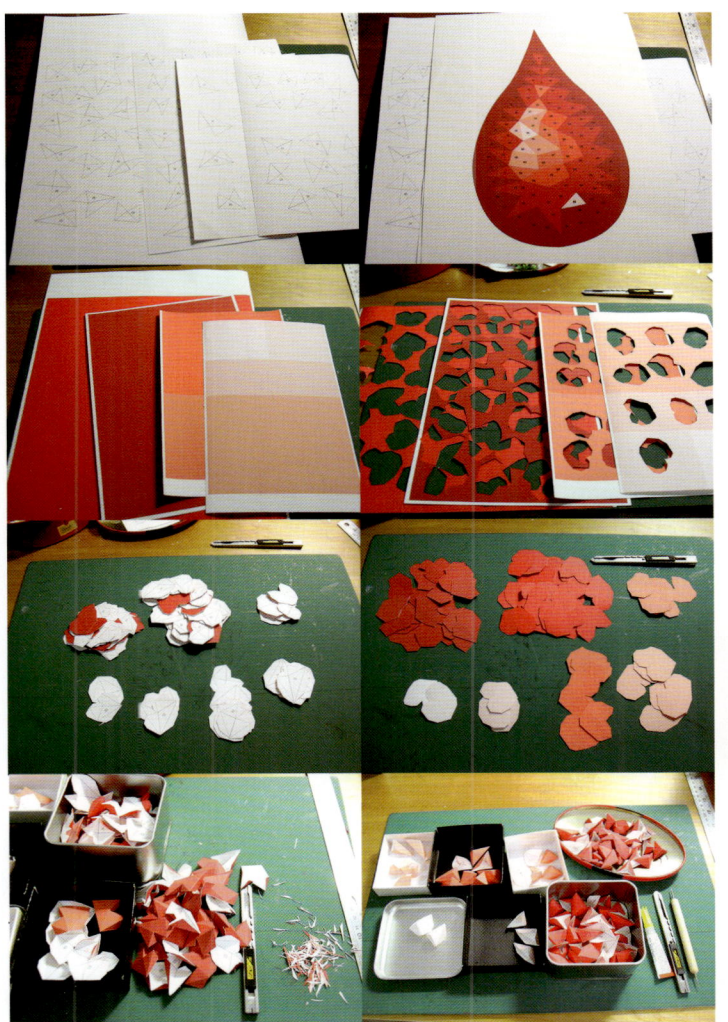

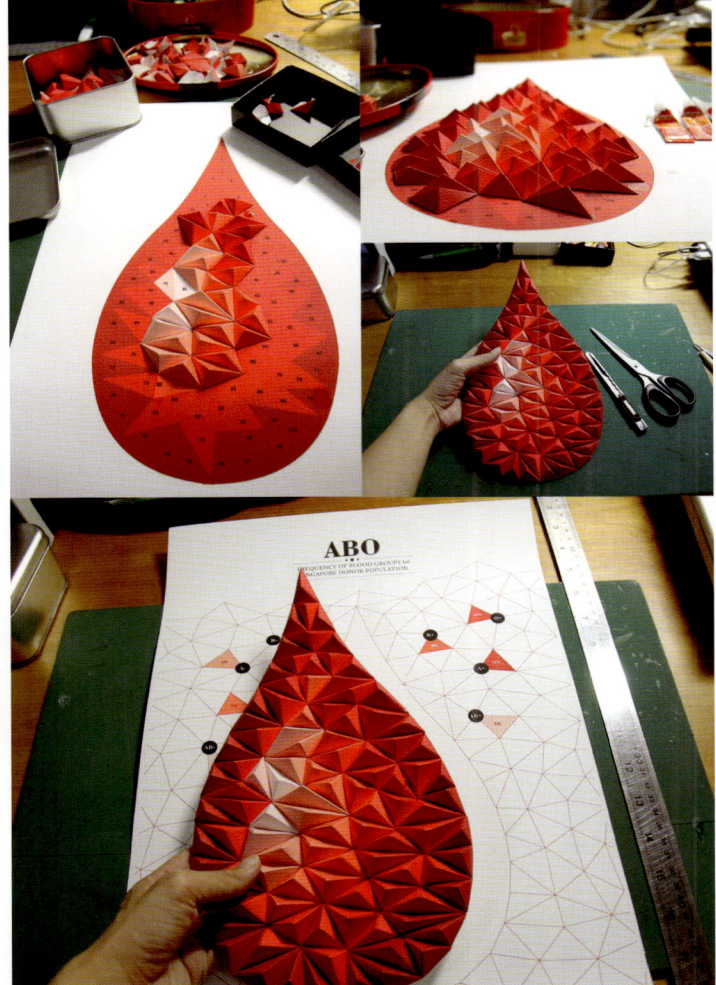

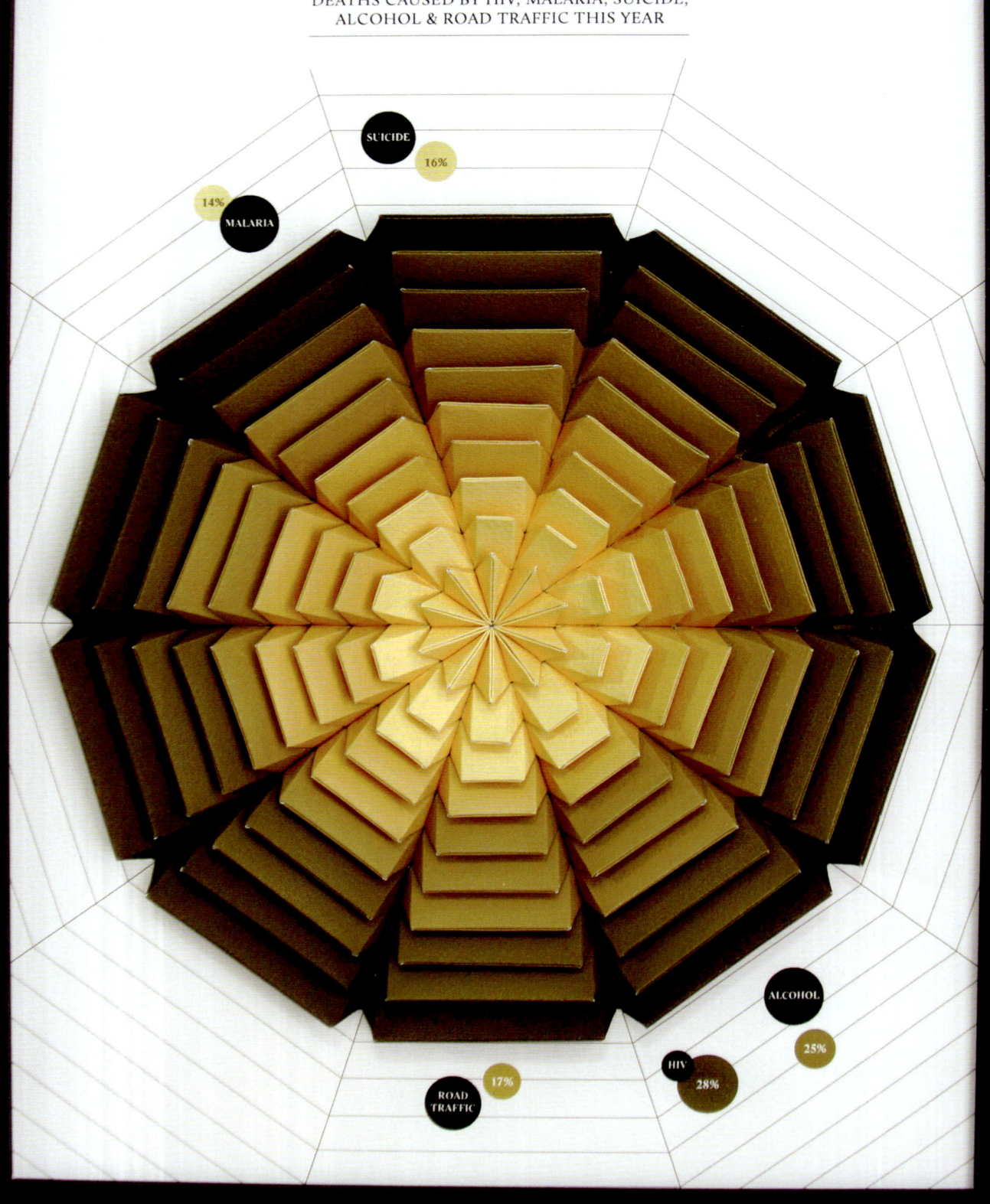

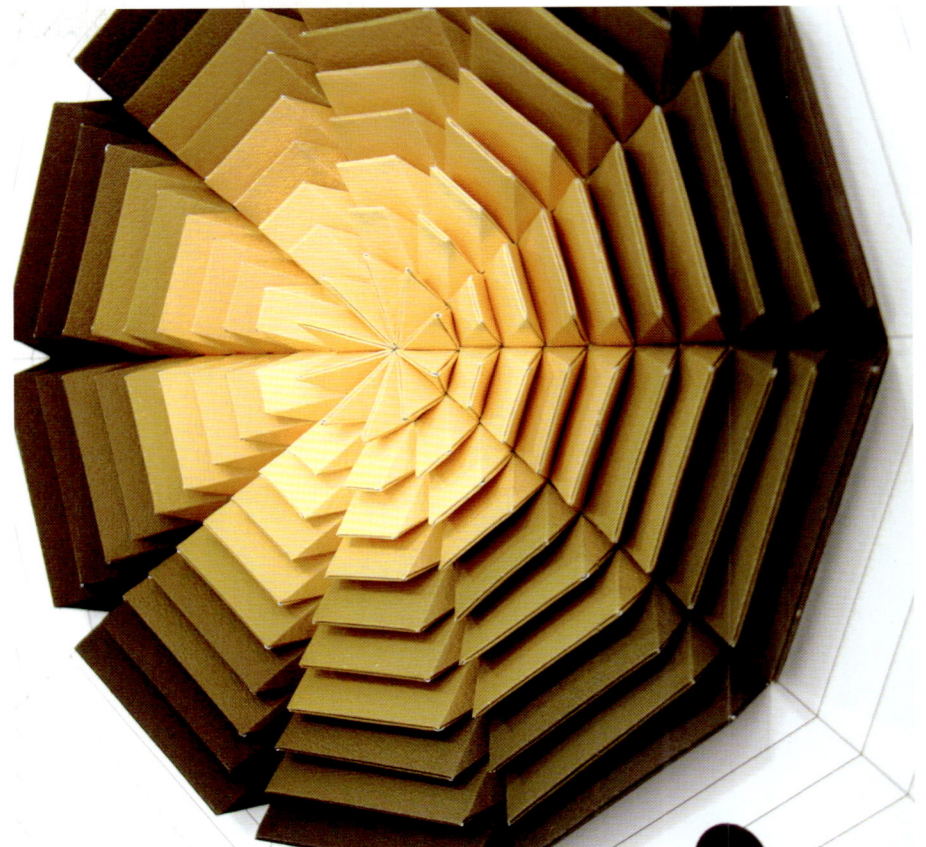

2. **DEATH**

Designer: Lim Siang Ching
Country: Singapore
Pattern Matters: An Experimental Design Response
Photographer: Lim Siang Ching

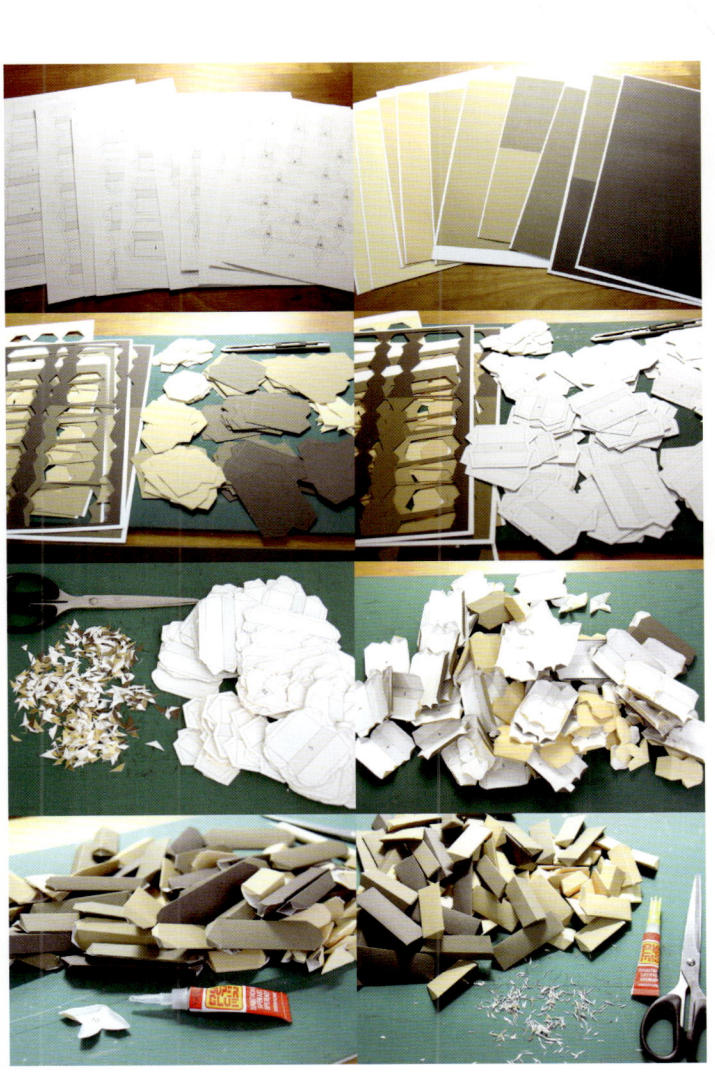

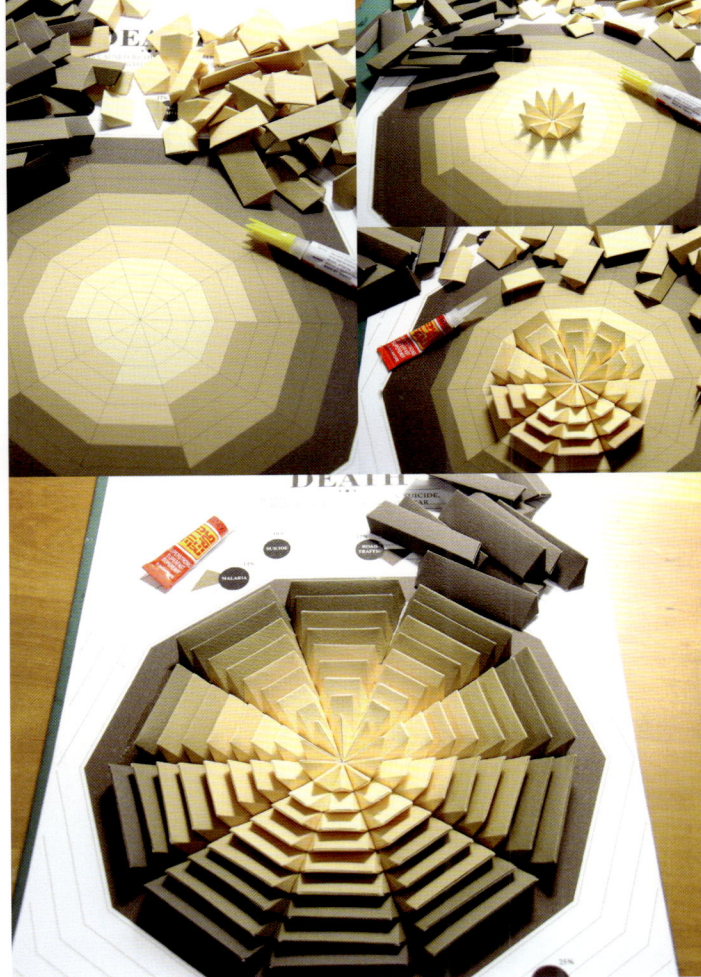

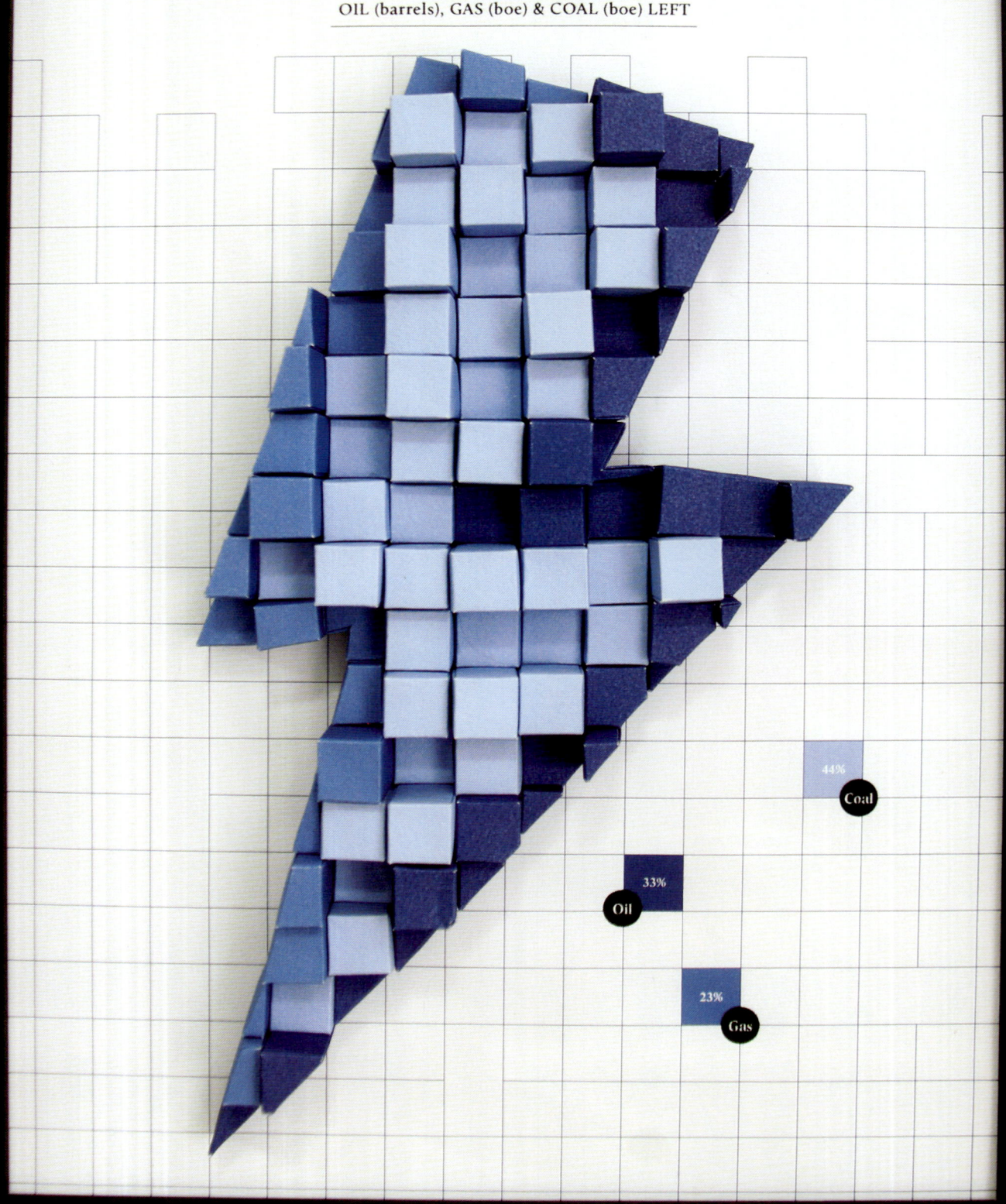

3. **ENERGY**

Designer: Lim Siang Ching
Country: Singapore
Pattern Matters: An Experimental Design Response
Photographer: Lim Siang Ching

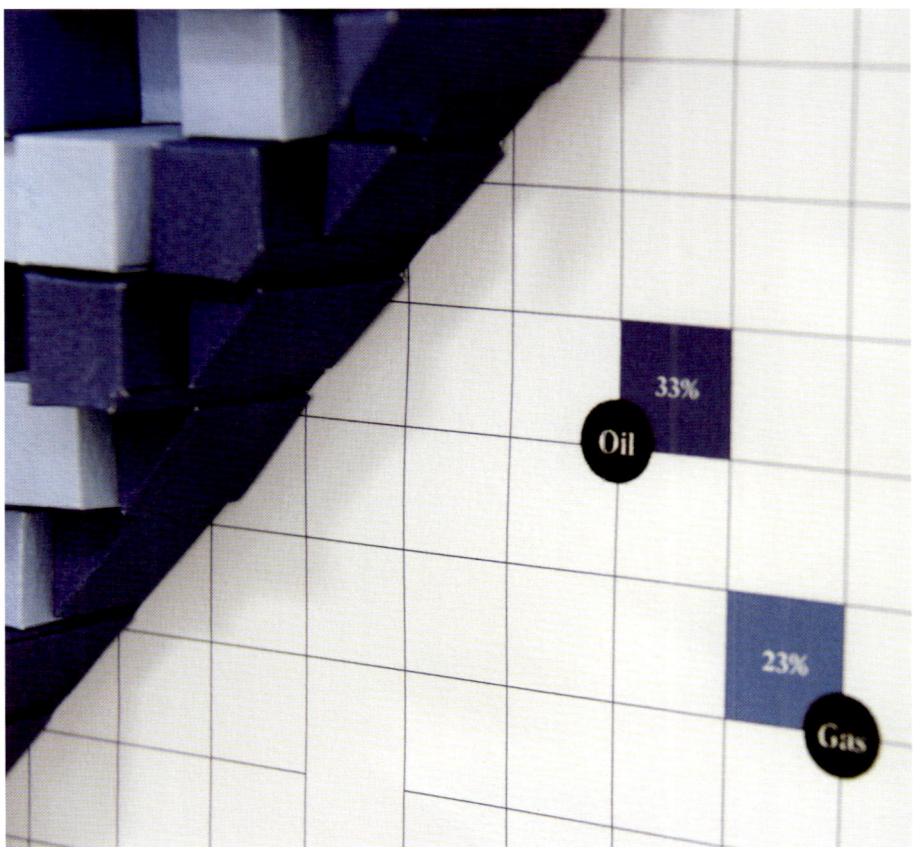
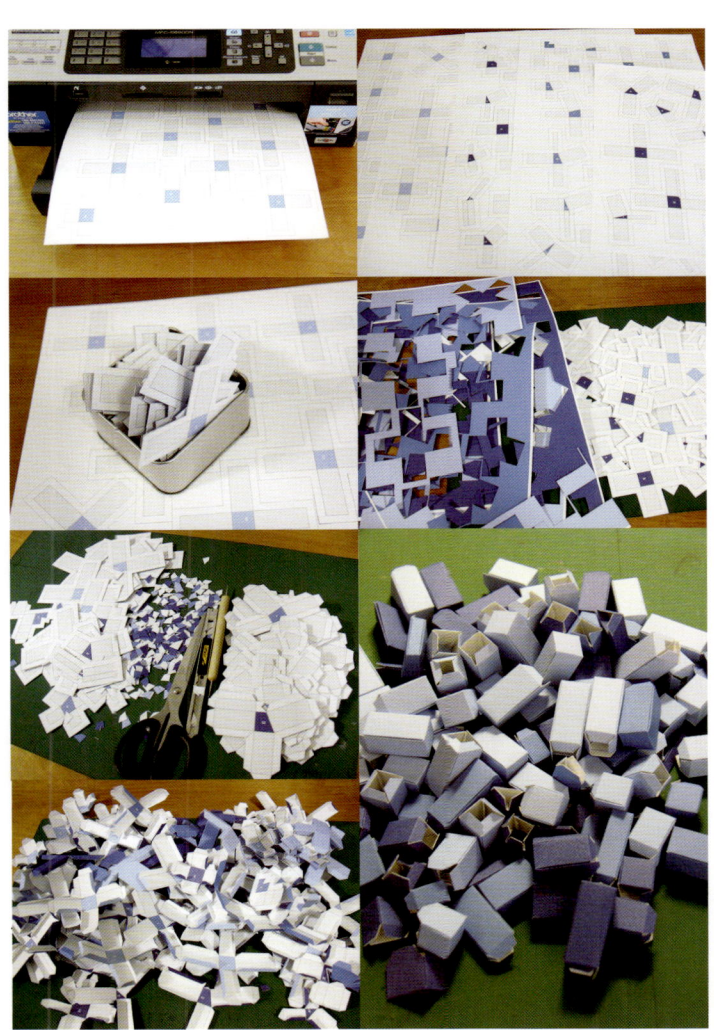
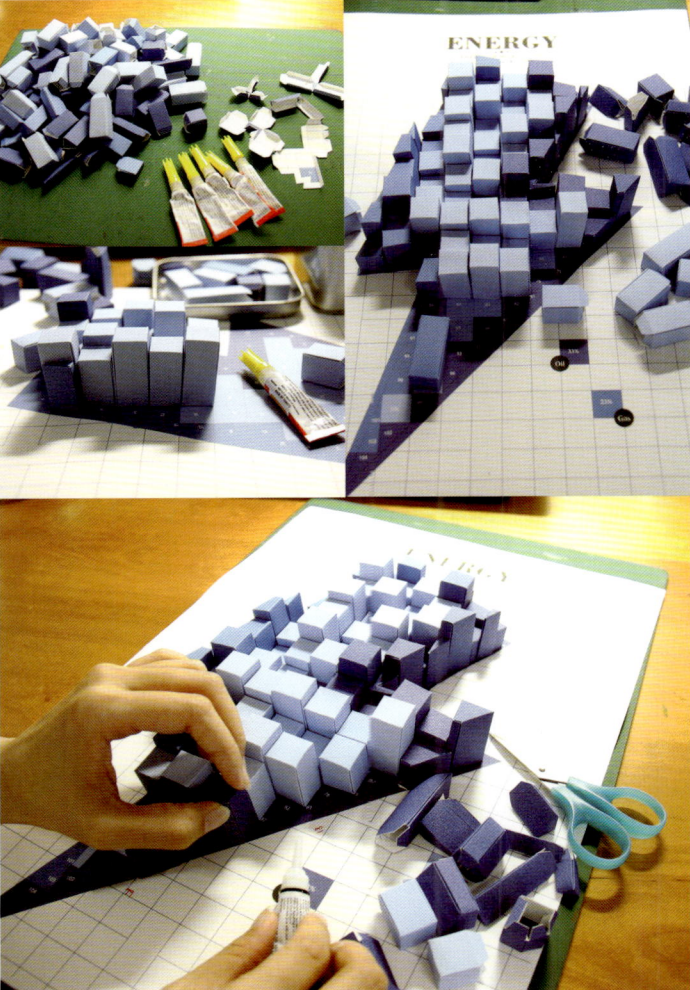

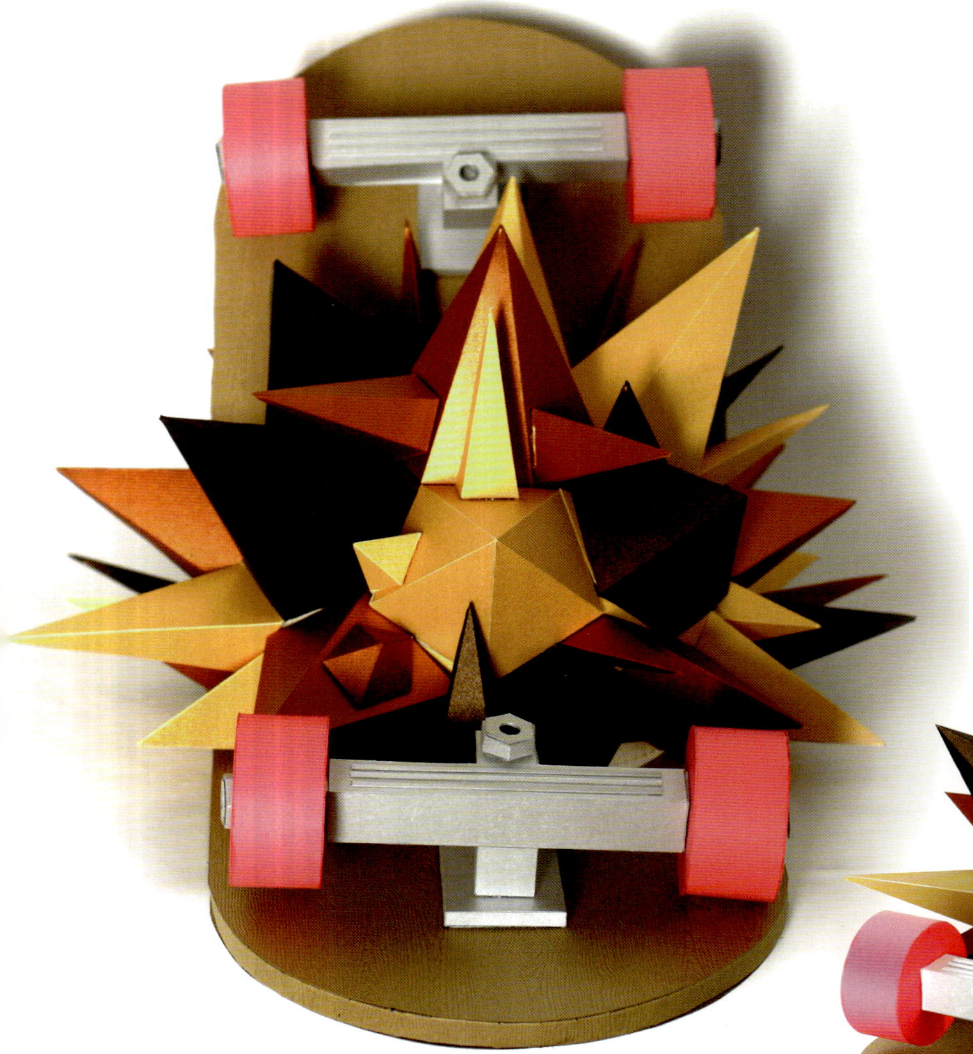

1. **New Era Cap**

Finalist cap for the New Era Introducing 2011.

Design Agency: Lobulo Design
Country: London, UK
Creative Director: Lobulo
Designer: Lobulo
Client: New Era
Photographer: Lobulo

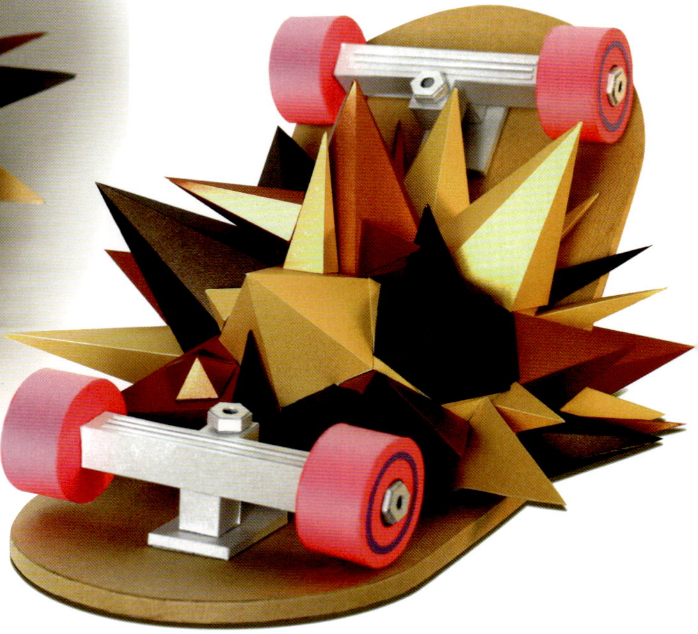

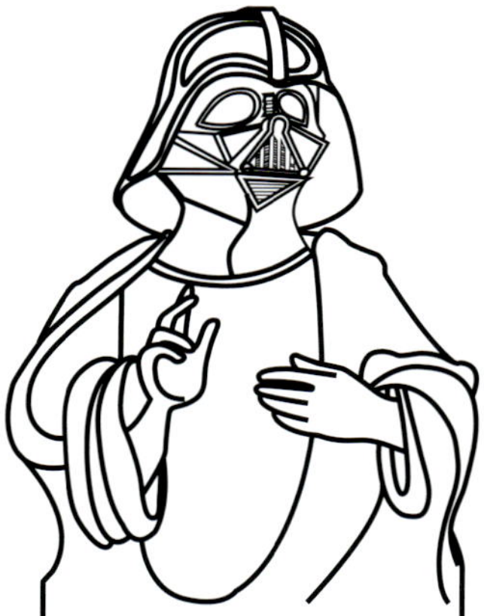

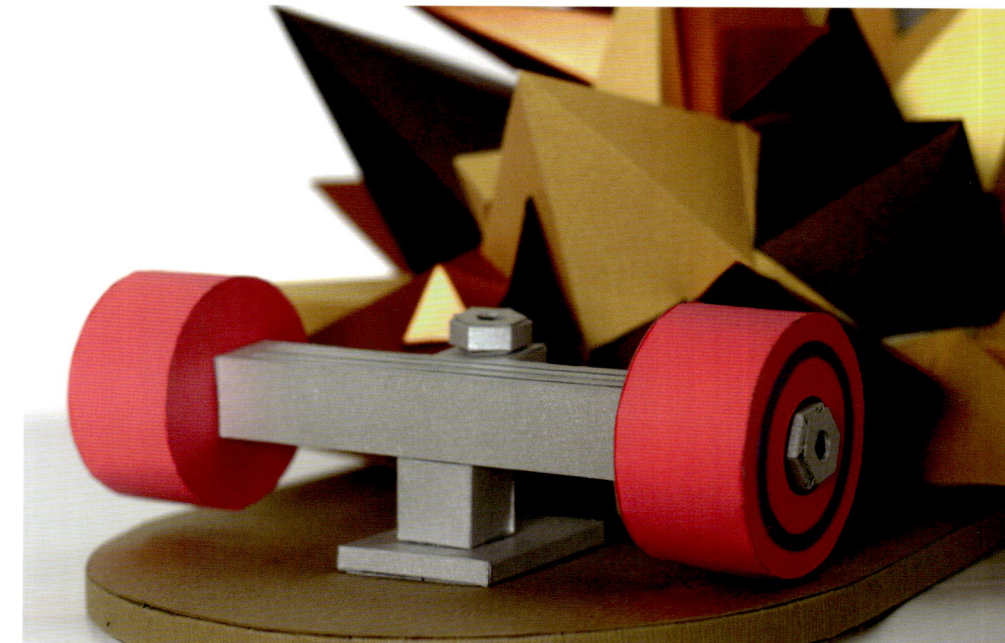

1. New Era Cap
2. El ingenioso Don Quijote de la Mancha
3. Paper Darth Project
4. H Magazine
5. Hospital / Icons
6. Casio G-Shock GA-110
7. Furniture Arthritis
8. Bcn 90's
9. LADY GAGA

---Lobulo Design

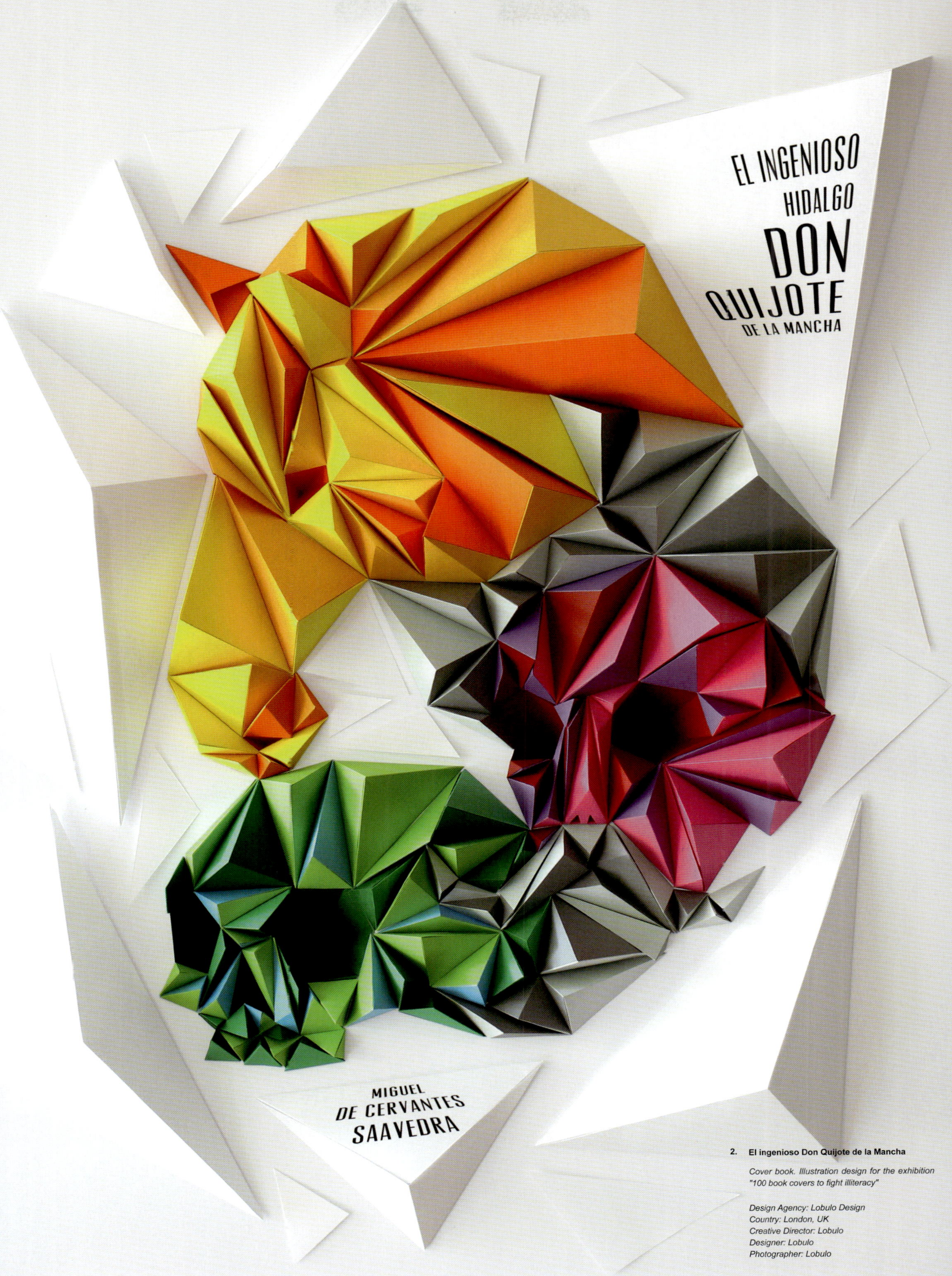

EL INGENIOSO
HIDALGO
**DON
QUIJOTE**
DE LA MANCHA

MIGUEL
DE CERVANTES
SAAVEDRA

2. El ingenioso Don Quijote de la Mancha

Cover book. Illustration design for the exhibition "100 book covers to fight illiteracy"

Design Agency: Lobulo Design
Country: London, UK
Creative Director: Lobulo
Designer: Lobulo
Photographer: Lobulo

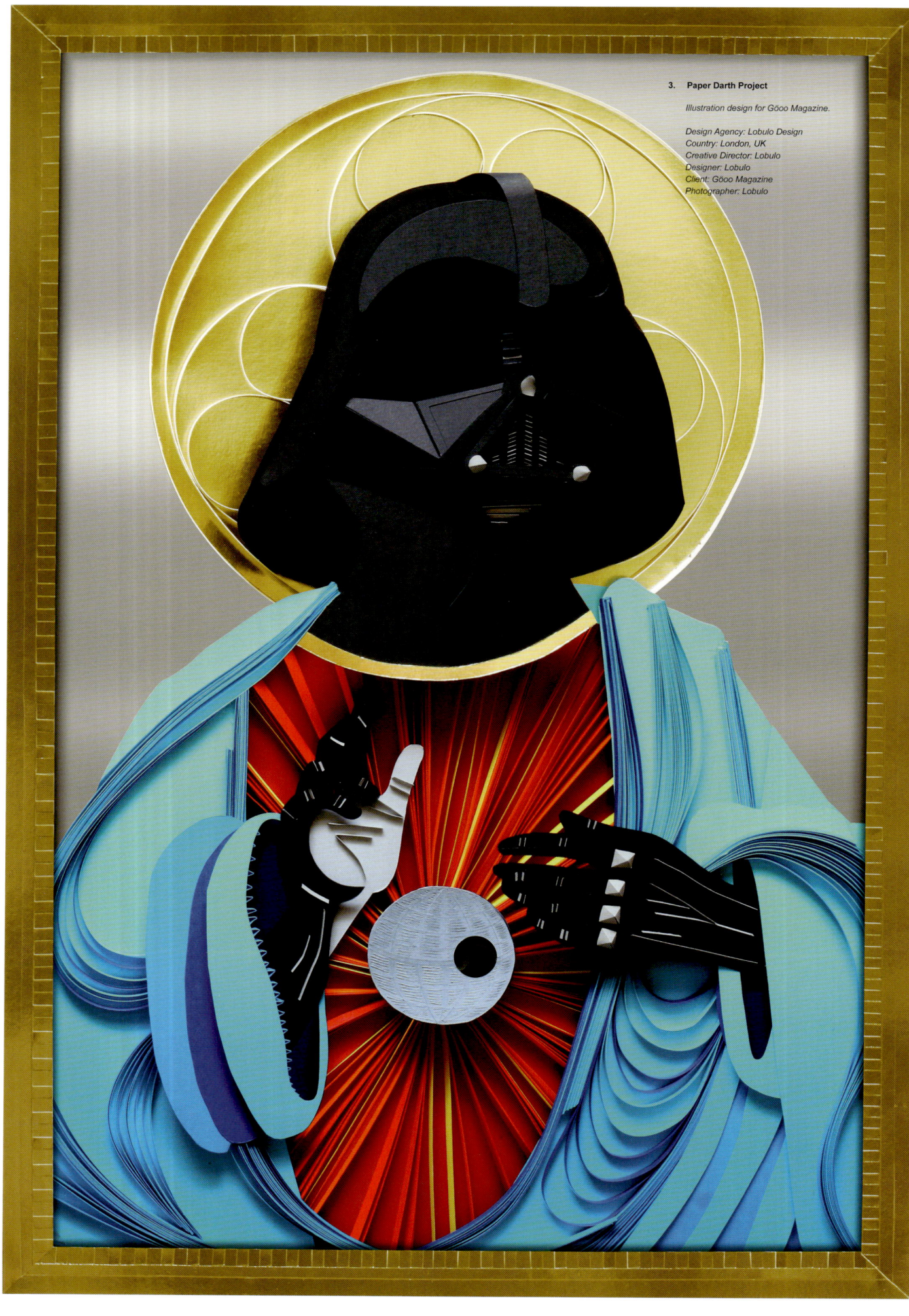

3. **Paper Darth Project**

Illustration design for Gōoo Magazine.

Design Agency: Lobulo Design
Country: London, UK
Creative Director: Lobulo
Designer: Lobulo
Client: Gōoo Magazine
Photographer: Lobulo

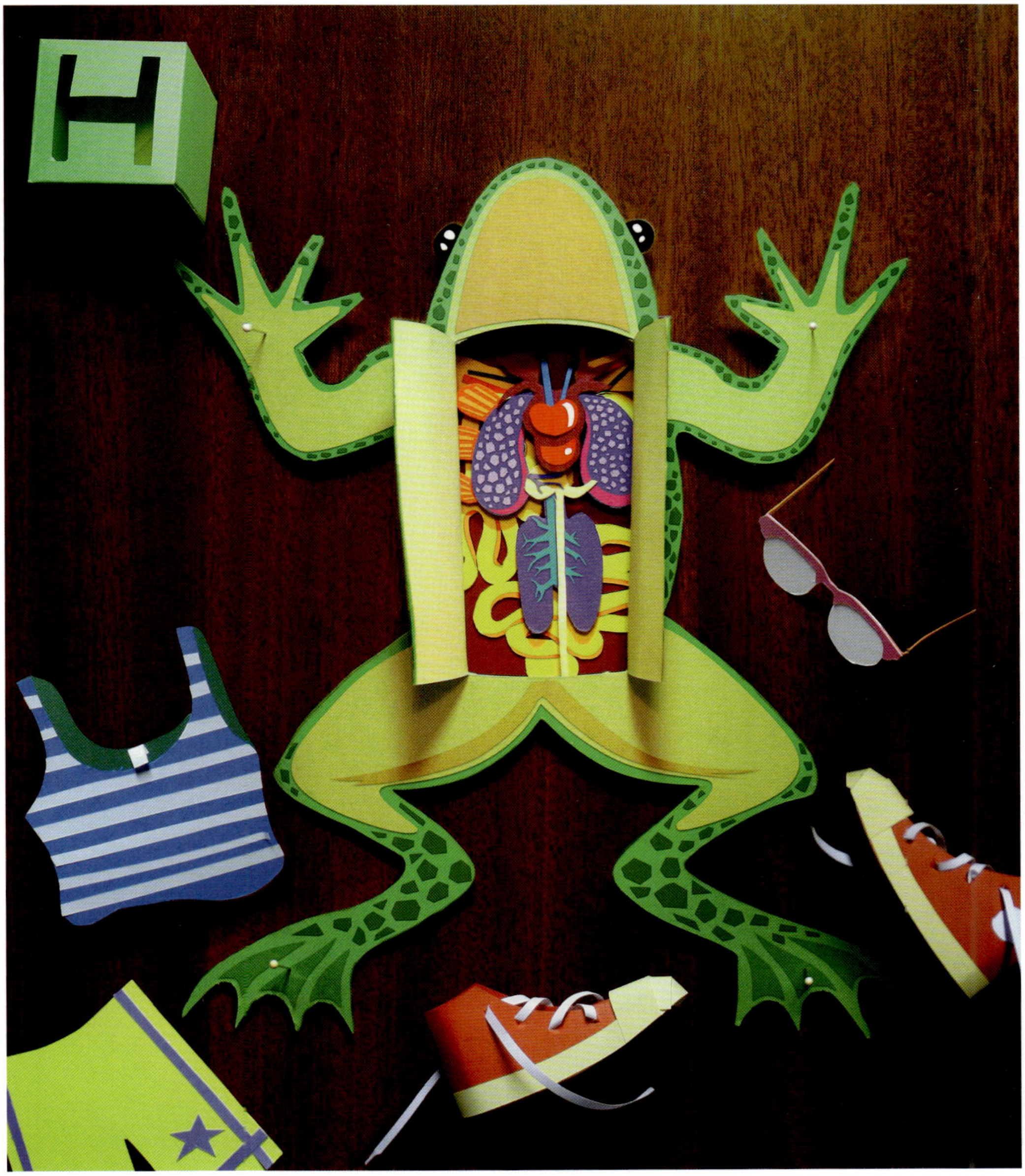

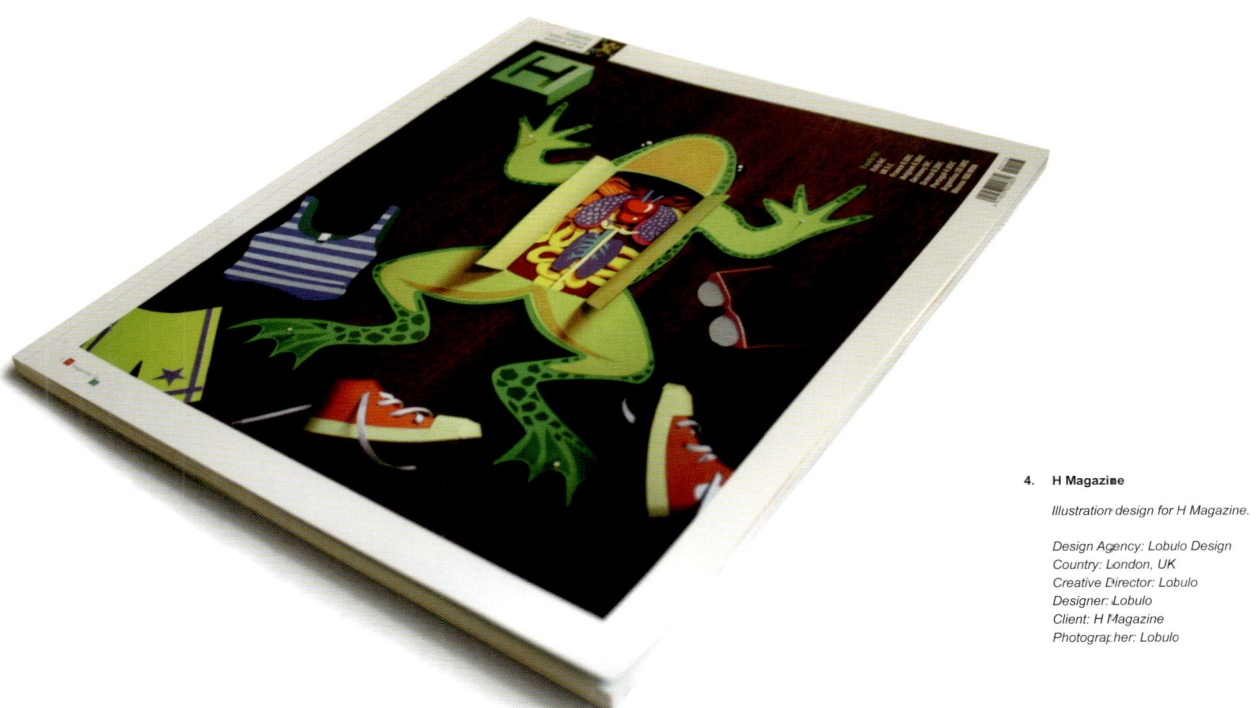

4. **H Magazine**

Illustration design for H Magazine.

Design Agency: Lobulo Design
Country: London, UK
Creative Director: Lobulo
Designer: Lobulo
Client: H Magazine
Photographer: Lobulo

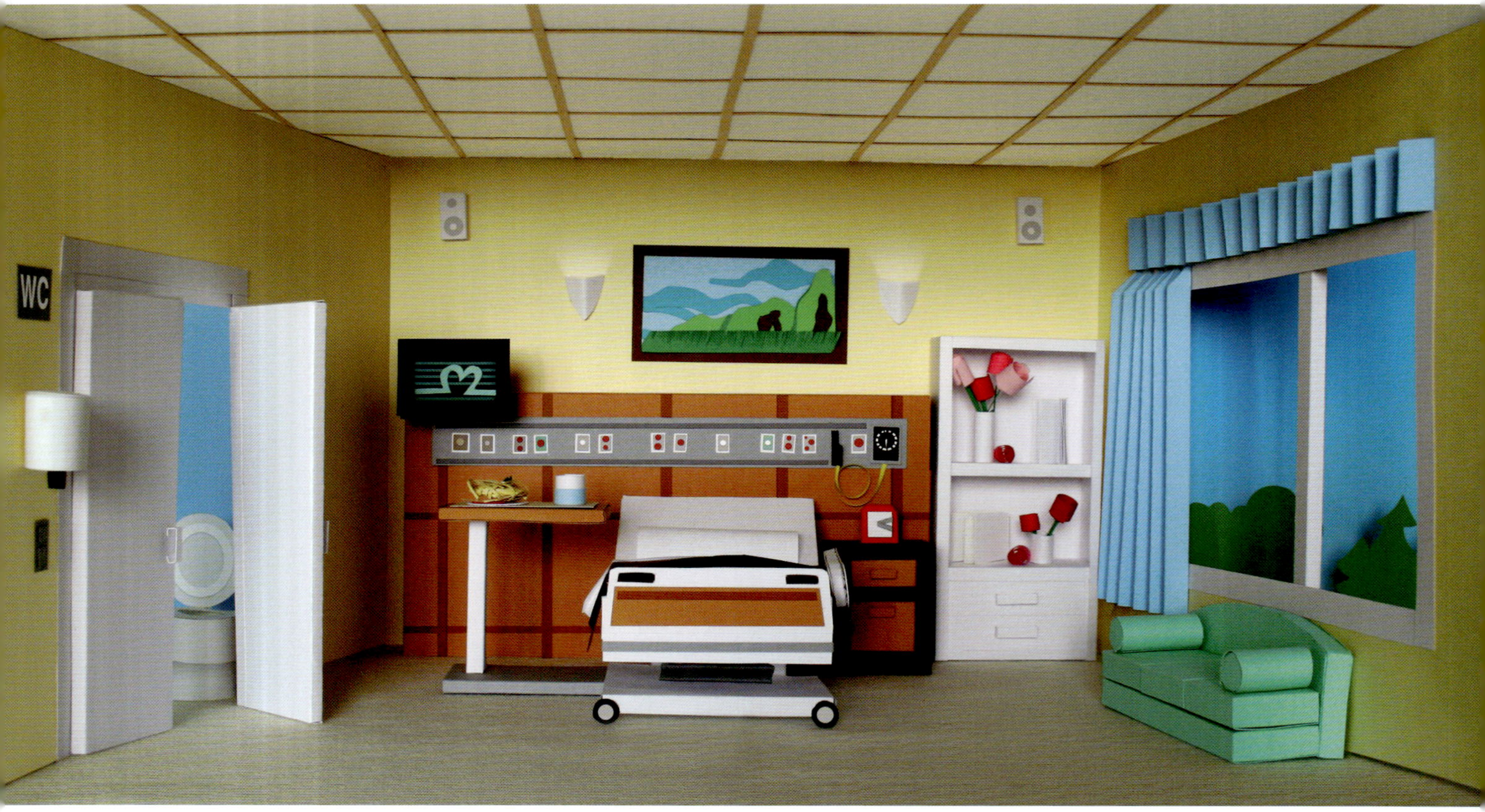

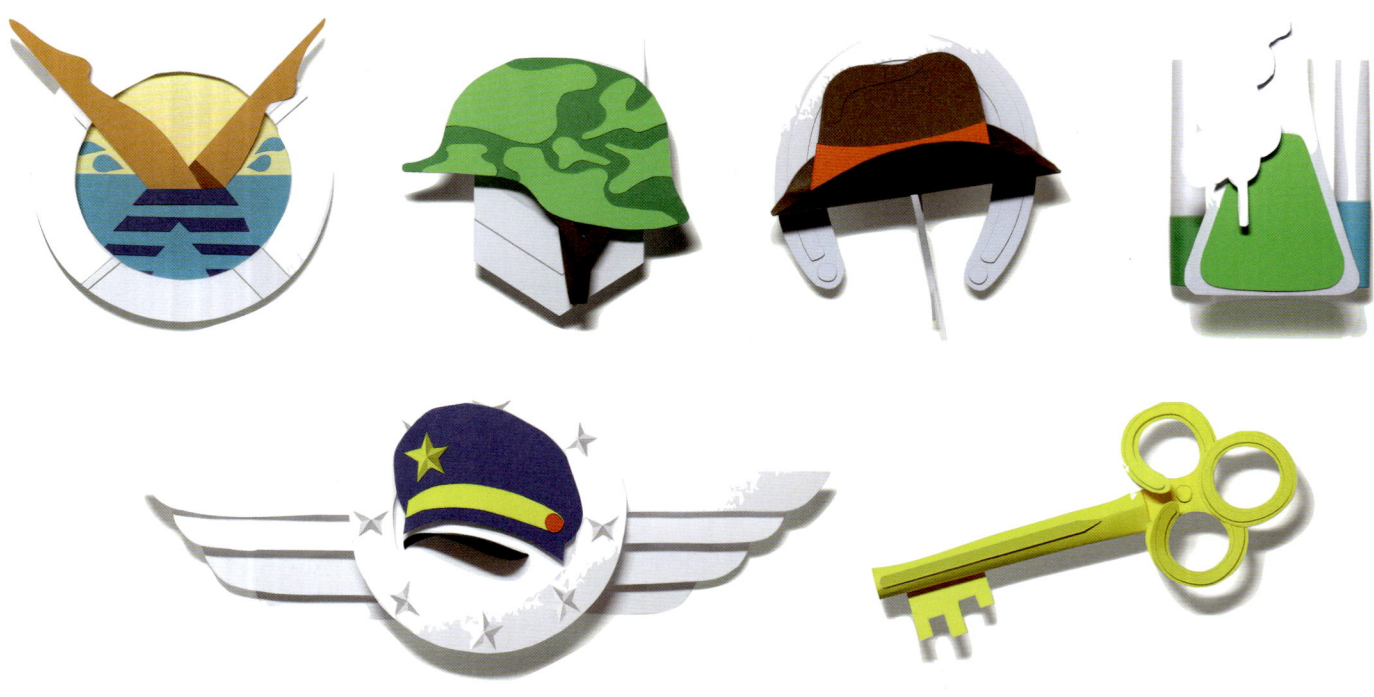

5. Hospital / Icons

Illustration design for O The Oprah Magazine.

Design Agency: Lobulo Design
Country: London, UK
Creative Director: Lobulo
Designer: Lobulo
Client: Oprah Magazine
Photographer: Lobulo

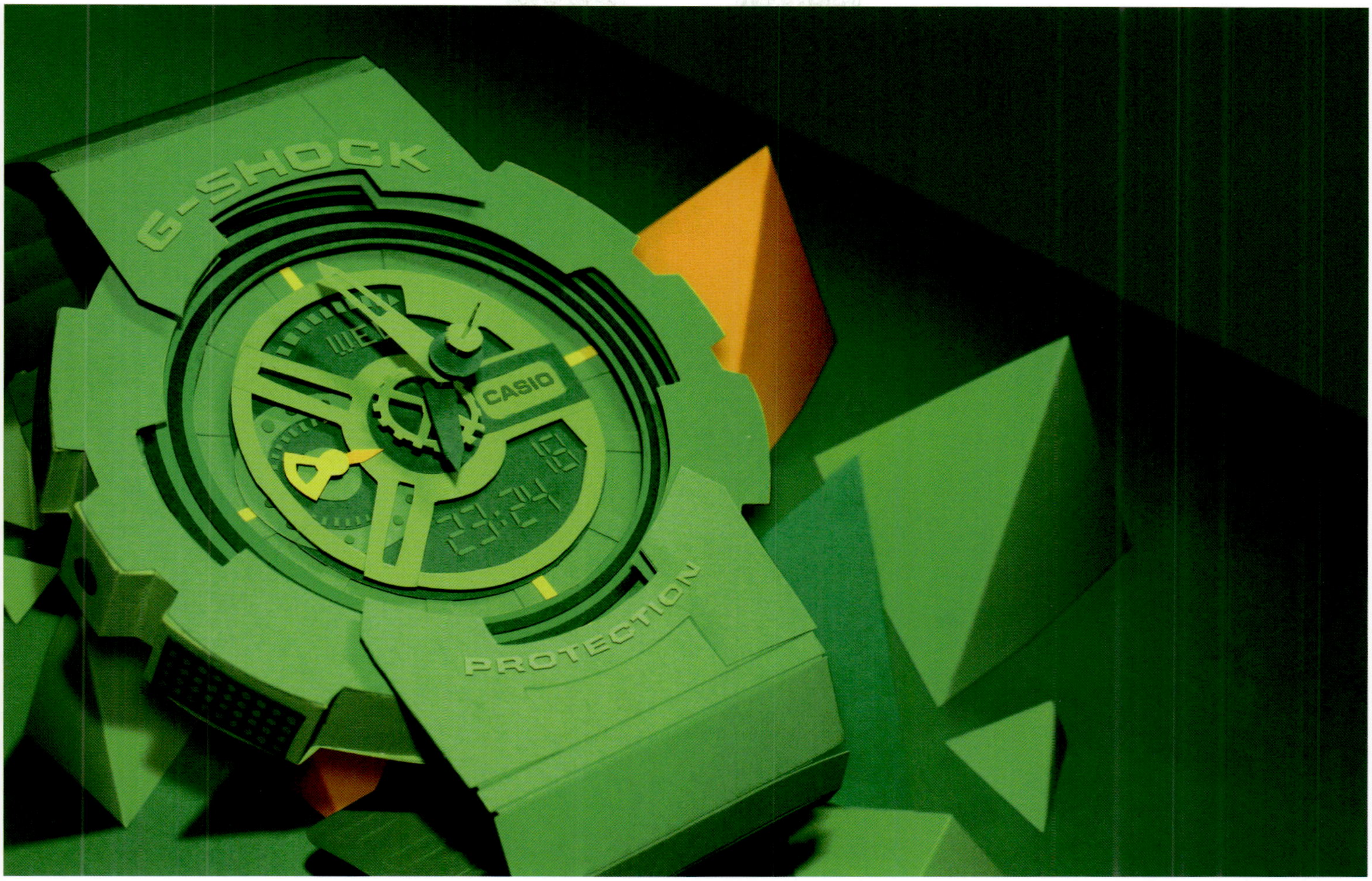

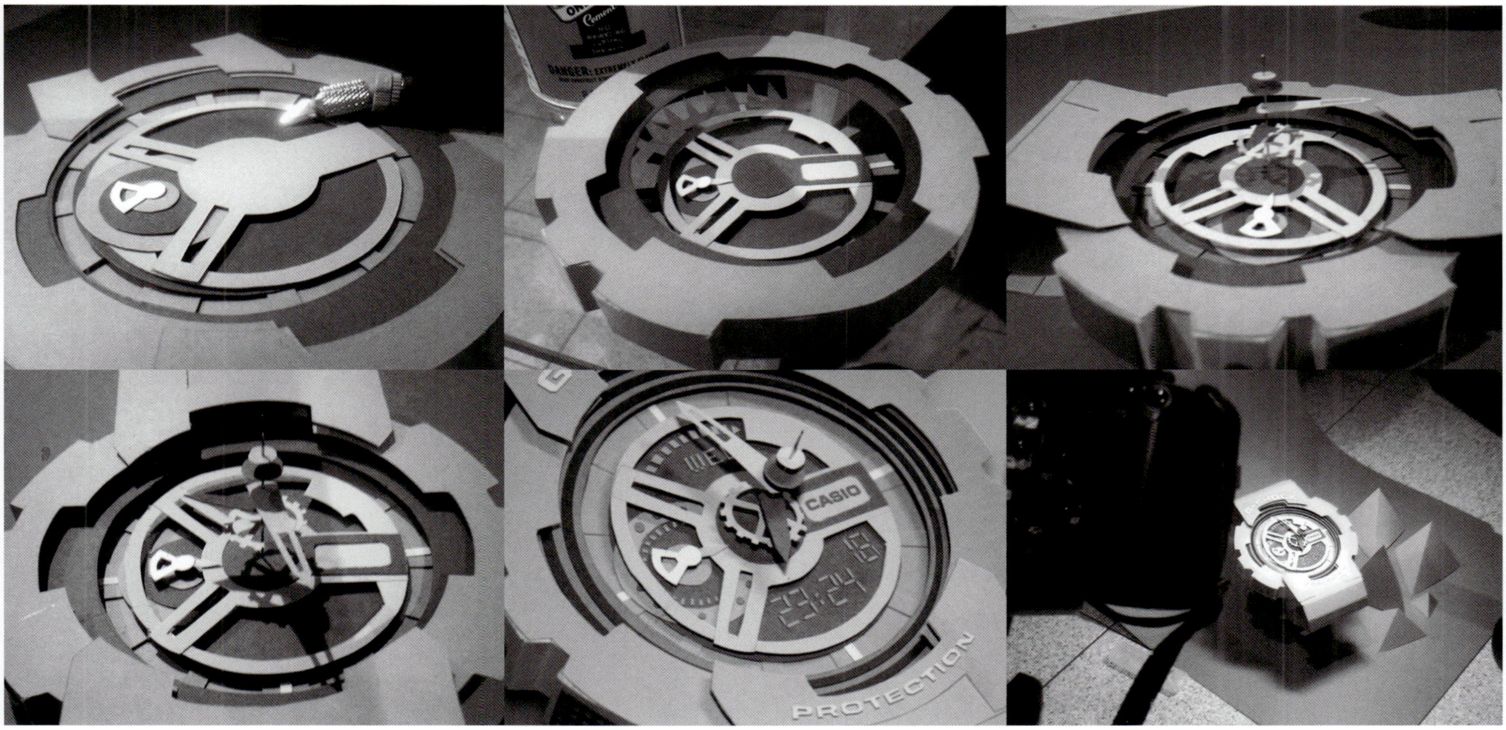

6. Casio G-Shock GA-110

   Illustration design for Casio.

   Design Agency: Lobulo Design
   Country: London, UK
   Creative Director: Lobulo
   Designer: Lobulo
   Client: Casio
   Photographer: Lobulo

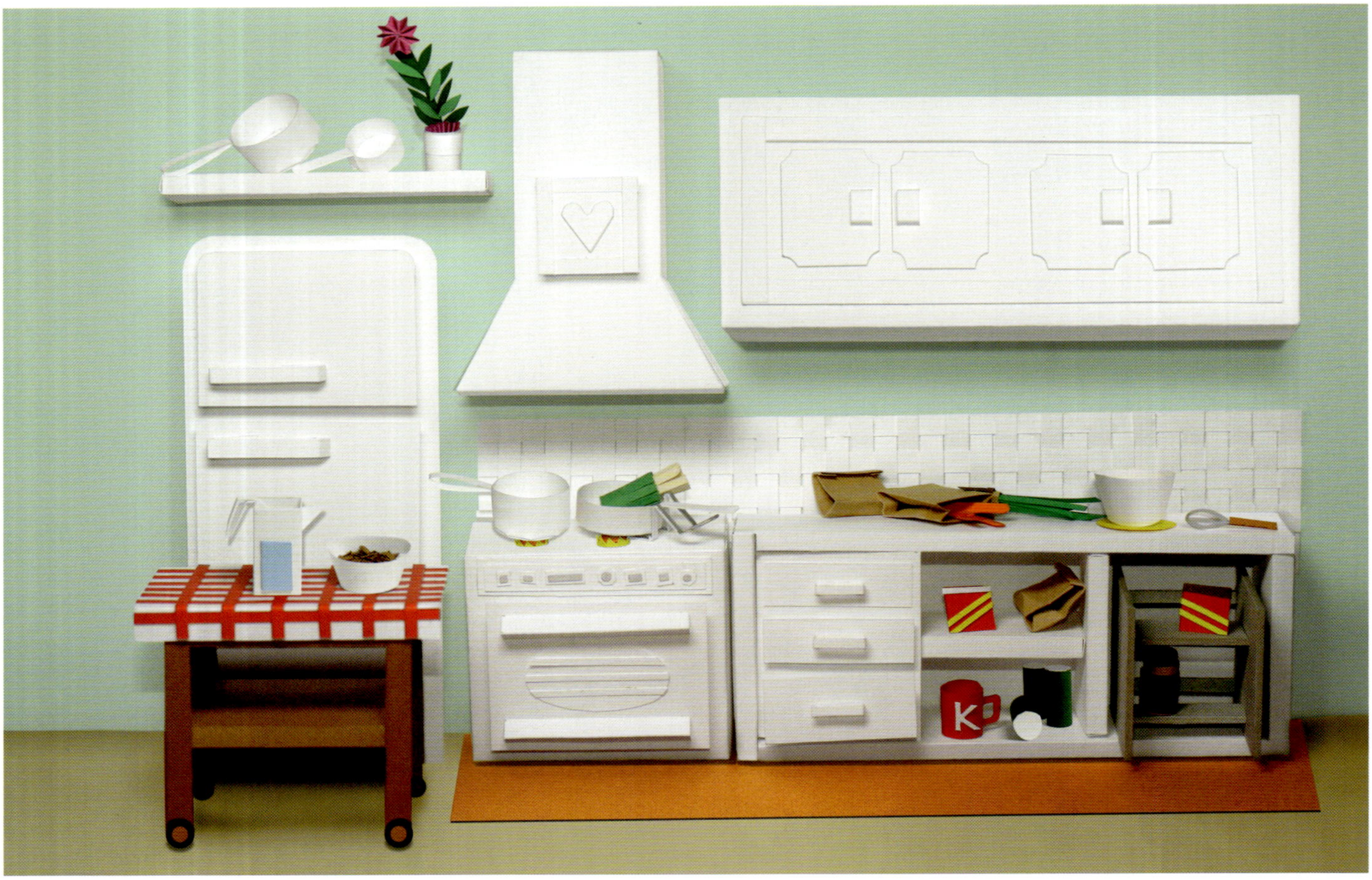

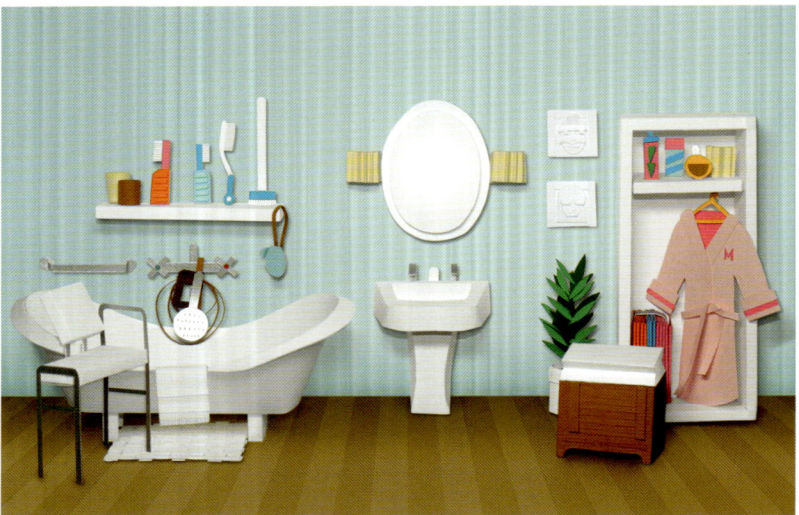
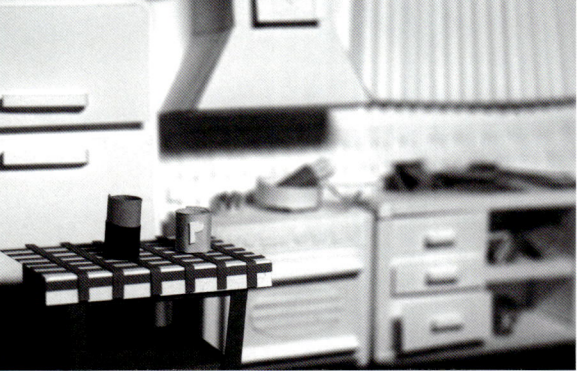
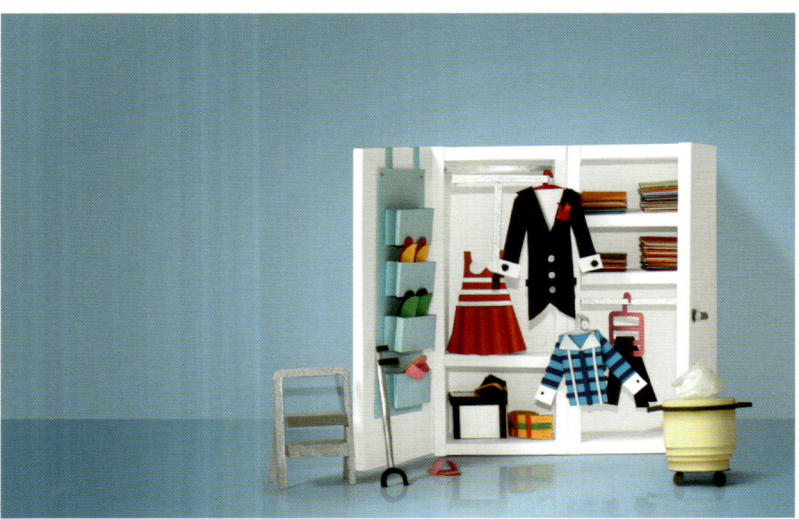
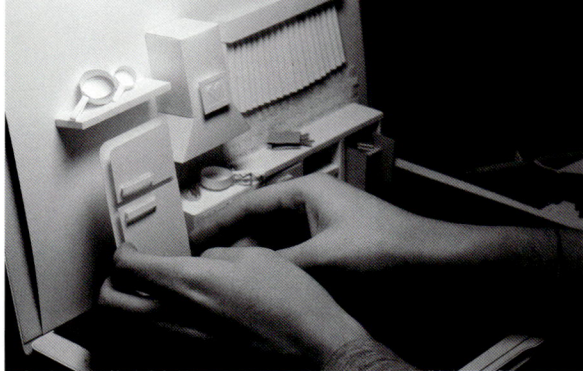

7. **Furniture Arthritis**

Illustration design for Arthritis Today, Lifestyle magazine.

Design Agency: Lobulo Design
Country: London, UK
Creative Director: Lobulo
Designer: Lobulo
Client: Arthritis Today
Photographer: Lobulo

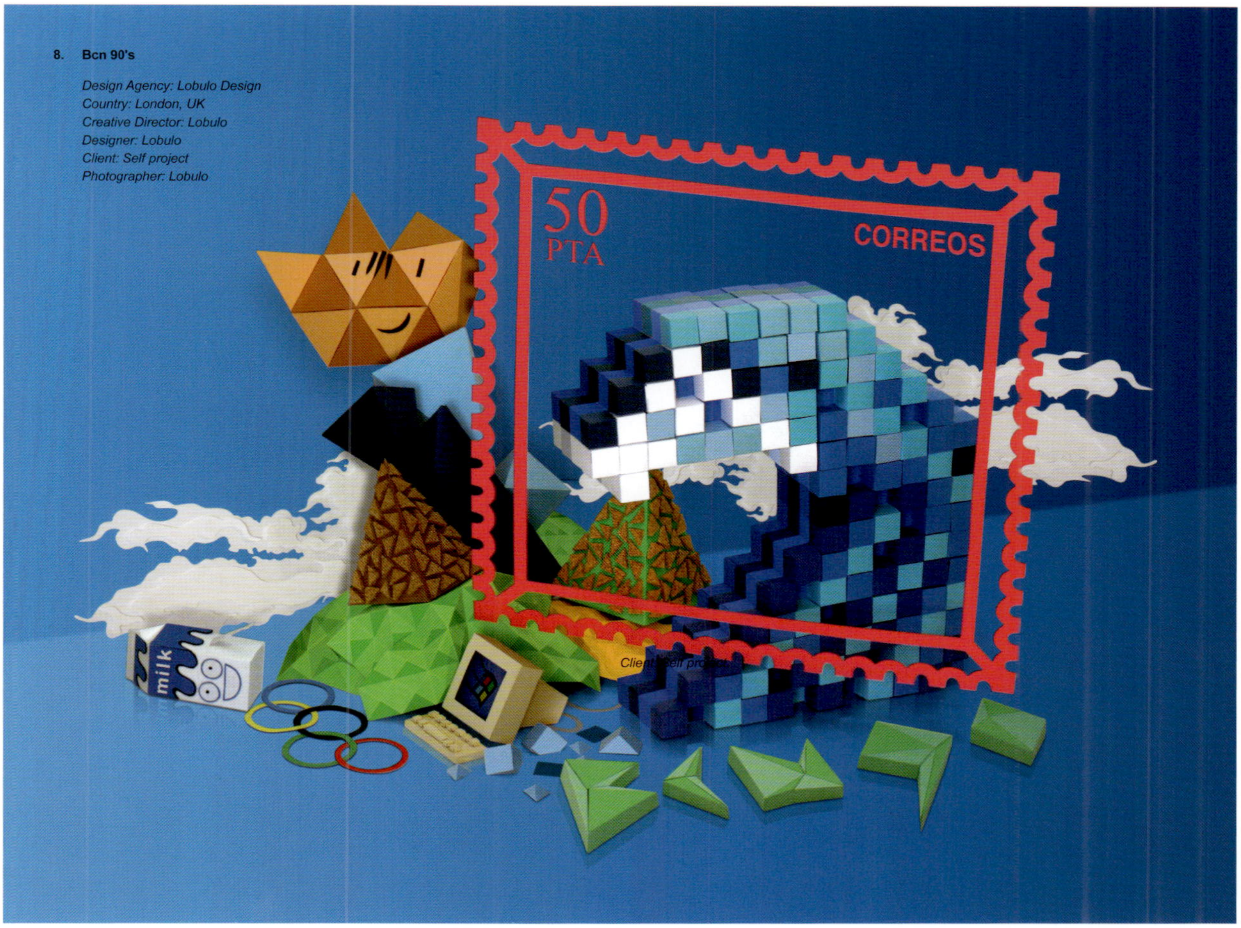

8. Bcn 90's

   Design Agency: Lobulo Design
   Country: London, UK
   Creative Director: Lobulo
   Designer: Lobulo
   Client: Self project
   Photographer: Lobulo

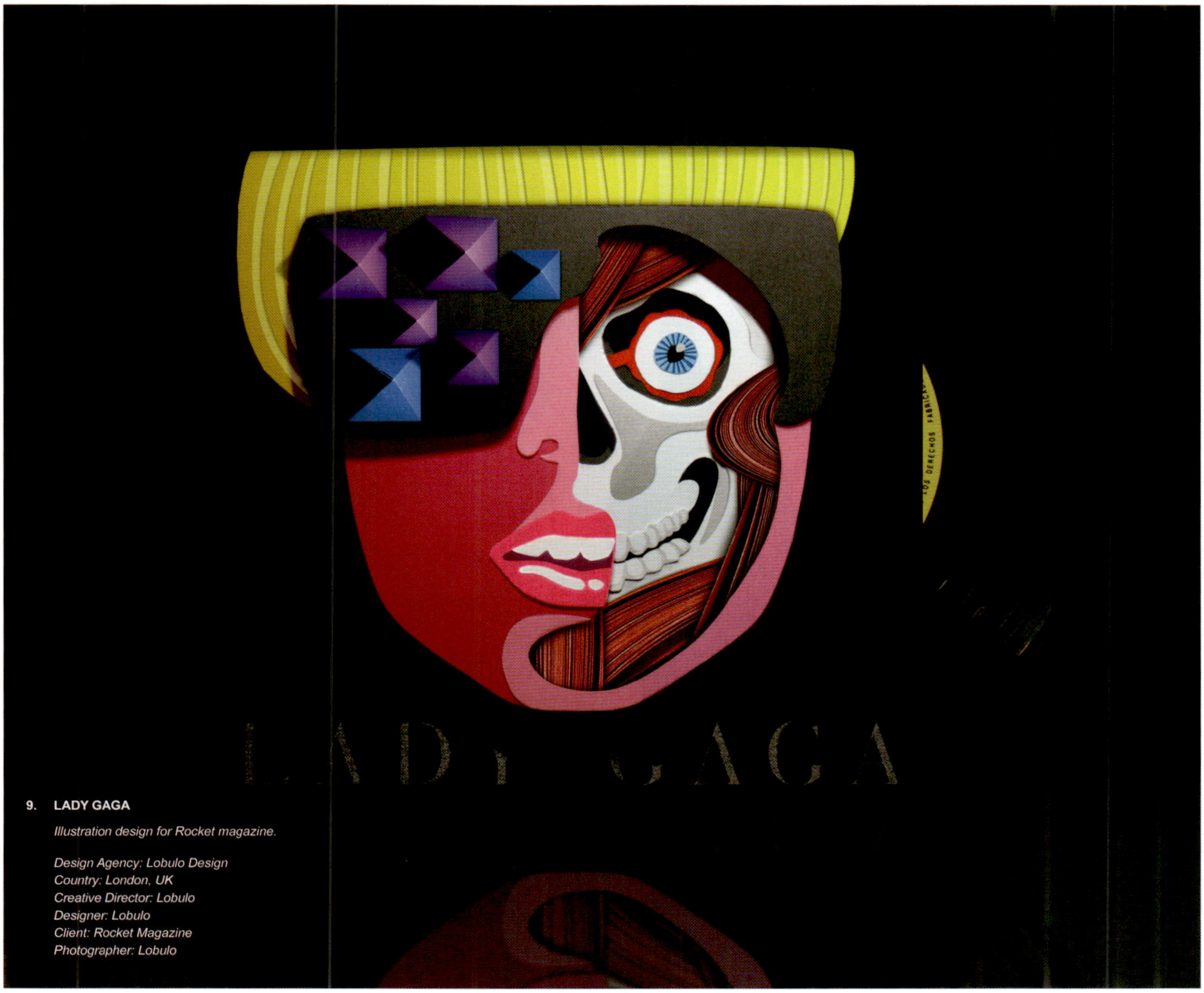

9. **LADY GAGA**

   Illustration design for Rocket magazine.

   Design Agency: Lobulo Design
   Country: London, UK
   Creative Director: Lobulo
   Designer: Lobulo
   Client: Rocket Magazine
   Photographer: Lobulo

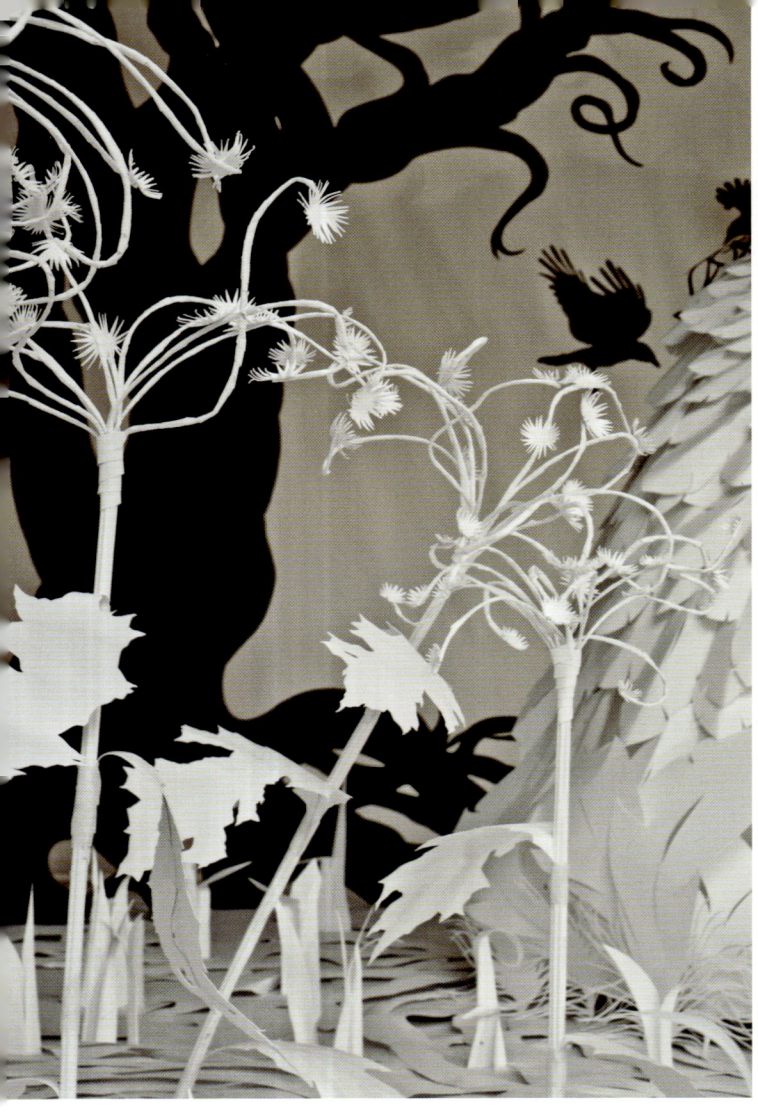
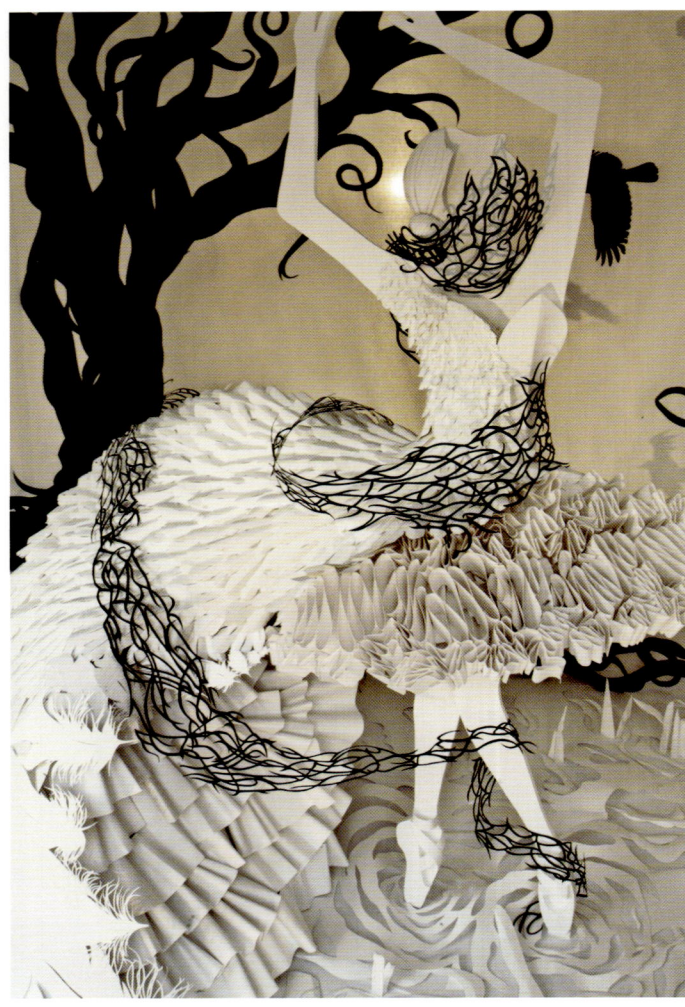
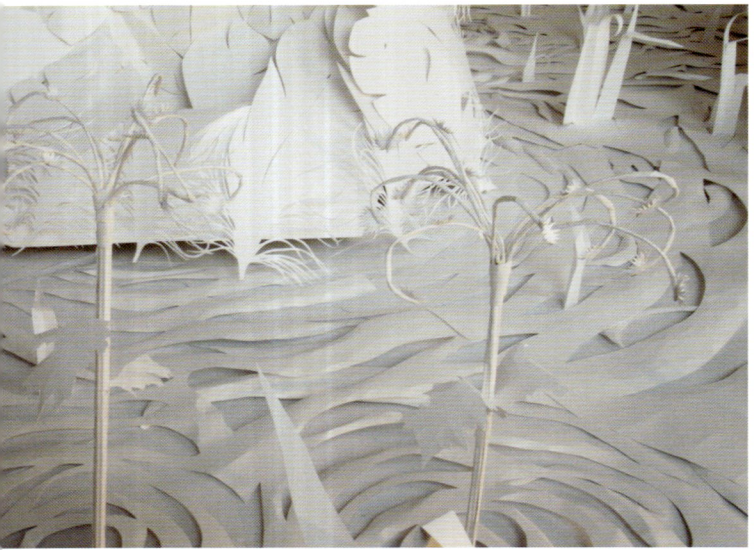
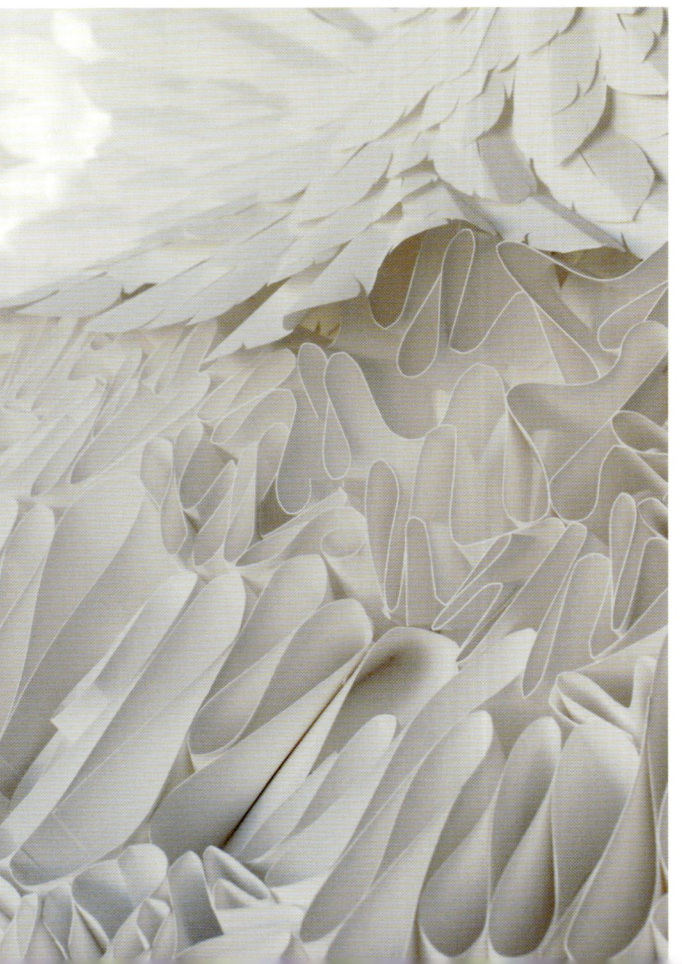

1. **Odette**

Mandy Smith is invited to create an installation for the festive period in 180 Amsterdam's space called Open. Playing with shadow, music and paper Mandy's twist on Swan lake is large scale display that reaches out to anyone who passes by.

Designer: Mandy Smith
Country: Amsterdam, Netherlands
Art Direction: Mandy Smith
Client: 180 Amsterdam

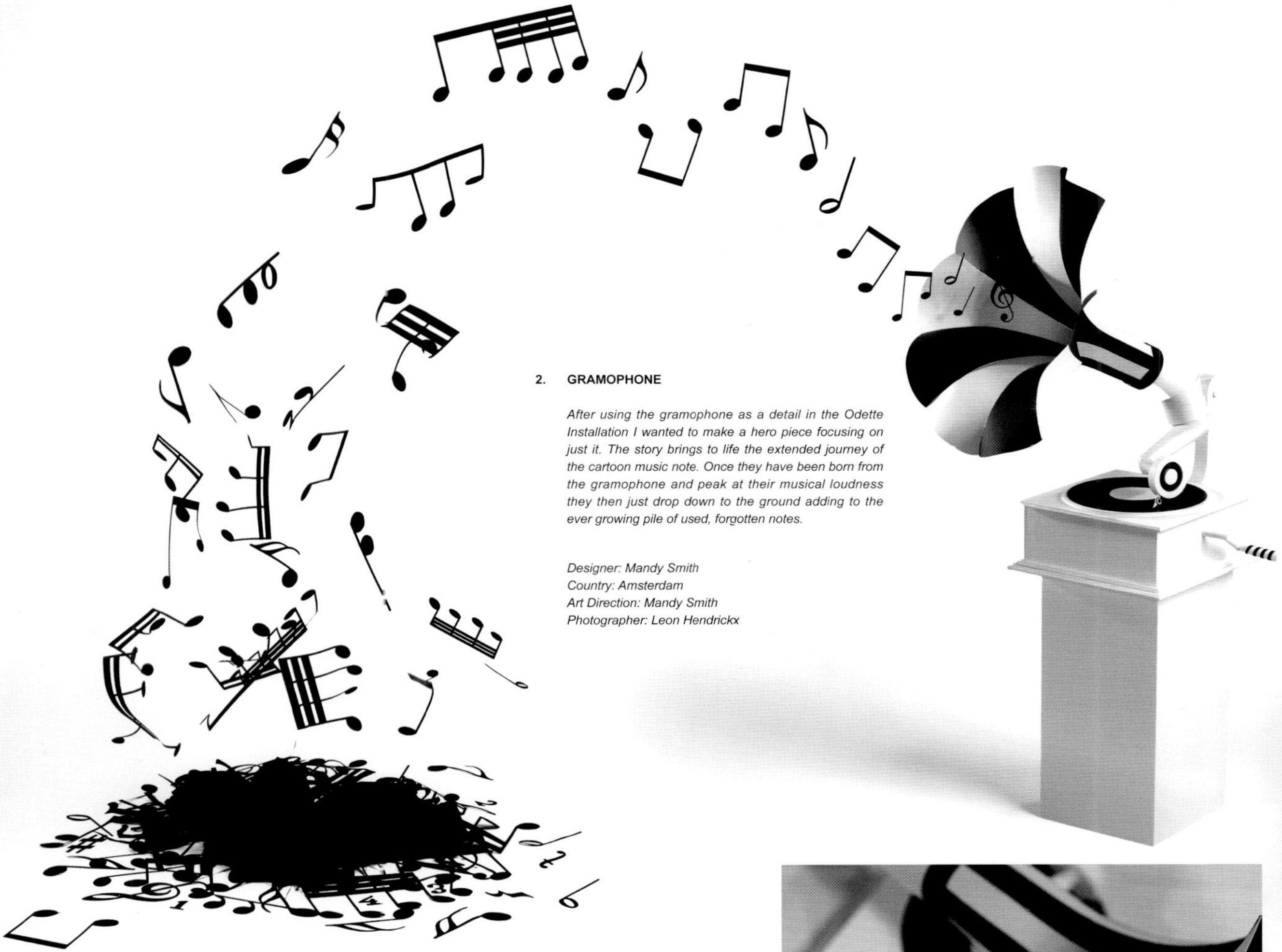

2. GRAMOPHONE

After using the gramophone as a detail in the Odette Installation I wanted to make a hero piece focusing on just it. The story brings to life the extended journey of the cartoon music note. Once they have been born from the gramophone and peak at their musical loudness they then just drop down to the ground adding to the ever growing pile of used, forgotten notes.

Designer: Mandy Smith
Country: Amsterdam
Art Direction: Mandy Smith
Photographer: Leon Hendrickx

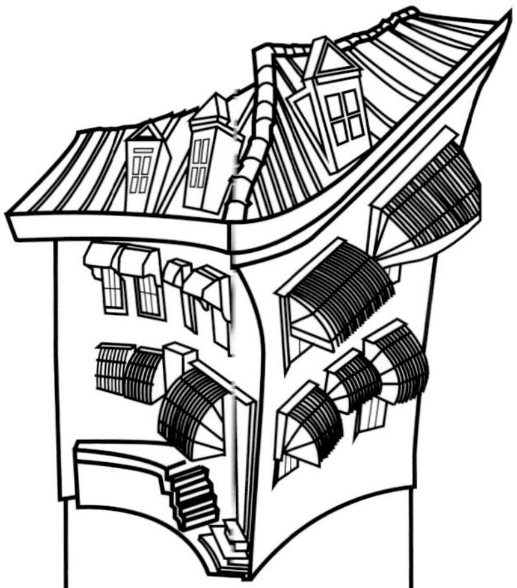

1. Odette
2. Gramophone
3. Pop Up
4. Rumpelstiltskin
5. The Move
6. Paper House
7. Waterstones

---Mandy Smith

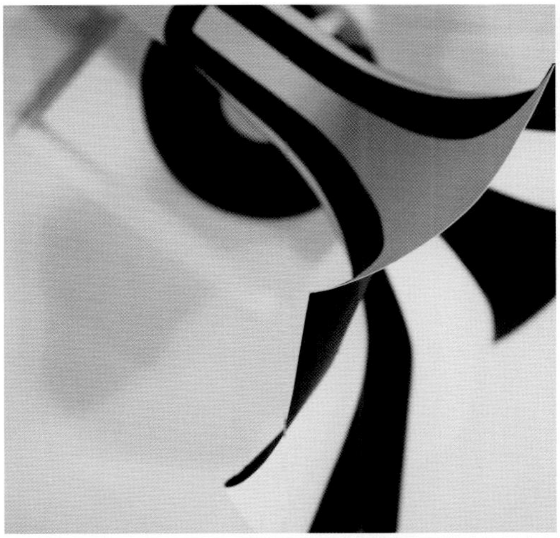

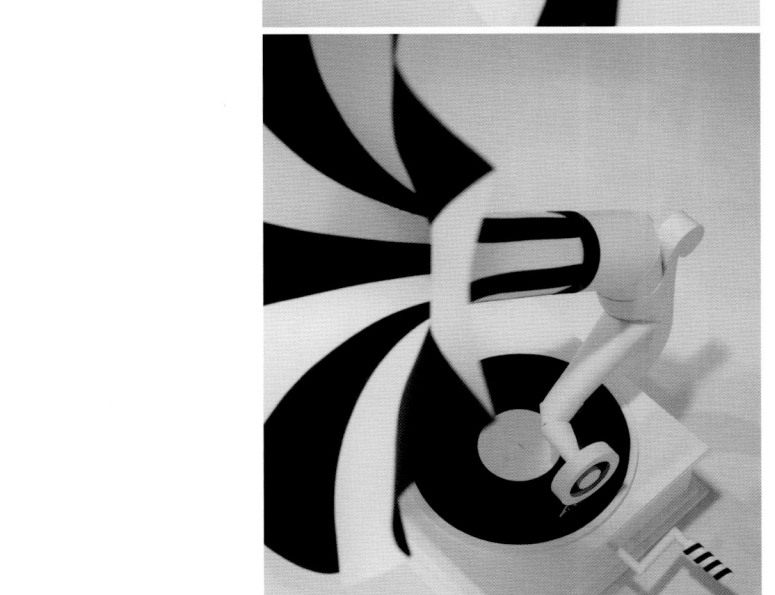

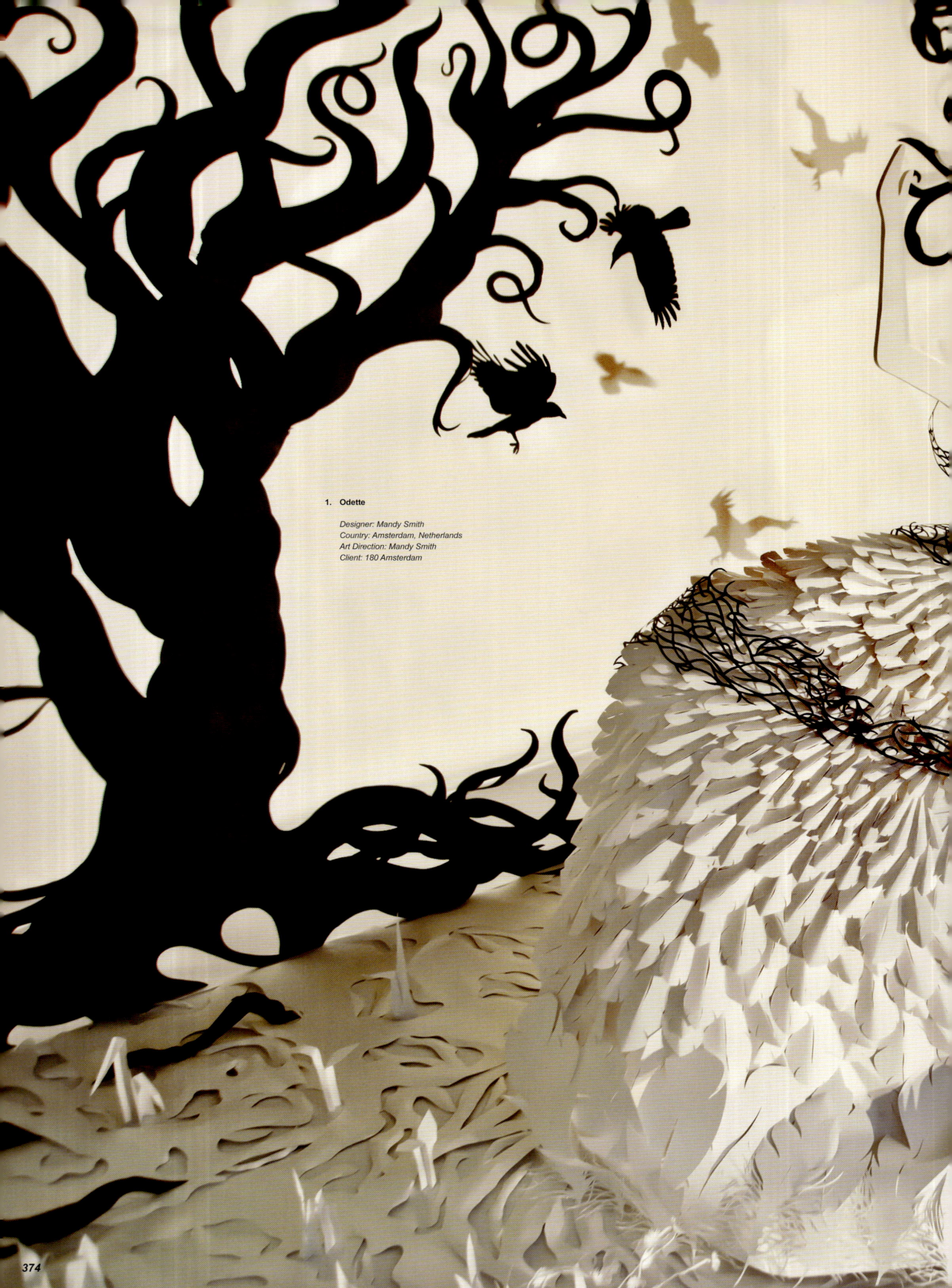

1. Odette

Designer: Mandy Smith
Country: Amsterdam, Netherlands
Art Direction: Mandy Smith
Client: 180 Amsterdam

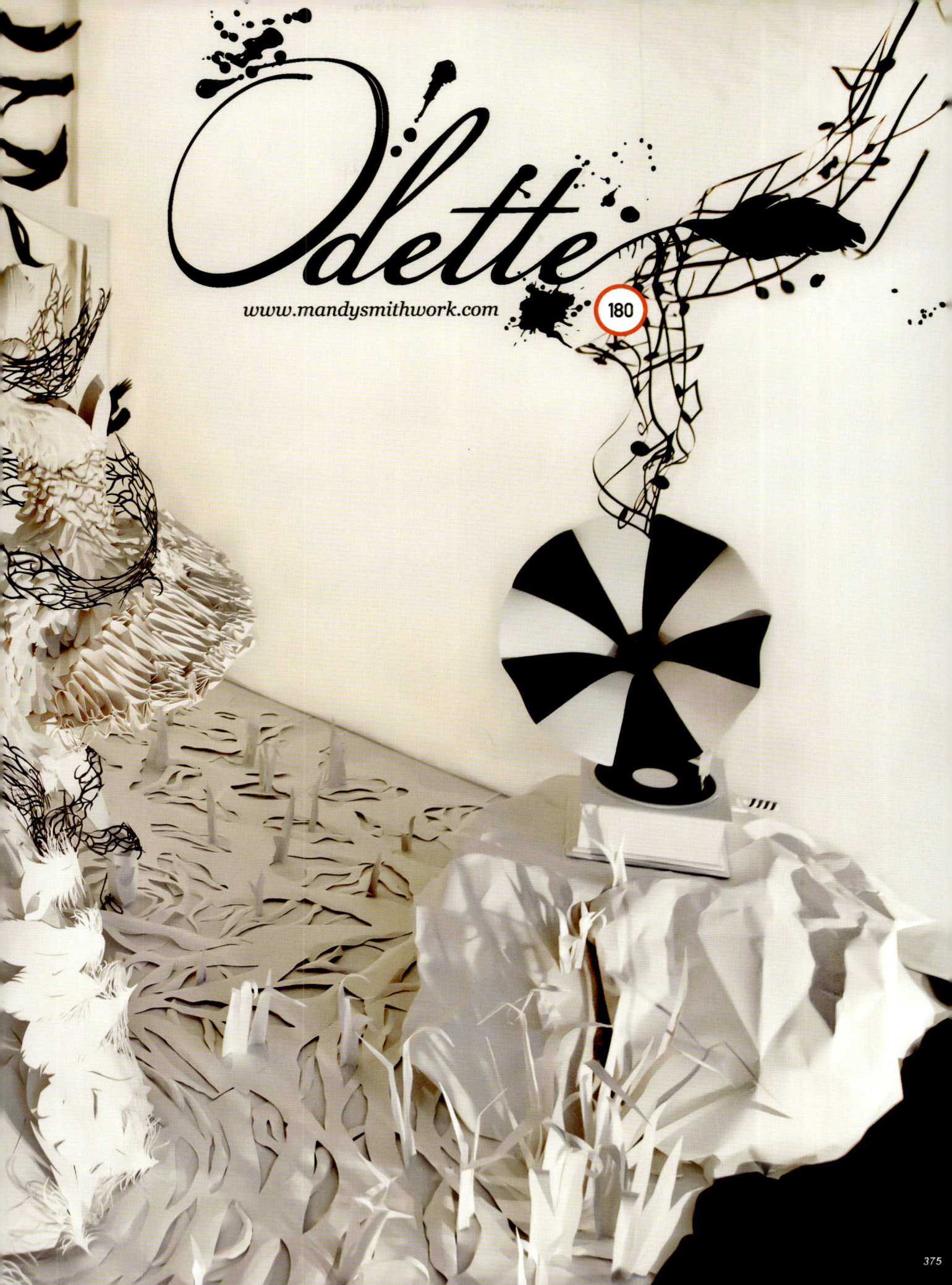

3. POP UP

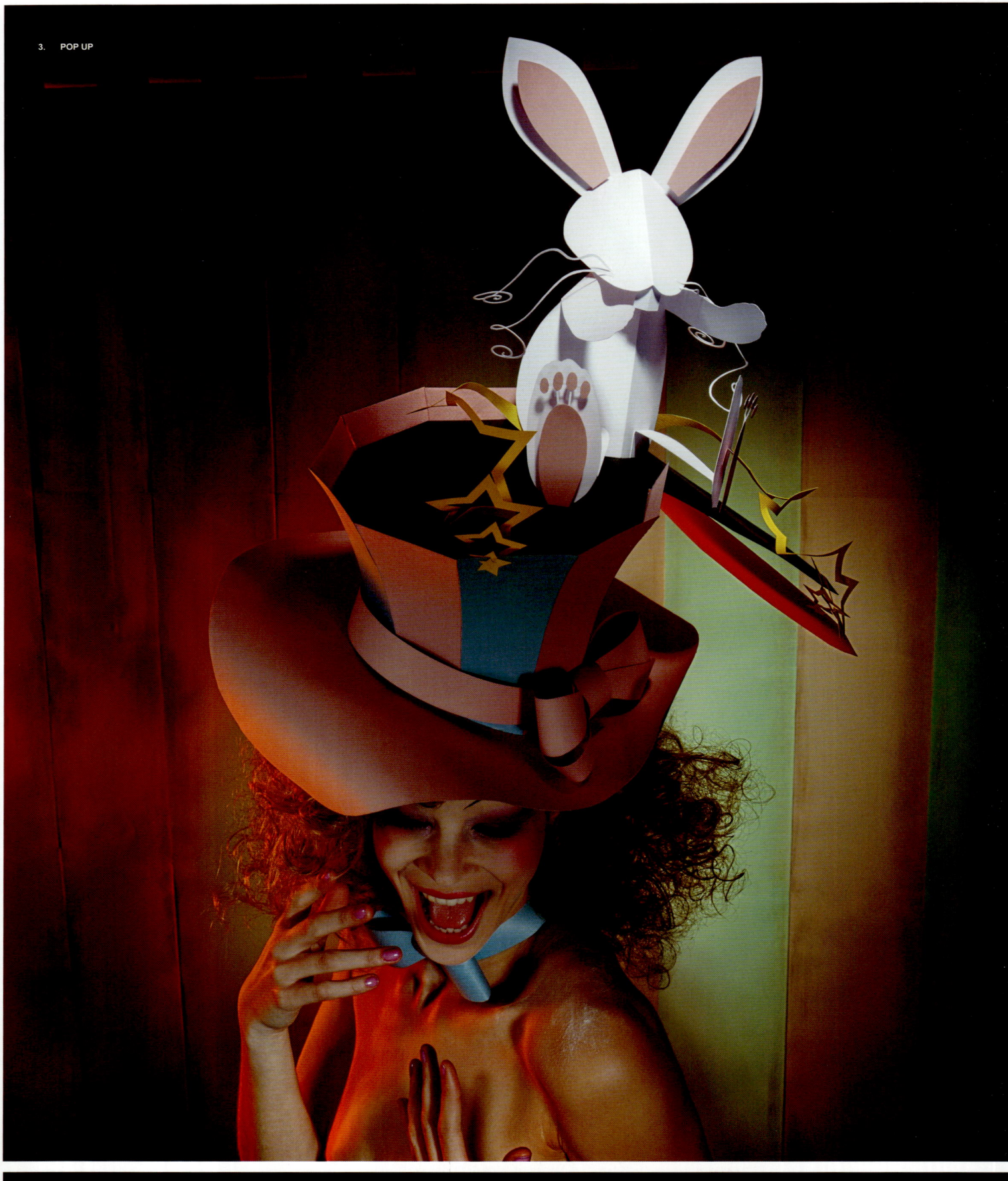

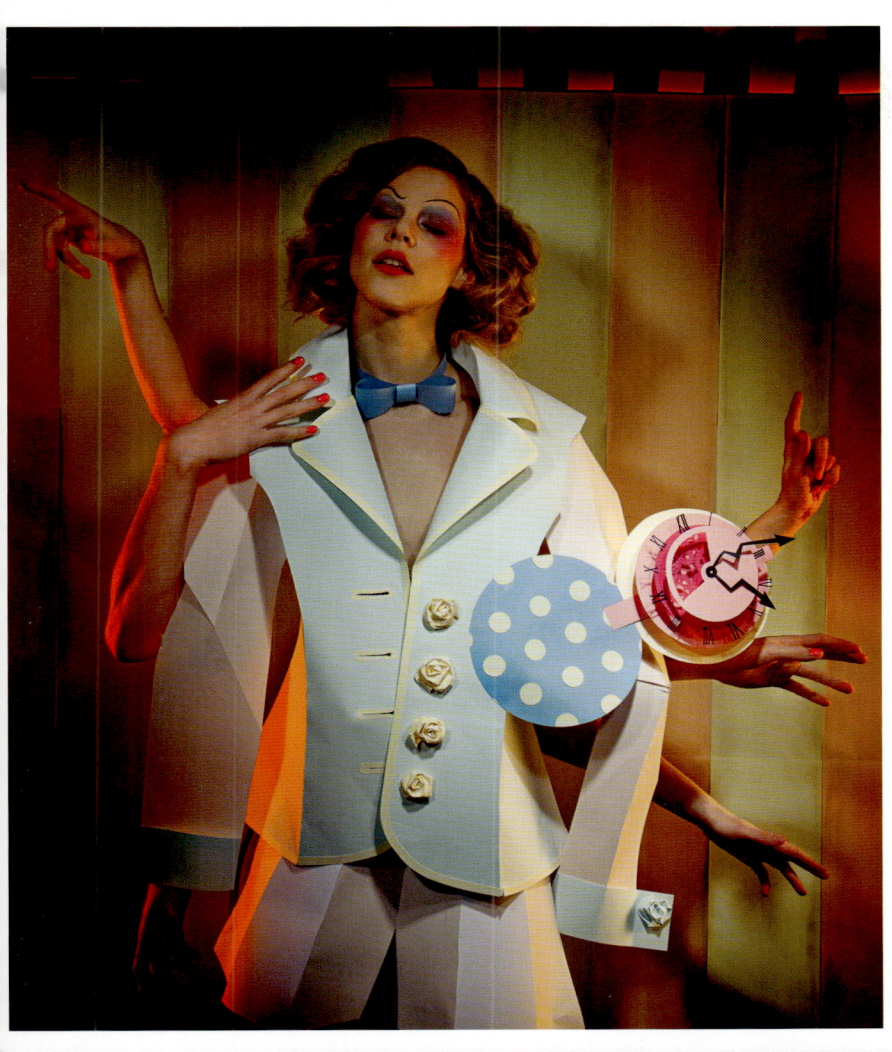

3. **Pop Up**

   Designer: Mandy Smith
   Country: Amsterdam, Netherlands
   Art Direction: Mandy Smith
   Photographer: Leon Hendrickx
   Model: Eke Bon
   Make-Up Artist: Corinne van der Heijden

4. **Rumpelstiltskin**

   Designer: Mandy Smith
   Country: Amsterdam, Netherlands
   Art Direction: Mandy Smith
   Photographer: Leon Hendrickx
   Model: Dorothy Bany
   Make-Up Artist: Anita Jolles

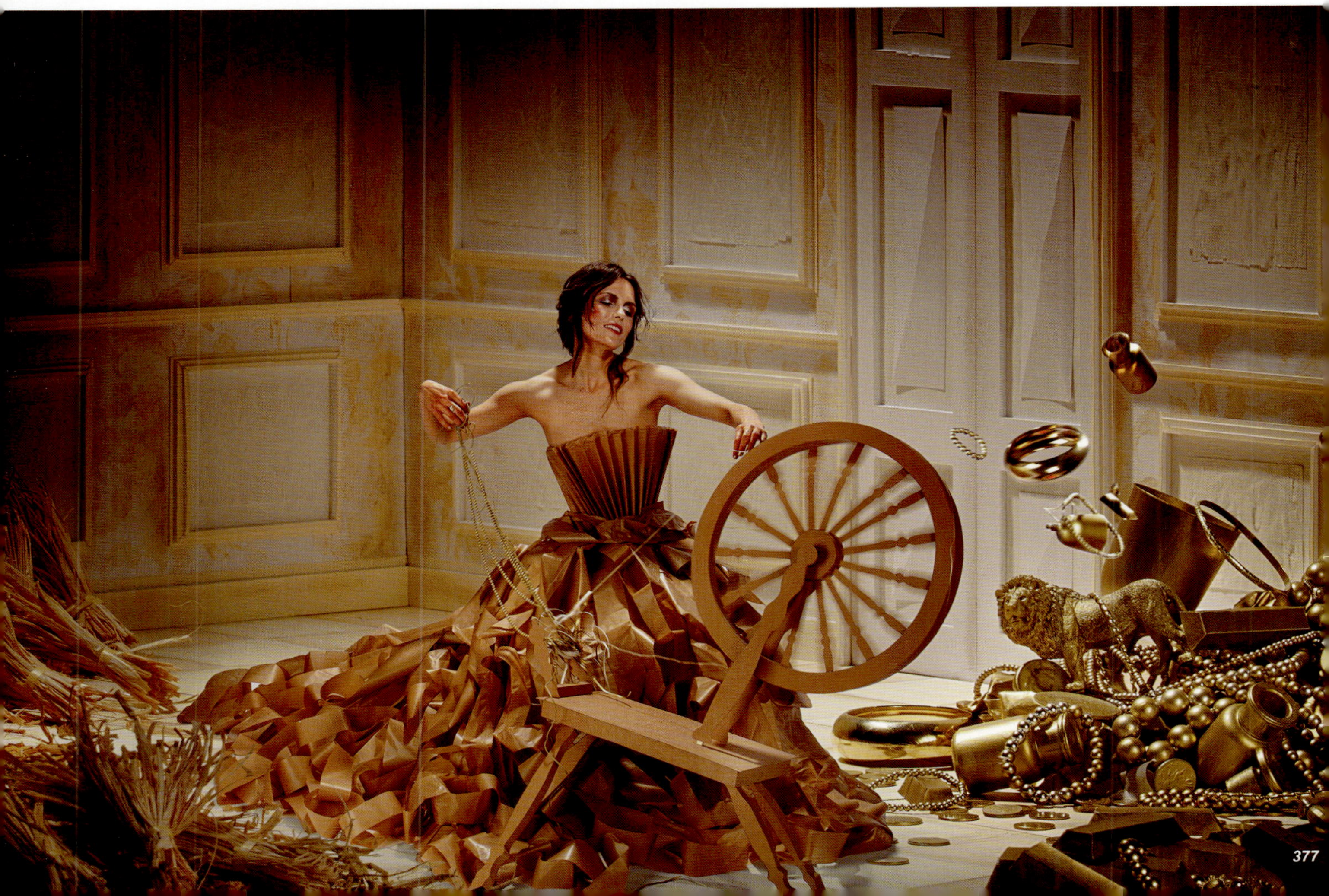

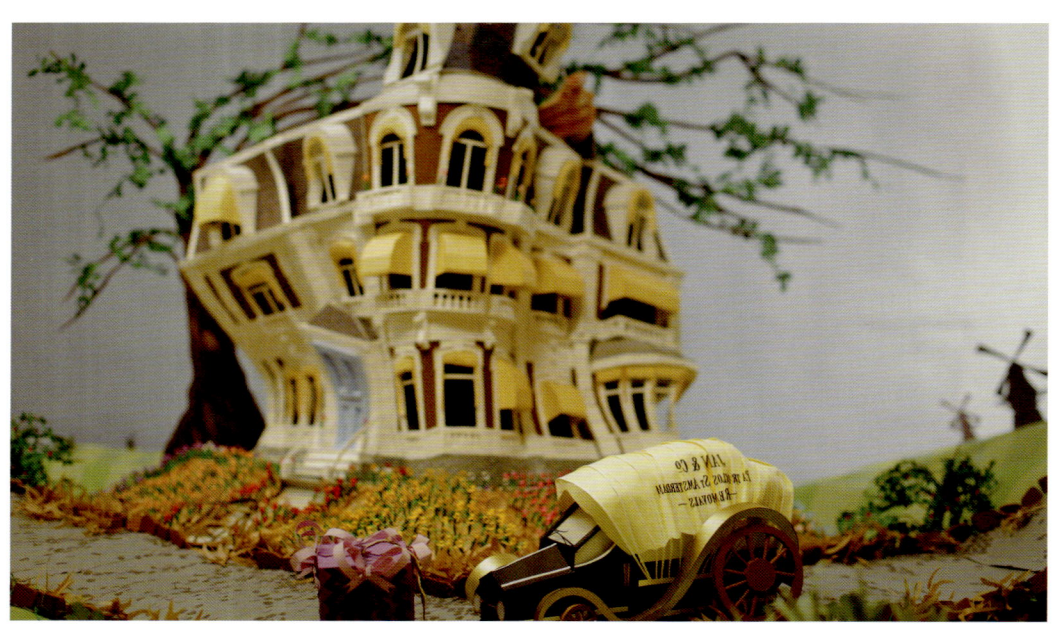

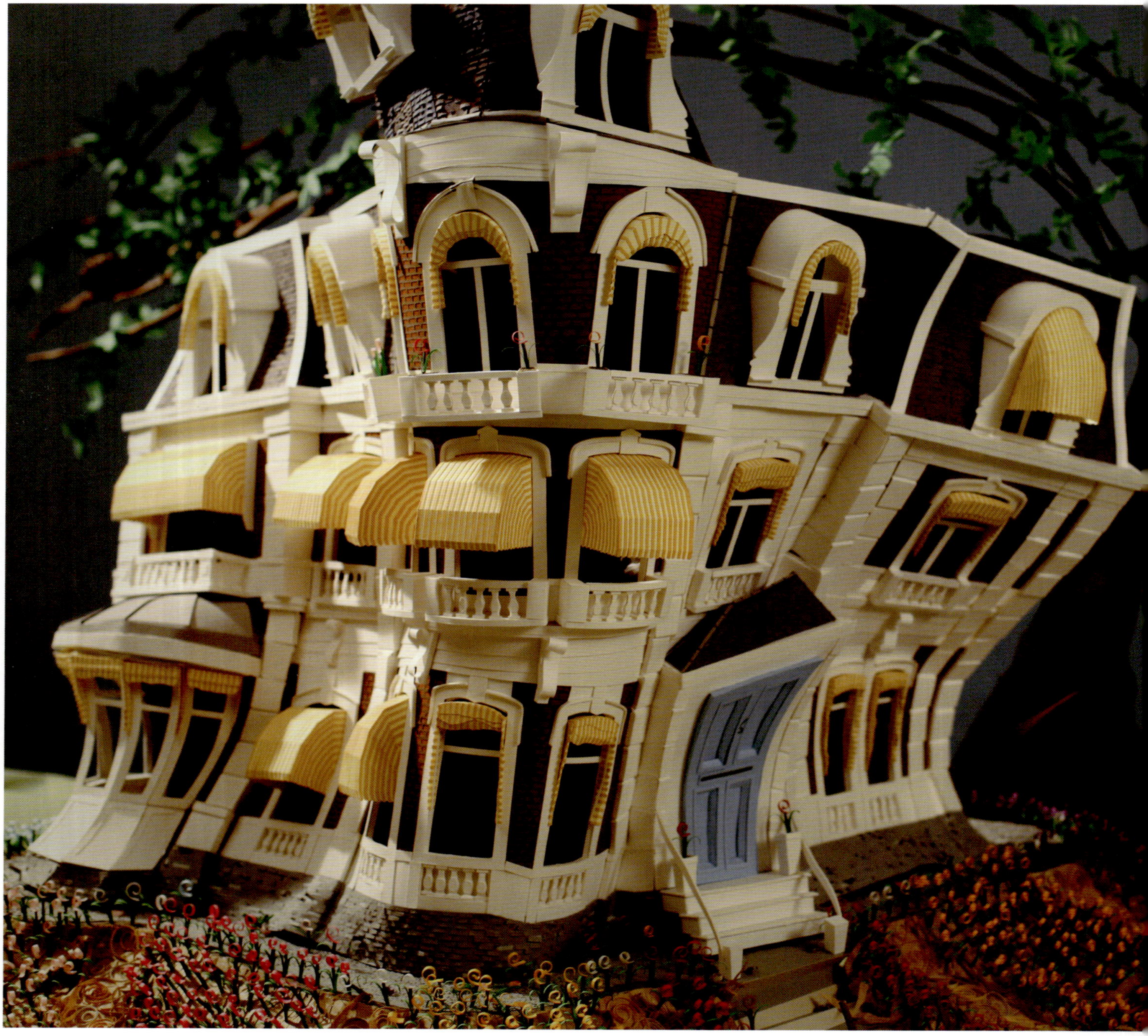

5. **The Move**

   Mandy Smith Directs and Art Directs her first short film, inspired by moving in Amsterdam. A self produced piece where everything was created by hand using colour paper.
   These pictures are a documentation of props and sets used to tell that were used in the animation.

   Designer: Mandy Smith
   Country: Amsterdam, Netherlands
   Art Direction: Mandy Smith

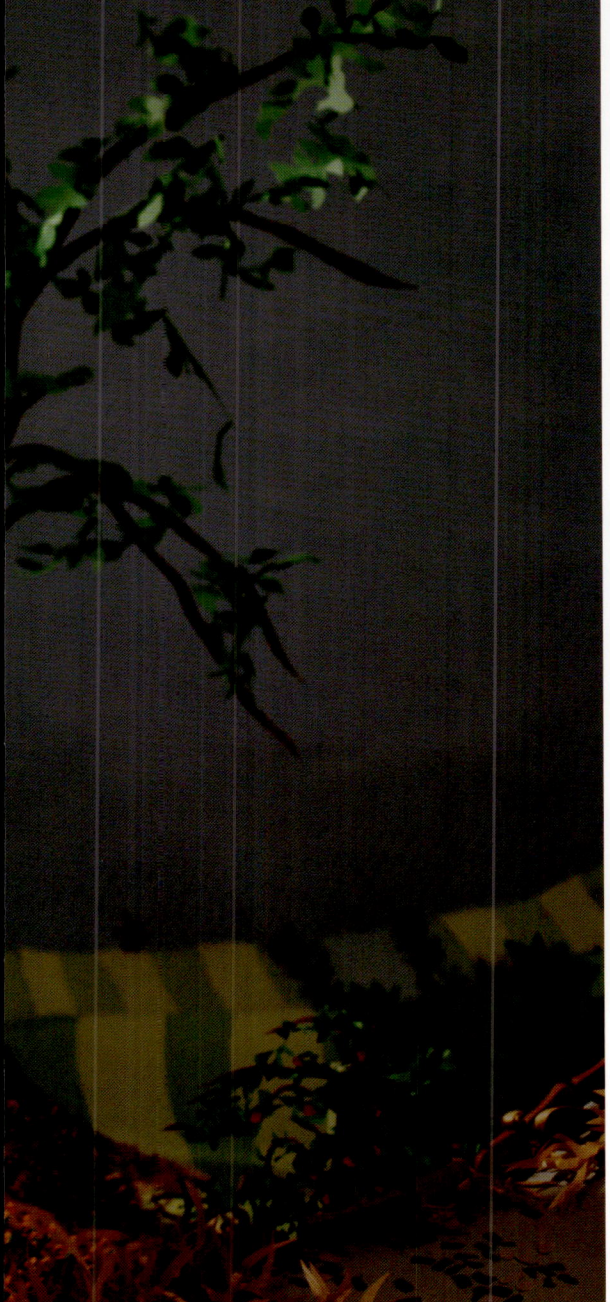
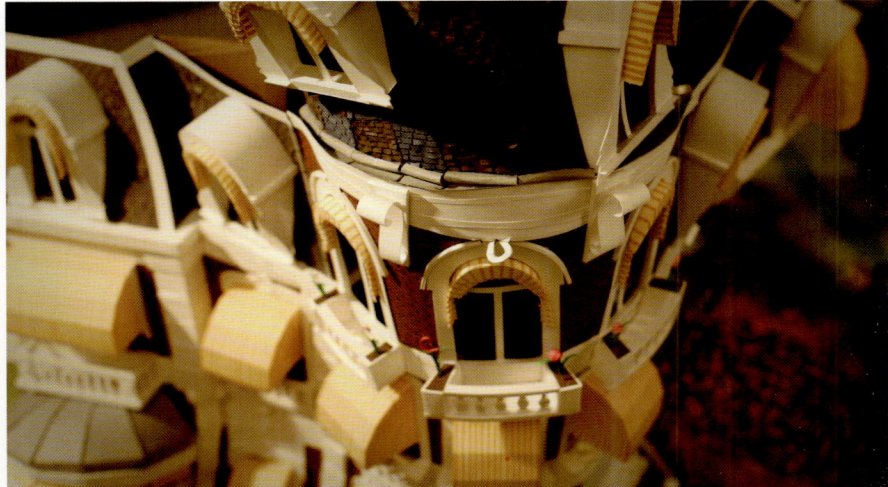
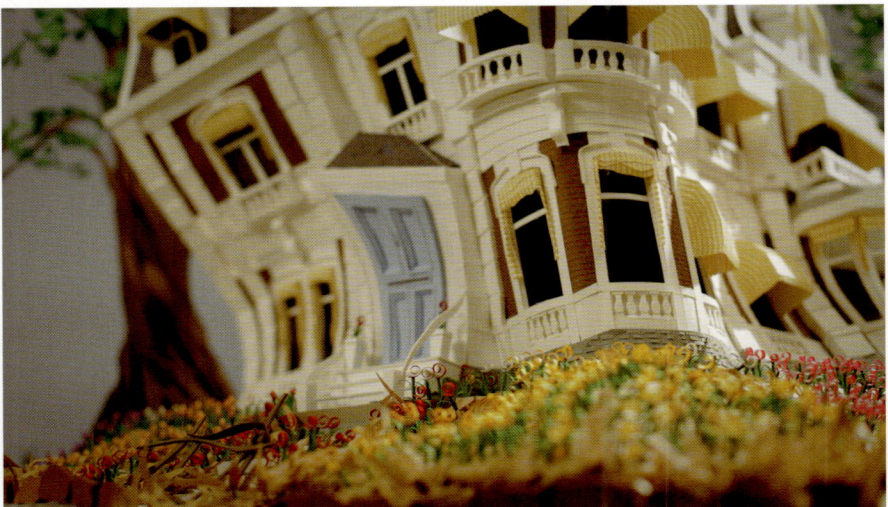

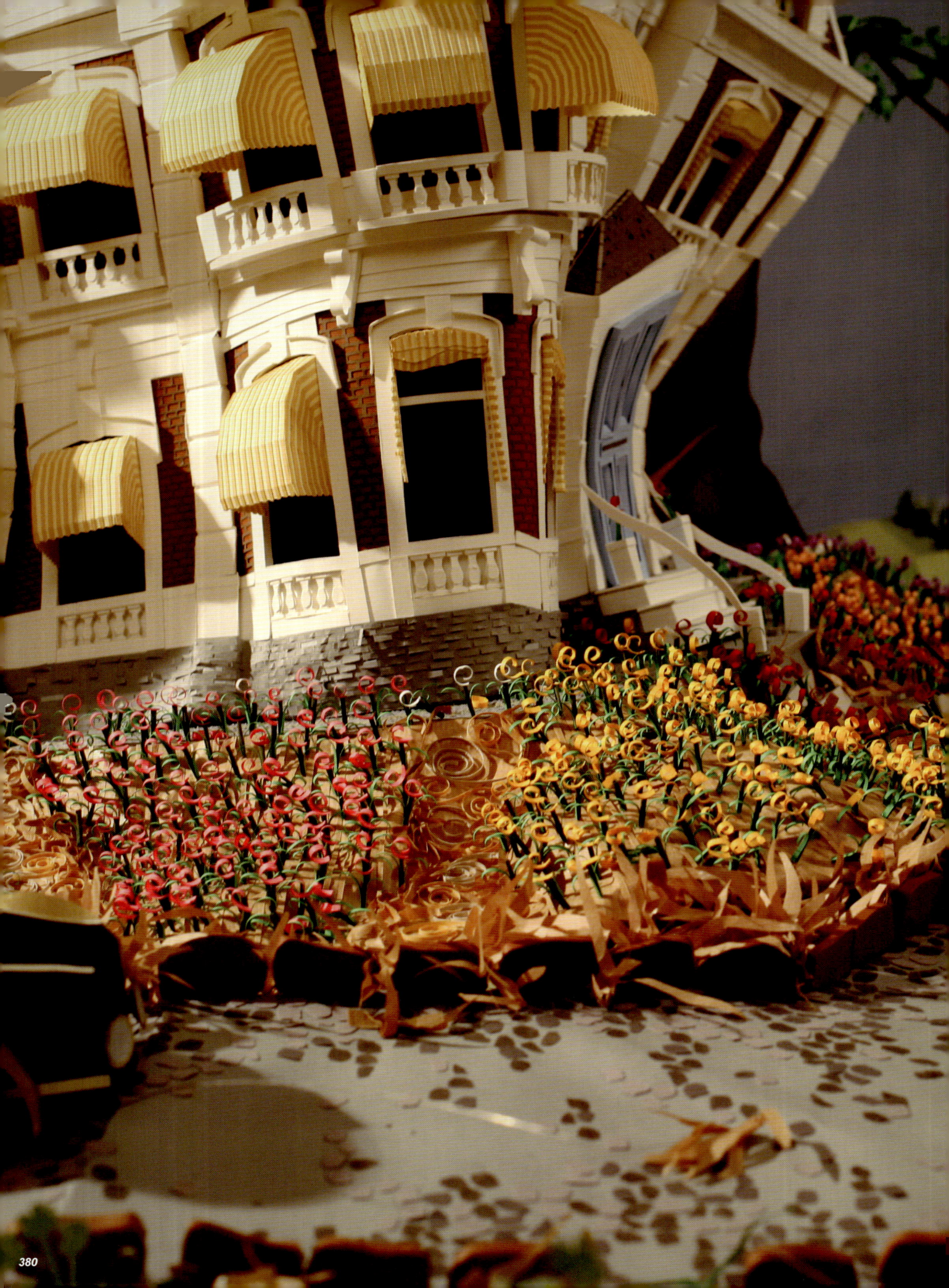

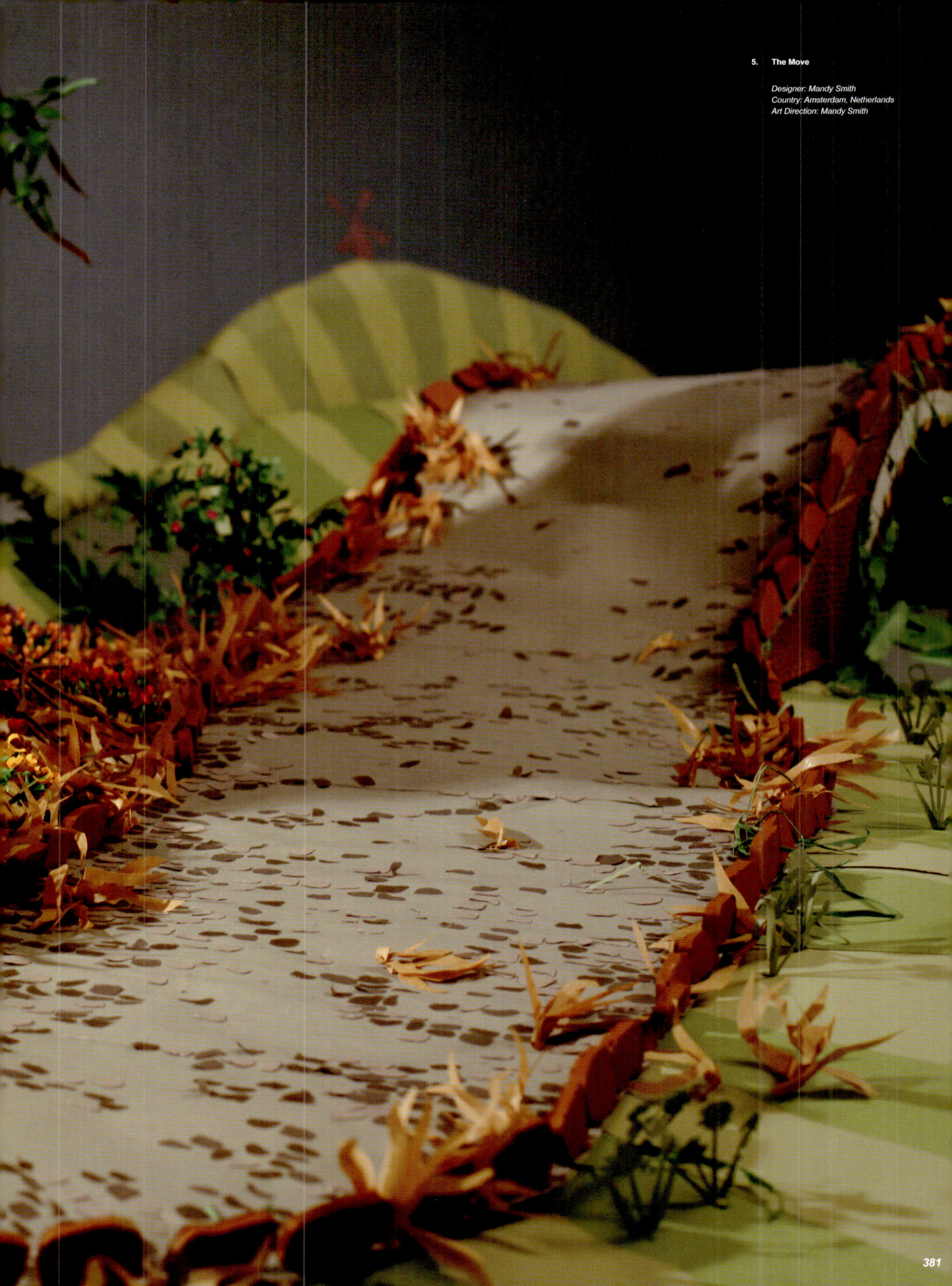

5. The Move

Designer: Mandy Smith
Country: Amsterdam, Netherlands
Art Direction: Mandy Smith

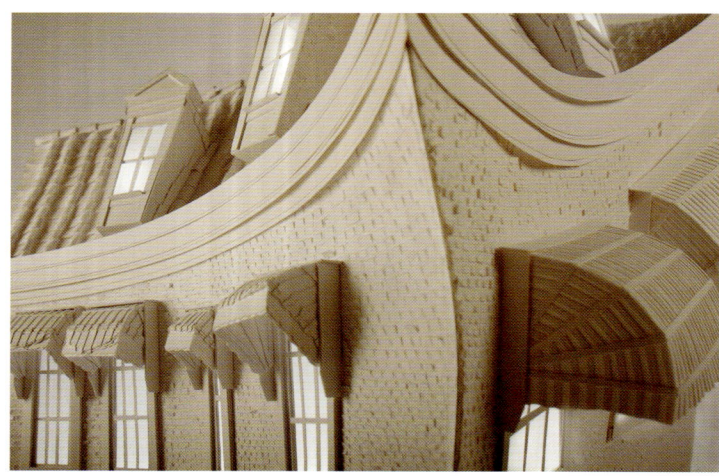

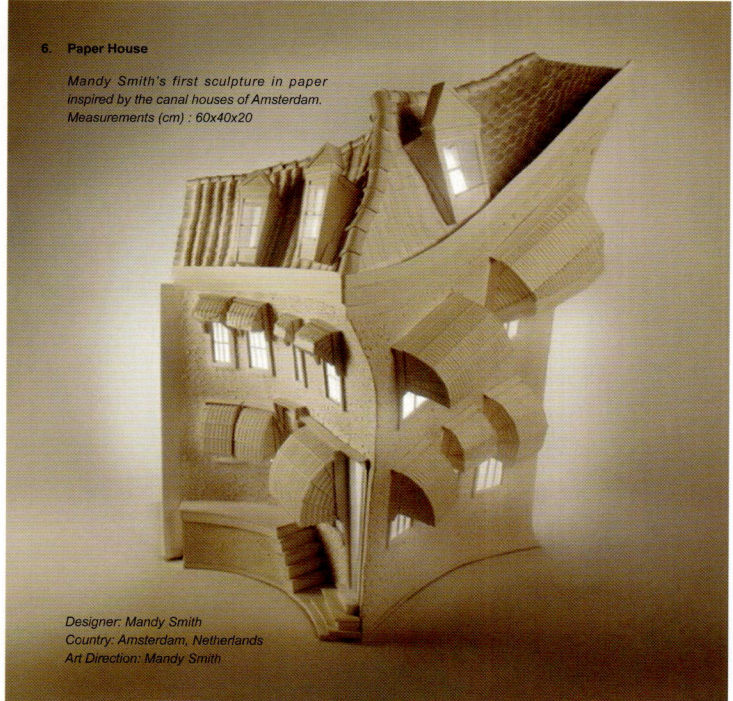

6. **Paper House**

*Mandy Smith's first sculpture in paper inspired by the canal houses of Amsterdam.
Measurements (cm) : 60x40x20*

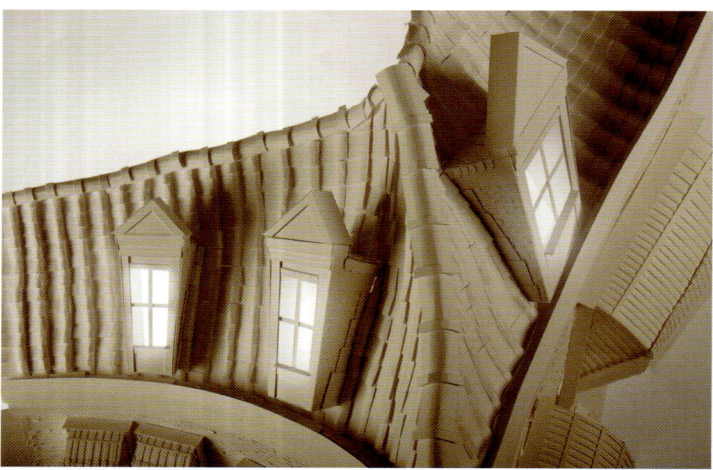

Designer: Mandy Smith
Country: Amsterdam, Netherlands
Art Direction: Mandy Smith

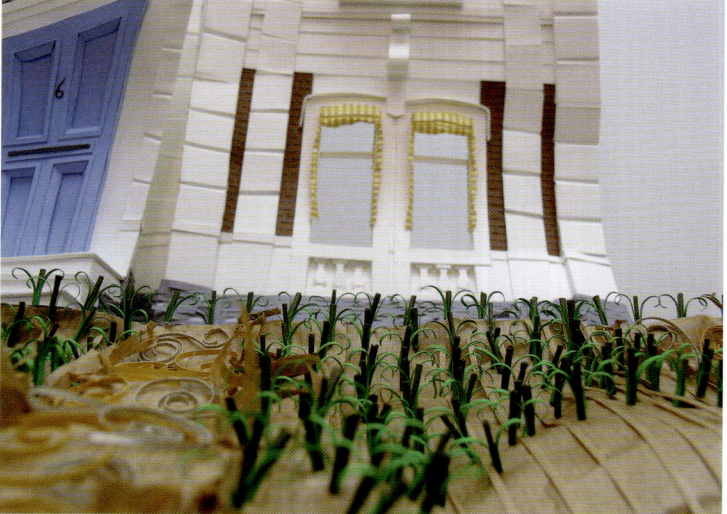

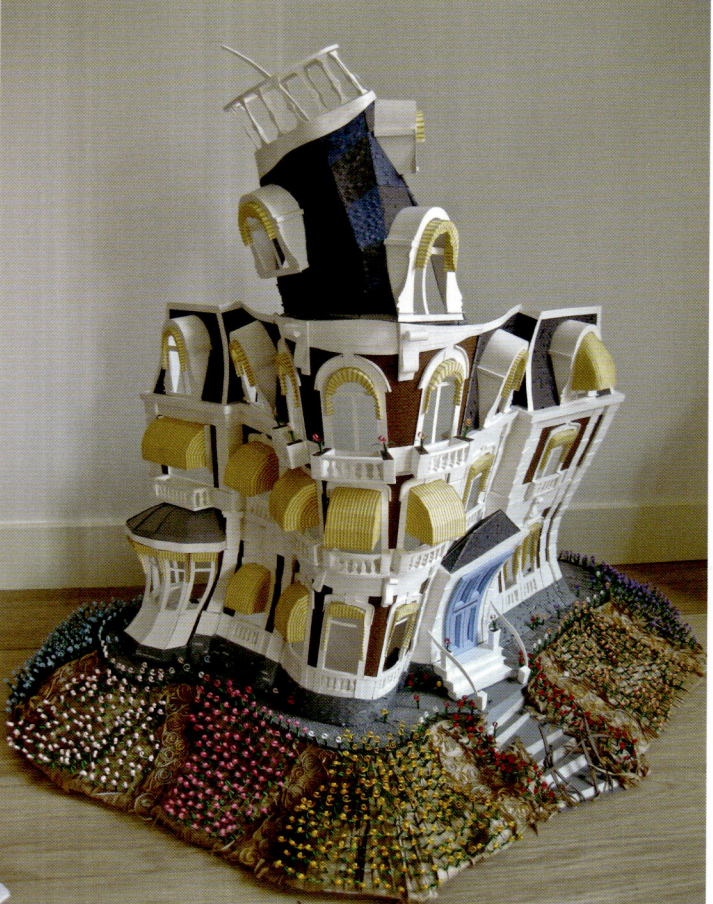

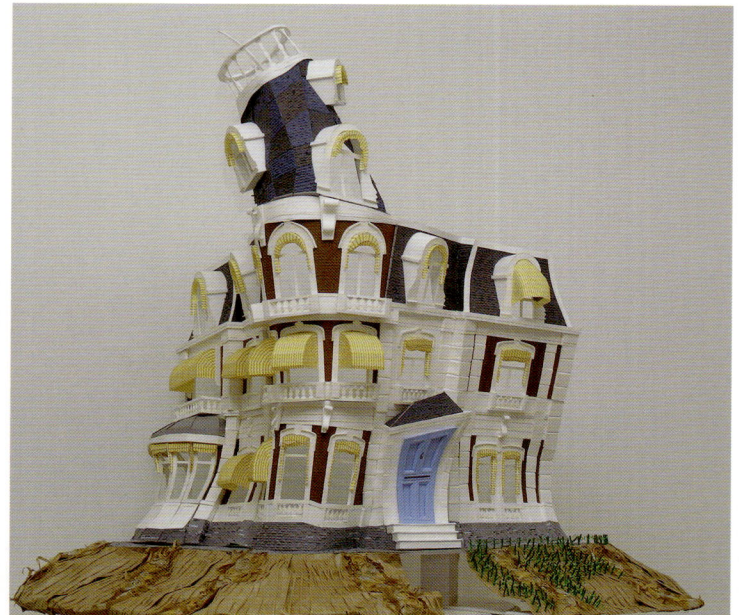

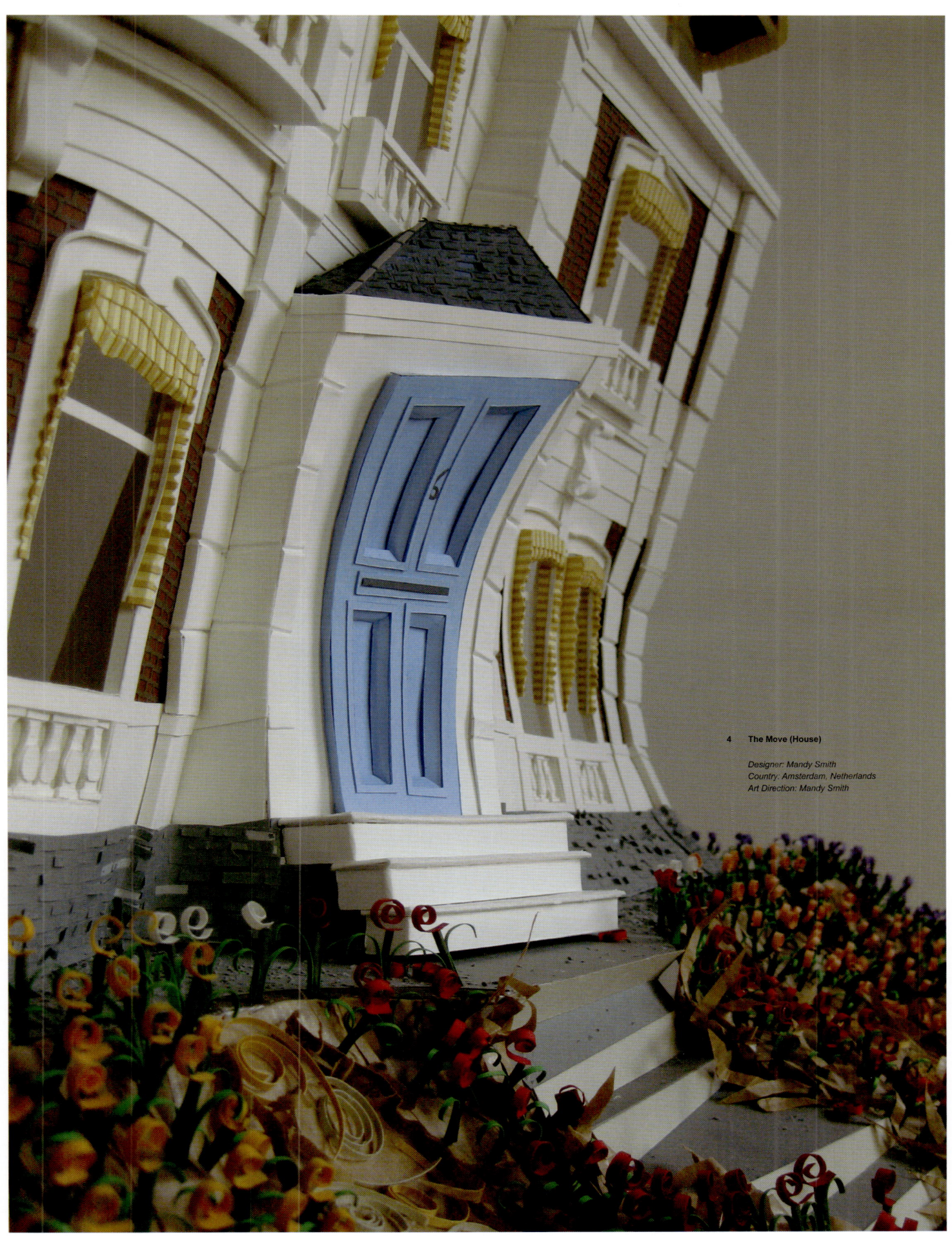

4   The Move (House)

Designer: Mandy Smith
Country: Amsterdam, Netherlands
Art Direction: Mandy Smith

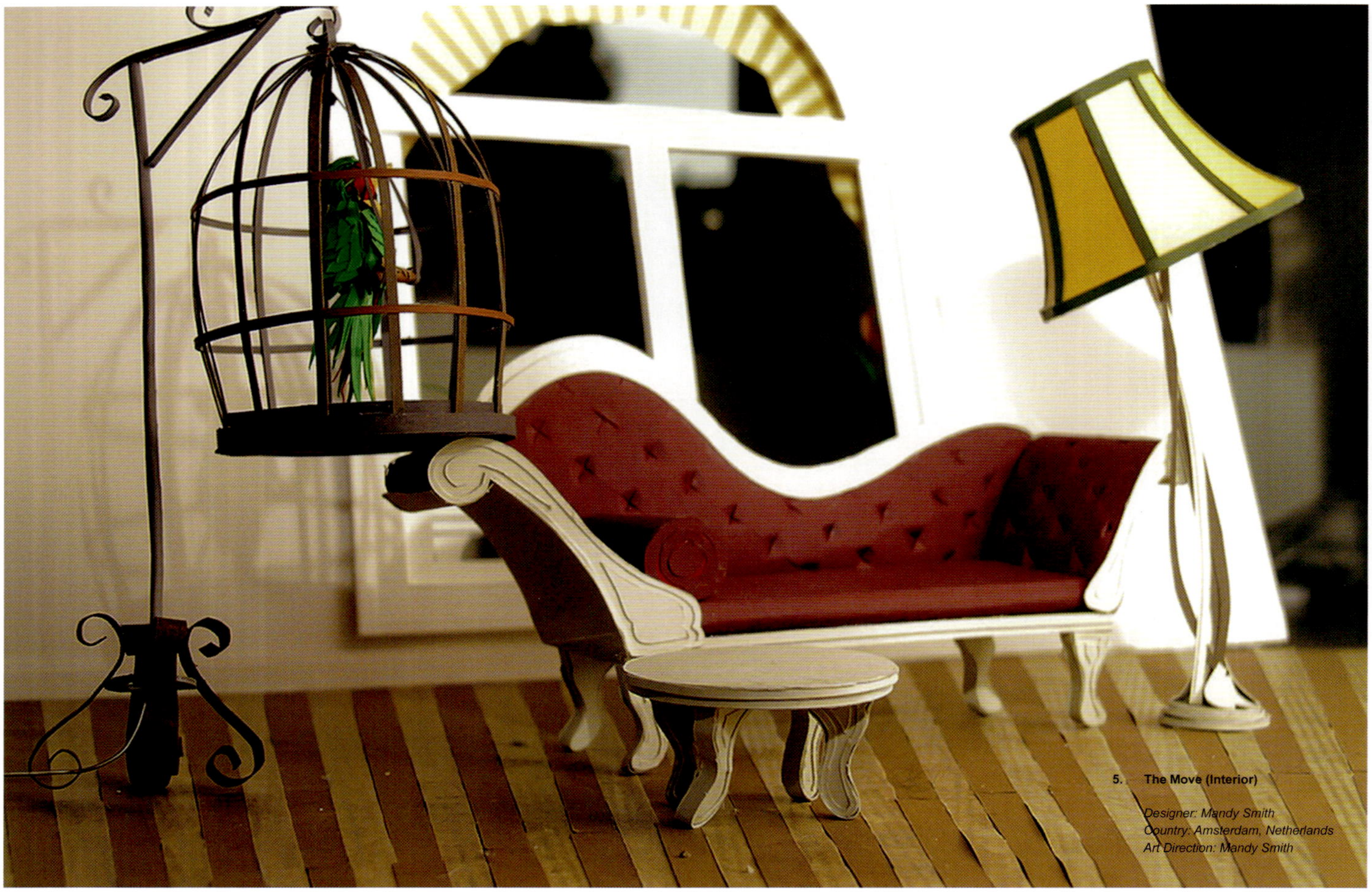

5. The Move (Interior)
Designer: Mandy Smith
Country: Amsterdam, Netherlands
Art Direction: Mandy Smith

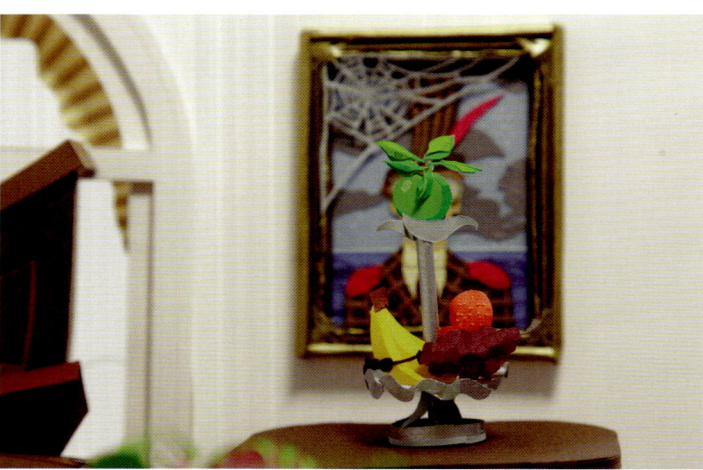
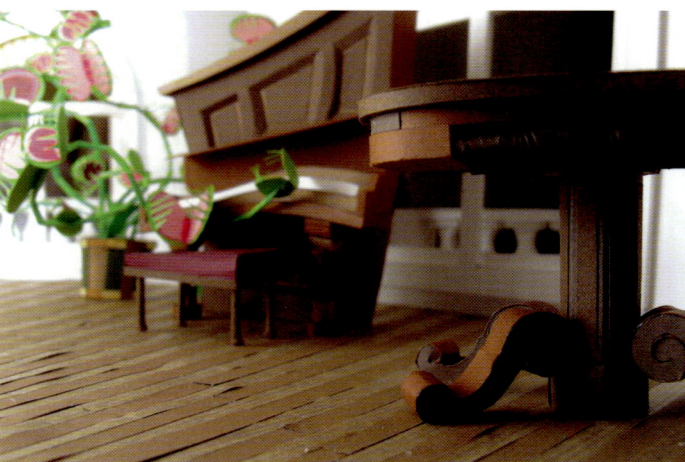
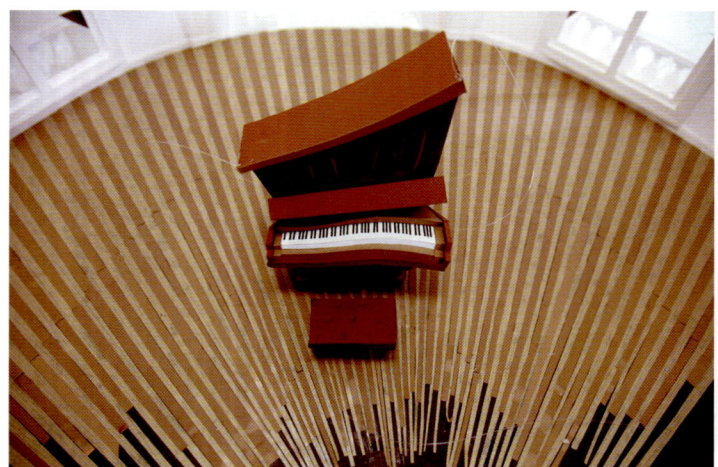
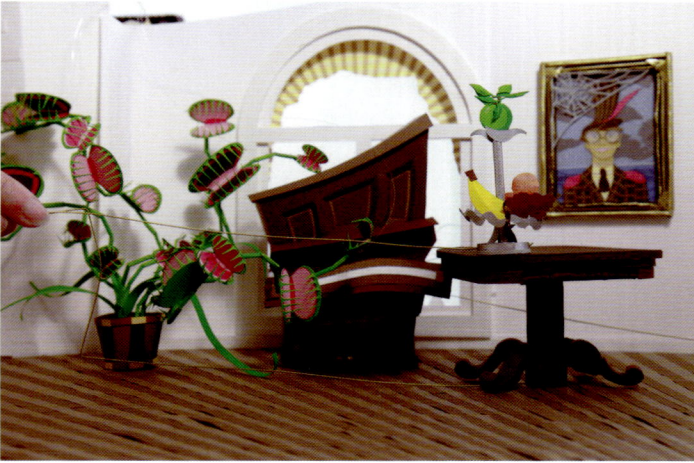

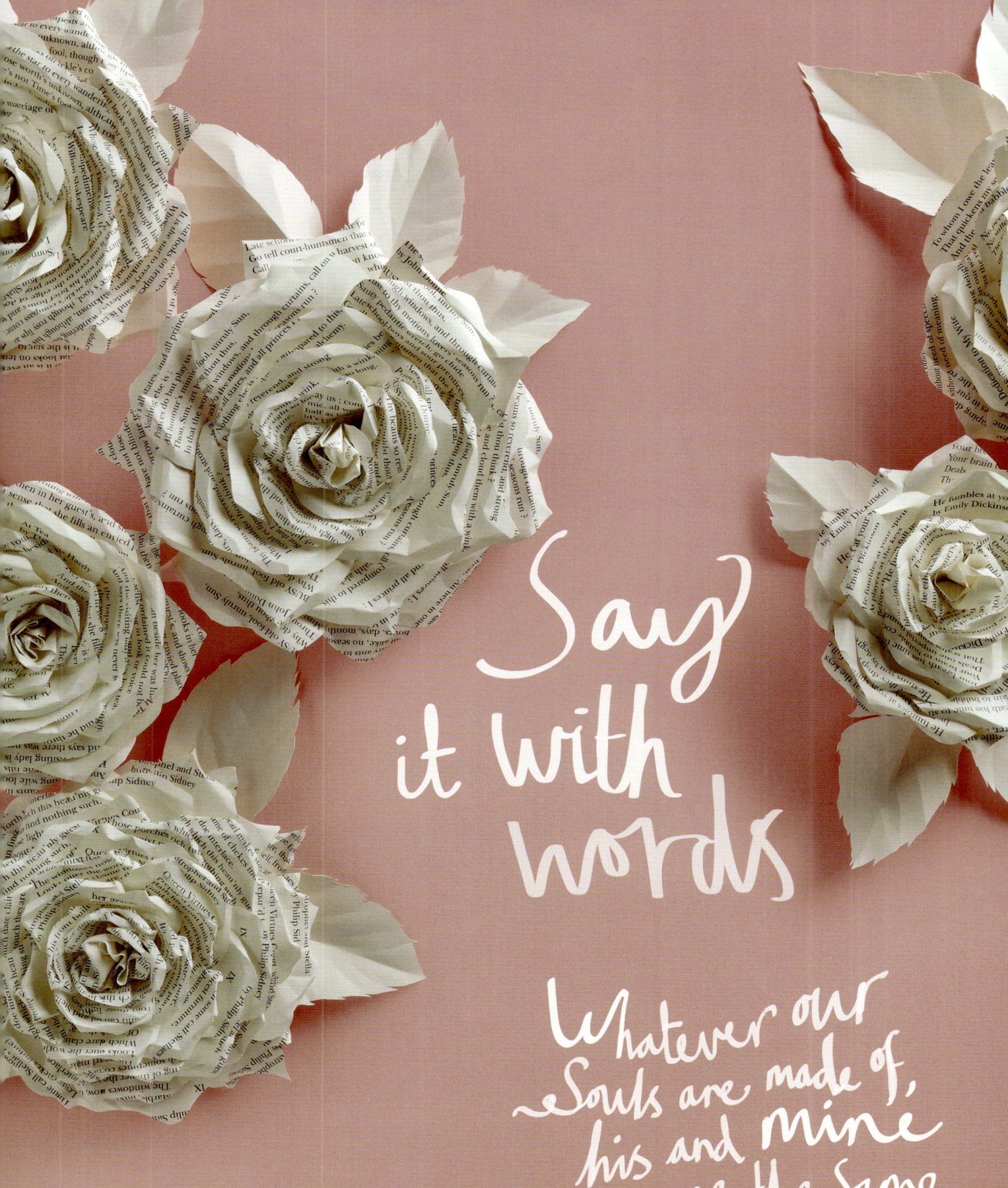

Say it with words

Whatever our souls are made of, his and mine are the same

7. Waterstones

Mandy Smith is commissioned to make roses out of selected poems to launch Valentines Day in Waterstones. Posters were used nationwide in their window displays and stores. Creative by VentureThree.

Designer: Mandy Smith
Country: Amsterdam, Netherlands
Design Agency: Venture Three (London)

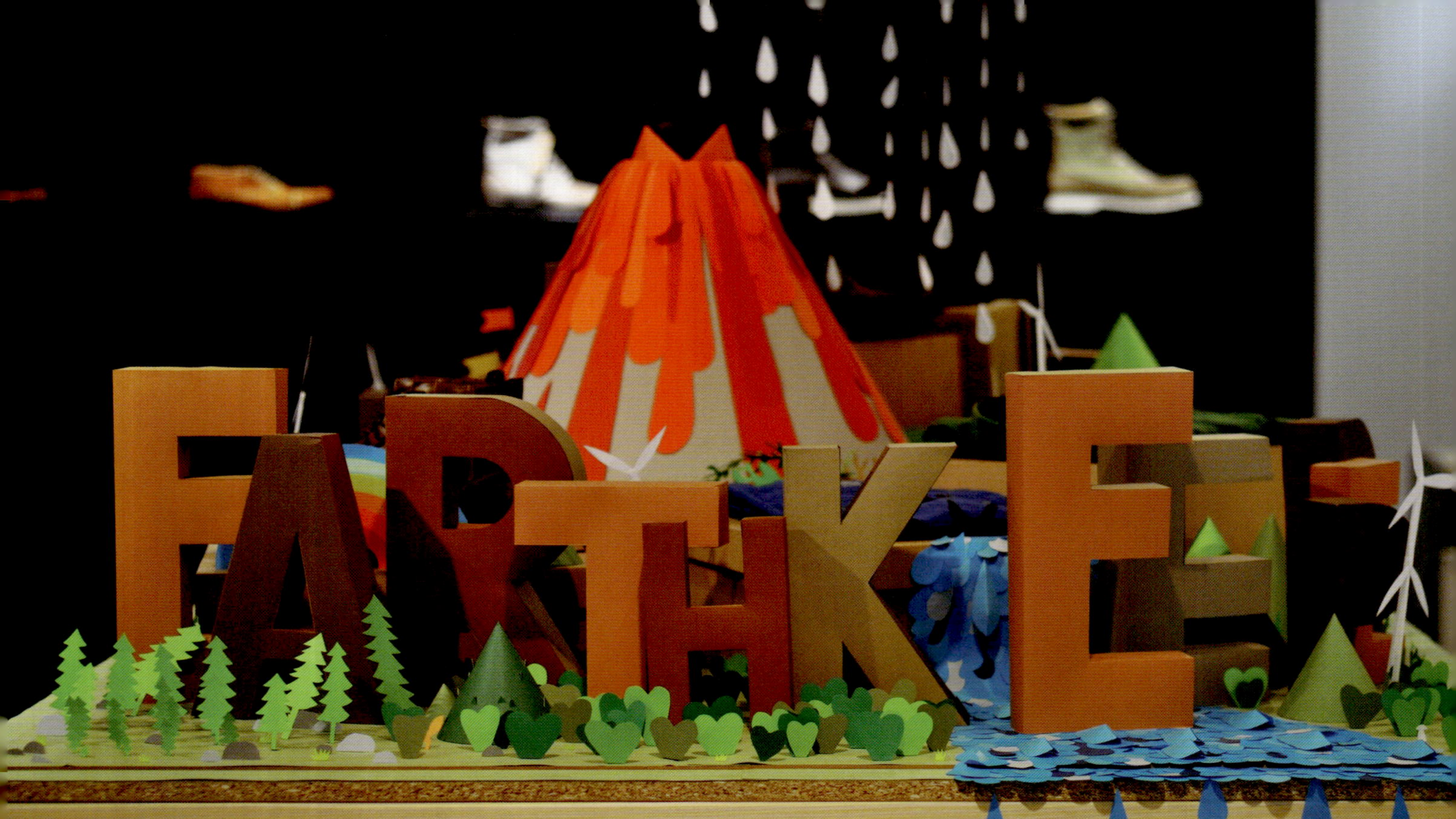

1. **Earthkeepers**

The brand asked me an installation for their ephemeral store in Paris dedicated to their new line of products ecologically taught. The keys words were "authenticity – ecology – urbanity - Nature ". They asked me also to use their cardboard shoes boxes and to integrate shoes and t-shirts.
To process, I first draw few propositions sketches to make sure that we agree with the client. I suggested creating a kind of universe full of details and little stories, positive and playful. Then, I started to make all the different elements, mountains, trees, windmills, etc…assembling them as one goes along. I changed often the composition until I get something satisfying. I use computer, scissors, cutters, scotch-tape, etc…
The inspiration behind the design came from the willing of creating something people spends time to discover, to see all the stories. It works actually! The shop was in front of a school and children were literally fascinated. Doing the installation, I imagined myself as a little character walking in and asked me what I would like to see. The better thing about this project was that actually I get the feeling to be paid to play Lego!

Designer: Mathilde Nivet   Country: France
Client: Timberland   Photographer: Valentin Bourdiol

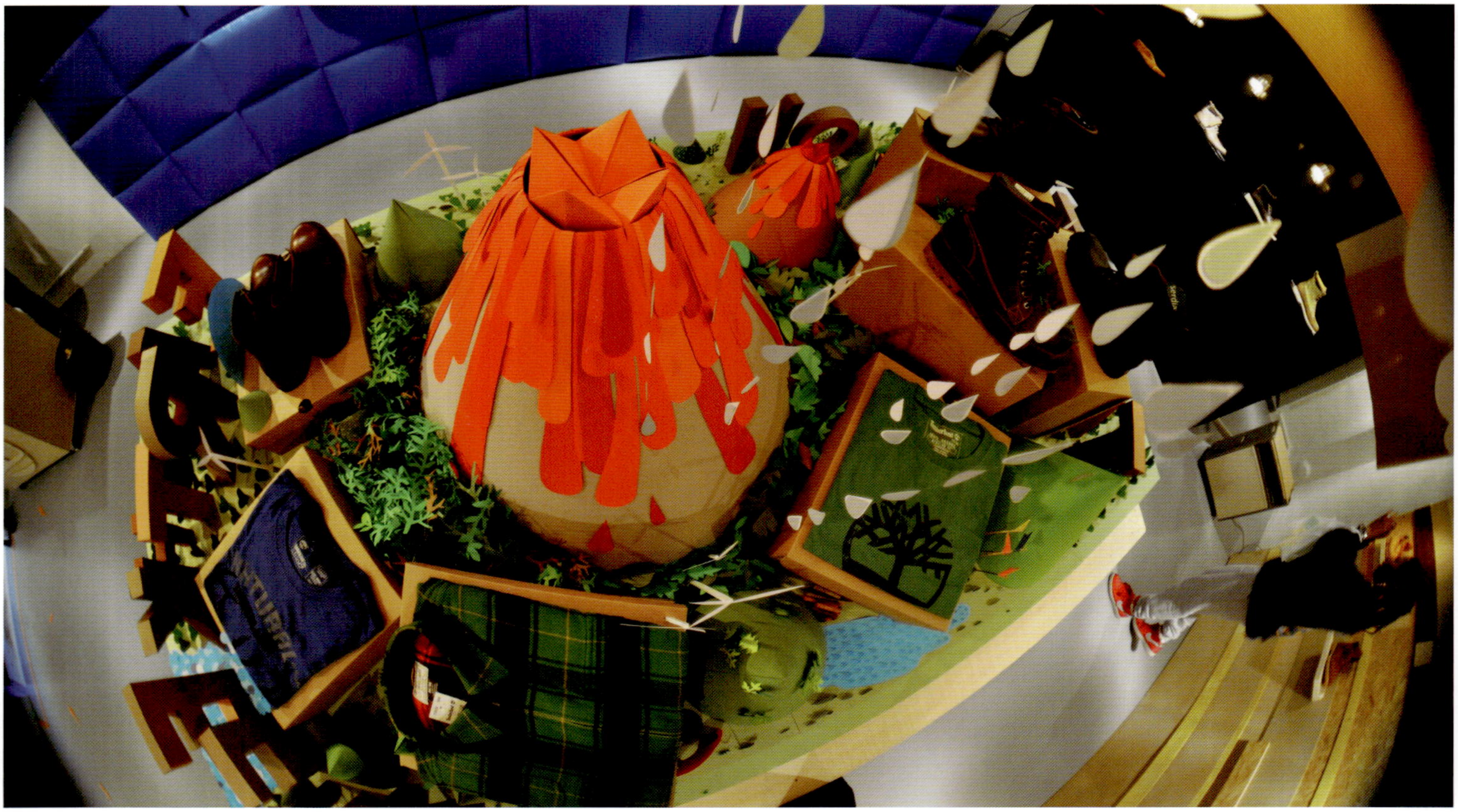

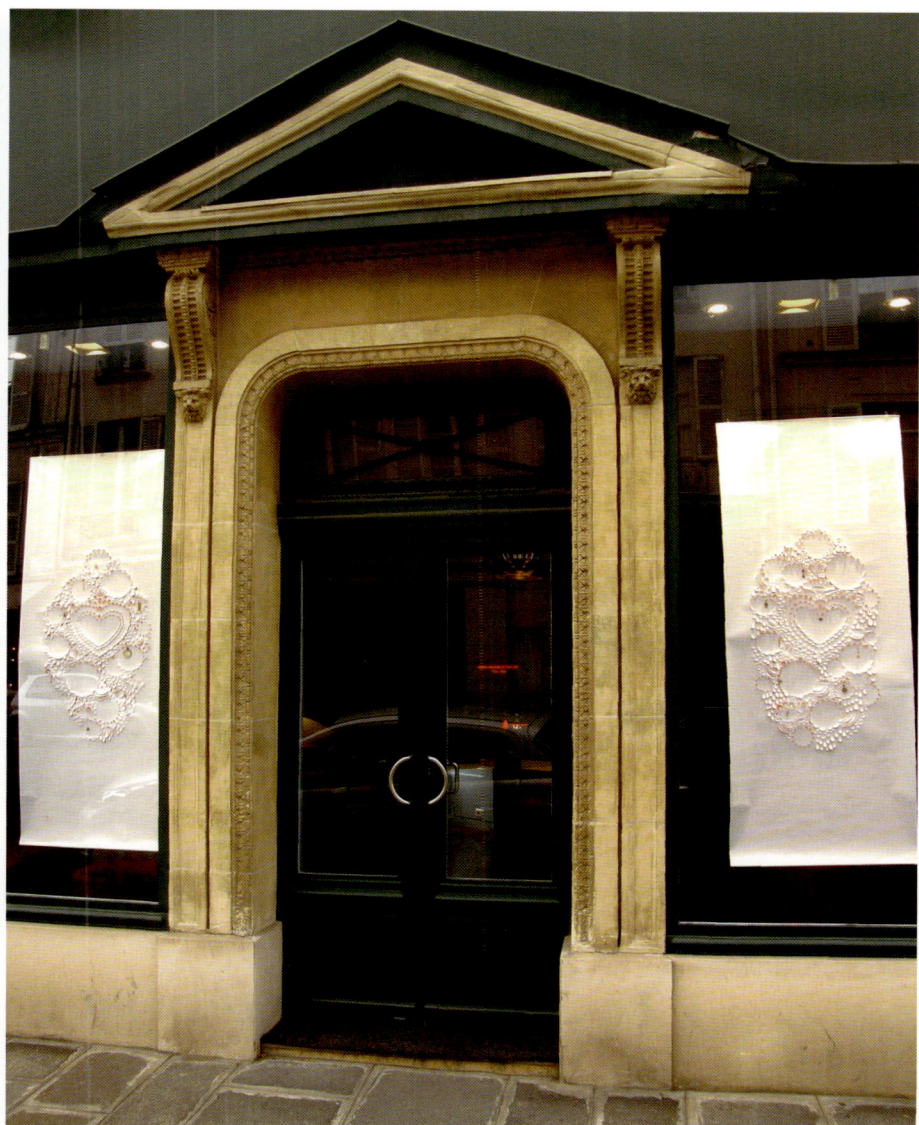
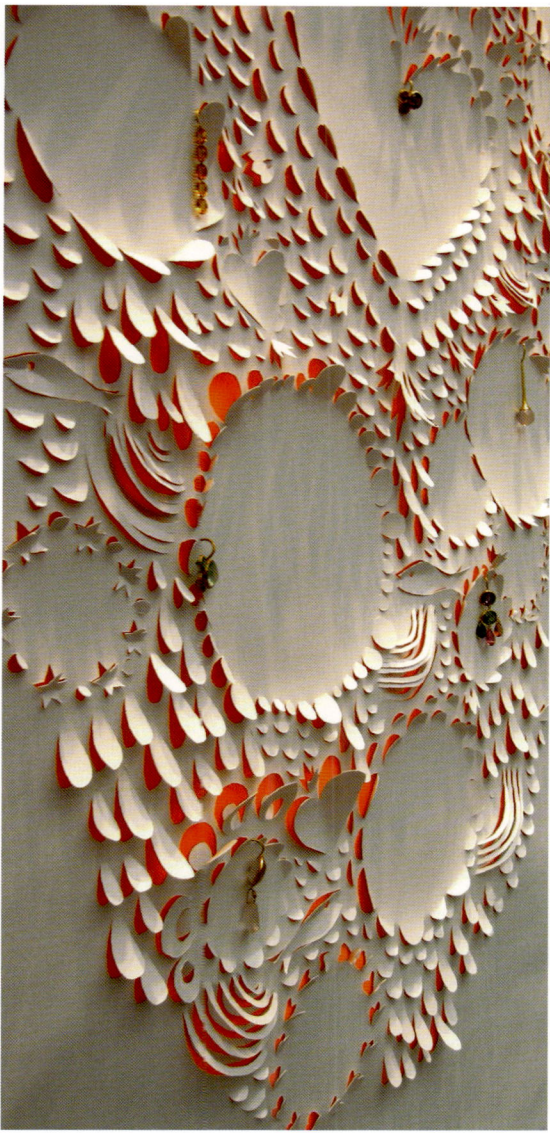

2. Marie-Hélène de Taillac Display

Windows display for show the new collection of jewellery of the brand Marie-Hélène de Taillac. The hand cut pattern is inspired from the classic patterns of the brand (hearts, fish, etc...). Enventually, it's looked like a delicate lace of paper.
The jewels hung on the cutted paper and could easily be removed. The light sprayed throught the cutted part.

Designer: Mathilde Nivet
Country: France
Client: Marie-Hélène de Taillac
Photographer: Mathilde Nivet

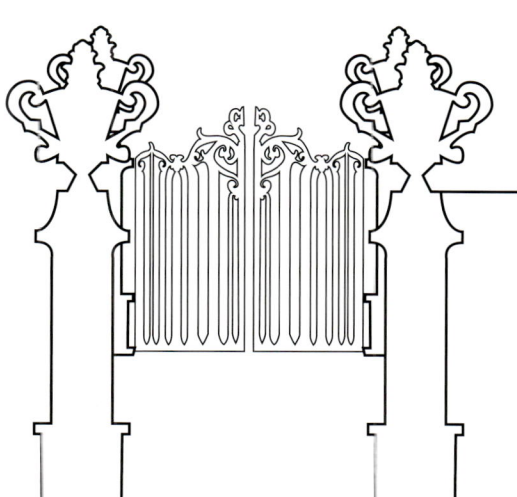

1. Earthkeepers
2. Marie-Hélène de Taillac Display
3. Christmas Display
4. Bulgari's New Perfum Lauch
5. The Necklace
6. Origami Jewellery Display
7. Paper Spring
8. Post Office Museum Shop Window Display
9. Dream City
10. Paris Marriage

---Mathilde Nivet

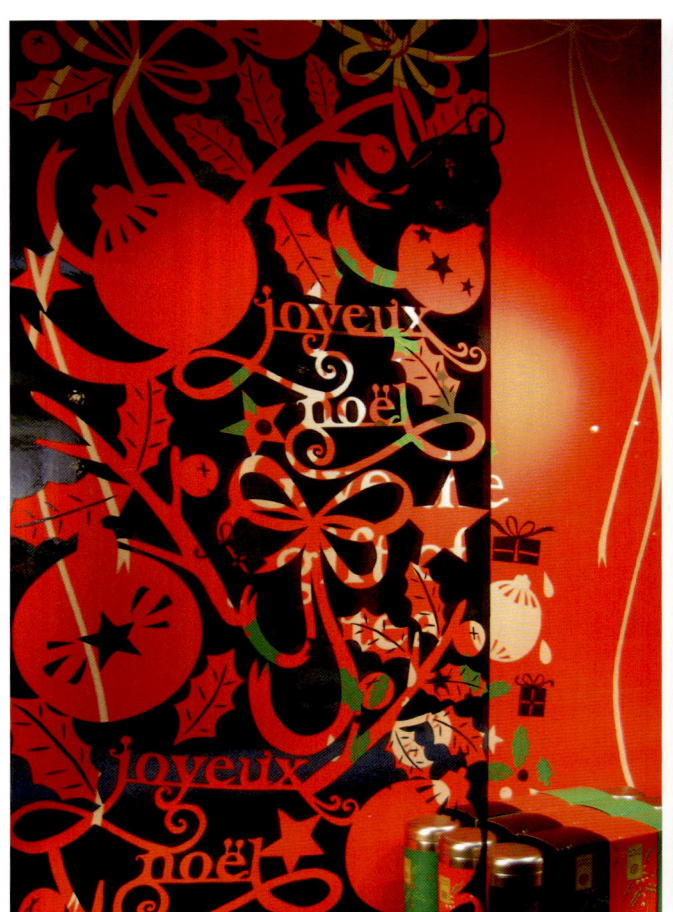
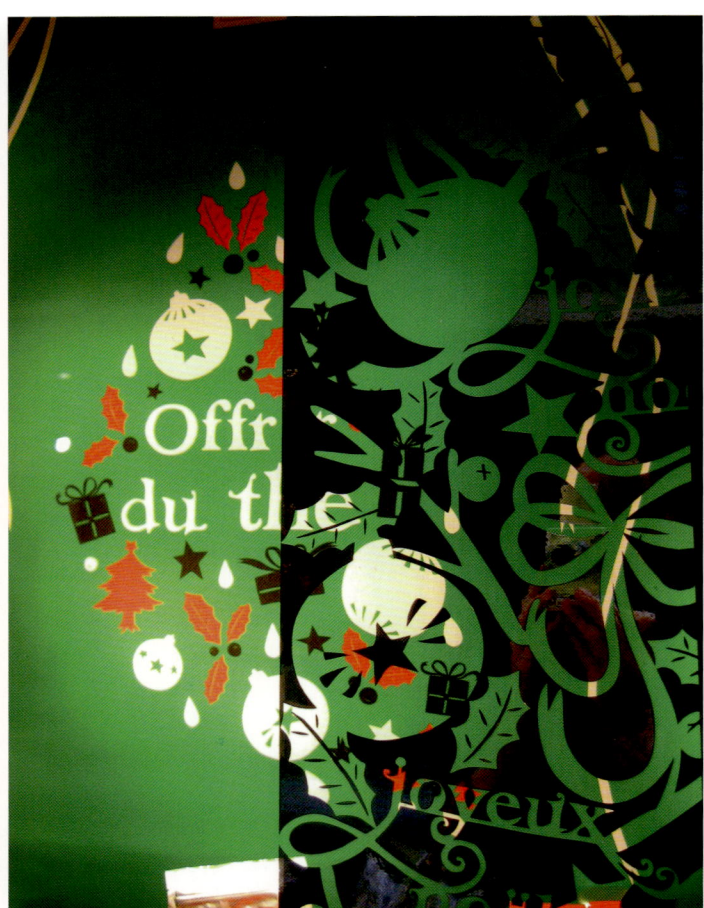
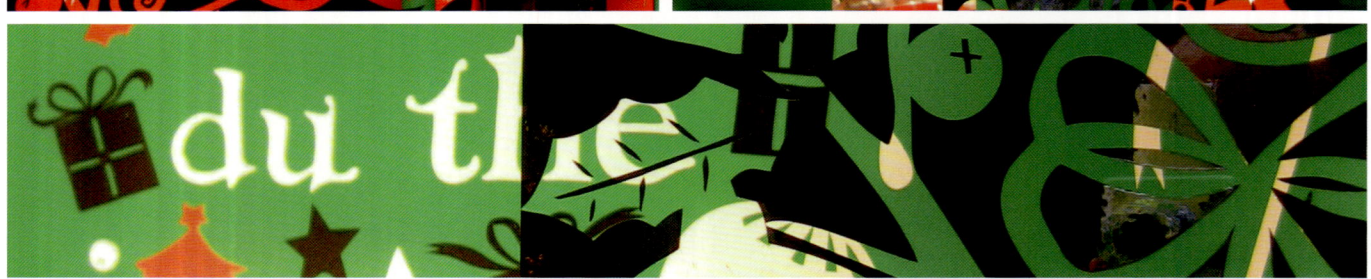
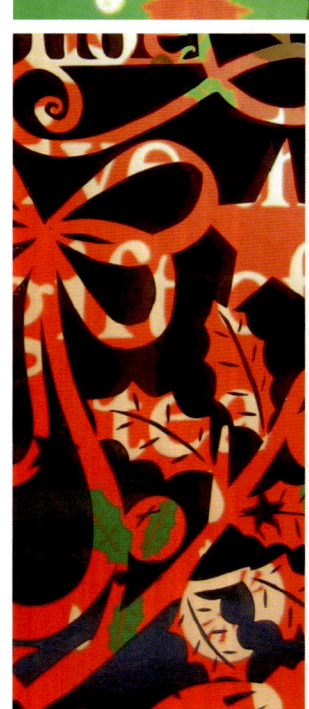
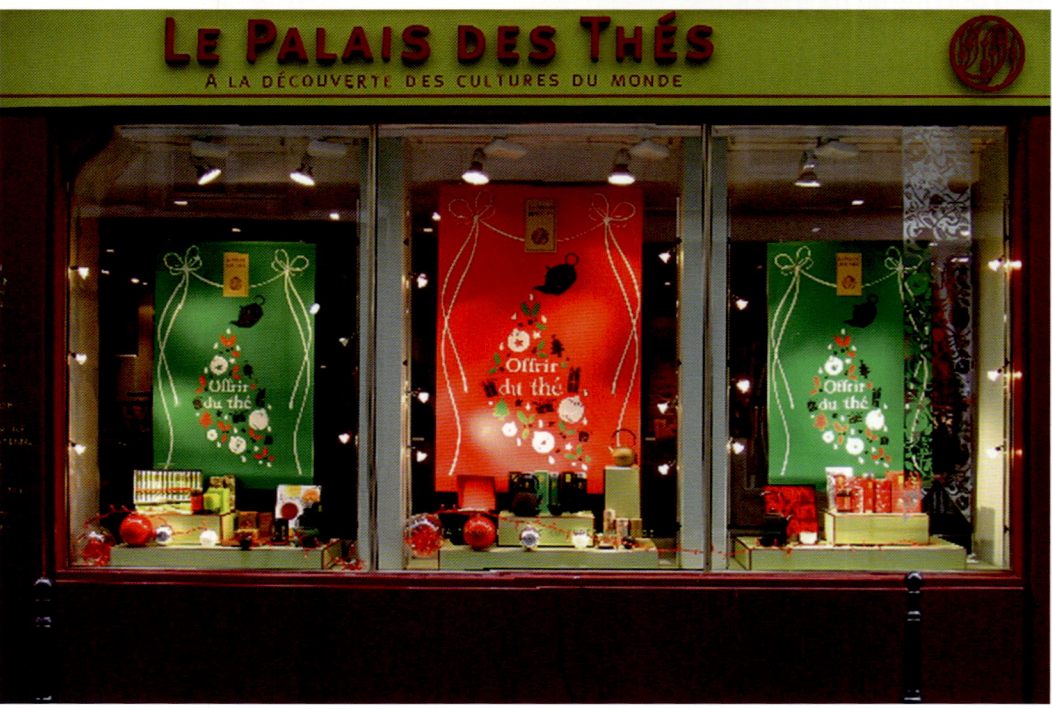

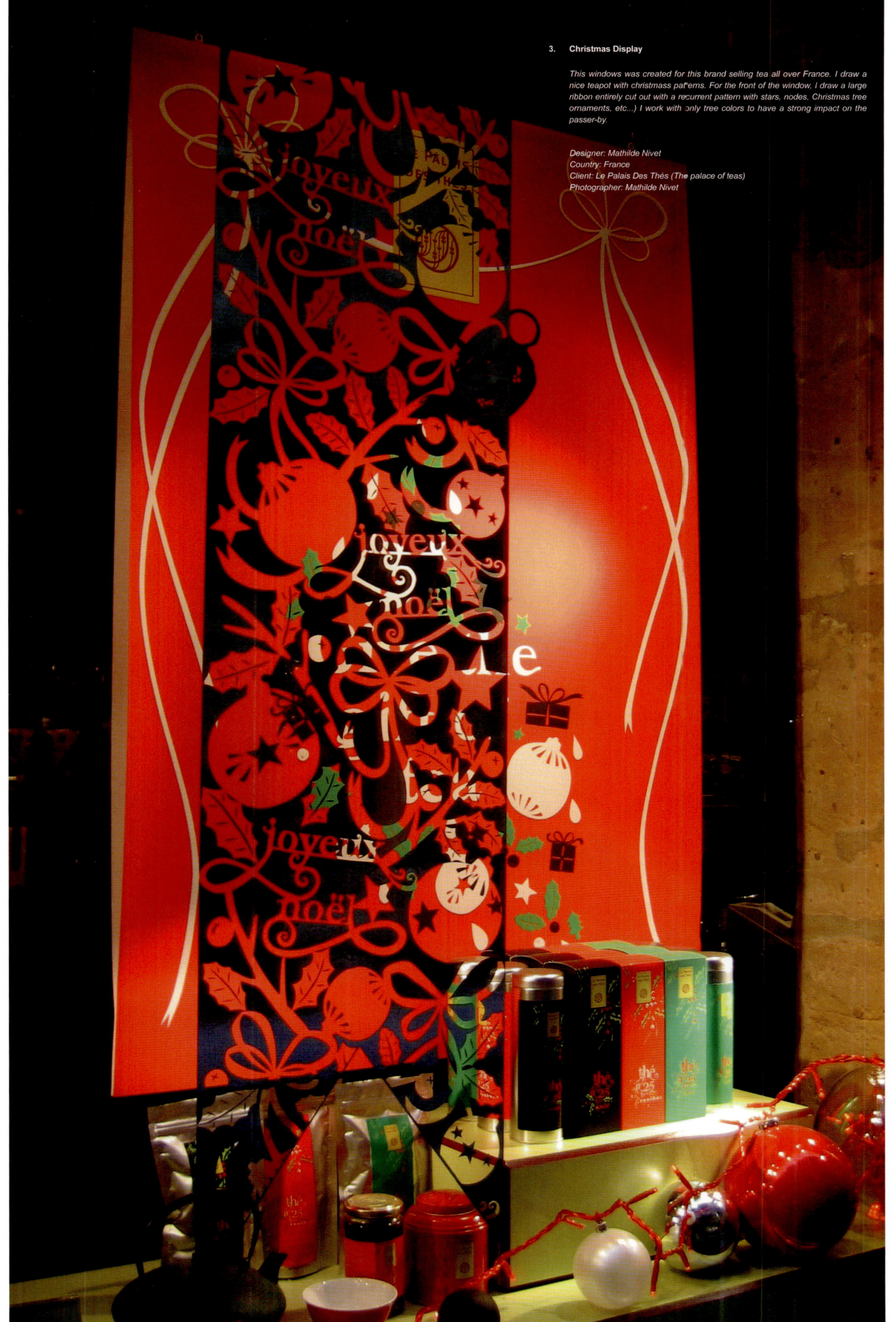

3. **Christmas Display**

This windows was created for this brand selling tea all over France. I draw a nice teapot with christmass patterns. For the front of the window, I draw a large ribbon entirely cut out with a recurrent pattern with stars, nodes, Christmas tree ornaments, etc...) I work with only tree colors to have a strong impact on the passer-by.

Designer: Mathilde Nivet
Country: France
Client: Le Palais Des Thés (The palace of teas)
Photographer: Mathilde Nivet

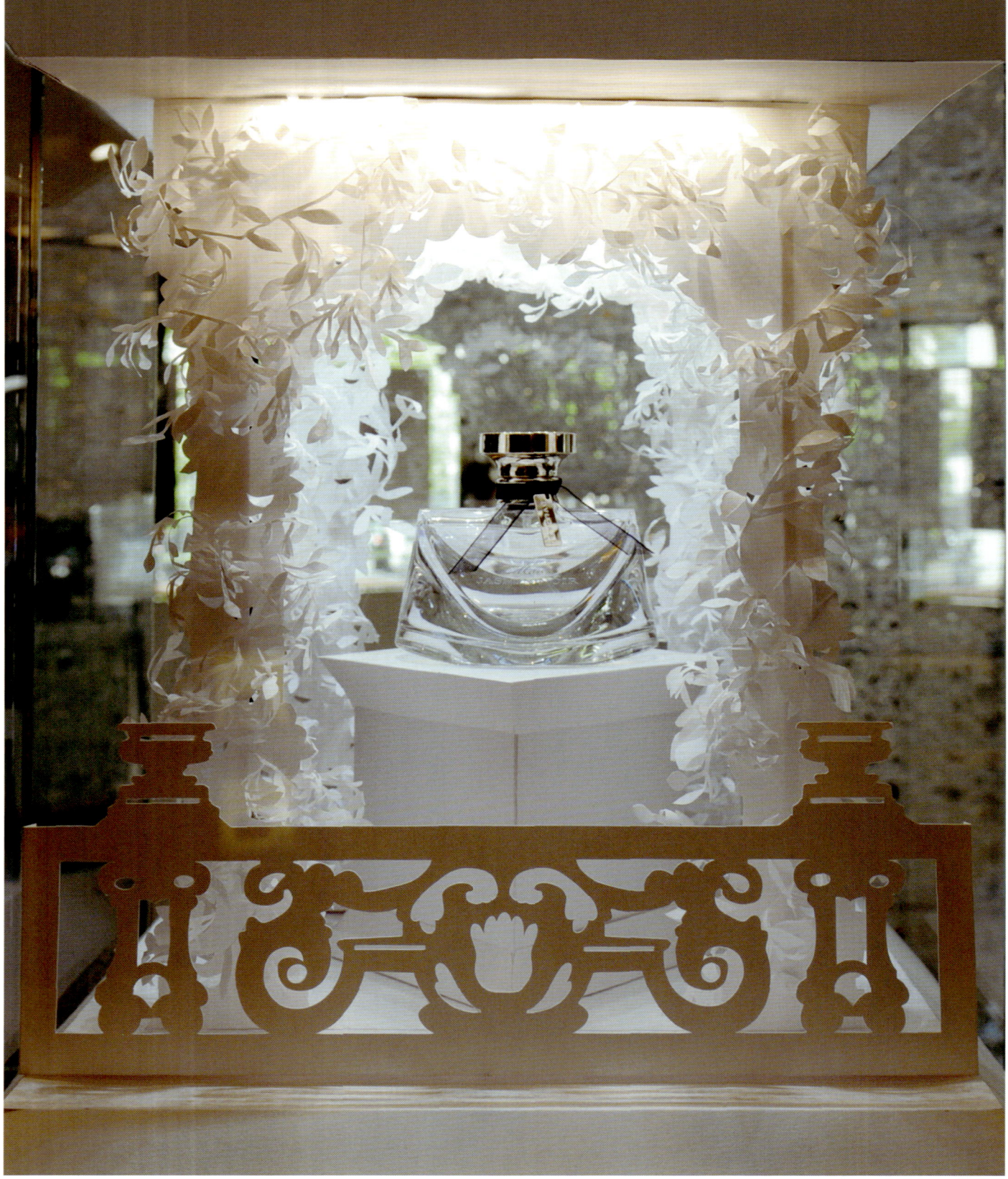

4. **Bulgari's New Perfum Lauch**

I created a whole setdesign for the press presentation of the parfum «Mon Jasmin Noir». In little square windows display, I recreated setting representing an Italian garden with sculpture and vegetation. I cut out floral patterns to present the jewell collection of the brand.
One hundred of nice and light paper flowers were also spreaded all over the boutique.

Designer: Mathilde Nivet
Country: France
Client: Say Hmm! / Bulgari
Photographer: Michaël Huard

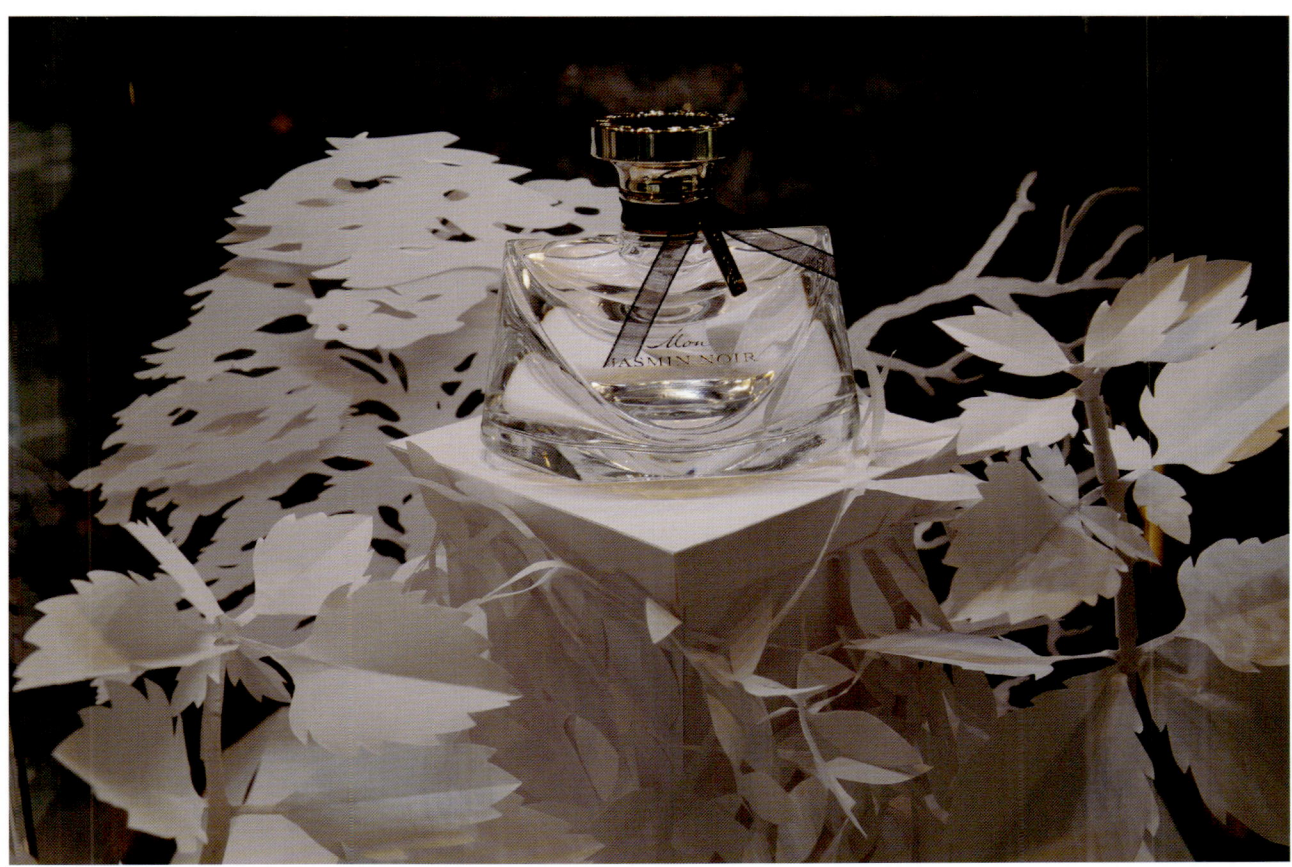
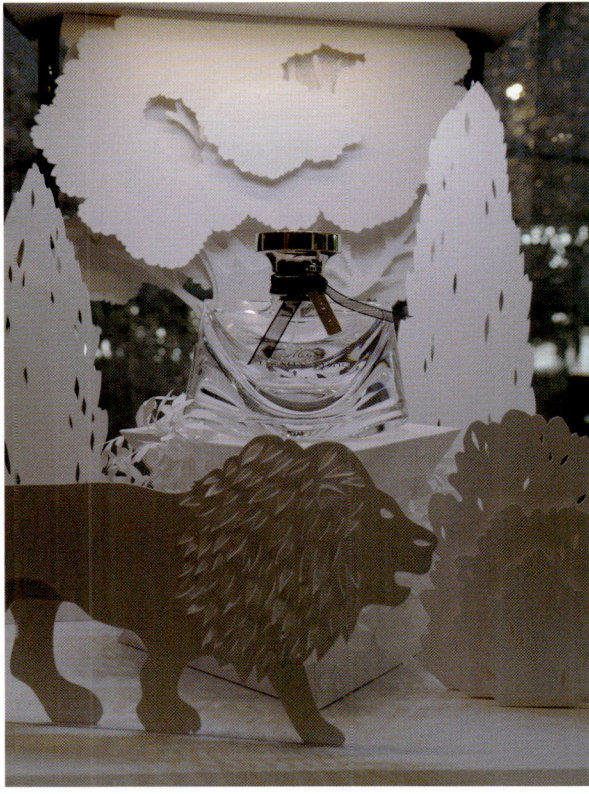
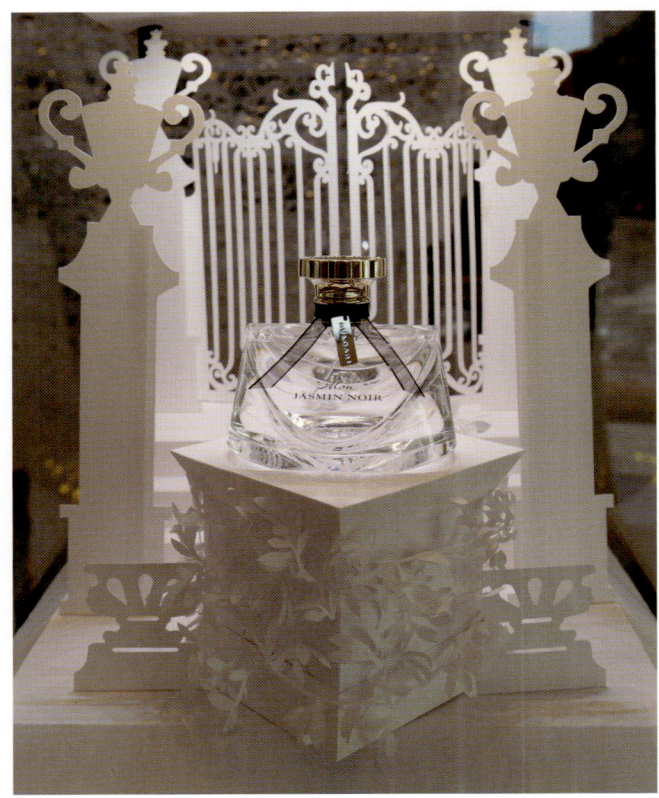

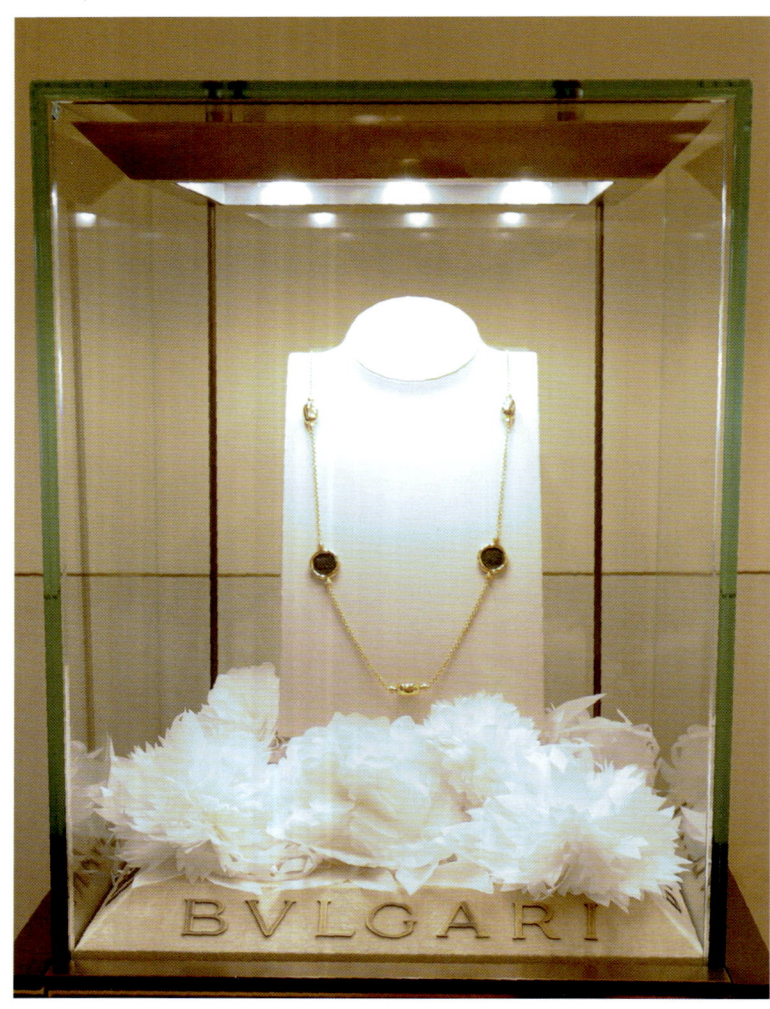
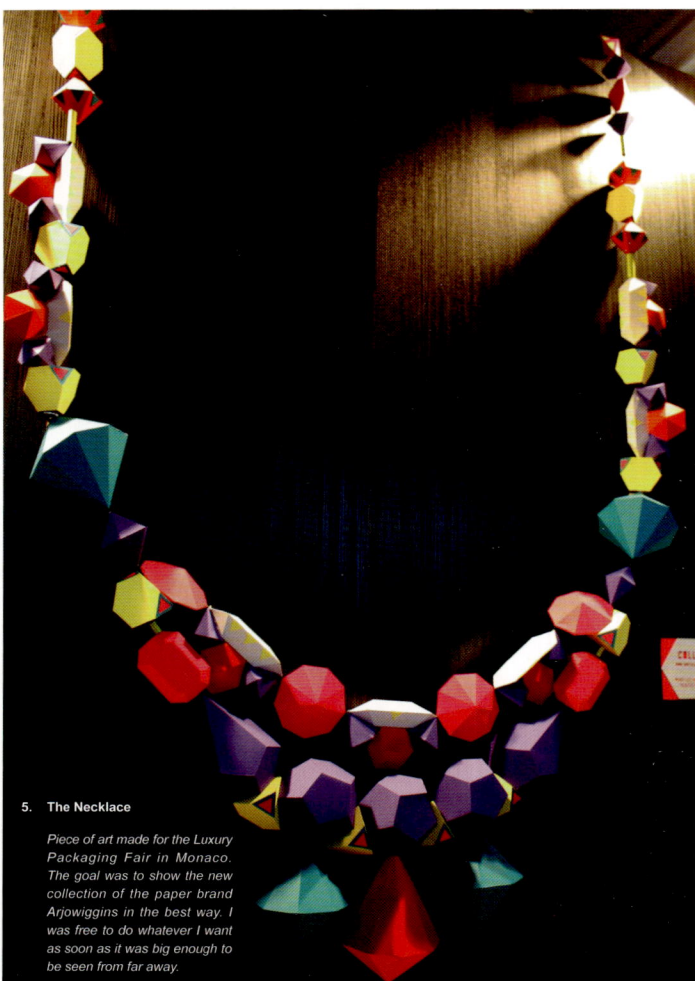

5. The Necklace

Piece of art made for the Luxury Packaging Fair in Monaco. The goal was to show the new collection of the paper brand Arjowiggins in the best way. I was free to do whatever I want as soon as it was big enough to be seen from far away.

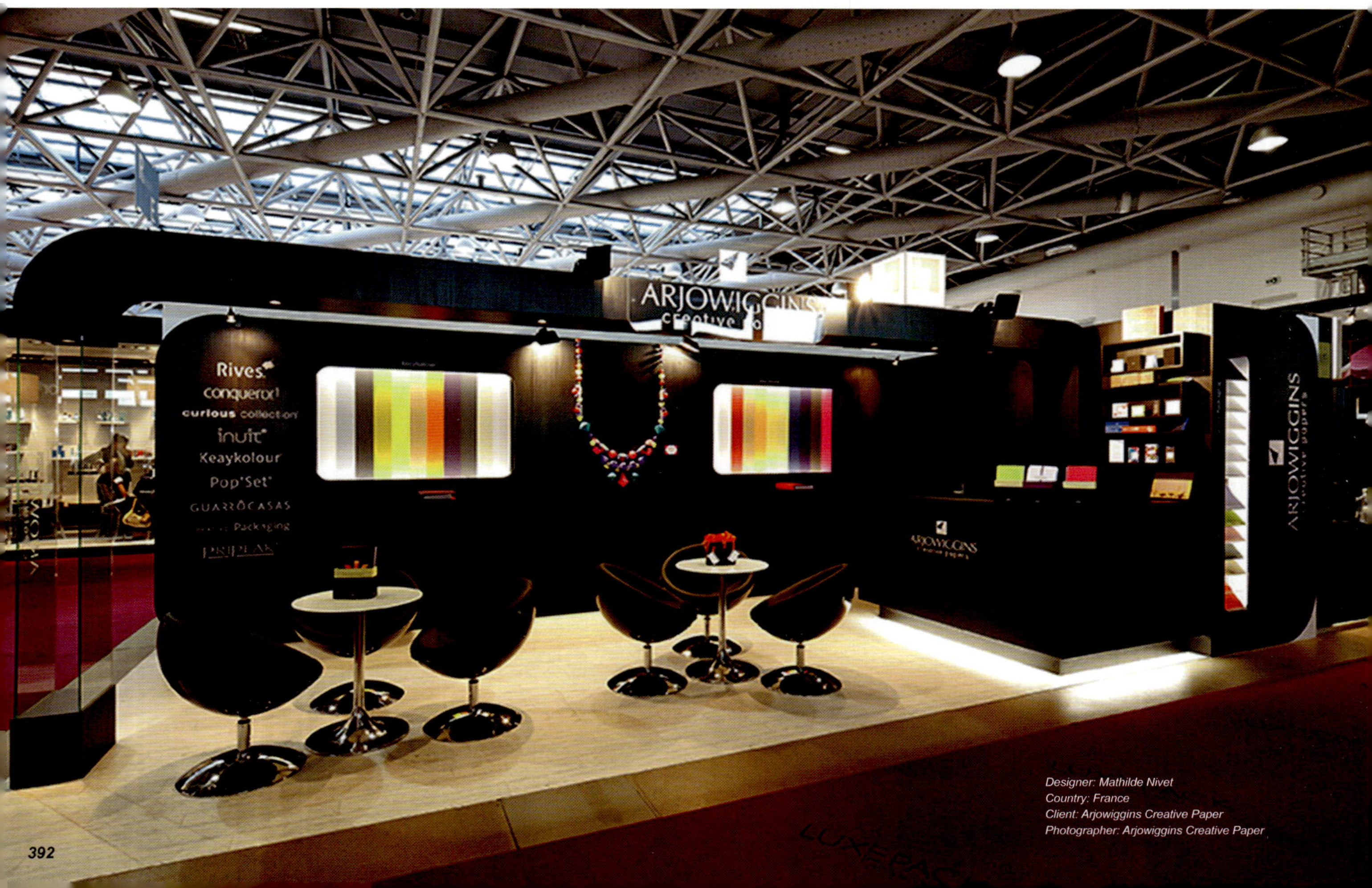

Designer: Mathilde Nivet
Country: France
Client: Arjowiggins Creative Paper
Photographer: Arjowiggins Creative Paper

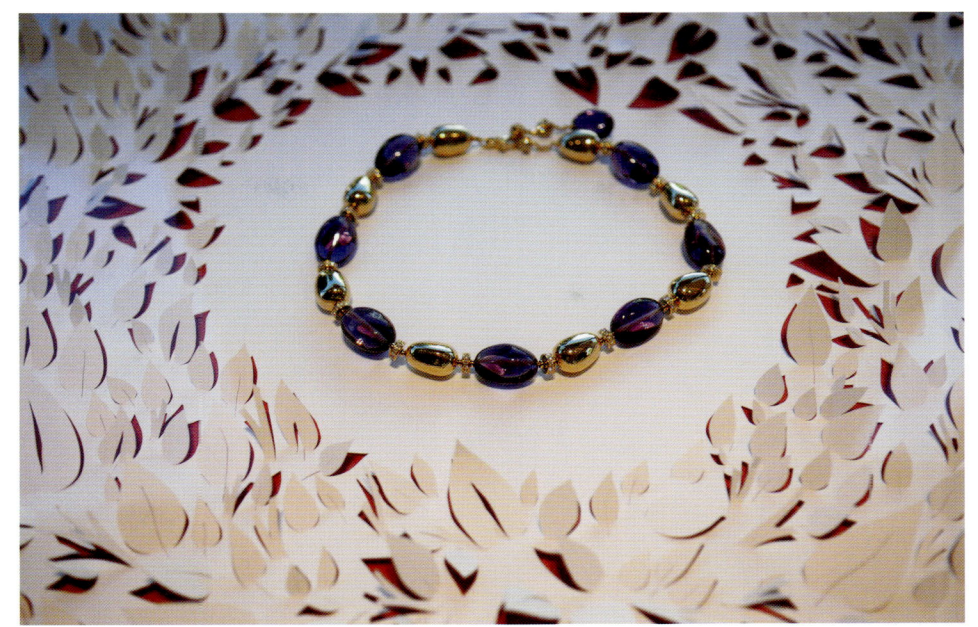
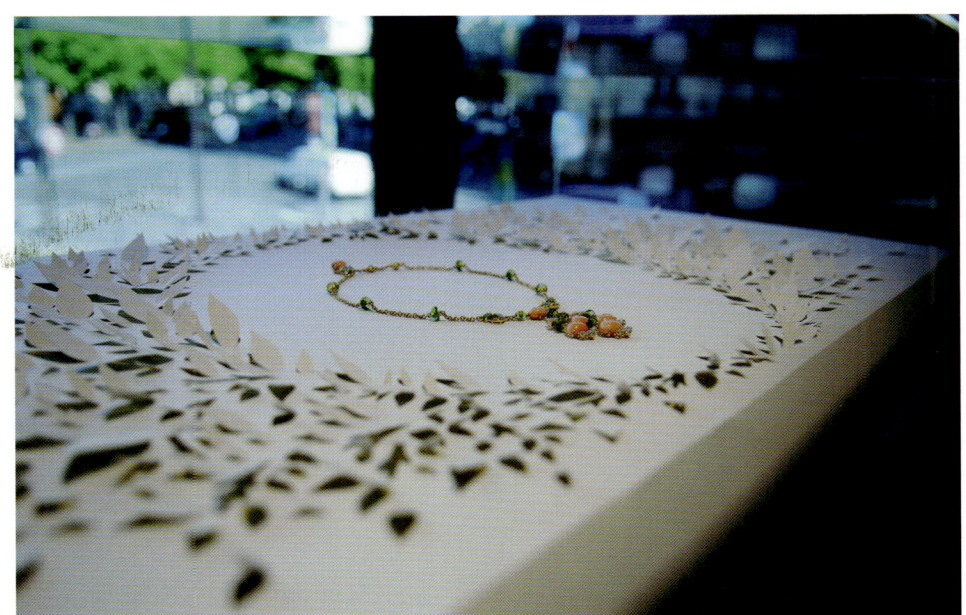
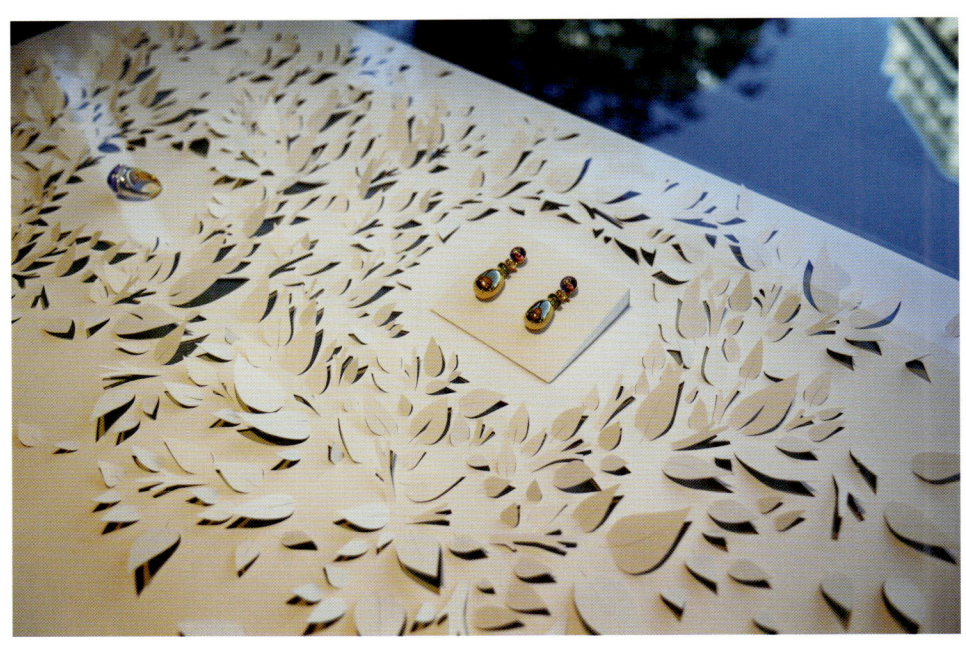

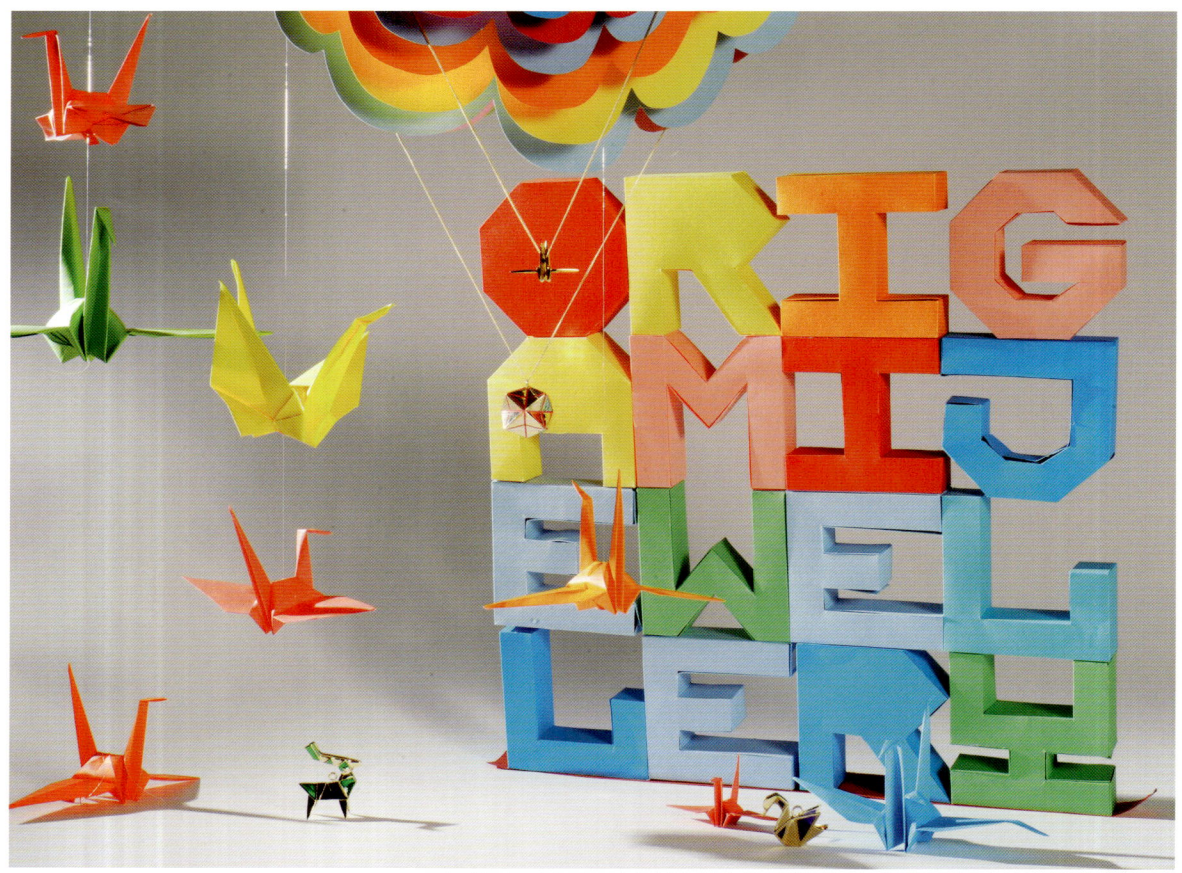
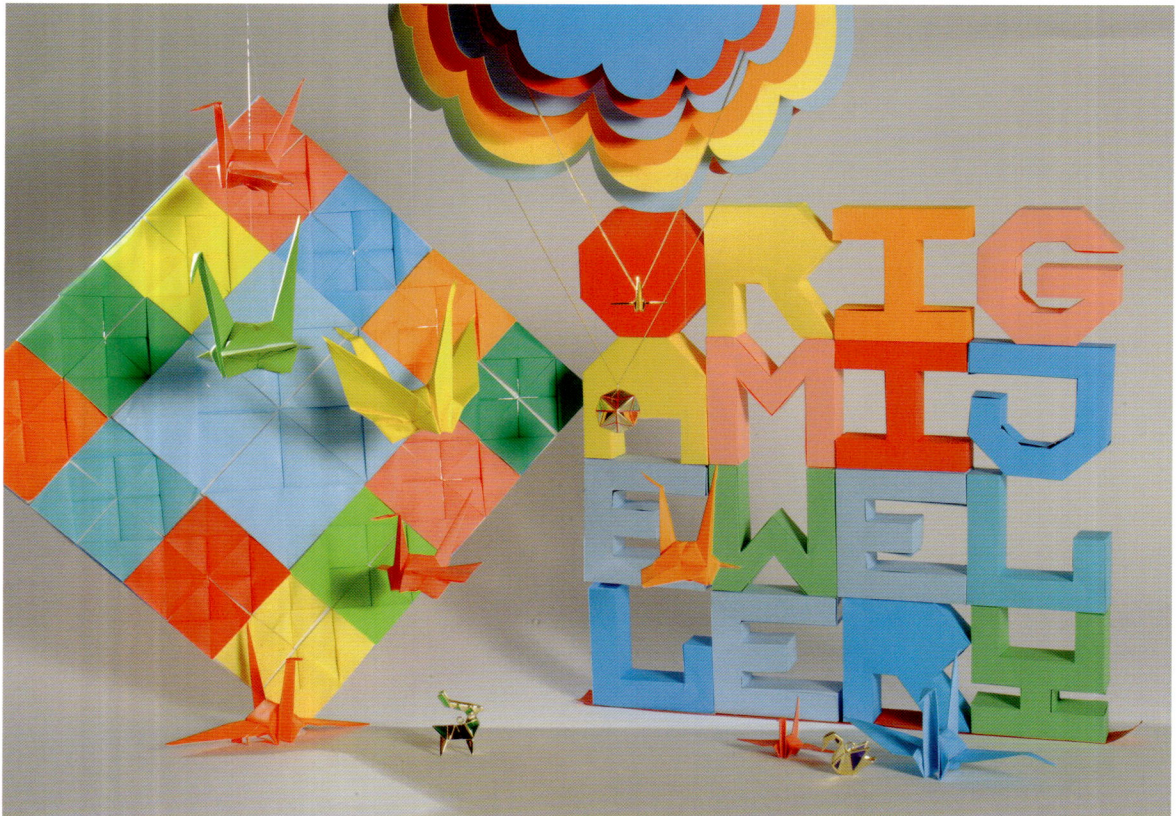

6. **Origami Jewellery Display**

The brand was having a space in a famous department store in Paris for Christmas. They had fiver little showcases and they asked me to create a paper installation for each one, colourfully and inspired by origami to present the jewels.
I made 3D letters and sticked all them together to do a square, like the logo of the brand.
The inspiration was coming from childish universe. I wanted something fun and flash to draw attention of the clients. The cloud was make to make the birds jewels actually fly and all the patterns where related with the design of the jewels.

Designer: Mathilde Nivet   Country: France   Client: Origami Jewellery   Photographer: Zoé Guilbert

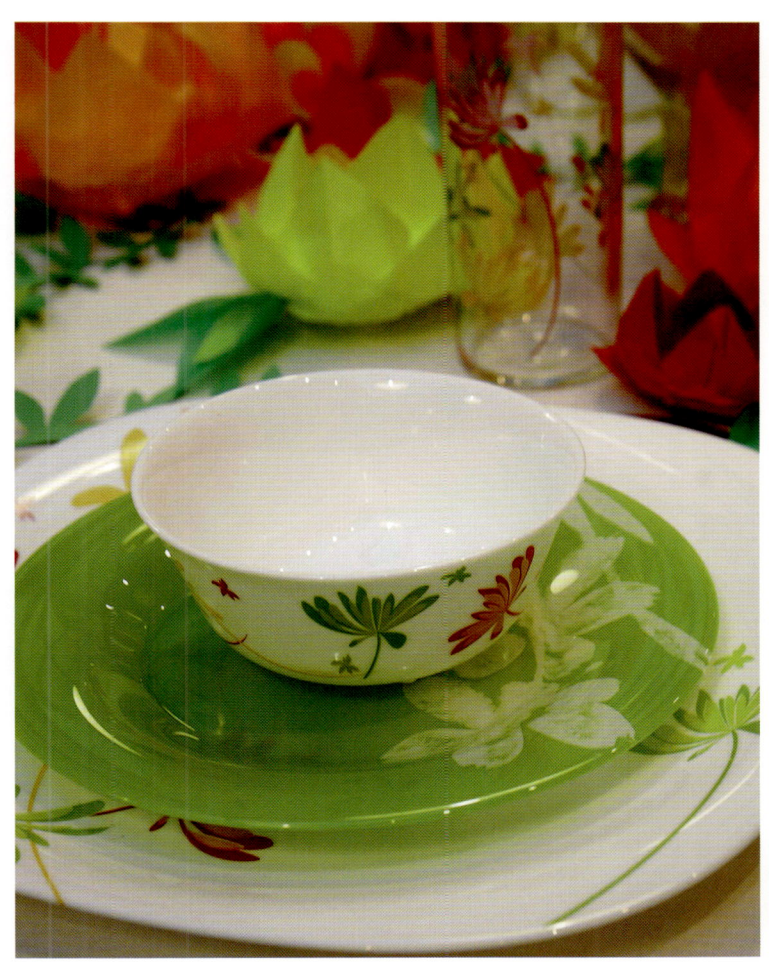
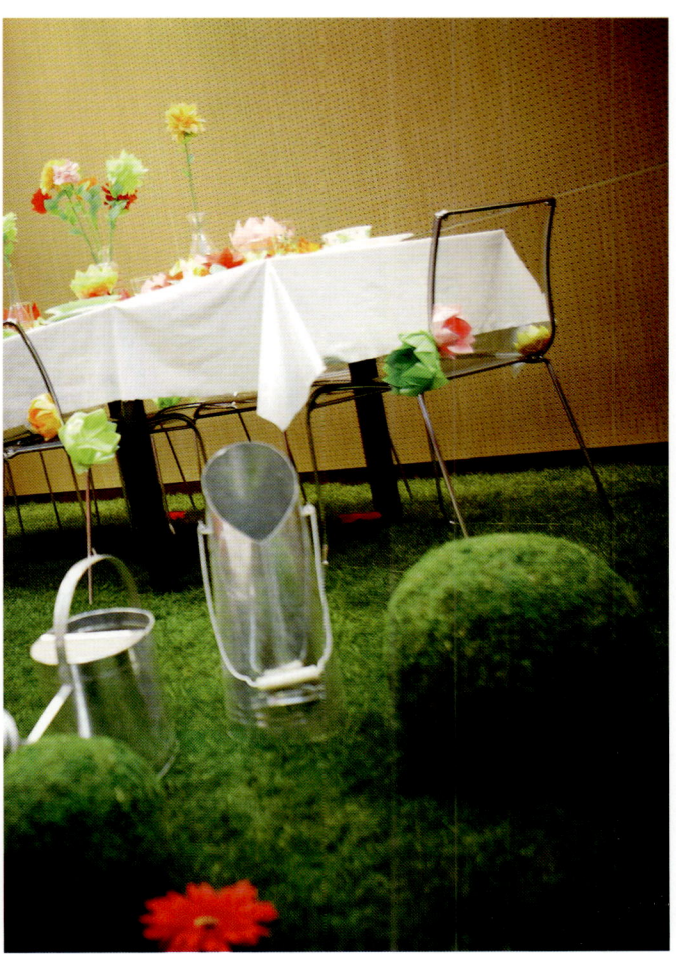

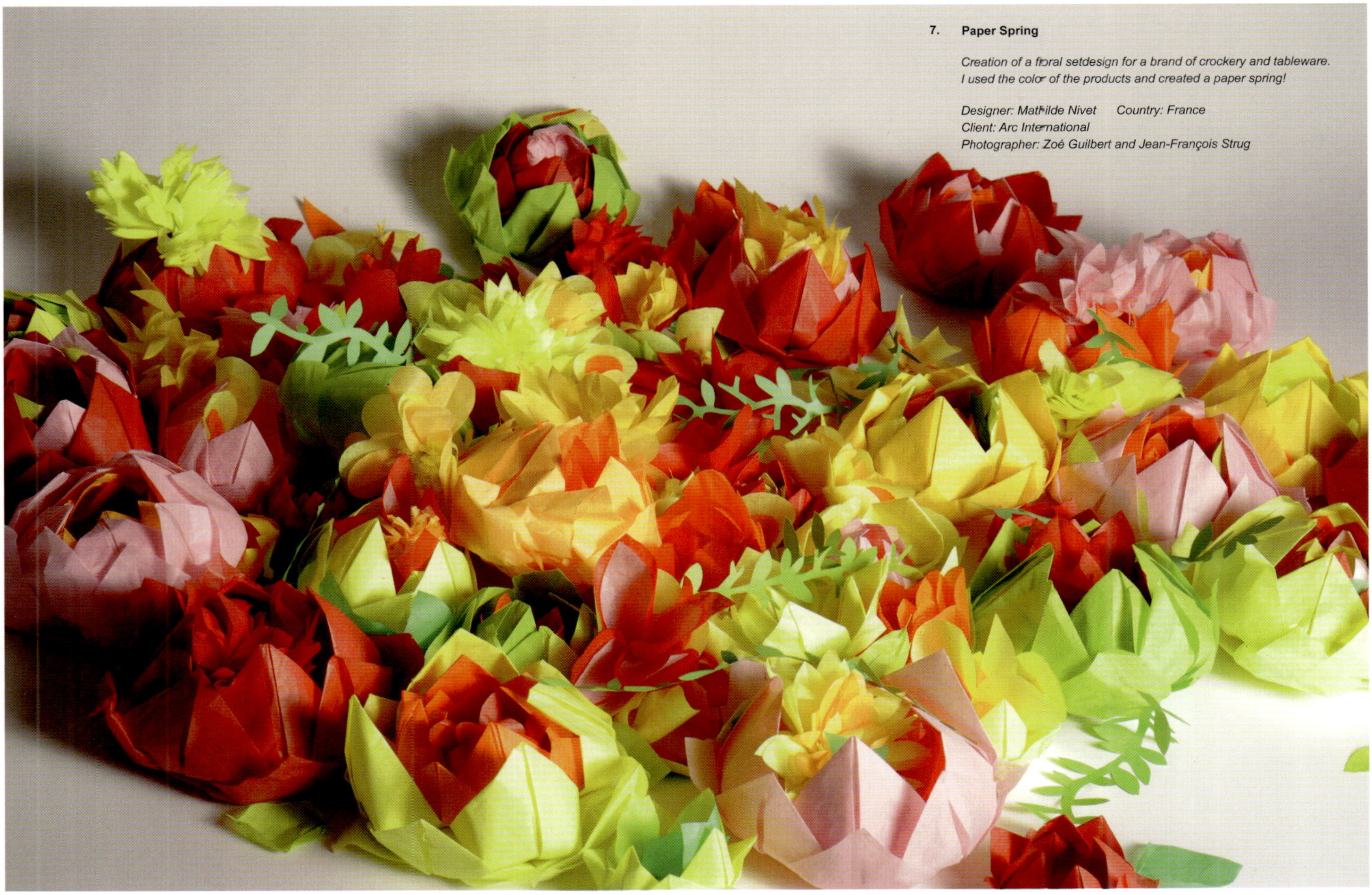

7. Paper Spring

Creation of a floral setdesign for a brand of crockery and tableware. I used the color of the products and created a paper spring!

Designer: Mathilde Nivet   Country: France
Client: Arc International
Photographer: Zoé Guilbert and Jean-François Strug

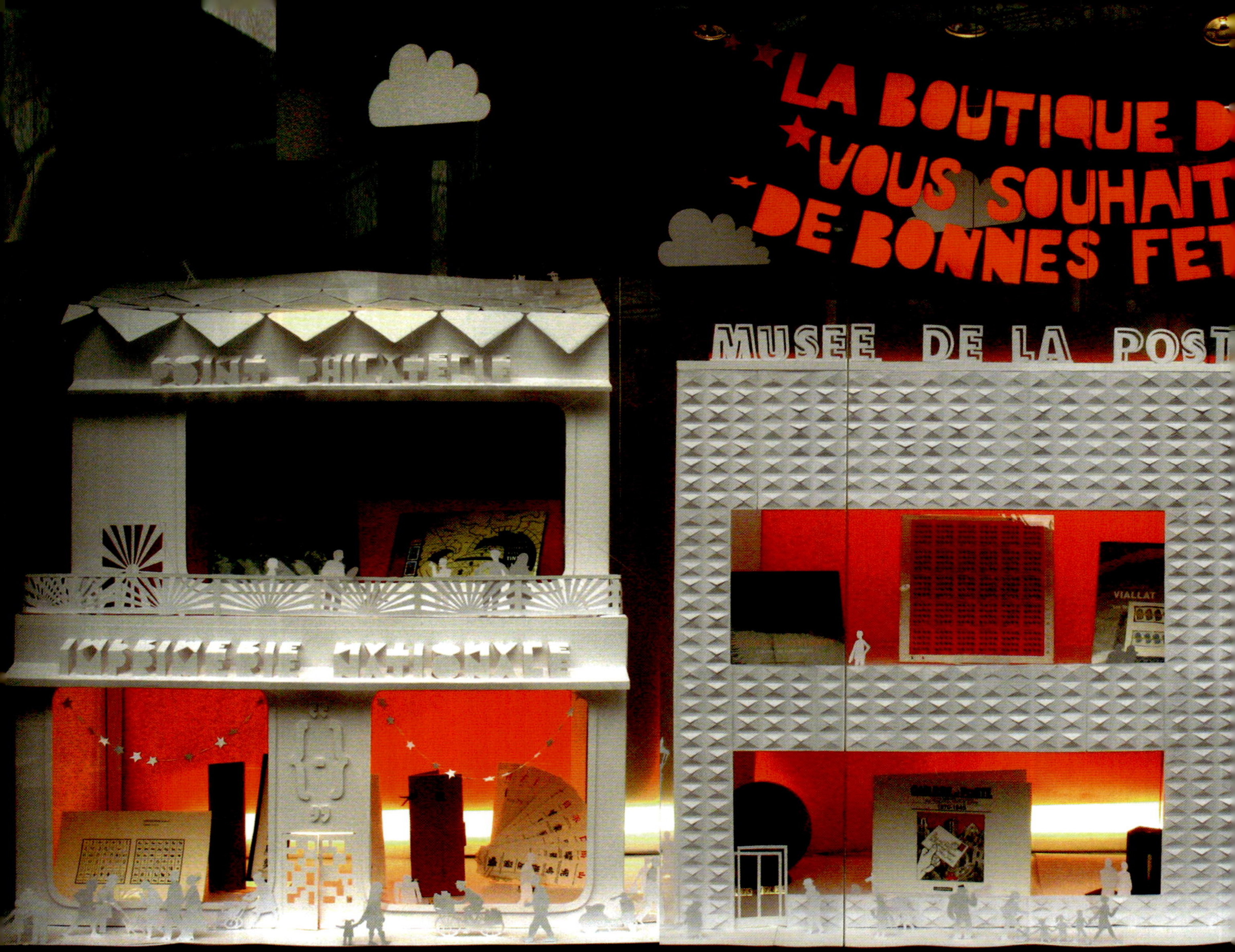

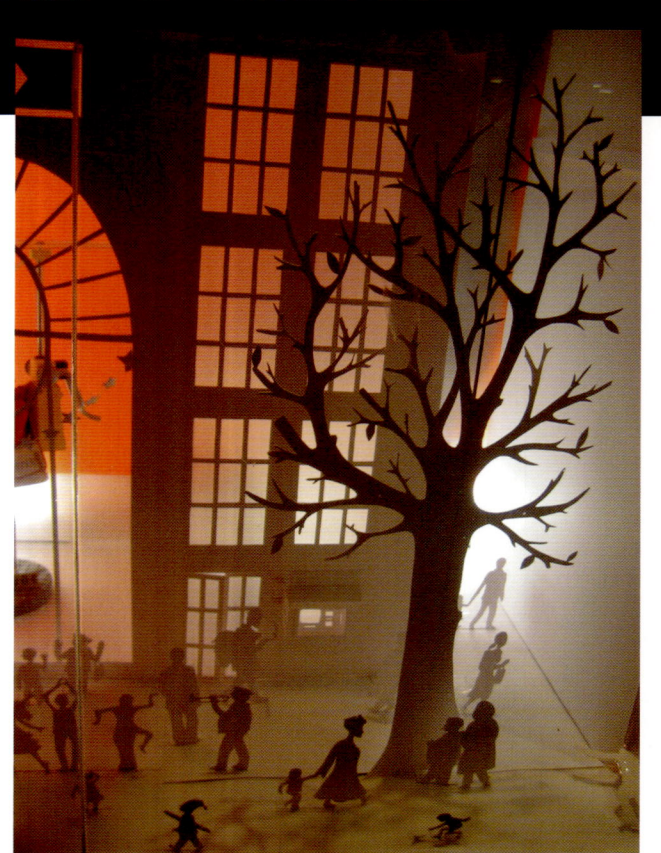
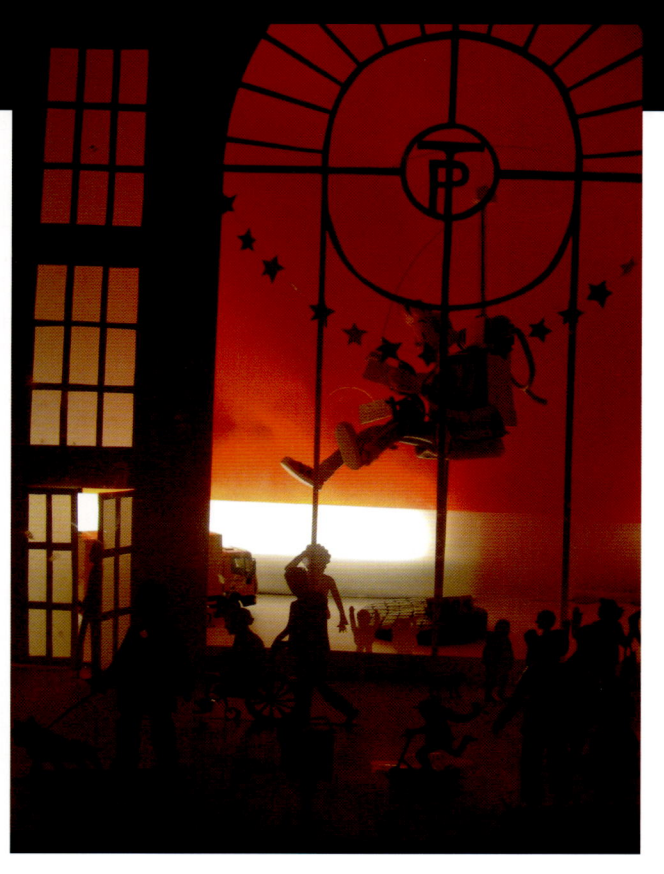

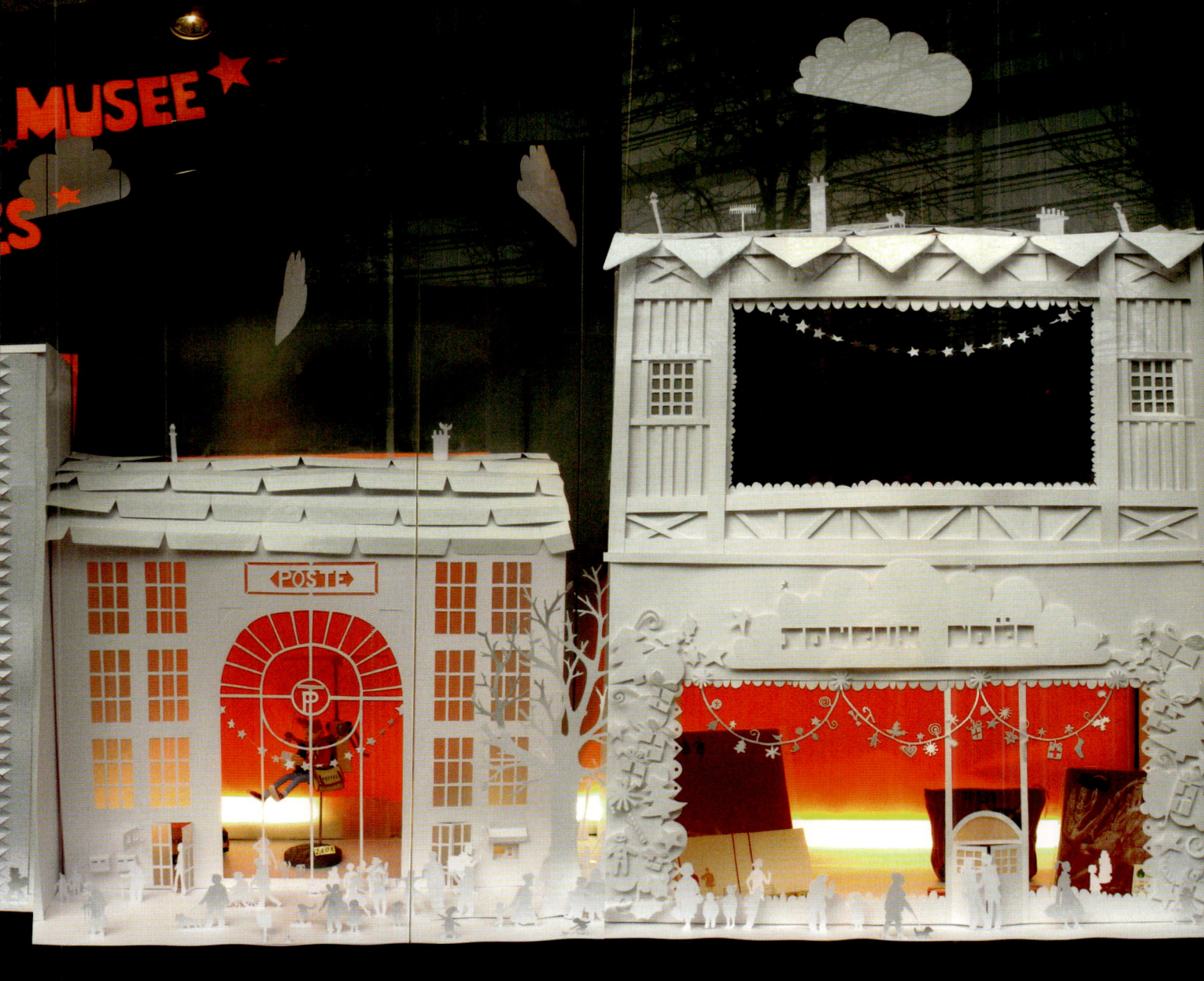

8. **Post Office Museum Shop Window Display**

Creation of a paper city. Four builing of 1m high using different technic linkend to paper: cutting, folding, assembling.
One hundred a little paper characters walk by this paper street, as a reflection of the street where the museum stays itself.

Designer: Mathilde Nivet   Country: France
Client: Post Office Museum   Photographer: Mathilde Nivet

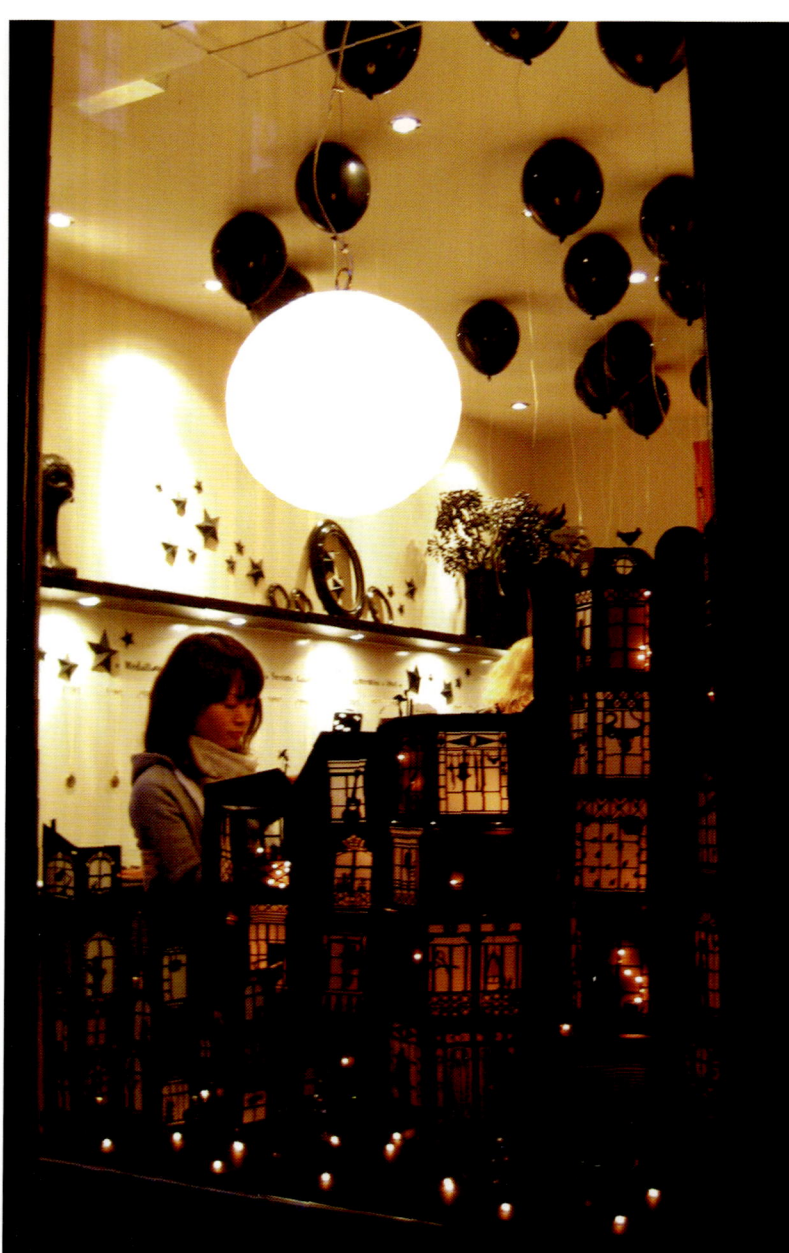
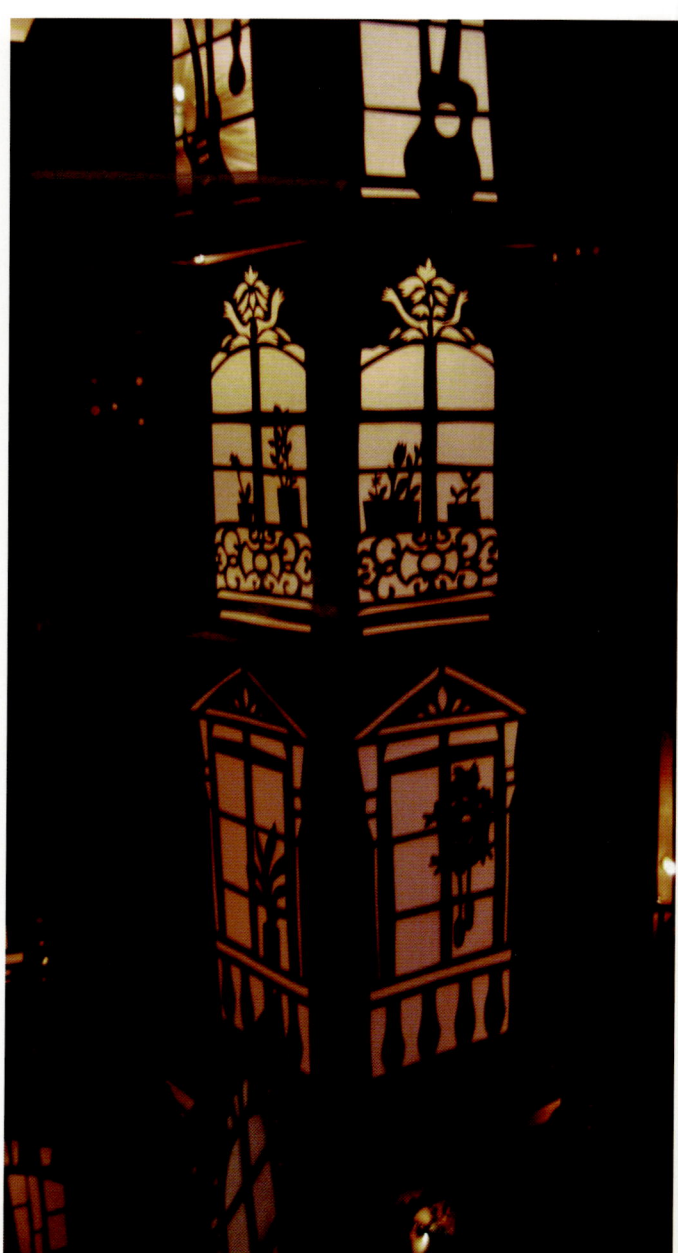
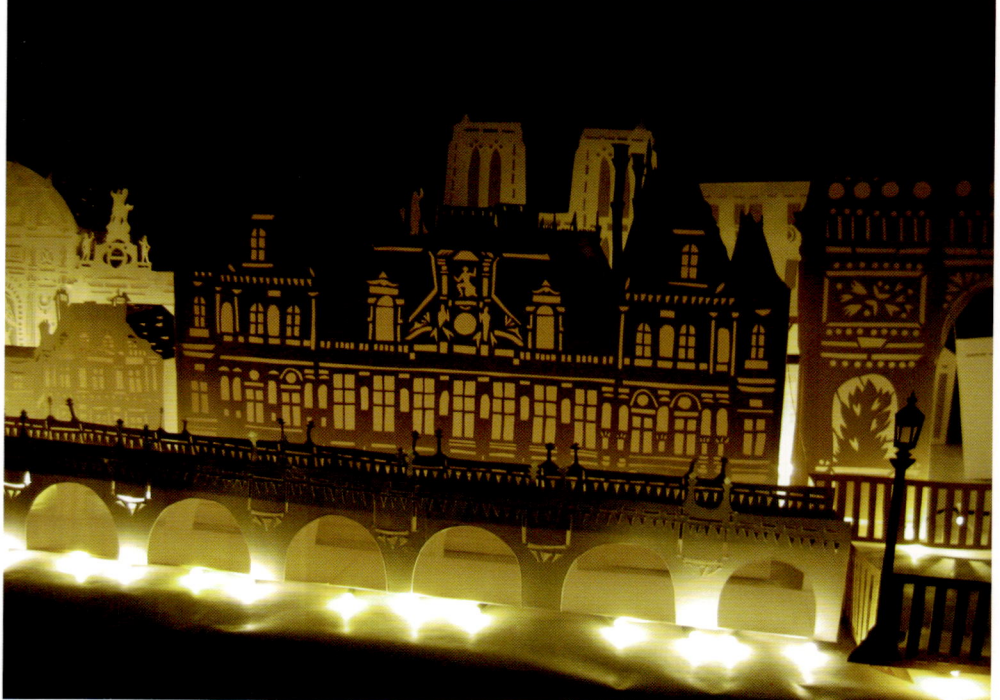
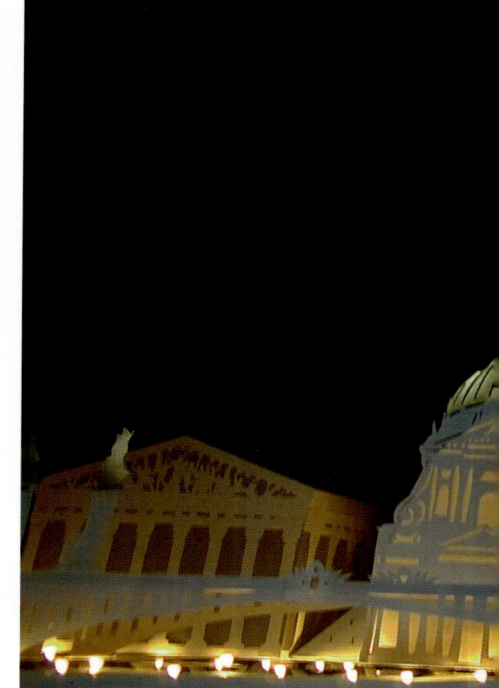

9. **Dream City**

Windows display for show the jewelry brand Servane Gaxotte.
I create a paper setdesign showing an imaginary street of Paris by night in a cosy area.
Strange details can be seen throught the windows, appearing as mini lit-up theatres.

Designer: Mathilde Nivet   Country: France
Client: Servane Gaxotte   Photographer: Mathilde Nivet

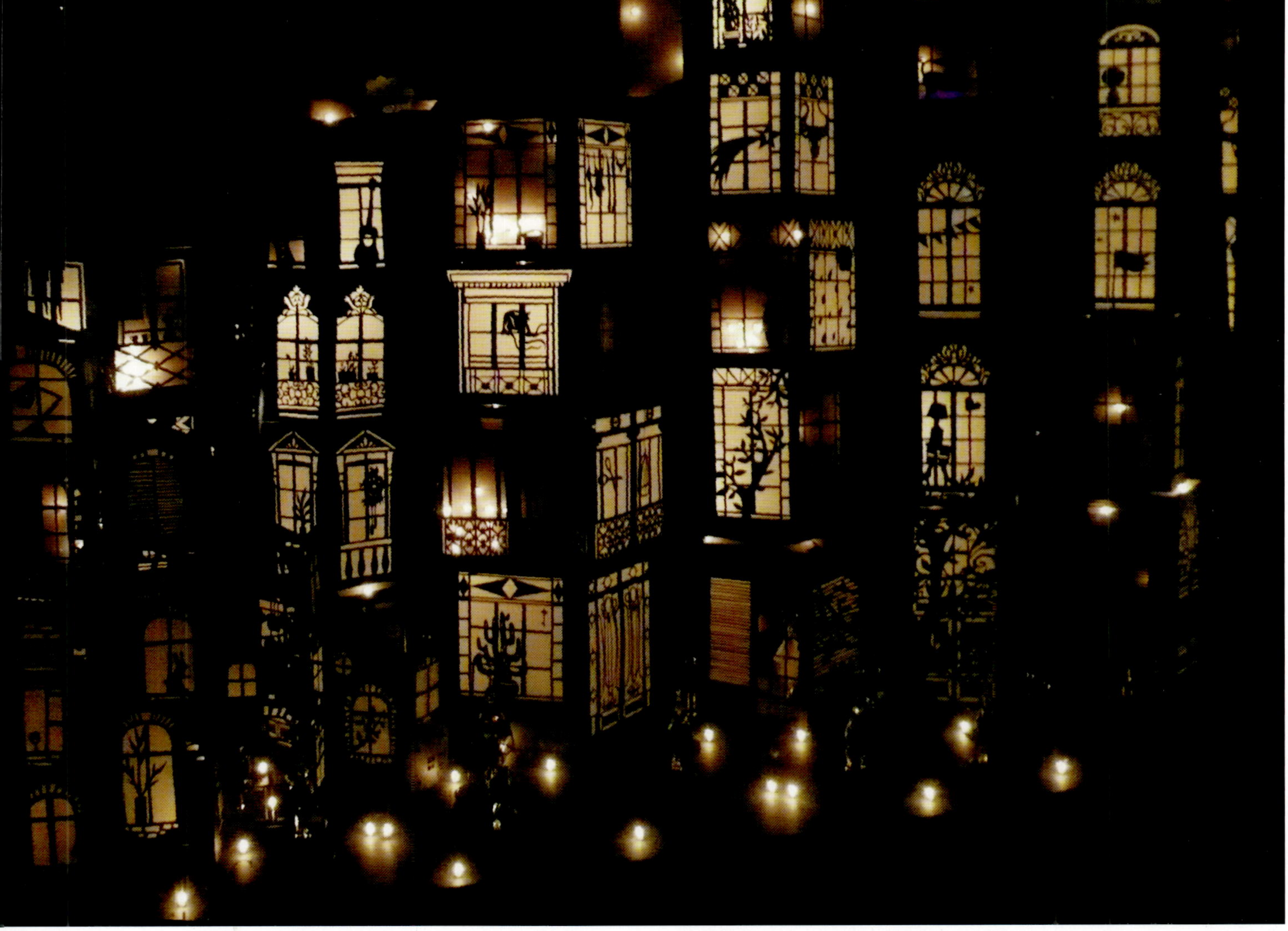

10. **Paris Marriage**

For a magnificent wedding in Paris, I created 20 famous monuments of Paris.
It was a very long and difficult work, with so many details but the result was quite enjoyable. The building where cut out in white paper and I applied golden leaf on the roofs and some parts of the monuments.

Designer: Mathilde Nivet   Country: France
Client: Akfa Family / My concierge Agency   Photographer: Laure Crubilé

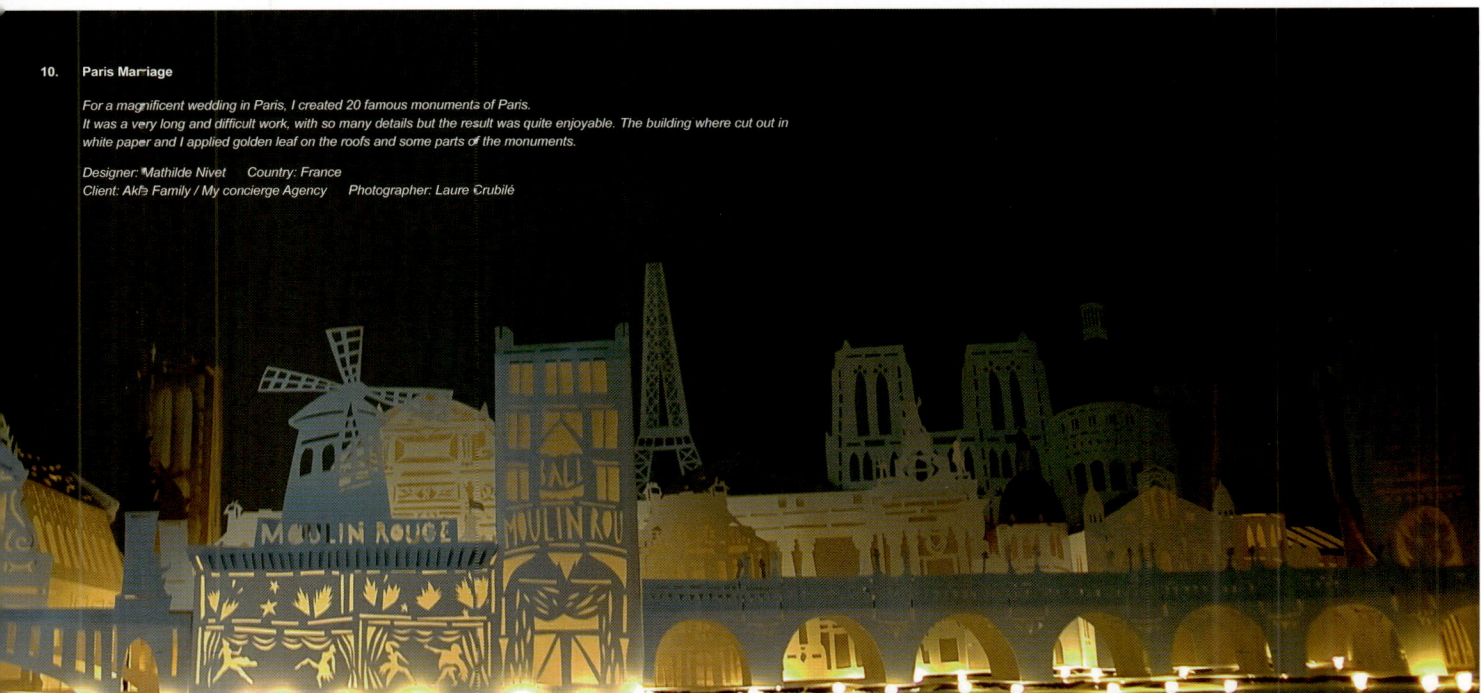

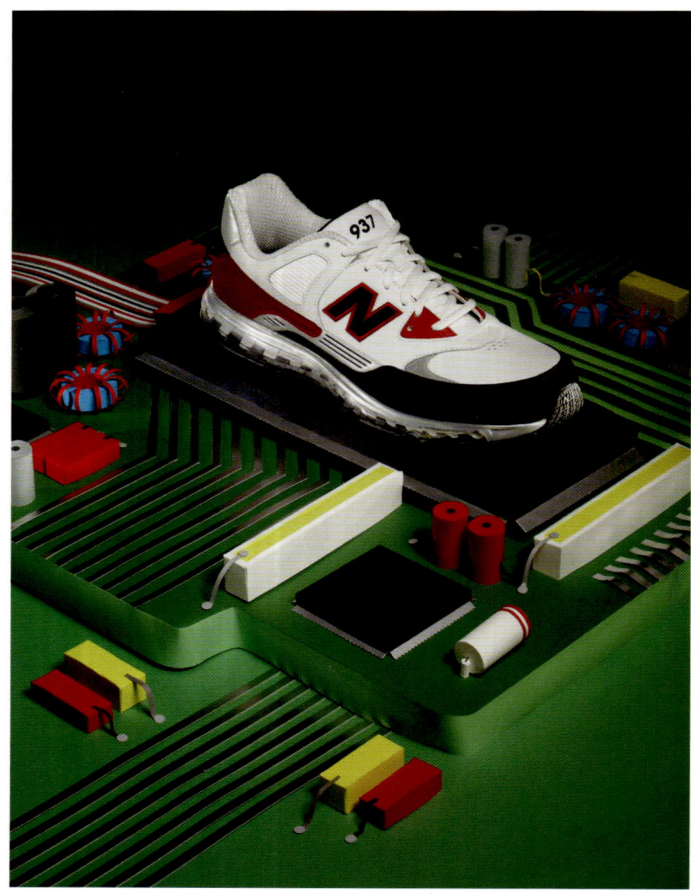
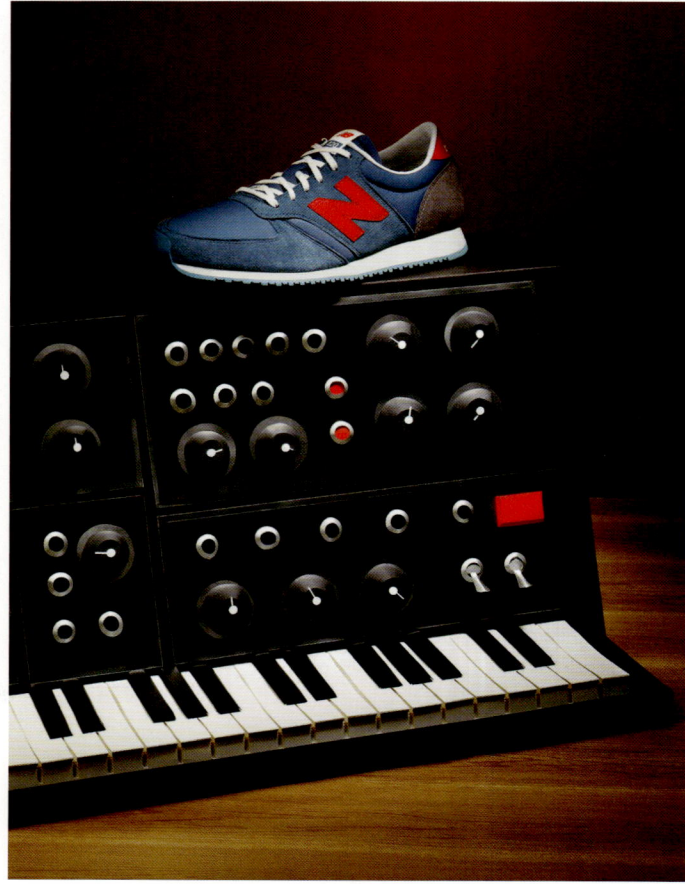
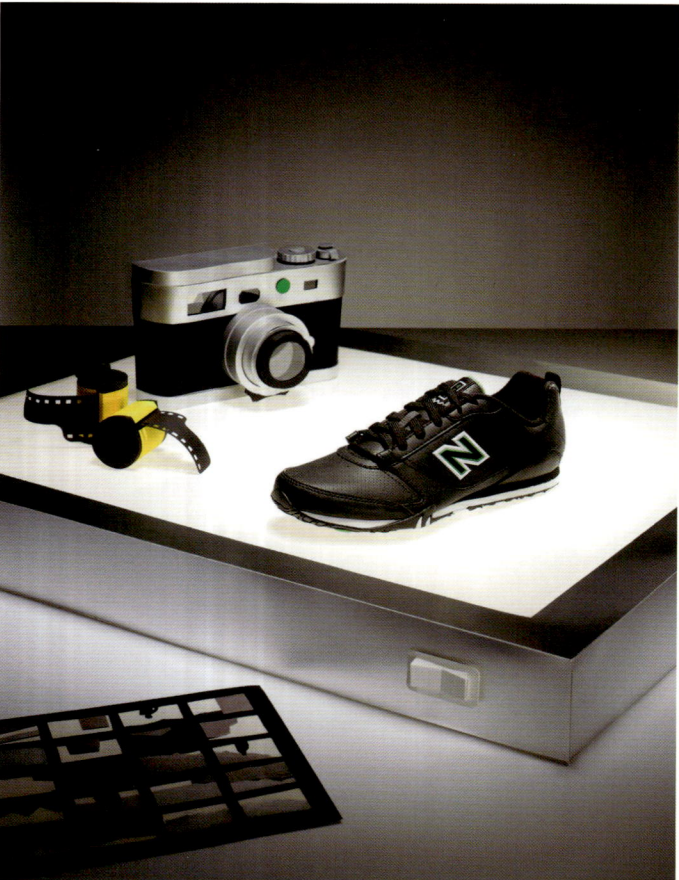
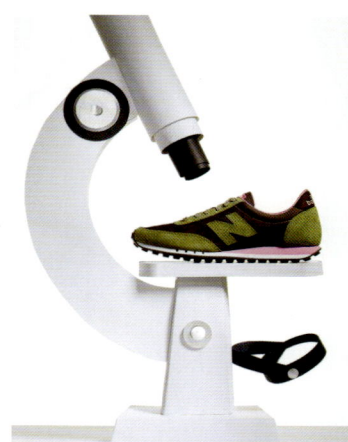
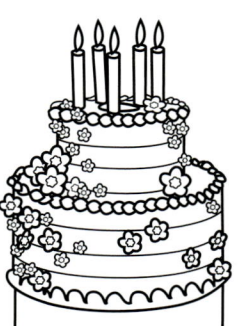

1. **New Balance Shoes**

   Paper scenery for internal catalog of shoes.
   These were done very very quickly. We had less than a week to make everything before the photo shoot. I had a great team helping me build everything. Stephen Lewis (photographer) made everything look great.

   Designer: Matthew Sporzynski
   Country: USA
   Design Agency: Mother
   Creative Director: Michael Kaye
   Client: New Balance Shoe
   Photographer: Stephen Lewis
   Art Director: Jed Grossman

1. New Balance Shoes
2. Town & Country Sea World
3. Sherwin Williams Paint Ads
4. In Style Weddings Leaf Background
5. Macy's First Impressions Ads
6. Jewelry Display for Fashion Event
7. Town & Country Winter Wonderland

---Matthew Sporzynski

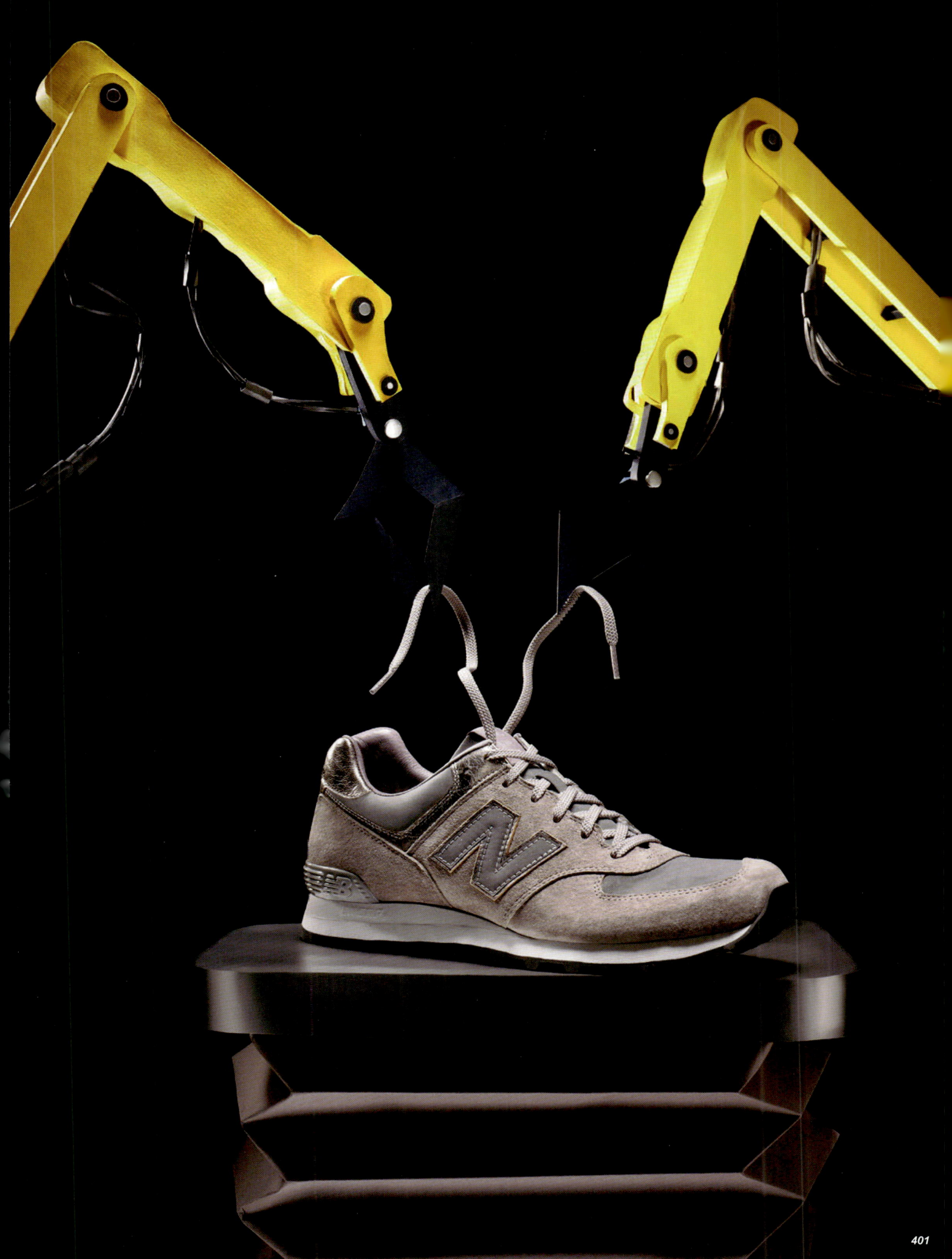

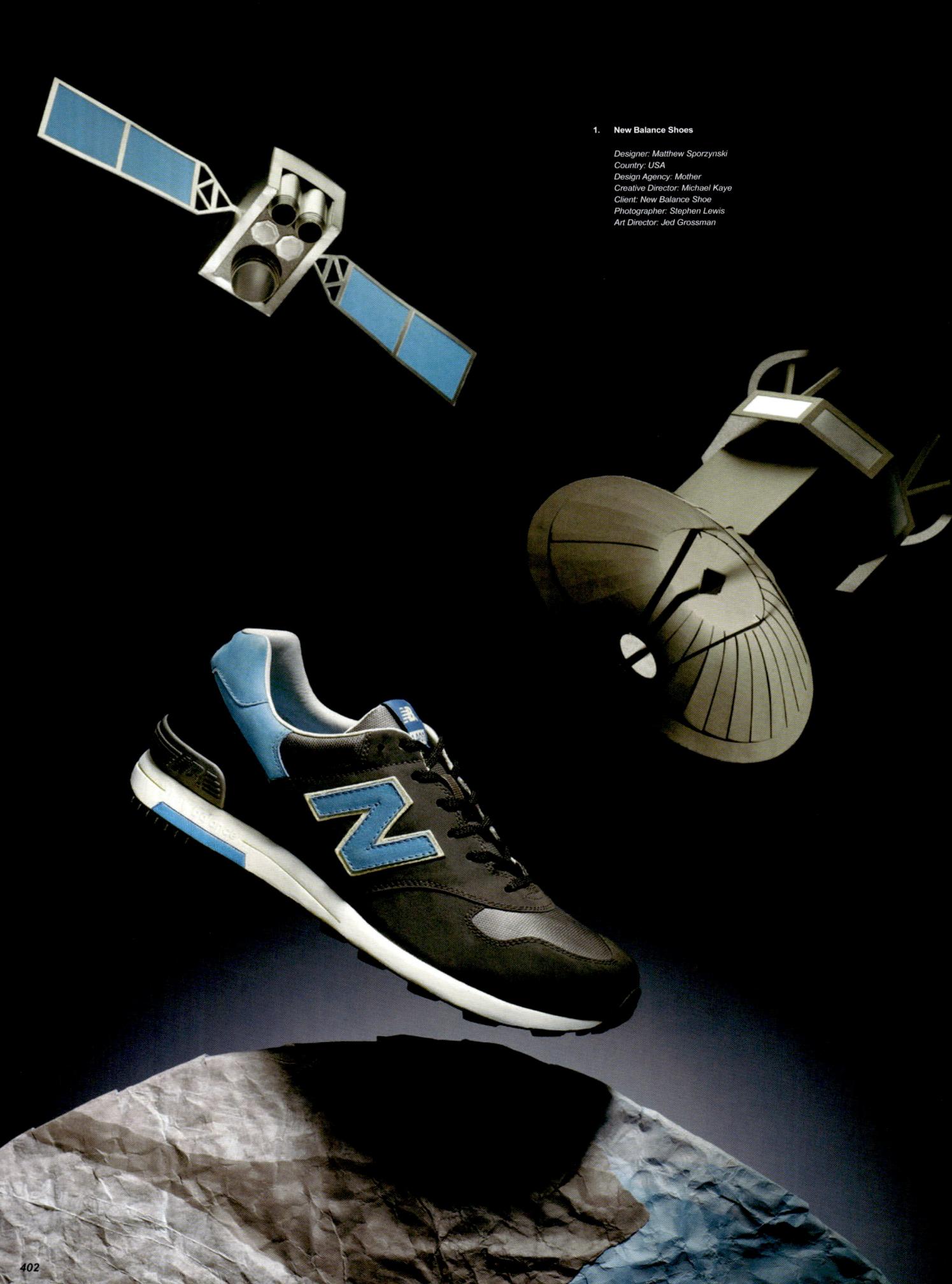

1. **New Balance Shoes**

   Designer: Matthew Sporzynski
   Country: USA
   Design Agency: Mother
   Creative Director: Michael Kaye
   Client: New Balance Shoe
   Photographer: Stephen Lewis
   Art Director: Jed Grossman

2. Town & Country Sea World

Paper scenery for magazine feature about luxe jewelry.
This is one of my favorite projects ever. The contrast between the paper constructions and the fine workmanship of the (very expensive) jewelry is nice. Sthephen Lewis lit and photographed everything beautifully.

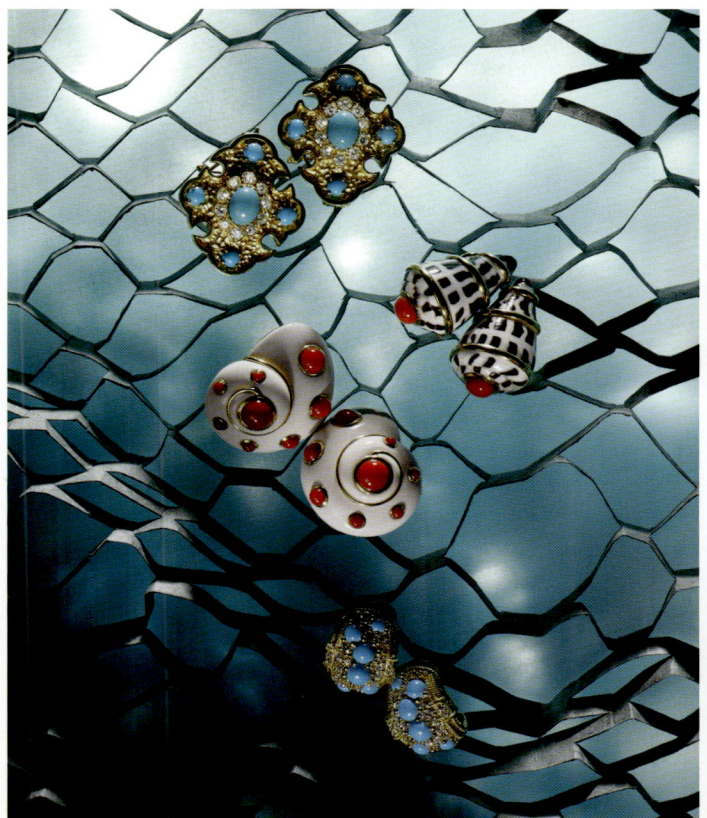
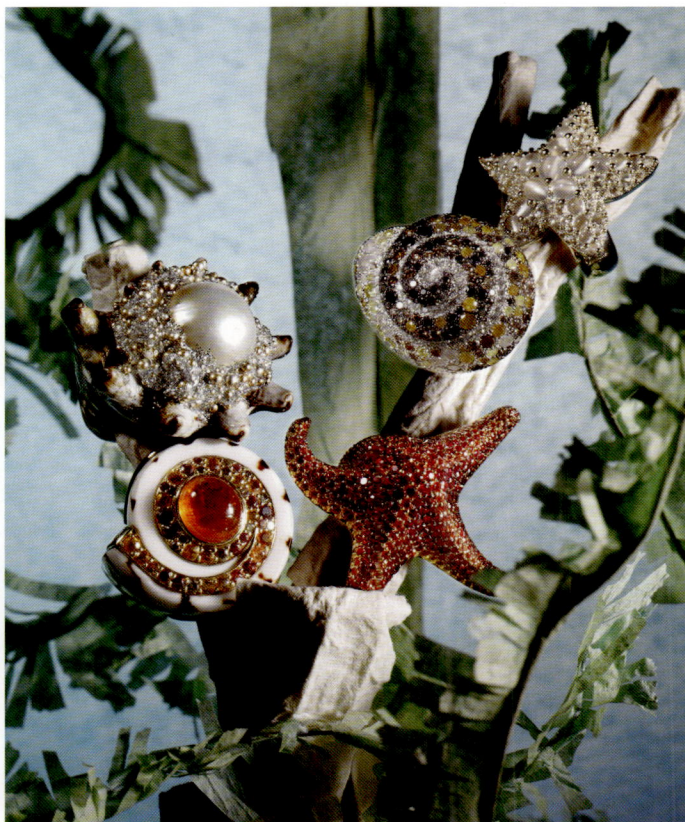
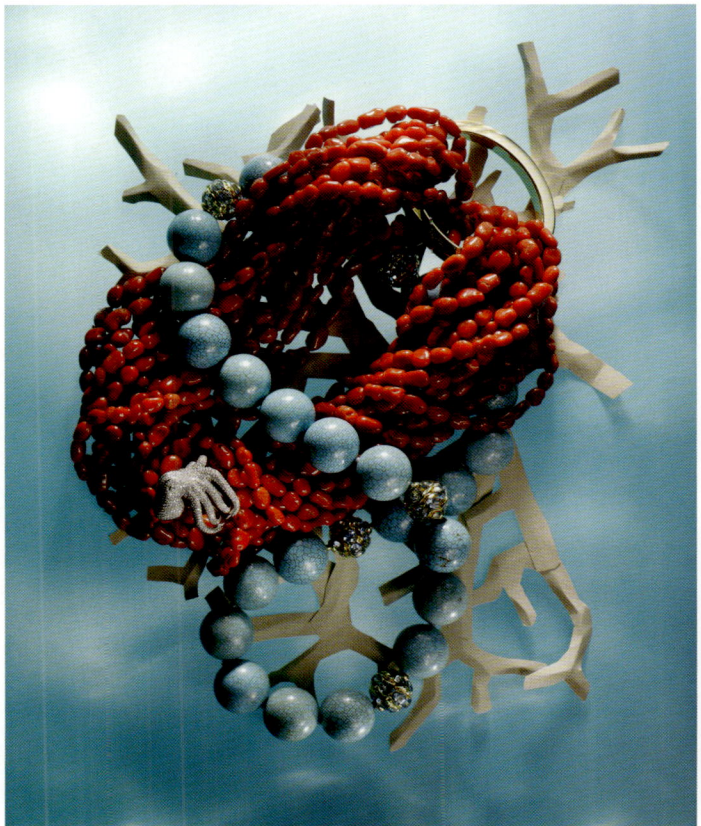
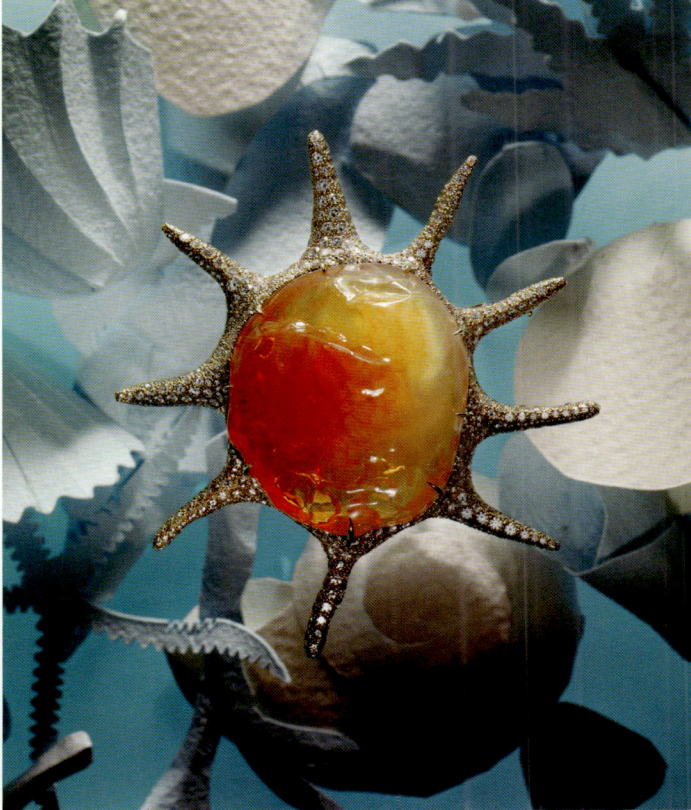

Designer: Matthew Sporzynski
Country: USA
Creative Director: Agnethe Glatved
Client: Town & Country Magazine
Photographer: Stephen Lewis

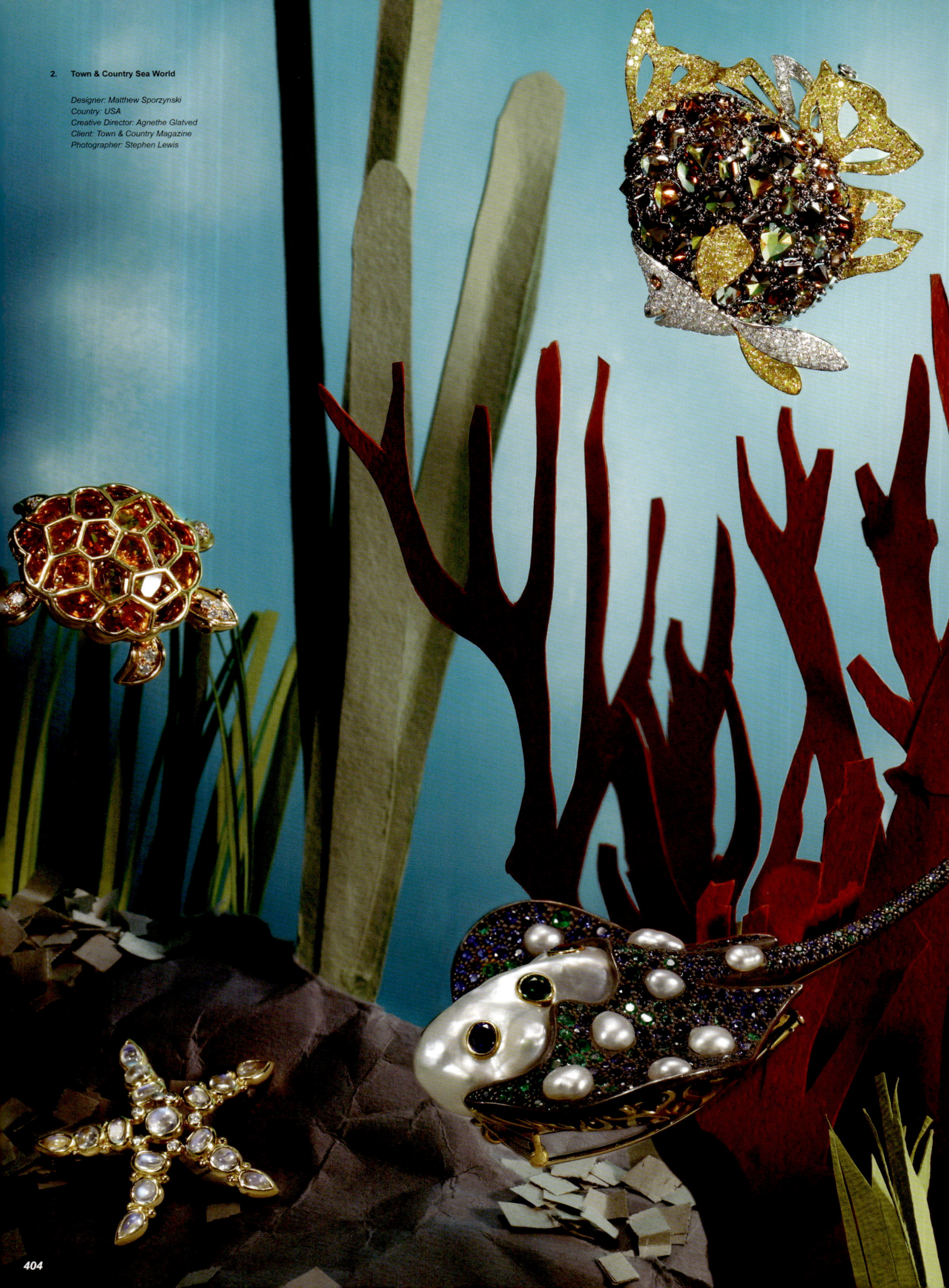

2. Town & Country Sea World

Designer: Matthew Sporzynski
Country: USA
Creative Director: Agnethe Glatved
Client: Town & Country Magazine
Photographer: Stephen Lewis

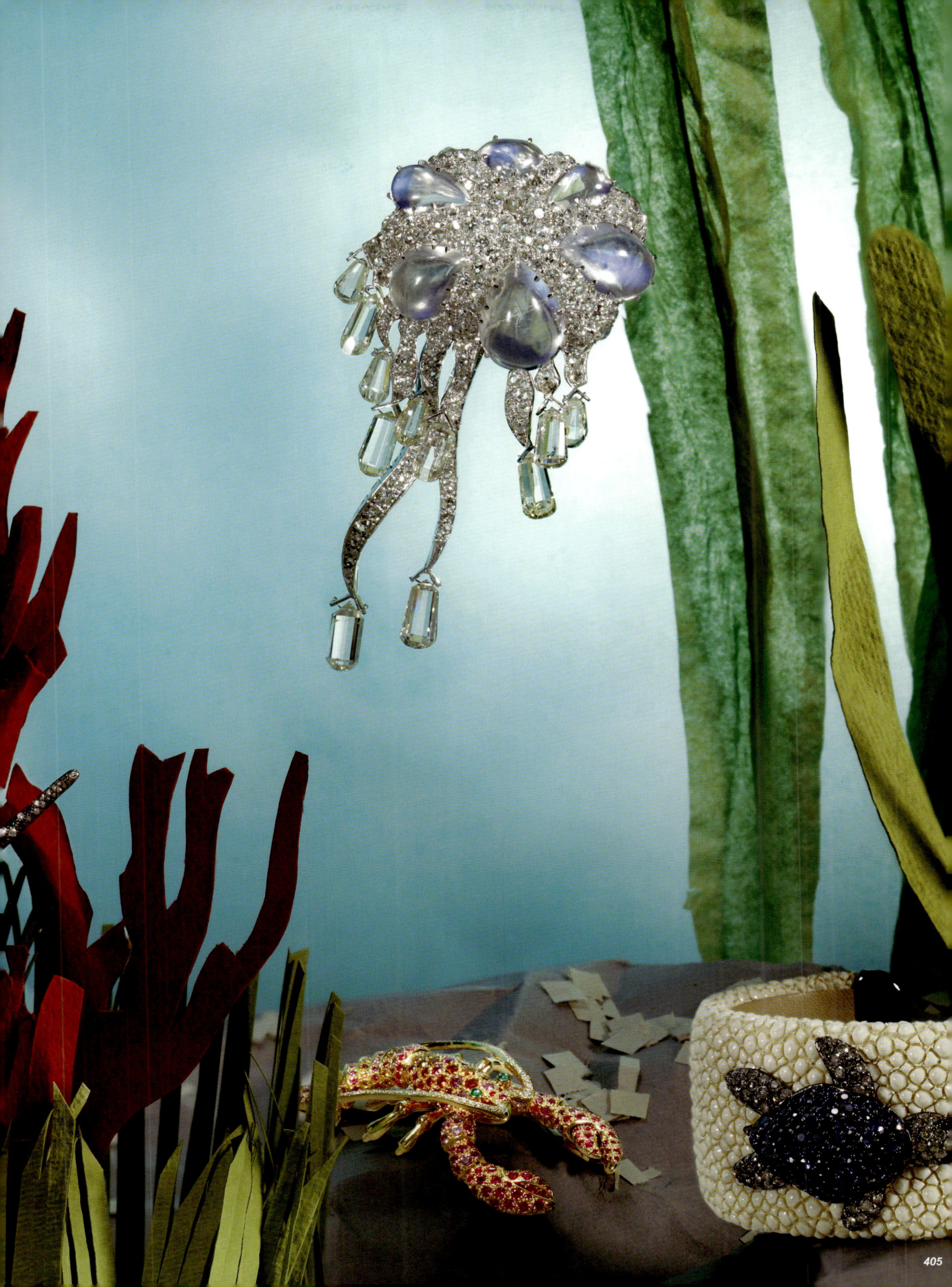

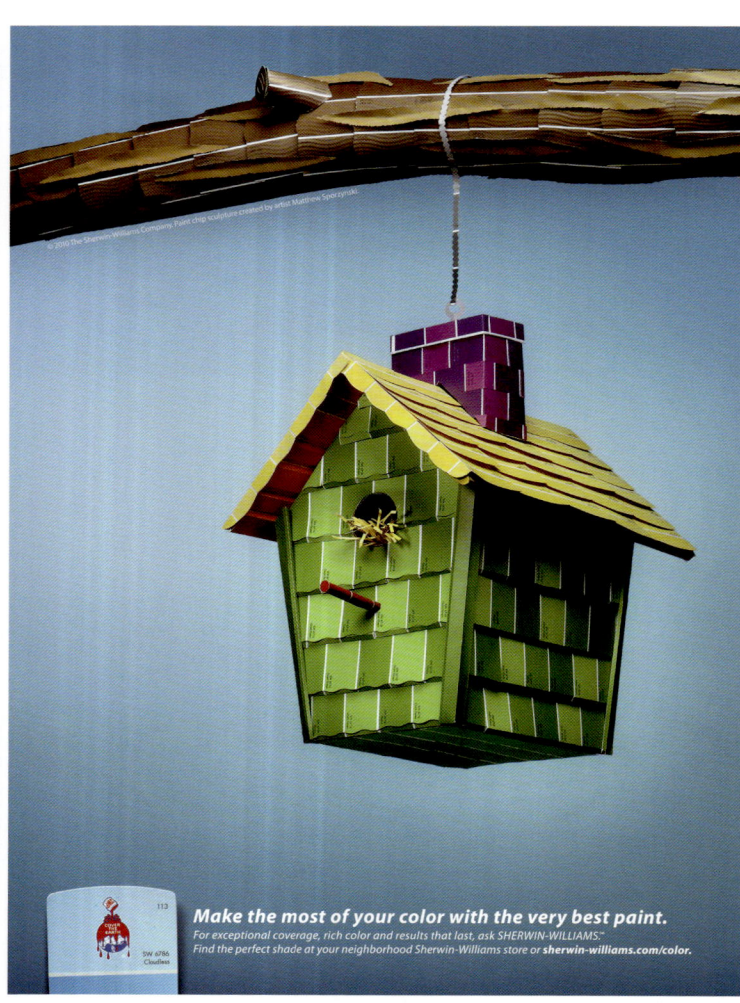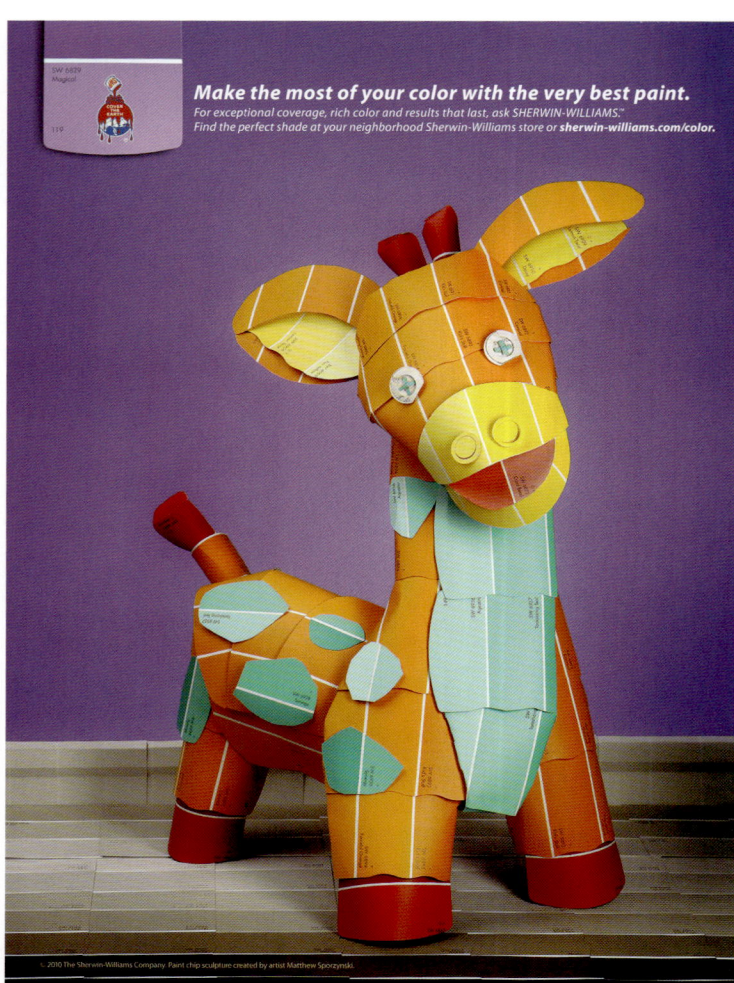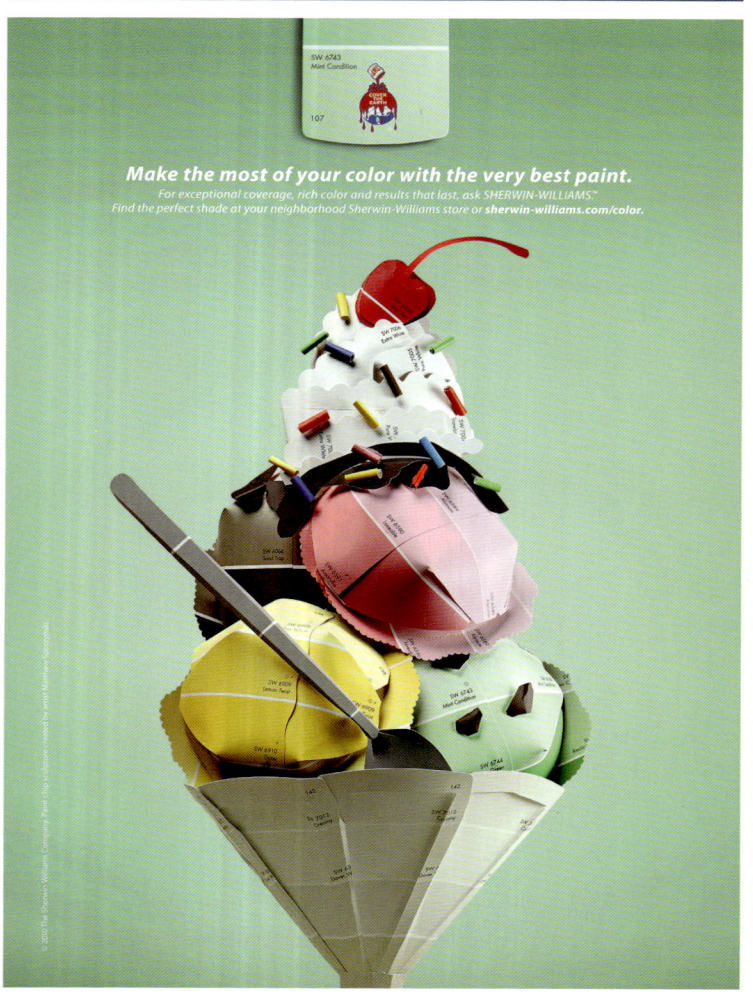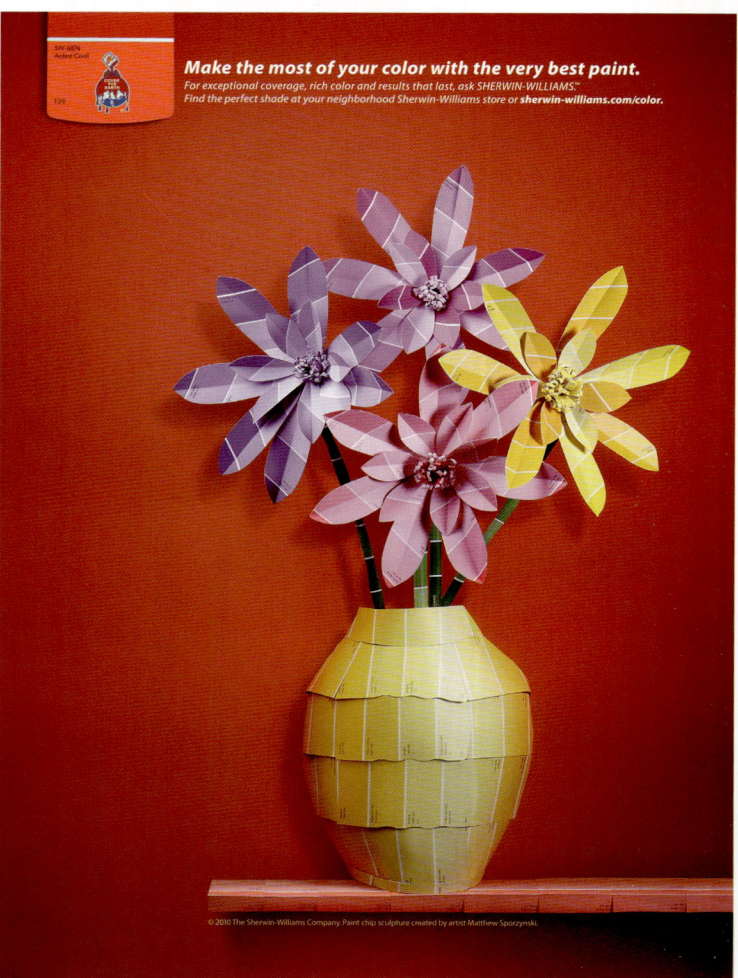

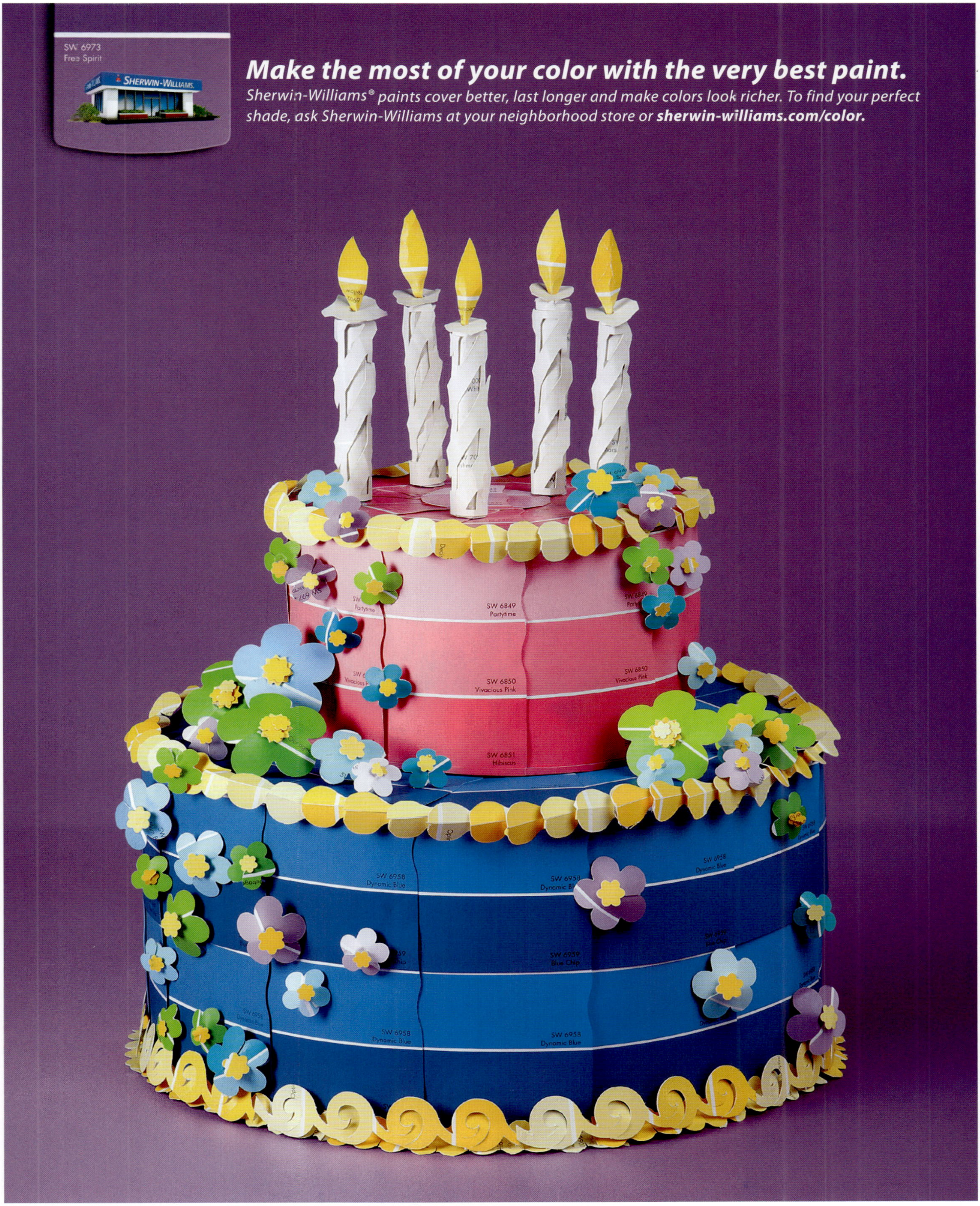

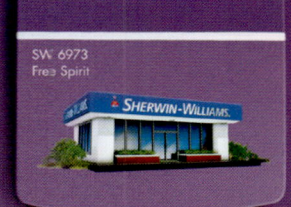

Make the most of your color with the very best paint.

Sherwin-Williams® paints cover better, last longer and make colors look richer. To find your perfect shade, ask Sherwin-Williams at your neighborhood store or **sherwin-williams.com/color**.

3. **Sherwin Williams Paint Ads**

Objects build out of paint chips for Sherwin Williams print ads.
The big challenge with these pictures was to get the objects to look like paint chips and to look like something else at the same time. I usually work with larger pieces of paper – using paint chips was like painting using a smaller brush. These are some of my most colorful work.

Designer: Matthew Sporzynski
Country: USA
Design Agency: McKinney
Creative Director: John Hagerty
Client: Sherwin Williams Paints
Photographer: Nicolai Grosell

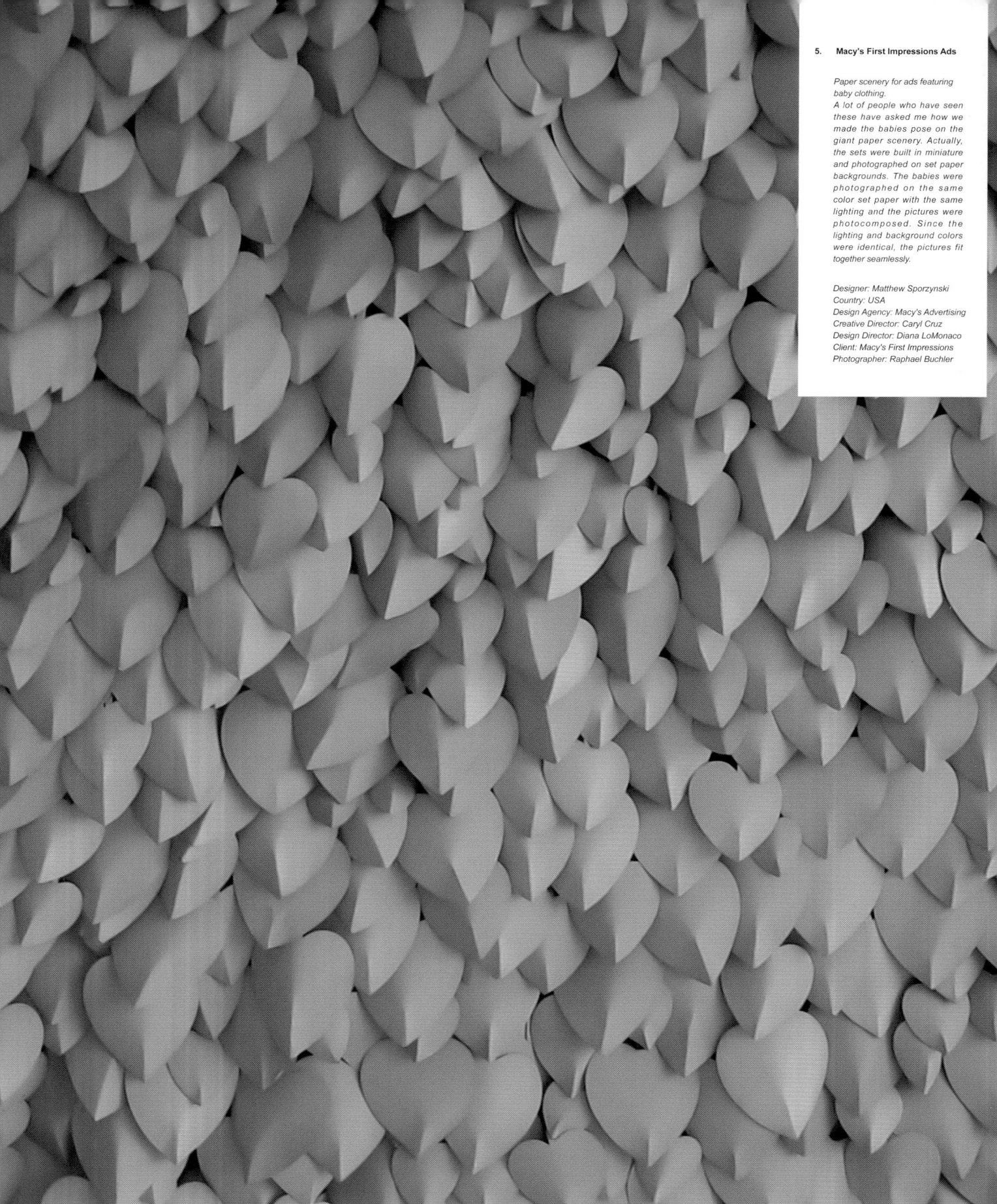

5. Macy's First Impressions Ads

Paper scenery for ads featuring baby clothing.
A lot of people who have seen these have asked me how we made the babies pose on the giant paper scenery. Actually, the sets were built in miniature and photographed on set paper backgrounds. The babies were photographed on the same color set paper with the same lighting and the pictures were photocomposed. Since the lighting and background colors were identical, the pictures fit together seamlessly.

Designer: Matthew Sporzynski
Country: USA
Design Agency: Macy's Advertising
Creative Director: Caryl Cruz
Design Director: Diana LoMonaco
Client: Macy's First Impressions
Photographer: Raphael Buchler

4. In Style Weddings Leaf Background

Background of paper leaves created for a magazine feature about wedding stationery.
In Style Weddings asked me to create something pretty to use as a backgrounds for a feature about wedding stationery. I had recently taken a lovely walk in Provincetown with my camera and my schnauzer Julius. I showed the editors photos from the walk and suggested making naturalistic backgrounds composed of leaves. This background was inspired by my neighbor Alice Brock's morning glory. I had the leaves die-cut from heavy all-cotton paper. The leaves were then dyed with Rit fabric dye. Each leaf absorbed the dye a little differently, giving a nice variation to the coloring.

Designer: Matthew Sporzynski
Country: USA
Client: In Style Weddings
Photographer: Matthew Sporzynski

5. Macy's First Impressions Ads

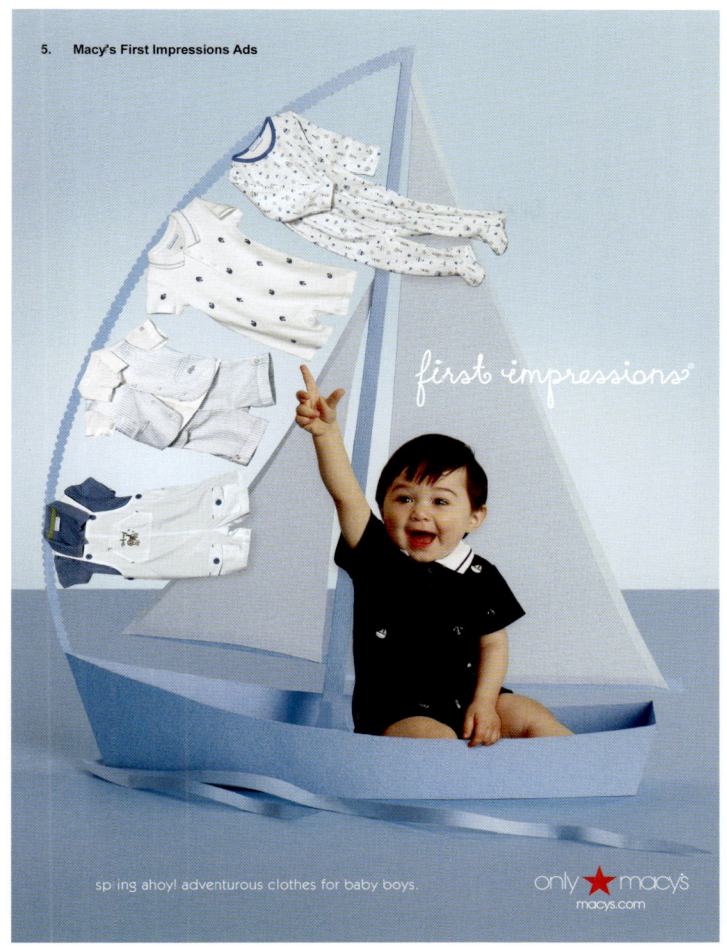
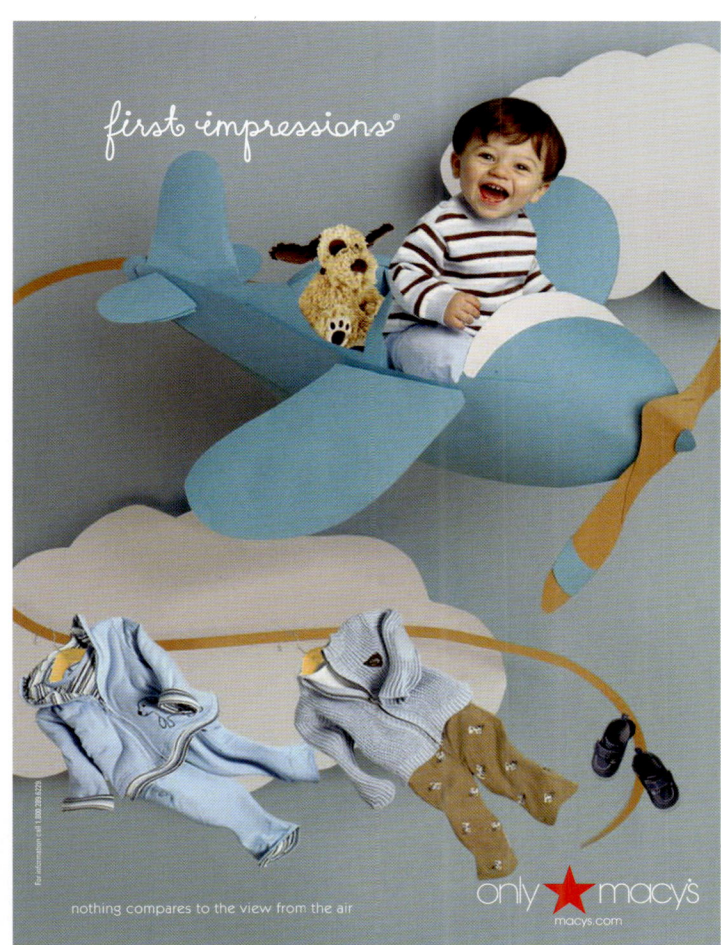
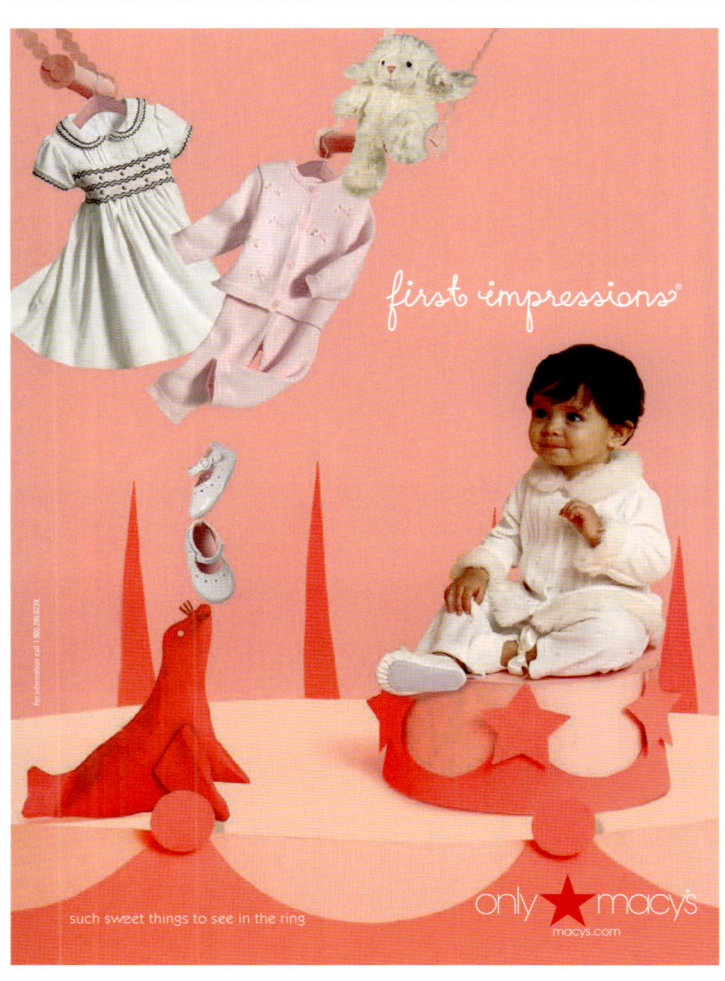
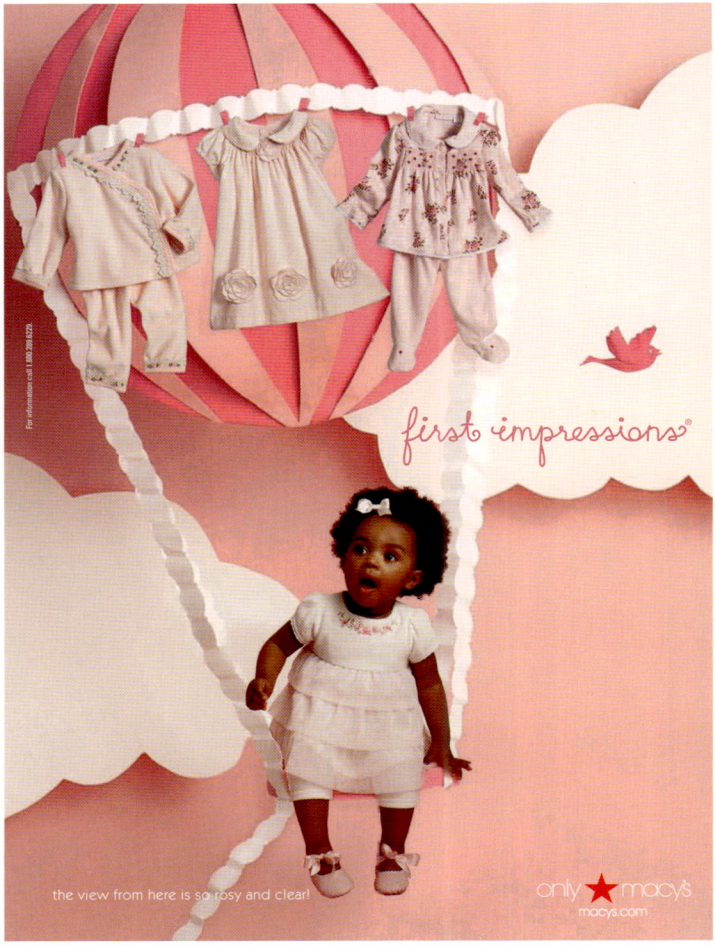

Winter Wonderland

Make your look sparkle with a sprinkling of bright white diamonds.

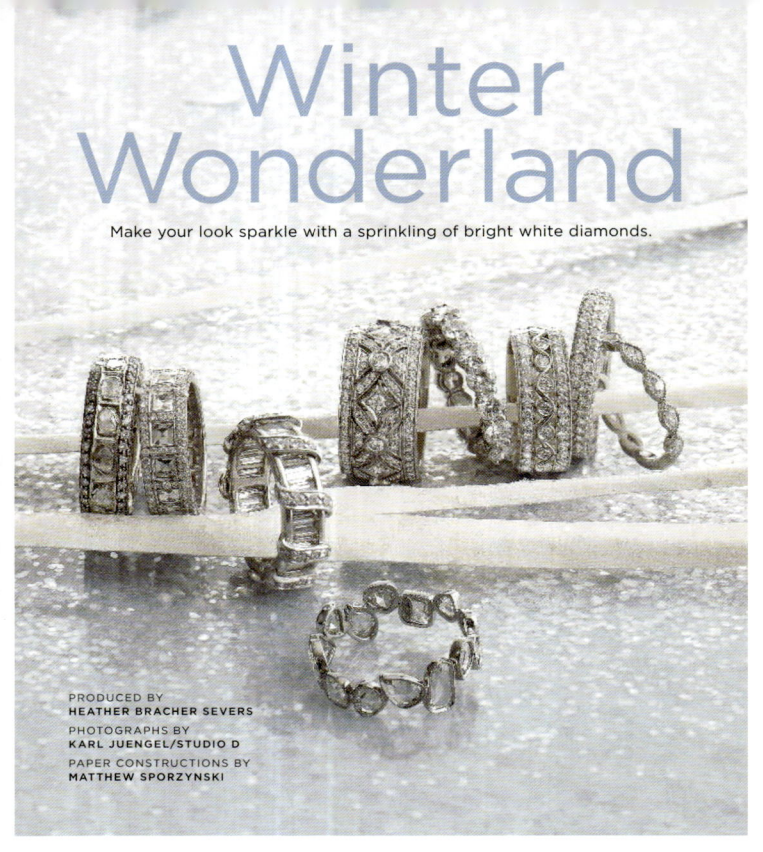

PRODUCED BY
HEATHER BRACHER SEVERS
PHOTOGRAPHS BY
KARL JUENGEL/STUDIO D
PAPER CONSTRUCTIONS BY
MATTHEW SPORZYNSKI

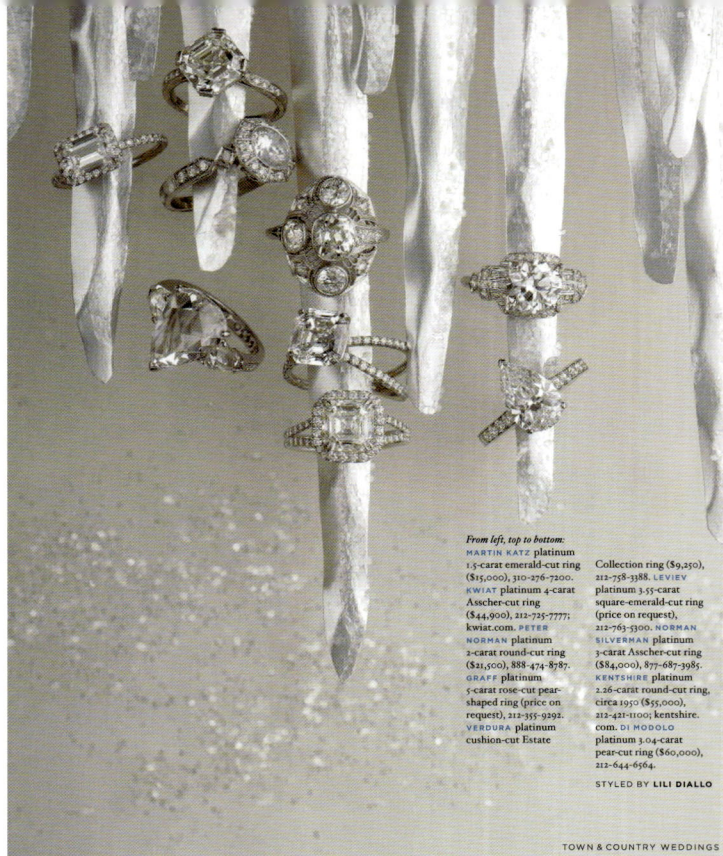

From left, top to bottom:
MARTIN KATZ platinum 1.5-carat emerald-cut ring ($15,000), 310-276-7200. **KWIAT** platinum 4-carat Asscher-cut ring ($44,900), 212-725-7777; kwiat.com. **PETER NORMAN** platinum 2-carat round-cut ring ($21,500), 888-474-8787. **GRAFF** platinum 5-carat rose-cut pear-shaped ring (price on request), 212-355-9292. **VERDURA** platinum cushion-cut Estate Collection ring ($9,250), 212-758-3388. **LEVIEV** platinum 3.55-carat square-emerald-cut ring (price on request), 212-763-5300. **NORMAN SILVERMAN** platinum 3-carat Asscher-cut ring ($84,000), 877-687-3985. **KENTSHIRE** platinum 2.26-carat round-cut ring, circa 1950 ($55,000), 212-421-1100; kentshire.com. **DI MODOLO** platinum 3.04-carat pear-cut ring ($60,000), 212-644-6564.

STYLED BY LILI DIALLO

TOWN & COUNTRY WEDDINGS

---

6. Jewelry Display for Fashion Event

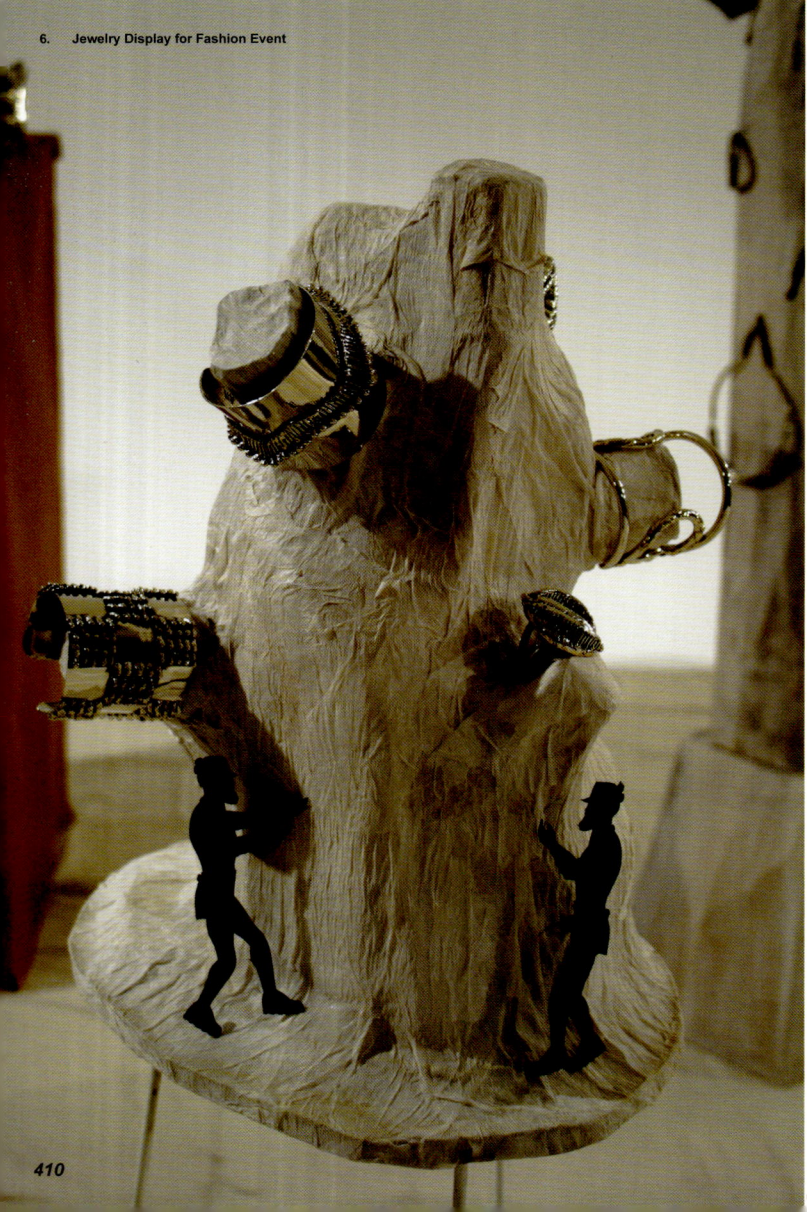

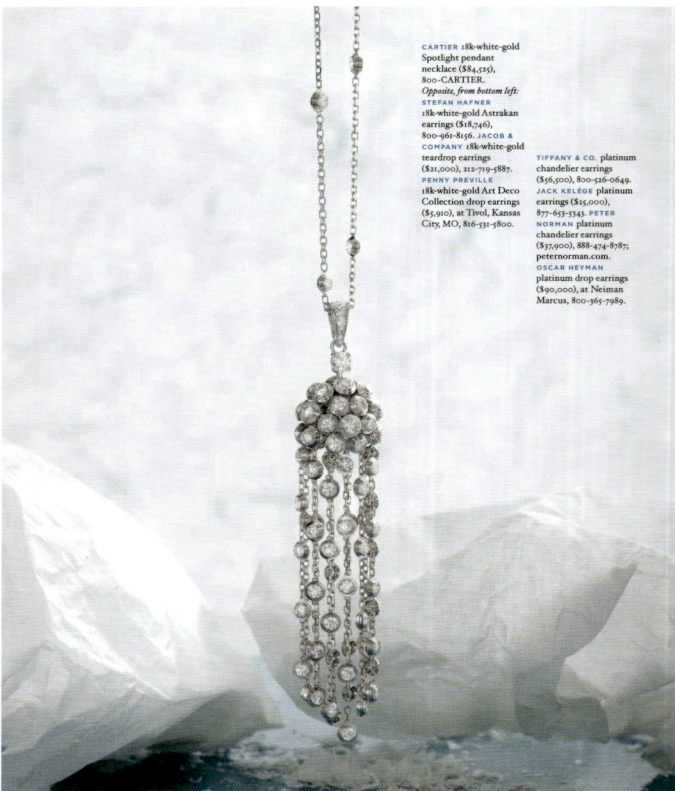

CARTIER 18k-white-gold Spotlight pendant necklace ($84,515), 800-CARTIER. *Opposite, from bottom left:* **STEFAN HAFNER** 18k-white-gold Astrakan earrings ($18,746), 800-961-8156. **JACOB & COMPANY** 18k-white-gold teardrop earrings ($21,000), 212-719-5887. **PENNY PREVILLE** 18k-white-gold Art Deco Collection drop earrings ($5,910), at Tivol, Kansas City, MO, 816-531-5800. **TIFFANY & CO.** platinum chandelier earrings ($56,000), 800-526-0649. **JACK KELEGE** platinum earrings ($35,000), 877-653-5343. **PETER NORMAN** platinum chandelier earrings ($37,900), 888-474-8787; peternorman.com. **OSCAR HEYMAN** platinum drop earrings ($90,000), at Neiman Marcus, 800-365-7989.

6. Jewelry Display for Fashion Event

Papier-mache display for bracelets with silhouette figures of Alpine men.
This was one of 10 large papier-mache sculptures I built for a press event/fashion week party for the jewelry line Anndra Neen. It was fun to build large abstract sculptures to display the jewelry. My friend fashion illustrator Linda Chamberlin drew silhouettes of tiny mountain climbers which I cut out, assembled and posed with the jewelry.

Designer: Matthew Sporzynski
Country: USA
Creative Director: Phoebe and Annette Stevens
Client: Anndra Neen
Photographer: Matthew Sporzynski
Silhouettes Drawn: Linda Chamberlin

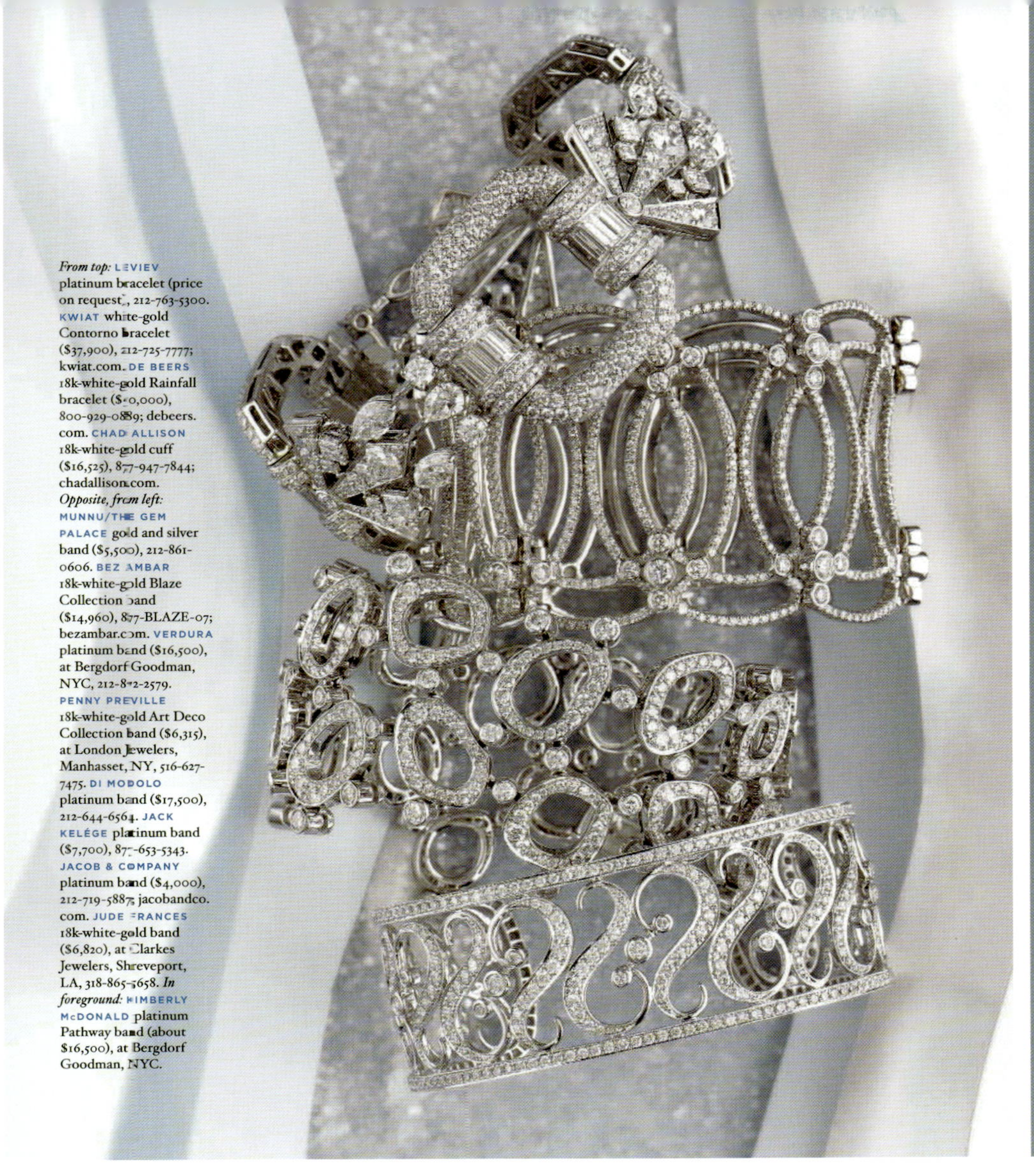

From top: **LEVIEV** platinum bracelet (price on request., 212-763-5300. **KWIAT** white-gold Contorno bracelet ($37,900), 212-725-7777; kwiat.com. **DE BEERS** 18k-white-gold Rainfall bracelet ($50,000), 800-929-0889; debeers.com. **CHAD ALLISON** 18k-white-gold cuff ($16,525), 877-947-7844; chadallison.com. *Opposite, from left:* **MUNNU/THE GEM PALACE** gold and silver band ($5,500), 212-861-0606. **BEZ AMBAR** 18k-white-gold Blaze Collection band ($14,960), 877-BLAZE-07; bezambar.com. **VERDURA** platinum band ($16,500), at Bergdorf Goodman, NYC, 212-872-2579. **PENNY PREVILLE** 18k-white-gold Art Deco Collection band ($6,315), at London Jewelers, Manhasset, NY, 516-627-7475. **DI MODOLO** platinum band ($17,500), 212-644-6564. **JACK KELEGE** platinum band ($7,700), 877-653-5343. **JACOB & COMPANY** platinum band ($4,000), 212-719-5887; jacobandco.com. **JUDE FRANCES** 18k-white-gold band ($6,820), at Clarkes Jewelers, Shreveport, LA, 318-865-5658. *In foreground:* **KIMBERLY McDONALD** platinum Pathway band (about $16,500), at Bergdorf Goodman, NYC.

7. Town & Country Winter Wonderland

Paper scenery for magazine feature about luxe wedding jewelry. Everything looks better with studio lightning and hundreds of thousands of dollars worth of jewelry!

Designer: Matthew Sporzynski
Country: USA
Creative Director: Agnethe Glatved
Design Director: Effie Tsu
Client: Town & Country Magazine
Photographer: Karl Juengel

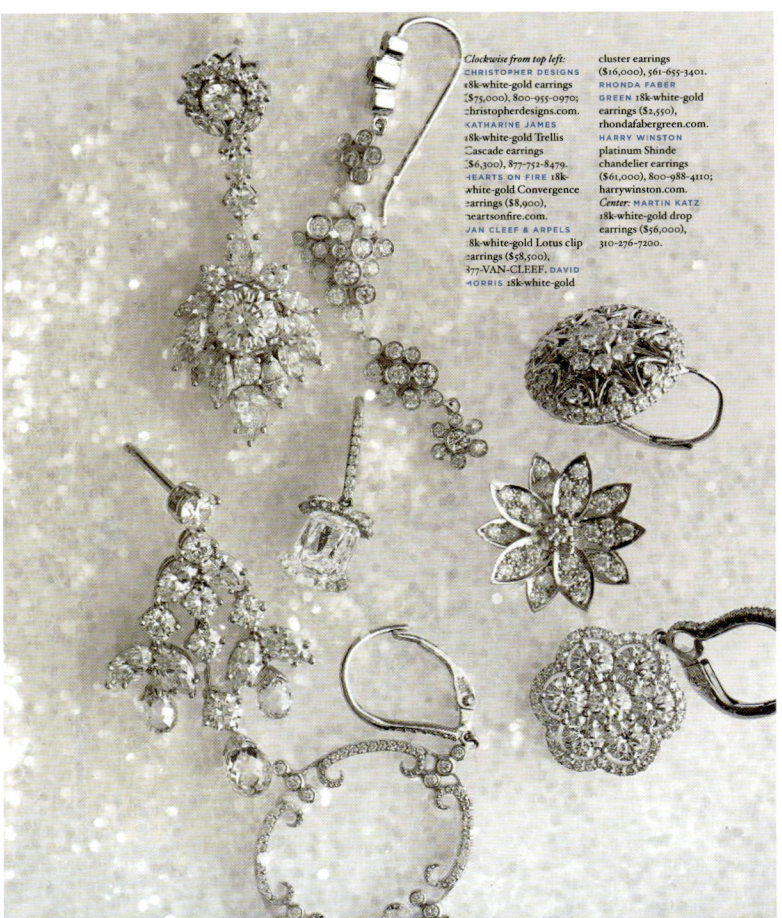

Clockwise from top left: **CHRISTOPHER DESIGNS** 18k-white-gold earrings ($75,000), 800-955-0970; christopherdesigns.com. **KATHARINE JAMES** 18k-white-gold Trellis Cascade earrings ($6,300), 877-712-8479. **HEARTS ON FIRE** 18k-white-gold Convergence earrings ($8,900), heartsonfire.com. **VAN CLEEF & ARPELS** 18k-white-gold Lotus clip earrings ($58,500), 877-VAN-CLEEF. **DAVID MORRIS** 18k-white-gold cluster earrings ($16,000), 561-655-3401. **RHONDA FABER GREEN** 18k-white-gold earrings ($2,550), rhondafabergreen.com. **HARRY WINSTON** platinum Shinde chandelier earrings ($61,000), 800-988-4110; harrywinston.com. *Center:* **MARTIN KATZ** 18k-white-gold drop earrings ($56,000), 310-276-7200.

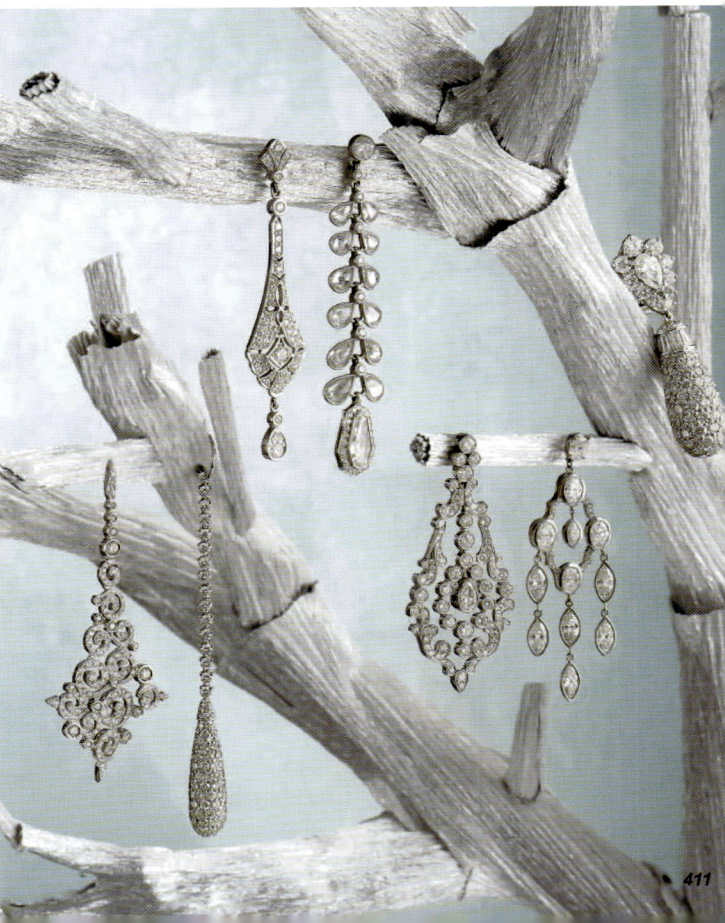

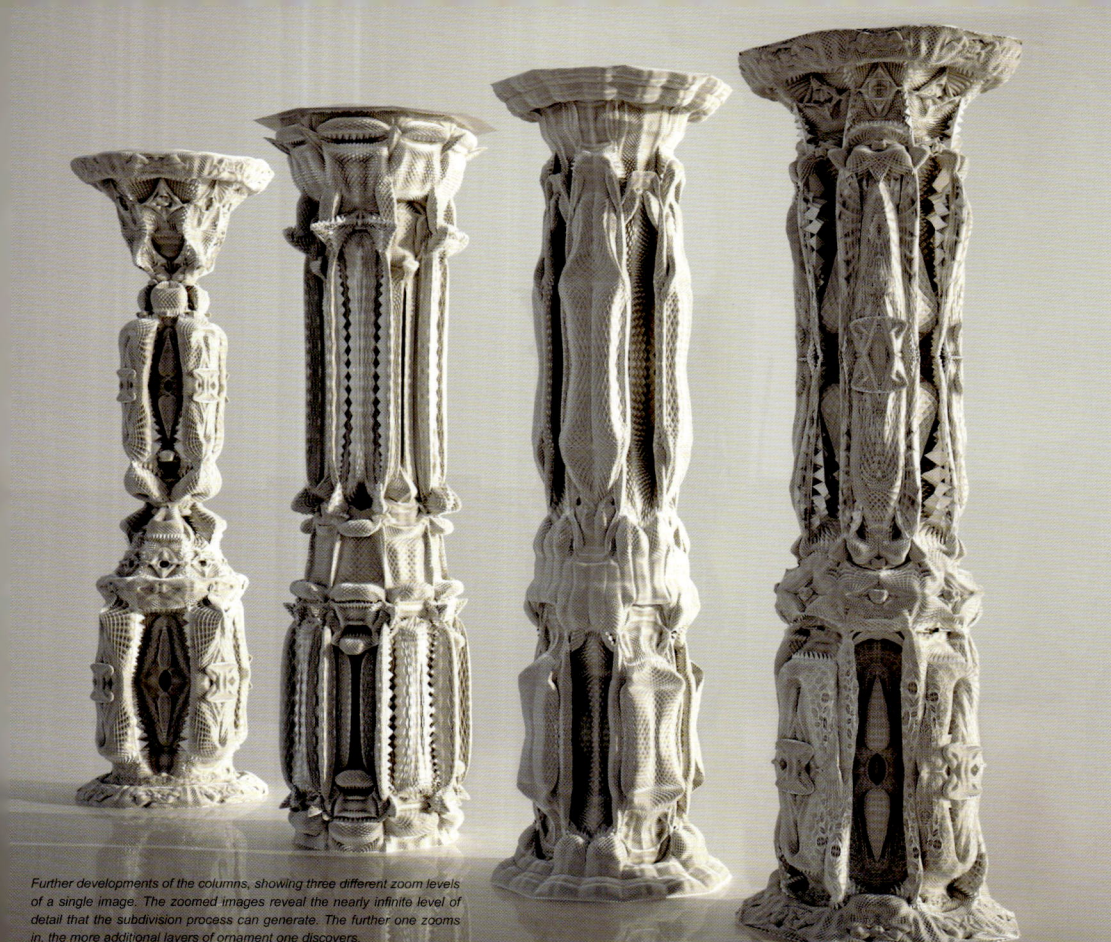

Further developments of the columns, showing three different zoom levels of a single image. The zoomed images reveal the nearly infinite level of detail that the subdivision process can generate. The further one zooms in, the more additional layers of ornament one discovers.

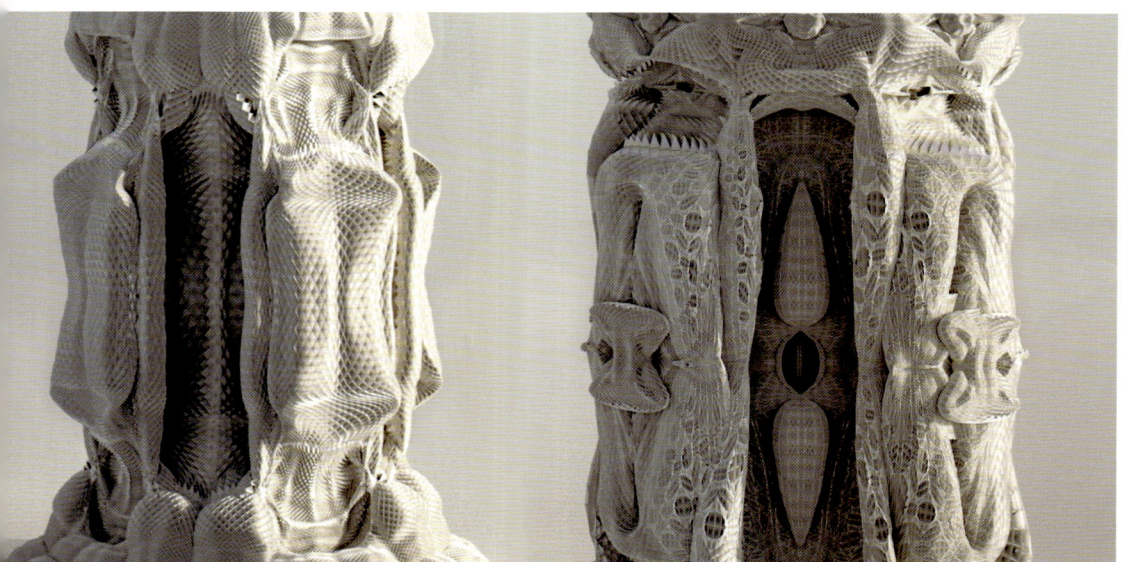

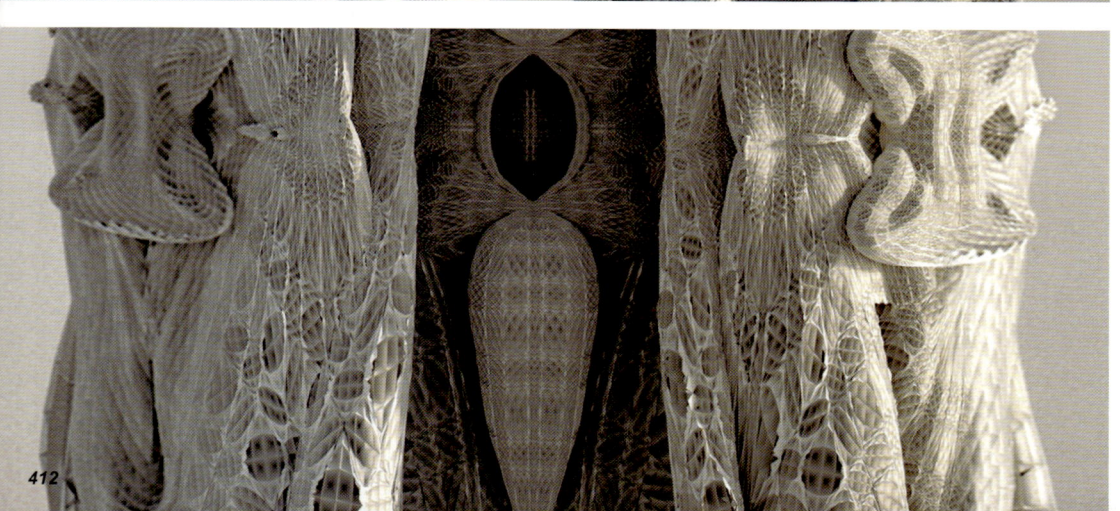

1. **Subdivided Column**

   Architect: Michael Hansmeyer

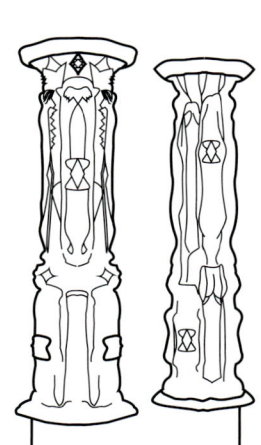

1. **Subdivided Column**
2. **The Sixth Order**

   ---Michael Hansmeyer

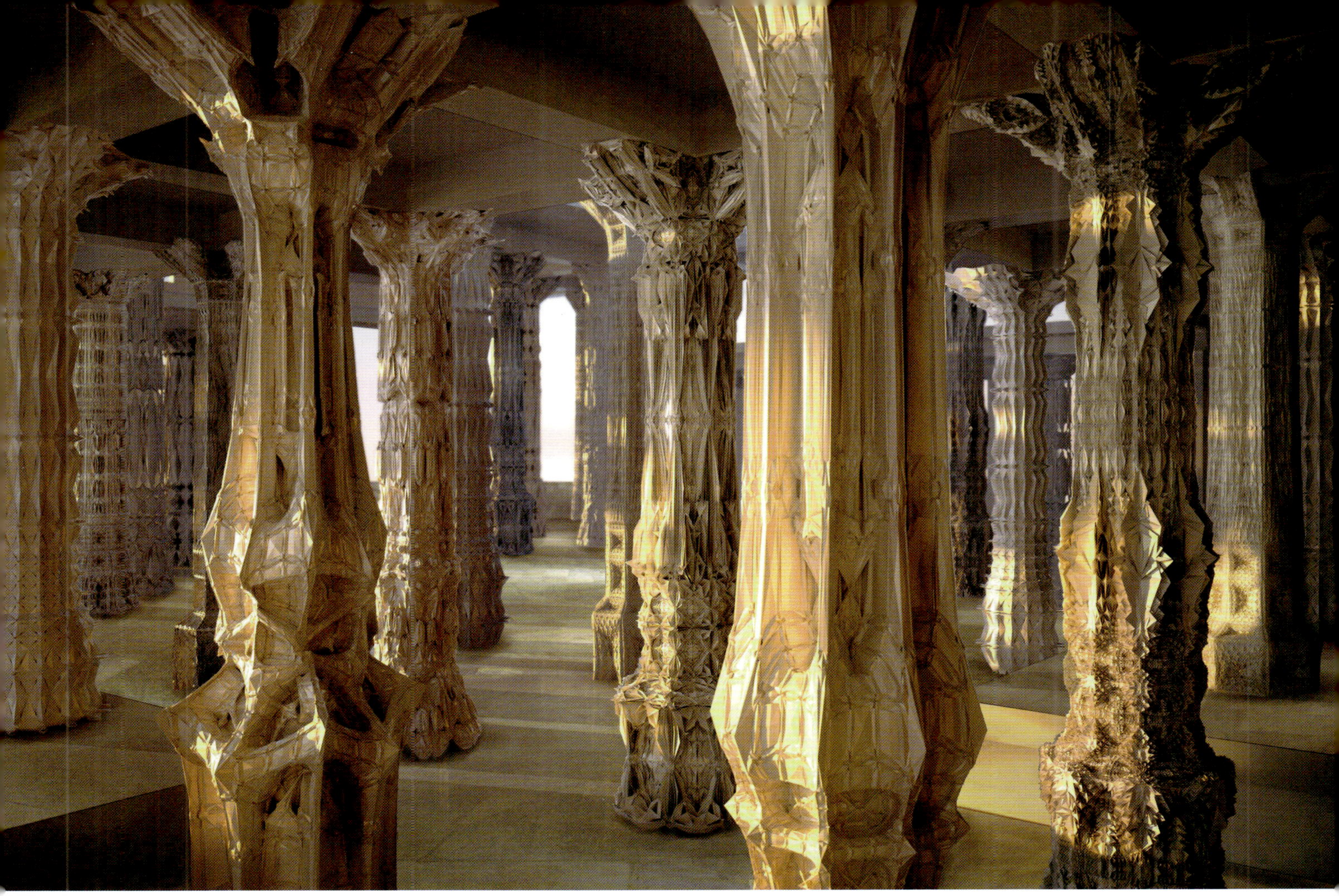

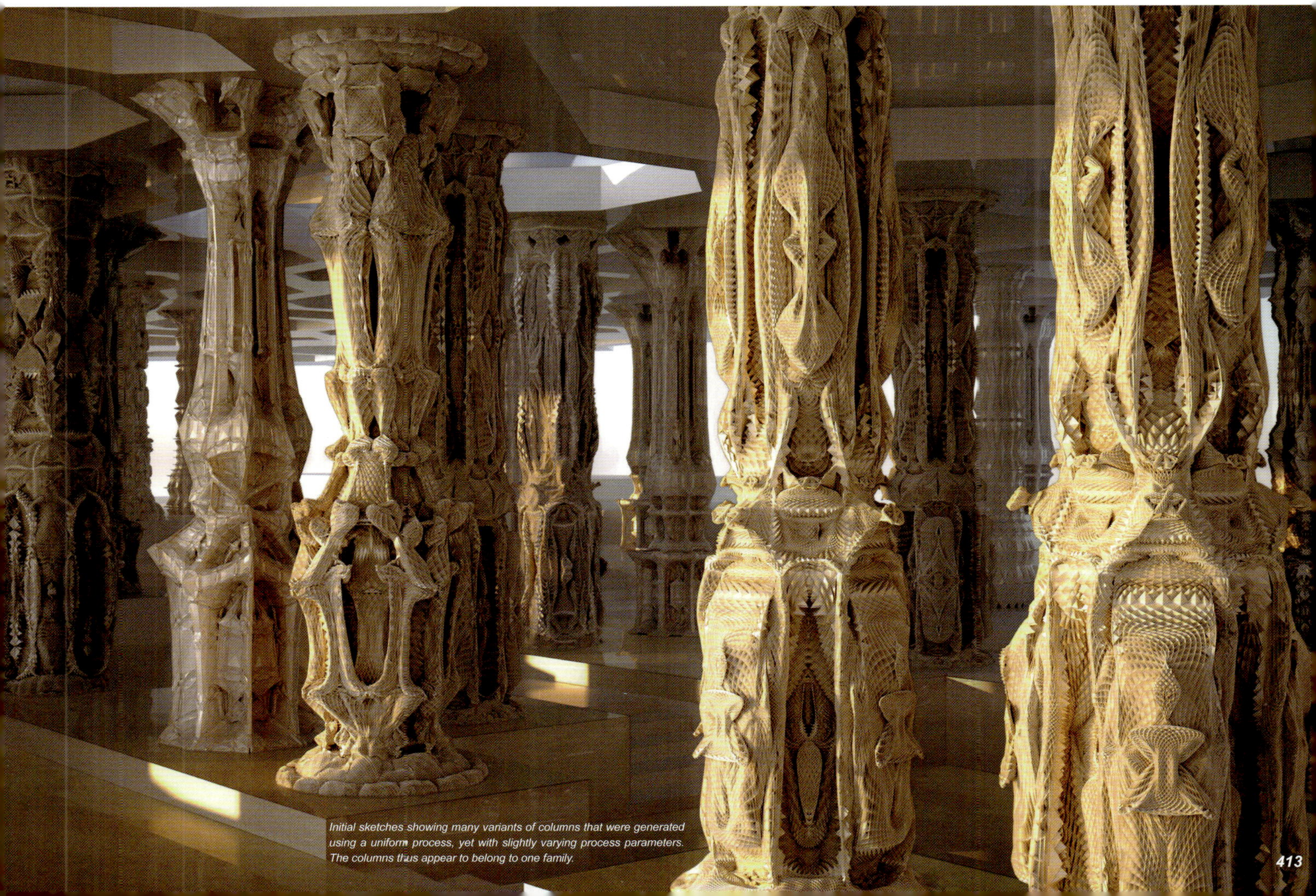

Initial sketches showing many variants of columns that were generated using a uniform process, yet with slightly varying process parameters. The columns thus appear to belong to one family.

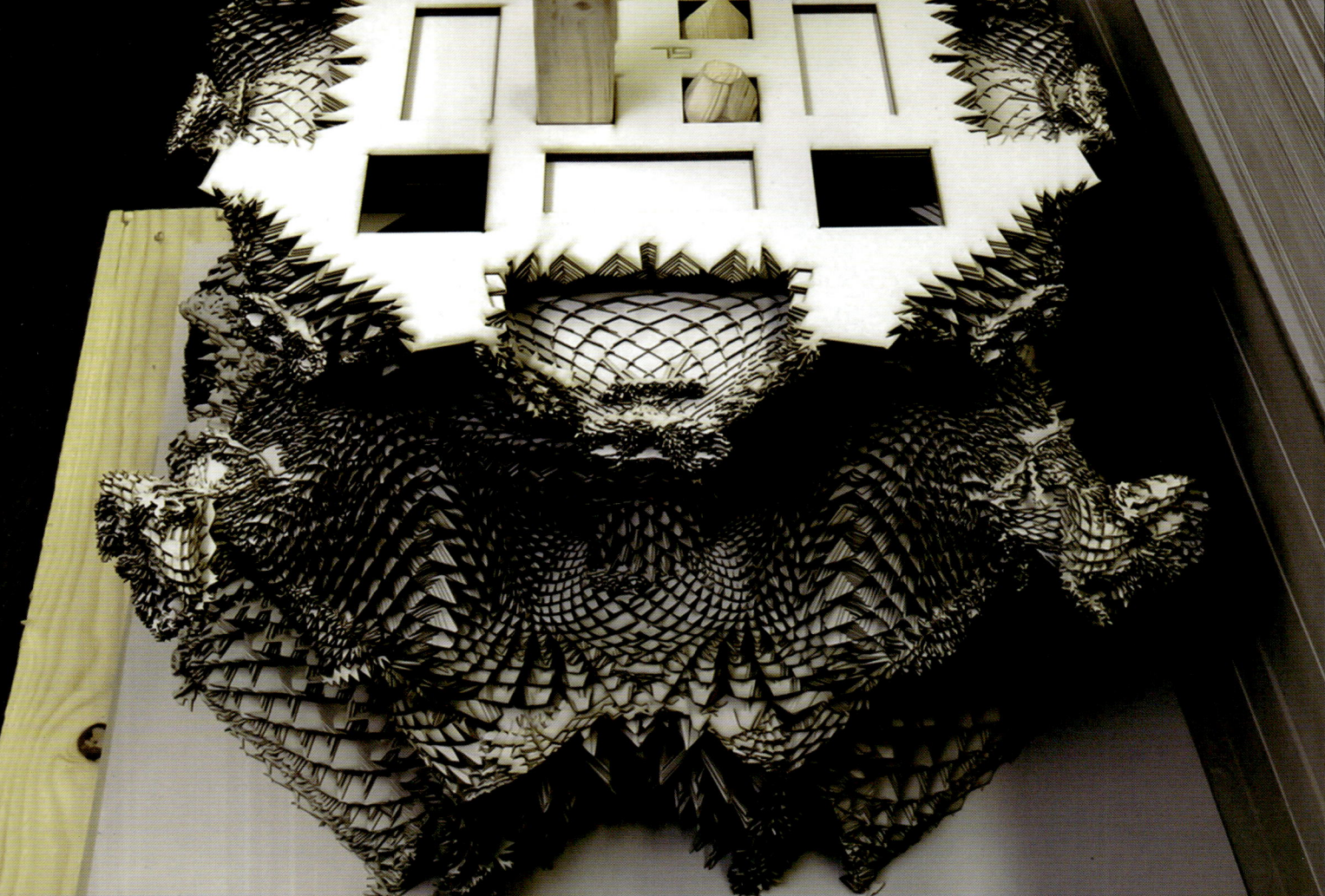

1. Subdivided Column

The Subdivided Columns project explores the use of algorithms to develop a new language of form. The columns are produced using customized subdivision processes. The allure of these processes is that despite using a very simple input, they can produce something that is extraordinarily complex.

In the case of these column prototypes, the input is an abstracted doric column. The process functions by taking each face (or facet) of this doric column and dividing it into four faces. The new faces in turn are further divided again and again until the final form emerges: an intricate column made of 16 million faces.

Each subdivision step adds further levels of detail (or "information") to the form. The first steps of the process influence the overall shape and its curvature, the next steps determine the surface development, while the final steps generate a minuscule texture on top of the broader surfaces.

The resulting columns have a distinct language of form unlike anything created by traditional processes. They exhibit both highly specific local conditions as well as an overall coherency and continuity. Their ornament is in continuous flow, yet it consist of very distinct local formations. The complexity of the columns contrasts with the simplicity of the their generative process and the their initial input.

It is difficult to deduce how these forms are created by looking at them. They appear to be come from a different world. Using this computational approach to architecture can - in the best case - create forms that could otherwise not even be imagined.

Materials: Greyboard, 1mm laser-cut sheet (2700 total), wood core
Dimensions: 40-70cm diameter, 270cm height, 650 kg weight

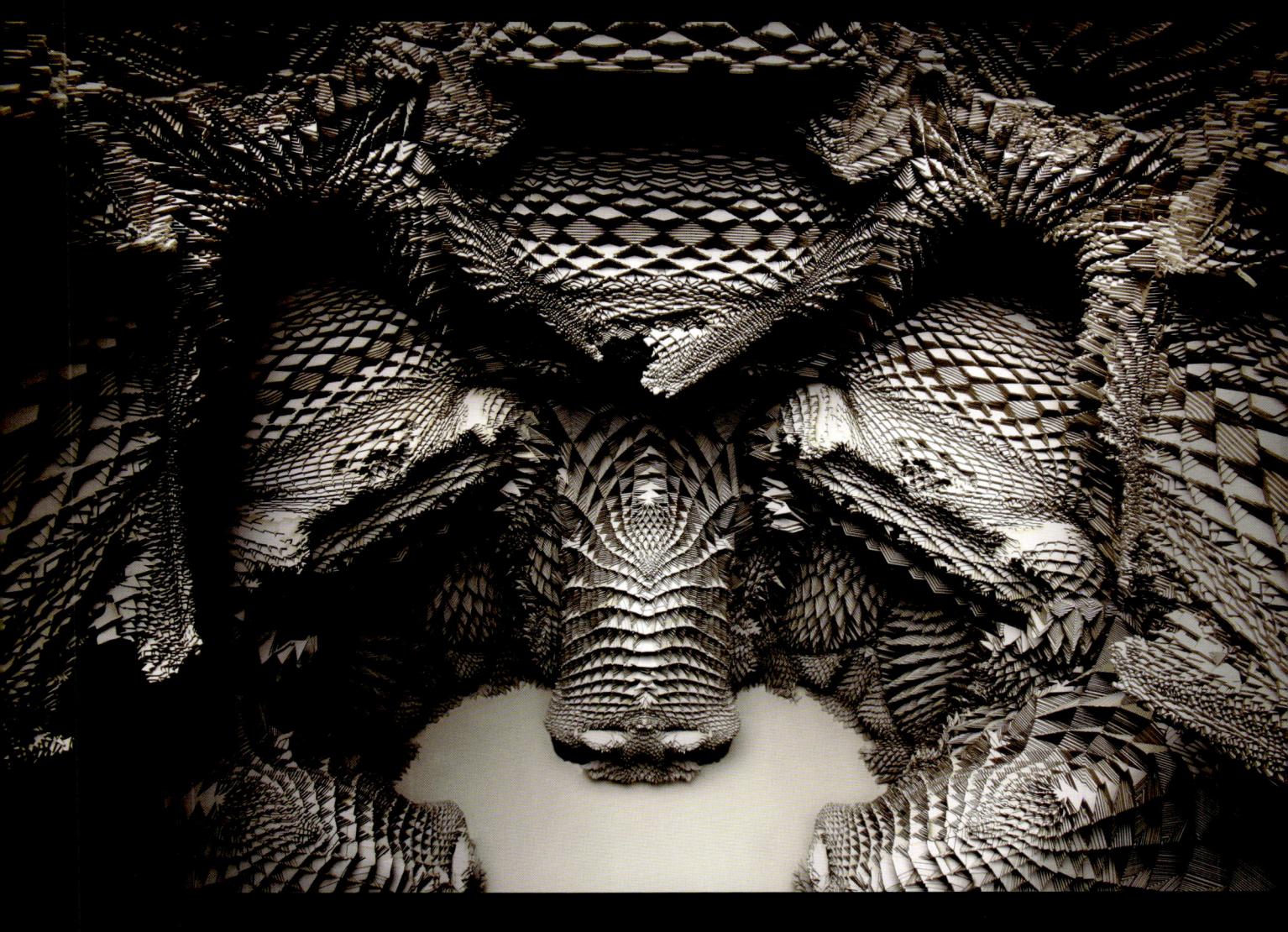

*Photo of the column negative,
i.e. the cardboard sheets that the column was cut out of.*

1. Subdivided Column

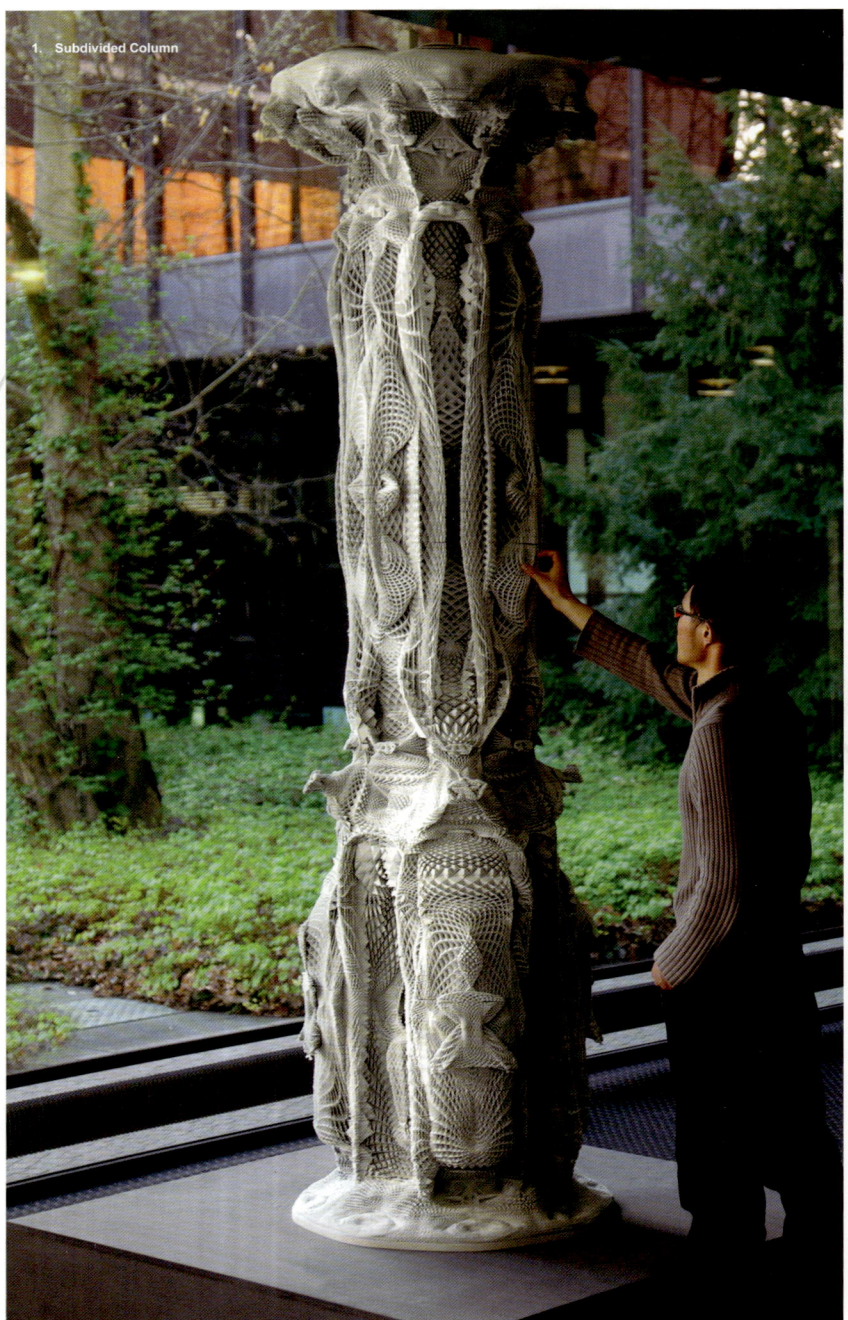
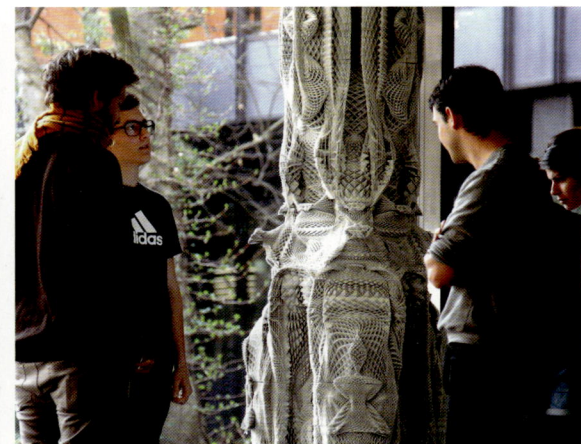
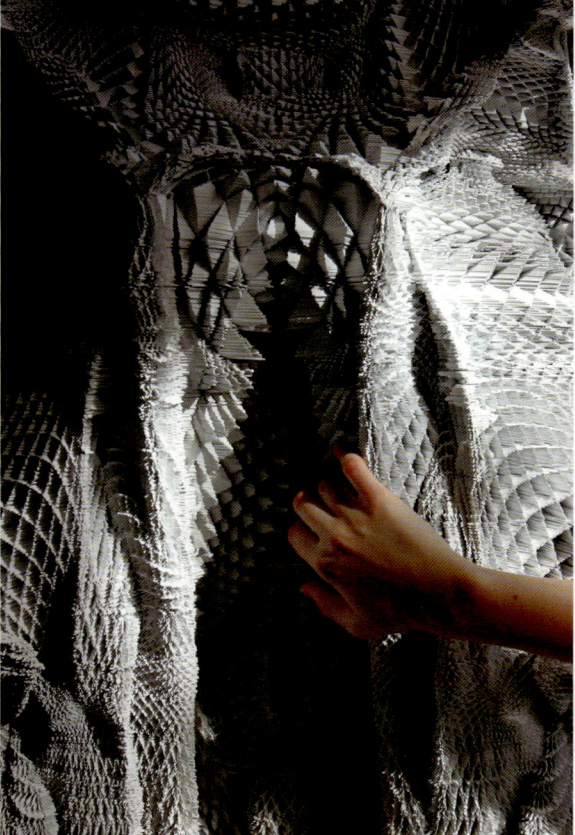
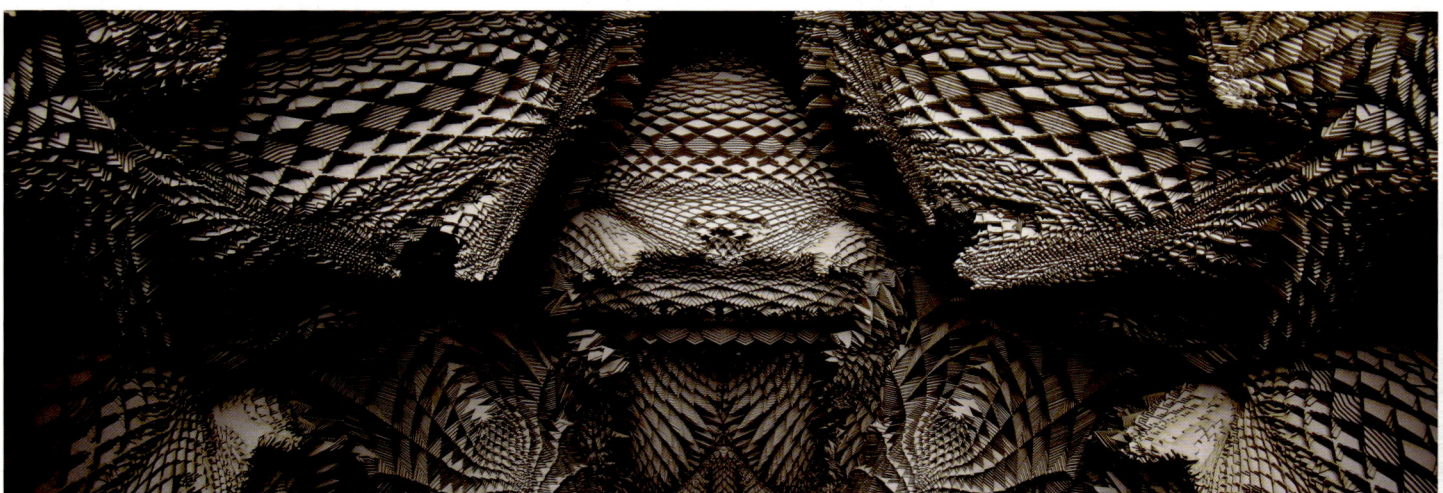

The final constructed column, made of 2700 sheets of 1mm laser-cut cardboard, standing 2.7 meters high. This prototype was initially exhibited at the Swiss Federal Institute of Technology (ETH) in Zurich.

Architect: Michael Hansmeyer

2. The Sixth Order

The Sixth Order installation by Michael Hansmeyer opens at the Gwangju Design Biennale 2011. The installation engages the main theme of the Biennale 'dogadobisando' (design is design is not design) by presenting not a designed object, but instead proposing the design of a process to generate objects.

The Sixth Order involves the development a column order based on subdivision processes. It explores how a procedural approach to form can define and embellish this column order with an elaborate system of ornament. This approach inherently shifts the focus from a single object to a family of objects: endless permutations of a theme can be generated. For the Gwangju Biennale, a single process was used to generate four individual columns. The resulting columns have not a single surface or motif in common, yet due to their shared constituent process, they form a coherent group.

When entering the exhibition room, the viewer at first perceives sixteen columns. This effect, created by the use of two floor-to-ceiling mirrors on adjoining walls, is intentionally accentuated by the columns' design. Thus the columns are symmetrical along only a single axis, and they have a different appearance when seen from the front or the back. In effect, two column permutations are united in a single column - with eight virtual models forming the four physical objects.

While the procedural approach to design enables this multiplicity of output, it also expands the solution space on the level of the single object. It thus allows the creation of objects that are otherwise undrawable - and perhaps even unimaginable - in terms of their detail and complexity.

Dimensions: Individual columns: 40-70 cm diameter, 270 cm height

Architect: Michael Hansmeyer
Photographer: Kyungsub Shin

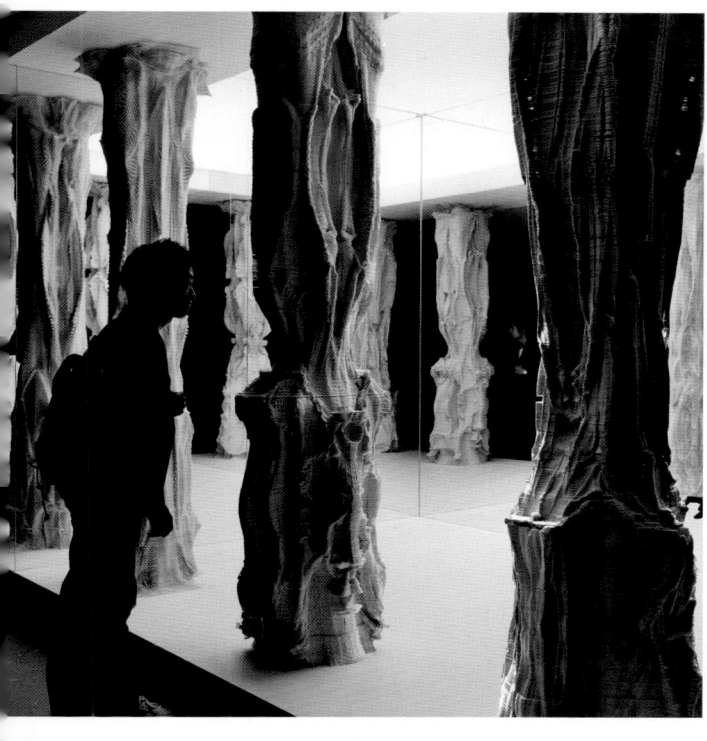
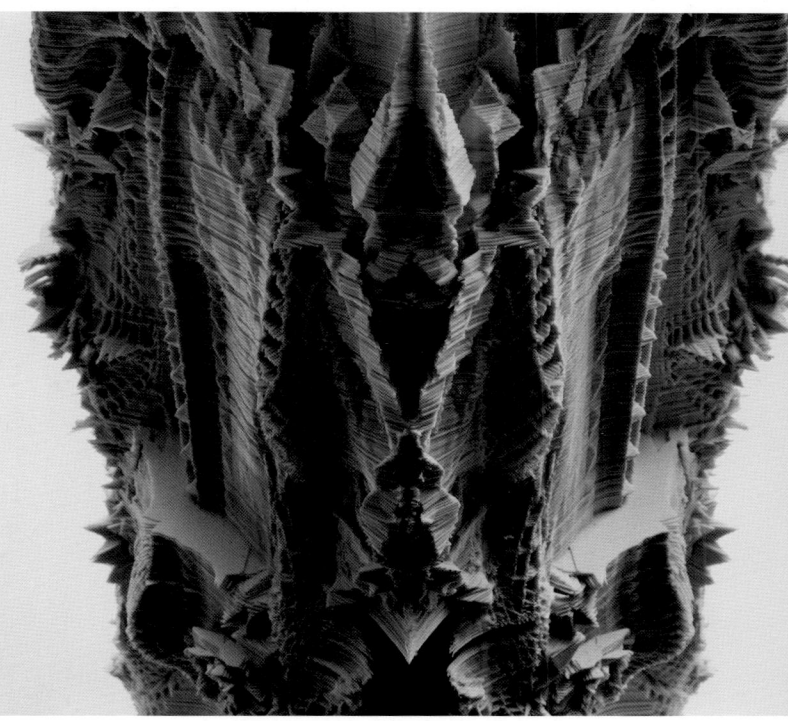

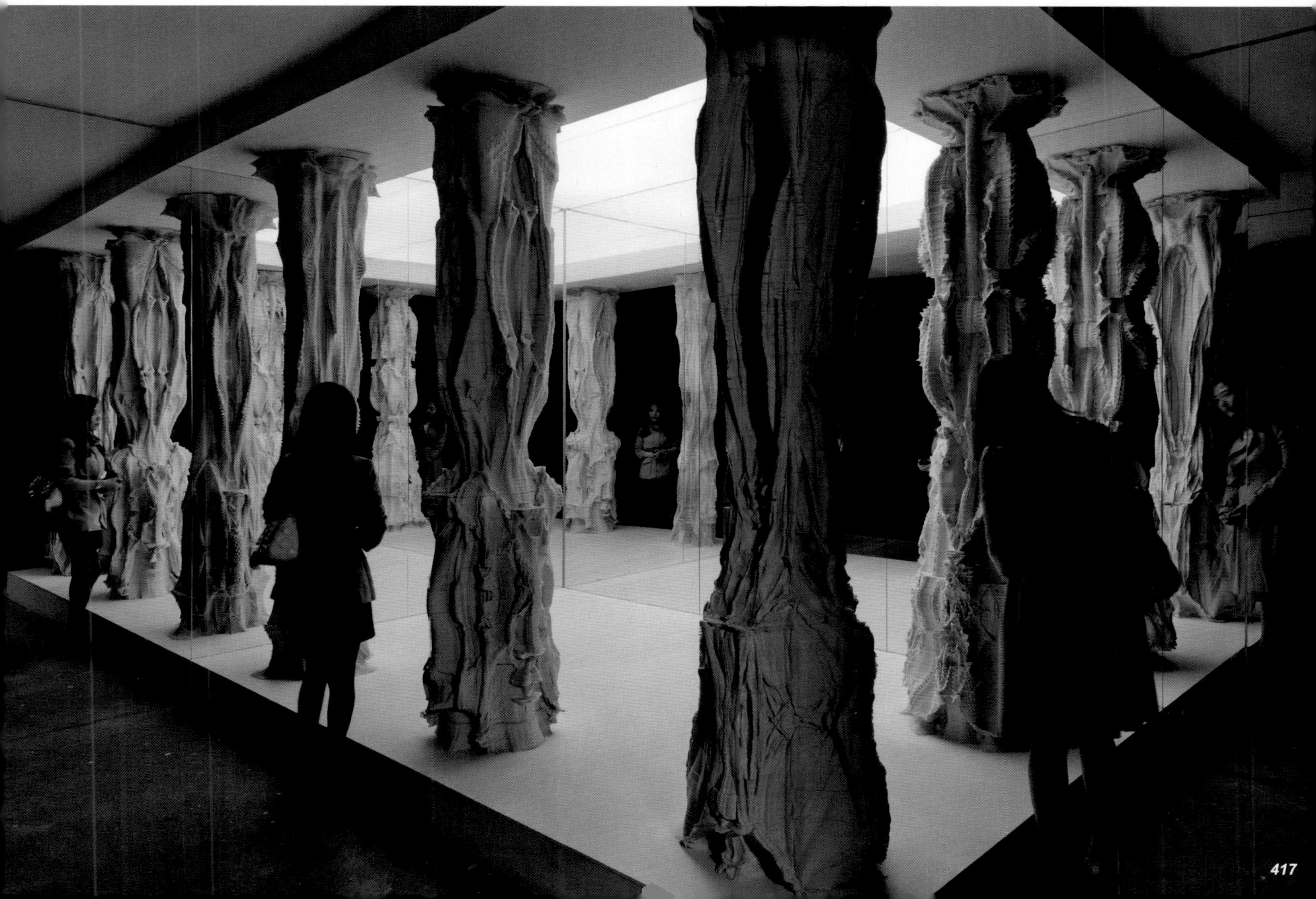

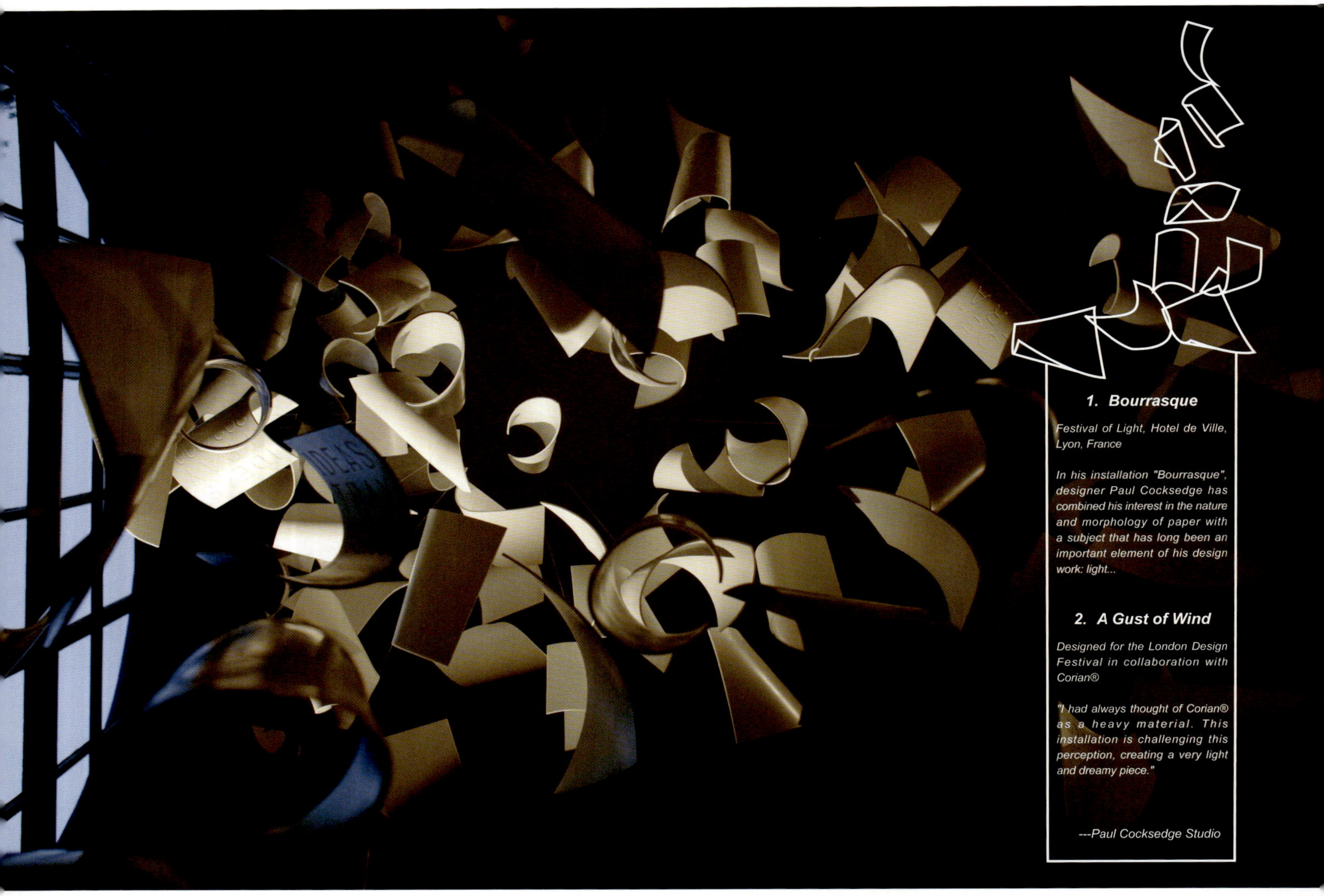

1. Bourrasque

Festival of Light, Hotel de Ville, Lyon, France

In his installation "Bourrasque", designer Paul Cocksedge has combined his interest in the nature and morphology of paper with a subject that has long been an important element of his design work: light...

2. A Gust of Wind

Designed for the London Design Festival in collaboration with Corian®

"I had always thought of Corian® as a heavy material. This installation is challenging this perception, creating a very light and dreamy piece."

---Paul Cocksedge Studio

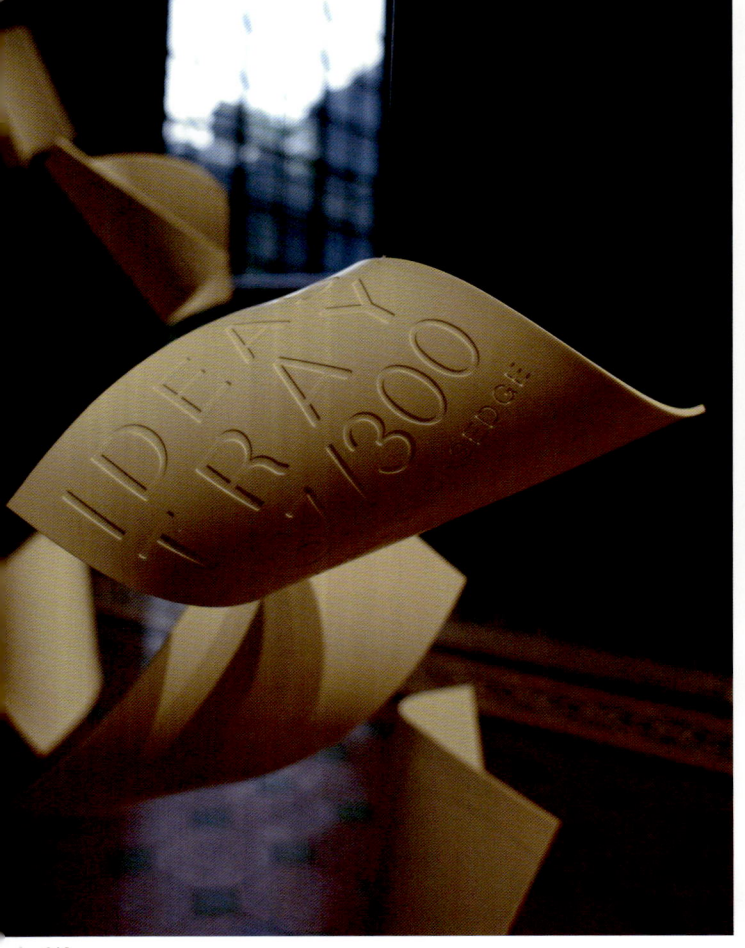

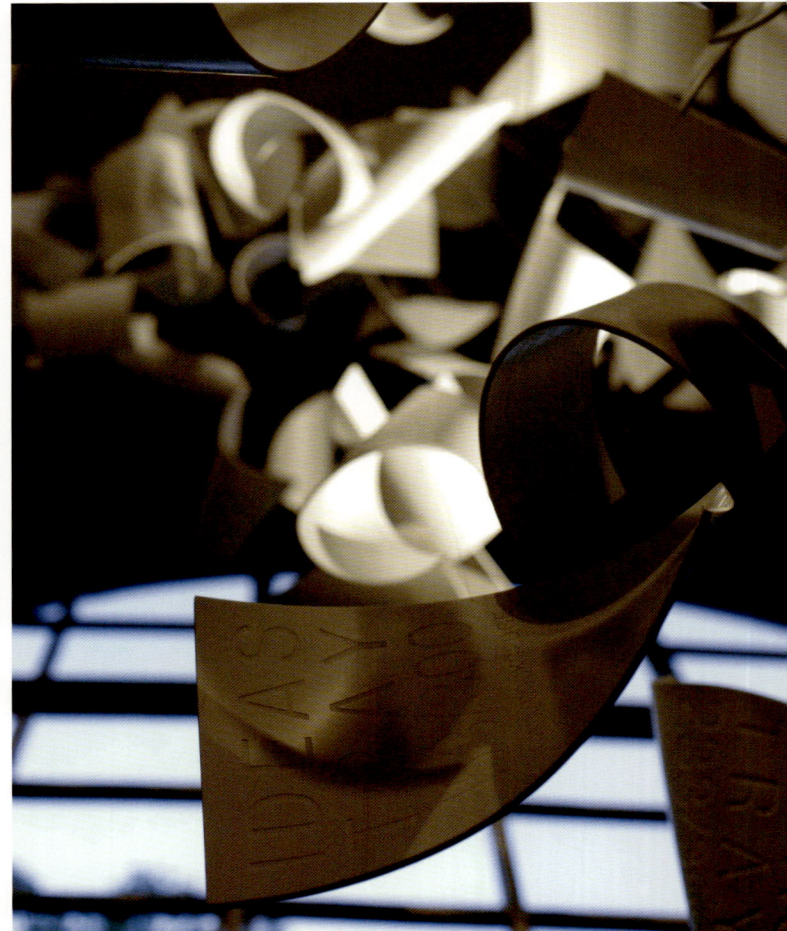

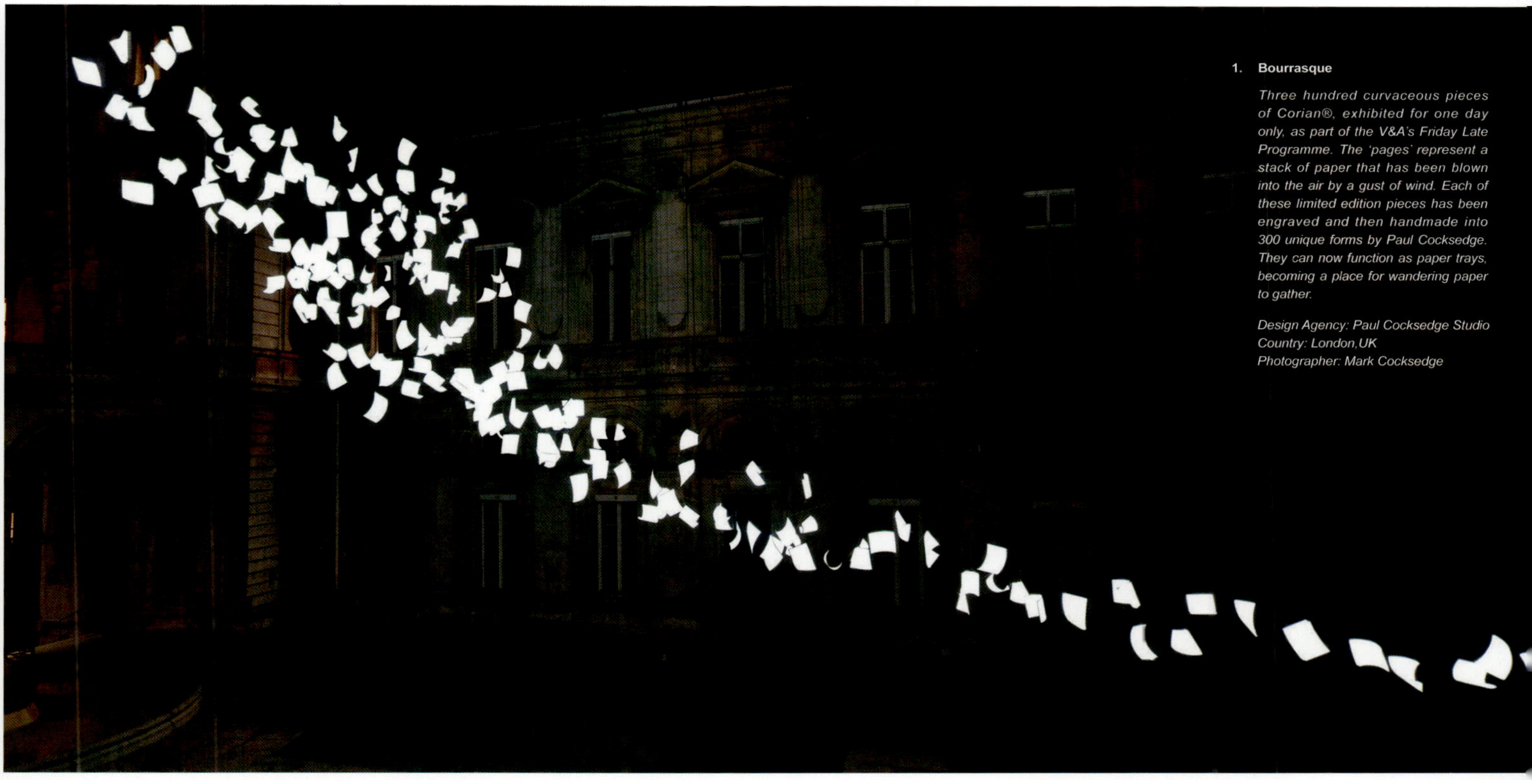

1. **Bourrasque**

Three hundred curvaceous pieces of Corian®, exhibited for one day only, as part of the V&A's Friday Late Programme. The 'pages' represent a stack of paper that has been blown into the air by a gust of wind. Each of these limited edition pieces has been engraved and then handmade into 300 unique forms by Paul Cocksedge. They can now function as paper trays, becoming a place for wandering paper to gather.

Design Agency: Paul Cocksedge Studio
Country: London, UK
Photographer: Mark Cocksedge

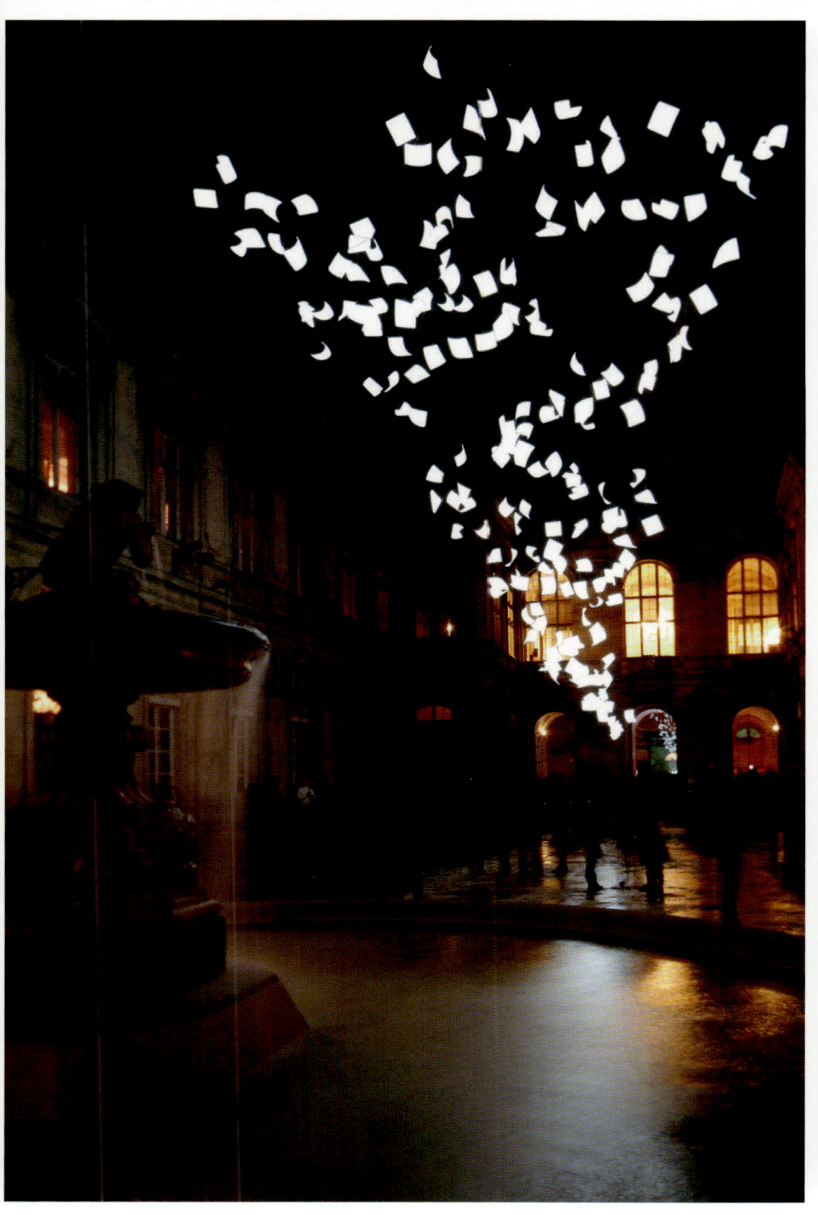
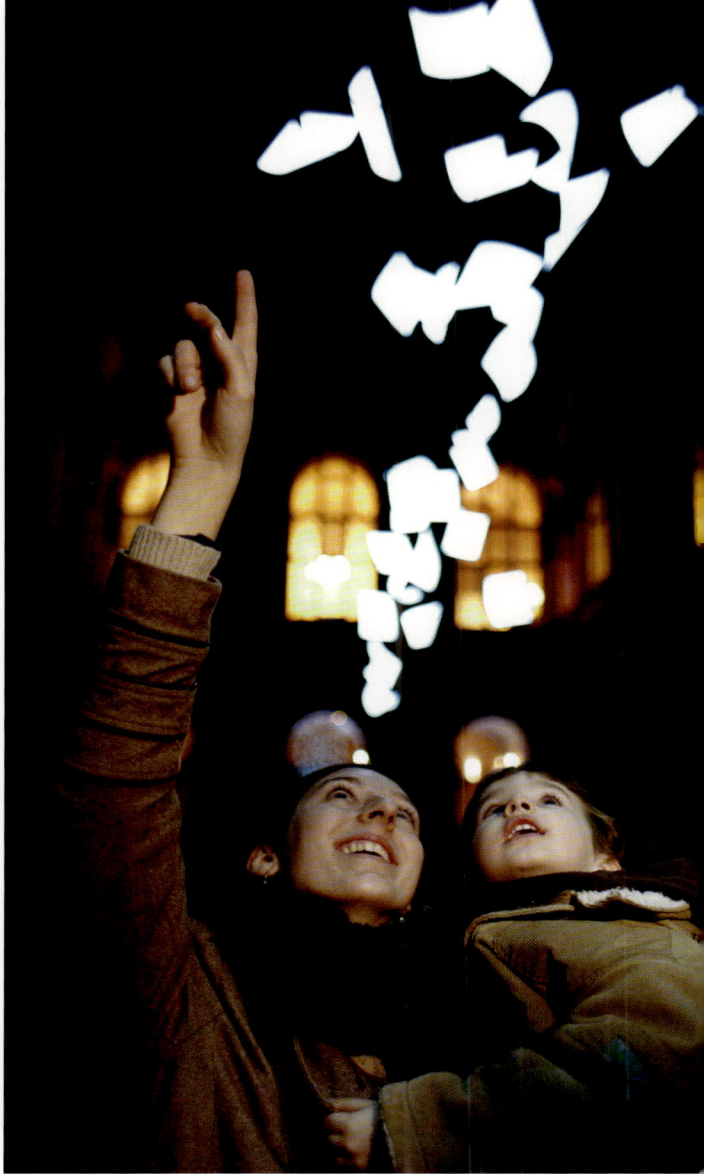

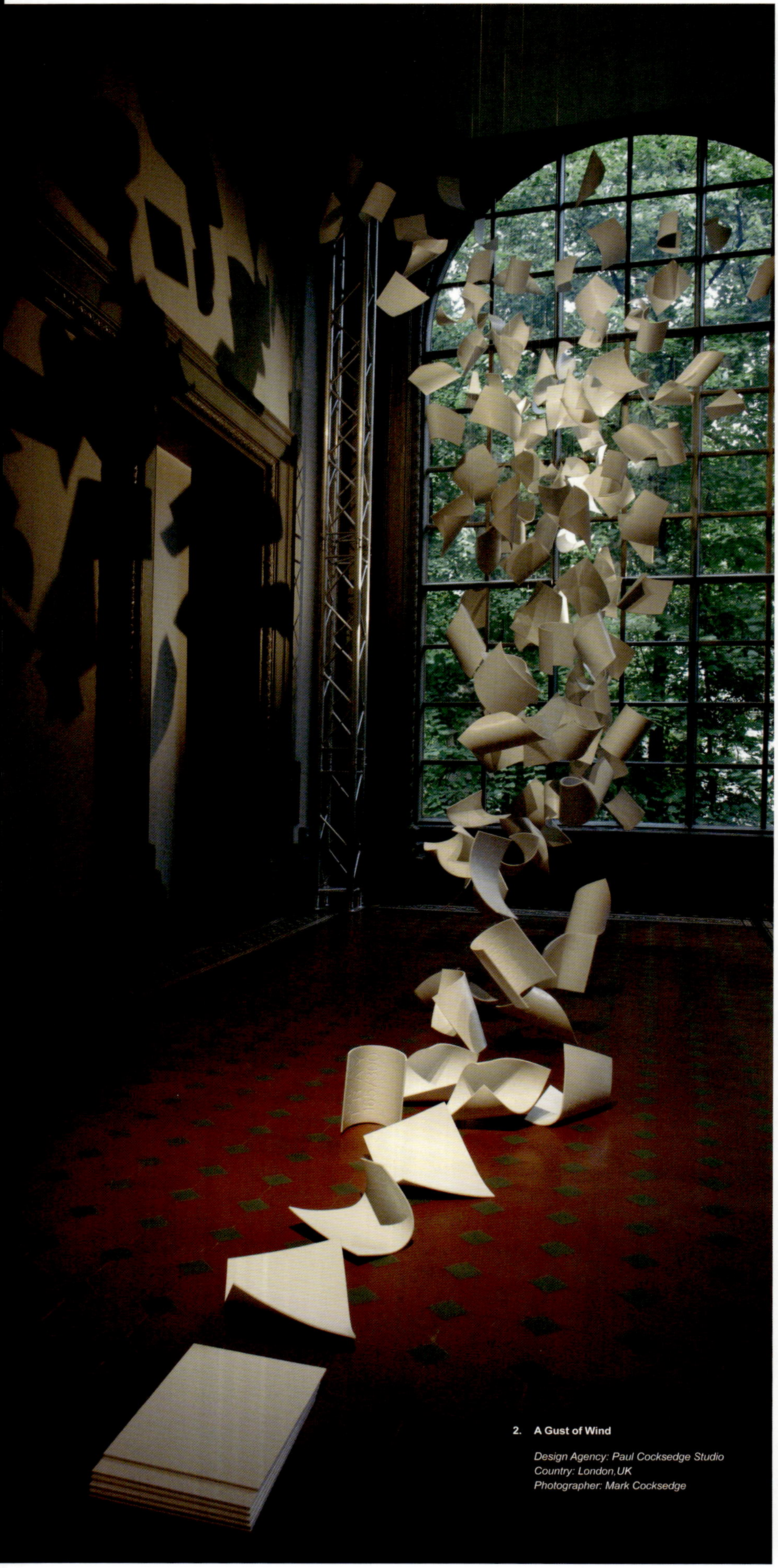

2. A Gust of Wind

Design Agency: Paul Cocksedge Studio
Country: London, UK
Photographer: Mark Cocksedge

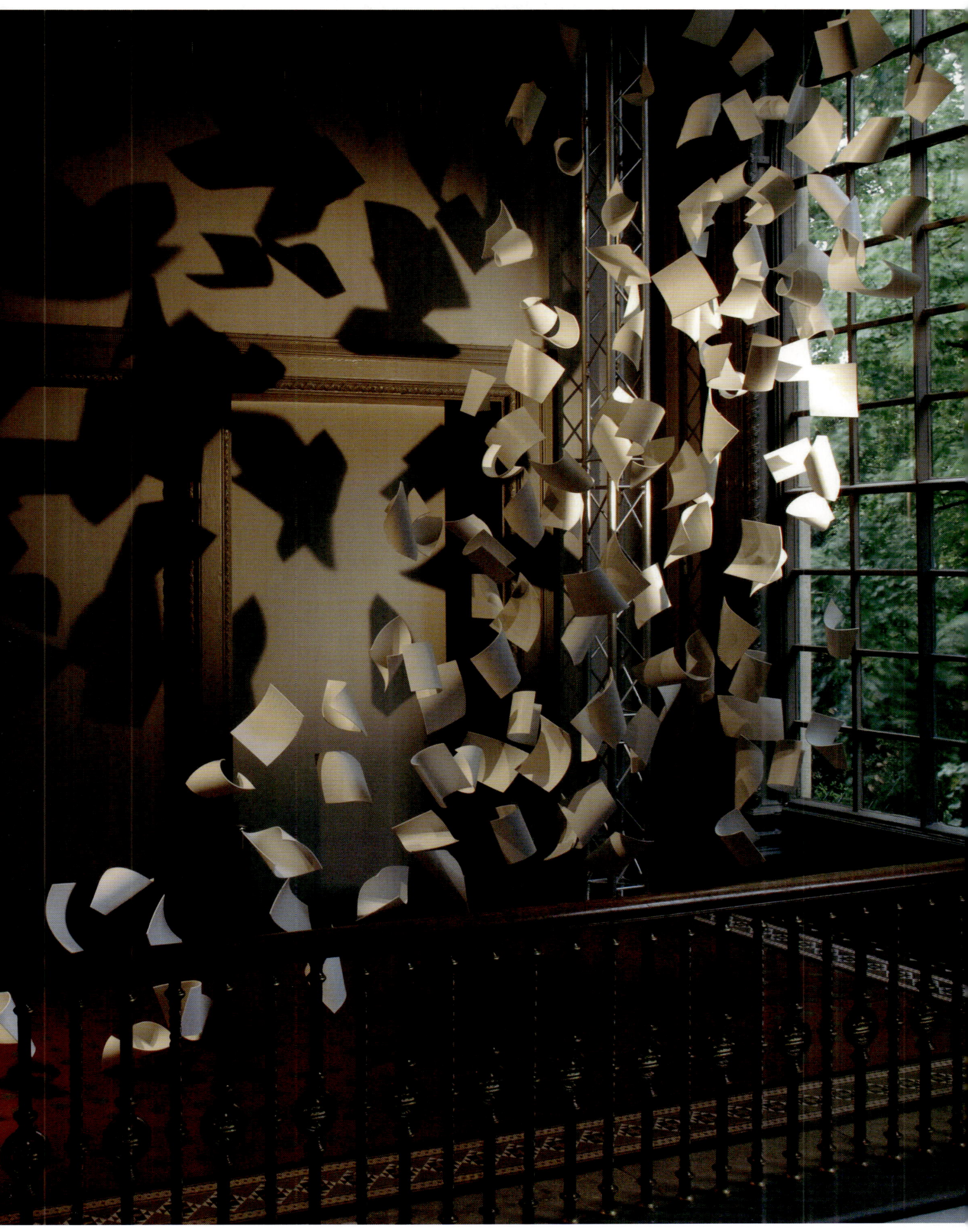

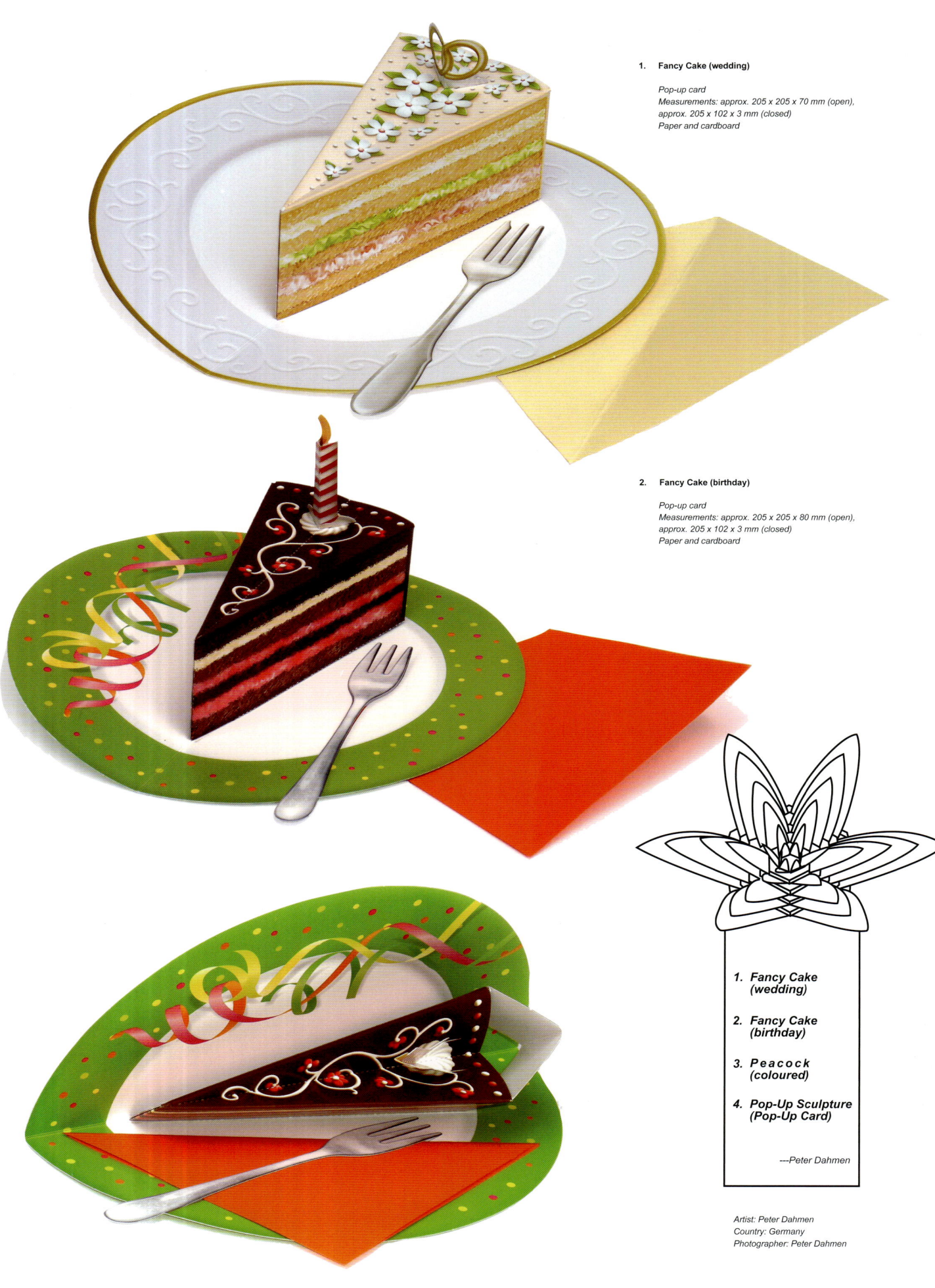

1. **Fancy Cake (wedding)**

   Pop-up card
   Measurements: approx. 205 x 205 x 70 mm (open),
   approx. 205 x 102 x 3 mm (closed)
   Paper and cardboard

2. **Fancy Cake (birthday)**

   Pop-up card
   Measurements: approx. 205 x 205 x 80 mm (open),
   approx. 205 x 102 x 3 mm (closed)
   Paper and cardboard

   1. Fancy Cake (wedding)
   2. Fancy Cake (birthday)
   3. Peacock (coloured)
   4. Pop-Up Sculpture (Pop-Up Card)

   ---Peter Dahmen

Artist: Peter Dahmen
Country: Germany
Photographer: Peter Dahmen

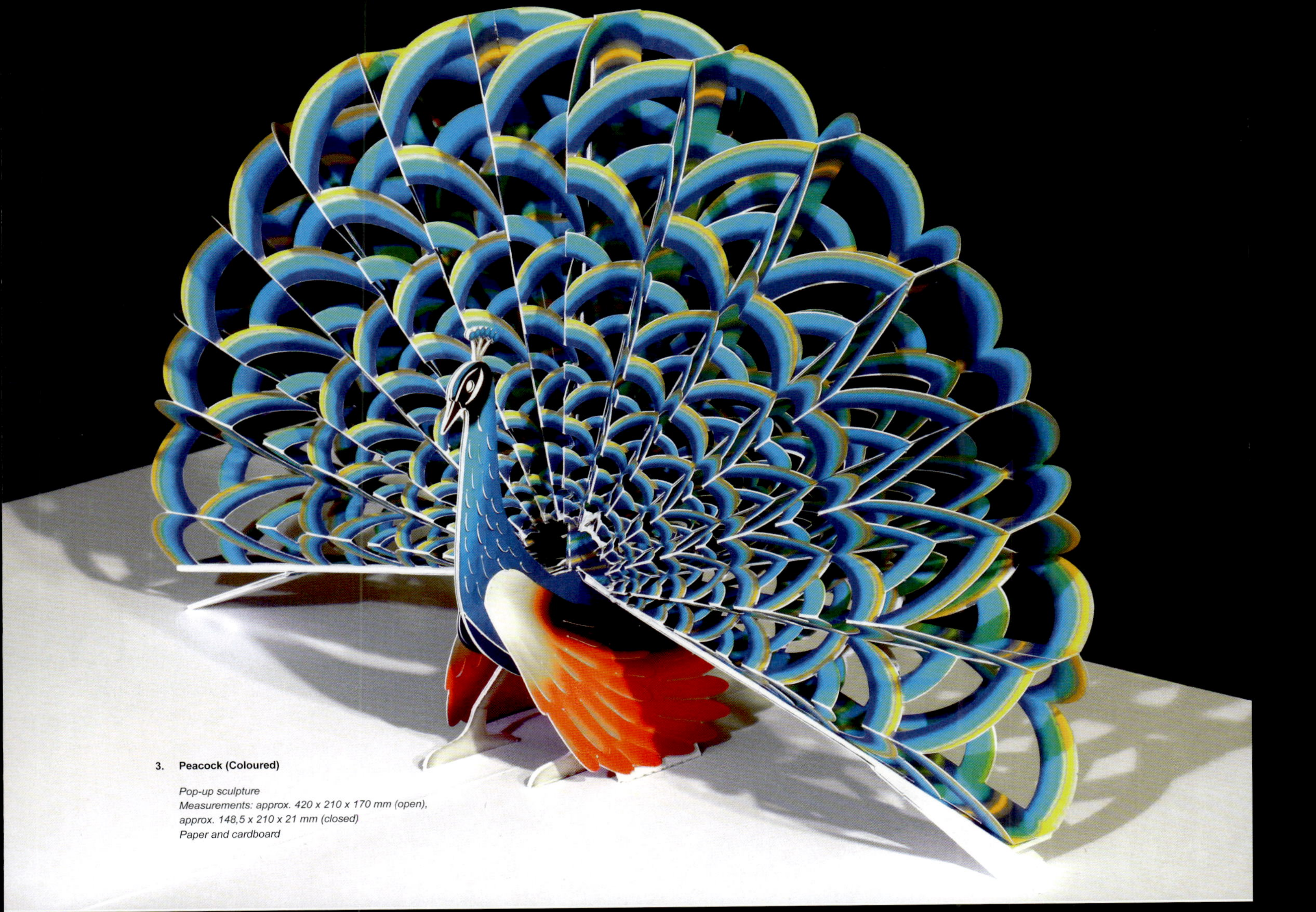

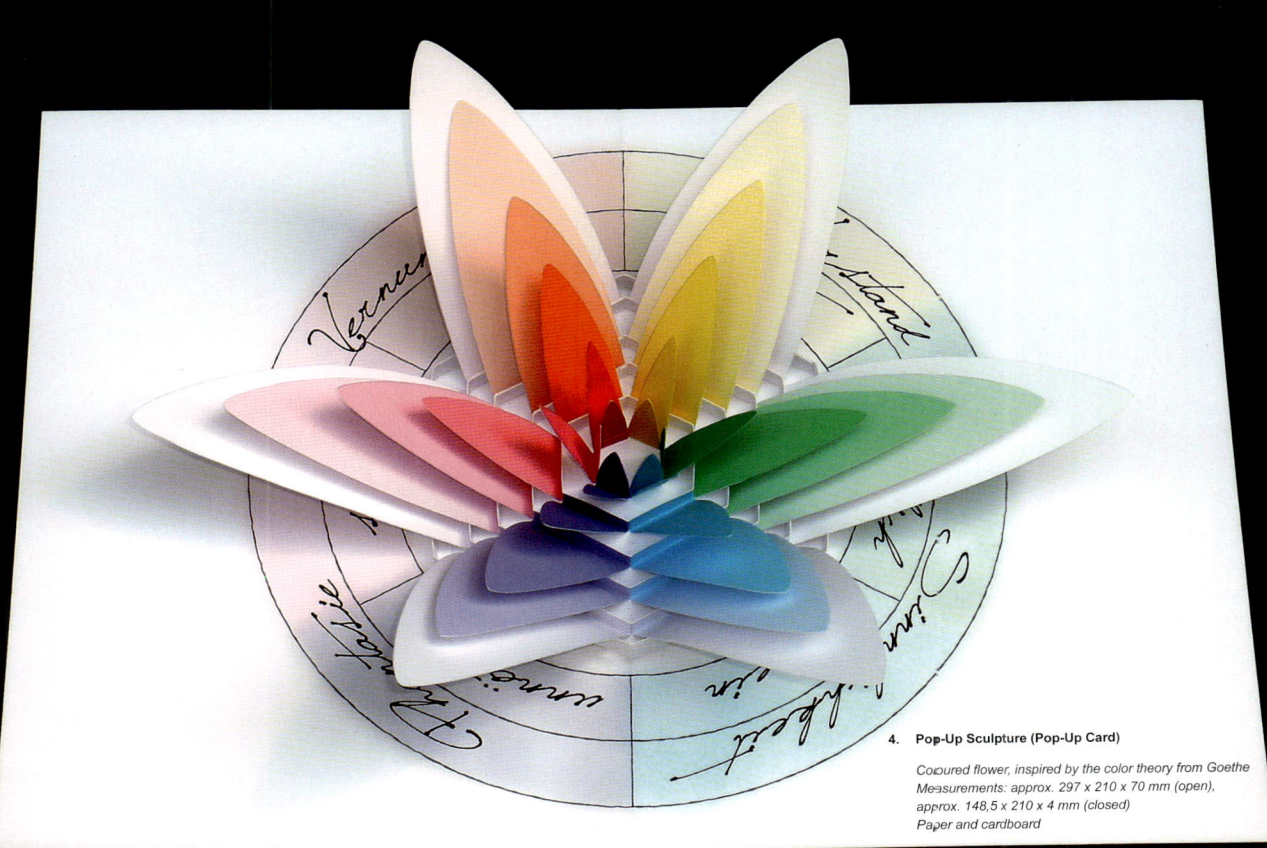

3. **Peacock (Coloured)**

   Pop-up sculpture
   Measurements: approx. 420 x 210 x 170 mm (open),
   approx. 148,5 x 210 x 21 mm (closed)
   Paper and cardboard

4. **Pop-Up Sculpture (Pop-Up Card)**

   Coloured flower, inspired by the color theory from Goethe
   Measurements: approx. 297 x 210 x 70 mm (open),
   approx. 148,5 x 210 x 4 mm (closed)
   Paper and cardboard

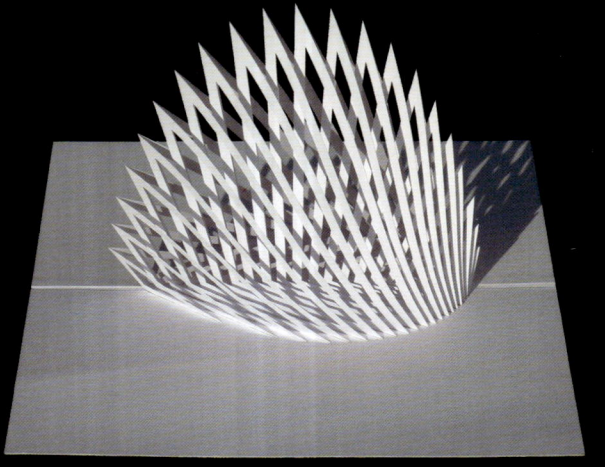

4. **Pop-Up Sculpture (Pop-Up Card)**
*Measurements: approx. 600 x 420 x 225 mm (open),
approx. 300 x 420 x 5 mm (closed)
Paper and cardboard*

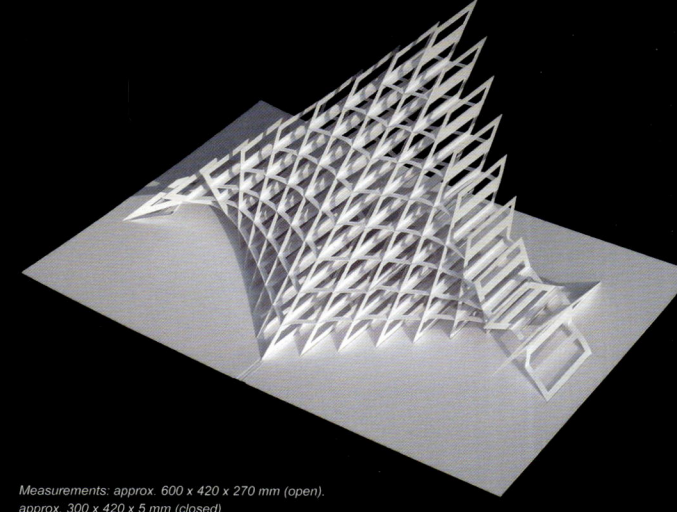

*Measurements: approx. 600 x 420 x 270 mm (open),
approx. 300 x 420 x 5 mm (closed)
Paper and cardboard*

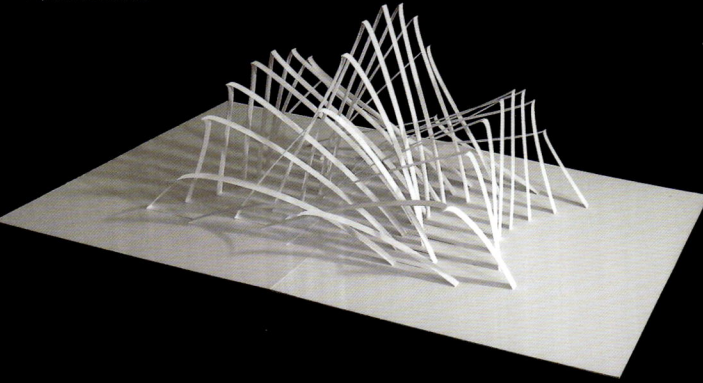

*Measurements: approx. 600 x 420 x 245 mm (open),
approx. 300 x 420 x 5 mm (closed)
Paper and cardboard*

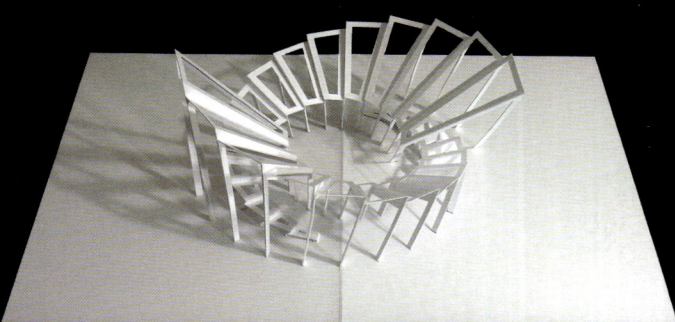

*Measurements: approx. 600 x 420 x 155 mm (open),
approx. 300 x 420 x 8 mm (closed)
Paper and cardboard*

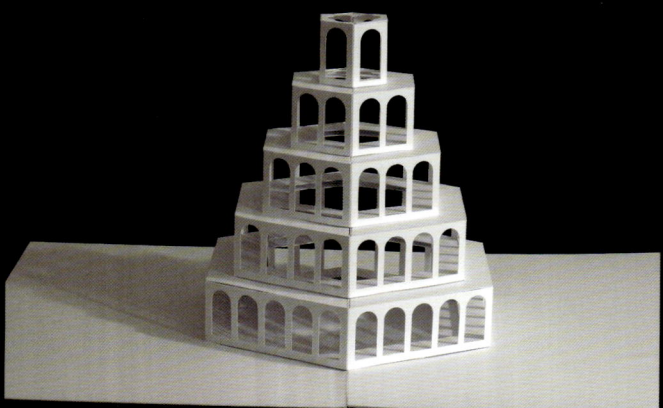

*Measurements: approx. 600 x 420 x 250 mm (open),
approx. 300 x 420 x 20 mm (closed)
Paper and cardboard*

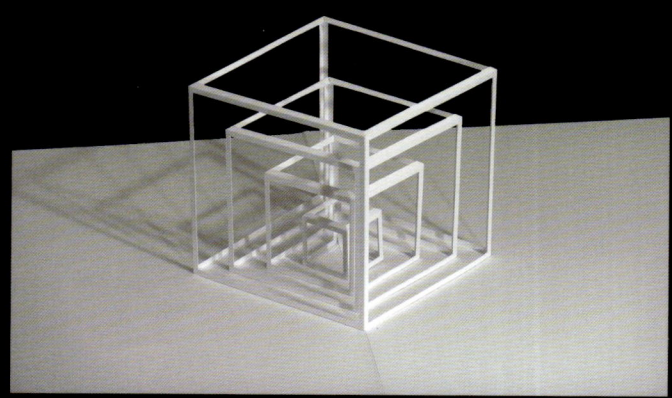

*Measurements: approx. 600 x 420 x 145 mm (open),
approx. 300 x 420 x 5 mm (closed)
Paper and cardboard*

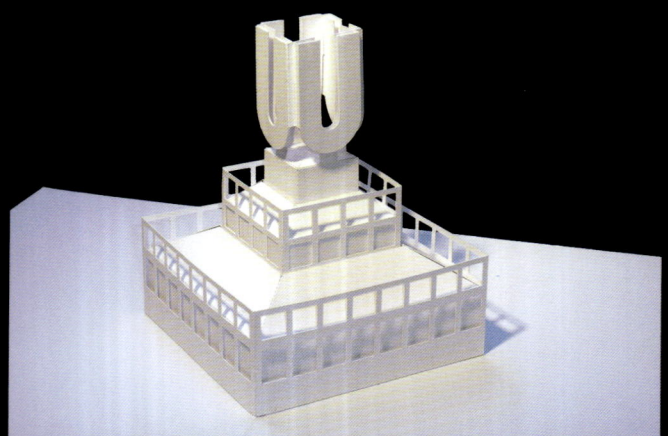

*Measurements: approx. 420 x 297 x 155 mm (open),
approx. 210 x 297 x 10 mm (closed)
Paper and cardboard*

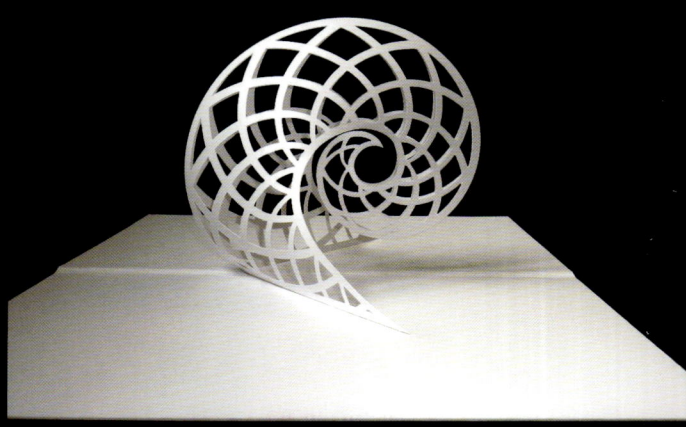

*Measurements: approx. 600 x 420 x 225 mm (open),
approx. 300 x 420 x 4 mm (closed)
Paper and cardboard*

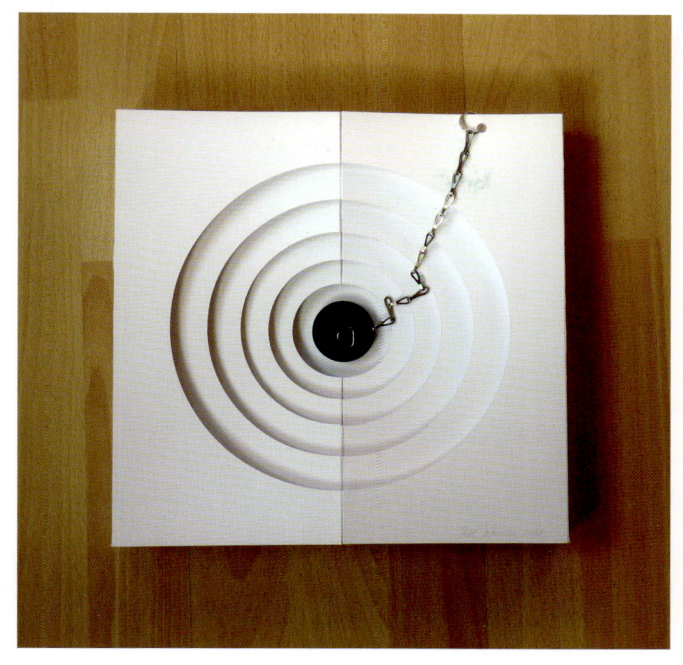
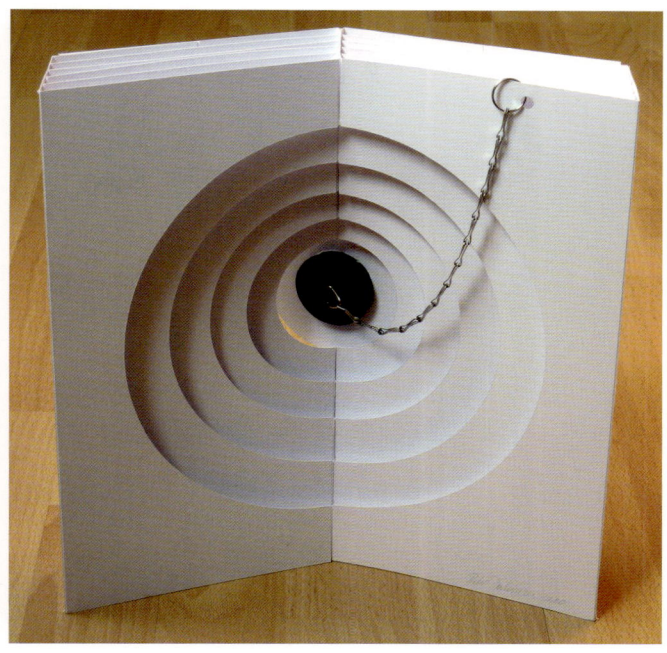
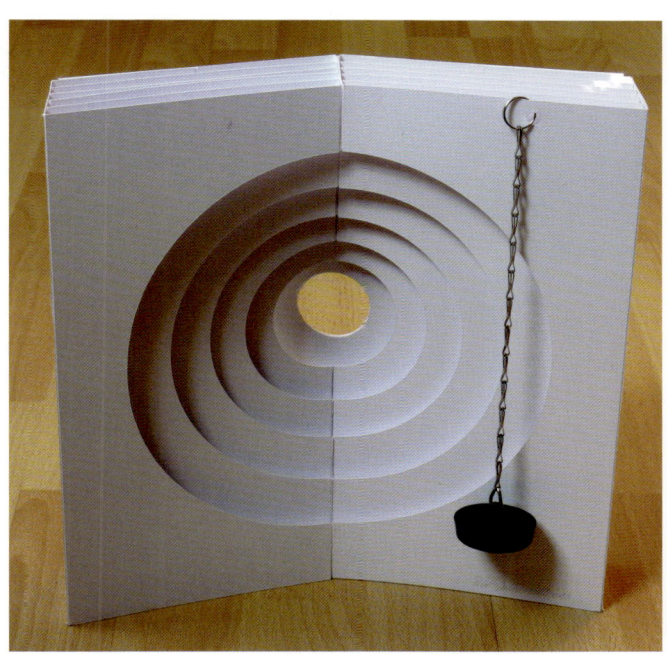
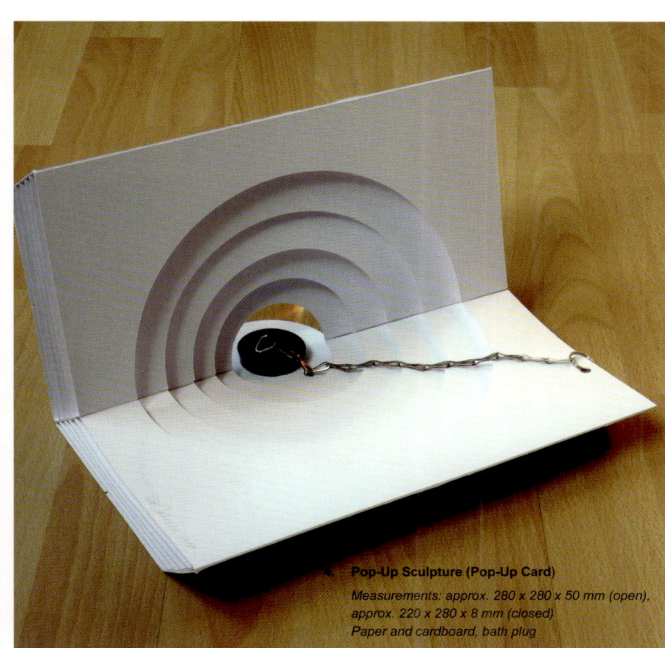

Pop-Up Sculpture (Pop-Up Card)
*Measurements: approx. 280 x 280 x 50 mm (open),
approx. 220 x 280 x 8 mm (closed)
Paper and cardboard, bath plug*

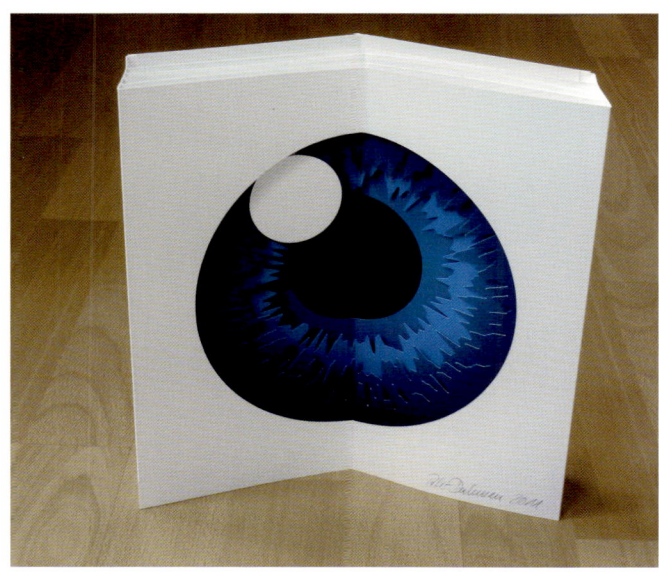
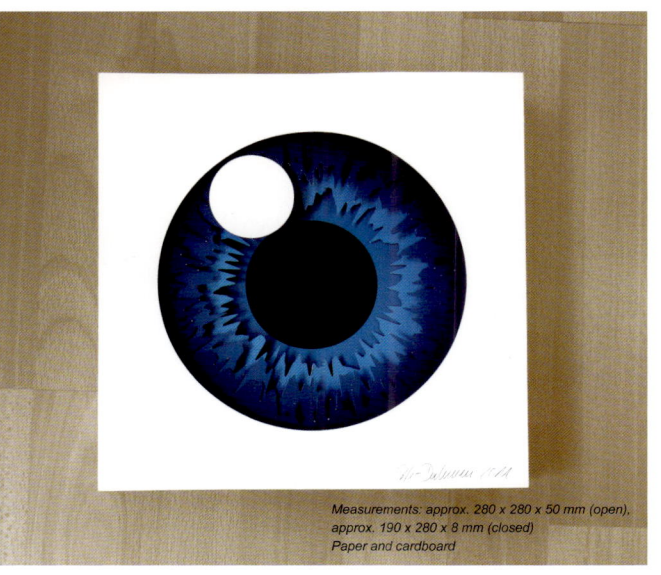

*Measurements: approx. 280 x 280 x 50 mm (open),
approx. 190 x 280 x 8 mm (closed)
Paper and cardboard*

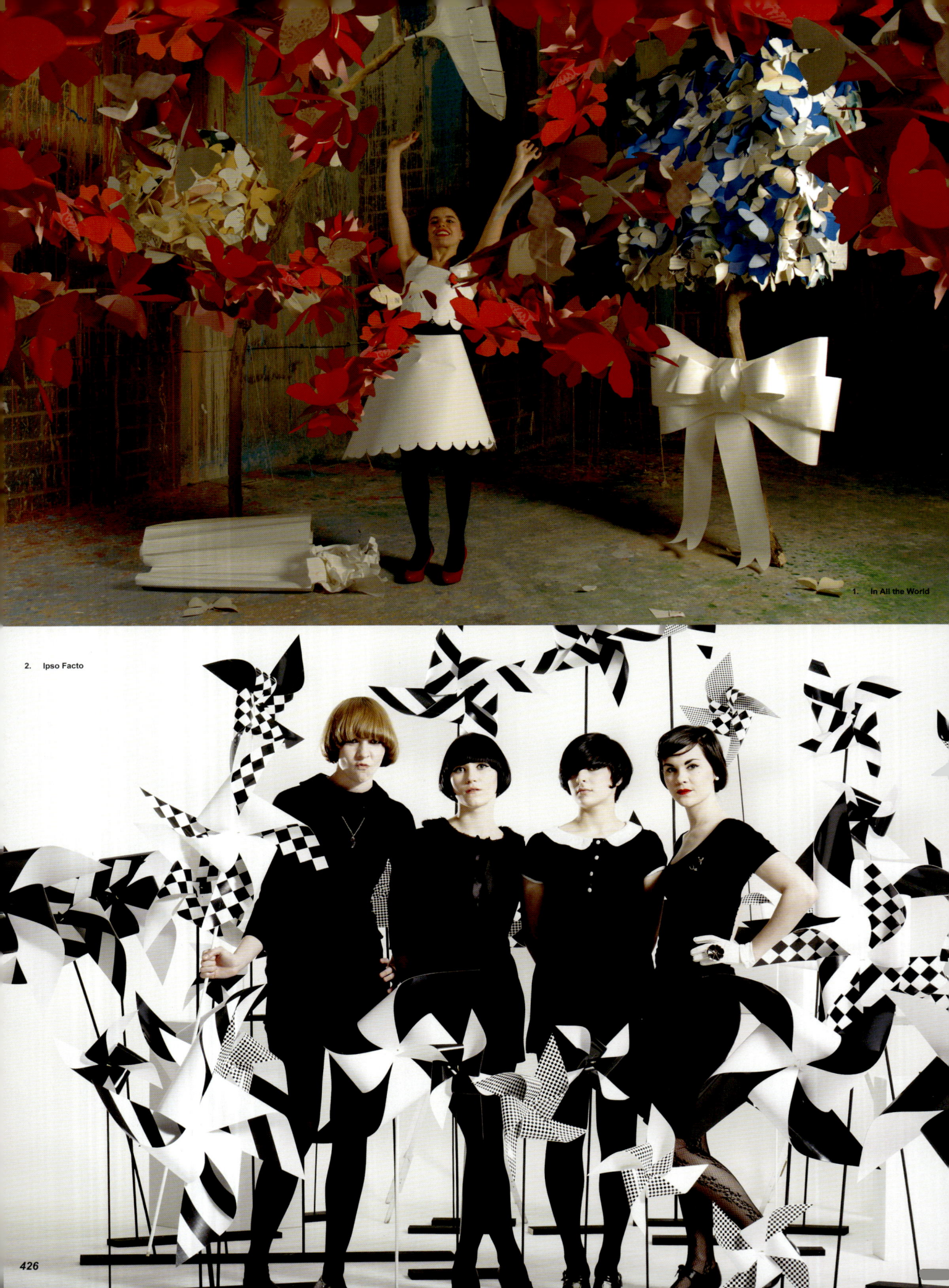

1. In All the World
2. Ipso Facto

1. **In All the World**

    Stills from "In All the World I Dream in Paper".
    Set Design & Styling: Petra Storrs
    Starring: Paloma Faith
    Music Composed: Pierre Conti.
    Photographer: James Champion

2. **Ipso Facto**

    Ipso facto NME editorial,
    Set Design: Petra Storrs
    Photographer: Dean Chalkley

3. **SOMA**

    Portrait for SOMA magazine.
    Set Design & Styling: Petra Storrs
    Photographer: Olivia Beasley

4. **Sublime**

    Paper garments for sublime magazine fashion editorial.
    Paper Garments by Petra Storrs
    Photographer: Rai Royal

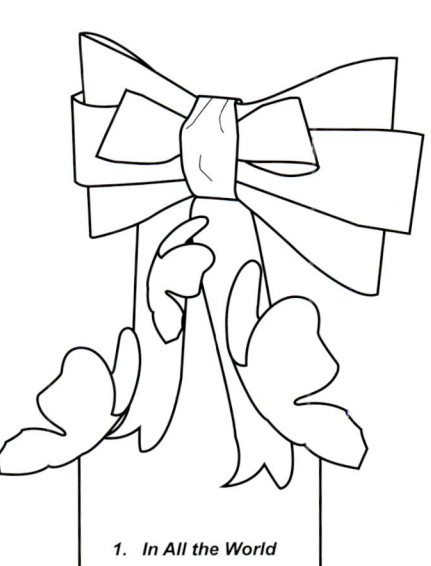

1. In All the World
2. Ipso Facto
3. SOMA
4. Sublime

---Petra Storrs

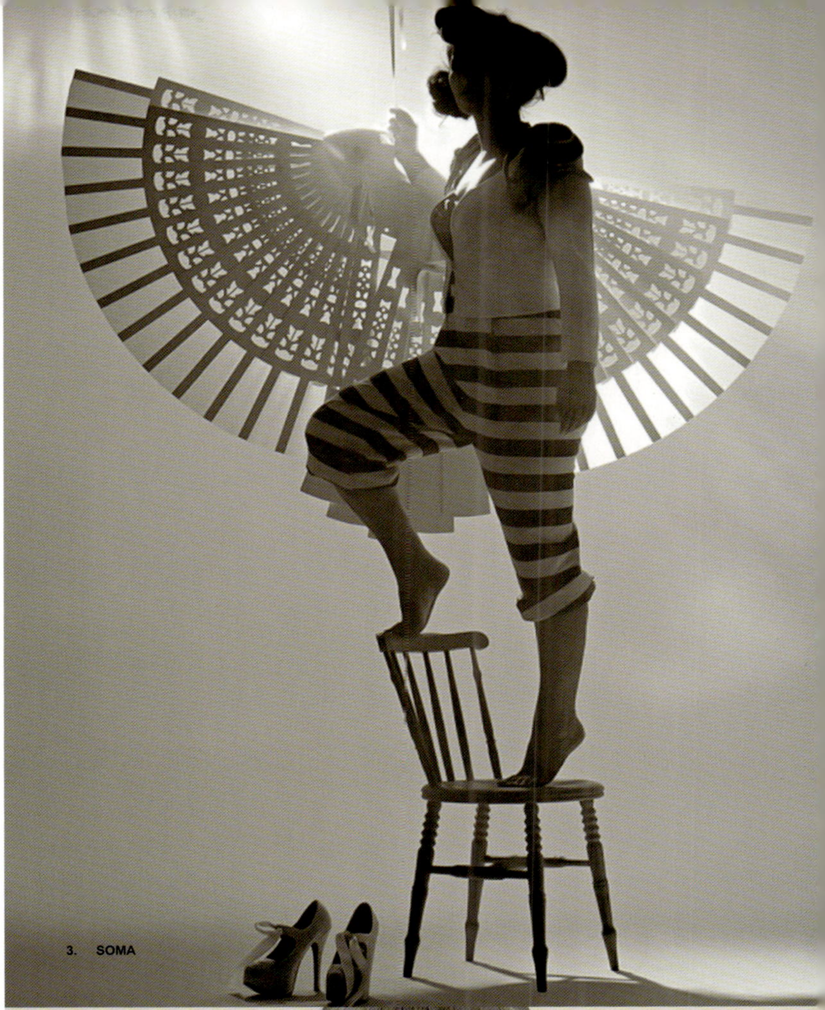

3. SOMA

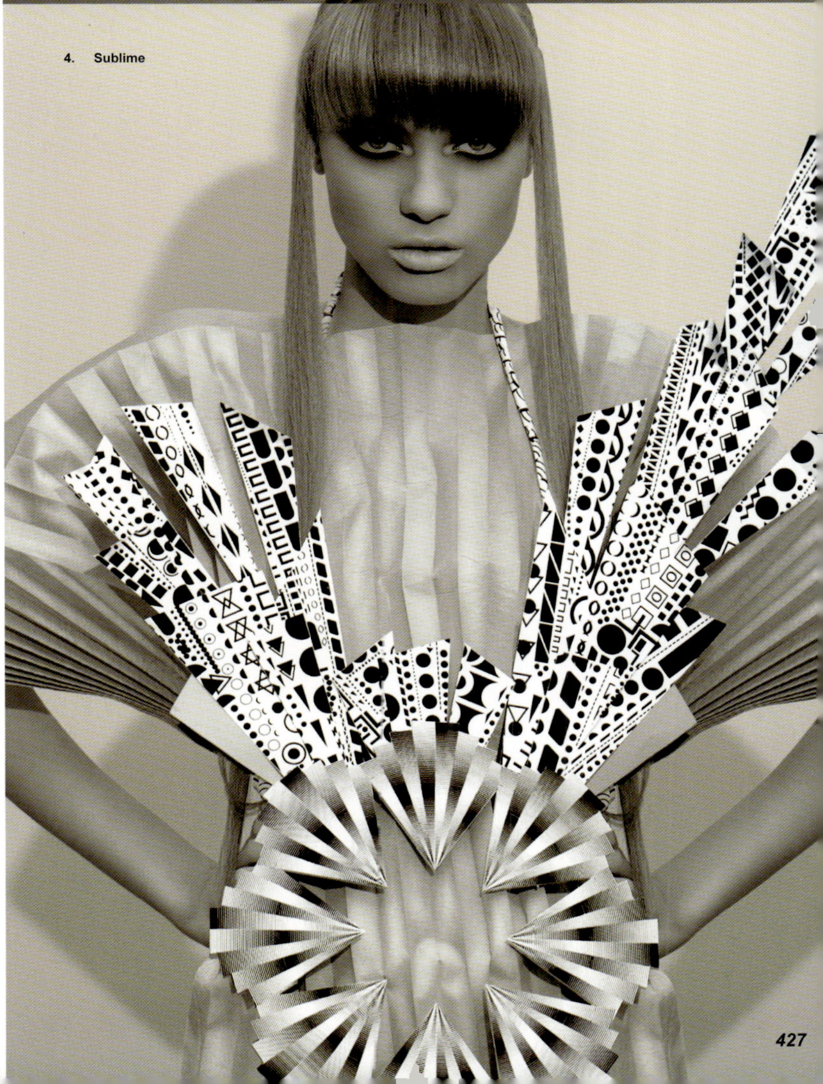

4. Sublime

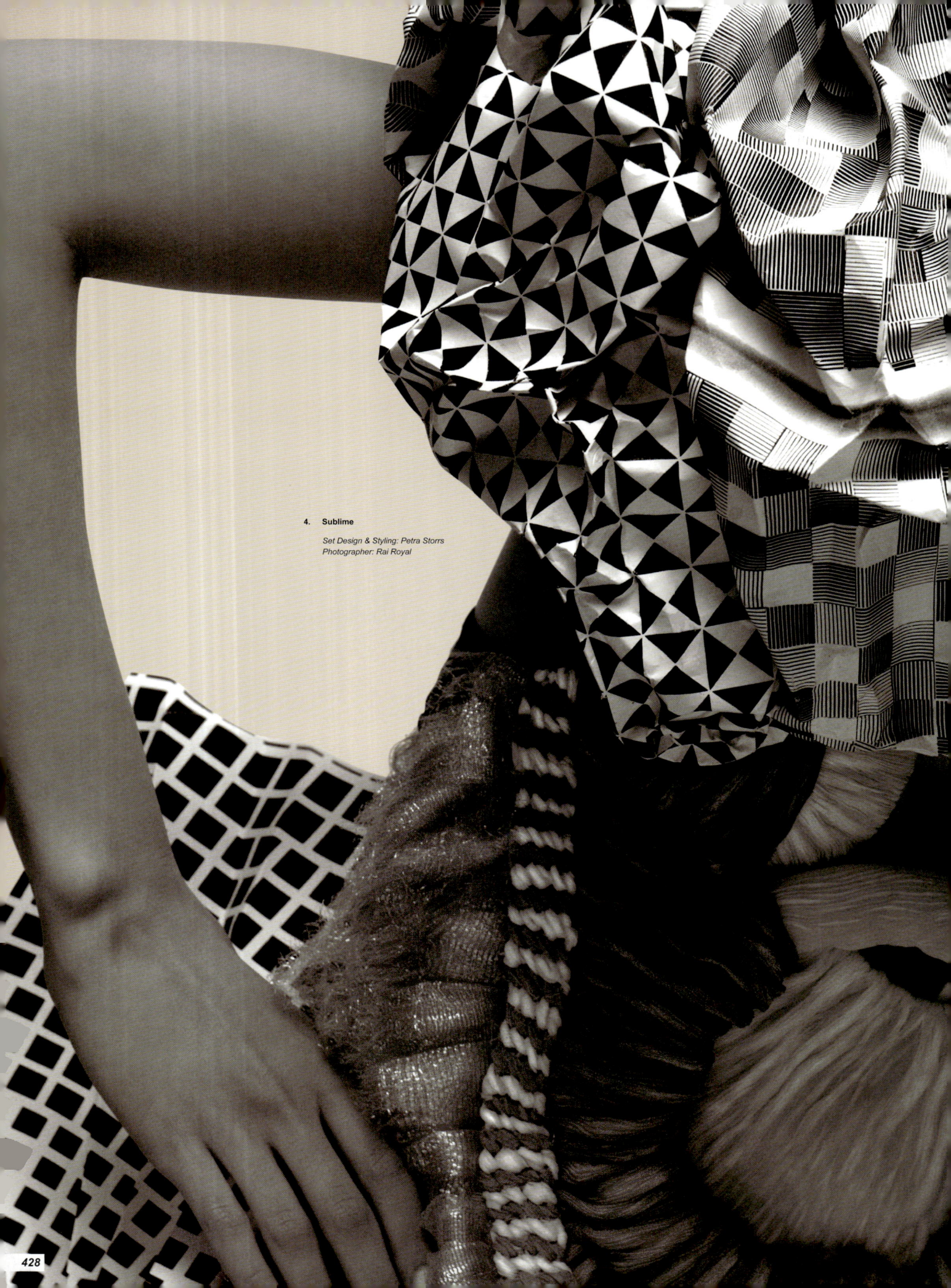

4. Sublime

Set Design & Styling: Petra Storrs
Photographer: Rai Royal

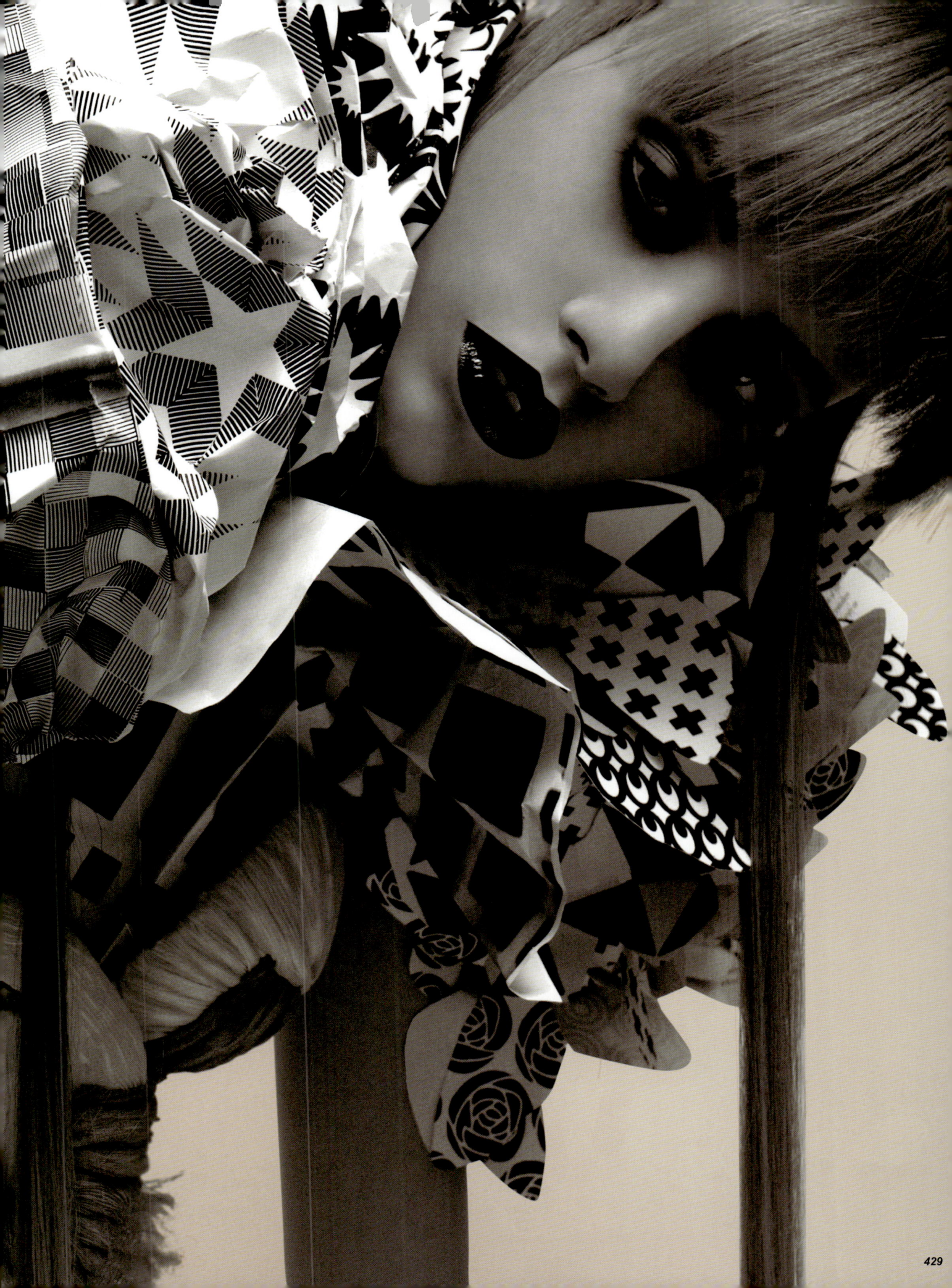

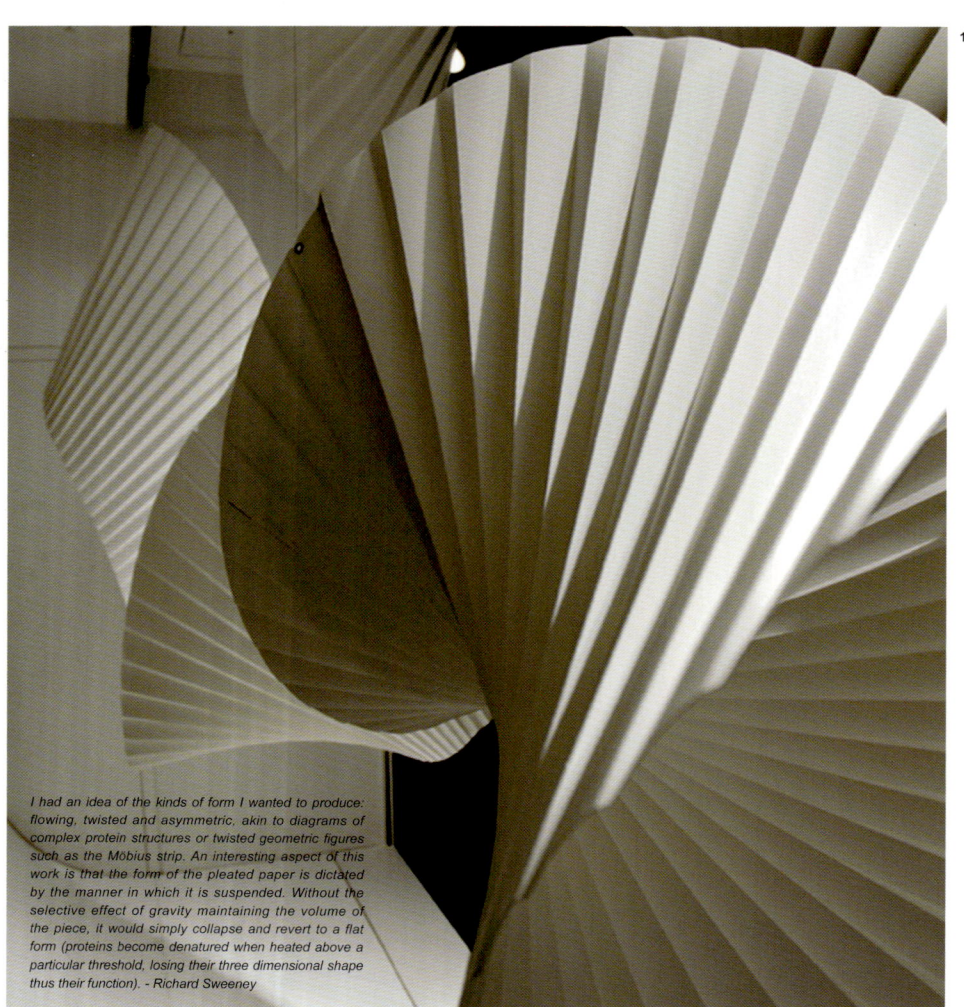

I had an idea of the kinds of form I wanted to produce: flowing, twisted and asymmetric, akin to diagrams of complex protein structures or twisted geometric figures such as the Möbius strip. An interesting aspect of this work is that the form of the pleated paper is dictated by the manner in which it is suspended. Without the selective effect of gravity maintaining the volume of the piece, it would simply collapse and revert to a flat form (proteins become denatured when heated above a particular threshold, losing their three dimensional shape thus their function). - Richard Sweeney

1. Mobius

A series of sculptural works in paper commissioned by Selfridges for display in the flagship store windows, Orchard Street, London.

Sweeney's interest lies in the manipulation of the material, taking a hands-on approach to the creation of form using paper folding techniques; of his method he says, "It is the tactile quality that drives me, I find it difficult to work with something unless I can hold it in my hands, touching and bending the material to feel how it behaves". Hand-made, paper models were used to generate the shape of the pleated paper pieces, combined with the use of computer modelling for further refinement. The virtual pleated form was then exported as a flat layout, printed and folded directly to create small prototypes for testing the composition of the work within a 1:10 scale model of the space.

After further tests with full scale models, the final layout was used to route an acrylic jig, which was used as a template for transferring the score-lines to the paper. A total of thirty six sheets were hand scored and pleated over three days. In the window space, the sheets were glued end-to-end to create continuous lengths. The tension in the sheets caused by the angled pleat allowed them to be suspended in a natural manner-that is to say they were not forced into any particular configuration, but arranged according to the behaviour of the sheet.

Designer: Richard Sweeney   Country: UK   Medium: Paper, Adhesive
Client: Selfridges, London   Photographer: Richard Sweeney / Andrew Meredith

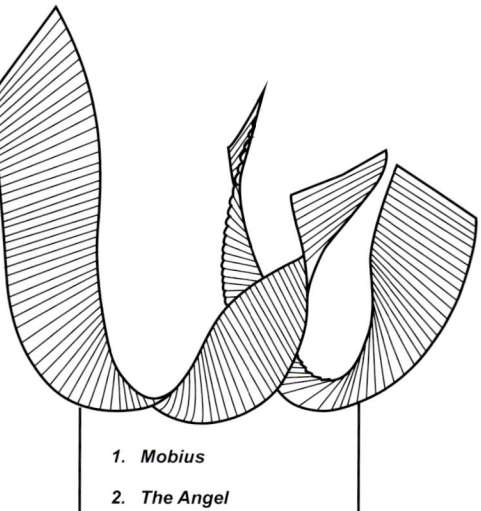

1. Mobius

2. The Angel

---Richard Sweeney

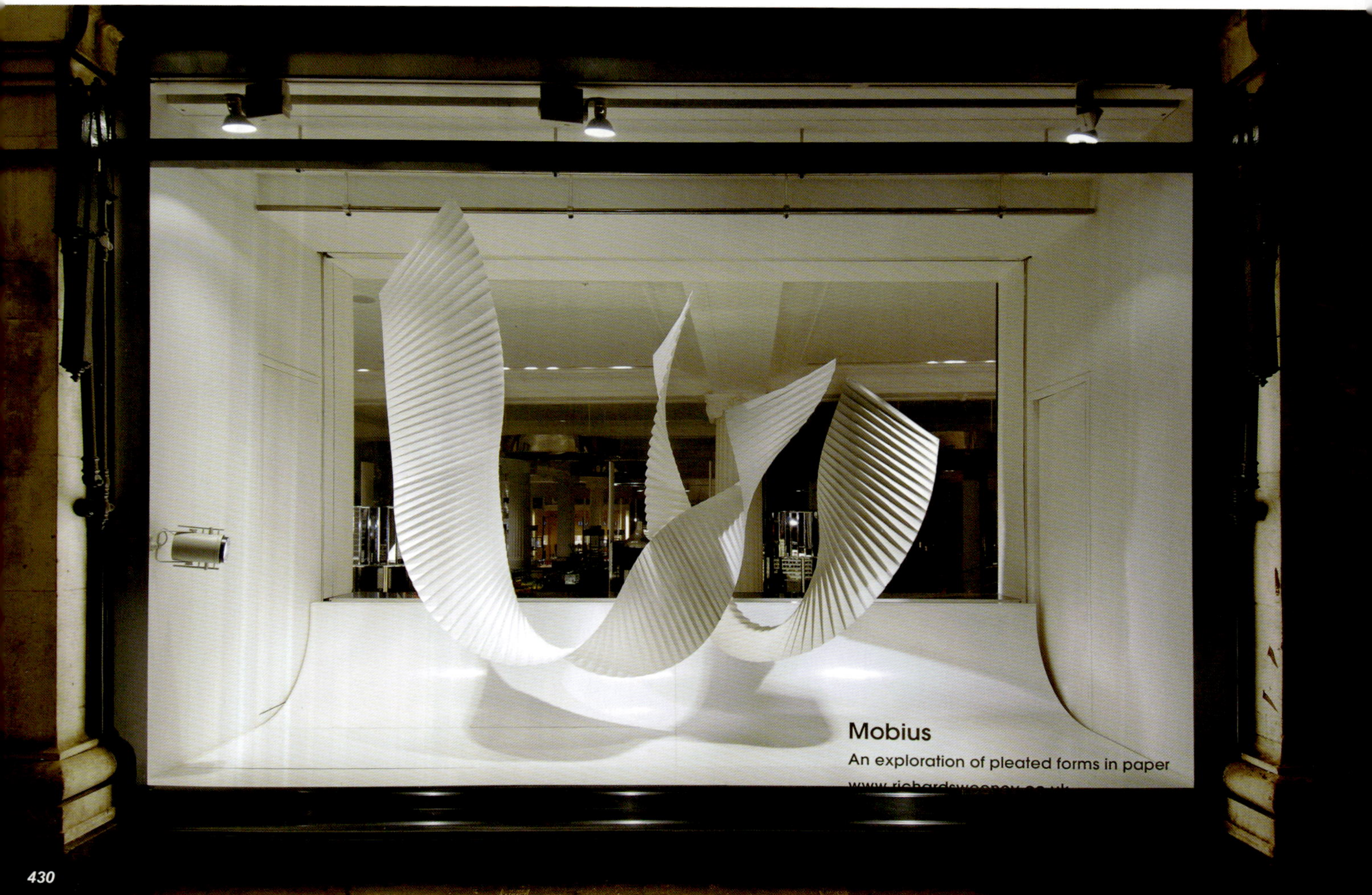

Mobius
An exploration of pleated forms in paper
www.richardsweeney.co.uk

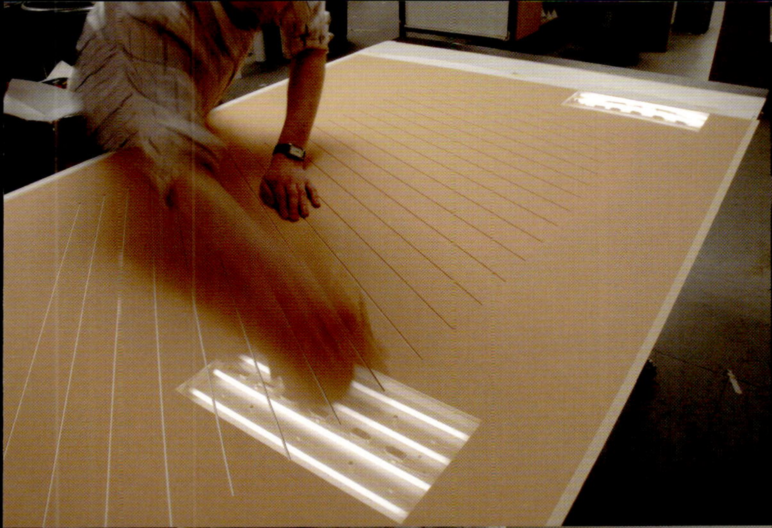

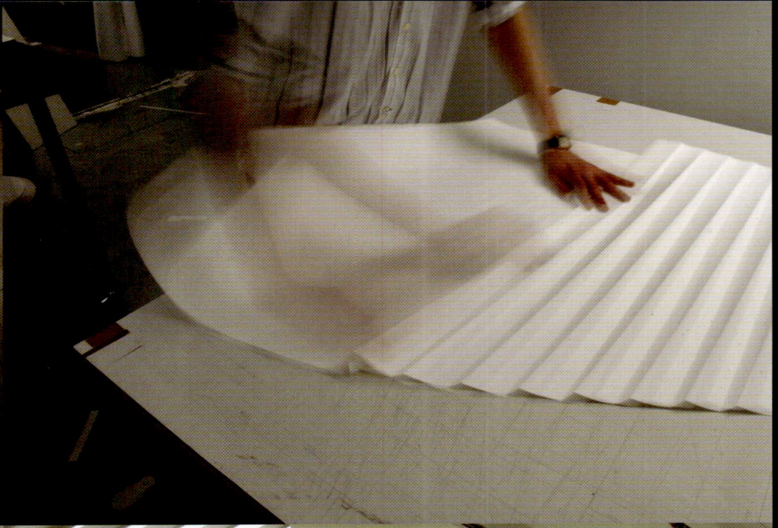

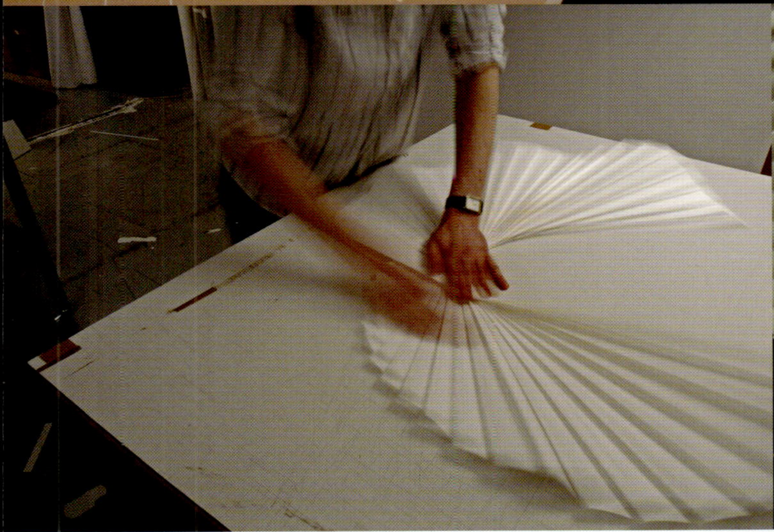

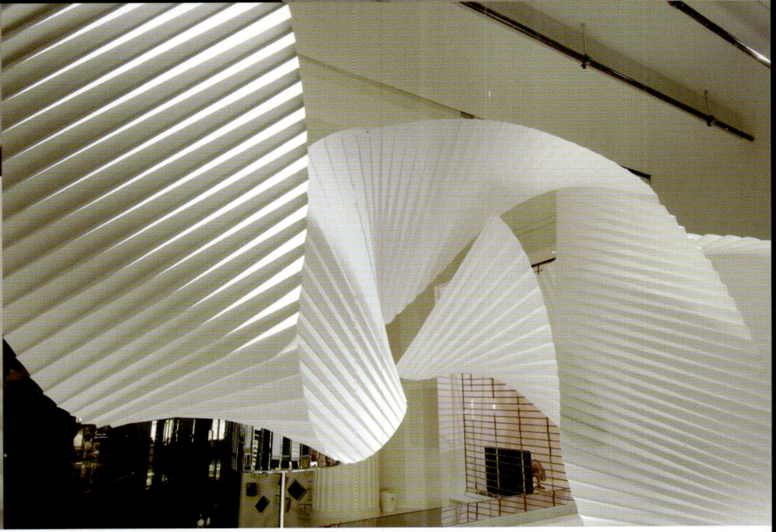

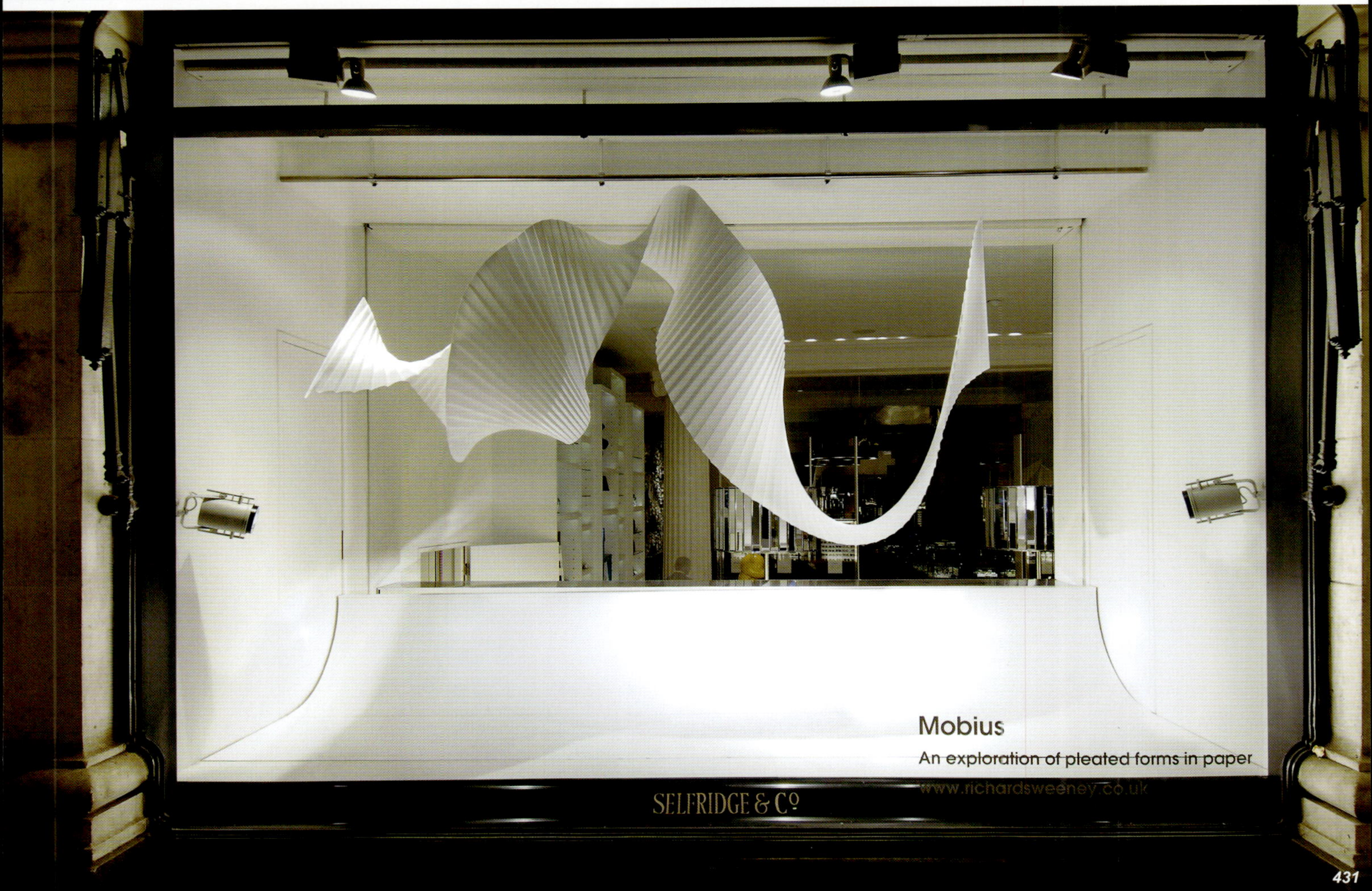

Mobius
An exploration of pleated forms in paper
www.richardsweeney.co.uk

SELFRIDGE & Cº

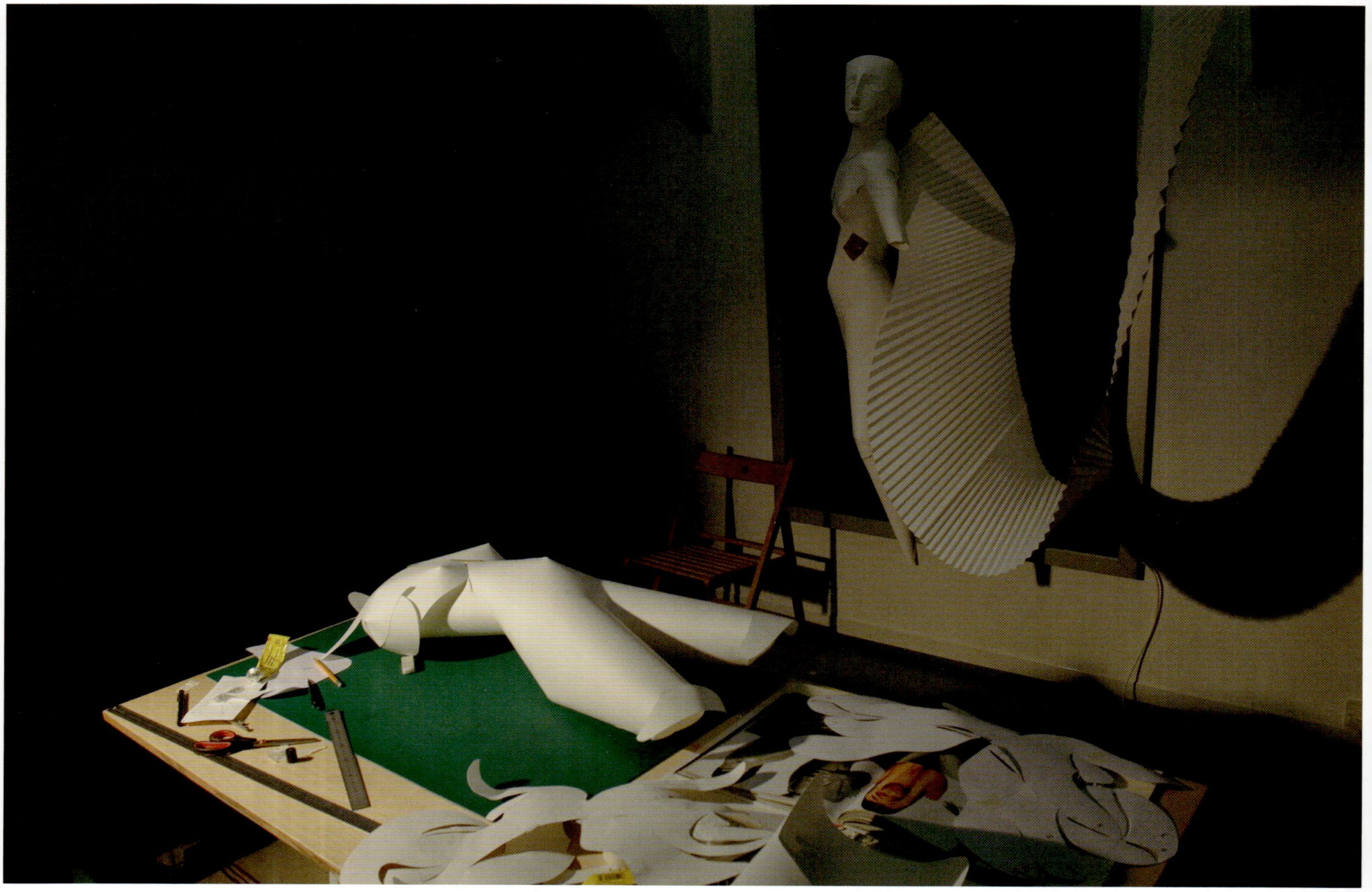

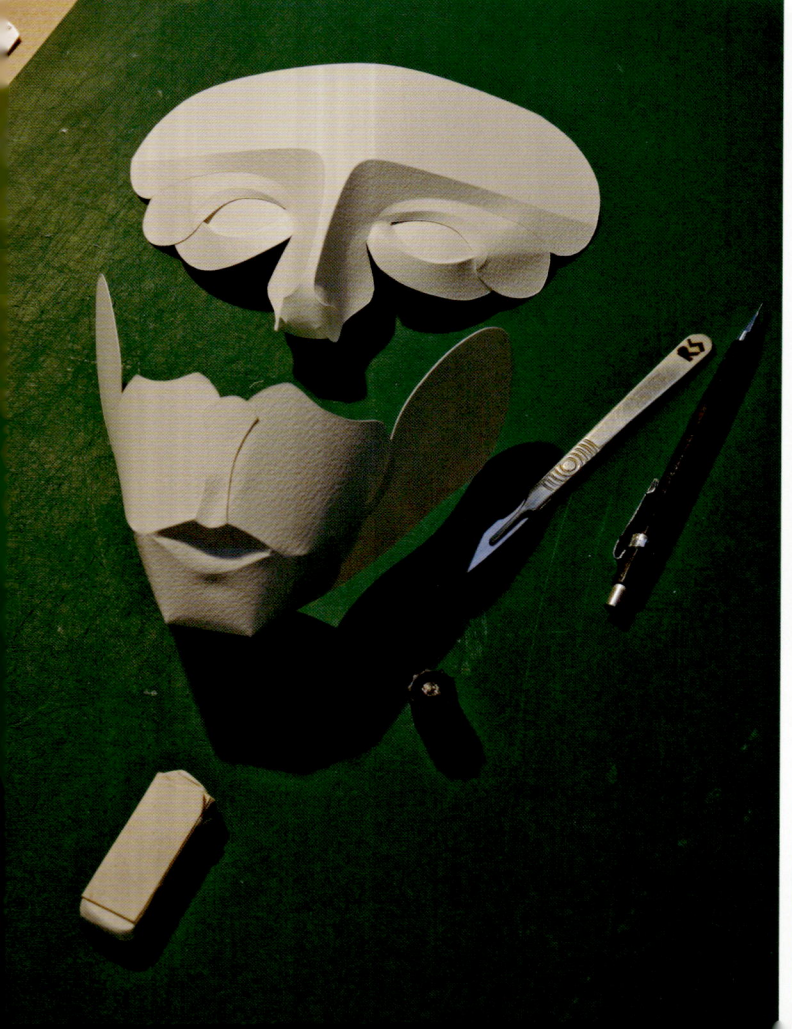
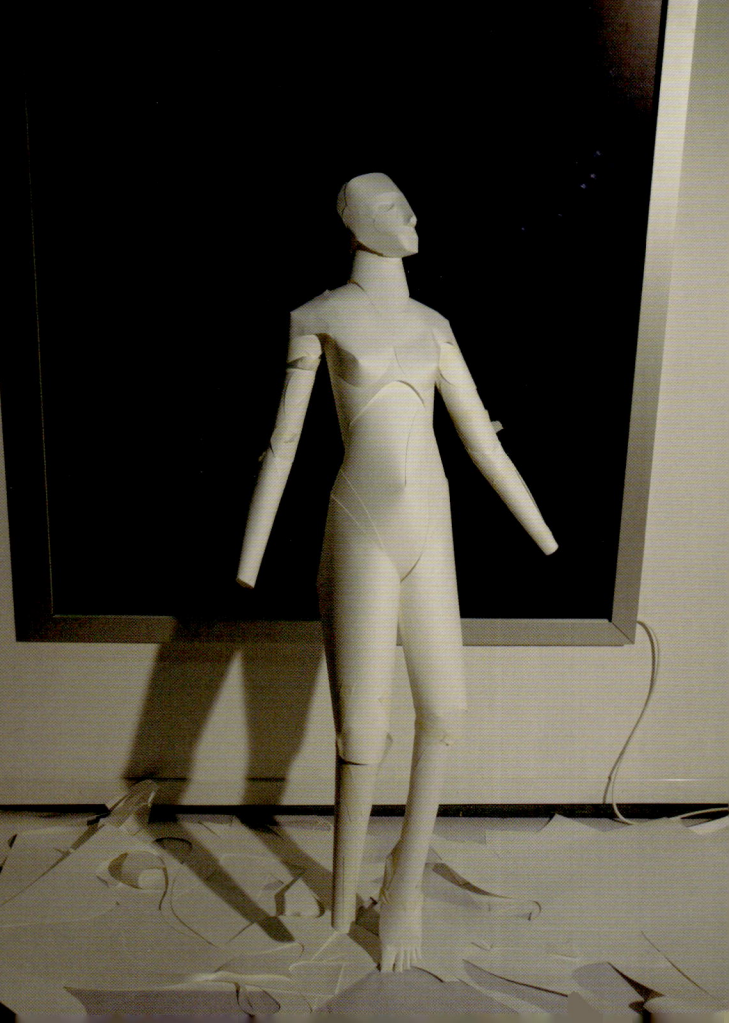

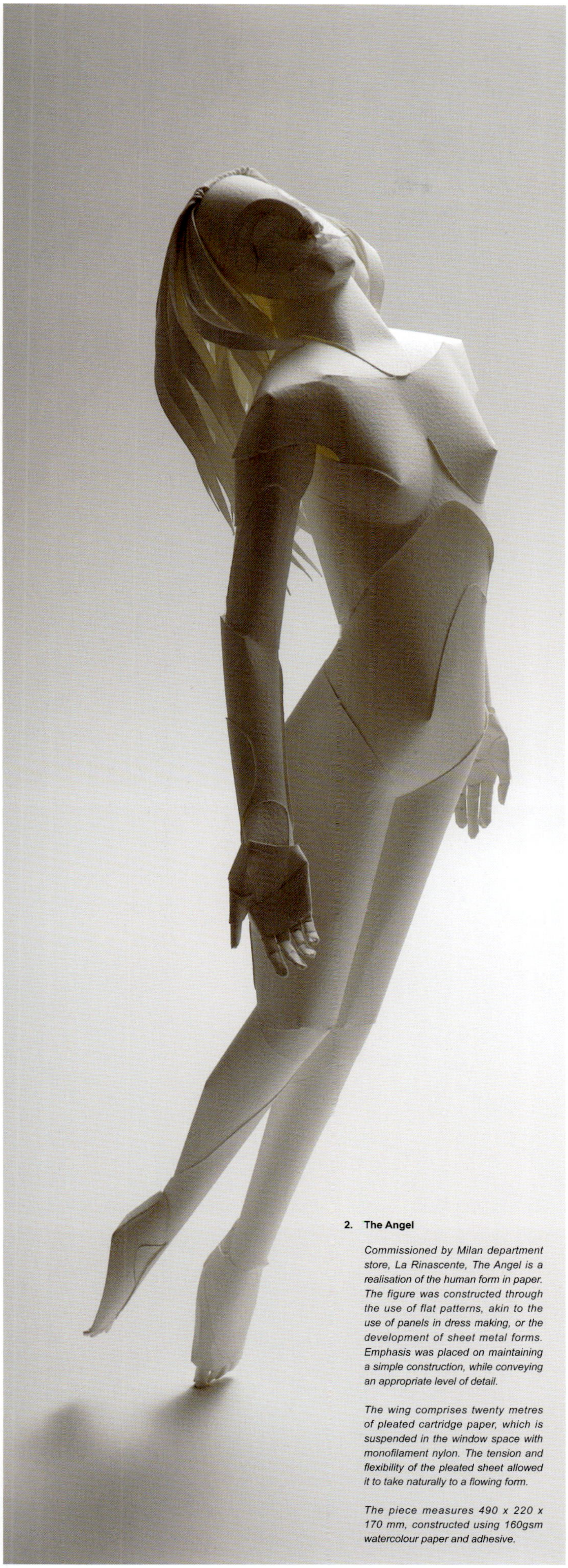

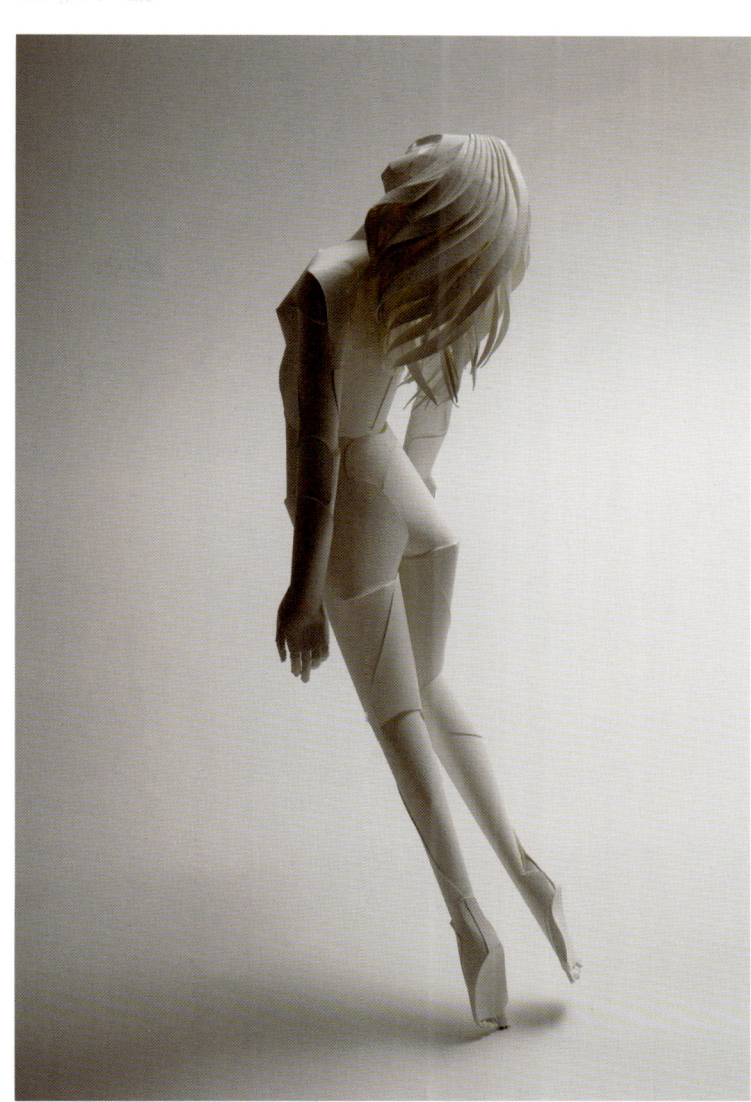

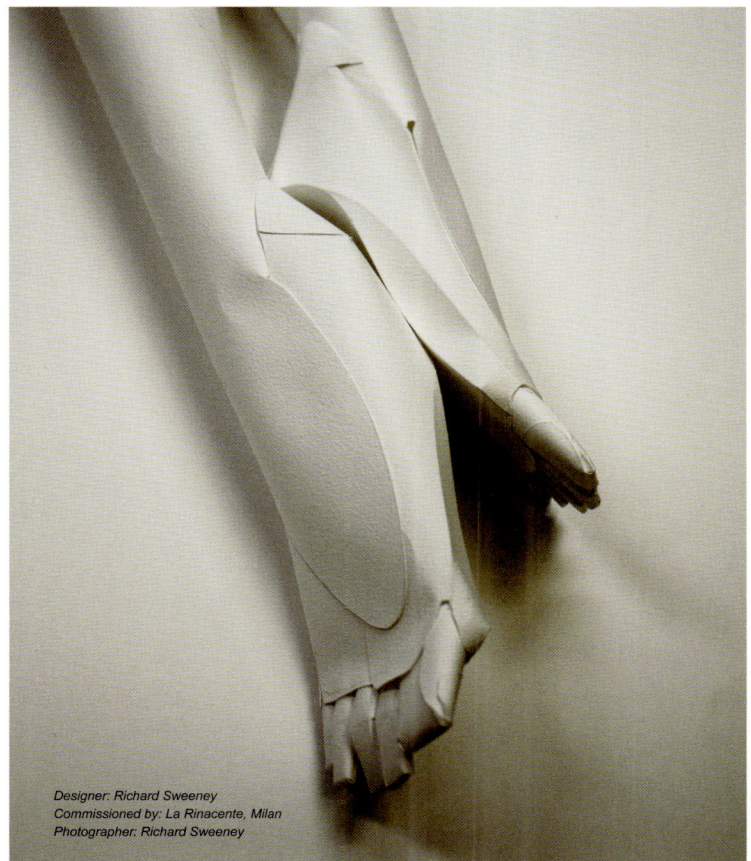

2. The Angel

Commissioned by Milan department store, La Rinascente, The Angel is a realisation of the human form in paper. The figure was constructed through the use of flat patterns, akin to the use of panels in dress making, or the development of sheet metal forms. Emphasis was placed on maintaining a simple construction, while conveying an appropriate level of detail.

The wing comprises twenty metres of pleated cartridge paper, which is suspended in the window space with monofilament nylon. The tension and flexibility of the pleated sheet allowed it to take naturally to a flowing form.

The piece measures 490 x 220 x 170 mm, constructed using 160gsm watercolour paper and adhesive.

Designer: Richard Sweeney
Commissioned by: La Rinacente, Milan
Photographer: Richard Sweeney

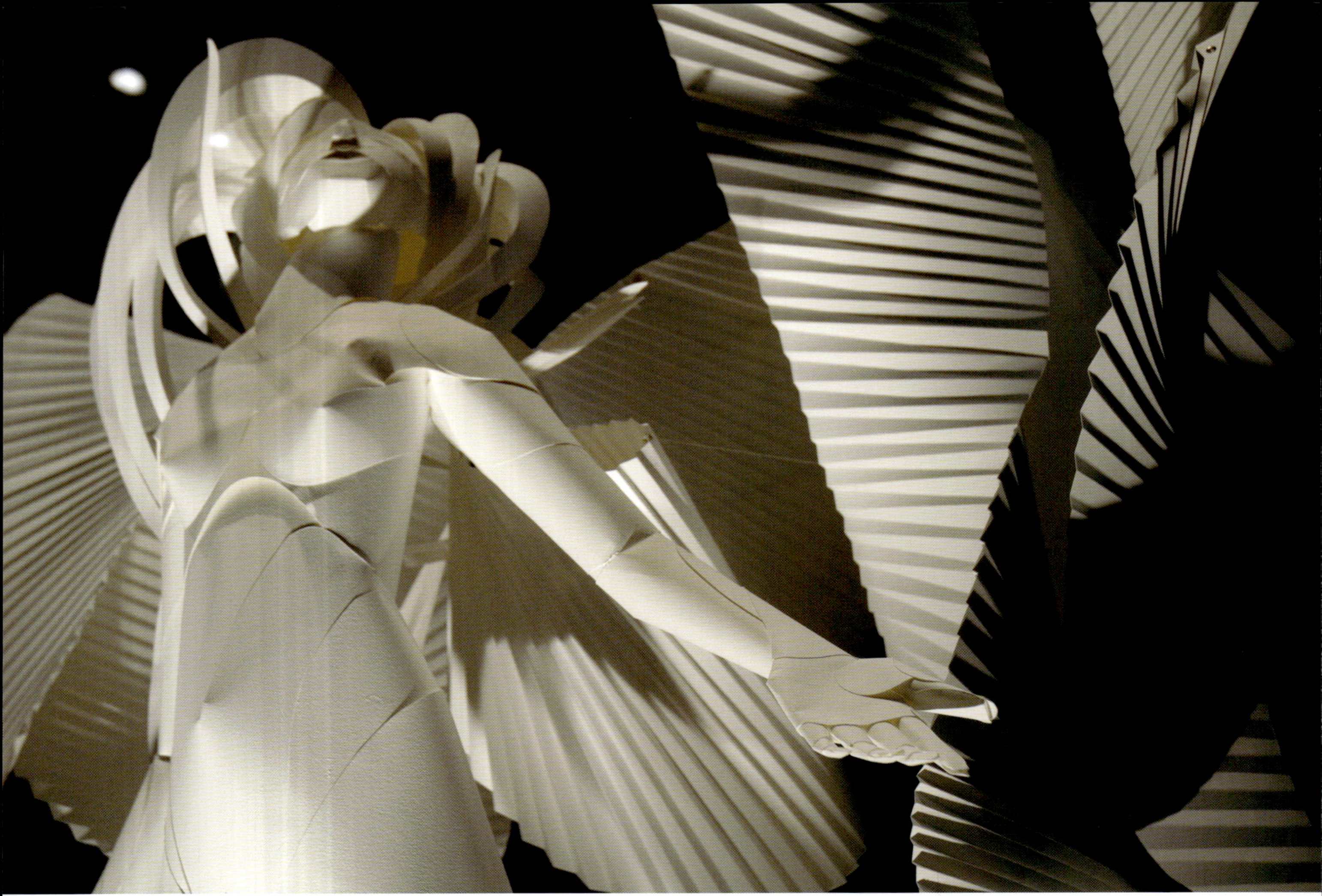

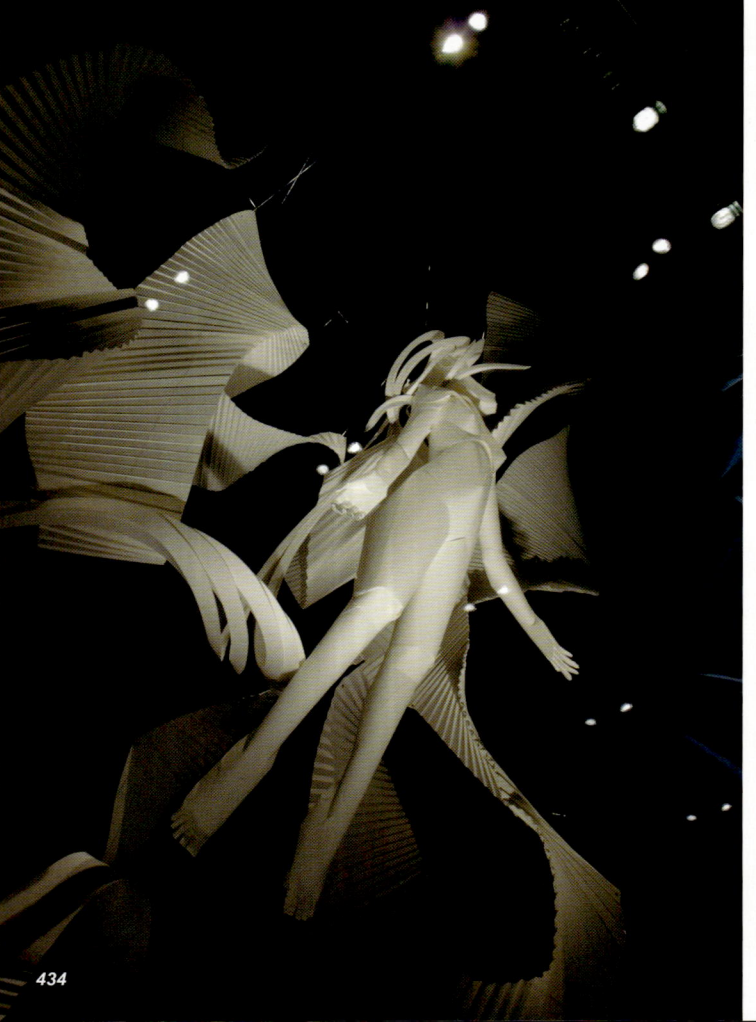
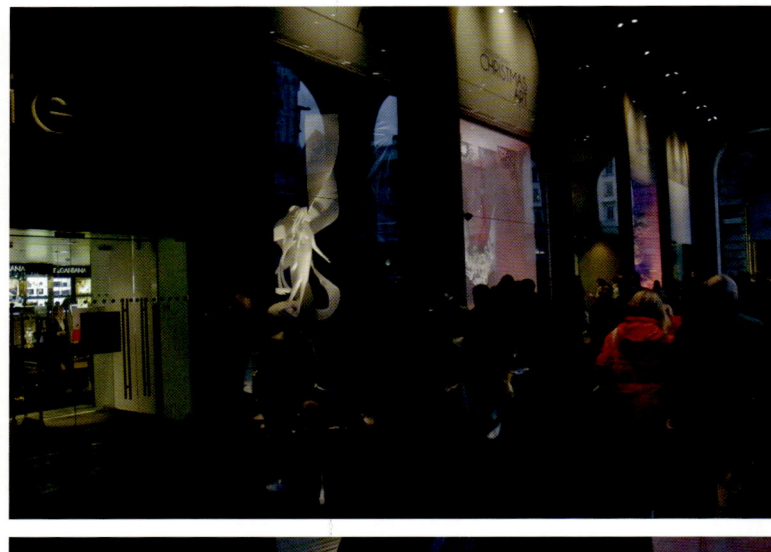
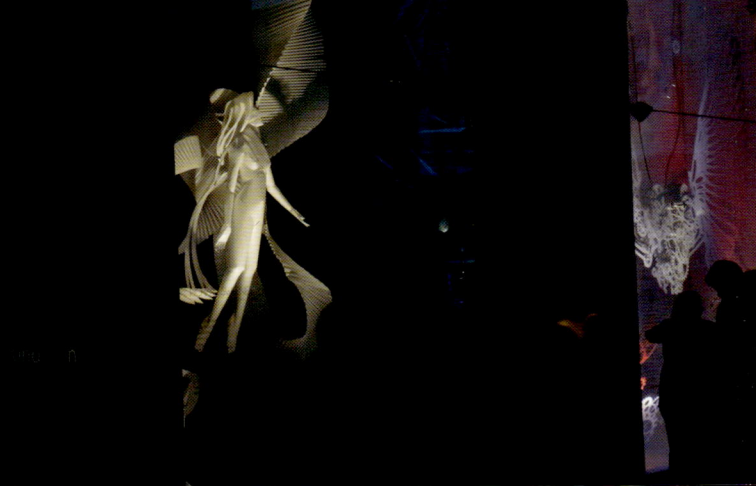

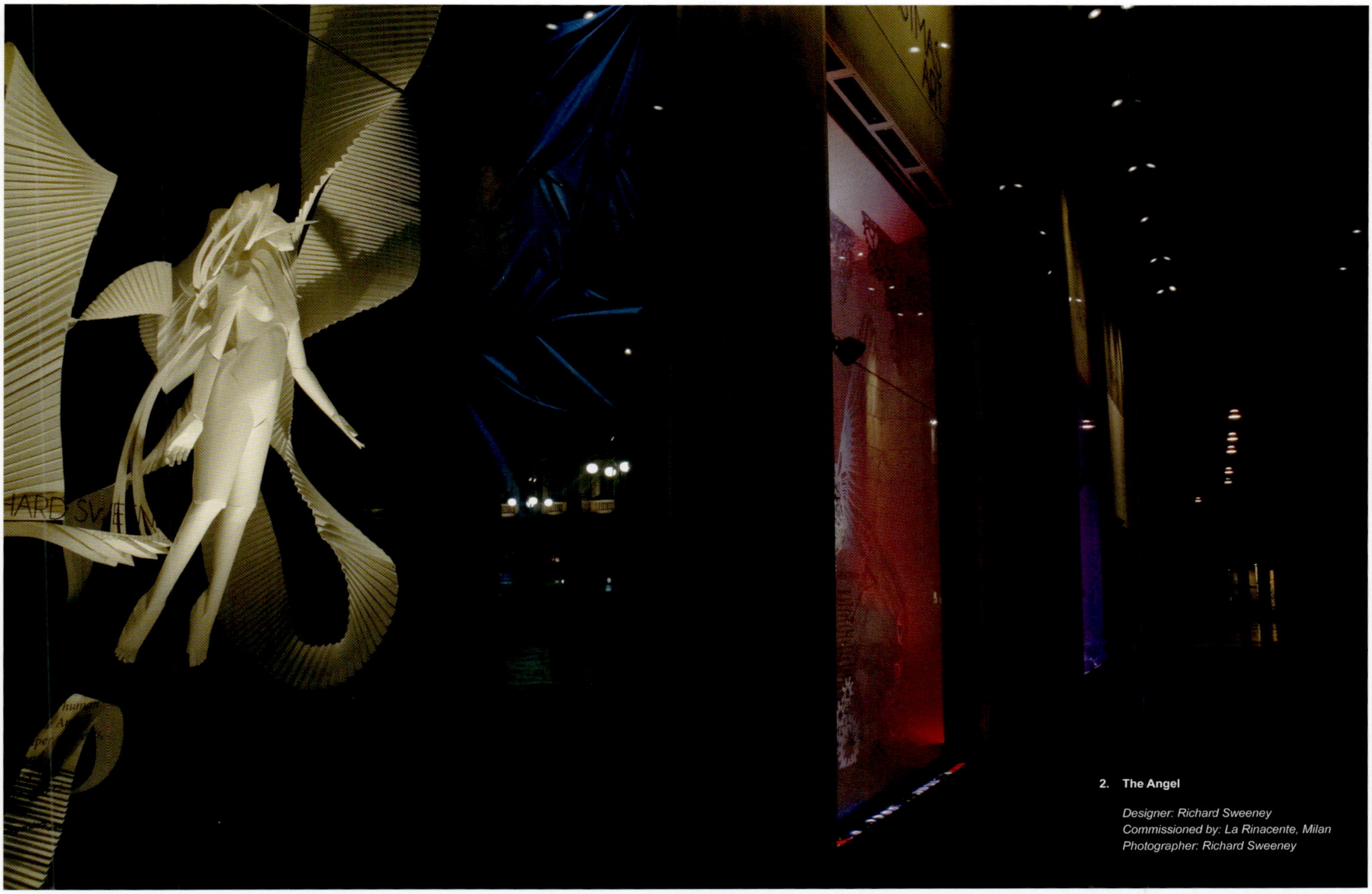

2. The Angel

Designer: Richard Sweeney
Commissioned by: La Rinacente, Milan
Photographer: Richard Sweeney

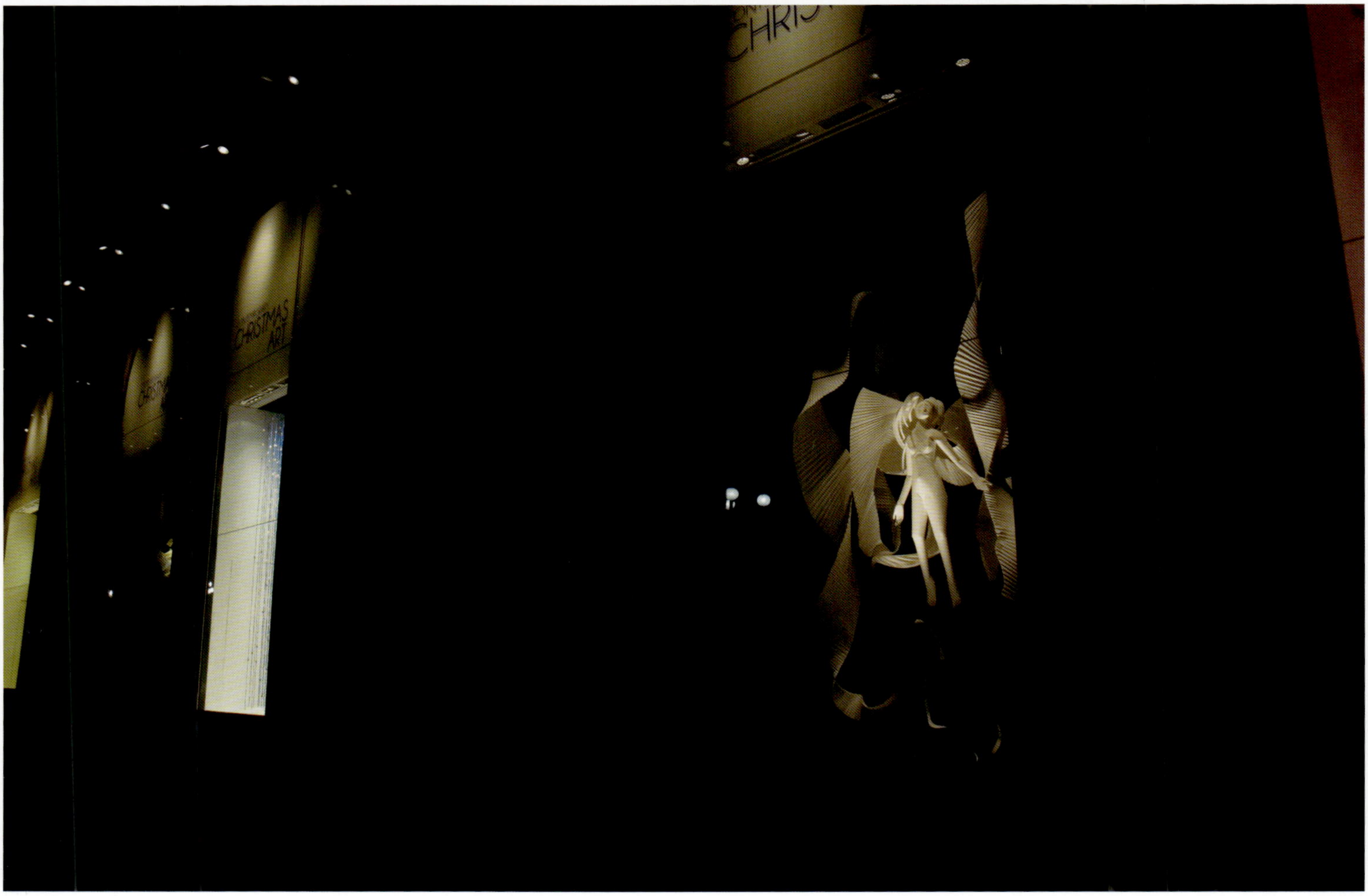

1. **Typography Design**
   Typography design made from strips of colored paper.
   Designer: Sabeena Karnik
   Country: India

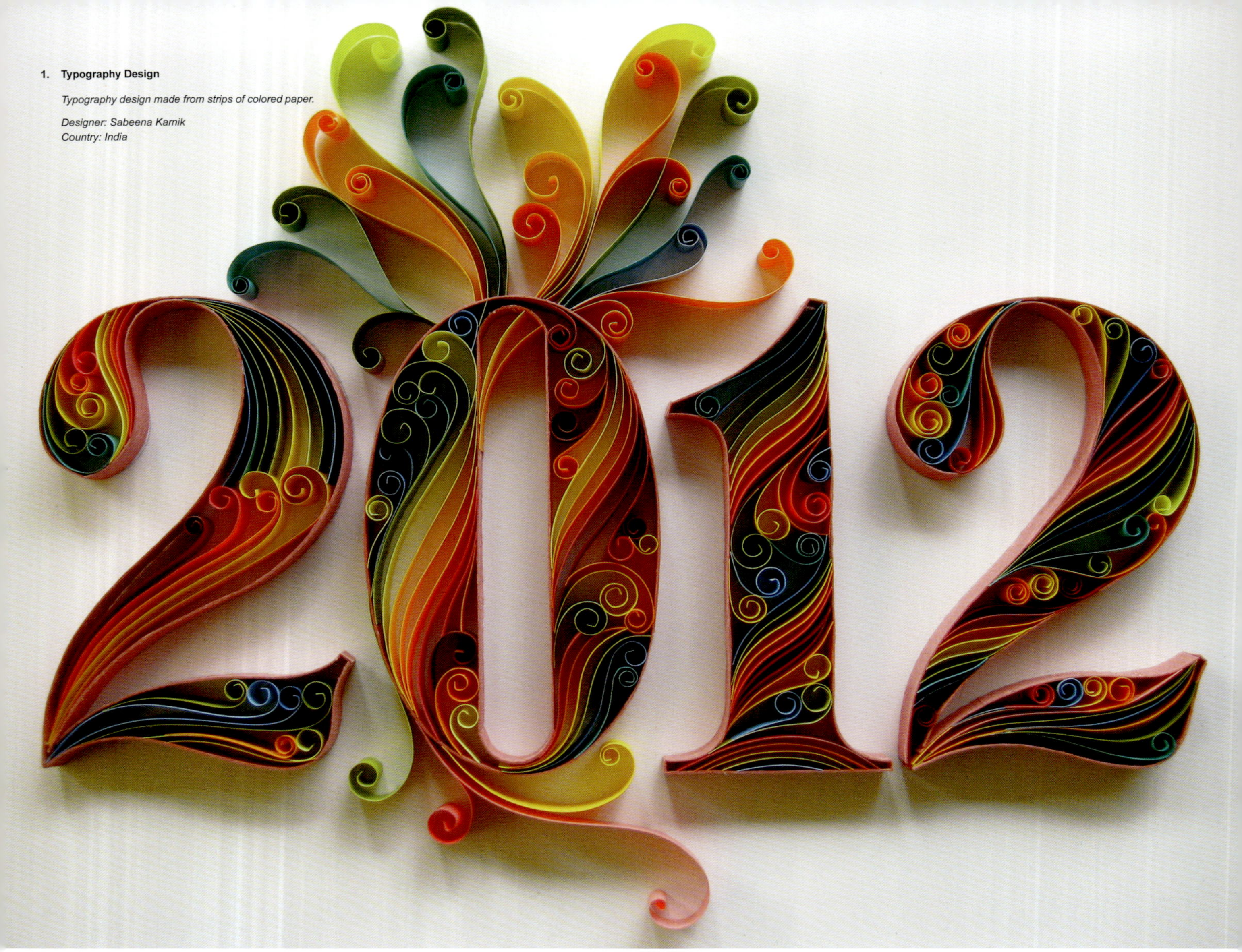

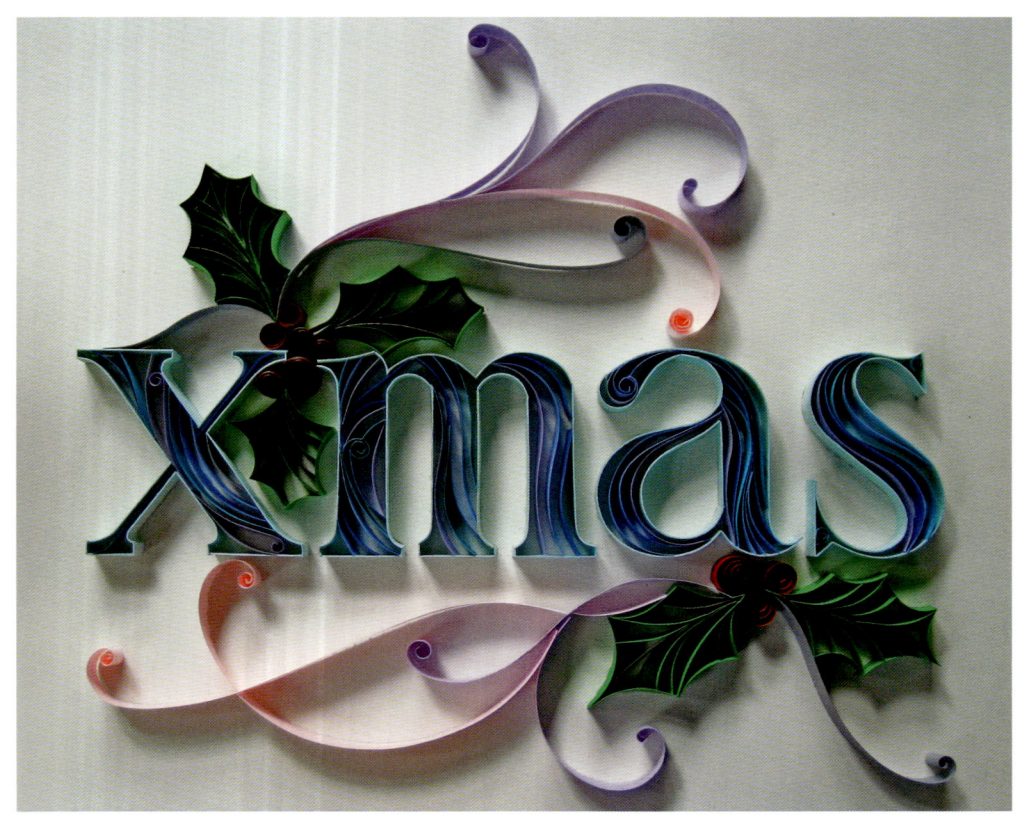

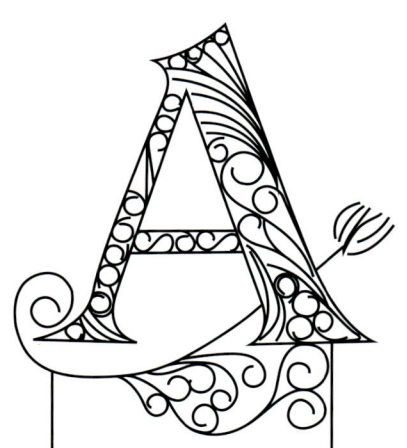

1. Typography Design
2. Typography Alphabet
3. Mia Collection for Tanishq

---Sabeena Karnik

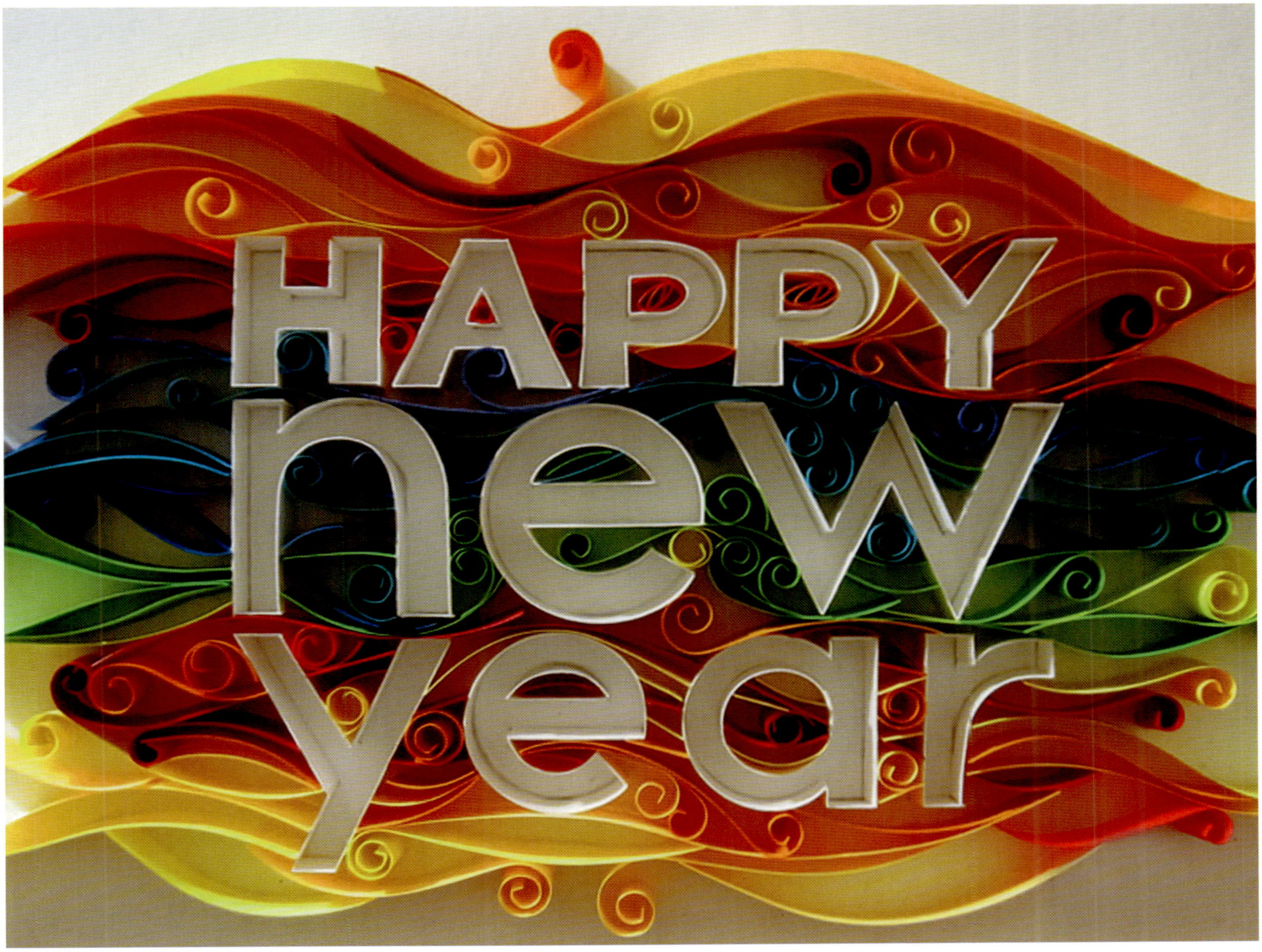

HAPPY new year

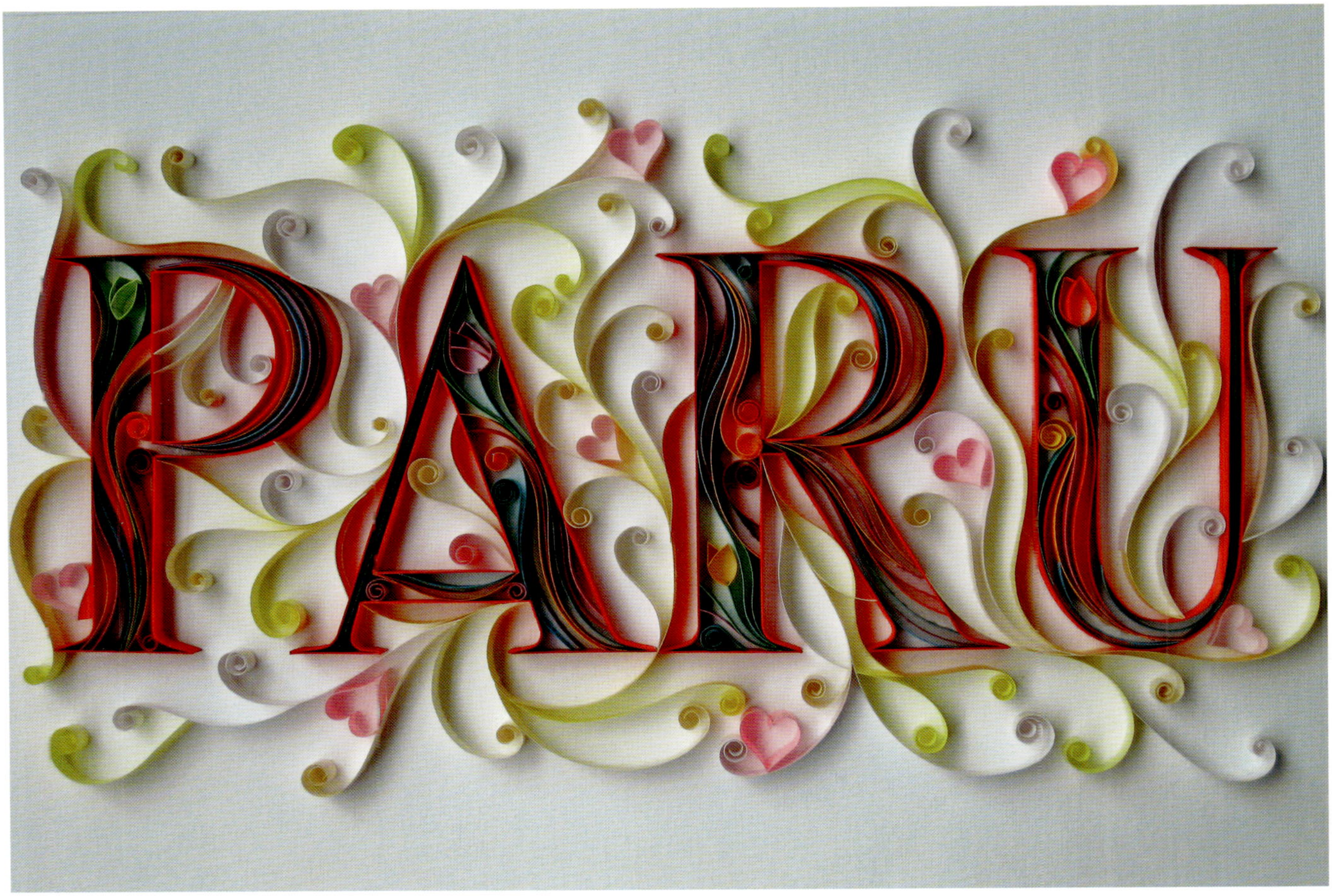

PARU

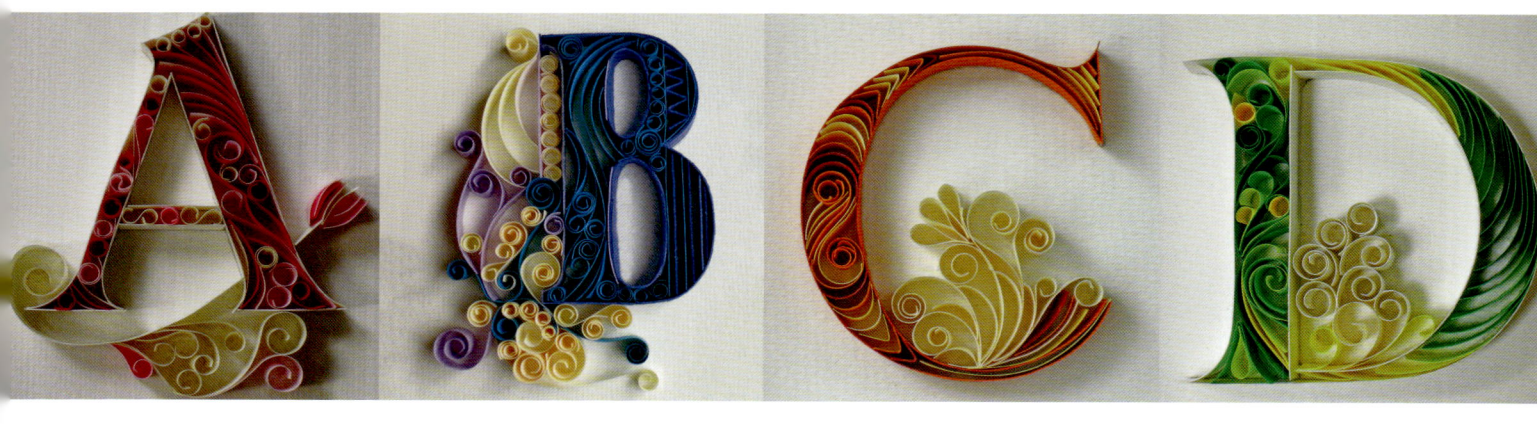
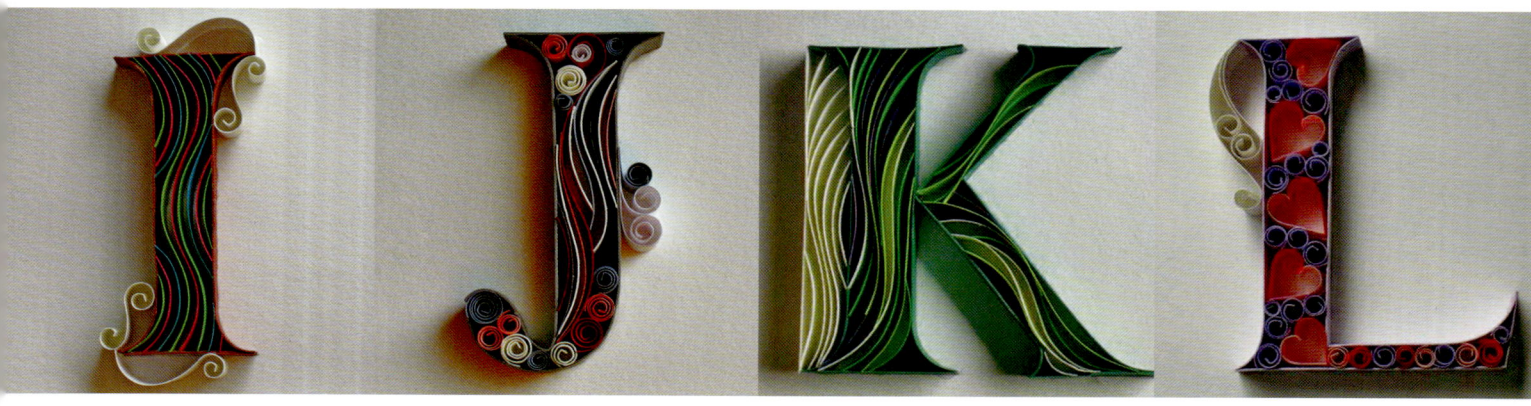
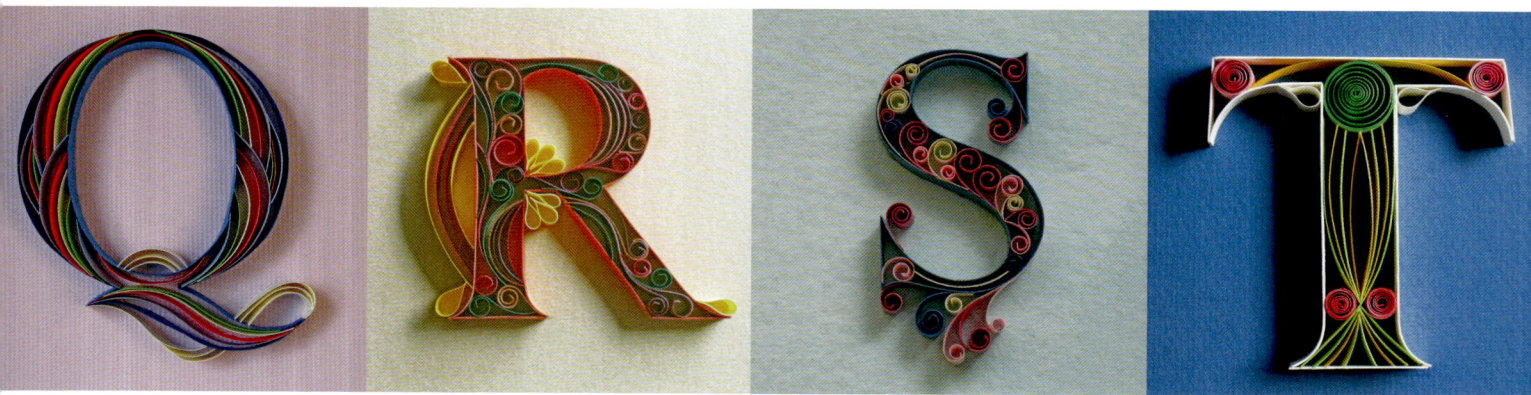
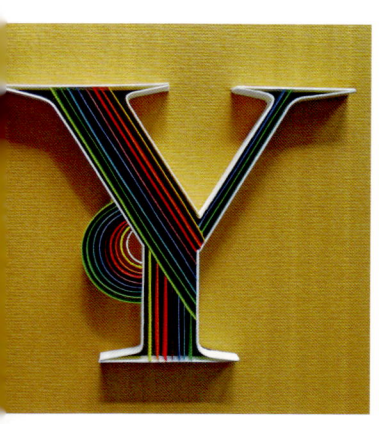

2. **Typography Alphabet**

Paper typography of the English alphabet using strips of colored paper.

Designer: Sabeena Karnik
Country: India

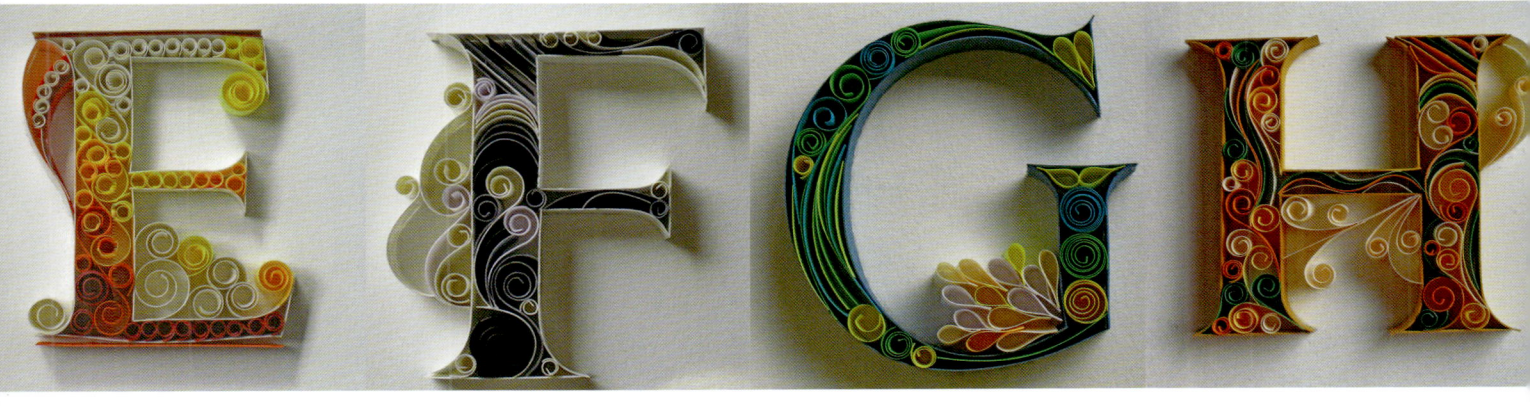
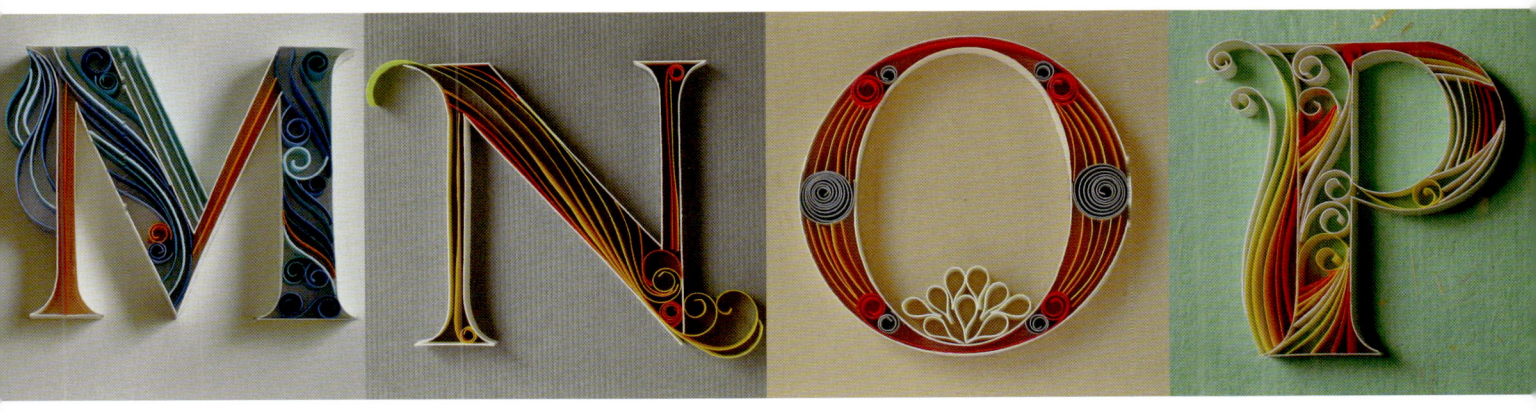
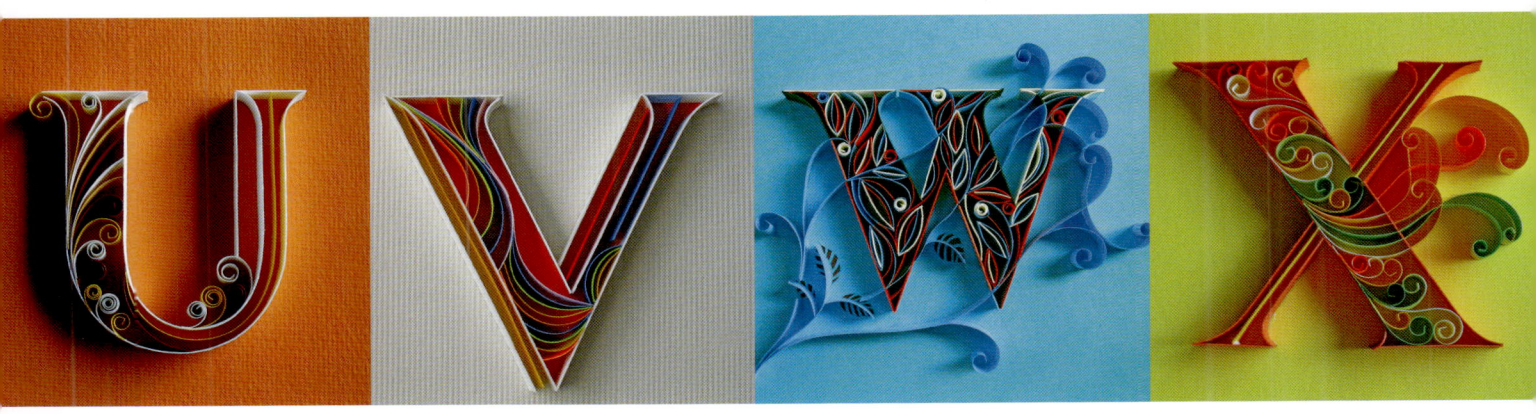
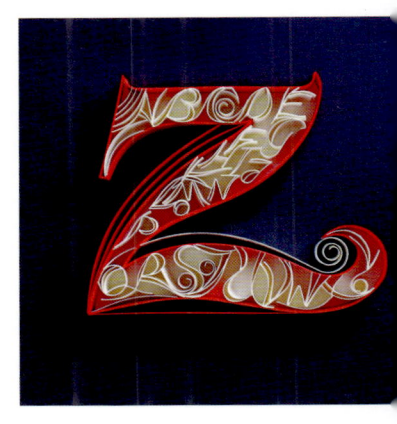

A **TATA** PRODUCT

3. Mia Collection for Tanishq
Paper typography done with strips of paper based on designs in the jewellery.
Designer: Sabeena Karnik
Country: India
Design Agency: Lowe Lintas
Client: Tanishq

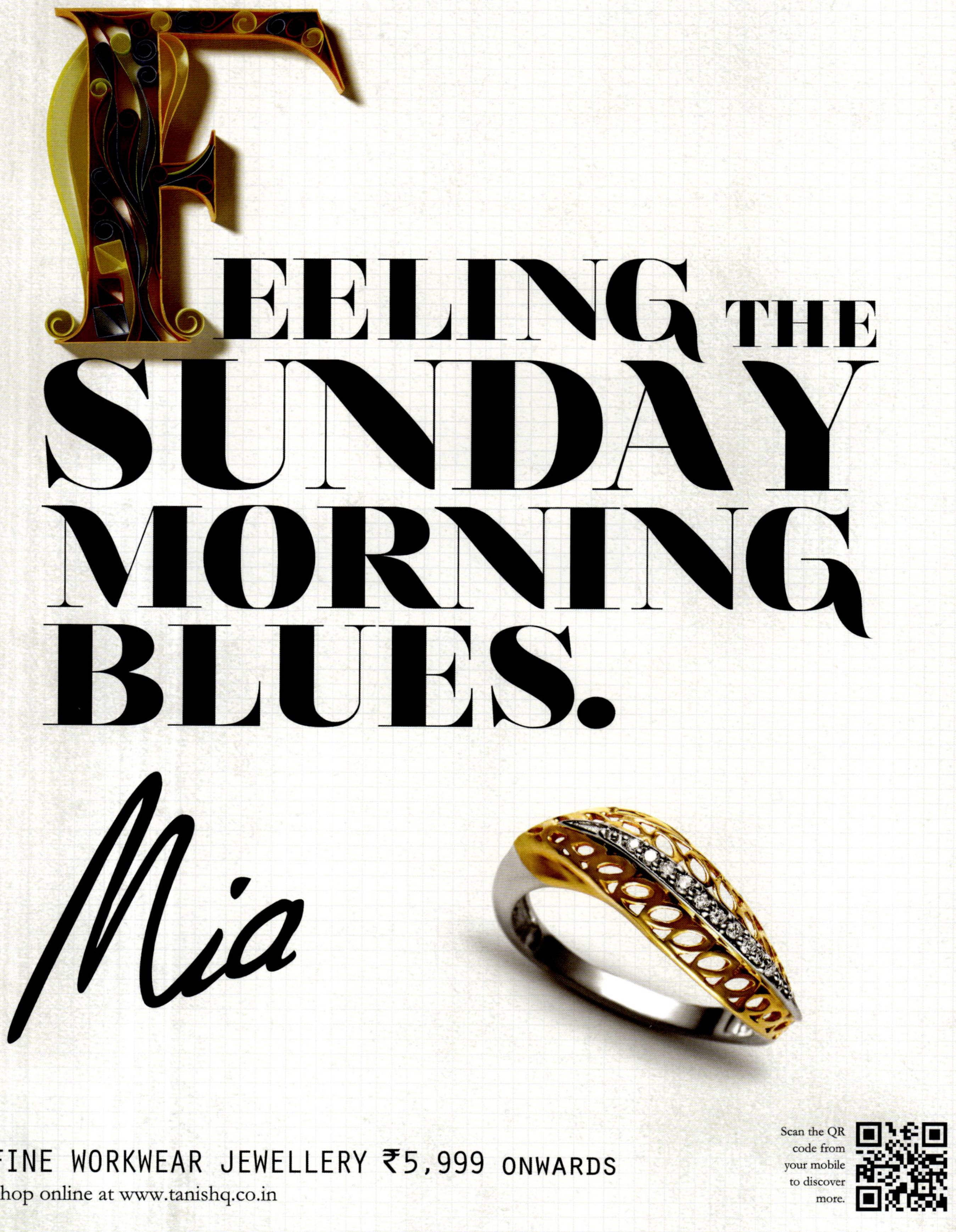

Feeling the Sunday Morning Blues.

Mia

FINE WORKWEAR JEWELLERY ₹5,999 ONWARDS
Shop online at www.tanishq.co.in

Scan the QR code from your mobile to discover more.

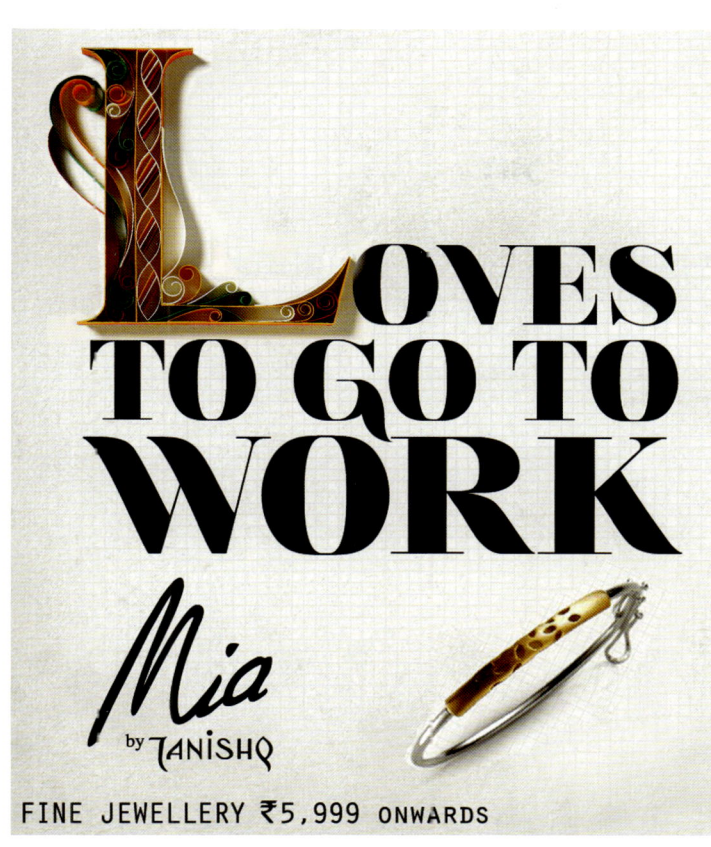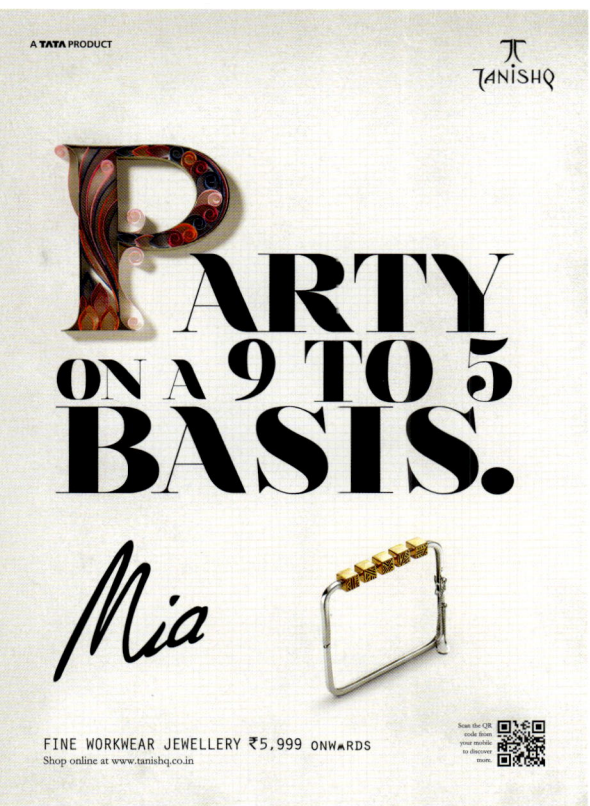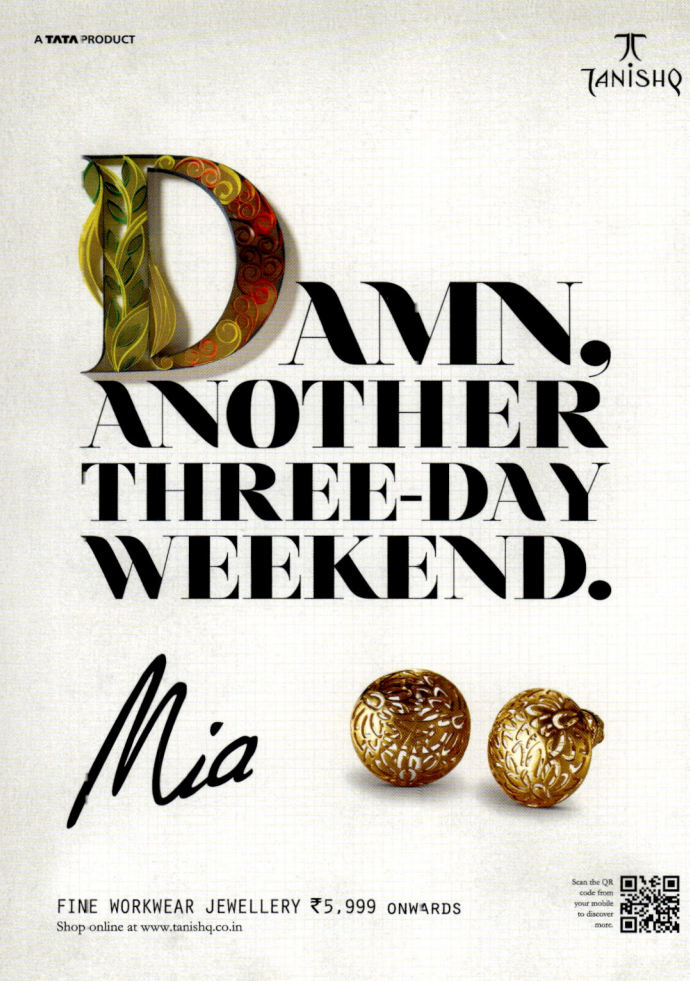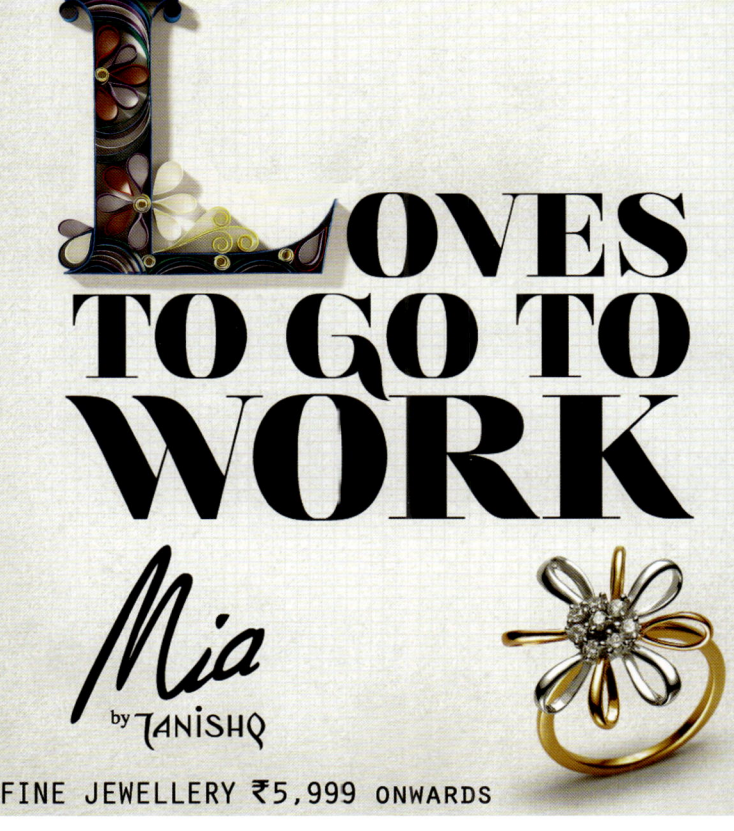

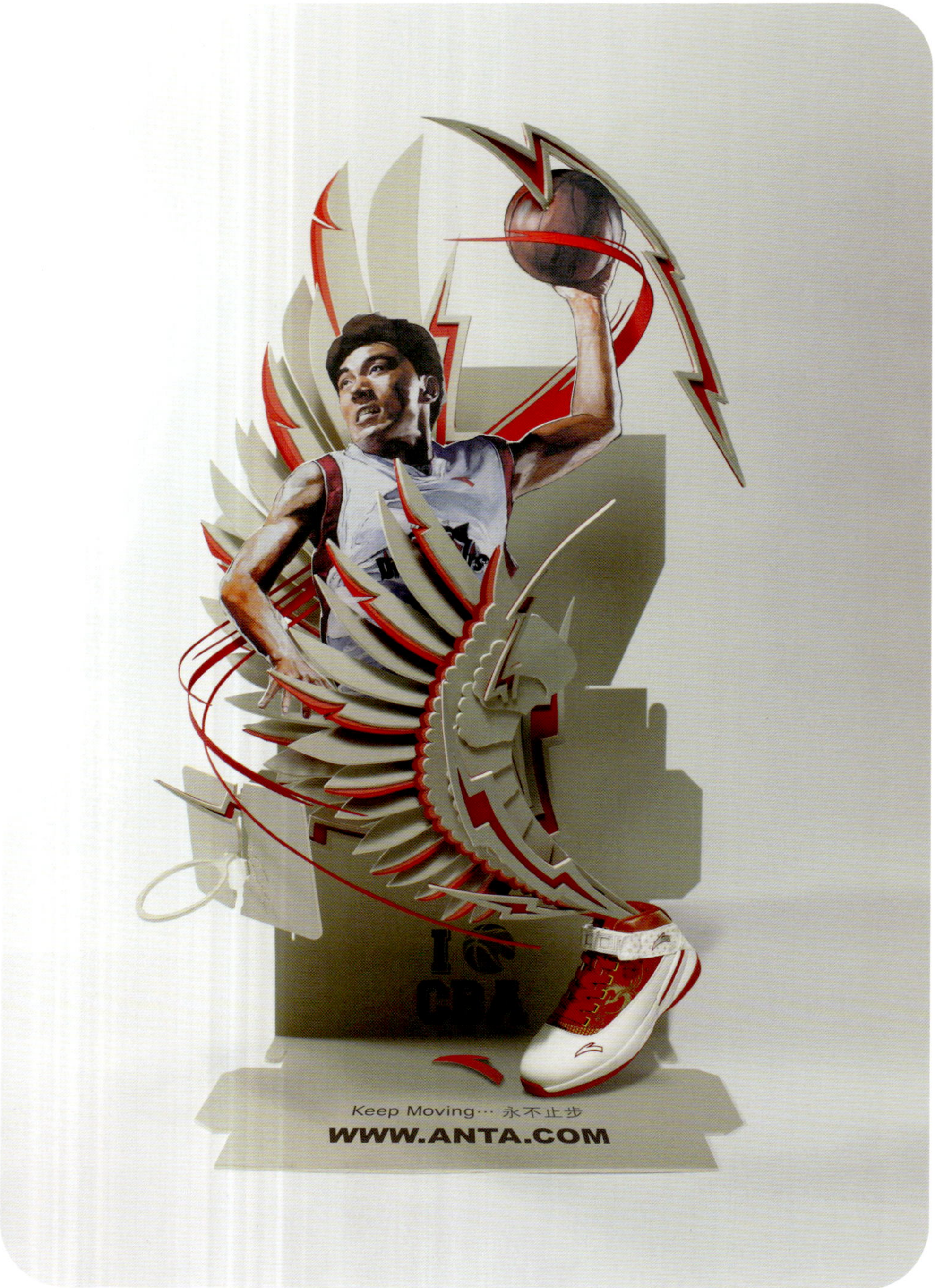

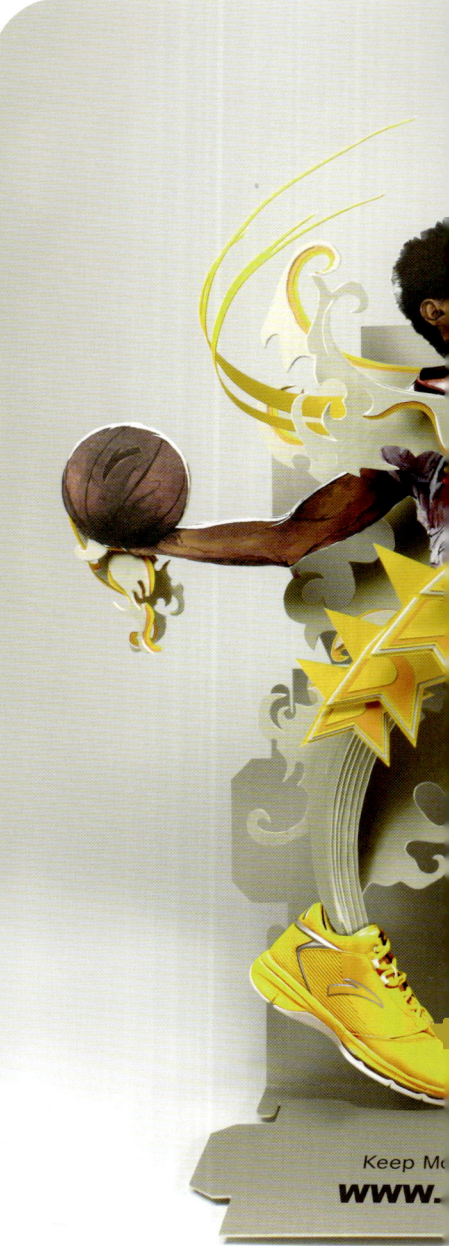

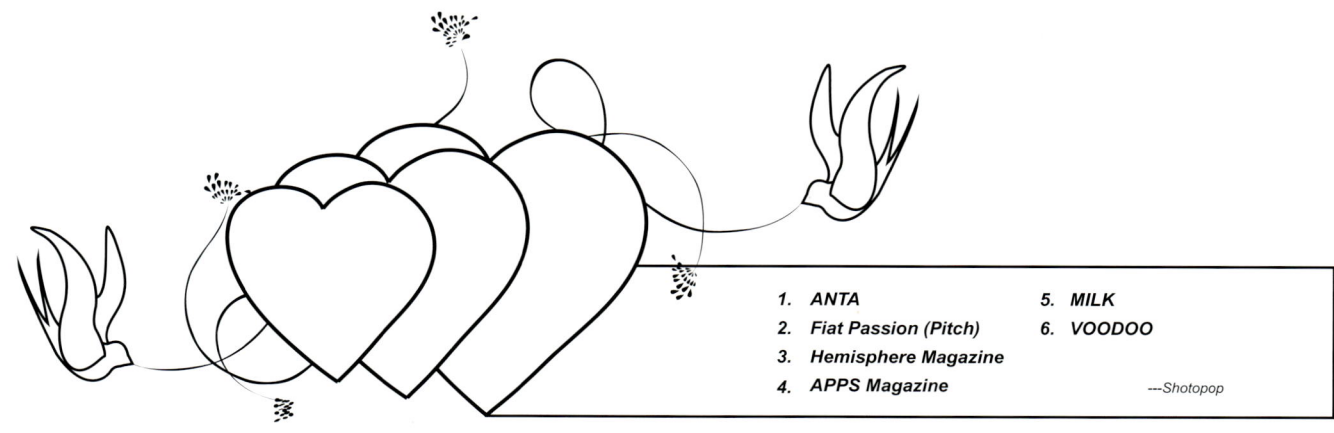

1. ANTA
2. Fiat Passion (Pitch)
3. Hemisphere Magazine
4. APPS Magazine
5. MILK
6. VOODOO

---Shotopop

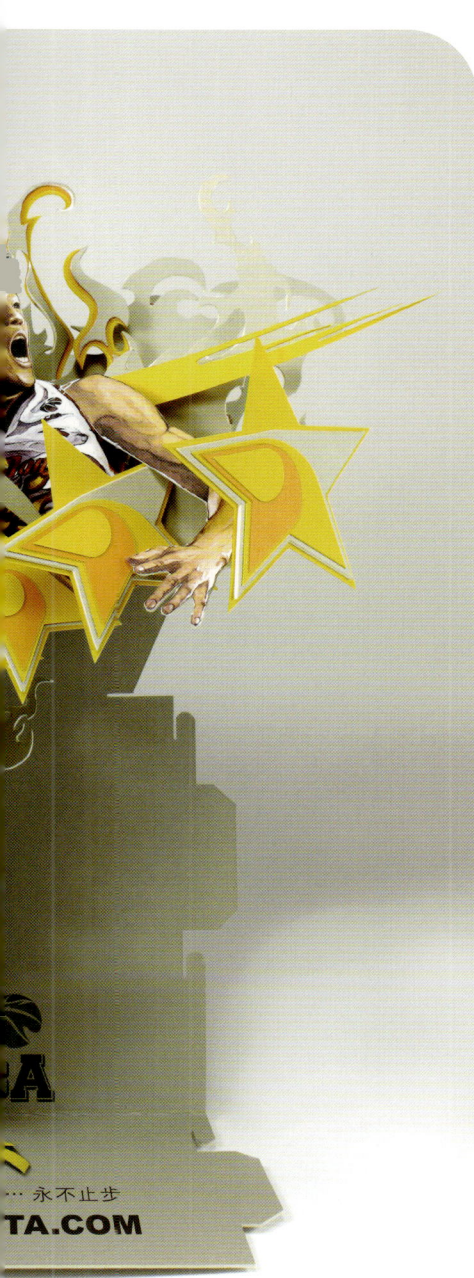

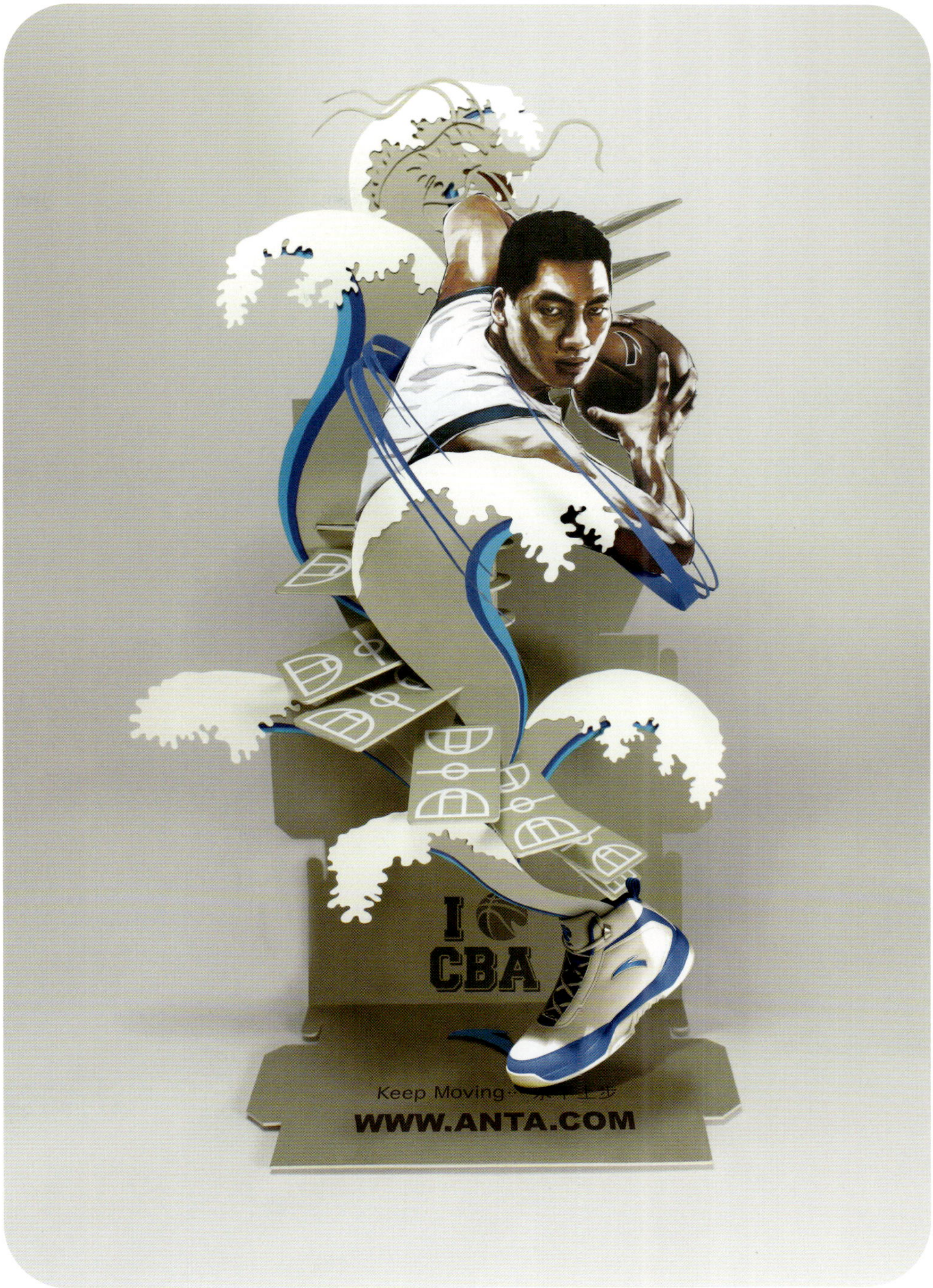

1. **ANTA**

   JWT Shanghai teamed up with Shotopop and set out to create an in-store display with a twist. The goal was to interpret the playing style and achievements of 3 CBA players, using ANTA shoe boxes. The final 3 pieces were used as in store sculptures in the ANTA Flagship store in Shanghai. The project won 2 Bronze Lions for "Outdoor" and "Design" at the 2011 Cannes Lions International Festival of Creativity and Awards.

   Design Agency: Shotopop
   Country: UK
   Creative Director: Yang Yeo / Elvis Chau
   Design Director: Carin Standford
   Designer: Carin Standford
   Client: ANTA
   Photographer: Casper Franken

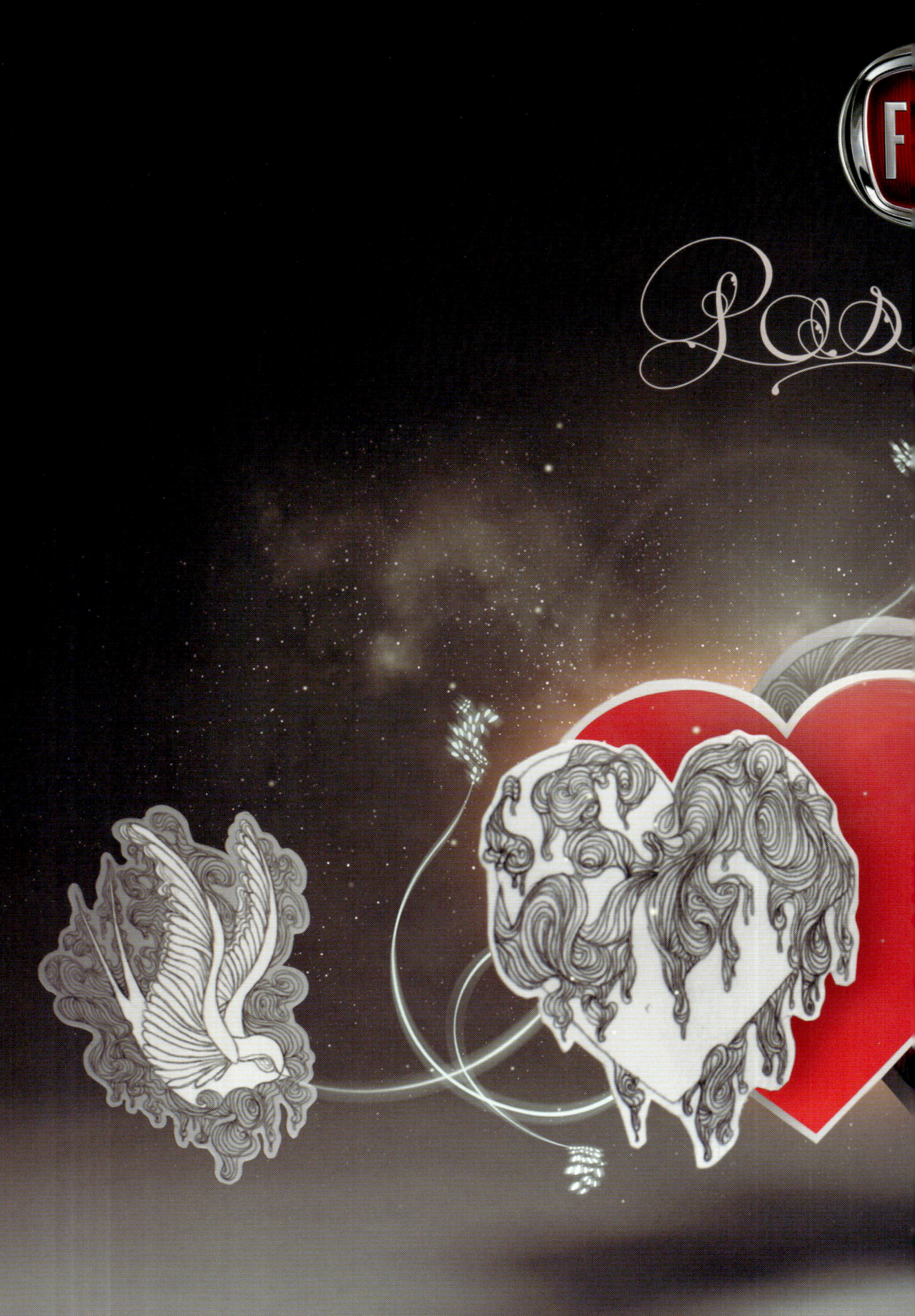

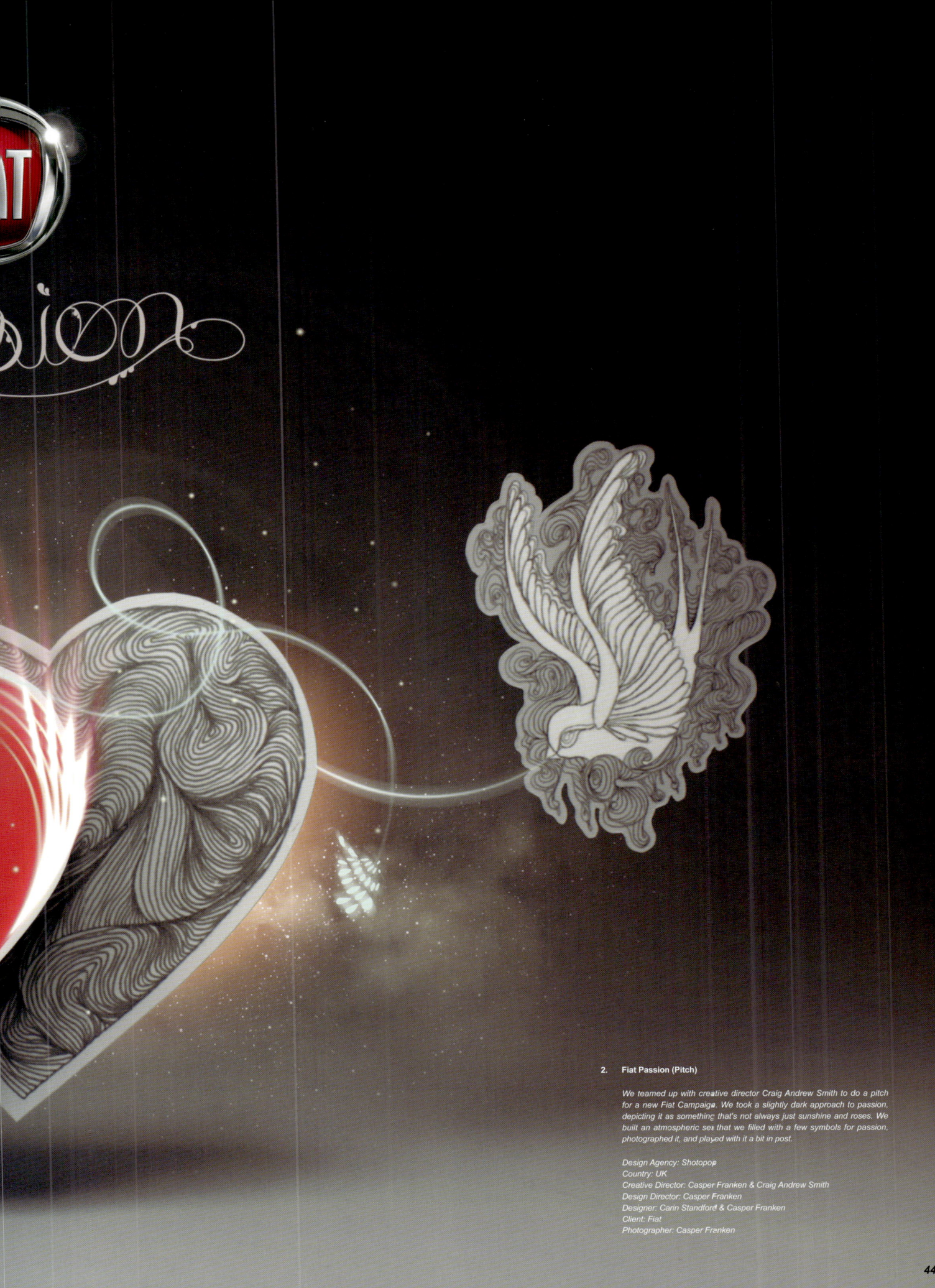

2. **Fiat Passion (Pitch)**

We teamed up with creative director Craig Andrew Smith to do a pitch for a new Fiat Campaign. We took a slightly dark approach to passion, depicting it as something that's not always just sunshine and roses. We built an atmospheric set that we filled with a few symbols for passion, photographed it, and played with it a bit in post.

Design Agency: Shotopop
Country: UK
Creative Director: Casper Franken & Craig Andrew Smith
Design Director: Casper Franken
Designer: Carin Standford & Casper Franken
Client: Fiat
Photographer: Casper Franken

3. Hemisphere Magazine

Editorial Illustration for Hemisphere Magazine.

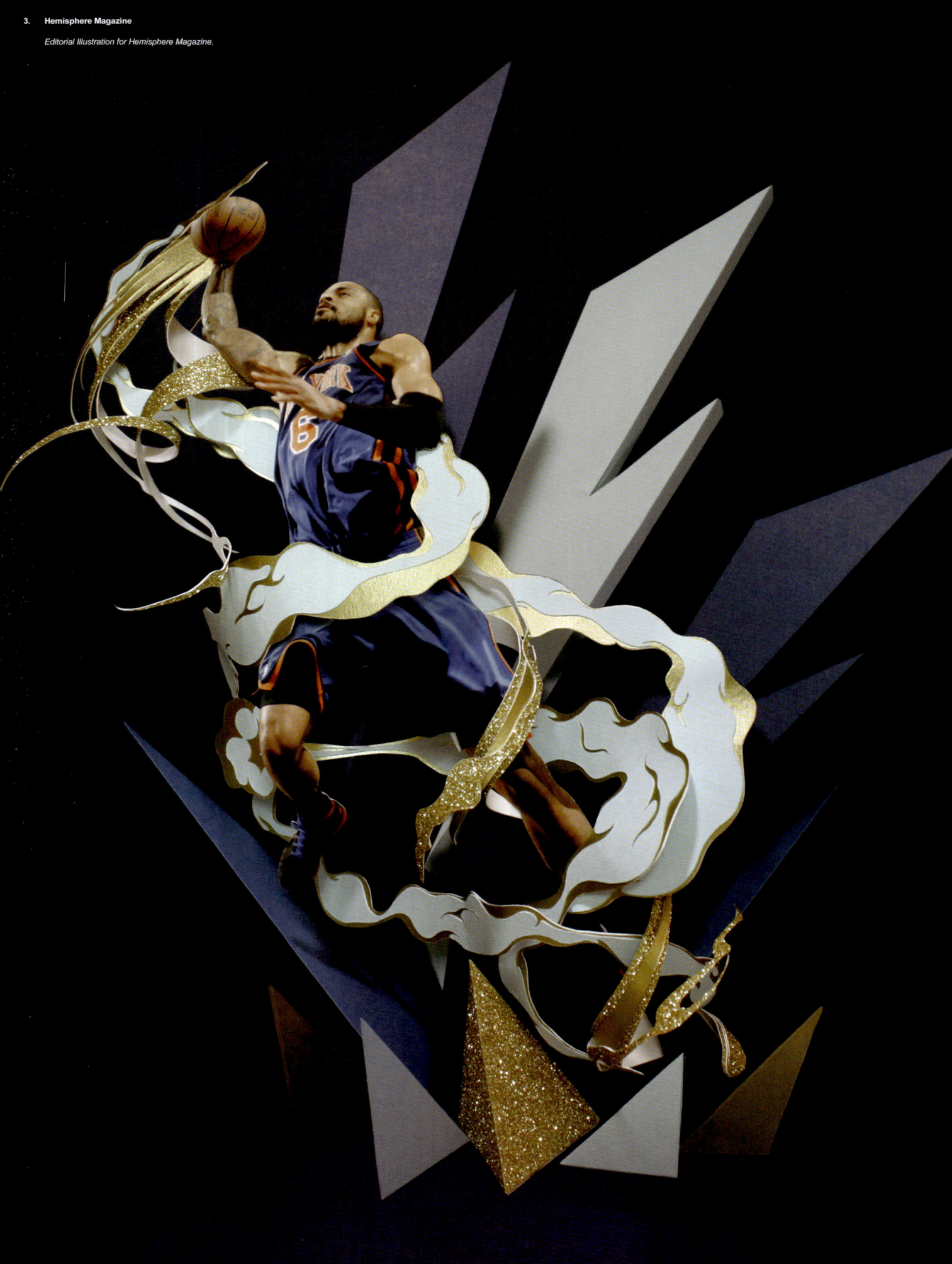

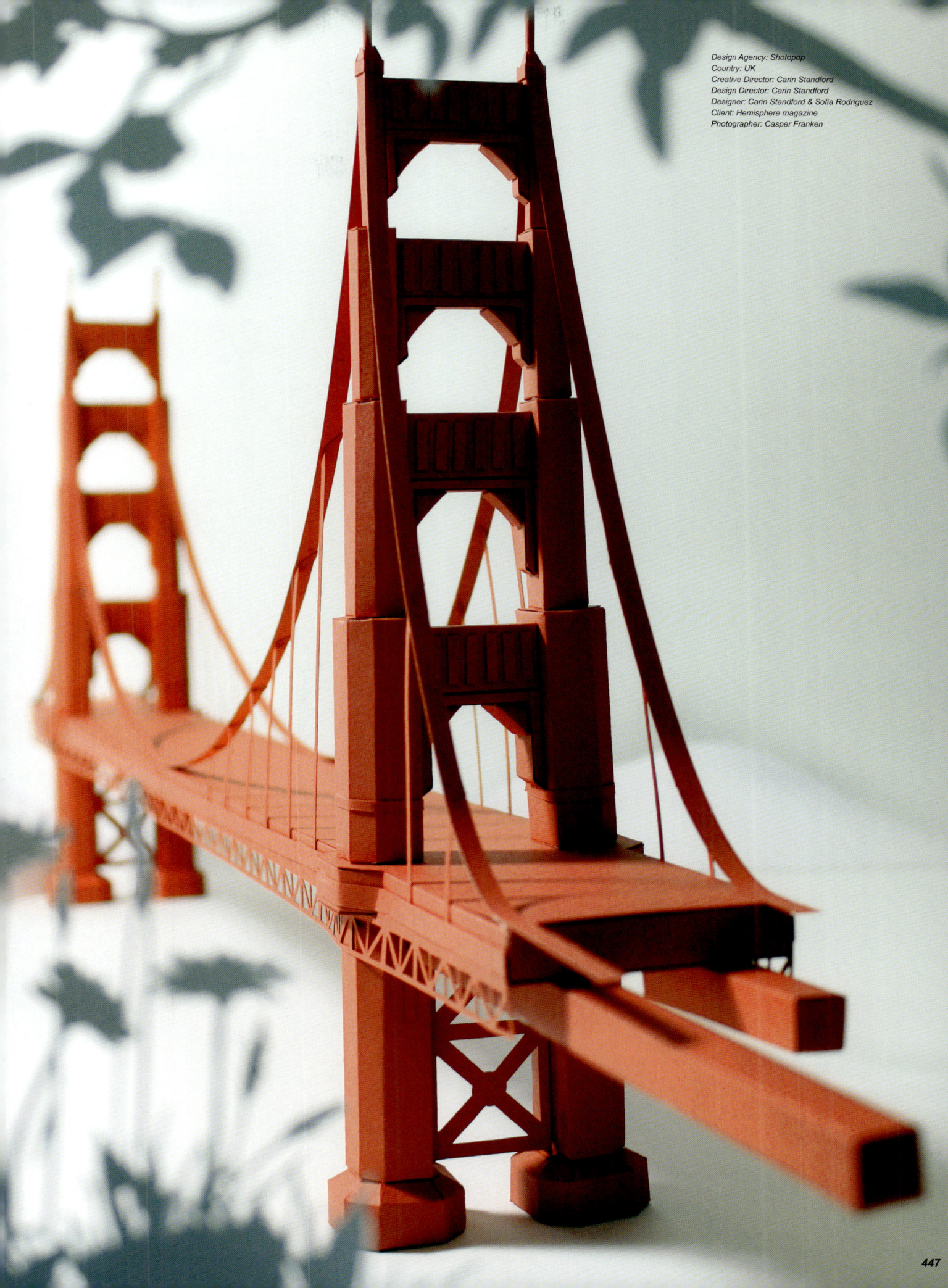

Design Agency: Shotopop
Country: UK
Creative Director: Carin Standford
Design Director: Carin Standford
Designer: Carin Standford & Sofia Rodriguez
Client: Hemisphere magazine
Photographer: Casper Franken

4. **APPS Magazine**
Editorial Illustration for Apps magazine, focussing on Mobile technologies.

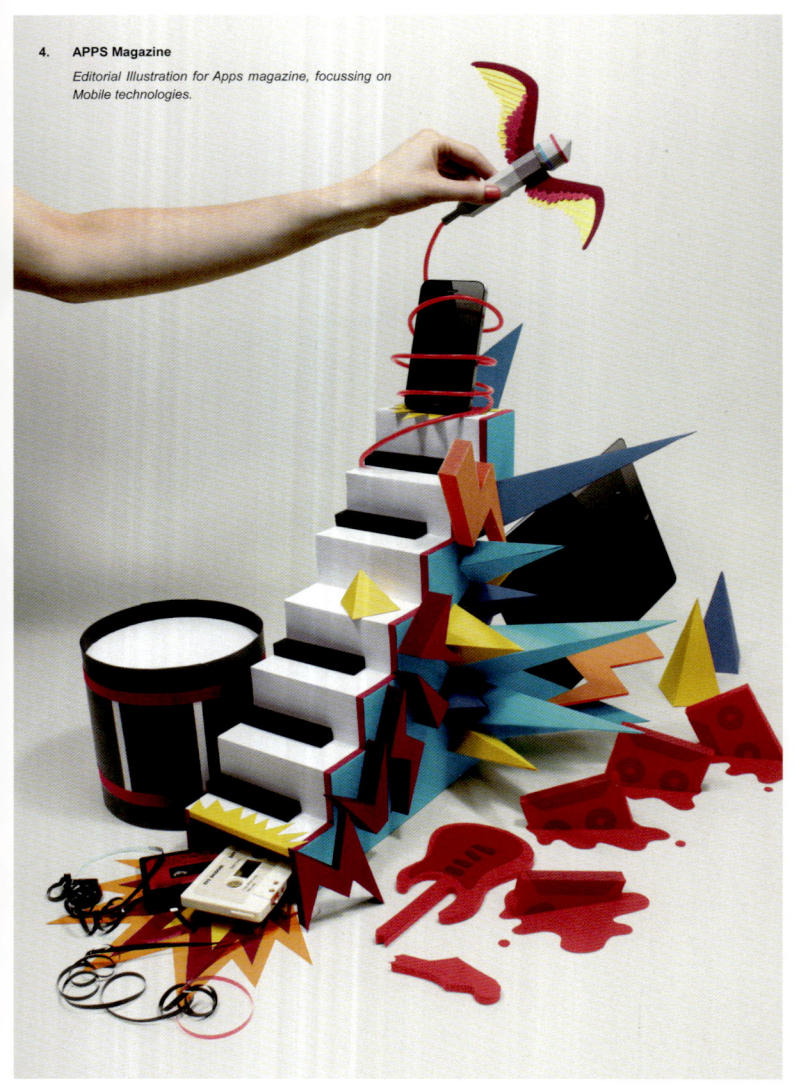

Design Agency: Shotopop
Country: UK
Creative Director: Carin Standford
Design Director: Carin Standford
Designer: Carin Standford & Sofia Rodriguez
Client: APPS magazine
Photographer: Casper Franken

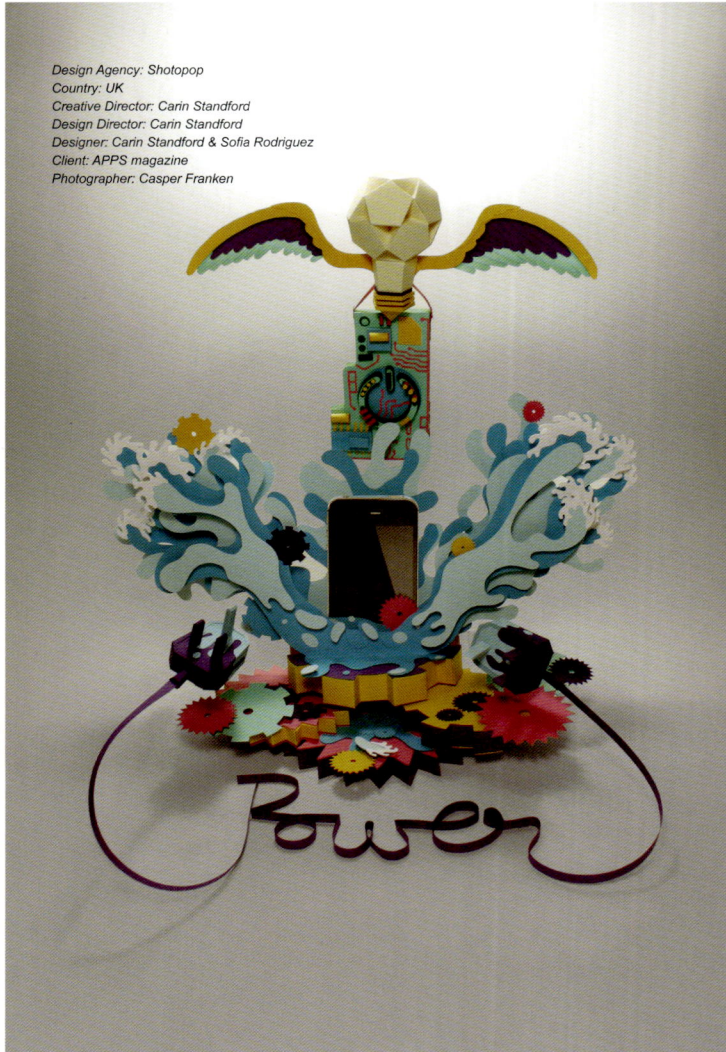

5. **MILK**
Pro-Active work With Paper.

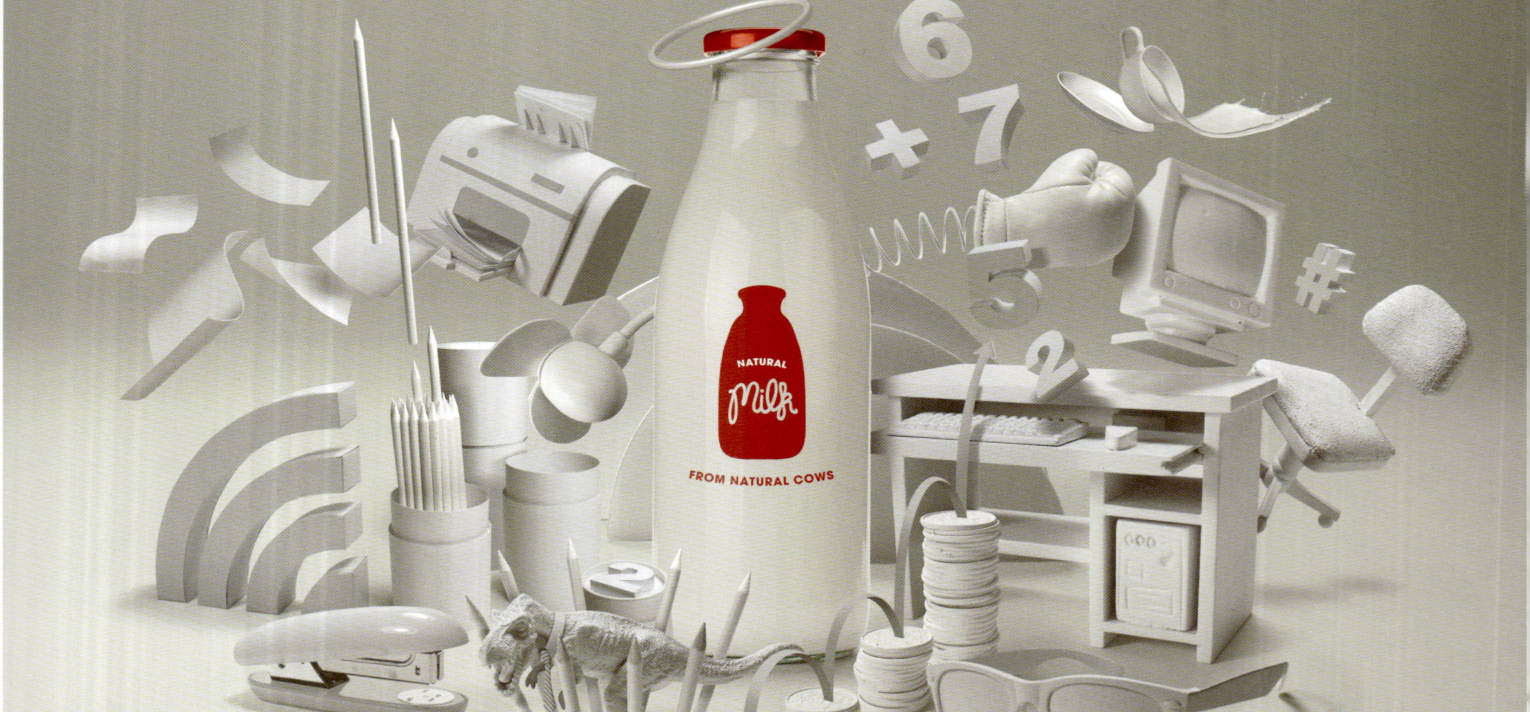

Design Agency: Shotopop
Country: UK
Creative Director: Carin Standford & Casper Franken
Design Director: Carin Standford & Casper Franken
Designer: Carin Standford & Sofia Rodriguez & Casper Franken
Client: Pro-Active
Photographer: Casper Franken

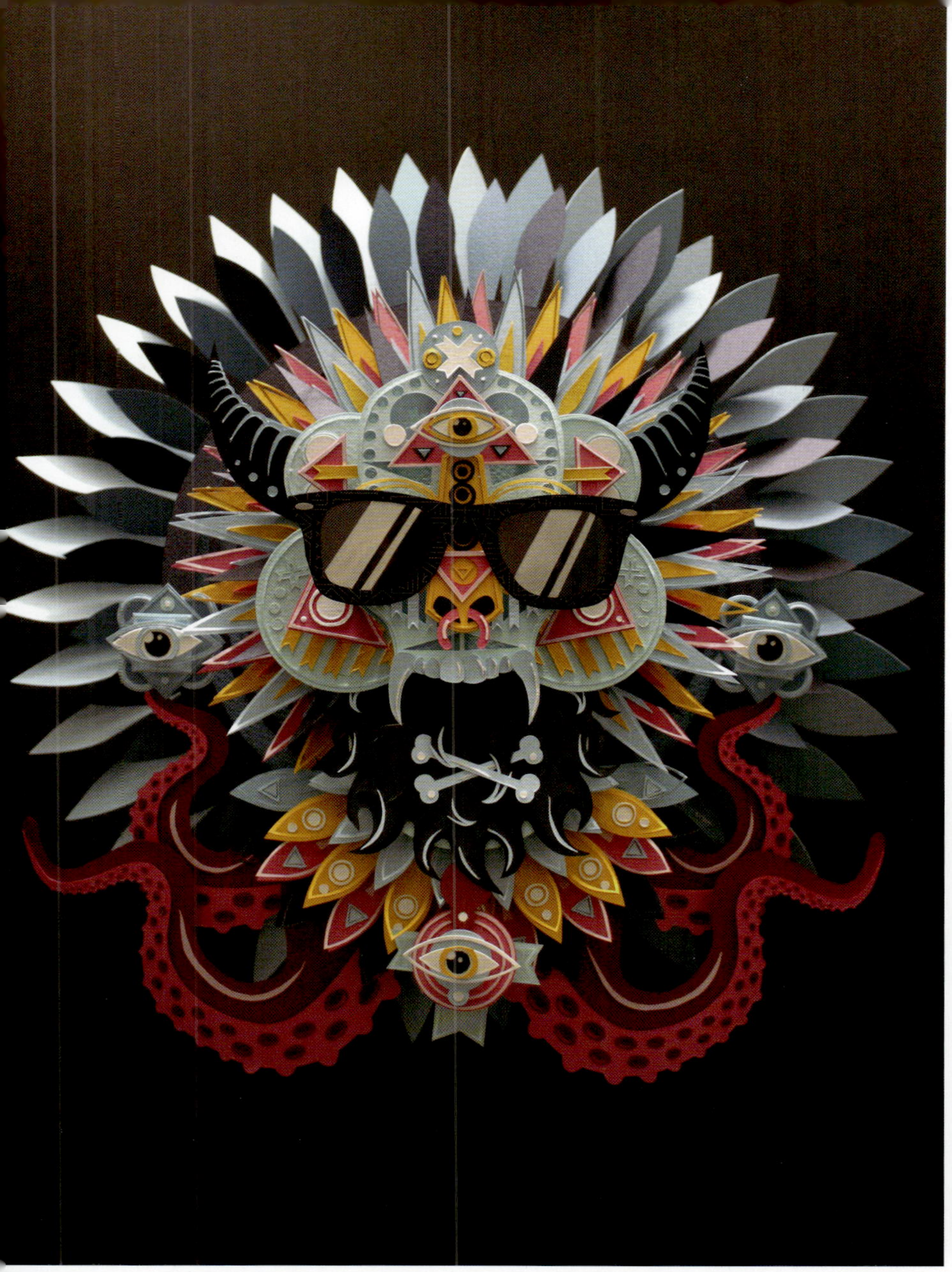

6. **VOODOO**

Pro-Active work With Paper.

Design Agency: Shotopop
Country: UK
Creative Director: Carin Standford & Casper Franken
Design Director: Carin Standford & Casper Franken
Designer: Carin Standford & Sofia Rodriguez & Casper Franken & MIKE CROZIER
Client: Pro-Active
Photographer: Casper Franken

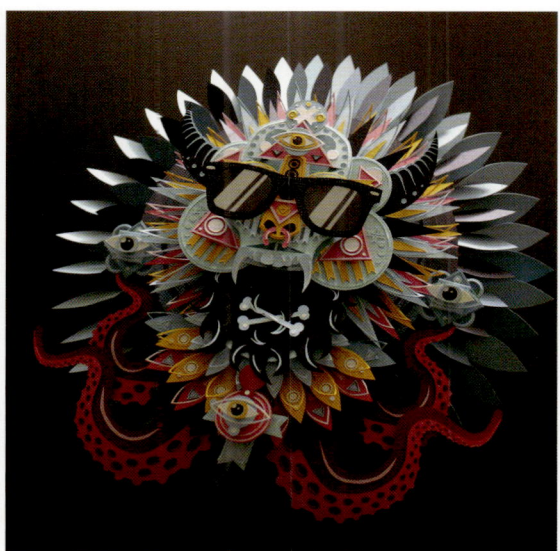
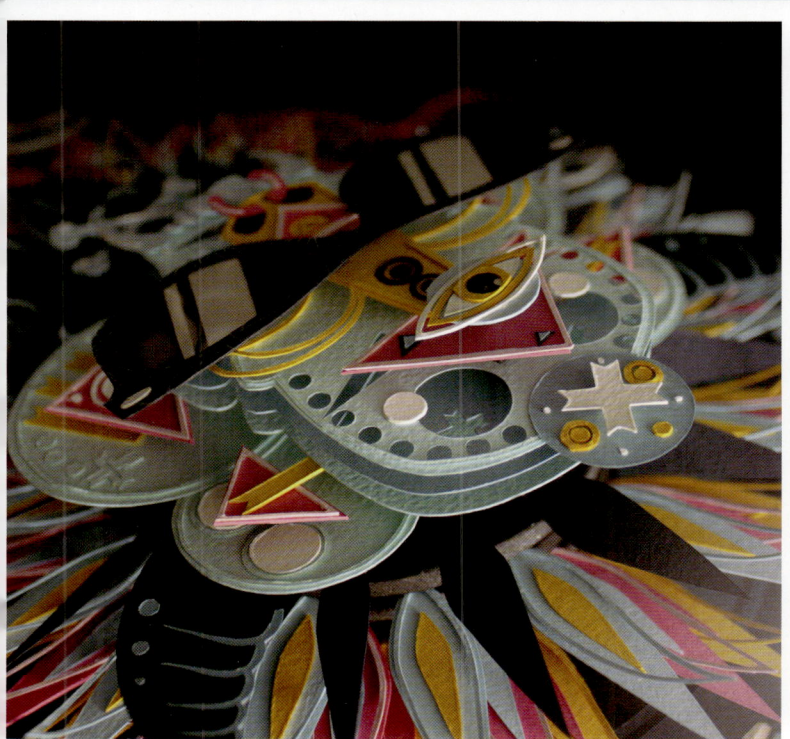
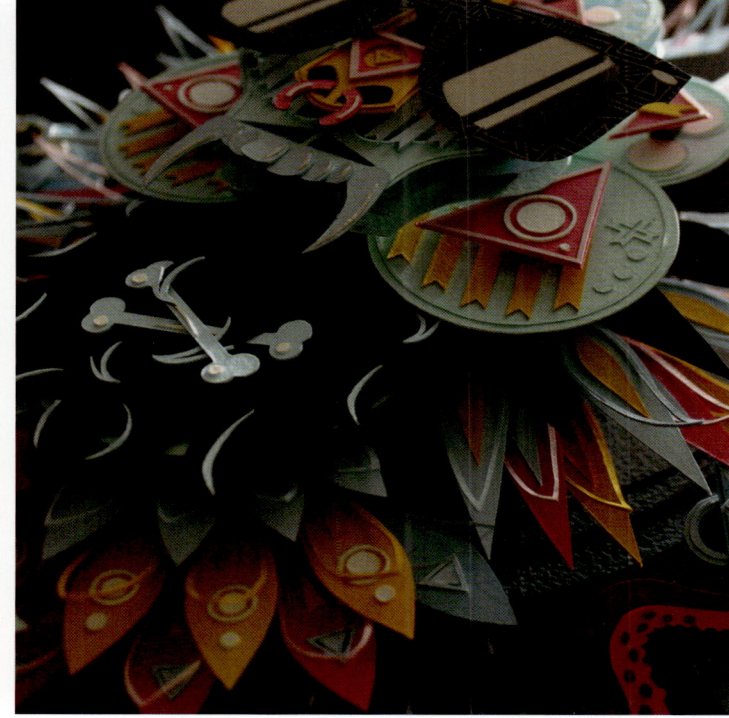

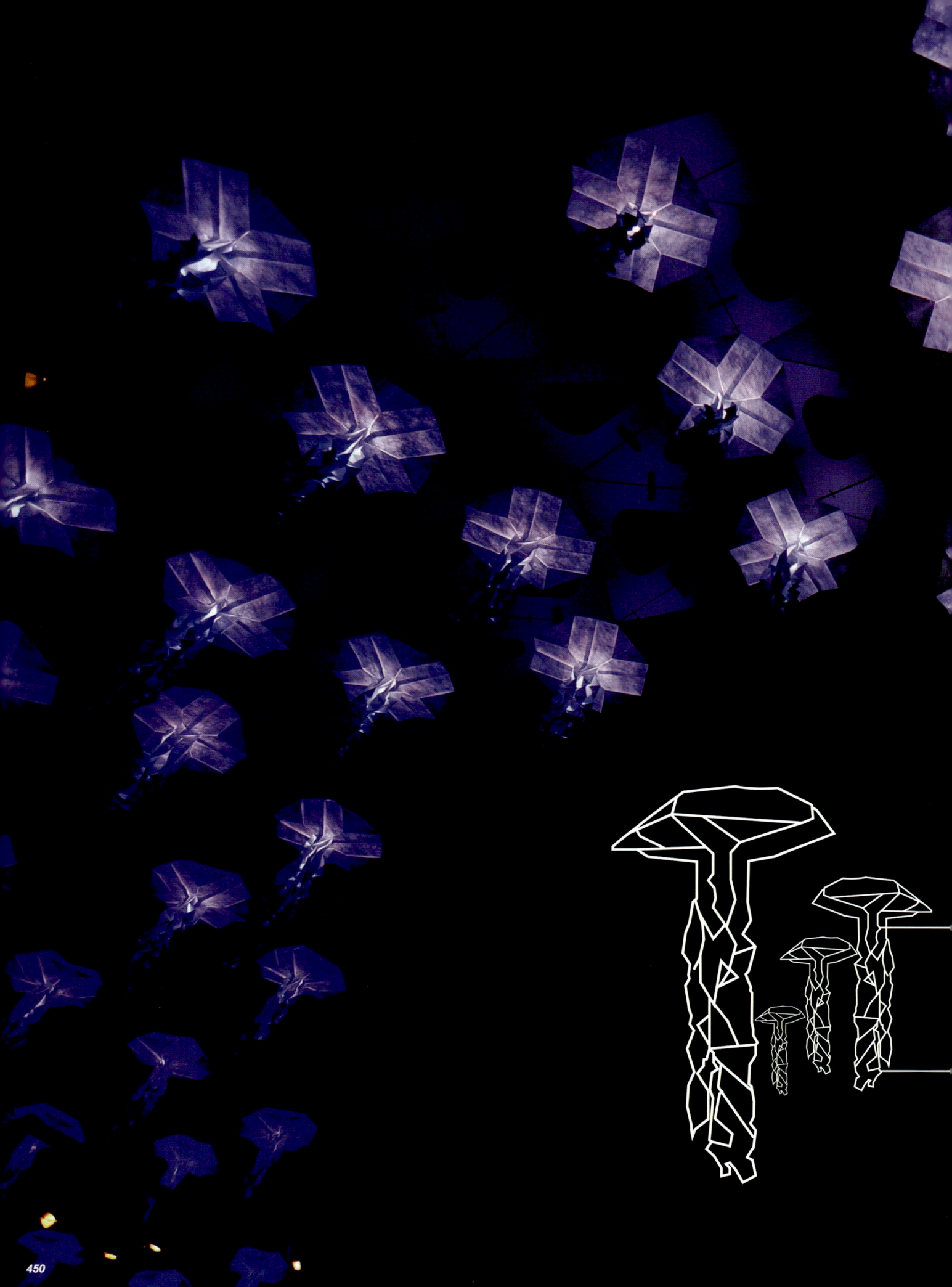

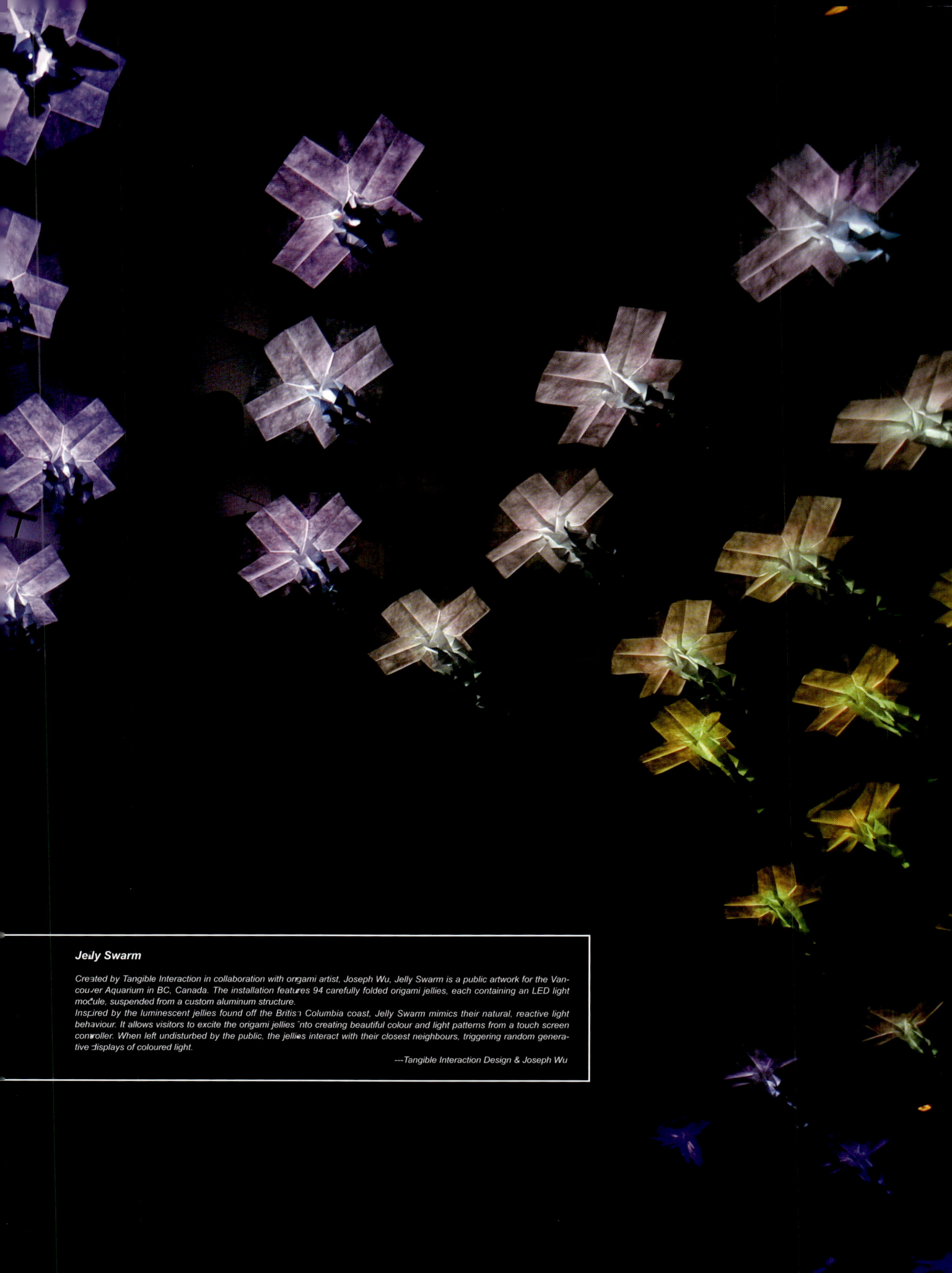

Jelly Swarm

Created by Tangible Interaction in collaboration with origami artist, Joseph Wu, Jelly Swarm is a public artwork for the Vancouver Aquarium in BC, Canada. The installation features 94 carefully folded origami jellies, each containing an LED light module, suspended from a custom aluminum structure.

Inspired by the luminescent jellies found off the British Columbia coast, Jelly Swarm mimics their natural, reactive light behaviour. It allows visitors to excite the origami jellies into creating beautiful colour and light patterns from a touch screen controller. When left undisturbed by the public, the jellies interact with their closest neighbours, triggering random generative displays of coloured light.

---Tangible Interaction Design & Joseph Wu

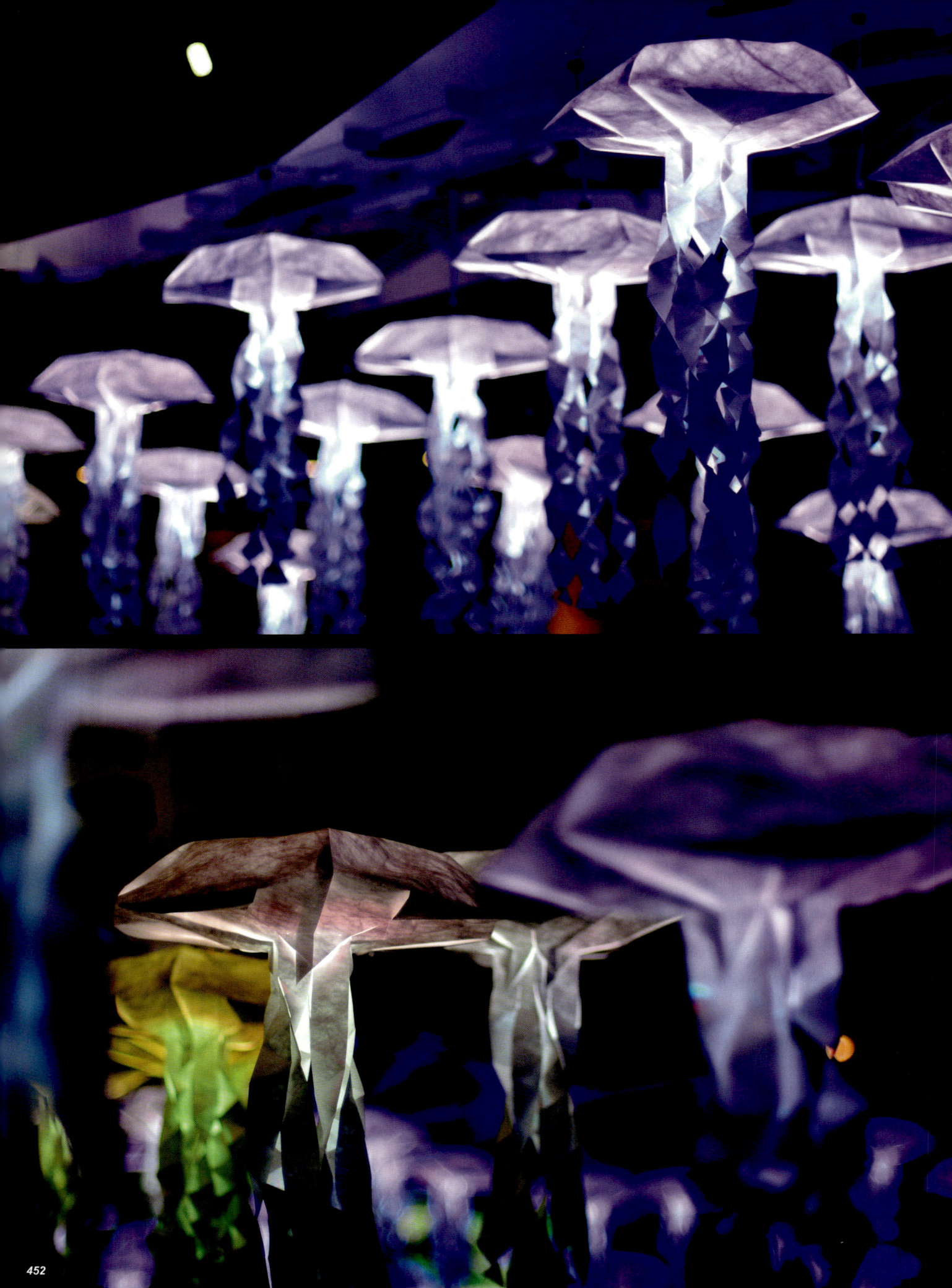

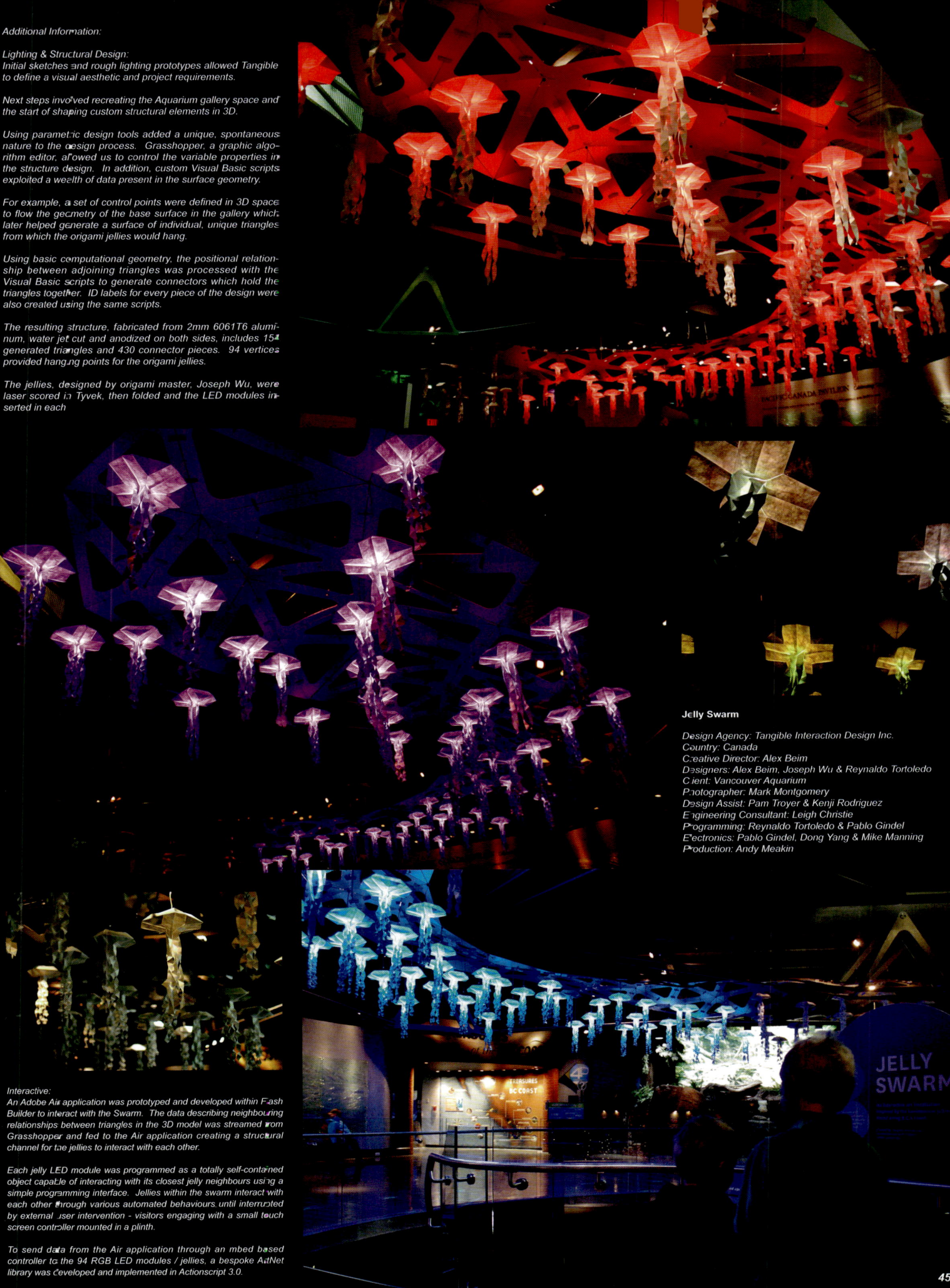

Additional Information:

Lighting & Structural Design:
Initial sketches and rough lighting prototypes allowed Tangible to define a visual aesthetic and project requirements.

Next steps involved recreating the Aquarium gallery space and the start of shaping custom structural elements in 3D.

Using parametric design tools added a unique, spontaneous nature to the design process. Grasshopper, a graphic algorithm editor, allowed us to control the variable properties in the structure design. In addition, custom Visual Basic scripts exploited a wealth of data present in the surface geometry.

For example, a set of control points were defined in 3D space to flow the geometry of the base surface in the gallery which later helped generate a surface of individual, unique triangles from which the origami jellies would hang.

Using basic computational geometry, the positional relationship between adjoining triangles was processed with the Visual Basic scripts to generate connectors which hold the triangles together. ID labels for every piece of the design were also created using the same scripts.

The resulting structure, fabricated from 2mm 6061T6 aluminum, water jet cut and anodized on both sides, includes 154 generated triangles and 430 connector pieces. 94 vertices provided hanging points for the origami jellies.

The jellies, designed by origami master, Joseph Wu, were laser scored in Tyvek, then folded and the LED modules inserted in each

Jelly Swarm

Design Agency: Tangible Interaction Design Inc.
Country: Canada
Creative Director: Alex Beim
Designers: Alex Beim, Joseph Wu & Reynaldo Tortoledo
Client: Vancouver Aquarium
Photographer: Mark Montgomery
Design Assist: Pam Troyer & Kenji Rodriguez
Engineering Consultant: Leigh Christie
Programming: Reynaldo Tortoledo & Pablo Gindel
Electronics: Pablo Gindel, Dong Yang & Mike Manning
Production: Andy Meakin

Interactive:
An Adobe Air application was prototyped and developed within Flash Builder to interact with the Swarm. The data describing neighbouring relationships between triangles in the 3D model was streamed from Grasshopper and fed to the Air application creating a structural channel for the jellies to interact with each other.

Each jelly LED module was programmed as a totally self-contained object capable of interacting with its closest jelly neighbours using a simple programming interface. Jellies within the swarm interact with each other through various automated behaviours until interrupted by external user intervention - visitors engaging with a small touch screen controller mounted in a plinth.

To send data from the Air application through an mbed based controller to the 94 RGB LED modules / jellies, a bespoke ArtNet library was developed and implemented in Actionscript 3.0.

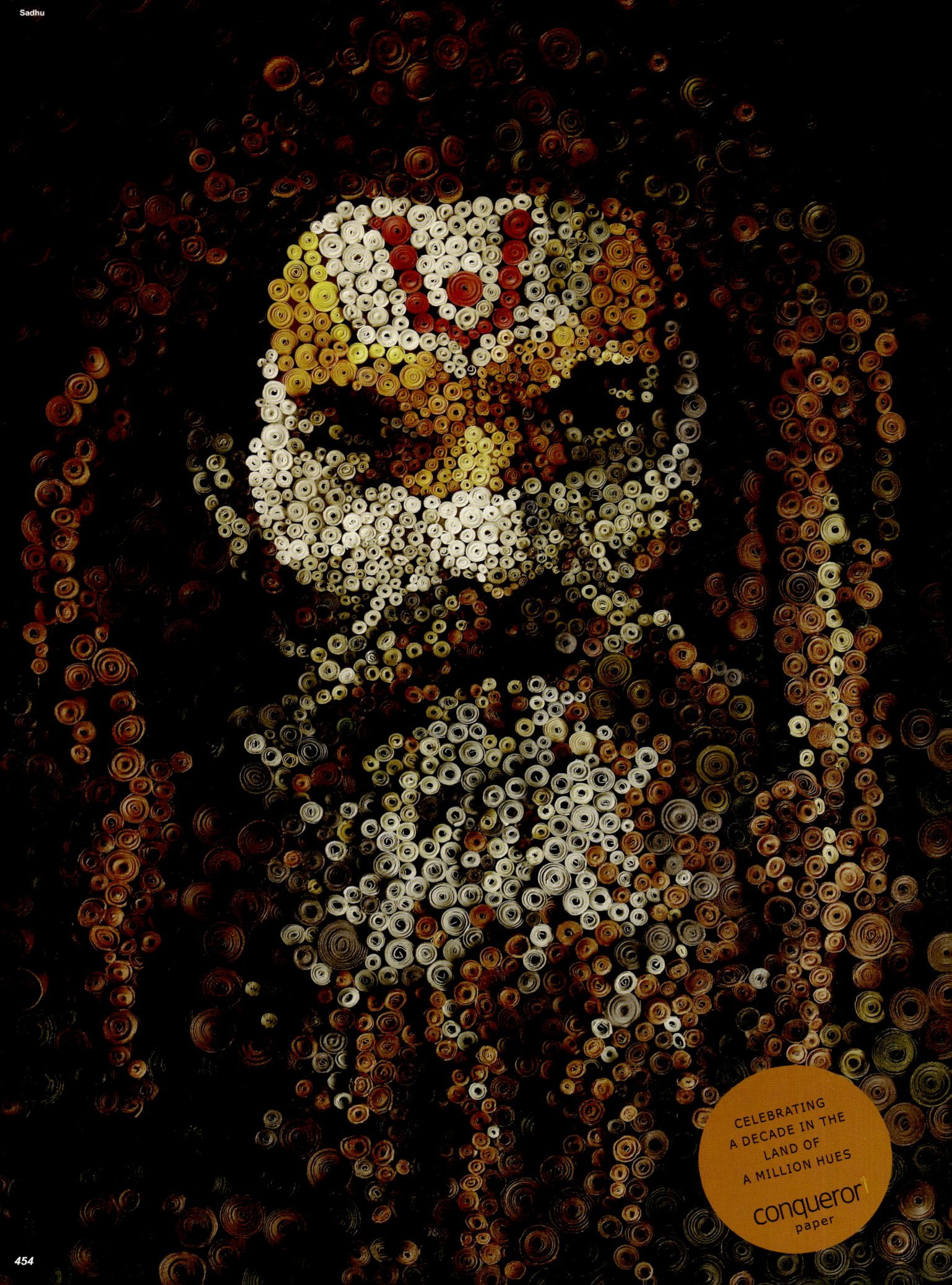

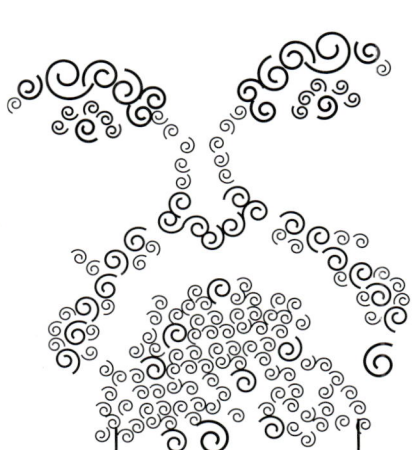

Colours of India

Conqueror Paper, a premium paper manufacturing brand, had just completed 10 years in India. They wanted to take the opportunity to pay a tribute to a culture and a market that has supported them all these years. Bridging the core category (all forms of base paper) and the vibrant, colourful country called India; we created an incredible though painstaking visual illustration that involved hundreds of rolled up mini-paper scrolls embedded on flat surface. The size and colour of each scroll created a breathtaking colourful mosaic of iconic Indian characters. Namely, the Kathakali Dancer, the Royal Rajput and the Spiritual Sadhu. These were released as magazine ads.

Design Agency: Taproot India Communication Pvt. Ltd.
Country: India
Creative Director: Santosh Padhi, Agnello Dias
Design Director: Santosh Padhi
Designer: Santosh Padhi
Client: Transasia Papers
Photographer: Amol Jadhav
Illustrator: Anant Nanvare
Digital Illustrator: Amol Kamble

--- Taproot India
      Communication Pvt. Ltd.

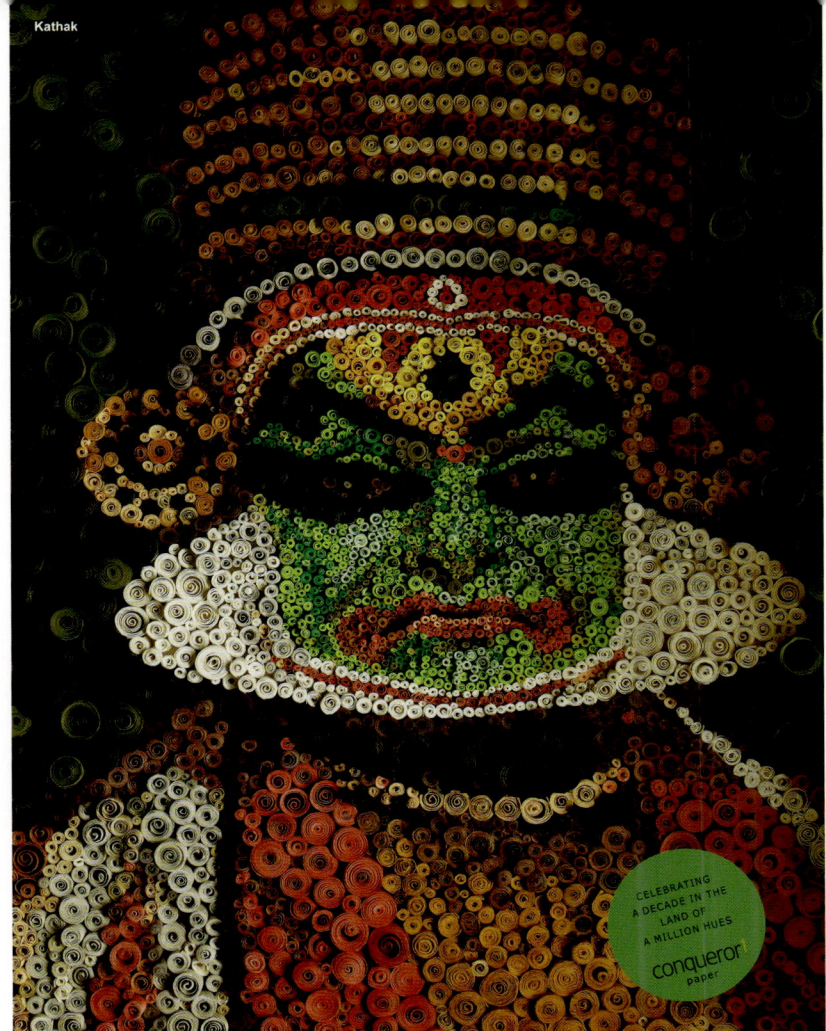

Kathak

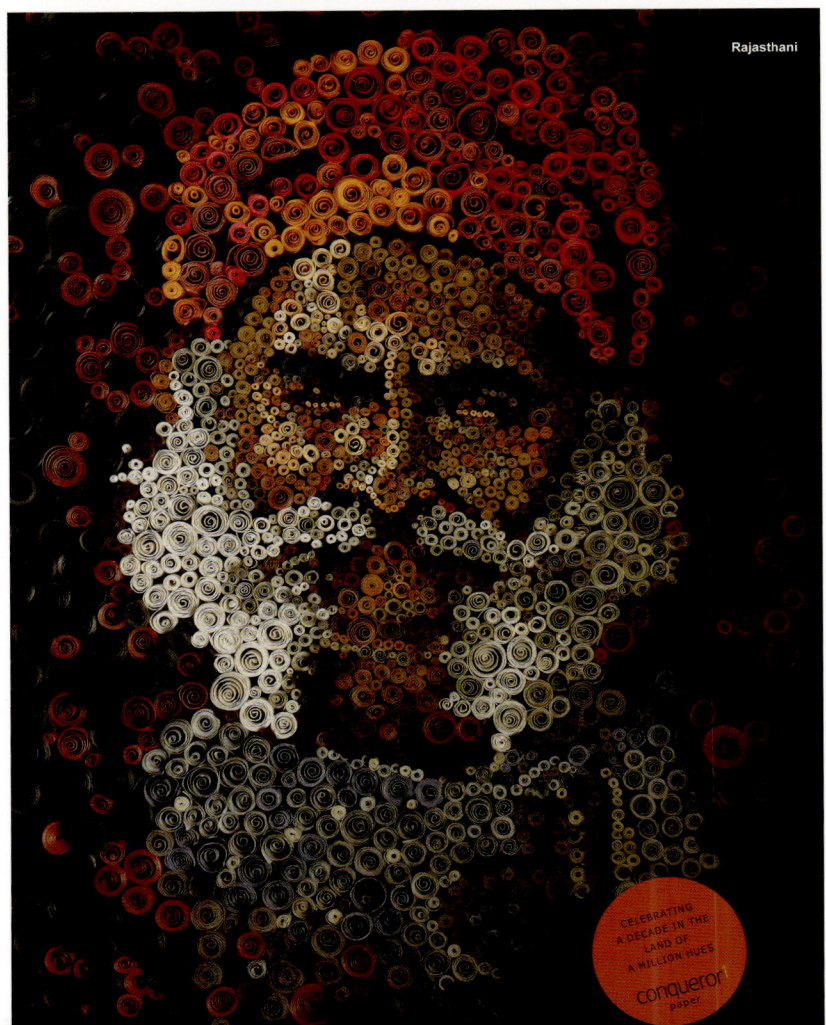

Rajasthani

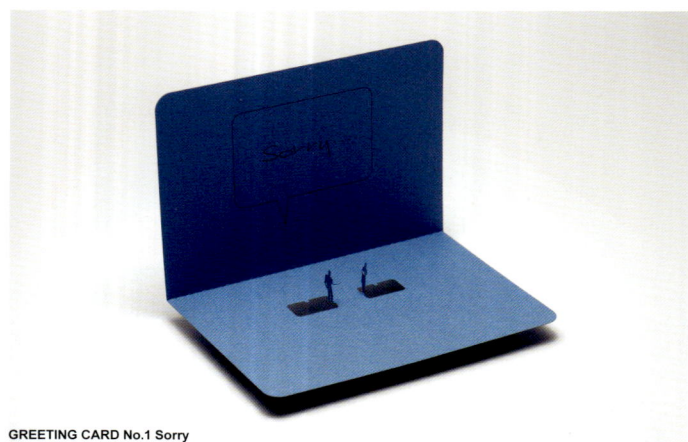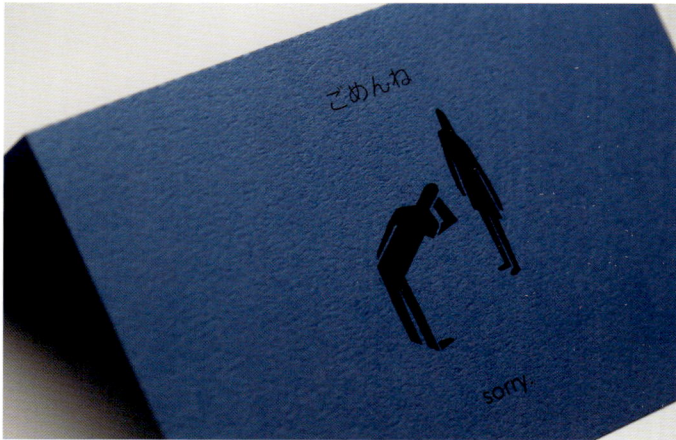

GREETING CARD No.1 Sorry
T's a greeting card with which you can have people at 1/100 scale convey their feelings on your behalf just by folding up the mat board and making a pose. Recording your message in the speech balloon, please send it to those important to you. No adhesive required. 1/100 scale. Based on the angle at which the mid-section is folded, the level of apology varies. A triple set of "Sorry", "I'm sorry" and "I'm really sorry". Let's hope the receiver will forgive you!

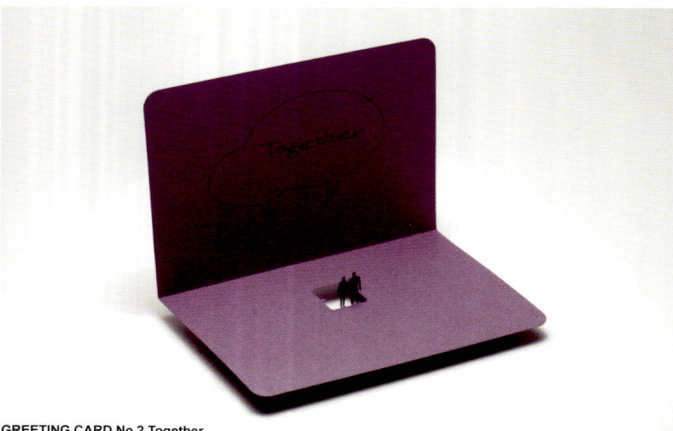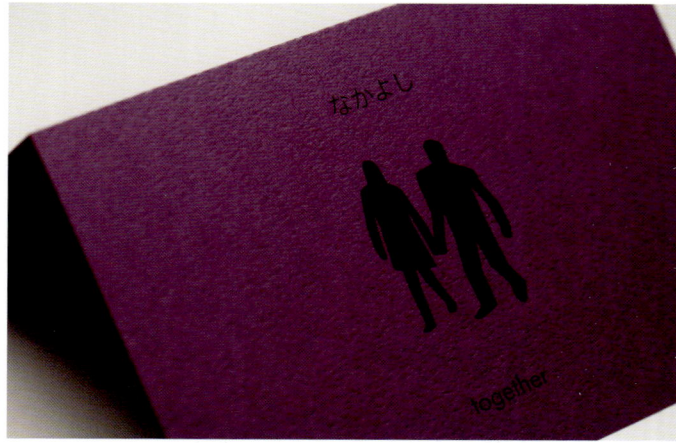

GREETING CARD No.2 Together
It's a greeting card with which you can have people at 1/100 scale convey their feelings on your behalf just by folding up the mat board and making a pose. Recording your message in the speech balloon, please send it to those important to you. No adhesive required. 1/100 scale. Somewhat exciting feelings have been immortalized in the shapes. A triple set of "date", "leisure time" and "princess-like carrying in arms". It's fun to dedicate slightly embarrassing memories to these shapes.

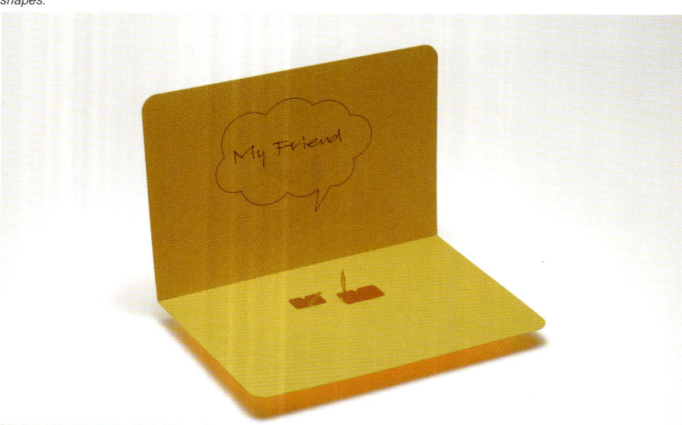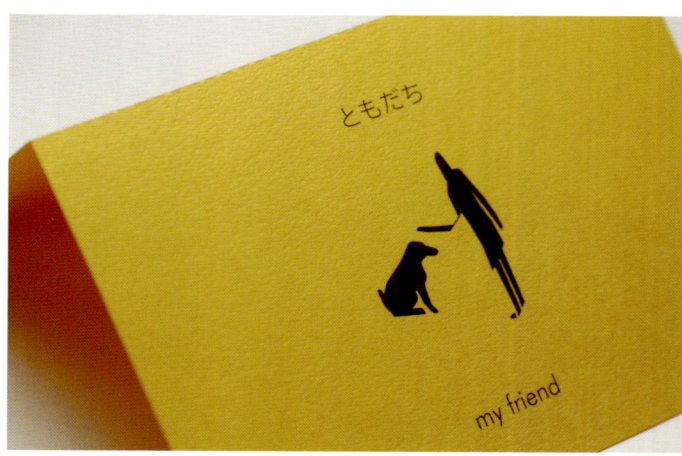

GREETING CARD No.3 My Friend
It's a greeting card with which you can have people at 1/100 scale convey their feelings on your behalf just by folding up the mat board and making a pose. Recording your message in the speech balloon, please send it to those important to you. No adhesive required. 1/100 scale. Much-loved feelings are passed on to the doggy. Daily feelings cannot be conveyed if not acted out. A triple set of "Give me your paw!", "Come" and "Hubba-hubba". It's always best to stay good friends, isn't it?

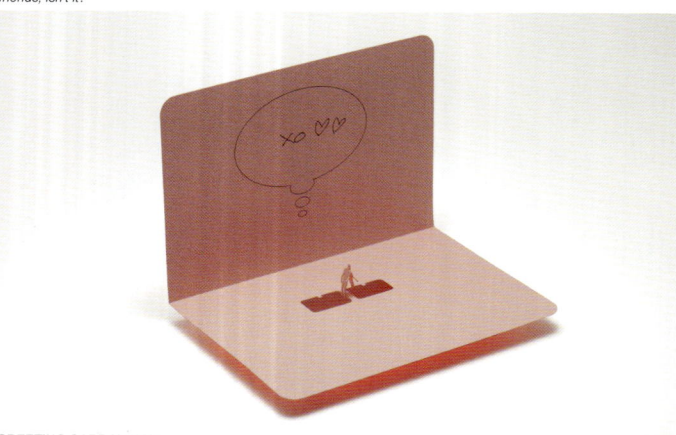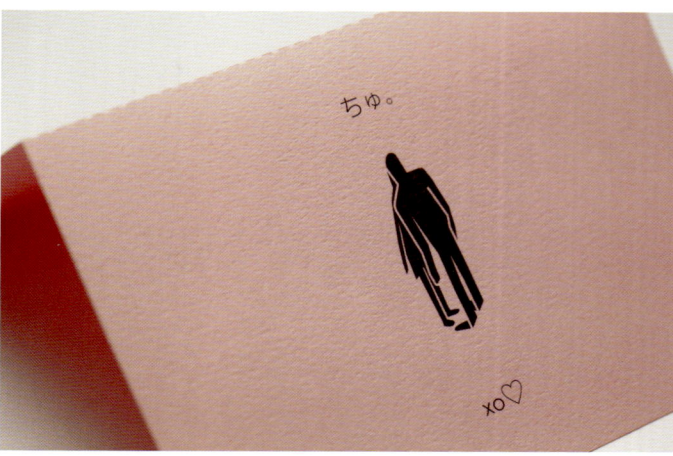

GREETING CARD No.4 Xo
It's a greeting card with which you can have people at 1/100 scale convey their feelings on your behalf just by folding up the mat board and making a pose. Recording your message in the speech balloon, please send it to those important to you. No adhesive required. 1/100 scale. Delusions have wings. Please use this card after reviewing your own situation. The four-piece set of "Kiss", "Please marry me", "Hug" and "Bitch slap". But maybe you should set the record straight instead of wallowing in delusion.

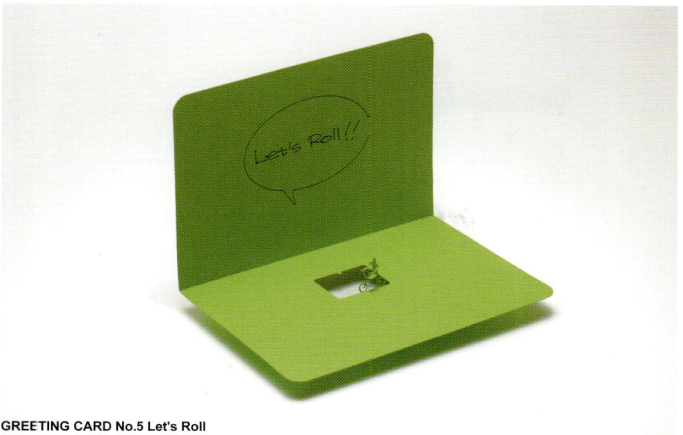 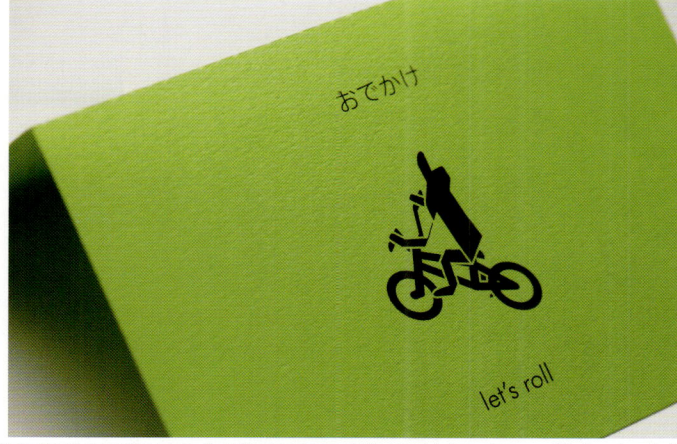

GREETING CARD No.5 Let's Roll

It's a greeting card with which you can have people at 1/100 scale convey their feelings on your behalf just by folding up the mat board and making a pose. Recording your message in the speech balloon, please send it to those important to you. No adhesive required. 1/100 scale. Pleasant outing! The weekend might be perfect for cycling. A triple set of "Cycling", "Hero" and "Acrobat". Please do not kick out the jams too much!

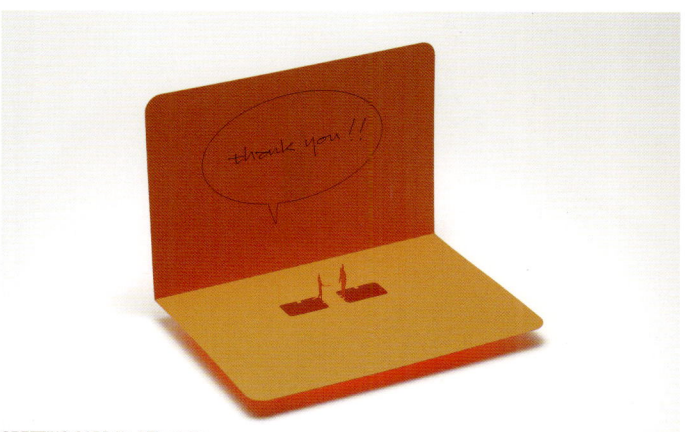 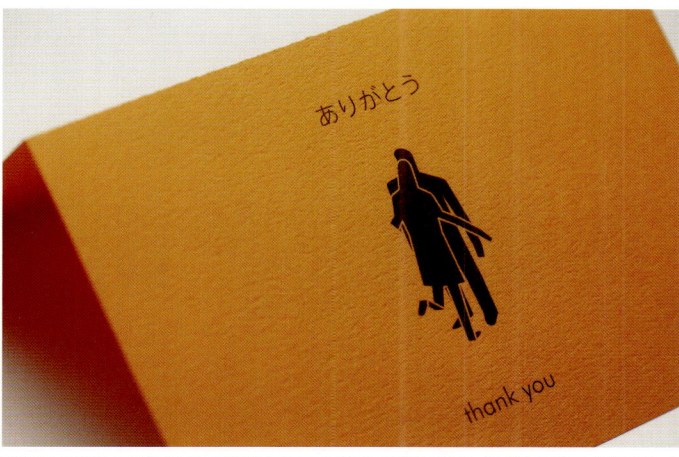

GREETING CARD No.6 Thank You

Simply fold the 1/100 scale figures on these greeting cards up to the desired angle and let them express your feelings for you. Add a message to the speech balloon and send it to a special someone. No glue required. 1/100 scale. A simple way to express your gratitude. Adjustable to three settings; 'thanks', 'thank you', and 'kiss'. Use these cards to express feelings you're too shy to say in person!

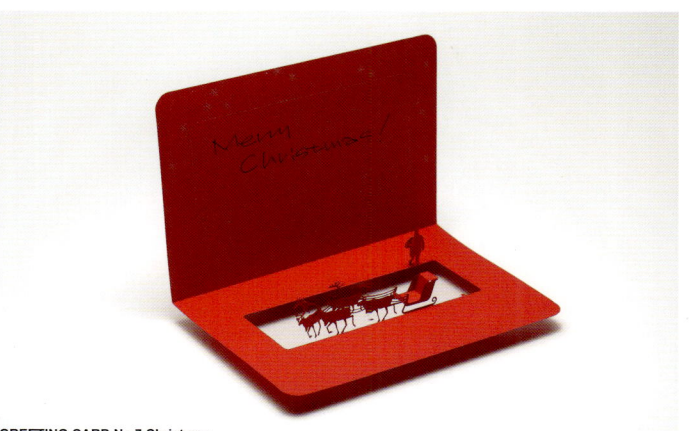 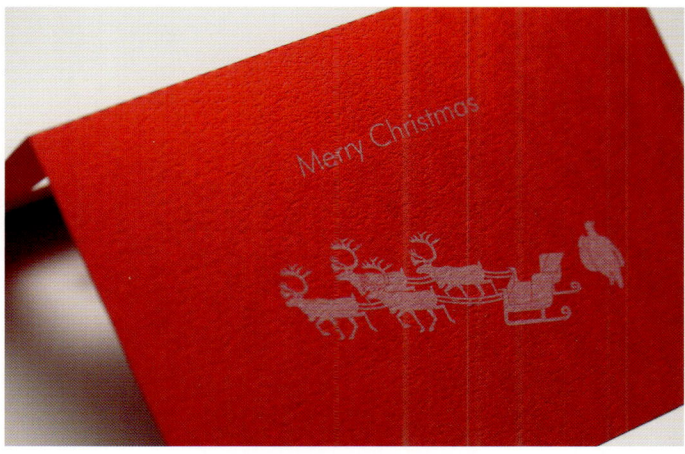

GREETING CARD No.7 Christmas

Simply fold the 1/100 scale figures on these greeting cards up to the desired angle and let them express your feelings for you. Add a message to the speech balloon and send it to a special someone. No glue required. 1/100 scale. These cards are perfect for adding a message to Christmas presents. Why not add a special touch to your Christmas gift this year.

1/100 ARCHITECTURAL MODEL ACCESSORIES SERIES

GREETING CARD No.1 Sorry
GREETING CARD No.2 Together
GREETING CARD No.3 My Friend
GREETING CARD No.4 Xo
GREETING CARD No.5 Let's Roll
GREETING CARD No.6 Thank You
GREETING CARD No.7 Christmas

JR East Railway Chuo Line Rapid Service 201 Series
No.6 New York
No.9 Orchestra
No.10 Street Tree
No.11 Cherry Blossom
No.13 The Seven Gods of Good Fortune
No.20 Food Stall

Design Agency: TERADA MOKEI   Country: Japan
Designer: Naoki Terada   Photographer: Kenji MASUNAGA

---TERADA MOKEI

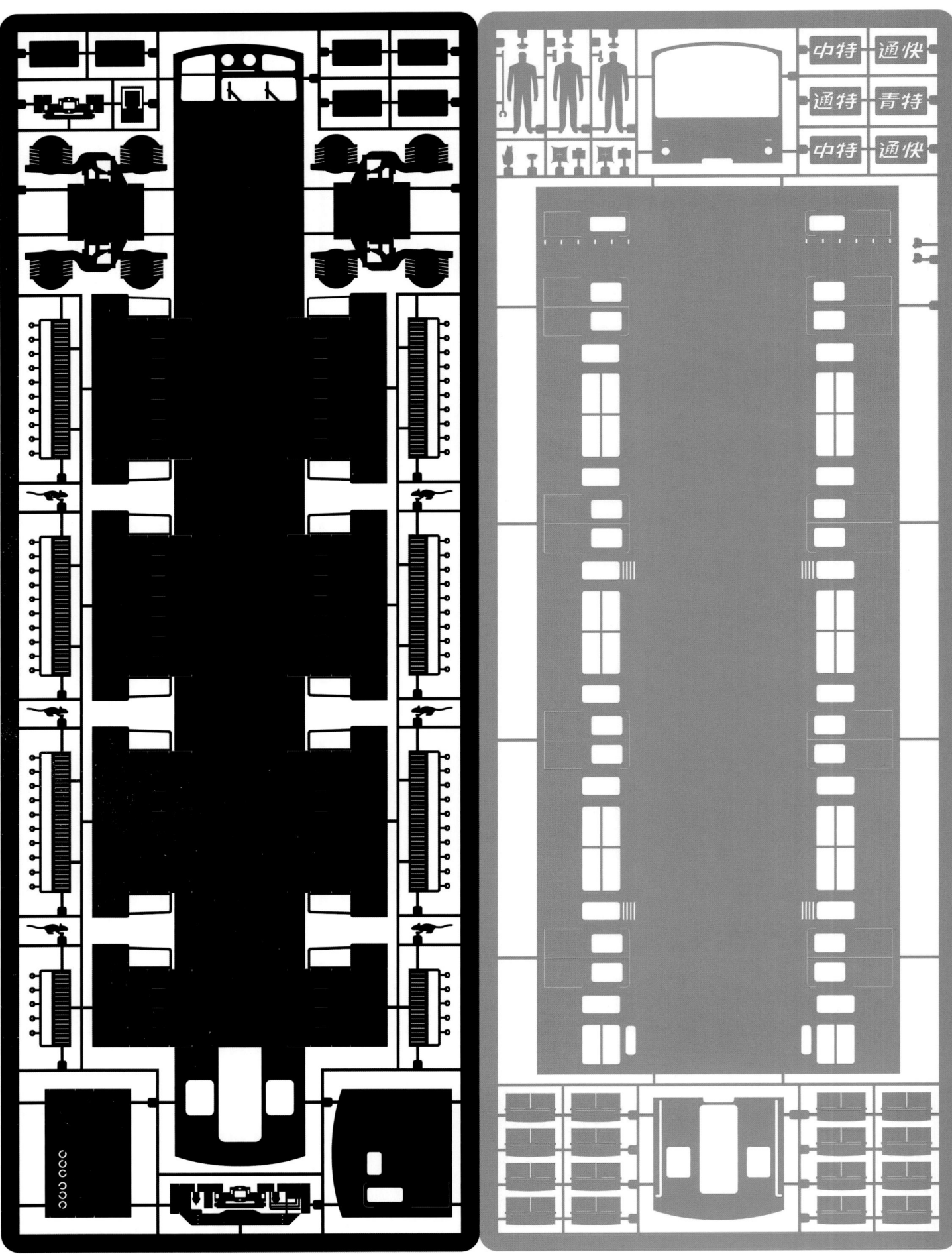

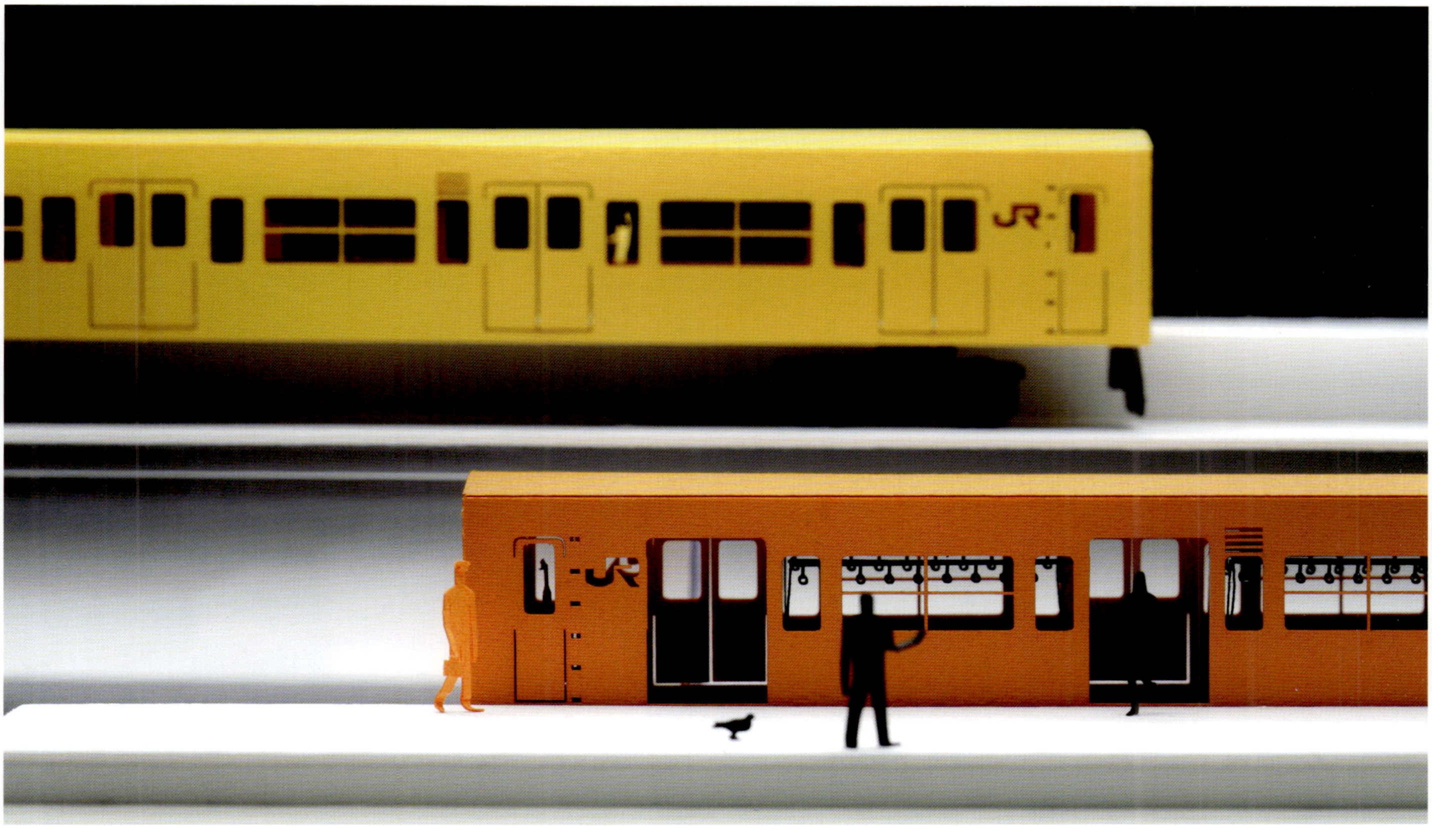

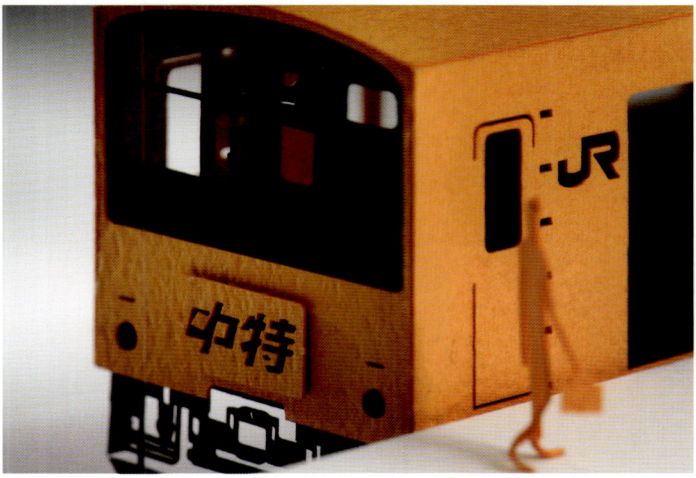
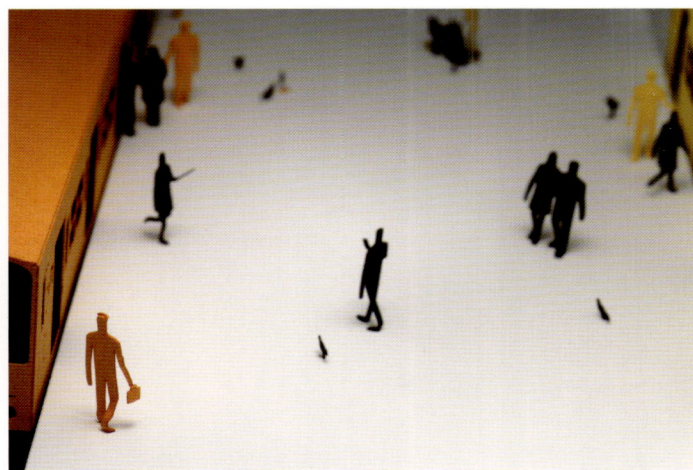

JR East Railway Chuo Line Rapid Service 201 Series

Good news for designing office staff who pull off all-nighters!! It's the JR 201 series, a special edition of the Architectural Model series, which you can easily assemble simply by tearing off the precut parts.
Lineup features the much loved but now retired orange Chuo-line 201 series, and the canary yellow Sobu-line 201 series trains. Includes miniature seats and hanging hand straps. Combine with other models to create various scenes such as rush hour trains. The Chuo-line version includes head plates for the Chuo Special Rapid service, Ome Special Rapid service, and Commuter Rapid service. The simple modeling which omits fine details is highly versatile and accentuates the sense of scale.

Including: JR201 Series lead car, driver, station attendant, a magic hand to pick up dropped items from the tracks, and more.

Design Agency: TERADA MOKEI Country: Japan Designer: Naoki Terada
Client: East Japan Railway trading Company Photographer: Kenji MASUNAGA

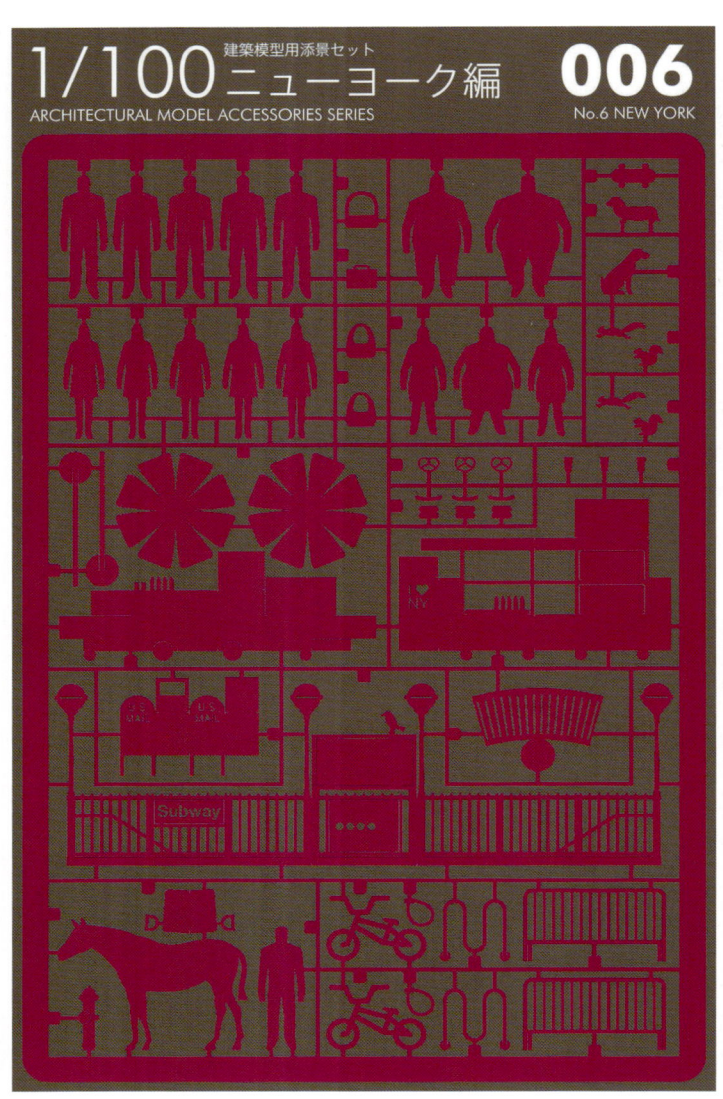
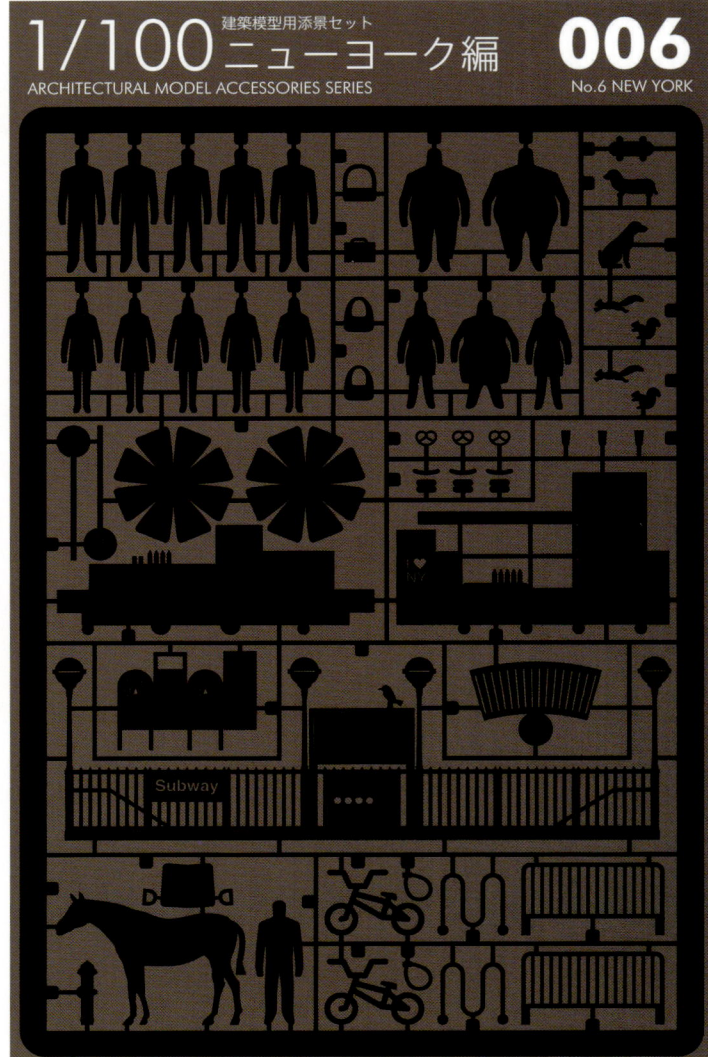

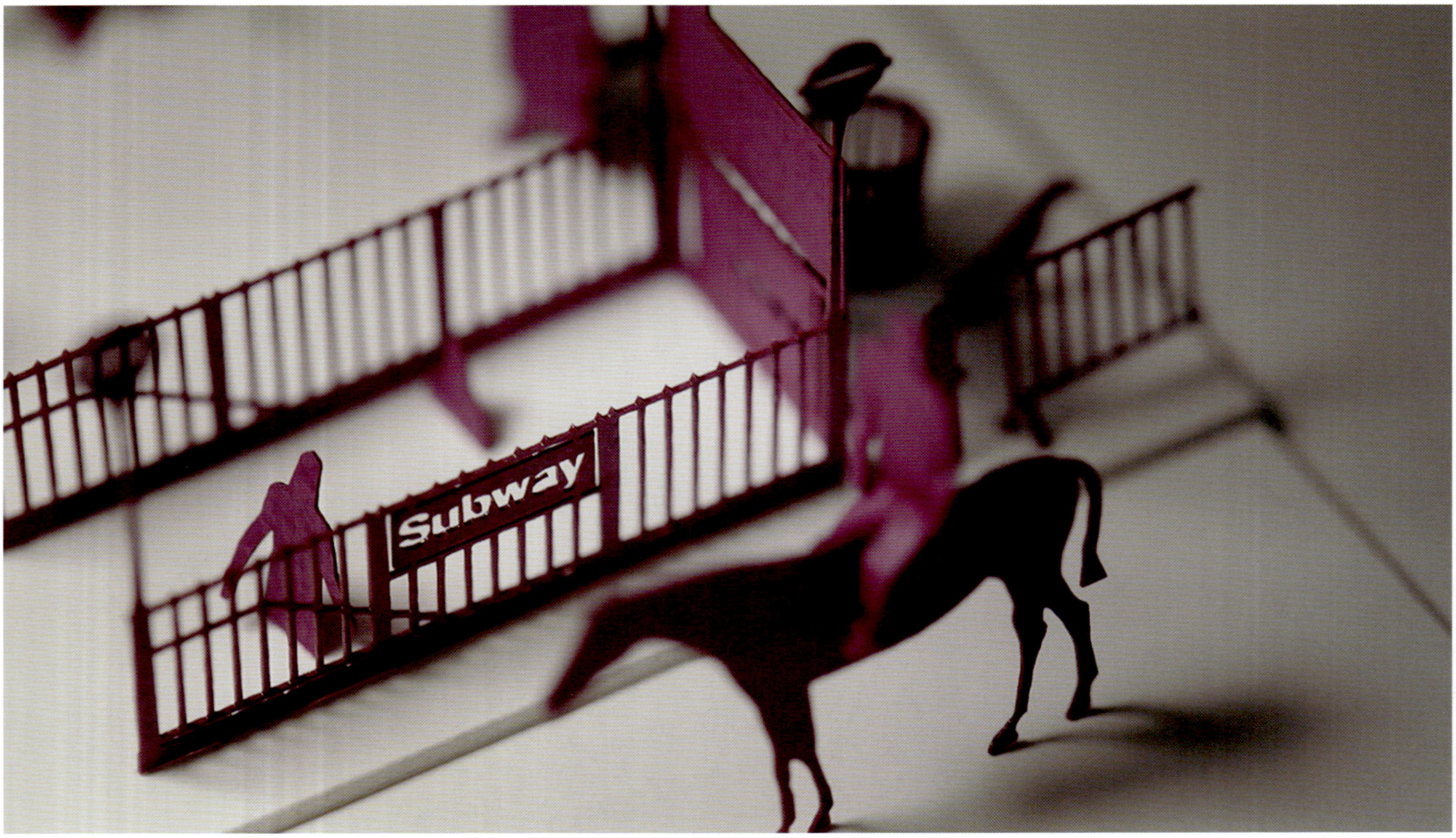

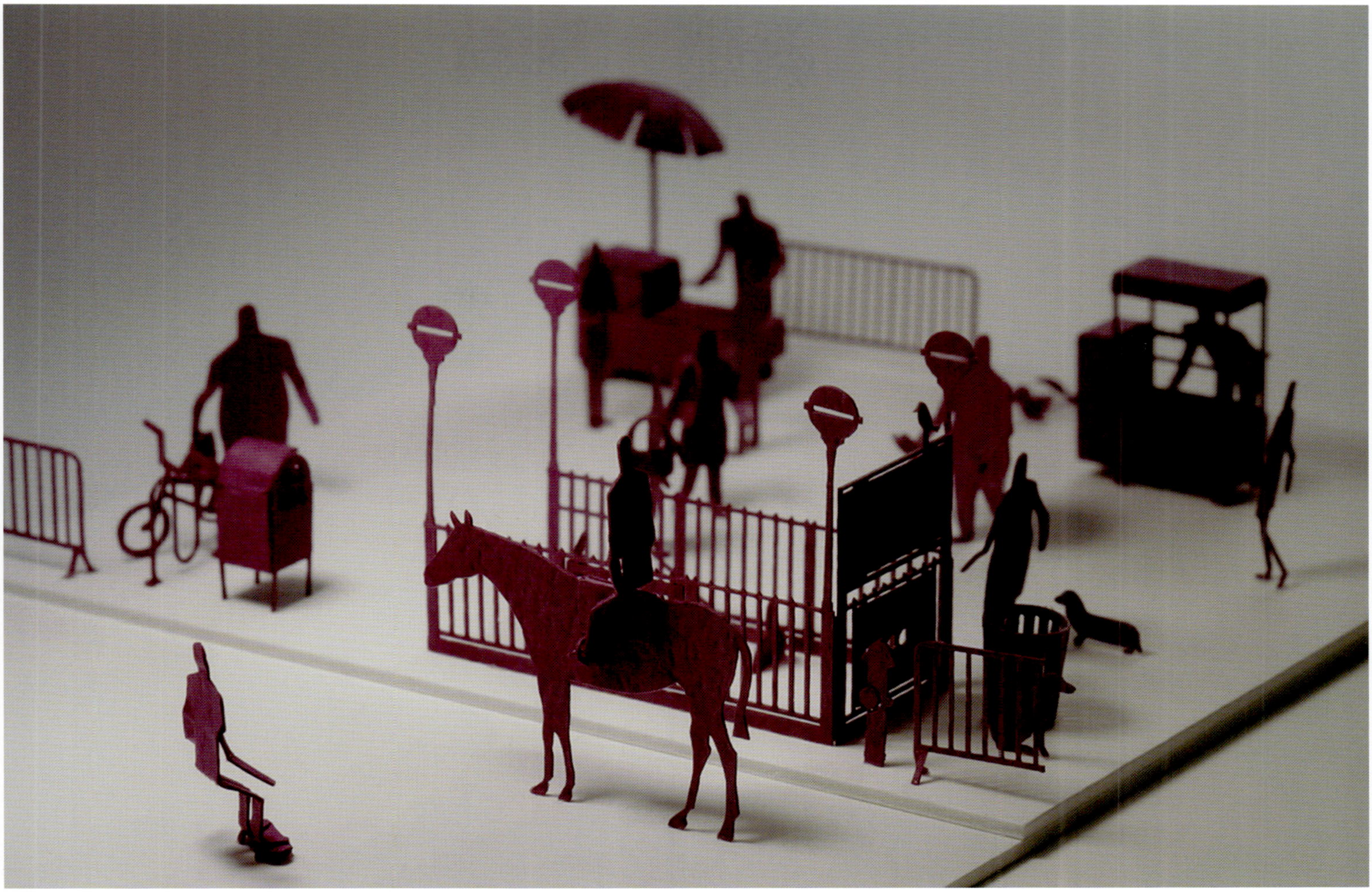

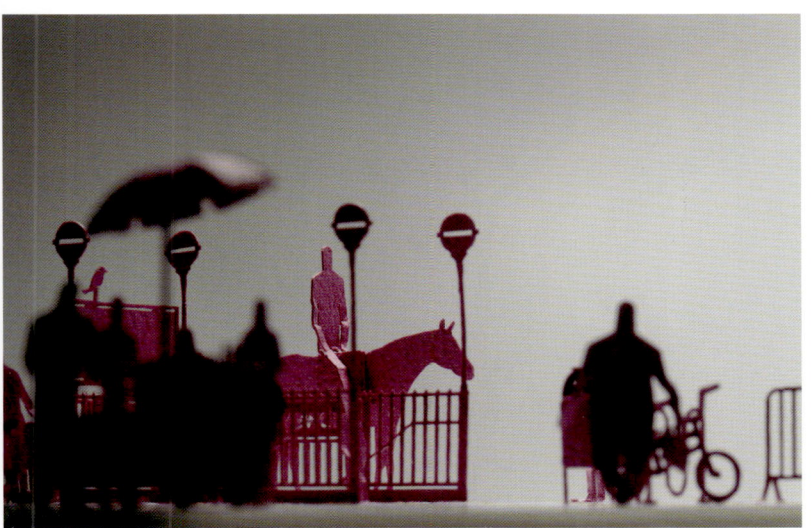
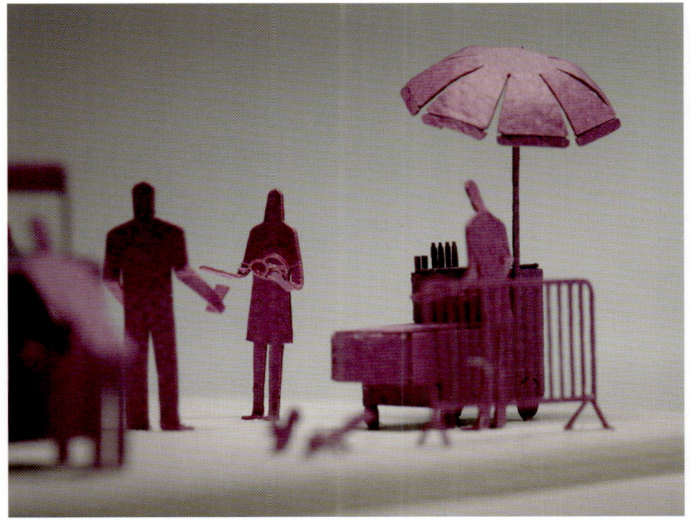

No.6 New York

Good news for designing office staff who pull off all-nighters!! It's a New York version, the sixth shot of the Architectural Model series, which you can easily assemble simply by tearing off the precut parts.
Items from the street corners of New York, the world's most exciting city and a melting pot of many races, have been carefully selected. The simple modeling, which omits fine details, is also highly versatile and complements the sense of scale. 1/100 scale.

Including:
Normal people, very fat people, dogs, squirrels, stands, hotdogs, pretzels, mailboxes, hydrants, subway exits, bicycles, bicycle stands, barricades, trash bins, mounted policemen and so on.

Design Agency: TERADA MOKEI   Country: Japan
Designer: Naoki Terada   Photographer: Kenji MASUNAGA

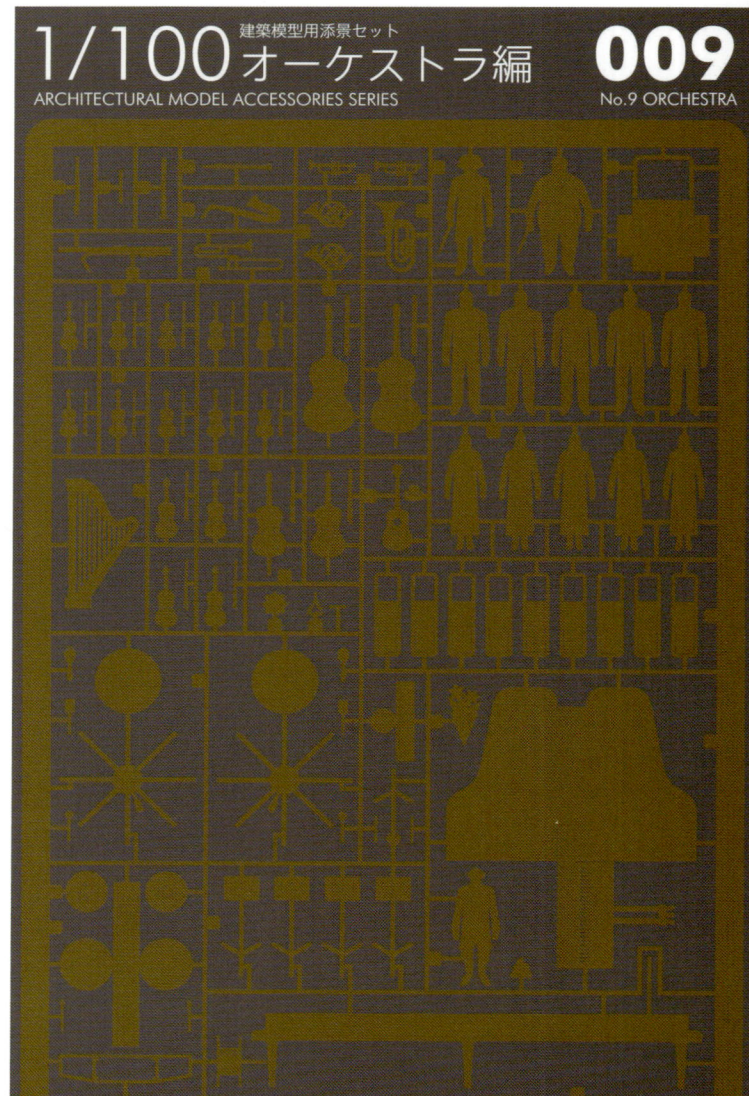

No.9 Orchestra

Good news for designing office staff who pull off all-nighters!! It's an orchestra version, the ninth shot of the Architectural Model series, which you can easily assemble simply by tearing off the precut parts. Instruments making up an orchestra are included. Depending on combinations, possible scenes include piano recitals, a string quartet and jazz session. The simple modeling, which omits fine details, is also highly versatile and complements the sense of scale.

Including:
flute, piccolo, oboe, clarinet, bassoon, horn, trumpet, trombone, tuba, violin, viola, cello, contrabass, timpani, cymbal, bass drum, snare drum, triangle, harp, piano, music stands and so on. To organize the orchestra, multiple sheets are required.

Design Agency: TERADA MOKEI   Country: Japan
Designer: Naoki Terada   Photographer: Kenji MASUNAGA

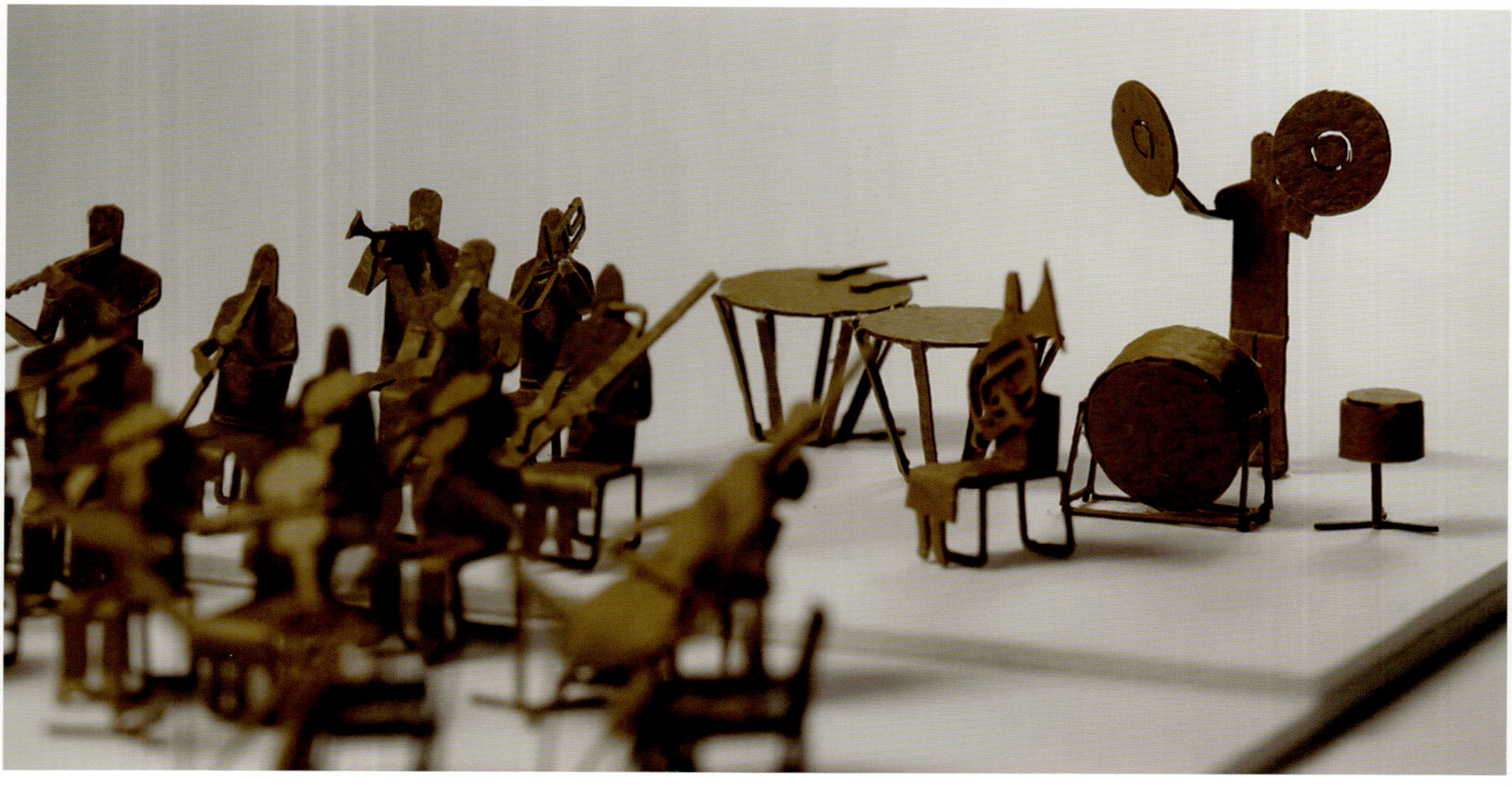

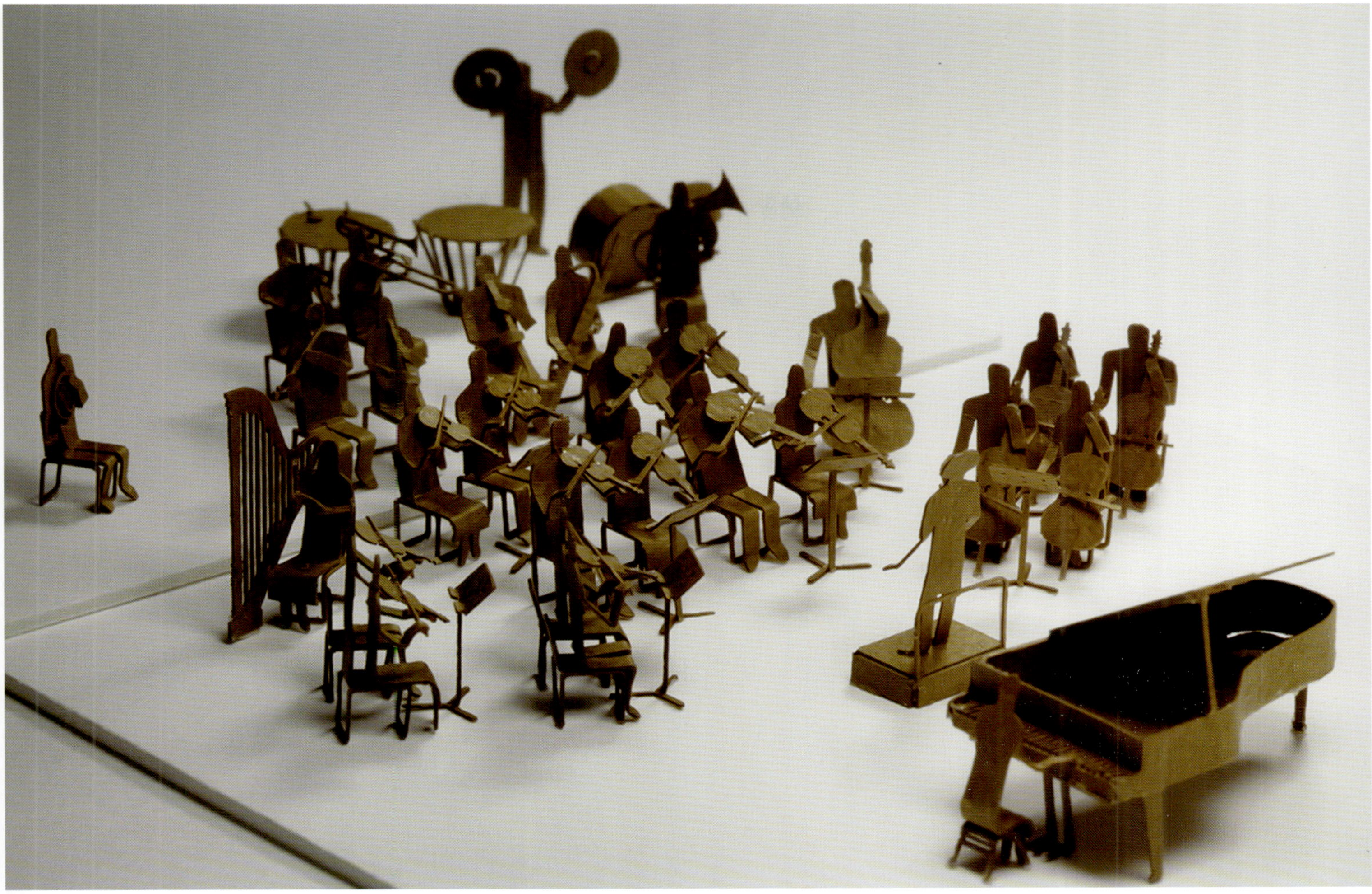

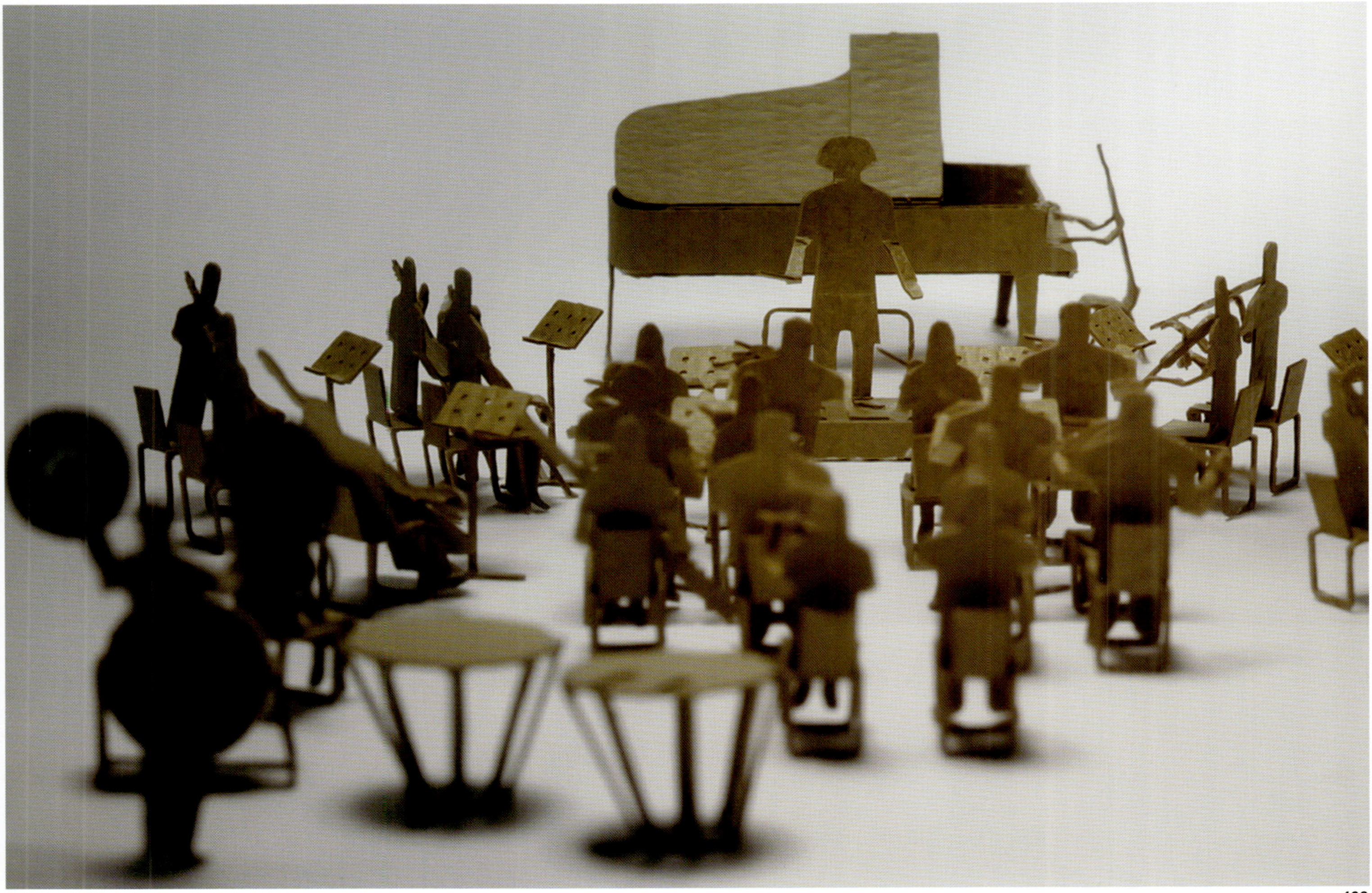

463

No.10 Street Tree

Good news for designing office staff who pull off all-nighters!! It's a street tree version, the tenth shot of the Architectural Model series, which you can easily assemble simply by tearing off the precut parts. 4 street trees inspired by zelkova are included. The leaves and branches are separated in parts, and the sense of the season can be created. The simple modeling, which omits fine details, is also highly versatile and complements the sense of scale.

Including:
Street trees, bench, crow, little birds, dogs, cats, bicycles and so on.

Design Agency: TERADA MOKEI   Country: Japan
Designer: Naoki Terada   Photographer: Kenji MASUNAGA

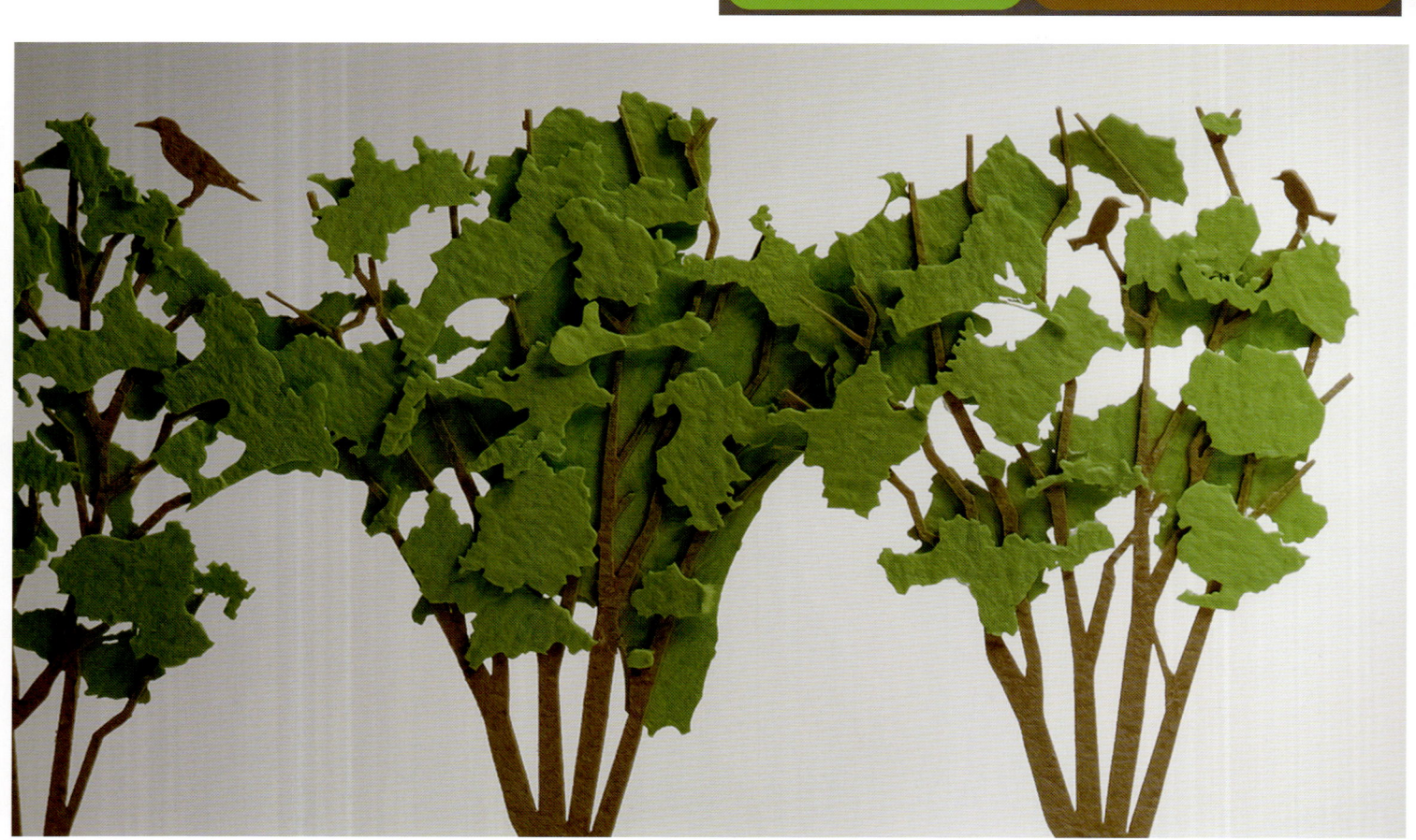

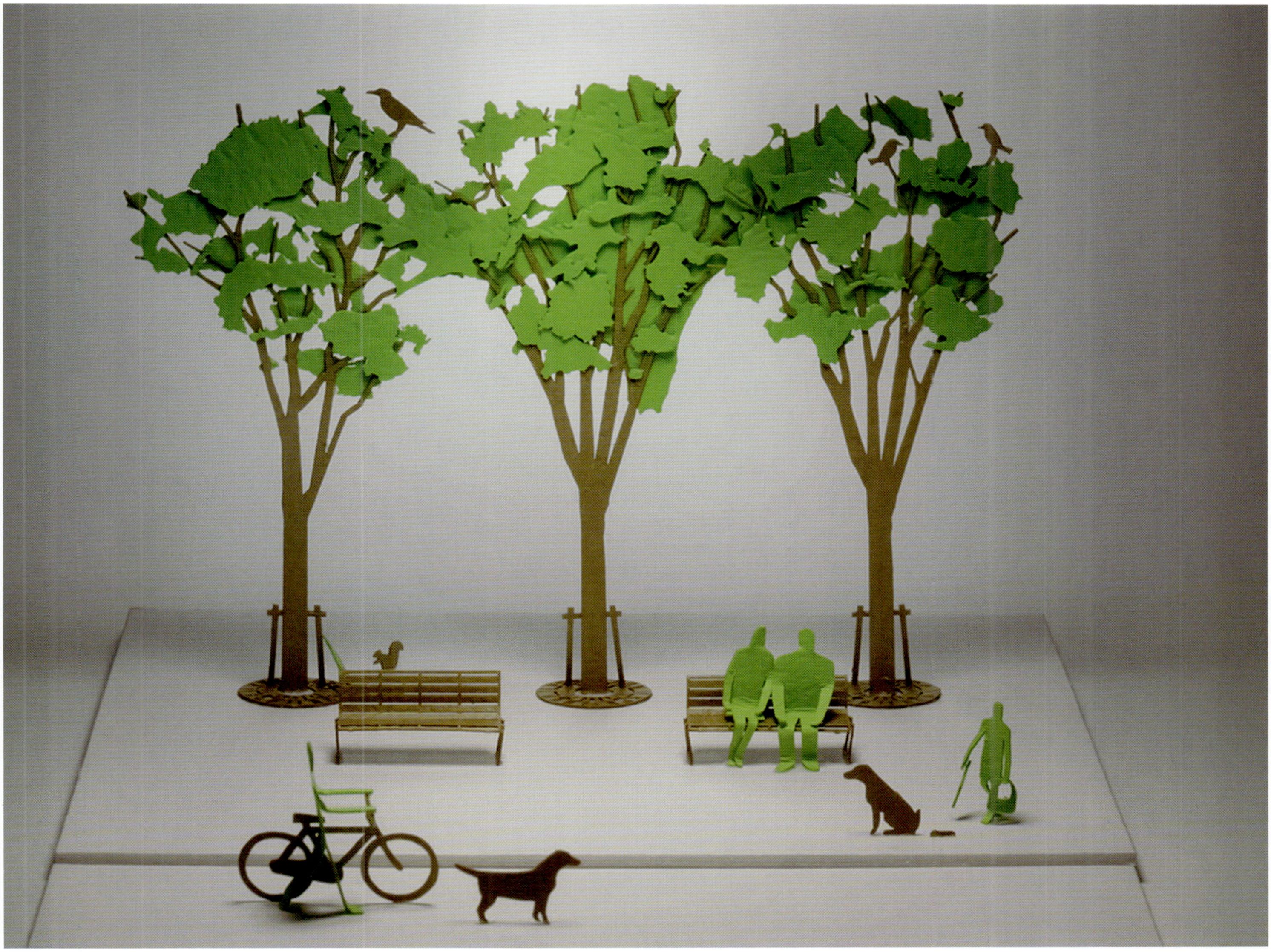

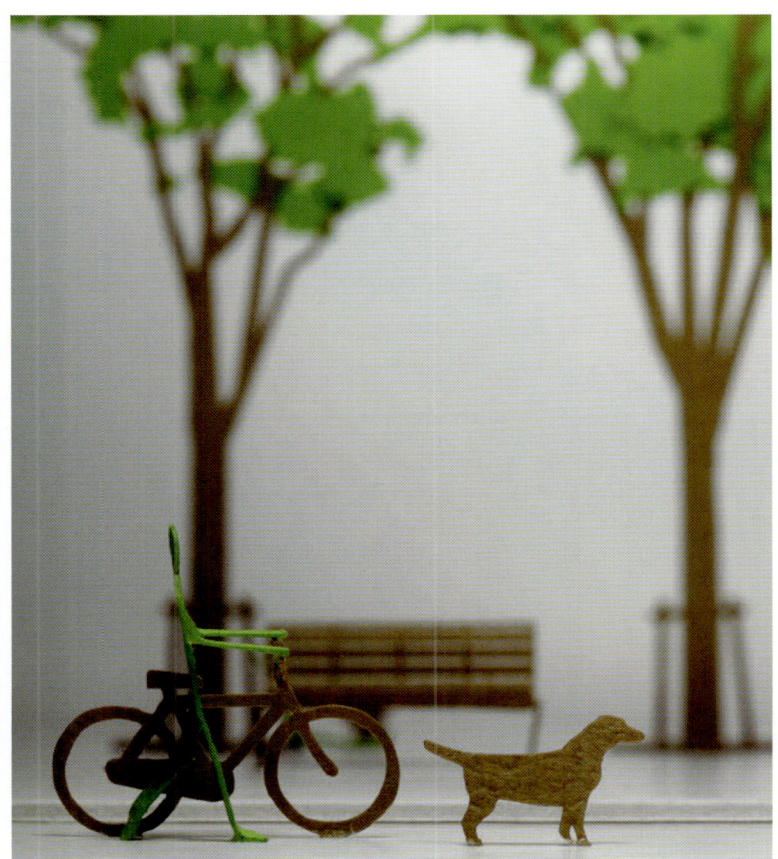
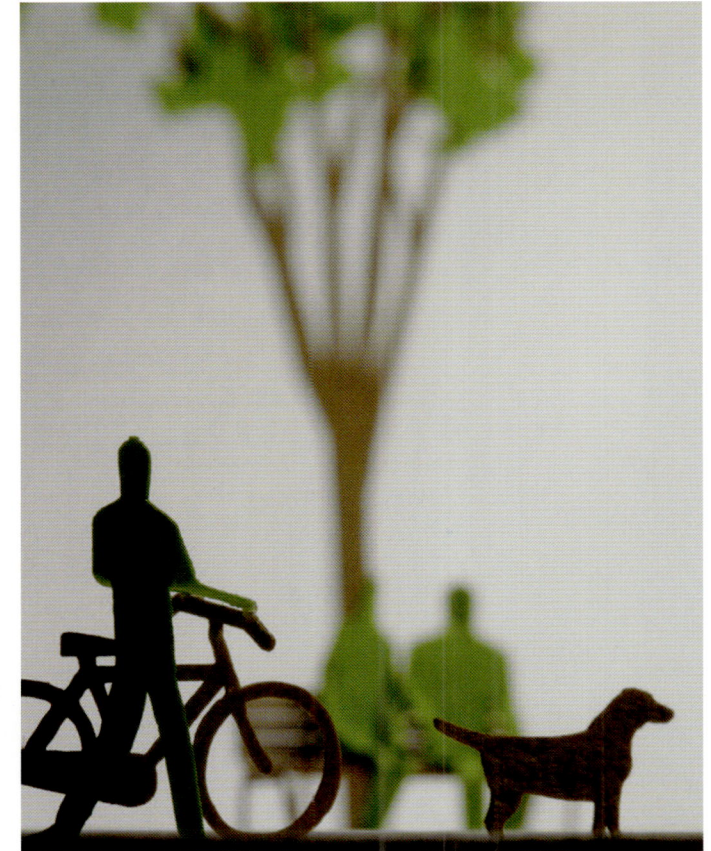

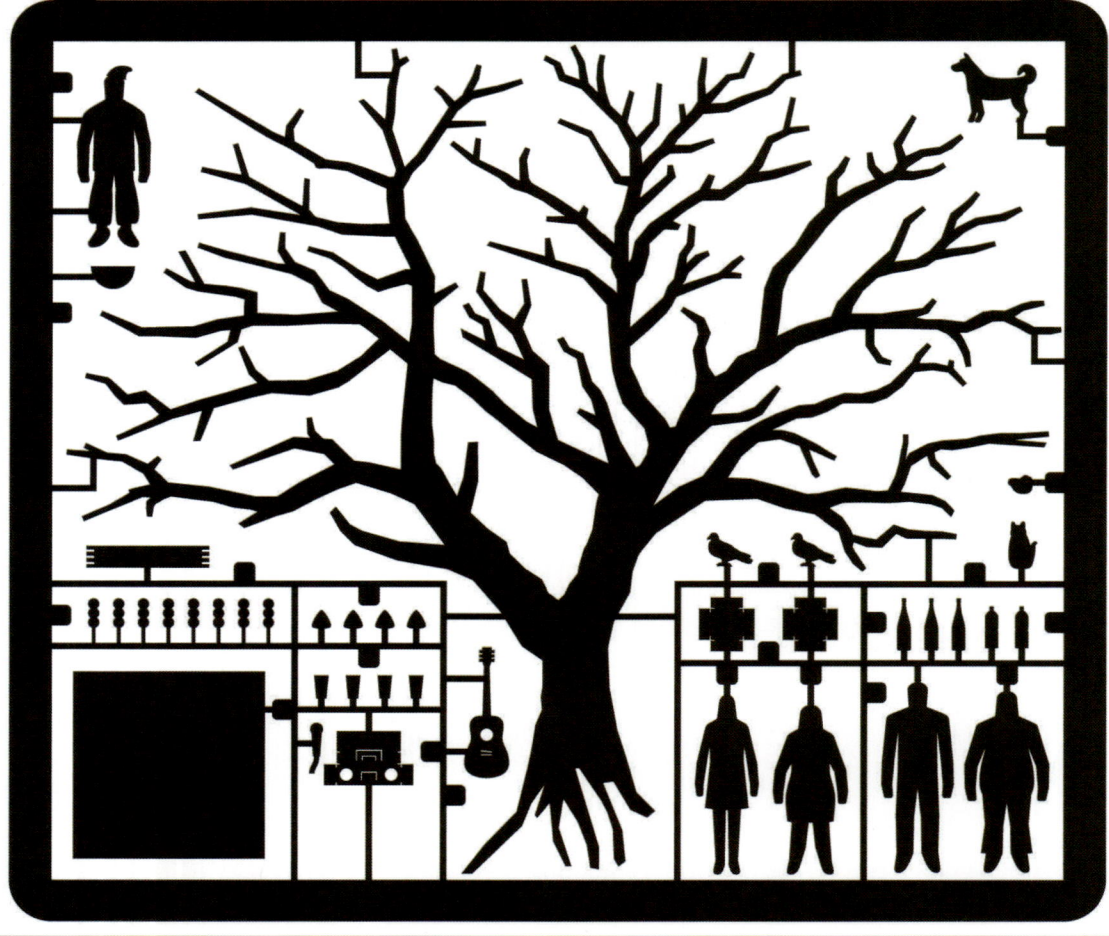

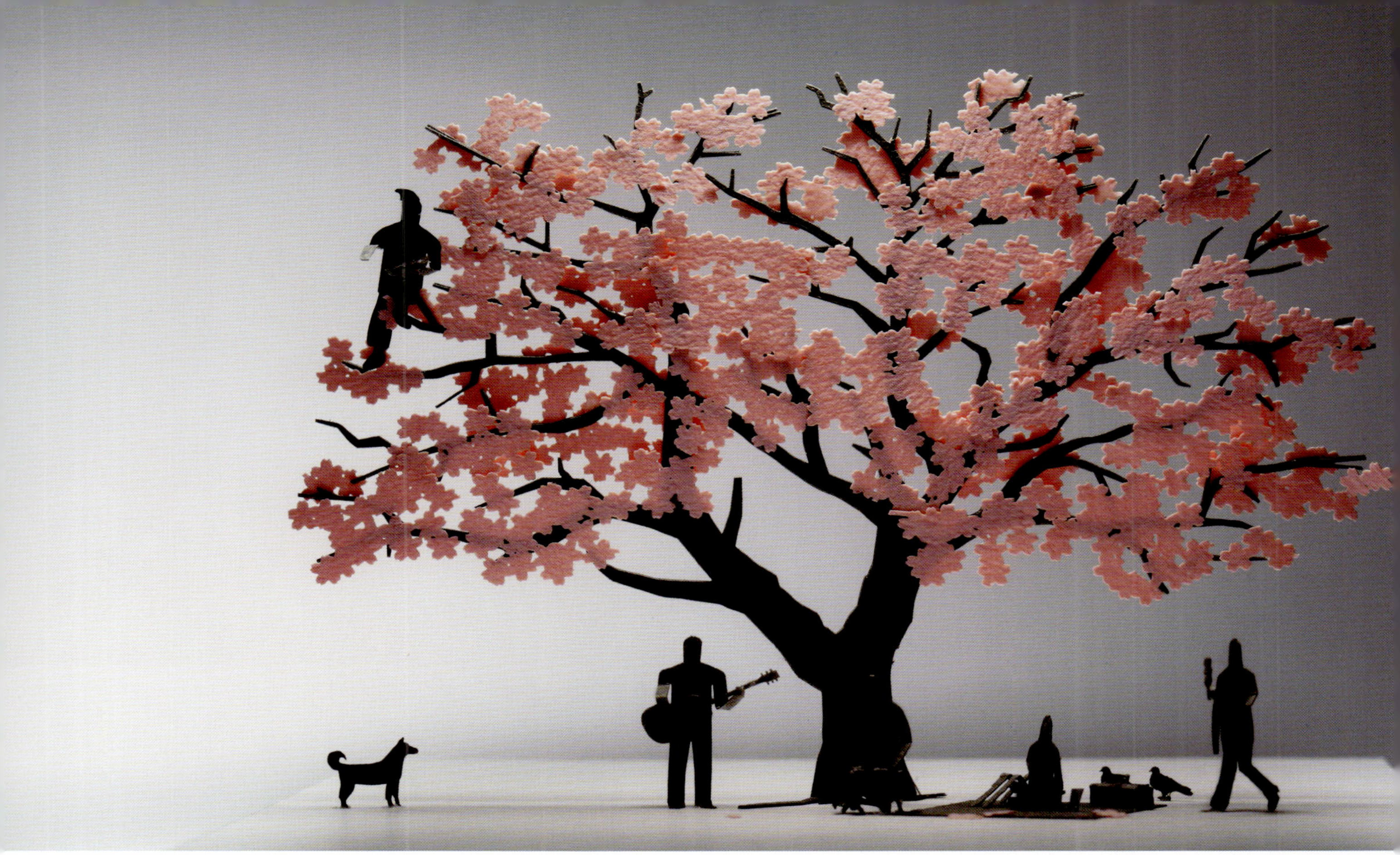

No.11 Cherry Blossom

Good news for designing office staff who pull off all-nighters!! It's a cherry blossom viewing version, the eleventh shot of the Architectural Model series, which you can easily assemble simply by tearing off the precut parts.

"Put some pretty blossoms on that old bare tree..." The trees and blossoms are made separately so you can enjoy bringing spring to your scene one blossom at a time. The simple modeling, which omits fine details, is also highly versatile and complements the sense of scale.

Including:
Hanasaka Grandpa, Pochi-the-dog, box lunch, bottle of sake, karaoke machine, picnic blanket, boss, otsubone (office 'grand dame'), new hire, etc.

Design Agency: TERADA MOKEI   Country: Japan
Designer: Naoki Terada   Photographer: Kenji MASUNAGA

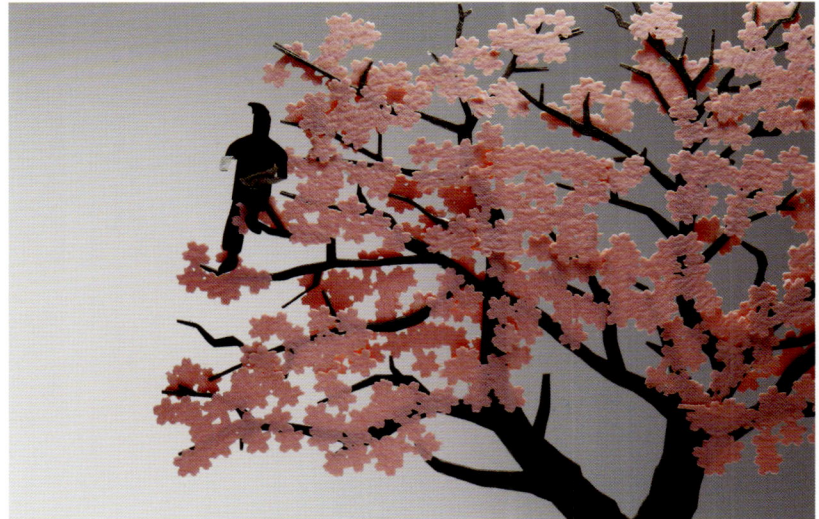

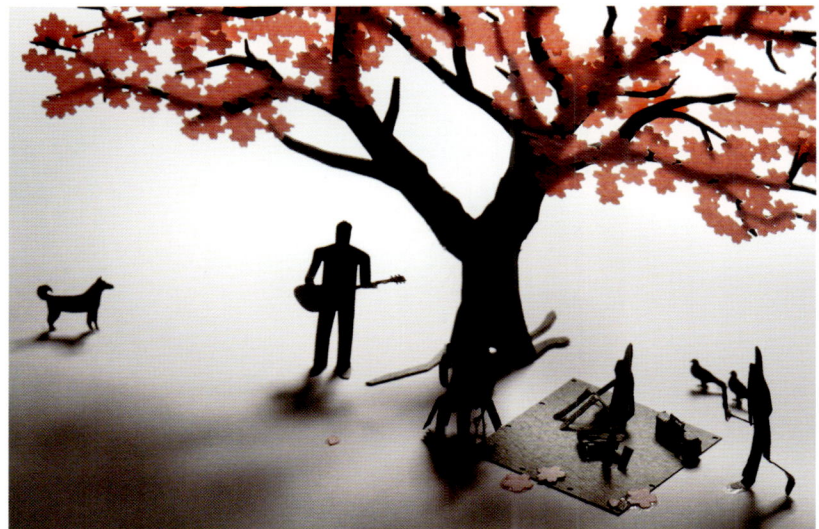

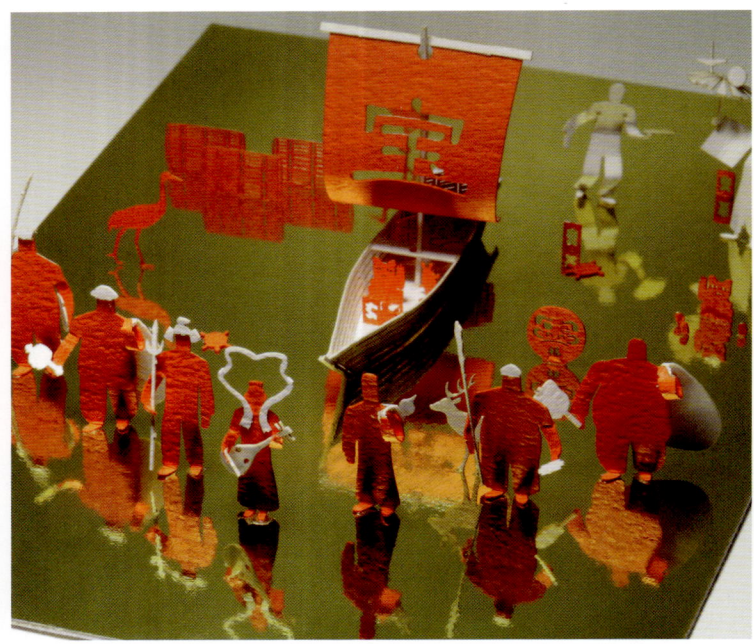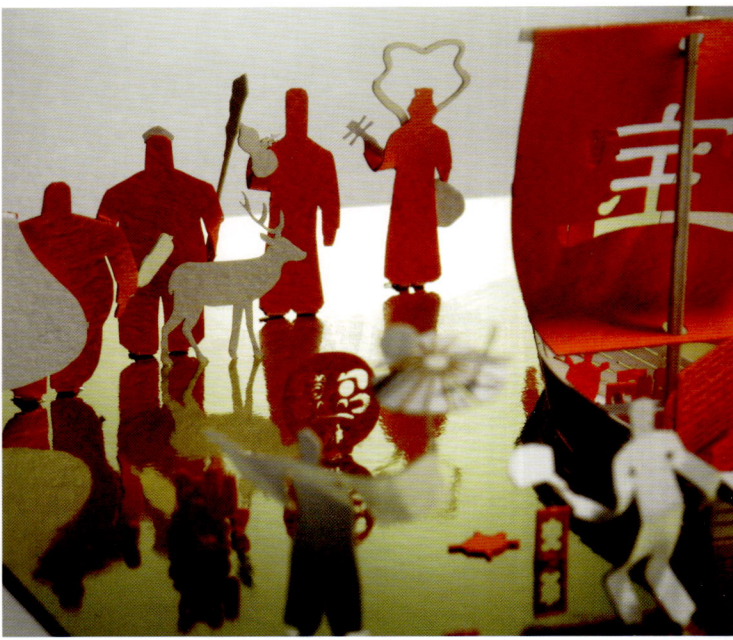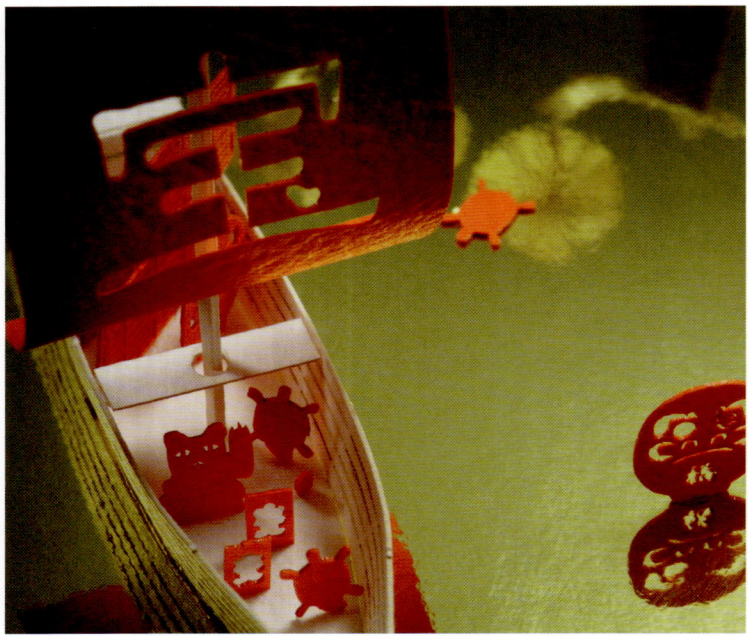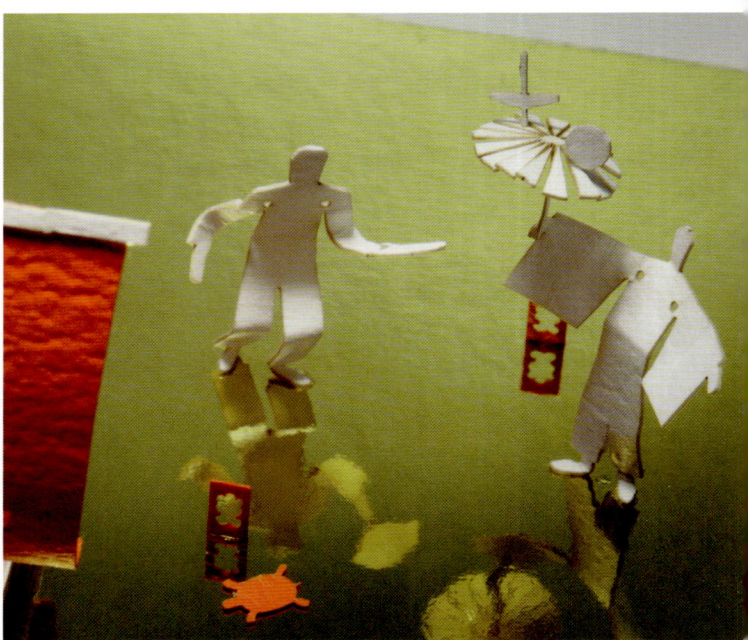

No.13 The Seven Gods of Good Fortune

Good news for designing office staff who pull off all-nighters!! It's the Seven Gods of Good Fortune version, the thirteenth shot of the Architectural Model series, which you can easily Prosperity in business, safety in the home, the fulfillment of true love, success in school, narrow escapes, lotteries, long life or whatever your desire, this set will encapsulate it into the world of 1/100 models. Quietly incorporate it into your architectural designs or business projects to bring success. Or slip it into your wallet for good luck.
The simple modeling, which omits fine details, is also highly versatile and complements the sense of scale.

Including:
the Seven Gods of Fortune, treasure ship, crane, turtle, bundles of rice, Daruma totem, Beckoning Cat, 'Koban' gold coin, and other items.

Design Agency: TERADA MOKEI   Country: Japan
Designer: Naoki Terada   Photographer: Kenji MASUNAGA

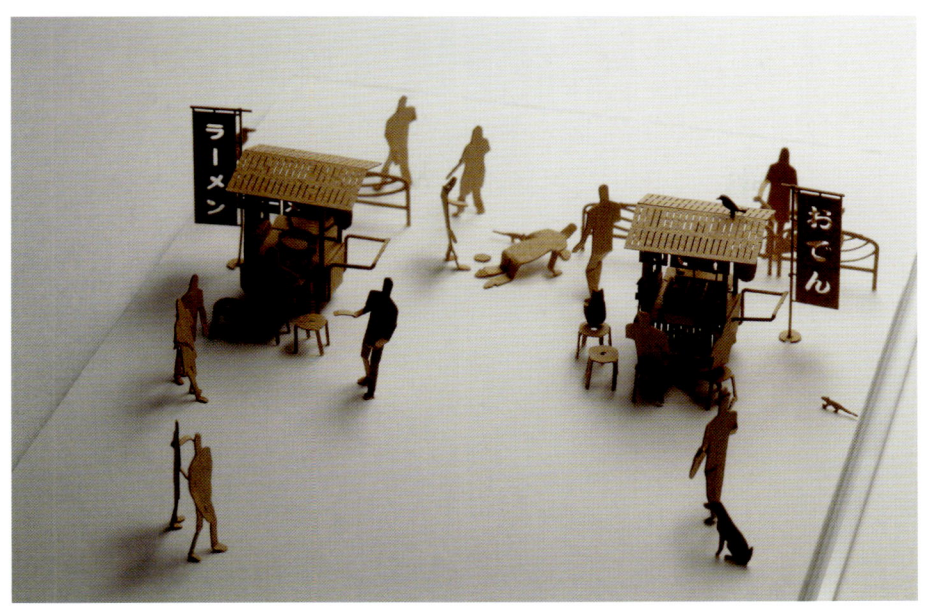

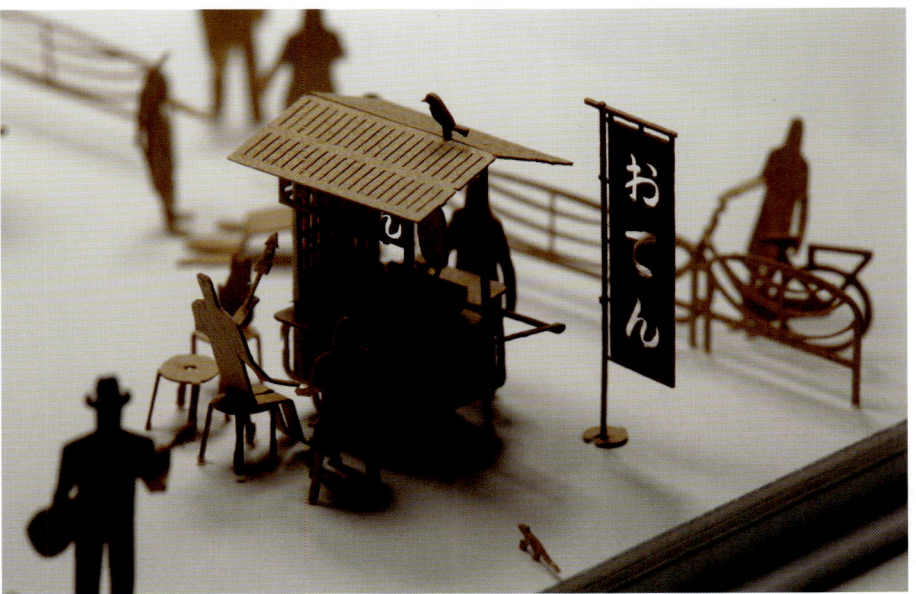

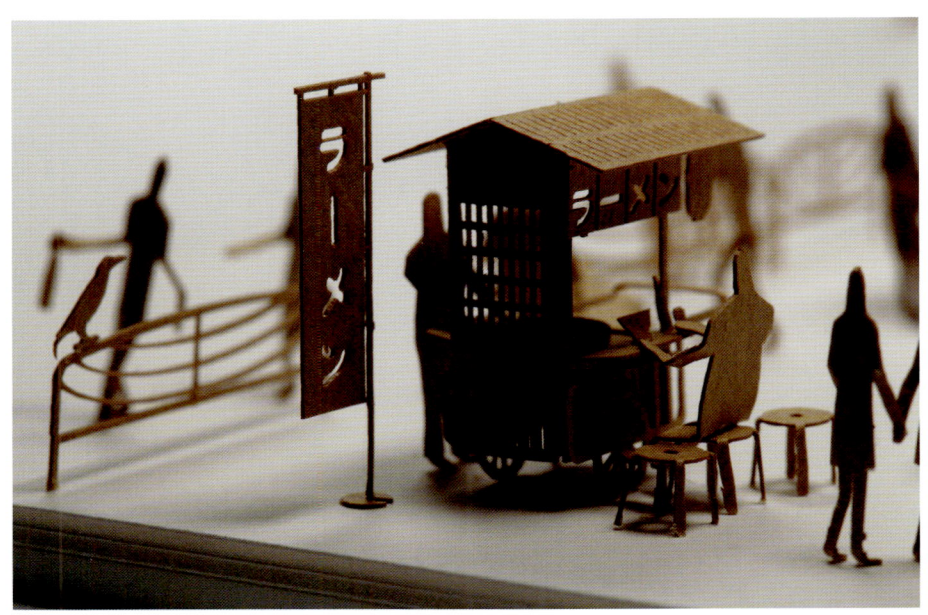

No.20 Food Stall

Good news for design office staff who pull off all-nighters!! Food Stall, the 20th installment of the pre-cut Architectural Model Series has arrived. Simply detach and assemble. Eating hot ramen noodles and stewed oden at street stalls snuggled shoulder to shoulder in the evening breeze is a heavenly pleasure. That scene has been shrunk to 1/100 scale in these models. Well, everything tastes good when you're drunk, doesn't it?! The simple modeling which omits fine details is highly versatile and accentuates the sense of scale.

Including: Food stall, flags, lanterns, stools, cat, dog, bicycle, guardrail, street musician, vomit, etc.

Design Agency: TERADA MOKEI   Country: Japan
Designer: Naoki Terada   Photographer: Kenji MASUNAGA

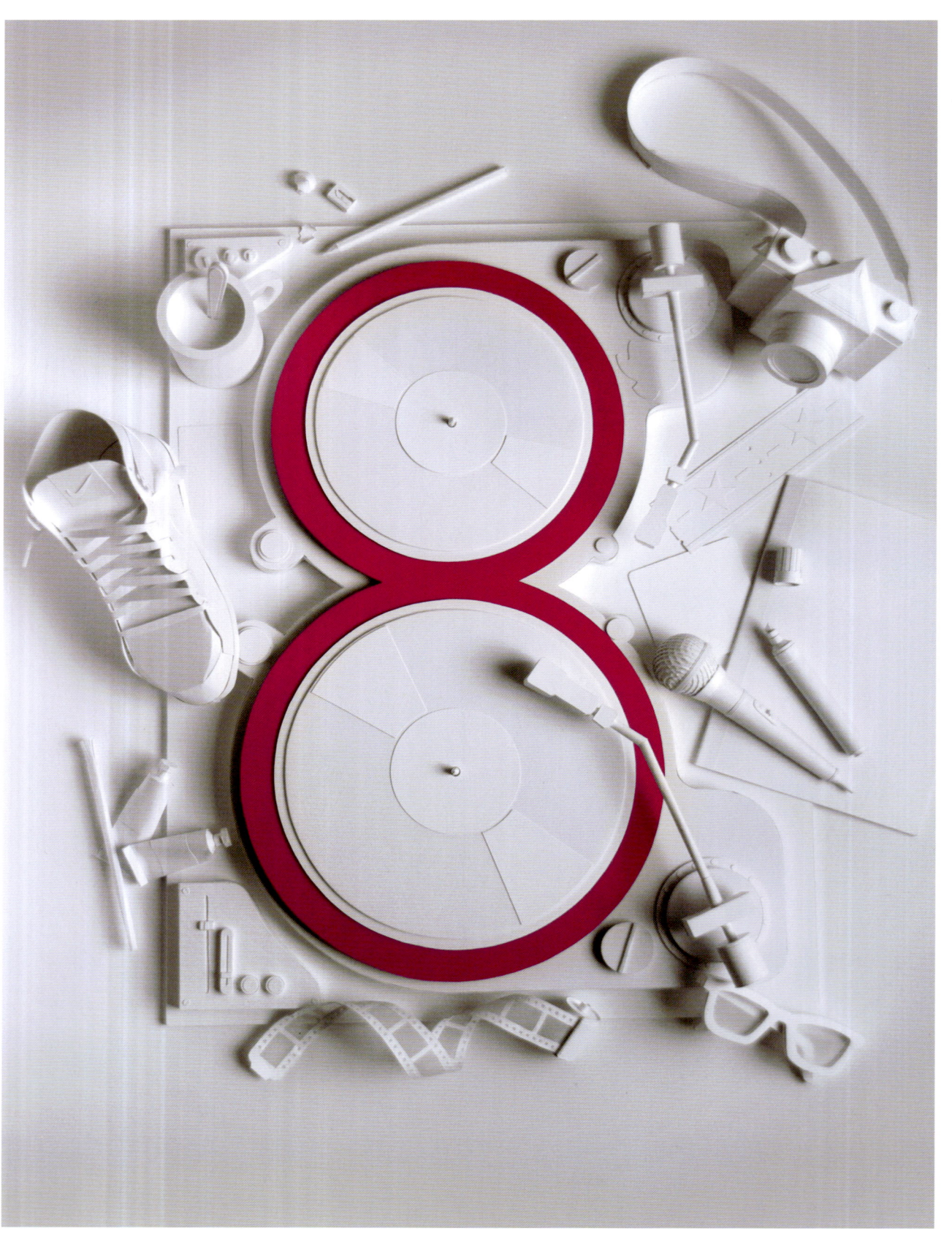

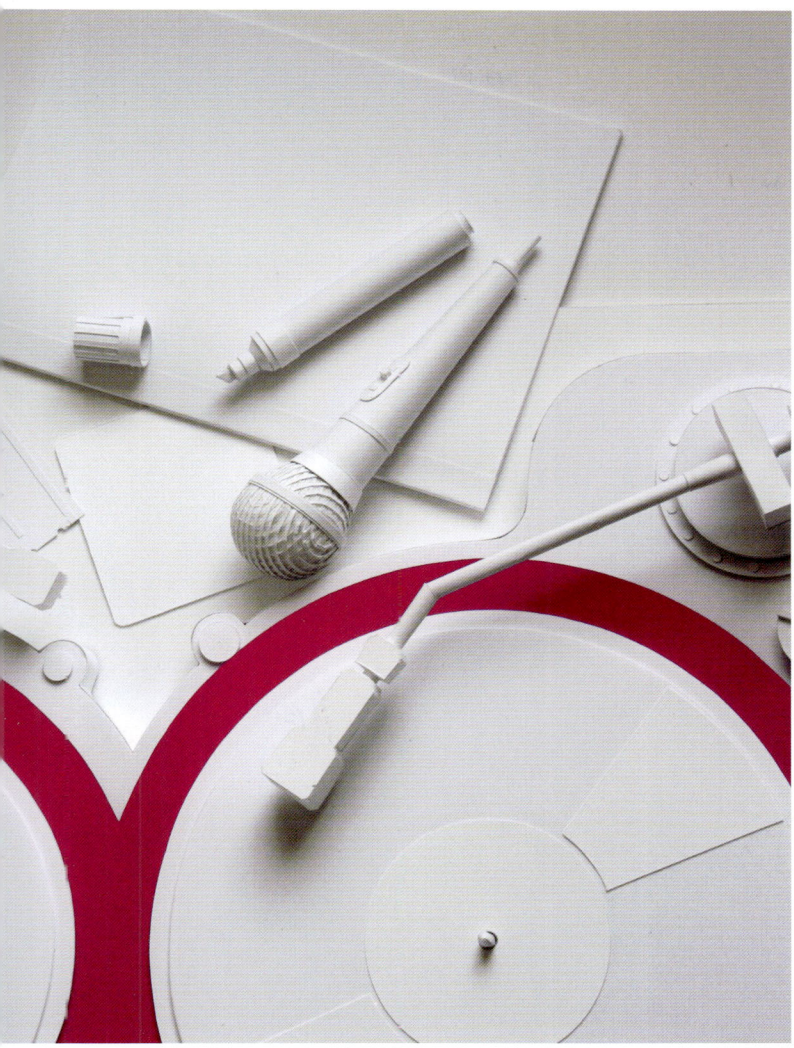

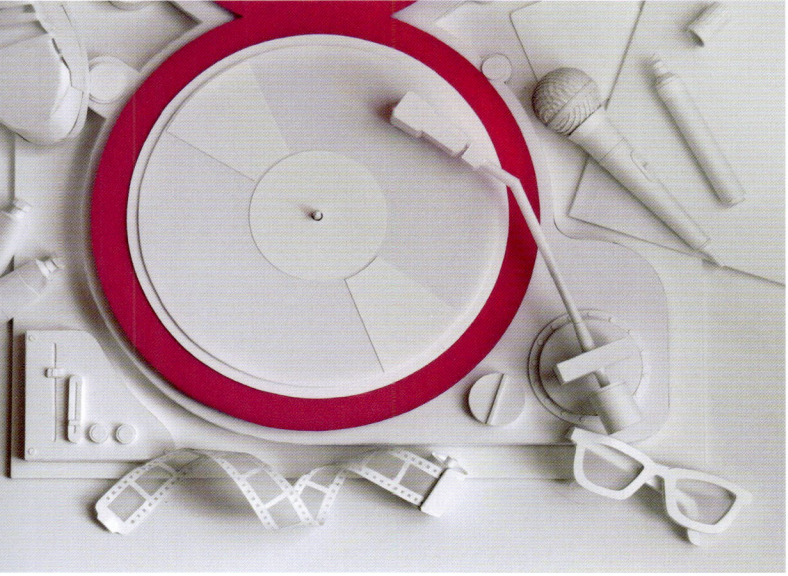

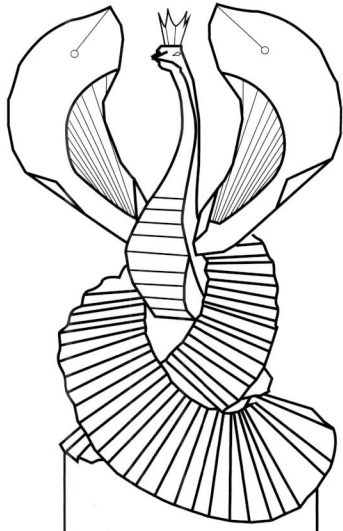

1. Female Cut Event
2. Fabriano Boutique Spring 2011
3. Atlas
4. BBDO Christmas Windows
5. BMW / Wallpaper*
6. Medusa
7. Freshfields 2012 Campaign
8. Hermes
9. Fabriano Collier
10. The Great Omar
11. The White Omar
12. Vogue Zodiac Issue
13. Vogue Gioiello Golden Dreams

---The Makerie Studio

1. **Female Cut Event**

We were commissioned by event organisers Female Cut Roma to create a cover piece for their key annual night, the 8th March. The event involved established and emerging photographers, filmmakers, artists and musicians; to showcase their variety of skills, as well as the key date of the event we used a clear typographic mechanism coupled with illustrative three-dimensional pieces.

Designer: The Makerie Studio
Country: UK
Client: Female Cut Roma (Italy)

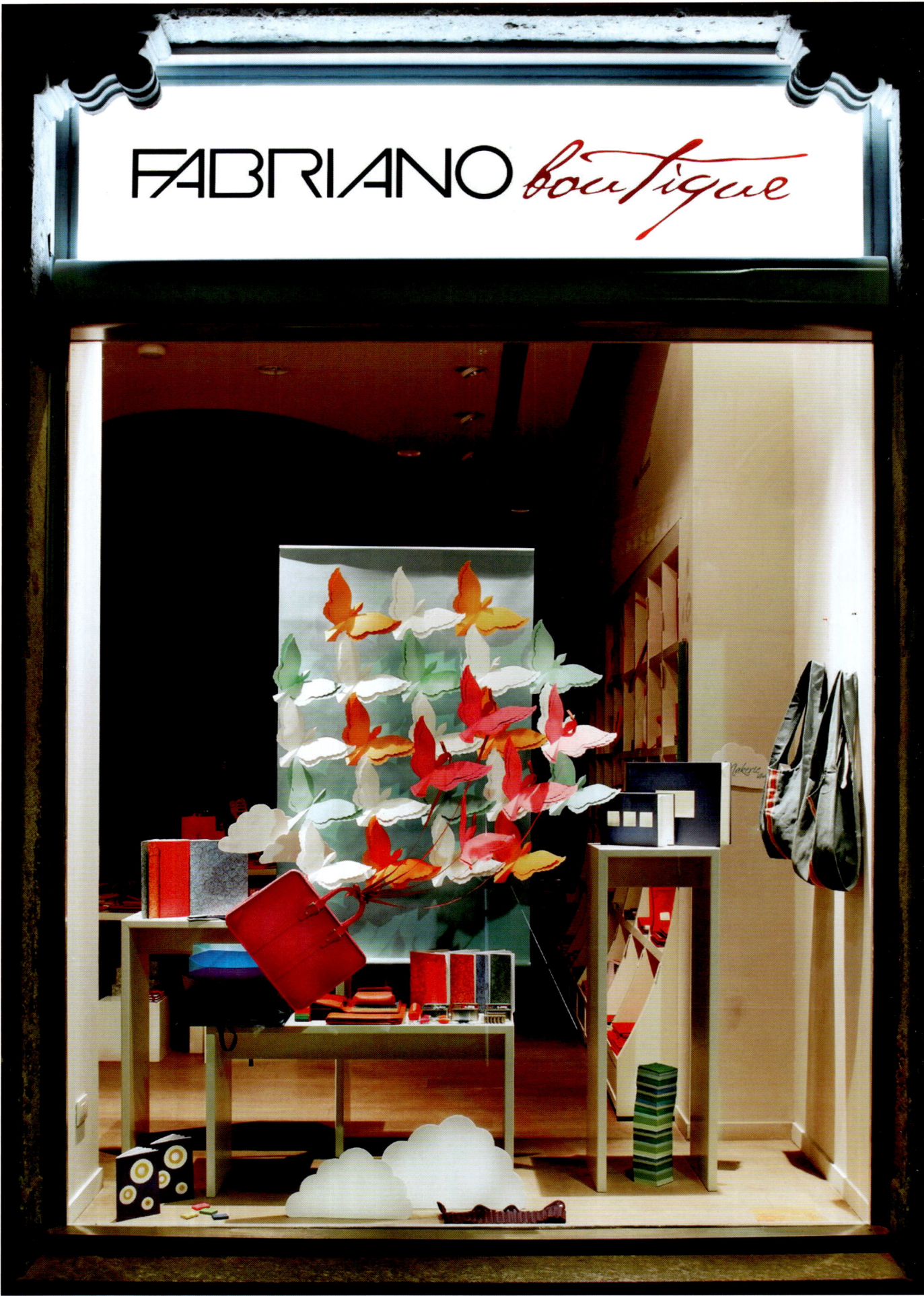

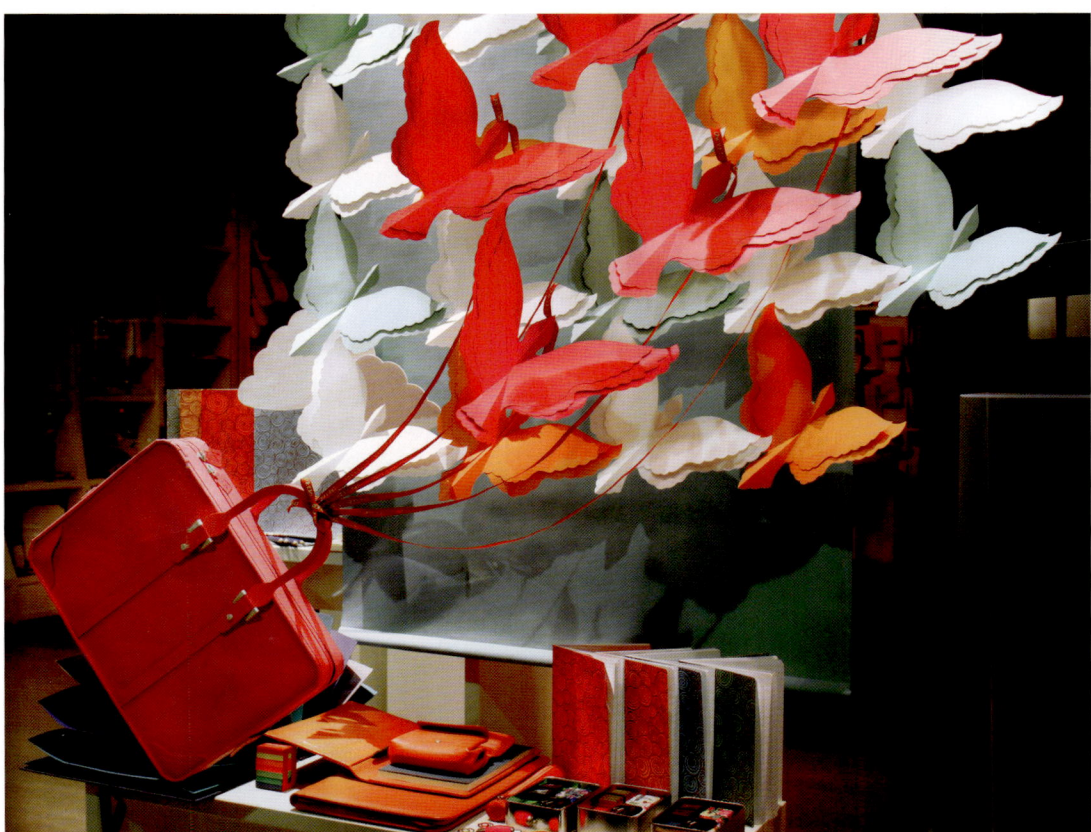

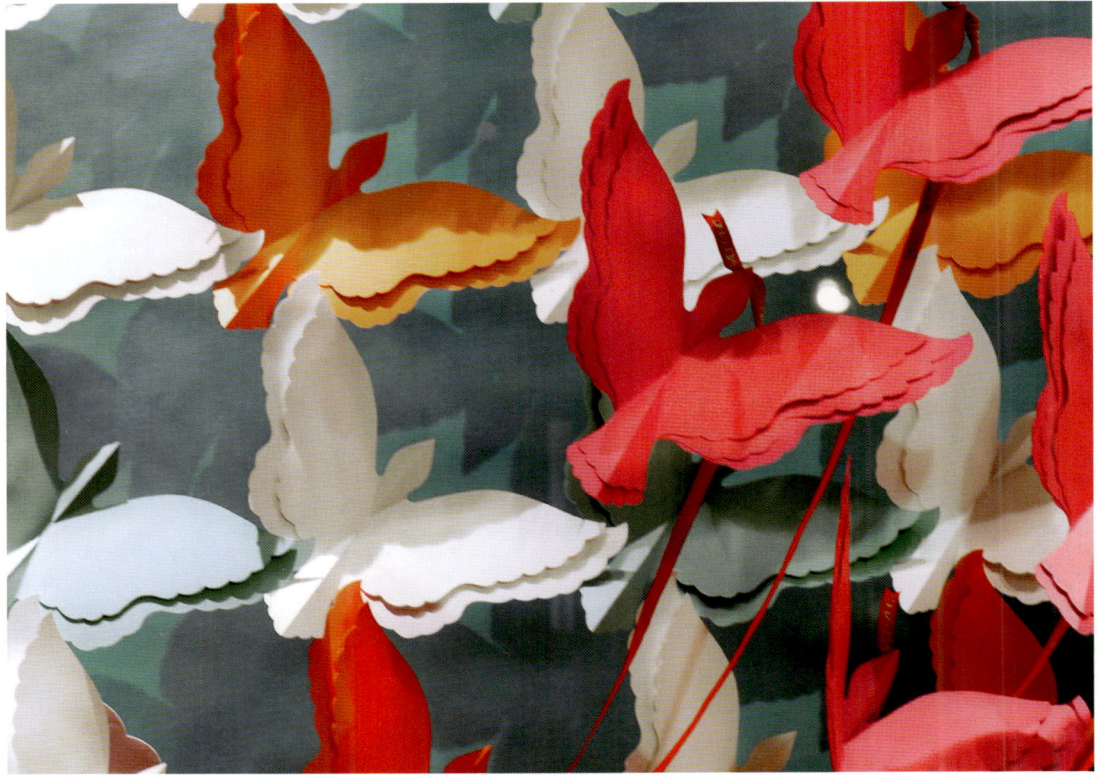

2. **Fabriano Boutique Spring 2011**

Window installations created for Fabriano Boutique's Spring 2011 collection and displayed in Milan, Rome, Florence and Munich. We created a bold scene of folded, layered and suspended birds carrying away a sculpted Fabriano bag. The unique backdrop is made up of interlocking birds that when closed fold completely flat, but open out to become a striking three-dimensional flock.

Designer: The Makerie Studio
Country: UK
Client: Fabriano Boutique
Photographer: Luigi Ziliani

Atlas

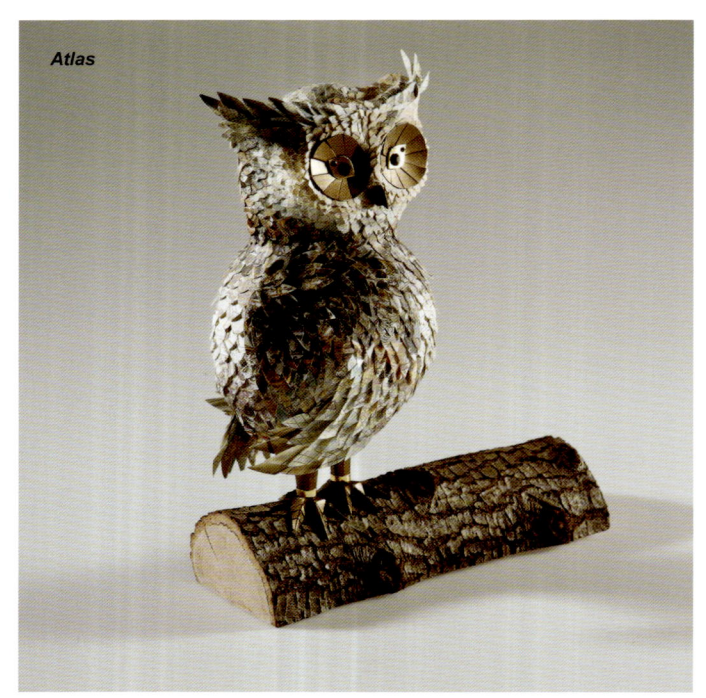
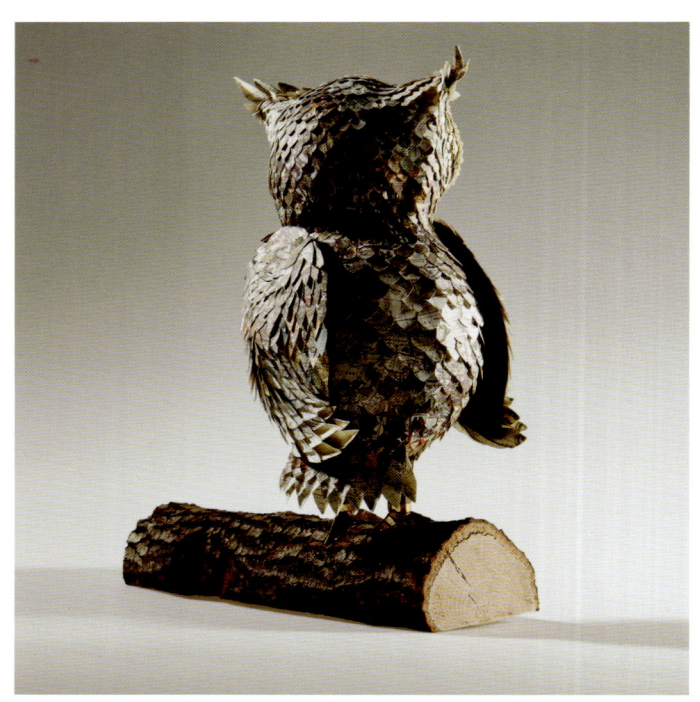

BBDO Christmas Windows

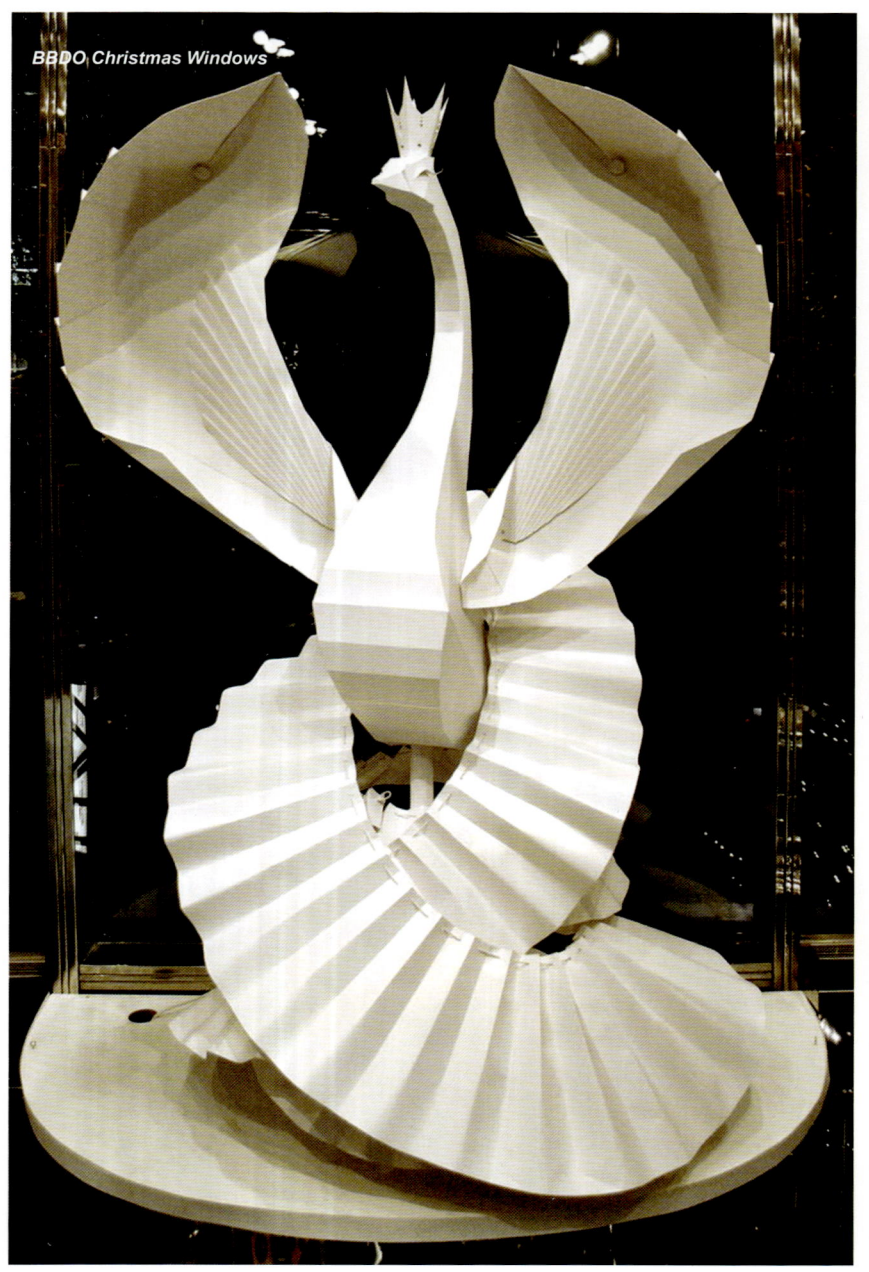
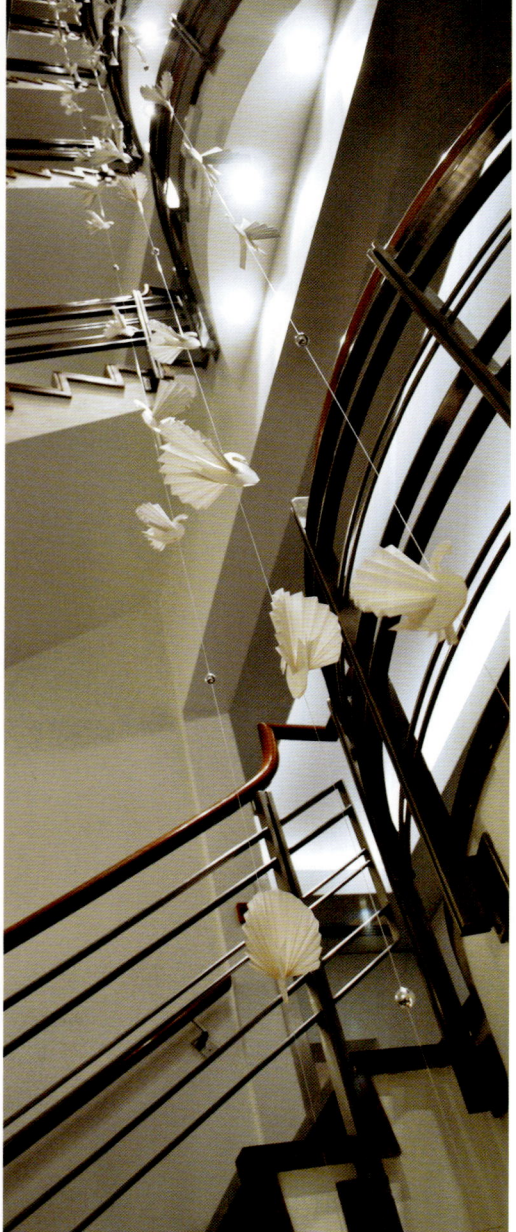

3. **Atlas**

   Life-size reproduction of a Whet Owl, created using papers printed with antique world atlases, provided by Carteria Tassotti Milano. The owl is finished using gold plated sheeting and black Swarowski crystals, with a base made from solid Italian oak

   Designer: The Makerie Studio
   Country: UK
   Photographer: Luigi Ziliani

4. **BBDO Christmas Windows**

   Christmas 2011 Window display for London's leading advertising agency; inspired by Swan Lake, we created a 3 metre-tall swan for the agency's foyer, as well as ballet shoes, baubles and a curtain of smaller swans for the 9-floor staircase.

   Designer: The Makerie Studio
   Country: UK
   Client: AMV BBDO London

5. **BMW / Wallpaper***

   BMW-i and Wallpaper magazine asked six design schools from major cities worldwide to explore the sustainable future of their environment, - and then asked The Makerie to help illustrate their designs by creating paper models of their solutions. Acetates, papers and card were used to pick out details of the designs as closely as possible.*

   Designer: The Makerie Studio
   Country: UK
   Client: Wallpaper Magazine*
   Photographer: Luke Kirwan

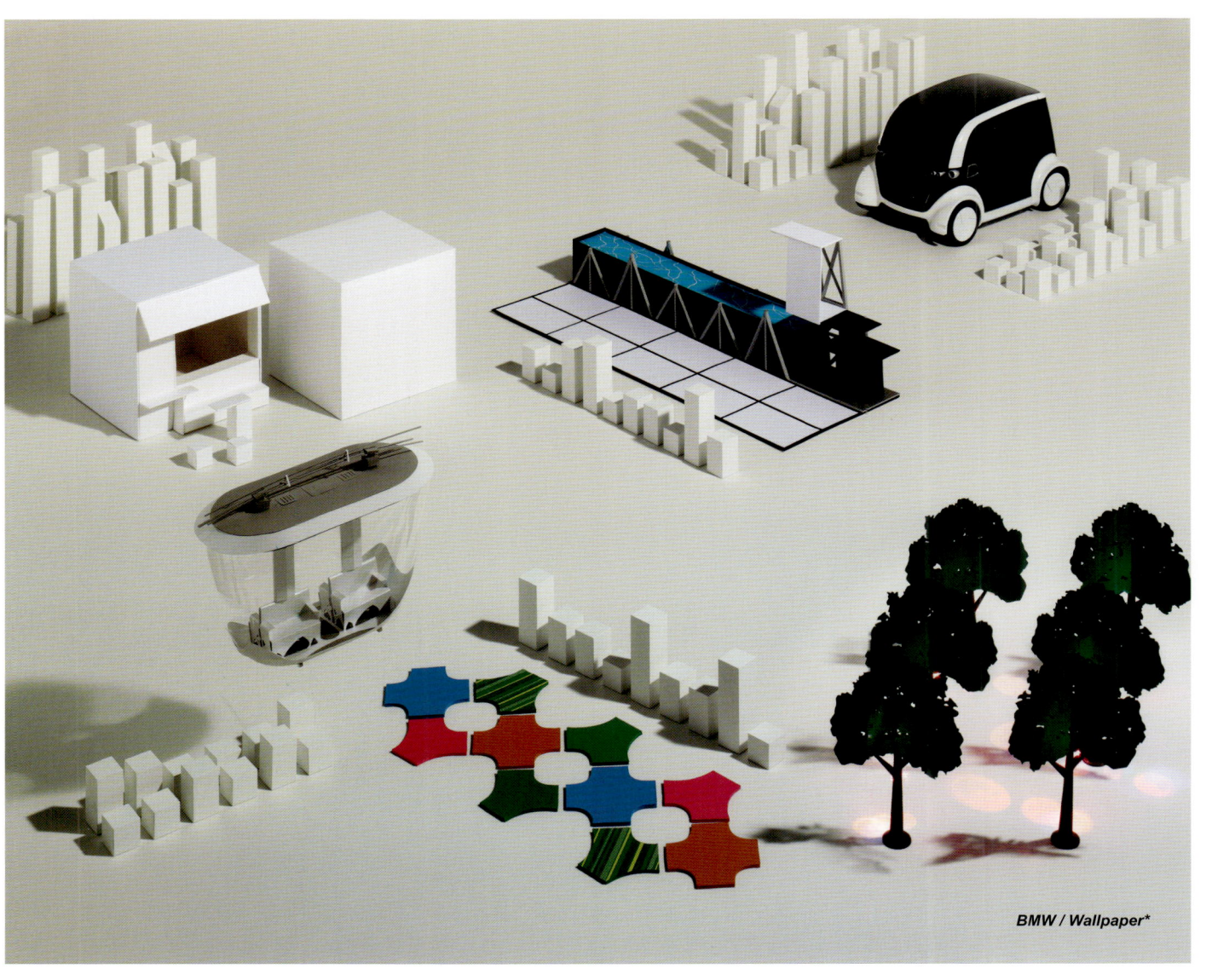

BMW / Wallpaper*

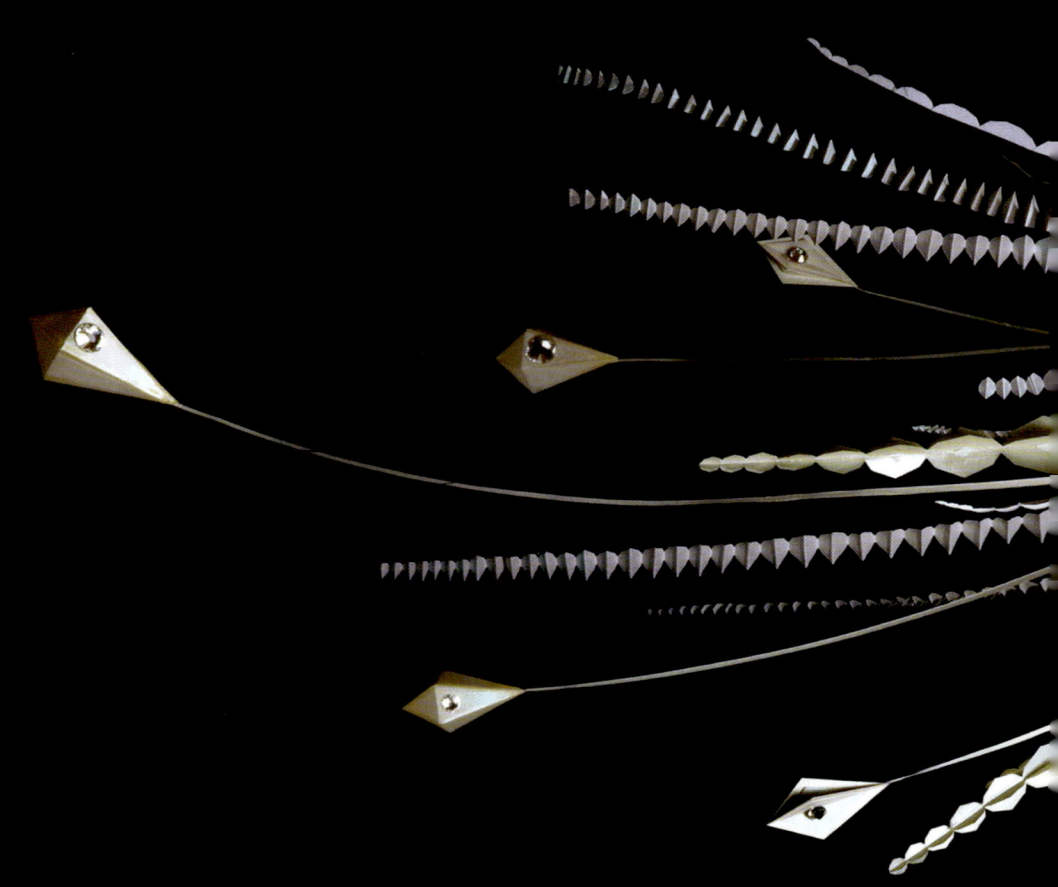

6. **Medusa**

Detailed jellyfish sculpture designed for Arjowiggins Creative Papers using their Curious Collection.
The exceptional qualities of the papers highlight and explore the nervous complexity and exquisite elegance of jellyfish.

Designer: The Makerie Studio
Country: UK
Client: Arjowiggins Creative Papers (Italy)
Photographer: Michele LaFiandra

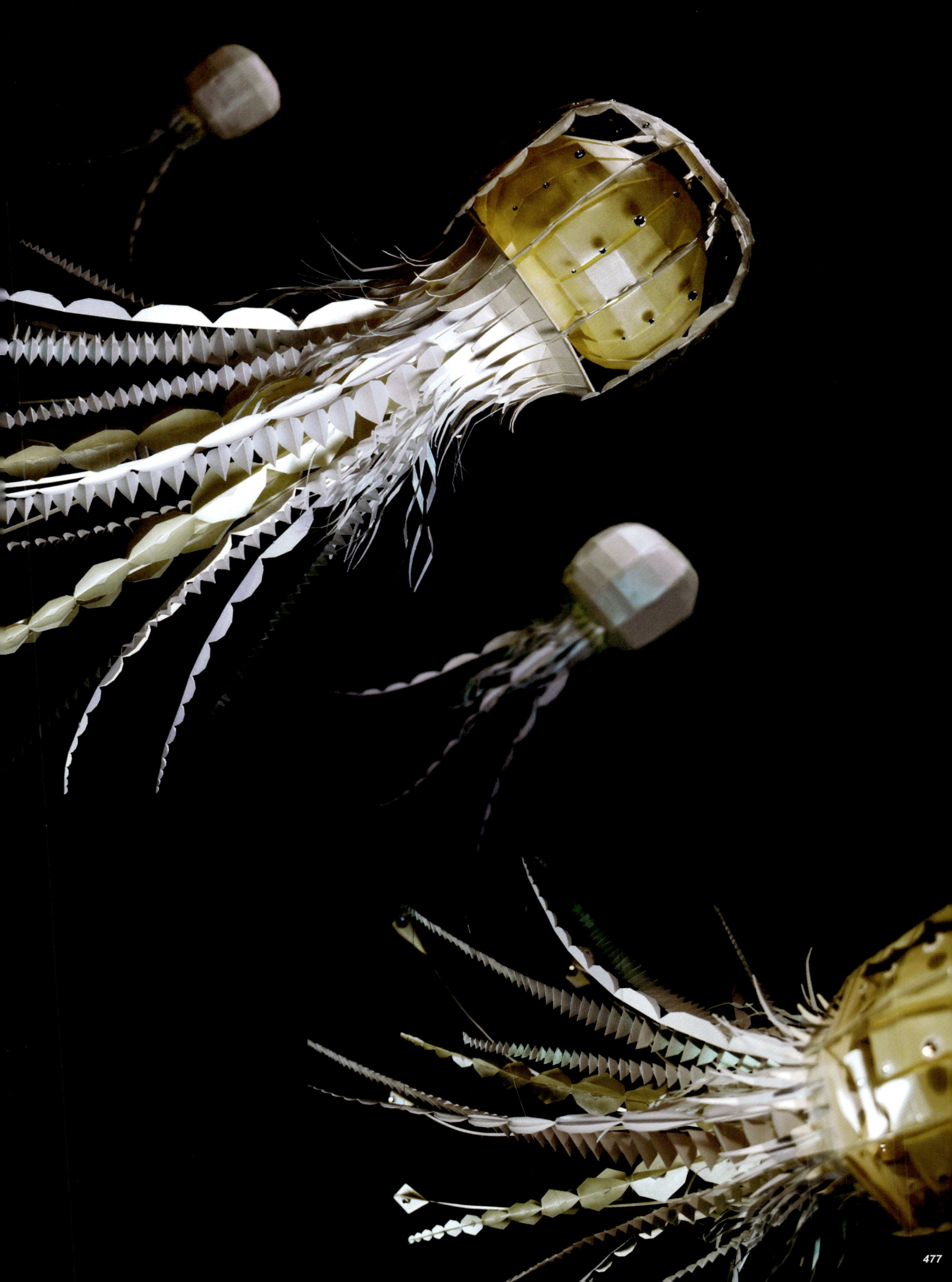

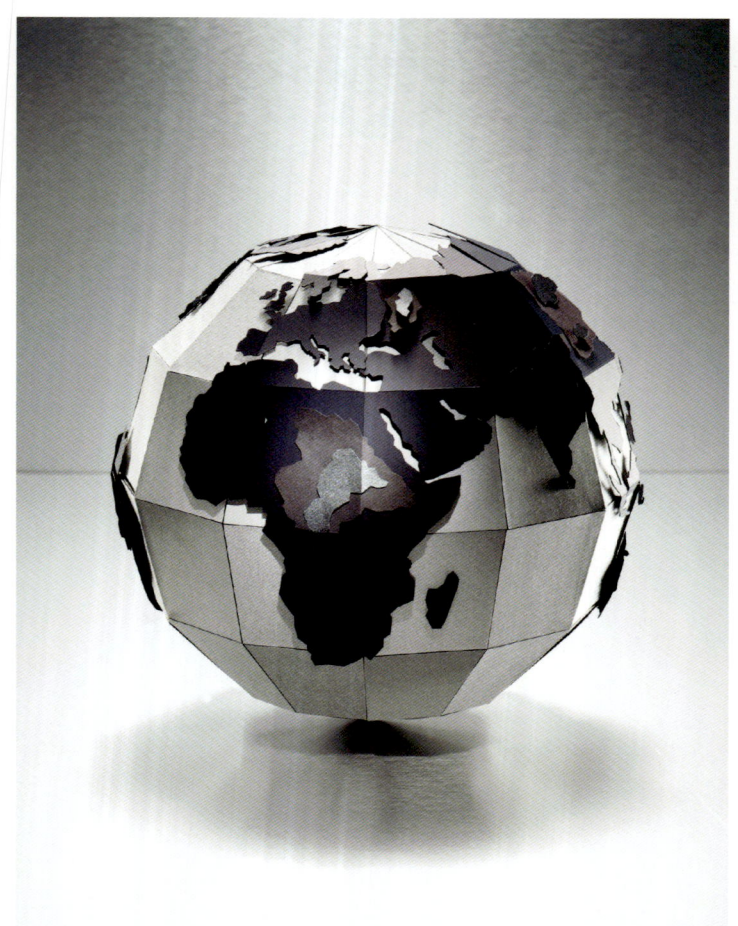
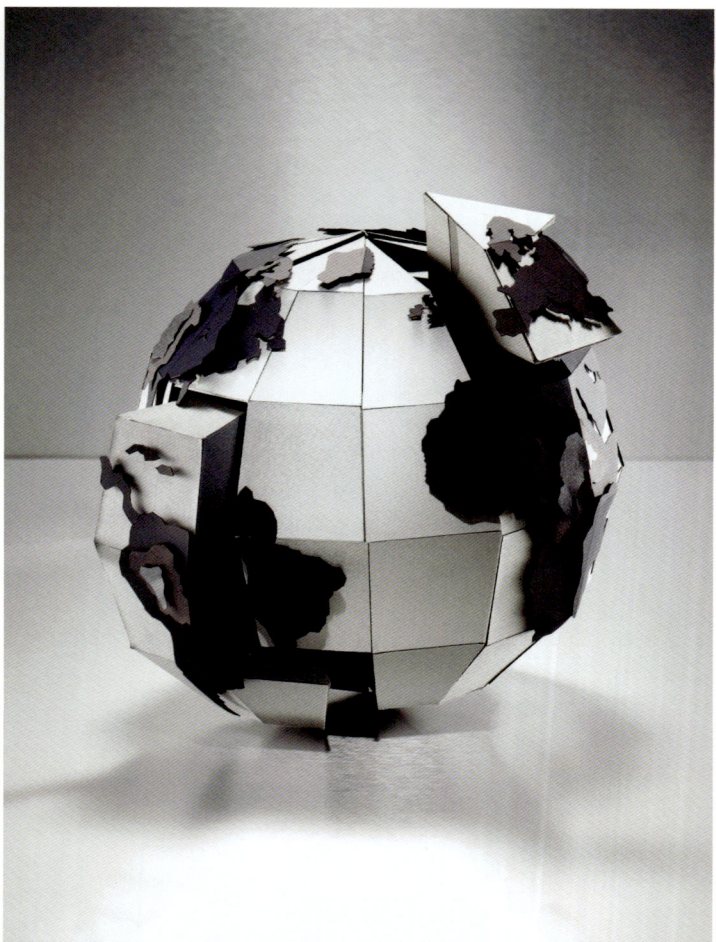
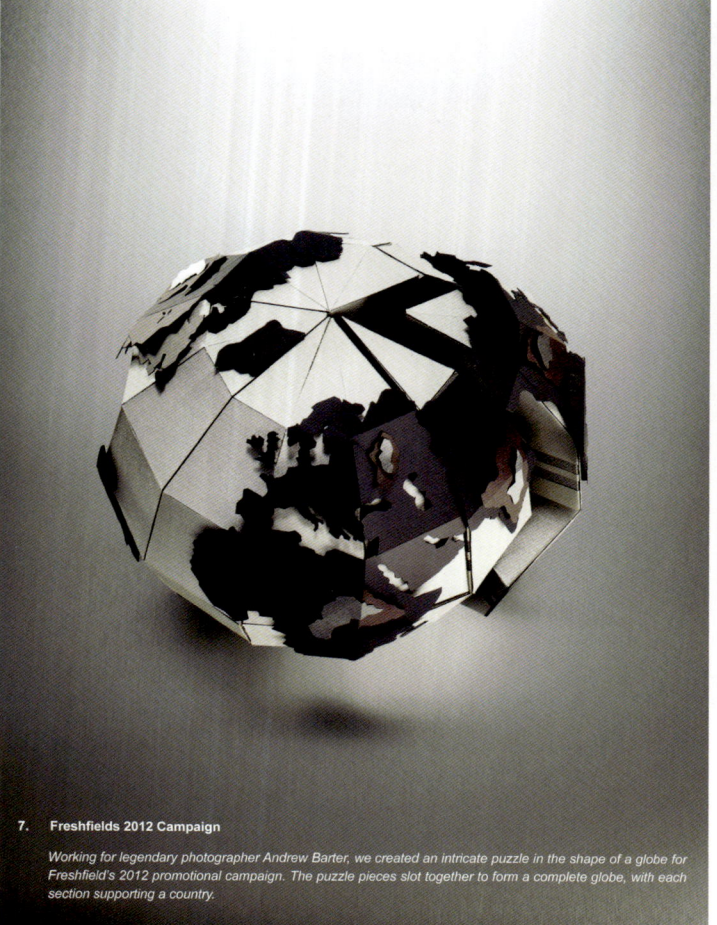
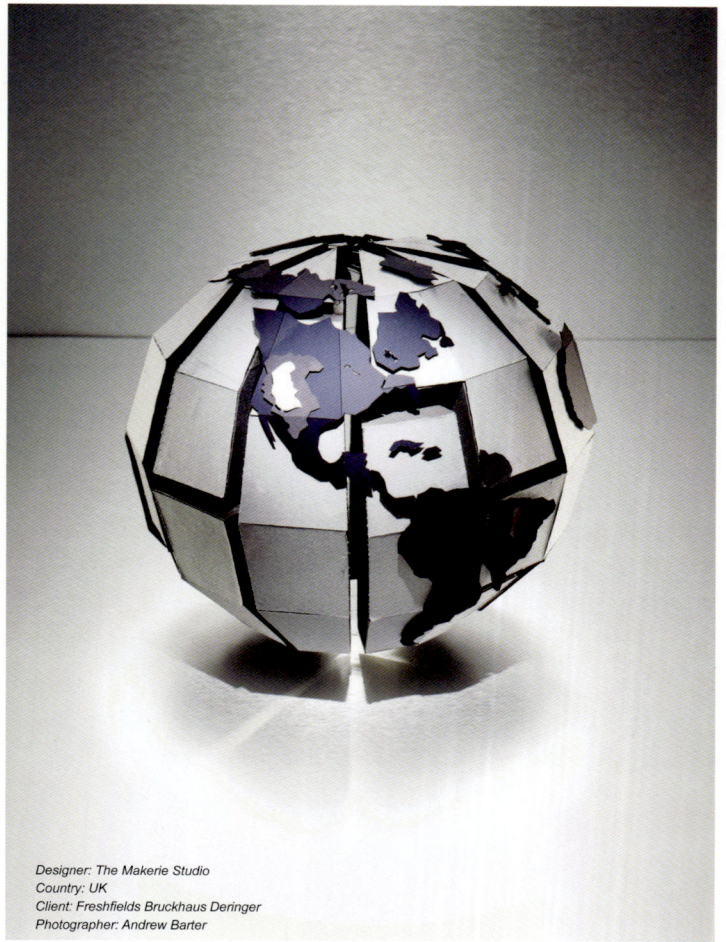

7. **Freshfields 2012 Campaign**

Working for legendary photographer Andrew Barter, we created an intricate puzzle in the shape of a globe for Freshfield's 2012 promotional campaign. The puzzle pieces slot together to form a complete globe, with each section supporting a country.

Designer: The Makerie Studio
Country: UK
Client: Freshfields Bruckhaus Deringer
Photographer: Andrew Barter

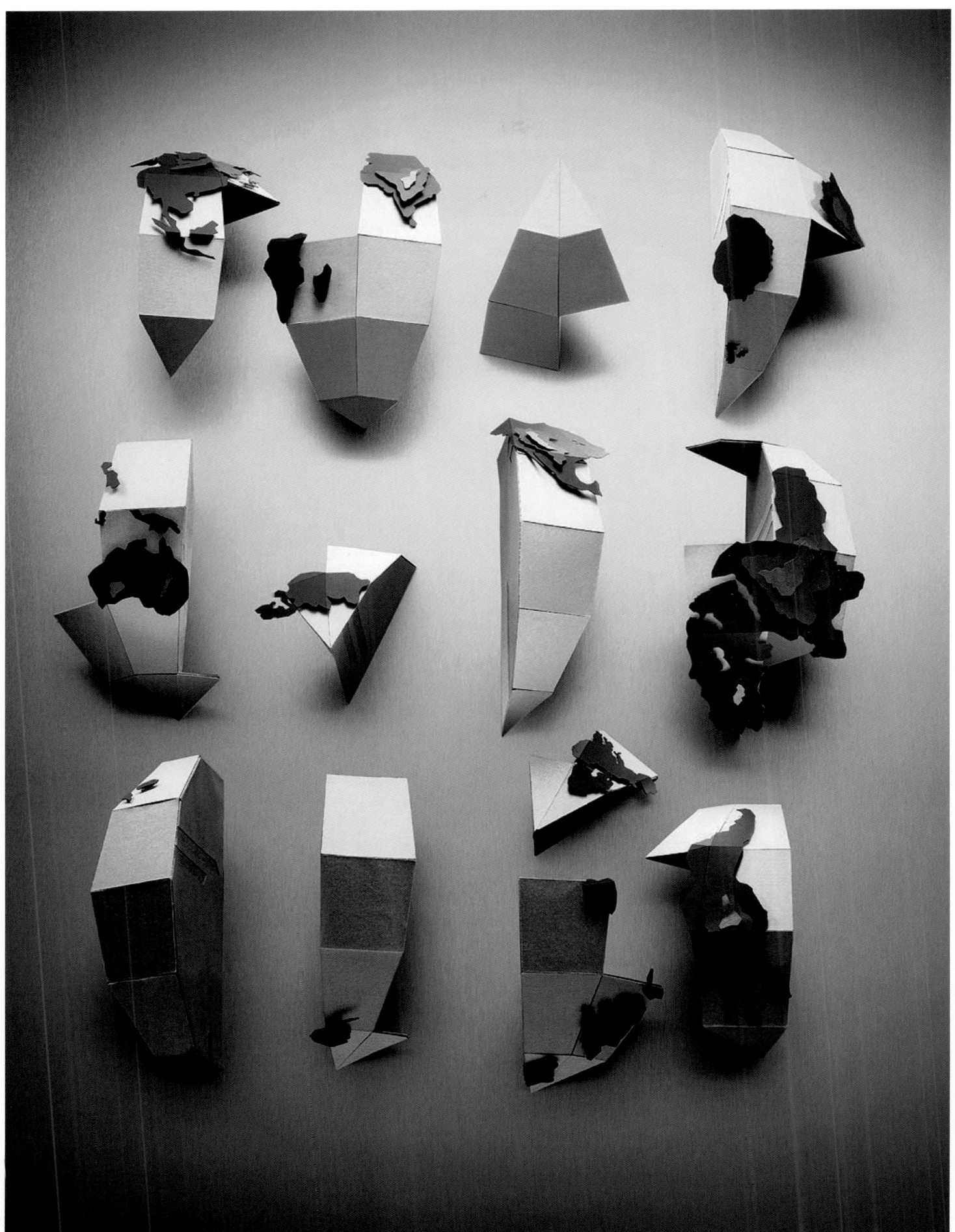

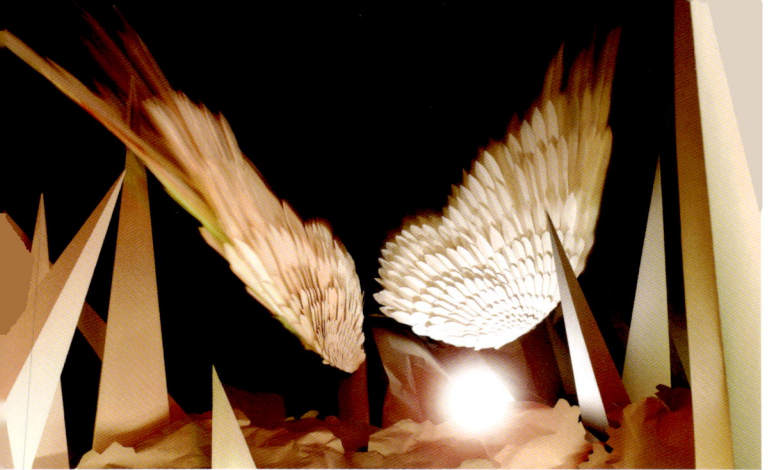

8. **Hermes**

Conceptual photo story created and shot with Luke Kirwan for the Olympian-themed issue of 125 Magazine, out March 2012. Inspired by Hermes, we created an enormous pair of white wings which were shot travelling through an abstract scenery, representing Hermes' journey into the underworld.

Designer: The Makerie Studio
Country: UK
Client: 125 Magazine
Photographer: Luke Kirwan

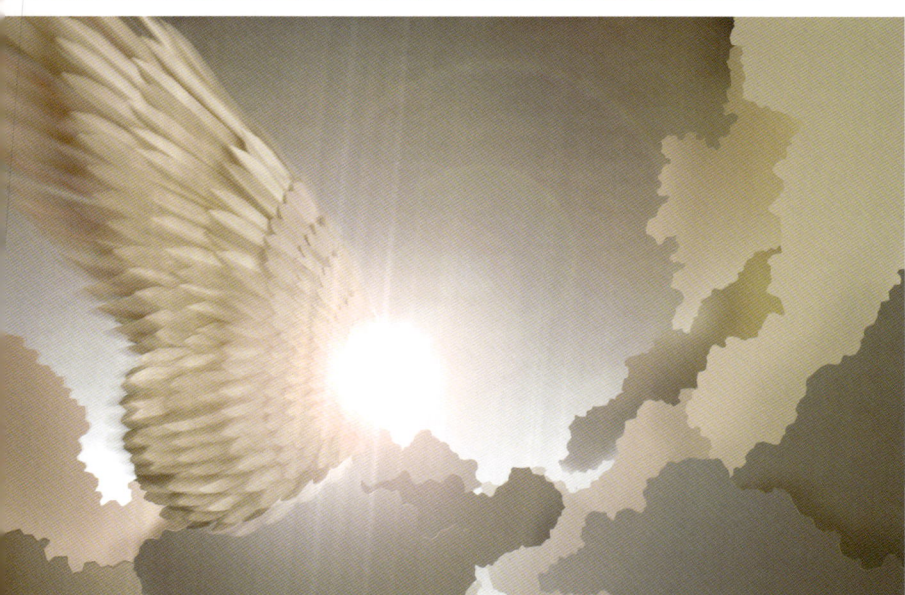
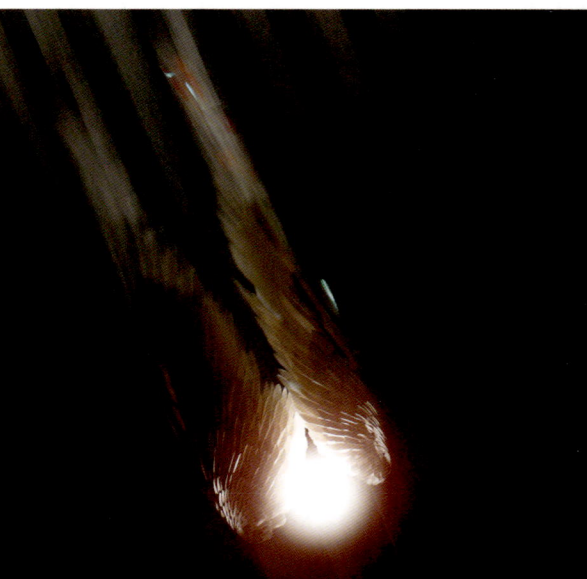

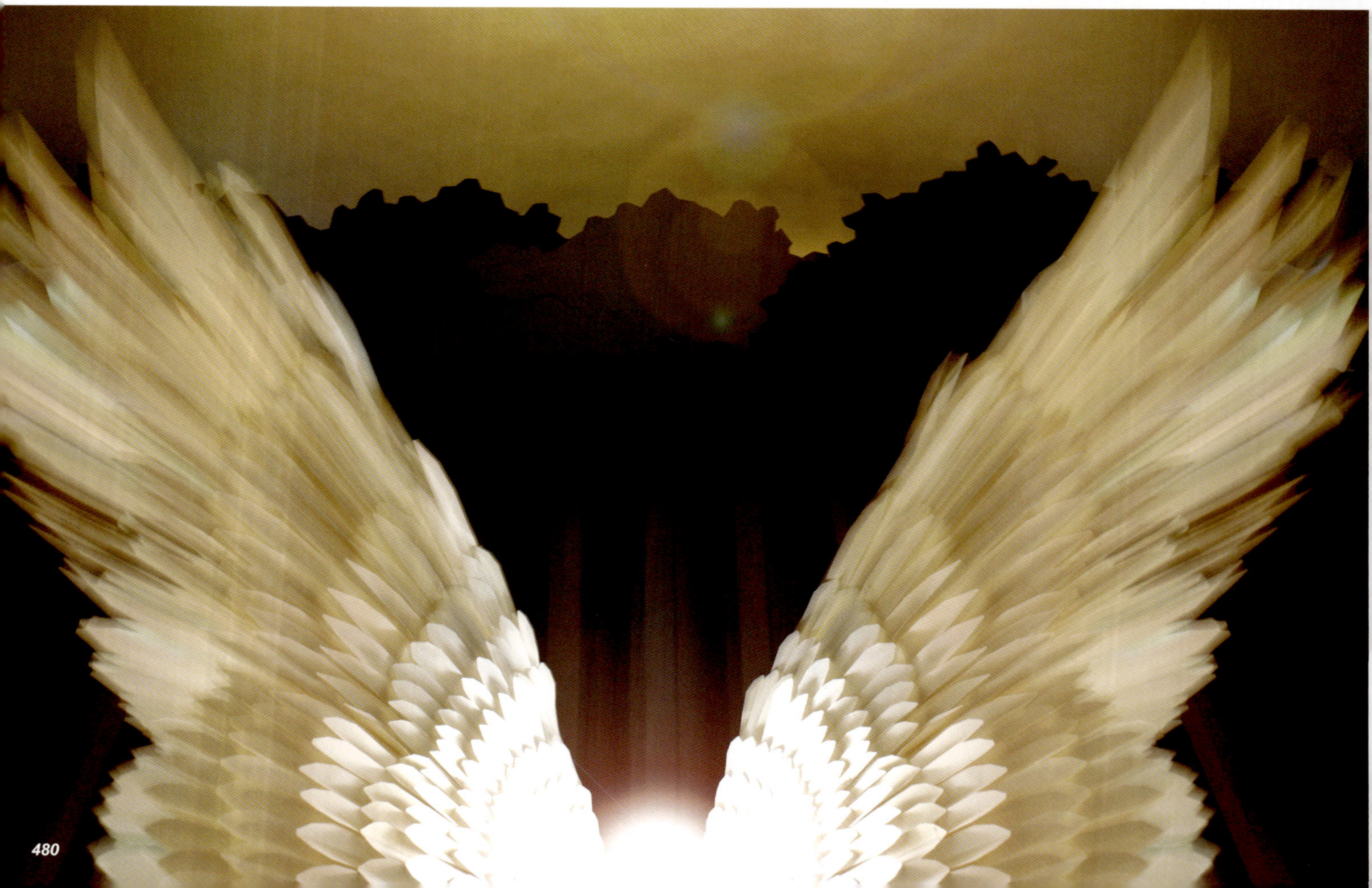

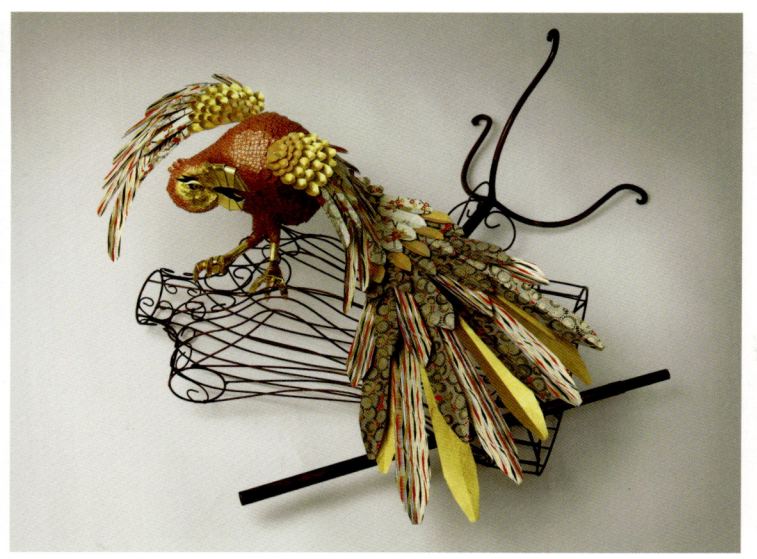
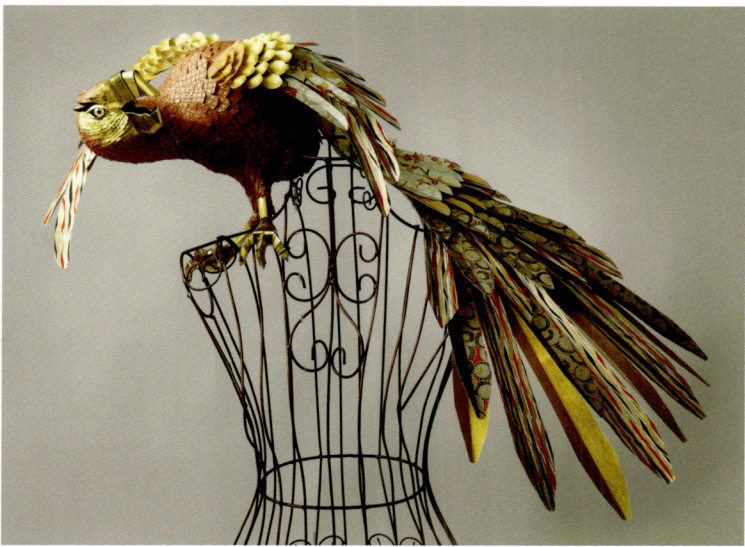

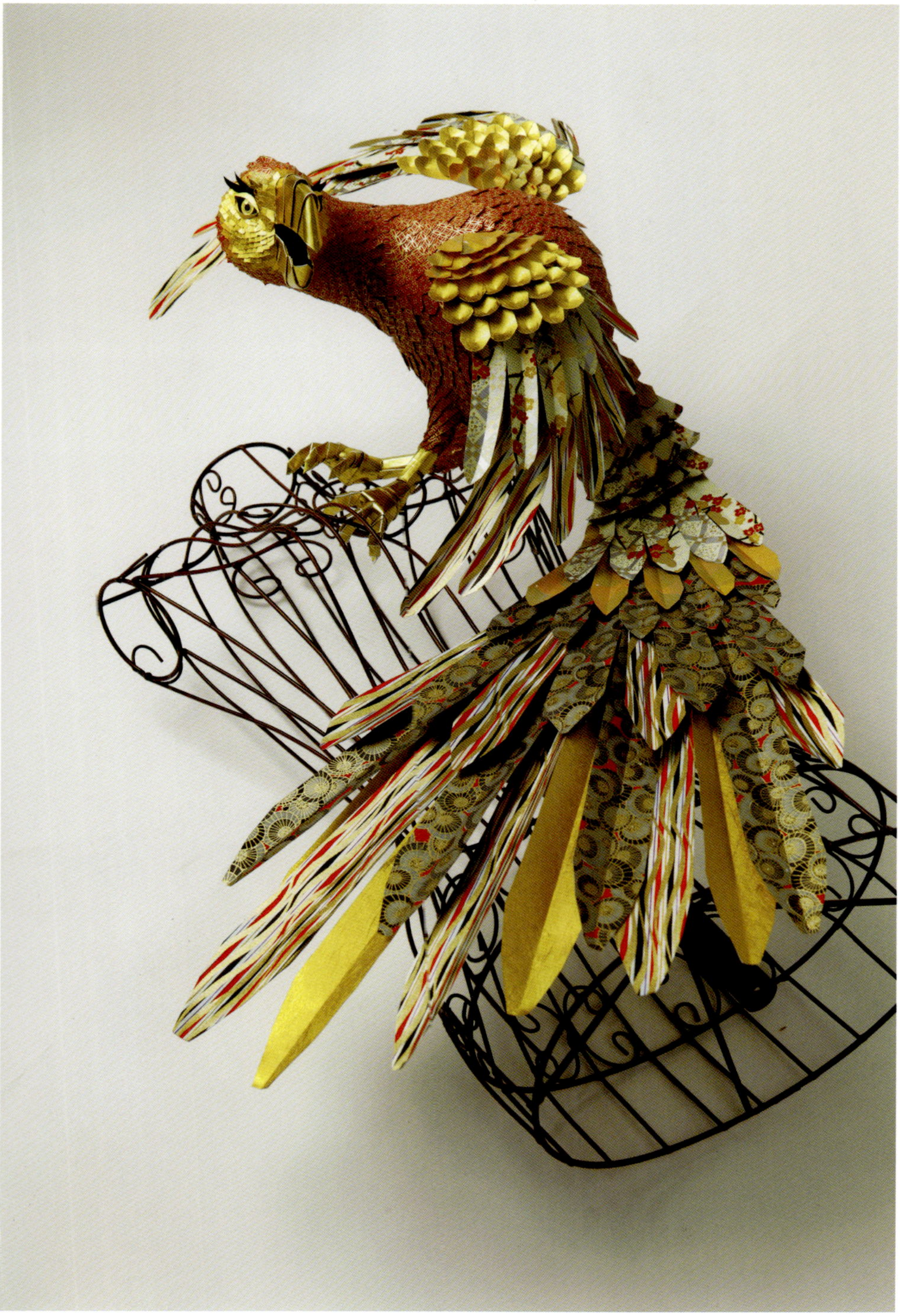

9. Fabriano Collier

Conceptual piece of jewellery design created for Fabriano's 2011 exhibition 'L'Arte é un Gioiello', held in the historical town where paper was born and featuring selected international artists. The piece is made using hand made oriental papers and gold foil detailing.

Designer: The Makerie Studio
Country: UK
Client: Fabriano (Italy)
Photographer: Nathan Gallagher

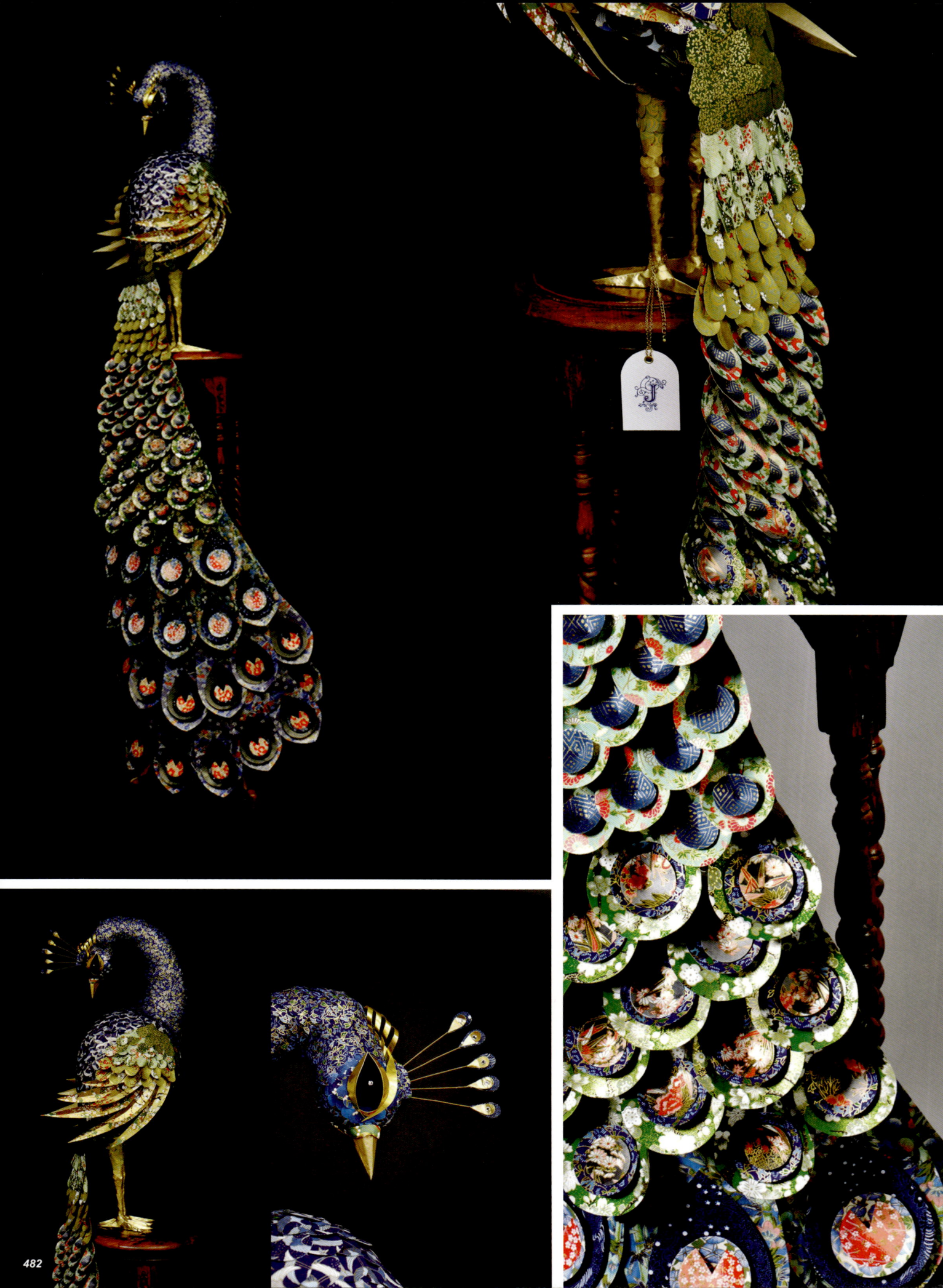

482

10. The Great Omar

Life size reproduction of a peacock inspired by the cover of The Great Omar, a collection of Persian poems known as the most precious volume ever bound. The sculpture was produced for London paper merchants Shepherds Bookbinders using papers from their range, and is currently displayed in their Holborn store.

Designer: The Makerie Studio
Country: UK
Client: Sangorski & Sutcliffe

11. The White Omar

The White Omar is a piece that explores the structure and form of patterns and shapes previously developed for an existing piece, The Great Omar, as a way of stripping back colour to highlight contours and light play across the surfaces. Currently being developed as a centre piece for a London boutique display.

Designer: The Makerie Studio
Country: UK
Photographer: Nathan Gallagher

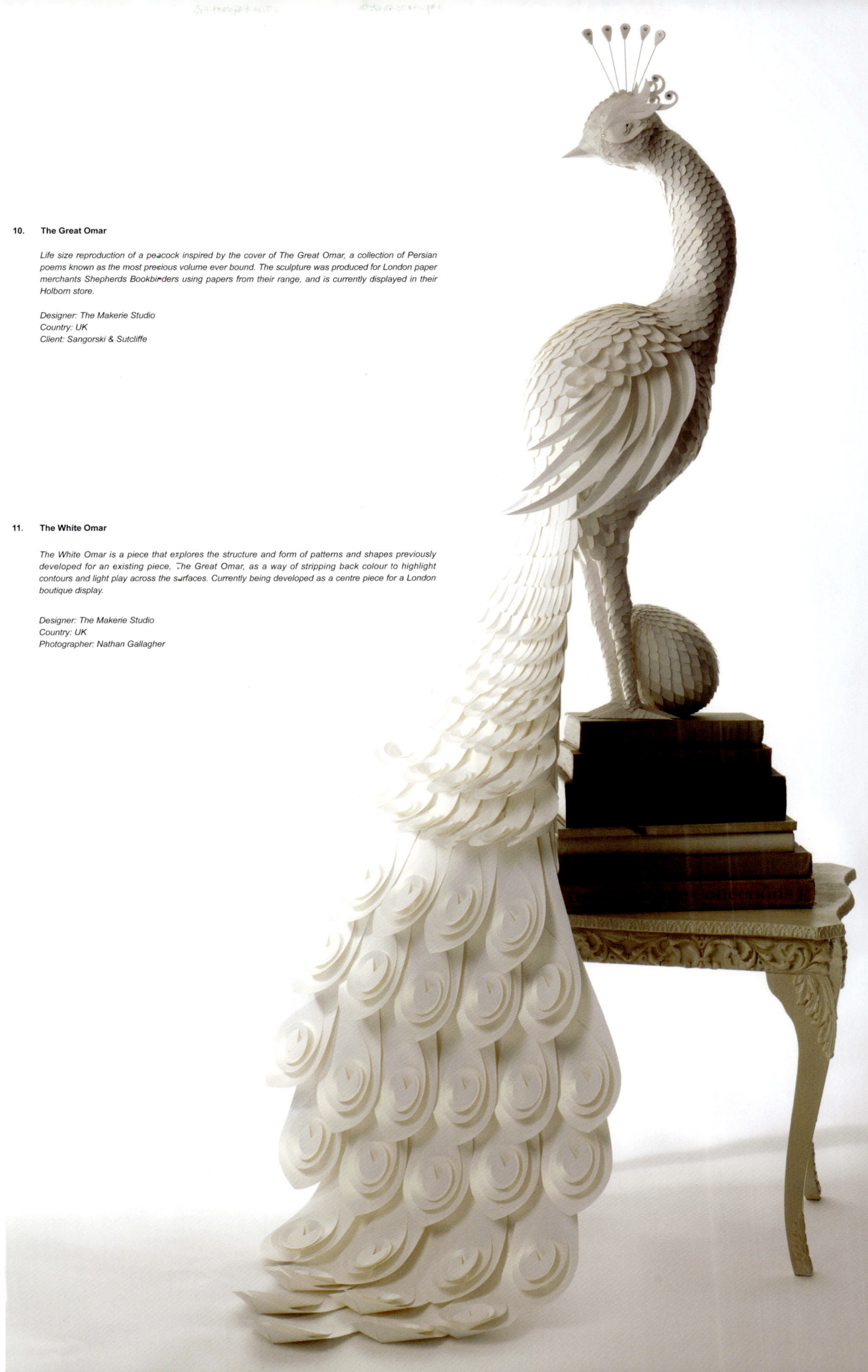

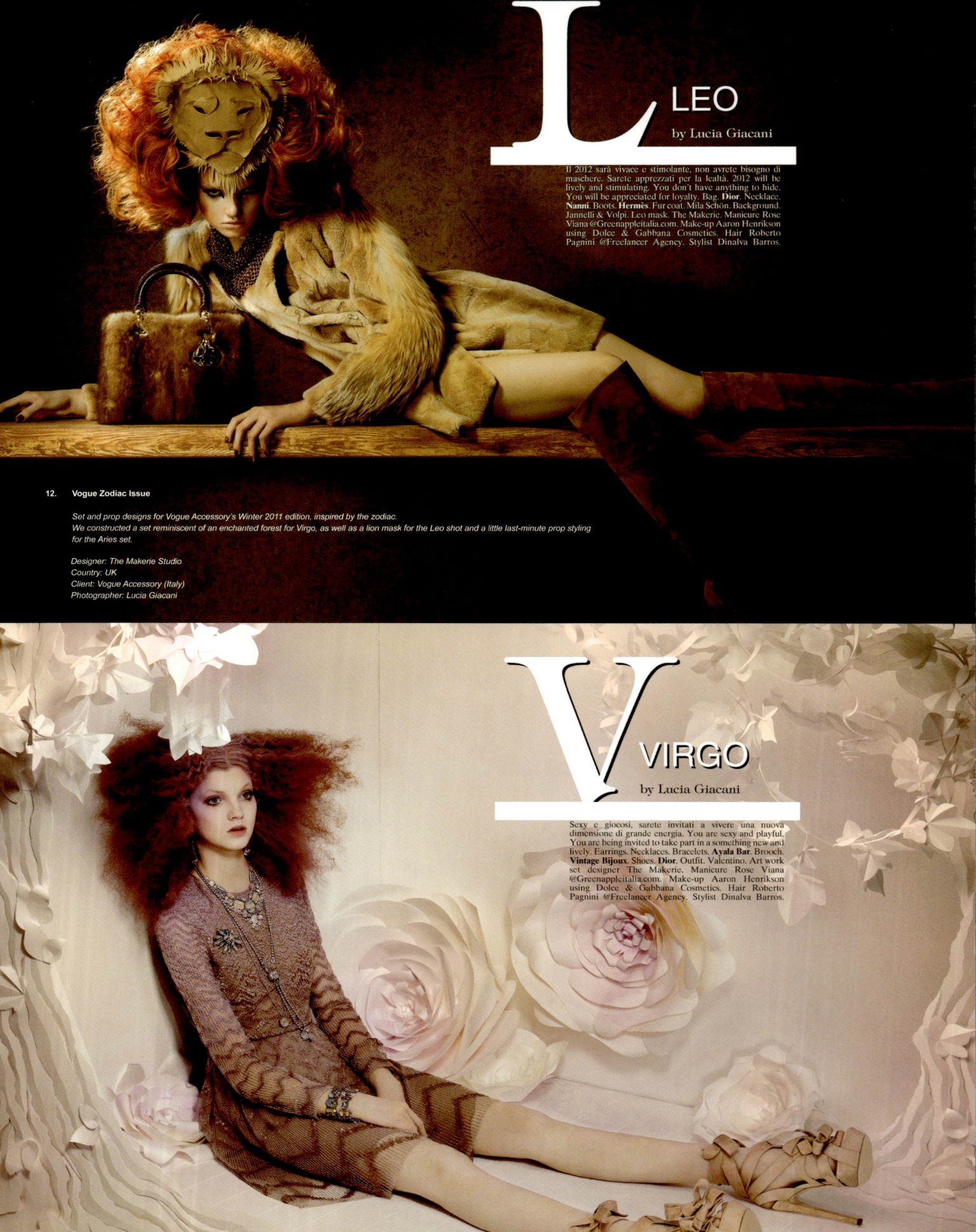

L LEO
by Lucia Giacani

Il 2012 sarà vivace e stimolante, non avrete bisogno di maschere. Sarete apprezzati per la lealtà. 2012 will be lively and stimulating. You don't have anything to hide. You will be appreciated for loyalty. Bag. **Dior**. Necklace. **Nanni**. Boots. **Hermès**. Fur coat. Mila Schön. Background. Jannelli & Volpi. Leo mask. The Makerie. Manicure Rose Viana @Greenappleitalia.com. Make-up Aaron Henrikson using Dolce & Gabbana Cosmetics. Hair Roberto Pagnini @Freelancer Agency. Stylist Dinalva Barros.

12. Vogue Zodiac Issue

Set and prop designs for Vogue Accessory's Winter 2011 edition, inspired by the zodiac.
We constructed a set reminiscent of an enchanted forest for Virgo, as well as a lion mask for the Leo shot and a little last-minute prop styling for the Aries set.

Designer: The Makerie Studio
Country: UK
Client: Vogue Accessory (Italy)
Photographer: Lucia Giacani

V VIRGO
by Lucia Giacani

Sexy e giocosi, sarete invitati a vivere una nuova dimensione di grande energia. You are sexy and playful. You are being invited to take part in a something new and lively. Earrings. Necklaces. Bracelets. **Ayala Bar**. Brooch. **Vintage Bijoux**. Shoes. **Dior**. Outfit. Valentino. Art work set designer The Makerie. Manicure Rose Viana @Greenappleitalia.com. Make-up Aaron Henrikson using Dolce & Gabbana Cosmetics. Hair Roberto Pagnini @Freelancer Agency. Stylist Dinalva Barros.

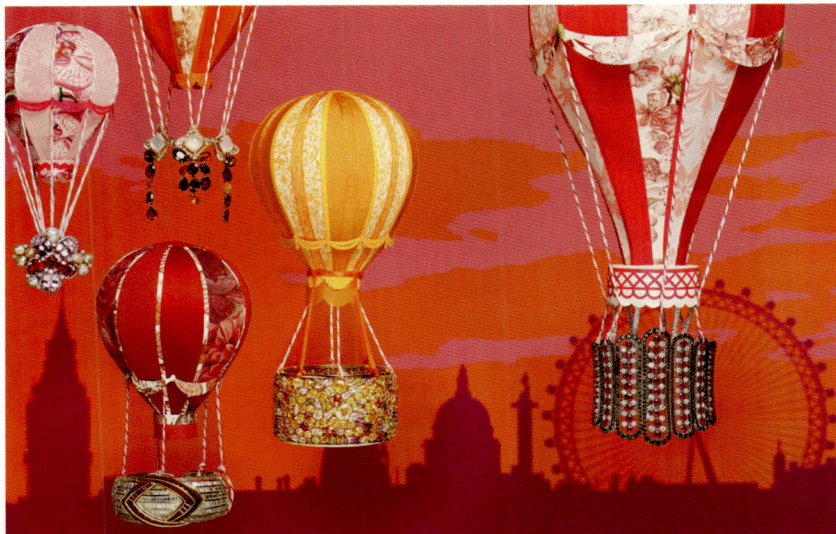
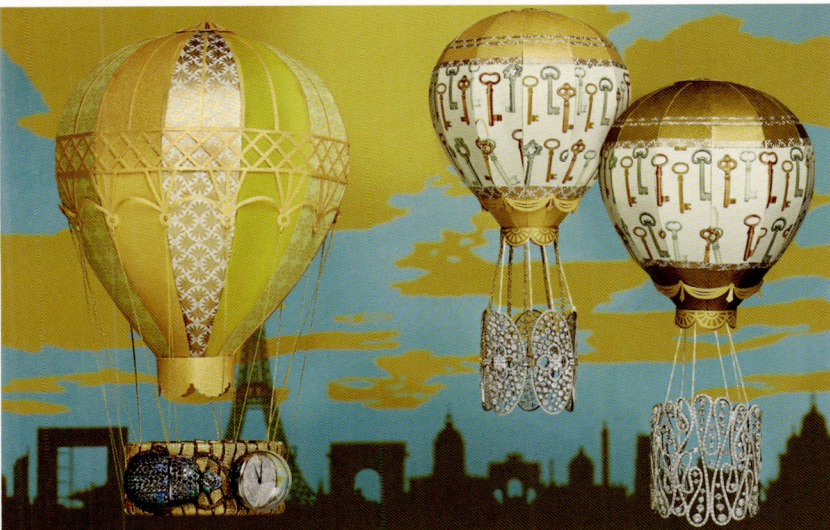
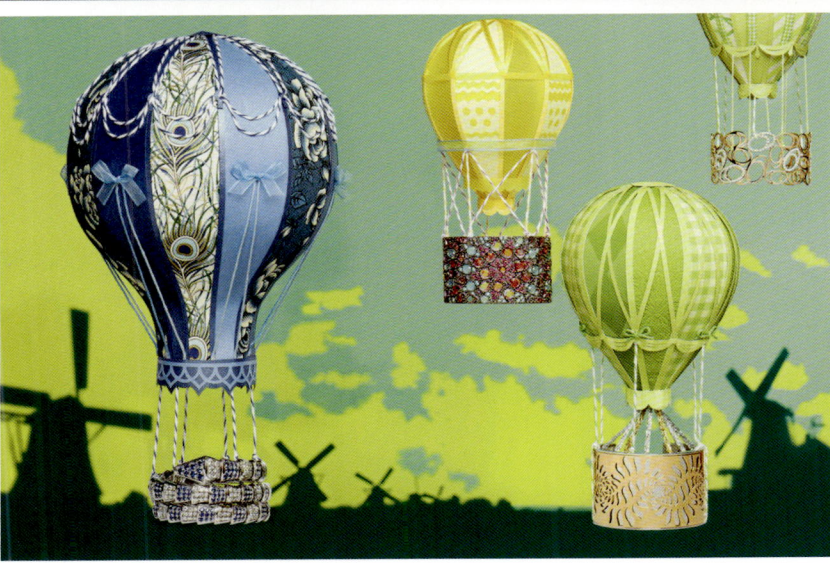
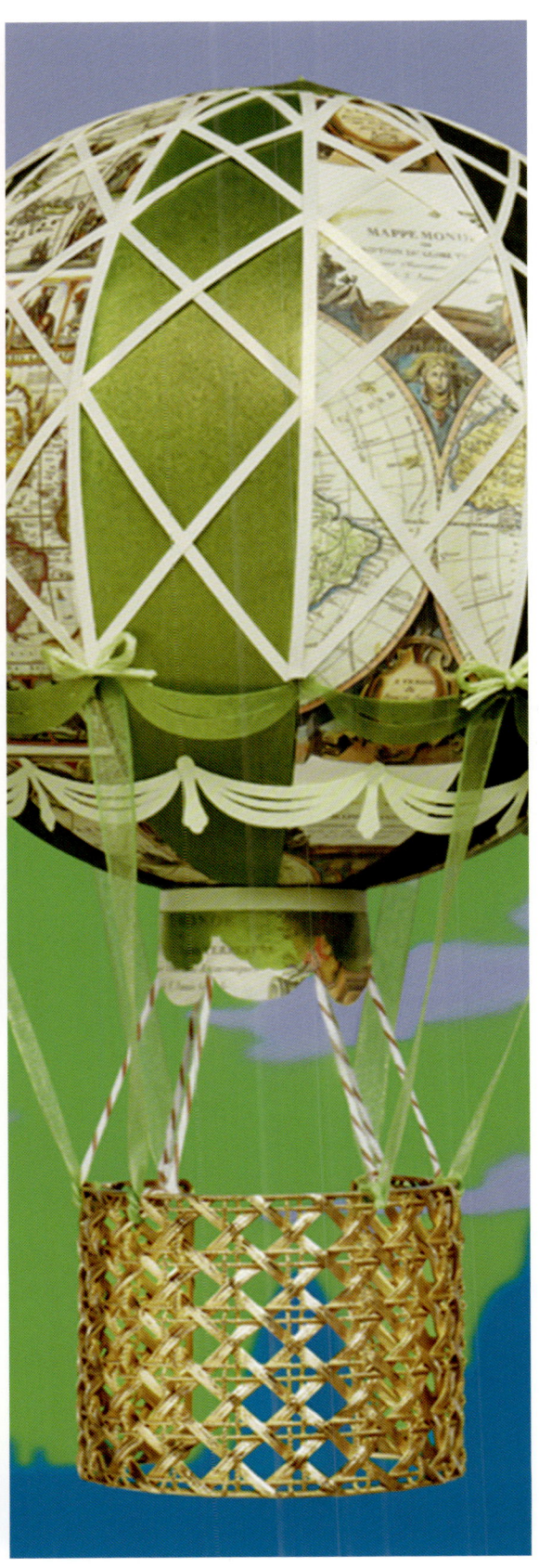

13. **Vogue Gioiello Golden Dreams**

Miniature hot air balloons created for Vogue Gioiello's May edition and featured as the cover story.
The balloons were created using patterned and textured papers as well as ribbons and divine twine, and beautifully photographed by the lovely Barbara Donninelli.

Designer: The Makerie Studio
Country: UK
Client: Vogue Gioiello (Italy)
Photographer: Barbara Donninelli

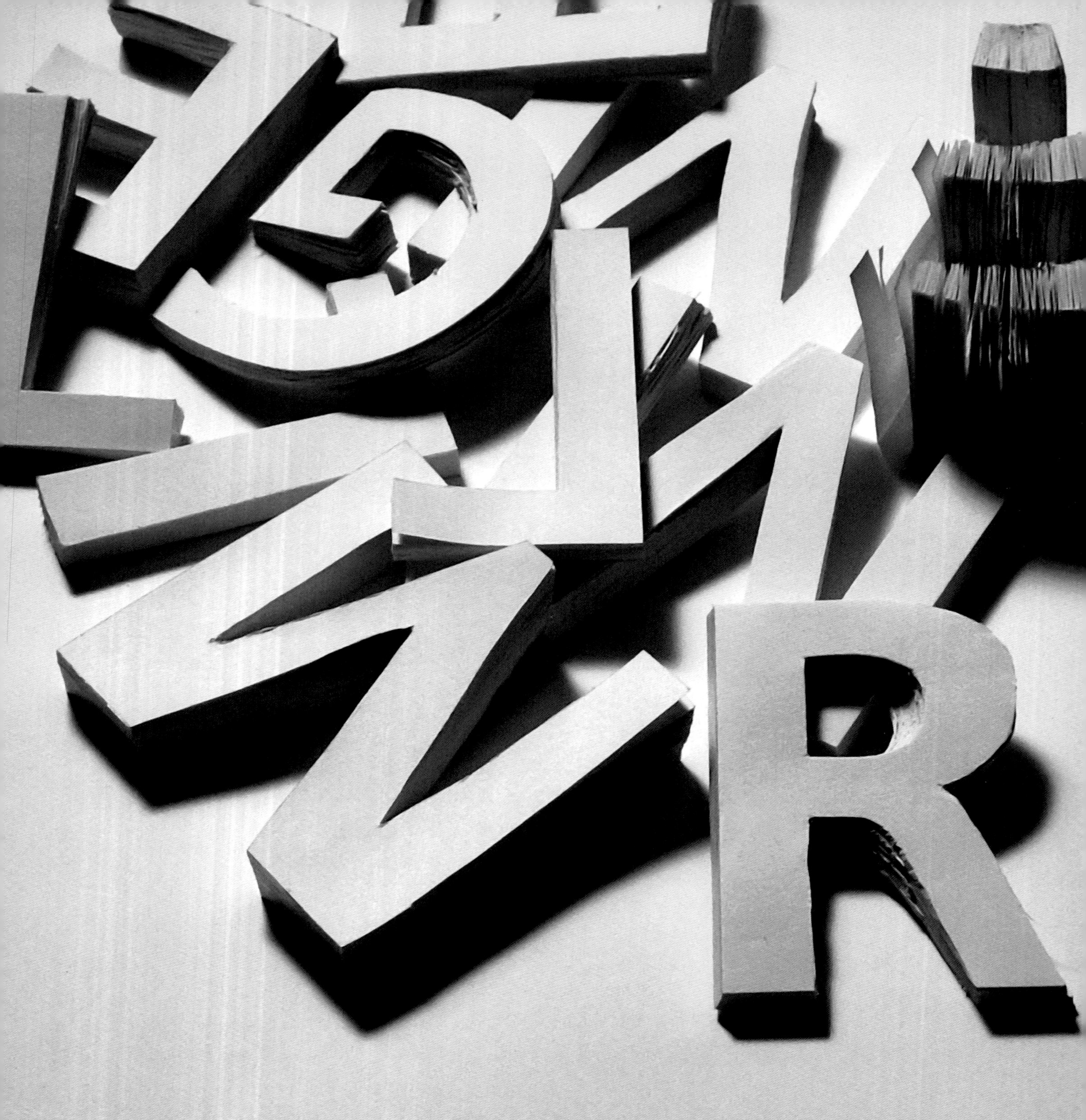

1. **Re-design of "Mérleg könyvek" book series**

My design consists in the re-design of 'Mérleg könyvek' (Balance Books) a book series composed mainly of essays in philosophy and aesthetics. The overall conception unifying the individual volumes is that every cover features a photograph of a hand-made (folded, crumpled, burnt-out etc.), paper-based letterform composition, making use of the optical possibilities offered by light/shadow effects. The individual compositions make thematic reference to the topics discussed in the books. The overall conception refers to the mutually facilitating dynamic of idea, letter and paper in the experience of reading.
Technique: Paper cutout, three-dimensional letterforms.

Designer: Tímea Andorka
Country: Hungary
Client: Non-realized Design
Photographer: Tímea Andorka, Ákos Polgárdi

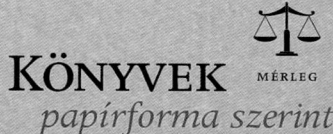

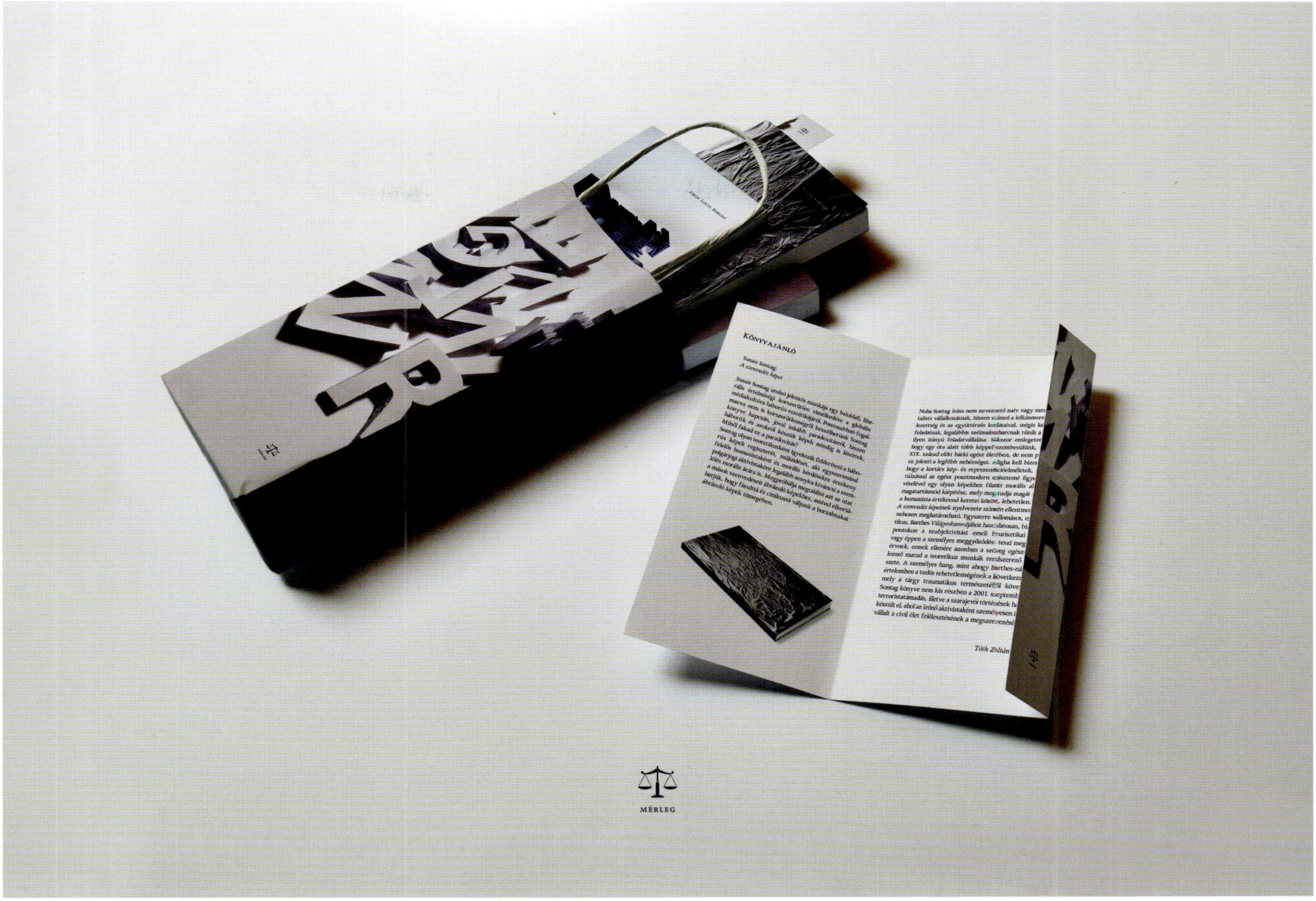

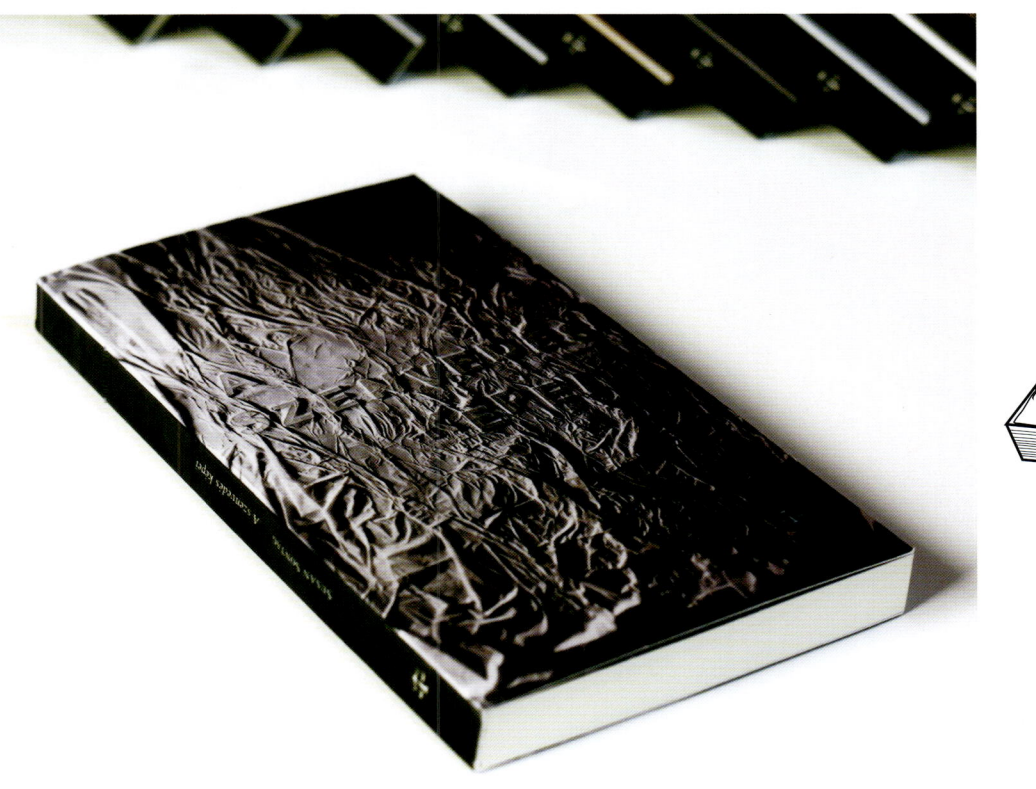
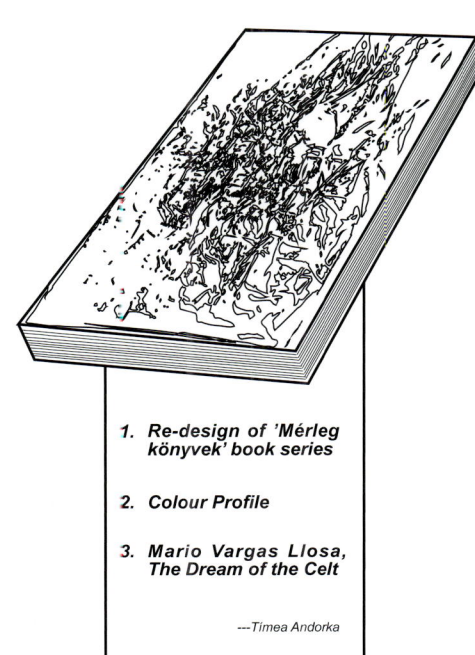

1. Re-design of 'Mérleg könyvek' book series
2. Colour Profile
3. Mario Vargas Llosa, The Dream of the Celt

---Tímea Andorka

1. Re-design of "Mérleg könyvek" book series

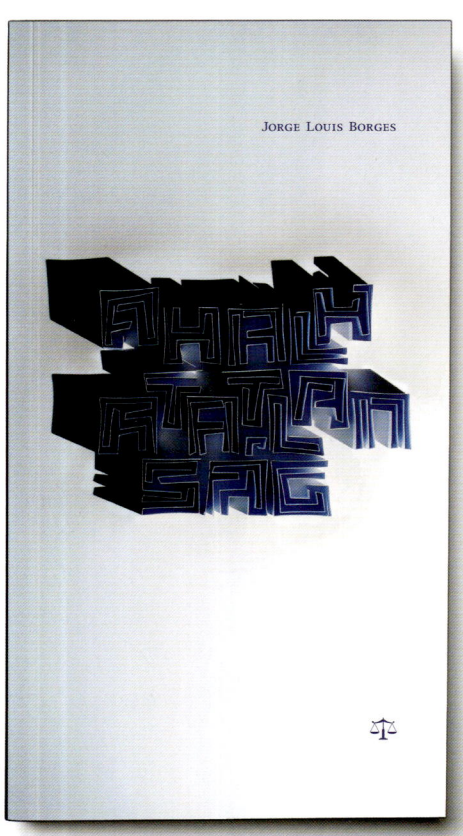

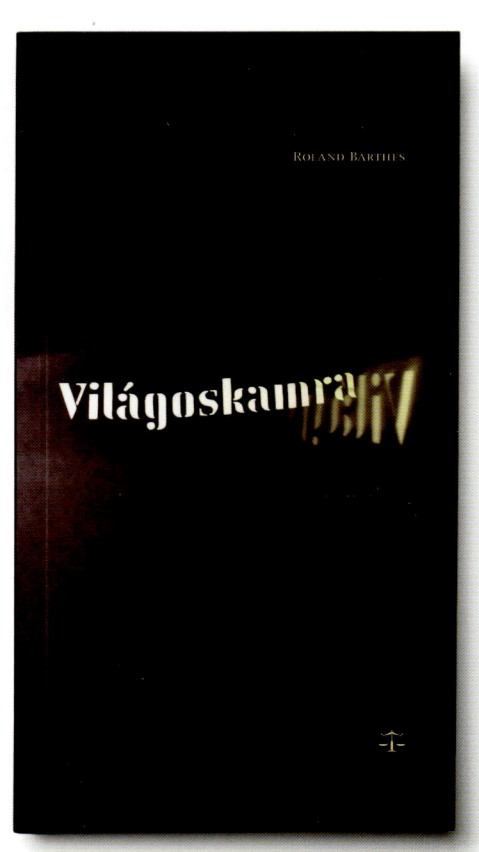

Designer: Timea Andorka
Country: Hungary
Client: Non-realized Design
Photographer: Timea Andorka, Akos Polgárdi

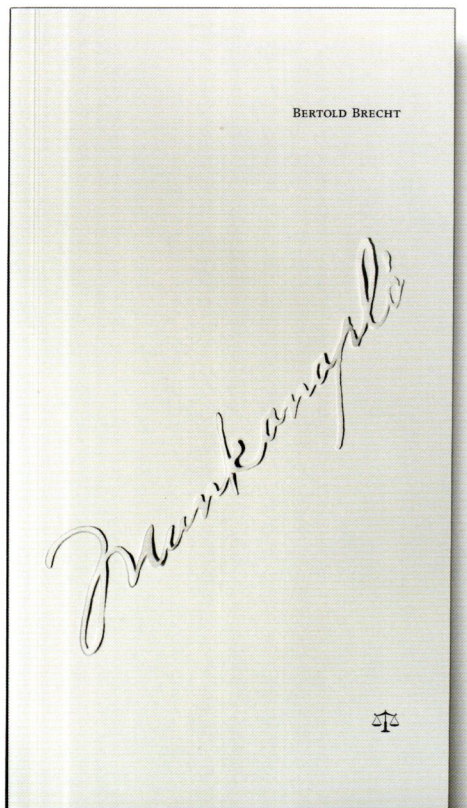

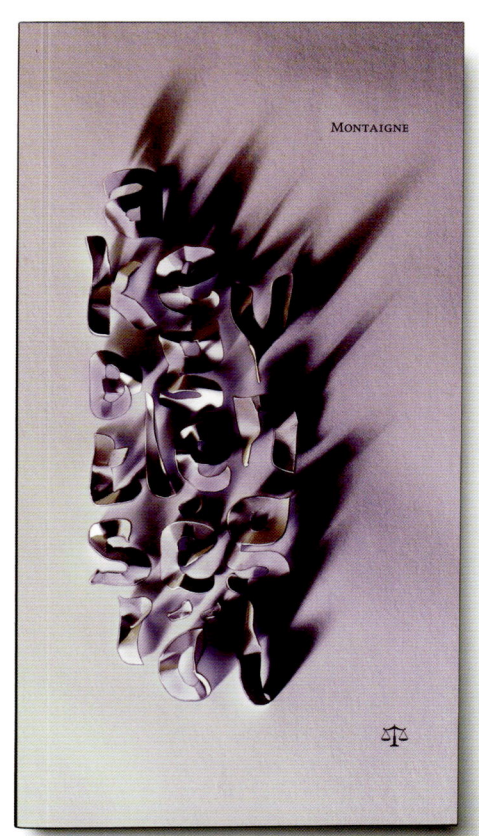

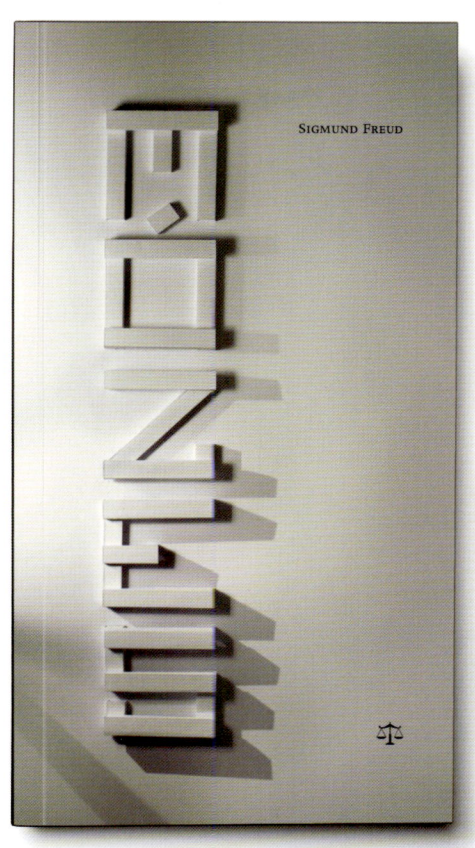
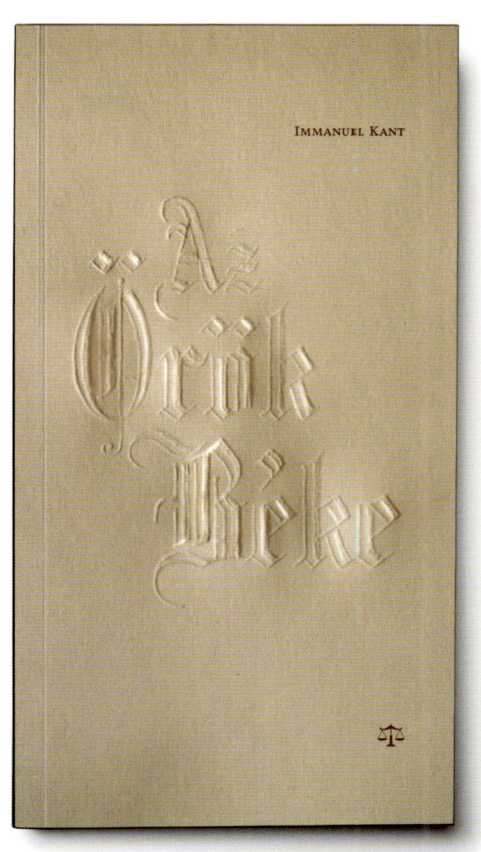
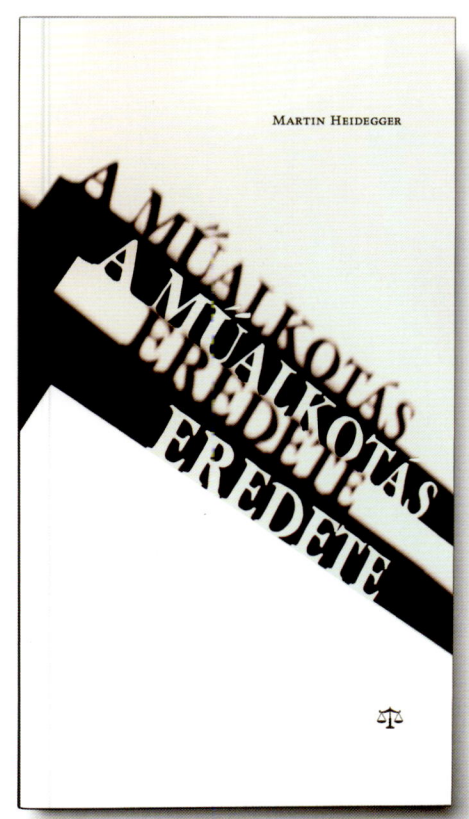
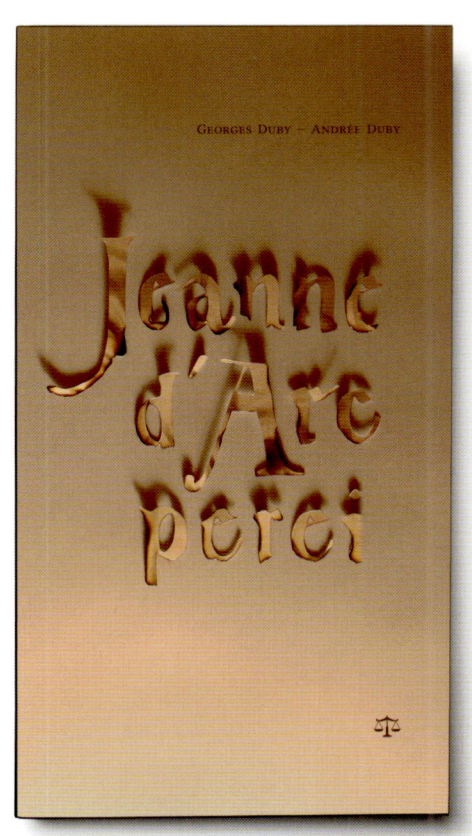

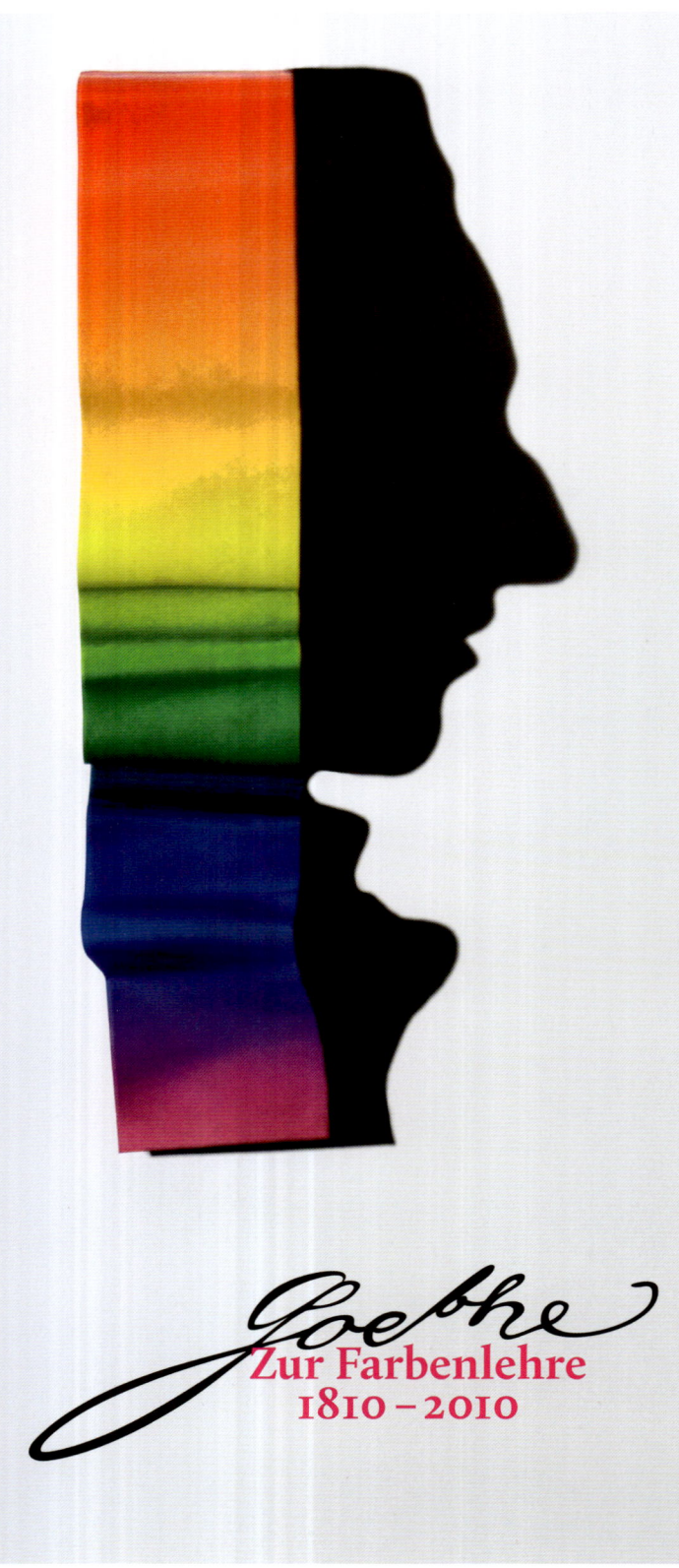

2. Colour Profile

On the occasion of the bicentennial anniversary of the first appearance of Goethe's 'Theory of Colours' the Society of Hungarian Graphic Designers and Typographers (MATT) announces an international design competition entitled 'Goetheorie'.

Goethe's interest in the experience of colour outlines his scientific profile – which is the metaphor elaborated on by the installation Colour Profile. In this case the figurative element of the composition is the shadow, traditionally conceived of as a lack of light and colour, which however appears and gives the impression of a bust only when the coloured stripe is lit from the appropriate angle.

Technique: folded colour paper strip, light, shadow.

Designer: Tímea Andorka
Country: Hungary

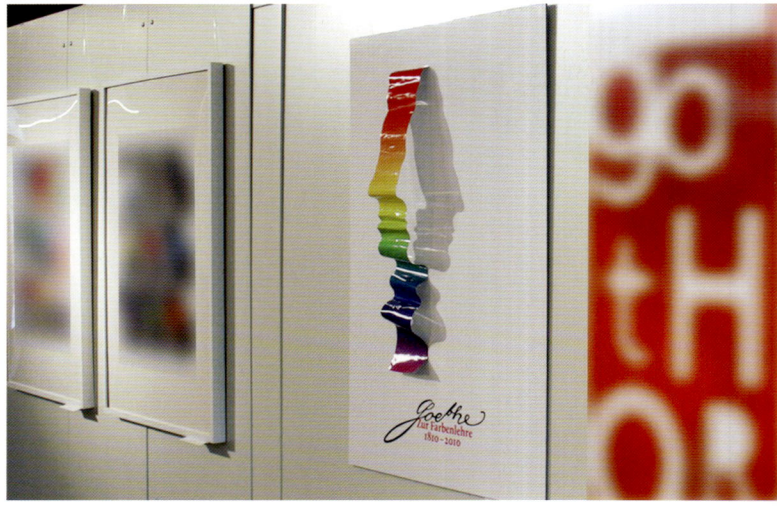

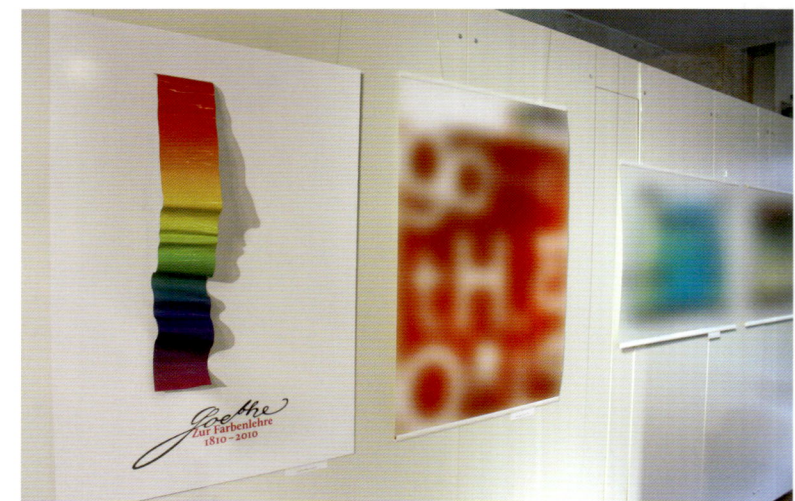

3. Mario Vargas Llosa, The Dream of the Celt

Cover design for the first volume of the new Vargas Llosa series edited in Hungary. The conception for the series consists in the combinative and thematically relevant use of the hand-cut paper layers. Here the layers of the cover-image expresses the different geographical and cultural dimensions of the narrative. Technique: paper cutting.

Designer: Tímea Andorka
Country: Hungary
Client: Európa Könyvkiadó (Európa Publishing House)
Photographer: Tímea Andorka

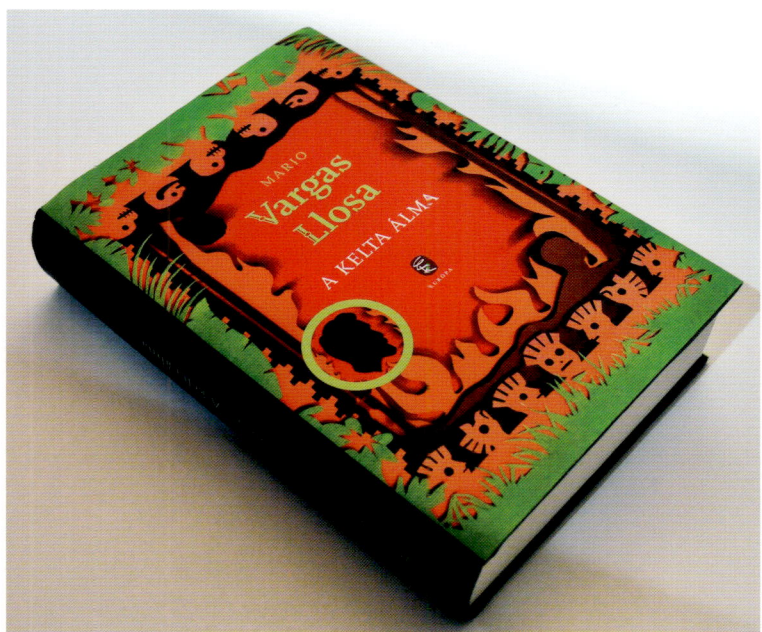
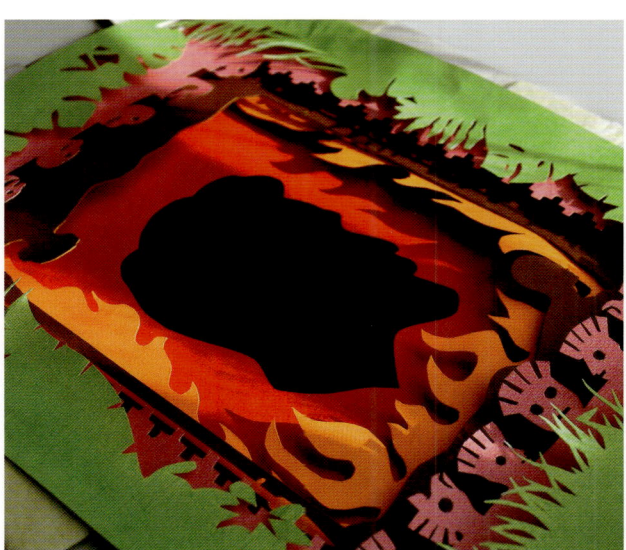
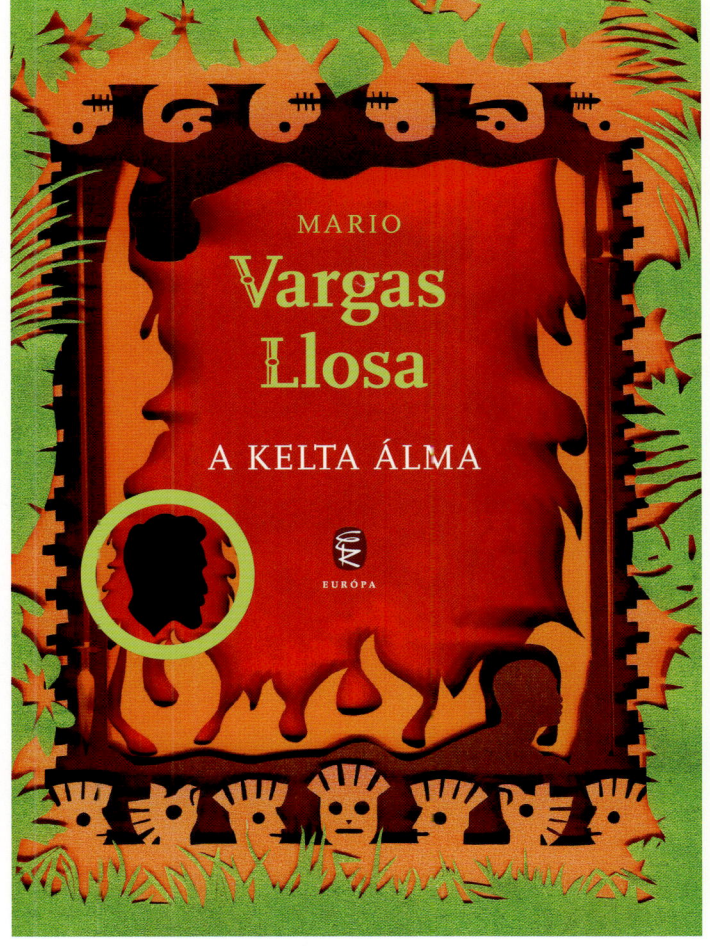
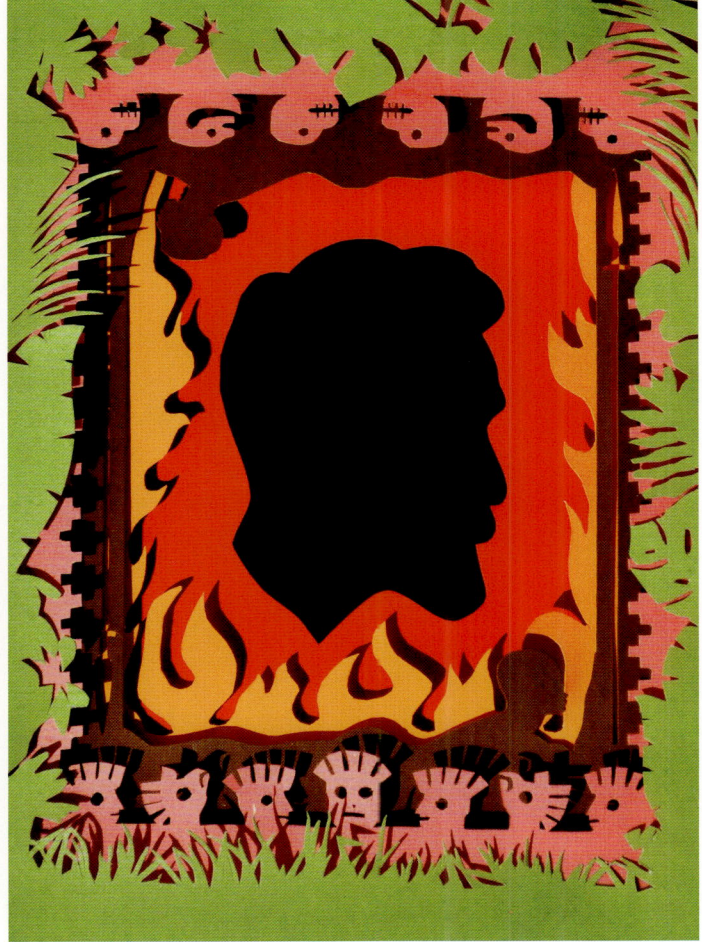

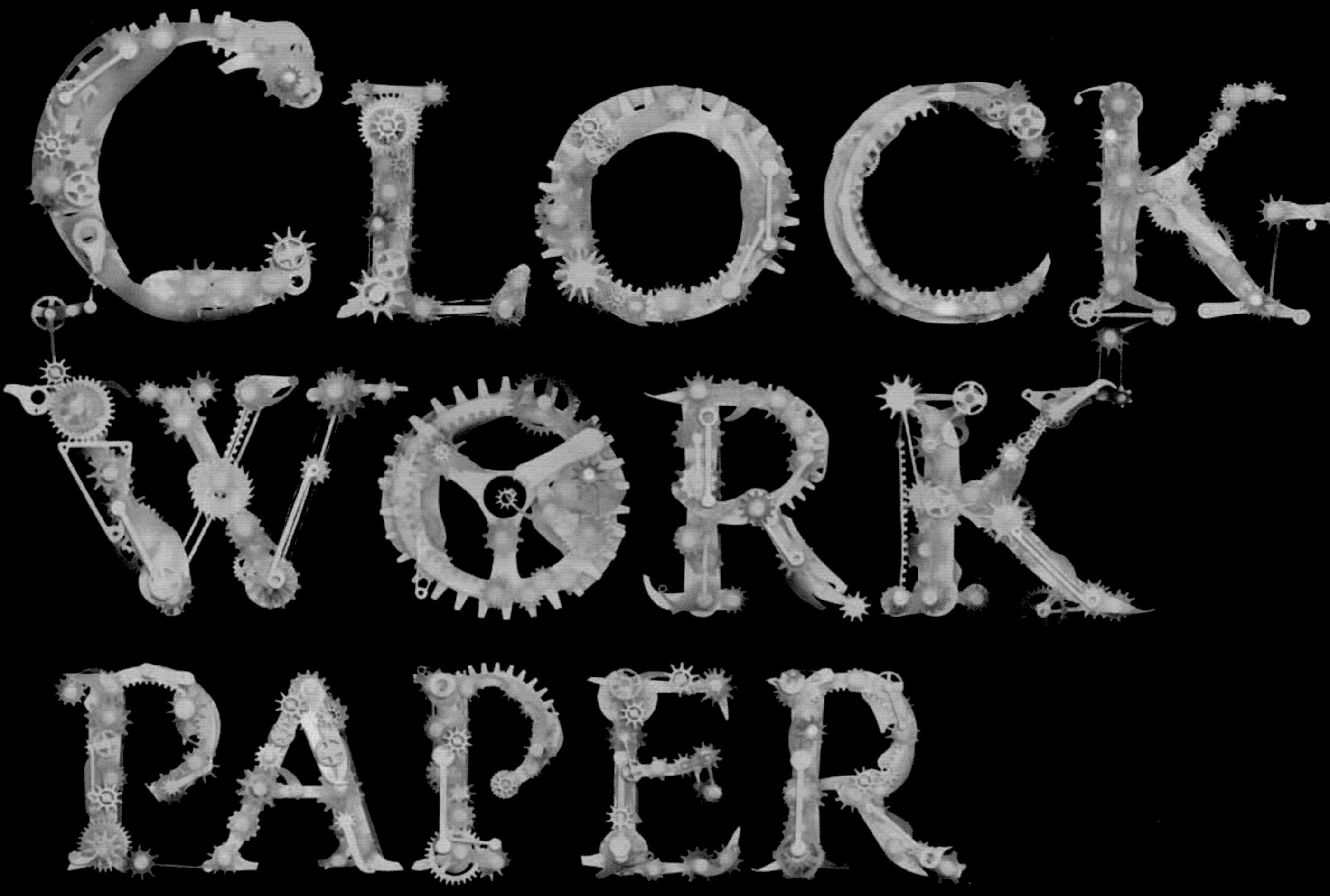

CLOCK-WORK PAPER

PDL Cigarette Papers stands for innovation,
experience and manufacturing process reliability.
The best guarantee for quality since 1920.

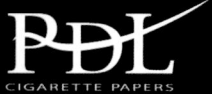

Roll Your Own, Cigarette paper
& Plug Wrap, LIP paper from
100% wood pulp to 100% flax.

www.pdlcigarettepapers.com

PDL PAPETERIES DU LÉMAN   B.P. 43   1080 Route Des Vignes Rouges   74 500 Publier, France
Global Account Manager   Francis Znidar   Tel +33 (0)4 50 17 05 79   Cell +33 (0)6 72 59 38 85   E-mail f.znidar@pdl.fr

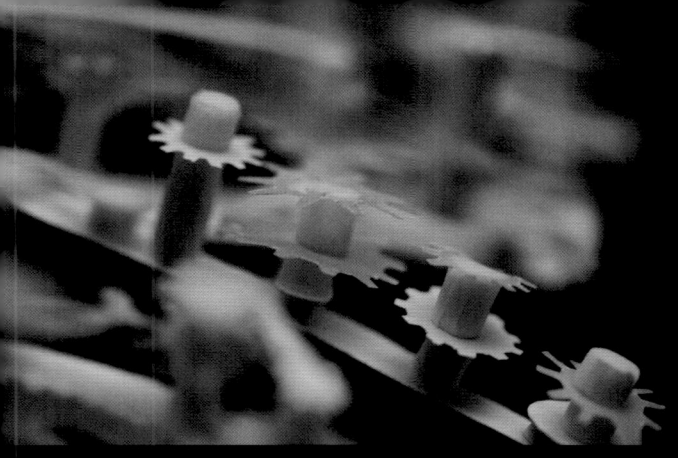
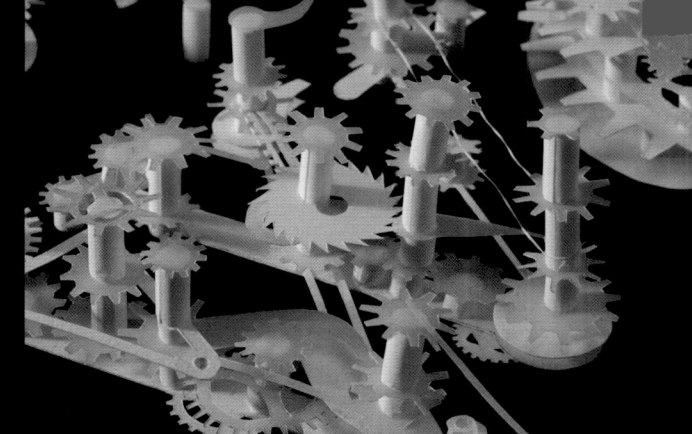
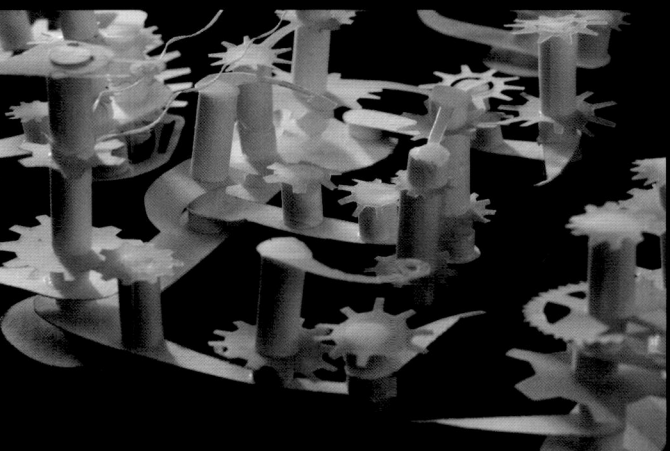
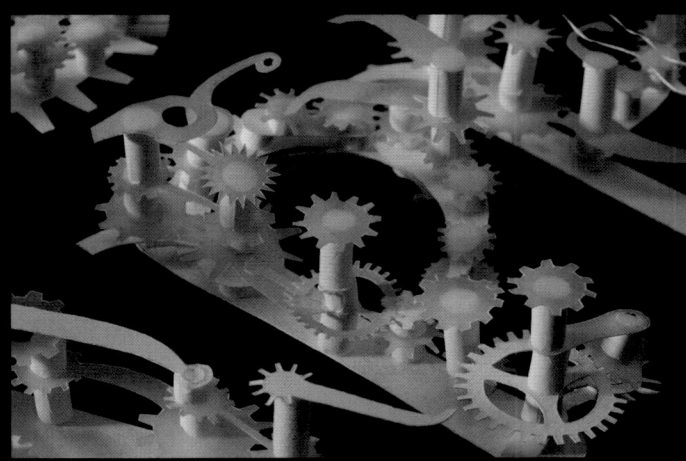
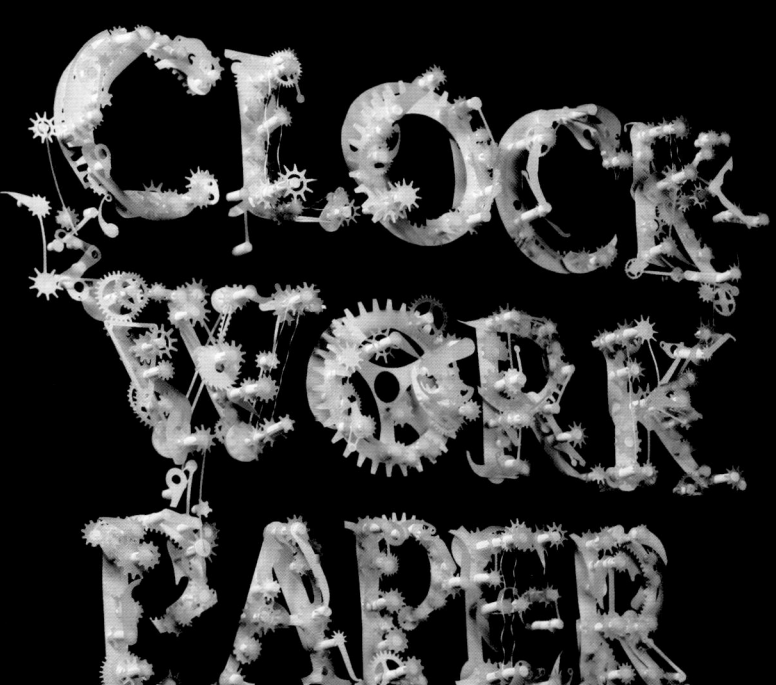
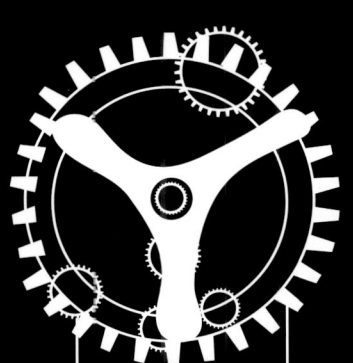

Clockwork Paper

Illustration work for PDL
Cigarette Papers advertisings
on specialized press.

Design Agency: United Fakes
Country: Spain
Creative Director: Marc Mallafré
(Agency Road)
Client: PDL Cigarette Papers

---United Fakes

1. Back to Basics

We've made those papercrafts for several reasons. At first it's a tribute to vintage technologies which marked the technological evolution of the last years, and all the nostalgia of the memories that each has with them. By getting these "obsolete" objects back to life, we tried to highlight the very fast evolution of our everyday possessions. The devices we use nowadays will in a few years be considered relics too. We decided to use paper because more than the fact that it's a basic material, accessible for everyone, it's a way to show the balance of power between digital and paper production. When today you can read a book on a screen, we needed to create "real" things. The aspect of craftmanship is really important for us. We wanted to turn an industrial object into a unique handmade craft. And the fact that the objects are not working places the user into a spectator position, a way to see the object out of its function.

Designer: Zim&Zou
Country: France

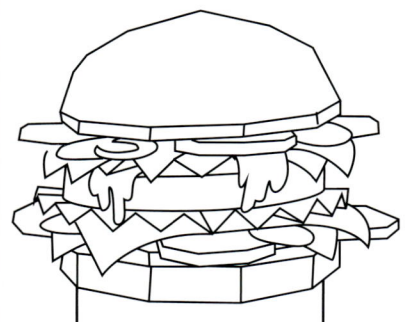

1. Back to Basics
2. New Tysons
3. Cabinet de Curiosités
4. Christmas Star
5. Dark Diamond
6. Lobster for Dinner
7. Coffee Dream
8. Low Gravity
9. Penguin Rider
10. Queensgate
11. The Future of Food

---Zim&Zou

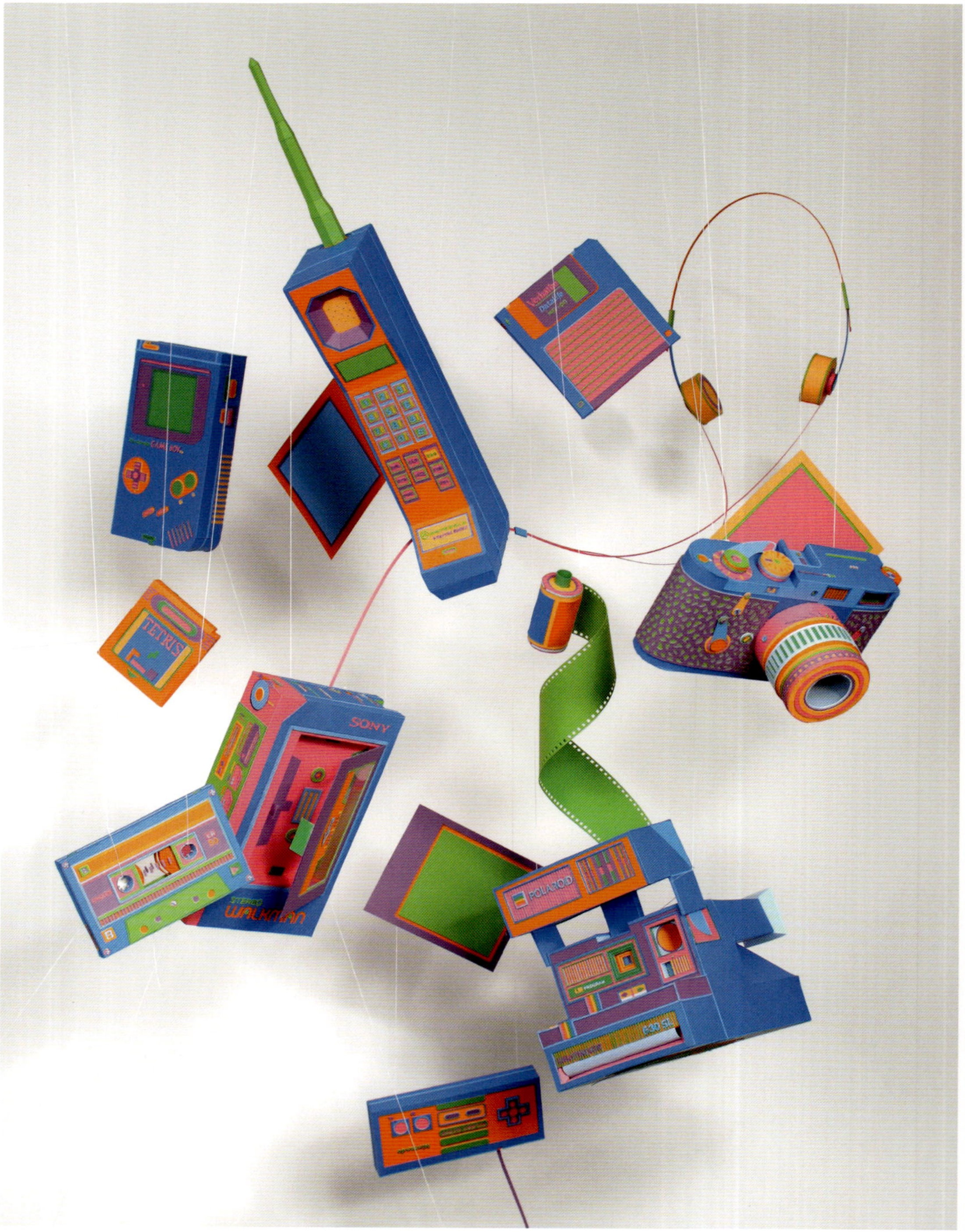

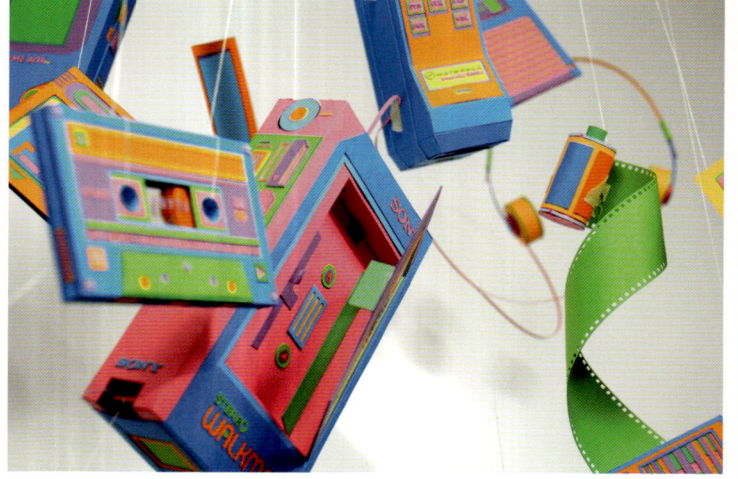

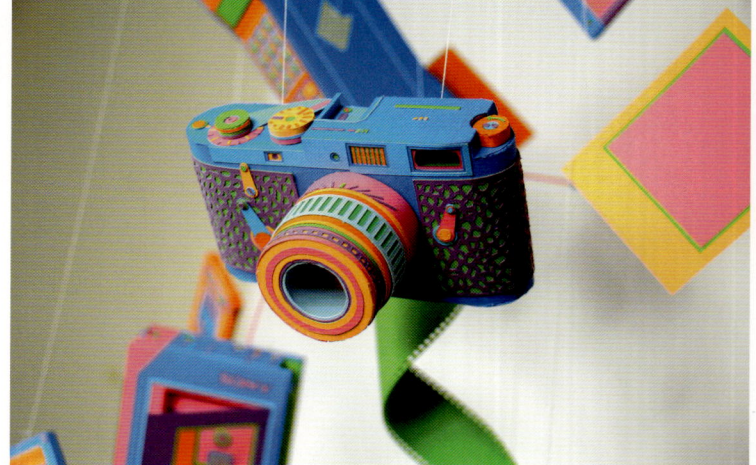

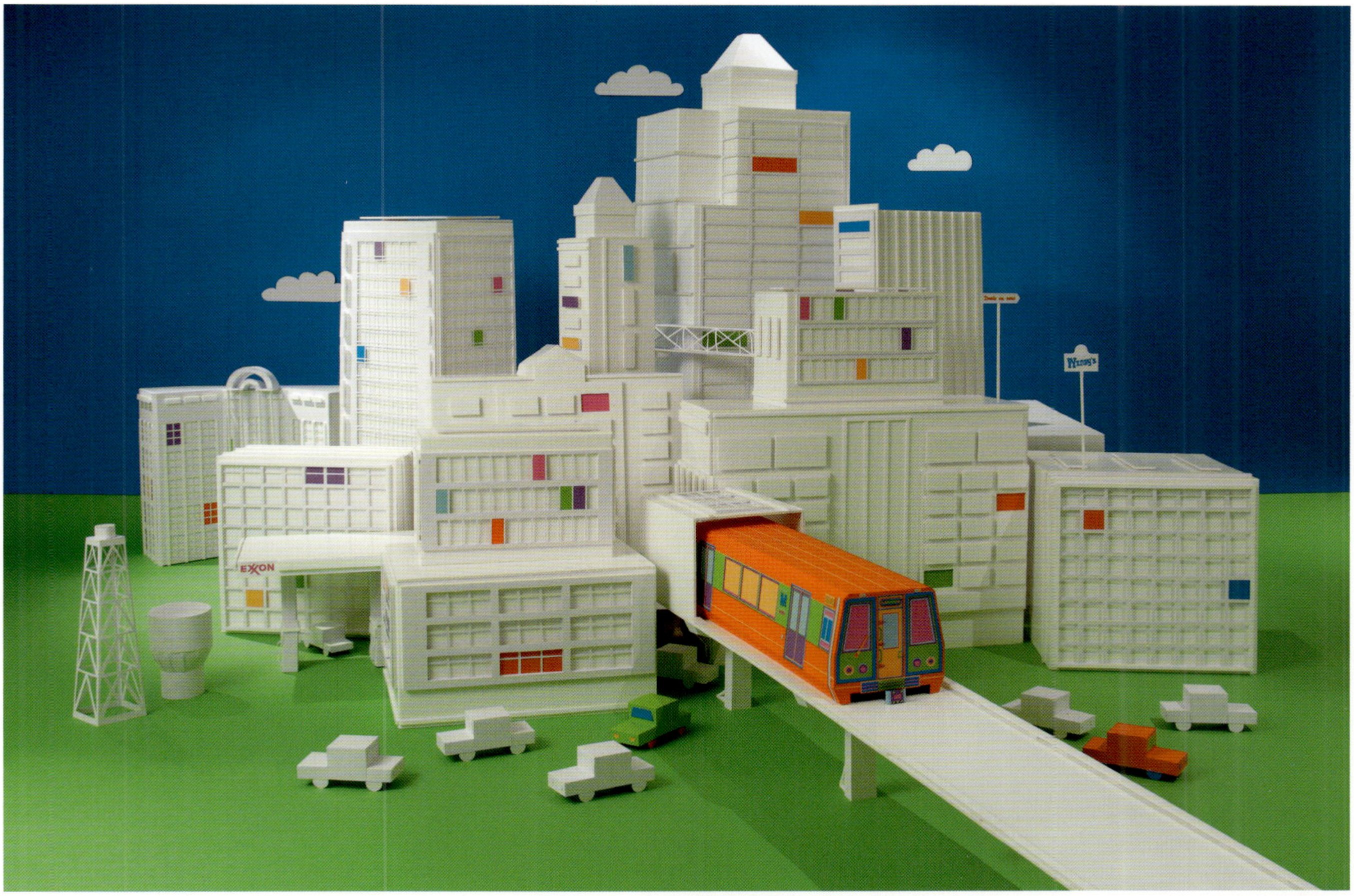

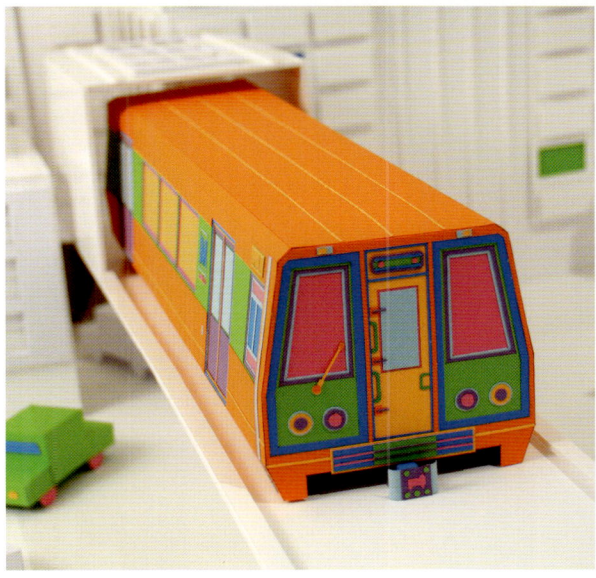

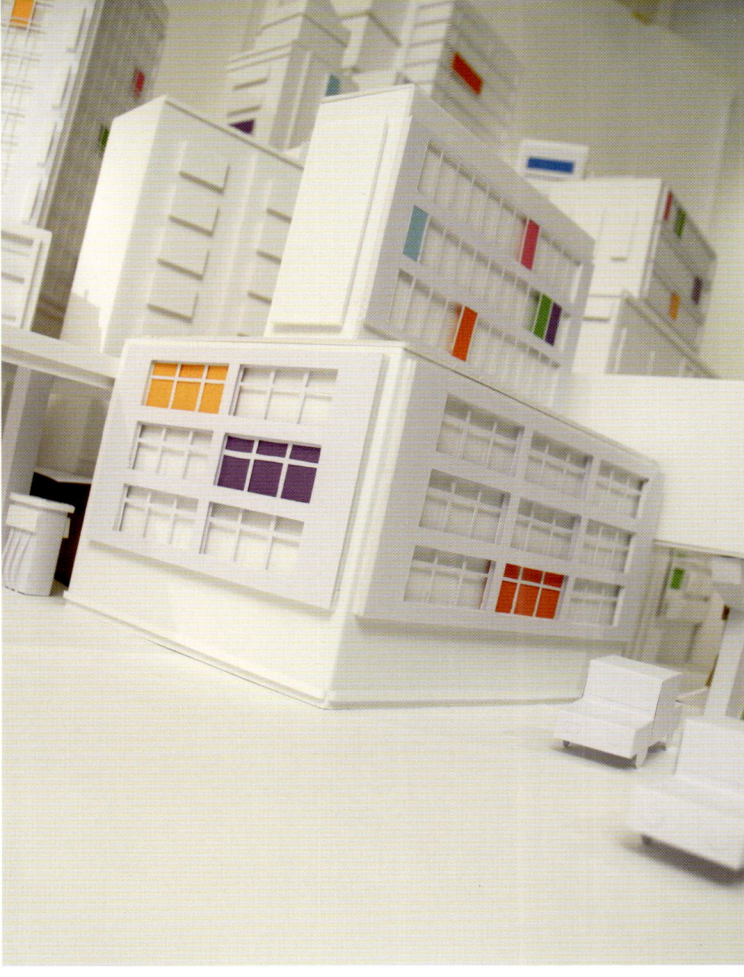

2. **New Tysons**

The story is about an area in the Washington DC suburbs, that is mainly offices, shopping and parking lots with tons and tons of cars. 4 metro stations will open out there. This car driven area will suddenly have more public transit. Right now it's kind of a soulless place, but they're hoping to make it more of a city. Hoping to add more pedestrian walkways, more apartments, more grocery stores - more of a place that people want to live, rather than just work.

Designer: Zim&Zou
Country: France
Client: Washington Post (USA)

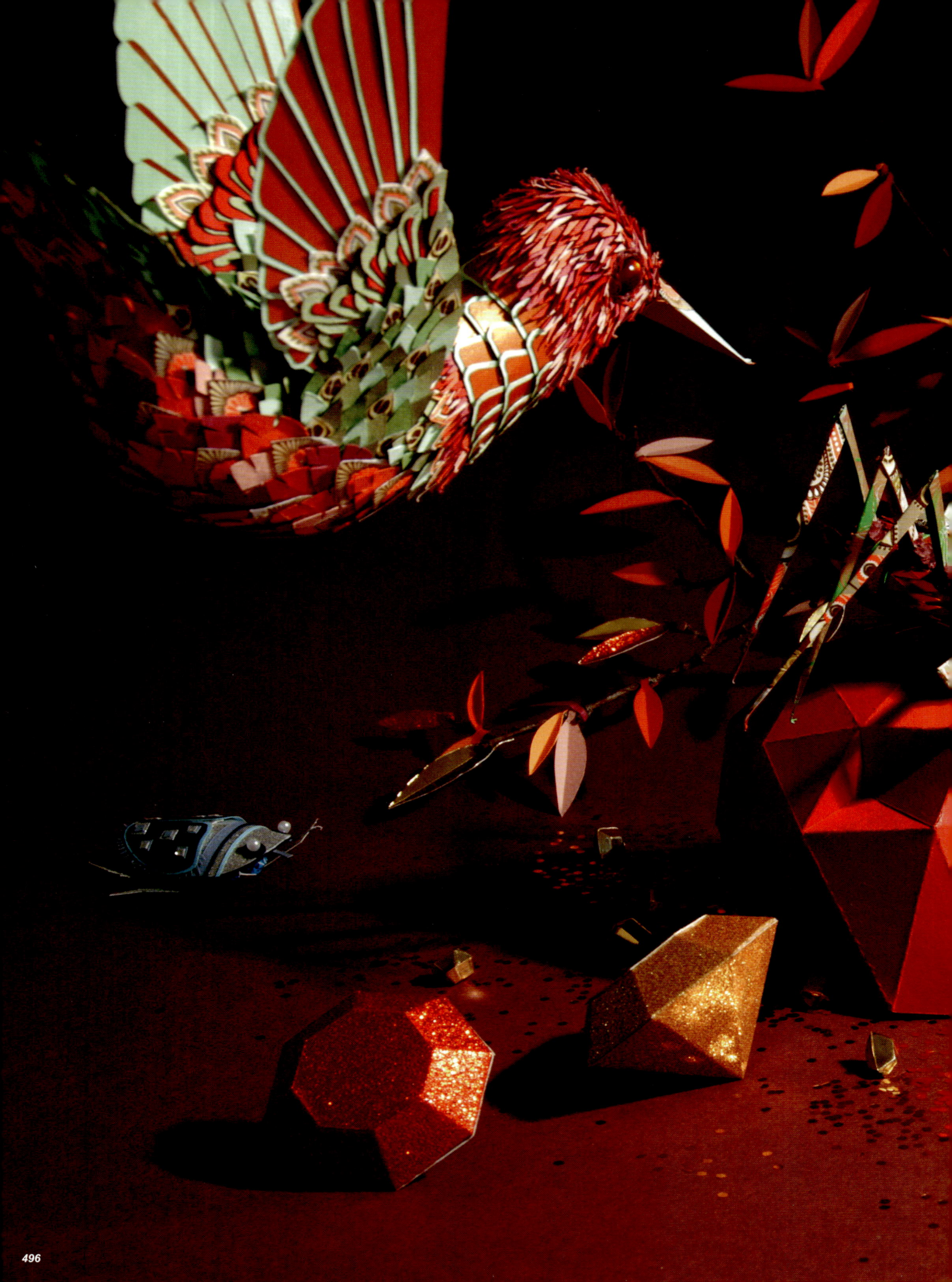

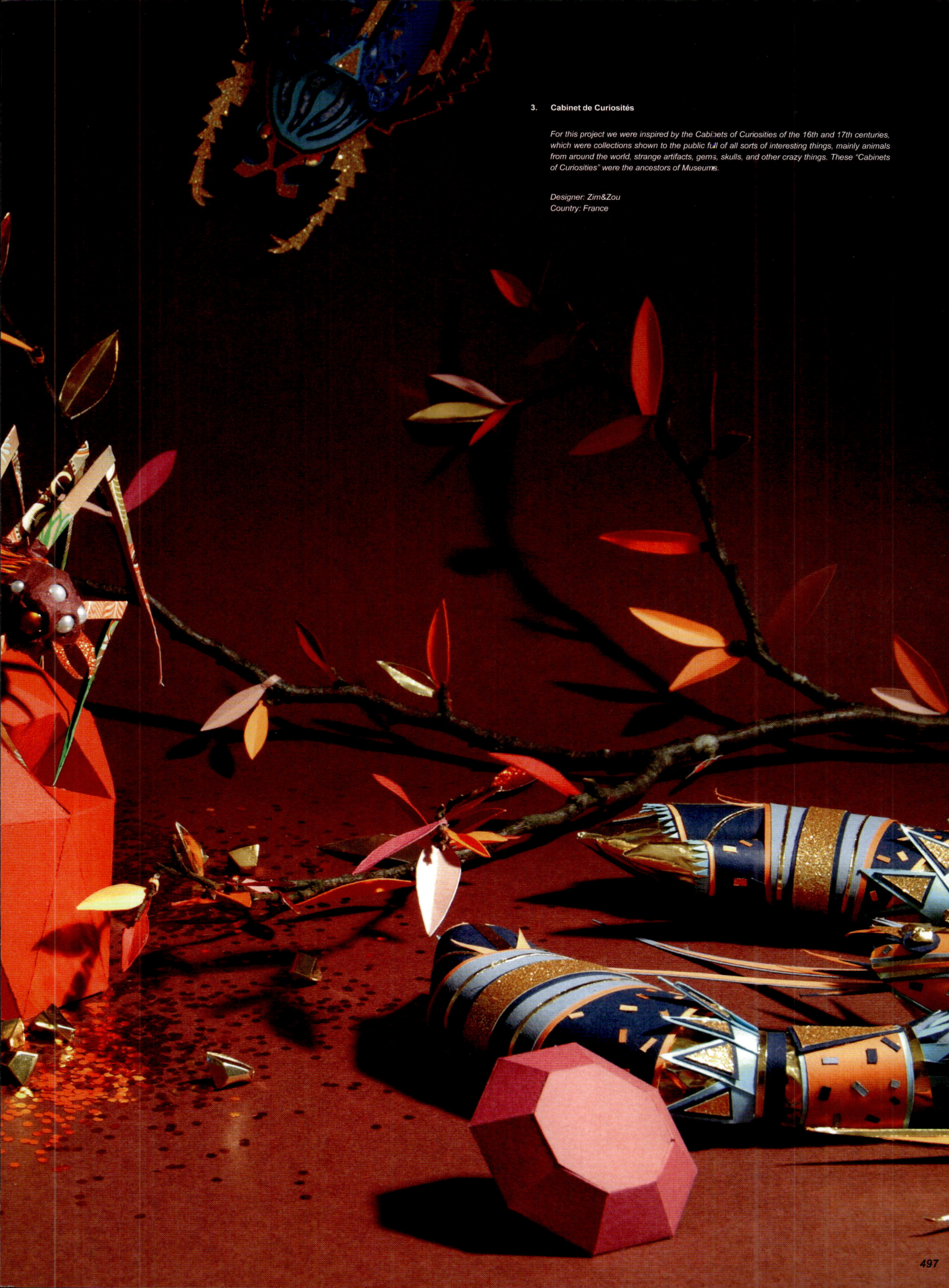

3. Cabinet de Curiosités

For this project we were inspired by the Cabinets of Curiosities of the 16th and 17th centuries, which were collections shown to the public full of all sorts of interesting things, mainly animals from around the world, strange artifacts, gems, skulls, and other crazy things. These "Cabinets of Curiosities" were the ancestors of Museums.

Designer: Zim&Zou
Country: France

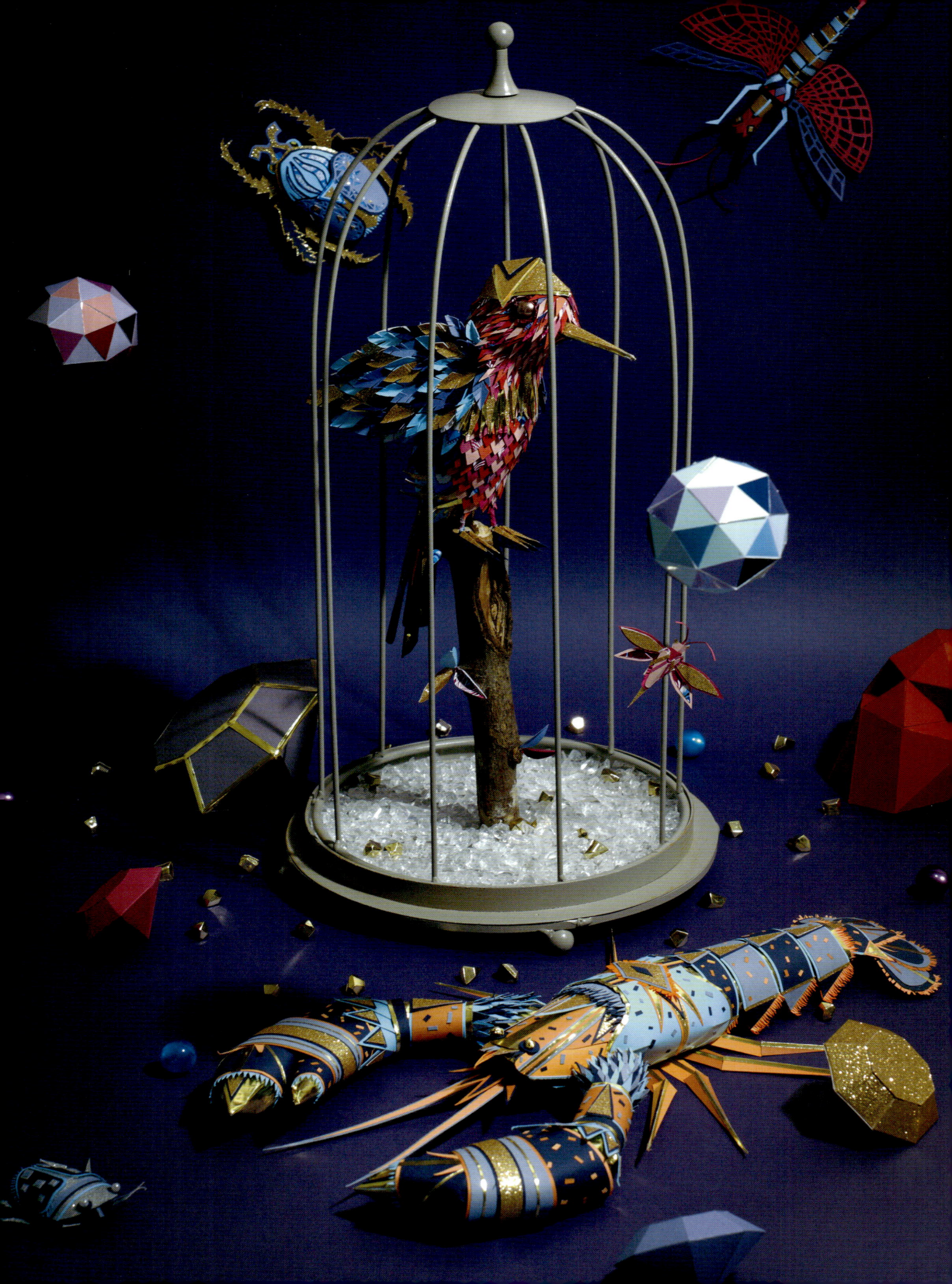

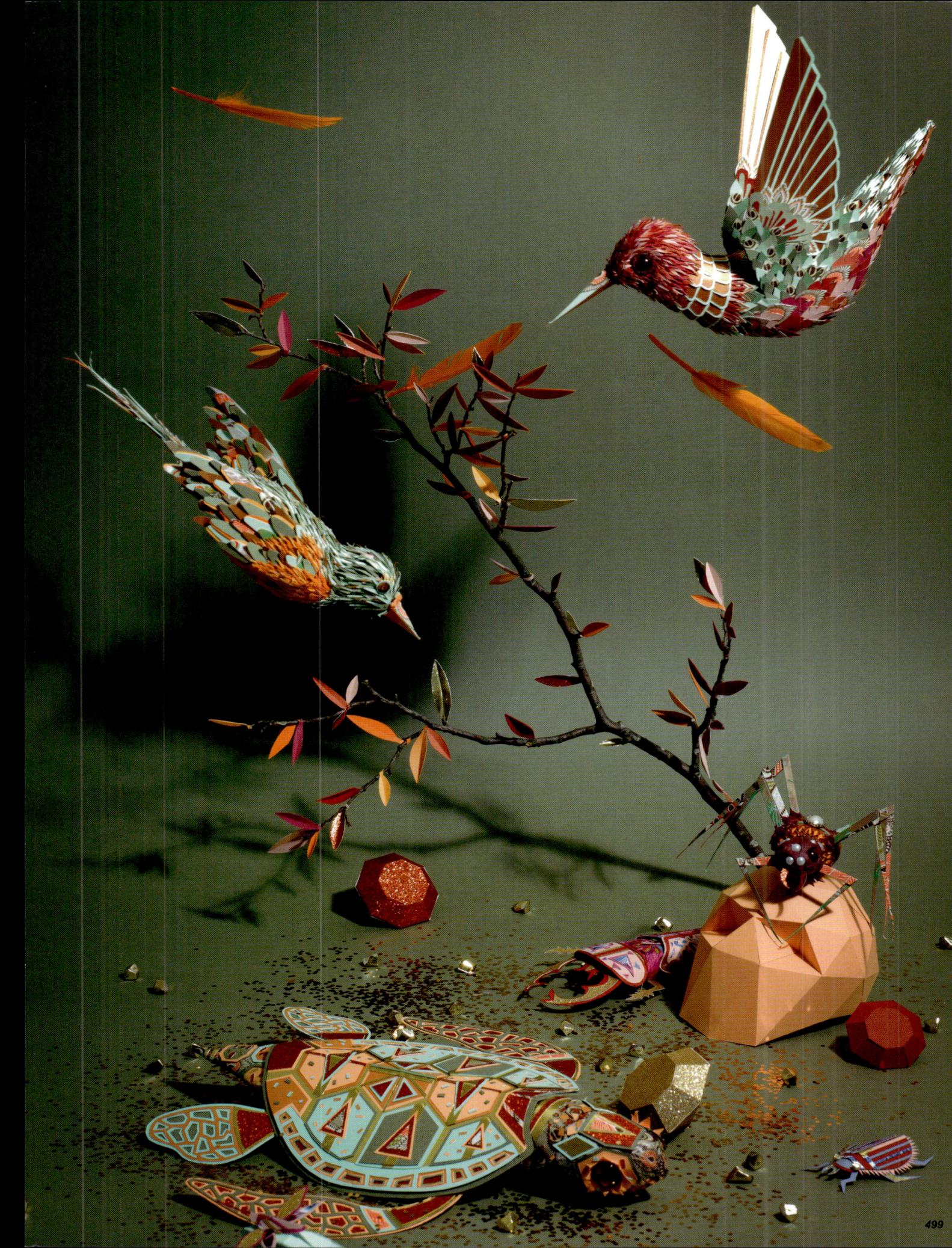

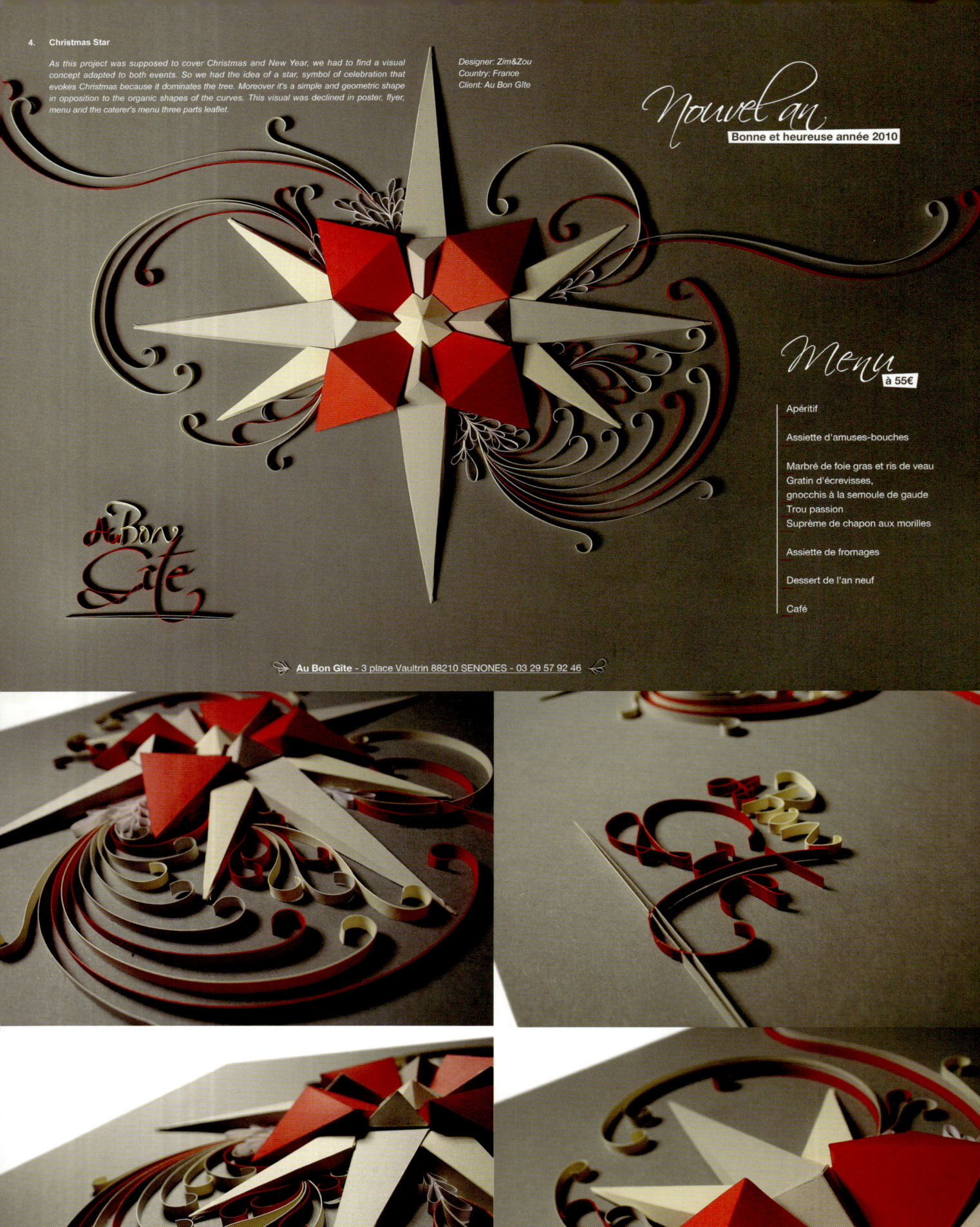

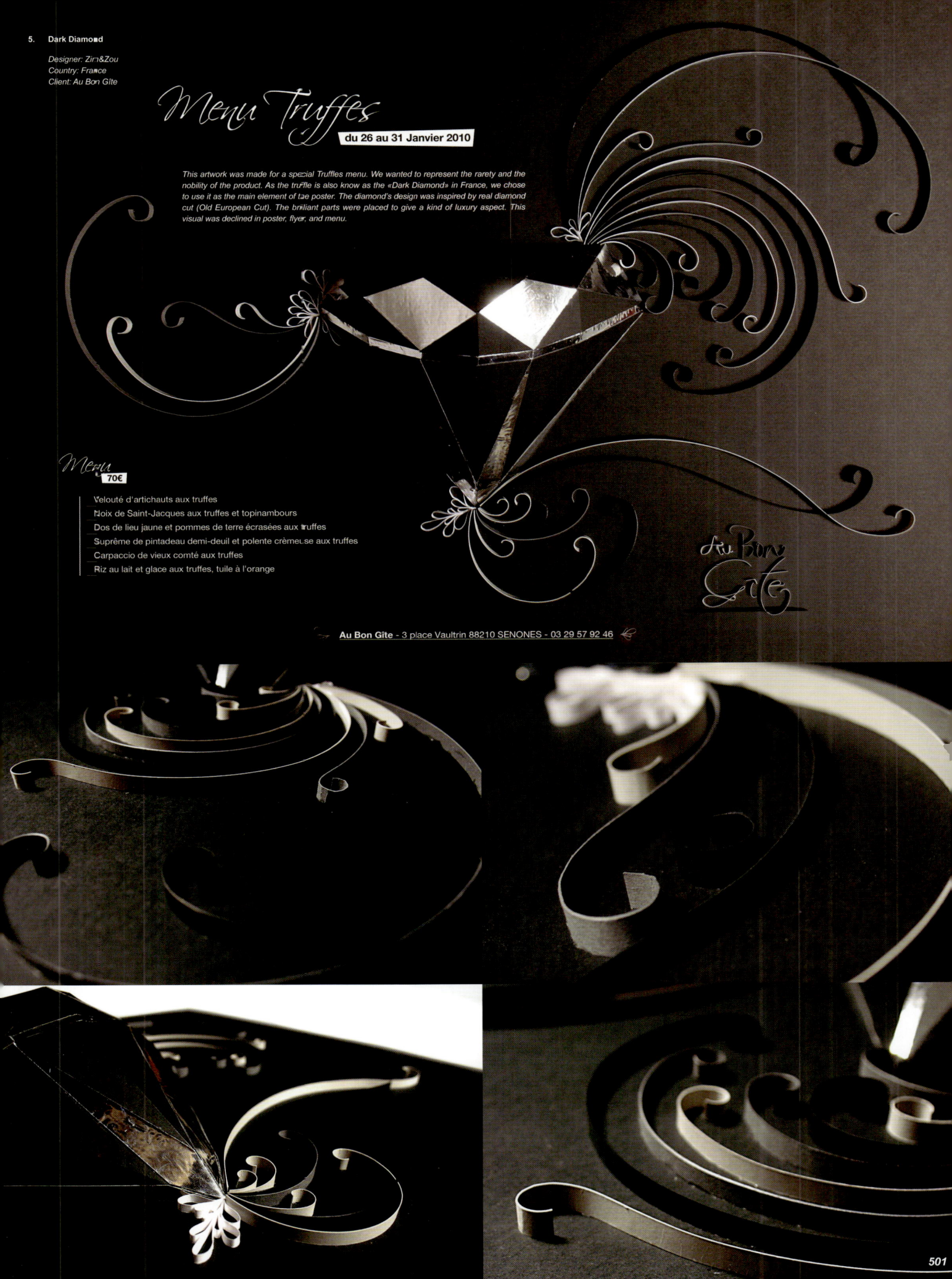

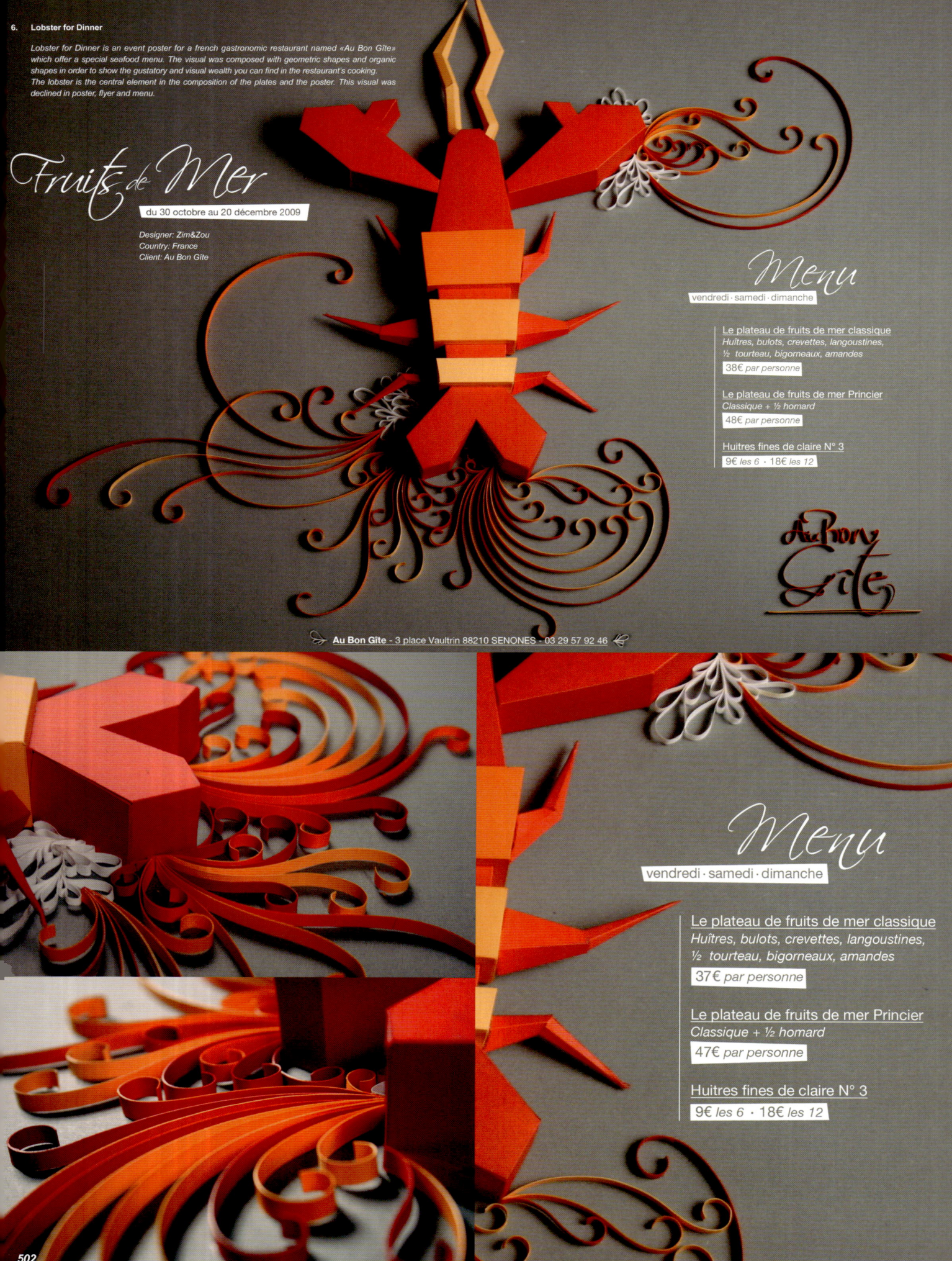

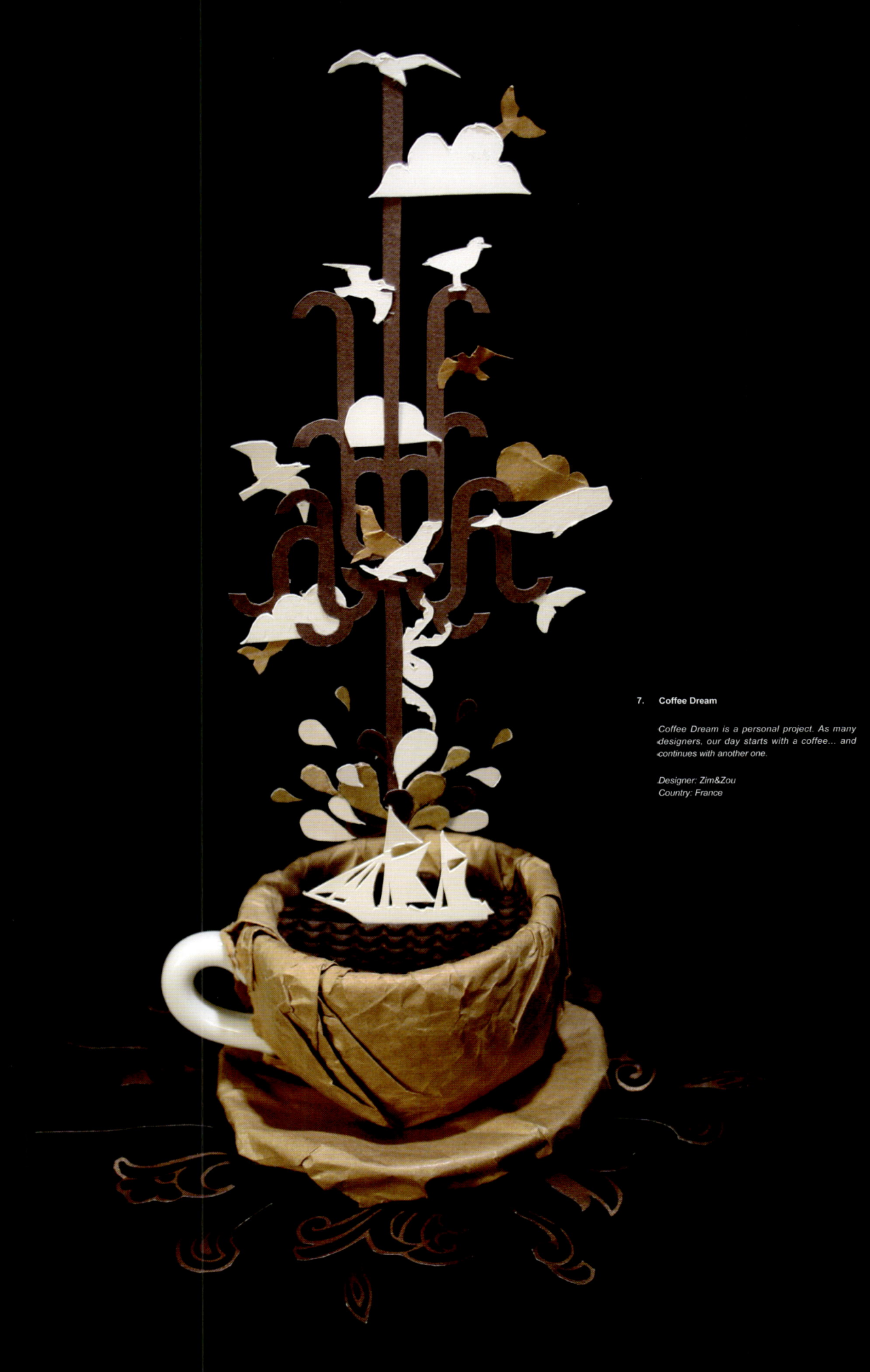

7. Coffee Dream

Coffee Dream is a personal project. As many designers, our day starts with a coffee... and continues with another one.

Designer: Zim&Zou
Country: France

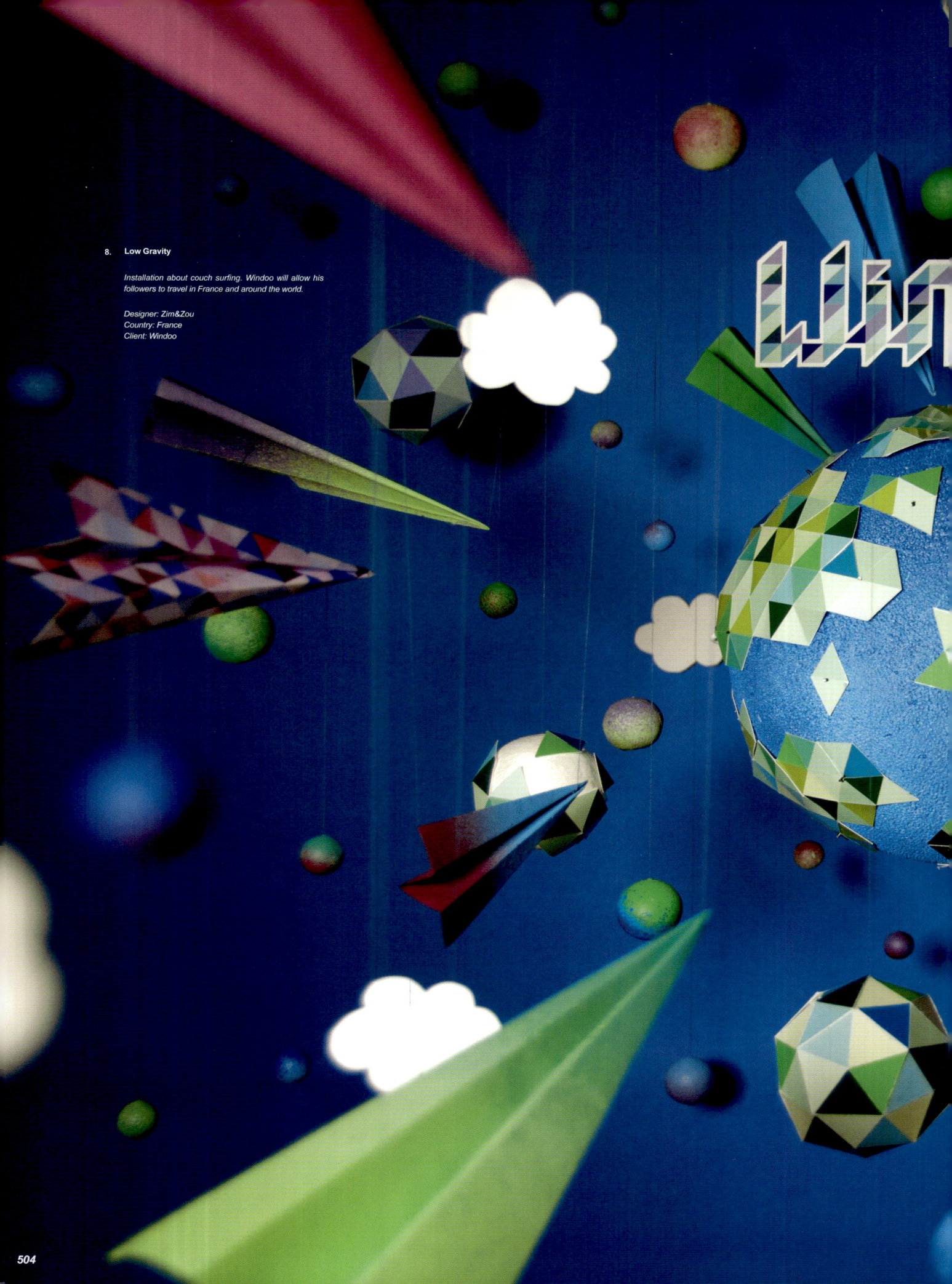

8. **Low Gravity**

Installation about couch surfing. Windoo will allow his followers to travel in France and around the world.

Designer: Zim&Zou
Country: France
Client: Windoo

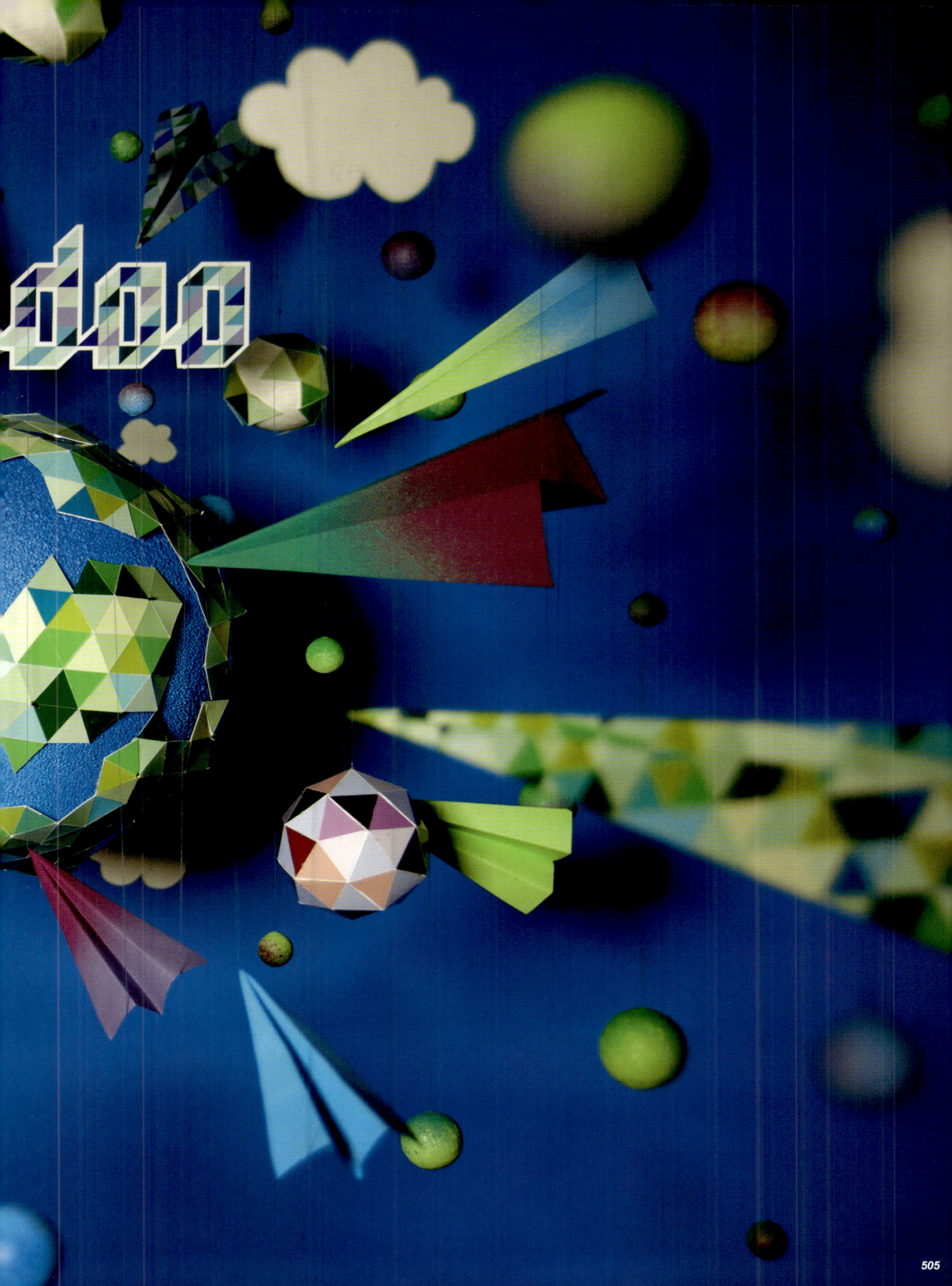

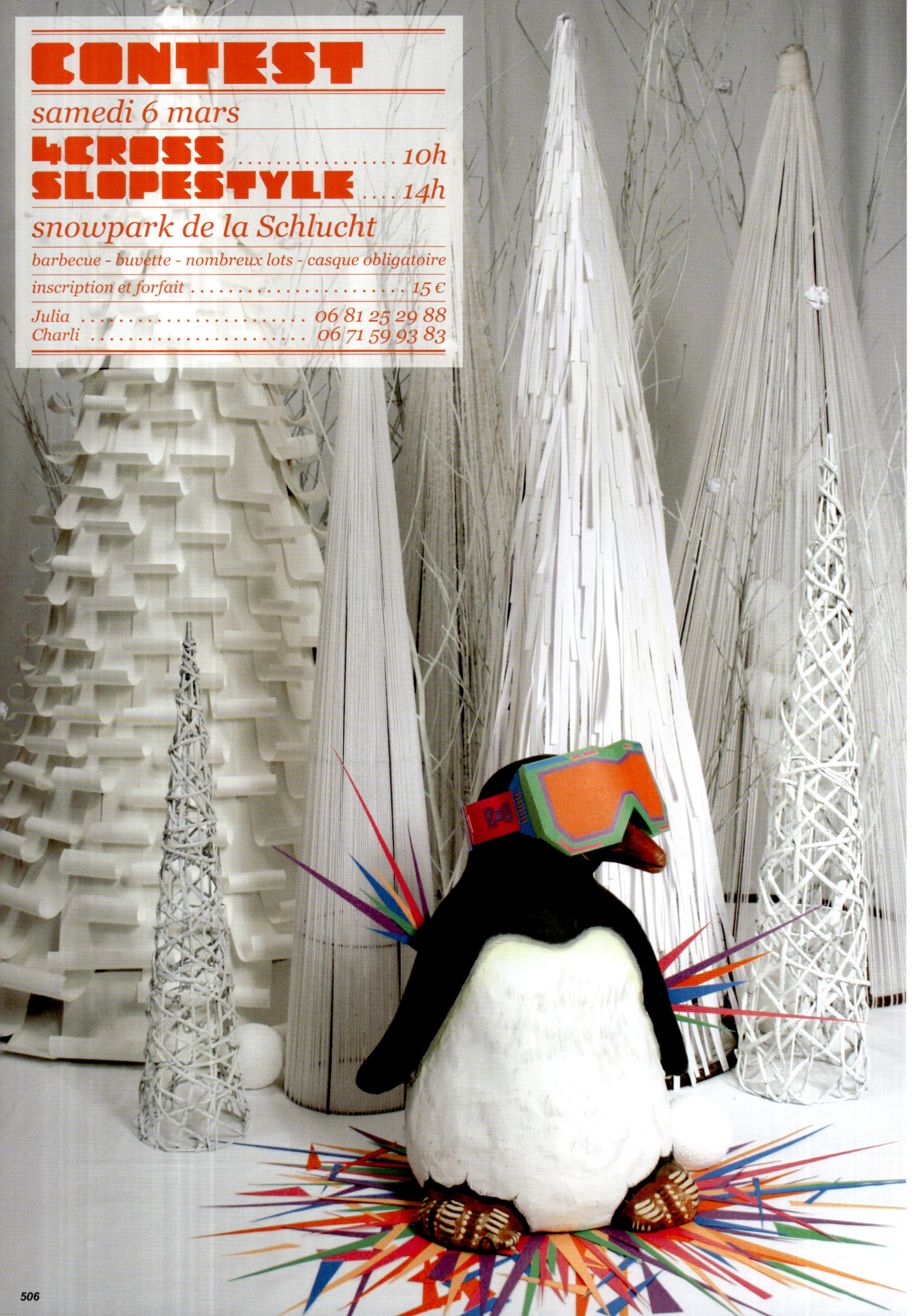

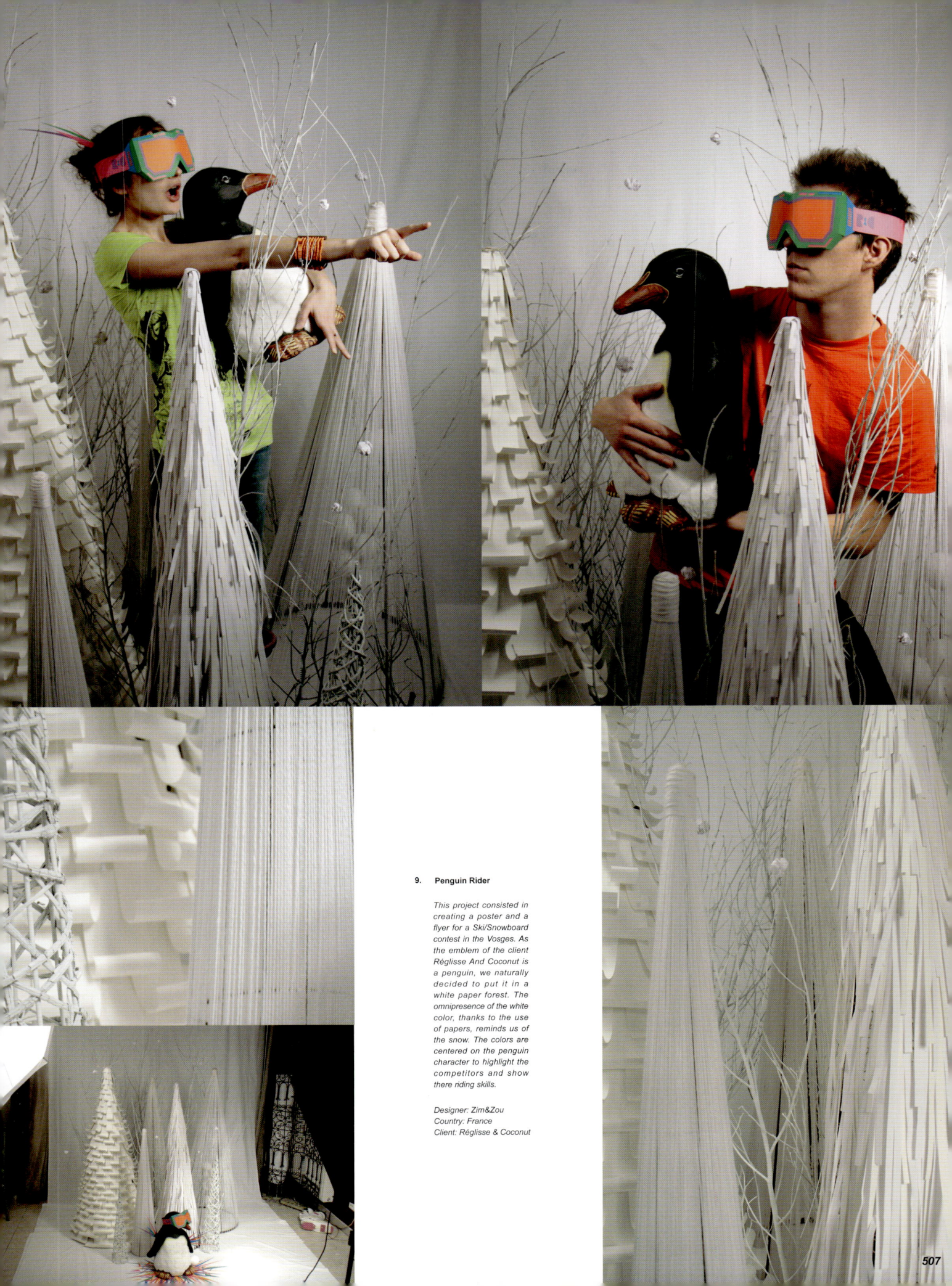

9. Penguin Rider

This project consisted in creating a poster and a flyer for a Ski/Snowboard contest in the Vosges. As the emblem of the client Réglisse And Coconut is a penguin, we naturally decided to put it in a white paper forest. The omnipresence of the white color, thanks to the use of papers, reminds us of the snow. The colors are centered on the penguin character to highlight the competitors and show there riding skills.

Designer: Zim&Zou
Country: France
Client: Réglisse & Coconut

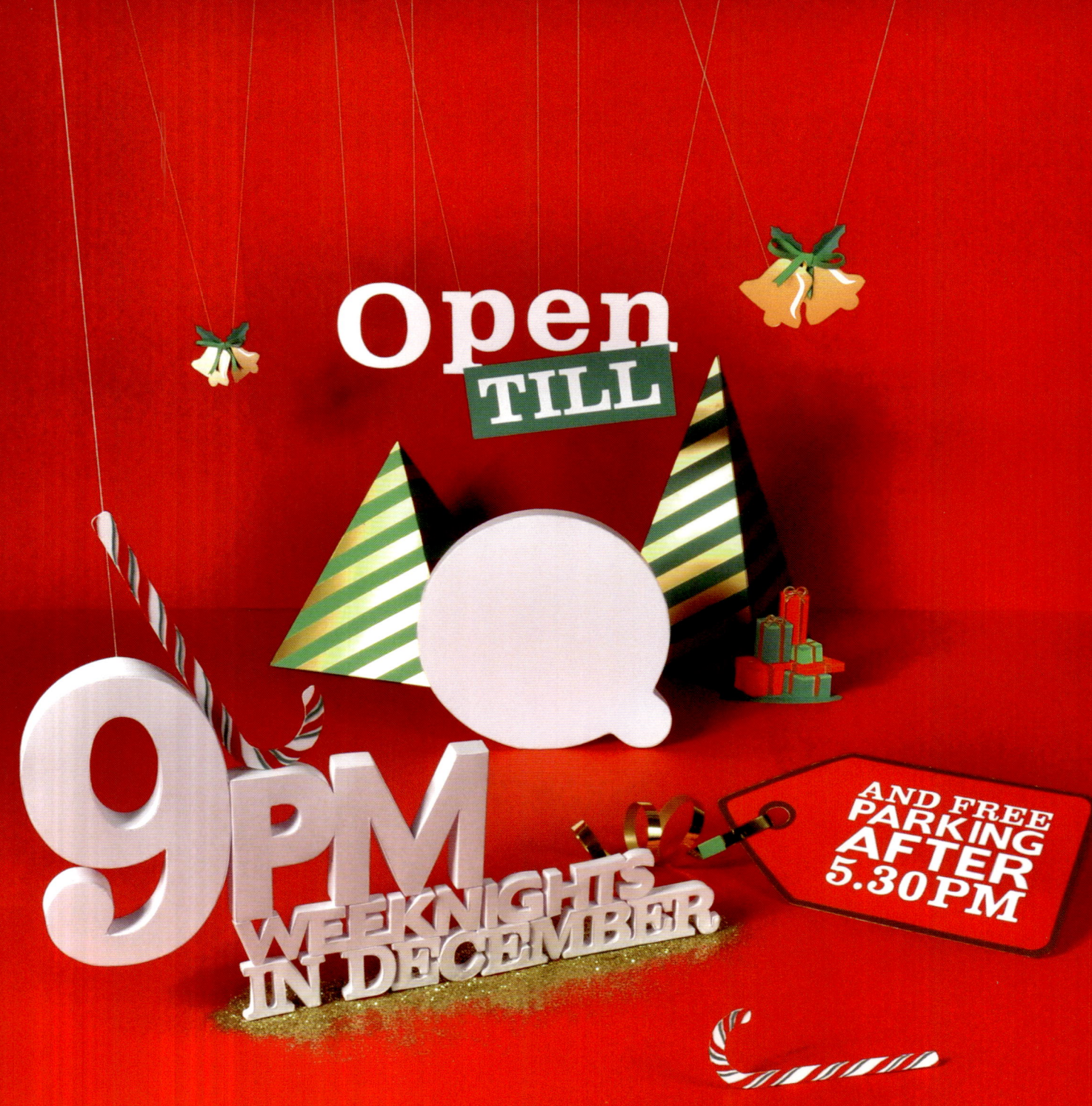

10. Queensgate

Posters for events at the Queensgate Shopping Center in Peterborough.

Designer: Zim&Zou
Country: France
Client: Queensgate Shopping Center (UK)

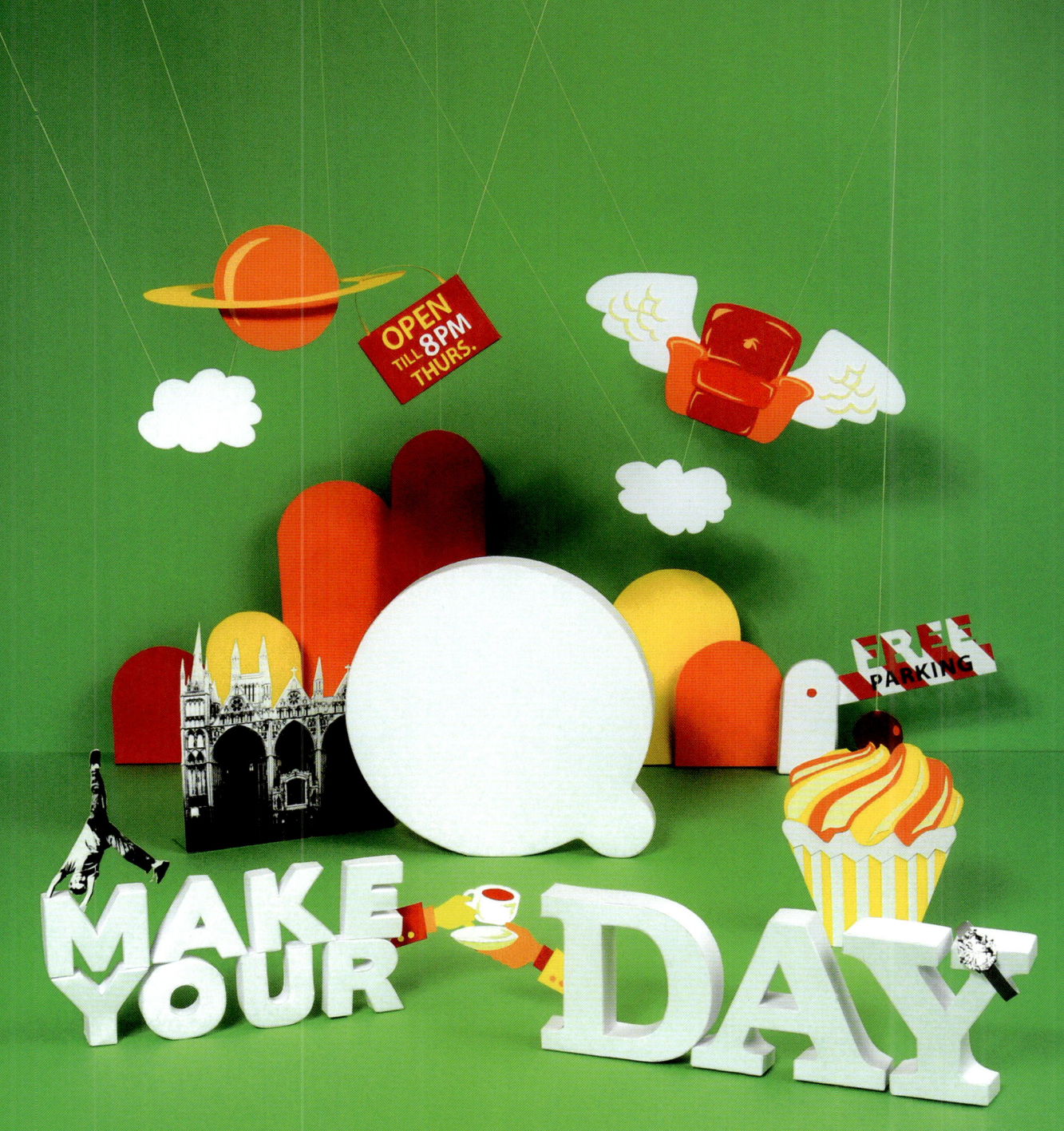

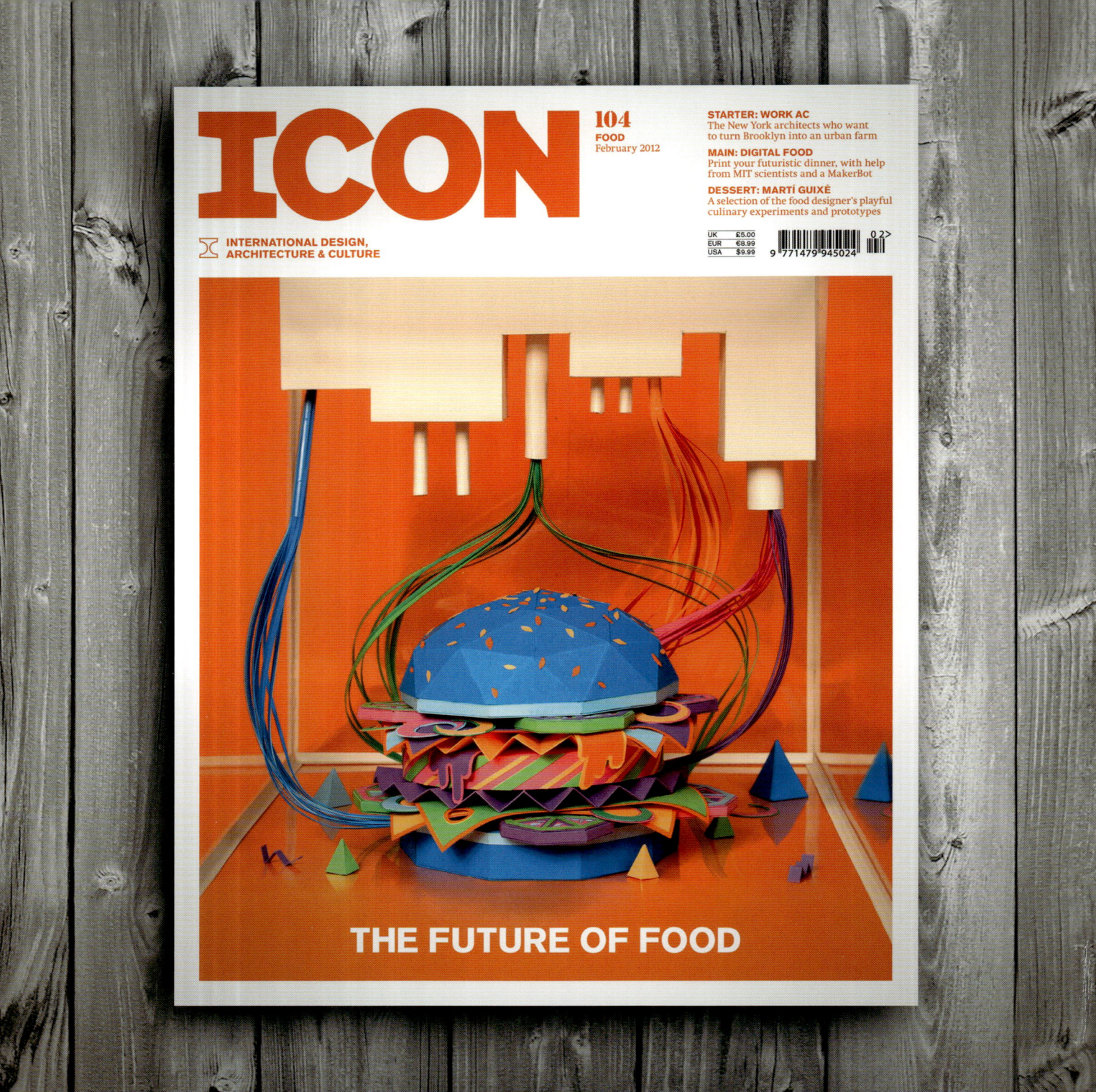

11. The Future of Food

The theme of the issue was Food. They were much looking at the future of food design, talking about 3d food printing (Digital food), how food is visualised and presented (Marti Guixe) and questionning what food should be. The brief was more about food and food design in general but we found the concept of the 3d food printing very interesting to work with. The cover had to be striking, vibrant and strong.

Designer: Zim&Zou
Country: France
Client: Icon Magazine (UK)

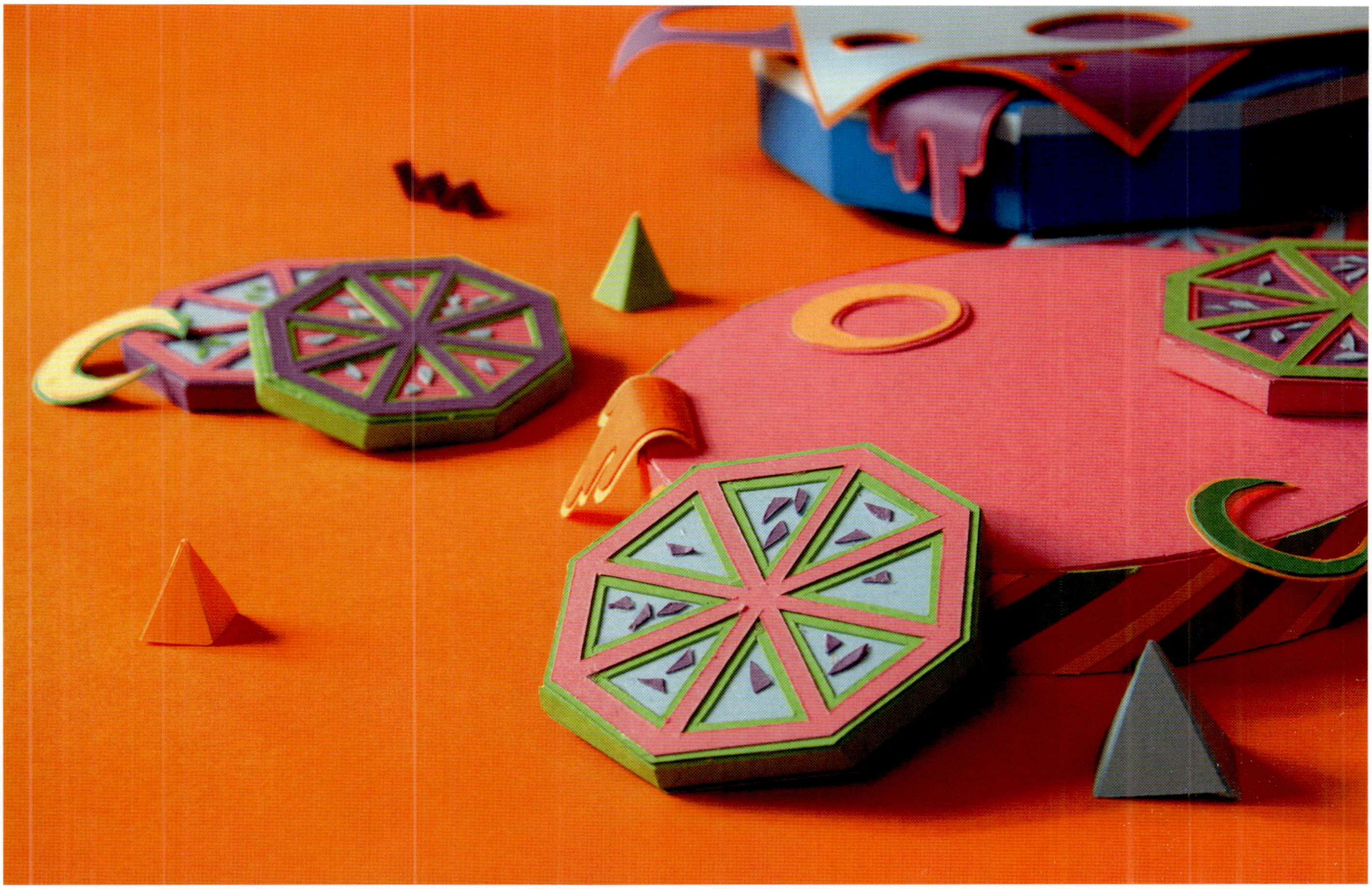

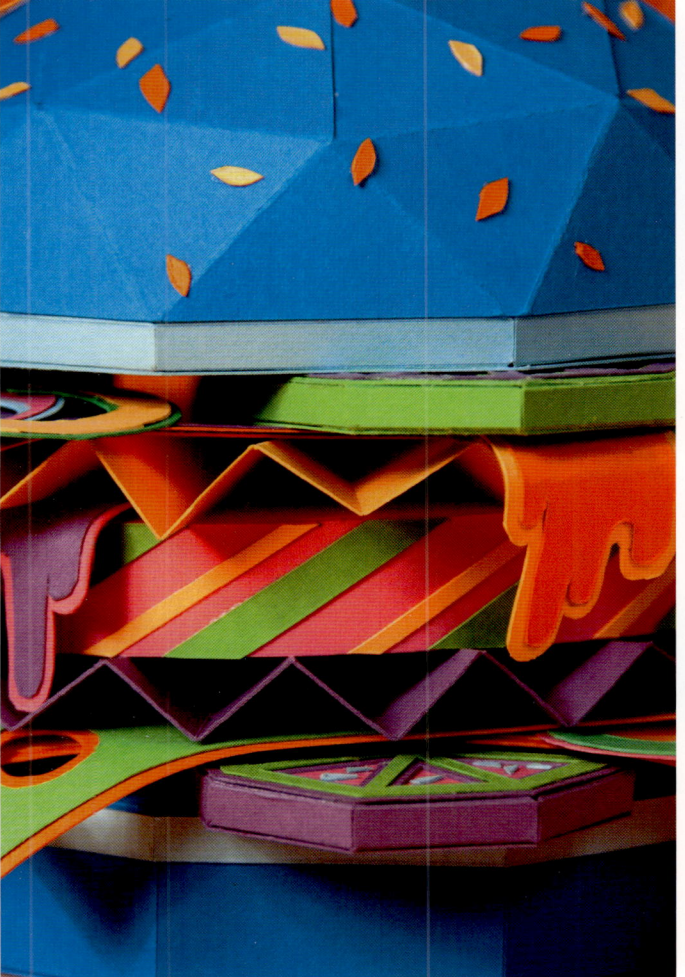
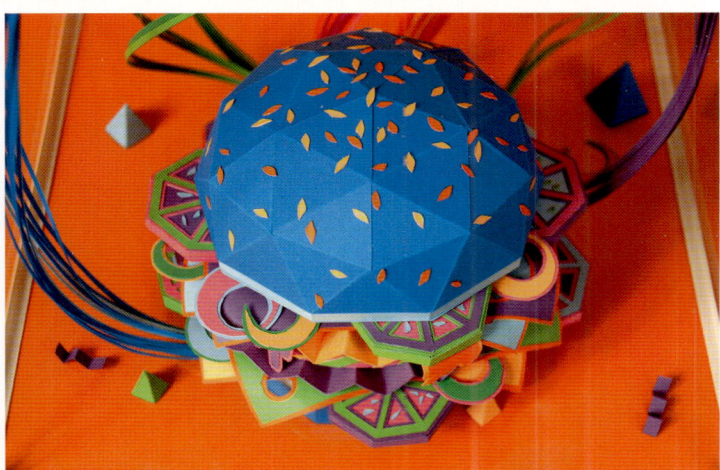
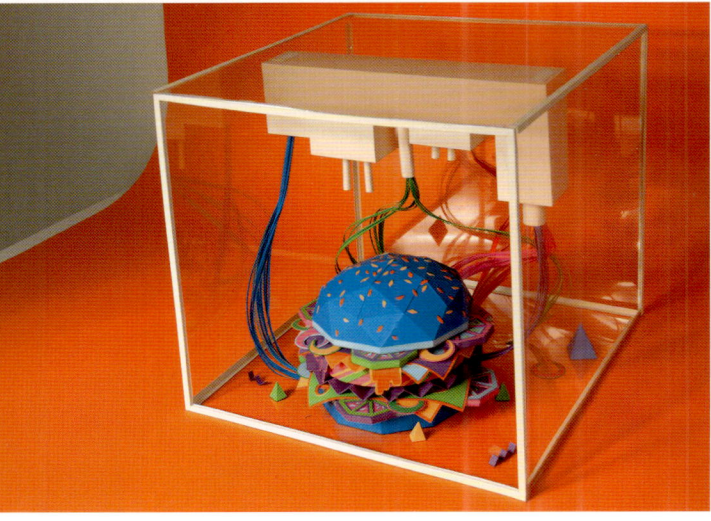

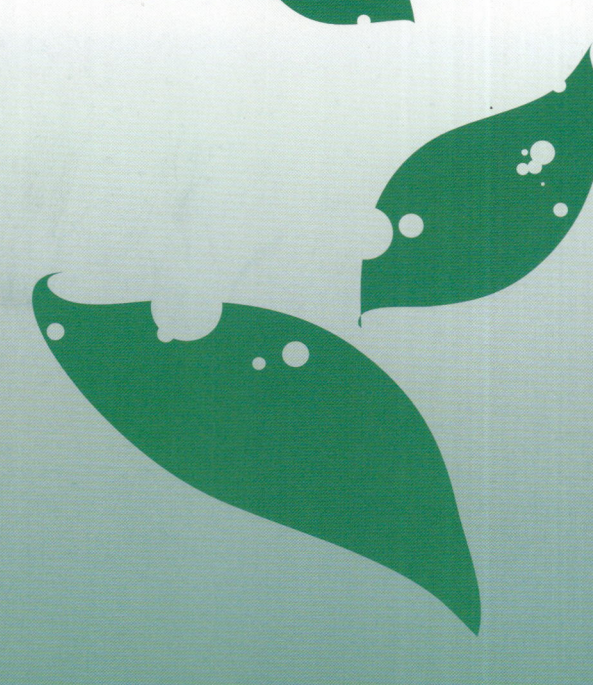

Organiger: Jianing Yuan(Yannick)
Editor: Jianing Yuan(Yannick)
Proofreader: Jianing Yuan(Yannick)
Art Director: Yang Liu(Amy)
Printing Specialist: Yang Liu(Amy)
Book Design: Yang Liu(Amy)
Layout: Tai Zhang

Publisher: DESIGNERBOOKS
Unit D, 16/F, Cheuk Nang 21st Century Plaza, 250 Hennessy Road,
Wanchai, Hong Kong
Tel: +852-2575-5186
Fax: +852-2891-1996
E-mail: edit@designerbooks.com.cn

Distributor:

DESIGNERBOOKS
A508/509, Tianhai Commercial plaza, 107#, North Street, Dongsi, Dongcheng District, Beijing, China
Tel: 0086-10-6400-3080 (Beijing) 0086-22-2341-1250 (Tianjin)
      0086-21-5596-7639 (Shanghai) 0086-571-8884-8576 (Hangzhou)
      0086-25-8483-9119 (Nanjing) 0086-23-6772-5751 (Chongqing)
      0086-755-8825-0425 (Shenzhen) 0086-20-8756-5010 (Guangzhou)
      0086-28-6465-8008 (Chengdu) 0086-27-6566-2067 (Wuhan)
Fax: 0086-10-64018430-822
E-mail: info@designerbooks.com.cn
http://www.designerbooks.com.cn

Printed in China

All rights reserved. No part of this publication may be reproduced in any form or by any means, graphic, electronic or mechanical, including photocopying and recording by an information storage and retrieval system without permission in writing from the publisher.

ISBN: 978-988-16075-4-6